Programming Microsoft® ADO.NET 2.0 Core Reference

David Sceppa

PUBLISHED BY
Microsoft Press
A Division of Microsoft Corporation
One Microsoft Way
Redmond, Washington 98052-6399

ISBN-13: 978-0-7356-2206-7
ISBN-10: 0-7356-2206-X
Library of Congress Control Number 2005939239

Printed and bound in the United States of America.

2 3 4 5 6 7 8 9   QWT   1 0 9 8 7

Distributed in Canada by H.B. Fenn and Company Ltd.

A CIP catalogue record for this book is available from the British Library.

Microsoft Press books are available through booksellers and distributors worldwide. For further information about international editions, contact your local Microsoft Corporation office or contact Microsoft Press International directly at fax (425) 936-7329. Visit our Web site at www.microsoft.com/mspress. Send comments to mspinput@microsoft.com.

Acquisitions Editor: Ben Ryan
Project Editor: Lynn Finnel
Technical Editors: Kurt Meyer; Jacqueline Richards
Copy Editor: Roger LeBlanc
Indexer: Seth Maislin

Body Part No. X11-53586

Contents at a Glance

Table of Contents

Part III   Working with Data Offline—The ADO.NET *DataSet*

Acknowledgments

First and foremost, I'd like to thank my mother, father, and sister for their constant support and patience through this project as well as through my life in general.

I'd like to thank Jackie Richards for her technical contributions to this book as a peer reviewer, for all of her support in this project, and for being an incredible person from whom I have learned so much.

I'd like to thank and congratulate the Microsoft Data Programmability team for developing the most powerful set of data access technologies that we've released to date.

Finally, thanks to Lynn Finnel, Kurt Meyer, Roger LeBlanc, and everyone at Microsoft Press who has played a role in getting this book onto the shelves.

David Sceppa

Introduction

Microsoft ADO.NET 2.0 includes a number of enhancements—new classes, such as the connection string builders, as well as new properties and methods on previously existing classes. This book will cover the new features in ADO.NET 2.0 as well as the features that existed in the initial release of the technology.

Although this book is the second edition of *Microsoft ADO.NET*, there are more changes to the text than just the coverage of the new features. For example, Chapters 12 and 13, which cover Microsoft Windows applications and Microsoft ASP.NET applications, respectively, contain updated information about new data binding features and scenarios. I've also updated other portions of the book to reflect what I've learned since writing the first edition.

Who This Book Is For

This book is intended for anyone writing data access code in a .NET application. Whether you're using .NET code to access a Microsoft SQL Server database from an ASP.NET application, or using .NET code with OLE DB to talk to a Microsoft Office Access database in a Windows application, you should interact with the database by using ADO.NET.

How This Book Is Organized

The book is divided into sections. Chapters 1 and 2 serve as an introduction to the technology as a whole. Chapters 3 through 5 explain how you can use connected ADO.NET classes (*SqlConnection*, *SqlConnectionStringBuilder*, *SqlCommand*, *SqlParameter*, and *SqlDataAdapter*) to talk to a SQL Server database. Chapters 6 through 12 cover ADO.NET disconnected features, which can store query results off line and support features such as sorting, searching, and filtering, as well as caching and submitting changes. Chapters 13 through 15 cover the basics for building effective applications by using Windows Forms, ASP.NET, and the SQL Server common language runtime (CLR). Appendix A explains how to use other .NET data providers, and Appendix B describes the relevant samples and tools that are available for download.

System Requirements

You'll need the following hardware and software to build and run the code samples for this book:

- Microsoft Windows XP with Service Pack 2, Microsoft Windows Server 2003 with Service Pack 1, or Microsoft Windows 2000 with Service Pack 4

- Microsoft Visual Studio 2005 Standard Edition or Microsoft Visual Studio 2005 Professional Edition

- Microsoft SQL Server 2005 Express (included with Visual Studio 2005) or Microsoft SQL Server 2005

- 600 MHz Pentium or compatible processor (1 GHz Pentium recommended)

- 192 MB RAM (256 MB or more recommended)

- Video monitor (800 × 600 or higher resolution) with at least 256 colors (1024 × 768 High Color 16-bit recommended)

- Microsoft mouse or compatible pointing device

Configuring SQL Server 2005 Express Edition

Some chapters of this book require that you have access to SQL Server 2005 Express Edition (or SQL Server 2005) to create and use the Northwind Traders database. Chapter 3 describes how to install the Northwind Traders database, and the majority of code snippets are written to work with the local installation of SQL Server Express 2005 Edition. If you are using SQL Server 2005 Express Edition, follow these steps to grant access to the user account that you will be using to perform the exercises in this book:

1. Log on to Windows on your computer by using an account with administrator privileges.

2. On the Windows Start menu, click All Programs, click Accessories, and then click Command Prompt to open a command prompt window.

3. In the command prompt window, type the following case-sensitive command:

   ```
   sqlcmd –S YourServer\SQLExpress –E
   ```

   Replace *YourServer* with the name of your computer.

   You can find the name of your computer by running the *hostname* command in the command prompt window before running the *sqlcmd* command.

4. At the 1> prompt, type the following command, including the square brackets, and then press Enter:

   ```
   sp_grantlogin [YourServer\UserName]
   ```

Replace *YourServer* with the name of your computer, and replace *UserName* with the name of the user account you will be using.

5. At the 2> prompt, type the following command and then press Enter:

    ```
    go
    ```

    If you see an error message, make sure that you have typed the `sp_grantlogin` command correctly, including the square brackets.

6. At the 1> prompt, type the following command, including the square brackets, and then press Enter:

    ```
    sp_addsrvrolemember [YourServer\UserName], dbcreator
    ```

7. At the 2> prompt, type the following command and then press Enter:

    ```
    go
    ```

    If you see an error message, make sure that you have typed the `sp_addsrvrolemember` command correctly, including the square brackets.

8. At the 1> prompt, type the following command and then press Enter:

    ```
    exit
    ```

9. Close the command prompt window.

10. Log out of the administrator account.

Code Samples

The downloadable code includes projects for most chapters that cover the code snippets and examples referenced in the chapter. All the code samples discussed in this book can be downloaded from the book's companion content page at the following address:

http://www.microsoft.com/mspress/companion/0-7356-2206-X/

At the time of publication, the samples and tools described in Appendix B are works in progress. All three tools are fairly ambitious projects, and I plan to periodically add new features and fix existing bugs in the months ahead. The downloadable code for the appendix includes the source code for each component as well as rudimentary documentation. Subsequent updates to the code and documentation will be available through my Web site at *http://www.DavidSceppa.net.*

Note   Please understand that my plans might be forced to change and that neither Microsoft Press nor I can promise to support the extra tools described in Appendix B.

Support for This Book

Every effort has been made to ensure the accuracy of this book and the companion content. Microsoft Press provides support for books and companion content at the following Web site:

http://www.microsoft.com/learning/support/books/

Questions and Comments

If you have comments or ideas regarding this book or the companion content or have questions that are not answered by visiting the preceding sites, please send them to Microsoft Press via e-mail to:

mspinput@microsoft.com

Or via postal mail to:

Microsoft Press
Attn: *Programming Microsoft ADO.NET 2.0* Editor
One Microsoft Way
Redmond, WA 98052-6399

Please note that Microsoft software product support is not offered through the preceding addresses.

Part I
Getting Started with Microsoft ADO.NET 2.0

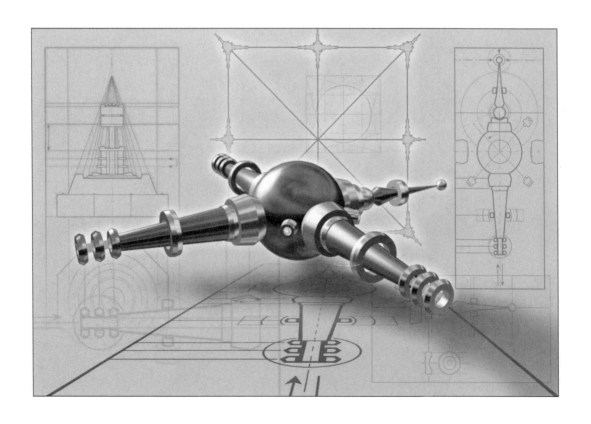

Chapter 1
Overview of ADO.NET

ADO.NET is a set of libraries included with the Microsoft .NET Framework that help you communicate with various data stores from .NET applications. The ADO.NET libraries include classes for connecting to a data source, submitting queries, and processing results. You can also use ADO.NET as a robust, hierarchical, disconnected data cache to work with data offline. The central disconnected object, the *DataSet*, allows you to sort, search, filter, store pending changes, and navigate through hierarchical data. The *DataSet* also includes a number of features that bridge the gap between traditional data access and XML development. Developers can now work with XML data through traditional data access interfaces and vice versa.

In short, if you're building a .NET application that accesses data, you should use ADO.NET.

Microsoft Visual Studio includes a suite of design-time data access features that can help you build data access applications more efficiently. Many of these features can save you time during the development process by generating large amounts of tedious code for you. Other features improve the performance of the applications you build by storing metadata and updating logic in your code rather than fetching this information at run time. Believe it or not, many of Visual Studio's data access features accomplish both tasks.

As we examine ADO.NET throughout this book, we'll also look at features in Visual Studio that you can use to save time and effort.

No New Object Model?!?

Visual Studio 2005 breaks new ground for Microsoft in that it is the first major release of Visual Studio that does not introduce a new data access object model. (Visual Studio 2003 doesn't count because it contained only minor enhancements to Visual Studio 2002.) Developers who have honed their ADO.NET skills using versions 1.0 and 1.1 of the .NET Framework can continue to enhance those skills in version 2.0 of the .NET Framework.

Many developers who are new to the .NET Framework may have had experience with Microsoft's previous data access technology—Active Data Object (ADO). ADO served many developers well, but it lacks key features that developers need to build more powerful applications. For example, more and more developers want to work with XML data. Although later versions of ADO added XML features, ADO was not *built* to work with XML data. For example, ADO does not allow you to separate the schema information from the actual data. Microsoft might add more XML features to future releases of ADO, but ADO will never handle XML data as efficiently as ADO.NET does because ADO.NET was designed with XML in mind and ADO was not. The ADO cursor engine makes it possible to pass disconnected ADO *Recordset* objects between different tiers in your application, but you cannot combine the contents of multiple *Recordset* objects. ADO allows you to submit cached changes to databases, but it does not give you control over the logic used to submit updates. Also, the ADO cursor engine does not, for example, provide a way to submit pending changes to your database via stored procedures. Because many database administrators allow users to modify the contents of the database only through stored procedures, many developers cannot submit updates through the ADO *Recordset* object.

Microsoft built ADO.NET to address these key scenarios, along with others that I'll discuss throughout this book.

ADO.NET is designed to combine the best features of its predecessors while adding features requested most frequently by developers—greater XML support, easier disconnected data access, more control over updates, and greater update flexibility.

The ADO.NET Object Model

Now that you understand the purpose of ADO.NET and where it fits into the overall Visual Studio architecture, it's time to take a closer look at the technology. In this chapter, we'll look briefly at the ADO.NET object model and see how it differs from previous Microsoft data access technologies.

ADO.NET is designed to help developers build efficient multi-tiered database applications across intranets and the Internet, and the ADO.NET object model provides the means. Figure 1-1 shows the classes that comprise the ADO.NET object model. A dotted line separates the object model into two halves. The objects to the left of the line are connected objects. These objects communicate directly with your database to manage the connection and transactions as well as to retrieve data from and submit changes to your database. The objects to the right of the line are disconnected objects that allow a user to work with data offline.

The objects that comprise the disconnected half of the ADO.NET object model do not communicate directly with the connected objects. This is a major change from previous Microsoft data access object models. In ADO, the *Recordset* object stores the results of your queries. You can call its *Open* method to fetch the results of a query and call its *Update* (or *UpdateBatch*) method to submit changes stored within the *Recordset* to your database.

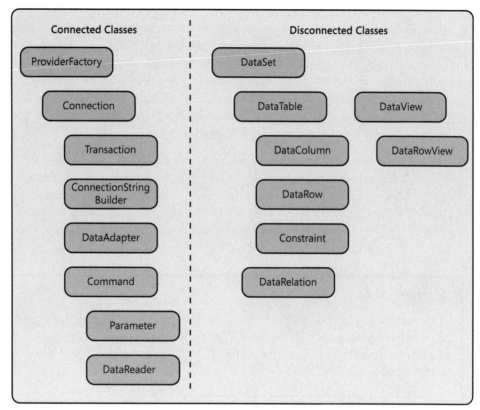

Figure 1-1   The ADO.NET object model

The ADO.NET *DataSet*, which we'll discuss shortly, is comparable in functionality to the ADO *Recordset*. However, the *DataSet* does not communicate with your database. To fetch data from your database into a *DataSet*, you pass the *DataSet* into the *Fill* method of a connected ADO.NET object—the *DataAdapter*. Similarly, to submit the pending changes stored in your *DataSet* to your database, you pass the *DataSet* to the *DataAdapter* object's *Update* method.

.NET Data Providers

A .NET data provider is a collection of classes designed to allow you to communicate with a particular type of data store. The .NET Framework includes four such providers, the SQL Client .NET Data Provider, the Oracle Client .NET Data Provider, the ODBC .NET Data Provider and the OLE DB .NET Data Provider. The SQL Client and Oracle Client .NET Data Providers are designed to talk to specific databases, SQL Server and Oracle, respectively. The ODBC and OLE DB .NET Data Providers are often called "bridge" components because they serve as a bridge to legacy technologies—ODBC and OLE DB. These providers let you communicate with various data stores through ODBC drivers and OLE DB providers, respectively.

Each .NET data provider implements the same basic classes—ProviderFactory, *Connection*, ConnectionStringBuilder, *Command*, *DataReader*, *Parameter*, and *Transaction*—although their actual names depend on the provider. For example, the SQL Client .NET Data Provider has a *SqlConnection* class, and the ODBC .NET Data Provider includes an *OdbcConnection* class. Regardless of which .NET data provider you use, the provider's *Connection* class implements the same basic features through the same basic interfaces. To open a connection to your data store, you create an instance of the provider's connection class, set the object's *ConnectionString* property, and then call its *Open* method.

Each .NET data provider has its own namespace. The four providers included in the .NET Framework are subsets of the *System.Data* namespace, where the disconnected objects reside. The SQL Client .NET Data Provider resides in the System.Data.SqlClient namespace, the ODBC .NET Data Provider resides in System.Data.Odbc, the OLE DB .NET Data Provider resides in the *System.Data.OleDb*, and the Oracle Client .NET Data Provider resides in *System.Data.OracleClient*.

Namespaces

A namespace is a logical grouping of objects. The .NET Framework is large, so to make developing applications with the .NET Framework a little easier, Microsoft has divided the objects into different namespaces. Figure 1-2 shows a portion of the hierarchy of namespaces in the .NET Framework.

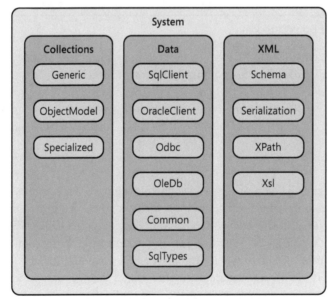

Figure 1-2   Namespaces in the .NET Framework

The most important reason for using namespaces is to prevent name collisions in assemblies. With different namespaces, programmers working on different components combined into a single solution can use the same names for different items. Because these names are separated, they don't interfere with each other at compile time. A more practical reason for namespaces is that grouping objects can make them easier to locate. Sometimes I forget the exact name of the class I'm looking for. If the classes in the .NET Framework were not broken out into smaller namespaces, I would have to find the desired class in an alphabetical list of all the classes in the framework. Thankfully, I can usually remember the namespace of the desired class. Finding the class within its namespace is simpler because there are fewer classes to examine.

For more information on using namespaces in the Microsoft .NET Framework or Visual Studio, see the .NET Framework SDK.

Because each .NET data provider implements the same basic features, the code you write will look fairly similar regardless of the provider you use. As you can see in the following code snippets, all you need to do to switch from using the ODBC .NET Data Provider to the SQL Client .NET Data Provider is to change the class you instantiate and the contents of the connection string to conform to the provider's standards.

Visual Basic

```
'Open and close an OdbcConnection
Dim cnOdbc As New OdbcConnection
cnOdbc.ConnectionString = "Driver={SQL Server};" & _
                          "Server=.\SQLExpress;" & _
                          "Database=Northwind;..."
cnOdbc.Open()
...
cnOdbc.Close()


'Open and close a SqlConnection
Dim cnSql As New SqlConnection
cnSql.ConnectionString = "Data Source=.\SQLExpress;" & _
                         "Initial Catalog=Northwind;..."
cnSql.Open()
...
cnSql.Close()
```

Visual C#

```
//Open and close an OdbcConnection
OdbcConnection cnOdbc = new OdbcConnection();
cnOdbc.ConnectionString =  "Driver={SQL Server};" +
                           @"Server=.\SQLExpress" +
                           "Database=Northwind;...";
cnOleDb.Open();
...
cnOleDb.Close();


//Open and close a SqlConnection
SqlConnection cnSql = new SqlConnection();
cnSql.ConnectionString = @"Data Source=.\SQLExpress;" +
                          "Initial Catalog=Northwind;...";
cnSql.Open();
...
cnSql.Close();
```

Why Use Separate Classes and Libraries?

No previous Microsoft data access technology has used separate libraries and classes for different data stores. Many developers have asked why Microsoft has made such a major change. There are three main reasons: performance, extensibility, and proliferation.

Better Performance

How does moving to .NET data providers improve performance? When you write ADO code, you're essentially using the ADO interfaces as middlemen when communicating with your data store. You tell ADO which provider you want to use, and ADO forwards your calls to the appropriate provider. The provider performs the requested action and returns the result to you through the ADO library.

.NET data providers don't involve a middle layer. You communicate directly with the data provider, which communicates with your data store using the data store's low-level programming interfaces. Communicating with SQL Server by using the SQL Client .NET Data Provider in ADO.NET is faster than using ADO and the SQL Server OLE DB provider because one less layer is involved.

Greater Extensibility

When SQL Server 2000 introduced XML features, the ADO development team faced an interesting challenge. To add features to ADO that would let developers retrieve XML data from SQL Server 2000, the ADO development team had to add new interfaces to the OLE DB API and to the SQL Server OLE DB provider.

.NET data providers are more easily extensible. They need to support only the same basic interfaces and can provide additional provider-specific features when appropriate. The SQL Client .NET Data Provider's *Command* object (*SqlCommand*) exposes all the same methods and properties that its OLE DB .NET Data Provider counterpart does, but it also adds a method to fetch the results of a query as XML.

SQL Server 2005 includes a suite of new features, including the ability to have applications use Notification Services to receive notifications when the results of a query change on the server. Rather than change the inner workings of ADO.NET's common classes, Microsoft simply introduced two new classes to the SQL Client .NET Data Provider to leverage these new SQL Server features.

Proliferation

Microsoft first shipped OLE DB providers for SQL Server, Microsoft Access, and Oracle with the release of the Microsoft Data Access Components (MDAC) version 2.0 in July 1998. Microsoft and other development teams have created native OLE DB providers to communicate with other data stores, but not a whole lot of OLE DB providers are available. If you're using

ADO but aren't using a Microsoft-built OLE DB provider, there's a high probability that you're using an ODBC (OLE DB's predecessor) driver instead. Many more ODBC drivers are available, primarily because they were easier to develop. Many developers simply found it too difficult to build their own OLE DB providers.

By comparison, a .NET data provider is simple to write. There are far fewer interfaces to implement. Microsoft simplified the process of building providers for ADO.NET so that developers can build .NET data providers more easily. The more .NET data providers there are, the more different data sources you can access via ADO.NET.

I wrote the previous two paragraphs for the first edition of this book. Since that time, .NET Data Providers have been developed by database vendors, independent software vendors and various open source projects. There are fewer and fewer teams producing new versions of OLE DB providers. At the time of writing the second edition of this book, most teams that are creating components to be used from Microsoft development technologies are focusing on producing .NET Data Providers, ODBC drivers, or both.

Coverage of .NET Data Providers in This Book

Because each .NET data provider implements the same base interfaces, there's no need for me to explain the use of these interfaces for every .NET data provider. Instead, I'll mostly focus on one provider: the SQL Client .NET Data Provider. In the first edition of the book, I focused on the OLE DB .NET Data Provider, but OLE DB providers have fallen out of vogue, as has the OLE DB .NET Data Provider. Plus, the SQL Client .NET Data Provider offers a ton of new features—asynchronous query execution, batch updating, query notifications, and bulk copy, to name just a few.

Appendix A discusses the features of the other three .NET data providers, as well as the common provider model. Chapter 12 addresses the SQL XML .NET Data Provider to demonstrate the use of some of ADO.NET's XML features. Because the SQL XML .NET Data Provider offers no new features and omits many classes included in other .NET data providers, it's generally not considered a full-fledged .NET data provider.

If I'm discussing a class that's common to all .NET data providers, I'll often refer to it by its provider-independent name—for example, *DataAdapter* rather than *SqlDataAdapter* or *OdbcDataAdapter*.

Connected Objects

The ADO.NET object model includes classes designed to help you communicate directly with your data source. I'll refer to such classes, which appear to the left of the dotted line in Figure 1-1 (shown earlier), as ADO.NET's "connected" classes. Most of these classes represent basic data access concepts such as the physical connection to the database, a query, and the query's results.

ProviderFactory Class

A *ProviderFactory* class is new to ADO.NET 2.0 and acts as an object factory, allowing you to create instances of other classes for your .NET data provider. Each *ProviderFactory* class offers a *Create* method that creates Connections, ConnectionStringBuilders, Commands, Parameters, DataAdapters and CommandBuilders.

Connection Class

A *Connection* object represents a connection to your data source. You can specify the type of data source, its location, and other attributes through the various properties of the *Connection* class. A *Connection* object is roughly equivalent to an ADO *Connection* object or a DAO *Database* object; you use it to connect to and disconnect from your database. A *Connection* object acts as a conduit through which other objects, such as *DataAdapter* and *Command* objects, communicate with your database to submit queries and retrieve results.

ConnectionStringBuilder Class

The *ConnectionStringBuilder* class is new to ADO.NET 2.0 and simplifies the process of building connection strings for a .NET data provider. Each *ConnectionStringBuilder* class exposes properties that correspond to options available in that .NET data provider's connection strings. For example, the *OdbcConnectionStringBuilder* class exposes a *Driver* property and the *OleDbConnectionStringBuilder* class exposes a *Provider* property. Once you've used your *ConnectionStringBuilder* to build your connection string, you can access the connection string by using the *ConnectionStringBuilder* object's *ConnectionString* property.

Command Class

Command objects are similar in structure to ADO *Command* or DAO *QueryDef* objects. They can represent a query against your database, a call to a stored procedure, or a direct request to return the contents of a specific table.

Databases support many types of queries. Some queries retrieve rows of data by referencing one or more tables or views or by calling a stored procedure. Other queries modify rows of data, and still others manipulate the structure of the database by creating or modifying objects such as tables, views, or stored procedures. You can use a *Command* object to execute any of these types of queries against your database.

Using a *Command* object to query your database is rather straightforward. You set the *Connection* property to a *Connection* object that connects to your database and then specify the text for your query in the *CommandText* property. You can supply a standard SQL query such as this one:

```
SELECT CustomerID, CompanyName, ContactName, Phone FROM Customers
```

You can also supply just the name of a table, view, or stored procedure and use the *Command* object's *CommandType* property for the type of query you want to execute. The *Command* class offers different ways to execute your query. If the query does not return rows, simply call the *ExecuteNonQuery* method. The *Command* class also has an *ExecuteReader* method, which returns a *DataReader* object that you can use to examine the rows returned by your query. If you only want to retrieve the first column of the first row returned by the query, you can save yourself a few lines of code by calling the *Command* object's *ExecuteScalar* method instead. The *SqlCommand* includes a fourth execution method, *ExecuteXmlReader*, that is similar to *ExecuteReader* but is designed to handle queries that return results in XML format.

DataReader Class

The *DataReader* class is designed to help you retrieve and examine the rows returned by your query as quickly as possible. You can use the *DataReader* class to examine the results of a query one row at a time. When you move forward to the next row, the contents of the previous row are discarded. The *DataReader* doesn't support updating. The data returned by the *DataReader* is read-only. Because the *DataReader* class supports such a minimal set of features, it's extremely fast and lightweight.

Developers with experience using cursors in previous data access technologies may recognize the DataReader as a forward-only read-only cursor, or a firehose cursor.

Transaction Class

At times, you might want to group a number of changes to your database and treat them as a single unit of work. In database programming, that unit of work is called a *transaction*. Let's say that your database contains banking information and has tables for checking and savings accounts and a user wants to transfer money from a savings account to a checking account. In your code, you'll want to make sure that the withdrawal from savings and the deposit to checking complete successfully as a single unit or that neither change occurs. You use a transaction to accomplish this.

The *Connection* class has a *BeginTransaction* method that you can use to create *Transaction* objects. You use a *Transaction* object to either commit or cancel the changes you make to your database during the lifetime of the *Transaction* object. In our banking example, the changes to both the savings and checking accounts would be included in a single transaction and, therefore, would be either committed or cancelled as a single unit of work.

Parameter Class

Say that you want to query your Orders table for all the orders for a particular customer. Your query will look something like this:

```
SELECT CustomerID, CompanyName, CompanyName, Phone FROM Customers
    WHERE CustomerID = 'ALFKI'
```

The value you use for the CustomerID column in the query's *WHERE* clause depends on the customer whose orders you want to examine. But if you use this type of query, you must modify the text for the query each time you want to examine the orders for a different customer.

To simplify the process of executing such queries, you can replace the value for the CustomerID column with a parameter marker, as shown in the following query:

```
SELECT CustomerID, CompanyName, CompanyName, Phone FROM Customers
    WHERE CustomerID = @CustomerID
```

Then, prior to executing the query, you supply a value for the parameter. Many developers rely heavily on parameterized queries because they can help simplify your programming and make for more efficient code.

To use a parameterized *Command* object, you create *Parameter* objects for each of the parameters in your query and append them to the *Command* object's *Parameters* collection. The ADO.NET *Parameter* class exposes properties and methods that let you define the data type and value for your parameters. To work with a stored procedure that returns data through output parameters, you set the *Parameter* object's *Direction* property to the appropriate value from the *ParameterDirection* enumeration.

DataAdapter Class

The *DataAdapter* class represents a new concept for Microsoft data access models; it has no true equivalent in ADO or DAO, although you can consider the ADO *Command* and DAO *QueryDef* objects to be its second cousins, once removed.

DataAdapter objects act as a bridge between your database and the disconnected objects in the ADO.NET object model. The *Fill* method, which is part of the *DataAdapter* object class, provides an efficient mechanism to fetch the results of a query into a *DataSet* or a *DataTable* so you can work with your data offline. You can also use *DataAdapter* objects to submit the pending changes stored in your *DataSet* objects to your database.

The ADO.NET *DataAdapter* class exposes a number of properties that are actually *Command* objects. For instance, the *SelectCommand* property contains a *Command* object that represents the query you'll use to populate your *DataSet* object. The *DataAdapter* class also has *UpdateCommand*, *InsertCommand*, and *DeleteCommand* properties that correspond to *Command* objects you use when you submit modified, new, or deleted rows to your database, respectively.

These *Command* objects provide updating functionality that was automatic (or "automagic," depending on your perspective) in the ADO and DAO *Recordset* objects. For example, when you run a query in ADO to generate a *Recordset* object, the ADO cursor engine asks the databases for metadata about the query to determine where the results came from. ADO then uses that metadata to build the updating logic to translate changes in your *Recordset* object into changes in your database.

So why does the ADO.NET *DataAdapter* class have separate *UpdateCommand*, *InsertCommand*, and *DeleteCommand* properties? To allow you to define your own updating logic. The updating functionality in ADO and DAO is fairly limited in the sense that both object models translate changes in *Recordset* objects into action queries that directly reference tables in your database. To maintain the security and integrity of the data, many database administrators restrict access to the tables in their databases so that the only way to change the contents of a table is to call a stored procedure. ADO and DAO don't know how to submit changes using a stored procedure; neither provides mechanisms that let you specify your own updating logic. The ADO.NET *DataAdapter* does.

With a *DataAdapter* object, you can set the *UpdateCommand*, *InsertCommand*, and *Delete-Command* properties to call the stored procedures that will modify, add, or delete rows in the appropriate table in your database. Then you can simply call the *Update* method on the *DataAdapter* object and ADO.NET will use the *Command* objects you've created to submit the cached changes in your *DataSet* to your database.

As I stated earlier, the *DataAdapter* class populates tables in the *DataSet* object and also reads cached changes and submits them to your database. To keep track of what goes where, a *DataAdapter* has some supporting properties. The *TableMappings* collection is a property used to track which table in your database corresponds to which table in your *DataSet* object. Each table mapping has a similar property for mapping columns, appropriately called a *ColumnMappings* collection.

Disconnected Classes

You've seen that you can use the connected classes in a .NET data provider to connect to a data source, submit queries, and examine their results. However, these connected classes let you examine data only as a forward-only, read-only stream of data. What if you want to sort, search, filter, or modify the results of your queries?

The ADO.NET object model includes classes to provide such functionality. These classes act as an offline data cache. Once you've fetched the results of your query into a *DataTable* (which we'll discuss shortly), you can close the connection to your data source and continue to work with the data. As mentioned earlier, because these classes do not require a live connection to your data source, we call them "disconnected" classes.

Let's look at the disconnected classes in the ADO.NET object model.

DataTable Class

The ADO.NET *DataTable* class is similar to the ADO and DAO *Recordset* classes. A *DataTable* object allows you to examine data through collections of rows and columns. You can store the results of a query in a *DataTable* by calling a *DataAdapter* object's *Fill* method, as shown in the following code snippet:

Visual Basic

```
Dim strConn, strSQL As String
strConn = "Data Source=.\SQLExpress;" & _
```

```
            "Initial Catalog=Northwind;Integrated Security=True;"
strSQL = "SELECT CustomerID, CompanyName FROM Customers"
Dim da As New SqlDataAdapter(strSQL, strConn)
Dim tbl As New DataTable()
da.Fill(tbl)
```

Visual C#

```
string strConn, strSQL;
strConn = @"Data Source=.\SQLExpress;" +
            "Initial Catalog=Northwind;Integrated Security=True;";
strSQL = "SELECT CustomerID, CompanyName FROM Customers";
SqlDataAdapter da = new SqlDataAdapter(strSQL, strConn);
DataTable tbl = new DataTable();
da.Fill(tbl);
```

Once you've fetched the data from your database and stored it in a *DataTable* object, that data is disconnected from the server. You can then examine the contents of the *DataTable* object without creating any network traffic between ADO.NET and your database. By working with the data offline, you no longer require a live connection to your database, but remember that you also won't see any changes made by other users after you've run your query.

The *DataTable* class contains collections of other disconnected objects, which I'll discuss shortly. You access the contents of a *DataTable* through its *Rows* property, which returns a collection of *DataRow* objects. If you want to examine the structure of a *DataTable*, you use its *Columns* property to retrieve a collection of *DataColumn* objects. The *DataTable* class also lets you define constraints, such as a primary key, on the data stored within the class. You can access these constraints through the *DataTable* object's *Constraints* property.

DataColumn Class

Each *DataTable* has a *Columns* collection, which is a container for *DataColumn* objects. As its name implies, a *DataColumn* object corresponds to a column in your table. However, a *DataColumn* object doesn't actually contain the data stored in your *DataTable*. Instead, it stores information about the structure of the column. This type of information, data about data, is commonly called *metadata*. For example, *DataColumn* exposes a *DataType* property that describes the data type (such as string or integer) that the column stores. The *Data-Column* class has other properties such as *ReadOnly*, *AllowDBNull*, *Unique*, *Default*, and *AutoIncrement* that allow you to control whether the data in the column can be updated, restrict what can be stored in the column, or dictate how values should be generated for new rows of data.

The *DataColumn* class also exposes an *Expression* property, which you can use to define how the data in the column is calculated. A common practice is to base a column in a query on an expression rather than on the contents of a column in a table in your database. For example, in the sample Northwind database that accompanies most Microsoft database-related products, each row in the Order Details table contains UnitPrice and Quantity columns. Traditionally, if you wanted to examine the total cost for the order item in your data structure, you would add a calculated column to the query. The following SQL example defines a calculated column called *ItemTotal*:

```
SELECT OrderID, ProductID, Quantity, UnitPrice,
     Quantity * UnitPrice AS ItemTotal
   FROM [Order Details]
```

The drawback to this technique is that the database engine performs the calculation only at the time of the query. If you modify the contents of the UnitPrice or Quantity columns in your *DataTable* object, the ItemTotal column doesn't change.

The ADO.NET *DataColumn* class defines an *Expression* property to handle this scenario more elegantly. When you check the value of a *DataColumn* object based on an expression, ADO.NET evaluates the expression and returns a newly calculated value. In this way, if you update the value of any column in the expression, the value stored in the calculated column is accurate. Here are two code snippets illustrating the use of the *Expression* property:

Visual Basic

```
Dim col As New DataColumn()
...
With col
   .ColumnName = "ItemTotal"
   .DataType = GetType(Decimal)
   .Expression = "UnitPrice * Quantity"
End With
```

Visual C#

```
DataColumn col = new DataColumn();
col.ColumnName = "ItemTotal";
col.DataType = typeof(Decimal);
col.Expression = "UnitPrice * Quantity";
```

The *Columns* collection and *DataColumn* objects can be roughly compared to the *Fields* collection and *Field* objects in ADO and DAO.

Constraint Class

The *DataTable* class also provides a way for you to place constraints on the data stored locally within a *DataTable* object. For example, you can build a *Constraint* object that ensures that the values in a column, or multiple columns, are unique within the *DataTable*. *Constraint* objects are maintained in a *DataTable* object's *Constraints* collection.

DataRow Class

To access the actual values stored in a *DataTable* object, you use the object's *Rows* collection, which contains a series of *DataRow* objects. To examine the data stored in a specific column of a particular row, use the *Item* property of the appropriate *DataRow* object to read the value for any column in that row. The *DataRow* class provides several overloaded definitions of its *Item* property. You can specify which column to view by passing the column name, index value, or associated *DataColumn* object to a *DataRow* object's *Item* property. Because *Item* is the default property of the *DataRow* class, you can use it implicitly, as shown in the following code snippets:

Visual Basic

```
Dim row As DataRow
row = tbl.Rows(0)
Console.WriteLine(row(0))
Console.WriteLine(row("CustomerID"))
Console.WriteLine(row(tbl.Columns("CustomerID")))
```

Visual C#

```
DataRow row;
row = tbl.Rows[0];
Console.WriteLine(row[0]);
Console.WriteLine(row["CustomerID"]);
Console.WriteLine(row[MyTable.Columns["CustomerID"]]);
```

Rather than return the data for just the current row, the *DataTable* makes all rows of data available through a collection of *DataRows*. This is a marked change in behavior from the ADO and DAO *Recordset* objects, which expose only a single row of data at a time, thereby requiring you to navigate through its contents by using methods such as *MoveNext*. The following code snippet is an example of looping through the contents of an ADO *Recordset*:

Visual Basic "Classic"

```
Dim strConn As String, strSQL As String
Dim rs As ADODB.Recordset
strConn = "Provider=SQLOLEDB;Data Source=.\SQLExpress;" & _
          "Initial Catalog=Northwind;Integrated Security=SSPI;"
strSQL = "SELECT CustomerID, CompanyName FROM Customers"
Set rs = New ADODB.Recordset
rs.CursorLocation = adUseClient
rs.Open strSQL, strConn, adOpenStatic, adLockReadOnly, adCmdText
Do While Not rs.EOF
    Debug.Print rs("CustomerID")
    rs.MoveNext
Loop
```

To examine the contents of an ADO.NET *DataTable*, you loop through the *DataRow* objects contained in the *DataTable* object's *Rows* property, as shown in the following code snippet:

Visual Basic

```
Dim strSQL, strConn As String
strConn = "Data Source=.\SQLExpress;" & _
          "Initial Catalog=Northwind;Integrated Security=True;"
strSQL = "SELECT CustomerID, CompanyName FROM Customers"
Dim da As New SqlDataAdapter(strSQL, strConn)
Dim tbl As New DataTable()
da.Fill(tbl)
For Each row As DataRow In tbl.Rows
    Console.WriteLine(row("CustomerID"))
Next row
```

Visual C#

```
string strSQL, strConn;
strConn = @"Data Source=.\SQLExpress;" +
           "Initial Catalog=Northwind;Integrated Security=True;";
strSQL = "SELECT CustomerID, CompanyName FROM Customers";
SqlDataAdapter da = new SqlDataAdapter(strSQL, strConn);
DataTable tbl = new DataTable();
da.Fill(tbl);
foreach (DataRow row in tbl.Rows)
    Console.WriteLine(row["CustomerID"]);
```

The *DataRow* class is also the starting point for your updates. For example, you can call the *BeginEdit* method of a *DataRow* object, change the value of some columns in that row through the *Item* property, and then call the *EndEdit* method to save the changes to that row. Calling a *DataRow* object's *CancelEdit* method lets you cancel the changes made in the current editing session. The *DataRow* class also exposes methods to delete or remove an item from the *Data-Table* object's collection of *DataRows*.

When you change the contents of a row, the *DataRow* caches those changes so that you can later submit them to your database. Thus, when you change the value of a column in a row, the *DataRow* maintains that column's original value as well as its current value to successfully update the database. The *Item* property of a *DataRow* object also allows you to examine the original value of a column when the row has a pending change.

DataSet Class

A *DataSet* object, as its name indicates, contains a set of data. You can think of a *DataSet* object as the container for a number of *DataTable* objects (stored in the *DataSet* object's *Tables* collection). Remember that ADO.NET was created to help developers build large multi-tiered database applications. At times, you might want to access a component running on a middle-tier server to retrieve the contents of many tables. Rather than having to repeatedly call the server in order to fetch that data one table at a time, you can package all the data into a *DataSet* object and return it in a single call. But a *DataSet* object does a great deal more than act as a container for multiple *DataTable* objects.

The data stored in a *DataSet* object is disconnected from your database. Any changes you make to the data are simply cached in each *DataRow*. When it's time to send these changes to your database, it might not be efficient to send the entire *DataSet* back to your middle-tier server. You can use the *GetChanges* method to extract just the modified rows from your *DataSet*. In this way, you pass less data between the different processes or servers.

The *DataSet* class also exposes a *Merge* method, which can act as a complement to the *GetChanges* method. The middle-tier server you use to submit changes to your database, using the smaller *DataSet* returned by the *Merge* method, might return a *DataSet* that contains newly retrieved data. You can use the *DataSet* class's *Merge* method to combine the contents of two *DataSet* objects into a single *DataSet*. This is another example that shows how ADO.NET was developed with multi-tiered applications in mind. Previous Microsoft data access models have no comparable feature.

You can create a *DataSet* object and populate its *Tables* collection with information without having to communicate with a database. In previous data access models, you generally need to query a database before adding new rows locally, and then later submit them to the database. With ADO.NET, you don't need to communicate with your database until you're ready to submit the new rows.

The *DataSet* class also has features that allow you to write it to and read it from a file or an area of memory. You can save just the contents of the *DataSet* object, just the structure of the *DataSet* object, or both. ADO.NET stores this data as an XML document. Because ADO.NET and XML are so tightly coupled, moving data back and forth between ADO.NET *DataSet* objects and XML documents is a snap. You can thus take advantage of one of the most powerful features of XML: its ability to easily transform the structure of your data. For example, you can use an Extensible Stylesheet Language (XSL) transformation template to convert data exported to an XML document into HTML.

DataRelation Class

The tables in your database are usually related in some fashion. For example, in the Northwind database, each entry in the Orders table relates to an entry in the Customers table, so you can determine which customer placed which orders. You'll probably want to use related data from multiple tables in your application. The ADO.NET *DataSet* class handles data from related DataTable objects with a little help from *DataRelation* class.

The DataSet class exposes a *Relations* property, which is a collection of *DataRelation* objects. You can use a *DataRelation* object to indicate a relationship between different *DataTable* objects in your *DataSet*. Once you've created your *DataRelation* object, you can use code such as the following to retrieve an array of *DataRow* objects for the orders that correspond to a particular customer:

Visual Basic
```
Dim ds As DataSet
Dim tblCustomers, tblOrders As DataTable
Dim rel As DataRelation

'The code for creating the DataSet goes here.

rel = ds.Relations.Add("Customers_Orders", _
                        tblCustomers.Columns("CustomerID"), _
                        tblOrders.Columns("CustomerID"))

For Each rowCustomer As DataRow In tblCustomers.Rows
    Console.WriteLine(rowCustomer("CompanyName"))
    For Each rowOrder As DataRow In rowCustomer.GetChildRows(rel)
        Console.WriteLine("  {0}", rowOrder("OrderID"))
    Next rowOrder
    Console.WriteLine()
Next rowCustomer
```

Visual C#

```
DataSet ds;
DataTable tblCustomers, tblOrders;
DataRelation rel;

//Create and initialize DataSet.

rel = ds.Relations.Add("Customers_Orders",
                       tblCustomers.Columns["CustomerID"],
                       tblOrders.Columns["CustomerID"]);

foreach (DataRow rowCustomer in tblCustomers.Rows) {
    Console.WriteLine(rowCustomer["CompanyName"]);
    foreach (DataRow rowOrder in rowCustomer.GetChildRows(rel))
        Console.WriteLine("  {0}", rowOrder["OrderID"]);
    Console.WriteLine();
}
```

DataRelation objects also expose properties that allow you to enforce referential integrity. For example, you can set a *DataRelation* object so that if you modify the value of the primary key field in the parent row, the change cascades down to the child rows automatically. You can also set your *DataRelation* object so that if you delete a row in one *DataTable*, the corresponding rows in any child *DataTable* objects, as defined by the relation, are automatically deleted as well.

DataView Class

Once you've retrieved the results of a query into a *DataTable* object, you can use a *DataView* object to view the data in different ways. If you want to sort the contents of a *DataTable* object based on a column, simply set the *DataView* object's *Sort* property to the name of that column. You can also set the *Filter* property on a *DataView* so that only the rows that match certain criteria are visible.

You can use multiple *DataView* objects to examine the same *DataTable* at the same time. For example, you can have two grids on a form, one showing all customers in alphabetical order, and the other showing the rows ordered by a different field, such as state or region. To show each view, you bind each grid to a different *DataView* object, but both *DataView* objects reference the same *DataTable*. This feature prevents you from having to maintain two copies of your data in separate structures. We'll discuss this in more detail in Chapter 8.

Metadata

ADO and DAO allow you to create a *Recordset* based on the results returned by your query. The data access engine examines the columns of data in the result set and populates the *Recordset* object's *Fields* collection based on this information, setting the name, data type, and so forth.

ADO.NET offers you a choice. You can use just a couple lines of code and let ADO.NET determine the structure of the results automatically, or you can use more code that includes metadata about the structure of the results of your query.

Why would you choose the option that involves writing more code? The main benefits are increased functionality and better performance. But how could having more code make your application run faster? That seems counterintuitive, doesn't it?

Unless you're writing an ad hoc query tool, you'll generally know what the structure of your query results will look like. For example, most ADO code looks something like the following:

```
Dim rs as Recordset
'Declare other variables here.
⋮
'Initialize variables and establish connection to database.
⋮
rs.Open strSQL, cnDatabase, adOpenStatic, adLockOptimistic, adCmdText
Do While Not rs.EOF
    List1.AddItem rs.Fields("UserName").Value
    rs.MoveNext
Loop
```

In this code snippet, the programmer knows that the query contains a column named UserName. The point is that as a developer, you generally know what columns your query will return and what data types those columns use. But ADO doesn't know in advance what the results of the query will look like. As a result, ADO has to query the OLE DB provider to ask questions such as "How many columns are there in the results of this query?" "What are the data types for each of those columns?" "Where did this data come from?" and "What are the primary key fields for each table referenced in this query?" The OLE DB provider can answer some of these questions, but in many cases it must call back to the database.

To retrieve the results of your query and store this data in a *DataSet* object, ADO.NET needs to know the answers to such questions. You can supply this information yourself or force ADO.NET to ask the provider for this information. Your code will run faster using the former option because asking the provider for this information at run time can result in a significant performance hit compared to supplying your own metadata through code.

Writing code to prepare the structure for your *DataSet* can become tedious, even if it improves the performance of your application. Thankfully, Visual Studio includes design-time data access features that offer the best of both worlds. For example, you can create a *DataSet* object based on a query, a table name, or a stored procedure, and then a configuration wizard will generate ADO.NET code to run the query and support submitting updates back to your database. We'll take a close look at many of these Visual Studio features in upcoming chapters.

Strongly Typed *DataSet* Classes

Visual Studio also helps you simplify the process of building data access applications by generating strongly typed *DataSet*. Let's say that we have a simple table named Orders that contains two columns, CustomerID and CompanyName. You don't have to write code such as the following.

Visual Basic
```
Dim ds As DataSet
'Create and fill DataSet.
Console.WriteLine(ds.Tables("Customers").Rows(0)("CustomerID"))
```

Visual C#
```
DataSet ds;
//Create and fill DataSet.
Console.WriteLine(ds.Tables["Customers"].Rows[0]["CustomerID"]);
```

Instead, we can write code like this:

Visual Basic
```
Dim ds As CustomersDataSet
'Create and fill DataSet.
Console.WriteLine(ds.Customers(0).CustomerID)
```

Visual C#
```
CustomersDataSet ds;
//Create and fill DataSet.
Console.WriteLine(ds.Customers[0].CustomerID);
```

The strongly typed *DataSet* is simply a class that Visual Studio builds with all the table and column information available through properties. Strongly typed *DataSet* objects also expose custom methods for such features as creating new rows. So instead of code that looks like the following:

Visual Basic
```
Dim ds as DataSet
'Code to create DataSet and customers DataTable
Dim rowNewCustomer As DataRow
rowNewCustomer = ds.Tables("Customers").NewRow()
rowNewCustomer("CustomerID") = "ALFKI"
rowNewCustomer("CompanyName") = "Alfreds Futterkiste"
ds.Tables("Customers").Rows.Add(rowNewCustomer)
```

Visual C#
```
DataSet ds;
//Code to create DataSet and customers DataTable
DataRow rowNewCustomer;
rowNewCustomer = ds.Tables["Customers"].NewRow();
rowNewCustomer["CustomerID"] = "ALFKI";
rowNewCustomer["CompanyName"] = "Alfreds Futterkiste";
ds.Tables["Customers"].Rows.Add(rowNewCustomer);
```

We can create and add a new row to our table in a single line of code, such as this:

```
ds.Customers.AddCustomersRow("ALFKI", "Alfreds Futterkiste")
```

We'll take a closer look at strongly typed *DataSet* objects in Chapter 9.

Questions That Should Be Asked More Frequently

Despite what its name implies, ADO.NET bears little resemblance to ADO. Although ADO.NET has classes that allow you to connect to your database, submit queries, and retrieve the results, the object model as a whole is very different from that of ADO. By now, you've probably picked up on many of those differences. In the coming chapters, we'll take a closer look at the main objects in the ADO.NET hierarchy. But before we do, it's worth addressing some of the questions that developers who are new to ADO.NET are likely to ask.

Q   Why didn't you mention cursors?

A   ADO.NET does not support server-side cursors. Future releases might include such functionality. Currently, no object in the ADO.NET hierarchy acts as an interface to a server-side cursor. The *DataSet* and *DataTable* classes most closely resemble a client-side ADO Recordset class. The *DataReader* class most closely resembles a server-side ADO *Recordset* class that uses a forward-only, read-only cursor.

Q   How do I set the current position in a *DataTable* using ADO.NET? Previous object models exposed such methods as *MoveFirst* and *MoveNext*. Where are the positional properties and move methods?

A   The *DataTable* class exposes a *Rows* collection (of *DataRow* objects) that you can use to reference any row in the table at any given time; therefore, the *DataTable* class has no concept of a current row. Because any row can be addressed directly, there is no need for positional properties or navigation methods such as *MoveFirst*, *MoveLast*, *MoveNext*, and *MovePrevious*.

These positional properties and move methods were used in ADO most often when displaying data on a form.

Chapter 2

Building Your First ADO.NET Application with Microsoft Visual Studio 2005

Many books for developers focus on snippets of code in several chapters before piecing together those snippets to construct a simple working application. Instead of following this standard approach, I'll use this chapter to show you how to build a quick and simple application that will illustrate some major features of Microsoft ADO.NET.

Everyone Loves a Demo

I've learned from the developer conferences I've attended and spoken at that everyone loves a good demo. It's so much easier to discuss features and look at code once you've seen that code in action. So I'll start this discussion with a demo.

The Data Form Wizard Has Been Deprecated

The first edition of this book used the Visual Studio 2002 Data Form Wizard to build a data-bound form in a few simple steps. That wizard walked you through a series of steps, prompting you for information. The wizard then used that information to create a new form and to add controls, other components, and a lot of code to the form. I use the past tense here to describe the wizard because it is no longer necessary.

The Visual Studio design-time data-access features have been completely overhauled in Visual Studio 2005. You can now build simple data-access applications without writing code and without using the Data Form Wizard. In this chapter, we'll walk through the steps necessary to create a simple data-access application that allows the user to retrieve, view, and modify data from a database and to send the changes back to the database. Along the way, we'll discuss some objects and concepts involved in creating this small application. We'll also look at the code generated automatically by Visual Studio. The sample application will also serve as a preview for many objects, features, and concepts covered in later chapters.

> **Note**   Many developers hate wizards. Well, maybe *hate* is too strong a word, but developers often don't trust wizards, especially ones that use "black-box technology." The Data Form Wizard created a new form, but you couldn't re-run the wizard to add more columns of data or a related table of information to a form the wizard already generated. The Data Source Configuration Wizard, which we'll discuss shortly, allows for more iterative programming.

This chapter will focus on the design-time data-access features built for Microsoft Windows Forms Applications, often called WinForms. There are also design-time data-access features for Web applications, powerful features that make building Web applications simpler than in previous versions of Microsoft Visual Studio. I've chosen to focus on the WinForms features because it's easier to peel back the layers in the designers and the code they generate—an approach that better lends itself to learning about ADO.NET.

This chapter is designed to help you create a simple application using the sample *Northwind* database. Products such as Microsoft SQL Server 2000 and most versions of Microsoft Access include this database. The structure of the *Northwind* database might vary slightly from one product or version to the next, but it always contains tables such as Customers, Orders, Products, and Employees.

This book assumes that you have access to a *Northwind* database. The various editions of Microsoft SQL Server 2005 no longer include this sample database. See the "SQL Server for the Masses! (Redux)" sidebar for code that will help create the *Northwind* database on SQL Server 2005 and SQL Server Express databases. The sidebar also discusses why this book uses the *Northwind* database rather than the more recently added SQL Server sample database named *AdventureWorks*.

Creating Your Data Access Form Without Code

Now, let's create a simple Windows application that will let us interact with data in a database.

Create the New Project

Launch Visual Studio, and use the Visual Studio menu (File | New | Project) to create a new project. Using the resulting dialog box, create a new Windows Application project, as shown in Figure 2-1. This chapter will assume the project is named Chapter02, but you can name your project whatever you'd like.

Now that we have a new project, let's start using the Visual Studio design-time data-access features to start building our project.

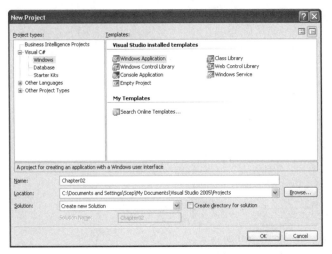

Figure 2-1   Creating a new Windows Application project

Add a New Data Source

On the Visual Studio menu, you'll see an item named Data. Select that menu item and you'll see a submenu that includes an item to add a new data source, as shown in Figure 2-2.

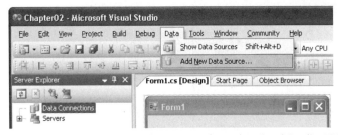

Figure 2-2   Adding a new data source from the Visual Studio 2005 menu

Visual Studio 2005 lets you quickly and easily create classes designed to contain data from a database, a Web service, or a collection of objects. Selecting the Add New Data Source sub-menu item launches the Data Source Configuration Wizard. You can use this wizard to quickly create a class designed to store multiple tables of information from your database. The first step in the wizard, shown in Figure 2-3, asks which type of data source you want to create. Select Database, and click Next.

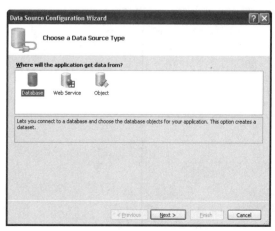

Figure 2-3   Specifying a database data source type

Choose Your Connection

Once you've specified that you want to create a data source based on a database, the Data Source Configuration Wizard asks for information about how to connect to your database, as shown in Figure 2-4.

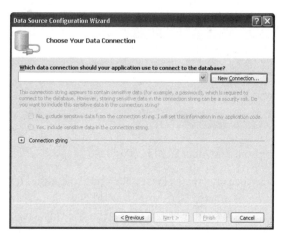

Figure 2-4   Choosing a connection

If you've already established connections to databases from Visual Studio, those connections are listed in the drop-down menu shown in Figure 2-4. If you select an item from the drop-down list, you can then use the options in the dialog box to examine the connection string (by clicking the + button) and to exclude sensitive data, such as password information, from the connection string.

To create a new connection, click the New Connection button. This action will launch a dialog box that will prompt you for information about how to connect to your database. Before you focus on that dialog box and the options available to you, take some time to read the sidebar titled "SQL Server for the Masses! (Redux)" for a brief overview of the new edition of Microsoft SQL Server.

SQL Server for the Masses! (Redux)

With the release of SQL Server 2005, Microsoft has created a new edition of SQL Server—Express. SQL Server Express is a royalty-free, redistributable database package.

This story might sound familiar and might also deserve a sidebar within a sidebar. You might recall that Microsoft released a product with similar goals and features called Microsoft Desktop Engine 2000 (MSDE). In fact, the first edition to this book had a sidebar called "SQL Server for the Masses!" dedicated to MSDE. Unfortunately, there were some minor problems with MSDE 2000—it contained no tool support and few developers seemed to know its limitations compared with the Standard edition. There are newsgroups littered with developers asking questions about how or whether queries were throttled on MSDE scenarios, and most of the "answers" are incorrect, including mine.

The SQL Server team has worked hard to address these issues. The SQL Server Express site includes clear guidelines that show how this new edition differs from its related editions: Workgroup, Standard, and Enterprise. If you already have the SQL Server 2005 tools (SQL Server Management Studio) installed, you can use them to access your SQL Server Express database. If not, you can download SQL Server Management Studio Express from the SQL Server Express site. For more information, see the SQL Server Express site at *http://www.microsoft.com/sql/editions/express/default.mspx*.

Like Microsoft Access databases, SQL Server Express is a royalty-free, redistributable database package. However, unlike Access databases and the Jet database engine, SQL Server Express is a true client/server database system, just like SQL Server. The database files you use for a SQL Server Express database can be used with other SQL Server versions. Also, like other SQL Server editions, SQL Server Express supports both standard and integrated security. SQL Server Express offers many of the same features of other SQL Server editions because it contains the same database engine. As a result, you can take an application built to work with SQL Server Express and move to the Workgroup, Standard, or Enterprise edition of SQL Server with minimal effort.

There are some important differences between SQL Server Express and other editions to keep in mind. SQL Server Express does not provide many of the same high-end features that are available in other editions. SQL Server Express supports databases up to 4 GB in size, whereas other editions can handle larger databases. Also, SQL Server Express does not support database partitioning, backup log shipping, failover clustering, full-text search, and other features associated with the higher-end editions of SQL Server.

The connection and query strings used throughout this book are written to communicate with the local instance of SQL Server 2005 Express, and they assume you've installed the sample *Northwind* and *pubs* databases. These databases are no longer included by default but, thankfully, they're easy to install using SQL Server Management Studio (or the Express edition). The install scripts for these databases (instnwind.sql for *Northwind* and instpubs.sql for *pubs*) are included with the .NET 2.0 SDK that comes with Visual Studio 2005, and they're installed to C:\Program Files\Microsoft Visual

Studio 8\SDK\v2.0\Samples\Setup. Open these files in SQL Server Management Studio (or the Express edition), as shown in Figure 2-5, and then click the Execute button.

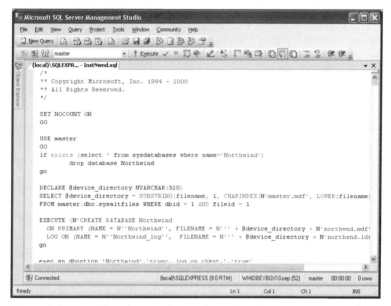

Figure 2-5 Installing the sample *Northwind* database using Microsoft SQL Server Management Studio Express

You can also execute these and other scripts through code using SQL Management Objects (SMO), a new object model designed to let you access and modify the structure of SQL Server programmatically. The sample code that follows shows how to use SMO to execute scripts to install the sample *Northwind* and *pubs* databases and then print a list of available databases, tables, and logins. For more information on SMO, see SQL Server Books Online.

The code assumes that you have references to the *Microsoft.SqlServer.Smo* and *Microsoft.SqlServer.ConnectionInfo* assemblies. The code is also written with the assumption that you're using the construct of choice for your language (*Imports* for Microsoft Visual Basic and *using* for Microsoft Visual C#) to access classes in the *System*, *System.IO*, and *Microsoft.SqlServer.Management.Smo* namespaces.

Visual Basic
```
Dim server As New Server(".\SQLExpress")
Dim dbMaster As Database = server.Databases("Master")
Dim strScriptDir As String
strScriptDir = "C:\Program Files\Microsoft Visual Studio 8\" & _
               "SDK\v2.0\Samples\Setup\"

If Not server.Databases.Contains("Northwind") Then
    Console.WriteLine("Creating Northwind database...")
    Dim rdr As New StreamReader(strScriptDir & "instnwnd.sql")
    dbMaster.ExecuteNonQuery(rdr.ReadToEnd())
End If

If Not server.Databases.Contains("pubs") Then
```

```
    Console.WriteLine("Creating pubs database...")
    Dim rdr As New StreamReader(strScriptDir & "instpubs.sql")
    dbMaster.ExecuteNonQuery(rdr.ReadToEnd())
End If

Console.WriteLine("Databases")
For Each db As Database In server.Databases
    Console.WriteLine("  {0}", db.Name)
    For Each tbl As Table In db.Tables
        Console.WriteLine("    {0}", tbl.Name)
    Next tbl
    Console.WriteLine()
Next db
```

Visual C#

```
Server server = new Server(@".\SQLExpress");
Database dbMaster = server.Databases["Master"];
string strScriptDir;
strScriptDir = @"C:\Program Files\Microsoft Visual Studio 8\" +
               @"SDK\v2.0\Samples\Setup\";

if (!server.Databases.Contains("Northwind"))
{
    Console.WriteLine("Creating Northwind database...");
    StreamReader rdr = new StreamReader(strScriptDir +
                                    "instnwnd.sql");
    dbMaster.ExecuteNonQuery(rdr.ReadToEnd());
}

if (!server.Databases.Contains("pubs"))
{
    Console.WriteLine("Creating pubs database...");
    StreamReader rdr = new StreamReader(strScriptDir +
                                    "instpubs.sql");
    dbMaster.ExecuteNonQuery(rdr.ReadToEnd());
}

Console.WriteLine("Databases");
foreach (Database db in server.Databases)
{
    Console.WriteLine("  {0}", db.Name);
    foreach (Table tbl in db.Tables)
        Console.WriteLine("    {0}", tbl.Name);
    Console.WriteLine();
}
```

Sample code in this book will continue to use the standard *Northwind* sample database that was included with SQL Server 2000 and 7.0, as well as most versions of Microsoft Access. SQL Server 2005 no longer includes this database or the old *pubs* database, although the scripts to create these databases are widely available. You can load and execute those scripts in SQL Server Management Studio for SQL Server 2005 or SQL Express Manager for SQL Express. You can also use the preceding code snippet.

The *AdventureWorks* sample database included with various editions of SQL Server 2005 and 2000 is a wonderful example of ways to partition and normalize your data, and the number of rows per table more closely resembles real-world scenarios. However, most developers I've spoken with have had a difficult time understanding the schema. Retrieving customer names and addresses, for example, requires a three-table join. The code snippets that appear in this text should be very easy to grasp conceptually. For that reason, this text will use the sample database with the more simplistic schema—*Northwind*.

I have one last note regarding SQL Server Express and Access databases. Many users ask, "Why would I want to build my application to talk to a SQL Server database? I've never had problems using Access databases in the past." Don't get me wrong. Access databases are great; they're simple, compact, and easy to redistribute with applications. However, they're not true client/server databases and are not appropriate for many applications. For example, the Jet engine used to access and modify the contents of an Access database is not thread-safe. I strongly caution against using an Access database as the data store for an ASP.NET or multitiered application.

Simply put, the Jet engine was intended for small numbers of simultaneous users and was not designed to handle larger multitiered, multithreaded applications. For example, when multiple users make changes to the same Access database, they each have a copy of the Jet engine loaded. They each query and modify the same .mdb file and also write to an .ldb file to keep track of which user has locked which records. The Jet engine might delay writing changes to the actual database file, keeping the changes cached locally. Postponing writing to the database file enhances performance for the user making the changes. The side effect to this behavior is that there will be a delay before the changes are visible to other users, which can cause problems in applications where many users might try to access and modify the same data. In other words, you should never build an airline reservation system using an Access database.

True client/server database systems such as SQL Server and Oracle take a different approach. Rather than having each application load a copy of the database engine and then forcing those engines to somehow synchronize access to the database files, the database is available through a centralized service that manages all the communication on various connections. The service then accesses and modifies the data files. Unless the transactions in use dictate otherwise, changes made on one connection are immediately available to all connections. Yes, this is a gross oversimplification of a client/server database system, but for those used to file-based databases such as Microsoft Access, Microsoft Visual FoxPro, and so on, it's a start.

Most client/server databases also include support for stored procedures, allowing you to execute additional code upon incoming changes to enforce validation rules, or take other actions such as sending mail to the purchasing department when an order for a product drops its quantity on hand below a certain level. Stored procedures offer you a central location for such logic, rather than forcing you to add such logic to all applications that interact with your data.

All right, enough of that rant. When we last left our hero, who was learning how to connect to a database...

Connect to Database

> **Note**   The samples in this text assume that you're working with a local installation of SQL Server Express with the *Northwind* sample database installed. See the sidebar titled "SQL Server for the Masses! (Redux)" for information on how to install the *Northwind* sample database.

The first time Visual Studio prompts you for connection information, you'll see the dialog box shown in Figure 2-6 that asks which type of database you want to use. The dialog box defaults to a Microsoft SQL Server database, but it provides other options such as a Microsoft SQL Server Database File, a Microsoft Access Database File, an Oracle Database, and so on.

Once you've chosen the type of database to use, you can choose that type of database as a default and prevent this dialog box from appearing in the future by selecting the Always Use This Selection check box before clicking the OK button. Even if you select this option, you can still return to this dialog box and use a different type of database later on. Once you click OK, Visual Studio will display a dialog box specifically designed to ask for more information about the type of database you've selected. This text assumes you're connecting to a SQL Server database.

Figure 2-6   Specifying the type of database to use

Once you've specified that you want to connect to a SQL Server database, you'll see the dialog box shown in Figure 2-7. This dialog box prompts you for information about the location of the SQL Server database, the credentials to use to connect to the database, and the initial catalog to use. To indicate that you're connecting to SQL Server Express running on the current machine, enter **.\SQLExpress** for the Server Name option in the dialog box. The "." character is a shortcut of sorts, which translates to "the local machine." You could supply the machine name or the "(local)" shortcut, but the "." character requires less typing and takes up less space in code snippets. The "\" character separates the machine name from the name of the SQL Server instance, and the name of the SQL Server Express instance is "SQLExpress".

Figure 2-7   Connecting to the local instance of SQL Server Express

The dialog box assumes you'll connect to the SQL Server database using Windows Authentication. By default, installations of SQL Server 2005 use the same default—requiring users to connect using their current Windows credentials rather than specifying a user name and password. If you want to log in using this second option, often called *SQL Server authentication*, select the Use SQL Server Authentication option and supply a user name and a password.

The dialog box also provides a drop-down list of available catalogs for the server. To connect to the *Northwind* database, select *Northwind* from this drop-down list. You could also select the Attach A Database File option to supply your own database file.

There's a wealth of other options available when connecting to SQL Server. Clicking the Advanced button allows you to set additional properties for the connection—such as packet size, connection pooling information, and so on—using the dialog box shown in Figure 2-8. You can also click the Test Connection button and the dialog box will attempt to connect to the database given the information you've provided.

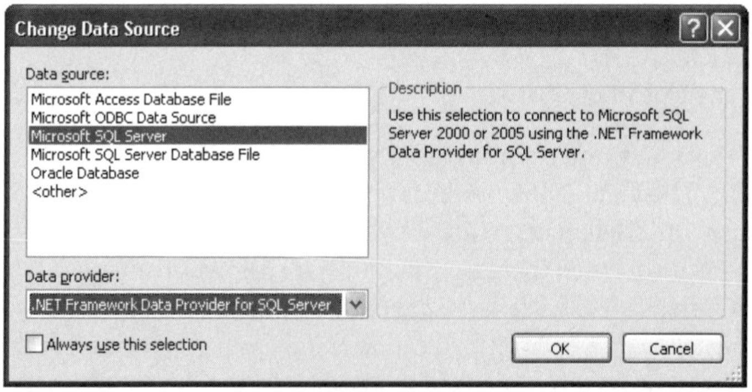

Figure 2-8   Advanced connection options

Once you've supplied information to connect to your database, click OK to accept the connection information in the dialog box, and then click the Next button in the Data Source Configuration Wizard to move on to the next option.

How Does This Relate to ADO.NET?   All this connection information is transformed into a single string, combining key words and values, separated by semicolons. Such a string is commonly called a *connection string*. For example, the information supplied in Figure 2-7 would be transformed into the following connection string:

```
Data Source=.\SQLExpress;Initial Catalog=Northwind;
Integrated Security=True;
```

The Visual Studio dialog boxes use ADO.NET classes to create this connection string. The dialog box shown in Figure 2-8 uses the *SqlConnectionStringBuilder* class, new in ADO.NET 2.0, which helps generate connection strings. This class is specifically designed to generate connection strings for SQL Server. The Test Connection button creates a new *SqlConnection* object, and it uses the connection string generated by the *SqlConnectionStringBuilder* to attempt to connect to your database. These classes are covered in more depth in Chapter 3.

The *SqlConnection* and *SqlConnectionStringBuilder* classes are part of a set of classes designed to communicate specifically with SQL Server. These classes reside in the *System.Data.SqlClient* namespace, and the set of classes is often called the SQL Client .NET Data Provider, or *SqlClient*. The generic term for a set of ADO.NET classes designed to communicate with a particular database or component is a .NET Data Provider. Version 2.0 of the .NET Framework also includes .NET Data Providers designed to talk to Oracle databases, as well as OLE DB providers and Open Database Connectivity (ODBC) drivers. In Appendix A, we'll examine how to use those .NET Data Providers and how they differ from *SqlClient*.

Connecting to Other Types of Databases   Visual Studio does not require that you work with a SQL Server database. If you want to connect to another type of database, you can click the Change button (shown in Figure 2-7), which will launch the dialog box previously shown in Figure 2-6. Visual Studio has some specialized connection information dialog boxes designed to interact with SQL Server, Access, Oracle, and ODBC data sources. You can select any of these options, and Visual Studio will launch the dialog box for that particular type of data source.

The options available in Figure 2-6 roughly translate to the different .NET Data Providers included in version 2.0 of the .NET Framework. However, Microsoft is not the only company who has built .NET Data Providers to talk to databases using ADO.NET. For example, both Oracle and IBM have produced their own .NET Data Providers designed to communicate with their databases. There's an entire community of third parties that build such components. While there is a plethora of third-party .NET Data Providers built for version 1.1 of the .NET Framework at the time of writing this text, as of yet there are no non-Microsoft .NET Data Providers built for version 2.0 of the .NET Framework.

If you have a third-party .NET Data Provider for version 2.0 of the .NET Framework installed and you want to use it to connect to your database, select <other> from the list of data sources shown in Figure 2-6, and then select the desired .NET Data Provider from the drop-down list and click OK.

Saving the Connection String

Once you've specified your connection information, the Data Source Configuration Wizard will display the dialog box shown in Figure 2-9 to ask whether you want to save the connection string in your application configuration file. Although there are many pros and cons to this approach, one key benefit is that it's a simple way to separate the connection information from the rest of your code.

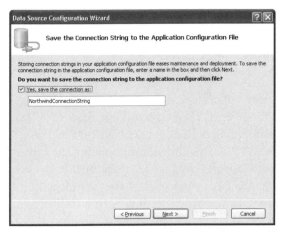

Figure 2-9   Saving the connection string in an application configuration file

Compiling the connection string into your application is, generally speaking, a bad idea. The location of your database might change after you've deployed your application. By storing the connection string in a resource that's external to your application's code, your application becomes more flexible.

If you leave the Yes, Save The Connection String As option selected in the dialog box, Visual Studio will store the connection string and the name you provide in the application configuration file for your project. Visual Studio will also add logic to your project's code to retrieve and use the connection string to communicate with your database.

Application configuration files are a standard way to store connection string information, and the classes designed to help you build and access configuration files in version 2.0 of the .NET Framework include features specifically designed for connection strings. For more information on configuration files in general, see the .NET Framework SDK. We'll cover using configuration files to store connection strings in more detail at the end of Chapter 3.

Select Tables and Columns to Display

After you've specified whether or not to store your connection string information in the application configuration file for the project, the Data Source Configuration Wizard will show all available tables, views, stored procedures, and functions in your database in the dialog box shown in Figure 2-10. You can then choose which structures you want to include in your new data source. You can also select just specific columns from tables and views.

Figure 2-10   Selecting tables and columns of information to retrieve from the database

Select the CustomerID, CompanyName, and ContactName columns from the Customers table by expanding the Customers node as shown in Figure 2-10, and select the OrderID, CustomerID, EmployeeID, and OrderDate columns from the Orders table. Choosing these columns will allow us to build a simple data-access application that demonstrates some of the more helpful features available in ADO.NET as well as helpful Visual Studio design-time data-access features.

At the bottom of the dialog box, there's an option for you to specify a name for the *DataSet*. By default, Visual Studio uses the name of the database to which you connected (*Northwind*, in our example) and appends "*DataSet*" to that name. You could change the name, but for the purposes of this walkthrough, stick with the default.

Now click the Finish button to complete the wizard and build the new data source.

How Does This Relate to ADO.NET?   The dialog box you see in Figure 2-10 uses the *GetSchema* method available on the *SqlConnection* class to get the lists of available columns, tables, views, stored procedures, and functions. There's a *GetSchema* method on the *Connection* class for each .NET Data Provider in version 2.0 of the .NET Framework, as shown in

Appendix A. The *GetSchema* method is a great way to retrieve information about the schema of your database, and it's discussed in Chapter 3.

What Did the Data Source Configuration Wizard Create?

Now that we've completed the Data Source Configuration Wizard, let's take a closer look at what the wizard has added to your project.

A New Project Item   If you look in the Solution Explorer window, you'll see a new entry in the project. If the Solution Explorer window is not visible, select View and then Server Explorer from the Visual Studio menu. The new project item, shown in Figure 2-11, contains the name specified in the dialog box shown in Figure 2-10. This new project item contains a definition of a class known as a "strongly typed *DataSet*."

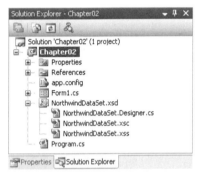

Figure 2-11   The new strongly typed *DataSet* class in the Solution Explorer window

Before we discuss strongly typed *DataSets*, let's briefly cover the standard *DataSet* class. The standard *DataSet* class contains a *DataTables* collection and a *DataRelations* collection. A *DataTable* contains collections of rows and columns of data, similar to a Microsoft Office Excel worksheet. The *DataRelation* class allows you to relate data between *DataTables*. For example, you could store separate *DataTables* of customer and order information and then use a *DataRelation* to locate the orders for a particular customer. These classes are covered in Chapter 6.

A strongly typed *DataSet* is a class that derives from a standard *DataSet*, and it makes the tables, rows, and columns of data stored in that *DataSet* available through strongly typed properties. These strongly typed properties allow you to write code such as the following:

Visual Basic
```
Dim rowCustomer As NorthwindDataSet.CustomersRow
rowCustomer = NorthwindDataSet.Customers(0)
txtCompanyName.Text = rowCustomer.CompanyName
```

Visual C#
```
NorthwindDataSet.CustomersRow rowCustomer;
rowCustomer = northwindDataSet.Customers[0];
txtCompanyName.Text = rowCustomer.CompanyName;
```

Writing code like that is preferable to writing it as follows:

Visual Basic
```
Dim rowCustomer As DataRow
rowCustomer = StandardDataSet.Tables("Customers").Rows(0)
txtCompanyName.Text = CStr(rowCustomer("CompanyName"))
```

Visual C#
```
DataRow rowCustomer;
rowCustomer = standardDataSet.Tables["Customers"].Rows[0];
txtCompanyName.Text = (string) rowCustomer["CompanyName"];
```

We'll take a closer look at strongly typed *DataSet*s in Chapter 9. For now, understand that strongly typed *DataSet*s simplify the process of writing code to access and modify the contents of a *DataSet*.

A New Connection in Server Explorer   Now look at the contents of the Server Explorer window. If you don't see it, select View and then Server Explorer from the Visual Studio menu. You should see an item in the Server Explorer tree view, shown in Figure 2-12, that corresponds to the connection you used in the Data Source Configuration Wizard.

Figure 2-12   The new connection available in Server Explorer

Server Explorer is a very helpful tool that, as its name implies, lets you explore servers. Server Explorer includes features specifically designed to interact with databases. You can use Server Explorer to examine the schema—such as tables, views, and stored procedures—in your database. You can also right-click in Server Explorer and select from options to create and execute a new query or to show the data in a table or view.

A New Data Source   Now let's look at the contents of the Data Source window to examine the structure of the Data Source we created using the wizard. If the Data Source window is not visible or you can't find it, select Data and then Show Data Sources from the Visual Studio menu. You'll see the data source you created using the wizard. If you expand each node in the tree view, the contents of your Data Source window will look like Figure 2-13.

Figure 2-13   Examining the structure of the new data source in the Data Source window

You'll see nodes for the tables you selected (Customers and Orders), with the columns you selected nested under the tables to which they belong. You might also notice that there are two distinct *Orders* nodes—one that's a child of the *NorthwindDataSet* node and one that's a child of the *Customers* node. We'll take a closer look at how these two nodes differ shortly.

Now let's learn how we can use the new data source.

Using the Data Source to Add Items to the Form

The Data Source window does more than simply let you examine the structure of your data source. You can also use the Data Source window to add items to a designer.

Adding the First Item to the Form

Select the *CustomerID* node that appears directly under the *Customers* node in the data source, and then drag the item onto the form, slightly below and to the right of the top-left corner of the form. Visual Studio will add a number of items to the form. The end result will look like Figure 2-14.

Now let's take a look at the various items that Visual Studio added to the form.

Label and **TextBox**   Visual Studio added a *Label* and *TextBox* to the form, and it set the properties of these controls based on the item you dragged onto the form. The *Label* control's *Text* property is based on the name of the column, CustomerID. Visual Studio analyzes the column name and assumes the change in casing means that "Customer" and "ID" should be separated. Visual Studio also set properties on the *TextBox* so that when you run the project, the *TextBox* will display values from the CustomerID column.

The *Name* property of both controls is also based on the item you dragged onto the form, although the actual values will depend on your language of choice. Visual Studio follows the commonly used patterns for the different languages, thus the Label's *Name* property is set to "*customerIDLabel*" if you're using Visual C# and "*CustomerIDLabel*" if you're using Visual Basic.

For more information on using controls such as *TextBox* to interact with your data, see Chapter 13.

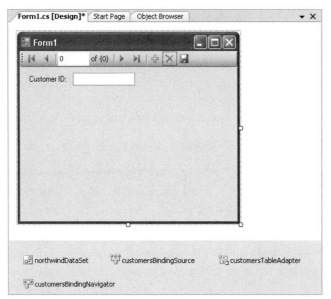

Figure 2-14   The result of dragging the *CustomerID* node onto the form

Navigation Control   You'll also notice that Visual Studio added a navigation control at the top of the form. This control is a *BindingNavigator* control, a class that's new to Windows Forms in version 2.0 of the .NET Framework. The *BindingNavigator* control allows the user to navigate back and forth through available results at run time. The control also has buttons that allow the user to add items to and remove items from the available results, as well as to submit pending changes.

Visual Studio sets the *Name* property of the *BindingNavigator* control by combining the name of the table in the data source, "Customers", with "BindingNavigator". As with the *Label* and *TextBox* controls, the first letter of the *BindingNavigator* control's *Name* property might or might not be capitalized, depending on your language of choice.

Beneath the form, you'll see a section called the Component Tray. In this section, you'll see another representation of the *BindingNavigator* control, along with a few other items.

For more information on using the *BindingNavigator* class to interact with your data, see Chapter 13.

Strongly Typed *DataSet*   You'll also see an item in the Component Tray named *Northwind-DataSet* or *northwindDataSet*, depending on your language of choice. This item is an instance of the strongly typed *DataSet*, which we briefly described earlier, designed to contain customer and order information retrieved from the database.

For more information on using strongly typed *DataSet*s, see Chapter 9.

BindingSource   There is also an item in the Component Tray named *CustomersBindingSource* or *customersBindingSource*, depending on your language of choice. This item is an instance of the *BindingSource* class, another addition to version 2.0 of the .NET Framework. The *Binding-Source* class is designed to interact with both a source of data, such as the strongly typed *DataSet*, and a consumer of data, such as the *TextBox* for the CustomerID column. This new class is helpful because you can bind controls to the *BindingSource* and then associate the *BindingSource* with different sources of data without having to change properties on the bound controls, a scenario that's very common if you're retrieving data from a Web service.

For more information on using the *BindingSource* class to interact with your data, see Chapter 13.

TableAdapter   There's one more item in the Component Tray, named *CustomersTable-Adapter* or *customersTableAdapter*, depending on your language of choice. As the name implies, this item is a *TableAdapter*, a new feature of Visual Studio. There is no *TableAdapter* class in the .NET Framework. *TableAdapter*s are a pure Visual Studio creation.

In the ADO.NET object model, a *DataAdapter* is the generic name for a class that contains logic to retrieve information from a database and to later submit pending changes back to the database. A *TableAdapter* is similar to a *DataAdapter*, but it's designed to interact with strongly typed *DataSet*s.

For more information on using *TableAdapter*s, see Chapter 9.

Adding Other Items to the Form

Now that we've taken a closer look at the items created by dragging the *CustomerID* item from the Data Sources window onto the form, let's add controls for other columns in the Customers table. Drag and drop the *CompanyName* and *ContactName* items onto the form beneath the *Label* and *TextBox* controls for the CustomerID column. You could *beautify* the form by lining up all the controls nicely, widening the *TextBox* controls, or doing both so that the *TextBox* controls are wide enough to accommodate values for the CompanyName and ContactName columns, but that's not really necessary.

Running the Project

At this point, we've added enough items and functionality to the form to allow the user to interact with customer data. It's time to run the project and see what happens. Build and run the project by pressing *F5* or the Start Debugging button on the standard toolbar, or build and run it by selecting Debug and then Start Debugging from the menu. You should see a form displayed that looks like the one shown in Figure 2-15.

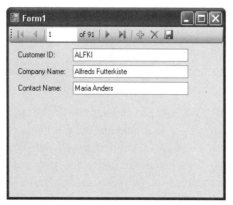

Figure 2-15   The running sample application

Customer Data Appears

When the form appears on your screen, it already contains customer information. The *TextBox* controls contain values for the CustomerID, CompanyName, and ContactName columns. The *BindingNavigator* control displays information about which customer entry appears on the form. The Customers table in SQL Server's sample *Northwind* database initially contains 91 rows.

Navigate Through the Available Customers

You can use the *BindingNavigator* control to navigate through the available customers. To move to the next customer, click the button that looks like ">." You can also use the button that looks like ">|" to move to the last customer. The first two buttons let you navigate to the first customer (|<) or the previous customer (<). These buttons are disabled when the first customer is displayed. Similarly, the buttons to move to the next customer and to the last customer are disabled when the last customer is displayed.

As you navigate through the available customers, the *TextBox* that's part of the *NavigationControl* responds to the changes, displaying the current position within the Customers table. You can change the current position within the Customers table by manually changing the value in the *TextBox* and pressing Enter.

Modify Data and Submit Changes

Use the *BindingNavigator* to move back to the first Customer, and then change the value of either the CompanyName or ContactName column. Now save the change by clicking the button that has an image of a floppy disk. If you don't remember what a floppy disk looks like, click the button whose ToolTip says "Save Data".

Verifying Your Changes Were Submitted

When you clicked the button to save your changes, there was no visual cue to indicate that anything happened. However, you can convince yourself that you successfully saved the changes to your database by closing the form and then re-running the project. The changes you made should be visible on the form.

Help! I Didn't See the Changes!

Depending on how you created the connection to your database, you might not see the changes you submitted. That doesn't necessarily mean that the project did not save the changes successfully.

If you're using an Access database file (*.mdb) or a SQL Server database file (*.mdf) in your project, Visual Studio might copy these files to the executable directory. If Visual Studio overwrites your database file the next time you build your solution, the changes you made to the customer data in the sample application will be lost. To determine how, or if, Visual Studio will copy the database file to the executable's directory, select the item in Solution Explorer and then look at the Copy To Output Directory entry in the Properties window.

Although copying database files is a well-intentioned feature, the end result has caused a great deal of confusion and frustration for many users. For more information, see the Visual Studio team's blog at *http://blogs.msdn.com/smartclientdata/archive/2005/08/26/456886.aspx*.

Adding Related Data to the Form

Let's make the sample application a little more useful by adding order information to the form. The goal will be to let the user view and modify order information for the currently visible customer.

Drag Orders onto the Form

In the Data Sources window, select the *Orders* node that's a child of the *Customers* node. Drag this node onto the form and position it below the *Label* and *TextBox* controls that already appear on the form. The result will look something like the form in Figure 2-16.

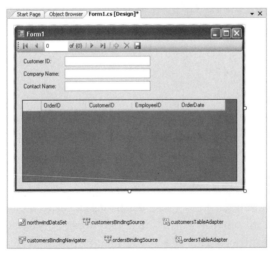

Figure 2-16   The result of dragging the child *Orders* node onto the form

What Was Added?

The most obvious addition to the form is the grid with columns for information from the Orders table. This grid is an instance of the *DataGridView* control, which is new in version 2.0 of the .NET Framework. The control is designed to display multiple rows of data at a time and allows the user to edit, add, or delete rows quickly and easily.

If you look at the Components Tray, you'll also see a new *TableAdapter* and a new *Binding-Source*, both designed to interact with the Orders table.

Re-Run the Project

Run the project and you'll see that the new *DataGridView* control displays just the order information for the currently displayed customer. If you use the *BindingNavigation* control to display a different customer, you'll see that the contents of the *DataGridView* remain synchronized, displaying the orders for the newly displayed customer.

Modifying Order Information

Now let's modify some order information and try to submit those changes. To simplify the process of verifying whether those changes were saved to the database, modify order information for the first available customer. Use the *BindingNavigation* control to display the initial customer.

In the *DataGridView* control, modify the contents of a column other than OrderID or CustomerID. These columns are special—the OrderID column is the key column in the Orders table, and the CustomerID column is used to associate the row in the Orders table with a row in the Customers table. Modify one of the other columns, either EmployeeID or OrderDate. Now click the Save Data button, close the form, and re-run the project to see whether the changes you made were saved to the database.

When you re-run the project, you'll see that the changes you made were *not* saved to the database. We'll discover why those changes were not saved later in the chapter.

Examining the Code Generated by Visual Studio

We've looked at the controls that Visual Studio added to the form and to the Components Tray. Now it's time to take a quick look at the code that Visual Studio added. Display the designer for the form, select View, and then select Code from the Visual Studio menu. You could also right-click the form's designer or the form node in Solution Explorer and select View Code from the context menu. Figures 2-17 and 2-18 show the sample code that Visual Studio generated for Visual Basic and Visual C#, respectively.

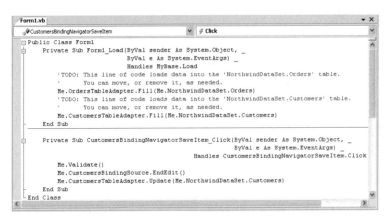

Figure 2-17   Visual Basic code generated by Visual Studio

```csharp
namespace Chapter02
{
    public partial class Form1 : Form
    {
        public Form1()...

        private void Form1_Load(object sender, EventArgs e)
        {
            // TODO: This line of code loads data into the 'northwindDataSet.Orders' table.
            //       You can move, or remove it, as needed.
            this.ordersTableAdapter.Fill(this.northwindDataSet.Orders);
            // TODO: This line of code loads data into the 'northwindDataSet.Customers' table.
            //       You can move, or remove it, as needed.
            this.customersTableAdapter.Fill(this.northwindDataSet.Customers);
        }

        private void customersBindingNavigatorSaveItem_Click(object sender, EventArgs e)
        {
            this.Validate();
            this.customersBindingSource.EndEdit();
            this.customersTableAdapter.Update(this.northwindDataSet.Customers);
        }
    }
}
```

Figure 2-18   Visual C# code generated by Visual Studio

Load Event

Looking at the code in the form's *Load* event will help explain why the form automatically displays customer and order information when the form appears. Looking at the code in Visual Studio or in Figures 2-17 and 2-18, you'll see that the form's *Load* event includes code that calls the *Fill* method on the *TableAdapters* for the Orders and Customers tables.

The *Fill* method executes the query stored in the *TableAdapter* and stores the results in the portion of the *DataSet* supplied. The code uses the strongly typed *DataSet* in both *Fill* events, but it references the *Orders* or *Customers* property on the strongly typed *DataSet* depending on which *TableAdapter*'s *Fill* method is called. Thanks to this code, the customer and order information is available in the form's strongly typed *DataSet* when the form appears and can be displayed in the *TextBox* and *DataGridView* controls.

SaveItem Click Event

There are three lines of code in the *Click* event for the *SaveItem* on the *BindingNavigator* for customer information. The first line of code calls the *Validate* method on the form, giving the controls a chance to validate the data the user has entered. The second line of code calls the *EndEdit* method on the *BindingSource* object for customer information, which tells the controls that are bound to this *BindingSource* to write any pending changes to the source of the data. Without this line of code, changes might still be cached in the controls and would not be sent to the database on the next line of code. The final line of code calls the *Update* method on the *TableAdapter* for customer information, submitting the pending changes in the *Customers* portion of the strongly typed *DataSet*.

Note that there is no code to submit the changes you've performed to order information. This explains why clicking the Save button did not submit the changes to the order information to the database.

You Can Write Better Data-Access Code Than the Designers!

The code that Visual Studio generates is very helpful, especially when you want to build a simple application quickly. However, the code Visual Studio generates is designed for simple scenarios and might not be the best approach for more robust applications. Let's take a look at two minor problems with the code that Visual Studio generated.

Load Event

As noted earlier, Visual Studio automatically adds code to the *Load* event to call the *Fill* method on the *TableAdapter* when you perform an action that adds a *TableAdapter* to the form's Components Tray. However, Visual Studio doesn't add this code in an "intelligent" way. The code retrieves order information before customer information.

The *Northwind* database contains a foreign-key constraint. Inserting an order that references a customer that does not exist in the database would violate the constraint.

The *DataSet* class also allows you to define foreign-key constraints to enforce referential integrity. Retrieving the order information before the customer information would violate such a foreign-key constraint if the constraint existed in the *DataSet*. Visual Studio does not add the foreign-key constraint to the *DataSet*, so you can retrieve data from tables in any order.

Although this approach is perfectly reasonable when simply retrieving data from a database—because in most cases the database has already validated the data—I would not recommend it for applications that modify data from related tables. For more information on this topic, see the discussion of foreign-key constraints in strongly typed *DataSet*s in Chapter 9.

SaveItem Click Event

As noted earlier, the *Click* event for the *SaveItem* button on the *BindingNavigator* control for customer information only called the *Update* method on the customers' *TableAdapter*. You could add code to call the *Update* method on the order's *TableAdapter* and pass the *Orders* property on the strongly typed *Northwind DataSet* as a parameter. But would you add this code before or after the call to the *Update* method on the customers' *TableAdapter*?

The answer isn't quite as simple as "before" or "after." In many cases, you'll need to submit new customers before new orders but submit deleted orders before deleted customers. For more information on submitting changes to related tables of data, see the "Submitting Hierarchical Changes" section in Chapter 11.

Questions That Should Be Asked More Frequently

You've now built a relatively simple application that uses ADO.NET, and you've seen some of the power available in the technology. We've discussed how some of the major features work by looking at the items and code that Visual Studio added to your form when dragging items from the Data Source window. This chapter is a starting point, but it's also a teaser. So instead of posing questions that developers might ask and then offering answers, as I do in the "Questions..." section of other chapters, here I will provide some background and reference other areas of the book that provide further information.

Q   When I added a new order on the form I generated, values automatically appeared for the *CustomerID* and *OrderID* fields before I submitted the new order to the database. How did ADO.NET generate these values?

A   The value for the CustomerID column is set based on the relationship between the Customer and Order tables in the database. The value of the CustomerID column for the currently visible customer is automatically assigned to the CustomerID column for the new order. This behavior is governed by the *DataRelation* class, which is covered in Chapter 7.

The new value for the OrderID column involves a slightly more complex explanation. This column in the *Northwind* database is called an AutoIncrement column. When you submit a new row to a table that contains an AutoIncrement column, the database generates a new value for that column. As noted earlier, changes made to the order information on the form are not submitted to the database. So this new value for the OrderID column did not come from the database. ADO.NET includes features to generate temporary *placeholder* values for AutoIncrement columns. If this form also allowed you to enter line items for pending orders, the placeholder values for the OrderID column would help you keep track of which line items were associated with which pending order.

By default, ADO.NET will generate a new value that's one larger than the largest value that ADO.NET contains for that column of that table. ADO.NET's autoincrement behavior is governed by the *DataColumn* class, which is covered in Chapter 6. There is also additional information about submitting changes involving AutoIncrement columns in Chapter 11.

Q   After I deleted a customer and clicked the Save button, I received an error saying that the DELETE statement conflicted with a column-reference constraint. What does that mean? How can I change the code to better handle this situation?

A   As noted earlier when we looked at the code that Visual Studio generated, the code in the *Click* event of the Save button only submitted changes to the customer information. The *Northwind* database contains a constraint that requires that if an order contains customer information (a value for the CustomerID column), it references a row in the Customers table. Attempting to delete a customer that has orders will violate that constraint. Prior to asking the database to delete a customer, you could issue a query to delete the related order information from the database. This process involves handling the *RowUpdating* event, discussed in Chapter 10, to determine when you're about to ask the database to delete a customer and executing a parameterized query, discussed in Chapter 4, to delete the related order information.

Q   What happens if another user modifies the contents of a row between the time I retrieve it and the time I submit the update?

A   You could simulate this scenario by running multiple instances of the sample application, modifying the same row in each instance, and then clicking the Save button in each instance. If you try this, you'll see that the first update attempt succeeds, and the second update attempt fails and displays the dialog box shown in Figure 2-19.

Dialog box thrown by the sample application if an update fails because of a concurrency exception

Notice, either by looking at the figure or by causing the failure yourself, that the dialog box calls the failure a *concurrency exception*. There is a *DBConcurrencyException* class in the *System.Data* namespace. If the *TableAdapter* determines that an update attempt failed because the contents of the row have changed, the call to the *Update* method will generate a *DBConcurrencyException*.

There are a variety of ways to handle the checks performed in updating logic, a topic that's covered in Chapter 10. There are also a variety of ways to react to a failed update attempt, a topic that's covered in Chapter 11.

Part II
Getting Connected: Using a .NET Data Provider

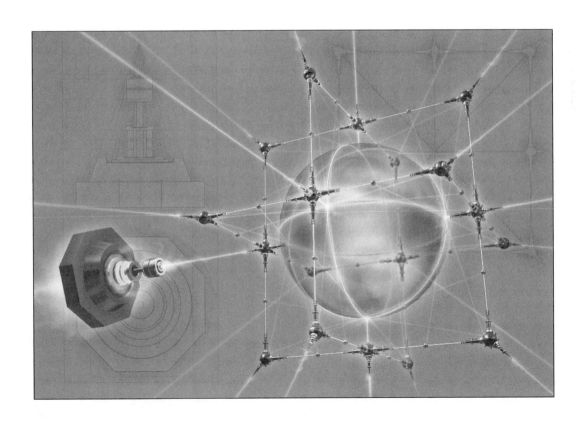

Chapter 3
Connecting to Your Database

Part of building a database application requires that you connect to your data source and manage that connection. In the ADO.NET object model, a Connection object represents a connection to your data source. Connection objects also serve as a starting point for creating queries and transactions.

This chapter will serve as your guide to using Connection objects by explaining the major features available in ADO.NET. We'll discuss how to open and close connections, connection pooling, and some new features available in ADO.NET 2.0 that let you control how ADO.NET tries to connect to your data source—connection string security and connection string builders. We'll also examine how to use another new ADO.NET feature, the *GetSchema* method, which lets us discover schema available on the database—listing the available tables, columns, and so on.

In the ADO.NET object model, all connection classes derive from the *DbConnection* class in the *System.Data.Common* namespace. Throughout the chapter, we'll focus on the class specifically designed to communicate with Microsoft SQL Server databases, the *SqlConnection* class. For information about working with other .NET Data Providers, see Appendix A. Unless otherwise noted, the features of the class are generic and apply to all Connection classes regardless of their .NET Data Provider.

Code snippets in this book assume that you have used the appropriate construct to reference the *System.Data* and *System.Data.SqlClient* namespaces. The following lines of code (Microsoft Visual Basic and Microsoft Visual C#, respectively) must appear at the beginning of your code modules. For more information about these constructs, please see the documentation for your language of choice.

In Visual Basic, the code looks like this:

```
Imports System.Data
Imports System.Data.SqlClient
```

In Visual C#, the code looks like this:

```
using System.Data;
using System.Data.SqlClient;
```

Creating *SqlConnection* Objects

There are two ways to create *SqlConnection* objects at run time. You can simply create an uninitialized *SqlConnection* object using the parameterless constructor, or you can use the constructor that accepts a connection string as shown here:

Visual Basic
```
Dim strConn As String
strConn = "Data Source=.\SQLExpress;" & _
          "Initial Catalog=Northwind;Integrated Security=True;"
Dim cn As New SqlConnection(strConn)
```

Visual C#
```
string strConn;
strConn = @"Data Source=.\SQLExpress;" +
          "Initial Catalog=Northwind;Integrated Security=True;";
SqlConnection cn = new SqlConnection(strConn);
```

If you haven't used ADO.NET or a similar data access technology before, you might look at this code and wonder what a connection string is. For now, a short explanation should suffice. A connection string consists of multiple name-value pairs that describe how ADO.NET should try to connect to your data source. In some ways, it's almost like a set of directions you'd follow to get to a friend's house. With this particular connection string, the directions say to look for a SQL Server instance named "SQLExpress" on the local machine, look for the catalog called "Northwind", and try to access that data store with a trusted connection using your Microsoft Windows credentials.

Later in this chapter, We'll take a much closer look at connection strings—discussing various connection string options, as well as ways to build and use them safely.

Opening *SqlConnection* Objects

When you create an instance of a *SqlConnection*, it's initialized in a "closed" state. In other words, despite its name, it's not actually connected to your data store. If you tried to execute a query on a *SqlConnection* without first opening the connection, you would receive an

InvalidOperationException saying that the method you called "requires an open and available Connection. The connection's current state is closed."

To connect to your data store, supply a valid connection string, either through the constructor or by setting the object's *ConnectionString* property, and then call the object's *Open* method.

Calling the *Open* method on a *SqlConnection* object that's already open will cause an *InvalidOperationException*. If you're unsure whether your *SqlConnection* is open, check the *SqlConnection* object's *State* property, which I discuss later in the "*SqlConnection* Object Reference" section.

Closing *SqlConnection* Objects

Closing a *SqlConnection* object is even easier than opening one. Simply call the object's *Close* method. If you use connection pooling, which We'll discuss in detail later in the chapter, the physical connection to the database is pooled rather than closed and can be reused later. If you're not using connection pooling, the physical connection to the database will be closed.

Calling the *Close* method on a *SqlConnection* object that is already closed will not cause an exception.

Cleaning Up After Yourself

Most developers know that the .NET Framework performs garbage collection, but many developers are unaware of how or when the garbage-collection process occurs. Although this text will not try to provide an in-depth explanation of the inner workings of garbage collection in .NET, it's important to understand that garbage collection is not performed immediately and how its timing can affect the behavior of your application.

Many .NET developers have experience with Visual Basic 6.0 and prior versions and know that those versions provide aggressive garbage collection. With these "classic" versions of Visual Basic, objects are cleaned up as soon as they fall out of scope or are released by setting the object variable to *Nothing*. Many Visual Basic classic developers relied on this behavior, whether they realized it or not, by leaving ADO Connection and Recordset objects open. Although they did not explicitly call the *Close* method on these objects, the Visual Basic classic garbage collector closed those objects as soon as they fell out of scope or the object variables were set to *Nothing*.

The biggest difference between .NET and Visual Basic classic garbage collection is that .NET garbage collection is less aggressive, releasing resources in the background using a process that I won't try to explain in this text. However, here is an important question to consider: What happens if you open a *SqlConnection* in the *Click* event of a *Button* object without calling the *SqlConnection* object's *Close* method?

When the .NET garbage collector cleans up the *SqlConnection* object, it will implicitly call the object's *Close* method. But when will the .NET garbage collector clean up the *SqlConnection* object? The correct, but vague, answer is, "Later."

Imagine that the user clicks the button on your form repeatedly—say, 10 times in five seconds due to an odd obsessive-compulsive disorder. Each time the *Click* event completes, the new *SqlConnection* falls out of scope. When the .NET garbage collector (eventually) disposes of the *SqlConnection*, ADO.NET will implicitly call the object's *Close* method and the physical connection to the database will be sent to the connection pool. Because the user repeatedly clicks the button before the .NET garbage collector cleans up the out-of-scope objects, your application will open 10 separate connections to your SQL Server database.

The important lesson to be learned here is to clean up after yourself. Do not rely on .NET garbage collection to manage the state of your database connections. In the previous example, explicitly calling the *Close* method on the *SqlConnection* object within the *Click* event will ensure that the application uses only a single physical connection to the SQL Server database.

Many classes in the ADO.NET object model, such as the *SqlConnection* class, expose a *Dispose* method. In general, calling this method on an object releases (or resets) its unmanaged resources. Calling this method on a *SqlConnection* object implicitly calls the *Close* method. As noted earlier, calling the *Close* method (implicitly or explicitly) on a *SqlConnection* object that's already closed will not cause an exception.

One simple way to make sure you've cleaned up your resources is to open short-lived resources inside of a *Using* block. In the example, where clicking the button opens a new *SqlConnection* object, we could perform that work in a *Using* block to ensure the *Close* method will be called implicitly at the end of the *Using* block, as shown in the following code:

Visual Basic

```
Private Sub Button1_Click(ByVal sender As System.Object, _
            ByVal e As System.EventArgs) Handles Button1.Click
    Dim strConn As String
    strConn = "Data Source=.\SQLExpress;" & _
            "Initial Catalog=Northwind;Integrated Security=True;"
    Using cn As New SqlConnection(strConn)
        cn.Open()
        'Execute a query
    End Using
End Sub
```

Visual C#

```
private void button1_Click(object sender, EventArgs e) {
    string strConn;
    strConn = @"Data Source=.\SQLExpress;" +
            "Initial Catalog=Northwind;Integrated Security=True;";
    using (SqlConnection cn = new SqlConnection(strConn))
    {
        cn.Open();
        //Execute a query
    }
}
```

Here, there is no need to explicitly call the *Close* method on the *SqlConnection* object. The *Using* block ensures that the *Dispose* method will be called at the end of the block, even if an unhandled exception occurs inside the *Using* block. I strongly recommend creating short-lived objects inside of *Using* blocks wherever possible.

With that said, you'll see many examples in this text that do *not* include *Using* blocks. Technical books, unfortunately, have limited real estate. If a code example uses a *SqlConnection*, *SqlCommand*, and *SqlDataReader* and a *Using* block for each of these objects, so much of the space is devoted to—well, blank space—that there's little room left for the rest of the code. Here's an example:

Visual Basic

```vb
Dim strConn, strSQL As String
strConn = "Data Source=.\SQLExpress;" & _
          "Initial Catalog=Northwind;Integrated Security=True;"
strSQL = "SELECT CustomerID, CompanyName FROM Customers"
Using cn As New SqlConnection(strConn)
    Try
        cn.Open()
    Catch ex As SqlException
        Console.WriteLine("Connect attempt failed")
        Console.WriteLine("    {0}", ex.Message)
        Return
    End Try

    Using cmd As New SqlCommand(strSQL, cn)
        Try
            Using rdr As SqlDataReader = cmd.ExecuteReader()
                Do While rdr.Read()
                    Console.WriteLine(rdr("CompanyName"))
                Loop
                rdr.Close()
            End Using
        Catch ex As SqlException
            Console.WriteLine("Query failed")
            Console.WriteLine("    {0}", ex.Message)
            Return
        End Try
    End Using

    cn.Close()
End Using
```

Visual C#

```csharp
string strConn, strSQL;
strConn = @"Data Source=.\SQLExpress;" +
          "Initial Catalog=Northwind;Integrated Security=True;";
strSQL = "SELECT CustomerID, CompanyName FROM Customers";
using (SqlConnection cn = new SqlConnection(strConn)) {
    try {
        cn.Open();
    } catch (SqlException ex) {
        Console.WriteLine("Connect attempt failed");
        Console.WriteLine("    {0}", ex.Message);
        return;
    }
```

```
using (SqlCommand cmd = new SqlCommand(strSQL, cn)) {
    try {
        using (SqlDataReader rdr = cmd.ExecuteReader()) {
            while (rdr.Read())
                Console.WriteLine(rdr["CompanyName"]);
            rdr.Close();
        }
    } catch (SqlException ex) {
        Console.WriteLine("Query failed");
        Console.WriteLine("    {0}", ex.Message);
        return;
    }
}

cn.Close();
}
```

Connection Strings

The previous code snippets have involved setting the *ConnectionString* property on *SqlConnection* objects through that class's constructor. However, we've yet to discuss what a connection string is.

What Is a Connection String?

In the previous code snippets, we supplied a connection string for our new *SqlConnection* objects. A connection string consists of a series of name-value pairs delimited by semicolons:

```
strConn = "Setting1=Value1;Setting2=Value2;..."
```

The settings and values depend on the data source you want to connect to, as well as on the technology you're using to connect to your data source.

The SQL Client .NET Data Provider is extremely flexible when it comes to connecting to databases, and it provides a variety of ways to build a connection string. You can use current keywords such as "Data Source" and "Initial Catalog" or older terms such as "Server" and "Database". Here are two simple examples of connection strings used to connect to a SQL Server database.

Connecting to the Local Default Instance of SQL Server

You can use a variety of special values to signify that you're connecting to the local machine—"(local)", "localhost", or "." (my personal preference). Simply specify the name of the machine you want to access in the "Data Source" for the connection string as shown here:

```
Data Source=.;
```

> **Note**   You can also use the older "Server" keyword instead of "Data Source".

Connecting to a Named Instance

You can have multiple instances of SQL Server installed on a particular machine. The previous examples access the default instance. If you want to access a named instance of SQL Server, add a backslash character (\) and then the name of the SQL Server instance to the value for the *Data Source*. The following code accesses the *SQLExpress* named instance on the local machine:

```
Data Source=.\SQLExpress;
```

> **Note**   The backslash character is a special character in Visual C#. If you're coding in Visual C#, you can either use a double backslash or precede the string with the @ symbol to indicate that the backslash is just a backslash.

Visual C#
```
string strConn;
strConn = "Data Source=.\\SQLExpress;";
//or
strConn = @"Data Source=.\SQLExpress;";
Console.WriteLine(strConn);
```

Either way, you'll see a single backslash character written to the Console window. This text will use the @ symbol in connection strings in Visual C# code snippets to allow you to focus on the contents of the strings rather than on escape sequences. Code snippets that do not denote a particular language will show the resulting string, so Visual C# developers must remember to modify the string appropriately for their code.

Specifying an Initial Catalog

Any instance of SQL Server can have multiple databases installed. When you connect to an instance of SQL Server, you can specify which database you want to access through the *Initial Catalog* keyword. If you want to access the Northwind database on the local default instance of SQL Server, you can use the following code:

```
Data Source=.\SQLExpress;Initial Catalog=Northwind;
```

> **Note**   You can also use the older *Database* keyword instead of *Initial Catalog*.

Connecting Using a Specific User Name and Password

Many databases allow you to log on to the data store by supplying a user name and password in the connection string. You can use these options for a *SqlConnection* by using the *User ID* and *Password* connection string keywords. Here is an example of such a connection string:

```
Data Source=.\SQLExpress;Initial Catalog=Northwind;
User ID=MyUserID;Password=MyPassword;
```

> **Note**   You can also use the older *UID* and *PWD* keywords instead of *User ID* and *Password*.

Connecting Using Integrated Security

Another connection option is to have SQL Server authenticate the user with the user's Windows credentials, rather than specify a user name and password in the connection string. Here's an example of using integrated security in a connection string:

```
Data Source=.\SQLExpress;Initial Catalog=Northwind;
Integrated Security=True;
```

> **Note**   You can also use the older *Trusted_Connection* keyword instead of *Integrated Security*.

Introducing Connection String Builders

Creating connection strings at design time or run time can get complex. Maybe you're having problems remembering the name of the connection string option that you want to use. Maybe you're not sure how to delimit the value. Maybe you're looking for help in ensuring that the input you receive from the user can't change the intentions of your connection string. ADO.NET 2.0 introduces connection string builder classes to help you address these issues when building connection strings.

Using a Connection String Builder

Connection string builders are easy to use. You can set or examine values through the class's indexer. Once you've supplied the desired values, use the builder's *ConnectionString* property to access the resulting connection string.

Here we've taken the example in which we want to generate a connection string based on various connection string options and modified it to use a *SqlConnectionStringBuilder*, which is the connection string builder class for *SqlConnection* objects. We simply set values for the different keywords through the indexer. Once you've built the desired connection string, access the *ConnectionString* property and hand the results to your *SqlConnection* object, as shown in the following code snippet:

Visual Basic
```
Dim bldr As New SqlConnectionStringBuilder()
bldr("Data Source") = ".\SQLExpress"
bldr("Initial Catalog") = "Northwind"
bldr("Integrated Security") = True

'Write the resulting connection string to the Console window
Console.WriteLine("Resulting connection string: {0}", bldr.ConnectionString)

'Use the resulting connection string with a SqlConnection
Dim cn As New SqlConnection(bldr.ConnectionString)
cn.Open()
```

Visual C#

```
SqlConnectionStringBuilder bldr = new SqlConnectionStringBuilder();
bldr["Data Source"] = @".\SQLExpress";
bldr["Initial Catalog"] = "Northwind";
bldr["Integrated Security"] = true;

//Write the resulting connection string to the Console window
Console.WriteLine("Resulting connection string: {0}", bldr.ConnectionString);

//Use the resulting connection string with a SqlConnection
SqlConnection cn = new SqlConnection(bldr.ConnectionString);
cn.Open();
```

You'll see that the connection string written to the Console window looks like this:

```
Data Source=.\SQLExpress;Initial Catalog=Northwind;Integrated Security=True
```

Of course, we already knew how to build this connection string. So we haven't really improved our code...yet.

Connection Strings, Meet IntelliSense; IntelliSense, Meet Connection Strings

I'll admit it. I have a tough time remembering some connection string keywords and values. I often write basic connection strings using old Open Database Connectivity (ODBC) syntax and hand that off to a *SqlConnection*, or I add *Driver={SQL Server}* or *Provider=SQLOLEDB* and hand off the result to an *OdbcConnection* or *OleDbConnection*, respectively. *Trusted_Connection=Yes* makes more sense to me than *Integrated Security=True*, and I can never remember the keywords for newer options. (No, I don't walk uphill both to and from work.) Apparently, I'm not the only person who has trouble remembering connection string options. In fact, there's an entire Web site devoted to connection string options.

Connection string builders simplify the process of building connection strings by exposing many commonly used options as properties. The connection string builder classes available in ADO.NET 2.0 include strongly typed properties that correspond to many of the available connection string options. In an earlier example, we set values for the *Data Source*, *Initial Catalog*, and *Integrated Security* connection string keywords through the default indexer. We can rewrite that code by accessing the *DataSource*, *InitialCatalog*, and *IntegratedSecurity* properties on a *SqlConnectionStringBuilder* class. Here's that same example, but this time it's using properties of the *SqlConnectionStringBuilder*.

Visual Basic

```
Dim bldr As New SqlConnectionStringBuilder()
bldr.DataSource = ".\SQLExpress"
bldr.InitialCatalog = "Northwind"
bldr.IntegratedSecurity = True

'Write the resulting connection string to the Console window
Console.WriteLine("Resulting connection string: {0}", bldr.ConnectionString)
```

```
'Use the resulting connection string with a SqlConnection
Dim cn As New SqlConnection(bldr.ConnectionString)
cn.Open()
```

Visual C#

```
SqlConnectionStringBuilder bldr = new SqlConnectionStringBuilder();
bldr.DataSource = @".\SQLExpress";
bldr.InitialCatalog = "Northwind";
bldr.IntegratedSecurity = true;

//Write the resulting connection string to the Console window
Console.WriteLine("Resulting connection string: {0}", bldr.ConnectionString);

//Use the resulting connection string with a SqlConnection
SqlConnection cn = new SqlConnection(bldr.ConnectionString);
cn.Open();
```

The code still generates the same connection string, but the code is now easier to write. Plus, if you make a typo when supplying the connection string keywords, you'll get a compile-time error. If you're writing your code in Microsoft Visual Studio and you have problems remembering connection string options, the options available on the *SqlConnectionStringBuilder* are readily available through the IntelliSense drop-down menus. Using those drop-down menus can also save a few keystrokes and prevent typos that you otherwise would not discover until testing your code.

Handling Complex Connection String Option Values

A secondary benefit to using connection string builders is that they prevent you from having to remember how to parse, escape, or delimit values in a connection string. Suppose that you need to supply a connection string value that includes a space. Do you need quotes around the keyword? Braces? Neither? Both?

If you're building your own connection strings by hand, there's no simple answer. In fact, the answer might depend on the .NET Data Provider you use. Developers who have used ODBC in the past might remember that ODBC driver names that included a space had to be delimited with braces: *"Driver={SQL Server}"*. By relying on connection string builders instead of building the connection string yourself, you needn't trouble yourself with such questions.

If, however, you're working with connection string builders, you can leave that logic to the builder. For example, you might want to use the connection string option to connect to a server and attach a database file in the process. The file you want to use may contain spaces or other characters in the path. Rather than worry about if or how to delimit the file name in the connection string, you can simply use the *SqlConnectionStringBuilder* class to create your connection string, as shown here:

Visual Basic

```
Dim bldr As New SqlConnectionStringBuilder()
bldr.DataSource = ".\SQLExpress"
bldr.IntegratedSecurity = True
bldr.AttachDBFilename = "C:\My Complex Path\AttachMe.mdf"
```

```
'Write the resulting connection string to the Console window
Console.WriteLine("Resulting connection string: {0}", bldr.ConnectionString)

'Use the resulting connection string with a SqlConnection
Dim cn As New SqlConnection(bldr.ConnectionString)
cn.Open()
```

Visual C#

```
SqlConnectionStringBuilder bldr = new SqlConnectionStringBuilder();
bldr.DataSource = @".\SQLExpress";
bldr.IntegratedSecurity = true;
bldr.AttachDBFilename = @"C:\My Complex Path\AttachMe.mdf";

//Write the resulting connection string to the Console window
Console.WriteLine("Resulting connection string: {0}", bldr.ConnectionString);

//Use the resulting connection string with a SqlConnection
SqlConnection cn = new SqlConnection(bldr.ConnectionString);
cn.Open();
```

If, for some reason, you're interested in how to delimit the file name properly in the connection string, the code snippet generates the following connection string:

```
Data Source=.\SQLExpress;AttachDbFilename="C:\My Complex Path\AttachMe.mdf";
Integrated Security=True
```

Malicious Connection String Input, Also Known as *Connection String Injection*

One of the most important rules in writing secure code is, "Never blindly trust user input." Parameterized queries, a topic we'll discuss in more detail in Chapter 4, are helpful for a variety of reasons, but one of the primary reasons is that they protect you from SQL injection. You can construct a parameterized query and assign user-supplied values to parameters without having to worry about whether the user input changed the structure of your query. Similar challenges exist when building connection strings.

You might decide to prompt the user for credentials—supplying text boxes that allow the user to supply a user name and a password—and then construct a connection string based on that input in a connection string with code such as the following:

Visual Basic

```
Dim strConn As String
strConn = "Data Source=.\SQLExpress;Initial Catalog=Northwind;" & _
        "User ID=" & txtUserID.Text & ";" & _
        "Password=" & txtPassword.Text & ";"
Console.WriteLine("Resulting connection string: {0}", strConn)
```

Visual C#

```
string strConn;
strConn = @"Data Source=.\SQLExpress;Initial Catalog=Northwind;" +
        "User ID=" + txtUserID.Text + ";" +
        "Password=" + txtPassword.Text + ";"
Console.WriteLine("Resulting connection string: {0}", strConn);
```

At first glance, this might seem like a safe and logical thing to do. Now consider a malevolent user who might want to change the connection string. Figure 3-1 illustrates one way such a user could change which server the application accesses. For lack of a better term, we'll call this approach "connection string injection."

Figure 3-1   A malevolent user attempts to change the server your application accesses through user input

Using the previous code snippet and the input shown in Figure 3-2, the resulting connection string is as follows:

```
Data Source=.\SQLExpress;Initial Catalog=Northwind;User ID=MyUserID;
Data Source=EvilServerName;Password=MyPassword;
```

As you can see, the *Data Source* keyword is specified twice. Which value wins if you use the resulting connection string—the first one (local machine) or the second one (the "evil" server)? Is there a way to manually inspect the user input to identify possible connection string injections such as these? Are the answers consistent across other connection string keywords or across other .NET Data Providers? What's a poor programmer to do?

Thankfully, connection string builders can help you handle input from mischievous or malevolent users.

Preventing Connection String Injection with Connection String Builders

When we rewrite the previous code snippet using the *SqlConnectionStringBuilder*, it looks like the following:

Visual Basic
```
Dim bldr As New SqlConnectionStringBuilder()
bldr.DataSource = ".\SQLExpress"
bldr.InitialCatalog = "Northwind"
bldr.UserID = txtUserID.Text
bldr.Password = txtPassword.Text
Console.WriteLine("Resulting connection string: {0}", bldr.ConnectionString)
```

Visual C#
```
SqlConnectionStringBuilder bldr = new SqlConnectionStringBuilder();
bldr.DataSource = @".\SQLExpress";
bldr.InitialCatalog = "Northwind";
bldr.UserID = txtUserID.Text;
bldr.Password = txtPassword.Text;
Console.WriteLine("Resulting connection string: {0}", bldr.ConnectionString);
```

By using the *SqlConnectionStringBuilder* with the malicious input in Figure 3-2 (that is, using "*MyUserID;Data Source=EvilServerName*" for the user ID and *MyPassword* for the password), you'll generate the following connection string:

```
Data Source=.\SQLExpress;Initial Catalog=Northwind;
User ID="MyUserID;Data Source=EvilServerName";Password=MyPassword
```

You'll notice that the value for the *User ID* keyword is delimited. This will cause ADO.NET to try to log on to the SQL Server database with a *User ID* of "*MyUserID;Data Source=EvilServerName*".

Recognizing Keyword Aliases

Because the *SqlConnectionStringBuilder* is built specifically for SQL Server, it recognizes older keyword aliases. You can supply current or legacy keywords to a *SqlConnectionStringBuilder* and the *ConnectionString* property will return the same value.

Visual Basic

```
Dim bldr As SqlConnectionStringBuilder

bldr = New SqlConnectionStringBuilder("Data Source=.\SQLExpress")
Console.WriteLine(bldr.ConnectionString)

bldr = New SqlConnectionStringBuilder("Server=.\SQLExpress")
Console.WriteLine(bldr.ConnectionString)
```

Visual C#

```
SqlConnectionStringBuilder bldr;

bldr = new SqlConnectionStringBuilder(@"Data Source=.\SQLExpress");
Console.WriteLine(bldr.ConnectionString);

bldr = new SqlConnectionStringBuilder(@"Server=.\SQLExpress");
Console.WriteLine(bldr.ConnectionString);
```

Regardless of which of the previous code snippets you execute, the *ConnectionString* property returns the following:

```
Data Source=.\SQLExpress
```

Creating a Connection-String Dialog Box with a Connection-String Builder

Previous technologies, such as OLE DB and ODBC, have included user-interface components that let developers prompt the user for connection information—for example, allowing the user to select an ODBC driver or an OLE DB provider from a drop-down list. There are countless newsgroup and forum posts where developers ask how to achieve similar functionality with ADO.NET. The short answer is that there is no simple control or dialog box to build ADO.NET connection strings. The long answer is that you can build your own dialog box to display connection string options fairly easily.

If you've already used Visual Studio 2005, you might have noticed that there are new dialog boxes for connecting to data stores in Server Explorer. There are different dialog boxes for

SQL Server, Microsoft Access, and Oracle databases, as well as ODBC data sources. Each of these dialog boxes is specialized for the database or technology selected. However, each dialog box also includes a button labeled Advanced. Clicking this button shows another dialog box that lists advanced options for that database or technology. Figure 3-2 shows the Advanced Properties dialog box for SQL Client connection strings.

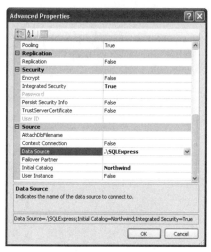

Figure 3-2   The Advanced Properties dialog box for SQL Client connection strings

If you want specialized dialog boxes for different .NET Data Providers, you have your work cut out for you. However, if you want to create a generic user interface that lists all the connection string options, you can achieve this functionality fairly easily thanks to the *PropertyGrid* control that's part of the .NET Framework. Simply set the *PropertyGrid* control's *SelectedObject* property to a *SqlConnectionStringBuilder* and you can generate a dialog box such as the one shown in Figure 3-2. The one remaining task is to trap for the *PropertyGrid* control's *PropertyValueChanged* event to update a textbox with the current value of the *SqlConnectionString* object's *ConnectionString* property, as you see with the dialog box shown in Figure 3-3.

Figure 3-3   A *PropertyGrid* control bound to a *SqlConnectionStringBuilder*

There's a reason the user interface in Figure 3-4 is similar to the one shown in Figure 3-3—Visual Studio is using *PropertyGrid* controls and connection string builders in its Advanced Properties dialog boxes.

Connection String Security

Let's say you wanted to use a simple connection string dialog box, like the one we just discussed with the *PropertyGrid* and *SqlConnectionStringBuilder*, but you wanted to allow only certain connection strings. For example, you might want to restrict the connection string to a specific server and initial catalog, while allowing any value for user ID and password, but no additional attributes. How would you write such code?

One approach would be to start with a *SqlConnectionStringBuilder* whose *DataSource* and *InitialCatalog* properties are set to the desired values. You could then build your own dialog box, allowing the user to enter values for user ID and password. Then you could assign these values to your *SqlConnectionStringBuilder* to avoid connection string injection.

In a very simple example such as the one described, this solution might suffice. But what if the options are more complex? Say, the user can connect to ServerA or ServerB, but a connection to ServerA required integrated security while a connection to ServerB required a user ID and password. The more complex the logistics, the more complicated the user interface and validation logic becomes. A simpler approach to validate the connection string is to use ADO.NET's new connection-string security features.

Using the *SqlClientPermission* Class to Restrict Data Access

The *SqlClientPermission* class derives from the *CodeAccessPermission* class in the *System.Security* namespace. You can use this class to restrict access to specific connection strings either programmatically, through attributes on classes and methods, or through code access security.

The code that follows is an example of how you could use the *SqlClientPermission* class to restrict access to a specific server name and initial catalog, while allowing any value for the User ID and Password within the connection string. The code snippet assumes a hypothetical "*myDialog*" that returns a connection string built using a *SqlConnectionStringBuilder* and a *PropertyGrid*, and it also assumes references to the *System.Security.Permissions* namespace:

Visual Basic

```
Dim perm As New SqlClientPermission(PermissionState.None)
perm.Add("Data Source=.\SQLExpress;Initial Catalog=Northwind;", _
        "User ID=;Password=;", _
        KeyRestrictionBehavior.AllowOnly)
perm.PermitOnly()

'Attempt to use connection string from hypothetical "myDialog"
Dim cn As New SqlConnection(myDialog.ConnectionString)
cn.Open()
...
```

Visual C#

```
SqlClientPermission perm;
perm = new SqlClientPermission(PermissionState.None);
perm.Add(@"Data Source=.\SQLExpress;Initial Catalog=Northwind;",
        "User ID=;Password=;",
        KeyRestrictionBehavior.AllowOnly);
perm.PermitOnly();

//Attempt to use connection string from hypothetical "myDialog"
SqlConnection cn = new SqlConnection();
cn.ConnectionString = myDialog.ConnectionString;
cn.Open();
...
```

The code snippet starts by creating a new instance of the *SqlClientPermission* class. The value of *PermissionState.None* in the constructor starts from a clean state, allowing no connection strings. You then add the connection strings that you want to allow by calling the *Add* method. The first argument contains a subset of the connection strings you want to permit, listing all required keys and values—in this case, the desired server name and initial catalog.

Connection strings that pass this security check must have the specified values for Data Source and Initial Catalog. The second argument is a semi-colon delimited list of optional connection string attributes, here listing the *User ID* and *Password* keywords. Connection strings can have any value for these keys and pass this security check. Connection strings that omit these keys will also pass this security check. The third and final argument controls whether you're granting or denying permission for the connection strings that match this pattern. Once the *PermitOnly* method is called, the security check will be enforced.

If the connection string supplied passes these checks, the *SqlConnection* will attempt to connect to the database. If the connection string supplied does not pass these checks, the *SqlConnection* will throw a *SecurityException* before even attempting to connect to the database.

Combining Permissions

The *SqlClientPermission* is not restricted to a single connection string. You can add multiple connections (and wildcards) to a *SqlClientPermission*. The call to *SqlConnection.Open* will not succeed unless the value in the *ConnectionString* property passes at least one of those checks.

Synonyms for Connection String Keywords

You might ask, "Does *SqlClientPermission* respect synonyms for connection string keywords?" The simple answer is "Yes."

For example, say you use the *Data Source* and *Initial Catalog* keywords with the *SqlClient-Permisssion* class. The SQL Client .NET Data Provider knows that Server and Database, respectively, are synonyms for those connection-string attributes. As long as the rest of the connection string passes the check, the *SqlClientPermission* will accept the connection string and allow you to (attempt to) connect to the SQL Server database.

Why You Shouldn't Start with Unrestricted AccessIn theory, if you wanted to allow connections to any SQL Server database except for the Northwind database on the local installation of SQL Server Express, you could start with unrestricted permissions and deny a specific connection string using the following code:

> **Note**   This is a very bad idea. Don't do this. You'll see why after the next code snippet.

Visual Basic

```
Dim perm As New SqlClientPermission(PermissionState.Unrestricted)
perm.Add("Data Source=.\SQLExpress;Initial Catalog=Northwind;", _
        "User ID=;Password=;", _
        KeyRestrictionBehavior.PreventUsage)
perm.Deny()

Dim strConn As String
strConn = "Data Source=.\SQLExpress;" & _
        "Initial Catalog=Northwind;User ID=...;Password=...;"
Dim cn As New SqlConnection(strConn)
cn.Open()
...
```

Visual C#

```
SqlClientPermission perm;
perm = new SqlClientPermission(PermissionState.Unrestricted);
perm.Add(@"Data Source=.\SQLExpress;Initial Catalog=Northwind;",
        "User ID=;Password=;",
        KeyRestrictionBehavior.PreventUsage);
perm.Deny();

string strConn;
strConn = @"Data Source=.\SQLExpress;" +
          "Initial Catalog=Northwind;User ID=...;Password=...;";
SqlConnection cn = new SqlConnection(strConn);
cn.Open();
...
```

This code will, as expected, throw a *SecurityException*. Problem solved? Not quite.

Starting with unrestricted permissions and trying to deny access to a single resource is generally easier said than done. What happens if you try the same code with the following connection string?

```
Data Source=(local)\SQLExpress;Initial Catalog=Northwind;
User ID=MyUserID;Password=MyPassword;
```

Unfortunately, the *SqlClientPermission* does not recognize that *.\SQLExpress* and *(local)\SQLExpress* refer to the same server. Thus, this passes the *SqlClientPermission*'s check and the *SqlConnection* will attempt to connect to SQL Server using this connection string, which is not what we wanted or expected. The *SqlClientPermission* would also allow you to connect to the database using the IP address for the server. That's not a knock on the *SqlClientPermission*. There are many ways to create a connection string to a single SQL Server database, and the logic required to determine that they're equivalent would be staggering. If *SqlClientPermission* did try to include that logic, you'd pay a significant performance penalty, plus there would be a good chance that *SqlClientPermission* would fail to successfully recognize *all* equivalent connection strings.

In other words, start with no permissions and allow specific strings rather than start with unrestricted permissions and trying to prevent access to specific resources.

Scoping Permissions

Say you have a function called *Function1* that uses a *SqlClientPermission* to restrict access to SQL Server databases. For how long are those restrictions enforced? If *Function1* calls *Function1A*, are those restrictions enforced? What if you call *Function2* after calling *Function1*? Are the restrictions enforced during *Function2*?

The restrictions are enforced for the lifetime of the function in which they're created. In the previous examples, they will be enforced in *Function1* and *Function1A* but not *Function2*.

Enforcing Connection String Security Through Procedure Attributes

Absolutely. You can apply attributes to a procedure to enforce connection string security. Here's a simple example:

Visual Basic

```
<SqlClientPermission( _
    SecurityAction.PermitOnly, _
    ConnectionString = "Server=.\SQLExpress;Initial Catalog=Northwind;" & _
                       "Integrated Security=True;", _
    KeyRestrictions = "", _
    KeyRestrictionBehavior = KeyRestrictionBehavior.AllowOnly)> _
Private Sub MyProcedure
    ...
End Sub
```

Visual C#

```
[SqlClientPermission(
    SecurityAction.PermitOnly,
    ConnectionString = @"Server=.\SQLExpress;Initial Catalog=Northwind;" +
                       "Integrated Security=True;",
    KeyRestrictions = "",
    KeyRestrictionBehavior = KeyRestrictionBehavior.AllowOnly)]
private void MyProcedure()
{
    ...
}
```

Connection Pooling

Like Microsoft's previous data access technology, ADO.NET includes built-in support for connection pooling.

Connection Handles and Physical Connections

If you're working with Visual Studio, you can examine some of the internal private properties of objects using the Visual Studio debugging tools. For example, write some code to open a *SqlConnection* and set a breakpoint on the call to the *Open* method. Add the object to the Watch window by right-clicking the object in your code and selecting Add Watch. In the Watch window, expand the area marked Non-Public Members. Scroll down and you'll see a private property called *InnerConnection*.

The contents of the *InnerConnection* property represent a very thin layer over the physical connection to the database. For the purposes of this discussion, the *InnerConnection* property and the physical connection to the database are interchangeable. As you step through your code, you'll see that the value of the *InnerConnection* property changes as you open and close your connection. When you call the *Open* method, the SQL Client .NET Data Provider associates the *SqlConnection* object with a physical connection to your database, so you can execute queries and return results.

Opening and closing database connections is expensive. To help save resources and improve performance, the .NET Data Providers in the .NET Framework all use connection pooling by default.

What Is Connection Pooling?

Connection pooling is a mechanism to improve the performance of applications when opening connections to your data store. When you call the *Close* method on your *SqlConnection* object, the SQL Client .NET Data Provider doesn't *actually* close the inner connection. Instead, the provider stores the inner connection in a pool so that it can be reused at a later time. The inner connection remains in the pool even after the *SqlConnection* object has been disposed of. If you later call the *Open* method on a *SqlConnection* object using the same connection string and credentials, you'll re-use the same inner connection to communicate with your database.

If you want to confirm that you're actually re-using the same inner connection, you can use functionality in .NET Reflection to programmatically access the contents of the private *InnerConnection* property. The following code, which requires a reference to the *System.Reflection* namespace, opens a *SqlConnection* in a *Using* block and stores the value of the *SqlConnection*'s *InnerConnection* property. By using a *Using* block, we implicitly dispose of the *SqlConnection* at the end of the block. The code then opens another *SqlConnection* in a *Using* block and stores the value of that *SqlConnection*'s *InnerConnection* property. Finally, the code compares the contents of the *InnerConnection* properties, confirming that they are in fact the same object.

Visual Basic
```
Dim strConn As String = "Data Source=.\SQLExpress;Integrated Security=True;"
Dim propInnerConn As PropertyInfo
propInnerConn = GetType(SqlConnection).GetProperty("InnerConnection", _
                        BindingFlags.NonPublic Or BindingFlags.Instance)
Dim objInnerConn1, objInnerConn2 As Object
Using cn As New SqlConnection(strConn)
    cn.Open()
```

```
        objInnerConn1 = propInnerConn.GetValue(cn, Nothing)
        cn.Close()
End Using
Using cn As New SqlConnection(strConn)
        cn.Open()
        objInnerConn2 = propInnerConn.GetValue(cn, Nothing)
        cn.Close()
End Using
Console.WriteLine(objInnerConn1 Is objInnerConn2)
```

Visual C#

```
string strConn = @"Data Source=.\SQLExpress;Integrated Security=True;";
PropertyInfo propInnerConn;
propInnerConn = typeof(SqlConnection).GetProperty("InnerConnection",
                              BindingFlags.NonPublic | BindingFlags.Instance);
object objInnerConn1, objInnerConn2;
using (SqlConnection cn = new SqlConnection(strConn))
{
    cn.Open();
    objInnerConn1 = propInnerConn.GetValue(cn, null);
    cn.Close();
}
using (SqlConnection cn = new SqlConnection(strConn))
{
    cn.Open();
    objInnerConn2 = propInnerConn.GetValue(cn, null);
    cn.Close();
}
Console.WriteLine(objInnerConn1 == objInnerConn2);
```

The two *SqlConnection* objects are created in separate *Using* blocks, so their resources are cleaned up at the end of each *Using* block. The contents of the *InnerConnection* property, and the physical connection that it encapsulates, are stored in a pool rather than disposed of so that they can be reused.

> **Note**   If you disable connection pooling in the connection string—and we'll explain how to do this shortly—you'll see that the inner connection is not reused.

How Connection Pooling Can Improve Your Code

Consider a typical ASP.NET or WebServices application that accesses a SQL Server database. Each time the client application needs to query the database, there's a round-trip to server-side code that opens a *SqlConnection* to execute the query. In many of these applications, this code connects to the same database, with the same credentials, over and over again. In theory, this means that every time the client application needs to execute a query, the server-side code needs to perform three operations—logging on to the database (which requires checking the supplied credentials), executing the query, and then logging out.

Connection pooling can really improve the performance of such applications. By storing the inner connection in a pool and re-using it later, you no longer pay the performance penalty associated with logging into and out of the database. The calls to the *Open* and *Close* methods of the *SqlConnection* objects return in a fraction of the time, thereby improving the performance and responsiveness of your code. (See Figure 3-4.)

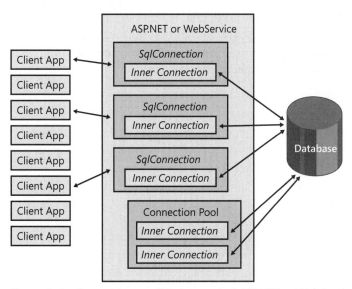

Figure 3-4   Connection pooling in a typical ASP.NET or WebServices application

Enabling Connection Pooling

Connection pooling is turned on by default in ADO.NET. The following code snippet opens and closes the same *SqlConnection* object five times. Because connection pooling is turned on by default, the actual connection to the database isn't actually closed when you call the *Close* method. Instead, the database connection is sent to the pool where it's later reused.

Visual Basic
```
Dim strConn As String
strConn = "Data Source=.\SQLExpress;Integrated Security=True;"
Dim cn As New SqlConnection(strConn)
For intCounter As Integer = 1 To 5
    cn.Open()
    cn.Close()
Next intCounter
```

Visual C#
```
string strConn;
strConn = @"Data Source=.\SQLExpress;Integrated Security=True;";
SqlConnection cn = new SqlConnection(strConn);
for (int intCounter = 1; intCounter <= 5; intCounter++)
{
    cn.Open();
    cn.Close();
}
```

When Will My Pooled Connection Be Closed?

When you call the *Close* method, *SqlClient* returns the connection to the pool. Assuming that connection is not re-used, it will be removed from the pool after approximately five minutes. There is no exact number of seconds involved. The behavior depends on random number generation and, if memory serves, the relative humidity at the time the pool was created. Of course, if the application exits while there are open pools, the connections will be closed and disposed of as part of the normal application cleanup.

Disabling Connection Pooling

You might not want to use connection pooling. For example, if you're working with a simple Windows application that communicates directly with the database, you might want to disable connection pooling. With this architecture, the individual client applications require their own connections. With connection pooling enabled, each application's connection is pooled and re-used if the connection is re-opened before the pool is cleared. So, if the application re-uses connections frequently, the call to *SqlConnection.Open* will return more quickly with connection pooling enabled. However, this approach leads to more active connections against the database at any given time. Disabling connection pooling would decrease the number of active connections against the database at any time, but it would force all calls to *SqlConnection.Open* to establish a new connection to the database.

If you want to disable connection pooling, you can do so on a per-connection basis by adding *Pooling=False* to the connection string.

Thankfully in ADO.NET 2.0, you do not need to memorize attributes like these. When in doubt, you can check the options on the *SqlConnectionStringBuilder* class. There, you'll find a *Pooling* property that takes a Boolean value. By default, this value is set to *True*. Setting the value to *False* will disable pooling on that connection. Then, when you call the *Close* method on your *SqlConnection* object, you'll close the actual connection to your database.

> **Note**   Using connection pooling in "occasionally connected" Windows applications can be helpful, depending on your application. If the application wants to reconnect to the database periodically, you could leverage connection pooling to keep the physical connection to the database open, at least temporarily. The pooling logic will re-use the physical connection to the database if the application attempts to reconnect to the database before the physical connection has been removed from the pool.

Answering Your Own Questions About Connection Pooling

The more developers learn about connection pooling, the more questions come to mind. For example, the most common question I hear regarding connection pooling is, "How can I figure out whether the physical connection to the database was truly closed or simply pooled?" Another common question is, "How can I tell whether a connection I just opened established a new physical connection or re-used a pooled one?"

There are many tools out there that can help you answer your own questions about connection pooling. Some are more elegant than others. I routinely use SQL Server Profiler to monitor connections as well as queries to my SQL Server databases. With the release of ADO.NET 2.0, you can also use the Performance Monitor in Windows.

The SQL Client .NET Data Provider in ADO.NET 2.0 includes performance counters for connection pooling. You can now use tools such as Performance Monitor to look at the number of pooled connections, active connections, free connections, active and inactive connection pools, and active and inactive connection pool groups. You can also gather information about connections and disconnections per second.

In some cases, maintaining performance counters can create a performance hit. For this reason, the SQL Client .NET Data Provider does not maintain performance counters for the number of active or free connections, or the number of pooled connections or disconnections per second. You can enable these performance counters in your application by adding an entry to your application's configuration file. For more information about using these performance counters, see the article "Using ADO.NET Performance Counters" on the MSDN Web site.

To make it easier for you to ask and answer your own connection pooling questions, I've built a sample application, which is shown in Figure 3-5 and is available as part of the downloadable sample code for this text. This application lets you create connection strings using the *SqlConnectionStringBuilder* / *PropertyGrid* dialog box shown previously in Figure 3-3. You can easily create new *SqlConnections*, open and close existing ones, and call the *ClearPool* and *ClearAllPool* methods. The sample also accesses the SQL Client performance counters without you having to manually add performance counters via Performance Monitor. The configuration file for the application includes the entry to enable the performance counters that are turned off by default. The performance counter information in the sample is updated every time you create, open, or close a *SqlConnection* or close either one or all connection pools.

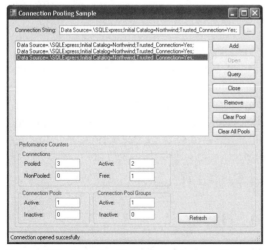

Figure 3-5   Investigating connection pooling

How ADO.NET Determines Whether to Use a Pooled Connection

Simply put, assuming pooling is not disabled, the SQL Client .NET Data Provider examines the *ConnectionString* when you call the *SqlConnection* object's *Open* method and determines whether or not there's an available connection in the pool. If there's an available connection, SQL Client uses it. Otherwise, it opens a new connection to the database.

Actually, there's a little more to it than that. Imagine an ASP.NET application where multiple users are logging into the same database with impersonation, each using their own credentials to access the SQL Server database. The connection string for each user is the same, but their credentials are very different. So, the logic used to determine which pooled connections can be used is a little more complex in that SQL Client takes user permissions into account.

Forcing ADO.NET to Use a New Pool

Occasionally, there are times when you might decide you no longer want to draw connections from an old pool and would prefer to establish a new pool. In such a case, the goal is to modify your connection string in a way that affects pooling, but not the rest of your application. The simplest way to accomplish this is to add a single space to the end of your connection string.

Manually Releasing Pooled Connections

The previous trick was handy with ADO.NET version 1.x because there were no features in the API to help you release pooled connections. In ADO.NET 2.0, there are two new static methods available on the *SqlConnection* class to help—*ClearPool* and *ClearAllPools*.

The *ClearPool* method takes a *SqlConnection* object and releases all pooled connections in the pool associated with that *SqlConnection*. Say you have 10 *SqlConnection* objects, all using the same connection string and credentials, with pooling enabled. You call the *Open* method on all 10 objects, and then call the *Close* method on three of the objects. A train then leaves Baltimore at 4:00 P.M., heading north at 200 kilometers per hour. On second thought, let's forget the train, at least for now.

There are 10 open connections to your SQL Server database. Seven of those connections are associated with the seven open *SqlConnection* objects. To use the terms used by the performance counters, these seven connections are "active." The remaining three connections reside in the connection pool. Again, using the performance counters' terms, these are "free" connections. Calling the *ClearPool* method will release those three free connections that reside in the pool, but it will not affect the active connections used by the seven open *SqlConnection* objects.

The *ClearAllPools* method takes no arguments and clears all free *SqlConnections*.

What Other Pooling Options Do I Have?

Let's quickly look at the other commonly used connection-pooling options. Each option is available through the *SqlConnectionStringBuilder* and through connection strings.

Connection Reset

If you've taken a close look at a SQL Profiler trace, you might have noticed a call to a stored procedure named *sp_reset_connection* and wondered when or why that stored procedure is called.

Simply re-using a pooled *SqlConnection* could have unexpected consequences. For lack of a better term, there's some "residue" associated with a pooled connection. Developers don't always clean up their messes to return the connection to its original state upon closing the connection. At the time the *Close* method was called, there might have been open cursors or transactions associated with the connection, or worse. If a query like "*USE AdventureWorks*" was issued, the connection might be associated with a different database than when the database was opened. If you specify the application role for a connection by calling *sp_setapprole*, those privileges are still applied to the connection until *sp_unsetapprole* is called, or until *sp_reset_connection* is called, or until the connection is truly closed (rather than simply pooled).

The SQL Client .NET Data Provider keeps track of which *SqlConnection*s use a connection retrieved from a connection pool. Rather than calling the *sp_reset_connection* stored procedure when you call the *Open* method, *SqlClient* executes this query just prior to the first activity on the connection.

If you're absolutely sure that you're not leaving any "residue" on the server for your pooled connections, you *could* add *Connection Reset=False;* to your connection string. This setting tells *SqlClient* that it does not need to call the *sp_reset_connection* stored procedure when re-using pooled connections. However, I would not recommend setting Connection Reset to False.

Min Pool Size

As its name might imply, *Min Pool Size* controls the minimum number of connections in a pool. By default, this attribute is set to *0*.

The *Min Pool Size* attribute can help you prepare a connection pool. Say you set the attribute to 5. Once you open your first connection, *SqlClient* will open another four connections on a background thread. There will always be at least five connections in the pool. Say your code creates 10 *SqlConnection* objects and opens them all. As before, when you open the first *SqlConnection*, *SqlClient* will open four more connections on a background thread. The next four *SqlConnection* objects will use the remaining connections from the pool. The remaining five *SqlConnection* objects will establish new connections.

Now, let's say you close eight of those 10 *SqlConnection* objects. All eight connections will be kept alive in the pool. When *SqlClient* cleans up the pool (approximately five minutes after the *SqlConnection*s are closed, assuming they are not re-used), it will make sure there are at least five connections (the *Min Pool Size* setting) still in the pool. This number includes the connections currently in use. Two connections are still in use. So three additional connections will stay in the pool. The five remaining connections will be discarded.

The main drawback to *Min Pool Size* is that the pool will keep at least that many connections active. These connections can get extremely stale in an ASP.NET application. You're better off leaving *Min Pool Size* at *0*.

Max Pool Size

The *Max Pool Size* setting is a little simpler to understand. The setting acts as a throttling feature, preventing you from opening more than the specified number of connections in a single pool. The default for *Max Pool Size* is *100*. Once you reach the maximum number of connections in the pool, the next attempt will try to open a connection for the time specified in the Connect Timeout setting before timing out with an *InvalidOperationException* saying, "Timeout expired. The timeout period elapsed prior to obtaining a connection from the pool. This may have occurred because all pooled connections were in use and max pool size was reached."

Using the *SqlConnection* as a Starting Point

Once you've connected to your SQL Server database, the *SqlConnection* object can serve as the starting point for a number of operations—creating commands, starting transactions, and retrieving schema.

Creating *SqlCommand*s

The *SqlCommand* class, which We'll explore in Chapter 4, is the class you use to execute queries against your database. To execute a query, you must set the *SqlCommand* object's *Connection* property to a *SqlConnection* object. The *SqlConnection* class provides a *Create-Command* method that you can use to simplify the process. This method returns a new *SqlCommand* object that's already initialized to use your *SqlConnection* object.

One benefit to the *CreateCommand* method is that it's available on all Connection classes in the .NET Framework. So this approach lets you create a Command on a given Connection in a generic fashion. I regularly write code to run with different .NET Data Providers to investigate or demonstrate features. That code often adds schema, data, or both prior to executing queries. Here's an example of this coding approach. Note that this code uses the *System.Data.Common* namespace. Each code snippet contains a commented-out reference to this namespace.

Visual Basic
```
'Imports System.Data.Common
Private Sub PrepDb(ByRef cn As DbConection)
    Using cmd As DbCommand = cn.CreateCommand
        cmd.CommandText = "CREATE TABLE MyTable ..."
        cmd.ExecuteNonQuery()
        cmd.CommandText = "INSERT INTO MyTable ..."
        cmd.ExecuteNonQuery()
    End Using
End Sub
```

Visual C#
```
//using System.Data.Common
private void PrepDb(DbConnection cn) {
    using (DbCommand cmd = cn.CreateCommand()) {
        cmd.CommandText = "CREATE TABLE MyTable ...";
        cmd.ExecuteNonQuery();
        cmd.CommandText = "INSERT INTO MyTable ...";
        cmd.ExecuteNonQuery();
    }
}
```

Starting *SqlTransactions*

You can also use a *SqlConnection* object to start transactions. The *SqlConnection* class's *Begin-Transaction* method returns a new open *SqlTransaction* object on your connection. I'll discuss the *SqlTransaction* object in detail in Chapter 10.

Here's some code that demonstrates how to start a transaction on a *SqlConnection* object:

Visual Basic
```
Dim strConn As String
strConn = "Data Source=.\SQLExpress;" & _
          "Initial Catalog=Northwind;Integrated Security=True;"
Dim cn As New SqlConnection(strConn)
cn.Open()
Dim txn As SqlTransaction = cn.BeginTransaction()
```

Visual C#
```
string strConn;
strConn = @"Data Source=.\SQLExpress;" +
          "Initial Catalog=Northwind;Integrated Security=True;";
SqlConnection cn = new SqlConnection(strConn);
cn.Open();
SqlTransaction txn = cn.BeginTransaction();
```

Retrieving Schema Information

In ADO.NET 1.x, the only way to query a *SqlConnection* for schema information was to construct and execute a query to request that information. For example, if you wanted to see the available tables, you'd need to execute a query against the system tables or the INFORMATION_SCHEMA.TABLES view. The latter query might look something like this:

```
SELECT TABLE_NAME FROM INFORMATION_SCHEMA.TABLES WHERE TABLE_TYPE = 'BASE TABLE'
```

Thankfully, in ADO.NET 2.0, there's now a way to retrieve this type of schema information from a *SqlConnection* object without having to scurry to the SQL Server Books Online for documentation on system tables or the INFORMATION_SCHEMA views. The *SqlConnection* class now exposes a *GetSchema* method that you can use to retrieve schema information from your database. The *GetSchema* method is overloaded in a way that might seem odd at first, but the overloads provide a simple, effective way to determine exactly what schemas and restrictions are available.

Say you want to use the *GetSchema* method to get a list of the tables available in your database. You could issue code such as the following:

Visual Basic
```
Dim strConn As String
strConn = "Data Source=.\SQLExpress;" & _
          "Initial Catalog=Northwind;Integrated Security=True;"
Dim cn As New SqlConnection(strConn)
cn.Open()

Dim tbl As DataTable = cn.GetSchema("Tables")
For Each row As DataRow In tbl.Rows
    Console.WriteLine(row("TABLE_NAME"))
Next row
```

Visual C#
```
string strConn;
strConn = @"Data Source=.\SQLExpress;" +
          "Initial Catalog=Northwind;Integrated Security=True;";
SqlConnection cn = new SqlConnection(strConn);
cn.Open();

DataTable tbl = cn.GetSchema("Tables");
foreach (DataRow row in tbl.Rows)
    Console.WriteLine(row["TABLE_NAME"]);
```

The *GetSchema* method returns a *DataTable* of information. I'll discuss the *DataTable* class in detail in Chapter 6. If you haven't used a *DataTable* before, think of it as a Microsoft Excel spreadsheet—a collection of columns and rows, designed to cache the results of a query. After calling *GetSchema*, the code walks through each of the rows available and prints out the value in the TABLE_NAME column.

The *GetSchema* call returns more than just the names of the tables. This information is a little easier to digest by displaying the full contents on a form. Figure 3-6 is a snapshot of this data, showing how the call to *GetSchema* also returns catalog and schema names, as well as whether the information represents a base table or a view.

You might look at this code and ask yourself, "How would I know to pass *Tables* into the *GetSchema* method?" Good question. There are a series of schemas that all .NET Data Providers support and they are listed in the *DbMetaDataCollectionNames* enumeration in the *System.Data.Common* namespace. The SQL Client .NET Data Provider lists the additional schemas it supports in the *SqlClientMetaDataCollectionNames* enumeration. So, rather than pass the literal string *Tables* into the *GetSchema* method, you could pass *SqlClientMetaData-CollectionNames.Tables*. However, there's another way to determine what schemas a particular .NET Data Provider supports.

Each Connection class has its own list of available schemas through the *DbConnection* class's *GetSchema* method. You can access this list by calling the overloaded *GetSchema* method that takes no parameters. The following code lists schemas supported by a *SqlConnection*, which includes Tables, Columns, Views, Procedures, Indexes, IndexColumns, and so on.

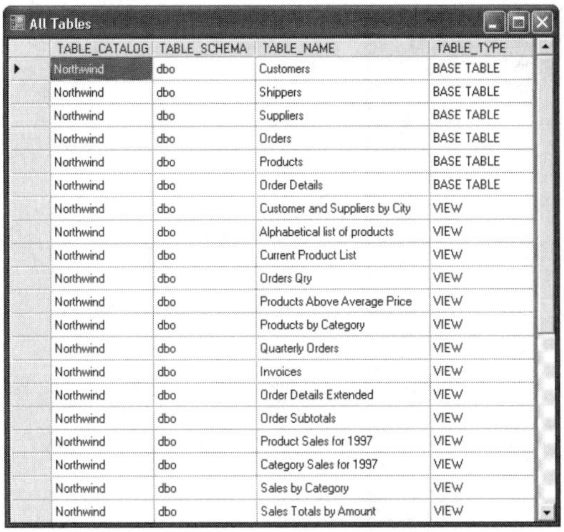

All Tables

TABLE_CATALOG	TABLE_SCHEMA	TABLE_NAME	TABLE_TYPE
Northwind	dbo	Customers	BASE TABLE
Northwind	dbo	Shippers	BASE TABLE
Northwind	dbo	Suppliers	BASE TABLE
Northwind	dbo	Orders	BASE TABLE
Northwind	dbo	Products	BASE TABLE
Northwind	dbo	Order Details	BASE TABLE
Northwind	dbo	Customer and Suppliers by City	VIEW
Northwind	dbo	Alphabetical list of products	VIEW
Northwind	dbo	Current Product List	VIEW
Northwind	dbo	Orders Qry	VIEW
Northwind	dbo	Products Above Average Price	VIEW
Northwind	dbo	Products by Category	VIEW
Northwind	dbo	Quarterly Orders	VIEW
Northwind	dbo	Invoices	VIEW
Northwind	dbo	Order Details Extended	VIEW
Northwind	dbo	Order Subtotals	VIEW
Northwind	dbo	Product Sales for 1997	VIEW
Northwind	dbo	Category Sales for 1997	VIEW
Northwind	dbo	Sales by Category	VIEW
Northwind	dbo	Sales Totals by Amount	VIEW

Figure 3-6 Table information returned by calling *SqlConnection.GetSchema("Tables")*

Visual Basic

```
Dim strConn As String
strConn = "Data Source=.\SQLExpress;" & _
          "Initial Catalog=Northwind;Integrated Security=True;"
Dim cn As New SqlConnection(strConn)
cn.Open()

Dim tbl As DataTable = cn.GetSchema()
For Each row As DataRow In tbl.Rows
    Console.WriteLine(row("CollectionName"))
Next row
```

Visual C#

```
string strConn;
strConn = @"Data Source=.\SQLExpress;" +
           "Initial Catalog=Northwind;Integrated Security=True;";
SqlConnection cn = new SqlConnection(strConn);
cn.Open();

DataTable tbl = cn.GetSchema();
foreach (DataRow row in tbl.Rows)
    Console.WriteLine(row["CollectionName"]);
```

Figure 3-7 shows the full contents of the data returned on a call to *SqlConnection.GetSchema* using a SQL Server Express database.

You can pass any of these collection names into the *GetSchema* method to understand what schema is available in your database. However, there are times when you might not want to examine all the information for a particular type of schema. For example, you might want to see information about the columns in your database, but only those columns that reside in a particular table.

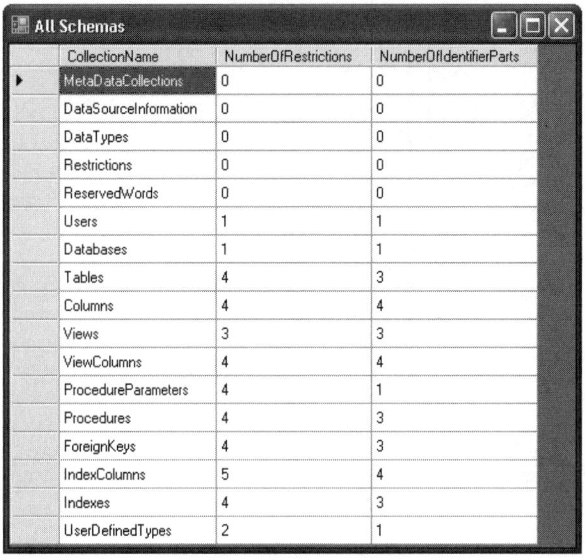

CollectionName	NumberOfRestrictions	NumberOfIdentifierParts
MetaDataCollections	0	0
DataSourceInformation	0	0
DataTypes	0	0
Restrictions	0	0
ReservedWords	0	0
Users	1	1
Databases	1	1
Tables	4	3
Columns	4	4
Views	3	3
ViewColumns	4	4
ProcedureParameters	4	1
Procedures	4	3
ForeignKeys	4	3
IndexColumns	5	4
Indexes	4	3
UserDefinedTypes	2	1

Figure 3-7 The list of available schemas returned by calling *SqlConnection.GetSchema()*

There's another overload for the *GetSchema* method, designed just for this purpose. You can pass a schema name and an array of strings to the *GetSchema* method. The strings are used as restrictions or filters in the query for schema information. The following code uses this approach to display just the column names from the Customers table:

Visual Basic

```
Dim strConn As String
strConn = "Data Source=.\SQLExpress;" & _
          "Initial Catalog=Northwind;Integrated Security=True;"
Dim cn As New SqlConnection(strConn)
cn.Open()

Dim restrictions = New String() { "Northwind", "dbo", _
                                  "Customers", Nothing }
Dim tbl As DataTable = cn.GetSchema("Columns", restrictions)
For Each row As DataRow In tbl.Rows
    Console.WriteLine(row("COLUMN_NAME"))
Next row
```

Visual C#

```
string strConn;
strConn = @"Data Source=.\SQLExpress;" +
          "Initial Catalog=Northwind;Integrated Security=True;";
SqlConnection cn = new SqlConnection(strConn);
cn.Open();

string[] restrictions;
restrictions = new string[] { "Northwind", "dbo", "Customers", null };
DataTable tbl = cn.GetSchema("Columns", restrictions);
foreach (DataRow row in tbl.Rows)
    Console.WriteLine(row["COLUMN_NAME"]);
```

Figure 3-8 shows this *DataTable* of information bound to a *DataGridView* control on a Windows form.

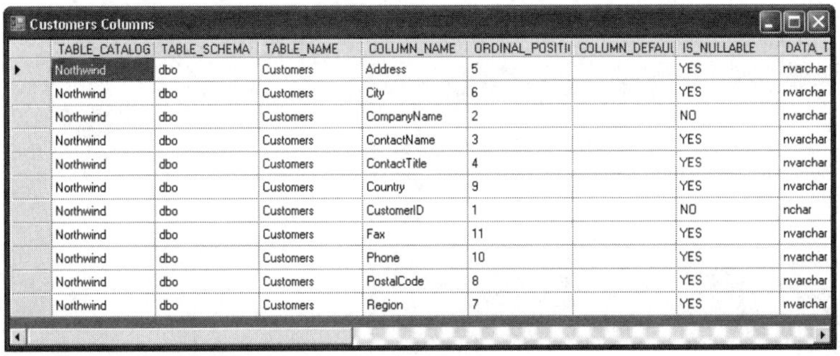

TABLE_CATALOG	TABLE_SCHEMA	TABLE_NAME	COLUMN_NAME	ORDINAL_POSITI	COLUMN_DEFAUL	IS_NULLABLE	DATA_T
Northwind	dbo	Customers	Address	5		YES	nvarchar
Northwind	dbo	Customers	City	6		YES	nvarchar
Northwind	dbo	Customers	CompanyName	2		NO	nvarchar
Northwind	dbo	Customers	ContactName	3		YES	nvarchar
Northwind	dbo	Customers	ContactTitle	4		YES	nvarchar
Northwind	dbo	Customers	Country	9		YES	nvarchar
Northwind	dbo	Customers	CustomerID	1		NO	nchar
Northwind	dbo	Customers	Fax	11		YES	nvarchar
Northwind	dbo	Customers	Phone	10		YES	nvarchar
Northwind	dbo	Customers	PostalCode	8		YES	nvarchar
Northwind	dbo	Customers	Region	7		YES	nvarchar

Figure 3-8 Retrieving schema information for the columns in a table via *SqlConnection.GetSchema*

Again, you might look at this code and wonder how you could figure out what the restrictions array should look like. How would anyone know to specify the name of the database as the first entry in the string array, the name of the schema as the second entry, the name of the table as the third entry, and *null* (or *Nothing*) as the fourth entry? Once again, you can use other overloads for the *GetSchema* method to figure out how to write your code.

There is a schema called Restrictions that you can use to examine the restrictions available on all schemas. The following code writes to the Console Window the collection name, restriction name, and restriction number for all available restrictions. The code also uses some *Console.WriteLine* formatting tricks to make the data a little easier to read.

Visual Basic

```
Dim strConn As String
strConn = "Data Source=.\SQLExpress;" & _
          "Initial Catalog=Northwind;Integrated Security=True;"
Dim cn As New SqlConnection(strConn)
cn.Open()

Dim tbl As DataTable = cn.GetSchema("Restrictions")
For Each row As DataRow In tbl.Rows
    Console.WriteLine("{0,-25} {1,-18} {2}", _
                      row("CollectionName"), _
                      row("RestrictionName"), _
                      row("RestrictionNumber"))
Next row
```

Visual C#

```
string strConn;
strConn = @"Data Source=.\SQLExpress;" +
          "Initial Catalog=Northwind;Integrated Security=True;";
SqlConnection cn = new SqlConnection(strConn);
cn.Open();

DataTable tbl = cn.GetSchema("Restrictions");
foreach (DataRow row in tbl.Rows)
```

```
Console.WriteLine("{0,-25} {1,-18} {2}",
                  row["CollectionName"],
                  row["RestrictionName"],
                  row["RestrictionNumber"]);
```

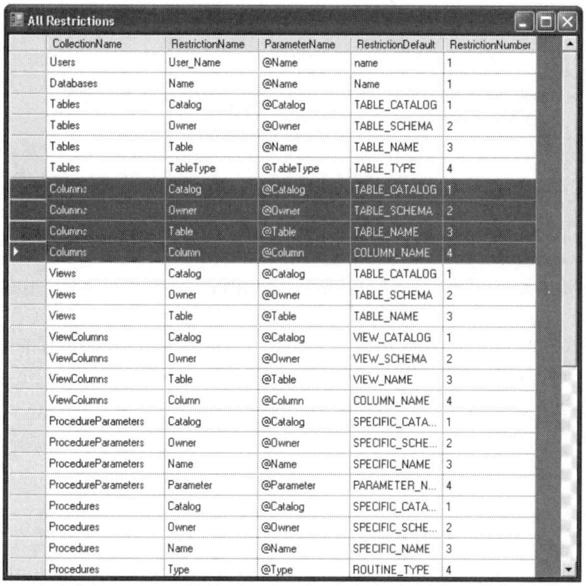

CollectionName	RestrictionName	ParameterName	RestrictionDefault	RestrictionNumber
Users	User_Name	@Name	name	1
Databases	Name	@Name	Name	1
Tables	Catalog	@Catalog	TABLE_CATALOG	1
Tables	Owner	@Owner	TABLE_SCHEMA	2
Tables	Table	@Name	TABLE_NAME	3
Tables	TableType	@TableType	TABLE_TYPE	4
Columns	Catalog	@Catalog	TABLE_CATALOG	1
Columns	Owner	@Owner	TABLE_SCHEMA	2
Columns	Table	@Table	TABLE_NAME	3
Columns	Column	@Column	COLUMN_NAME	4
Views	Catalog	@Catalog	TABLE_CATALOG	1
Views	Owner	@Owner	TABLE_SCHEMA	2
Views	Table	@Table	TABLE_NAME	3
ViewColumns	Catalog	@Catalog	VIEW_CATALOG	1
ViewColumns	Owner	@Owner	VIEW_SCHEMA	2
ViewColumns	Table	@Table	VIEW_NAME	3
ViewColumns	Column	@Column	COLUMN_NAME	4
ProcedureParameters	Catalog	@Catalog	SPECIFIC_CATA...	1
ProcedureParameters	Owner	@Owner	SPECIFIC_SCHE...	2
ProcedureParameters	Name	@Name	SPECIFIC_NAME	3
ProcedureParameters	Parameter	@Parameter	PARAMETER_N...	4
Procedures	Catalog	@Catalog	SPECIFIC_CATA...	1
Procedures	Owner	@Owner	SPECIFIC_SCHE...	2
Procedures	Name	@Name	SPECIFIC_NAME	3
Procedures	Type	@Type	ROUTINE_TYPE	4

Figure 3-9 Retrieving schema restriction information via *SqlConnection.GetSchema*

Figure 3-9 shows this same information bound to a *DataGridView* control on a Windows form. Notice that there are four entries with a *CollectionName* of "Columns." This means that there are four parameters available for restricting the information returned on a call to get column schema information. This explains why we used a string array that contained four elements on the call to *GetSchema* in the previous code snippet. Take another look at the figure and you'll see that the third restriction for Columns corresponds to the table name. This explains why we used the value *Customers* in the third element in the array. For portions of the array where you do not want to apply a restriction, supply no value for those entries in the array. For Visual Basic developers, that means using the *Nothing* keyword. For C# developers, that means using the *null* keyword.

The *GetSchema* methods return robust information–there's a lot more than just table and column names. For example, the columns schema also includes column ordinals, data types, sizes, and defaults. If you need to dynamically retrieve schema information from your database at run time, there's a wealth of information available through *GetSchema*.

Visual Studio Design-Time Features

The Visual Studio development environment includes features that make it easy to create connections to your database at design time and use those connections at run time.

Working with Connections in Server Explorer

The ADO.NET development team built ADO.NET to help you build fast, scalable database applications. The Visual Studio development team built a number of features into Visual Studio to help you build those database applications faster. One such feature is Server Explorer, which lets you examine various operating system services and integrate them into your applications. Server Explorer has additional support for database connectivity.

You can use Server Explorer to connect to SQL Server, as well as to other databases, from within Visual Studio. Once you've created a connection to your database, Server Explorer lets you examine the schema for that database—including tables (and columns), views, stored procedures and so on. If you're connecting to a SQL Server 2005 or SQL Express database, as shown in Figure 3-10, you'll also see additional schema—namely, types and assemblies.

Figure 3-10 Visual Studio Server Explorer

If you want to execute a query on a particular connection, right-click on that connection in Server Explorer and select New Query, which will launch the graphical query tool shown in Figure 3-11. Here, you can create your query quickly and easily. To execute the query and view the results, select Execute SQL from the menu, context menu, or toolbar.

If you're working with a SQL Server database, you can also use Server Explorer to change the schema of your database. Server Explorer allows you to create, modify, or drop tables, views, stored procedures, and so on for your SQL Server database. There's no need to create data-definition-language (DDL) queries such as CREATE TABLE. Instead, Server Explorer lets you modify schema through a simple but powerful user interface, shown in Figure 3-12.

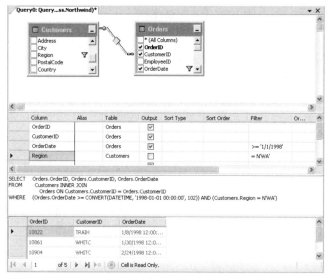

Figure 3-11   Visual Studio Query Designer

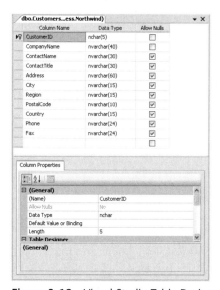

Figure 3-12   Visual Studio Table Designer

Adding a Data Connection to Server Explorer

You can add a data connection to Server Explorer by clicking the button at the top of Server Explorer that shows a yellow cylinder with an electrical cord attached. This will launch the dialog box shown in Figure 3-13, which lets you specify the information needed to connect to a SQL Server database.

Figure 3-13   Connecting to a SQL Server database from Server Explorer

If you want to connect to a different database, such as an Access or Oracle database, click the button marked Change near the top of this dialog box. This will dismiss the SQL Server–specific dialog box and launch the dialog box shown in Figure 3-14, which lets you choose a different type of data source.

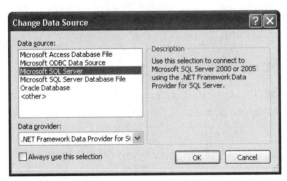

Figure 3-14   Selecting the type of data source for a connection

> **Note**   In diagrams, databases are represented almost universally by cylinders. I'm not entirely sure why, but Dail Magee, Jr., the technical editor for the first edition of this book, informed me that this is "likely because a cylinder is the old flowchart symbol for mass storage—chosen because long, long ago random-access, mass-storage devices used drums rather than disks." He also claimed not to be old enough to remember such drives before saying, "Now go away and let me drink my Geritol in peace." He gets a little cranky when he hasn't had his afternoon nap.

What Happened to the Drag-and-Drop Features?

If you've used previous versions of Visual Studio, you might have noticed a change in the Server Explorer drag-and-drop functionality. Namely, you can't drag schema items (connections, tables, stored procedures, and so on) from Server Explorer onto many designer surfaces (such as Windows and Web Forms) in Visual Studio 2005 the way you could in previous versions. Most of this functionality has moved to the strongly typed *DataSet* feature, which we'll explain in Chapter 9.

If you want to have *SqlConnection* and *SqlCommand* objects in the component tray of your designers, you might have noticed that these classes are no longer available with standard controls in the Toolbox window. However, you can add these classes to the toolbox. Right-click in the Toolbox window and select Choose Items, and then select the desired components from the resulting dialog box. This will not re-enable the drag-and-drop functionality, but it will add the desired components to the toolbox. You can then drag and drop these components onto your designer surfaces and set their properties using the Properties window.

SqlConnection Object Reference

You now understand the role of the *SqlConnection* class in database applications and are comfortable using its major features. The following section is intended to fill in some of the blanks and cover the less-frequently-used but still important features of the class. Read it now or save it for later. This reference material does not introduce new characters, nor does it contain any unexpected plot twists that will affect your ability to understand subsequent chapters.

Let's take a closer look at the properties and methods of the *SqlConnection* object.

Properties of the *SqlConnection* Class

Table 3-1 contains the properties you'll use most often when working with a *SqlConnection* object. The majority of these properties can be set only through the *ConnectionString* property and cannot be modified directly.

Table 3-1 Commonly Used Properties of the *SqlConnection* Class

Property	Data Type	Description
ConnectionString	*String*	Controls how the *SqlConnection* object will connect to your data source.
ConnectionTimeout	*Int32*	Specifies how long, in seconds, the *SqlConnection* will try to connect to your data source (read-only).
Database	*String*	Returns the name of the database you are, or will be, connected to (read-only).
DataSource	*String*	Returns the location of the database you are, or will be, connected to (read-only).
FireInfoMessageEvent-OnUserErrors	*Boolean*	Controls whether or not the *InfoMessage* event fires on user errors. By default, this property is set to *False*. This property can be changed on both closed and open *SqlConnections*.

Table 3-1   Commonly Used Properties of the *SqlConnection* Class

Property	Data Type	Description
PacketSize	Int32	Returns the packet size used when communicating with SQL Server (read-only).
ServerVersion	String	Returns the version of your data source (read-only).
State	ConnectionState	Indicates the current state of the *SqlConnection* object (read-only).
StatisticsEnabled	Boolean	Controls whether or not statistics are enabled for the connection. By default, this property is set to *False*. This property can be modified on closed and open *SqlConnections*.
WorkstationId	String	Returns the name of the database client. By default, this property is set to the machine name (read-only).

ConnectionString Property

The *ConnectionString* property controls how the *SqlConnection* object will attempt to connect to your data source. You can set this property only when your *SqlConnection* is not connected to your data source. When it's connected to your data source, the property is read-only.

ConnectionTimeout Property

The *ConnectionTimeout* property indicates the amount of time, in seconds, that the SQL Client provider will wait for an attempt to connect to your data source before timing out.

This property is read-only and can be set only through the *SqlConnection* class's *ConnectionString* property. There are two options for setting the connection timeout in a connection string—use a *SqlConnectionStringBuilder* with *ConnectTimeout* set to the desired value, or use the *Connect Timeout* keyword in your connection string.

Database and *DataSource* Properties

The terms *database* and *data source* are often used interchangeably, but the *SqlConnection* class exposes each as a separate property. So how do they differ? An instance of SQL Server is a data source, which might have different databases installed.

Let's assume that you're using a connection string such as the following:

```
"Data Source=.\SQLExpress;Initial Catalog=Northwind;Integrated Security=True;"
```

With this connection string, a *SqlConnection* object would return ".*SQLExpress*" in the *DataSource* property and "*Northwind*" in the *Database* property.

Both properties are read-only and can be set through the *SqlConnection*'s *ConnectionString* property.

The *DataSource* property can be set by setting the *DataSource* property on a *SqlConnectionStringBuilder* or by using the *Data Source* or *Server* keyword in a connection string.

The *Database* property can be set through the *SqlConnectionStringBuilder*'s *InitialCatalog* property or by using the *Initial Catalog* or *Database* keyword in a connection string.

FireInfoMessageEventOnUserErrors Property

If you try to query a table that does not exist, you'll generate a *SqlException*. If you set the *FireInfoMessageEventOnUserErrors* property to *True* (its default is *False*), user errors will be reported through the *SqlConnection*'s *InfoMessageEvent* instead. I'll discuss the *InfoMessageEvent* later in this chapter and include an example that demonstrates the *FireInfoMessageEventOnUserErrors* property.

The *FireInfoMessageEventOnUserErrors* property is read-write on *SqlConnections*, regardless of whether the connection is open or closed, and it might be the longest property name in ADO.NET.

PacketSize Property

The *PacketSize* property returns the size of network packets, in bytes, used to communicate with SQL Server. This *SqlConnection* property is read-only and can be set only through the *ConnectionString* property, either by using the *SqlConnectionStringBuilder*'s *PacketSize* property or the *Packet Size* keyword in a connection string.

The *SqlConnection* supports packet sizes between 512 and 32768 bytes. Attempts to set a packet size outside these boundaries will result in an *ArgumentException*.

ServerVersion Property

Most database systems introduce new features with each successive version. SQL Server 2005, for example, supports many features that SQL Server 2000 did not, such as multiple active resultsets on a single connection and the XML data type. You can check the *ServerVersion* property to ensure you don't make unsupported calls to a server.

The *SourceVersion* property returns a string containing the version of the database to which you're connected. Developers with a SQL Server background might be familiar with the SELECT @@Version query. The *SourceVersion* property returns a subset of the information returned by SELECT @@Version—the database's version number.

Let's say your application expects to communicate with SQL Server 2005 but needs to programmatically verify that the *SqlConnection* is talking to a SQL Server 2005 database (or later). The string returned by the *ServerVersion* property will start with "09" if you're connecting to a SQL Server 2005 database. So you could use the following code to verify that you've connected to a SQL Server 2005 (or later) database:

Visual Basic
```
Dim strConn As String = "Data Source=.\SQLExpress;Integrated Security=True;"
Dim cn As New SqlConnection(strConn)
cn.Open()
```

```
If String.Compare(cn.ServerVersion, "09") >= 0 Then
    'You're working with SQL Server 2005 or later.
Else
    'You're working with an earlier version of SQL Server
End If
```

Visual C#

```
string strConn = @"Data Source=.\SQLExpress;Integrated Security=True;";
SqlConnection cn = new SqlConnection(strConn);
cn.Open();
if (string.Compare(cn.ServerVersion, "09") >= 0) {
    //You're working with SQL Server 2005 or later.
} else {
    //You're working with an earlier version of SQL Server
}
```

The *ServerVersion* property is available only on open connections. Accessing the *ServerVersion* property on a closed connection will cause an *InvalidOperationException*.

State Property

The *SqlConnection* class's *State* property returns the current state of the connection as a member of the *ConnectionState* enumeration in the *System.Data* namespace. As of ADO.NET 2.0, *SqlConnection.State* will return either *Open* or *Closed*. Other values might be used in a future release of ADO.NET.

You can use the *SqlConnection* object's *StateChange* event to determine when the value of the *State* property changes.

WorkstationId Property

If you've used SQL Server's tracing features in the past, you might have noticed a column in the trace called "HostName," which generally contains the name of the client machine connected to SQL Server. The *SqlConnection* class's *WorkstationId* property returns the same information. This property is read-only and is, by default, set to the machine name. You can control the value this property returns by using the *Workstation ID* keyword in your connection string or by using the *WorkstationId* property on a *SqlConnectionStringBuilder*.

Methods of the *SqlConnection* Class

Table 3-2 lists the *SqlConnection* class's methods. Methods such as *GetType* and *ToString* that are common to most objects in the .NET Framework are omitted. Take a look at the table to familiarize yourself with these methods.

Table 3-2   Commonly Used Methods of the *SqlConnection* Object

Method	Description
BeginTransaction	Begins a transaction on the connection
ChangeDatabase	Changes the current database on an open connection
ClearAllPools	Clears free connections in all *SqlConnection* pools (Static)

Table 3-2   Commonly Used Methods of the *SqlConnection* Object

Method	Description
ClearPool	Clears free connections in the connection pool associated with the supplied *SqlConnection* (Static)
Close	Closes the connection
CreateCommand	Creates a *SqlCommand* for the current connection
EnlistDistributedTransaction	Manually enlists the connection on a COM+ distributed transaction
EnlistTransaction	Manually enlists the connection on a System.Transactions transaction
GetSchema	Returns schema information for the connection
Open	Opens the connection
ResetStatistics	Resets statistics for the current connection
RetrieveStatistics	Returns statistics for the current connection

BeginTransaction Method

If you want to start a transaction on your connection—to lock data or to ensure that you can commit or roll back a series of changes to your data store—call the *BeginTransaction* method on the *SqlConnection* object. This method returns a new *SqlTransaction* object, a class I'll discuss in depth in Chapter 10 when I discuss updating your database.

> **Note**   Developers who've used the connection objects in ADO, RDO, or DAO might expect methods of the *SqlConnection* object to commit or roll back a transaction. In the ADO.NET object model, the *BeginTransaction* method generates a new *SqlTransaction* object. When you want to commit or roll back a transaction, call *Commit* or *Rollback* on the *SqlTransaction* object.

Because *BeginTransaction* creates a new transaction, associates it with the connection that created it, and initializes the transaction, using this method of the *SqlConnection* object can simplify your code slightly. The following code snippets are functionally equivalent:

Visual Basic
```
Dim txn As SqlTransaction = cn.BeginTransaction()
```

This code is equivalent to

```
Dim txn As New SqlTransaction()
txn.Connection = cn
txn.Begin()
```

Visual C#
```
SqlTransaction txn = cn.BeginTransaction();
```

This code is equivalent to

```
SqlTransaction txn = new SqlTransaction();
txn.Connection = cn;
txn.Begin();
```

ChangeDatabase Method

Earlier in the chapter, we talked about SQL Server's ability to support multiple databases on a single server. You can change the database you're communicating with by executing a query such as this one:

```
USE Northwind
```

ADO.NET also offers a method for changing the database. The *SqlConnection* class has a *ChangeDatabase* method that simplifies the process. The following code snippets are equivalent:

Visual Basic
```
Dim cn As New SqlConnection(strConn)
cn.Open()
...
cn.ChangeDatabase("Northwind")
```

This code is equivalent to

```
Dim cn As New SqlConnection(strConn)
cn.Open()
...
Dim cmd As SqlCommand = cn.CreateCommand()
cmd.CommandText = "USE Northwind"
cmd.ExecuteNonQuery()
```

Visual C#
```
SqlConnection cn = new SqlConnection(strConn);
cn.Open();
...
cn.ChangeDatabase("Northwind");
```

This code is equivalent to

```
SqlConnection cn = new SqlConnection(strConn);
cn.Open();
...
SqlCommand cmd = cn.CreateCommand();
cmd.CommandText = "USE Northwind";
cmd.ExecuteNonQuery();
```

ClearPool and *ClearAllPools* Methods

To manually clear a pool of connections, call the *SqlConnection* class's static *ClearPool* method and pass in a *SqlConnection* object. To clear all *SqlConnection* pools rather than just a single pool, call the *SqlConnection* class's *ClearAllPools* method.

Remember that only connections that currently reside in the pool will be released. Connections that are currently in use will not be affected by calling either of these methods.

Close Method

To close a *SqlConnection*, call the object's *Close* method. Remember that if you're using connection pooling, you're simply sending the physical connection to your data source to the pool. For more detail, see the earlier discussion in this chapter regarding connection pooling.

Calling the *Close* method on a *SqlConnection* object that's already marked as closed will not generate an exception. Disposing of a *SqlConnection* object implicitly calls the *Close* method.

CreateCommand Method

You can create new *SqlCommand* objects by using the *SqlConnection* class's *CreateCommand* method. This method accepts no arguments and returns a new *SqlCommand* object whose *Connection* property is set to the *SqlConnection* object that created it.

The following code snippets are functionally equivalent:

Visual Basic
```
Dim cn As New SqlConnection(strConn)
Dim cmd As SqlCommand = cn.CreateCommand()
```

This code is equivalent to

```
Dim cn As New SqlConnection(strConn)
Dim cmd As New SqlCommand()
cmd.Connection = cn
```

Visual C#
```
SqlConnection cn = new SqlConnection(strConn);
SqlCommand cmd = cn.CreateCommand();
```

This code is equivalent to

```
SqlConnection cn = new SqlConnection(strConn);
SqlCommand cmd = new SqlCommand();
cmd.Connection = cn;
```

EnlistDistributedTransaction Method

SqlConnection objects are automatically enlisted in COM+ distributed transactions by default. If, however, you need to manually enlist a *SqlConnection* object in a COM+ distributed transaction, use the *EnlistDistributedTransaction* method. Cast the current context's *Transaction* property to the *ITransaction* interface, and pass that to the *SqlConnection* object's *EnlistDistributedTransaction* method as shown in the following code, which assumes a reference to *System.Enterprise-Services*.

> **Note**   This code doesn't actually create a COM+ transaction, so it will not run. See the .NET Framework documentation for information about creating COM+ transactions in .NET code.

Visual Basic

```vb
'Imports System.EnterpriseServices
Dim strConn As String
strConn = "Data Source=.\SQLExpress;" & _
          "Initial Catalog=Northwind;Integrated Security=True;"
Using cn As New SqlConnection(strConn)
    cn.Open()
    Dim txn As ITransaction = CType(ContextUtil.Transaction, ITransaction)
    Try
        cn.EnlistDistributedTransaction(txn)
        'Perform work and commit the transaction
        ContextUtil.SetComplete()
    Catch ex As Exception
        'Handle exception and roll back the transaction
        ContextUtil.SetAbort()
    Finally
        'Release connection from distributed transaction
        cn.EnlistDistributedTransaction(Nothing)
    End Try
End Using
```

Visual C#

```csharp
//Imports System.EnterpriseServices
string strConn;
strConn = @"Data Source=.\SQLExpress;" +
          "Initial Catalog=Northwind;Integrated Security=True;";
using (SqlConnection cn = new SqlConnection(strConn)) {
    cn.Open();
    ITransaction txn = (ITransaction) ContextUtil.Transaction;
    try {
        cn.EnlistDistributedTransaction(txn);
        //Perform work and commit the transaction
        ContextUtil.SetComplete();
    } catch (Exception ex) {
        //Handle exception and roll back the transaction
        ContextUtil.SetAbort();
    } finally {
        //Release connection from distributed transaction
        cn.EnlistDistributedTransaction(null);
    }
}
```

> **Note**   Remember to clean up after yourself. Once you've committed or rolled back the distributed transaction, release the *SqlConnection* from the distributed transaction by calling *EnlistDistributedTransaction* and passing a null *ITransaction*.

EnlistTransaction Method

The *EnlistTransaction* method is nearly identical to the *EnlistDistributedTransaction* method, except the *EnlistTransaction* method is designed to work with *System.Transactions* transactions–new to version 2.0 of the .NET Framework. The following code snippet assumes a reference to the *System.Transactions* namespace.

Visual Basic

```vb
'Imports System.Transactions
Dim strConn As String
strConn = "Data Source=.\SQLExpress;" & _
        "Initial Catalog=Northwind;Integrated Security=True;"
Using cn As New SqlConnection(strConn)
    cn.Open()
    Using txn As CommittableTransaction = New CommittableTransaction()
        Try
            cn.EnlistTransaction(txn)
            'Perform work and commit the transaction
            txn.Commit()
        Catch ex As Exception
            'Handle exception and roll back the transaction
            txn.Rollback()
        Finally
            'Release connection from distributed transaction
            cn.EnlistTransaction(Nothing)
        End Try
    End Using
End Using
```

Visual C#

```csharp
//using System.Transactions;
string strConn;
strConn = @"Data Source=.\SQLExpress;" +
        "Initial Catalog=Northwind;Integrated Security=True;";
using (SqlConnection cn = new SqlConnection(strConn)) {
    cn.Open();
    using (CommittableTransaction txn = new CommittableTransaction()) {
        try {
            cn.EnlistTransaction(txn);
            //Perform work and commit the transaction
            txn.Commit();
        } catch (Exception ex) {
            //Handle exception and roll back the transaction
            txn.Rollback();
        } finally {
            //Release connection from distributed transaction
            cn.EnlistDistributedTransaction(null);
        }
    }
}
```

> **Note**   As with the *EnlistDistributedTransaction* method, remember to clean up after yourself.
> If you manually enlist a *SqlConnection* in a *System.Transactions* transaction, you should dis-
> charge the *SqlConnection* from the distributed transaction when you're done by calling *Enlist-*
> *Transaction* and passing a null *Transaction*.

GetSchema Method

The *GetSchema* method can help you programmatically examine your database's schema. The
GetSchema method returns a *DataTable* of schema information and is overloaded. Use the
parameter-less method to retrieve a list of available schemas. To retrieve a specific schema,
such as a list of columns, use the overloaded *GetSchema* method that takes a string parameter
for the schema name. To apply restrictions—so that you get just the columns in a particular
table, for example—use the overloaded *GetSchema* method that takes a string for the schema
name and an array of strings for the restriction values. For more information about using the
GetSchema method, see the discussion earlier in the chapter.

Open Method

To open a connection to your data source, call the *SqlConnection* object's *Open* method. The
SqlConnection object will attempt to connect to your data source based on the information
provided in the object's *ConnectionString* property. If the attempt to connect fails, the *Sql-*
Connection object will throw an exception.

Visual Basic

```
Dim strConn As String = "Data Source=.\SQLExpress;" & _
                        "Initial Catalog=Northwind;Integrated Security=True;"
Dim cn As New SqlConnection(strConn)
Try
    cn.Open()
Catch ex As Exception
    Console.WriteLine("Attempt to connect failed! - {0}", ex.Message)
End Try
```

Visual C#

```
string strConn = @"Data Source=.\SQLExpress;" +
                 "Initial Catalog=Northwind;Integrated Security=True;";
SqlConnection cn = new SqlConnection(strConn);
try {
    cn.Open();
} catch (Exception ex) {
    Console.WriteLine("Attempt to connect failed! - {0}", ex.Message);
}
```

Calling the *Open* method on a *SqlConnection* object that's already open will throw an *Invalid-*
OperationException.

RetrieveStatistics and *ResetStatistics* Methods

The *SqlConnection* class now lets you retrieve statistics about your current connection. You might want to know how long you've been connected, how many bytes you've passed to the server, how many bytes you've received, and so on.

The *RetrieveStatistics* method returns a set of keys and values. Though the method signature merely says *IDictionary*, the method really returns a *Hashtable*. These collections are part of the *System.Collections* namespace and the code includes commented-out references to those namespaces. You can use the following code to retrieve and display those statistics, which are shown in Figure 3-15:

Visual Basic

```
'Imports System.Collections
Dim strConn As String = "Data Source=.\SQLExpress;" & _
                        "Initial Catalog=Northwind;Integrated Security=True;"
Dim cn As New SqlConnection(strConn)
cn.Open()
cn.StatisticsEnabled = True
'Perform some work on the connection
Dim stats As IDictionary = cn.RetrieveStatistics()
For Each key As Object In stats.Keys
    Console.WriteLine("{0}: {1}", key, stats(key))
Next key
```

Visual C#

```
//using System.Collections;
string strConn = @"Data Source=.\SQLExpress;" +
                  "Initial Catalog=Northwind;Integrated Security=True;";
SqlConnection cn = new SqlConnection(strConn);
cn.Open();
cn.StatisticsEnabled = true;
//Perform some work on the connection
IDictionary stats = cn.RetrieveStatistics();
foreach (object key in stats.Keys)
    Console.WriteLine("{0}: {1}", key, stats[key]);
```

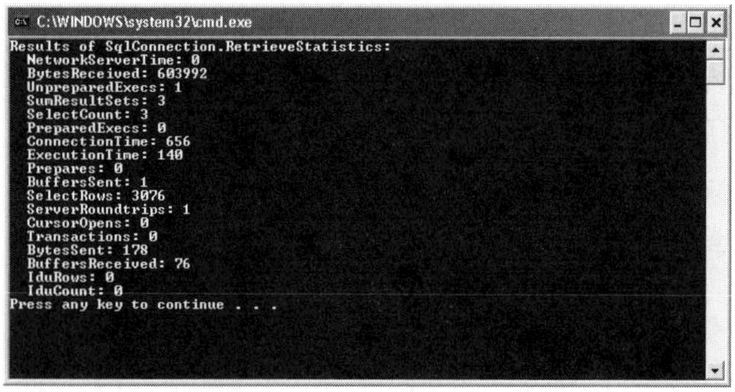

Figure 3-15   Statistics returned using *SqlConnection.RetrieveStatistics*

You can reset the statistics on a connection by calling the *ResetStatistics* method.

> **Note**   If you find that all values returned using *RetrieveStatistics* are set to *0*, you likely forgot to enable statistics on the *SqlConnection*, which can be done by setting the *StatisticsEnabled* property to *True*.

Events of the *SqlConnection* Class

The *SqlConnection* class exposes two events, *InfoMessage* and *StateChange*, as described in Table 3-3.

Table 3-3   Events of the *SqlConnection* Class

Event	Description
InfoMessage	Fires when the connection receives an informational message from the data source
StateChange	Fires when the *State* property of the connection changes

InfoMessage Event

Some database systems, such as SQL Server, support informational messages. SQL Server lets you send messages to the client via the PRINT command. These messages are not returned as errors, nor are they included with the results of a query.

You can use the *SqlConnection* class's *InfoMessage* event to trap for such messages. The following code snippet shows how you can log informational messages. You can also force the *Sql-Connection* to indicate query errors, such as trying to query a table that does not exist, through the *InfoMessage* event rather than through an exception by setting the *FireInfoMessageEvent-OnUserErrors* property on the *SqlConnection* to *True*.

Visual Basic
```
Dim strConn As String = "Data Source=.\SQLExpress;" & _
                        "Initial Catalog=Northwind;Integrated Security=True;"
Dim cn As New SqlConnection(strConn)
AddHandler cn.InfoMessage, AddressOf cn_InfoMessage
cn.Open()
Dim cmd As SqlCommand = cn.CreateCommand()
cmd.CommandText = "PRINT 'Hello, ADO.NET!'"
cmd.ExecuteNonQuery()

Public Sub cn_InfoMessage(ByVal sender As Object, _
                          ByVal e As SqlInfoMessageEventArgs)
    Console.WriteLine("InfoMessage event occurred")
    Console.WriteLine("  Message received: {0}", e.Message)
End Sub
```

Visual C#

```csharp
string strConn = @"Data Source=.\SQLExpress;" +
                 "Initial Catalog=Northwind;Integrated Security=True;";
SqlConnection cn = new SqlConnection(strConn);
cn.InfoMessage += new SqlInfoMessageEventHandler(cn_InfoMessage);
cn.Open();
SqlCommand cmd = cn.CreateCommand();
cmd.CommandText = "PRINT 'Hello, ADO.NET'";
cmd.ExecuteNonQuery();

static void cn_InfoMessage(object sender, SqlInfoMessageEventArgs e)
{
    Console.WriteLine("InfoMessage event occurred");
    Console.WriteLine("  Message received: {0}", e.Message);
}
```

> **Note**   SQL Server also supports generating informational messages using the RAISERROR command. Errors created with this command are treated as informational messages if the error's severity level is 10 or below. For more information, see SQL Server Books Online.

StateChange Event

The *SqlConnection* class's *StateChange* event fires whenever the value of its *State* property changes. This event can prove handy if you display the current state of your connection in, say, a status bar at the bottom of your application's main form.

Visual Basic

```vb
Dim strConn As String = "Data Source=.\SQLExpress;" & _
                        "Initial Catalog=Northwind;Integrated Security=True;"
Dim cn As New SqlConnection(strConn)
AddHandler cn.StateChange, AddressOf cn_StateChange
cn.Open()
cn.Close()

Public Sub cn_StateChange(ByVal sender As Object, _
                          ByVal e As StateChangeEventArgs)
    Console.WriteLine("StateChange from {0} to {1}", _
                      e.OriginalState, e.CurrentState)
End Sub
```

Visual C#

```csharp
string strConn = @"Data Source=.\SQLExpress;" +
                 "Initial Catalog=Northwind;Integrated Security=True;";
SqlConnection cn = new SqlConnection(strConn);
cn.StateChange += new StateChangeEventHandler(cn_StateChange);
cn.Open();
cn.Close();

static void cn_StateChange(object sender, StateChangeEventArgs e) {
    Console.WriteLine("StateChange from {0} to {1}",
                      e.OriginalState, e.CurrentState);
}
```

Questions That Should Be Asked More Frequently

Q Where should I store my connection strings?

A That's a bit of a loaded question. Some developers want to separate the connection string from the rest of the application in case they want to reconfigure the connection string without having to change the code in the application. Other developers' primary goal is to keep the connection information a secret. To see how to accomplish either goal, read the next two Q&As.

Q How should I store my connection strings to isolate them from the rest of the code in my application?

A Configuration files are a great way to isolate this information from the rest of your application. They're easy to create and modify using simple tools. The .NET Framework offers configuration files at the machine level, the application level (both Windows and Web applications), or the user level. Those configuration files are combined automatically through the ConfigurationManager class.

Connection string entries are now first-class citizens in configuration files in version 2.0 of the .NET Framework. You can store connection strings and names of connection strings in configuration file and access them quickly and easily.

Version 2.0 of the .NET Framework makes it even easier to modify configuration files programmatically—accessing, adding, or editing entries in the configuration file for the whole machine, the entire application, or just the application settings for only the current user.

You could use the following code to look for an entry in the connection strings section of the combined configuration file. If the code does not find the desired entry, it opens the configuration file for the application and adds the desired connection string. That particular portion of the code could be helpful in the application's installer.

Visual Basic

```
Dim strConnectionName As String = "Local SQLExpress"
Dim setting As ConnectionStringSettings
setting = ConfigurationManager.ConnectionStrings(strConnectionName)

If setting Is Nothing Then
    'Create new entry in app.config
    setting = New ConnectionStringSettings()
    setting.Name = strConnectionName
    setting.ConnectionString = "Data Source=.\SQLExpress;" & _
                                "Initial Catalog=Northwind;" & _
                                "Integrated Security=True;"

    Dim config As Configuration
    config = ConfigurationManager.OpenExeConfiguration(ConfigurationUserLevel.None)
    config.ConnectionStrings.ConnectionStrings.Add(setting)
    config.Save()
End If
```

```
Using cn As SqlConnection = New SqlConnection(setting.ConnectionString)
    Try
        cn.Open()
        Console.WriteLine("Success!")
    Catch ex As Exception
        Console.WriteLine(ex.Message)
    End Try
End Using
```

Visual C#

```csharp
string strConnectionName = "Local SQLExpress";
ConnectionStringSettings setting;
setting = ConfigurationManager.ConnectionStrings[strConnectionName];

if (setting == null)
{
    //Create new entry in app.config
    setting = new ConnectionStringSettings();
    setting.Name = strConnectionName;
    setting.ConnectionString = @"Data Source=.\SQLExpress;" +
                                "Initial Catalog=Northwind;" +
                                "Integrated Security=True;";

    Configuration config;
    config = ConfigurationManager.OpenExeConfiguration(ConfigurationUserLevel.None);
    config.ConnectionStrings.ConnectionStrings.Add(setting);
    config.Save();
}

using (SqlConnection cn = new SqlConnection(setting.ConnectionString)) {
    try {
        cn.Open();
        Console.WriteLine("Success!");
    }
    catch (Exception ex) {
        Console.WriteLine(ex.ToString());
    }
}
```

Q   How should I store my connection strings if I don't want the application user to be able to find out where the data is stored?

A   You can now encrypt sections of a .NET configuration file programmatically. In the previous code snippet, we could add the following line of code to invoke the default option for encrypting configuration files—the *RSACryptoServiceProvider* class.

Visual Basic

```vb
config.ConnectionStrings.SectionInformation.ProtectSection(Nothing)
```

Visual C#

```csharp
config.ConnectionStrings.SectionInformation.ProtectSection(null);
```

For more information about this and other encryption options, see the .NET Framework SDK.

If the user opens the configuration file in Internet Explorer or Notepad, the contents will look similar to Figure 3-16:

```
<?xml version="1.0" encoding="utf-8" ?>
- <configuration>
  - <connectionStrings configProtectionProvider="RsaProtectedConfigurationProvider">
    - <EncryptedData Type="http://www.w3.org/2001/04/xmlenc#Element"
        xmlns="http://www.w3.org/2001/04/xmlenc#">
        <EncryptionMethod Algorithm="http://www.w3.org/2001/04/xmlenc#tripledes-cbc" />
      - <KeyInfo xmlns="http://www.w3.org/2000/09/xmldsig#">
        - <EncryptedKey xmlns="http://www.w3.org/2001/04/xmlenc#">
            <EncryptionMethod Algorithm="http://www.w3.org/2001/04/xmlenc#rsa-1_5" />
          - <KeyInfo xmlns="http://www.w3.org/2000/09/xmldsig#">
              <KeyName>Rsa Key</KeyName>
            </KeyInfo>
          - <CipherData>
              <CipherValue>cOOgR+NYYu7kXJd+aBdOqlONrc2U5xvbpAbz1X1+KQspE9wORnRUVxHw2pmhoXI
            </CipherData>
          </EncryptedKey>
        </KeyInfo>
      - <CipherData>
          <CipherValue>v4XcTjltMjgTAgPhRfFZ2AS8WuZnORM9P2Q/UzXK9BHwLU5vPw53+H462a8GGThF8IKI
        </CipherData>
      </EncryptedData>
    </connectionStrings>
  </configuration>
```

Figure 3-16   The contents of an application's configuration file with the connection string section encrypted

While the application user won't be able to determine the connection string based on the contents of the configuration file, your application's code can still easily access the contents of the configuration file using the code in the previous example. However, the connection string is now in memory, and there are tools available that the application user could utilize to try to find the connection string in memory.

If you absolutely, positively want your application to retrieve data while leaving no possible trace of the connection information, have the application access data through a Web service and let the Web service component manage the connection to the database.

Q   When I add a data connection to Server Explorer, I can shut down and restart, and Visual Studio will remember my settings. Where does Server Explorer store those settings?

A   Server Explorer stores its settings on a per-user basis. This file, called DefaultView.SEView, resides in a subfolder in a user's Settings folder. The full path will look something like this:

```
<System Drive>\Documents and Settings\<User Name>\
    Application Data\Microsoft\VisualStudio\8.0\ServerExplorer\DefaultView.SEView
```

Visual Studio encrypts the connection strings, so they are not readily available to anyone who has access to that directory.

Q   I'm building an application that will use SQL Server as the back-end database. Should I use standard or integrated security?

A   This is a complex issue. The appropriate solution might depend on the architecture of your application and how you choose to manage security on your SQL Server database. I prefer using integrated security in two-tier applications and standard security in multi-tiered applications.

Using integrated security prevents you from having to prompt the user for credentials or hard-code them into the application. Using standard security in a multitiered application (where your data access code runs in a Web service or COM+ component) lets you take advantage of connection pooling. In this architecture, the component determines the user's credentials. That might sound like a cop-out, and in some ways it is. However, I think it's also a totally valid solution.

What if the only point at which your middle-tier component validates the user's credentials is in the data access code? If the database says that the user doesn't have access, that generally means you didn't want the user to access this feature of the middle-tier object in the first place. If that's the case, you're wasting time and might be compromising security by letting the user run the code in the component that precedes the call to connect to your database.

You're better off setting up security so that the user must have the proper credentials to access the component. You can then have the component use a standard connection string. Because all clients will use the same connection string, your component will be able to use all their connections with a single pool. If all your users connect to your database using different credentials, you're not taking advantage of pooling.

For more information about using SQL Server with standard and integrated security, see SQL Server Books Online.

Q   For security purposes, the *SqlConnection* that I'm using in my application has limited access to my database. However, I still want to take advantage of some of the database-administration features in Server Explorer, such as creating or modifying the structure of my tables. How do I balance the security of the connection I'm using in my application at run time with the functionality I want to use at design time?

A   Use multiple connections in Server Explorer. You can simply add a new connection to Server Explorer that uses an account with more database privileges. If you don't actually use the connection in your application, it won't be included in your application.

Chapter 4
Querying Your Database

In Chapter 3, you learned how to connect to a database using the Microsoft ADO.NET *SqlConnection* class. Now it's time to learn how to execute queries against your database. In the ADO.NET object model, you execute queries using the *SqlCommand* class.

In this chapter, I'll focus first on specific tasks that involve the *SqlCommand* class. I'll examine how to execute queries that retrieve results and queries that modify, rather than return, data. We'll take a close look at parameterized queries, which can help simplify your code and prevent users from changing the intent of your query. This chapter also explores some new features in ADO.NET and Microsoft SQL Server—multiple active resultsets (often called MARS) and asynchronous queries.

I'll also introduce two other ADO.NET classes: the *SqlDataReader* and *SqlParameter* classes. *SqlDataReader* objects allow you to examine the results of your queries, and *SqlParameter* objects allow you to execute parameterized queries. Finally, I'll examine the properties, methods, and events of the *SqlCommand, SqlDataReader,* and *SqlParameter* classes.

Using *SqlCommand* Objects in Code

SqlCommand objects let you execute many different types of queries. Some *SqlCommand* objects retrieve data in the form of a resultset, and others modify the content or structure of the data store. Let's look at how to create *SqlCommand* objects and use them to perform a variety of tasks.

Creating a *SqlCommand* Object

You can create a *SqlCommand* object in three ways. The first way is simply to create an instance of an object using the new keyword and then set the appropriate properties. Second, you can use one of the available constructors to specify the query string and a *SqlConnection* object.

The third way is to call the *CreateCommand* method of the *SqlConnection* class (which we examined in Chapter 3). The three approaches are shown here:

Visual Basic

```
Dim strConn, strSQL As String
strConn = "Data Source=.\SQLExpress;" & _
          "Initial Catalog=Northwind;Trusted_Connection=Yes;"
strSQL = "SELECT CustomerID, CompanyName FROM Customers"
Dim cn As New SqlConnection(strConn)
cn.Open()

Dim cmd As SqlCommand

'Use the parameter-less constructor
cmd = New SqlCommand()
cmd.Connection = cn
cmd.CommandText = strSQL

'Use the parameterized constructor
cmd = New SqlCommand(strSQL, cn)

'Use the Connection object's CreateCommand method
cmd = cn.CreateCommand()
cmd.CommandText = strSQL
```

Visual C#

```
string strConn, strSQL;
strConn = @"Data Source=.\SQLExpress;" +
           "Initial Catalog=Northwind;Trusted_Connection=Yes;";
strSQL = "SELECT CustomerID, CompanyName FROM Customers";
SqlConnection cn = new SqlConnection(strConn);
cn.Open();
SqlCommand cmd;

//Use the parameter-less constructor
cmd = new SqlCommand();
cmd.Connection = cn;
cmd.CommandText = strSQL;

//Use the parameterized constructor
cmd = new SqlCommand(strSQL, cn);

//Use the Connection object's CreateCommand method
cmd = cn.CreateCommand();
cmd.CommandText = strSQL;
```

Using a *SqlCommand* to Execute Queries

Now that you understand how to create a *SqlCommand* object, let's look at the basic scenarios in which you'll use a *SqlCommand* to execute queries.

Executing a Row-Returning Query

The most common use for a *SqlCommand* is to execute a query that returns results. You might want to retrieve some information about orders that shipped to a particular country, perhaps Canada, using a query such as the following one:

```
SELECT OrderID, CustomerID, OrderDate, ShippedDate, ShipCity
  FROM Orders WHERE ShipCountry = 'Canada'
```

To execute this query, you'll first need to set the *SqlCommand* object's *CommandText* property to a string that contains the text of the query. Then call the *SqlCommand* object's *ExecuteReader* method as shown in the following code:

Visual Basic

```
Dim strConn, strSQL As String
strConn = "Data Source=.\SQLExpress;" & _
          "Initial Catalog=Northwind;Integrated Security=True;"
strSQL = "SELECT OrderID, CustomerID, OrderDate, ShippedDate, ShipCity" & _
          " FROM Orders WHERE ShipCountry = 'Canada'"

Dim cn As New SqlConnection(strConn)
cn.Open()

Dim cmd As SqlCommand = cn.CreateCommand()
cmd.CommandText = strSQL
Dim rdr As SqlDataReader = cmd.ExecuteReader()
```

Visual C#

```
string strConn, strSQL;
strConn = @"Data Source=.\SQLExpress;" +
            "Initial Catalog=Northwind;Trusted_Connection=Yes;";
strSQL = "SELECT OrderID, CustomerID, OrderDate, ShippedDate, ShipCity" +
          " FROM Orders WHERE ShipCountry = 'Canada'";

SqlConnection cn = new SqlConnection(strConn);
cn.Open();

SqlCommand cmd = cn.CreateCommand();
cmd.CommandText = strSQL;
SqlDataReader rdr = cmd.ExecuteReader();
```

As you can see in the code, the *ExecuteReader* method returns a *SqlDataReader* object. It's this object that lets you examine the results of the query. We'll discuss the *SqlDataReader* in depth shortly, but rather than leave you hanging or force you to jump around in the book, we'll explain the basics here.

The *SqlDataReader* lets you examine the results of the query using a stream-based approach. You can look at the results one row of data at a time. Once you move to the next row, the contents of the previous row are no longer available. There are a number of ways to access the value for a particular column—string-based and ordinal-based lookups, and untyped and strongly typed accessors. For now, we'll use the simplest approach.

The following code walks through the rows returned by the query, and it writes the values of the OrderID, CustomerID, and OrderDate columns to the *Console* window before closing the *SqlDataReader*. The dates stored in the database do not include any time-of-day information. The code also specifies ":d" in the call to *Console.WriteLine* to use the "short date" format to simplify the output and make it easier to read.

> **Note**   The code snippets in the chapter assume that your code has references to the *System.Data* and *System.Data.SqlClient* namespaces. Make sure you're referencing the *System.Data.dll* assembly in your project, and include the following references to the *System.Data* and *System.Data.SqlClient* namespaces.
>
> **Visual Basic**
>
> Imports System.Data
>
> Imports System.Data.SqlClient
>
> **Visual C#**
>
> using System.Data;
>
> using System.Data.SqlClient;

Visual Basic

```vbnet
Dim strConn, strSQL As String
strConn = "Data Source=.\SQLExpress;" & _
          "Initial Catalog=Northwind;Integrated Security=True;"
strSQL = "SELECT OrderID, CustomerID, OrderDate" & _
         "  FROM Orders WHERE ShipCountry = 'Canada'"

Dim cn As New SqlConnection(strConn)
cn.Open()

Dim cmd As New SqlCommand(strSQL, cn)
Dim rdr As SqlDataReader = cmd.ExecuteReader()

Do While rdr.Read
      Console.WriteLine("{0} {1} {2:d}", rdr("OrderID"), _
                        rdr("CustomerID"), rdr("OrderDate"))
Loop
rdr.Close()
```

Visual C#

```csharp
string strConn, strSQL;
strConn = @"Data Source=.\SQLExpress;" +
          "Initial Catalog=Northwind;Trusted_Connection=Yes;";
strSQL = "SELECT OrderID, CustomerID, OrderDate" +
         "  FROM Orders WHERE ShipCountry = 'Canada'";

SqlConnection cn = new SqlConnection(strConn);
cn.Open();

SqlCommand cmd = new SqlCommand(strSQL, cn);
SqlDataReader rdr = cmd.ExecuteReader();
```

```
while (rdr.Read())
    Console.WriteLine("{0} {1} {2:d}", rdr["OrderID"],
                      rdr["CustomerID"], rdr["OrderDate"]);
rdr.Close();
```

In the preceding code snippet, calling the *Read* method accomplishes two tasks at once. First, the *Read* method positions the *SqlDataReader* to the next row in the resultset. Second, the method returns a *Boolean* value that indicates whether there is an available row. So, the code continually calls the *Read* method in a loop, displaying results as long as the *Read* method returns *True*. Once the *Read* method returns *False*, the code exits the loop and calls the *Close* method on the *SqlDataReader*.

To display the contents of the currently available row of data, the code uses the *SqlDataReader* class's default indexer. Pass the name of the column to the default indexer and the *SqlData-Reader* returns the contents of that column using the generic *Object* data type.

Retrieving a Single Value

There might be times when you want to execute a query to return a single value. Perhaps you want to execute a simple query to determine how many rows exist in a table or something more complex—such as the total of all orders placed by a particular customer—with a query that looks something like the following:

```
SELECT SUM([Order Details].UnitPrice * [Order Details].Quantity)
  FROM Orders INNER JOIN [Order Details]
    ON Orders.OrderID = [Order Details].OrderID
  WHERE Orders.CustomerID = 'ALFKI'
```

Queries such as this are common in many applications. The following code snippet executes the query and writes the order total to the *Console* window. Here, creating a *SqlDataReader*, calling *Read*, retrieving the contents of the first column of the first row, and closing the *Sql-DataReader* just to retrieve that single value seems like a lot of overhead. This code also includes a formatting trick. Because the query returns an order total, the code uses ":c" in the call to *Console.WriteLine* to format the output using the system's currency format.

Visual Basic

```
Dim strConn, strSQL As String
strConn = "Data Source=.\SQLExpress;" & _
          "Initial Catalog=Northwind;Integrated Security=True;"
strSQL = "SELECT SUM(UnitPrice * Quantity) " & _
         "  FROM Orders INNER JOIN [Order Details]" & _
         "    ON Orders.OrderID = [Order Details].OrderID" & _
         "  WHERE CustomerID = 'ALFKI'"
Dim cn As New SqlConnection(strConn)
cn.Open()
Dim cmd As New SqlCommand(strSQL, cn)

Dim rdr As SqlDataReader = cmd.ExecuteReader()
```

```
rdr.Read()
Dim decOrderTotal As Decimal = CDec(rdr(0))
rdr.Close()
Console.WriteLine("Order Total: {0:c}", decOrderTotal)
```

Visual C#

```
string strConn, strSQL;
strConn = @"Data Source=.\SQLExpress;" +
        "Initial Catalog=Northwind;Trusted_Connection=Yes;";
strSQL = "SELECT SUM(UnitPrice * Quantity) " +
        "  FROM Orders INNER JOIN [Order Details]" +
        "    ON Orders.OrderID = [Order Details].OrderID" +
        "  WHERE CustomerID = 'ALFKI'";
SqlConnection cn = new SqlConnection(strConn);
cn.Open();
SqlCommand cmd = new SqlCommand(strSQL, cn);

SqlDataReader rdr = cmd.ExecuteReader();
rdr.Read();
decimal decOrderTotal = (decimal)rdr[0];
rdr.Close();
Console.WriteLine("Order Total: {0:c}", decOrderTotal);
```

To help simplify such scenarios, the *SqlCommand* class exposes an *ExecuteScalar* method. Rather than return a *SqlDataReader*, the *ExecuteScalar* method returns the first value from the first row in the generic *Object* data type. Such methods are commonly called "syntactic sugar," at least where I work. In other words, calling *ExecuteScalar* effectively creates a *SqlDataReader* and retrieves the desired information for you without your having to write all the code. *Execute-Scalar* then closes and disposes of the *SqlDataReader*.

Here's that same code snippet, but using the *ExecuteScalar* method instead:

Visual Basic

```
Dim strConn, strSQL As String
strConn = "Data Source=.\SQLExpress;" & _
        "Initial Catalog=Northwind;Integrated Security=True;"
strSQL = "SELECT SUM(UnitPrice * Quantity) " & _
        "  FROM Orders INNER JOIN [Order Details]" & _
        "    ON Orders.OrderID = [Order Details].OrderID" & _
        "  WHERE CustomerID = 'ALFKI'"
Dim cn As New SqlConnection(strConn)
cn.Open()
Dim cmd As New SqlCommand(strSQL, cn)

Dim decOrderTotal As Decimal = CDec(cmd.ExecuteScalar())
Console.WriteLine("Order Total: {0:c}", decOrderTotal)
```

Visual C#

```
string strConn, strSQL;
strConn = @"Data Source=.\SQLExpress;" +
        "Initial Catalog=Northwind;Trusted_Connection=Yes;";
strSQL = "SELECT SUM(UnitPrice * Quantity) " +
        "  FROM Orders INNER JOIN [Order Details]" +
```

```
        "     ON Orders.OrderID = [Order Details].OrderID" +
        "   WHERE CustomerID = 'ALFKI'";
SqlConnection cn = new SqlConnection(strConn);
cn.Open();
SqlCommand cmd = new SqlCommand(strSQL, cn);

decimal decOrderTotal = (decimal)cmd.ExecuteScalar();
Console.WriteLine("Order Total: {0:c}", decOrderTotal);
```

Executing a Query That Does Not Return a Resultset

Queries that don't return resultsets are generally referred to as *action queries*—a term we'll use occasionally in this text. There are two main categories of action queries:

- **Data manipulation language (DML) queries**   Also known as *query-based updates* (*QBUs*), these modify the contents of your database. Here are a few examples:

```
INSERT INTO Customers (CustomerID, CompanyName)
       VALUES ('NewID', 'NewCustomer')

UPDATE Customers SET CompanyName = 'NewCompanyName'
       WHERE CustomerID = 'ALFKI'

DELETE FROM Customers WHERE CustomerID = 'ALFKI'
```

- **Data definition language (DDL) queries**   These modify the structure of your database, as shown in the following examples:

```
CREATE TABLE Table1 (Field1 int NOT NULL
                       CONSTRAINT PK_Table1 PRIMARY KEY,
                       Field2 varchar(32))

ALTER VIEW View1 AS SELECT Field1, Field2 FROM Table1

DROP PROCEDURE StoredProcedure1
```

You could execute these queries by calling the *ExecuteReader* method on the *SqlCommand*. However, because these queries don't return any rows, that seems like unnecessary overhead. Thankfully, there's a simpler way. The *SqlCommand* class exposes an *ExecuteNonQuery* method that executes the query without returning a *SqlDataReader* object. Here's an example that demonstrates how you can use this feature:

Visual Basic
```
Dim strConn, strSQL As String
strConn = "Data Source=.\SQLExpress;" & _
          "Initial Catalog=Northwind;Trusted_Connection=Yes;"
strSQL = "UPDATE Customers SET CompanyName = 'NewValue' " & _
          "WHERE CustomerID = 'ALFKI'"

Dim cn As New SqlConnection(strConn)
cn.Open()
```

```
Dim cmd As New SqlCommand(strSQL, cn)
cmd.ExecuteNonQuery()
```

Visual C#

```
string strConn, strSQL;
strConn = @"Data Source=.\SQLExpress;" +
          "Initial Catalog=Northwind;Trusted_Connection=Yes;";
strSQL = "UPDATE Customers SET CompanyName = 'NewValue' " +
         "WHERE CustomerID = 'ALFKI'";

SqlConnection cn = new SqlConnection(strConn);
cn.Open();
SqlCommand cmd = new SqlCommand(strSQL, cn);
cmd.ExecuteNonQuery();
```

> **Note**   Despite what the *ExecuteNonQuery* method's name implies, action queries are valid queries. They simply don't return rows. I'm not entirely sure why the method is called *ExecuteNonQuery*.

However, executing an action query is often only half the battle.

When you execute the following query, there are two possible outcomes, success or failure:

```
CREATE TABLE NewTable (NewTableID int NOT NULL
                       CONSTRAINT PK_NewTable PRIMARY KEY,
                       OtherField varchar(32))
```

The query either successfully creates your new table or fails. Possible reasons for failure are that a table of the same name already exists, you didn't use the right syntax for the query, or you don't have an open connection to your database. The point here is that if you execute the query and it doesn't generate an error, you successfully created your new table.

With action queries that are designed to modify or delete an existing row, you need to do more than simply execute the query successfully. Let's take another look at the query we executed in a code snippet on the previous page (to change the company name for a specific customer):

```
UPDATE Customers SET CompanyName = 'NewValue'
       WHERE CustomerID = 'ALFKI'
```

There's a specific expectation here: that executing this query modifies the corresponding row in the Customers table. In some cases, executing this query might not modify that customer's company name. For example, another user might have deleted this row from the table or changed the value of the CustomerID column. In such cases, the database will execute the query, but because no rows satisfy the criteria in the WHERE clause, the query will not modify any rows.

To the database, this outcome does not constitute failure. The database did as it was asked without any true failure—there's still a table named Customers with fields named CompanyName and CustomerID. No rows satisfied the criteria in the WHERE clause, so the database didn't modify any rows.

So how can you tell whether the query modified one row? If you submit this query using a tool such as Microsoft SQL Server Query Analyzer, you'll see a message such as this one:

```
(1 row(s) affected)
```

The *SqlCommand* lets you retrieve this information by returning the number of rows affected by your query as the return value of the *ExecuteNonQuery* method. If you expected the query to modify one row, you could use the *ExecuteNonQuery* method and trap for its return value to determine success or failure, as shown here:

Visual Basic
```
Dim strConn, strSQL As String
strConn = "Data Source=.\SQLExpress;" & _
          "Initial Catalog=Northwind;Trusted_Connection=Yes;"
strSQL = "UPDATE Customers SET CompanyName = 'NewValue' " & _
         "WHERE CustomerID = 'ALFKI'"

Dim cn As New SqlConnection(strConn)
cn.Open()
Dim cmd As New SqlCommand(strSQL, cn)
Dim intRecordsAffected As Integer = cmd.ExecuteNonQuery()
If intRecordsAffected = 1 Then
    Console.WriteLine("Update succeeded")
Else
    'Assume intRecordsAffected = 0
    Console.WriteLine("Update failed")
End If
```

Visual C#
```
string strConn, strSQL;
strConn = @"Data Source=.\SQLExpress;" +
           "Initial Catalog=Northwind;Trusted_Connection=Yes;";
strSQL = "UPDATE Customers SET CompanyName = 'NewValue' " +
         "WHERE CustomerID = 'ALFKI'";
SqlConnection cn = new SqlConnection(strConn);
cn.Open();

SqlCommand cmd = new SqlCommand(strSQL, cn);
int intRecordsAffected = cmd.ExecuteNonQuery();
if (intRecordsAffected == 1)
    Console.WriteLine("Update succeeded");
else
    //Assume intRecordsAffected = 0
    Console.WriteLine("Update failed");
```

In the code, we assume that if the query didn't modify one row, it modified zero rows. But there are other possible return values from *ExecuteNonQuery*. If you execute anything other than a DML query, *ExecuteNonQuery* will return –1. There are also situations in which a DML query will modify more than one row.

However, in the code snippet, we used the table's primary key field in the WHERE clause. Because the Customer table uses the *CustomerID* field as its primary key, no two rows can have the same value for the *CustomerID* field. We therefore know that the query cannot modify more than one row.

Like the *ExecuteScalar* method, the *ExecuteNonQuery* method is also "syntactic sugar." You can achieve the same functionality by calling the *SqlDataReader*, but this approach requires more code—call *ExecuteReader*, check the value of the *SqlDataReader*'s *RecordsAffected* property, and then close the *SqlDataReader*. If I know I'm executing an action query, I'll use the *ExecuteNonQuery* method instead.

Executing Batches of Action Queries

Suppose that you want to issue a series of action queries in a batch. For example, let's say that you have a Products table and you want to change the unit price for some products based on the product category, marking some prices down while marking others up. You could batch the following queries together and execute them all at once:

```
UPDATE Products SET UnitPrice = UnitPrice * 0.85 WHERE CategoryID = 3;
UPDATE Products SET UnitPrice = UnitPrice * 1.15 WHERE CategoryID = 4;
UPDATE Products SET UnitPrice = UnitPrice * 0.75 WHERE CategoryID = 5;
```

What if you want to know how many rows each query affected? Ideally, you'd like to call a simple method such as *ExecuteNonQuery* and have that method return an array of values in which the entries in the array correspond to the number of rows modified by the individual queries in the batch.

Neither the *ExecuteReader* nor the *ExecuteNonQuery* methods on their own can get you *all* the way there. Both methods allow you to execute the batch of queries, but neither will tell you how many rows each query modified. The *ExecuteNonQuery* method's return value will tell you how many rows the entire batch modified, but that information might not be enough to suit your needs.

The (new and) improved *SqlCommand* in ADO.NET 2.0 exposes a *StatementCompleted* event that you can use to gather this information. The main argument for the *StatementCompleted* event has a single interesting property, *RecordCount*, but thankfully that's the information we're looking for. The following code snippet demonstrates how you can use this event to determine the number of rows modified by individual queries in the batch. The code includes a procedure to handle the *StatementCompleted* event. If you're copying and pasting the code, you'll need to paste that procedure separately.

Visual Basic

```
Dim strConn, strSQL As String
strConn = "Data Source=.\SQLExpress;" & _
          "Initial Catalog=Northwind;Trusted_Connection=Yes;"
Dim cn As New SqlConnection(strConn)
cn.Open()
strSQL = "UPDATE Products SET UnitPrice = UnitPrice * 0.85 " & _
         "  WHERE CategoryID = 3;" & _
```

```
            "UPDATE Products SET UnitPrice = UnitPrice * 1.15 " & _
            "    WHERE CategoryID = 4;" & _
            "UPDATE Products SET UnitPrice = UnitPrice * 0.75 " & _
            "    WHERE CategoryID = 5;"
Dim cmd As New SqlCommand(strSQL, cn)
AddHandler cmd.StatementCompleted, _
            AddressOf HandleStatementCompleted
Dim intTotalRowsAffected As Integer = cmd.ExecuteNonQuery()
Console.WriteLine("TotalRowsAffected: {0} row(s)", intTotalRowsAffected)
cn.Close()
...
Public Sub HandleStatementCompleted(ByVal sender As Object, _
                                    ByVal e As StatementCompletedEventArgs)
    Console.WriteLine("Statement Affected {0} row(s)", e.RecordCount)
End Sub
```

Visual C#

```
string strConn, strSQL;
strConn = @"Data Source=.\SQLExpress;" +
            "Initial Catalog=Northwind;Trusted_Connection=Yes;";
SqlConnection cn = new SqlConnection(strConn);
cn.Open();
strSQL = "UPDATE Products SET UnitPrice = UnitPrice * 0.85 " +
         "    WHERE CategoryID = 3;" +
         "UPDATE Products SET UnitPrice = UnitPrice * 1.15 " +
         "    WHERE CategoryID = 4;" +
         "UPDATE Products SET UnitPrice = UnitPrice * 0.75 " +
         "    WHERE CategoryID = 5;";
SqlCommand cmd = new SqlCommand(strSQL, cn);
cmd.StatementCompleted +=
            new StatementCompletedEventHandler(HandleStatementCompleted);
int intTotalRowsAffected = cmd.ExecuteNonQuery();
Console.WriteLine("TotalRowsAffected: {0} row(s)", intTotalRowsAffected);
cn.Close();
...
static void HandleStatementCompleted(object sender,
                                     StatementCompletedEventArgs e) {
    Console.WriteLine("Statement Affected {0} row(s)", e.RecordCount);
}
```

Executing a Query to Retrieve XML Data

SQL Server supports queries that return data in a stream of XML. If you're working with this type of a query, you can call the *ExecuteXmlReader* method on your *SqlCommand* to get the results through an *XmlReader* rather than a *SqlDataReader*. We'll examine this scenario in more detail in Chapter 12.

Executing a Query in a Transaction

The *SqlCommand* class has a *Transaction* property that you must set to execute your *SqlCommand* within a *SqlTransaction*. In the previous chapter, you saw how to create a *SqlTransaction* object using the *SqlConnection* class's *BeginTransaction* method.

If you start a *SqlTransaction* on your *SqlConnection*, you must associate all queries with that transaction. Otherwise, you'll receive an *InvalidOperationException* with a message saying something like: "*ExecuteNonQuery* requires the command to have a transaction when the connection assigned to the command is in a pending local transaction. The *Transaction* property of the command has not been initialized."

There are two ways to associate a *SqlCommand* with a *SqlTransaction*. You can set the *Transaction* property of the *SqlCommand* to the *SqlTransaction*, or you can pass the *SqlTransaction* into *Sql-Command*'s constructor. The following code uses the second approach. After executing the query and determining how many rows the query affected, the code calls the rollback method on the *SqlTransaction* to prevent the database from committing the changes.

Visual Basic

```
Dim strConn, strSQL As String
strConn = "Data Source=.\SQLExpress;" & _
          "Initial Catalog=Northwind;Trusted_Connection=Yes;"
strSQL = "UPDATE Products SET UnitPrice = UnitPrice * .7 " & _
         "  WHERE CategoryID = 1"
Dim cn As New SqlConnection(strConn)
cn.Open()
Using txn As SqlTransaction = cn.BeginTransaction()
    Dim cmd As New SqlCommand(strSQL, cn, txn)
    Dim intRecordsAffected As Integer = cmd.ExecuteNonQuery()
    Console.WriteLine("Query affected {0} row(s)", intRecordsAffected)
    txn.Rollback()
End Using
cn.Close()
```

Visual C#

```
string strConn, strSQL;
strConn = @"Data Source=.\SQLExpress;" +
           "Initial Catalog=Northwind;Trusted_Connection=Yes;";
strSQL = "UPDATE Products SET UnitPrice = UnitPrice * .7 " +
         "  WHERE CategoryID = 1";
SqlConnection cn = new SqlConnection(strConn);
cn.Open();
using (SqlTransaction txn = cn.BeginTransaction()) {
    SqlCommand cmd = new SqlCommand(strSQL, cn, txn);
    int intRecordsAffected = cmd.ExecuteNonQuery();
    Console.WriteLine("Query affected {0} row(s)", intRecordsAffected);
    txn.Rollback();
}
cn.Close();
```

Tip   To ensure that you don't leave your transactions open for too long, consider using *SqlTransaction* objects in a *Using* block, as shown in the preceding code snippet. The longer the transaction remains open, the longer the database needs to maintain the locks for the transaction, and the greater the chances are that multiple users will try to lock the same rows. If the *SqlTransaction* has not been committed or rolled back at the end of the *Using* block, the *Rollback* method is called implicitly.

Executing a Query Asynchronously

In ADO.NET 2.0, the *SqlCommand* now includes support for asynchronous queries. Some queries return almost instantaneously; others take a while to execute. If you're working with queries that might take a while to execute, and you want to perform other tasks while SQL Server processes the query, consider using asynchronous queries. This feature works with SQL Server 2005, SQL Server 2000, and SQL Server 7.0.

Why would you want to execute a query asynchronously? When you execute a query using the standard synchronous mode, the call will not complete until SQL Server has processed the query and returns the first available row in the resultset. You might have other work that you want to perform while waiting for SQL Server to respond, such as executing a query against another database or calling out to a Web service to retrieve other information.

If you're working with other asynchronous features in the .NET Framework, the *SqlCommand* class's support for asynchronous queries will look familiar. The *SqlCommand* class exposes *Begin* and *End* methods for the *ExecuteReader*, *ExecuteNonQuery*, and *ExecuteXmlReader* methods. For example, there's a *BeginExecuteReader* method and an *EndExecuteReader* method.

Each *Begin* method returns an object that implements the *IAsyncResult* interface. This returned object is a handle to the status of your query. The *IAsyncResult* interface is part of the .NET Framework pattern for asynchronous methods. It is designed to help you determine whether the operation has completed, block the current thread if you need to wait for the operation to complete, and serve as your handle to the results of the method call. In the upcoming examples that demonstrate how you can execute queries asynchronously using *SqlCommand*, we'll also demonstrate these features of the *IAsyncResult* interface.

To simulate a long-running query in our examples, we'll precede a simple query with a SQL Server "WAITFOR DELAY" query. The following query waits for 10 seconds before returning the contents of the Customers table:

```
WAITFOR DELAY '00:00:10'; SELECT * FROM Customers
```

The asynchronous feature is not enabled by default. To enable asynchronous queries on your *SqlConnection*, include the following in your connection string:

```
Asynchronous Processing=True;
```

> **Tip**   As with other connection string options, if you have trouble remembering the keyword, the *SqlConnectionStringBuilder* can help.

Execute a Query Asynchronously and Wait for Results

Let's say that we want to execute a query asynchronously, performing a series of other operations. Once those operations have completed, we then wait until the results are available. The code samples assume a reference (*using* or *Imports*, depending on your choice of language) to the *System.Threading* namespace.

Visual Basic

```vb
Dim strConn, strSQL As String
strConn = "Data Source=.\SQLExpress;" & _
          "Initial Catalog=Northwind;Trusted_Connection=Yes;" & _
          "Asynchronous Processing=True;"
strSQL = "WAITFOR DELAY '00:00:10'; SELECT * FROM Customers"

Dim cn As New SqlConnection(strConn)
cn.Open()
Dim cmd As New SqlCommand(strSQL, cn)
Dim iar As IAsyncResult = cmd.BeginExecuteReader()

'Perform other operations

Dim rdr As IAsyncResult = cmd.EndExecuteReader(iar)
Do While rdr.Read()
    Console.WriteLine(rdr("CustomerID"))
Loop
rdr.Close()
cn.Close()
```

Visual C#

```csharp
string strConn, strSQL;
strConn = @"Data Source=.\SQLExpress;" +
          "Initial Catalog=Northwind;Trusted_Connection=Yes;" +
          "Asynchronous Processing=True;";
strSQL = "WAITFOR DELAY '00:00:10'; SELECT * FROM Customers";

SqlConnection cn = new SqlConnection(strConn);
cn.Open();
SqlCommand cmd = new SqlCommand(strSQL, cn);
IAsyncResult iar = cmd.BeginExecuteReader();

//Perform other operations

SqlDataReader rdr = cmd.EndExecuteReader(iar);
while (rdr.Read())
    Console.WriteLine(rdr["CustomerID"]);
rdr.Close();
cn.Close();
```

We could have checked the *IsCompleted* property on the *IAsyncResult* interface to see whether the *BeginExecuteReader* call had completed. This check can be helpful if you have made multiple asynchronous requests and want to see which ones have completed and handle the results of those first. In this case, if the call to *BeginExecuteReader* had not completed, there is no other work to perform. So we would want to wait for the call to complete anyway, and that's the default behavior of the *End* methods. If you call an *End* method, it will not return until the *Begin* method has completed.

You could also use the *IAsyncResult* interface to wait for the call to complete by calling *IAsync-Result.AsyncWaitHandle.WaitOne*. Calling the *WaitOne* method that accepts parameters lets you wait for a specified amount of time (in milliseconds), after which you could check the *IsCompleted* method to determine whether the call has completed. With the *WaitOne* method, you can construct "AreWeThereYet" logic, in which the code asks whether the operation has completed every three seconds, as in the following code:

Visual Basic

```
...
Dim iar As IAsyncResult = cmd.BeginExecuteReader()
Console.Write("Are we there yet?  ")
Do While Not iar.IsCompleted
    Console.WriteLine("No!")
    iar.AsyncWaitHandle.WaitOne(3000, True)
    Console.Write("Are we there yet?  ")
Loop
Console.WriteLine("Yes!")
```

Visual C#

```
...
IAsyncResult iar = cmd.BeginExecuteReader();
Console.Write("Are we there yet?  ");
while (!iar.IsCompleted) {
    Console.WriteLine("No!");
    iar.AsyncWaitHandle.WaitOne(3000, true);
    Console.Write("Are we there yet?  ");
}
Console.WriteLine("Yes!");
```

Execute Multiple Queries Asynchronously and Wait for One to Complete

An even more helpful asynchronous query scenario involves ASP.NET pages that need to execute queries against multiple databases. Using the asynchronous methods on multiple *SqlCommand*s, you can issue a series of queries asynchronously. You can then use the *WaitOne* method described in the previous example to wait for a particular query to complete.

However, do you really know which query will complete first? You can process the results in the order in which you executed the queries, but is there any guarantee that the first query you execute will be the first query to complete? If you process the results in this order and the second query completes before the first query, you're not serving up your pages as quickly as possible.

An even more powerful option is to use the .NET Framework Threading features and wait for *any* of the queries to complete. The *WaitHandle* class, in the *System.Threading* namespace, exposes a static *WaitAny* method and a static *WaitAll* method to help you handle this type of scenario. These methods each accept an array of *WaitHandles*. The *WaitAny* method returns as soon as any of the asynchronous operations associated with those *WaitHandles* has completed. The method returns the index of the *WaitHandle* whose asynchronous operation has completed. The *WaitAll* method behaves in the same way, except that it waits for all the asynchronous operations to complete.

We'll use the *WaitAny* method in an example shortly.

Passing Additional State to the *Begin* Method

The *Begin* methods include overloads that let you pass in a *StateObject* parameter. This parameter accepts any object and will assign this object to the *AsyncState* property on the resulting *IAsync-Result* interface.

The following code snippet demonstrates how you can use this feature in your code. The code snippet opens two *SqlConnections*—one to retrieve customer information and one to retrieve order information. They use the same connection string to simplify the scenario. In a real application, they could work with the same SQL Server or different SQL Servers. The code executes an asynchronous query on each *SqlConnection*. That's where the fun starts.

Once the code executes the two queries asynchronously, it uses the *WaitAny* method on the *WaitHandle* class to wait for either of the queries to complete. The *WaitAny* method accepts an array of *WaitHandles* and returns the index of the *WaitHandle* whose operation has completed. The challenge at that point is to determine what that index *means*. Which query completed? The one that returns customer information or the one that returns order information?

One approach would be to hard-code that the first item in the array corresponds to the customer query and the second item in the array corresponds to the order query. You could then check the return value of *WaitAny* in a *Case* or *switch* block to determine the *SqlCommand* whose *EndExecuteReader* method you'll call.

A second approach is to pass some additional state information into the *BeginExecuteReader* method. You could pass strings such as *Customers* and *Orders* into the *BeginExecuteReader* methods. In this code snippet, we pass the actual *SqlCommand* objects into the *BeginExecuteReader* methods. This way, the *SqlCommand* object is available through the *IAsyncResult* object's *AsyncState* property. So, when the *WaitAny* call returns, we access the corresponding *IAsyncResult* object and simply cast the *AsyncState* property to a *SqlCommand*, process the results, and close that *SqlCommand*'s *Connection*.

Visual Basic

```
'Imports System.Threading
Dim strConn, strSQL As String
Dim cnCustomers, cnOrders As SqlConnection
Dim cmdCustomers, cmdOrders As SqlCommand
Dim iasyncresults(1) As IAsyncResult()
Dim waithandles(1) As WaitHandle()

strConn = "Data Source=.\SQLExpress;" & _
          "Initial Catalog=Northwind;Integrated Security=True;" & _
          "Asynchronous Processing=True;"
cnCustomers = New SqlConnection(strConn)
cnCustomers.Open()
cnOrders = New SqlConnection(strConn)
cnOrders.Open()
```

```vb
strSQL = "WAITFOR DELAY '00:00:10'; " & _
         "SELECT TOP 10 CustomerID FROM Customers"
cmdCustomers = New SqlCommand(strSQL, cnCustomers)
iasyncresults(0) = cmdCustomers.BeginExecuteReader(Nothing, cmdCustomers, _
                                    CommandBehavior.CloseConnection)
waithandles(0) = iasyncresults(0).AsyncWaitHandle

strSQL = "WAITFOR DELAY '00:00:05'; SELECT TOP 10 OrderID FROM Orders"
cmdOrders = New SqlCommand(strSQL, cnOrders)
iasyncresults(1) = cmdOrders.BeginExecuteReader(Nothing, cmdOrders, _
                                    CommandBehavior.CloseConnection)
waithandles(1) = iasyncresults(1).AsyncWaitHandle

For intCounter As Integer = 0 To waithandles.Length - 1
    Dim intIndex As Integer = WaitHandle.WaitAny(waithandles)
    Dim cmd As SqlCommand
    cmd = CType(iasyncresults(intIndex).AsyncState, SqlCommand)
    Console.WriteLine(cmd.CommandText)
    Using rdr As SqlDataReader _
            = cmd.EndExecuteReader(iasyncresults(intIndex))
        Do While rdr.Read()
            Console.WriteLine(rdr(0))
        Loop
        rdr.Close()
    End Using
Next intCounter
```

Visual C#

```csharp
//using System.Threading;
string strConn, strSQL;
SqlConnection cnCustomers, cnOrders;
SqlCommand cmdCustomers, cmdOrders;
IAsyncResult[] iasyncresults = new IAsyncResult[2];
WaitHandle[] waithandles = new WaitHandle[2];

strConn = @"Data Source=.\SQLExpress;" +
            "Initial Catalog=Northwind;Integrated Security=True;" +
            "Asynchronous Processing=True;";
cnCustomers = new SqlConnection(strConn);
cnCustomers.Open();
cnOrders = new SqlConnection(strConn);
cnOrders.Open();

strSQL = "WAITFOR DELAY '00:00:10'; " +
         "SELECT TOP 10 CustomerID FROM Customers";
cmdCustomers = new SqlCommand(strSQL, cnCustomers);
iasyncresults[0] = cmdCustomers.BeginExecuteReader(null, cmdCustomers,
                                    CommandBehavior.CloseConnection);
waithandles[0] = iasyncresults[0].AsyncWaitHandle;
strSQL = "WAITFOR DELAY '00:00:05'; SELECT TOP 10 OrderID FROM Orders";
cmdOrders = new SqlCommand(strSQL, cnOrders);
iasyncresults[1] = cmdOrders.BeginExecuteReader(null, cmdOrders,
                                    CommandBehavior.CloseConnection);
waithandles[1] = iasyncresults[1].AsyncWaitHandle;
for (int intCounter = 0; intCounter < waithandles.Length; intCounter++)
```

```
{
    int intIndex = WaitHandle.WaitAny(waithandles);
    SqlCommand cmd = (SqlCommand) iasyncresults[intIndex].AsyncState;
    Console.WriteLine(cmd.CommandText);
    using (SqlDataReader rdr =
                    cmd.EndExecuteReader(iasyncresults[intIndex]))
    {
        while (rdr.Read())
            Console.WriteLine(rdr[0]);
        rdr.Close();
    }
}
```

Tip   The preceding code snippet uses *CommandBehavior.CloseConnection* when executing queries. When this option is specified on the call to *ExecuteReader* (or *BeginExecuteReader*), closing the resulting *SqlDataReader* will also close the corresponding *SqlConnection*. Using *CommandBehavior.CloseConnection* can help you write more reliable code, especially if the code that consumes the *SqlDataReader* does not have access to the *SqlConnection*.

Executing a Query Asynchronously with a Callback Function

You might have noticed that in the preceding code snippet, we pass no data to the first parameter in *BeginExecuteReader*. The first parameter in this overload accepts a callback function. If you pass a callback function into this method, that function will be invoked when the asynchronous operation completes. You can then call the *EndExecuteReader* method from within your function. For more information about callback functions, see the .NET Framework software development kit (SDK).

The following code demonstrates using a callback function. Unlike other examples, this example is not intended for basic Console applications. If you ran the code from within a Console application, the "main" code block would complete before the query completed and the application would end before the callback function is called. To better understand this scenario, create a Windows application, add a button to the form, copy the main code into the *Click* event of a button and set a breakpoint on the call to *BeginExecuteReader*. Copy the *MyCallback* function separately and set a breakpoint on the call to *EndExecuteReader*. Then run the code. You'll see that the callback function is called approximately 10 seconds after the call to *BeginExecuteReader*, which is the time delay specified in the query.

Visual Basic

```
Dim strConn, strSQL As String
strConn = "Data Source=.\SQLExpress;" & _
        "Initial Catalog=Northwind;Integrated Security=True;" & _
        "Asynchronous Processing=True;"
Dim cn As New SqlConnection(strConn)
cn.Open()

strSQL = "WAITFOR DELAY '00:00:10'; " & _
        "SELECT TOP 10 CustomerID FROM Customers"
```

```
Dim cmd As New SqlCommand(strSQL, cn)
Dim callback As New AsyncCallback(AddressOf MyCallback)
cmd.BeginExecuteReader(callback, cmd, CommandBehavior.CloseConnection)

Private Sub MyCallback(ByVal Result As IAsyncResult)
    Dim cmd As SqlCommand = CType(Result.AsyncState, SqlCommand)
    Using rdr As SqlDataReader = cmd.EndExecuteReader(Result)
        Do While rdr.Read()
            Console.WriteLine(rdr(0))
        Loop
        rdr.Close()
    End Using
End Sub
```

Visual C#

```
string strConn, strSQL;
strConn = @"Data Source=.\SQLExpress;" +
          "Initial Catalog=Northwind;Integrated Security=True;" +
          "Asynchronous Processing=True;";
SqlConnection cn = new SqlConnection(strConn);
cn.Open();

strSQL = "WAITFOR DELAY '00:00:10'; " +
         "SELECT TOP 10 CustomerID FROM Customers";
SqlCommand cmd = new SqlCommand(strSQL, cn);
AsyncCallback callback = new AsyncCallback(MyCallback);
cmd.BeginExecuteReader(callback, cmd, CommandBehavior.CloseConnection);
private void MyCallback(IAsyncResult result)
{
    SqlCommand cmd = (SqlCommand)result.AsyncState;
    using (SqlDataReader rdr = cmd.EndExecuteReader(result))
    {
        while (rdr.Read())
            Console.WriteLine(rdr[0]);
        rdr.Close();
    }
}
```

Asynchronous queries and Windows applications   I've talked with a lot of developers about ADO.NET's new asynchronous features. Their eyes generally light up at the thought of using callback functions for their Windows applications. However, using this approach in Windows applications might prove to be more trouble than it's worth.

In the previous code sample, we used a function called *MyCallback* to process the results of the query. This procedure is executed on a background thread, which means that there are severe limitations if you try to interact with the user interface from within the procedure. For example, if you load the results of your query in a *DataTable* and then try to bind a *DataGrid-View* to the *DataTable*, you'll receive an *InvalidOperationException* saying that the control cannot be accessed from a thread other than the thread on which it was created.

You can create and invoke a delegate from your callback function to interact with the controls. In fact, there's a topic in the .NET Framework SDK that demonstrates this approach and discusses delegates in more depth. As of this writing, you can find that example in the documentation for either overload of the *BeginExecuteReader* method that takes a callback function.

A simpler approach is to use a new feature for Windows Forms in version 2.0 of the .NET Framework—the *BackgroundWorker* class. We'll address this topic in detail in Chapter 13, when we discuss building Windows applications in more depth.

Working with the *SqlDataReader*

The *SqlCommand* class is designed to help you construct your queries. As shown earlier in the chapter, calling the *ExecuteReader* method on a *SqlCommand* object returns a *SqlDataReader* object, which you can use to retrieve the rows returned by those queries.

The *SqlDataReader* class is similar to other reader classes in the .NET Framework, such as the *XmlReader*, *TextReader*, and *StreamReader* classes. Each of these classes provides an efficient, lightweight object that lets you examine (in a read-only fashion) the data that the object exposes. The *TextReader* class, for example, has methods that let you read the contents of a text file one line at a time. Similarly, the *SqlDataReader* exposes properties and methods that let you loop through the results of your query.

Developers who've worked with Remote Data Objects (RDOs) and Active Data Objects (ADOs) or the lower-level Open Database Connectivity (ODBC) and OLE DB API might be familiar with the term *firehose cursor*. This is the mechanism that databases use to return the results of a query as quickly as possible. Firehose cursors forgo functionality in favor of performance. Once you've read one row from the resultset and moved on to the next row, the previous row is no longer available. The results come at you fast and furiously, like water from a fire hose—hence the name. The ADO.NET *SqlDataReader* lets you access the firehose cursor directly. To create a *SqlDataReader*, you simply call the *ExecuteReader* method on a *SqlCommand* object.

Examining the Results of Your Query

The following code snippet shows how to examine the results of a simple query using a *SqlDataReader* object:

Visual Basic
```
Dim strConn, strSQL As String
strConn = "Data Source=.\SQLExpress;" & _
        "Initial Catalog=Northwind;Trusted_Connection=Yes;"
strSQL = "SELECT CustomerID, CompanyName FROM Customers"
Dim cn As New SqlConnection(strConn)
cn.Open()
Dim cmd As New SqlCommand(strSQL, cn)
Dim rdr As SqlDataReader = cmd.ExecuteReader()
While rdr.Read()
    Console.WriteLine("{0}: {1}", _
                    rdr("CustomerID"), rdr("CompanyName"))
End While
rdr.Close()
```

Visual C#
```
string strConn, strSQL;
strConn = @"Data Source=.\SQLExpress;" +
            "Initial Catalog=Northwind;Trusted_Connection=Yes;";
strSQL = "SELECT CustomerID, CompanyName FROM Customers";
SqlConnection cn = new SqlConnection(strConn);
cn.Open();
SqlCommand cmd = new SqlCommand(strSQL, cn);
SqlDataReader rdr = cmd.ExecuteReader();
while (rdr.Read())
    Console.WriteLine("{0}: {1}",
                        rdr["CustomerID"], rdr["CompanyName"]);
rdr.Close();
```

Note that the code calls the *Read* method before reading the first row of the resultset because the first row is not available immediately after you call *ExecuteReader*. This represents a change from previous object models such as ADO. The *SqlDataReader* that the *SqlCommand* object returns does not make the first row of data available until you call the *Read* method.

The first time you call the *Read* method, the *SqlDataReader* moves to the first row in the resultset. Subsequent calls to the *Read* method move to the next row. The method also returns a *Boolean* value to indicate whether the *SqlDataReader* has another row available. So, if *Read* returns *True*, the *SqlDataReader* moved to the next available row. When the *Read* method returns *False*, you've reached the end of the results.

When there's an available row of data, you can simply call into the *SqlDataReader*'s indexer, passing in the name of the column. The *SqlDataReader* returns the contents of that column using the generic *Object* data type. Although this is not the most efficient way to retrieve data, it serves as a simple starting point.

Closing Your *SqlDataReader*

In Chapter 3, we briefly mentioned the importance of closing *SqlConnection* objects. It's every bit as important to close your *SqlDataReader* objects. Imagine that you've built a simple Windows application in which the application opens a single *SqlConnection* that it uses throughout the lifetime of the application.

In the *Click* event of a *Button*, you execute a query and retrieve results using the *SqlDataReader*. However, you neglect to close the *SqlDataReader*. If the user clicks the *Button* more than once, the code will likely encounter an *InvalidOperationException* with a message stating, "There is already an open *DataReader* associated with this Command which must be closed first." As the message suggests, the first *SqlDataReader* was never closed.

SQL Server 2005 supports multiple active resultsets (commonly referred to as MARS) but this feature is disabled by default. I'll discuss MARS in more detail later in the chapter. SQL Server, by default, supports only a single active resultset on a connection. The connection is blocked until you close that resultset. In this case, the "abandoned" but open *SqlDataReader* blocks the *SqlConnection*, preventing you from using it to execute other queries.

Developers who have some experience with ADO might be surprised by this restriction, but those who've used RDO should not be. Different Microsoft data access technologies have handled this scenario differently.

If you try to open two firehose cursors against a SQL Server database using ADO, everything will work and you won't receive an error. This is because the OLE DB specification states that when the current connection is blocked, the OLE DB provider will perform the requested action on a new connection.

RDO developers might recognize the error message, "Connection is busy with results from another hstmt." ODBC does not do any behind-the-scenes work to try to help you out. If you try to use a connection that's busy, you'll simply receive an error message.

Which of these approaches (raising an error or performing the desired action on a new connection) is better? Developers, both inside and outside Microsoft, can't seem to agree. In fact, each successive Microsoft data access technology has handled the scenario differently from its predecessor: VBSQL raises an error, DAO/Jet creates a new connection, RDO raises an error, ADO creates a new connection, and ADO.NET raises an error. As they say in New England, "If you don't like the weather, just wait a while."

> **Note**   I believe VBSQL predates DAO/Jet, but carbon dating is difficult and the results are not 100 percent accurate.

The *SqlDataReader* is built for performance. Regardless of the restriction that an open *SqlData-Reader* blocks a *SqlConnection*, you should pull the results of your query off the wire as quickly as possible after issuing the query. If you need to move back and forth between the results of separate queries, you should use a *DataSet* or consider storing the results of your queries in a business object of some sort.

Thankfully, *SqlDataReader*s implement *IDisposable*, so they can be cleaned up easily and automatically within a *Using* block. Calling *Dispose* on a *SqlDataReader* implicitly calls the object's *Close* method. You can call the *Close* method directly through code, but I still prefer and recommend *Using* blocks because they ensure cleanup even in the case of an unhandled exception.

> **Note**   Most code snippets included in this text omit *Using* blocks, *Try/Catch* blocks, and many other recommended coding practices. Although I'm a strong fan of good coding practices, having multiple *Using* and *Try/Catch* blocks in a code snippet can take up so much space on a printed page that there's little room left to cover the ADO.NET features. For example, in the following code snippet, we've used nearly one-third the width of the page by the time we access the contents of the current row in the *SqlDataReader*. Many code snippets in this text will not use *Using* or *Try/Catch* blocks to conserve space.

Visual Basic

```vb
Dim strConn, strSQL As String
strConn = "Data Source=.\SQLExpress;" & _
          "Initial Catalog=Northwind;Integrated Security=True;"
strSQL = "SELECT CustomerID, CompanyName FROM Customers"
Using cn As New SqlConnection(strConn)
    Try
        cn.Open()
    Catch ex As SqlException
        Console.WriteLine("Connect attempt failed")
        Console.WriteLine("    {0}", ex.Message)
    End Try

    Using cmd As New SqlCommand(strSQL, cn)
        Try
            Using rdr As SqlDataReader = cmd.ExecuteReader()
                Do While rdr.Read()
                    Console.WriteLine(rdr("CompanyName"))
                Loop
                rdr.Close()
            End Using
        Catch ex As SqlException
            Console.WriteLine("Query failed")
            Console.WriteLine("    {0}", ex.Message)
        End Try
    End Using

    cn.Close()
End Using
```

Visual C#

```csharp
string strConn, strSQL;
strConn = @"Data Source=.\SQLExpress;" +
          "Initial Catalog=Northwind;Integrated Security=True;";
strSQL = "SELECT CustomerID, CompanyName FROM Customers";
using (SqlConnection cn = new SqlConnection(strConn)) {
    try {
        cn.Open();
    } catch (SqlException ex) {
        Console.WriteLine("Connect attempt failed");
        Console.WriteLine("    {0}", ex.Message);
    }

    using (SqlCommand cmd = new SqlCommand(strSQL, cn)) {
        try {
            using (SqlDataReader rdr = cmd.ExecuteReader()) {
                while (rdr.Read())
                    Console.WriteLine(rdr["CompanyName"]);
                rdr.Close();
            }
        } catch (SqlException ex) {
            Console.WriteLine("Query failed");
            Console.WriteLine("    {0}", ex.Message);
        }
    }

    cn.Close();
}
```

Examining the Schema of Your Resultset

You might not know the schema of your resultset at the time you write your code. For example, you might have created an ad hoc query tool in which the user defines the query, or you might be using SELECT * FROM queries and the database administrator might have added more columns to the table you're querying.

Regardless of the reason, if you don't know the schema of your resultset ahead of time, you can use various methods on the *SqlDataReader* object to determine the resultset's schema.

Determining the Number of Available Fields

The *SqlDataReader* class offers a *FieldCount* property that you can check to determine how many fields your query returned. Remember that some queries (UPDATE, CREATE TABLE, and so on) do not return any fields.

> **Note**   Field versus Column: The debate rages on. ADO.NET is not consistent about how it classifies query results. The *SqlDataReader* class uses the term *field* in its methods and properties, whereas the *DataTable* instead uses the term *column*. The terms are interchangeable as far as I'm concerned.

Determining the Number of Rows Returned

There is no property to indicate the number of rows available in a *SqlDataReader*. The *SqlDataReader* represents a stream of data, and there is no way for the *SqlDataReader* to know ahead of time how many rows the query will return.

Determining the Name of the Field

If you need to determine the name of a field, call the *SqlDataReader*'s *GetName* method. This method accepts an integer, specifying the field's ordinal and returns the name in a string.

Determining the .NET Data Type for a Field

To determine the .NET data type used to store the contents of a particular field, call the *SqlDataReader*'s *GetFieldType* method. Like the *GetName* method, *GetFieldType* accepts an integer, specifying the field's ordinal. The *GetFieldType* method returns the data type in a *Type* object.

Determining the Database Data Type for a Field

If you need to determine the database data type for a field, call the *SqlDataReader* class's *Get-DataTypeName* method. The method accepts the field's ordinal as an integer, and it returns a string with the name of the field's data type in the database.

The following code snippet uses the overloaded *ExecuteReader* method to return schema but no rows, and then it uses the *GetName*, *GetFieldType*, and *GetDataTypeName* methods to display information about the resultset's schema.

Visual Basic

```
Dim strConn, strSQL As String
strConn = "Data Source=.\SQLExpress;" & _
          "Initial Catalog=Northwind;Trusted_Connection=Yes;"
strSQL = "SELECT OrderID, CustomerID, OrderDate, Freight " & _
          "FROM Orders"
Dim cn As New SqlConnection(strConn)
cn.Open()
Dim cmd As New SqlCommand(strSQL, cn)
Dim rdr As SqlDataReader = cmd.ExecuteReader(CommandBehavior.SchemaOnly)
For intField As Integer = 0 To rdr.FieldCount - 1
    Console.WriteLine("Field #{0}", intField)
    Console.WriteLine("  Name:              {0}", rdr.GetName(intField))
    Console.WriteLine("  .NET data type:    {0}", _
                    rdr.GetFieldType(intField).Name)
    Console.WriteLine("  Database data type: {0}", _
                    rdr.GetDataTypeName(intField))
    Console.WriteLine()
Next intField
rdr.Close()
```

Visual C#

```
string strConn, strSQL;
strConn = @"Data Source=.\SQLExpress;" +
           "Initial Catalog=Northwind;Trusted_Connection=Yes;";
strSQL = "SELECT OrderID, CustomerID, OrderDate, Freight " +
          "FROM Orders";
SqlConnection cn = new SqlConnection(strConn);
cn.Open();
SqlCommand cmd = new SqlCommand(strSQL, cn);
SqlDataReader rdr = cmd.ExecuteReader(CommandBehavior.SchemaOnly);
for (int intField = 0; intField < rdr.FieldCount; intField++)
{
    Console.WriteLine("Field #{0}", intField);
    Console.WriteLine("  Name:              {0}", rdr.GetName(intField));
    Console.WriteLine("  .NET data type:    {0}",
                    rdr.GetFieldType(intField).Name);
    Console.WriteLine("  Database data type: {0}",
                    rdr.GetDataTypeName(intField));
    Console.WriteLine();
}
rdr.Close();
```

Determining the Ordinal for a Field

If you know the name of the field you want to access but don't know the ordinal for that field, use the *SqlDataReader*'s *GetOrdinal* method. This method accepts a string for the field name and returns the ordinal for that column.

Additional Resultset Schema Information

You might have a plethora of other questions about your resultset schema. Is the column read-only? What's the length of the field? Can the field contain null? Is this field part of the key?

What table did this field come from? Is this an autoincrement field? Is this a rowversion field? What is the scale and precision for the field?

The *SqlDataReader* does not offer a method to address each of these questions. Instead, the *SqlDataReader* lets you retrieve this additional schema information and place it into a *Data-Table*, a class I'll discuss in more depth in Chapter 6. For now, understand that a *DataTable* is similar to a Microsoft Office Excel spreadsheet—a collection of rows and columns of data. The *DataTable*'s columns represent schema properties—*ColumnName*, *DataType*, *AllowDBNull*, *IsAutoIncrement*, and so forth. Each row in the *SqlDataReader*'s resultset corresponds to a column in the *DataTable*.

The simplest way to view the schema information returned by *GetSchemaTable* is to bind the resulting *DataTable* to a Windows *DataGridView* control and scroll through the information. Figure 4-1 shows an example of this data being returned.

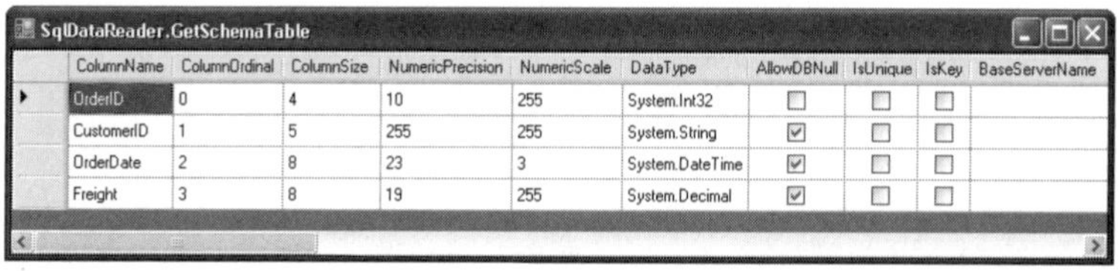

SqlDataReader.GetSchemaTable

ColumnName	ColumnOrdinal	ColumnSize	NumericPrecision	NumericScale	DataType	AllowDBNull	IsUnique	IsKey	BaseServerName
OrderID	0	4	10	255	System.Int32	☐	☐	☐	
CustomerID	1	5	255	255	System.String	☑	☐	☐	
OrderDate	2	8	23	3	System.DateTime	☑	☐	☐	
Freight	3	8	19	255	System.Decimal	☑	☐	☐	

Figure 4-1 Schema returned by *SqlDataReader.GetSchemaTable* displayed in a Windows *DataGridView*

As you work with the schema information returned by *GetSchemaTable*, you might notice that some key pieces of schema information are omitted—such as *IsKey* and *BaseTableName*. See the following discussion of *CommandBehavior* for more information about how to control the schema table returned with the resultset.

Using *CommandBehavior*

The *SqlCommand* class's *ExecuteReader* method is overloaded. You can pass in a value from the *CommandBehavior* enumeration in the *System.Data* namespace to control what data is returned. If you use the parameterless *ExecuteReader* method, the *SqlDataReader* returned will contain the results of the query and basic schema information—resultset field names and data types.

SchemaOnly If you want to retrieve resultset schema information but no rows, pass *CommandBehavior.SchemaOnly* into the *ExecuteReader* method. All the schema information will still be available through the *SqlDataReader*, but the *SqlDataReader* will not contain any rows of data.

KeyInfo By default, SQL Server returns basic schema information with the resultset—column names and data types. SQL Server does not indicate which column (or columns) represents a key for the resultset or the base table (or tables) from which the data was retrieved. If you need access to this information, include *CommandBehavior.KeyInfo* in your call to *SqlCommand.ExecuteReader*.

If you request this additional key information, SQL Server will tell you the table and column name for each column in the resultset, and note which column or columns can be used as a key for the resultset. SQL Server will not return all schema information. For example, if you query a table that contains a primary key and three unique keys, and the resultset contains all columns for all these constraints, only the primary key columns will return *True* for *IsKey*.

Fetching Data Faster with Ordinal-Based Lookups

Now let's look at ways that we can improve the performance of the previous code snippet.

In the previous code snippets, we supplied the name of the column in our code snippet. To return the value stored in that column, the *SqlDataReader* must locate the column in its internal structure based on the string we supplied. Remember that in our code snippet, we ask the *SqlDataReader* to perform that string-based lookup for each row in the resultset. That means we're paying the performance penalty for a string-based lookup for every call to retrieve a value from the *SqlDataReader*. There are more efficient ways to perform such lookups.

We can improve the performance of our code by supplying the index, or ordinal, for the column rather than its name. This coding technique can be applied to almost all objects that expose collections. I've recommended this technique to many developers who were writing ADO code and looking for ways to improve performance. Most developers have agreed that this technique would improve performance, but some have hesitated for fear it might limit their flexibility.

In the majority of applications, you can hard-code the index values for each column into your application without encountering problems. The order of the columns in your resultset won't change unless you change the query string or you make a change to the structure of your database object (table, view, or stored procedure) and you're retrieving all columns that your database object returns.

However, you might encounter situations where you'll know the column name but not its index. As noted earlier in the chapter, the *SqlDataReader*'s *GetOrdinal* method accepts a string that represents the column name and returns an integer to denote that column's ordinal. This method is a welcome addition to the ADO.NET object model because it can help you improve performance without losing the flexibility that comes with string-based lookups.

The following code snippet improves on our original *SqlDataReader* code snippet. It uses the *GetOrdinal* method to get the ordinal values for the two columns we want to examine and then uses those values to examine the contents of each row. This improves performance because we perform a string-based search of the collection only once per column. In our original code snippet, we performed the string-based search each time we fetched data from a column.

Visual Basic

```
Dim strConn, strSQL As String
strConn = "Data Source=.\SQLExpress;" & _
          "Initial Catalog=Northwind;Trusted_Connection=Yes;"
```

```
strSQL = "SELECT CustomerID, CompanyName FROM Customers"
Dim cn As New SqlConnection(strConn)
cn.Open()
Dim cmd As New SqlCommand(strSQL, cn)
Dim rdr As SqlDataReader = cmd.ExecuteReader()
Dim intCustomerIDOrdinal, intCompanyNameOrdinal As Integer
intCustomerIDOrdinal = rdr.GetOrdinal("CustomerID")
intCompanyNameOrdinal = rdr.GetOrdinal("CompanyName")
While rdr.Read()
    Console.WriteLine("{0}: {1}", _
                        rdr(intCustomerIDOrdinal), _
                        rdr(intCompanyNameOrdinal))
End While
rdr.Close()
```

Visual C#
```
string strConn, strSQL;
strConn = @"Data Source=.\SQLExpress;" +
            "Initial Catalog=Northwind;Trusted_Connection=Yes;";
strSQL = "SELECT CustomerID, CompanyName FROM Customers";
SqlConnection cn = new SqlConnection(strConn);
cn.Open();
SqlCommand cmd = new SqlCommand(strSQL, cn);
SqlDataReader rdr = cmd.ExecuteReader();
int intCustomerIDOrdinal, intCompanyNameOrdinal;
intCustomerIDOrdinal = rdr.GetOrdinal("CustomerID");
intCompanyNameOrdinal = rdr.GetOrdinal("CompanyName");
while (rdr.Read())
    Console.WriteLine("{0}: {1}",
                        rdr[intCustomerIDOrdinal],
                        rdr[intCompanyNameOrdinal]);
rdr.Close();
```

That's great, but we can go even faster...

Strongly Typed Getters

The *SqlDataReader* also exposes a series of methods that return data in the different .NET Framework data types (such as string, 32-bit integer, decimal, and double). Currently, our code snippet implicitly uses the *Item* property, which returns the contents of the specified column in the generic *Object* data type. This process is referred to as *boxing*. Extracting the value back from the *Object* data type is referred to as *unboxing*. Boxing and unboxing are expensive operations. They're also unnecessary.

The *SqlDataReader* class exposes *Get* methods for many basic .NET data types—*GetString*, *GetInt32*, *GetDateTime*, and so on. These methods are generally called the *strongly typed getters*. You can avoid the performance penalty incurred by boxing and unboxing by calling the appropriate *Get* method on the *SqlDataReader*. For example, the CustomerID and CompanyName columns contain string data. So we can use the *GetString* method of the *SqlDataReader* to return the contents of those columns as a string, as shown in the following code. Although the output appears the same, this code runs faster than the previous code snippet.

Visual Basic

```
...
Dim rdr As SqlDataReader = cmd.ExecuteReader()
Dim intCustomerIDOrdinal, intCompanyNameOrdinal As Integer
intCustomerIDOrdinal = rdr.GetOrdinal("CustomerID")
intCompanyNameOrdinal = rdr.GetOrdinal("CompanyName")
While rdr.Read()
    Console.WriteLine("{0}: {1}", _
                    rdr.GetString(intCustomerIDOrdinal), _
                    rdr.GetString(intCompanyNameOrdinal))
End While
rdr.Close()
```

Visual C#

```
...
SqlDataReader rdr = cmd.ExecuteReader();
int intCustomerIDOrdinal, intCompanyNameOrdinal;
intCustomerIDOrdinal = rdr.GetOrdinal("CustomerID");
intCompanyNameOrdinal = rdr.GetOrdinal("CompanyName");
while (rdr.Read())
    Console.WriteLine("{0}: {1}",
                    rdr.GetString(intCustomerIDOrdinal),
                    rdr.GetString(intCompanyNameOrdinal));
rdr.Close();
```

You should always use the appropriate strongly typed getter that corresponds to the data returned by the column in the resultset. As noted earlier, the strongly typed getters offer better performance. Calling the "wrong" strongly typed getter results in an *InvalidCastException*. During development, if you're unsure which strongly typed getter to call, try calling the *GetFieldType* method, passing in the ordinal for the desired column.

Handling Null Values

Let's say you're retrieving information about a series of orders—OrderID, CustomerID, Order-Date, and ShippedDate—using the *SqlDataReader* and the strongly typed *Get* methods and your code looks something like the following:

Visual Basic

```
Dim rdr As SqlDataReader
Dim orders As New List(Of Order)
Dim order As Order
...
Do While rdr.Read()
    order = New Order()
    order.OrderID = rdr.GetInt32(0)
    order.CustomerID = rdr.GetString(1)
    order.OrderDate = rdr.GetDateTime(2)
    order.ShippedDate = rdr.GetDateTime(3)
    orders.Add(order)
Loop
```

Visual C#

```csharp
SqlDataReader rdr;
List<Order> orders = new List<Order>();
Order order;
...
while (rdr.Read())
{
    order = new Order();
    order.OrderID = rdr.GetInt32(0);
    order.CustomerID = rdr.GetString(1);
    order.OrderDate = rdr.GetDateTime(2);
    order.ShippedDate = rdr.GetDateTime(3);
    orders.Add(order);
}
```

You run this code and find that on the call to retrieve the contents of the ShippedDate column you receive an exception saying, "Data is Null. This method or property cannot be called on Null values." What happened?

First, let's talk about handling null values in .NET code. Let's say that you want to work with the contents of a string, perhaps to check its length, but there's a chance that the string might not be initialized. You'd use code like the following to make sure the string was initialized before working with the contents of the string:

Visual Basic

```vb
Dim str As String
Dim intLength As Integer
...
If str Is Nothing Then
    Console.WriteLine("Un-initialized string!")
Else
    intLength = str.Length;
End If
```

Visual C#

```csharp
string str;
...
if (str == null)
    Console.WriteLine("Un-initialized string!");
else
    intLength = str.Length;
```

The same rules apply for any reference data type in .NET. Before working with the variable, make sure that it has been initialized. Databases support the same concept. If you do not supply a value for a column in a new row, and the database will not automatically supply a value through a default or other such construct, the value for that column is null. Depending on the definition for a database table, the column might accept nulls, or it might not. If you're retrieving data from a column that might contain a null value, check for that value before trying to access it.

DBNull.Value

If the database value for a column is null and you call one of the strongly typed getters on the *SqlDataReader* that returns a .NET data type (*String*, *DateTime*, *Int32*, and so on), you'll get a *SqlNullValueException*. However, you can still use the default indexer, passing the column name or ordinal with code like the following:

Visual Basic
```
Dim ShippedDate As Object = rdr("ShippedDate")
```

Visual C#
```
object ShippedDate = rdr["ShippedDate"];
```

Again, assuming the database value is null, if you check the contents of your object variable you'll seethat it's an instance of the *DBNull* type. Specifically, it's set to *DBNull.Value*. You could follow this process to check for null values, but there's an easier way.

Using the *IsDBNull* Method

The *SqlDataReader* exposes an *IsDBNull* method. Use this method to determine whether a column contains a null value before fetching the contents of the column. The *IsDBNull* method only accepts an integer for the column ordinal and, as its name implies, returns true if the column's value is null and false otherwise.

In the initial example, the mythical *Order* class's *ShippedDate* property used the *DateTime* type. Because the ShippedDate column can be null, to indicate an order that has not yet shipped, a better choice would be to use the *IsDBNull* method in conjunction with the *Nullable* class that's new to version 2.0 of the .NET Framework.

ADO.NET 2.0 does not directly support *Nullable* types. The *SqlDataReader* does not have a *GetNullableDateTime* or a generic method that lets you indicate that you want to retrieve a *Nullable DateTime*. However, you can use the *IsDBNull* method in conjunction with a *Nullable* class. Let's say that you created an *Order* class, with *OrderID*, *CustomerID*, *OrderDate*, and *ShippedDate* properties using *Int32*, *String*, *DateTime*, and *Nullable DateTime* data types, respectively. The *ShippedDate* property is a *Nullable DateTime* to represent unshipped orders. You could use a *SqlDataReader* to create instances of that *Order* class and handle potential null values in the ShippedDate column by making your code look like the following:

Visual Basic
```
Dim rdr As SqlDataReader
Dim orders As New List(Of Order)
Dim order As Order
...
Do While rdr.Read()
    order = New Order()
    order.OrderID = rdr.GetInt32(0)
    order.CustomerID = rdr.GetString(1)
    order.OrderDate = rdr.GetDateTime(2)
```

```
    If rdr.IsDBNull(3) Then
        order.ShippedDate = Nothing
    Else
        order.ShippedDate = rdr.GetDateTime(3)
    End If
    orders.Add(order)
Loop
```

Visual C#

```csharp
SqlDataReader rdr;
List<Order> orders = new List<Order>();
Order order;
...
while (rdr.Read()) {
    order = new Order();
    order.OrderID = rdr.GetInt32(0);
    order.CustomerID = rdr.GetString(1);
    order.OrderDate = rdr.GetDateTime(2);
    if (rdr.IsDBNull(3))
        order.ShippedDate = null;
    else
        order.ShippedDate = rdr.GetDateTime(3);
    orders.Add(order);
}
```

SqlTypes

When you retrieve the results of a query, the *SqlDataReader* looks at the data type for the SQL Server column and converts the data to the appropriate .NET data type. However, there are some differences between those data types. For example, the *SqlDataReader* returns the SQL Server *Decimal* data type as a .NET *Decimal*. Although the names match up, the SQL Server *Decimal* can hold more data than the .NET *Decimal*. If you call the un-typed getter or the *GetDecimal* method to return this data as a .NET *Decimal*, you'll receive an *OverflowException*.

The SQL Client .NET Data Provider addresses these type incompatibilities by offering a series of specialized classes designed to match their corresponding SQL Server data types–the *Sql-Types*. These classes are available in the *System.Data.SqlTypes* namespace. A *SqlDecimal*, for example, is designed to handle all possible values for SQL Server's *Decimal* data type. This class exposes a *Value* property that returns a .NET *Decimal*. There are other ways to examine the contents of a *SqlDecimal*, which help when you can't convert the data to a .NET *Decimal*. You can simply convert the data to a string, using the *ToString* method. *SqlDecimal* also exposes a *ToDouble* method that returns its contents in a .NET *Double*, which can hold values beyond the range of a .NET *Decimal*. And, if you really want to get down to the 1s and 0s, you can also examine the contents of a *SqlDecimal* as an array of integers using the *Data* property or as a byte array using the *BinData* property.

The *SqlTypes* offer a variety of constructors. For example, you can create a *SqlDecimal* based on a .NET *Decimal*, *double*, *int*, or *long*. You can also use the static *Parse* method to create a *Sql-Decimal* based on a string.

The *SqlDataReader* offers additional *Get* methods that can return *SqlTypes*. If you want to retrieve the contents of a SQL Server decimal column as a *SqlDecimal*, simply call the *GetSql-Decimal* method.

Keep in mind that the *SqlTypes* are immutable. Once you create one, you can't change its internal value. The *Value* property for each class is read-only, but you can create new *SqlTypes* based on values in existing *SqlTypes*. For example, the following code creates a new *SqlInt32* as the sum of two existing *SqlInt32*s:

Visual Basic

```
'Imports System.Data.SqlTypes
Dim x, y, z As SqlInt32
x = New SqlInt32(3)
y = New SqlInt32(5)
z = SqlInt32.Add(x, y)
Console.WriteLine(z)
```

Visual C#

```
//using System.Data.SqlTypes;
SqlInt32 x, y, z;
x = new SqlInt32(3);
y = new SqlInt32(5);
z = SqlInt32.Add(x, y);
Console.WriteLine(z);
```

Note   All code snippets that use *SqlTypes* require a reference to the *System.Data.SqlTypes* namespace, as shown in the preceding code snippet.

The other major benefit to using the *SqlTypes* is that they're designed to handle null values. You don't have to use the *IsDBNull* method to check for a null value before calling a method such as *GetSqlInt32*. Each class in the *SqlTypes* namespace offers an *IsNull* property that you can use to check whether the *SqlType* contains a null value. To create a *SqlType* and set it to null, use the parameterless constructor for that *SqlType*, as shown in the following code:

Visual Basic

```
'Imports System.Data.SqlTypes
Dim nullint As New SqlInt32()
Console.WriteLine(nullint.IsNull)
```

Visual C#

```
//using System.Data.SqlTypes;
SqlInt32 nullint = new SqlInt32();
Console.WriteLine(nullint.IsNull);
```

Handling Multiple Resultsets from a Query

Some databases, such as SQL Server, allow you to execute a batch of queries that return multiple results. Let's say that we want to issue the following query against the sample

Northwind database:

```
SELECT CustomerID, CompanyName FROM Customers;
SELECT OrderID, OrderDate FROM Orders;
SELECT OrderID, ProductID FROM [Order Details]
```

In our previous *SqlDataReader* code snippets, we looped through the results of our query until the *Read* method returned *False*. That code loops through only the first resultset returned by the query. If we used that code with the batch query just shown, we would retrieve data from the Customers table but not from the Orders or Order Details tables.

The *SqlDataReader* exposes a *NextResult* method that lets you move to the results of the next row-returning query. The *NextResult* method is similar to the *Read* method in that it returns a *Boolean* value to indicate whether there are more results. However, unlike with the *Read* method, you should not call this method initially.

When the *Read* method returns *False*, you can check to see whether there are additional results to fetch by calling the *NextResult* method. When the *NextResult* method returns *False*, there are no more resultsets. The following code snippet shows how to use the *NextResult* method to fetch the results of a batch query:

Visual Basic

```
...
cn.Open()
Dim strSQL As String
strSQL = "SELECT CustomerID, CompanyName FROM Customers;" & _
         "SELECT OrderID, OrderDate FROM Orders;" & _
         "SELECT OrderID, ProductID FROM [Order Details]"
Dim cmd As New SqlCommand(strSQL, cn)
Dim rdr As SqlDataReader = cmd.ExecuteReader()
Do
    Do While rdr.Read()
        Console.WriteLine("{0} - {1}", rdr(0), rdr(1))
    Loop
    Console.WriteLine()
Loop While rdr.NextResult()
```

Visual C#

```
...
cn.Open();
string strSQL;
strSQL = "SELECT CustomerID, CompanyName FROM Customers;" +
         "SELECT OrderID, OrderDate FROM Orders;" +
         "SELECT OrderID, ProductID FROM [Order Details]";
SqlCommand cmd = new SqlCommand(strSQL, cn);
SqlDataReader rdr = cmd.ExecuteReader();
do {
    while (rdr.Read())
        Console.WriteLine("{0} - {1}", rdr[0], rdr[1]);
    Console.WriteLine();
} while (rdr.NextResult());
```

SQL Server 2005 and Multiple Active Resultsets

Prior to the release of SQL Server 2005, connections that had an open firehose cursor (*Sql-DataReader* in ADO.NET terms) were blocked. You could not execute other queries on that connection until you closed the open firehose cursor. In other words, you could have only a single active request for your session.

SQL Server 2005 introduces support for multiple active resultsets (often referred to as MARS) or multiple requests on a single connection. By enabling this feature on your connections to SQL Server 2005, your connection is no longer blocked if there's an open *SqlDataReader* associated with the *SqlConnection*. You can still execute other queries—SELECT, UPDATE, CREATE TABLE, and so on—on your *SqlConnection* even though you've yet to close the currently open *SqlDataReader*.

First, let's set up a basic scenario. You've issued a query for order information, perhaps the orders for a particular customer. As you're examining the results of the query, you need to retrieve related information, perhaps the order details for that order.

Life before MARS

So what did developers working with non-MARS connections do if they needed to execute a query on a connection with a firehose cursor open? The following sections explain.

Use an off-line data cache   If you're constructing your own queries to retrieve this information, there are some obvious workarounds, such as querying for the order details information first, and storing the results in an off-line cache. Then, as you retrieve the order information, you can query your off-line cache for the related order details. Some object relational management technologies use this approach.

You can adopt the same approach by creating your own data cache, or by storing the results in *DataTable*s, which we'll briefly introduce in Chapter 5 and then cover in more detail in Chapter 6.

However, this approach might not be feasible if you have no way to construct a query to retrieve the related "child" data ahead of time. Perhaps both queries are stored procedure calls and your database administrator will let you retrieve order detail information only one order at a time, despite your repeated pleas.

Use server-side cursors   The single active resultset restriction applies only to firehose cursors. You can have multiple non-firehose cursors open on a single connection to SQL Server. Previous data access technologies (such as ADO and RDO) support these other cursor types. However, ADO.NET does not, at least not yet. So let's not discuss this any further. In fact, forget I even mentioned server-side cursors. As a wise old Jedi once said, "This is not the approach you're looking for."

Perform the work on another connection   If you absolutely need to query the database and your connection to the database has a firehose cursor open, you can always open another connection to the database and perform the work on the new connection. As noted earlier in the chapter, the SQL Server OLE DB provider will implicitly create new connections to handle queries if the current connection is currently blocked.

While spawning additional connections does incur some overhead, this approach allows for parallelism—the server can handle the requests independently.

Enabling MARS

The MARS functionality of SQL Server 2005 is disabled by default. You enable this feature on a per-connection basis by adding the following to your connection string:

```
MultipleActiveResultSets=True;
```

> **Tip**   As with other connection string options, if you have trouble remembering the keyword, the *SqlConnectionStringBuilder* can help.

> **Note**   At the time of this writing, using this option in a connection string for SQL Server 2000 did not throw an exception when opening the connection. Of course, later trying to execute a query on the *SqlConnection* with an open *SqlDataReader* threw an *InvalidOperation-Exception*. If you want to use MARS and there's a chance the server you're connecting to might not be running SQL Server 2005, you should check the *ServerVersion* property of the *SqlConnection* object after opening your connection.

Why Is MARS Disabled by Default?

Initial betas of SQL Server 2005 enabled MARS by default. Late in the development cycle, the SQL Server team made the decision to change the behavior and disable it by default. Why?

When you're executing multiple queries using MARS, SQL Server does not handle the queries in parallel. Instead, SQL Server interleaves execution, switching back and forth between the different queries. Generally speaking, SQL Server executes each query atomically. In other words, if you execute a long-running UPDATE query and then try to execute a second query while waiting for the first one to complete, SQL Server will complete the first query before starting the second. You can, however, execute a SELECT query and then execute an additional query and SQL Server temporarily halts execution of the SELECT query to work on another query. Only data-reading queries (such as SELECT, READTEXT, and bulk insert) support interleaving prior to the completion of the query.

If you're working with simple SELECT queries, MARS can be a powerful and helpful feature. However, if you're working with more complex operations—batches of queries, stored procedure calls, or transactions—you might encounter unexpected results.

The way SQL Server interleaves execution of multiple queries on a MARS-enabled connection can lead to nondeterministic behavior. Say that you execute two separate requests, either batches or stored procedure calls, on a MARS-enabled connection. Each request returns a resultset but also executes additional queries. You can't truly know when SQL Server will interleave execution between the two requests unless you execute one and handle all the results before executing the other.

Transactional scenarios become more complex with MARS. With MARS-enabled connections, you can execute multiple requests within a single transaction. If you start a transaction and execute multiple long-running batches, one batch might modify data that has already been viewed or modified in another batch because they're running within the same transaction, which is behavior you might not have expected. SQL Server will return an error on calls to create or roll back to savepoints, as well as to calls to commit the transaction if there is more than one active request in the transaction.

You might have stored procedures that execute the USE query to switch to a different database (from Northwind to Pubs, for example). What if you have multiple active requests that involve such context switching?

To put it bluntly, things that are simple on a non-MARS-enabled connection are more complex on MARS-enabled connections. As a result, the SQL Server team felt that MARS should be an opt-in feature rather than something that's enabled by default.

> **Note**   Is MARS a SQL Server feature or an ADO.NET feature? It's a SQL Server feature that has to be explicitly enabled by client technologies such as *SqlClient* or the new SQL Server OLE DB provider (SQLNCLI).

Should I Use MARS?

MARS is a very powerful and helpful feature. If you're processing the results of a simple SELECT query (or stored procedure call that consists of a simple SELECT query) using a *SqlData-Reader* and absolutely need to execute a second query, intelligent use of MARS can really simplify your code.

> **Warning**   Danger, Will Robinson! Before you consider using MARS for anything other than simple SELECT queries, I strongly recommend going to Microsoft's MSDN site and reading the articles and whitepapers dedicated to explaining the inner workings of MARS.

Keep in mind that when you call the *ExecuteReader* on your *SqlCommand*, SQL Server places the results of the query in server-side buffers. Those resources are tied up until you consume the contents of the *SqlDataReader*. As a general rule, you should retrieve the results as quickly as possible to release those resources. Pausing momentarily to retrieve the results of a second query probably won't cause problems. However, pausing and waiting on input from the user might needlessly tie up resources on the server. If you need to prompt the user for information, or perform other potentially long-running operations that would prevent you from examining the remaining results, consider storing the results in an off-line cache such as a *DataTable* before performing that other operation.

Using MARS

Now that we've addressed all the appropriate warnings regarding MARS, let's look at a brief snippet of code that demonstrates this feature. The code retrieves order information for a customer through a *SqlDataReader*. Upon examining the information for each order, the code executes a parameterized query to retrieve the order details for the current order and prints the interleaved results to the Console window.

Visual Basic

```
Dim strSQL, strConn As String
strConn = "Data Source=.\SQLExpress;Initial Catalog=Northwind;" & _
          "Integrated Security=True;MultipleActiveResultSets=True;"
Dim cn As New SqlConnection(strConn)
Dim cmdOrders, cmdDetails As SqlCommand
Dim pCustID, pOrderID As SqlParameter
Dim rdrOrders, rdrDetails As SqlDataReader
cn.Open()

strSQL = "SELECT OrderID, OrderDate FROM Orders " & _
         "WHERE CustomerID = @CustomerID"
cmdOrders = New SqlCommand(strSQL, cn)
pCustID = cmdOrders.Parameters.Add("@CustomerID", SqlDbType.NChar, 5)

strSQL = "SELECT ProductID, Quantity, UnitPrice " & _
         "FROM [Order Details] WHERE OrderID = @OrderID"
cmdDetails = New SqlCommand(strSQL, cn)
pOrderID = cmdDetails.Parameters.Add("@OrderID", SqlDbType.Int)

pCustID.Value = "ALFKI"
Console.WriteLine("Orders for {0}", pCustID.Value)
Console.WriteLine("===================")
rdrOrders = cmdOrders.ExecuteReader()
Do While rdrOrders.Read()
    Console.WriteLine("OrderID: {0}  OrderDate: {1:d}", _
                      rdrOrders("OrderID"), rdrOrders("OrderDate"))

    pOrderID.Value = rdrOrders("OrderID")
    rdrDetails = cmdDetails.ExecuteReader()
    Do While rdrDetails.Read()
        Console.WriteLine("   ProductID: {0}  Quantity: {1}  " & _
                          "UnitPrice: {2:c}", rdrDetails("ProductID"), _
                          rdrDetails("Quantity"), rdrDetails("UnitPrice"))
    Loop
    rdrDetails.Close()

    Console.WriteLine()
```

```
Loop
rdrOrders.Close()

cn.Close()
```

Visual C#

```csharp
string strSQL, strConn;
strConn = @"Data Source=.\SQLExpress;Initial Catalog=Northwind;" +
            "Integrated Security=True;MultipleActiveResultSets=True;";
SqlConnection cn = new SqlConnection(strConn);
SqlCommand cmdOrders, cmdDetails;
SqlParameter pCustID, pOrderID;
SqlDataReader rdrOrders, rdrDetails;
cn.Open();

strSQL = "SELECT OrderID, OrderDate FROM Orders " +
          "WHERE CustomerID = @CustomerID";
cmdOrders = new SqlCommand(strSQL, cn);
pCustID = cmdOrders.Parameters.Add("@CustomerID", SqlDbType.NChar, 5);

strSQL = "SELECT ProductID, Quantity, UnitPrice " +
          "FROM [Order Details] WHERE OrderID = @OrderID";
cmdDetails = new SqlCommand(strSQL, cn);
pOrderID = cmdDetails.Parameters.Add("@OrderID", SqlDbType.Int);

pCustID.Value = "ALFKI";
Console.WriteLine("Orders for {0}", pCustID.Value);
Console.WriteLine("===================");
rdrOrders = cmdOrders.ExecuteReader();
while (rdrOrders.Read()) {
    Console.WriteLine("OrderID: {0}  OrderDate: {1:d}",
                        rdrOrders["OrderID"], rdrOrders["OrderDate"]);

    pOrderID.Value = rdrOrders["OrderID"];
    rdrDetails = cmdDetails.ExecuteReader();
    while (rdrDetails.Read())
        Console.WriteLine("    ProductID: {0}  Quantity: {1}  " +
                            "UnitPrice: {2:c}", rdrDetails["ProductID"],
                            rdrDetails["Quantity"], rdrDetails["UnitPrice"]);
    rdrDetails.Close();

    Console.WriteLine();
}
rdrOrders.Close();

cn.Close();
```

Working with Parameterized Queries

There are many scenarios in which you might want to use parameterized queries, but the most common scenario occurs when you need user input in your query.

Formatting User Input in a Query String

Let's say that you're building an application that lets a user examine the orders placed by a particular customer. The application user will specify customer information while the application is running, whether that be the company name or some other information. You'll likely want to construct a "base" query, apply the user's input, and execute the query.

There are two basic approaches you could follow. First, you could look for a way to embed the user input into your query string, perhaps using the *String.Format* function in the .NET Framework. The second approach is to construct a parameterized query, which we'll discuss shortly. I strongly caution developers who might feel the urge to follow the first approach. Simply put, formatting values in a query is difficult.

String values might be the least of your worries from a formatting standpoint. Properly formatting date values is a challenge, especially if you're building a multicultural application. Should the date format depend on the regional settings for the database or the client, or should you use a standard format?

In theory, you can handle all these formatting issues given a thorough understanding of the query syntax of the database or databases you want to query and liberal use of the *String.Format* function in the .NET Framework. That's not to say that you aren't up to the challenge, from a technical standpoint. Instead, I'd argue that it's not worth trying to construct queries this way. The process is too time-consuming, and it's very easy to mishandle scenarios and not even realize it until after you've deployed your application. More importantly, the consequences of mishandling user input can be severe—much more severe than a query failing to execute.

Query Construction and SQL Injection

The most common mistake developers make is to forget to look for single quotes in the input from the user. The classic example is that the developer stores user names and passwords in a table and prompts the user for his or her user name and password when the application launches. The application then queries the database for the specified user name and password. If the query returns a row, the application assumes the user must have supplied a valid user name and password.

The developer starts with a base query such as the following one:

```
SELECT COUNT(*) FROM UserInfo
  WHERE UserName = '{0}' AND Password = '{0}'
```

The developer then applies input from the user to construct a query such as this one:

```
SELECT COUNT(*) FROM UserInfo
  WHERE UserName = 'MyUserName' AND Password = 'MyPassword'
```

The developer writing this code might have anticipated simple input, such as *MyUserName* and *MyPassword*. But what happens if the user has some understanding of the query being executed and instead enters the following: *NonUser' OR 1 = 1 --*? The query that the code generates and executes is now this:

```
SELECT COUNT(*) FROM UserInfo
  WHERE UserName = 'NonUser' OR 1 = 1 --' AND Password = 'MyPassword'
```

The double hyphen has a special significance in SQL Server's query syntax. It signifies that the rest of the line in the query is a comment. In other words, *AND Password = 'MyPassword'* is ignored. Now, there might be no entry in the UserName column for *NonUser*, but the other half of the WHERE clause (*1 = 1*) is true for all rows. Thus, this query executes successfully and returns all rows in the table. The application assumes the user supplied a valid user name and password and continues.

Sure, this is an extreme example, but the point is that trying to properly format user input in a query string is challenging and mishandling even a single scenario can cause major problems for your application. Thankfully, there's a simpler and more effective solution—using parameterized queries.

Parameterized Queries

Let's revisit the initial scenario, the one in which you want to retrieve order information for a particular customer. We can construct a query against the Orders table and specify that the CustomerID column must equal the value in a parameter, for which the user will supply a value at run time. Here's the query:

```
SELECT OrderID, CustomerID, OrderDate, EmployeeID FROM Orders
  WHERE CustomerID = @CustomerID
```

> **Note** The SQL Client .NET Data provider supports only named parameters and does not support the generic parameter marker (*?*). The OLE DB and ODBC .NET Data Providers support only the generic parameter marker (*?*). The Oracle Client .NET Data Provider supports named parameters, like the SQL Client .NET Data Provider, but its parameters use the colon character (:) rather than the "at" character (@).
>
> I'll discuss executing parameterized queries with the other .NET data providers in more detail in Appendix A.

To execute a parameterized query in the ADO.NET object model, you add a *Parameter* object to the *Command* object's *Parameters* collection. When using the SQL Client .NET Data Provider, the *Parameter* class you'll use is *SqlParameter*. The simplest way to create a *SqlParameter* is to call the *AddWithValue* method on a *SqlCommand* object's *Parameters* collection, as shown in the following code:

Visual Basic
```
Dim strConn, strSQL As String
strConn = "Data Source=.\SQLExpress;" & _
        "Initial Catalog=Northwind;Integrated Security=True;"
```

```
strSQL = "SELECT OrderID, CustomerID, OrderDate, EmployeeID " & _
         "FROM Orders WHERE CustomerID = @CustomerID"
Dim cn As New SqlConnection(strConn)
cn.Open()
Dim cmd As New SqlCommand(strSQL, cn)

'Create the new parameter
cmd.Parameters.AddWithValue("@CustomerID", "ALFKI")

Dim rdr As SqlDataReader = cmd.ExecuteReader()
Do While rdr.Read()
    Console.WriteLine("OrderID: {0}    OrderDate: {1:d}", _
                      rdr.GetInt32(0), rdr.GetDateTime(2))
Loop
```

Visual C#

```
string strConn, strSQL;
strConn = @"Data Source=.\SQLExpress;" +
          "Initial Catalog=Northwind;Integrated Security=True;";
strSQL = "SELECT OrderID, CustomerID, OrderDate, EmployeeID " +
         "FROM Orders WHERE CustomerID = @CustomerID";
SqlConnection cn = new SqlConnection(strConn);
cn.Open();
SqlCommand cmd = new SqlCommand(strSQL, cn);

//Create the new parameter
cmd.Parameters.AddWithValue("@CustomerID", "ALFKI");

SqlDataReader rdr = cmd.ExecuteReader();
while (rdr.Read())
    Console.WriteLine("OrderID: {0}    OrderDate: {1:d}",
                      rdr.GetInt32(0), rdr.GetDateTime(2));
rdr.Close();
```

The *AddWithValue* method is another syntactic sugar method. *AddWithValue* creates a new *SqlParameter* object and sets the *ParameterName* and *Value* properties on that new object. The following code snippets are equivalent:

Visual Basic

```
Dim cmd As New SqlCommand()
Dim p As SqlParameter

p = cmd.Parameters.AddWithValue("@CustomerID", "ALFKI")

p = New SqlParameter()
p.ParameterName = "@CustomerID"
p.Value = "ALFKI"
cmd.Parameters.Add(p)
```

Visual C#

```
SqlCommand cmd = new SqlCommand();
SqlParameter p;
p = cmd.Parameters.AddWithValue("@CustomerID", "ALFKI");
```

```
p = new SqlParameter();
p.ParameterName = "@CustomerID";
p.Value = "ALFKI";
cmd.Parameters.Add(p);
```

Parameter Data Types

You can set the *SqlDbType* property on a *SqlParameter* object to control the data type used when passing parameter information to your SQL Server database. This property accepts values from the *SqlDbType* enumeration. If you're familiar with the data types available on SQL Server columns, the values in the *SqlDbType* enumeration should look familiar: *NVar-Char*, *Int*, *DateTime*, *Bit*, *Money*, *Text*, *Image*, and so on.

For some data types, you might need to do more than simply specify a data type. The SQL Server *Decimal* and *Numeric* data types, for example, support different values for scale and precision. The SQL Server *string* and *binary* data types support different values for length. If you're working with these data types, you can set the appropriate properties on your *Sql-Parameter* object—*Size* to control the size of *string* and *binary* data, or *Precision* and *Scale* to control the precision and scale for *Decimal* or *Numeric* data.

Inferring the data type   Some developers who have had experience working with ADO.NET or other data access models might look at that preceding sample and wonder, "How did ADO.NET determine the SQL Server data type for the parameter?" The simple answer is that the *SqlParameter* object inferred the data type based on the contents of the *Value* property.

Because we set the *Value* property to a string, which in .NET is a series of Unicode characters, the *SqlParameter* implicitly set the *SqlDbType* property to *SqlDbType.NVarChar* and the *Size* property to 5, because we set the *Value* property to a five-character Unicode string.

Explicitly setting the data type   If implicitly setting the *SqlDbType* property scares you, there's no need to worry. You are not forced to rely on this behavior. You can explicitly set the *SqlDbType* property as you see fit, along with *Size*, *Precision*, and *Scale* if you so choose. In fact, there are a series of *SqlParameter* constructors that allow you to set the *SqlDbType* property, as well as other commonly used properties.

Here, we've modified the previous example (querying the Orders table for orders from a particular customer) so that we explicitly set the *SqlDbType* and *Size* properties of the *SqlParameter*.

Visual Basic

```
...
Dim cmd As New SqlCommand(strSQL, cn)
Dim p As SqlParameter
p = New SqlParameter("@CustomerID", SqlDbType.NVarChar, 5)
p.Value = "ALFKI"
cmd.Parameters.Add(p)
```

Visual C#

```
...
SqlCommand cmd = new SqlCommand(strSQL, cn);
SqlParameter p;
p = new SqlParameter("@CustomerID", SqlDbType.NVarChar, 5);
p.Value = "ALFKI";
cmd.Parameters.Add(p);
```

For those interested in writing code in as few lines as possible, the *SqlParameterCollection*'s *Add* method offers a similar overload.

> **Note** If you want to use *SqlParameters* with *SqlTypes* (*SqlDecimal*, *SqlString*, and so on) rather than .NET types, use the *SqlValue* property instead of the *Value* property.

Parameter Direction

In the previous examples, we used the parameter in the query to pass data to the database. This is an example of an input parameter. You can also use parameters to retrieve data from the database. For example, you might want to retrieve data from a single row in your database through output parameters rather than by examining a row through the *SqlDataReader*. Returning this data through output parameters is faster because parameters involve less overhead than resultsets.

The following query looks up a row in the Products table based on the ProductName column using an input parameter, and it returns the values of the UnitPrice and UnitsInStock columns through output parameters:

```
SELECT @UnitPrice = UnitPrice, @UnitsInStock = UnitsInStock
    FROM Products WHERE ProductName = @ProductName
```

The following code uses this query to retrieve the unit price and number of units in stock for a particular product through output parameters:

Visual Basic

```
Dim strConn, strSQL As String
strConn = "Data Source=.\SQLExpress;" & _
        "Initial Catalog=Northwind;Integrated Security=True;"
strSQL = "SELECT @UnitPrice = UnitPrice, @UnitsInStock = UnitsInStock " & _
        "FROM Products WHERE ProductName = @ProductName"
Dim cn As New SqlConnection(strConn)
cn.Open()
Dim cmd As New SqlCommand(strSQL, cn)

Dim pUnitPrice, pInStock, pProductName As SqlParameter
pUnitPrice = cmd.Parameters.Add("@UnitPrice", SqlDbType.Money)
pUnitPrice.Direction = ParameterDirection.Output
pInStock = cmd.Parameters.Add("@UnitsInStock", SqlDbType.NVarChar, 20)
pInStock.Direction = ParameterDirection.Output
```

```
pProductName = cmd.Parameters.Add("@ProductName", SqlDbType.NVarChar, 40)
pProductName.Value = "Chai"

cmd.ExecuteNonQuery()

Console.WriteLine("Unit Price:  {0}", pUnitPrice.Value)
Console.WriteLine("In Stock:    {0}", pInStock.Value)
```

Visual C#

```csharp
string strConn, strSQL;
strConn = @"Data Source=.\SQLExpress;" +
          "Initial Catalog=Northwind;Integrated Security=True;";
strSQL = "SELECT @UnitPrice = UnitPrice, @UnitsInStock = UnitsInStock " +
         "FROM Products WHERE ProductName = @ProductName";
SqlConnection cn = new SqlConnection(strConn);
cn.Open();
SqlCommand cmd = new SqlCommand(strSQL, cn);

SqlParameter pUnitPrice, pInStock, pProductName;
pUnitPrice = cmd.Parameters.Add("@UnitPrice", SqlDbType.Money);
pUnitPrice.Direction = ParameterDirection.Output;
pInStock = cmd.Parameters.Add("@UnitsInStock", SqlDbType.NVarChar, 20);
pInStock.Direction = ParameterDirection.Output;
pProductName = cmd.Parameters.Add("@ProductName", SqlDbType.NVarChar, 40);
pProductName.Value = "Chai";

cmd.ExecuteNonQuery();

Console.WriteLine("Unit Price:  {0}", pUnitPrice.Value);
Console.WriteLine("In Stock:    {0}", pInStock.Value);
```

You might wonder what would happen if no rows in the Products table matched the criteria specified in the WHERE clause. In that case, the query executes successfully but the *Value* property for each output parameter is set to *DBNull.Value*. So, if we wanted to determine whether the criteria matched a row in the Products table, we could include a check after calling *ExecuteNonQuery*, as shown here:

Visual Basic

```
...
Dim cmd As New SqlCommand(strSQL, cn)
Dim pUnitPrice, pInStock, pProductName As SqlParameter
...

cmd.ExecuteNonQuery()

If pUnitPrice.Value Is DBNull.Value Then
    Console.WriteLine("No product found named {0}", pProductName.Value)
Else
    Console.WriteLine("Unit Price:  {0}", pUnitPrice.Value)
    Console.WriteLine("In Stock:    {0}", pInStock.Value)
End If
```

Visual C#

```
...
SqlCommand cmd = new SqlCommand(strSQL, cn);
SqlParameter pUnitPrice, pUnitsInStock, pProductName;
...

cmd.ExecuteNonQuery();

if (pUnitPrice.Value == DBNull.Value) {
    Console.WriteLine("No product found named {0}", pProductName.Value);
} else {
    Console.WriteLine("Unit Price:  {0}", pUnitPrice.Value);
    Console.WriteLine("In Stock:    {0}", pInStock.Value);
}
```

Stored Procedures

Let's take a quick look at how you could call a stored procedure in SQL Server's toolset—
Query Analyzer or Management Studio, depending on the version of SQL Server you're using.
The simple answer is that you use the T-SQL EXEC command, followed by the stored procedure
name, as shown here:

```
EXEC MyStoredProc
```

If you want to pass values into parameters for the stored procedure, you can supply the values
in the same order as their corresponding parameters, or you can specify the parameter name
prior to each parameter value, as shown here:

```
EXEC MyStoredProc @Param2 = 'Value 2', @Param1 = 'Value 1'
```

If you're interested in retrieving values from return or output parameters, things get more
complex. You need to declare variables to store the values of these parameters, call the stored
procedure with the correct syntax (using the OUT keyword for input/output or output
parameters), and then query for values of the desired variables.

```
DECLARE @retval int, @inval varchar(32), @outval int
SET @inval = 'Input Value'
EXEC @retval = MyStoredProc @inval, @outval OUT
SELECT @retval, @outval
```

With *SqlCommand* objects, calling stored procedures is simple. Set the *CommandText* property
to the name of the stored procedure. Set the *CommandType* property to *CommandType.Stored-
Procedure*. Add *SqlParameters* to the *Parameters* collection, with the *Direction* property set
appropriately. Then simply call the stored procedure using the appropriate method on your
SqlCommand—ExecuteReader if you want to examine rows returned, *ExecuteScalar* if you want
to retrieve only a single value, or *ExecuteNonQuery* if you want to retrieve the number of rows
modified or if you aren't interested in the data returned.

Populating the *Parameters* Collection

You can ask for help when populating the *Parameters* collection for a stored procedure call. The *SqlCommandBuilder* class, which we'll explain in more depth in Chapter 10, exposes a static *DeriveParameters* method. You can call this method and pass in a *Sql-Command* object whose *CommandType* property is set to *CommandType.StoredProcedure*, and the *SqlCommandBuilder* will query the SQL Server database for information about that stored procedure's parameters and populate the *SqlCommand*'s *Parameters* collection based on that information.

The *DeriveParameters* method is extremely handy when you're writing your code but struggling to get the right data types and sizes for your parameters. However, you should avoid using this method at run time if at all possible. In most cases, the stored procedure already exists as you're writing your application, and you have code to access the parameters collection—supplying values for input parameters and checking values for output parameters. There's a performance hit involved with querying for this schema information. There should be no need to pay that performance penalty each time you want to populate the *Parameters* collection. Although populating the *Parameters* collection directly (using *Parameters.Add*) requires more code than a call to *DeriveParameters*, populating the *Parameters* collection yourself yields much better performance.

> **Note**   In SQL Server's stored procedure declarations, there is no way to denote whether a parameter is output-only or input/output. If you call *SqlCommandBuilder.DeriveParameters*, the *SqlCommandBuilder* assumes all parameters whose definitions include the OUT keyword are input/output parameters. If you leave the *Direction* property of these *SqlParameters* as *Input-Output* and do not supply a value, you'll receive an exception. If the parameters are truly output-only, you'll need to change the *Direction* property of these parameters to *Output*.

Microsoft Visual Studio Design-Time Features

Visual Studio offers some design-time features that are handy when you're working with *Sql-Commands*. As shown in Figure 4-2, the Server Explorer window gives you the ability to create and execute queries against your database easily at design-time.

You can also use Server Explorer to examine your database's schema. When you're writing your ADO.NET code, you can use Server Explorer to check the names of tables, columns, and stored procedures easily by drilling down into your connection. You can also examine data types of columns in your tables and views, and parameters on your stored procedures. Simply select the desired column or parameter in Server Explorer and then examine its properties in the Properties window, as shown in Figure 4-3.

Figure 4-2 The Server Explorer window

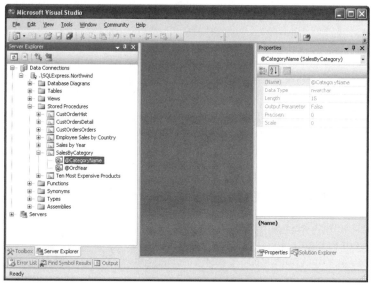

Figure 4-3 Examining properties of a stored procedure parameter in the Properties Window

What Happened to the Drag-and-Drop Features?

As noted in Chapter 3, the drag-and-drop design-time data access features have changed in moving from Visual Studio 2002/2003 to Visual Studio 2005. You can no longer drag and drop tables, views, or stored procedures onto design surfaces to create queries.

Object Reference for *SqlCommand, SqlDataReader,* and *SqlParameter*

Now that we've examined the major features of the *SqlCommand, SqlDataReader,* and *Sql-Parameter* classes, let's examine the properties and methods of each object.

Properties of the *SqlCommand* Class

Table 4-1 lists the properties of the *SqlCommand* class that you're most likely to use.

Table 4-1   Commonly Used Properties of the *SqlCommand* Class

Property	Data Type	Description
CommandText	*String*	The text of the query that you want to execute.
CommandTimeout	*Int32*	Time (in seconds) that the adapter will wait for the query to execute before timing out. (Default = *30* seconds.)
CommandType	*CommandType*	Specifies the type of query to execute. (Default = *Text.*)
Connection	*SqlConnection*	The connection to your data store that the *SqlCommand* will use to execute the query.
Notification	*SqlNotificationRequest*	Contains the *SqlNotificationRequest* object bound to the *SqlCommand.* (See Chapter 14.)
NotificationAutoEnlist	*Boolean*	Determines whether the query will automatically receive SQL Notifications from the *Sql-Dependency* object. (Default = *True.*)
Parameters	*SqlParameterCollection*	A collection of parameters for the query.
Transaction	*SqlTransaction*	Specifies the transaction to use for the query.
UpdatedRowSource	*UpdateRowSource*	Controls how the results of the query will affect the current *DataRow* if the *Command* is used by calling the *Update* method of a *Sql-DataAdapter.* (Default = *Both.*) See Chapter 11 for more information about using this property when submitting pending changes to your database.

CommandText Property

The *CommandText* property contains the text of the query the *SqlCommand* will execute when you call one of the available methods to execute the query—*ExecuteReader*, *ExecuteScalar*, *Execute-NonQuery*, or *ExecuteXmlReader*.

CommandTimeout Property

The *CommandTimeout* property determines how long, in seconds, the *Command* will wait for the first row of the results of your query before timing out. By default, this property is set to *30*. If the query does not complete by the time specified in the *CommandTimeout* property, the *Command* will throw an exception.

Keep in mind that once the query starts returning results, the query won't time out. Let's say that you want to use a *SqlDataAdapter* to fetch the contents of a table into a *DataSet*. For the sake of argument, let's imagine that your table is so absurdly large that the process of fetching its contents takes more than 30 seconds, the default value for the *SqlCommand* object's *CommandTimeout* property. Because the *SqlCommand* that the *SqlDataAdapter* uses retrieved the first row in less than the time specified in the *CommandTimeout* property, the query won't time out no matter how long it takes to retrieve the contents of the table—whether it's a minute, a day, or a year.

CommandType Property

By default, the *CommandType* property is set to *Text*, which will cause the *SqlCommand* to execute just the query specified in the *CommandText* property. If you try to set a *SqlCommand* object's *CommandType* property to *TableDirect*, you'll receive an *ArgumentOutOfRangeException*. (*TableDirect* was a concept introduced by OLE DB to make it simpler to retrieve all rows and all columns in a table by just specifying the table name and a table type of *TableDirect*.)

Setting the *CommandType* property to *StoredProcedure* can prove very handy when calling stored procedures. If you want to call a stored procedure and leave the *CommandType* property as the default of *Text*, you'll need the T-SQL syntax for calling stored procedures, which gets fairly complex if you're interested in retrieving values from output or return parameters.

When you execute a *SqlCommand* whose *CommandType* property is set to *StoredProcedure*, the *SqlCommand* will assume that the *CommandText* property contains the name of a stored procedure. If the stored procedure you want to call contains a space or is a reserved word, you'll need to enclose the stored procedure name in square brackets. So for a stored procedure called *My Stored Proc*, you would set *CommandText* to *[My Stored Proc]*. If the stored procedure name includes a closing square bracket character, you'll need to replace it with double closing square brackets. So for a stored procedure called *My[Stored]Proc*, you would set *CommandText* to *[My[Stored]]Proc]*. Note that only the closing square bracket is doubled.

Of course, the key lesson here is that your stored procedure names should not be reserved words, and they should not contain spaces or square brackets.

Connection Property

The *Connection* property contains the *SqlConnection* object that the *SqlCommand* will use to execute the query specified.

Notification Property

The *Notification* property contains the *SqlNotificationRequest* object bound to the *SqlCommand*. This property is used for SQL Server 2005 query notifications, a feature we'll discuss in more detail in Chapter 14.

NotificationAutoEnlist Property

The *NotificationAutoEnlist* property is also related to SQL Server 2005 query notifications. This property controls whether the query will automatically receive query notifications from a *SqlDependency* object.

Parameters Property

The *Parameters* property returns a *SqlParameterCollection*, which contains a collection of *SqlParameter* objects. We'll examine the properties and methods of the *SqlParameter* class later in this chapter.

Transaction Property

You use the *SqlCommand* object's *Transaction* property to execute your *SqlCommand* within a transaction. If you've opened a *SqlTransaction* object on your *SqlConnection* and try to execute your *SqlCommand* without associating it with that *SqlTransaction* using this property, the *Execute* method will generate an exception.

UpdatedRowSource Property

The *UpdatedRowSource* property is designed to help you refetch data for the row you're updating using a *SqlDataAdapter* and *SqlCommand* objects that contain updating logic. Table 4-2 lists the values accepted by *UpdatedRowSource*. We'll discuss the use of this property in Chapter 11.

Table 4-2   Members of the *UpdateRowSource* Enumeration

Constant	Value	Description
Both	3	*Command* will fetch new data for the row through both the first returned record and output parameters.
FirstReturnedRecord	2	*Command* will fetch new data for the row through the first returned record.
None	0	*Command* will not fetch new data for the row upon execution.
OutputParameters	1	*Command* will fetch new data for the row through output parameters.

Methods of the *SqlCommand* Class

Now let's take a look at the methods of the *SqlCommand* object, which are listed in Table 4-3.

Table 4-3   Commonly Used Methods of the *SqlCommand* Class

Method	Description
BeginExecuteNonQuery, BeginExecuteReader, Begin-ExecuteXmlReader	Starts the asynchronous execution of a query.
Cancel	Cancels the execution of the query.
Clone	Returns a copy of the *SqlCommand*.
CreateParameter	Creates a new parameter for the query.
EndExecuteNonQuery, End-ExecuteReader, EndExecute-XmlReader	Finishes the asynchronous execution of the query.
ExecuteNonQuery	Executes the query (for queries that do not return rows).
ExecuteReader	Executes the query and retrieves the results in a *SqlDataReader*.
ExecuteScalar	Executes the query and retrieves the first column of the first row. Designed for singleton queries such as "SELECT COUNT(*) FROM MyTable WHERE..."
Prepare	Creates a prepared version of the query in the data store.
ResetCommandTimeout	Resets the *CommandTimeout* property to its default of 30 seconds.

BeginExecuteReader, *BeginExecuteNonQuery*, and *BeginExecuteXmlReader* Methods

These *Begin* methods can be used to start the asynchronous execution of a query. Each method corresponds to one of the SqlCommand class's *Execute* methods. In other words, *BeginExecuteNonQuery* behaves like *ExecuteNonQuery*, but it executes asynchronously.

Cancel Method

You can use the *Cancel* method to cancel the execution of a query. If the *SqlCommand* object whose *Cancel* method you've called is not currently executing a query, the *Cancel* method does nothing.

The *Cancel* method also causes the *SqlCommand* object to discard any unread rows on a *SqlDataReader* object. The following sample code fetches the results of a simple query. The code displays the results, followed by the number of rows retrieved. In the code, there's a call to the *SqlCancel* method that's commented out. Remove the comment character or characters, and re-run the code to demonstrate that the *Cancel* method discards the results of the query.

Visual Basic

```
Dim strConn, strSQL As String
strConn = "Data Source=.\SQLExpress;" & _
          "Initial Catalog=Northwind;Integrated Security=True;"
strSQL = "SELECT CustomerID FROM Customers"
Dim cn As New SqlConnection(strConn)
cn.Open()
Dim cmd As New SqlCommand(strSQL, cn)
Dim rdr As SqlDataReader = cmd.ExecuteReader()
Dim intRowsRetrieved As Integer
'cmd.Cancel()
Do While rdr.Read
    Console.WriteLine(rdr.GetString(0))
    intRowsRetrieved += 1
Loop
Console.WriteLine("{0} row(s) retrieved", intRowsRetrieved)
rdr.Close()
cn.Close()
```

Visual C#

```
string strConn, strSQL;
strConn = @"Data Source=.\SQLExpress;" +
          "Initial Catalog=Northwind;Integrated Security=True;";
string strSQL = "SELECT CustomerID FROM Customers";
SqlConnection cn = new SqlConnection(strConn);
cn.Open();
SqlCommand cmd = new SqlCommand(strSQL, cn);
SqlDataReader rdr = cmd.ExecuteReader();
int intRowsRetrieved = 0;
//cmd.Cancel();
while (rdr.Read())
{
    Console.WriteLine(rdr.GetString(0));
    intRowsRetrieved++;
}
Console.WriteLine("{0} row(s) retrieved", intRowsRetrieved);
rdr.Close();
cn.Close();
```

Clone Method

The *Clone* method creates and returns a new copy of the existing *SqlCommand* object.

CreateParameter Method

The *CreateParameter* method creates a new *SqlParameter* object.

EndExecuteReader, *EndExecuteNonQuery*, and *EndExecuteXmlReader* Methods

These *End* methods can be used to complete the asynchronous execution of a query. Each method corresponds to one of the *SqlCommand* class's *Execute* methods. In other words,

EndExecuteNonQuery returns the same data that *ExecuteNonQuery* does, but it is used for asynchronous query execution in conjunction with *BeginExecuteNonQuery*.

ExecuteNonQuery Method

Speaking of *ExecuteNonQuery*, the *ExecuteNonQuery* method executes the query without returning a *SqlDataReader* to examine the rows returned by the query. Use *ExecuteNonQuery* if you want to issue an action query or don't want to examine the rows returned by the query. Values for return and output parameters are available upon completion of the call to *Execute-NonQuery*.

ExecuteNonQuery returns an integer to indicate the number of rows modified by the query you've executed. If you're using batch queries, see the discussion of batch queries and the return value of *ExecuteNonQuery* earlier in this chapter.

ExecuteReader Method

If you want to examine the row or rows returned by a query, use the *SqlCommand* object's *ExecuteReader* method to return that data in a new *SqlDataReader* object. I discussed the basic use of this method earlier in the chapter. However, there are some interesting options on the method.

The *Command* object's *ExecuteReader* method is overloaded and can accept a value from the *CommandBehavior* enumeration. Table 4-4 describes each of these options.

ResetCommandTimeout Method

Calling the *ResetCommandTimeout* method resets the *Command* object's *CommandTimeout* property to its default value of 30 seconds. If you find yourself wondering, "Why would I need a property to do that?" you're not alone. The *ResetCommandTimeout* method enables Visual Studio to reset the *CommandTimeout* property for a *Command* from within the designer.

Table 4-4   Members of the *CommandBehavior* Enumeration

Constant	Value	Description
CloseConnection	32	Closing the *SqlDataReader* will close the connection.
KeyInfo	4	This constant causes the *SqlCommand* to fetch primary key information for the columns in the resultset.
SchemaOnly	2	The *SqlDataReader* will contain only column information without actually running the query.
SequentialAccess	16	Values in the columns will be available only sequentially. For example, after you examine the contents of the third column, you won't be able to examine the contents of the first two columns.
SingleResult	1	The *SqlDataReader* will fetch the results of only the first row-returning query.
SingleRow	8	The *SqlDataReader* will fetch only the first row of the first row-returning query.

CloseConnection   If you supply *CloseConnection* when calling the *ExecuteReader* method, when you call the *Close* method on the *SqlDataReader*, the *SqlDataReader* will call the *Close* method on the *SqlConnection* with which it is associated.

This feature can be extremely handy if you're building business objects and passing data from one object to another. You might encounter situations in which you want a business object to return a *SqlDataReader* to the calling object rather than returning the data in a *DataTable* or some other structure. In such cases, you might want the calling object to be able to close the *SqlConnection* object after it's done reading the results of the query from the *SqlDataReader*.

But what if you don't trust the calling object? You might not want to hand it a direct connection to the database. Using *CloseConnection* can simplify this scenario without compromising the security and architecture of your application.

KeyInfo and **SchemaOnly**   These enumerations return metadata about the columns in the *SqlDataReader*–column names, data types, and so on. Such information can be helpful if you're building code-generation tools. If you're going to use the *SqlDataReader* object's *GetSchemaTable* method, you should also look at the *KeyInfo* and *SchemaOnly* options of the *SqlCommand*'s *ExecuteReader* method.

If you call *ExecuteReader* and use the *SchemaOnly* value in the *Options* parameter, you'll retrieve schema information about the columns but you won't actually execute the query.

Using *KeyInfo* in the *Options* parameter forces the *SqlCommand* to fetch additional schema information from your data source to indicate whether the columns in the resultset are part of the key columns in the tables in your data source.

SequentialAccess   If you use the *SequentialAccess* option when calling *ExecuteReader*, the columns of data will be available only sequentially through the *SqlDataReader*. For example, if you look at the contents of the second column, the contents of the first column will no longer be available.

Use of the *SequentialAccess* value might increase the performance of your *SqlDataReader* slightly, depending on the data source you're using.

SingleRow and **SingleResult**   If you're interested in examining only the first row or first resultset returned by your query, you might want to use *SingleRow* or *SingleResult* when calling *ExecuteReader*.

Supplying *SingleRow* in the *Options* parameter will create a *SqlDataReader* that contains, at most, one row of data. If you issue a query that returns 10 rows of data but you use *SingleRow* in your call to *ExecuteReader*, only the first row of data will be available through the *SqlData-Reader*. All other rows will be discarded. Similarly, using *SingleResult* causes subsequent result-sets to be discarded.

ExecuteScalar Method

The *ExecuteScalar* method is similar to *ExecuteReader* except that it returns the first column of the first row of the resultset in a generic *Object* data type. If the query returns more than one cell of data, the additional data is discarded.

If your query returns a single cell of data, like the following query does, you can improve the performance of your code by using *ExecuteScalar*.

```
SELECT COUNT(*) FROM MyTable
```

Prepare Method

The *Prepare* method is an artifact from bygone days, the heyday of ODBC, when database administrators walked uphill through snow to and from work, before SQL Server effectively cached query plans. In those days, explicitly asking SQL Server to prepare and cache a query plan before executing the query repeatedly could improve performance. Thankfully, those days are gone.

In scenarios I've tested, using the *Prepare* method did not improve performance of query scenarios, even before repeatedly executing a parameterized query. I welcome and encourage you to perform your own testing to see whether the *Prepare* method can improve the performance of your scenarios.

Event of the *SqlCommand* Class

Now let's look at the commonly used event of the *SqlCommand* class (which is described in Table 4-5).

Table 4-5   Event of the *SqlCommand* Class

Event	Description
StatementCompleted	Fires upon the completion of each query within a batch

StatementCompleted Event

As shown earlier in this chapter, the *StatementCompleted* event was added to the *SqlCommand* class in ADO.NET 2.0 to help you determine the number of rows affected by individual queries within a batch.

Properties of the *SqlDataReader* Class

Now let's look at the properties of the *SqlDataReader*, which are listed in Table 4-6.

Table 4-6   Commonly Used Properties of the *SqlDataReader* Class

Property	Data Type	Description
Depth	Int32	Indicates the depth of nesting for the current row (read-only)
FieldCount	Int32	Returns the number of fields contained by the *DataReader* (read-only)
HasRows	Boolean	Indicates whether the *SqlCommand*'s query returned rows (read-only)
IsClosed	Boolean	Indicates whether the *DataReader* is closed (read-only)
Item	Object	Returns the contents of a column for the current row (read-only)
RecordsAffected	Int32	Indicates the number of records affected by the queries submitted (read-only)

Depth Property (and *GetData* Method)

The *Depth* property and the *GetData* method are reserved for queries that return hierarchical data. These features are not supported in the current release of ADO.NET.

FieldCount Property

The *FieldCount* property returns an integer to indicate the number of fields of data in the resultset.

HasRows Property

You can check the *HasRows* property to determine whether the query you executed returned rows. This property is handy when you need to execute different code depending on whether the query returned any rows.

IsClosed Property

The *IsClosed* property returns a *Boolean* value to indicate whether the *SqlDataReader* object is closed.

Item Property

The *SqlDataReader* class's *Item* property is similar, in form and function, to the *DataRow* class's *Item* property. You can supply the name of a field as a string or the integer position of a field, and the property will return the value stored in that column in the generic object data type.

If you know the data type of the field, you'll get better performance by calling the *Get<DataType>* method (such as *GetInteger* or *GetString*) instead.

RecordsAffected Property

You can use the *RecordsAffected* property to determine the number of rows that your action query (or queries) modified. If you want to execute a single action query, use the *ExecuteNonQuery* method of the *SqlCommand* object instead. The *ExecuteNonQuery* method returns the number of rows the action query affected.

If you're executing a batch of queries and you want to determine the number of rows affected, see the section about batch queries earlier in the chapter.

Methods of the *SqlDataReader* Class

And now for your programming pleasure, Table 4-7 presents the methods of the *SqlData-Reader* that you're most likely to encounter.

Table 4-7   Commonly Used Methods of the *SqlDataReader* Class

Method	Description
Close	Closes the *SqlDataReader*.
Get<DataType>	Returns the contents of a field in the current row as the specified type based on its ordinal.
GetBytes	Retrieves an array of bytes from a field in the current row.
GetChars	Retrieves an array of characters from a field in the current row.
GetData	Returns a new *SqlDataReader* from a field.
GetDataTypeName	Returns the name of the data type for a field based on its ordinal.
GetFieldType	Returns the .NET data type for a field based on its ordinal.
GetName	Returns the name of a field based on its ordinal.
GetOrdinal	Returns the ordinal of a field based on its name.
GetProviderSpecificField-Type	Similar to *GetFieldType*, but returns the *SqlType* for a field based on its ordinal.
GetProviderSpecificValue	Similar to *GetValue*, but returns the value of a field, based on its ordinal, as a *SqlType*.
GetProviderSpecificValues	Similar to *GetValues*, but for an array of *SqlType* objects rather than .NET objects.
GetSchemaTable	Returns the schema information (field names and data types) of the *SqlDataReader* as a *DataTable*.
GetSqlValue	Returns the value of a field, based on its ordinal, as a *SqlType*.
GetValue	Returns the value of a field, based on its ordinal, as a .NET data type.
GetValues	Accepts an array that the *SqlDataReader* will use to return the contents of the current row. This call returns a 32-bit integer that indicates the number of entries returned in the array.
IsDBNull	Indicates whether a field contains a *Null* value.
NextResult	Moves to the next result.
Read	Moves to the next row.

Read Method

The *Read* method accesses the next row of data. Remember that the first row in the resultset will not be available through the *SqlDataReader* until you call the *Read* method. The first time you call the *Read* method, the *SqlDataReader* will move to the first row in the resultset. Subsequent calls to *Read* will move to the next row of data.

The *Read* method also returns a *Boolean* value to indicate whether there are any more results for the query. The sample code we examined earlier continually examines results until the *Read* method returns *False*.

GetValue, *GetSqlValue*, and *GetProviderSpecificValue* Methods

The *GetValue* method is similar to the *Item* property. Supply an integer, and the *GetValue* method will return the contents of that field in the generic object type.

The *GetValue* method and the various *Get<DataType>* methods accept only integers for the field index and do not perform string-based lookups such as the *Item* property. The *SqlDataReader* is designed for speed; referencing an item in a collection by its ordinal value is faster than having the collection locate the item by its name.

The *GetSqlValue* and *GetProviderSpecificValue* methods behave like the *GetValue* method, except that they return the data in a specialized *SqlType* rather than a generic .NET type.

Get<DataType> Methods

The *SqlDataReader* also offers methods that return specific data types. If you know that a field contains string data, you can call the *GetValue* method of the *SqlDataReader* and cast the data to a string or simply call the *GetString* method. Of the two approaches, using the strongly typed getter gives better performance. Both approaches are shown in the following code snippet:

Visual Basic
```
Dim strCompanyName As String
Dim rdr As SqlDataReader
...
strCompanyName = rdr.GetString(intCompanyNameIndex)
'or
strCompanyName = CStr(rdr.GetValue(intCompanyNameIndex))
```

Visual C#
```
string strCompanyName;
SqlDataReader rdr;
...
strCompanyName = rdr.GetString(intCompanyNameIndex);
//or
strCompanyName = (string) rdr.GetValue(intCompanyNameIndex);
```

The *SqlDataReader* has methods to return data types available in the .NET Framework that correspond to database data types—*GetByte*, *GetChar*, *GetDateTime*, and so on. The *SqlData-Reader* class also has methods to return the data types in the *SqlTypes* namespace—*GetSql-Decimal*, *GetSqlString*, and so on.

GetValues, *GetSqlValues*, and *GetProviderSpecificValues* Methods

The *GetValues* method lets you store the contents of a row in an array. If you want to retrieve the contents of each field as quickly as possible, using the *GetValues* method will provide better performance than checking the value of each column separately.

> **Note**   The *SqlDataAdapter* uses a *SqlDataReader* to fetch data from your database to store the results in *DataTables*. To provide the best performance possible, the *DataAdapter* classes that are part of the .NET Framework use the *GetValues* method on the corresponding *Data-Reader* classes.

Here's a simple example of how to use *GetValues*:

Visual Basic
```
Dim rdr As SqlDataReader = cmd.ExecuteReader()
Dim aData(rdr.FieldCount - 1) As Object
Do While rdr.Read
    rdr.GetValues(aData)
    Console.WriteLine(aData(0).ToString())
Loop
```

Visual C#
```
SqlDataReader rdr = cmd.ExecuteReader();
object[] aData = new object[rdr.FieldCount];
while (rdr.Read())
{
    rdr.GetValues(aData);
    Console.WriteLine(aData[0].ToString());
}
```

> **Note**   Visual Basic and Visual C# create arrays differently. The preceding code snippets take this difference into account. For example, *Dim aData(4) As Object* creates an array of length 5 (0 to 4) in Visual Basic, but *object[] aData = new object[4];* creates an array of length 4 (0 to 3) in Visual C#.

The *GetSqlValues* and *GetProviderSpecificValues* methods are similar to the *GetValues* method, but they work with *SqlTypes* rather than the basic .NET data types.

NextResult Method

If you're working with batch queries that return multiple resultsets, use the *NextResult* method to move to the next set of results. Like the *Read* method, *NextResult* returns a Boolean value to indicate whether there are more results.

The sample code on page 162 shows how to use a *SqlDataReader* to examine the contents of a batch query. It also shows how to use the *NextResult* method in a loop.

Close Method

When you're using *SqlDataReader* objects, it's important that you loop through the results and close the *SqlDataReader* as quickly as possible. Unless your *SqlConnection* object is MARS-enabled, it is blocked from performing any other work while a live firehose cursor is open on the connection. If you try to use a non-MARS-enabled *SqlConnection* that has an open *Sql-DataReader* on it, you'll receive an exception that states that the operation "requires an open and available connection."

See the discussion of MARS earlier in the chapter for more information.

GetName, *GetOrdinal*, and *GetDataTypeName* Methods

The *SqlDataReader* has methods that you can use to learn more about the results returned by your query. If you want to determine the name of a particular field, you can call the *GetName* method. If you already know the field name you want to access but don't know its ordinal position within the resultset, you can pass the field name into the *GetOrdinal* method to retrieve its ordinal position. The *GetDataTypeName* method accepts an integer denoting the ordinal position of the field and returns as a string the name of the SQL Server data type (*nvarchar*, *int*, and so forth) for that field.

GetFieldType and *GetProviderSpecificFieldType* Methods

The *GetFieldType* method behaves like the *GetDataTypeName* method, except that it returns the .NET data type used to store the contents of the field. This method can be helpful if you're unsure of which strongly typed *Get* method to call—*GetString*, *GetDateTime*, and so on.

The *GetProviderSpecificFieldType* property behaves the same way, except that it returns the *SqlType* used to store the contents of the field. This method can be helpful if you're unsure of which method to call to return the contents of the field as a *SqlType*—*GetSqlString*, *GetSqlDateTime*, and so on.

GetSchemaTable Method

The *SqlDataReader* class's *GetSchemaTable* method is similar to the *DataAdapter* object's *FillSchema* method. Each method lets you create a *DataTable* containing *DataColumn* objects that correspond to the columns returned by your query. The *GetSchemaTable* method accepts no parameters and returns a new *DataTable*.

The data that *GetSchemaTable* returns might be a little difficult to grasp initially. The *GetSchema-Table* method returns a *DataTable* with a predefined structure. Each *DataRow* in the *DataTable* returned by this method corresponds to a different field in the query results, and the *DataColumn* objects represent properties or attributes for those fields.

The following code snippet prints the name and database data type for each field the query returns to the Console window. The easiest way to really understand the data returned by *GetSchemaTable* is to display it in a Windows Forms *DataGrid*, as shown in Figure 4-1 earlier in the chapter.

Visual Basic

```
Dim strConn, strSQL As String
strConn = "Data Source=.\SQLExpress;" & _
          "Initial Catalog=Northwind;Integrated Security=True;"
strSQL = "SELECT OrderID, CustomerID, EmployeeID, OrderDate FROM Orders"
Dim cn As New SqlConnection(strConn)
cn.Open()
Dim cmd As New SqlCommand(strSQL, cn)
Dim rdr As SqlDataReader = cmd.ExecuteReader
Dim tbl As DataTable = rdr.GetSchemaTable
For Each row As DataRow In tbl.Rows
    Console.WriteLine("{0} - {1}", row("ColumnName"), _
                      CType(row("ProviderType"), SqlDbType))
Next row
```

Visual C#

```
string strConn, strSQL;
strConn = @"Data Source=.\SqlExpress;" +
          "Initial Catalog=Northwind;Integrated Security=True;";
strSQL = "SELECT OrderID, CustomerID, EmployeeID, OrderDate FROM Orders";
SqlConnection cn = new SqlConnection(strConn);
cn.Open();
SqlCommand cmd = new SqlCommand(strSQL, cn);
SqlDataReader rdr = cmd.ExecuteReader();
DataTable tbl = rdr.GetSchemaTable();
foreach (DataRow row in tbl.Rows)
    Console.WriteLine("{0} - {1}", row["ColumnName"],
                      (SqlDbType) row["ProviderType"]);
```

Note   The code snippet for each language converts the integer stored in the ProviderType column to the *SqlDbType* enumeration.

Additional schema is available in the *DataTable* returned by *GetSchemaTable* if you pass *CommandBehavior.KeyInfo* to the call to *SqlCommand.ExecuteDataReader*.

GetData Method (and *Depth* Property)

The *Depth* property and the *GetData* method are reserved for queries that return hierarchical data. These features are not supported in the current release of ADO.NET.

Creating *SqlParameter* Objects

The *SqlParameter* class has seven constructors. The *SqlParameterCollection* has four overloaded *Add* methods that you can use to create a *SqlParameter* and append it to the collection, as well as a new *AddWithValue* method. You can also use the *CreateParameter* method on the *SqlCommand*. So many choices.

Which method of creating a *SqlParameter* is right for you? That depends on which properties on the *SqlParameter* you want to set. One constructor for *SqlParameter* lets you supply values for the *ParameterName*, *SqlDbType*, *Size*, *Direction*, *IsNullable*, *Precision*, *Scale*, *SourceColumn*, *SourceVersion*, and *Value* properties. Think about the properties you want to set and then use the constructor that provides the functionality you need.

Properties of the *SqlParameter* Class

Table 4-8 lists the commonly used properties of the *SqlParameter* class.

Table 4-8   Commonly Used Properties of the *SqlParameter* Class

Property Name	Data Type	Description
DbType	DbType	Specifies the database data type for the parameter.
Direction	ParameterDirection	Specifies the direction for the parameter—input, output, input/output, or return.
IsNullable	Boolean	Indicates whether the parameter can accept *Null*.
ParameterName	String	Specifies the name of the parameter.
Precision	Byte	Specifies the precision for the parameter.
Scale	Byte	Specifies the numeric scale for the parameter.
Size	Int32	Specifies the size of the parameter.
SourceColumn	String	Specifies the name of the column in the *DataSet* that this parameter references. See Chapter 10 for more information about binding query parameters to *DataSet* objects.
SourceColumn-NullMapping	Boolean	Used in special cases for handling null values in *SqlDataAdapter* updating logic. See Chapter 10 for more information about binding query parameters to *DataSet* objects.
SourceVersion	DataRowVersion	Specifies version (current or original) of the column in the *DataSet* that this parameter references. See Chapter 10 for more information about binding query parameters to *DataSet* objects.
SqlDbType	SqlDbType	Specifies the SQL data type for the parameter.
SqlValue	Object	Specifies the value for the parameter using a *SqlType*.
Value	Object	Specifies the value for the parameter.

Table 4-8   Commonly Used Properties of the *SqlParameter* Class

Property Name	Data Type	Description
XmlSchemaCollection-Database, XmlSchema-CollectionName, XmlSchemaCollection-OwningSchema	*String*	Used for handling *SqlXml* values in parameters. See Chapter 12 for more information about using SQL Server's XML features in ADO.NET.

ParameterName Property

The *SqlCommand* supports named parameters only. You cannot use a *SqlCommand* with parameter markers as you can in OLE DB and ODBC. Thus, the *ParameterName* property should match the corresponding parameter as it appears in your query.

Direction Property

If you're calling a stored procedure and you want to use output or return parameters, you should set the *Direction* property of your *Parameter* to one of the values listed in Table 4-9. Because the default value for *Direction* is *Input*, you need to explicitly set this property only on *SqlParameter* objects that are not input-only.

Table 4-9   Members of the *ParameterDirection* Enumeration

Constant	Value	Description
Input	1	Default value. The parameter is input-only.
Output	2	The parameter is output-only.
InputOutput	3	The parameter is input/output.
ReturnValue	6	The parameter will contain the return value of a stored procedure.

Most code generation tools will query your database for parameter information, including the direction of the parameters. Even if you're using a robust code-generation tool, such as the ones included in Visual Studio, you might still need to modify the *Direction* value of your *SqlParameter* objects in some cases.

Why, you ask? Most databases support the use of input, output, and input-output parameters on stored procedures, but not all databases have language constructs to let you explicitly specify the direction for your stored procedure parameters. SQL Server, for example, supports the OUTPUT keyword in stored procedure definitions to specify that the parameter can return a value. However, the definition of the parameter in the stored procedure is the same regardless of whether the parameter is input/output or output-only. As a result, code-generation tools cannot determine whether the parameter is input/output or output-only. The Visual Studio tools assume that the parameter is input/output. If you want an output-only parameter, you must explicitly set the direction in your code.

Value and *SqlValue* Properties

Use the *Value* property to check or set the value of your *SqlParameter*. This property contains an *Object* data type. As a result, you might need to convert the data to store it in a data type such as a *string* or *integer*.

The *SqlValue* property behaves like the *Value* property, except that it's used for *SqlTypes* rather than basic .NET data types.

SourceColumn, *SourceVersion*, and *SourceColumnNullMapping* Properties

The *SourceColumn*, *SourceVersion*, and *SourceColumnNullMapping* properties control how the *SqlParameter* fetches data from a *DataRow* when you submit pending changes to your database by calling the *Update* method on the *DataAdapter*.

I'll discuss these properties in more depth in Chapter 10, when we examine updating your database.

DbType and *SqlDbType* Properties

The *DbType* property is available on all *Parameter* classes—*SqlParameter*, *OracleParameter*, *OdbcParameter*, and so on. This property takes a value from the *DbType* enumeration, an enumeration that lists various general database data types like *AnsiString*, *DateTime*, *Int16*, *Int32*, *String*, and so on.

The *SqlDbType* property is similar to the *DbType* property, except that it uses SQL Server terms to define the data types (*VarChar* instead of *AnsiString*, *SmallInt* instead of *Int16*, *NVarChar* instead of *String*, and so on) and adds entries that have no equivalent in *DbType* (*NText*, *Image*, *Timestamp*, and so on).

Set the *DbType* property only if you're writing code to work with different types of *Parameters*—*SqlParameters*, *OracleParameters*, and so on. If you're working with just *SqlParameters*, use the *SqlDbType* property instead because the values in that enumeration are intended specifically for SQL Server.

You can set the *SqlDbType* property on a *SqlParameter* directly, or you can rely on "type inference" to set the *SqlDbType* property. If you create a *SqlParameter* by calling the *AddWithValue* method on a *SqlParameterCollection*, *SqlClient* uses the value you've supplied to implicitly set the *SqlDbType* property on the new *SqlParameter*. You can also set the *SqlDbType* property implicitly by setting the *Value* property on a *SqlParameter*.

Generally speaking, *SqlClient* will choose an appropriate *SqlDbType* once you set the *Value* property. For output parameters, set the value for the *SqlDbType* property directly.

Precision, Scale, and *Size* Properties

When you define the structure for a table in a database, some data types require that you specify additional information beyond simply the name of the data type. Binary and character-based columns often have a maximum size. If you're using a *SqlParameter* with such data, you must set the *Size* property to the desired size. Numeric data types often let you specify the scale (number of digits) and precision (number of digits to the right of the decimal point).

Questions That Should Be Asked More Frequently

Q   How can I determine the values of the *SqlDbType, Length, Scale,* and *Precision* properties for a *SqlParameter* that matches up with a column in my table.

A   There are a couple simple ways to determine this information. The easiest way to check these properties for your column is to select the column in the Server Explorer window and check the *Data Type, Length, Scale,* and *Precision* properties in the Properties window. You can also create a *SqlCommand* to query for that column, call *ExecuteReader* with a *CommandBehavior* of *SchemaOnly* so that the *SqlDataReader* you receive contains only schema, no results. Then call *GetSchemaTable* and check the values of the *SqlDbType, Length, Scale,* and *Precision* properties for a *SqlParameter* that matches up with a column in my table.

Visual Basic

```
Dim strConn, strSQL As String
strConn = "Data Source=.\SQLExpress;" & _
        "Initial Catalog=Northwind;Trusted_Connection=Yes;"
strSQL = "SELECT * FROM Orders"
Dim cn As New SqlConnection(strConn)
cn.Open()
Dim cmd As New SqlCommand(strSQL, cn)
Dim rdr As SqlDataReader = cmd.ExecuteReader(CommandBehavior.SchemaOnly)
Dim tbl As DataTable = rdr.GetSchemaTable()
rdr.Close()
cn.Close()

Console.WriteLine("ColumnName      SqlDbType  Length  Precision  Scale")
Console.WriteLine("==========      =========  ======  =========  =====")
For Each row As DataRow In tbl.Rows
    Console.WriteLine("{0,-15} {1,-10}  {2,3}        {3,3}       {4,3}", _
                    row("ColumnName"), _
                    CType(row("ProviderType"), SqlDbType), _
                    row("ColumnSize"), row("NumericPrecision"), _
                    row("NumericScale"))
Next row
```

Visual C#

```
string strConn, strSQL;
strConn = @"Data Source=.\SQLExpress;" +
        "Initial Catalog=Northwind;Trusted_Connection=Yes;";
strSQL = "SELECT * FROM Orders";
SqlConnection cn = new SqlConnection(strConn);
```

```
cn.Open();
SqlCommand cmd = new SqlCommand(strSQL, cn);
SqlDataReader rdr = cmd.ExecuteReader(CommandBehavior.SchemaOnly);
DataTable tbl = rdr.GetSchemaTable();
rdr.Close();
cn.Close();

Console.WriteLine("ColumnName        SqlDbType  Length  Precision  Scale");
Console.WriteLine("==========        =========  ======  =========  =====");
foreach (DataRow row in tbl.Rows)
    Console.WriteLine("{0,-15} {1,-10}  {2,3}        {3,3}       {4,3}",
                      row["ColumnName"], (SqlDbType) row["ProviderType"],
                      row["ColumnSize"], row["NumericPrecision"],
                      row["NumericScale"]);
```

Q   I called a stored procedure that returns a set of rows. Everything seems to work except that the output and return parameters are empty. Why is that?

A   Think of a stored procedure as a function in your code. The function doesn't return a value until it has executed all its code. If the stored procedure returns results and you haven't finished processing these results, the stored procedure hasn't really finished executing. Until you've closed the *SqlDataReader*, the return and output parameters of your *SqlCommand* won't contain the values returned by your stored procedure.

Let's say that we have the stored procedure

```
CREATE PROCEDURE RowsAndOutput (@OutputParam int OUTPUT) AS
    SELECT @OutputParam = COUNT(*) FROM Customers
    SELECT CustomerID, CompanyName, ContactName, Phone FROM Customers
```

and we call it with the following code:

Visual Basic

```
Dim strConn As String
strConn = "Data Source=.\SQLExpress;" & _
          "Initial Catalog=Northwind;Integrated Security=True;"
Dim cn As New SqlConnection(strConn)
cn.Open()
Dim cmd As New SqlCommand("RowsAndOutput", cn)
cmd.CommandType = CommandType.StoredProcedure
Dim param As SqlParameter
param = cmd.Parameters.Add("@OutputParam", SqlDbType.Int)
param.Direction = ParameterDirection.Output
Dim rdrCustomers As Sqlmd.CommandType = CommandType.StoredProcedureproperty, except that
it's used for SqlTypes rather than generic n OLE DB and ODBC.DataReader = cmd.ExecuteReader
Console.WriteLine("After execution - {0}", param.Value)
Do While rdrCustomers.Read
Loop
Console.WriteLine("After reading rows - {0}", param.Value)
Do While rdrCustomers.NextResult()
Loop
Console.WriteLine("After reading all results - {0}", param.Value)
rdrCustomers.Close()
Console.WriteLine("After closing DataReader - {0}", param.Value)
```

Visual C#

```
string strConn;
strConn = @"Data Source=.\SQLExpress;" +
          "Initial Catalog=Northwind;Integrated Security=True;";
SqlConnection cn = new SqlConnection(strConn);
cn.Open();

SqlCommand cmd = new SqlCommand("RowsAndOutput", cn);
cmd.CommandType = CommandType.StoredProcedure;
SqlParameter param;
param = cmd.Parameters.Add("@OutputParam", SqlDbType.Int);
param.Direction = ParameterDirection.Output;
SqlDataReader rdrCustomers = cmd.ExecuteReader();
Console.WriteLine("After execution - {0}", param.Value);
while (rdrCustomers.Read()) {}
Console.WriteLine("After reading rows - {0}", param.Value);
while (rdrCustomers.NextResult()) {}
Console.WriteLine("After reading all results - {0}", param.Value);
rdrCustomers.Close();
Console.WriteLine("After closing DataReader - {0}", param.Value);
```

Even though the stored procedure sets the value of the output parameter before running the query that returns rows from the Customers table, the value of the output parameter is not available until after the *SqlDataReader* is closed.

Q   I'm trying to migrate code from ADO to ADO.NET. My old program used the *Refresh* method on an ADO *Parameters* collection. Doesn't the ADO.NET *SqlParameterCollection* class have a *Refresh* method?

A   There is no *Refresh* method on the ADO.NET *SqlParameterCollection* class, at least not yet. As of the initial release, there is no way to use the ADO.NET object model to "auto-magically" supply parameter information for a generic parameterized query. Unless you're working with an ad hoc query tool, you should know the data types and directions for the parameters in your queries. Specifying the parameter information in code is more performant and more reliable than asking the database or data access technology to guess for you. I've seen developers complain that a previous technology didn't select the correct data type for a query that included "? = ?" in the WHERE clause.

Chapter 5

Retrieving Data Using *SqlDataAdapter* Objects

As you learned in the previous chapter, you can use *SqlCommand* objects and *SqlDataReader* objects to execute queries and examine their results. But what if you want to store the results of a query using ADO.NET's off-line cache, the *DataSet* class?

You could execute your query and then populate a *DataSet* with new rows by looping through the data available in a *SqlDataReader* until the *SqlDataReader*'s *Read* method returns *False*. (And don't forget to close the *SqlDataReader*!) Another option is to use the *Load* method that has been added to the *DataSet* and *DataTable* classes in ADO.NET 2.0, as shown in the following example:

Visual Basic
```vb
'Connect and execute the query
Dim strConn, strSQL As String
strConn = "Data Source=.\SQLExpress;" & _
          "Initial Catalog=Northwind;Integrated Security=True"
strSQL = "SELECT CustomerID, CompanyName FROM Customers"
Dim cn As New SqlConnection(strConn)
cn.Open()
Dim cmd As New SqlCommand(strSQL, cn)
Dim rdr As SqlDataReader
rdr = cmd.ExecuteReader(CommandBehavior.CloseConnection)

'Store the results off-line
Dim ds As New DataSet()
Dim tbl As DataTable = ds.Tables.Add("Customers")
tbl.Load(rdr)

'Close the data reader (and connection)
rdr.Close()
```

Visual C#

```csharp
//Connect and execute the query
string strConn, strSQL;
strConn = @"Data Source=.\SQLExpress;" +
        "Initial Catalog=Northwind;Integrated Security=True";
strSQL = "SELECT CustomerID, CompanyName FROM Customers";
SqlConnection cn = new SqlConnection(strConn);
cn.Open();
SqlCommand cmd = new SqlCommand(strSQL, cn);
SqlDataReader rdr;
rdr = cmd.ExecuteReader(CommandBehavior.CloseConnection);

//Store the results off-line
DataSet ds = new DataSet();
DataTable tbl = ds.Tables.Add("Customers");
tbl.Load(rdr);

//Close the data reader (and connection)
rdr.Close();
```

This case is rather simplistic. If the columns in the DataTable and the SqlDataReader did not match up, the code would be a good deal more complex.

In this example, we're executing a standard SELECT query. If you don't like the choice of column names, you could "alias" them within the query. For example, if the columns in the table were CID and CName, you could issue the following query to change the column names to friendlier names such as CustomerID and CustomerName:

```
SELECT CID AS CustomerID, CName AS CustomerName FROM Customers
```

What if, instead of a SELECT query, we were calling a stored procedure? If the stored procedure's resultset contains column names such as CID and CName, there's no way to apply aliases to columns after the fact. If you wanted to retrieve the results of that stored procedure query and store the results in a *DataSet* using friendly column names, your code would look like the following:

Visual Basic

```vb
'Prepare the DataSet
Dim ds As New DataSet()
Dim tbl As DataTable = ds.Tables.Add("Customers")
tbl.Columns.Add("CustomerID")
tbl.Columns.Add("CompanyName")

'Connect and execute the query
Dim strConn As String
strConn = "Data Source=.\SQLExpress;" & _
        "Initial Catalog=Northwind;Integrated Security=True"
Dim cn As New SqlConnection(strConn)
cn.Open()
Dim cmd As New SqlCommand("MyStoredProc", cn)
cmd.CommandType = CommandType.StoredProcedure
Dim rdr As SqlDataReader
rdr = cmd.ExecuteReader(CommandBehavior.CloseConnection)
```

```
'Store the results off-line
Dim row As DataRow
Do While rdr.Read()
    row = tbl.NewRow()
    row("CustomerID") = rdr("CID")
    row("CompanyName") = rdr("CName")
    tbl.Rows.Add(row)
Loop
tbl.AcceptChanges()

'Close the data reader (and connection)
rdr.Close()
```

Visual C#

```
//Prepare the DataSet
DataSet ds = new DataSet()
DataTable tbl = ds.Tables.Add("Customers");
tbl.Columns.Add("CustomerID");
tbl.Columns.Add("CompanyName");

//Connect and execute the query
string strConn;
strConn = @"Data Source=.\SQLExpress;" +
          "Initial Catalog=Northwind;Integrated Security=True";
SqlConnection cn = new SqlConnection(strConn);
cn.Open();
SqlCommand cmd = new SqlCommand("MyStoredProc", cn);
cmd.CommandType = CommandType.StoredProcedure;
SqlDataReader rdr;
rdr = cmd.ExecuteReader(CommandBehavior.CloseConnection);

//Store the results off-line
DataRow row;
while (rdr.Read()) {
    row = tbl.NewRow();
    row["CustomerID"] = rdr["CID"];
    row["CompanyName"] = rdr["CName"];
    tbl.Rows.Add(row);
}
tbl.AcceptChanges();

//Close the data reader (and connection)
rdr.Close();
```

Yikes! Storing the results of your query in a *DataSet* should be simple. This code isn't simple, and it certainly isn't rapid application development (RAD). Who wants to write code like that?

Thankfully, you don't have to. The ADO.NET object model offers a more elegant solution: using the *SqlDataAdapter* class. In this chapter, you'll learn how to use this class to store the results of queries in *DataSet* objects and *DataTable* objects.

What Is a *SqlDataAdapter* Object?

The *SqlDataAdapter* class acts as a bridge between the connected and disconnected halves of the ADO.NET object model. You can use a *SqlDataAdapter* to pull data from your database and store it in your *DataSet*. The *SqlDataAdapter* can also take the cached updates stored in your *DataSet* and submit them to your database. Chapter 10 will cover updating your database with *SqlDataAdapter* objects. In this chapter, we will focus on using *SqlDataAdapter* objects to fetch data from your database.

How the *SqlDataAdapter* Differs from Other Query Objects

When I describe the *SqlDataAdapter* class to database programmers, most nod their heads and say that it sounds similar to the ADO *Command* object, the RDO *rdoQuery* object, and the DAO *QueryDef* object—all of which let you submit queries to your database and store the results in a separate object. However, there are some major differences between the *DataAdapter* and its predecessors, as I'll detail in the following sections.

The *SqlDataAdapter* Is Designed to Work with Disconnected Data

ADO, RDO, and DAO all support disconnected data. Each object model can store the results of a query in a disconnected structure. For example, you can use an ADO *Command* object to fetch data and store it in a *Recordset* that's disconnected from the *Connection* object. However, none of these object models provided disconnected functionality in their initial release. As a result, their query-based objects were never truly designed for disconnected data.

The *SqlDataAdapter* is designed to work with disconnected data. Perhaps the best example of this design is the *Fill* method. You don't even need a live connection to your database to call the *Fill* method. If you call the *Fill* method on a *SqlDataAdapter* whose connection to your database is not currently open, the *SqlDataAdapter* opens that connection, queries the database, fetches the results of the query, stores it in your *DataSet*, and then closes the connection to your database.

There Is No Direct Connection Between the *DataAdapter* and the *DataSet*

You fill a *DataTable* in your *DataSet* by passing your *DataSet* as a parameter to the *SqlData-Adapter* object's *Fill* method, as shown here:

Visual Basic
```
Dim strConn, strSQL As String
strConn = "Data Source=.\SQLExpress;" & _
          "Initial Catalog=Northwind;Integrated Security=True"
strSQL = "SELECT CustomerID, CompanyName FROM Customers"
Dim ds As New DataSet()
Dim da As New SqlDataAdapter(strSQL, strConn)
da.Fill(ds)

'Display the customer information retrieved
For Each row As DataRow In ds.Tables(0).Rows
    Console.WriteLine("{0} - {1}", row("CustomerID"), _
                      row("CompanyName"))
Next row
```

Visual C#

```csharp
string strConn, strSQL;
strConn = @"Data Source=.\SQLExpress;" +
          "Initial Catalog=Northwind;Integrated Security=True";
strSQL = "SELECT CustomerID, CompanyName FROM Customers";
DataSet ds = new DataSet();
SqlDataAdapter da = new SqlDataAdapter(strSQL, strConn);
da.Fill(ds);

//Display the customer information retrieved
foreach (DataRow row in ds.Tables[0].Rows)
    Console.WriteLine("{0} - {1}", row["CustomerID"],
                      row["CompanyName"]);
```

Once this call completes, there is no connection between the two objects. The *DataSet* does not maintain a reference, internally or externally, to the *SqlDataAdapter*, and the *SqlData-Adapter* does not maintain a reference to the *DataSet*. Also, the *DataSet* contains no information indicating where the data originated—no connection string, no table name. The *DataSet* does contain the column names, by default, but these column names do not need to match the names of the columns in your database table. Thus, you can pass *DataSet* objects from your middle-tier server to your client applications without divulging any information about the location or structure of your database.

The *SqlDataAdapter* Contains the Updating Logic to Submit Changes Stored in Your *DataSet* Back to Your Database

The *SqlDataAdapter* class acts as a two-way street. You can use a *SqlDataAdapter* to submit a query and store its results in a *DataSet*, and you can use it to submit pending changes back to your database. This is a major change from previous data-access models.

For example, in ADO, you use a *Command*, explicitly or implicitly, to fetch the results of your query and store them in your *Recordset* object. When you want to update your database, you call the *Update* method of the *Recordset*. The *Command* object is not involved in the update process.

With ADO.NET, you use the *SqlDataAdapter*'s *Update* method to submit the changes stored in your *DataSet* to your database. When you call the *Update* method, you supply the *DataSet* as a parameter. The *DataSet* can cache changes, but it's the *SqlDataAdapter* object that contains your updating logic.

You Control the Updating Logic in the *SqlDataAdapter*

That statement bears repeating: You control the updating logic in the *SqlDataAdapter*. As far as I'm concerned, this is the number one reason to move from ADO, DAO, or RDO to ADO.NET. You can use your own custom INSERT, UPDATE, and DELETE queries or submit updates using stored procedures. The first time I noticed this feature while examining the structure for the *SqlDataAdapter*, three thoughts ran through my mind: "Wow!" "I can't wait to see developers' reactions to this feature!" and "Why didn't we think of this earlier?"

Because none of the previous data access models offer this level of control over updating logic, many developers have been unable to use many of the RAD features offered by those object models. Many database administrators will permit users to modify data in the database only by calling a stored procedure. Users don't have permissions to modify data by running UPDATE, INSERT INTO, or DELETE queries. However, these are the queries that DAO, RDO, and ADO generate to translate changes made to *Recordset* and *rdoResultset* objects into changes in your database. This means that developers building a database application with ADO cannot take advantage of the *Recordset*'s ability to submit changes to the database.

I spoke to one developer during the beta testing of the initial release of the .NET Framework who was skeptical about moving to ADO.NET. As if attempting to dismiss the new object model, he asked, "Can I use stored procedures to update my database?" He looked shocked when I smiled and responded, "Yes." I could almost hear the wheels in his brain turning for a moment or two before he asked, "How?"

Part of the reason he was so perplexed is that database administrators create separate stored procedures for updating, inserting, and deleting rows and there's no simple way for a technology like ADO.NET to determine what stored procedures to use to submit changes given a SELECT query. So, for a data access object model to support submitting updates using stored procedures in a RAD way, the data access model must let you specify separate stored procedures for updates, inserts, and deletes.

And that's exactly the level of flexibility the *SqlDataAdapter* class offers. The *SqlDataAdapter* has four properties that contain *Command* objects—one for the query to fetch data, one for submitting pending updates, one for submitting pending insertions, and one for submitting pending deletions. You can specify your own action queries or stored procedures for each of these *SqlCommand* objects, as well as parameters that can move data from your *DataSet* to your stored procedure and back.

Developers can be a difficult bunch. (As a developer, I'm allowed to make that observation.) We like control and performance, but we also like ease of use. The *SqlDataAdapter* offers all of the above. You can provide your own updating logic, or you can request that ADO.NET generate action queries similar to the ones that ADO and DAO automatically generate behind the scenes. You can even use Visual Studio 2005 to generate the updating logic at design time, an option that combines ease of use with control and performance.

We'll look at sample updating code and discuss the actual mechanics of updating your database using the *SqlDataAdapter* in Chapter 10. In this chapter, we'll focus on the structure of the *SqlDataAdapter* and how to use it to fetch the results of your queries.

Anatomy of the *SqlDataAdapter* Class

Now that you understand a little more about what the *SqlDataAdapter* does, let's look at the structure of the object to understand how it works.

The *SqlDataAdapter* class is designed to help you store the results of your query in *DataSet* and *DataTable* objects. As you learned in Chapter 4, the *SqlCommand* class lets you examine the results of your query through a *SqlDataReader* object. The *SqlDataAdapter* class consists of a series of *SqlCommand* objects and a collection of mapping properties that determines how the *SqlDataAdapter* will communicate with your *DataSet*. Figure 5-1 shows the structure of the *SqlDataAdapter*.

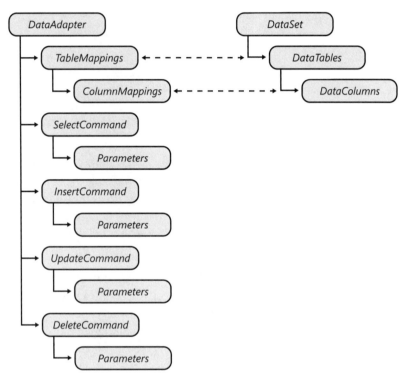

Figure 5-1   The structure of the *SqlDataAdapter* class

Child Commands

When you use a *SqlDataAdapter* to store the results of a query in a *DataSet*, the *SqlDataAdapter* uses a *SqlCommand* and *SqlConnection* to communicate with your database. (You can see the *SqlCommand* by examining the *SqlDataAdapter*'s *SelectCommand* property and the *SqlConnection* by examining that *SqlCommand* object's *Connection* property.) Internally, the *SqlDataAdapter* uses a *SqlDataReader* to fetch the results and then copies that information into new rows in your *DataSet*. This process is roughly similar to the second snippet of code shown at the start of this chapter.

The *SqlDataAdapter* class also has other properties that contain *SqlCommand* objects—*Insert-Command*, *UpdateCommand*, and *DeleteCommand*. The *SqlDataAdapter* uses these *SqlCommand* objects to submit the changes stored within your *DataSet* to your database. We'll look closely at how the *SqlDataAdapter* uses these *SqlCommand* objects to submit updates to your database in Chapter 10.

TableMappings Collection

By default, the *SqlDataAdapter* assumes that the columns in the *SqlDataReader* match up with columns in your *DataSet*. However, you might encounter situations in which you want the schema of your *DataSet* to differ from the schema in your database. You might want to use a different name for a particular column in your *DataSet*. Traditionally, developers have renamed columns within the query by using an alias. For example, if your Employees table had columns named EmpID, LName, and FName, you could use aliases within the query to change the column names to EmployeeID, LastName, and FirstName within the results, as shown in the following query:

```
SELECT EmpID AS EmployeeID, LName AS LastName, FName AS FirstName
    FROM Employees
```

The *SqlDataAdapter* offers a mechanism for mapping the results of your query to the structure of your *DataSet*: the *TableMappings* collection.

The preceding query describes a table with column names such as EmpID, LName, and FName. Let's take this example a step further and say that the name of the table in the database is Emp. We want to map that data to a table in our *DataSet* named Employees that contains friendlier column names such as EmployeeID, LastName, and FirstName. The *SqlDataAdapter* class's *TableMappings* collection allows you to create such a mapping layer between your database and the *DataSet*.

The *TableMappings* property returns a *DataTableMappingsCollection* object that contains a collection of *DataTableMapping* objects. Each object lets you create a mapping between a table (or view or stored procedure) in your database and the corresponding table name in your *DataSet*. The *DataTableMapping* object also has a *ColumnMappings* property that returns a *DataColumnMappingsCollection* object, which consists of a collection of *Data-ColumnMapping* objects. Each *DataColumnMapping* object maps a column in your database to a column in your *DataSet*. These mapping classes reside in the *System.Data.Common* namespace.

> **Note**   The *DataColumnMappingCollection* class has the longest name I've encountered so far. Thanks to the wonders of Microsoft IntelliSense and statement completion, you don't have to type the entire class name when working in Visual Studio 2005.

Figure 5-2 shows how the *SqlDataAdapter* class's *TableMappings* collection maps the employee data structure from our database table to the corresponding structure in our *DataSet*.

In the figure, we're mapping the database's Emp table to the *DataSet* object's Employees table, but the mapping information implies that it's mapping "Table" to "Employees". This is because the *SqlDataAdapter* really has no idea which table it's communicating with in the database. The *SqlDataAdapter* can retrieve column names from the result of the query using the

SqlDataReader but has no way of determining the table name. As a result, the *SqlDataAdapter* assumes that the table name is "Table". Thus, the entry in the *TableMappings* collection map is "Table" to "Employees".

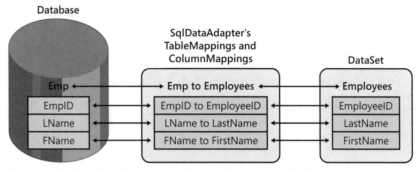

Figure 5-2   The *DataAdapter* class's *TableMappings* collection

The following code sample shows how you can populate a *SqlDataAdapter* object's *TableMappings* collection:

Visual Basic

```
'Imports System.Data.Common
Dim da As New SqlDataAdapter()
'Initialize DataAdapter.
Dim tableMap As DataTableMapping
Dim columnMap As DataColumnMapping
tableMap = da.TableMappings.Add("Table", "Employees")
columnMap = tableMap .ColumnMappings.Add("EmpID", "EmployeeID")
columnMap = tableMap .ColumnMappings.Add("LName", "LastName")
columnMap = tableMap .ColumnMappings.Add("FName", "FirstName")
```

Visual C#

```
//using System.Data.Common;
SqlDataAdapter da = new SqlDataAdapter();
//Initialize DataAdapter.
DataTableMapping tableMap;
DataColumnMapping columnMap;
tableMap = da.TableMappings.Add("Table", "Employees");
columnMap = tableMap.ColumnMappings.Add("EmpID", "EmployeeID");
columnMap = tableMap.ColumnMappings.Add("LName", "LastName");
columnMap = tableMap.ColumnMappings.Add("FName", "FirstName");
```

Creating and Using *SqlDataAdapter* Objects

You now know what a *SqlDataAdapter* is and what it can do for you, so let's examine how to create and use one.

Creating a *SqlDataAdapter*

When you create a *SqlDataAdapter*, you generally want to set its *SelectCommand* property to a valid *SqlCommand* object. The following code sample sets the *SelectCommand* for a new *SqlDataAdapter*:

Visual Basic

```
Dim strConn, strSQL As String
strConn = "Data Source=.\SQLExpress;" & _
          "Initial Catalog=Northwind;Integrated Security=True;"
strSQL = "SELECT CustomerID, CompanyName FROM Customers"
Dim cn As New SqlConnection(strConn)
Dim cmd As New SqlCommand(strSQL, cn)
Dim da As New SqlDataAdapter()
da.SelectCommand = cmd
```

Visual C#

```
string strConn, strSQL;
strConn = @"Data Source=.\SQLExpress;" +
          "Initial Catalog=Northwind;Integrated Security=True;";
strSQL = "SELECT CustomerID, CompanyName FROM Customers";
SqlConnection cn = new SqlConnection(strConn);
SqlCommand cmd = new SqlCommand(strSQL, cn);
SqlDataAdapter da = new SqlDataAdapter();
da.SelectCommand = cmd;
```

SqlDataAdapter Constructors

The *SqlDataAdapter* class has three constructors that you can use to simplify the process of creating a *SqlDataAdapter*, as shown in the following code. One constructor accepts a query string and a connection string.

Visual Basic

```
Dim strConn, strSQL As String
strConn = "Data Source=.\SQLExpress;" & _
          "Initial Catalog=Northwind;Integrated Security=True;"
strSQL = "SELECT CustomerID, CompanyName FROM Customers"
Dim da As New SqlDataAdapter(strSQL, strConn)
```

Visual C#

```
string strConn, strSQL;
strConn = @"Data Source=.\SQLExpress;" +
          "Initial Catalog=Northwind;Integrated Security=True;";
strSQL = "SELECT CustomerID, CompanyName FROM Customers";
SqlDataAdapter da = new SqlDataAdapter(strSQL, strConn);
```

There's a potential drawback to this approach. Say that you're going to use a series of *SqlData-Adapter* objects in your application. Creating your *SqlDataAdapter* objects in this fashion will create a new *SqlConnection* object for each *SqlDataAdapter*. You can ensure that your *SqlData-Adapter* objects use the same *SqlConnection* object by using the *SqlDataAdapter* constructor that accepts a query string and a *SqlConnection* object. The following code sample creates two *SqlDataAdapter* objects, each using the same *SqlConnection* object:

Visual Basic

```
Dim strConn, strSQL As String
strConn = "Data Source=.\SQLExpress;" & _
          "Initial Catalog=Northwind;Integrated Security=True;"
Dim cn As New SqlConnection(strConn)
Dim daCustomers, daOrders As SqlDataAdapter
strSQL = "SELECT CustomerID, CompanyName FROM Customers"
daCustomers = New SqlDataAdapter(strSQL, cn)
strSQL = "SELECT OrderID, CustomerID, OrderDate FROM Orders"
daOrders = New SqlDataAdapter(strSQL, cn)
```

Visual C#

```
string strConn, strSQL;
strConn = @"Data Source=.\SQLExpress;" +
          "Initial Catalog=Northwind;Integrated Security=True;";
SqlConnection cn = new SqlConnection(strConn);
SqlDataAdapter daCustomers, daOrders;
strSQL = "SELECT CustomerID, CompanyName FROM Customers";
daCustomers = new SqlDataAdapter(strSQL, cn);
strSQL = "SELECT OrderID, CustomerID, OrderDate FROM Orders";
daOrders = new SqlDataAdapter(strSQL, cn);
```

The *SqlDataAdapter* also offers a third constructor that accepts a *SqlCommand* object. If you've already created a *SqlCommand* object and want to create a *SqlDataAdapter* that uses that *Sql-Command* object to populate a *DataSet*, you can use the following code:

Visual Basic

```
Dim strConn, strSQL As String
strConn = "Data Source=.\SQLExpress;" & _
          "Initial Catalog=Northwind;Integrated Security=True;"
strSQL = "SELECT CustomerID, CompanyName FROM Customers"
Dim cn As New SqlConnection(strConn)
Dim cmd As New SqlCommand(strSQL, cn)
Dim da As New SqlDataAdapter(cmd)
```

Visual C#

```
string strConn, strSQL;
strConn = @"Data Source=.\SQLExpress;" +
          "Initial Catalog=Northwind;Integrated Security=True;";
strSQL = "SELECT CustomerID, CompanyName FROM Customers";
SqlConnection cn = new SqlConnection(strConn);
SqlCommand cmd = new SqlCommand(strSQL, cn);
SqlDataAdapter da = new SqlDataAdapter(cmd);
```

Retrieving Results from a Query

Now that we've looked at a few ways to create a *SqlDataAdapter* programmatically, let's look at how to use one to store the results of a query in a *DataSet*. First let's create a simple *SqlData-Adapter* to fetch data from the Customers table in the *Northwind* database.

Using the *Fill* Method

Calling the *SqlDataAdapter* class's *Fill* method executes the query stored in the *SqlDataAdapter* object's *SelectCommand* property and stores the results in a *DataSet*. The following code calls the *Fill* method and displays the results stored in the *DataSet*:

Visual Basic

```
Dim strConn, strSQL As String
strConn = "Data Source=.\SQLExpress;" & _
          "Initial Catalog=Northwind;Integrated Security=True;"
strSQL = "SELECT CustomerID, CompanyName FROM Customers"
Dim da As New SqlDataAdapter(strSQL, strConn)
Dim ds As New DataSet()
da.Fill(ds)

For Each row As DataRow In ds.Tables(0).Rows
    Console.WriteLine("{0} - {1}", row("CustomerID"), _
                      row("CompanyName"))
Next row
```

Visual C#

```
string strConn, strSQL;
strConn = @"Data Source=.\SQLExpress;" +
          "Initial Catalog=Northwind;Integrated Security=True;";
strSQL = "SELECT CustomerID, CompanyName FROM Customers";
SqlDataAdapter da = new SqlDataAdapter(strSQL, strConn);
DataSet ds = new DataSet();
da.Fill(ds);

foreach (DataRow row in ds.Tables[0].Rows)
    Console.WriteLine("{0} - {1}", row["CustomerID"],
                      row["CompanyName"]);
```

In this code sample, calling the *Fill* method creates a new *DataTable* in the *DataSet*. The new *DataTable* contains columns that correspond to the columns returned by the query–CustomerID and CompanyName.

Retrieving Results Using *SqlTypes*

The *DataSet* class is now fully equipped to handle the various *SqlType* classes in the *System.Data.SqlTypes* namespace. You might recall that in Chapter 4 we discussed retrieving *SqlTypes* using the *SqlDataReader*. In ADO.NET 2.0, you can use a *SqlDataAdapter* to store the results of your query using *SqlTypes* rather than the standard .NET data types by setting a *SqlDataAdapter* object's *ReturnProviderSpecificTypes* property to *True* prior to calling *Fill*.

You could modify the previous code sample to return *SqlTypes* and the rest of the code will still run successfully. The one difference is that the *DataColumn* objects you implicitly create will have their *DataType* properties set to *SqlString* rather than *String*.

Creating *DataTable* and *DataColumn* Objects Using the *Fill* Method

Calling the *Fill* method in the previous example created a new *DataTable* in the *DataSet*. The new *DataTable* has columns named CustomerID, CompanyName, ContactName, and Phone, but the name of the *DataTable* object is *Table,* not *Customers*.

You might ask, "Why is the *SqlDataAdapter* able to determine appropriate names for the *Data-Columns* it creates, but not for the *DataTable*?" Remember that the *SqlDataAdapter* implicitly creates a *SqlDataReader* to retrieve the results of the query. Before the *SqlDataAdapter* examines the first row, it gathers information from the *SqlDataReader*'s schema features to determine column names and data types. As we saw in Chapter 4, the table name that the query references is not available through the *SqlDataReader*'s schema, by default. If you check the *TableName* property of the *DataTable* the *SqlDataReader* created in the previous example, you'll see that it was given the rather nondescript value of "Table".

However, you can add schema to the *SqlDataAdapter* itself so that it knows to associate the results of the query with a *DataTable* named "Customers". We already touched on this behavior when we discussed the *SqlDataAdapter* class's *TableMappings* collection. We can add an item to this collection to inform the *SqlDataAdapter* that we want to map the results of the query to a *DataTable* named Customers, as shown here:

Visual Basic

```
Dim strConn, strSQL As String
strConn = "Data Source=.\SQLExpress;" & _
          "Initial Catalog=Northwind;Integrated Security=True;"
strSQL = "SELECT CustomerID, CompanyName FROM Customers"
Dim da As New SqlDataAdapter(strSQL, strConn)
da.TableMappings.Add("Table", "Customers")
Dim ds As New DataSet()
da.Fill(ds)

'Display the new table name
Console.WriteLine("New TableName = {0}", ds.Tables(0).TableName)
```

Visual C#

```
string strConn, strSQL;
strConn = @"Data Source=.\SQLExpress;" +
          "Initial Catalog=Northwind;Integrated Security=True;";
strSQL = "SELECT CustomerID, CompanyName FROM Customers";
SqlDataAdapter da = new SqlDataAdapter(strSQL, strConn);
da.TableMappings.Add("Table", "Customers");
DataSet ds = new DataSet();
da.Fill(ds);

//Display the new table name
Console.WriteLine("New TableName = {0}", ds.Tables[0].TableName);
```

We'll cover the *TableMappings* collection in more detail shortly.

Using Overloaded *Fill* Methods

There's more than one way to use a *SqlDataAdapter* object's *Fill* method to fill a *DataSet*. Let's look at the available *Fill* methods in groups.

Specifying the *DataTable*   The *SqlDataAdapter* offers two *Fill* methods that give you more control over the *DataTable* that it will use.

Rather than having to add an entry to the *SqlDataAdapter* object's *TableMappings* collection, you can specify a table name in the *Fill* method:

```
SqlDataAdapter.Fill(DataSet, "MyTableName")
```

I often use this *Fill* method to fill a table in my *DataSet* without having to use the *TableMappings* collection.

You can also specify a *DataTable* instead of a *DataSet* when calling the *Fill* method:

```
SqlDataAdapter.Fill(DataTable)
```

This *Fill* method is useful when you've already created the *DataTable* you want to populate. Here's an example:

Visual Basic
```
Dim strConn, strSQL As String
strConn = "Data Source=.\SQLExpress;" & _
          "Initial Catalog=Northwind;Integrated Security=True;"
strSQL = "SELECT CustomerID, CompanyName FROM Customers"
Dim da As New SqlDataAdapter(strSQL, strConn)
Dim tbl As New DataTable()
da.Fill(tbl)

For Each row As DataRow In tbl.Rows
    Console.WriteLine("{0} - {1}", row("CustomerID"), _
                      row("CompanyName"))
Next row
```

Visual C#
```
string strConn, strSQL;
strConn = @"Data Source=.\SQLExpress;" +
          "Initial Catalog=Northwind;Integrated Security=True;";
strSQL = "SELECT CustomerID, CompanyName FROM Customers";
SqlDataAdapter da = new SqlDataAdapter(strSQL, strConn);
DataTable tbl = new DataTable();
da.Fill(tbl);

foreach (DataRow row in tbl.Rows)
    Console.WriteLine("{0} - {1}", row["CustomerID"],
                      row["CompanyName"]);
```

Paging with the *SqlDataAdapter* class's *Fill* method   You've browsed through product catalogs online that display items one page at a time. If the catalog has a hundred items, the Web site might display 20 of the items per page. The *SqlDataAdapter* has a *Fill* method that you can use to fetch only a portion of the results of your query, as shown here:

```
SqlDataAdapter.Fill(DataSet, intStartRecord, intNumRecords,
                    "TableName")
```

Remember that the parameter for the starting record is zero based. So the following code example fetches the first 20 rows:

```
SqlDataAdapter.Fill(DataSet, 0, 20, "Products")
```

It's also important to keep in mind that using this *Fill* method affects only the rows stored in your *DataSet*. Let's say you're querying a table that contains 1000 rows and you're fetching this data in pages of 20 records each. The following call stores the last 20 rows from the query in your *DataSet*:

```
DataAdapter.Fill(DataSet, 980, 20, "Products")
```

However, the actual query still returns 1000 rows. The *SqlDataAdapter* executes the *Sql-Command* in its *SelectCommand* property and then calls the *Read* method on the resulting *SqlDataReader* 980 times to "skip" the first 49 pages of data.

Although this *Fill* method can make it easy to break your query into pages, it's not terribly efficient. There are more efficient (but more complex) ways to achieve paging with *DataSet* and *SqlDataReader* objects, which we'll discuss in Chapter 14 when I explain how to build efficient Web applications.

Opening and Closing Connections

In the code samples that showed how to use the *Fill* method, you might have noticed a major difference between how the *SqlDataAdapter* and the *SqlCommand* handle *SqlConnection* objects. In Chapter 4, before calling one of the *SqlCommand* object's execute methods, we opened the *SqlConnection* object associated with the *SqlCommand*. Otherwise, the *SqlCommand* would throw an exception. The *SqlDataAdapter* has no such requirement.

If you call a *SqlDataAdapter* object's *Fill* method and the *SelectCommand* property's *SqlConnection* is closed, the *SqlDataAdapter* will open the connection, submit the query, fetch the results, and then close the connection. You might say that the *SqlDataAdapter* is very tidy. It always returns the *SelectCommand* property's *SqlConnection* to its initial state. If you open the *SqlConnection* before calling the *Fill* method, the *SqlConnection* will still be open afterwards.

The way the *SqlDataAdapter* handles *SqlConnection* objects can come in handy because you're not required to open your *SqlConnection*. However, there are times when you should write code to open your *SqlConnection* explicitly.

Let's say that as your application starts up, you use multiple *SqlDataAdapter* objects to populate your *DataSet* with the results of a few queries. You've already learned how to use one of the

SqlDataAdapter class's constructors to force each *SqlDataAdapter* to use the same *SqlConnection* object. So your code looks something like this:

Visual Basic

```
Dim strConn, strSQL As String
strConn = "Data Source=.\SQLExpress;" & _
          "Initial Catalog=Northwind;Integrated Security=True;"
Dim cn As New SqlConnection(strConn)
Dim daCustomers, daOrders As SqlDataAdapter
strSQL = "SELECT CustomerID, CompanyName FROM Customers"
daCustomers = New SqlDataAdapter(strSQL, cn)
strSQL = "SELECT OrderID, CustomerID, OrderDate FROM Orders"
daOrders = New SqlDataAdapter(strSQL, cn)
Dim ds As New DataSet()
daCustomers.Fill(ds, "Customers")
daOrders.Fill(ds, "Orders")
```

Visual C#

```
string strConn, strSQL;
strConn = @"Data Source=.\SQLExpress;" +
          "Initial Catalog=Northwind;Integrated Security=True;";
SqlConnection cn = new SqlConnection(strConn);
SqlDataAdapter daCustomers, daOrders;
strSQL = "SELECT CustomerID, CompanyName FROM Customers";
daCustomers = new SqlDataAdapter(strSQL, cn);
strSQL = "SELECT OrderID, CustomerID, OrderDate FROM Orders";
daOrders = new SqlDataAdapter(strSQL, cn);
DataSet ds = new DataSet();
daCustomers.Fill(ds, "Customers");
daOrders.Fill(ds, "Orders");
```

You're actually opening and closing the *SqlConnection* object twice, once each time you call a *SqlDataAdapter* object's *Fill* method. To keep from opening and closing the *SqlConnection* object, call the *SqlConnection* object's *Open* method before you call the *Fill* method on the *SqlDataAdapter* objects. If you want to close the *SqlConnection* afterwards, you call the *Close* method as shown here:

```
cn.Open()
daCustomers.Fill(ds, "Customers")
daOrders.Fill(ds, "Orders")
cn.Close()
```

> **Note**   Another option would be to use a single *SqlDataAdapter* with a batch query to return data from both the Customers and Orders tables, but let's not get too far ahead of ourselves.

Making Multiple Calls to the *Fill* Method

What do you do if you want to refresh the data in your *DataSet*? Maybe your *SqlDataAdapter* fetches the contents of a table when your application starts up and you want to add a feature so that the user can see more timely data. The simple solution is to clear your *DataSet* (or *DataTable*) and then call the *SqlDataAdapter* object's *Fill* method again.

Hypothetically speaking, let's say that you didn't realize that this was the best way to go. Instead, you just called the *SqlDataAdapter* object's *Fill* method a second time, as shown here:

Visual Basic

```
Dim strConn, strSQL As String
strConn = "Data Source=.\SQLExpress;" & _
          "Initial Catalog=Northwind;Integrated Security=True;"
strSQL = "SELECT CustomerID, CompanyName FROM Customers"
Dim da As New SqlDataAdapter(strSQL, strConn)
Dim ds As New DataSet()
da.Fill(ds, "Customers")
...
da.Fill(ds, "Customers")
```

Visual C#

```
string strConn, strSQL;
strConn = @"Data Source=.\SQLExpress;"
            "Initial Catalog=Northwind;Integrated Security=True;";
strSQL = "SELECT CustomerID, CompanyName FROM Customers";
SqlDataAdapter da = new SqlDataAdapter(strSQL, strConn);
DataSet ds = new DataSet();
da.Fill(ds, "Customers");
...
da.Fill(ds, "Customers");
```

By calling the *Fill* method twice, you're asking the *SqlDataAdapter* to execute the specified query and to store the results in the *DataSet* twice. The first call to the *Fill* method creates a new table within the *DataSet* called Customers. The second call to the *Fill* method appends the results of the query into that same table in the *DataSet*. Thus, each customer will appear twice in the *DataSet*. With only this code sample, neither the *SqlDataAdapter* nor the *DataTable* has any way to know which customers are duplicates.

Database administrators generally define primary keys on tables in a database. One of the benefits of this practice is that it prevents users from creating duplicate rows. The *DataTable* object has a *PrimaryKey* property. If the *DataTable* that the *SqlDataAdapter* is filling has a primary key, the *DataTable* will use this key to determine which rows are duplicates. For more information on setting the *PrimaryKey* property of a *DataTable*, see the "Fetching Schema Information" section later in the chapter, as well as the discussion of the *DataTable* object's *PrimaryKey* property in Chapter 6.

Getting back to the example at hand, if we define a primary key on the Customers *DataTable* in the *DataSet* before we call the *SqlDataAdapter* object's *Fill* method the second time, the *DataTable* will locate the duplicate rows and discard the old values.

For example, say a customer's company name has changed in the database. Calling the *Fill* method again will retrieve this new information. The *DataTable* will use its primary key to determine whether the row for this particular customer already exists. If the customer already exists within the *DataTable*, the newly retrieved information will be applied to the row that already exists in the *DataTable*. However, rows deleted from the database will not be removed from your *DataTable*.

Say that a particular customer was in the database the first time you called the *SqlDataAdapter* object's *Fill* method and the *SqlDataAdapter* added that customer to your *DataTable*. Later, someone realized that the customer was a deadbeat and purged the customer from your database. If you call the *SqlDataAdapter* a second time, the *SqlDataAdapter* will not find information for that customer in the results of your query but will not remove the row from your *DataTable*.

Now we've come full circle. If you need to refresh all the data, you should clear the *DataSet* or *DataTable* prior to calling the *SqlDataAdapter* object's *Fill* method. Using this methodology ensures that you will not have duplicate rows (even if you haven't defined a primary key for your *DataTable*) and that you will not see rows in your *DataSet* that no longer exist in your database.

Mapping the Results of Your Query to Your *DataSet*

Earlier in the chapter, I described the role of the *SqlDataAdapter* class's *TableMappings* collection. Now it's time to take a closer look at how to use this collection in code.

The *SqlDataAdapter* Class's *TableMappings* Collection

The *TableMappings* collection controls how the *SqlDataAdapter* maps your *DataSet* to your database. If you leave a *SqlDataAdapter* object's *TableMappings* collection empty, call the *Fill* method, and then supply a *DataSet* as a parameter without specifying a table name, the *SqlDataAdapter* will assume that you want to work with a *DataTable* called "Table".

The *TableMappings* property returns a *DataTableMappingCollection* object. This object contains a collection of *DataTableMapping* objects. Adding the following line of code adds a *DataTableMapping* object to the *TableMappings* collection to tell the *SqlDataAdapter* that it should communicate with a *DataTable* called "Employees" instead:

```
SqlDataAdapter.TableMappings.Add("Table", "Employees")
```

Once you've created a *DataTableMapping* object, you can create column mappings for the table. In an example earlier in the chapter, we mapped columns in the database named EmpID, LName, and FName to columns in the *DataSet* named EmployeeID, LastName, and FirstName using the following code:

Visual Basic
```
Dim da As SqlDataAdapter
'Initialize DataAdapter.
Dim tableMap As DataTableMapping
tableMap = da.TableMappings.Add("Table", "Employees")
tableMap.ColumnMappings.Add("EmpID", "EmployeeID")
tableMap.ColumnMappings.Add("LName", "LastName")
tableMap.ColumnMappings.Add("FName", "FirstName")
```

Visual C#

```
SqlDataAdapter da;
//Initialize DataAdapter.
DataTableMapping tableMap;
tableMap = da.TableMappings.Add("Table", "Employees");
tableMap.ColumnMappings.Add("EmpID", "EmployeeID");
tableMap.ColumnMappings.Add("LName", "LastName");
tableMap.ColumnMappings.Add("FName", "FirstName");
```

Both the *DataTableMappingCollection* and *DataColumnMappingCollection* objects have an *AddRange* method that you can use to add an array of mappings to the collection in a single call, as shown here:

Visual Basic

```
Dim da As New SqlDataAdapter()
'Initialize DataAdapter.
Dim tableMap As DataTableMapping
Dim columnMaps As DataColumnMapping()
tableMap = da.TableMappings.Add("Table", "Employees")
columnMaps = New DataColumnMapping() _
                {New DataColumnMapping("EmpID", "EmployeeID"), _
                 New DataColumnMapping("LName", "LastName"), _
                 New DataColumnMapping("FName", "FirstName")}
tableMap.ColumnMappings.AddRange(columnMaps)
```

Visual C#

```
SqlDataAdapter da = new SqlDataAdapter();
//Initialize DataAdapter.
DataTableMapping tableMap;
DataColumnMapping[] columnMaps;
tableMap = da.TableMappings.Add("Table", "Employees");
columnMaps = new DataColumnMapping[]
                {new DataColumnMapping("EmpID", "EmployeeID"),
                 new DataColumnMapping("LName", "LastName"),
                 new DataColumnMapping("FName", "FirstName")};
tableMap.ColumnMappings.AddRange(columnMaps);
```

The *MissingMappingAction* Property

You now understand how to populate a *SqlDataAdapter* object's *TableMappings* collection with table and column information. However, you might have noticed that you don't have to supply this information. Earlier in the chapter, you saw examples that used a *SqlDataAdapter* object's *Fill* method to create and fill a new *DataTable* even though the *SqlDataAdapter* had no column mapping information.

In most cases, developers use the same column names in the *DataSet* as in the database. The ADO.NET development team wisely realized that developers would not appreciate having to populate the *SqlDataAdapter* object's *TableMappings* collection with identical database and *DataSet* column names in order to fetch data into their *DataSet*. When the *SqlDataAdapter* examines the results of your query and finds a column that does not exist in its mappings collection, it checks its *MissingMappingAction* property to determine what to do with those columns.

The *MissingMappingAction* property accepts values from the *MissingMappingAction* enumeration in the *System.Data* namespace. By default, this property is set to *Passthrough*. When the *MissingMappingAction* property is set to this value, the *SqlDataAdapter* assumes that columns that do not appear in the mappings collection should still be mapped to your *DataSet*, using the column names from the resultset. Setting this property to *Ignore* tells the *SqlDataAdapter* to ignore columns that don't appear in the mappings collection. You can also set the *MissingMappingAction* property to *Error*, which will cause the *SqlDataAdapter* to throw an exception if it detects a column in the results of your query that does not exist in the mappings collection.

Working with Batch Queries

All the queries in the chapter so far have retrieved a single set of results. Some databases, such as Microsoft SQL Server, let you submit a batch of queries that return multiple resultsets, as shown here:

```
SELECT CustomerID, CompanyName, ContactName, Phone
       FROM Customers WHERE CustomerID = 'ALFKI';
SELECT OrderID, CustomerID, EmployeeID, OrderDate
       FROM Orders WHERE CustomerID = 'ALFKI'
```

If you build a *SqlDataAdapter* with the preceding query, fetch the results, and store them in a *DataSet* using the following code, you'll fetch the results and store them in two *DataTable* objects within the *DataSet*:

```
SqlDataAdapter.Fill(DataSet)
```

The results of the first portion of the query, which references the Customers table, will be stored in a *DataTable* named "Table". The results of the second portion, which references the Orders table, will be stored in a *DataTable* named "Table1". You might want to choose more descriptive names for your *DataTable* objects.

The *SqlDataAdapter* class's *TableMappings* collection can contain multiple *DataTableMapping* objects. You can add entries to the collection to control the table names that the *SqlData-Adapter* will use to store the results of the batch query. The following code fetches the results of the batch queries and stores them in two *DataTable* objects, named "Customers" and "Orders", within the *DataSet*:

Visual Basic
```
Dim strConn, strSQL As String
strConn = "Data Source=.\SQLExpress;" & _
          "Initial Catalog=Northwind;Integrated Security=True;"
strSQL = "SELECT CustomerID, CompanyName, ContactName " & _
         "    FROM Customers WHERE CustomerID = 'ALFKI'; " & _
         "SELECT OrderID, CustomerID, OrderDate " & _
         "    FROM Orders WHERE CustomerID = 'ALFKI'"
Dim da As New SqlDataAdapter(strSQL, strConn)
da.TableMappings.Add("Table", "Customers")
```

```
da.TableMappings.Add("Table1", "Orders")
Dim ds As New DataSet()
da.Fill(ds)

For Each tbl As DataTable In ds.Tables
    Console.WriteLine("TableName = {0}", tbl.TableName)
Next tbl
```

Visual C#

```
string strConn, strSQL;
strConn = @"Data Source=.\SQLExpress;" +
          "Initial Catalog=Northwind;Integrated Security=True;";
strSQL = "SELECT CustomerID, CompanyName, ContactName " +
         "   FROM Customers WHERE CustomerID = 'ALFKI'; " +
         "SELECT OrderID, CustomerID, OrderDate " +
         "   FROM Orders WHERE CustomerID = 'ALFKI'";
SqlDataAdapter da = new SqlDataAdapter(strSQL, strConn);
da.TableMappings.Add("Table", "Customers");
da.TableMappings.Add("Table1", "Orders");
DataSet ds = new DataSet();
da.Fill(ds);

foreach (DataTable tbl in ds.Tables)
    Console.WriteLine("TableName = {0}", tbl.TableName);
```

Retrieving Rows from a Stored Procedure

If you have stored procedures that return resultsets, you can use a *SqlDataAdapter* to fetch those results and store them in a *DataSet* or *DataTable*. Say that you have the following stored procedure definition:

```
CREATE PROCEDURE GetAllCustomers AS
    SELECT CustomerID, CompanyName, ContactName FROM Customers
RETURN
```

You can fetch the results of the stored procedure call and store them in a *DataSet* by using the following query string:

```
EXEC GetAllCustomers
```

You can also base the *SqlDataAdapter* on a *SqlCommand* with a *CommandType* of *StoredProcedure*. For more information on using *SqlCommand* objects with *CommandType* values other than the default, see the discussion of the *SqlCommand* object's *CommandType* property in Chapter 4.

Fetching Schema Information

The *DataTable* class, which we'll discuss in detail in the following chapter, is designed to enforce constraints on your data such as a primary key, maximum length of string fields, and nullability constraints. Fetching this information at run time can be costly, and in many cases developers have no need to retrieve this information. So, by default, the *SqlDataAdapter* does not fetch this information. However, if you encounter a situation in which you're willing to pay the performance penalty to retrieve additional schema information about your results, you can use a couple of key features of the *SqlDataAdapter*: the *MissingSchemaAction* property and the *FillSchema* method.

The *MissingSchemaAction* Property

You might have noticed that, so far, all the examples that use the *SqlDataAdapter* class's *Fill* method use *DataSet* and *DataTable* objects that contain no schema information. By default, the *SqlDataAdapter* will add columns to store the results of your query if those columns do not already exist in your *DataSet* or *DataTable*. This behavior is governed by the *MissingSchemaAction* property.

This property accepts values from the *MissingSchemaAction* enumeration in the *System.Data* namespace. The default value for this property is *Add*. As with *MissingMappingAction*, you can ignore missing columns by setting the property to *Ignore* or throw an exception in such circumstances by setting the property to *Error*.

There's another value in the *MissingSchemaAction* enumeration: *AddWithKey*. The name of this value is slightly misleading. If you set the property to this value and the *SqlDataAdapter* encounters a column that does not exist in your *DataSet* or *DataTable*, the *SqlDataAdapter* adds the column and sets two additional schema attributes of the property: *MaxLength* and *AllowDBNull*. If the *DataTable* does not yet exist or does not contain any columns, this value also causes the *SqlDataAdapter* to query the database for primary key information.

The *FillSchema* Method

The *SqlDataAdapter* also has a *FillSchema* method that you can use to fetch only schema information and store it in your *DataSet* or *DataTable*. The *FillSchema* method's signatures mirror the basic *Fill* signatures. You can supply a *DataSet*, *DataTable*, or *DataSet* and table name in the *FillSchema* method.

Each *FillSchema* method also requires a value from the *SchemaType* attribute: *Mapped* or *Source*. The value you specify in this parameter determines whether the *SqlDataAdapter* will apply the settings in its *TableMappings* collection to the results of the query. If you call the *FillSchema* method and use *Source* as the *SchemaType*, the *SqlDataAdapter* will use the column names that the query returns. Using *Mapped* as the *SchemaType* will cause the *SqlDataAdapter* to apply the settings in its *TableMappings* to the columns returned by the query.

FillSchema will set the *AutoIncrement*, *AllowDBNull*, and *MaxLength* properties on the columns returned and will also create a primary key on the resulting *DataTable* if the database indicates that the results of your query contain a column or set of columns that represents a primary or unique key.

Visual Studio 2005 Design-Time Features

Visual Studio 2005 offers some design-time features that are handy when you're working with *SqlDataAdapters*. As noted in Chapter 3, the Server Explorer window gives you the ability to easily create and execute queries against your database at design time.

You can also use Server Explorer to examine your database's schema, as described in Chapter 4. When you're writing your ADO.NET code, you can easily use Server Explorer to check the names of tables, columns, and stored procedures by drilling down into your connection. You can also examine data types of columns in your tables and views, and parameters on your stored procedures. Simply select the desired column or parameter in Server Explorer, and then examine its properties in the Properties window, as shown in Figure 5-3.

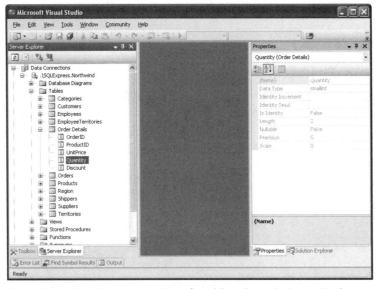

Figure 5-3   Examining properties of a table column in Server Explorer using the Properties window

What Happened to the Drag-and-Drop Features?

As noted in Chapter 3, the drag-and-drop design-time data access features have changed in moving from Visual Studio .NET 2002/2003 to Visual Studio 2005. You can no longer drag and drop tables, views, or stored procedures onto design surfaces to create *SqlDataAdapters* or *SqlCommands*.

The design-time *SqlDataAdapter* story has changed dramatically. Queries are now associated with strongly typed *DataSets*. The queries are now strongly typed, a feature that Visual Studio 2005 refers to as "TableAdapters." For more information on this feature, see the discussion of TableAdapters in Chapter 9.

SqlDataAdapter Reference

The *SqlDataAdapter* class offers properties, methods, and events to meet your every need. Let's meet them now.

Properties of the *SqlDataAdapter* Class

You can divide the *SqlDataAdapter* class's properties into two groups—those that control communication with the data store, and those that control communication with the *DataSet*.

The properties that control communication with the data store are the ones that contain *SqlCommand* objects: the *SelectCommand*, *UpdateCommand*, *InsertCommand*, and *Delete-Command* properties. These properties contain *SqlCommand* objects that the *SqlDataAdapter* executes when you want to move information back and forth between a *DataSet* and your data store—to retrieve rows into your *DataSet* or to submit changes stored in a *DataSet* to your data store. Table 5-1 describes the properties.

Table 5-1   Properties of the *SqlDataAdapter* Class

Property	Data Type	Description
AcceptChangesDuringFill	*Boolean*	Determines the *RowState* of the rows retrieved by the *SqlDataAdapter*. (Default = *True*.)
AcceptChangesDuringUpdate	*Boolean*	Determines whether the *SqlDataAdapter* will implicitly call *AcceptChanges* after submitting the pending changes in a *DataRow*. (Default = *True*.)
ContinueUpdateOnError	*Boolean*	Controls whether the *SqlDataAdapter* will continue to submit changes if it encounters an error. (Default = *False*.)
DeleteCommand	*SqlCommand*	*SqlCommand* used to submit pending deletions.
FillLoadOption	*LoadOption*	Controls how the *DataTable* handles loading rows that already exist in the *DataTable*. (Requires the *DataTable*'s *PrimaryKey* property to be set; Default = *OverwriteChanges*.)
InsertCommand	*SqlCommand*	*SqlCommand* used to submit pending insertions.
MissingMappingAction	*MissingMappingAction*	Controls the *SqlDataAdapter* object's behavior when fetching columns that do not appear in the *TableMappings* collection. (Default = *Passthrough*.)
MissingSchemaAction	*MissingSchemaAction*	Controls the *SqlDataAdapter* object's behavior when fetching columns that do not appear in the *DataTable* object's *Columns* collection. (Default = *Add*.)

Table 5-1   Properties of the *SqlDataAdapter* Class

Property	Data Type	Description
ReturnProviderSpecificTypes	*Boolean*	Controls whether the *SqlDataAdapter* uses standard .NET data types or provider-specific types (in this case, *SqlTypes*) to store the results of the query. (Default = *False*.)
SelectCommand	*SqlCommand*	*SqlCommand* used to query database and to fetch results and store them in a *DataSet* or *DataTable*.
TableMappings	*DataTableMappingCollection*	Collection of information the *SqlDataAdapter* uses to map the results of the query to the *DataSet*.
UpdateBatchSize	*Int32*	Controls how many *DataRows* the *SqlDataAdapter* submits per batch. (Default = 1.)
UpdateCommand	*SqlCommand*	*SqlCommand* used to submit pending updates.

SelectCommand, *UpdateCommand*, *InsertCommand*, and *DeleteCommand*

Each of these properties of the *SqlDataAdapter* stores a *SqlCommand* object. The specific object type will depend on the .NET Data Provider you're using. For example, a *SqlDataAdapter* object's *SelectCommand* property contains a *SqlCommand* object, and an *OleDbDataAdapter* object's *SelectCommand* property contains an *OleDbCommand* object. (The *SqlCommand* object is discussed in more detail in Chapter 4.)

If you supply a query string in the constructor for the *SqlDataAdapter*, this query string will become the *CommandText* property for the *SqlDataAdapter* object's *SelectCommand*. If you supply a *SqlCommand* rather than just a query string, that *SqlCommand* will be assigned to the *SqlDataAdapter* object's *SelectCommand* property.

If you supply a *SqlConnection* in the *SqlDataAdapter*'s constructor, that *SqlDataAdapter*'s *SelectCommand* will have its *Connection* property set to that *SqlConnection*. If you supply a connection string, the *SqlDataAdapter* will create a new *SqlConnection*, set its *ConnectionString* property to the string you supplied, and then assign the new *SqlConnection* to the *Connection* property of the *SqlDataAdapter* object's *SelectCommand*.

TableMappings Property

Earlier in the chapter, you learned that the *SqlDataAdapter* and the *DataSet* are completely disconnected from each other in the ADO.NET object model. So how does the *SqlDataAdapter* know how to communicate with the *DataSet*? What if the *DataSet* supplied in the *Fill* method contains multiple *DataTable* objects? How will the *SqlDataAdapter* know which *DataTable* to examine?

The *SqlDataAdapter* class has a *TableMappings* property that contains a collection of *DataTableMapping* objects. Each *DataTableMapping* object has a *ColumnMappings* property that returns a collection of *DataColumnMapping* objects. This hierarchy of objects corresponds to the collection of *DataTable* objects and *DataColumn* objects in your *DataSet*.

When the *SqlDataAdapter* retrieves data from your data store, it uses the information in the *TableMappings* collection to determine where in your *DataSet* to store the results of your query. Generally speaking, if you fetch the results of the query

```
SELECT CustomerID, CompanyName, ContactName, Phone FROM Customers
```

you'll want to create a *DataTable* named Customers that contains *DataColumn* objects whose names correspond to the columns in the results of the query. If you want to provide alternative names for the *DataTable* or any of its *DataColumn* objects, you'll want to populate the *SqlDataAdapter* object's *TableMappings* collection with the desired mapping information.

The following code is an example of populating a *SqlDataAdapter* object's *TableMappings* collection based on the query. With each *DataTableMapping* and *DataColumnMapping*, the first string corresponds to the name of the item that the *SqlDataAdapter* retrieves from the database, and the second string corresponds to the name of the item in the *DataSet*.

In this example, we'll query the authors table in the sample *pubs* database. This table has columns named "au_id", "au_lname", and "au_fname". Here, we'll use the *TableMappings* collection to rename those columns "AuthorID", "FirstName", and "LastName", respectively.

Visual Basic

```
Dim strConn, strSQL As String
strConn = "Data Source=.\SQLExpress;" & _
          "Initial Catalog=pubs;Integrated Security=True;"
strSQL = "SELECT au_id, au_fname, au_lname FROM authors"
Dim da As New SqlDataAdapter(strSQL, strConn)
Dim tableMap As DataTableMapping
tableMap = da.TableMappings.Add("Table", "Authors")
tableMap.ColumnMappings.Add("au_id", "AuthorID")
tableMap.ColumnMappings.Add("au_fname", "FirstName")
Dim ds As New DataSet()
da.Fill(ds)

'Display the names of the newly created objects
Console.WriteLine("TableName = {0}", ds.Tables(0).TableName)
For Each col As DataColumn In ds.Tables(0).Columns
    Console.WriteLine("  ColumnName = {0}", col.ColumnName)
Next col
```

Visual C#

```
string strConn, strSQL;
strConn = @"Data Source=.\SQLExpress;" +
          "Initial Catalog=pubs;Integrated Security=True;";
strSQL = "SELECT au_id, au_fname, au_lname FROM authors";
SqlDataAdapter da = new SqlDataAdapter(strSQL, strConn);
DataTableMapping tableMap;
tableMap = da.TableMappings.Add("Table", "Authors");
```

```
tableMap.ColumnMappings.Add("au_id", "AuthorID");
tableMap.ColumnMappings.Add("au_fname", "FirstName");
tableMap.ColumnMappings.Add("au_lname", "LastName");
DataSet ds = new DataSet();
da.Fill(ds);

//Display the names of the newly created objects
Console.WriteLine("TableName = {0}", ds.Tables[0].TableName);
foreach (DataColumn col in ds.Tables[0].Columns)
    Console.WriteLine("  ColumnName = {0}", col.ColumnName);
```

You can also use the *AddRange* method of the *DataTableMappingCollection* or *DataColumn-MappingCollection* object to add an array of *ColumnMappings* to the collection in a single call, as shown here:

Visual Basic

```
Dim tableMap As DataTableMapping
Dim columnMaps As DataColumnMapping()
tableMap = da.TableMappings.Add("Table", "Authors")
columnMaps = New DataColumnMapping() _
    {New DataColumnMapping("au_id", "AuthorID"), _
     New DataColumnMapping("au_fname", "FirstName")}
tableMap.ColumnMappings.AddRange(columnMaps)
```

Visual C#

```
DataTableMapping tableMap;
DataColumnMapping[] columnMaps;
tableMap = da.TableMappings.Add("Table", "Authors");
columnMaps = new DataColumnMapping[]
    {new DataColumnMapping("au_id", "AuthorID"),
     new DataColumnMapping("au_fname", "FirstName")};
tableMap.ColumnMappings.AddRange(columnMaps);
```

What if the query the *SqlDataAdapter* executes contains information that does not appear in the *SqlDataAdapter* object's *TableMappings* collection for the *DataTable* in your *DataSet*? By default, the *SqlDataAdapter* will assume that you want to retrieve this information and store it in your table.

MissingMappingAction and *MissingSchemaAction* Properties

When the *SqlDataAdapter* fetches the results of your query, it looks for corresponding tables and columns in its *TableMappings* collection. The *MissingMappingAction* property of the *SqlDataAdapter* controls its behavior in situations where the *SqlDataAdapter* retrieves tables or columns that don't correspond to entries in the *TableMappingsCollection*. By default, this property is set to *Passthrough*, but you can set it to the other values in the *MissingMappingAction* enumeration, which is in the *System.Data* namespace. Setting *MissingMappingAction* to *Ignore* will cause the *SqlDataAdapter* to ignore tables and columns that do not appear in the *TableMappings* collection. If you set *MissingMappingAction* to *Error*, you'll receive an exception if the query contains tables or columns that do not appear in the *SqlDataAdapter* object's *TableMappings* collection.

The *SqlDataAdapter* also has a *MissingSchemaAction* property that controls the behavior of the *SqlDataAdapter* if the tables or columns in the results of the query do not appear in the destination *DataSet*. By default, *MissingSchemaAction* is set to *Add*, which forces the *SqlData-Adapter* to add the expected tables and columns to the *DataSet*. You can set the property to other values in the *MissingSchemaAction* enumeration in *System.Data*–such as *AddWithKey*, *Ignore*, and *Error*. Setting *MissingSchemaAction* to *Ignore* causes the *SqlDataAdapter* to ignore tables and columns that do not appear in the *DataSet*, and setting the property to *Error* will generate an exception in the same scenario, just as the *MissingMappingAction* property does.

Setting *MissingSchemaAction* to *AddWithKey* will add the missing tables and columns to the *DataSet* but will also add key information for the table. This behavior is similar to calling the *FillSchema* method of the *SqlDataAdapter*, a feature we'll cover shortly.

AcceptChangesDuringFill and *AcceptChangesDuringUpdate* Properties

When I worked as a support engineer helping developers who were having problems using ADO, I was amazed at how many developers were trying to use ADO as some sort of data synchronization tool. They would query one database and then point their *Recordset* at a different database and call *Update*, expecting that ADO would synchronize the tables in the two databases. ADO could not do that. ADO.NET can . . . sort of.

The *SqlDataAdapter* class has an *AcceptChangesDuringFill* property that accepts a Boolean value. This property, which is set to *True* by default, controls the *RowState* of the rows retrieved by the *SqlDataAdapter*. If the property is set to *True*, the new *DataRow* objects will each have a *RowState* of *Unchanged*. Setting *AcceptChangesDuringFill* to *False* causes the new *DataRow* objects to have a *RowState* of *Added*.

This means that if you set *AcceptChangesDuringFill* to *False*, you can query a table in one data-base, pass the *DataSet* to a *SqlDataAdapter* that's set to communicate with another database, and then insert all the newly retrieved rows into this other database.

The *AcceptChangesDuringUpdate* property is somewhat similar. When you submit a pending change in a *DataRow* by calling *SqlDataAdapter.Update*, a process we'll cover in detail in Chapter 10, the *SqlDataAdapter* implicitly calls *AcceptChanges* on the *DataRow*. This process marks the *DataRow* as *Unchanged*, indicating that the *DataRow* no longer contains pending changes. If you don't want the *SqlDataAdapter* to call *AcceptChanges* after submitting pending changes, set *AcceptChangesDuringUpdate* to *False*.

ContinueUpdateOnError Property

If you use a *SqlDataAdapter* to submit updates to your database, you're relying on optimistic updating. If you fetch the contents of a row, modify that row in your *DataSet*, and then submit the pending change to the database using a *SqlDataAdapter*, your update attempt might fail if another user has already changed the contents of the same row in your database. Don't worry; we'll discuss this functionality in depth in Chapter 10 and Chapter 11. For now, just know that when you're optimistic, things don't always work out the way you'd like.

The *SqlDataAdapter* class's *ContinueUpdateOnError* property controls how the *SqlDataAdapter* reacts when it detects that an attempt to submit the pending changes stored in a *DataRow* fails. By default, this property is set to *False*, which means that the *SqlDataAdapter* will stop when it encounters a failed update attempt. If you want the *SqlDataAdapter* to continue under such circumstances and try to submit the changes stored in the remaining pending *DataRows*, set this property to *True*.

Why would you want the *SqlDataAdapter* to stop when it encounters a failed update attempt? Imagine that the pending changes in your *DataSet* represent an order and the customer does not want to submit a partial order. It's an all-or-nothing proposition. So you start a transaction before submitting the changes, and if one update fails, you roll back the transaction. Under these circumstances, there's no reason to attempt to submit the rest of the changes if, while submitting changes for a prior row, an error occurs.

ReturnProviderSpecificTypes Property

By default, the *SqlDataAdapter* will store the results of your query in a *DataSet* or *DataTable* using basic .NET data types—*String*, *DateTime*, and so on. If you want to store the results using *SqlTypes*—*SqlString*, *SqlDateTime*, and so on—set the *SqlDataAdapter* object's *ReturnProvider-SpecificTypes* property to *True*.

FillLoadOption Property

The *FillLoadOption* property controls how a *DataTable* will handle query results that match a row that already exists in the *DataTable*. The property accepts a value from the *LoadOption* enumeration and defaults to *OverwriteChanges*. As its name implies, this value will cause the *DataTable* to overwrite any changes currently stored in the *DataRow*. The *DataTable* will write values retrieved by the *SqlDataAdapter* into both the "current" and "original" values in the corresponding *DataRow*. Setting the *FillLoadOption* property to *PreserveChanges* will preserve the current changes in the *DataRow*, writing values retrieved by the *SqlDataAdapter* into only the "original" values in the corresponding *DataRow*.

The *Upsert* option might be familiar for those who have worked with SQL Server's SQLXML features. The term *upsert* is a combination of *update* and *insert*, and it loosely translates to, "If the row exists, treat this action as an update; otherwise, treat it as an insert." If you set the *FillLoadOption* to *Upsert*, it will assign values retrieved by the *SqlDataAdapter* to the "current" values in *DataRows* that already exist. If no corresponding *DataRow* already exists in the *DataTable*, the new row will be marked as a pending insert.

UpdateBatchSize Property

By default, the *SqlDataAdapter* submits pending changes to your SQL Server database one *DataRow* at a time. ADO.NET 2.0 allows you to submit multiple rows at a time. To enable batch updating, set the *UpdateBatchSize* property to the desired batch size. This property is set to *1* by default.

We'll discuss submitting pending changes to your SQL Server database in more detail in Chapters 10 and 11.

Methods of the *SqlDataAdapter* Class

The *SqlDataAdapter* has many properties, but it has just four methods, as described in Table 5-2.

Table 5-2   Methods of the *SqlDataAdapter* Class

Method	Description
Fill	Executes the query stored in the *SelectCommand* and stores the results in a *DataTable*.
FillSchema	Retrieves schema information for the query stored in the *SelectCommand*.
GetFillParameters	Returns an array containing the parameters for the *SelectCommand*.
Update	Submits changes stored in your *DataSet* (or *DataTable* or *DataRows*) to your database.

Fill Method

Calling the *Fill* method on a *SqlDataAdapter* executes the query stored in the *SqlDataAdapter* object's *SelectCommand* property and stores the results in a *DataTable* in your *DataSet*. The *Fill* method also returns a 32-bit integer that indicates the number of rows the *SqlDataAdapter* retrieved.

This sample code shows how to use the *Fill* method:

Visual Basic
```
Dim strConn, strSQL As String
strConn = "Data Source=.\SQLExpress;" & _
          "Initial Catalog=Northwind;Integrated Security=True;"
strSQL = "SELECT CustomerID, CompanyName FROM Customers"
Dim da As New SqlDataAdapter(strSQL, strConn)
Dim ds As New DataSet()
Dim intRowsRetrieved As Integer = da.Fill(ds)
Console.WriteLine("{0} row(s) retrieved", intRowsRetrieved)
For Each row As DataRow In ds.Tables(0).Rows
    Console.WriteLine("{0} - {1}", row("CustomerID"), _
                      row("CompanyName"))
Next row
```

Visual C#
```
string strConn, strSQL;
strConn = @"Data Source=.\SQLExpress;" +
          "Initial Catalog=Northwind;Integrated Security=True;";
strSQL = "SELECT CustomerID, CompanyName FROM Customers";
SqlDataAdapter da = new SqlDataAdapter(strSQL, strConn);
DataSet ds = new DataSet();
int intRowsRetrieved = da.Fill(ds);
Console.WriteLine("{0} row(s) retrieved", intRowsRetrieved);
foreach (DataRow row in ds.Tables[0].Rows)
    Console.WriteLine("{0} - {1}", row["CustomerID"],
                      row["CompanyName"]);
```

The *SqlDataAdapter* examines the contents of its *TableMappings* collection to determine which *DataTable* and *DataColumn* object or objects to use in the *DataSet* you supply. If the *SqlData-Adapter* does not find the expected schema information in its *TableMappings* collection or within the *DataSet*, it checks its *MissingMappingAction* and *MissingSchemaAction* properties to determine how to react.

The *SqlDataAdapter* class's *Fill* method is overloaded. You can supply a *DataTable* rather than a *DataSet*, or you can supply a *DataSet* and a string for the name of the *DataTable* you want to populate or create, as shown here:

Visual Basic

```
Dim strConn, strSQL As String
strConn = "Data Source=.\SQLExpress;" & _
        "Initial Catalog=Northwind;Integrated Security=True;"
strSQL = "SELECT CustomerID, CompanyName FROM Customers"
Dim da As New SqlDataAdapter(strSQL, strConn)
Dim ds As New DataSet()
Dim intRowsRetrieved As Integer
intRowsRetrieved = da.Fill(ds, "Customers")
Console.WriteLine("{0} row(s) retrieved", intRowsRetrieved)
For Each row As DataRow In ds.Tables("Customers").Rows
    Console.WriteLine("{0} - {1}", row("CustomerID"), _
                        row("CompanyName"))
Next row
```

Visual C#

```
string strConn, strSQL;
strConn = @"Data Source=.\SQLExpress;" +
            "Initial Catalog=Northwind;Integrated Security=True;";
strSQL = "SELECT CustomerID, CompanyName FROM Customers";
SqlDataAdapter da = new SqlDataAdapter(strSQL, strConn);
DataSet ds = new DataSet();
int intRowsRetrieved;
intRowsRetrieved = da.Fill(ds, "Customers");
Console.WriteLine("{0} row(s) retrieved", intRowsRetrieved);
foreach (DataRow row in ds.Tables["Customers"].Rows)
    Console.WriteLine("{0} - {1}", row["CustomerID"],
                        row["CompanyName"]);
```

The *SqlDataAdapter* also has a *Fill* method overload that can come in handy if you're building a Web application that has to support paging. Let's say you want to allow users to view the contents of your product catalog 10 items at a time. You can supply a starting row number and the number of rows to retrieve in the *SqlDataAdapter* object's *Fill* method:

Visual Basic

```
Dim strConn, strSQL As String
strConn = "Data Source=.\SQLExpress;" & _
        "Initial Catalog=Northwind;Integrated Security=True;"
strSQL = "SELECT CustomerID, CompanyName FROM Customers"
Dim da As New SqlDataAdapter(strSQL, strConn)
Dim ds As New DataSet()
Dim intStartingRow As Integer = 10
Dim intRowsToRetrieve As Integer = 10
```

```
Dim intRowsRetrieved As Integer
intRowsRetrieved = da.Fill(ds, intStartingRow, _
                        intRowsToRetrieve, "Customers")
Console.WriteLine("{0} row(s) retrieved", intRowsRetrieved)
For Each row As DataRow In ds.Tables("Customers").Rows
    Console.WriteLine("{0} - {1}", row("CustomerID"), _
                    row("CompanyName"))
Next row
```

Visual C#

```
string strConn, strSQL;
strConn = @"Data Source=.\SQLExpress;" +
            "Initial Catalog=Northwind;Integrated Security=True;";
strSQL = "SELECT CustomerID, CompanyName FROM Customers";
SqlDataAdapter da = new SqlDataAdapter(strSQL, strConn);
DataSet ds = new DataSet();
int intStartingRow = 10;
int intRowsToRetrieve = 10;
int intRowsRetrieved = da.Fill(ds, intStartingRow,
                            intRowsToRetrieve, "Customers");
Console.WriteLine("{0} row(s) retrieved", intRowsRetrieved);
foreach (DataRow row in ds.Tables["Customers"].Rows)
    Console.WriteLine("{0} - {1}", row["CustomerID"],
                    row["CompanyName"]);
```

The *SqlDataAdapter* submits the query, and if you say that you want to start fetching at row 10 (as shown in the example), the *SqlDataAdapter* will simply discard the first 10 rows. The *SqlDataAdapter* will then fetch the number of rows you've requested. If the query (ignoring the discarded rows) does not contain the number of rows you've requested, the *SqlData-Adapter* will simply fetch all remaining rows without throwing an exception.

Is this the best way to break up the results of a query into pages? No. Let's say your query returns 100 rows and you break it up into 10 pages of 10 rows each. When you fetch the first page, you simply fetch the first 10 rows. When you fetch the second page, you discard the first 10 rows and fetch the second set of 10 rows. Keep in mind that the database returns 20 rows in order for you to fetch the second page. When you fetch the tenth page, the database has to return all 100 rows. The *SqlDataAdapter* simply discards the first 90. If that sounds inefficient, that's because it is. So why does the *SqlDataAdapter* support this feature? Because it's simple.

A more complex but much more efficient way to achieve the same functionality is to store the key value or values for the last row from the previous page. Say you fetch the first set of 10 rows using the following query:

```
SELECT TOP 10 CustomerID, CompanyName, ContactName, Phone
        FROM Customers ORDER BY CustomerID
```

If the tenth customer has a CustomerID of "BSBEV", the following query retrieves the next 10 rows:

```
SELECT TOP 10 CustomerID, CompanyName, ContactName, Phone
        FROM Customers ORDER BY CustomerID
        WHERE CustomerID > "BSBEV"
```

Using this type of architecture will improve the performance of your database because it will fetch fewer rows. Your data access code will run faster because it won't need to discard an initial set of rows to get to the desired rows and because the database will perform better.

FillSchema Method

The *FillSchema* method lets you retrieve schema information about your query before executing it. Like the *Fill* method, the *FillSchema* method retrieves names and data types for each of the columns in your query. *FillSchema* also retrieves information on whether a column can accept *Null* values and sets the *AllowDBNull* property of the *DataColumn* objects it creates accordingly.

When you call *FillSchema*, the *SqlDataAdapter* looks for a primary key or unique index in the available resultset. If it finds one, the *DataTable*'s *PrimaryKey* property is set to that *Data-Column* or array of *DataColumns*.

Using the *FillSchema* method is rather straightforward and will remind you of the *Fill* method, with one slight difference. As with the *Fill* method, you can supply a *DataSet*, a *DataSet* and table name, or a *DataTable*. The slight difference is that the *FillSchema* method adds a parameter to let you control whether to retrieve schema information straight from the data source or apply the *SqlDataAdapter* object's *TableMappings* to the schema information the *SqlData-Adapter* retrieves.

You can specify either value from the *SchemaType* enumeration in *System.Data—Source* or *Mapped*. If you specify *Source*, the *SqlDataAdapter* will generate schema information using just the column names retrieved from the data source. Specifying *Mapped* will force the *SqlData-Adapter* to apply the contents of its *TableMappings* collection, the same way the *SqlData-Adapter* maps the columns when you call the *Fill* method. Here are examples of all three ways to call *FillSchema*:

Visual Basic

```
Dim strConn, strSQL As String
strConn = "Data Source=.\SQLExpress;" & _
        "Initial Catalog=Northwind;Integrated Security=True;"
strSQL = "SELECT CustomerID, CompanyName FROM Customers"
Dim da As New SqlDataAdapter(strSQL, strConn)
Dim ds As New DataSet()

'Supply a DataSet and a SchemaType.
da.FillSchema(ds, SchemaType.Source)
'Returns no rows but creates a DataTable named "Table"
'and creates DataColumns for each column returned by the query
Console.WriteLine("Table Name: {0}", ds.Tables(0).TableName)
Console.WriteLine("Returned {0} rows", ds.Tables(0).Rows.Count)
For Each col As DataColumn In ds.Tables(0).Columns
    Console.WriteLine("Column Name: {0}", col.ColumnName)
Next col

'Supply a DataSet, a SchemaType, and a table name.
da.FillSchema(ds, SchemaType.Source, "Customers")
```

```
'Creates the same column names
'but the new DataTable will have a TableName of "Customers"
Console.WriteLine("Table Name: {0}", ds.Tables(0).TableName)

Dim tbl As New DataTable()
'Supply a DataTable and a SchemaType.
da.FillSchema(tbl, SchemaType.Source)
'Returns the same schema as the first FillSchema call
```

Visual C#

```
string strConn, strSQL;
strConn = @"Data Source=.\SQLExpress;" +
            "Initial Catalog=Northwind;Integrated Security=True;";
strSQL = "SELECT CustomerID, CompanyName FROM Customers";
SqlDataAdapter da = new SqlDataAdapter(strSQL, strConn);
DataSet ds = new DataSet();

//Supply a DataSet and a SchemaType.
da.FillSchema(ds, SchemaType.Source);
//Returns no rows but creates a DataTable named "Table"
//and creates DataColumns for each column returned by the query
Console.WriteLine("Table Name: {0}", ds.Tables[0].TableName);
Console.WriteLine("Returned {0} rows", ds.Tables[0].Rows.Count);
foreach (DataColumn col in ds.Tables[0].Columns)
    Console.WriteLine("Column Name: {0}", col.ColumnName);

//Supply a DataSet, a SchemaType, and a table name.
da.FillSchema(ds, SchemaType.Source, "Customers");
//Creates the same column names
//but the new DataTable will have a TableName of "Customers"
Console.WriteLine("Table Name: {0}", ds.Tables[0].TableName);

DataTable tbl = new DataTable();
//Supply a DataTable and a SchemaType.
da.FillSchema(tbl, SchemaType.Source);
//Returns the same schema as the first FillSchema call
```

The *FillSchema* method returns an array of *DataTable* objects that contains the *DataTable* objects that the *FillSchema* method populated.

You can call the *FillSchema* method and reference a *DataTable* that already exists. In this scenario, the *SqlDataAdapter* will not overwrite the columns that already appear in the *DataTable* but will add new columns if the columns that the query returns do not already appear in the *DataTable*.

GetFillParameters Method

The *GetFillParameters* method acts as a shortcut to the *Parameters* collection of the *SqlData-Adapter* object's *SelectCommand*, with one minor difference. *GetFillParameters* returns the parameter information as an array of *IParameter* objects rather than the *Parameter* type for the specific .NET Data Provider (such as *OleDbParameter* or *SqlParameter*). Unless you need to check or set the parameters' size, precision, or scale properties, you'll be able to access your parameters using the *GetFillParameters* method, as shown here:

Visual Basic

```vb
Dim strConn, strSQL As String
strConn = "Data Source=.\SQLExpress;" & _
          "Initial Catalog=Northwind;Integrated Security=True;"
strSQL = "SELECT CustomerID, CompanyName FROM Customers " & _
          "WHERE CustomerID LIKE @CustomerID"
Dim da As New SqlDataAdapter(strSQL, strConn)
da.SelectCommand.Parameters.Append("@CustomerID", _
                                   SqlDbType.NVarChar, 10)
da.GetFillParameters(0).Value = "A%"
Dim ds As New DataSet()
da.Fill(ds)

'Display the results
For Each row As DataRow In ds.Tables(0).Rows
    Console.WriteLine("{0} - {1}", row("CustomerID"), _
                      row("CompanyName"))
Next row
```

Visual C#

```csharp
string strConn, strSQL;
strConn = @"Data Source=.\SQLExpress;" +
           "Initial Catalog=Northwind;Integrated Security=True;";
strSQL = "SELECT CustomerID, CompanyName FROM Customers " +
          "WHERE CustomerID LIKE @CustomerID";
SqlDataAdapter da = new SqlDataAdapter(strSQL, strConn);
da.SelectCommand.Parameters.Append("@CustomerID",
                                   SqlDbType.NVarChar, 10);
da.GetFillParameters[0].Value = "A%";
DataSet ds = new DataSet();
da.Fill(ds);

//Display the results
foreach (DataRow row in ds.Tables[0].Rows)
    Console.WriteLine("{0} - {1}", row["CustomerID"],
                      row["CompanyName"]);
```

For more information on the *SqlCommand* and *SqlParameter* classes, see Chapter 4.

Update Method

To submit the pending changes stored in a *DataTable* or *DataSet* to your data store, you use the *SqlDataAdapter* class's *Update* method.

As with the *Fill* and *FillSchema* methods, you can pass a *DataSet*, a *DataSet* and table name, or a *DataTable* to the *Update* method. The *Update* method offers another overloaded method–you can also pass an array of *DataRow* objects to the *Update* method. This option can come in handy if you want to pass a subset of rows in a table based on a filter or a relation.

The *Update* method returns an integer that indicates the number of rows you successfully updated in your data store. We'll discuss how the *Update* method submits changes to your data store in detail in Chapter 10. You can use any of the following overloads:

```
SqlDataAdapter.Update(DataSet)
SqlDataAdapter.Update(DataSet, "TableName")
SqlDataAdapter.Update(DataTable)
SqlDataAdapter.Update(DataRowArray)
```

Events of the *SqlDataAdapter* Class

The *SqlDataAdapter* class offers only three events, all of which are listed in Table 5-3.

Table 5-3   Events of the *SqlDataAdapter* Class

Event	Description
FillError	Fires when the *SqlDataAdapter* encounters an error filling your *DataSet* or *DataTable*
RowUpdating	Fires before submitting a modified row to your database
RowUpdated	Fires after submitting a modified row to your database

FillError Event

If the *SqlDataAdapter* encounters an error when filling your *DataSet* or *DataTable*, you might be able to trap for that error using the *FillError* event. The following code example fires the *FillError* event because the *SqlDataAdapter*'s *MissingSchemaAction* property is set to *Error* and one of the columns in the resultset (EmployeeID) does not appear in the *DataTable*:

Visual Basic

```
Dim strConn, strSQL As String
strConn = "Data Source=.\SQLExpress;" & _
          "Initial Catalog=Northwind;Integrated Security=True;"
strSQL = "SELECT OrderID, CustomerID, EmployeeID FROM Orders"
Dim da As New SqlDataAdapter(strSQL, strConn)
da.MissingSchemaAction = MissingSchemaAction.Error
AddHandler da.FillError, AddressOf da_FillError
Dim tbl As New DataTable("Orders")
tbl.Columns.Add("OrderID", GetType(Integer))
tbl.Columns.Add("CustomerID", GetType(String))
da.Fill(tbl)
...
Public Sub da_FillError(ByVal sender As Object, _
                        ByVal e As FillErrorEventArgs)
    Console.WriteLine(e.Errors.Message)
    e.Continue = True
End Sub
```

Visual C#

```
string strConn, strSQL;
strConn = @"Data Source=.\SQLExpress;" +
          "Initial Catalog=Northwind;Integrated Security=True;";
strSQL = "SELECT OrderID, CustomerID, EmployeeID FROM Orders";
```

```
SqlDataAdapter da = new SqlDataAdapter(strSQL, strConn);
da.MissingSchemaAction = MissingSchemaAction.Error;
da.FillError += new FillErrorEventHandler(da_FillError);
DataTable tbl = new DataTable("Orders");
tbl.Columns.Add("OrderID", typeof(int));
tbl.Columns.Add("CustomerID", typeof(string));
da.Fill(tbl);
...
static void da_FillError(object sender, FillErrorEventArgs e) {
    Console.WriteLine(e.Errors.Message);
    e.Continue = true;
}
```

As far as I can tell, you cannot use the *FillError* event to trap for situations where the data retrieved by the *SqlDataAdapter* violates a constraint in your *DataSet* or *DataTable*.

RowUpdating and *RowUpdated* Events

The *SqlDataAdapter* also fires events when submitting pending changes to your database via the *SqlDataAdapter.Update* method. If you want to examine the pending changes in your row prior to submitting the change, use the *SqlRowUpdating* event. If you want to execute code immediately after submitting a change, use the *SqlRowUpdated* event.

The following code sample demonstrates how to use both of the events:

Visual Basic

```
Dim strConn, strSQL As String
strConn = "Data Source=.\SQLExpress;" & _
          "Initial Catalog=Northwind;Integrated Security=True;"
strSQL = "SELECT TOP 1 OrderID, EmployeeID FROM Orders"
Dim da As New SqlDataAdapter(strSQL, strConn)
Dim cb As New SqlCommandBuilder(da)
AddHandler da.RowUpdated, AddressOf da_RowUpdated
AddHandler da.RowUpdating, AddressOf da_RowUpdating
Dim tbl As New DataTable("Orders")
da.Fill(tbl)
tbl.Rows(0)("EmployeeID") = CInt(tbl.Rows(0)("EmployeeID")) + 1
da.Update(tbl)
tbl.Rows(0)("EmployeeID") = CInt(tbl.Rows(0)("EmployeeID")) - 1
da.Update(tbl)
...
Public Sub da_RowUpdating(ByVal sender As Object, _
                          ByVal e As SqlRowUpdatingEventArgs)
    Console.WriteLine("RowUpdating Event: {0}", e.StatementType)
    Console.WriteLine("  OrderID: {0}", e.Row("OrderID"))
    Console.WriteLine("  EmployeeID from {0} to {1}", _
                e.Row("EmployeeID", DataRowVersion.Original), _
                e.Row("EmployeeID"))
    Console.WriteLine()
End Sub

Public Sub da_RowUpdated(ByVal sender As Object, _
                         ByVal e As SqlRowUpdatedEventArgs)
    Console.WriteLine("RowUpdated Event: {0}", e.StatementType)
```

```
        Console.WriteLine("  OrderID: {0}", e.Row("OrderID"))
        If e.Status = UpdateStatus.ErrorsOccurred Then
            Console.WriteLine("  Errors occurred")
        Else
            Console.WriteLine("  Success!")
        End If
        Console.WriteLine()
End Sub
```

Visual C#

```
string strConn, strSQL;
strConn = @"Data Source=.\SQLExpress;" +
          "Initial Catalog=Northwind;Integrated Security=True;";
strSQL = "SELECT TOP 1 OrderID, EmployeeID FROM Orders";
SqlDataAdapter da = new SqlDataAdapter(strSQL, strConn);
SqlCommandBuilder cb = new SqlCommandBuilder(da);
da.RowUpdated += new SqlRowUpdatedEventHandler(da_RowUpdated);
da.RowUpdating += new SqlRowUpdatingEventHandler(da_RowUpdating);
DataTable tbl = new DataTable("Orders");
da.Fill(tbl);
tbl.Rows[0]["EmployeeID"] = (int) tbl.Rows[0]["EmployeeID"] + 1;
da.Update(tbl);
tbl.Rows[0]["EmployeeID"] = (int) tbl.Rows[0]["EmployeeID"] - 1;
da.Update(tbl);
...
static void da_RowUpdating(object sender,
                          SqlRowUpdatingEventArgs e) {
    Console.WriteLine("RowUpdating Event: {0}", e.StatementType);
    Console.WriteLine("  OrderID: {0}", e.Row["OrderID"]);
    Console.WriteLine("  EmployeeID from {0} to {1}",
                e.Row["EmployeeID", DataRowVersion.Original],
                e.Row["EmployeeID"]);
    Console.WriteLine();
}

static void da_RowUpdated(object sender,
                          SqlRowUpdatedEventArgs e) {
    Console.WriteLine("RowUpdated Event: {0}", e.StatementType);
    Console.WriteLine("  OrderID: {0}", e.Row["OrderID"]);
    if (e.Status == UpdateStatus.ErrorsOccurred)
        Console.WriteLine("  Errors occurred");
    else
        Console.WriteLine("  Success!");
    Console.WriteLine();
}
```

With basic (nonbatched) updating, the *SqlDataAdapter* submits the changes to the database one row at a time. The *RowUpdating* event fires, the *SqlDataAdapter* submits the pending change, and then the *RowUpdated* event fires.

The behavior of these events changes slightly when using the *SqlDataAdapter*'s batch updating feature. Prior to submitting a batch of changes, the *SqlDataAdapter* fires the *RowUpdating* event for each pending row in the batch. The *SqlDataAdapter* submits the batch of changes and then fires the *RowUpdated* event *once*.

If you want to examine the rows that the *SqlDataAdapter* submitted through the *RowUpdated* event, you'll need to do a little more work. The *SqlRowUpdatedEventArgs* event argument can help. The *StatementType* property will return *Batch* if the *RowUpdated* event contains a batch of updates. Use the *RowCount* property to determine the number of changes submitted to SQL Server in the batch. Then use the *CopyToRows* method to access the individual rows, as shown in the following code sample:

Visual Basic

```
Dim strConn, strSQL As String
strConn = "Data Source=.\SQLExpress;" & _
          "Initial Catalog=Northwind;Integrated Security=True;"
strSQL = "SELECT OrderID, EmployeeID FROM Orders " & _
          "WHERE CustomerID = 'ALFKI'"
Dim da As New SqlDataAdapter(strSQL, strConn)
da.UpdateBatchSize = 10
Dim cb As New SqlCommandBuilder(da)
AddHandler da.RowUpdated, AddressOf da_RowUpdated
AddHandler da.RowUpdating, AddressOf da_RowUpdating
Dim tbl As New DataTable("Orders")
da.Fill(tbl)

For Each row As DataRow In tbl.Rows
    row("EmployeeID") = CInt(row("EmployeeID")) + 1
Next row
da.Update(tbl)

For Each row As DataRow In tbl.Rows
    row("EmployeeID") = CInt(row("EmployeeID")) - 1
Next row
da.Update(tbl)
...
Public Sub da_RowUpdating(ByVal sender As Object, _
                          ByVal e As SqlRowUpdatingEventArgs)
    Console.WriteLine("RowUpdating Event: {0}", e.StatementType)
    Console.WriteLine("  OrderID: {0}", e.Row("OrderID"))
    Console.WriteLine("  EmployeeID from {0} to {1}", _
                e.Row("EmployeeID", DataRowVersion.Original), _
                e.Row("EmployeeID"))
    Console.WriteLine()
End Sub

Public Sub da_RowUpdated(ByVal sender As Object, _
                         ByVal e As SqlRowUpdatedEventArgs)
    Console.WriteLine("RowUpdated Event: {0}", e.StatementType)
    Console.WriteLine("  Changes submitted: {0}", e.RowCount)
    Dim rows(e.RowCount - 1) As DataRow
    e.CopyToRows(rows)
    For Each row As DataRow in rows
        Console.WriteLine("    OrderID: {0}", row("OrderID"))
    Next row
    If e.Status = UpdateStatus.ErrorsOccurred Then
        Console.WriteLine("  Errors occurred")
    Else
```

```
        Console.WriteLine("  Success!")
    End If
    Console.WriteLine()
End Sub
```

Visual C#

```csharp
string strConn, strSQL;
strConn = @"Data Source=.\SQLExpress;" +
          "Initial Catalog=Northwind;Integrated Security=True;";
strSQL = "SELECT OrderID, EmployeeID FROM Orders " +
         "WHERE CustomerID = 'ALFKI'";
SqlDataAdapter da = new SqlDataAdapter(strSQL, strConn);
da.UpdateBatchSize = 10;
SqlCommandBuilder cb = new SqlCommandBuilder(da);
da.RowUpdated += new SqlRowUpdatedEventHandler(da_RowUpdated);
da.RowUpdating += new SqlRowUpdatingEventHandler(da_RowUpdating);
DataTable tbl = new DataTable("Orders");
da.Fill(tbl);

foreach (DataRow row in tbl.Rows)
    row["EmployeeID"] = (int) row["EmployeeID"] + 1;
da.Update(tbl);

foreach (DataRow row in tbl.Rows)
    row["EmployeeID"] = (int) row["EmployeeID"] - 1;
da.Update(tbl);
...
static void da_RowUpdating(object sender,
                           SqlRowUpdatingEventArgs e) {
    Console.WriteLine("RowUpdating Event: {0}", e.StatementType);
    Console.WriteLine("  OrderID: {0}", e.Row["OrderID"]);
    Console.WriteLine("  EmployeeID from {0} to {1}",
                e.Row["EmployeeID", DataRowVersion.Original],
                e.Row["EmployeeID"]);
    Console.WriteLine();
}

static void da_RowUpdated(object sender,
                          SqlRowUpdatedEventArgs e) {
    Console.WriteLine("RowUpdated Event: {0}", e.StatementType);
    Console.WriteLine("  Changes submitted: {0}", e.RowCount);
    DataRow[] rows = new DataRow[e.RowCount];
    e.CopyToRows(rows);
    foreach (DataRow row in rows)
        Console.WriteLine("    OrderID: {0}", row["OrderID"]);
    if (e.Status == UpdateStatus.ErrorsOccurred)
        Console.WriteLine("  Errors occurred");
    else
        Console.WriteLine("  Success!");
    Console.WriteLine();
}
```

Questions That Should Be Asked More Frequently

Q   Of my three options for creating *DataTable* objects, which should I use?

- Creating them using code before populating them using a *SqlDataAdapter*

- Creating them implicitly by calling *SqlDataAdapter.Fill*

- Creating them by calling *SqlDataAdapter.FillSchema*

A   I strongly recommend the first option. As of this writing, creating tables using code is about 20 times faster than calling the *FillSchema* method of the *SqlDataAdapter*.

Q   I created my *DataTable* objects in code, as you recommended, but now the code that fills my *DataTable* objects runs much more slowly. Why is that?

A   I'm so glad you asked. You'll see this slowdown if your *DataTable* objects have constraints. As you retrieve data from your data store and add rows to your *DataTable* objects, ADO.NET will validate each new row based on these constraints. Also, constraints (such as primary keys and unique constraints) require ADO.NET to examine your *DataTable* to ensure that each new row you create does not violate these constraints. This means that you will pay a greater performance penalty as you add more rows to the *DataTable*.

Generally speaking, the constraints you create in your *DataTable* objects also exist in your database. Assuming that's the case, your database has already validated the data that you're going to pull into your *DataTable* objects. There's no reason to validate the data again. Is there some sort of middle ground that lets you create constraints on your *DataTable* objects but not pay the performance penalty that comes with validating the data you retrieve using *DataAdapter.Fill*?

You could build your *DataTable* objects without constraints, populate them using *SqlDataAdapter.Fill*, and *then* add your constraints, but that's an inelegant solution at best.

Ah, but the ADO.NET development team anticipated this scenario and provided a more elegant solution. The *DataSet* class has an *EnforceConstraints* property. By default, it's set to *True*, which means that ADO.NET will enforce the constraints in the *DataSet*. However, you can set this property to *False* just before you call the *Fill* method on your *SqlDataAdapter* objects and then set the property back to *True*, as shown here:

Visual Basic

```
Dim ds As DataSet
Dim da1, da2 As SqlDataAdapter
...
ds.EnforceConstraints = False
da1.Fill(ds.Tables("Table1"))
da2.Fill(ds.Tables("Table2"))
ds.EnforceConstraints = True
```

Visual C#

```
DataSet ds;
SqlDataAdapter da1, da2;
...
ds.EnforceConstraints = false;
da1.Fill(ds.Tables["Table1"]);
da2.Fill(ds.Tables["Table2"]);
ds.EnforceConstraints = true;
```

Now the *Fill* method will retrieve data as quickly as if you had no constraints on your *Data-Table* objects.

Part III
Working with Data Offline—
The ADO.NET *DataSet*

Chapter 6
Working with *DataSet* Objects

In the previous three chapters, I explained the basic functionality of the connected classes in the ADO.NET object model, which compose a .NET data provider. Now it's time to discuss the disconnected half—the classes that ADO.NET uses to provide a feature-rich, relational, disconnected data cache. In this chapter, I'll discuss the basics of storing data in the *DataSet* class and many of the classes that reside in a *DataSet* object.

This chapter briefly addresses the major features of the *DataSet* and then focuses on examples of how you could use a *DataSet* object. Along the way, the chapter introduces other classes (*DataTable, DataRow, DataColumn, DataRelation, UniqueConstraint,* and *ForeignKeyConstraint*) when the scenarios presented require use of those classes. As a result of the number of classes I discuss, this is a large chapter. Here is a list of the major *DataSet* scenarios the chapter will explore before discussing how to create *DataSet* objects using Microsoft Visual Studio and presenting the reference information for the classes discussed:

- Creating a *DataSet* Object
- Examining the Structure Created by Calling *SqlDataAdapter.Fill*
- Examining the Data Returned by a *SqlDataAdapter*
- Validating Data in Your *DataSet*
- Creating *DataTable* Objects in Code
- Modifying the Contents of a *DataTable*
- ADO.NET 2.0 *DataSet* Serialization and Remoting Options

Features of the *DataSet* Class

At its core, a *DataSet* object is a set of data. When developers picture the results returned by a query, they generally picture data in a grid, much like a Microsoft Office Excel spreadsheet.

You can use a *DataSet* to store the results of a query, but a *DataSet* more closely resembles an Excel workbook because it can hold the results of multiple queries.

But the ADO.NET object model already lets you examine the results of a query through the *SqlDataReader* class. Why would you need another class?

In Chapter 4, you learned about the *SqlDataReader*, which is a fast and efficient structure that lets you retrieve the results of a query. The *SqlDataReader* is built for speed because it supports very limited functionality. The data in the *SqlDataReader* is read-only, and once you've moved on to read the next row, there's no going back to reexamine previous rows.

The *DataSet* class provides much more powerful functionality. Let's look at some features available through the *DataSet* class.

Working with Disconnected Data

The data in your *DataSet* is disconnected from your database. Once you fetch the results of a query and store those results in a *DataSet* using a *SqlDataAdapter* object, there is no longer a connection between your *DataSet* and your database. Changes you make to the contents of the *DataSet* will not directly affect your database. If other users modify data in your database that corresponds to the data in your *DataSet*, you will not see those changes in your *DataSet*.

Working with disconnected data structures definitely has its benefits. The primary benefit of working with disconnected data is that it does not require a live connection to your database. Once you've fetched the results of your query and put them into a *DataSet* object, you can close the connection to your database and continue to work with the data in your *DataSet*.

Disconnected data structures such as *DataSets* are also helpful when you build multitiered applications. If your application uses business objects running on a middle-tier server to access your database, your business object needs to pass disconnected data structures to your client application. The *DataSet* class is designed for use in such situations. You can pass the contents of a *DataSet* from one component to another. The component that receives the data can work with the information as a *DataSet* (if the component is built using the Microsoft .NET Framework) or as an XML document.

Scrolling, Sorting, Searching, and Filtering

The *DataSet* class lets you examine the contents of any row in your *DataSet* at any time. You can loop back and forth through the results of your query as often as you like. This makes *DataSet* objects ideal for scenarios in which your code needs to loop through data, such as in reporting routines, or in which a user needs to scroll back and forth through the results of a query.

DataSet objects also let you change the way you view the results of queries. You can sort the data in a *DataSet* based on a column or a series of columns. You can search for a row of data based on simple search criteria. You can also apply a filter to the data in your *DataSet* so that only rows that satisfy the desired criteria are visible. We'll examine these features in more depth in Chapter 8.

Working with Hierarchical Data

DataSet objects are designed to work with hierarchical data. In Chapter 2, we used various features of Visual Studio to build a simple Windows application that let us retrieve information from two tables—customers and orders. When you ran the application, the form let you scroll through the customer data. As you moved from one customer to the next, the form displayed only the orders for the current customer.

The *DataSet* class lets you define relationships between the tables of data stored in the *DataSet*. Visual Studio automatically built this relationship for us based on a foreign key constraint defined between the two tables in the database. The *DataGridView* control was configured to use the relationship in the *DataSet* to show only the orders for the current customer. (We'll take a closer look at the *DataRelation* class in the next chapter.)

Caching Changes

Working with read-only data is easy. One of the bigger challenges in building a database application is to transform the user's input into changes to the contents of your database. Building such logic into a multitiered application can present an even greater challenge if your application needs to cache changes and submit them to your database all at once.

The *DataSet* class lets you cache changes to a row of data so that you can submit the changes to your database using a *SqlDataAdapter*. You can also examine modified rows in your *DataSet* to determine how the row has changed (has the row been inserted, modified, or deleted?) as well as to compare both the original and current values for each row.

In this chapter, you'll learn about modifying the contents of a *DataSet*. I'll discuss submitting pending changes to your database using the *SqlDataAdapter* class in Chapter 10 and Chapter 11.

XML Integration

The ADO.NET *DataSet* was built from the ground up to work with XML. You can save and load the contents of a *DataSet* to and from files as XML documents. The *DataSet* also lets you separate the schema information (table, column, and constraint information) into an XML schema file.

In ADO.NET, *DataSet* objects and XML documents are almost interchangeable. It's easy to move from one data structure to the other. This duality allows developers to use the interfaces with which they're most comfortable. XML programmers can work with *DataSet* objects as XML documents, and database programmers can work with XML documents as *DataSet* objects.

We'll take a closer look at the *DataSet* class's XML features in Chapter 12.

Uniform Functionality

Developers who have worked with ADO might be aware that the *Recordset* class has features similar to those of the *DataSet*. The ADO *Recordset* class supports features such as filtering, searching, sorting, and caching updates. However, the manner in which you open a *Recordset* plays a large part in determining what functionality is available in the *Recordset*.

For example, if you use just the default settings to create ADO *Recordset* and *Connection* objects, you cannot get an accurate count of the number of rows in the *Recordset*. The *Recordset* class has a *Supports* method that developers often use to determine the functionality available. You can use the *Supports* method in code to answer such questions as: Can I modify the contents of the *Recordset*? If I update a row, will the *Recordset* send the change to the database immediately or will it be cached? Can I bind my *Recordset* to a grid? Can I move to the previous row?

The reason that not all *Recordset* objects support the same functionality is that the *Recordset* class tries to be everything to everyone. Whether you're working with a firehose cursor, a server-side cursor, or disconnected data in ADO, you're using a *Recordset* object.

The ADO.NET *DataSet* class does not require such integration because it's designed strictly for disconnected data. As a result, ADO.NET developers will never have to post questions to a forum asking, "Why is the *RecordCount* for my *Recordset* −1?" or "What does 'The rowset is not bookmarkable' mean?"

Using *DataSet* Objects

In some ways, the *DataSet* and its related classes resemble matryoshka—those nested wooden Russian dolls. A *DataSet* contains *DataTable* objects and *DataRelation* objects. A *DataTable* contains *DataRow*, *DataColumn*, and *Constraint* objects. Each of these classes resides in the *System.Data* namespace.

Rather than try to explain how each class is used one at a time, I will illustrate the basic functionality of the *DataSet* in this chapter by working through simple examples. Along the way, you'll learn a little about each of the other classes I've just mentioned.

Creating a *DataSet* Object

Instantiating a *DataSet* object in code is straightforward. You simply use the *New* keyword in your language of choice. The *DataSet* class has one optional constructor that you can use to set the *DataSetName* property of the *DataSet*:

Visual Basic

```
Dim ds As New DataSet("DataSetName")
Console.WriteLine(ds.DataSetName)
```

Visual C#

```
DataSet ds = new DataSet("DataSetName");
Console.WriteLine(ds.DataSetName);
```

Examining the Structure Created by Calling *SqlDataAdapter.Fill*

In Chapter 5, you learned how to fetch the results of a query and put them into a *DataSet* using the *SqlDataAdapter* class's *Fill* method, as shown here:

Visual Basic

```
Dim strConn, strSQL As String
strConn = "Data Source=.\SQLExpress;" & _
        "Initial Catalog=Northwind;Integrated Security=True;"
strSQL = "SELECT CustomerID, CompanyName FROM Customers"
Dim da As New SqlDataAdapter(strSQL, strConn)
Dim ds As New DataSet()
da.Fill(ds, "Customers")
```

Visual C#

```
string strConn, strSQL;
strConn = @"Data Source=.\SQLExpress;" +
            "Initial Catalog=Northwind;Integrated Security=True;";
strSQL = "SELECT CustomerID, CompanyName FROM Customers";
SqlDataAdapter da = new SqlDataAdapter(strSQL, strConn);
DataSet ds = new DataSet();
da.Fill(ds, "Customers");
```

Before we examine the results of the query, let's take a quick look at the structure that the *SqlDataAdapter* created to store those results.

DataTable Objects

The *SqlDataAdapter* stores the results of your query in a *DataTable*, an object similar to the *SqlDataReader* object we discussed in Chapter 4. You can use either object to examine the results of a query. Each object exposes the results as a collection of rows and columns.

As you might recall, the *SqlDataReader* is tuned for performance. It lets you tear through the results of your query quickly but offers little functionality beyond that. You already know that you can't modify the data in the *SqlDataReader* and that you can't move back to a previous row. The *DataTable* class is designed for more durable data and thus provides more robust functionality than the *SqlDataAdapter*. You can modify, sort, and filter the data in a *DataTable*– features not available through the *SqlDataReader*.

To handle this more durable data, the *DataTable* exposes a more durable structure for the data it contains. Each *DataTable* object has a *Columns* property that returns a collection of *DataColumn* objects. Each *DataColumn* corresponds to a column in the results of your query.

This structure will be familiar to programmers with DAO and ADO experience because the *Recordset* classes in DAO and ADO each have a *Fields* property that returns a collection of *Field* objects.

DataColumn Objects

Simply put, *DataColumn* objects define the schema for your *DataTable*. When you use the *SqlDataAdapter* class's *Fill* method to create a new *DataTable*, the *SqlDataAdapter* also creates a *DataColumn* object for each column in the results of your query. The new *DataColumn* objects that the *SqlDataAdapter* creates will have only their most basic properties set—*Name*, *Ordinal*, and *DataType*.

Here's a quick sample that displays basic information about the *DataColumn* objects created by calling *SqlDataAdapter.Fill*:

Visual Basic
```
Dim strConn, strSQL As String
strConn = "Data Source=.\SQLExpress;" & _
          "Initial Catalog=Northwind;Integrated Security=True;"
strSQL = "SELECT OrderID, CustomerID FROM Orders"
Dim da As New SqlDataAdapter(strSQL, strConn)
Dim ds As New DataSet()
da.Fill(ds, "Orders")

For Each col As DataColumn In ds.Tables("Orders").Columns
    Console.WriteLine("{0} - {1}", col.ColumnName, col.DataType)
Next col
```

Visual C#
```
string strConn, strSQL;
strConn = @"Data Source=.\SQLExpress;" +
           "Initial Catalog=Northwind;Integrated Security=True;";
strSQL = "SELECT OrderID, CustomerID FROM Orders";
SqlDataAdapter da = new SqlDataAdapter(strSQL, strConn);
DataSet ds = new DataSet();
da.Fill(ds, "Orders");

foreach (DataColumn col in ds.Tables["Orders"].Columns)
    Console.WriteLine("{0} - {1}", col.ColumnName, col.DataType);
```

There's a lot more information available in a *DataColumn* object than name and data type. But for now, we'll take a quick break from *DataColumn* objects and learn how to examine the data that the *SqlDataAdapter* placed in our new *DataTable*.

Examining the Data Returned by a *SqlDataAdapter*

At this point, the *DataTable* takes a sharp right turn from previous data access object models. The *Recordset* classes in both ADO and DAO, RDO's *rdoResultset* class, and ADO .NET's *SqlDataReader* all support the concept of a "current row" of data. Each class lets you examine the results of your query one row at a time. The *Recordset* and *rdoResultset* classes let you control the currently available row using methods such as *MoveFirst*, *MovePrevious*, *MoveNext*, and *MoveLast*.

The ADO.NET *DataTable* class takes a different approach that is more in line with XML documents, in which you can access any node in the tree at any given time. With the *DataTable*, all rows are available all the time—24 hours a day, 7 days a week, 365 (and change) days a year, and...well, you get the general idea.

The *DataTable* class exposes a *Rows* property that returns the collection of *DataRow* objects available in your *DataTable*. Now let's look at how you can use *DataRow* objects to examine the results of your query.

DataRow Objects

The *DataRow* class lets you examine and modify the contents of a row in your *DataTable*. To access the *DataRow* object for a particular row in the *DataTable*, you use the *DataTable* class's *Rows* property. This property returns a *DataRowCollection* object that contains a collection of *DataRow* objects. Like most collection classes, the *DataRowCollection* class lets you specify an integer to indicate the item you want to access.

The following code snippet uses the *SqlDataAdapter* class's *Fill* method to fetch the results of a query and put them into a new *DataTable* object. The code then accesses the first row returned and displays the contents of two of the columns in the row.

Visual Basic
```
Dim strConn, strSQL As String
strConn = "Data Source=.\SQLExpress;" & _
        "Initial Catalog=Northwind;Integrated Security=True;"
strSQL = "SELECT OrderID, CustomerID FROM Orders"
Dim da As New SqlDataAdapter(strSQL, strConn)
Dim ds As New DataSet()
da.Fill(ds, "Orders")

Dim row As DataRow = ds.Tables("Orders").Rows(0)
Console.WriteLine("OrderID = {0}", row("OrderID"))
Console.WriteLine("CustomerID = {0}", row("CustomerID"))
```

Visual C#
```
string strConn, strSQL;
strConn = @"Data Source=.\SQLExpress;" +
        "Initial Catalog=Northwind;Integrated Security=True;";
strSQL = "SELECT OrderID, CustomerID FROM Orders";
SqlDataAdapter da = new SqlDataAdapter(strSQL, strConn);
DataSet ds = new DataSet();
da.Fill(ds, "Orders");

DataRow row = ds.Tables["Orders"].Rows[0];
Console.WriteLine("OrderID = {0}", row["OrderID"]);
Console.WriteLine("CustomerID = {0}", row["CustomerID"]);
```

As you can see, once you've referenced a *DataRow* object in the *DataTable*, accessing the value of a particular column is similar to accessing data in a *SqlDataReader*. The *DataRow* class has a parameterized *Item* property that returns the contents of the specified column. You can supply a column name, as shown in the preceding code snippet, or an integer that represents the column's ordinal position in the *DataTable*. As with the *SqlDataReader*, using an index-based lookup will return data more quickly than a string-based lookup. I've used column names to make the code snippet easier to follow. You can use constants in your code to achieve both goals.

Examining the Data Stored in a *DataRow*

What if you want to write a more generic routine to display the contents of a *DataRow*? Let's say that you want to write a procedure that accepts a *DataRow* object and displays the column names and values contained in that *DataRow*.

If you were writing code using the *DataReader* class, you could check its *FieldCount* property to determine the number of columns. You could then use the *GetName* and *Item* properties to retrieve the name and value for each column. However, the *DataRow* does not have a counterpart to the *DataReader* class's *FieldCount* property.

Instead, the *DataRow* class exposes a *Table* property. This property returns the *DataTable* whose *DataRowCollection* contains the *DataRow*. You can use this property to get back to the *DataTable* to retrieve the total number of columns as well as the name of each column. Here's a sample that uses this property of the *DataRow* class to display the contents of a *DataRow*, including column names:

Visual Basic
```
Private Sub DisplayRow(ByVal row As DataRow)
    For Each col As DataColumn In row.Table.Columns
        Console.WriteLine("  {0}: {1}", col.ColumnName, row(col))
    Next col
End Sub
```

Visual C#
```
static void DisplayRow(DataRow row)
{
    foreach (DataColumn col in row.Table.Columns)
        Console.WriteLine("  {0}: {1}", col.ColumnName, row[col]);
}
```

The preceding code snippet demonstrates a third way to examine the contents of a particular column. The *DataRow* class's *Item* method accepts a *DataColumn* object. The *Item* property does not actually appear in the preceding code snippet because it is the default property on the *DataRowCollection* class. As of this writing, fetching the contents of a row by supplying a *DataColumn* slightly outperforms (by about 6 percent) ordinal-based lookups.

Examining the *DataRow* Objects in a *DataTable*

You can loop through the *DataRow* objects in a *DataTable* as easily as with any other collection in the .NET Framework. You use a *foreach* loop or a *For Each* loop in your language of choice. The following code snippet loops through the contents of the *DataTable* created by calling *SqlDataAdapter.Fill*, and it relies on the *DisplayRow* procedure developed in the previous snippet:

Visual Basic

```
Dim strConn, strSQL As String
strConn = "Data Source=.\SQLExpress;" & _
          "Initial Catalog=Northwind;Integrated Security=True;"
strSQL = "SELECT OrderID, CustomerID FROM Orders"
Dim da As New SqlDataAdapter(strSQL, strConn)
Dim ds As New DataSet()
da.Fill(ds, "Orders")

Dim tbl As DataTable = ds.Tables("Orders")
For Each row As DataRow In tbl.Rows
    Console.WriteLine("Contents of row #{0}", _
                      tbl.Rows.IndexOf(row))
    DisplayRow(row)
Next row
```

Visual C#

```
string strConn, strSQL;
strConn = @"Data Source=.\SQLExpress;" +
           "Initial Catalog=Northwind;Integrated Security=True;";
strSQL = "SELECT OrderID, CustomerID FROM Orders";
SqlDataAdapter da = new SqlDataAdapter(strSQL, strConn);
DataSet ds = new DataSet();
da.Fill(ds, "Orders");

DataTable tbl = ds.Tables["Orders"];
foreach (DataRow row in tbl.Rows)
{
    Console.WriteLine("Contents of row #{0}",
                      tbl.Rows.IndexOf(row));
    DisplayRow(row);
}
```

Validating Data in Your *DataSet*

Databases offer different mechanisms that you can use to ensure that the data in your database is valid. The sample Northwind database has many rules and constraints defined. The CustomerID column in the Customers table must be populated with a string of up to five characters, and that value must be unique within the table. The Orders table generates a new OrderID value for each row and requires that the CustomerID value for each row refer to an existing entry in the Customers table.

Sometimes you'll want to apply similar rules to validate data in your application before submitting changes to your database. For example, let's say that you're shopping online and reach the page where you purchase the items in your basket. Most Web sites will make sure that you've entered information into each of the required fields before they submit your order information to the appropriate database.

This type of logic might seem redundant because the database probably has similar validation rules defined. However, adding validation rules to your application can improve its performance. If a user fails to enter a credit card number, either by accident or in the hope that the system programmers were extremely lazy, the code for the Web page can easily determine that it can't successfully submit the order without having to contact the database. The other benefits of this approach are a slight reduction of network traffic and a lighter load on your database.

To keep you from having to write validation logic that mirrors basic database constraints, the ADO.NET *DataSet* offers many of the same data validation mechanisms available in database systems. You can separate these validation mechanisms, also called *constraints*, into two categories—column-level restrictions and table-level restrictions.

Validation Properties of the *DataColumn*

The *DataColumn* class exposes a number of properties that you can use to validate your data:

- **ReadOnly**   The simplest way to ensure that your data is valid is to not let users modify it. If you want to make the data in a *DataColumn* read-only, set the *ReadOnly* property of the *DataColumn* to *True*.

- **AllowDBNull**   Some database columns require values, while others accept empty, or null, values. The *DataColumn* class exposes an *AllowDBNull* property that you can set to control whether the column in your *DataSet* accepts null values.

- **MaxLength**   Many databases place restrictions on the size of a string in a column. In the Customers table, for example, the CustomerID column accepts a string of up to 5 characters and the CompanyName column accepts up to 40 characters. You can place similar restrictions on a *DataColumn* using the *MaxLength* property.

- **Unique**   The *DataColumn* lets you specify which values in a column are unique using the *Unique* property. When you set this property to *True* on a *DataColumn*, ADO.NET will examine the value stored in this column of each row in your *DataTable*. If you add or modify a row in your *DataTable* to create a duplicate value in a unique column, ADO.NET will throw a *ConstraintException*.

The *DataTable* Class's *Constraints* Collection

You can also validate data in your *DataSet* by setting properties of the *DataTable* objects in the *DataSet*. The ADO.NET object model includes two classes that you can use to define constraints in a *DataTable*. These classes, *UniqueConstraint* and *ForeignKeyConstraint*, are derived from the *Constraint* class. They are listed below. The *DataTable* exposes a *Constraints* property that you can use to add to, modify, or examine the constraints on the *DataTable*.

- **UniqueConstraint**   If you set the *Unique* property of a *DataColumn* to *True*, you've defined a unique constraint in the *DataTable* that contains that column. At the same time, you've also added a *UniqueConstraint* object to the *DataTable* class's *Constraints* collection. Setting the *Unique* property of a *DataColumn* is simpler than creating a new *UniqueConstraint* in a *DataTable* class's *Constraints* collection. However, there are times when you'll want to explicitly create a *UniqueConstraint*, such as when you need to ensure that the combinations of values from multiple columns are unique.

- **PrimaryKey**   The *DataTable* class allows you to define a primary key for the *DataTable* through the *PrimaryKey* property, but there is no *PrimaryKey* class. The *DataTable*'s *PrimaryKey* property contains an array of *DataColumn* objects, which the *DataTable* uses to construct a *UniqueConstraint* to enforce the primary key constraint. The ADO.NET *DataRowCollection* object has a *Find* method that you can use to locate a row in your *DataTable* by the value or values in its primary key column, as shown here. (I'll discuss the *Find* method in detail in Chapter 8.)

  ```
  row = MyTable.Rows.Find("ALFKI")
  ```

  A *DataTable* can have multiple unique constraints but can contain at most one primary key. You can set or examine a *DataTable* object's primary key using its *PrimaryKey* property.

- **ForeignKeyConstraint**   You can also add foreign constraints to a *DataTable*. I described an example of a foreign key constraint just a couple of pages back. Each order in the Northwind database's Orders table must have a value for its CustomerID column that is used in the Customers table. You can place similar restrictions on the data in your *DataSet* by creating a *ForeignKeyConstraint* and adding it to the table whose rows you want to validate.

You generally won't need to explicitly create a *ForeignKeyConstraint*. Creating a *DataRelation* between two *DataTable* objects within your *DataSet* creates a *ForeignKeyConstraint* in the process. In the next chapter, I'll discuss the *DataRelation* object and how you can use it to work with relational data.

Note   ADO.NET does not know what data resides in your database. Constraints you define on columns and tables within your *DataSet* are valid only within that *DataSet*. This is an important point to keep in mind. Here's why.

Say that you define a *UniqueConstraint* based on the CustomerID column in your *DataTable*. If you add a row with a CustomerID of *ZZZZZ*, ADO.NET will throw an exception only if another row in your *DataTable* has that same value for the CustomerID column.

Foreign key constraints are enforced in a similar fashion. If you define a foreign key on your orders *DataTable* object based on the CustomerID column in your orders and customers *DataTable* objects, ADO.NET will let you add only orders with a value for the CustomerID column that appears in your customers *DataTable*. ADO.NET will throw an exception if you add a new order with a CustomerID that is used in your database but that does not reside in your customers *DataTable*.

Retrieving Schema Information Using *SqlDataAdapter.FillSchema*

Validating data takes time. In many scenarios, you don't want to set validation properties on your *DataSet*, so the *SqlDataAdapter* does not set validation properties on *DataColumn* objects or add constraints to a *DataTable* object's *Constraints* collection when it creates the *DataTable* in the *SqlDataAdapter* class's *Fill* method unless you make an explicit request.

There are two ways to tell the *SqlDataAdapter* that you want to retrieve this schema information from your database when adding columns to your *DataTable*–by setting the *SqlDataAdapter* object's *MissingSchemaAction* property to *AddWithKey* or by calling the *SqlDataAdapter* object's *FillSchema* method. (I addressed these features of the *SqlDataAdapter* in Chapter 5.)

Try This at Home, But Only at Home

ADO.NET has a few features that you should avoid using in your applications whenever possible. Fetching schema information for your *DataSet* through the *SqlDataAdapter* is one of them.

Using the *SqlDataAdapter* to gather schema information can save time during the design process. In fact, Visual Studio uses the *SqlDataAdapter* to generate your *DataSet* objects at design time (as you'll discover in Chapter 9). If you're building a small sample or a proof-of-concept application, you might find that using the *SqlDataAdapter* to gather schema information reduces the amount of code you have to write.

But unless your application is an ad-hoc query tool, you should know which columns your queries return, so you should have no need to use features such as *SqlDataAdapter.Fill-Schema* in your full-blown applications.

If you ask your *SqlDataAdapter* to fetch additional schema information using these features, the *SqlDataAdapter* will query your database for schema information beyond the name and data type for each new *DataColumn* it creates. Examine any of these *DataColumn* objects and you'll find that the *ReadOnly*, *AllowDBNull*, *MaxLength*, and *ReadOnly* properties are set correctly.

The *SqlDataAdapter* will also attempt to generate a primary key for your *DataTable*. Microsoft SQL Server can return this information quickly and easily, compared to other databases. Through the *SqlClient .NET Data Provider*, you can also request this information by calling *SqlCommand.ExecuteReader* and specifying a *CommandBehavior* of *KeyInfo*. The *SqlClient .NET* Data Provider simply passes this request along to SQL Server without having to perform any client-side parsing of your query. However, requesting this information incurs an additional performance hit. Here's why.

When SQL Server parses the query you supply, it determines which table or tables your query references, and then gathers the information necessary to construct the results. If you ask for key information for the query results, SQL Server has to perform additional work.

After determining the table, or tables, your query references, SQL Server must also gather primary key information for the table or tables. If your query references a table that does not contain primary key information, SQL Server looks for a unique constraint. Assuming that SQL Server finds a primary (or unique) key to identify the columns in your table, it then checks to see whether the query references the entire key. For example, the primary key for the Order Details table consists of both the OrderID and ProductID columns. A query that references just the OrderID column references only part of the primary key. In such cases, SQL Server does not mark the OrderID column as part of the key in the resultset, and the *SqlDataAdapter* does not mark this column as part of the *DataTable*'s primary key.

As you can see, a simple call to *SqlDataAdapter.FillSchema* requires a nontrivial amount of work. Your code will execute much faster if you supply the schema for your *DataTables* and *DataSets* through your own code. We'll examine creating *DataTable* objects shortly. If you're looking for an in-depth example, you'll find a large code snippet later in the chapter that creates a *DataSet* with *DataTables* for the Customers, Orders, and Order Details tables in the sample Northwind database.

> **Note**   The *SqlDataAdapter* will also set the *AutoIncrement* property of new *DataColumn* objects. I'll discuss this property briefly later in this chapter. For more in-depth information about using this property, see Chapter 11.

Creating *DataTable* Objects in Code

You've learned how to create *DataTable* objects using the *Fill* and *FillSchema* methods of the *SqlDataAdapter*. You've also learned that you should create your own *DataTable* objects, especially if you want to validate your data using column or table-level restrictions. Now it's time to learn how to build *DataTable* objects using code.

Creating a *DataTable* Object

You can create a *DataTable* object the same way that you create a *DataSet* object. The *DataTable* has an optional constructor that you can use to set the *TableName* property of the new *DataTable* object, as shown here:

Visual Basic
```
Dim tbl As New DataTable("TableName")
Console.WriteLine(tbl.TableName)
```

Visual C#
```
DataTable tbl = new DataTable("TableName");
Console.WriteLine(tbl.TableName);
```

Adding Your *DataTable* to a *DataSet* Object's *Tables* Collection

Once you've created a *DataTable*, you can add it to an existing *DataSet* object's *Tables* collection using the *DataTableCollection* class's *Add* method, as shown here:

Visual Basic

```
Dim ds As New DataSet()
Dim tbl As New DataTable("Customers")
ds.Tables.Add(tbl)
```

Visual C#

```
DataSet ds = new DataSet();
DataTable tbl = new DataTable("Customers");
ds.Tables.Add(tbl);
```

That's not much code, but the always-clever developers at Microsoft have actually provided a simpler way of adding a new *DataTable* to a *DataSet* object's *Tables* collection by overloading the *DataTableCollection* class's *Add* method. You can create a new *DataTable* and add it to an existing *DataSet* object's *Tables* collection in a single call, as shown in the following code snippet:

Visual Basic

```
Dim ds As New DataSet()
Dim tbl As DataTable = ds.Tables.Add("Customers")
```

Visual C#

```
DataSet ds = new DataSet();
DataTable tbl = ds.Tables.Add("Customers");
```

You can determine whether a *DataTable* resides within a *DataSet* by checking the *DataTable* object's *DataSet* property. If the *DataTable* resides in a *DataSet* object's *Tables* collection, the *DataSet* property returns that *DataSet*. Otherwise, the property returns *Nothing* or *null*, depending on your language of choice. The *DataSet* property of the *DataTable* object is read-only.

It is also worth noting that a *DataTable* can reside in at most one *DataSet*. If you want to add a *DataTable* to multiple *DataSet* objects, you must use either the *Copy* or *Clone* method. The *Copy* method creates a new *DataTable* with the same structure that contains the same set of rows as the original *DataTable*. The *Clone* method creates a new *DataTable* with the same structure, just as the *Copy* method does, but it creates a *DataTable* that contains no rows.

Adding Columns to Your *DataTable*

It's time to add some meat to the structure of our new *DataTable*. To store the results of a query, the *DataTable* needs to have columns. Earlier in the chapter, you saw how the *SqlDataAdapter* can create new *DataColumn* objects for you. As noted in Chapter 5, calling *SqlDataAdapter.Fill* can add *DataColumns* to your *DataTable*, but those *DataColumns* have few properties set. The *DataColumns* created by calling *SqlDataAdapter.FillSchema* have more properties set, but calling *SqlDataAdapter.FillSchema* incurs a significant performance hit. Your best bet is to create your own *DataColumn* objects.

We can add *DataColumn* objects to a *DataTable* object's *Columns* collection by using code that's almost identical to the code we used to add a new *DataTable* to a *DataSet* object's *Tables* collection:

Visual Basic

```
Dim ds As New DataSet()
Dim tbl As DataTable = ds.Tables.Add("Customers")
Dim col As DataColumn = tbl.Columns.Add("CustomerID")
```

Visual C#

```
DataSet ds = new DataSet();
DataTable tbl = ds.Tables.Add("Customers");
DataColumn col = tbl.Columns.Add("CustomerID");
```

Specifying a Data Type for a *DataColumn*

When you create a new *DataColumn*, you'll also want to specify the data type that the *DataColumn* contains. You can use the *DataType* property of the *DataColumn* to set or check the data type that the column will contain. The *DataColumn* class's *DataType* property is read-write until you add data to the *DataTable* object's *Rows* collection.

Although the data type you select for your *DataColumn* will depend on the data type for that column in your database, there isn't a one-to-one mapping between database data types and *DataColumn* data types.

For example, Microsoft SQL Server lets you choose from a number of data types for string-based data. When you define the structure of a table in a SQL Server database, you can specify whether you want to store your string-based data as a fixed-length or variable-length string. You can also control whether SQL Server stores that data as single-byte (ANSI) or double-byte (Unicode) characters.

However, as far as ADO.NET is concerned, a string is a string. Regardless of whether the database data type is fixed-length or variable-length, single-byte or double-byte, the data type for the *DataColumn* is simply *string*. The *DataType* property of the *DataColumn* class works with .NET data types rather than database data types.

By default, *DataColumn* objects have a *DataType* property of *string*. The *DataColumn* has a constructor that allows you to specify a data type, as well as a column name, for the new column you're creating. Similarly, the *DataColumnCollection* class's *Add* method is overloaded to let you specify values for the *ColumnName* and *DataType* properties for your new *DataTable* object's new *DataColumn*, as shown here:

Visual Basic

```
Dim ds As New DataSet()
Dim tbl As DataTable = ds.Tables.Add("Orders")
Dim col As DataColumn = tbl.Columns.Add("OrderID", GetType(Integer))
```

Visual C#

```csharp
DataSet ds = new DataSet();
DataTable tbl = ds.Tables.Add("Orders");
DataColumn col = tbl.Columns.Add("OrderID", typeof(int));
```

The data type for the *DataType* property is *Type*. The preceding code snippet demonstrates how to get a *Type* value that corresponds to the integer data type in each language. Microsoft Visual Basic and Visual C# use different functions to generate types for backward-compatibility reasons. Prior to .NET, both C++ and Visual Basic included a *typeof* function, although the function did not return the same information in each language. As a result, Visual Basic includes a *GetType* function to return type information.

Adding a Primary Key

I gave a bit of a lecture earlier in the chapter extolling the virtues of using validation features of the *DataColumn* and *DataTable* in your own code rather than relying on the *SqlDataAdapter* to query your database for this information. That lecture would ring hollow without an explanation of how to set validation properties on your *DataColumn* and *DataTable* objects.

Just before that lecture, you learned about the *AllowDBNull*, *ReadOnly*, *MaxLength*, and *Unique* properties of the *DataColumn* object and how to use them to validate the data stored in your columns. Setting those properties in your code is simple:

Visual Basic

```vb
Dim ds As New DataSet()
Dim tbl As DataTable = ds.Tables.Add("Customers")
Dim col As DataColumn = tbl.Columns.Add("CustomerID")
col.AllowDBNull = False
col.ReadOnly = False
col.MaxLength = 5
col.Unique = True
```

Visual C#

```csharp
DataSet ds = new DataSet();
DataTable tbl = ds.Tables.Add("Customers");
DataColumn col = tbl.Columns.Add("CustomerID");
col.AllowDBNull = false;
col.ReadOnly = false;
col.MaxLength = 5;
col.Unique = true;
```

Setting the primary key for a *DataTable* is slightly more complicated. The *PrimaryKey* property contains an array of *DataColumn* objects. So you can't simply set the property to the name of the column or columns that you want to use for your primary key.

Some of the *DataTable* objects you create will rely on single columns as their primary keys; others will rely on combinations of columns. The following code snippet includes code for each scenario. The Customers table uses a single column, CustomerID, while the Order Details table uses a combination of two columns, OrderID and ProductID. In both cases, you must create an array of *DataColumn* objects and assign that array to the *DataTable* object's *PrimaryKey* property:

Visual Basic
```vb
Dim ds As New DataSet()
'Create the Customers DataTable.
With ds.Tables.Add("Customers")
    .Columns.Add("CustomerID", GetType(String))
    '...
    .PrimaryKey = New DataColumn() {.Columns("CustomerID")}
End With

'Create the Order Details DataTable.
With ds.Tables.Add("Order Details")
    .Columns.Add("OrderID", GetType(Integer))
    .Columns.Add("ProductID", GetType(Integer))
    '...
    .PrimaryKey = New DataColumn() {.Columns("OrderID"), _
                                    .Columns("ProductID")}
End With
```

Visual C#
```csharp
DataSet ds = new DataSet();
DataTable tbl;
//Create the Customers DataTable.
tbl = ds.Tables.Add("Customers");
tbl.Columns.Add("CustomerID", typeof(string));
//...
tbl.PrimaryKey = new DataColumn[] {tbl.Columns["CustomerID"]};

//Create the Order Details DataTable.
tbl = ds.Tables.Add("Order Details");
tbl.Columns.Add("OrderID", typeof(int));
tbl.Columns.Add("ProductID", typeof(int));
//...
tbl.PrimaryKey = new DataColumn[] {tbl.Columns["OrderID"],
                                   tbl.Columns["ProductID"]};
```

> **Note**   When you set the primary key for your *DataTable*, ADO.NET automatically sets the *AllowDBNull* property of the *DataColumn* object or objects referenced in your primary key to *False*.

Adding Other Constraints

Primary keys are the most widely used constraint, but you can also add unique key and foreign key constraints to a *DataTable*. The *DataTable* class's *Constraints* collection has an overloaded *Add* method that you can use to add new primary key, unique key, and foreign key constraints.

You can classify the overloaded *Add* method into different categories. The *ConstraintCollection* class's *Add* method accepts any object that inherits from the *Constraint* object, so you can supply either a *UniqueConstraint* object or a *ForeignKeyConstraint* object. So you can execute code such as the following:

```
DataTable.Constraints.Add(New UniqueConstraint(...))
DataTable.Constraints.Add(New ForeignKeyConstraint(...))
```

As you can with the *Add* methods for the *DataTableCollection* and *DataColumnCollection* classes, you can create your constraint as you add it to the collection. You can use this method to add both unique and foreign key constraints and both single-column and multiple-column constraints.

First, let's look at an example that creates unique constraints by using the *Add* method. The first parameter contains the name of the new unique constraint. The second parameter contains the *DataColumn* (or array of *DataColumns*) that constitute the unique constraint. The third parameter is a Boolean value that determines whether the new constraint will be used for the *DataTable*'s primary key.

Visual Basic

```
Dim ds As New DataSet()
Dim tblCustomers As DataTable = ds.Tables.Add("Customers")
tblCustomers.Columns.Add("CustomerID", GetType(String))
tblCustomers.Columns.Add("CompanyName", GetType(String))
'...
tblCustomers.Constraints.Add("PK_CustomerID", _
                            tblCustomers.Columns("CustomerID"), _
                            True)
tblCustomers.Constraints.Add("UK_CompanyName", _
                            tblCustomers.Columns("CompanyName"), _
                            False)
```

Visual C#

```
DataSet ds = new DataSet()
DataTable tblCustomers = ds.Tables.Add("Customers");
tblCustomers.Columns.Add("CustomerID", typeof(string));
tblCustomers.Columns.Add("CompanyName", typeof(string));
//...
tblCustomers.Constraints.Add("PK_CustomerID",
                            tblCustomers.Columns["CustomerID"],
                            true);
tblCustomers.Constraints.Add("UK_CompanyName",
                            tblCustomers.Columns["CompanyName"],
                            false);
```

The *Add* method is overloaded so you can also use it to create foreign key constraints. The method signature looks very similar. The first parameter contains the name of the new foreign key constraint. The second parameter contains the *DataColumn* (or array of *DataColumns*) from the parent table. The third parameter contains the *DataColumn* (or array of *DataColumns*) from the child table.

Visual Basic

```
Dim ds As New DataSet()
Dim tblCustomers As DataTable = ds.Tables.Add("Customers")
```

```
Dim tblOrders As DataTable = ds.Tables.Add("Orders")
tblCustomers.Columns.Add("CustomerID", GetType(String))
'...
tblOrders.Columns.Add("OrderID", GetType(Integer))
tblOrders.Columns.Add("CustomerID", GetType(String))
'...
tblOrders.Constraints.Add("FK_Customers_Orders", _
                    tblCustomers.Columns("CustomerID"), _
                    tblOrders.Columns("CustomerID"))
```

Visual C#

```
DataSet ds = new DataSet();
DataTable tblCustomers = ds.Tables.Add("Customers");
DataTable tblOrders = ds.Tables.Add("Orders");
tblCustomers.Columns.Add("CustomerID", typeof(string));
//...
tblOrders.Columns.Add("OrderID", typeof(int));
tblOrders.Columns.Add("CustomerID", typeof(string));
//...
tblOrders.Constraints.Add("FK_Customers_Orders",
                    tblCustomers.Columns["CustomerID"],
                    tblOrders.Columns["CustomerID"]);
```

I prefer explicitly creating constraints and adding them to the collection. I find the code for the overloaded *Add* methods to be too difficult to read and maintain. Unless you're prefacing your constraint names with codes like "PK", "UK", and "FK", it requires too much work to determine what type of constraint the *Add* method creates.

Working with Autoincrement Columns

There are benefits and drawbacks to using autoincrement columns to generate key values for your database. The main benefit is that you're using central logic to generate simple, unique integers that serve as key values for your new rows. The main drawback is that you won't know the key values for your new rows until you submit them to the database. Some developers and database administrators prefer using *Guids* to generate unique keys prior to submitting the rows to the database.

If you're using autoincrement columns in your database, ADO.NET's autoincrement features can help you keep your pending inserts straight prior to submitting those new rows to your database. ADO.NET includes support for autoincrement columns through three properties of the *DataColumn*: *AutoIncrement*, *AutoIncrementSeed*, and *AutoIncrementStep*.

If you want ADO.NET to generate such autoincrement values for new rows in your *DataTable*, set the *AutoIncrement* property of your *DataColumn* to *True*, as shown here:

Visual Basic

```
Dim ds As New DataSet()
Dim tbl As DataTable = ds.Tables.Add("Orders")
Dim col As DataColumn = tbl.Columns.Add("OrderID", GetType(Integer))
col.AutoIncrement = True
```

```
col.AutoIncrementSeed = -1
col.AutoIncrementStep = -1
col.ReadOnly = True
```

Visual C#
```
DataSet ds = new DataSet();
DataTable tbl = ds.Tables.Add("Orders");
DataColumn col = tbl.Columns.Add("OrderID", typeof(int));
col.AutoIncrement = true;
col.AutoIncrementSeed = -1;
col.AutoIncrementStep = -1;
col.ReadOnly = true;
```

The preceding code snippet marked the OrderID column as autoincrement, but it also set the *AutoIncrementSeed* and *AutoIncrementStep* properties to −1. I strongly recommend setting these two properties to −1, which causes negative autoincrement values to be generated, whenever you set *AutoIncrement* to *True*. Allow me to explain why.

The *AutoIncrementSeed* and *AutoIncrementStep* properties control how ADO.NET generates new values. When you're working with an empty table, ADO.NET will assign the value stored in *AutoIncrementSeed* to the autoincrement column for your first row. ADO.NET will use the *AutoIncrementStep* property to generate subsequent autoincrement values. For example, if you set *AutoIncrement* to *True* and set both *AutoIncrementSeed* and *AutoIncrementStep* to 2, ADO.NET will generate the following values for the autoincrement column of your first five rows: 2, 4, 6, 8, 10.

This behavior changes slightly if you add rows to your *DataTable* by calling *SqlDataAdapter* *.Fill*. Say that you're working with a *DataTable* whose structure matches the Orders table in the Northwind database and that you've set the *AutoIncrementSeed* and *AutoIncrementStep* properties to 5 for the OrderID *DataColumn*. If you add new rows to this *DataTable* while it's empty, those new rows will have values of 5, 10, 15, 20, and so on for the OrderID column. However, if you add rows to the *DataTable* from your database using *SqlDataAdapter.Fill* and then add new rows using *DataTable.Rows.Add*, the new values you generate for the OrderID column will depend on the data you fetched from your database. ADO.NET will generate subsequent autoincrement values based on the largest autoincrement value that appears in the *DataTable* and the value of the *AutoIncrementStep* properties.

Let's say that, in this example, the largest current value for the OrderID column in your *Data-Table* is 973. If you generate a new row at this point, ADO.NET will add the value stored in the *AutoIncrementStep* property (5) to the largest current value in the *DataTable* (973) for a new OrderID of 978.

It is extremely important to keep in mind that ADO.NET is aware only of data that exists in your *DataTable*. It does not know what your database will generate for the next autoincrement value. I said that the largest value for the OrderID column that appears in our *DataTable* based on the results of our query was 973. Maybe the query fetched orders only for a particular customer:

```
SELECT OrderID, CustomerID, OrderDate FROM Orders
    WHERE CustomerID = 'ALFKI'
```

The database might contain larger values for the OrderID column than the ones that appear in the *DataTable*. ADO.NET has no way to know, so it might generate autoincrement values for new rows in your *DataTable*, but those autoincrement values might already be in use in your database.

During the development of ADO.NET and the .NET Framework as a whole, a developer asked me whether there was any way to achieve paging in a *DataTable* (that is, he wanted to return or display just a portion of the contents of a *DataTable*). Rather than try to count the rows and construct elaborate filters based on search criteria and row ordering, you can achieve paging in a much simpler way by letting ADO.NET count the rows as they're added to the *DataTable*, thanks to the autoincrement features in ADO.NET.

The following code snippet fills a *DataTable* based on the results of a simple query. Before filling the table, the code adds an autoincrement column to the table. Because the query does not return data for this autoincrement column, ADO.NET generates new values for the column for each row returned by the query.

The code snippet uses the *DataView* and *DataRowView* objects. We'll discuss these objects in Chapter 8, but in this sample their use should be self-explanatory. Once we've filled the *DataTable* based on the results of the query, we'll use the *DataView*'s *RowFilter* property to view just one "page" of the *DataTable* and write the contents of that page to the screen.

Yes, I know that I used the *FillSchema* method to create the structure of my *DataTable* despite what I said in Chapter 5 and earlier in this chapter about the performance hit incurred by calling the method, but I used it only to compress the code snippet. I would not have used it in a real-world application. Scout's honor.

Visual Basic

```
'Create the SqlDataAdapter and retrieve schema for the query
Dim strConn, strSQL As String
strConn = "Data Source=.\SQLExpress;" & _
          "Initial Catalog=Northwind;Integrated Security=True;"
strSQL = "SELECT CustomerID, CompanyName FROM Customers"
Dim da As New SqlDataAdapter(strSQL, strConn)
Dim tbl As DataTable = New DataTable("Customers")
da.FillSchema(tbl, SchemaType.Source)

'Add a DataColumn that will number the rows 1, 2, 3, ...
Dim col As DataColumn = tbl.Columns.Add("RowNum", GetType(Integer))
col.AutoIncrement = True
col.AutoIncrementSeed = 1
col.AutoIncrementStep = 1

'Retrieve the results of the query
da.Fill(tbl)

'Create a new DataView that will show rows 21 - 30
Dim intPageSize As Integer = 10
Dim intPageNum As Integer = 3
Dim vue As New DataView(tbl)
vue.RowFilter = String.Format("RowNum > {0} AND RowNum <= {1}", _
```

```
                            (intPageNum - 1) * intPageSize, _
                            intPageNum * intPageSize)


'Print the contents of the rows visible through the DataView
For Each row As DataRowView In vue
    Console.WriteLine("{0}: {1} - {2}", row("RowNum"), _
                    row("CustomerID"), row("CompanyName"))
Next row
```

Visual C#

```
//Retrieve the data
string strConn, strSQL;
strConn = @"Data Source=.\SQLExpress;" +
          "Initial Catalog=Northwind;Integrated Security=True;";
strSQL = "SELECT CustomerID, CompanyName FROM Customers";
SqlDataAdapter da = new SqlDataAdapter(strSQL, strConn);
DataTable tbl = new DataTable("Customers");
da.FillSchema(tbl, SchemaType.Source);

//Add a DataColumn that will number the rows 1, 2, 3, ...
DataColumn col = tbl.Columns.Add("RowNum", typeof(int));
col.AutoIncrement = true;
col.AutoIncrementSeed = 1;
col.AutoIncrementStep = 1;

//Retrieve the results of the query
da.Fill(tbl);

//Create a new DataView that will show rows 21 - 30
int intPageSize = 10;
int intPageNum = 3;
DataView vue = new DataView(tbl);
vue.RowFilter = String.Format("RowNum > {0} AND RowNum <= {1}",
                    (intPageNum - 1) * intPageSize,
                    intPageNum * intPageSize);

//Print the contents of the rows visible through the DataView
foreach(DataRowView row in vue)
    Console.WriteLine("{0}: {1} - {2}", row["RowNum"],
                    row["CustomerID"], row["CompanyName"]);
```

Should you use this approach to achieve paging in your Web applications? Probably not. The approach is not very scalable because it requires retrieving all rows, even though you might wind up displaying just a fraction of the rows on your page. We'll discuss other ways to achieve paging in Chapter 14. I've included this sample strictly to demonstrate that you can solve some interesting problems using the ADO.NET autoincrement features.

Autoincrement Do's and Don'ts

Here's a quick list of autoincrement do's and don'ts:

Do: Use the ADO.NET autoincrement features if you're using autoincrement columns in your database of choice.

Do: Set the autoincrement properties prior to adding rows to the *DataTable*. Otherwise, the values of those properties will not affect the autoincrement values that the *DataTable* generates.

Don't: Submit autoincrement values that ADO.NET generates to your database. The values that ADO.NET generates are merely placeholders. Let the database generate the real new values. Chapter 11 includes examples that show how to let the database generate values as well as how to fetch these new values and place them into the corresponding rows in your *DataTable*.

Don't: Display autoincrement values for new rows that have not been submitted to the database. The database will probably generate different values from the ones ADO.NET generates. The user of your application might not be aware that the autoincrement value that ADO.NET generated for a new row is just a placeholder. If your application is an order-entry system, do you really want to take the chance that the user, who is taking orders over the phone from customers, might mistakenly assume that the value ADO.NET generated for the Order ID is accurate—and then read that value to the customer?

Do: Set the *AutoIncrementSeed* and *AutoIncrementStep* properties to −1 prior to adding rows to your *DataTable*. Doing so ensures that you're generating placeholder values such as −1, −2, −3, and so on. Assuming that you've set the autoincrement seed in your database to the default (1), ADO.NET is generating placeholder values that can not appear in your database. Even if you display this value in your application, it will prevent users from mistakenly assuming that the autoincrement values that ADO.NET generates will be the same as the ones the database will generate.

I've included this information to help you understand how the ADO.NET autoincrement features work. Armed with this information, you should be able to make intelligent decisions about when and how to generate new autoincrement values using ADO.NET.

Adding an Expression-Based Column

Database administrators generally avoid including data in their databases that can be derived from data that already exists within the database. For example, the Order Details table in the Northwind database contains columns that store the unit price and quantity for each line item in an order, but it does not contain a column for the total cost of the line item. Users don't care whether the total cost of the line item is stored in the database as long as they can see the total cost of the line item.

Most databases support expressions in their query language so that you can include calculated columns in the results of your query. If you want the database to calculate and return the total cost of a line item in the result set, you could use the following query:

```
SELECT OrderID, ProductID, UnitPrice, Quantity,
    UnitPrice * Quantity AS ItemTotal FROM [Order Details]
```

If you fill a *DataTable* with the results of this query, you'll have a column that contains the results of the desired expression. But if you change the contents of the UnitPrice or Quantity column in a row in your *DataTable*, the contents of the calculated column will remain unchanged. That's because the definition for the calculated column appears in the query itself. The database performs the actual calculation, and you simply retrieve the results of the query. Once you've retrieved the results of the query, the contents of the calculated column will not change.

ADO.NET lets you create expression-based *DataColumn* objects. Rather than include an expression such as the preceding one in your query, you can set the *Expression* property of a *DataColumn* to an expression. When you examine the contents of the column, ADO.NET will evaluate the expression and return the results. You can then modify an order item by changing the UnitPrice or Quantity in the order, and when you check the contents of the ItemTotal column, you'll see that the column value has been recalculated to include the change you've made.

The following code snippet adds a column to our order detail *DataTable* that will contain the total cost of the order item:

Visual Basic

```
Dim ds As New DataSet()
Dim tbl As DataTable = ds.Tables.Add("Order Details")
'...
tbl.Columns.Add("Quantity", GetType(Integer))
tbl.Columns.Add("UnitPrice", GetType(Decimal))
tbl.Columns.Add("ItemTotal", GetType(Decimal), _
                "Quantity * UnitPrice")
```

Visual C#

```
DataSet ds = new DataSet();
DataTable tbl = ds.Tables.Add("Order Details");
//...
tbl.Columns.Add("Quantity", typeof(int));
tbl.Columns.Add("UnitPrice", typeof(Decimal));
tbl.Columns.Add("ItemTotal", typeof(Decimal),
                "Quantity * UnitPrice");
```

> **Note**   This isn't actually the proper way to calculate the total cost of a line item for an order in the Northwind database. The Order Details table contains a Discount column that is used to compute discounts on line items. The column accepts values between 0 and 1. If a line item has a value of .25 in the discount column, there's a 25 percent discount on the total cost of the line item. Thus, the true way to calculate the total cost of a line item is as follows:
>
> ```
> Quantity * UnitPrice * (1 - Discount)
> ```
>
> I simplified the process in the earlier code snippets because I wanted to focus on creating calculated columns rather than having to digress about the structure of the Northwind database.

The *Expression* property supports a wide variety of functions, including aggregate functions that can reference data in other *DataTable* objects in the *DataSet*. We'll create expression-based columns that use aggregate functions in the next chapter when we discuss working with relational data. For more information about the list of functions that the *Expression* property supports, see the MSDN documentation on the *Expression* property.

Creating *DataTable* Objects for the Customers, Orders, and Order Details Tables

We've explored a lot of features of the *DataSet*, *DataTable*, and *DataColumn* classes. Now let's tie them all together into a single *DataSet*. The following code snippet creates a new *DataSet* that contains three *DataTable* objects. (Smaller snippets shown earlier in the chapter demonstrated how to create pieces of each of these *DataTable* objects.) In the process, the code sets properties on the *DataColumn* objects (including *DataType*, *AllowDBNull*, and *AutoIncrement*) and creates both primary key and foreign key constraints.

The *DataSet* that this code snippet creates mirrors the one that we created in Chapter 2 when we used the Data Source Configuration Wizard, except for a few key differences beyond the fact that it includes the Order Details table. This code adds a couple more refined settings to our *DataSet* and sets the *AutoIncrementStep* and *AutoIncrementSeed* values on the OrderID column in the Orders *DataTable* to obtain more control over the autoincrement values that ADO.NET generates for new orders. It also sets the *MaxLength* property of the string-based columns.

The code creates foreign key constraints but does not populate the *DataSet* object's *Relations* collection. (I'll discuss the *DataRelation* class in the next chapter.)

The Data Source Configuration Wizard creates a strongly typed *DataSet*. I'll discuss strongly typed *DataSet* objects in Chapter 9. For now, think of a strongly typed *DataSet* as a class that has all the features of a *DataSet* but also exposes structures such as *DataTable* objects and *DataColumn* objects as well-defined properties rather than as simple collections. The code that follows creates a *DataSet* that's not strongly typed.

Visual Basic

```
Dim ds As New DataSet()
Dim col As DataColumn
Dim fk As ForeignKeyConstraint

'Create the customers table.
With ds.Tables.Add("Customers")
    .Columns.Add("CustomerID", GetType(String)).MaxLength = 5
    .Columns.Add("CompanyName", GetType(String)).MaxLength = 40
    .Columns.Add("ContactName", GetType(String)).MaxLength = 30
    .Columns.Add("Phone", GetType(String)).MaxLength = 24
    .PrimaryKey = New DataColumn() {.Columns("CustomerID")}
End With
```

```
'Create the orders table.
With ds.Tables.Add("Orders")
    col = .Columns.Add("OrderID", GetType(Integer))
    col.AutoIncrement = True
    col.AutoIncrementSeed = -1
    col.AutoIncrementStep = -1
    col.ReadOnly = True
    col = .Columns.Add("CustomerID", GetType(String))
    col.AllowDBNull = False
    col.MaxLength = 5
    .Columns.Add("EmployeeID", GetType(Integer))
    .Columns.Add("OrderDate", GetType(DateTime))
    .PrimaryKey = New DataColumn() {.Columns("OrderID")}
End With

'Create the order details table.
With ds.Tables.Add("Order Details")
    .Columns.Add("OrderID", GetType(Integer))
    .Columns.Add("ProductID", GetType(Integer))
    .Columns.Add("UnitPrice", GetType(Decimal)).AllowDBNull = False
    col = .Columns.Add("Quantity", GetType(Integer))
    col.AllowDBNull = False
    col.DefaultValue = 1
    .Columns.Add("Discount", GetType(Decimal)).DefaultValue = 0
    .Columns.Add("ItemTotal", GetType(Decimal), _
                "UnitPrice * Quantity * (1 - Discount)")
    .PrimaryKey = New DataColumn() {.Columns("OrderID"), _
                                    .Columns("ProductID")}
End With

'Create the foreign key constraints.
fk = New ForeignKeyConstraint("FK_Customers_Orders", _
                              ds.Tables("Customers").Columns("CustomerID"), _
                              ds.Tables("Orders").Columns("CustomerID"))
ds.Tables("Orders").Constraints.Add(fk)
fk = New ForeignKeyConstraint("FK_Orders_OrderDetails", _
                              ds.Tables("Orders").Columns("OrderID"), _
                              ds.Tables("Order Details").Columns("OrderID"))
ds.Tables("Order Details").Constraints.Add(fk)
```

Visual C#

```
DataSet ds = new DataSet();
DataTable tbl;
DataColumn col;
ForeignKeyConstraint fk;

//Create the customers table.
tbl = ds.Tables.Add("Customers");
tbl.Columns.Add("CustomerID", typeof(string)).MaxLength = 5;
tbl.Columns.Add("CompanyName", typeof(string)).MaxLength = 40;
tbl.Columns.Add("ContactName", typeof(string)).MaxLength = 30;
tbl.Columns.Add("Phone", typeof(string)).MaxLength = 24;
tbl.PrimaryKey = new DataColumn[] {tbl.Columns["CustomerID"]};
```

```
//Create the orders table.
tbl = ds.Tables.Add("Orders");
col = tbl.Columns.Add("OrderID", typeof(int));
col.AutoIncrement = true;
col.AutoIncrementSeed = -1;
col.AutoIncrementStep = -1;
col.ReadOnly = true;
col = tbl.Columns.Add("CustomerID", typeof(string));
col.AllowDBNull = false;
col.MaxLength = 5;
tbl.Columns.Add("EmployeeID", typeof(int));
tbl.Columns.Add("OrderDate", typeof(DateTime));
tbl.PrimaryKey = new DataColumn[] {tbl.Columns["OrderID"]};

//Create the order details table.
tbl = ds.Tables.Add("Order Details");
tbl.Columns.Add("OrderID", typeof(int));
tbl.Columns.Add("ProductID", typeof(int));
tbl.Columns.Add("UnitPrice", typeof(Decimal)).AllowDBNull = false;
col = tbl.Columns.Add("Quantity", typeof(int));
col.AllowDBNull = false;
col.DefaultValue = 1;
tbl.Columns.Add("Discount", typeof(Decimal)).DefaultValue = 0;
tbl.Columns.Add("ItemTotal", typeof(Decimal),
                "UnitPrice * Quantity * (1 - Discount)");
tbl.PrimaryKey = new DataColumn[] {tbl.Columns["OrderID"],
                                   tbl.Columns["ProductID"]};

//Create the foreign key constraints.
fk = new ForeignKeyConstraint("FK_Customers_Orders",
                              ds.Tables["Customers"].Columns["CustomerID"],
                              ds.Tables["Orders"].Columns["CustomerID"]);
ds.Tables["Orders"].Constraints.Add(fk);
fk = new ForeignKeyConstraint("FK_Orders_OrderDetails",
                              ds.Tables["Orders"].Columns["OrderID"],
                              ds.Tables["Order Details"].Columns["OrderID"]);
ds.Tables["Order Details"].Constraints.Add(fk);
```

Modifying the Contents of a *DataTable*

You now know how to create *DataSet*, *DataTable*, and *DataColumn* objects, and you know how to use a *SqlDataAdapter* to store the results of a query into *DataTable* objects. You also know how to examine the contents of a *DataTable*. Now let's look at how to add, modify, and delete *DataRow* objects.

Adding a New *DataRow*

Now that we have a *DataSet*, let's add some data to it. In Chapter 5, you learned how to use *SqlDataAdapter* objects to fill a *DataTable* with data from a database. You can also load data from an XML file, a feature we'll examine in Chapter 12. For now, we'll focus on loading data on a row-by-row basis.

Each *DataTable* object has a *Rows* property that returns a *DataRowCollection* object, which contains a collection of *DataRow* objects. As with most collections, you can use the *DataRowCollection* class's *Add* method to add a new object to the collection. However, *DataRow* objects differ from other ADO.NET objects in how you create them.

Let's say that you want to programmatically add 10 *DataRow* objects to a *DataTable* that contains 10 *DataColumn* objects. To add a row to the table, you create a new *DataRow*, assign values to each of the columns, and add the new *DataRow* to the *DataTable*'s *Rows* collection.

If you look closely at the Visual Studio Object Browser, you might notice that there is no public constructor on the *DataRow* class. Although this might seem counterintuitive, it makes sense. How would the *DataRow* determine its structure—that is, which columns it contains? Because the *DataTable* already contains that schema, it's the natural starting point for creating new *DataRows*.

The *DataTable* class has a *NewRow* method that returns a new *DataRow* object that contains information about each of the columns in the table. Once you've created your new *DataRow*, you can populate the various columns using its *Item* property. You can also use the *Item* property to examine the contents of a column in your row. The *Item* property is the default property of the *DataRow* class, so you don't even need to explicitly call *Item* to use it. To set the value of a column in a *DataRow*, you supply the name of the column (or its index or the *DataColumn* itself) and then assign the desired value.

The *NewRow* method of the *DataTable* creates a new row, but it does not add that row to the *DataTable*. Generally speaking, you don't want to add your new row as soon as you've created it because, at that point, it's empty. The values in the columns are set to the appropriate default values or to *Null* if they don't have defaults. By creating the new *DataRow* but not adding it to the *Rows* collection, you can assign values to your columns before making the new *DataRow* part of your *DataTable*. The CustomerID column of our Customers table does not accept *Null* values but does not have a default value. Say that you have a Customers *DataTable* that has a primary key based on the CustomerID column. If you try to add a new *Customers* row to the table without assigning a value to the CustomerID column, you'll generate an exception.

Once you've supplied values for all the desired columns in your new row and you're ready to add it to the *DataTable*, you use the *Add* method of the *DataRowCollection* and supply your new row, as shown here:

Visual Basic
```
Dim tbl As New DataTable("Customers")
tbl.Columns.Add("CustomerID", GetType(String))
tbl.Columns.Add("CompanyName", GetType(String))
Dim row As DataRow = tbl.NewRow()
row("CustomerID") = "NEWCO"
row("CompanyName") = "New Customer"
tbl.Rows.Add(row)
```

Visual C#

```
DataTable tbl = new DataTable("Customers");
tbl.Columns.Add("CustomerID", typeof(string));
tbl.Columns.Add("CompanyName", typeof(string));
DataRow row = tbl.NewRow();
row["CustomerID"] = "NEWCO";
row["CompanyName"] = "New Customer";
tbl.Rows.Add(row);
```

The *DataRowCollection* class's *Add* method is overloaded, so you create a new *DataRow*, whose *RowState* will be set to *Added*, by supplying a list of column values for the new row as shown here:

Visual Basic

```
Dim tbl As New DataTable("Customers")
tbl.Columns.Add("CustomerID", GetType(String))
tbl.Columns.Add("CompanyName", GetType(String))
tbl.Rows.Add("NEWCO", "New Customer")
```

Visual C#

```
DataTable tbl = new DataTable("Customers");
tbl.Columns.Add("CustomerID", typeof(string));
tbl.Columns.Add("CompanyName", typeof(string));
tbl.Rows.Add("NEWCO", "New Customer");
```

The *DataTable* class offers a third way to add a new row to the table: the *LoadDataRow* method. This method is similar to the overloaded *Add* method that lets you supply the list of values for the new *DataRow*, but it also lets you control the *RowState* for the new *DataRow*. To use this method, you supply an array of values in the first parameter. The items in the array correspond to columns in the table. The second parameter of the *LoadDataRow* method, *AcceptChanges*, lets you control the value of the *RowState* property of the new *DataRow*. Passing a value of *False* for this parameter, as shown in the following code snippet, causes the new row to have a *RowState* of *Added*, just as if you'd added the row by using *DataTable* .*NewRow* and *Rows.Add*, as in the earlier examples.

Visual Basic

```
Dim tbl As New DataTable("Customers")
tbl.Columns.Add("CustomerID", GetType(String))
tbl.Columns.Add("CompanyName", GetType(String))
tbl.LoadDataRow(New Object() {"NEWCO", "New Customer"}, False)
```

Visual C#

```
DataTable tbl = new DataTable("Customers");
tbl.Columns.Add("CustomerID", typeof(string));
tbl.Columns.Add("CompanyName", typeof(string));
tbl.LoadDataRow(new object[] {"NEWCO", "New Customer"}, false);
```

When you submit changes to your database by calling the *Update* method of a *SqlDataAdapter* object, the *SqlDataAdapter* examines the *RowState* of each *DataRow* to determine how to update the database—by modifying an existing row, adding a new row, or deleting an existing row. If you pass a value of *True* to the second parameter in *LoadDataRow*, the new *DataRow*

will have a *RowState* of *Unchanged*, which means that the row does not contain a pending
change that the *SqlDataAdapter* would submit to the database. We'll discuss the *DataRow*
class's *RowState* property and updating your database in more detail in Chapter 10.

Modifying an Existing Row

There are three ways to modify the contents of a row programmatically. Let's start with the
simplest.

Once you have a *DataRow* object, you can set the value of a column using the *DataRow* object's
Item property. Earlier in the chapter, you saw how to use this property to check the contents
of a column. The property is read/write, so you can also use it to set the value of a column. The
code snippets that follow use the *Rows* collection's *Find* method to locate a row in the Customers
DataTable and then change the values in the CompanyName and ContactName columns.
We'll discuss the *Find* method in more detail in Chapter 8. For now, consider this a preview.

Visual Basic

```
Dim tbl As New DataTable("Customers")
tbl.Columns.Add("CustomerID", GetType(String))
tbl.Columns.Add("CompanyName", GetType(String))
tbl.PrimaryKey = New DataColumn() {tbl.Columns("CustomerID")}
tbl.LoadDataRow(New Object() {"NEWCO", "New Customer"}, False)

Dim row As DataRow = tbl.Rows.Find("NEWCO")
If row Is Nothing Then
    'Customer not found!
Else
    row("CompanyName") = "New Value"
End If
```

Visual C#

```
DataTable tbl = new DataTable("Customers");
tbl.Columns.Add("CustomerID", typeof(string));
tbl.Columns.Add("CompanyName", typeof(string));
tbl.PrimaryKey = new DataColumn[] {tbl.Columns["CustomerID"]};
tbl.LoadDataRow(new object[] {"NEWCO", "New Customer"}, false);

DataRow row = tbl.Rows.Find("NEWCO");
if (row == null)
    //Customer not found!
else
    row["CompanyName"] = "New Value";
```

The second way to update a row is similar to the first, except that you add calls to the *DataRow*
class's *BeginEdit* and *EndEdit* methods:

Visual Basic

```
Dim row As DataRow = tbl.Rows.Find("NEWCO")
If row Is Nothing Then
    'Customer not found!
Else
```

```
    row.BeginEdit()
    row("CompanyName") = "New Value"
    row.EndEdit()
End If
```

Visual C#

```
DataRow row = tbl.Rows.Find("NEWCO");
if (row == null)
    //Customer not found!
else {
    row.BeginEdit();
    row["CompanyName"] = "New Value";
    row.EndEdit();
}
```

Using *BeginEdit* and *EndEdit* lets you buffer the changes to the row. Calling *EndEdit* saves the changes to the row. If you decide that you don't want to keep the changes, you can call *CancelEdit* instead to undo the changes and the row will revert to its state at the time you called *BeginEdit*.

There's another difference between these two ways of modifying a row. The *DataTable* has events such as *RowChanging*, *RowChanged*, *ColumnChanging*, and *ColumnChanged* that you can use to examine the changes to a row or column. When, or if, these events fire depends on how you modify a row—with or without calling *BeginEdit* and *EndEdit*.

In the first example, the contents of the row changed each time we modified a column in the row. The *DataTable* class's events fire each time you modify the contents of a column. Using *BeginEdit* blocks the events from occurring until you call *EndEdit*. (If you call *CancelEdit* instead of *EndEdit*, the buffered changes will be discarded, and because the row is not updated, the events will not fire.)

The third way to modify the contents of a row is by using the *ItemArray* property. Like the *Item* property, this property can be used to retrieve or modify the contents of the row. The difference between the properties is that the *Item* property works with one column at a time and the *ItemArray* property returns and accepts an array in which each item corresponds to a column.

The *ItemArray* property is handy if you you want to retrieve or modify multiple column values in a single line of code. If you want to modify just a subset of the values available in a row, use *null* or *Nothing* (depending on your language of choice) to indicate that you do not want to override the value of that column in the *DataRow*. For example, the following code snippet uses the *ItemArray* property to leave the value for CustomerID (first column) untouched but modify the value for CompanyName (second column):

Visual Basic

```
Dim row As DataRow = tbl.Rows.Find("NEWCO")
row.ItemArray = New Object() {Nothing, "New Value"}
```

Visual C#
```csharp
DataRow row = tbl.Rows.Find("NEWCO");
row.ItemArray = new object[] {null, "New Value"};
```

> **Note**   Modifying the contents of a row does not automatically modify the contents of the
> corresponding row in your database. The changes you make to the row are considered
> pending changes that you can later submit to your database using the *SqlDataAdapter* class.
> We'll discuss this process in more detail in Chapter 10 and Chapter 11.

So which method should you use to modify rows in your *DataTable*? I prefer using *BeginEdit*
and *EndEdit* because it forces me to write code that's better structured, easier to read, and
easier to maintain. Plus, this approach allows me to cancel the entire set of updates to a row if
an unexpected problem occurs.

In this book, however, I'll generally avoid using the *BeginEdit* and *EndEdit* methods, which will
allow me to make the code snippets more concise.

Working with *Null* Values in a *DataRow*

During the beta for the initial release of the .NET Framework, developers asked a lot of
questions about setting database values to *Null* or checking database values for *Null*.
Determining whether a column in a row contains a *Null* value is actually very simple.

The *DataRow* class has an *IsNull* method that you can use to check whether a column contains
a *Null* value. Like the *DataRow* class's *Item* method, the *IsNull* method accepts a column name,
an integer that represents the index for the column, or a *DataColumn* object.

The following code snippet demonstrates the use of the *DataRow* class's *IsNull* method.

Visual Basic
```vbnet
Dim row As DataRow = tbl.Rows.Find("NEWCO")
If row.IsNull("CompanyName") Then
    Console.WriteLine("It's Null")
Else
    Console.WriteLine("It's not Null")
End If
```

Visual C#
```csharp
DataRow row = tbl.Rows.Find("NEWCO");
if (row.IsNull("CompanyName"))
    Console.WriteLine("It's Null");
else
    Console.WriteLine("It's not Null");
```

When you want to set the value of a column to a null value, don't use the *Null* keyword from
your programming language of choice. The .NET Framework includes a class in the *System*

namespace called *DBNull*. To set the value of a column in a *DataRow* to a null value, use the *Value* property of the *DBNull* class, as shown here:

Visual Basic

```
Dim row As DataRow = tbl.Rows.Find("NEWCO")
row("CompanyName") = DBNull.Value
```

Visual C#

```
DataRow row = tbl.Rows.Find("NEWCO");
row["CompanyName"] = DBNull.Value;
```

Deleting a *DataRow*

Deleting a row is simpler than modifying one. You simply call the *Delete* method on the *DataRow*. However, deleting the row does not remove it from the *DataTable*. Instead, ADO.NET marks the row as a pending deletion. Why doesn't ADO.NET just remove the *DataRow* from the table?

Remember that the data storage objects in the ADO.NET object model act as a data cache so that you can retrieve data from your database, modify that data in a disconnected mode, and later submit the pending changes. When you call the *Delete* method on the *DataRow*, you're not deleting the corresponding row in your database. Instead, you're marking the row as a pending deletion so that you can later submit that pending change to the database. If you completely remove the row from your *DataTable*, you will not delete the corresponding row in your database when you submit the pending changes stored in your *DataSet* or *DataTable*.

We'll examine submitting pending changes to your database in Chapter 10.

Removing a *DataRow*

If you really want to remove a row from your *DataTable* rather than mark it as a pending deletion, you can use the *Remove* or *RemoveAt* method on the *DataRowCollection* class, as shown in the following code snippet. Use the *Remove* method if you have a reference to the *DataRow* you want to remove. If you have the index number for the *DataRow*, use the *RemoveAt* method instead.

Visual Basic

```
Dim row As DataRow = tbl.Rows.Find("NEWCO")
tbl.Rows.Remove(row)

'or

tbl.Rows.RemoveAt(tbl.Rows.IndexOf(row))
```

Visual C#

```
DataRow row = tbl.Rows.Find("NEWCO");
tbl.Rows.Remove(row);

//or

tbl.Rows.RemoveAt(tbl.Rows.IndexOf(row));
```

Note that the *RemoveAt* example calls the *IndexOf* method on the *DataRowCollection* class, which is new to ADO.NET 2.0. The *RemoveAt* method is used implicitly by the Windows data-binding features. When you select a row in a *DataGrid* or *DataGridView* and press the Delete key, that action is translated into a call to *RemoveAt*.

In addition, the *DataSet* and *DataTable* classes each have a *Clear* method that you can use to remove all *DataRow* objects from the *DataSet* or *DataTable* while preserving its structure.

Using the *DataRow.RowState* Property

The *DataSet*, *DataTable*, and *DataRow* objects act as an off-line data cache. You can query your database and store the results in these objects. As you've just learned, you can add, modify, and delete rows. Because these ADO.NET objects are not connected to your database, the changes you make will not affect the contents of your database. Of course, modifying data offline isn't very useful if you can't submit those changes to your database later.

ADO.NET supports submitting changes back to your database. In Chapter 10, I'll explain this functionality in depth. For now, I'll review some of the basics of how the *DataSet* supports this functionality. To cache a change to a *DataRow* so that ADO.NET can later submit the change to your database, ADO.NET must remember what type of change you've made to the row. Why, you ask?

One way to update the data stored in your database is to issue action queries such as this:

```
INSERT INTO MyTable (Field1, Field2, ... FieldN)
          VALUES (Value1, Value2, ... ValueN)
```

or this:

```
UPDATE MyTable SET FieldToModify = NewValue
      WHERE PKField = PKValue AND FieldToModify = OriginalValue
```

or this:

```
DELETE FROM MyTable WHERE PKField = PKValue
```

You can also use stored procedures to perform updates in a similar fashion.

The point is that the logic used to insert a row is different from the logic used to modify a row and the logic used to delete a row. Therefore, ADO.NET must keep track of what kind of change you've made to your *DataRow* in order to successfully submit the change to your database later.

ADO.NET stores this information in a property of the *DataRow* called *RowState*, which uses the values in the *DataRowState* enumeration. (See Table 6-1.) By checking this property, you can determine whether the row has been changed, along with the type of change (insertion, modification, or deletion) the row contains.

Table 6-1   The *DataRowState* Enumeration

Constant	Value	Description
Unchanged	2	The row does not contain any pending changes.
Detached	1	The row is not a member of a *DataTable*.
Added	4	The row has been added to the *DataTable* but does not exist in the database.
Modified	16	The row contains pending changes.
Deleted	8	The row is a pending deletion.

The list of possible values might lead you to believe that the *RowState* property can return a combination of values from *DataRowState*, but the *RowState* property always returns a value from the enumeration. Table 6-2 provides a few scenarios and the resulting value.

Table 6-2   *RowState* Examples

Example	DataRowState

Newly created but detached row:
`row = tbl.NewRow`
`row("ColX") = "InitValue"`
	Detached

Adding the new row to a *DataTable*: `tbl.Rows.Add(row)`	*Added*
Newly retrieved row: `row = tbl.Rows(0)`	*Unchanged*

After an edit:
`row.BeginEdit()`
`row("ColX") = "NewValue1"`
`row.EndEdit()`
	Modified

After deleting a row: `row.Delete()`	*Deleted*

Controlling the *RowState* of your *DataRow*

We've looked at how various actions can affect the *RowState* of your *DataRows*, but what if you want to change the value of the *RowState* property? For example, you might have a *DataRow* whose *RowState* is *Unchanged*, but you really want its *RowState* to be *Added*.

We already discussed the *Delete* method, which marks the row as a pending deletion and sets the *DataRow*'s *RowState* to *Deleted*.

The *DataRow* class has an *AcceptChanges* method that you can use to accept the pending changes stored in the *DataRow*. The *SqlDataAdapter* class implicitly calls the *AcceptChanges* method after successfully submitting the pending change stored in a *DataRow*. This method purges the pending changes stored in a *DataRow* and implicitly sets the *DataRow*'s *RowState*. Calling *AcceptChanges* will set the *RowState* of an *Added* or *Modified DataRow* to *Unchanged*. Calling *AcceptChanges* on a *Deleted DataRow* removes the *DataRow* from the *DataTable*'s collection of rows and sets the *DataRow*'s *RowState* to *Detached*.

The *DataRow* class also has a *RejectChanges* method that you can use to undo the changes stored in the *DataRow*. The *RejectChanges* method resets the *DataRow*'s current values based on its original values, purging the pending changes that it previously contained. As with *AcceptChanges*, the resulting *RowState* of the *DataRow* depends on the initial *RowState*. Calling *RejectChanges* on a *Modified* or *Deleted DataRow* returns the *RowState* to *Unchanged*. Calling *RejectChanges* on an *Added DataRow* removes the *DataRow* from the *DataTable*'s collection of rows and sets the *DataRow*'s *RowState* to *Detached*.

There are also new methods in ADO.NET 2.0 that can help you control the *RowState* of your *DataRows*: *SetAdded* and *SetModified*. As its name implies, the *SetAdded* method sets a *DataRow*'s *RowState* to *Added*. Similarly, the *SetModified* method sets a *DataRow*'s *RowState* to *Modified*. However, these methods are available only on *DataRows* whose *RowState* is *Unmodified*. Calling either method on a *DataRow* whose *RowState* is not *Unmodified* (meaning *Added*, *Modified*, *Deleted*, and so on) will throw an *InvalidOperationException*.

Why are these methods available only for unmodified *DataRows*? Say that you have a *DataRow* whose *RowState* is *Modified*, and you want to set its *RowState* to *Added*. In most cases, you'd want to do this so that you can insert this row into your database. What values would you want to insert—the original values or the current values in the *DataRow*? If you want to insert the current values, call *AcceptChanges* prior to *SetAdded*. If you want to insert the original values, call *RejectChanges* prior to *SetAdded*.

Examining the Pending Changes in a *DataRow*

Let's say that we've looped through the contents of your *DataTable* and, thanks to the *RowState* property, we've located a modified row. You've seen how to use the *Item* property of the *DataRow* to examine the contents of the columns in the row. You can also use the *Item* property to determine what the contents of the columns were before you modified the row.

The *Item* property accepts a second optional parameter from the *DataRowVersion* enumeration, as described in Table 6-3.

Table 6-3   The *DataRowVersion* Enumeration

Constant	Value	Description
Current	512	The current value stored in the column
Original	256	The original value stored in the column
Proposed	1024	The proposed value for the column (valid only while editing a row using *BeginEdit*)
Default	1536	Default action

Generally speaking, the *DataRow* has two "versions"—what's currently stored in the row, and what was originally stored in the row. You'll usually need both sets of information to locate the row. After you've updated a row, you can check the current contents of a column as well as the original contents of a column. The following code changes the contents of the CompanyName column in a *DataRow* and then retrieves both the current (new) value and the original value of the column. Note that this code passes in *True* on the call to *LoadDataRow*, so the row is added to the *DataTable* in an unmodified state. There is no "original" state for rows marked as pending insertions.

Visual Basic

```
Dim tbl As New DataTable("Customers")
tbl.Columns.Add("CustomerID", GetType(String))
tbl.Columns.Add("CompanyName", GetType(String))
tbl.PrimaryKey = New DataColumn() {tbl.Columns("CustomerID")}
tbl.LoadDataRow(New Object() {"NEWCO", "Initial Value"}, True)

Dim row As DataRow = tbl.Rows.Find("NEWCO")
row("CompanyName") = "New Value"
Console.WriteLine("DataRowVersion.Current = {0}", _
                  row("CompanyName", DataRowVersion.Current))
Console.WriteLine("DataRowVersion.Original = {0}", _
                  row("CompanyName", DataRowVersion.Original))
```

Visual C#

```
DataTable tbl = new DataTable("Customers");
tbl.Columns.Add("CustomerID", typeof(string));
tbl.Columns.Add("CompanyName", typeof(string));
tbl.PrimaryKey = new DataColumn[] {tbl.Columns["CustomerID"]};
tbl.LoadDataRow(new object[] {"NEWCO", "Initial Value"}, true);

DataRow row = tbl.Rows.Find("NEWCO");
row["CompanyName"] = "New Value";
Console.WriteLine("DataRowVersion.Current = {0}",
                  row["CompanyName", DataRowVersion.Current]);
Console.WriteLine("DataRowVersion.Original = {0}",
                  row["CompanyName", DataRowVersion.Original]);
```

When you edit a row using *BeginEdit* and *EndEdit*, you might want to examine another version of the column: the "proposed" version. Once you call *EndEdit*, the changes will be stored in the current version of the row. Before then, however, the changes you make to the row will only be pending because you can still cancel the changes by calling *CancelEdit*.

While you're editing a row, you can check the proposed value of a column by checking its *Item* property and supplying the *Proposed* constant from the *DataRowVersion* enumeration. Using the *Current* constant will return the value of the column before *BeginEdit* is called—which is not necessarily the original value of the column.

Let's look at the various states of a *DataRow* and the different values the *Item* property returns based on the value of *DataRowVersion* you use. (This is sort of like how a bill becomes a law, but without the Saturday morning cartoon animation.)

Table 6-4 lists the values returned by the *Item* property, depending on the *DataRowVersion* enumeration specified and the current state of the row. Entries marked as *[Exception]* represent scenarios in which calling the *Item* property with the *DataRowVersion* enumeration specified will throw an exception.

Table 6-4   Values of Various Versions of a Column in a *DataRow*

Example	Current	Original	Proposed	Default

Newly created but detached row:
 	
`row = tbl.NewRow`
`row("ColumnX") = "InitValue"`
	InitialValue	*[Exception]*	*[Exception]*	*NewValue*

Adding the new row to a *DataTable*: `Tbl.Rows.Add(row)`	*InitialValue*	*[Exception]*	*[Exception]*	*NewValue*
Newly retrieved row: `row = tbl.Rows(0)`	*Retrieved-Value*	*Retrieved-Value*	*[Exception]*	*Retrieved-Value*

During first edit:
 	
`row.BeginEdit()`
`row("ColX") = "NewValue1"`
	Retrieved-Value	*Retrieved-Value*	*NewValue1*	*NewValue1*

After first edit: `row.EndEdit()`	*NewValue1*	*Retrieved-Value*	*[Exception]*	*NewValue1*

During second edit:
 	
`row.BeginEdit()`
`row("ColX") = "NewValue2"`
	NewValue1	*Retrieved-Value*	*NewValue2*	*NewValue2*

After second edit: `row.EndEdit()`	*NewValue2*	*Retrieved-Value*	*[Exception]*	*NewValue2*

After canceled edit:
 	
`row.BeginEdit()`
`row("ColX") = "ValueToCan-cel"`
`row.CancelEdit()`
	NewValue2	*Retrieved-Value*	*[Exception]*	*NewValue2*

After deleting a row: `row.Delete()`	*[Exception]*	*Retrieved-Value*	*[Exception]*	*[Exception]*

> **Note**   Performing a successful edit changes the current value but does not affect the original value. Calling *CancelEdit* resets the current value to the value before *BeginEdit* is called, which is not necessarily the same as the original value.
>
> After you've deleted a row, you'll receive an exception if you try to examine its current values, but you can still access its original values.

We've discussed three of the four values in the *DataRowVersion* enumeration. Now let's discuss the *Default* value. Using this value in the *Item* property will not return the default value for the column. That's the *DefaultValue* property's job. This *Default* value in the enumeration represents the default value for the *DataRowVersion* parameter on the *DataRow* object's *Item* property.

Earlier in the chapter, I mentioned that the *Item* property returns the current value of a column in the row. The accuracy of that statement might depend on your definition of "current."

If you're not in the process of editing a row, calling *Item* and omitting the optional parameter or specifying *Default* for this parameter is equivalent to supplying the *DataRowVersion.Current* constant for the optional parameter. However, if you're in the process of editing a row and you omit the optional parameter on the *Item* property or specify *Default*, you'll receive the "proposed" version for the column.

ADO.NET 2.0 *DataSet* Serialization and Remoting Options

ADO.NET 2.0 includes new options that can give you more control and better performance in a Web service or multitiered applications that serialize or remote *DataSets*.

Serializing and Remoting *DataTables*

You can now serialize and remote *DataTables* in ADO.NET 2.0 as easily as you could serialize *DataSets* in ADO.NET 1.x. Many of the XML features previously associated with just the *DataSet* (*ReadXml*, *ReadXmlSchema*, *WriteXml*, and *WriteXmlSchema*) are now available on the *DataTable* as well. The one requirement is that you must set the *DataTable*'s *TableName* property prior to using these features.

DataColumn.DateTimeMode

In version 2.0 of the .NET Framework, the *DateTime* data type has been enhanced so that you can tell whether the *DateTime* value represents the local or coordinated universal time (UTC) by checking the *Kind* property on the *DateTime* object. This property returns a value from the *DateTimeKind* enumeration: *Local*, *Utc*, or *Unspecified*. The *DateTimeMode* property on the *DataColumn* class controls how ADO.NET serializes *DateTime* values in that *DataColumn*.

The following example will display the current date and time according to your machine's time zone settings as well as the corresponding UTC date and time. Note that the *Kind* property indicates whether the *DateTime* contains local or UTC date/time information.

Visual Basic

```
DateTime nowLocal = DateTime.Now;
DateTime nowUtc = TimeZone.CurrentTimeZone.ToUniversalTime(nowLocal);
Console.WriteLine("Kind: {0,-5}  DateTime: {1}", nowLocal.Kind, nowLocal);
Console.WriteLine("Kind: {0,-5}  DateTime: {1}", nowUtc.Kind, nowUtc);
```

Visual C#

```
DateTime nowLocal = DateTime.Now;
DateTime nowUtc = TimeZone.CurrentTimeZone.ToUniversalTime(nowLocal);
Console.WriteLine("Kind: {0,-5}  DateTime: {1}", nowLocal.Kind, nowLocal);
Console.WriteLine("Kind: {0,-5}  DateTime: {1}", nowUtc.Kind, nowUtc);
```

This functionality can prove invaluable if you're building a personal information manager (PIM) application, such as Microsoft Outlook. You can store all appointments in the central store in UTC format and then display those appointments in the application based on the user's local time zone.

For the purposes of this discussion, let's assume that the PIM application uses a Windows Forms client to interact with a Web service. The machine on which the Web service is running is located in Boston, Mass., and the Windows Forms client application client is running in Seattle, Wash. And though the client and server are close to the same highway, they are three time zones apart. While it's 6:00 P.M. in Seattle, it's 9:00 P.M. in Boston.

By default, when you serialize a value in a *DateTime DataColumn* in a *DataSet*, ADO.NET writes that *DateTime* value and includes the time zone information in the form of a UTC offset. If we stored the current *DateTime* on the server in Boston (9:00 P.M., Eastern Time, which is five hours behind UTC time at the time of this writing) in a *DataSet* and serialized that *DataSet* as XML, you would see the following information:

```
<DateTimeCol>2005-11-27T21:00:00.00-05:00</DateTimeCol>
```

If the client application in Seattle receives this information, it will automatically translate this value, based on the Windows settings for the local time zone. The real work here is actually handled by the *DateTime* class's *Parse* method, which can handle the date-time format shown earlier, which includes the UTC offset. The *DateTime* value in the *DataSet* on the client in Seattle will be translated to 6:00 P.M. Pacific Time. However, the *Kind* property on the *DateTime* will be set to *Unspecified*.

In ADO.NET 2.0, the *DataSet* class has also added enhancements to give you more control as to how *DateTime* values are serialized and deserialized with the new *DateTimeMode* property on the *DataColumn* class. To better understand the effect this property can have on your application, let's look at how the property could be used in our theoretical PIM application.

The *DateTimeMode* property affects the *Kind* property of *DateTime* values generated by deserializing a *DataSet*. As we discussed earlier, the *Kind* property was set to *DateTime-Kind.Unspecified* for the *DateTime* value generated in the client application when it receives a *DataSet* from the Web service. This is the expected behavior when the *DataColumn*'s *DateTimeMode* property is set to *UnspecifiedLocal* (the default) or *Unspecified*. If you want the *DateTime* values in the deserialized *DataSet* to have their *Kind* properties set to *DateTimeKind.Local*, set the *DataColumn*'s *DateTimeMode* property to *DataSetDateTime .Local*. Setting the *DataColumn*'s *DateTimeMode* property to *DataSetDateTime.Utc* will cause the *DateTime* values in the deserialized *DataSet* to have their *Kind* properties set to *DateTimeKind.Utc*.

You can also use the *DateTimeMode* property to control the data that's serialized along with your *DataSet*. When a *DateTimeMode* is set to the default of *UnspecifiedLocal*, the *DateTime* value is written along with the current time zone's UTC offset information:

```
<DateTimeCol>2005-11-27T21:00:00.00-05:00</DateTimeCol>
```

Some developers might have written *DateTime* values in a similar format using the *ToString* method and a custom format such as "yyyy-MM-ddTHH:mm:ss.FFFFFFFzzz".

Setting the *DateTimeMode* property to *Unspecified* will cause the *DateTime* values in that *Data-Column* to be serialized using a similar format ("yyyy-MM-ddTHH:mm:ss.FFFFFFF") that omits the time zone offset.

Setting the *DateTimeMode* property to *Local* will include the full *DateTime* information, including the time zone offset, but *DateTime* values whose *Kind* property is *Utc* will be translated to the local time zone prior to serialization.

Setting the *DateTimeMode* property to *Utc* will cause ADO.NET to serialize the *DateTime* value in the UTC format shown here:

```
<DateTimeCol>2005-11-28T02:00:00.00Z</DateTimeCol>
```

You could write data the same way by using the custom format "yyyy-MM-ddTHH:mm:ss.FFFFFFFZ". *DateTime* values whose *Kind* property is set to *Local* are translated to UTC. *DateTime* values whose *Kind* property is set to *Unspecified* are not translated. They are assumed to be UTC *DateTimes* already.

Let's return to our theoretical PIM application. If you store the dates and times of appointments in your database using the current time zone information on the server, do the applications that access the data need to be aware of that time zone information for their queries and user interfaces? What happens if you need to change the location of the server, or if you need to replicate the data to a server in another time zone?

Many developers prefer to store the data in their database using UTC values. Setting the *DateTimeMode* property on your *DateTime DataColumns* to *DataSetDateTime.Utc* can help. Say that you create an appointment in the client portion of our PIM application using the local time zone—Pacific Time, in our example. When the *DataSet* is sent to the Web service, the *DateTime* value will be translated to the UTC date and time without having to perform any manual translations, before submitting the new value to the database.

DataSet.SchemaSerializationMode

Visual Studio makes it easy to build Web services that return query results using strongly typed *DataSets*. We'll discuss strongly typed *DataSets* in detail in Chapter 9. For now, the key point to understand is that a strongly typed *DataSet* derives from a basic *DataSet* and includes schema information about the *DataSet* describing its tables, columns, and relations.

Here's some simple code I put together for a Web method that accepts a *CustomerID* and returns basic information for that customer in a strongly typed *DataSet*:

Visual Basic

```
<WebMethod()> _
Public Function GetACustomer(ByVal CustomerID As String) As TinyDataSet
    Dim ds As New TinyDataSet()
    Dim strConn, strSQL As String
    strConn = "Data Source=.\SQLExpress;" & _
                "Initial Catalog=Northwind;Integrated Security=True;"
    strSQL = "SELECT CustomerID, CompanyName FROM Customers " & _
            "WHERE CustomerID = @CustomerID"
    Using cn As New SqlConnection(strConn)
        Using cmd As New SqlCommand(strSQL, cn)
            cmd.Parameters.AddWithValue("@CustomerID", CustomerID)
            cn.Open()
            Using rdr As SqlDataReader = cmd.ExecuteReader()
                ds.Customers.Load(rdr)
            End Using
        End Using
    End Using

    Return ds
End Function
```

Visual C#

```
[WebMethod]
public TinyDataSet GetACustomer(string CustomerID) {
    TinyDataSet ds = new TinyDataSet();
    string strConn, strSQL;
    strConn = @"Data Source=.\SQLExpress;" +
                "Initial Catalog=Northwind;Integrated Security=True;";
    strSQL = "SELECT CustomerID, CompanyName FROM Customers " +
            "WHERE CustomerID = @CustomerID";
    using (SqlConnection cn = new SqlConnection(strConn)) {
        using (SqlCommand cmd = new SqlCommand(strSQL, cn)) {
            cmd.Parameters.AddWithValue("@CustomerID", CustomerID);
            cn.Open();
            using (SqlDataReader rdr = cmd.ExecuteReader()) {
                ds.Customers.Load(rdr);
            }
        }
    }

    return ds;
}
```

You can run the Web service inside Visual Studio and call the Web method from an Internet Explorer window to see the strongly typed *DataSet* returned, shown in Figure 6-1:

```
<?xml version="1.0" encoding="utf-8" ?>
- <TinyDataSet xmlns="http://tempuri.org/">
  - <xs:schema id="TinyDataSet" targetNamespace="http://tempuri.org/TinyDataSet.xsd" xmlns:mstns="http://tempuri.org/T
    - <xs:element name="TinyDataSet" msdata:IsDataSet="true" msdata:UseCurrentLocale="true">
      - <xs:complexType>
        - <xs:choice minOccurs="0" maxOccurs="unbounded">
          - <xs:element name="Customers">
            - <xs:complexType>
              - <xs:sequence>
                - <xs:element name="CustomerID">
                  - <xs:simpleType>
                    - <xs:restriction base="xs:string">
                        <xs:maxLength value="5" />
                      </xs:restriction>
                    </xs:simpleType>
                  </xs:element>
                - <xs:element name="CompanyName">
                  - <xs:simpleType>
                    - <xs:restriction base="xs:string">
                        <xs:maxLength value="40" />
                      </xs:restriction>
                    </xs:simpleType>
                  </xs:element>
                </xs:sequence>
              </xs:complexType>
            </xs:element>
          </xs:choice>
        </xs:complexType>
      - <xs:unique name="Constraint1" msdata:PrimaryKey="true">
          <xs:selector xpath=".//mstns:Customers" />
          <xs:field xpath="mstns:CustomerID" />
        </xs:unique>
      </xs:element>
    </xs:schema>
  - <diffgr:diffgram xmlns:msdata="urn:schemas-microsoft-com:xml-msdata" xmlns:diffgr="urn:schemas-microsoft-com:xml-d
    - <TinyDataSet xmlns="http://tempuri.org/TinyDataSet.xsd">
      - <Customers diffgr:id="Customers1" msdata:rowOrder="0">
          <CustomerID>ALFKI</CustomerID>
          <CompanyName>Alfreds Futterkiste</CompanyName>
        </Customers>
      </TinyDataSet>
    </diffgr:diffgram>
  </TinyDataSet>
```

Figure 6-1   Viewing a strongly typed *DataSet* returned from a Web method in Internet Explorer

If you take a close look at Figure 6-1, you'll see that there's very little data in this *DataSet*. The majority of the information returned is schema information.

One of the more powerful features of Web services is that Web methods are self-describing. A client can examine the .wsdl file for the Web service to understand the parameters and return value for Web methods. In this case, that metadata includes the *DataSet*'s schema. As a result, many clients already have the *DataSet*'s schema information prior to calling the Web method. In other words, for most client applications, the schema information you see in Figure 6-1 is redundant.

ADO.NET 2.0 lets you omit this schema information when you serialize your *DataSets*. Simply set the *SchemaSerializationMode* property to *SchemaSerializationMode.ExcludeSchema* inside the Web method and the schema will be omitted, as shown in Figure 6-2. As you can see by comparing the figures, excluding the schema drastically reduces the amount of data returned. In fact, excluding the schema in Figure 6-2 allowed me to use a more legible font size.

```
<?xml version="1.0" encoding="utf-8" ?>
- <TinyDataSet msdata:SchemaSerializationMode="ExcludeSchema" xmlns:msdata="urn:schemas-microsoft-com:x
    xmlns="http://tempuri.org/">
  - <xs:schema id="TinyDataSet" targetNamespace="http://tempuri.org/TinyDataSet.xsd"
      xmlns:mstns="http://tempuri.org/TinyDataSet.xsd" xmlns="http://tempuri.org/TinyDataSet.xsd"
      xmlns:xs="http://www.w3.org/2001/XMLSchema" xmlns:msdata="urn:schemas-microsoft-com:xml-msda
      attributeFormDefault="qualified" elementFormDefault="qualified">
    - <xs:element name="TinyDataSet" msdata:IsDataSet="true" msdata:UseCurrentLocale="true">
      - <xs:complexType>
          <xs:choice minOccurs="0" maxOccurs="unbounded" />
        </xs:complexType>
      </xs:element>
    </xs:schema>
  - <diffgr:diffgram xmlns:msdata="urn:schemas-microsoft-com:xml-msdata" xmlns:diffgr="urn:schemas-micros
      diffgram-v1">
    - <TinyDataSet xmlns="http://tempuri.org/TinyDataSet.xsd">
      - <Customers diffgr:id="Customers1" msdata:rowOrder="0">
          <CustomerID>ALFKI</CustomerID>
          <CompanyName>Alfreds Futterkiste</CompanyName>
        </Customers>
      </TinyDataSet>
    </diffgr:diffgram>
  </TinyDataSet>
```

Figure 6-2   The same *DataSet* from Figure 6-1 with *SchemaSerializationMode.ExcludeSchema*

Excluding the schema can make a major difference in the performance of your application. By excluding the schema, you're serializing less data with your *DataSet*. You're also skipping the step of writing the schema information to and reading the schema information from the serialization stream.

I created two simple *DataSet* serialization scenarios—one that retrieved just a *CustomerID* and *CompanyName* for a single *Customer*, and one that retrieved all Categories, Customers, Employees, Order Details, Orders, Products, Regions, Shippers, Suppliers, and Territories. For each scenario, I created a simple Web service and a Console application and timed thousands of calls to the Web service. I started the timer inside the Web service after filling the *DataSet*, just prior to returning the *DataSet*, and stopped it immediately after the call to the Web service. For both scenarios, excluding the schema information improved performance by approximately 30 percent. Of course, the difference in performance will largely depend on the amount of data you're returning. For small amounts of data, the schema represents a larger proportion of bits, but for large amounts of data the schema info becomes proportionally smaller.

This schema serialization feature was designed for strongly typed *DataSet*s rather than untyped *DataSet*s. The logic to determine whether to include the schema is built into strongly typed *DataSet*s rather than the *DataSet* class. If you create a simple *DataSet* and try to set the *Schema-SerializationMode* to *SchemaSerializationMode.ExcludeSchema*, you'll receive an *InvalidOperation-Exception* stating, "*SchemaSerializationMode* property can be set only if it is overridden by derived *DataSet*."

The strongly typed *DataSet* overrides the *SchemaSerializationMode* property and includes custom serialization code that checks the property before determining whether to serialize the schema information. The property is available on the *DataSet* class because there is no common class or interface between the *DataSet* class and the strongly typed *DataSet*s.

DataSet.RemotingFormat

As you saw in Figures 6-1 and 6-2, *DataSet*s are serialized as XML. This is a flexible and easy-to-understand format because it's self-describing. However, XML is not always the best format to use. For example, the row of data in Figures 6-1 and 6-2 contains elements (CustomerID, CompanyName) in the contents of the file. Those element names appear on each row in the *DataSet* when it's serialized as XML. That information is redundant. For small *DataSet*s, the XML format is fine. For larger *DataSet*s, that redundancy might constitute a significant performance hit.

ADO.NET 2.0 now lets you control the format used to remote a *DataSet*. By default, *DataSet*s are still remoted as XML. However, you can set the *RemoteFormat* property of your *DataSet* to *SerializationFormat.Binary* to use a binary format instead. Which format should you use? That depends on how much data you're working with.

For very small *DataSets*, the XML format conserves space and provides better performance. When I used a query that returned *CustomerID* and *CompanyName* for one Customer, the XML format required 1645 bytes and the serializing/deserializing process took an average of 2 milliseconds. Using the same query, the binary format required 6362 bytes and the serialization/deserialization process took an average of 3 milliseconds.

For very large *DataSets*, the binary format is preferable. I used a batch query that returned all entries from the Customers, Orders, Order Details, Products, and Employees tables into separate *DataTables*—a total of 11,620 entries (sum of rows * columns). The binary format here was much more compact—141,887 bytes for binary and 444,231 bytes for XML. The performance of the binary format was also superior—serializing and deserializing took an average of 45 milliseconds for the binary format and 160 milliseconds for the XML format.

The tipping point was "SELECT * FROM Customers". Running this query on my machine returned 1001 entries. Here, the binary and XML formats achieved nearly the same size and performance. In other words, stick with the XML format if you're working with small *DataSets*, those with at most a few hundred entries. If you're working with larger *DataSets*, use the binary format.

You can and should perform your own tests to measure performance in your scenarios. You can use the following code snippet to remote a *DataSet* to a file stream, and then read that file stream to re-create the *DataSet*. I started with this approach and added code to determine the size of the stream and the time required to serialize and deserialize the *DataSet* to and from the file.

Visual Basic

```vb
'Imports System.IO
'Imports System.Runtime.Serialization
'Imports System.Runtime.Serialization.Formatters.Binary
Private Function SerializeAndDeserialize(dsInput As DataSet) As DataSet
    Dim dsOutput As DataSet = Nothing
    Dim strTempFile As String = Path.GetTempFileName()
    Using stream As New FileStream(strTempFile, FileMode.Open)
        Dim formatter As IFormatter = new BinaryFormatter()
        formatter.Serialize(stream, dsInput)

        stream.Flush()
        stream.Position = 0

        dsOutput = CType(formatter.Deserialize(stream), DataSet)
    End Using
    File.Delete(strTempFile)
    Return dsOutput
End Function
```

Visual C#

```csharp
//using System.IO;
//using System.Runtime.Serialization;
//using System.Runtime.Serialization.Formatters.Binary;
```

```
static DataSet SerializeAndDeserialize(DataSet dsInput)
{
    DataSet dsOutput = null;
    string strTempFile = Path.GetTempFileName();
    using (FileStream stream = new FileStream(strTempFile, FileMode.Open))
    {
        IFormatter formatter = new BinaryFormatter();
        formatter.Serialize(stream, dsInput);

        stream.Flush();
        stream.Position = 0;

        dsOutput = (DataSet)formatter.Deserialize(stream);
    }
    File.Delete(strTempFile);
    return dsOutput;
}
```

Working with *DataSet* Objects in Visual Studio

You now know a great deal about the structure of *DataSet* objects and how to create them in code. But, man, that's a lot of code to write! Let's look at some features of the Visual Studio development environment that you can use to create *DataSet* objects with a lot less effort.

Creating Strongly Typed *DataSets* in Visual Studio

If you've used previous versions of Visual Studio and you're trying to create a strongly typed *DataSet* in Visual Studio 2005, you might be a bit confused initially. For example, the Generate *DataSet* option in the main menu and context menus is gone. The functionality still exists, but it has been moved, renamed, and retooled. We'll discuss strongly typed *DataSet*s and creating them in depth in Chapter 9.

Creating an Untyped *DataSet*

You can still use Visual Studio 2005 to create simple untyped *DataSet*s using simple dialog boxes at design time, rather than using ADO.NET code at run time. Visual Studio will then translate your input into ADO.NET code and store that code in the designer files.

To add an untyped *DataSet* to a designer, such as a Windows form, drag and drop the *DataSet* item from the Visual Studio toolbox onto the designer surface. This action will launch the dialog box shown in Figure 6-3. Select Untyped *DataSet* from the dialog box and click OK to add the new untyped *DataSet* to your designer. You'll see your new *DataSet* in your designer's components tray.

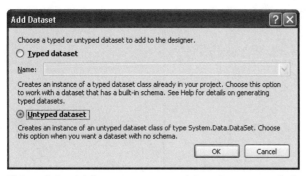

Figure 6-3   Adding a new untyped *DataSet* to your designer

Select the *DataSet* in the components tray, and you'll see its properties listed in the Properties window. To add *DataTable* objects to the *DataSet*, select the *Tables* property in the Properties window and then click the ellipsis button to the right. Doing so will launch the Visual Studio Collection Editor. Many components within Visual Studio use the Collection Editor. Figure 6-4 shows how the Collection Editor appears when it is used to modify the *DataTable* objects within a *DataSet*.

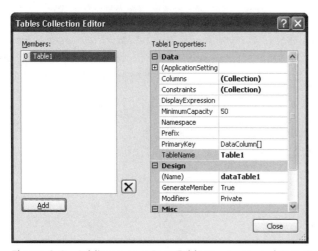

Figure 6-4   Adding a new *DataTable* to an untyped *DataSet*

You'll also see the same editor when you add *DataColumn* objects to your new *DataTable*. To add *DataColumn* objects, select the *DataTable* to which you want to add columns in the Collection Editor. Then select the *Columns* collection in the window to the right and click the ellipsis button. You'll launch a new Collection Editor, shown in Figure 6-5, which is used for building *DataColumn* objects.

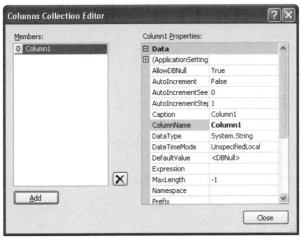

Figure 6-5   Adding a new *DataColumn* to a *DataTable*

Once you've added your *DataColumn* objects, you might want to specify a primary key for your *DataTable*. Select your *DataTable* in the Collection Editor, and you'll see *PrimaryKey* listed as a property in the window on the right. Select this property, and then click the arrow to the right. You'll see the list of columns that appear in the *DataTable*, as shown in Figure 6-6. Select the *DataColumn*(s) you want to use for the *DataTable* object's primary key, and then dismiss the drop-down list by clicking elsewhere in the Collection Editor. As Figure 6-6 shows, the designer makes it simple to build primary keys that are based on multiple columns.

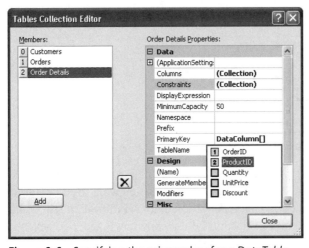

Figure 6-6   Specifying the primary key for a *DataTable*

You can also add items to the *Constraints* collection of your *DataTable* objects. Click the *Constraints* property for your *DataTable* in the *DataTable*'s Collection Editor, and then click the ellipsis button to launch another Collection Editor. This new Collection Editor, shown in

Figure 6-7, lets you modify the contents of your *DataTable* object's *Constraints* collection. If you already have a primary key defined on your *DataTable*, you'll see that there's already an item in the *Constraints* collection.

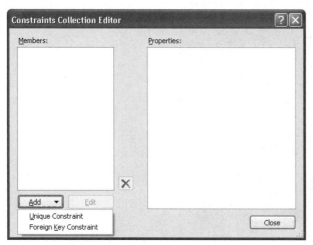

Figure 6-7   Adding constraints to a *DataTable*

As Figure 6-7 implies, you can use the Collection Editor to add unique or foreign key constraints. Click the Add button, and you'll see a shortcut menu asking which type of constraint you want to add. Figure 6-8 shows the user interface for adding new unique constraints. The interface is pretty straightforward. You simply select the *DataColumn* object you want to include in the new unique key. You can also specify a name for the key and indicate whether this unique key should also be the *DataTable* object's primary key.

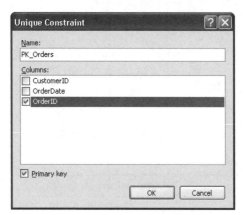

Figure 6-8   Adding a new *UniqueConstraint* to a *DataTable*

Figure 6-9 shows the user interface for adding new foreign key constraints. Supply a name for the foreign key constraint, and select the parent *DataTable*. Then select the parent and child *DataColumns* for the new foreign key constraint. There are also drop-down options that allow you to specify values for other properties on the new *ForeignKeyConstraint*—*UpdateRule*, *DeleteRule*, and *CascadeRule*. By default, these properties are set to the ADO.NET defaults when creating a *ForeignKeyConstraint* object—*Cascade*, *Cascade*, and *None*, respectively. We'll explore these properties in more detail in Chapter 7 when we discuss *DataRelations*.

Figure 6-9 Adding a new *ForeignKeyConstraint* to a *DataTable*

DataSet, DataTable, DataColumn, DataRow, UniqueConstraint, and *ForeignKeyConstraint* Class Reference

Now that you understand how to use the basic features of the *DataSet* and its related classes, let's look at each of the properties, events, and methods that those classes expose.

Properties of the *DataSet* Class

The commonly used properties of the *DataSet* class are shown in Table 6-5.

Table 6-5   Properties of the *DataSet* Class

Property	Data Type	Description
CaseSensitive	*Boolean*	Controls whether string comparisons are case sensitive
DataSetName	*String*	Returns the name of the *DataSet*
DefaultViewManager	*DataViewManager*	Returns the default *DataViewManager* for the *DataSet*
DesignMode	*Boolean*	Indicates whether the *DataSet* is in design mode

Table 6-5 Properties of the *DataSet* Class

Property	Data Type	Description
EnforceConstraints	Boolean	Controls whether the *DataSet* will enforce the constraints that it contains
ExtendedProperties	PropertyCollection	Contains a collection of dynamic properties and values
HasErrors	Boolean	Indicates whether the *DataSet* contains errors
IsInitialized	Boolean	Indicates whether the *DataSet* has been initialized
Locale	CultureInfo	Controls the locale that the *DataSet* will use to compare strings
Namespace	String	Contains the namespace that ADO.NET will use when writing the contents of your *DataSet* to XML or when loading XML data into your *DataSet*
Prefix	String	Contains the prefix for the namespace that ADO.NET will use when writing the contents of your *DataSet* to XML or when loading XML data into your *DataSet*
Relations	DataRelationCollection	Contains the collection of *DataRelation* objects for your *DataSet*
RemotingFormat	SerializationFormat	Controls the serialization format used to remote the *DataSet*
SchemaSerializationMode	SchemaSerializationMode	Controls whether the *DataSet*'s schema will be included when the *DataSet* is serialized
Tables	DataTableCollection	Contains the collection of *DataTable* objects for your *DataSet*

CaseSensitive Property

The *CaseSensitive* property of the *DataSet* controls whether string comparisons within the *DataSet* are case sensitive. The default value for this property is *False*.

Changing the value of the *CaseSensitive* property of the *DataSet* will change the value of the *CaseSensitive* property of *DataTable* objects within the *DataSet* whose *CaseSensitive* property has not been set.

The *DataTable* class also exposes a *CaseSensitive* property.

DataSetName Property

The *DataSetName* property contains the name of the *DataSet*. You can specify a value for this property in the *DataSet* object's constructor. If you do not specify a value in the constructor, this property will be set to *NewDataSet*.

If you write the contents of your *DataSet* to an XML document, the *DataSetName* property controls the name of the root node for the XML document. The *DataSetName* property also controls the name of the class you'll generate if you use the XSD.exe utility to generate a class file that's based on the contents of an XML schema file.

DefaultViewManager Property

The *DefaultViewManager* property returns a *DataViewManager* object, which you can use to control the default *DataView* of each *DataTable* in your *DataSet*. We'll discuss *DataView*s in more detail in Chapter 8.

DesignMode Property

The *DesignMode* property of the *DataSet* class returns a Boolean value that indicates whether the *DataSet* is in design mode. This property can be useful when you write code in a user control. If the *DataSet* is being used at design time within a component, *DesignMode* will return *True*. Otherwise, it will return *False*.

The *DataTable* object also exposes a *DesignMode* property. This property is read-only for both classes.

EnforceConstraints Property

You can use the *EnforceConstraints* property to control whether the *DataSet* will enforce the constraints that it contains. By default, this property is set to *True*. If you want to temporarily turn off constraints, you can set *EnforceConstraints* to *False*.

Setting the property to *True* will throw a *ConstraintException* if the current contents of the *DataSet* violate any of its constraints.

ExtendedProperties Property

You can use the *DataSet* class's *ExtendedProperties* property to store miscellaneous information. The property returns a *PropertyCollection* object, which is designed to store various objects. Although you can store objects within the *DataSet* object's *ExtendedProperties* collection, you should probably stick with simple strings. When you save the contents of a *DataSet* object's schema to a file or a stream, ADO.NET will write the contents of the *ExtendedProperties* collection as strings.

The *DataTable*, *DataColumn*, *DataRelation*, and *Constraint* classes also expose an *Extended-Properties* property.

The following code shows how to add entries to a *DataSet* object's *ExtendedProperties* collection, as well as how to access the contents of the collection. Because the code uses an *IDictionaryEnumerator*, it requires a reference to the *System.Collections* namespace.

Visual Basic

```vb
'Imports System.Collections
Dim ds As New DataSet()

'Add extended properties.
ds.ExtendedProperties.Add("Prop1", "Value1")
ds.ExtendedProperties.Add("Prop2", "Value2")
ds.ExtendedProperties.Add("Prop3", "Value3")

'Retrieve the value of an extended property.
Console.WriteLine(ds.ExtendedProperties("Prop2"))

'Retrieve and enumerate all extended properties.
Dim objEnum As IDictionaryEnumerator
objEnum = ds.ExtendedProperties.GetEnumerator()
Do While objEnum.MoveNext()
    Console.WriteLine("{0} = {1}", objEnum.Key, objEnum.Value)
Loop
```

Visual C#

```csharp
//using System.Collections;
DataSet ds = new DataSet();

//Add extended properties.
ds.ExtendedProperties.Add("Prop1", "Value1");
ds.ExtendedProperties.Add("Prop2", "Value2");
ds.ExtendedProperties.Add("Prop3", "Value3");

//Retrieve the value of an extended property.
Console.WriteLine(ds.ExtendedProperties["Prop2"]);

//Retrieve and enumerate all extended properties.
IDictionaryEnumerator objEnum;
objEnum = ds.ExtendedProperties.GetEnumerator();
while (objEnum.MoveNext())
    Console.WriteLine("{0} = {1}", objEnum.Key, objEnum.Value);
```

> **Note**   Some databases, such as SQL Server and Microsoft Access, support extended properties on tables and columns. As a result, some developers have expected that those extended properties would immediately appear in their *DataSet* after calling the *Fill* or *FillSchema* method on their *SqlDataAdapter* or *OleDbDataAdapter*. To make a long story short, there is no direct way to retrieve these extended properties from your database and place them into your *DataSet* using a method in the ADO.NET API. If you want to retrieve this information, you'll have to write a database-specific query and then add those properties to the *ExtendedProperties* collection.

HasErrors Property

The *HasErrors* property returns a Boolean value that indicates whether any *DataRow* objects within the *DataSet* contain errors. If you're submitting batches of changes to your database and you've set the *ContinueUpdateOnError* property of your *SqlDataAdapter* objects to

True, you should check the *HasErrors* property of your *DataSet* after submitting changes to determine whether any of the update attempts failed.

The *DataTable* and *DataRow* classes also expose a *HasErrors* property.

For more information about handling failed update attempts, see Chapter 11.

IsInitialized Property

The *DataSet* class supports the *IsInitialized* property as part of its implementation of the *ISupportInitializeNotification* interface. For more information, see the sidebar that describes the *ISupportInitializeNotification* interface following the *BeginInit* and *EndInit* methods of the *DataSet* class.

Locale Property

Different languages and cultures employ different rules when comparing the contents of strings. By default, the *DataSet* will use your system's current culture information to compare strings. You can change this behavior by setting the *Locale* property of your *DataSet*.

This property accepts a *CultureInfo* object, which resides in the *System.Globalization* namespace. For more information about the *CultureInfo* class, see the MSDN documentation.

Like the *CaseSensitive* property, the *Locale* property also exists on the *DataTable* class. Setting the *Locale* property of a *DataSet* will change the *Locale* property of all *DataTable* objects in the *DataSet* whose *Locale* property has not been set.

The following code snippet shows how to set the *Locale* property of the *DataSet* to *English (Australia)*:

Visual Basic
```
Dim ds As New DataSet()
ds.Locale = New System.Globalization.CultureInfo("en-AU")
Console.WriteLine(ds.Locale.DisplayName)
```

Visual C#
```
DataSet ds = new DataSet();
ds.Locale = new System.Globalization.CultureInfo("en-AU");
Console.WriteLine(ds.Locale.DisplayName);
```

Namespace and *Prefix* Properties

You can use the *DataSet* class's *Namespace* and *Prefix* properties to specify an XML namespace and prefix for your *DataSet*. ADO.NET will use these settings when it writes the contents of your *DataSet* to XML and when it loads data from an XML document into your *DataSet*.

The *DataTable* and *DataColumn* classes also expose *Namespace* and *Prefix* properties.

For more information about XML namespaces, see the MSDN documentation.

Relations Property

The *Relations* property returns a *DataRelationCollection* object, which contains the *DataRelation* objects that reside in the *DataSet*. You can use this property to examine existing *DataRelation* objects as well as to add, modify, or remove *DataRelation* objects.

For more information about the *DataRelation* class, see Chapter 7.

RemotingFormat Property

As noted earlier in the chapter, ADO.NET 2.0 gives you the option to choose a binary remoting format. By default, *DataSet*s are remoted as XML. However, you can set the *RemotingFormat* property to *SerializationFormat.Binary* to have your *DataSet* remoted in binary format.

The *DataTable* class also exposes a *RemotingFormat* property.

SchemaSerializationMode Property

As noted earlier in the chapter, the *SchemaSerializationMode* property controls whether the *DataSet*'s schema is included when the *DataSet* is serialized. This property is intended for derived *DataSet*s that override the property (in other words, strongly typed *DataSet*s). Attempts to set this property on a *DataSet* that does not override the property will cause an *InvalidOperationException*.

By default, the *DataSet*'s schema is included in the serialized data. Excluding the schema, by setting the property to *SchemaSerializationMode.ExcludeSchema*, can greatly improve the performance of applications accessing strongly typed *DataSet*s from Web services.

Tables Property

You can use the *Tables* property to examine existing *DataTable* objects as well as to add, modify, or remove *DataTable* objects. This property returns a *DataTableCollection* object, which contains the *DataTable* objects that reside in the *DataSet*.

You can access a *DataTable* using the *Tables* property by supplying either the desired *DataTable* object's *TableName* property or its index within the collection. Accessing a *DataTable* based on its index will yield better performance.

Methods of the *DataSet* Class

The commonly used methods of the *DataSet* class are shown in Table 6-6.

Table 6-6   Methods of the *DataSet* Class

Method	Description
AcceptChanges	Accepts all pending changes within the *DataSet*
BeginInit	Used by the Visual Studio designers before adding schema information to the *DataSet*

Table 6-6   Methods of the *DataSet* Class

Method	Description
Clear	Removes all *DataRow* objects from the *DataSet*
Clone	Creates a new *DataSet* object with the same schema but with no *DataRow* objects
Copy	Creates a new *DataSet* object with the same schema and the same *DataRow* objects
CreateDataReader	Returns a *DataTableReader* that contains the data available in the *DataTable*(s) specified in the call to the method
EndInit	Used by the Visual Studio designers after adding schema information to the *DataSet*
GetChanges	Returns a new *DataSet* with the same structure and that contains all modified rows from the original *DataSet*
GetXml	Returns the contents of the *DataSet* as an XML string
GetXmlSchema	Returns the schema for the *DataSet* as an XML string
HasChanges	Returns a Boolean value that indicates whether any *DataRow* objects in the *DataSet* contain pending changes
InferXmlSchema	Loads schema information from an XML schema, and allows you to supply a list of namespaces whose elements you want to exclude from the *DataSet* object's schema
Load	Loads data from a *DataReader* into the *DataTable*
Merge	Merges data from another *DataSet*, *DataTable*, or array of *DataRow* objects into the existing *DataSet*
ReadXml	Reads XML data into your *DataSet* from a file, a *Stream*, a *TextReader*, or an *XmlReader*
ReadXmlSchema	Reads XML schema information into your *DataSet* from a file, a *Stream*, a *TextReader*, or an *XmlReader*
RejectChanges	Rejects all pending changes within the *DataSet*
Reset	Resets your *DataSet* to its original, uninitialized state
WriteXml	Writes the contents of your *DataSet* as XML to a file, a *Stream*, a *TextReader*, or an *XmlReader*
WriteXmlSchema	Writes the schema of your *DataSet* as XML to a file, a *Stream*, a *TextReader*, or an *XmlReader*

AcceptChanges and *RejectChanges* Methods

You can use the *AcceptChanges* and *RejectChanges* methods to accept or reject all pending changes within your *DataSet*.

When you modify the contents of a *DataRow* object, ADO.NET will mark the *DataRow* object as having a pending change and set the *RowState* property of the *DataRow* object to the appropriate value—*Added*, *Modified*, or *Deleted*. ADO.NET will also maintain both the original values and the current values for the contents of the *DataRow*.

If you call the *AcceptChanges* method on your *DataSet*, ADO.NET will accept all pending changes stored in the *DataRow* objects in your *DataSet*. Any rows whose *RowState* property is set to *Added* or *Modified* will have their *RowState* property set to *Unchanged*. Doing this will also reset the "original" values for the *DataRow* to the current contents of the *DataRow*. Any *DataRow* objects marked as *Deleted* will be removed from your *DataSet* when you call *AcceptChanges*.

When the *SqlDataAdapter* object successfully submits pending changes stored in a *DataRow* object, it implicitly calls the *AcceptChanges* method on that *DataRow*.

Calling the *RejectChanges* method on your *DataSet* will cancel any pending changes within your *DataSet*. Any *DataRow* objects marked as *Added* will be removed from your *DataSet*. Other modified *DataRow* objects (that is, *RowState* is *Modified* or *Deleted*) will return to their previous states.

The *DataTable* and *DataRow* objects also expose *AcceptChanges* and *RejectChanges* methods.

BeginInit and *EndInit* Methods

The *DataSet* and *DataTable* classes support the *BeginInit* and *EndInit* methods as part of their implementation of the *IsupportInitializeNotification* interface. For more information, see the following sidebar.

DataSet, *DataTables*, and the *ISupportInitializeNotification* Interface

When you add *DataTables*, *DataColumns* and *Constraints* to a *DataSet*, you may have to add the items in a particular order to successfully construct the *DataSet*. For example, if you add an expression-based *DataColumn*, you must add the *DataColumns* that the expression references before you add the expression-based *DataColumn*. In the following code snippet, the line of code that tries to create an expression-based column will fail, raising an *EvaluateException* whose *Message* property states "Cannot find column [Quantity]" because the Quantity *Data-Column* does not yet exist in the *DataTable*.

Visual Basic
```
Dim tbl As New DataTable("OrderDetails")
tbl.Columns.Add("OrderID", GetType(Integer))
tbl.Columns.Add("ProductID", GetType(Integer))
tbl.Columns.Add("ItemTotal", GetType(Decimal), "Quantity * UnitPrice")
tbl.Columns.Add("Quantity", GetType(Short))
tbl.Columns.Add("UnitPrice", GetType(Decimal))
```

Visual C#
```
DataTable tbl = new DataTable("OrderDetails");
tbl.Columns.Add("OrderID", typeof(int));
tbl.Columns.Add("ProductID", typeof(int));
tbl.Columns.Add("ItemTotal", typeof(decimal), "Quantity * UnitPrice");
tbl.Columns.Add("Quantity", typeof(short));
tbl.Columns.Add("UnitPrice", typeof(decimal));
```

The *DataSet* and *DataTable* classes implement the *ISupportInitializeNotification* interface so designers like Visual Studio can construct the objects without having to worry about the order of operations required. For classes that support *ISupportInitializeNotification* (or *ISupportInitialize*, which represents a subset of the functionality available through *ISupport-InitializeNotification*), Visual Studio can call the wrap the code that sets properties and calls methods on an object in calls to *BeginInit* and *EndInit*, as shown in the following code:

Visual Basic

```
Dim tbl As New DataTable("OrderDetails")
tbl.BeginInit()
tbl.Columns.Add("OrderID", GetType(Integer))
tbl.Columns.Add("ProductID", GetType(Integer))
tbl.Columns.Add("ItemTotal", GetType(Decimal), "Quantity * UnitPrice")
tbl.Columns.Add("Quantity", GetType(Short))
tbl.Columns.Add("UnitPrice", GetType(Decimal))
tbl.EndInit()
```

Visual C#

```
DataTable tbl = new DataTable("OrderDetails");
tbl.BeginInit();
tbl.Columns.Add("OrderID", typeof(int));
tbl.Columns.Add("ProductID", typeof(int));
tbl.Columns.Add("ItemTotal", typeof(decimal), "Quantity * UnitPrice");
tbl.Columns.Add("Quantity", typeof(short));
tbl.Columns.Add("UnitPrice", typeof(decimal));
tbl.EndInit();
```

Note that this code snippet resembles the previous snippet with two major differences. The first difference is that in the second code snippet, the code that constructs the *DataColumns* appears between calls to the *BeginInit* and *EndInit* methods. The second difference is that the second code snippet populates the *DataTable*'s *Columns* collection successfully. When the code calls the *DataTable* object's *BeginInit* method, the *DataTable* delays evaluating the *DataColumns* constructed until the *EndInit* method is called.

As the code demonstrates, this "batched initialization" approach allows Visual Studio to generate code that can construct *DataSets* and *DataTables* successfully without having to worry about the order of operations.

The *ISupportInitializeNotification* interface provides two additional features—the *IsInitialized* property and the *Initialized* event. The *IsInitialized* property indicates whether the object has been initialized. *IsInitialized* returns *True* by default. Once the *BeginInit* method is called, the *IsInitialized* property returns *False* until the *EndInit* method is called. Calling the *EndInit* method also fires the object's *Initialized* event.

Clear Method

You can use the *DataSet* class's *Clear* method to remove all *DataRow* objects from a *DataSet*. Using this method is faster than releasing a *DataSet* and then creating a new *DataSet* with the same structure.

The *DataTable* class also exposes a *Clear* method.

Clone and *Copy* Methods

You use the *Copy* method to create a new *DataSet* that contains the same structure and the same set of rows as the original *DataSet*. If you want to create a new *DataSet* object that contains the same structure but doesn't contain any rows, use the *Clone* method instead.

The *DataTable* class also exposes *Clone* and *Copy* methods.

CreateDataReader Method

For developers who want to access the contents of a *DataSet* using the *DataReader* interface, the *DataSet* class exposes a *CreateDataReader* method. This method returns an instance of a *DataTableReader* class, which behaves like a *SqlDataReader* object. The following code snippet fills a *DataSet* with the results of two queries and uses the *CreateDataReader* method to display the contents of the *DataSet*:

Visual Basic
```
Dim strConn, strSQL As String
strConn = "Data Source=.\SQLExpress;" & _
          "Initial Catalog=Northwind;Integrated Security=True;"
strSQL = "SELECT OrderID, CustomerID FROM Orders " & _
         " WHERE CustomerID = 'ANTON'" & _
         ";SELECT CustomerID, CompanyName FROM Customers " & _
         " WHERE CustomerID = 'ANTON';"
Dim da As New SqlDataAdapter(strSQL, strConn)
Dim ds As New DataSet()
da.Fill(ds)
Using rdr As DataTableReader = ds.CreateDataReader()
    Do
        Do While rdr.Read()
            Console.WriteLine("{0} - {1}", rdr(0), rdr(1))
        Loop
        Console.WriteLine()
    Loop While rdr.NextResult()
End Using
```

Visual C#
```
string strConn, strSQL;
strConn = @"Data Source=.\SQLExpress;" +
          "Initial Catalog=Northwind;Integrated Security=True;";
strSQL = "SELECT OrderID, CustomerID FROM Orders " +
         " WHERE CustomerID = 'ANTON'" +
         ";SELECT CustomerID, CompanyName FROM Customers " +
         " WHERE CustomerID = 'ANTON';";
SqlDataAdapter da = new SqlDataAdapter(strSQL, strConn);
DataSet ds = new DataSet();
da.Fill(ds);
using (DataTableReader rdr = ds.CreateDataReader()) {
    do {
```

```
        while (rdr.Read())
            Console.WriteLine("{0} - {1}", rdr[0], rdr[1]);
        Console.WriteLine();
    } while (rdr.NextResult());
}
```

The *CreateDataReader* method is overloaded. You can pass an array of *DataTable*s into the method to control which *DataTable*s of information are available through the reader, as well as the order of those *DataTable*s. For example, in the previous code snippet, the query returned Order information before Customer information. We could pass an array of *DataTable*s into the *CreateDataReader* method to change which of the *DataTable*s are available in the *DataTableReader*. The following code does the trick:

Visual Basic

```
...
Dim tables As DataTable() = New DataTable() {ds.Tables(1), ds.Tables(0)}
Using rdr As DataTableReader = ds.CreateDataReader(tables)
...
```

Visual C#

```
...
DataTable[] tables = new DataTable[] {ds.Tables[1], ds.Tables[0]};
using (DataTableReader rdr = ds.CreateDataReader(tables))
...
```

The *DataTable* class also exposes a *CreateDataReader* method.

GetChanges Method

The *DataSet* class's *GetChanges* method returns a new *DataSet* with the same structure as the original *DataSet* and also includes all rows from the original *DataSet* that contain pending changes. We'll discuss this feature in more depth in Chapter 11.

The *DataTable* class also exposes a *GetChanges* method.

Note The new *DataSet* object returned by the *GetChanges* method might also include some unmodified *DataRow* objects to conform to referential integrity constraints in the *DataSet*. If you have a modified child row but the parent row is unmodified, the parent row will be included in the new *DataSet*. If the new *DataSet* were to contain the child row but not the parent row, it would violate the referential integrity constraint.

GetXml and GetXmlSchema Methods

You can use the *GetXml* method to retrieve the contents of your *DataSet*, including its schema, and place it into a string in XML format. If you want to retrieve only the schema information, use the *GetXmlSchema* method instead.

I'll discuss the ADO.NET XML features in more depth in Chapter 12.

HasChanges Method

The *HasChanges* method returns a Boolean value that indicates whether the *DataSet* has *DataRow* objects that contain pending changes.

If you're building an application that allows users to modify data in a *DataSet* and submit the changes to the database using a *SqlDataAdapter*, you might want to check the *HasChanges* method. There's no reason to try to submit changes to your database if the *DataSet* does not contain any pending changes.

Load Method

In ADO.NET 2.0, the *DataSet* class now exposes a *Load* method you can use to load data from a *SqlDataReader* into your *DataSet*.

In ADO.NET 1.0 and 1.1, the only way to load the results of a query into a *DataSet* (without having to add the data on a row-by-row basis) was to use the *Fill* method on a *DataAdapter*. Many developers wanted access to the same features, but for a *DataReader* rather than a *Data-Adapter*. The *Load* method is designed to provide this functionality.

Here's a quick example that executes a batch of queries and stores the results in a new *DataSet*. The first parameter in the *Load* method accepts a *SqlDataReader*, or any class that implements *IDataReader*. The second parameter controls the *RowState* of the rows stored in the *DataSet* and corresponds to the *SqlDataAdapter*'s *FillLoadOption* property. In the following example, the third parameter contains an array of strings to control the names of the *DataTables* used or created, like the *SqlDataAdapter TableMappingsCollection*.

Visual Basic

```vb
Dim ds As New DataSet
'Connect and execute the query
Dim strConn, strSQL As String
strConn = "Data Source=.\SQLExpress;" & _
          "Initial Catalog=Northwind;Integrated Security=True;"
strSQL = "SELECT CustomerID, CompanyName FROM Customers " & _
         " WHERE CustomerID = 'ANTON';" & _
         "SELECT OrderID, CustomerID FROM Orders " & _
         " WHERE CustomerID = 'ANTON'"
Using cn As New SqlConnection(strConn)
    Using cmd As New SqlCommand(strSQL, cn)
        cn.Open()
        Using rdr As SqlDataReader = cmd.ExecuteReader

            'Load the data
            ds.Load(rdr, LoadOption.PreserveChanges, _
                    New String() {"Customers", "Orders"})
        End Using
    End Using
End Using

'Examine the contents of the DataSet
```

```
For Each tbl As DataTable In ds.Tables
    Console.WriteLine(tbl.TableName)
    For Each row As DataRow In tbl.Rows
        Console.WriteLine("  {0} - {1}", row(0), row(1))
    Next row
    Console.WriteLine()
Next tbl
```

Visual C#

```
DataSet ds = new DataSet();
//Connect and execute the query
string strConn, strSQL;
strConn = @"Data Source=.\SQLExpress;" +
            "Initial Catalog=Northwind;Integrated Security=True;";
strSQL = "SELECT CustomerID, CompanyName FROM Customers " +
         " WHERE CustomerID = 'ANTON';" +
         "SELECT OrderID, CustomerID FROM Orders " +
         " WHERE CustomerID = 'ANTON'";
using (SqlConnection cn = new SqlConnection(strConn)) {
    using (SqlCommand cmd = new SqlCommand(strSQL, cn)) {
        cn.Open();
        using (SqlDataReader rdr = cmd.ExecuteReader()) {

            //Load the data
            ds.Load(rdr, LoadOption.PreserveChanges,
                    new String[] {"Customers", "Orders"});
        }
    }
}

//Examine the contents of the DataSet
foreach (DataTable tbl in ds.Tables) {
    Console.WriteLine(tbl.TableName);
    foreach (DataRow row in tbl.Rows)
        Console.WriteLine("  {0} - {1}", row[0], row[1]);
    Console.WriteLine();
}
```

> **Note** In the previous code snippet, when the *Load* method completes, it will implicitly close the *SqlDataReader*. However, if you're going to use the *Load* method to load data from a data reader, you should always work with that data reader in a *Using* block. If the call to *Load* data throws an exception, perhaps because the data loaded into the *DataSet* violates a constraint, the *Load* method will not close the data reader. Here, the *Using* block ensures that the *SqlDataReader* will be closed even if an unhandled exception occurs.

There's an overload for the *Load* method that accepts an array of *DataTables* instead of an array of strings. This *Load* method is helpful if your *DataSet* contains the *DataTables* you want to fill.

Finally, there's a *Load* method that accepts an error handler in case you want to trap for errors—such as the *SqlDataAdapter*'s *FillError* event—while loading data.

The *DataTable* class also exposes a *Load* method.

Merge Method

The *DataSet* class's *Merge* method allows you to load data from another *DataSet* or *DataTable* or load an array of *DataRow* objects into your existing *DataSet*.

I'll discuss the *Merge* method in detail in Chapter 11.

ReadXml and *WriteXml* Methods

You can use the *ReadXml* method to load XML data into your *DataSet* from a file, a *TextReader*, a *Stream*, or an *XmlReader*. You can also control how the *DataSet* will read the XML using the *mode* parameter. This parameter accepts values from the *XmlReadMode* enumeration and allows you to specify options such as whether you want to read a full XML document or just an XML fragment and whether to read or ignore the XML schema.

The *DataSet* class also exposes a *WriteXml* method so that you can write the contents of your *DataSet* as XML. The *WriteXml* method offers all the same options as the *ReadXml* method.

I'll discuss the ADO.NET XML features in more depth in Chapter 12.

ReadXmlSchema, *WriteXmlSchema*, and *InferXmlSchema* Methods

The *ReadXmlSchema* and *WriteXmlSchema* methods are similar to their counterparts *ReadXml* and *WriteXml*, but they're designed to work with XML schemas. Like the *ReadXml* and *WriteXml* methods, these methods accept a *TextReader*, a *Stream*, an *XmlReader*, or a string that contains a filename for your XML data.

The *InferXmlSchema* method is similar to the *ReadXmlSchema* method, but it provides an added level of control. It lets you specify a list of namespaces whose elements you want to ignore. For more information about this difference between the features, see "Loading DataSet Schema Information from XML" in the MSDN documentation.

I'll discuss the ADO.NET XML features in more depth in Chapter 12.

Reset Method

The *DataSet* class's *Reset* method returns the *DataSet* to its original, uninitialized state. If you want to discard an existing *DataSet* and start working with a new *DataSet*, use the *Reset* method rather than creating a new instance of a *DataSet*.

Events of the *DataSet* Class

The most commonly used events of the *DataSet* class are shown in Table 6-7.

Table 6-7   Event of the *DataSet* Class

Event	Description
Initialized	Fires when the *EndInit* method of the *DataSet* is called
MergeFailed	Fires if the *Merge* method of the *DataSet* generates an exception

Initialized Event

The *DataSet* class supports the *Initialized* event as part of its implementation of the *ISupport-InitializeNotification* interface. For more information, see the sidebar that describes the *ISupportInitializeNotification* interface following the *BeginInit* and *EndInit* methods of the *DataSet* class.

The *DataTable* class also exposes an *Initialize* event.

MergeFailed Event

The *DataSet*'s *MergeFailed* event will fire under very specific, and somewhat obscure, conditions.

For example, the *DataSet* will fire the *MergeFailed* event if the you're merging a *DataTable* into your *DataSet*, the *DataSet* already contains a *DataTable* of that name, the *PrimaryKey* properties of the corresponding *DataTable*s do not match, and *MissingSchemaAction.Add* is used on the call to *Merge*.

Properties of the *DataTable* Class

The commonly used properties of the *DataTable* class are shown in Table 6-8.

Table 6-8   Properties of the *DataTable* Class

Property	Data Type	Description
CaseSensitive	*Boolean*	Controls whether string comparisons are case sensitive
ChildRelations	*DataRelationCollection*	Returns the *DataRelation* objects that contain child data for the *DataTable*
Columns	*DataColumnCollection*	Contains the collection of *DataColumn* objects for the *DataTable*
Constraints	*ConstraintCollection*	Contains the collection of *Constraint* objects for the *DataTable*
DataSet	*DataSet*	Returns the *DataSet* to which the *DataTable* belongs
DefaultView	*DataView*	Returns the *DataView* object that bound controls will receive for the *DataTable*
DesignMode	*Boolean*	Indicates whether the *DataTable* is in design mode
ExtendedProperties	*PropertyCollection*	Contains a collection of dynamic properties and values
HasErrors	*Boolean*	Indicates whether the *DataTable* contains errors
IsInitialized	*Boolean*	Indicates whether the *DataTable* is currently being initialized

Table 6-8   Properties of the *DataTable* Class

Property	Data Type	Description
Locale	*CultureInfo*	Controls the locale that the *DataTable* will use to compare strings
MinimumCapacity	*Integer*	Controls how much memory, in rows, that the *DataTable* will reserve initially
Namespace	*String*	Contains the namespace that ADO.NET will use when it writes the contents of your *DataTable* to XML or when it loads XML data into your *DataTable*
ParentRelations	*DataRelationCollection*	Returns the *DataRelation* objects that contain parent data for the *DataTable*
Prefix	*String*	Contains the prefix for the namespace that ADO.NET will use when it writes the contents of your *DataTable* to XML or when it loads XML data into your *DataTable*
PrimaryKey	Array of *DataColumn* objects	Contains information about the primary key for the *DataTable*
RemotingFormat	*SerializationFormat*	Controls whether the *DataTable* is remoted in XML or binary format
Rows	*DataRowCollection*	Contains the collection of *DataColumn* objects for the *DataTable*
TableName	*String*	Contains the name of the *DataTable*

CaseSensitive Property

The *CaseSensitive* property of the *DataTable* controls whether string comparisons within the *DataTable* are case sensitive. The *DataSet* class also exposes a *CaseSensitive* property.

By default, the *DataTable* class's *CaseSensitive* property contains the same value as the *Case-Sensitive* property of the parent *DataSet* object. If you set the *CaseSensitive* property of your *DataTable*, this value will override the setting for the parent *DataSet* object.

The default value of the *CaseSensitive* property for a *DataTable* that does not reside in a *DataSet* is *False*.

ChildRelations and *ParentRelations* Properties

The *ChildRelations* and *ParentRelations* properties let you examine the *DataRelation* objects that contain child or parent relations for the current *DataTable*.

Suppose that you're working with a hierarchy of customers, orders, and order details data and you have a reference to the *DataTable* that contains order information. The *ParentRelations* collection will contain the *DataRelation* that relates the order *DataTable* to the customer *DataTable*. The *ChildRelations* collection will contain the *DataRelation* that relates the order *DataTable* to the order details *DataTable*.

Columns Property

You can use the *Columns* property to examine existing *DataColumn* objects as well as to add, modify, or remove *DataColumn* objects. This property returns a *DataColumnCollection* object, which contains the *DataColumn* objects that reside in the *DataTable*.

You can access a *DataColumn* using the *Columns* property by supplying the desired *DataColumn* object's *Ordinal* property or *ColumnName* property. As with most searches, accessing a *Data-Column* based on its *Ordinal* property will yield better performance.

Constraints Property

The *Constraints* property lets you examine the constraints defined for your *DataTable*. Like the *Columns* property, you can use the *Constraints* collection to add, modify, or remove constraints from the *DataTable*. This property returns a *ConstraintCollection* object.

You can access a *Constraint* using the *Columns* property by supplying either the desired *Constraint* object's *ConstraintName* property or its index within the collection. Performing the search using the desired *Constraint* object's index will yield better performance.

DataSet Property

The *DataSet* property returns the *DataSet* in which the *DataTable* resides. If the *DataTable* does not reside in a *DataSet*, the *DataSet* property returns an uninitialized object.

The *DataSet* property is read-only.

DefaultView Property

If you bind a control to your *DataTable*, the control will actually bind to the *DataView* object returned by the *DataTable* object's *DefaultView* property. For example, you can use the following code to apply a filter so that only the customers from Spain appear in the *DataGrid* bound to the *DataTable*. The *DataTable* will still contain all customers, regardless of the filter.

Visual Basic
```
tblCustomers.DefaultView.RowFilter = "Country = 'Spain'"
gridCustomers.DataSource = tblCustomers
```

Visual C#
```
tblCustomers.DefaultView.RowFilter = "Country = 'Spain'";
gridCustomers.DataSource = tblCustomers;
```

I'll discuss the *DataView* object in more detail in Chapter 8.

DesignMode Property

The *DesignMode* property of the *DataTable* class returns a Boolean value that indicates whether the *DataTable* is in design mode. This property can be useful when you write code in a user control. If the *DataTable* is being used at design time within a component, *DesignMode* will return *True*. Otherwise, it will return *False*.

The *DataSet* class also exposes a *DesignMode* property.

The *DesignMode* property is read-only.

ExtendedProperties Property

The *DataTable* class's *ExtendedProperties* property returns a *PropertyCollection* object, which is designed to store various objects.

The *DataSet*, *DataColumn*, *DataRelation*, and *Constraint* classes also expose an *ExtendedProperties* property.

For more information, including a code example, see the information about the *Extended-Properties* property in the "Properties of the *DataSet* Class" section earlier in the chapter.

HasErrors Property

The *HasErrors* property returns a Boolean value that indicates whether any *DataRow* objects within the *DataTable* contain errors. If you're submitting batches of changes to your database and you've set the *ContinueUpdateOnError* property of your *DataAdapter* objects to *True*, you should check the *HasErrors* property of your *DataSet* after you submit changes to determine whether any of the update attempts failed.

The *DataSet* and *DataRow* classes also expose a *HasErrors* property.

For more information about handling failed update attempts, see Chapter 11.

IsInitialized Property

The *DataTable* class supports the *IsInitialized* property as part of its implementation of the *ISupportInitializeNotification* interface. For more information, see the sidebar that describes the *ISupportInitializeNotification* interface following the *BeginInit* and *EndInit* methods of the *DataSet* class.

The *DataSet* class also exposes an *IsInitialized* property.

Locale Property

The *Locale* property controls how ADO.NET will compare strings within your *DataTable*.

The *DataSet* class also exposes a *Locale* property.

For more information, including a code example, see the information about the *Locale* property in the "Properties of the *DataSet* Class" section earlier in the chapter.

MinimumCapacity Property

If you know approximately how many rows your *DataTable* will contain, you can improve the performance of your code by setting the *DataTable* object's *MinimumCapacity* property prior to filling your *DataTable* with the results of a query.

By default, the *MinimumCapacity* property is set to 50, which means that ADO.NET will reserve enough memory for your *DataTable* to hold 50 rows of data. You might be able to improve the performance of your code by setting the *MinimumCapacity* property to a more a value that matches the number of rows your *DataTable* will contain. Setting this property to a lower value when you work with *DataTable* objects will also reduce the memory footprint of your application.

If you add more rows to the *DataTable*, you won't receive an out-of-memory error. ADO.NET will simply request more memory.

Namespace and *Prefix* Properties

You can use the *DataTable* class's *Namespace* and *Prefix* properties to specify an XML namespace and prefix for your *DataTable*. ADO.NET will use these settings when it writes the contents of your *DataTable* to XML and when it loads data from an XML document into your *DataTable*.

The *DataSet* and *DataColumn* classes also expose *Namespace* and *Prefix* properties.

For more information about XML namespaces, see the MSDN documentation.

PrimaryKey Property

The *PrimaryKey* property contains an array of *DataColumn* objects that constitute the primary key for your *DataTable*.

This primary key serves two purposes. First it acts as a unique constraint. No two *DataRow* objects can have the same values in the primary key columns. For example, say that you have a *DataTable* of customer information and you define the primary key based on the CustomerID *DataColumn*. If you add a new *DataRow* to your *DataTable* object's *Rows* collection and the new *DataRow* has a value for the CustomerID *DataColumn* that already exists in your *DataTable*, you'll receive an exception.

You can also locate a *DataRow* in a *DataTable* based on its primary key values using the *Find* method of the *DataTable* object's *Rows* collection. I'll discuss this feature in more detail when I discuss sorting, searching, and filtering in Chapter 8.

The following code snippet shows an example of setting the *PrimaryKey* property of a *DataTable*.

Visual Basic
```
Dim tbl As New DataTable("Customers")
tbl.Columns.Add("CustomerID", GetType(String))
tbl.Columns.Add("CompanyName", GetType(String))
tbl.PrimaryKey = New DataColumn() {tbl.Columns("CustomerID")}
```

Visual C#

```csharp
DataTable tbl = new DataTable("Customers");
tbl.Columns.Add("CustomerID", typeof(string));
tbl.Columns.Add("CompanyName", typeof(string));
tbl.PrimaryKey = new DataColumn[] {tbl.Columns["CustomerID"]};
```

RemotingFormat Property

As noted earlier in the chapter, ADO.NET 2.0 gives you the option to choose a binary remoting format. By default, *DataTable*s are remoted as XML. However, you can set the *RemotingFormat* property to *SerializationFormat.Binary* to have your *DataTable* remoted in binary format.

The *DataSet* class also exposes a *RemotingFormat* property.

Rows Property

The *DataTable* class's *Rows* property returns a *DataRowCollection* object that contains the *DataRow* objects in the *DataTable*. You can use the *Rows* property to add a *DataRow* object to the *DataTable*, as well as to access any of the existing *DataRow* objects.

You can use only the *DataRowCollection* object to locate a *DataRow* based on its ordinal value within the *DataTable*. If you want to locate *DataRow* objects based on their primary key values or other search criteria, you can use the various methods described in Chapter 8.

TableName Property

The *TableName* property contains the name for the *DataTable* object. You can set this property in the *DataTable* class's constructor.

When you store the contents of your *DataSet* as XML, ADO.NET uses the *TableName* property of each *DataTable* as the element tag for each row of data in the *DataTable*.

Methods of the *DataTable* Class

The commonly used methods of the *DataTable* class are shown in Table 6-9.

Table 6-9   Methods of the *DataTable* Class

Method	Description
AcceptChanges	Accepts all pending changes within the *DataTable*
BeginInit	Used by the Visual Studio designers before adding schema information to the *DataTable*
BeginLoadData	Turns off constraints while loading data
Clear	Removes all *DataRow* objects from the *DataTable*
Clone	Creates a new *DataTable* object with the same schema but with no *DataRow* objects

Table 6-9   Methods of the *DataTable* Class

Method	Description
Compute	Returns the value of an aggregate expression, based on the contents of your *DataTable*
Copy	Creates a new *DataTable* object with the same schema and the same *DataRow* objects
CreateDataReader	Creates a *DataTableReader* that contains the contents of the *DataTable*
EndInit	Used by the Visual Studio designers after adding schema information to the *DataSet*
EndLoadData	Reenables constraints after you've loaded data
GetChanges	Returns a new *DataTable* with the same structure and that contains all modified rows from the original *DataTable*
GetErrors	Returns an array that contains the *DataRow* objects that contain errors
ImportRow	Imports an existing *DataRow* into your *DataTable*
Load	Loads data from the supplied *DataReader*
LoadDataRow	Adds a new *DataRow* to your *DataTable* based on the contents of an array
NewRow	Returns a new *DataRow* object for your *DataTable*
ReadXml	Reads XML data into your *DataTable* from a file, a *Stream*, a *TextReader*, or an *XmlReader*
ReadXmlSchema	Reads XML schema information into your *DataTable* from a file, a *Stream*, a *TextReader*, or an *XmlReader*
RejectChanges	Rejects all pending changes within the *DataTable*
Reset	Resets your *DataTable* to its original, uninitialized state
Select	Returns an array of *DataRow* objects based on the specified search criteria
WriteXml	Writes the contents of your *DataTable* as XML to a file, a *Stream*, a *TextReader*, or an *XmlReader*
WriteXmlSchema	Writes the schema of your *DataTable* as XML to a file, a *Stream*, a *TextReader*, or an *XmlReader*

AcceptChanges and *RejectChanges* Methods

You can use the *AcceptChanges* and *RejectChanges* methods to accept or reject all pending changes within your *DataTable*, respectively.

The *DataSet* and *DataRow* objects also expose *AcceptChanges* and *RejectChanges* methods. For more information about these methods, see the "Methods of the *DataSet* Class" section earlier in the chapter.

BeginInit and *EndInit* Methods

The *DataTable* class supports the *BeginInit* and *EndInit* methods as part of its implementation of the *ISupportInitializeNotification* interface. For more information, see the sidebar that describes the *ISupportInitializeNotification* interface following the *BeginInit* and *EndInit* methods of the *DataSet* class.

The *DataSet* object also exposes *BeginInit* and *EndInit* methods.

BeginLoadData and *EndLoadData* Methods

If you're adding a series of *DataRow* objects to your *DataTable* object, you might be able to improve the performance of your code by using the *BeginLoadData* and *EndLoadData* methods.

Calling the *BeginLoadData* method turns off constraints for the *DataTable*. You can enable the constraints again by calling *EndLoadData*. If the *DataTable* contains rows that violate the constraints, you'll receive a *ConstraintException* when you call *EndLoadData*. To determine which rows caused the exception, you can examine the rows returned by the *GetErrors* method.

Clear Method

You can use the *DataTable* class's *Clear* method to remove all *DataRow* objects from the *Data-Table*. Using this method is faster than releasing a *DataTable* and then creating a new *DataTable* with the same structure.

The *DataSet* class also exposes a *Clear* method.

Clone and *Copy* Methods

You can use the *Copy* method to create a new *DataTable* that contains the same structure and the same set of rows. If you want to create a new *DataTable* object that contains the same structure but doesn't contain any rows, use the *Clone* method instead.

The *DataSet* class also exposes *Clone* and *Copy* methods.

Compute Method

You can use the *Compute* method to perform an aggregate query on a single column in your *DataTable* that's based on the search criteria you specify.

The following code snippet demonstrates using the *Compute* method to count the number of orders that include chai. The code snippet also computes the total number of chai units ordered.

Visual Basic
```
Dim strSQL, strConn As String
strConn = "Data Source=.\SQLExpress;" & _
        "Initial Catalog=Northwind;Integrated Security=True;"
strSQL = "SELECT OrderID, ProductID, Quantity " & _
        " FROM [Order Details]"
Dim da As New SqlDataAdapter(strSQL, strConn)
Dim tbl As New DataTable("Order Details")
da.Fill(tbl)
Dim intNumChaiOrders As Integer
```

```
Dim lngNumChaiUnits As Long
intNumChaiOrders = CInt(tbl.Compute("COUNT(OrderID)", _
                                    "ProductID = 1"))
lngNumChaiUnits = CLng(tbl.Compute("SUM(Quantity)", _
                                    "ProductID = 1"))
Console.WriteLine("# of orders that include chai: {0}", _
                  intNumChaiOrders)
Console.WriteLine("Total number of chai units ordered: {0}", _
                  lngNumChaiUnits)
```

Visual C#

```
string strSQL, strConn;
strConn = @"Data Source=.\SQLExpress;" +
            "Initial Catalog=Northwind;Integrated Security=True;";
strSQL = "SELECT OrderID, ProductID, Quantity " +
         "  FROM [Order Details]";
SqlDataAdapter da = new SqlDataAdapter(strSQL, strConn);
DataTable tbl = new DataTable("Order Details");
da.Fill(tbl);
int intNumChaiOrders = (int) tbl.Compute("COUNT(OrderID)",
                                         "ProductID = 1");
Int64 intNumChaiUnits = (Int64) tbl.Compute("SUM(Quantity)",
                                            "ProductID = 1");
Console.WriteLine("# of orders that include chai: {0}",
                  intNumChaiOrders);
Console.WriteLine("Total number of chai units ordered: {0}",
                  intNumChaiUnits);
```

You cannot use the *Compute* method to compute an aggregate that involves multiple columns, such as *SUM(Quantity * UnitPrice)*. However, you can use an expression-based column to perform the calculation between the two columns and then use that expression-based column in the *Count* method: *SUM(ItemTotal)*.

The *Compute* method returns its results using the generic *Object* data type. When you perform a calculation using the *Compute* method, the data type that the *Compute* method uses to store the results might surprise you. For example, the *DataType* property for the *Quantity* column is a 16-bit integer, but the call to the *Compute* method returns a 64-bit integer.

If you're unsure what data type to use to store the results of the *Compute* method, you can use code such as the following:

Visual Basic

```
Dim objRetVal As Object = tbl.Compute("SUM(Quantity)", _
                                      "ProductID = 1")
Console.WriteLine(objRetVal.GetType().ToString())
```

Visual C#

```
object objRetVal = tbl.Compute("SUM(Quantity)",
                               "ProductID = 1");
Console.WriteLine(objRetVal.GetType().ToString());
```

CreateDataReader Method

For developers who want to access the contents of the *DataTable* using a *DataReader* interface, the *DataTable* class exposes a *CreateDataReader* method. This method returns an instance of a *DataTableReader* class, which behaves like a *SqlDataReader* object. The following code snippet fills a *DataTable* with the results of a query and uses the *CreateDataReader* method to display the contents of the *DataTable*.

Visual Basic

```
Dim strConn, strSQL As String
strConn = "Data Source=.\SQLExpress;" & _
          "Initial Catalog=Northwind;Integrated Security=True;"
strSQL = "SELECT CustomerID, CompanyName FROM Customers"
Dim da As New SqlDataAdapter(strSQL, strConn)
Dim tbl As New DataTable()
da.Fill(tbl)
Using rdr As DataTableReader = tbl.CreateDataReader()
    Do While rdr.Read()
        Console.WriteLine("{0} - {1}", rdr(0), rdr(1))
    Loop
End Using
```

Visual C#

```
string strConn, strSQL;
strConn = @"Data Source=.\SQLExpress;" +
           "Initial Catalog=Northwind;Integrated Security=True;";
strSQL = "SELECT CustomerID, CompanyName FROM Customers";
SqlDataAdapter da = new SqlDataAdapter(strSQL, strConn);
DataTable tbl = new DataTable();
da.Fill(tbl);
using (DataTableReader rdr = tbl.CreateDataReader())
{
    while (rdr.Read())
        Console.WriteLine("{0} - {1}", rdr[0], rdr[1]);
}
```

The *DataSet* class also exposes a *CreateDataReader* method.

GetChanges Method

The *DataSet* class's *GetChanges* method returns a new *DataTable* with the same structure and also includes all rows from the original *DataTable* that contain pending changes. I'll discuss this feature in more depth in Chapter 11.

The *DataSet* class also exposes a *GetChanges* method.

GetErrors Method

You can use the *GetErrors* method to access the *DataRow* objects that contain errors, whether those errors constitute constraint violations or failed update attempts. The *GetErrors* method returns an array of *DataRow* objects.

ImportRow, *LoadDataRow*, and *NewRow* Methods

The *ImportRow* method accepts a *DataRow* object and adds that row of data to the *DataTable*.

The *LoadDataRow* method accepts an array as its first argument. Each item in the array corresponds to an item in the *DataTable* object's *Columns* collection. The second argument in the *LoadDataRow* method takes a Boolean value to control the *RowState* of the new *DataRow* object. You can supply *False* for this parameter if you want the new *DataRow* to have a *RowState* of *Added*, and you can supply *True* if you want a *RowState* of *Unmodified*. The *Load-DataRow* method also returns the newly created *DataRow* object.

The *NewRow* method returns a new *DataRow* object for the *DataTable*. The new *DataRow* will not reside in the *DataTable* object's *Rows* collection at this point. You'll need to add the item to the *Rows* collection after you've populated the desired columns on the *DataRow*.

So which of these three methods should you use? Here are some guidelines:

- Use the *ImportRow* method if you want to import a row from a different *DataTable*.

- Use the *LoadDataRow* method if you want to add a number of new rows at a time, perhaps based on the contents of a file. Adding a row to a *DataTable* using *LoadDataRow* requires fewer lines of code than using the *NewRow* method.

- Otherwise, use the *NewRow* method.

Load Method

In ADO.NET 2.0, the *DataTable* class now exposes a *Load* method you can use to load data from a *SqlDataReader* into your *DataTable*.

In ADO.NET 1.0 and 1.1, the only way to load the results of a query into a *DataTable* (without having to add the data on a row-by-row basis) was to use the *Fill* method on a *DataAdapter*. Many developers wanted access to the same features, but for a *DataReader* rather than a *Data-Adapter*. The *Load* method is designed to provide this functionality.

Here's a quick example that executes a query and stores the results in a new *DataTable*, passing a *SqlDataReader* into the *Load* method:

Visual Basic
```
Dim tbl As New DataTable
'Connect and execute the query
Dim strConn, strSQL As String
strConn = "Data Source=.\SQLExpress;" & _
        "Initial Catalog=Northwind;Integrated Security=True;"
strSQL = "SELECT CustomerID, CompanyName FROM Customers"
Using cn As New SqlConnection(strConn)
    Using cmd As New SqlCommand(strSQL, cn)
        cn.Open()
        Using rdr As SqlDataReader = cmd.ExecuteReader

            'Load the data
```

```
        tbl.Load(rdr)
      End Using
    End Using
End Using


'Examine the contents of the DataSet
For Each row As DataRow In tbl.Rows
    Console.WriteLine("  {0} - {1}", row(0), row(1))
Next row
```

Visual C#

```csharp
DataTable tbl = new DataTable();
//Connect and execute the query
string strConn, strSQL;
strConn = @"Data Source=.\SQLExpress;" +
          "Initial Catalog=Northwind;Integrated Security=True;";
strSQL = "SELECT CustomerID, CompanyName FROM Customers";
using (SqlConnection cn = new SqlConnection(strConn)) {
    using (SqlCommand cmd = new SqlCommand(strSQL, cn)) {
        cn.Open();
        using (SqlDataReader rdr = cmd.ExecuteReader()) {

            //Load the data
            ds.Load(rdr);
        }
    }
}


//Examine the contents of the DataSet
foreach (DataRow row in tbl.Rows)
    Console.WriteLine("  {0} - {1}", row[0], row[1]);
```

> **Note**   In the previous code snippet, when the *Load* method completes, it will implicitly close the *SqlDataReader*. However, if you're going to use the *Load* method to load data from a data reader, you should always work with that data reader in a *Using* block. If the call to *Load* data throws an exception, perhaps because the data loaded into the *DataSet* violates a constraint, the *Load* method will not close the data reader. Here, the *Using* block ensures that the *Sql-DataReader* will be closed even if an unhandled exception occurs.

There's an overload for the *Load* method that also accepts a value from the *LoadOption* enumeration to control the *RowState* of the rows added or modified during the *Load* operation. This value corresponds to the *SqlDataAdapter*'s *FillLoadOption* property. There's also a *Load* method that accepts an error handler in case you want to trap for errors—such as the *SqlDataAdapter*'s *FillError* event—while loading data.

The *DataSet* class also exposes a *Load* method.

ReadXml, *ReadXmlSchema*, *WriteXml*, and *WriteXmlSchema* Methods

In ADO.NET 2.0, the *DataTable* class now exposes *ReadXml*, *ReadXmlSchema*, *WriteXml*, and *WriteXmlSchema* methods just like the *DataSet* class.

I'll discuss the ADO.NET XML features in more depth in Chapter 12.

Reset Method

The *DataTable* class's *Reset* method returns the *DataTable* object to its original, uninitialized state. If you want to discard an existing *DataTable* and start working with a new *DataTable*, use the *Reset* method rather than creating a new instance of a *DataTable*.

The *DataSet* class also exposes a *Reset* method.

Select Method

You can use the *Select* method to locate a row or multiple rows in a *DataTable* based on various search criteria. The *Select* method returns an array of *DataRow* objects that satisfy the specified criteria.

I'll take a closer look at the *Select* method when I discuss sorting, searching, and filtering in Chapter 8.

Events of the *DataTable* Class

The commonly used events of the *DataTable* class are shown in Table 6-10.

Table 6-10   Events of the *DataTable* Class

Event	Description
ColumnChanged	Fires after the contents of a column have changed
ColumnChanging	Fires just before the contents of a column change
Initialized	Fires when the *DataTable*'s *EndInit* method is called
RowChanged	Fires after the contents of a row have changed
RowChanging	Fires just before the contents of a row change
RowDeleted	Fires after a row has been deleted
RowDeleting	Fires just before a row is deleted
TableCleared	Fires just after a *DataTable* is cleared
TableClearing	Fires just before a *DataTable* is cleared
TableNewRow	Fires when the *DataTable*'s *NewRow* method is called

ColumnChanged and *ColumnChanging* Events

The *ColumnChanged* and *ColumnChanging* events fire each time the contents of a column in a row change. You can use these events to validate your data, enable or disable controls, and so forth.

The events include an argument of type *DataColumnChangeEventArgs*, which has properties such as *Row* and *Column* that you can use to determine which row and column have been changed.

Remember that if you use the events to modify the contents of the row, you might cause an infinite loop.

Initialized Event

The *DataTable* class supports the *Initialized* event as part of its implementation of the *ISupport-InitializeNotification* interface. For more information, see the sidebar that describes the *ISupport-InitializeNotification* interface following the *BeginInit* and *EndInit* methods of the *DataSet* class.

The *DataSet* class also exposes an *Initialize* event.

RowChanged and *RowChanging* Events

The *RowChanged* and *RowChanging* events fire when a *DataRow* object's contents change or its *RowState* property changes.

You can determine why the event fired by checking the *Action* property of the *DataRowChange-EventArgs* argument of the event. You can also access the row that's being modified using the *Row* property of the same argument.

RowDeleted and *RowDeleting* Events

The *RowDeleted* and *RowDeleting* events expose the same arguments and properties as the *RowChanged* and *RowChanging* arguments do. The only difference is that these events fire when a row is deleted from the *DataTable*.

TableClearing and *TableCleared* Events

If you call the *Clear* method on a *DataTable*, the *TableClearing* event will fire before the rows are cleared, and the *TableCleared* event will fire after the rows have been cleared. Both events use the same event handler structure and argument type—*DataTableClearEventHandler* and *DataTableClearEventArgs*, respectively.

TableNewRow Event

The *TableNewRow* event fires when you call the *DataTable*'s *NewRow* method. This event can prove helpful if you're looking to programmatically generate default values for columns in new *DataRows*. You can also use the *TableNewRow* event to generate values in Windows applications that use bound controls because Windows data binding relies on the *DataTable*'s *NewRow* method to create a new *DataRows*.

The following example shows how you can use the *TableNewRow* event to generate a default value for a column like *OrderDate*.

Visual Basic
```
'Create the DataTable's schema
Dim tbl As New DataTable("Orders")
Dim colOrderID As DataColumn = tbl.Columns.Add("OrderID", GetType(Integer))
colOrderID.AutoIncrement = True
colOrderID.AutoIncrementSeed = -1
```

```
colOrderID.AutoIncrementStep = -1
tbl.Columns.Add("CustomerID", GetType(String))
tbl.Columns.Add("OrderDate", GetType(DateTime))

'Add a handler for the event
AddHandler tbl.TableNewRow, AddressOf HandleTableNewRow

'This call will fire the event
Dim row As DataRow = tbl.NewRow()

'Confirm that the event was used to generate a new order date
Console.WriteLine(row("OrderDate"))


'Event handler
Private Sub HandleTableNewRow(ByVal sender As Object, _
                             ByVal e As DataTableNewRowEventArgs)
    e.Row("OrderDate") = DateTime.Today
End Sub
```

Visual C#

```
//Create the DataTable's schema
DataTable tbl = new DataTable("Orders");
DataColumn colOrderID = tbl.Columns.Add("OrderID", typeof(int));
colOrderID.AutoIncrement = true;
colOrderID.AutoIncrementSeed = -1;
colOrderID.AutoIncrementStep = -1;
tbl.Columns.Add("CustomerID", typeof(string));
tbl.Columns.Add("OrderDate", typeof(DateTime));

//Add a handler for the event
tbl.TableNewRow += new DataTableNewRowEventHandler(HandleTableNewRow);

//This call will fire the event
DataRow row = tbl.NewRow();

//Confirm that the event was used to generate a new order date
Console.WriteLine(row["OrderDate"]);


//Event handler
static void HandleTableNewRow(object sender,
                             DataTableNewRowEventArgs e)
{
    e.Row["OrderDate"] = DateTime.Today;
}
```

> **Note**   The major drawback to the *TableNewRow* event is that it fires only for new rows added via *DataTable.NewRow*. The event does not fire for new rows generated by calling *DataTable.LoadDataRow, DataTable.Rows.Add, DataTable.Load,* or *SqlDataAdapter.Fill.*

Properties of the *DataColumn* Class

The commonly used properties of the *DataColumn* class are shown in Table 6-11.

Table 6-11   Properties of the *DataColumn* Class

Property	Data Type	Description
AllowDBNull	Boolean	Controls whether the column will accept null values
AutoIncrement	Boolean	Controls whether ADO.NET will generate new autoincrement values for the column
AutoIncrementSeed	Integer	Controls what value ADO.NET will use for the first new autoincrement value
AutoIncrementStep	Integer	Controls the value ADO.NET will use to generate subsequent autoincrement values
Caption	String	Controls the caption for the column. Note: This will not set the caption for the column in bound controls such as a *DataGrid*
ColumnMapping	MappingType	Controls how ADO.NET will store the contents of the column in an XML document
ColumnName	String	Contains the name of the *DataColumn* object
DataType	Type	Controls the data type that ADO.NET will use to store the contents of the column
DateTimeMode	DataSetDateTime	Controls the serialization format for *DateTime* columns
DefaultValue	Object	Controls the default value that ADO.NET will use to populate this column for new rows
Expression	String	Controls how ADO.NET will generate values for expression-based columns
ExtendedProperties	PropertyCollection	Contains a collection of dynamic properties and values
MaxLength	Integer	Specifies the maximum length of the string that the column can contain
Namespace	String	Contains the namespace that ADO.NET will use when it writes the contents of the *DataSet* to XML or when it loads XML data into your *DataSet*
Ordinal	Integer	Returns the index of the *DataColumn* within the *DataTable* object's *Columns* collection
Prefix	String	Contains the prefix for the namespace that ADO.NET will use when it writes the contents of your *DataSet* to XML or when it loads XML data into your *DataSet*
ReadOnly	Boolean	Controls whether the contents of the column are read-only

Table 6-11   Properties of the *DataColumn* Class

Property	Data Type	Description
Table	*DataTable*	Returns the *DataTable* to which the *DataColumn* belongs
Unique	*Boolean*	Controls whether ADO.NET requires that the values for the column be unique within the *DataTable*

AllowDBNull Property

You can use the *AllowDBNull* property to control whether the *DataColumn* will accept null values. By default, this property is set to *True* when you create new *DataColumn* objects.

Using a *SqlDataAdapter* object's *Fill* method to create new *DataColumn* objects will not set the *AllowDBNull* property to *True* even if the corresponding column in the database does not accept null values. The *SqlDataAdapter* will not fetch this schema information from your database when you call the *Fill* method. Calling the *FillSchema* method instead will fetch this information and apply it to new columns in your *DataTable*.

AutoIncrement, *AutoIncrementSeed*, and *AutoIncrementStep* Properties

You can use these properties to control how or whether ADO.NET will generate new auto-increment values for the column.

Setting the *AutoIncrement* property to *True* will force ADO.NET to generate new autoincrement values for your column. By default, this property is set to *False*. As with the *AllowDBNull* property, you must call the *SqlDataAdapter* object's *FillSchema* method to set the *AutoIncrement* property to *True* for *DataColumn* objects that correspond to autoincrement columns in your database.

If you set the *AutoIncrement* property to *True*, ADO.NET will use the values in the *AutoIncrementSeed* and *AutoIncrementStep* properties to generate new autoincrement values. By default, *AutoIncrementSeed* is set to 0 and *AutoIncrementStep* is set to 1. For reasons stated earlier in the chapter, I prefer to set both of these properties to −1 when I use ADO.NET to generate new autoincrement values. Using the *FillSchema* method of the *SqlDataAdapter* will not set the *AutoIncrementSeed* or *AutoIncrementStep* properties on new autoincrement *DataColumn* objects.

Earlier in the chapter, I also explained that although you can use ADO.NET to generate placeholder values for autoincrement columns in your *DataSet*, you should not try to submit these placeholder values to your database. Instead, let the database handle generating the actual values.

Caption Property

The name of the *Caption* property implies that the value of this property will determine the text in the header for the column in a *DataGrid* or *DataGridView* control. Unfortunately, that's not the case. I'm sure someone will correct me on this, but I'm not aware of any use of the

Caption property. If you do not set the *Caption* property, it does default to the same value as the *DataColumn*'s *ColumnName* property.

ColumnMapping Property

You can use the *ColumnMapping* property to control how ADO.NET will write the contents of the column when returning the data in your *DataSet* as XML.

The *ColumnMapping* property accepts values from the *MappingType* enumeration in the *System.Data* namespace. By default, the *ColumnMapping* property is set to *Element*, which means that the value of each column within your *DataRow* will appear in an element tag. You can also set *ColumnMapping* to *Attribute*, *Hidden*, or *SimpleContent*.

The following examples show the difference between using elements and attributes for data within your *DataSet*:

Using Column.ColumnMapping = MappingType.Element
```
<MyDataSet>
  <Customers>
    <CustomerID>ABCDE</CustomerID>
    <CompanyName>New Customer</CompanyName>
    <ContactName>New Contact</ContactName>
    <Phone>425 555-1212</Phone>
  </Customers>
</MyDataSet>
```

Using Column.ColumnMapping = MappingType.Attribute
```
<MyDataSet>
  <Customers CustomerID="ABCDE" CompanyName="New Customer"
             ContactName="New Contact" Phone="425 555-1212" />
</MyDataSet>
```

For more information about using the ADO.NET XML features, see Chapter 12.

ColumnName Property

The *ColumnName* property contains the name of the *DataColumn*. You can set this property in the *DataColumn* class's constructors.

DataType Property

The *DataType* property controls the data type that ADO.NET will use to store the contents of the column. By default, this property is set to store a string.

ADO.NET stores the data using a .NET data type. Previous data access models such as ADO store the results of queries in a data type designed to mirror the one that the database uses.

For example, SQL Server has different data types for fixed-length strings and variable-length strings, and for strings that contain single-byte characters and those that contain double-byte characters. ADO treats all these data types differently. As far as the ADO.NET *DataColumn* is concerned, a string is a string is a string.

The *DataType* property accepts a value of type *Type*. The following code snippet shows how to set a *DataColumn* object's *DataType* property directly and use the *Add* method of the *DataColumnCollection* object:

Visual Basic
```
Dim col As New DataColumn("NewColumn")
col.DataType = GetType(Decimal)

Dim tbl As New DataTable("Products")
tbl.Columns.Add("ProductID", GetType(Integer))
tbl.Columns.Add("ProductName", GetType(String))
tbl.Columns.Add("UnitPrice", GetType(Decimal))
```

Visual C#
```
DataColumn col = new DataColumn("NewColumn");
col.DataType = typeof(Decimal);

DataTable tbl = new DataTable("Products");
tbl.Columns.Add("ProductID", typeof(int));
tbl.Columns.Add("ProductName", typeof(string));
tbl.Columns.Add("UnitPrice", typeof(Decimal));
```

DateTimeMode Property

The *DateTimeMode* property controls how *DateTime* values in a *DataColumn* are serialized. For an in-depth look at this property, see the discussion in the "ADO.NET 2.0 *DataSet* Serialization and Remoting Options" section earlier in the chapter.

DefaultValue Property

You can use the *DefaultValue* property to generate a default value for the column in each new *DataRow* object.

SQL Server lets you define default values for columns in your tables. However, the *DefaultValue* property of the *DataColumn* object doesn't work quite the same way as the SQL Server feature.

When you define a default value for a SQL Server column, you supply a string that contains an expression. SQL Server evaluates that expression each time it assigns a default value to a column.

The *DefaultValue* property accepts a static value via the generic *Object* data type. For example, say that you're working with order dates. You can use the *DefaultValue* property to specify the default value for an OrderDate column. However, the default value is static. It will return the same value tomorrow as it does today.

The *DefaultValue* property is handy but not nearly as flexible as the corresponding SQL Server feature. The *TableNewRow* event can help bridge a portion of this gap.

Expression Property

You can store an expression in the *Expression* property, and ADO.NET will evaluate that expression any time you request the contents of the column. Setting the *Expression* property of a *DataColumn* to anything other than the default empty string will automatically set the *ReadOnly* property of the *DataColumn* to *True*.

The following code snippet demonstrates how to set the *Expression* property of a *DataColumn* to return the product of two other columns in the *DataTable*–*Quantity* and *UnitPrice*. The code also adds a new *DataRow* to the *DataTable* and displays the contents of the expression-based column in the Console window.

Visual Basic

```
Dim tbl As New DataTable("Order Details")
tbl.Columns.Add("OrderID", GetType(Integer))
tbl.Columns.Add("ProductID", GetType(Integer))
tbl.Columns.Add("Quantity", GetType(Integer))
tbl.Columns.Add("UnitPrice", GetType(Decimal))
Dim col As New DataColumn("ItemTotal", GetType(Decimal))
col.Expression = "Quantity * UnitPrice"
tbl.Columns.Add(col)
Dim row As DataRow = tbl.NewRow()
row("OrderID") = 1
row("ProductID") = 1
row("Quantity") = 6
row("UnitPrice") = 18
tbl.Rows.Add(row)
Console.WriteLine(row("ItemTotal"))
```

Visual C#

```
DataTable tbl = new DataTable("Order Details");
tbl.Columns.Add("OrderID", typeof(int));
tbl.Columns.Add("ProductID", typeof(int));
tbl.Columns.Add("Quantity", typeof(int));
tbl.Columns.Add("UnitPrice", typeof(Decimal));
DataColumn col = new DataColumn("ItemTotal", typeof(Decimal));
col.Expression = "Quantity * UnitPrice"
tbl.Columns.Add(col);
DataRow row = tbl.NewRow();
row["OrderID"] = 1;
row["ProductID"] = 1;
row["Quantity"] = 6;
row["UnitPrice"] = 18;
tbl.Rows.Add(row);
Console.WriteLine(row["ItemTotal"]);
```

In Chapter 7, you'll learn how to reference the contents of other *DataTable* objects in an expression-based column. For more information about the functions you can use in the *Expression* property, see the MSDN documentation.

ExtendedProperties Property

The *DataColumn* class's *ExtendedProperties* property returns a *PropertyCollection* object, which is designed to store various objects.

The *DataSet*, *DataTable*, *DataRelation*, and *Constraint* classes also expose an *ExtendedProperties* property.

For more information, including a code sample, see the *ExtendedProperties* property in the "Properties of the *DataSet* Class" section earlier in the chapter.

MaxLength Property

You can use the *MaxLength* property to make sure that a user does not enter a longer string into your *DataColumn* than the database will allow.

By default, the *MaxLength* property is set to *−1*, which means that there is no maximum length for the column. As with the *AllowDBNull* and *AutoIncrement* properties, the *SqlDataAdapter* will not set the *MaxLength* property of *DataColumn* objects that it creates via the *Fill* method. However, you can use the *SqlDataAdapter* class's *FillSchema* method to set this property.

Namespace and *Prefix* Properties

You can use the *DataSet* class's *Namespace* and *Prefix* properties to specify an XML namespace and prefix for your *DataSet*. ADO.NET will use these settings when it writes the contents of your *DataSet* to XML and when it loads data from an XML document into your *DataSet*.

The *DataSet* and *DataTable* classes also expose *Namespace* and *Prefix* properties.

For more information about XML namespaces, see the MSDN documentation.

Ordinal Property

The *Ordinal* property returns the position of the *DataColumn* within the *DataTable* object's *Columns* collection. This property is read-only and will return −1 if the *DataColumn* object is not part of a *DataTable* class's *Columns* collection.

ReadOnly Property

You can use the *ReadOnly* property to control whether the contents of the column are read-only. By default, this property is set to *False*.

If you set the *Expression* property of a *DataColumn*, the *ReadOnly* property will be automatically set to *True*. At that point, the *ReadOnly* property becomes read-only.

If you attempt to change the value of a column whose *ReadOnly* property is set to *True*, ADO.NET will throw a *ReadOnlyException*. But even though the *ReadOnly* property is set to

True, you can still modify the contents of the column before adding it to a *DataTable* object's *Rows* collection.

Like the *AllowDBNull* and *AutoIncrement* properties, the *ReadOnly* property is one of the properties that the *SqlDataAdapter* will set via the *FillSchema* method but not via the *Fill* method.

Table Property

The *Table* property returns the *DataTable* to which the *DataColumn* object belongs. This property is read-only and returns an uninitialized *DataTable* if the *DataColumn* does not reside in a *DataTable* object's *Columns* collection.

Unique Property

You can use the *Unique* property to ensure that all values for a column within a *DataTable* are unique. By default, the *Unique* property is set to *False*.

Setting the *Unique* property to *True* will implicitly create a *UniqueConstraint* object for the *DataTable* in which the column resides. Similarly, adding a *UniqueConstraint* based on a single column will set the *Unique* property of that *DataColumn* to *True*.

If you create a unique constraint or a primary key on a collection of columns, the *Unique* property of each *DataColumn* will not be set to *True* because the values within the column are not necessarily unique. For example, the Order Details table in the Northwind database has a primary key based on the combination of the OrderID and ProductID columns. Neither column on its own is unique because there can be multiple entries in the table for an order and multiple orders can include the same product.

Like the *AllowDBNull* and *AutoIncrement* properties, the *Unique* property is one of the properties that the *SqlDataAdapter* will set via the *FillSchema* method but not via the *Fill* method.

Properties of the *DataRow* Class

The commonly used properties of the *DataRow* class are shown in Table 6-12.

Table 6-12   Properties of the *DataRow* Class

Property	Data Type	Description
HasErrors	*Boolean*	Indicates whether the current row contains errors
Item	*Object*	Returns or sets the contents of a column
ItemArray	Array of *Objects*	Returns or sets the contents of the row
RowError	*String*	Returns or sets error information for the row
RowState	*DataRowState*	Returns the state of the row
Table	*DataTable*	Returns the *DataTable* to which the row belongs

HasErrors Property

You can use the *HasErrors* property to determine whether the row contains errors. The *HasErrors* property returns a Boolean value and is read-only.

Item Property

The *Item* property allows you to examine or modify the contents of a column of information in the row. You can access the contents of the column by specifying the ordinal for the column, its name, or the *DataColumn* object itself.

The *Item* property also lets you supply a value from the *DataRowVersion* enumeration so that you can choose which version of the column you want to see. For example, you might want to view the original contents of a column for a row that has changed.

ItemArray Property

You can retrieve or set values for all columns in your row by using the *ItemArray* property. This property returns or accepts an array of type *Object*, where each item in the array corresponds to a column in the *DataTable*.

When you use the *ItemArray* property to change the contents of a row, you can use the appropriate keyword for your language of choice to keep from modifying certain fields. For example, Visual Basic programmers would use *Nothing* and Visual C# programmers would use *null*.

The following line of code modifies the contents of the second, third, and fourth columns in the row but does not modify the contents of the first or last columns. Such code is necessary when you work with *DataTable* objects that contain read-only columns.

Visual Basic
```
row.ItemArray = New Object() {Nothing, 2, 3, 4, Nothing}
```

Visual C#
```
row.ItemArray = new object[] {null, 2, 3, 4, null};
```

RowError Property

The *RowError* property returns a string that contains error information for the row. You can set the *RowError* property to a string to indicate that the row has an error.

The *DataRow* class's *HasErrors* property might return *True* even if the *RowError* property is empty. For more information, see the documentation for *SetColumnError* later in the chapter.

RowState Property

The *RowState* property returns a value from the *DataRowState* enumeration to indicate the current state of the row. This property is read-only.

I discussed the various values that the *RowState* property can return earlier in the chapter.

Table Property

The *Table* property returns the *DataTable* to which the *DataRow* object belongs. This property is read-only.

There are times when a *DataRow* object does not reside in a *DataTable* object's *Rows* collection—for example, after the *DataRow* is created using *DataTable.NewRow* but before it is added to the *DataTable* object's *Rows* collection. However, the *DataRow* object's *Table* property will always return the *DataTable* to which the *DataRow* belongs.

Methods of the *DataRow* Class

The commonly used methods of the *DataRow* class are shown in Table 6-13.

Table 6-13   Methods of the *DataRow* Class

Method	Description
AcceptChanges	Accepts the pending changes stored in the *DataRow*
BeginEdit	Starts the editing process for the *DataRow*
CancelEdit	Cancels the changes made since the *BeginEdit* method was called
ClearErrors	Clears the errors for the *DataRow*
Delete	Marks the *DataRow* as deleted
EndEdit	Commits the changes made since the *BeginEdit* method was called
GetChildRows	Returns an array of child *DataRow* objects for the current *DataRow* based on a *DataRelation*
GetColumnError	Retrieves error information for a particular column
GetColumnsInError	Returns an array of *DataColumn* objects that contain errors for the current row
GetParentRow	Returns the parent *DataRow* for the current *DataRow* based on a *DataRelation*
GetParentRows	Returns an array of parent *DataRow* objects for the current *DataRow* based on a *DataRelation*
HasVersion	Returns a Boolean value to indicate whether the *DataRow* can return that version of data
IsNull	Indicates whether a particular column in the row contains a *Null* value
RejectChanges	Discards the pending changes stored in the *DataRow*
SetAdded	Sets the *DataRow*'s *RowState* to *Added*
SetColumnError	Sets error information for a particular column in the row
SetModified	Sets the *DataRow*'s *RowState* to *Modified*
SetParentRow	Changes the parent *DataRow* for the current *DataRow* based on a *DataRelation*

AcceptChanges and *RejectChanges* Methods

The *DataRow* stores pending changes so that you can later submit those changes to the database. The *AcceptChanges* and *RejectChanges* methods let you accept or discard those changes, respectively.

By default, when you successfully submit pending changes to your database using a *SqlData-Adapter*, the *SqlDataAdapter* will implicitly call the *AcceptChanges* method on the *DataRow* object. The *DataRow* will then have a *RowState* of *Unmodified*.

You can discard the pending changes stored in a *DataRow* by calling its *RejectChanges* method. As with the *AcceptChanges* method, the *DataRow* object's *RowState* will then return *Unmodified*.

Say that you have a row of customer data that contains a pending change. The CompanyName column originally contained *"Initial CompanyName"* but now contains *"New CompanyName"*.

If you call the *AcceptChanges* method, the *DataRow* will no longer maintain the old original value of *"Initial CompanyName"*. The *DataRow* will return *"New CompanyName"* regardless of whether you request the current or original value using the *DataRow* object's *Item* method.

If, instead, you call the *RejectChanges* method, the *DataRow* will no longer maintain the *"New CompanyName"* value. The *DataRow* will return *"Initial CompanyName"* regardless of whether you request the current or original value using the *DataRow* object's *Item* method.

To gain a better understanding of how ADO.NET uses the original values for a *DataRow* to submit changes to your database, see Chapter 10 and Chapter 11.

BeginEdit, CancelEdit, and *EndEdit* Methods

The *BeginEdit, CancelEdit,* and *EndEdit* methods allow you to store or cancel a series of changes to the *DataRow*. For example, you might want to let the user modify the contents of a row and then display a dialog box that gives the user the chance to accept or cancel those changes.

CancelEdit and *EndEdit* behave differently from *AcceptChanges* and *RejectChanges*. The best way to explain the difference between the sets of methods is to show some sample code. The following code snippet creates a new *DataRow* and modifies its contents. It then calls *BeginEdit*, modifies the contents of the row again, and displays the various versions of the row:

Visual Basic
```
Dim tbl As New DataTable("Customers")
tbl.Columns.Add("CustomerID", GetType(String))
tbl.Columns.Add("CompanyName", GetType(String))
Dim row As DataRow

'Create a new row using the LoadDataRow method.
row = tbl.LoadDataRow(New Object() {"NEWCO", _
                                    "Initial CompanyName"}, True)
```

```
'Modify the contents of the DataRow.
'row.RowState will now return Modified.
'The 'Original' value for the column is "Initial CompanyName".
row("CompanyName") = "New CompanyName"

'Call BeginEdit and modify the CompanyName column again.
row.BeginEdit()
row("CompanyName") = "Even Newer CompanyName!"

'Display the different versions of the column.
Console.WriteLine("Proposed: {0}", _
                row("CompanyName", DataRowVersion.Proposed))
Console.WriteLine("Current:  {0}", _
                row("CompanyName", DataRowVersion.Current))
Console.WriteLine("Original: {0}", _
                row("CompanyName", DataRowVersion.Original))
```

Visual C#

```csharp
DataTable tbl = new DataTable("Customers");
tbl.Columns.Add("CustomerID", typeof(string));
tbl.Columns.Add("CompanyName", typeof(string));
DataRow row;

//Create a new row using the LoadDataRow method.
row = tbl.LoadDataRow(new object[] {"NEWCO",
                                "Initial CompanyName"}, true);

//Modify the contents of the DataRow.
//row.RowState will now return Modified.
//The 'Original' value for the column is "Initial CompanyName."
row["CompanyName"] = New CompanyName";

//Call BeginEnit and modify the CompanyName column again.
row.BeginEdit();
row["CompanyName"] = "Even Newer CompanyName!";

//Display the different versions of the column.
Console.WriteLine("Proposed: {0}",
                row["CompanyName", DataRowVersion.Proposed]);
Console.WriteLine("Current:  {0}",
                row["CompanyName", DataRowVersion.Current]);
Console.WriteLine("Original: {0}",
                row["CompanyName", DataRowVersion.Original]);
```

Run the code, and you'll see that the proposed value for the column is *"Even Newer CompanyName!"*, the current value is *"New CompanyName"*, and the original value is *"Initial CompanyName"*.

You can call the *EndEdit* method to accept the edit. The current value of the column will be set to the proposed value. The original value for the column will remain the same.

You can call the *CancelEdit* method to discard the edit. The current and original values of the column will remain the same.

Keep in mind that while you're editing the contents of a row after using the *BeginEdit* method, the *Item* method will return the proposed values for the columns by default. For more information about this behavior, see the "Examining the Pending Changes in a *DataRow*" section earlier in this chapter.

ClearErrors Method

To clear all errors in a *DataRow*, call the object's *ClearErrors* method. The method clears the error information for the *DataRow* object as a whole as well as for each column in the row.

Delete Method

The *Delete* method does not actually remove a *DataRow* from its table's *Rows* collection. When you call a *DataRow* object's *Delete* method, ADO.NET marks the row as deleted so that you can later remove the corresponding row in your database by calling the *DataAdapter* object's *Update* method.

If you want to completely remove the *DataRow*, you can call its *Delete* method and then call its *AcceptChanges* method. You can also use the *Remove* method of the *DataRowCollection* object to accomplish the same task in a single line of code.

GetChildRows Method

You can use the *GetChildRows* method to access the child rows for the current *DataRow*. To use the *GetChildRows* method, you must supply a *DataRelation* or the name of a *DataRelation*. You can also supply a value from the *DataRowVersion* enumeration to control the version of the child data that you retrieve.

The *GetChildRows* method returns child data in an array of *DataRow* objects.

GetColumnError and *SetColumnError* Methods

To set or examine error information for a particular column in a row, you can use the *GetColumnError* and *SetColumnError* methods. You can supply a column name, its ordinal position within the *DataTable*, or the *DataColumn* object itself with either method.

You can also use *SetColumnError* to clear the error information for a particular column by passing an empty string as the second parameter.

GetColumnsInError Method

If a *DataRow* object's *HasErrors* property returns *True*, you can use the *GetColumnsInError* method to determine which column (or columns) in the *DataRow* contains error information.

The following code snippet demonstrates how you can use the *GetColumnsInError* method in conjunction with the *GetColumnError* method to return error information for a particular *DataRow*:

Visual Basic

```
Dim row As DataRow
'...
If row.HasErrors Then
    Console.WriteLine("The row contains the following errors:")
    Console.WriteLine("RowError: {0}", row.RowError)
    For Each colError As DataColumn In row.GetColumnsInError
        Console.WriteLine("  Error in {0}: {1}",
                            colError.ColumnName, _
                            row.GetColumnError(colError))
    Next colError
Else
    Console.WriteLine("The row does not contain errors")
End If
```

Visual C#

```
DataRow row;
//...
if (row.HasErrors) {
    Console.WriteLine("The row contains the following errors:");
    Console.WriteLine("RowError: {0}", row.RowError);
    foreach (DataColumn colError in row.GetColumnsInError())
        Console.WriteLine("  Error in {0}: {1}",
                            colError.ColumnName,
                            row.GetColumnError(colError));
}
else
    Console.WriteLine("The row does not contain errors");
```

GetParentRow, *GetParentRows*, and *SetParentRow* Methods

The *GetParentRow* and *SetParentRow* methods provide an easy way for you to examine or set the parent row of the current row in a *DataRelation* object, respectively.

Like the *GetChildRows* method, the *GetParentRow* method accepts relation information—either the name of the *DataRelation* or the object itself—as well as a value from the *DataRowVersion* enumeration to control the version of the row that the method returns. The *GetParentRow* method returns a *DataRow* object.

If the current *DataRow* can have multiple parent rows via a relation, you can use the *GetParent-Rows* method to access those rows. This method accepts the same parameters as the *GetParent-Row* method, except that it returns an array of *DataRow* objects.

The *SetParentRow* method allows you to change a row's parent row in a relation. To use the method, you simply pass the row's new parent. If the current row's *DataTable* is the child table in multiple relations within the *DataSet*, you should use the overloaded method that allows you to pass the *DataRelation* object as the second parameter so that the *SetParentRow* method will know which relation you want to reference.

We'll discuss these methods again in Chapter 7 when we examine the *DataRelation* class.

HasVersion Method

We've discussed some of the versions of data that a *DataRow* object maintains—current, original, and proposed. The *DataRow* object does not maintain values for all these versions all the time.

You might have code that's going to check the current or original value of a column in your *DataRow*. Prior to executing that code, you could check the *DataRow*'s *RowState* to make sure checking that version of a column in your *DataRow* will not throw an exception. For example, a *DataRow* whose *RowState* is *Added* will have a current version but not an original version. A *DataRow* whose *RowState* is *Deleted* will have an original version but not a current version.

A simpler approach is to call the *HasVersion* method. The *HasVersion* method accepts a value from the *DataRowVersion* enumeration and returns a Boolean value that indicates whether the *DataRow* currently maintains that version of data.

IsNull Method

Say that you're working with a *DataRow* that contains customer information and you want to retrieve the contents of the ContactName column and place it into a string variable. If you use the following code, you might run into problems if the ContactName column contains a null value:

Visual Basic
```
Dim row As DataRow
'...
Dim strContactName As String
strContactName = CStr(row("ContactName"))
```

Visual C#
```
DataRow row;
//...
string strContactName;
strContactName = (string) row["ContactName"];
```

To avoid such problems, you can do one of two things: set up your database and *DataSet* so that the column does not support *null* values, or check the contents of the column for *null* values before accessing its contents.

The *IsNull* method can simplify the second of these options. This method accepts the name of a column, its ordinal position, or the *DataColumn* object itself, and it returns a Boolean value to indicate whether the column contains a *null* value.

We can change our previous code snippet to use the *IsNull* method, as shown here:

Visual Basic

```
Dim row As DataRow
'...
Dim strContactName As String
If row.IsNull("ContactName") Then
    strContactName = "<Null>"
Else
    strContactName = CStr(row("ContactName"))
End If
```

Visual C#

```
DataRow row;
//...
string strContactName;
if (row.IsNull("ContactName"))
    strContactName = "<Null>";
else
    strContactName = (string) row["ContactName"];
```

You might also encounter *null* values when checking different versions of values in a *DataRow*. The *IsNull* method also supports a fourth overloaded method that accepts a *DataColumn* object and a value from the *DataRowVersion* enumeration. You can use this method to determine whether a particular version of a column contains a *null* value.

SetAdded and SetModified Methods

In ADO.NET 2.0, the *DataRow* class now exposes *SetAdded* and *SetModified* methods. You can call either of these methods to set the *DataRow*'s *RowState* to the row state that corresponds to the name of the method. In other words, the *SetAdded* method sets the *DataRow*'s *RowState* to *Added* and the *SetModified* method sets the *DataRow*'s *RowState* to *Modified*. These methods are available only on *DataRows* whose *RowState* is *Unmodified*. Calling either method on a *DataRow* whose *RowState* is not *Unmodified* will result in an exception.

Properties of the *UniqueConstraint* Class

The commonly used properties of the *UniqueConstraint* class are shown in Table 6-14.

Table 6-14   Properties of the *UniqueConstraint* Class

Property	Data Type	Description
Columns	Array of *DataColumn* objects	Returns the columns that are part of the constraint
ConstraintName	*String*	Contains the name of the constraint
ExtendedProperties	*PropertyCollection*	Contains a collection of dynamic properties and values
IsPrimaryKey	*Boolean*	Indicates whether the constraint constitutes the primary key for the *DataTable*
Table	*DataTable*	Returns the *DataTable* to which the constraint belongs

Columns Property

The *Columns* property returns an array of *DataColumn* objects that contains the columns that make up the constraint. This property is read-only.

ConstraintName Property

You can use the *ConstraintName* property to examine or set the name of the *UniqueConstraint*.

ExtendedProperties Property

The *UniqueConstraint* class's *ExtendedProperties* property returns a *PropertyCollection* object, which is designed to store various objects.

The *DataSet*, *DataColumn*, *DataRelation*, and *ForeignKeyConstraint* classes also expose an *ExtendedProperties* property.

For more information, including a code sample, see the *ExtendedProperties* property in the "Properties of the *DataSet* Class" section earlier in the chapter.

IsPrimaryKey Property

The *IsPrimaryKey* property returns a Boolean value that indicates whether the *Unique-Constraint* object is the primary key for the *DataTable*.

The *IsPrimaryKey* property is read-only. The *UniqueConstraint* class only lets you specify whether the constraint is a *DataTable* object's primary key through its constructors.

You can also set a *DataTable* object's primary key through its *PrimaryKey* property.

Table Property

The *Table* property returns the *DataTable* to which the *UniqueConstraint* belongs. This property is read-only.

Properties of the *ForeignKeyConstraint* Class

The commonly used properties of the *ForeignKeyConstraint* class are shown in Table 6-15.

Table 6-15   Properties of the *ForeignKeyConstraint* Class

Property	Data Type	Description
AcceptRejectRule	*AcceptRejectRule*	Controls whether the effects of a call to a parent row's *AcceptChanges* or *RejectChanges* method cascade to the child rows
Columns	Array of *DataColumn* objects	Returns the columns in the child table that make up the constraint
ConstraintName	*String*	Contains the name of the constraint

Table 6-15   Properties of the *ForeignKeyConstraint* Class

Property	Data Type	Description
DeleteRule	*Rule*	Controls how or whether a deletion of a parent row cascades to the child rows
ExtendedProperties	*PropertyCollection*	Contains a collection of dynamic properties and values
RelatedColumns	Array of *DataColumns*	Returns the columns in the parent table that make up the constraint
RelatedTable	*DataTable*	Returns the parent table for the constraint
Table	*DataTable*	Returns the child table for the constraint
UpdateRule	*Rule*	Controls how or whether changes to the parent row cascade to the child rows

AcceptRejectRule, DeleteRule, and *UpdateRule* Properties

The *AcceptRejectRule*, *DeleteRule*, and *UpdateRule* properties control how or whether changes to a parent row cascade to the child rows.

The *AcceptRejectRule* property accepts values from the *AcceptRejectRule* enumeration. By default, the *AcceptRejectRule* property is set to *None*, which means that if you call the *AcceptChanges* or *RejectChanges* method on a row, its child rows will not be affected. If you set the *AcceptRejectRule* property to *Cascade*, the action will cascade down to the child rows defined by the *ForeignKeyConstraint* object.

The *DeleteRule* and *UpdateRule* properties behave in a similar fashion, but they accept values from the *Rule* enumeration. By default, both properties are set to *Cascade*, which means that the changes you make to a parent row will automatically cascade down to the child rows.

For example, if you call the *Delete* method on a *DataRow*, you're implicitly calling the *Delete* method on its child rows as well. Similarly, if you change the value of a key column in a *DataRow*, you'll implicitly change the contents of the corresponding column in the child rows.

You can set the *DeleteRule* and *UpdateRule* properties to *None* if you don't want to cascade changes. You can also set the properties to *SetDefault* or *SetNull*. Setting the properties to *SetNull* will assign *null* values to the related columns in child rows if the parent row is deleted or if the contents of its related columns change. The *SetDefault* value causes similar behavior, except that the contents of the related columns in child rows will be set to their default values.

Columns and *RelatedColumns* Properties

The *Columns* property returns an array of *DataColumn* objects that contain the columns in the child table that are part of the constraint. The *RelatedColumns* property returns the same information for the parent table.

Both properties are read-only.

ConstraintName Property

You can use the *ConstraintName* property to examine or set the name of the *ForeignKeyConstraint*.

ExtendedProperties Property

The *ForeignKeyConstraint* class's *ExtendedProperties* property returns a *PropertyCollection* object, which is designed to store various objects.

The *DataSet*, *DataColumn*, *DataRelation*, and *UniqueConstraint* classes also expose an *Extended-Properties* property.

For more information, including a code sample, see the *ExtendedProperties* property in the "Properties of the *DataSet* Class" section earlier in the chapter.

RelatedTable and *Table* Properties

The *Table* property returns the child *DataTable* for the constraint. The *RelatedTable* property returns the parent *DataTable* for the constraint. Both properties are read-only.

Questions That Should Be Asked More Frequently

Q   Do I need to use a *DataSet* if I want to work with only a few rows of data?

A   In this situation, you can use just a *DataTable* object without using a *DataSet*. In ADO.NET 2.0, the *DataTable* class now lets you read and write data to and from files and streams and offers support for XML features. If you need to work with data from various *DataTable*s, you might consider using a *DataSet*.

Q   I added a row to my *DataTable*, and when I submitted the new row to my database, I received an error that said the new row violated the primary key constraint on the table. Why didn't I receive this error when I added the row to the *DataTable*?

A   ADO.NET enforces the constraints you create based on the data in your *DataSet*. The new row that you created will not violate the primary key constraint on your *DataTable* unless the *DataTable* already contains a row with the same values in the primary key columns. ADO.NET does not have any inherent knowledge of what data exists in your database.

Q   How do I examine the contents of a deleted row?

A   Use *DataRowVersion.Original* for the optional parameter on the *Item* property.

Q   Is there any way to undo the changes I've made to my rows?

A   Yes. You can call the *RejectChanges* method on a *DataRow*, *DataTable*, or *DataSet* to discard any pending changes in the affected rows.

Q   How can I tell whether a *DataTable* has a primary key defined?

A   You can use the following snippet of code:

Visual Basic

```vb
If tbl.PrimaryKey.Length > 0 Then
    'DataTable has a primary key.
Else
    'DataTable has no primary key.
End If
```

Visual C#

```csharp
if (tbl.PrimaryKey.Length > 0)
    //DataTable has a primary key.
else
    //DataTable has no primary key.
```

Q   Does calling the *Dispose* method on the *DataSet* also dispose the *DataTables* and *DataColumns* contained in that *DataSet*?

A   In short, no.

The *DataSet*, *DataTable*, and *DataColumn* classes are each derived from the *MarshalByValueComponent* class, which exposes both a *Dispose* method and a *Disposed* event. You can use the *Dispose* method to release an object's resources. You can also trap for an object's *Disposed* event if you want to execute code when the object's *Dispose* method executes.

However, a call to the *Dispose* method of any of these classes does not cascade down to the objects it contains. In other words, calling the *Dispose* method of a *DataSet* object does not implicitly call the *Dispose* method of the *DataTable* objects of the *DataSet*. The following code snippet uses the *Dispose* event on the *DataSet*, *DataTable*, and *DataColumn* objects to demonstrate that calling *Dispose* on the *DataSet* (implicitly, through the use of the *Using* block) does not call the *Dispose* method on the *DataTables* and *DataColumns* contained by that *DataSet*:

Visual Basic

```vb
Dim strConn, strSQL As String
strConn = "Data Source=.\SQLExpress;" & _
          "Initial Catalog=Northwind;Integrated Security=True;"
strSQL = "SELECT CustomerID, CompanyName FROM Customers;" & _
         "SELECT OrderID, CustomerID, OrderDate FROM Orders;" & _
         "SELECT OrderID, ProductID, Quantity, UnitPrice " & _
         "FROM [Order Details]"
Dim da As New SqlDataAdapter(strSQL, strConn)
Using ds As New DataSet("Northwind")
    da.Fill(ds)

    AddHandler ds.Disposed, AddressOf Log_Disposed
    For Each tbl As DataTable In ds.Tables
    AddHandler tbl.Disposed, AddressOf Log_Disposed
        For Each col As DataColumn In tbl.Columns
            AddHandler col.Disposed, AddressOf Log_Disposed
```

```
            Next col
        Next tbl

        Console.WriteLine("Calling DataSet.Dispose")
    End Using
    Console.WriteLine("Done calling DataSet.Dispose")

    Private Sub Log_Disposed(ByVal sender As Object, ByVal e As EventArgs)
        If TypeOf sender Is DataSet Then
            Console.WriteLine("  Disposing DataSet")
        ElseIf TypeOf sender Is DataTable Then
            Console.WriteLine("    Disposing DataTable {0}", _
                              CType(sender, DataTable).TableName)
        ElseIf TypeOf sender Is DataColumn Then
            Console.WriteLine("      Disposing DataColumn {0}", _
                              CType(sender, DataColumn).ColumnName)
        End If
    End Sub
```

Visual C#

```
string strConn, strSQL;
strConn = @"Data Source=.\SQLExpress;" +
            "Initial Catalog=Northwind;Integrated Security=True;";
strSQL = "SELECT CustomerID, CompanyName FROM Customers;" +
         "SELECT OrderID, CustomerID, OrderDate FROM Orders;" +
         "SELECT OrderID, ProductID, Quantity, UnitPrice " +
         "FROM [Order Details]";
SqlDataAdapter da = new SqlDataAdapter(strSQL, strConn);
using (DataSet ds = new DataSet("Northwind"))
{
    da.Fill(ds);

    ds.Disposed += new EventHandler(Log_Disposed);
    foreach (DataTable tbl in ds.Tables)
    {
        tbl.Disposed += new EventHandler(Log_Disposed);
        foreach (DataColumn col in tbl.Columns)
            col.Disposed += new EventHandler(Log_Disposed);
    }

    Console.WriteLine("Calling DataSet.Dispose");
}
Console.WriteLine("Done calling DataSet.Dispose");

static void Log_Disposed(object sender, EventArgs e)
{
    if (sender is DataSet)
        Console.WriteLine("  Disposing DataSet");
    else if (sender is DataTable)
        Console.WriteLine("    Disposing DataTable {0}",
                          ((DataTable)sender).TableName);
    else if (sender is DataColumn)
        Console.WriteLine("      Disposing DataColumn {0}",
                          ((DataColumn)sender).ColumnName);
}
```

If you really want to dispose of the contents of the *DataSet*, you could still call the *Dispose* method (implicitly through the *Using* block or explicitly) and then handle the *DataSet*'s *Disposed* event, using the event to call the *Dispose* methods of all *DataColumns* and *DataTables*, as shown in the following modification to the preceding code snippet:

Visual Basic

```vb
Dim strConn, strSQL As String
strConn = "Data Source=.\SQLExpress;" & _
          "Initial Catalog=Northwind;Integrated Security=True;"
strSQL = "SELECT CustomerID, CompanyName FROM Customers;" & _
         "SELECT OrderID, CustomerID, OrderDate FROM Orders;" & _
         "SELECT OrderID, ProductID, Quantity, UnitPrice " & _
         "FROM [Order Details]"
Dim da As New SqlDataAdapter(strSQL, strConn)
Using ds As New DataSet("Northwind")
    da.Fill(ds)

    AddHandler ds.Disposed, AddressOf Handle_DataSet_Disposed

    AddHandler ds.Disposed, AddressOf Log_Disposed
    For Each tbl As DataTable In ds.Tables
    AddHandler tbl.Disposed, AddressOf Log_Disposed
        For Each col As DataColumn In tbl.Columns
            AddHandler col.Disposed, AddressOf Log_Disposed
        Next col
    Next tbl

    Console.WriteLine("Calling DataSet.Dispose")
End Using
Console.WriteLine("Done calling DataSet.Dispose")


Private Sub Handle_DataSet_Disposed(ByVal sender As Object, ByVal e As EventArgs)
    Dim ds As DataSet = CType(sender, DataSet)
    For Each tbl As DataTable In ds.Tables
        For Each col As DataColumn In tbl.Columns
            col.Dispose()
        Next col
        tbl.Dispose()
    Next tbl
End Sub

Private Sub Log_Disposed(ByVal sender As Object, ByVal e As EventArgs)
    If TypeOf sender Is DataSet Then
        Console.WriteLine("  Disposing DataSet")
    ElseIf TypeOf sender Is DataTable Then
        Console.WriteLine("    Disposing DataTable {0}", _
                            CType(sender, DataTable).TableName)
    ElseIf TypeOf sender Is DataColumn Then
        Console.WriteLine("      Disposing DataColumn {0}", _
                            CType(sender, DataColumn).ColumnName)
    End If
End Sub
```

Visual C#

```csharp
string strConn, strSQL;
strConn = @"Data Source=.\SQLExpress;" +
            "Initial Catalog=Northwind;Integrated Security=True;";
strSQL = "SELECT CustomerID, CompanyName FROM Customers;" +
         "SELECT OrderID, CustomerID, OrderDate FROM Orders;" +
         "SELECT OrderID, ProductID, Quantity, UnitPrice " +
         "FROM [Order Details]";
SqlDataAdapter da = new SqlDataAdapter(strSQL, strConn);
using (DataSet ds = new DataSet("Northwind"))
{
    da.Fill(ds);

    ds.Disposed += new EventHandler(Handle_DataSet_Disposed);

    ds.Disposed += new EventHandler(Log_Disposed);
    foreach (DataTable tbl in ds.Tables)
    {
        tbl.Disposed += new EventHandler(Log_Disposed);
        foreach (DataColumn col in tbl.Columns)
            col.Disposed += new EventHandler(Log_Disposed);
    }

    Console.WriteLine("Calling DataSet.Dispose");
}
Console.WriteLine("Done calling DataSet.Dispose");

static void Handle_DataSet_Disposed(object sender, EventArgs e)
{
    DataSet ds = (DataSet)sender;
    foreach (DataTable tbl in ds.Tables)
    {
        foreach (DataColumn col in tbl.Columns)
            col.Dispose();
        tbl.Dispose();
    }
}

static void Log_Disposed(object sender, EventArgs e)
{
    if (sender is DataSet)
        Console.WriteLine("  Disposing DataSet");
    else if (sender is DataTable)
        Console.WriteLine("    Disposing DataTable {0}",
                          ((DataTable)sender).TableName);
    else if (sender is DataColumn)
        Console.WriteLine("      Disposing DataColumn {0}",
                          ((DataColumn)sender).ColumnName);
}
```

Chapter 7
Working with Relational Data

Database tables are rarely independent structures. If you look at the tables in the Microsoft SQL Server sample Northwind database, shown in Figure 7-1, you'll see that they're all interrelated. Notice that no table stands alone.

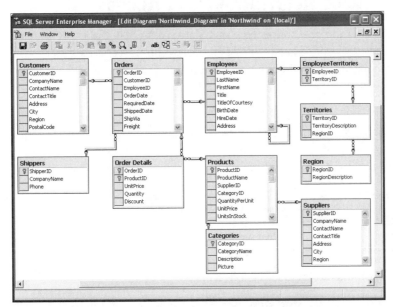

Figure 7-1 Relations between tables in the Northwind database

Not all databases have such a high percentage of related tables, but most contain tables that are related. When you build applications, you'll encounter scenarios in which you want to display or programmatically access data from related tables in your database.

When you're working with data from multiple *DataTable* objects, you're likely to need four types of features—those for navigation, validation, aggregation, and cascadation. OK, *cascadation* isn't really a word. Even though this is a technical book, I'm still entitled to a little artistic license once in awhile.

Users will want to navigate between different tables of information to locate related rows easily, such as the orders for a particular customer. They'll want to validate their data to make sure that they don't create *orphaned* rows in the database. Applications will often require users to gather aggregate information—for example, to display the number of items in, and total cost of, an order. And when a parent row is modified, you might want the changes to cascade down to child rows—for example, if an order is deleted, you'll probably want the items associated with that order to be deleted as well.

In this chapter, we'll look at how to use the ADO.NET *DataRelation* class to work with data from related *DataTable* objects. I'll also discuss in more detail some of the features of the *ForeignKeyConstraint* class, which I introduced in Chapter 6. We'll look at how you can use *DataRelations* to navigate between rows and to generate aggregate information with expression-based *DataColumns*. We'll also look at how you can use the *ForeignKeyConstraint* class to validate data and cascade changes.

A Brief Overview of Relational Data Access

Obviously, ADO.NET did not pioneer relational data access. ADO.NET was predated by other ways of processing data from related tables. Let's review the most common methods of working with data from related tables and quickly compare them to using the *DataRelation* object.

Join Queries

Join queries predate all Microsoft data access technologies. They're a simple, standard way to retrieve data from multiple tables in a single query. The following query retrieves data from the Customers, Orders, and Order Details tables in the Northwind database:

```
SELECT C.CustomerID, C.CompanyName, C.ContactName, C.Phone,
       O.OrderID, O.EmployeeID, O.OrderDate,
       D.ProductID, D.Quantity, D.UnitPrice
    FROM Customers C, Orders O, [Order Details] D
    WHERE C.CustomerID = O.CustomerID AND O.OrderID = D.OrderID
```

The benefits of join queries include the following:

- **They're a widely accepted standard.** Every database programmer knows how to use join queries.

- **They return results in a single structure.**

- **They're easy to filter.** If you want data only for customers from a particular country, you can simply add a filter to the query and the query will return data for only those customers.

The drawbacks include the following:

- **They can return redundant data.** If a customer has 100 orders, the same customer information will be returned for every order. (See Figure 7-2.)

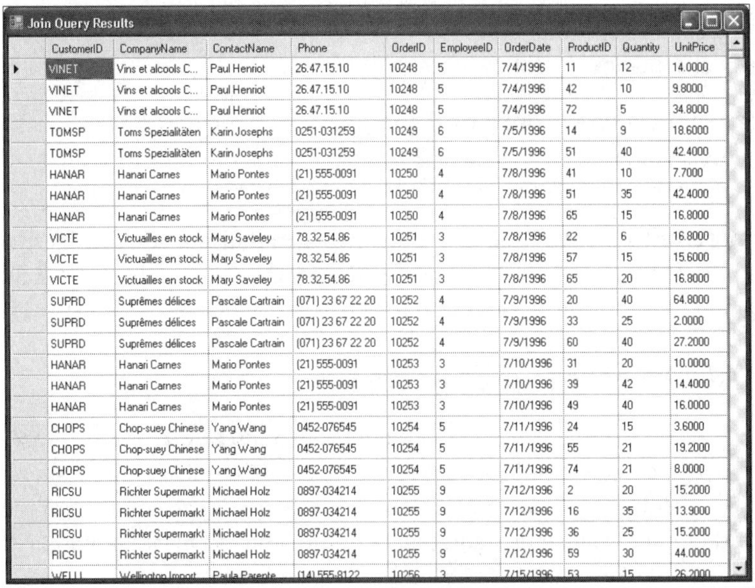

CustomerID	CompanyName	ContactName	Phone	OrderID	EmployeeID	OrderDate	ProductID	Quantity	UnitPrice
VINET	Vins et alcools C...	Paul Henriot	26.47.15.10	10248	5	7/4/1996	11	12	14.0000
VINET	Vins et alcools C...	Paul Henriot	26.47.15.10	10248	5	7/4/1996	42	10	9.8000
VINET	Vins et alcools C...	Paul Henriot	26.47.15.10	10248	5	7/4/1996	72	5	34.8000
TOMSP	Toms Spezialitäten	Karin Josephs	0251-031259	10249	6	7/5/1996	14	9	18.6000
TOMSP	Toms Spezialitäten	Karin Josephs	0251-031259	10249	6	7/5/1996	51	40	42.4000
HANAR	Hanari Carnes	Mario Pontes	(21) 555-0091	10250	4	7/8/1996	41	10	7.7000
HANAR	Hanari Carnes	Mario Pontes	(21) 555-0091	10250	4	7/8/1996	51	35	42.4000
HANAR	Hanari Carnes	Mario Pontes	(21) 555-0091	10250	4	7/8/1996	65	15	16.8000
VICTE	Victuailles en stock	Mary Saveley	78.32.54.86	10251	3	7/8/1996	22	6	16.8000
VICTE	Victuailles en stock	Mary Saveley	78.32.54.86	10251	3	7/8/1996	57	15	15.6000
VICTE	Victuailles en stock	Mary Saveley	78.32.54.86	10251	3	7/8/1996	65	20	16.8000
SUPRD	Suprêmes délices	Pascale Cartrain	(071) 23 67 22 20	10252	4	7/9/1996	20	40	64.8000
SUPRD	Suprêmes délices	Pascale Cartrain	(071) 23 67 22 20	10252	4	7/9/1996	33	25	2.0000
SUPRD	Suprêmes délices	Pascale Cartrain	(071) 23 67 22 20	10252	4	7/9/1996	60	40	27.2000
HANAR	Hanari Carnes	Mario Pontes	(21) 555-0091	10253	3	7/10/1996	31	20	10.0000
HANAR	Hanari Carnes	Mario Pontes	(21) 555-0091	10253	3	7/10/1996	39	42	14.4000
HANAR	Hanari Carnes	Mario Pontes	(21) 555-0091	10253	3	7/10/1996	49	40	16.0000
CHOPS	Chop-suey Chinese	Yang Wang	0452-076545	10254	5	7/11/1996	24	15	3.6000
CHOPS	Chop-suey Chinese	Yang Wang	0452-076545	10254	5	7/11/1996	55	21	19.2000
CHOPS	Chop-suey Chinese	Yang Wang	0452-076545	10254	5	7/11/1996	74	21	8.0000
RICSU	Richter Supermarkt	Michael Holz	0897-034214	10255	9	7/12/1996	2	20	15.2000
RICSU	Richter Supermarkt	Michael Holz	0897-034214	10255	9	7/12/1996	16	35	13.9000
RICSU	Richter Supermarkt	Michael Holz	0897-034214	10255	9	7/12/1996	36	25	15.2000
RICSU	Richter Supermarkt	Michael Holz	0897-034214	10255	9	7/12/1996	59	30	44.0000
WELLI	Wellington Import	Paula Parente	(14) 555-8122	10256	3	7/15/1996	53	15	26.2000

Figure 7-2 Data returned by a join query

- **Their results are difficult to update.** It's difficult for a data access model such as ADO.NET to know how to interpret changes to the results of a join query. For example, if you delete a row, does that mean you want to delete just the corresponding row in the child table or do you want to delete the row in the parent tables as well? If you add a new row, does that mean you want to add a new row to just the child table or do you want to add a new row to the parent tables as well?
- **Their results are difficult to keep in sync.** If you modify a parent row—by changing the contact name for a customer, for example—you have to submit the change to the database and then execute the entire query again to see that change in all related rows in the resultset.

Separate Queries

Because join query results have always been notoriously difficult to update using data access technologies such as DAO and ADO, many developers use separate queries to retrieve data from each table and place it into separate structures.

The benefits of using separate queries include the following:

- **They return less total data than join queries do.**

- **They're more suitable for updates.** Because you're modifying a structure, such as a *Recordset*, that corresponds to a single table, it's easy for a technology such as ADO to interpret that change and modify the data in your database accordingly.

- **They're suitable for multiple data sources.** You can use this approach if the related tables exist on different database systems.

The drawbacks include the following:

- **They require synchronization code.** To locate the orders for a particular customer, you must apply a filter to the child *Recordset* and write code to keep the *Recordset* objects in sync with each other.

- **They're difficult to filter.** Constructing queries against child tables that retrieve only the rows that relate to the rows retrieved from the parent table can be challenging. We'll examine this topic further later in the chapter.

Hierarchical ADO *Recordset* Objects

ADO 2.0 introduced the concept of a hierarchical *Recordset*. You can use a special provider and a special query syntax to combine the results of multiple queries into a single structure. The following Microsoft Visual Basic 6.0 code snippet retrieves the contents of the Customers, Orders, and Order Details tables and places it into a hierarchical *Recordset*:

```
Dim rsCustomers As ADODB.Recordset, rsOrders As ADODB.Recordset
Dim rsOrderDetails As ADODB.Recordset
Dim strConn As String, strSQL As String
strConn = "Provider=MSDataShape;Data Provider=SQLOLEDB;" & _
          "Data Source=.\SQLExpress;Initial Catalog=Northwind;" & _
          "Trusted_Connection=Yes;"
strSQL = "SHAPE {SELECT CustomerID, CompanyName, ContactName, " & _
          "ContactTitle FROM Customers} AS Customers APPEND " & _
          "((SHAPE {SELECT OrderID, CustomerID, EmployeeID, OrderDate " & _
          "FROM Orders} AS Orders APPEND ({SELECT OrderID, ProductID, " & _
          "UnitPrice, Quantity FROM [Order Details]} AS OrderDetails " & _
          "RELATE 'OrderID' TO 'OrderID') AS OrderDetails) AS Orders " & _
          "RELATE 'CustomerID' TO 'CustomerID') AS Orders"
Set rsCustomers = New ADODB.Recordset
rsCustomers.Open strSQL, strConn, adOpenStatic, adLockBatchOptimistic
Set rsOrders = rsCustomers.Fields("Orders").Value
Set rsOrderDetails = rsOrders.Fields("OrderDetails").Value
```

The *Recordset* has three object variables, but they all reference data that's maintained in a single structure. As you navigate through the top-level *Recordset*, only the related data will be visible in the child *Recordset* objects.

The benefits of using hierarchical *Recordset* objects include the following:

- **They return less total data than join queries do.**

- **They return data in a single structure.**

- **They don't require complex synchronization code.**

- **They're suitable for simple updates.** However, even though hierarchical *Recordset* objects handle simple updates well, they have limitations. Submitting pending changes against multiple tables can be problematic at best.

The drawbacks include these:

- **The query syntax is hideous.** Look at that query! I like to consider myself an ADO expert, but I never bothered to learn the SHAPE syntax.

- **They offer limited control.** You have to define the relationship in your query.

- **You can query only a single data source.**

- **They're difficult to filter.**

ADO.NET *DataRelation* Objects

The ADO.NET *DataRelation* is very different in structure from hierarchical *Recordset* objects. *DataRelation* objects do not require an additional provider, and no abominable SHAPE query syntax is required. *DataRelation* objects are considered part of the *DataSet* object's schema.

Quite simply, the *DataRelation* combines the best features of the separate query and hierarchical *Recordset* approaches to managing data from related tables, and it eliminates nearly all of their drawbacks. The following lists of the pros and cons should whet your appetite for now.

The benefits of using *DataRelation* objects include the following:

- **They return less total data than join queries do.**

- **They simplify locating related data.**

- **They don't require complex synchronization code.**

- **They can handle advanced updating scenarios.** For example, you can submit new customers before new orders but also delete existing orders before deleting existing customers. Or, if you have a series of pending orders and order details, you can fetch server-generated autoincrement values for your new orders before submitting their new order details. I'll discuss both scenarios in detail in Chapter 11.

- **They're dynamic.** You can create, modify, and delete *DataRelation* objects programmatically before or after you query the related database tables.

- **They support cascading changes.** You can control whether changes to a row cascade down to child rows by using properties of the foreign key constraint associated with the *DataRelation*.

- **They support creating hierarchies from different data sources.** Need to relate the results of a customer query against a SQL Server database and an order query against an Oracle database? No problem.

The primary drawback to using *DataRelation* objects is:

- **They're difficult to filter.** Unfortunately, *DataRelation* objects do not simplify fetching only child rows that correspond to the desired parent rows. I'll discuss ways of handling such scenarios later in the chapter.

Working with *DataRelation* Objects in Code

You can navigate through multiple tables of data, validate data, aggregate data, and cascade changes using your own code, but you can perform all these functions quickly and easily with the help of the ADO.NET *DataRelation* object. Let's look at how to create and use *DataRelation* objects in code.

Creating *DataRelation* Objects

The *DataRelation* class has a few important properties, which you can set in its constructors. When you create a *DataRelation*, you should provide a name so that you can locate the object in its collection as well as specify the parent and child columns on which to base the relationship. To simplify creation, the *DataRelation* has separate constructors that accept single *DataColumn* objects and arrays of *DataColumn* objects.

The standard example of creating a relationship relies on *DataTable* objects that contain customer and order information, such as that shown in Figure 7-3 on page 323. You can use the following code snippet to create that *DataRelation*. We'll look at code shortly that can use the *DataRelation* to navigate between related *DataRows* to output data as shown in the preceding figure.

Visual Basic
```
'Create a new DataSet and add DataTable and DataColumn objects.
Dim ds As New DataSet()
Dim tbl As DataTable
tbl = ds.Tables.Add("Customers")
tbl.Columns.Add("CustomerID", GetType(String))
tbl.Columns.Add("CompanyName", GetType(String))

tbl = ds.Tables.Add("Orders")
tbl.Columns.Add("OrderID", GetType(Integer))
tbl.Columns.Add("CustomerID", GetType(String))
tbl.Columns.Add("OrderDate", GetType(DateTime))

'Add a DataRelation between the two tables.
Dim rel As DataRelation
rel = New DataRelation("Customers_Orders", _
                        ds.Tables("Customers").Columns("CustomerID"), _
                        ds.Tables("Orders").Columns("CustomerID"))
ds.Relations.Add(rel)
```

Visual C#
```csharp
//Create a new DataSet and add DataTable and DataColumn objects.
DataSet ds = new DataSet();
DataTable tbl;
tbl = ds.Tables.Add("Customers");
tbl.Columns.Add("CustomerID", typeof(string));
tbl.Columns.Add("CompanyName", typeof(string));

tbl = ds.Tables.Add("Orders");
tbl.Columns.Add("OrderID", typeof(int));
tbl.Columns.Add("CustomerID", typeof(string));
tbl.Columns.Add("OrderDate", typeof(DateTime));

//Add a DataRelation between the two tables.
DataRelation rel;
rel = new DataRelation("Customers_Orders",
                       ds.Tables["Customers"].Columns["CustomerID"],
                       ds.Tables["Orders"].Columns["CustomerID"]);
ds.Relations.Add(rel);
```

If you want to define a relationship that's based on multiple columns, you can use a constructor of the *DataRelation* that accepts arrays of *DataColumn* objects, as shown in the following code snippet:

Visual Basic
```vbnet
'Create a new DataSet and add DataTable and DataColumn objects.
Dim ds As New DataSet()
Dim tblParent, tblChild As DataTable
tblParent = ds.Tables("ParentTable")
tblParent.Columns.Add("ParentColumn1", GetType(String))
tblParent.Columns.Add("ParentColumn2", GetType(String))
tblChild = ds.Tables("ChildTable")
tblChild.Columns.Add("ChildColumn1", GetType(String))
tblChild.Columns.Add("ChildColumn2", GetType(String))

'Create arrays that reference the DataColumn objects
'on which we'll base the new DataRelation.
Dim colsParent, colsChild As DataColumn()
colsParent = New DataColumn() {tblParent.Columns("ParentColumn1"), _
                              tblParent.Columns("ParentColumn2")}
colsChild = New DataColumn() {tblChild.Columns("ChildColumn1"), _
                             tblChild.Columns("ChildColumn2")}
'Create the new DataRelation.
Dim rel As DataRelation
rel = New DataRelation("MultiColumnRelation", colsParent, colsChild)
ds.Relations.Add(rel)
```

Visual C#
```csharp
//Create a new DataSet and add DataTable and DataColumn objects.
DataSet ds = new DataSet();
DataTable tblParent, tblChild;
tblParent = ds.Tables("ParentTable");
tblParent.Columns.Add("ParentColumn1", typeof(string));
```

```
tblParent.Columns.Add("ParentColumn2", typeof(string));
tblChild = ds.Tables("ChildTable");
tblChild.Columns.Add("ChildColumn1", typeof(string));
tblChild.Columns.Add("ChildColumn2", typeof(string));

//Create arrays that reference the DataColumn objects
//on which we'll base the new DataRelation.
DataColumn[] colsParent, colsChild;
colsParent = new DataColumn[] {tblParent.Columns["ParentColumn1"],
                                  tblParent.Columns["ParentColumn2"]};
colsChild = new DataColumn[] {tblChild.Columns["ChildColumn1"],
                                 tblChild.Columns["ChildColumn2"]};

//Create the new DataRelation.
DataRelation rel;
rel = new DataRelation("MultiColumnRelation", colsParent, colsChild);
ds.Relations.Add(rel);
```

The *DataRelation* also has a pair of constructors whose signatures match the ones we just examined but which also expose a fourth parameter to indicate whether to create constraints to enforce referential integrity based on the new relation. By default, creating a new *DataRelation* adds constraints to your *DataTable* objects if such constraints do not already exist. We'll take a closer look at this functionality shortly.

Once you've created a new *DataRelation*, you should append it to the *Relations* collection of your *DataSet*. As with creating new *DataTable* objects and *DataColumn* objects, you can create a new *DataRelation* and append it to a *DataSet* object's *Relations* collection in a single call using code such as the following:

Visual Basic
```
'Create a new DataSet and add DataTable and DataColumn objects.
Dim ds As New DataSet()
Dim tbl As DataTable
tbl = ds.Tables.Add("Customers")
tbl.Columns.Add("CustomerID", GetType(String))
tbl.Columns.Add("CompanyName", GetType(String))

tbl = ds.Tables.Add("Orders")
tbl.Columns.Add("OrderID", GetType(Integer))
tbl.Columns.Add("CustomerID", GetType(String))
tbl.Columns.Add("OrderDate", GetType(DateTime))

'Add a DataRelation between the two tables.
ds.Relations.Add("Customers_Orders", _
                ds.Tables("Customers").Columns("CustomerID"), _
                ds.Tables("Orders").Columns("CustomerID"))
```

Visual C#
```
//Create a new DataSet and add DataTable and DataColumn objects.
DataSet ds = new DataSet();
tbl = ds.Tables.Add("Customers");
tbl.Columns.Add("CustomerID", typeof(string));
```

```
tbl.Columns.Add("CompanyName", typeof(string));

tbl = ds.Tables.Add("Orders");
tbl.Columns.Add("OrderID", typeof(int));
tbl.Columns.Add("CustomerID", typeof(string));
tbl.Columns.Add("OrderDate", typeof(DateTime));

//Add a DataRelation between the two tables.
ds.Relations.Add("Customers_Orders",
                  ds.Tables["Customers"].Columns["CustomerID"],
                   ds.Tables["Orders"].Columns["CustomerID"]);
```

Locating Related Data

One of the main uses of the *DataRelation* class is to locate related data in different *DataTable* objects. However, the *DataRelation* class does not handle this task, at least not directly. This functionality is actually available through the *DataRow* object's *GetChildRows*, *GetParentRow*, and *GetParentRows* methods. How does the *DataRelation* enter into the equation? When you call any of these methods on the *DataRow* object, you specify a *DataRelation* as a parameter of the method. Let's take a closer look at these methods and how to use them.

The *DataRow* Class's *GetChildRows* Method

Locating a row's related child rows in another *DataTable* is rather straightforward: Simply call the *GetChildRows* method of your *DataRow* and supply the name of the *DataRelation* object that defines the relationship between your *DataTable* objects. You can also supply the actual *DataRelation* object instead of the object's name. The *GetChildRows* method returns the related data as an array of *DataRow* objects.

The following code snippet constructs a *DataSet* with basic customer and order information with a *DataRelation*, fills the *DataSet* via a *SqlDataAdapter*, and calls the *GetChildRows* method and loops through the data it returns. The *GetChildRows* method allows us to display customer and order information in the Console window as shown in Figure 7-3:

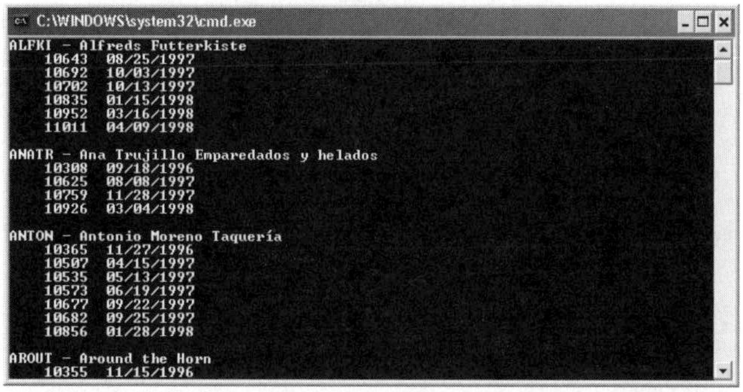

Figure 7-3   Displaying related information using a *DataRelation* and *DataRow.GetChildRows*

Visual Basic

```vb
'Create a new DataSet and add DataTable and DataColumn objects.
Dim ds As New DataSet()
Dim tbl As DataTable
tbl = ds.Tables.Add("Customers")
tbl.Columns.Add("CustomerID", GetType(String))
tbl.Columns.Add("CompanyName", GetType(String))

tbl = ds.Tables.Add("Orders")
tbl.Columns.Add("OrderID", GetType(Integer))
tbl.Columns.Add("CustomerID", GetType(String))
tbl.Columns.Add("OrderDate", GetType(DateTime))

'Add a DataRelation between the two tables.
Dim rel As DataRelation
rel = ds.Relations.Add("Customers_Orders", _
                        ds.Tables("Customers").Columns("CustomerID"), _
                        ds.Tables("Orders").Columns("CustomerID"))


'Fill the DataSet
Dim strConn, strSQL As String
strConn = "Data Source=.\SQLExpress;" & _
          "Initial Catalog=Northwind;Integrated Security=True;"
strSQL = "SELECT CustomerID, CompanyName FROM Customers " & _
         "  WHERE CustomerID LIKE 'A%';" & _
         "SELECT OrderID, CustomerID, OrderDate FROM Orders " & _
         "  WHERE CustomerID LIKE 'A%'"
Dim da As New SqlDataAdapter(strSQL, strConn)
da.TableMappings.Add("Table", "Customers")
da.TableMappings.Add("Table1", "Orders")
da.Fill(ds)

'Loop through the customers.
Dim rowCustomer, rowOrder As DataRow
For Each rowCustomer In ds.Tables("Customers").Rows
    Console.WriteLine("{0} - {1}", rowCustomer("CustomerID"), _
                      rowCustomer("CompanyName"))
    'Loop through the related orders.
    For Each rowOrder In rowCustomer.GetChildRows(rel)
        Console.WriteLine("  {0}  {1:MM/dd/yyyy}", rowOrder("OrderID"), _
                          rowOrder("OrderDate"))
    Next rowOrder
    Console.WriteLine()
Next rowCustomer
```

Visual C#

```csharp
//Create a new DataSet and add DataTable and DataColumn objects.
DataSet ds = new DataSet();
DataTable tbl;
tbl = ds.Tables.Add("Customers");
tbl.Columns.Add("CustomerID", typeof(string));
tbl.Columns.Add("CompanyName", typeof(string));

tbl = ds.Tables.Add("Orders");
tbl.Columns.Add("OrderID", typeof(int));
```

```
tbl.Columns.Add("CustomerID", typeof(string));
tbl.Columns.Add("OrderDate", typeof(DateTime));

//Add a DataRelation between the two tables.
DataRelation rel;
rel = ds.Relations.Add("Customers_Orders",
                       ds.Tables["Customers"].Columns["CustomerID"],
                       ds.Tables["Orders"].Columns["CustomerID"]);

//Fill the DataSet
string strConn, strSQL;
strConn = @"Data Source=.\SQLExpress;" +
          "Initial Catalog=Northwind;Integrated Security=True;";
strSQL = "SELECT CustomerID, CompanyName FROM Customers " +
         "  WHERE CustomerID LIKE 'A%';" +
         "SELECT OrderID, CustomerID, OrderDate FROM Orders " +
         "  WHERE CustomerID LIKE 'A%'";
SqlDataAdapter da = new SqlDataAdapter(strSQL, strConn);
da.TableMappings.Add("Table", "Customers");
da.TableMappings.Add("Table1", "Orders");
da.Fill(ds);

//Loop through the customers.
foreach (DataRow rowCustomer in ds.Tables["Customers"].Rows) {
    Console.WriteLine("{0} - {1}", rowCustomer["CustomerID"],
                      rowCustomer["CompanyName"]);
    //Loop through the related orders.
    foreach (DataRow rowOrder in rowCustomer.GetChildRows(rel))
        Console.WriteLine("  {0}  {1:MM/dd/yyyy}", rowOrder["OrderID"],
                          rowOrder["OrderDate"]);
    Console.WriteLine();
}
```

The *DataRow* Class's *GetParentRow* Method

DataRelation objects let you not only drill down through a hierarchy but also travel upstream. The *DataRow* class exposes a *GetParentRow* method that you can call to locate that row's parent row based on a *DataRelation* within the *DataSet*. Like the *GetChildRows* method, *GetParentRow* accepts a *DataRelation* object or a string that contains the name of the *DataRelation* you want to use. The following code walks through the child rows (orders) and displays information from the corresponding parent row (customer) and, for the sake of brevity, assumes the code from the previous example to create and fill the *DataSet*:

Visual Basic

```
Dim rowCustomer, rowOrder As DataRow
'Loop through the orders.
For Each rowOrder In ds.Tables("Orders").Rows
    'Locate the related parent row.
    rowCustomer = rowOrder.GetParentRow("Customers_Orders")
    Console.WriteLine("{0}  {1:MM/dd/yyyy}  {2}", rowOrder("OrderID"), _
                      rowOrder("OrderDate"), rowCustomer("CompanyName"))
Next rowOrder
```

Visual C#

```csharp
DataRow rowCustomer;
//Loop through the orders.
foreach (DataRow rowOrder in ds.Tables["Orders"].Rows) {
    //Locate the related parent row.
    rowCustomer = rowOrder.GetParentRow("Customers_Orders");
    Console.WriteLine("{0}  {1:MM/dd/yyyy}  {2}", rowOrder["OrderID"],
                      rowOrder["OrderDate"], rowCustomer["CompanyName"]);
}
```

Using the *DataRow* Class's *GetParentRows* Method to Access Multiple Parent Rows

In most situations, a *DataRow* will have at most one parent row in the related *DataTable*. However, if you are not enforcing constraints in your *DataTable*, one row in the child table might reference multiple rows in the parent *DataTable*. If you're working with such a scenario and you want to access all parent *DataRows*, the *GetParentRows* method accepts the same parameters as the *GetParentRow* and *GetChildRows* methods, but it returns an array of *DataRows*.

The following code snippet is an example of how you could use this feature. Because there is no relation between tables in the SQL Server sample databases that naturally lends itself to this feature, we'll bend one to suit our needs. We'll invert the standard customers/orders relationship so that the customer is the child table and the *GetParentRows* method returns multiple orders.

Visual Basic

```vbnet
'Create a new DataSet and add DataTable and DataColumn objects.
Dim ds As New DataSet()
Dim tbl As DataTable
tbl = ds.Tables.Add("Customers")
tbl.Columns.Add("CustomerID", GetType(String))
tbl.Columns.Add("CompanyName", GetType(String))

tbl = ds.Tables.Add("Orders")
tbl.Columns.Add("OrderID", GetType(Integer))
tbl.Columns.Add("CustomerID", GetType(String))
tbl.Columns.Add("OrderDate", GetType(DateTime))

'Add a DataRelation between the two tables.
Dim rel As DataRelation
rel = ds.Relations.Add("Customers_Orders", _
                    ds.Tables("Orders").Columns("CustomerID"), _
                    ds.Tables("Customers").Columns("CustomerID"), False)

'Fill the DataSet
Dim strConn, strSQL As String
strConn = "Data Source=.\SQLExpress;" & _
          "Initial Catalog=Northwind;Integrated Security=True;"
strSQL = "SELECT CustomerID, CompanyName FROM Customers " & _
```

```vbnet
                    "  WHERE CustomerID LIKE 'A%';" & _
                    "SELECT OrderID, CustomerID, OrderDate FROM Orders " & _
                    "  WHERE CustomerID LIKE 'A%'"
Dim da As New SqlDataAdapter(strSQL, strConn)
da.TableMappings.Add("Table", "Customers")
da.TableMappings.Add("Table1", "Orders")
da.Fill(ds)

'Loop through the customers.
Dim rowCustomer, rowOrder As DataRow
For Each rowCustomer In ds.Tables("Customers").Rows
    Console.WriteLine("{0} - {1}", rowCustomer("CustomerID"), _
                        rowCustomer("CompanyName"))
    'Loop through the related orders.
    For Each rowOrder In rowCustomer.GetParentRows(rel)
        Console.WriteLine("  {0}  {1:MM/dd/yyyy}", rowOrder("OrderID"), _
                            rowOrder("OrderDate"))
    Next rowOrder
    Console.WriteLine()
Next rowCustomer
```

Visual C#

```csharp
//Create a new DataSet and add DataTable and DataColumn objects.
DataSet ds = new DataSet();
DataTable tbl;
tbl = ds.Tables.Add("Customers");
tbl.Columns.Add("CustomerID", typeof(string));
tbl.Columns.Add("CompanyName", typeof(string));

tbl = ds.Tables.Add("Orders");
tbl.Columns.Add("OrderID", typeof(int));
tbl.Columns.Add("CustomerID", typeof(string));
tbl.Columns.Add("OrderDate", typeof(DateTime));

//Add a DataRelation between the two tables.
ds.Relations.Add("Customers_Orders",
                ds.Tables["Orders"].Columns["CustomerID"],
                ds.Tables["Customers"].Columns["CustomerID"], false);

//Fill the DataSet
string strConn, strSQL;
strConn = @"Data Source=.\SQLExpress;" +
            "Initial Catalog=Northwind;Integrated Security=True;";
strSQL = "SELECT CustomerID, CompanyName FROM Customers " +
        "  WHERE CustomerID LIKE 'A%';" +
        "SELECT OrderID, CustomerID, OrderDate FROM Orders " +
        "  WHERE CustomerID LIKE 'A%'";
SqlDataAdapter da = new SqlDataAdapter(strSQL, strConn);
da.TableMappings.Add("Table", "Customers");
da.TableMappings.Add("Table1", "Orders");
da.Fill(ds);

//Loop through the customers.
foreach (DataRow rowCustomer in ds.Tables["Customers"].Rows) {
    Console.WriteLine("{0} - {1}", rowCustomer["CustomerID"],
                        rowCustomer["CompanyName"]);
```

```
    //Loop through the related orders.
    foreach (DataRow rowOrder
                    in rowCustomer.GetParentRows("Customers_Orders"))
        Console.WriteLine("  {0}  {1:MM/dd/yyyy}", rowOrder["OrderID"],
                        rowOrder["OrderDate"]);
    Console.WriteLine();
}
```

Choosing the Version of Data to View

Imagine that you've already built an application that allows users to retrieve data from your database and modify that data. But the employees who'll use that application are prone to making mistakes. So the application uses some functionality exposed by the *DataSet* to store changes in a file rather than submit them to the database. (We'll discuss this feature further in Chapter 12.)

As a result, you must create a second application that allows supervisors to review the pending changes entered by employees using the first application. This auditing application will display both the original and proposed values for the modified rows in your *DataSet*.

In Chapter 6, you learned that you could use the *DataRow* class's *Item* method to examine either the original or current version of the data in a particular column of that row. The *DataRow* object's *GetChildRows*, *GetParentRow*, and *GetParentRows* methods also let you supply a value from the *DataRowVersion* enumeration to indicate which version of the data you want to access.

So, if you want to loop through the customers and display the original values for each order that the customer has placed, you can replace the code from the previous snippet that displayed customer and order information with the following:

Visual Basic
```
'Loop through the customers.
Dim rowCustomer, rowOrder As DataRow
For Each rowCustomer In ds.Tables("Customers").Rows
    Console.WriteLine("{0} - {1}", rowCustomer("CustomerID"), _
                    rowCustomer("CompanyName"))
    'Display the original state of the related child orders.
    For Each rowOrder In _
            rowCustomer.GetChildRows(rel, DataRowVersion.Original)
        Console.WriteLine("  {0}  {1:MM/dd/yyyy}", rowOrder("OrderID"), _
                        rowOrder("OrderDate"))
    Next rowOrder
    Console.WriteLine()
Next rowCustomer
```

Visual C#
```
//Loop through the customers.
foreach (DataRow rowCustomer in ds.Tables["Customers"].Rows) {
    Console.WriteLine("{0} - {1}", rowCustomer["CustomerID"],
                    rowCustomer["CompanyName"]);
```

```
    //Display the original state of the related child orders.
    foreach (DataRow rowOrder in
            rowCustomer.GetChildRows(rel, DataRowVersion.Original))
        Console.WriteLine("  {0}  {1:MM/dd/yyyy}", rowOrder["OrderID"],
                        rowOrder["OrderDate"]);
    Console.WriteLine();
}
```

> **Note**   If you use the methods that do not take a value from *DataRowVersion*, you'll view the current version of the data.

Using *DataRelation* Objects to Validate Your Data

Now that you've learned how to use *DataRelation* objects to navigate through data from related *DataTable* objects, let's look at one of the other major functions of the *DataRelation* object—validating data.

When you define a relationship between two *DataTable* objects, you generally want to make sure that you don't allow *orphaned* data in the child *DataTable*—that is, you want to prevent users from entering a row into the Orders table that does not correspond to a row in the Customers table. You can use a *DataRelation* object to enforce constraints on the related *DataTable* objects.

Creating Constraints

By default, when you create a *DataRelation*, you also create a *UniqueConstraint* on the parent *DataTable* and a *ForeignKeyConstraint* on the child *DataTable*. The following code snippet creates a *DataRelation* and then displays the number of constraints defined on the parent and child *DataTables*:

Visual Basic

```
'Create a new DataSet and add DataTable and DataColumn objects.
Dim ds As New DataSet()
Dim tbl As DataTable
tbl = ds.Tables.Add("Customers")
tbl.Columns.Add("CustomerID", GetType(String))
tbl.Columns.Add("CompanyName", GetType(String))

tbl = ds.Tables.Add("Orders")
tbl.Columns.Add("OrderID", GetType(Integer))
tbl.Columns.Add("CustomerID", GetType(String))
tbl.Columns.Add("OrderDate", GetType(DateTime))

'Add a DataRelation between the two tables
ds.Relations.Add("Customers_Orders", _
                ds.Tables("Customers").Columns("CustomerID"), _
                ds.Tables("Orders").Columns("CustomerID"))
```

```
Console.WriteLine("The parent DataTable has {0} constraint(s)", _
                ds.Tables("Customers").Constraints.Count)
Console.WriteLine("The child DataTable has {0} constraint(s)", _
                ds.Tables("Orders").Constraints.Count)
```

Visual C#
```
//Create a new DataSet and add DataTable and DataColumn objects.
DataSet ds = new DataSet();
DataTable tbl;
tbl = ds.Tables.Add("Customers");
tbl.Columns.Add("CustomerID", typeof(string));
tbl.Columns.Add("CompanyName", typeof(string));

tbl = ds.Tables.Add("Orders");
tbl.Columns.Add("OrderID", typeof(int));
tbl.Columns.Add("CustomerID", typeof(string));
tbl.Columns.Add("OrderDate", typeof(DateTime));

//Add a DataRelation between the two tables.
ds.Relations.Add("Customers_Orders",
                ds.Tables["Customers"].Columns["CustomerID"],
                ds.Tables["Orders"].Columns["CustomerID"]);

Console.WriteLine("The parent DataTable has {0} constraint(s)",
                ds.Tables["Customers"].Constraints.Count);
Console.WriteLine("The child DataTable has {0} constraint(s)",
                ds.Tables["Orders"].Constraints.Count);
```

Using Existing Constraints

If the *DataSet* already contains constraints that match the *UniqueConstraints* and *ForeignKey-Constraints* that the *DataRelation* would otherwise create implicitly, the *DataRelation* simply uses the pre-existing constraints. The following code snippet creates constraints prior to the creation of the *DataRelation*. You'll notice that after the creation of the *DataRelation*, there is still just one constraint defined per *DataTable*.

Visual Basic
```
'Create a new DataSet and add DataTable and DataColumn objects.
'Create constraints prior to creating the DataRelation
Dim ds As New DataSet()
Dim tbl As DataTable
tbl = ds.Tables.Add("Customers")
tbl.Columns.Add("CustomerID", GetType(String))
tbl.Columns.Add("CompanyName", GetType(String))
    tbl.PrimaryKey = New DataColumn() {tbl.Columns("CustomerID")}
tbl = ds.Tables.Add("Orders")
tbl.Columns.Add("OrderID", GetType(Integer))
tbl.Columns.Add("CustomerID", GetType(String))
tbl.Columns.Add("OrderDate", GetType(DateTime))
Dim fk As ForeignKeyConstraint
fk = New ForeignKeyConstraint("FK_Customers_Orders", _
                ds.Tables("Customers").Columns("CustomerID"), _
                tbl.Columns("CustomerID"))
```

```
tbl.Constraints.Add(fk)

ds.Relations.Add("Customers_Orders", _
                ds.Tables("Customers").Columns("CustomerID"), _
                ds.Tables("Orders").Columns("CustomerID"))

'Verify that only one constraint exists per table
Console.WriteLine("The parent DataTable has {0} constraint(s)", _
                ds.Tables("Customers").Constraints.Count)
Console.WriteLine("The child DataTable has {0} constraint(s)", _
                ds.Tables("Orders").Constraints.Count)
```

Visual C#

```
//Create a new DataSet and add DataTable and DataColumn objects.
'Create constraints prior to creating the DataRelation

DataSet ds = new DataSet();
DataTable tbl;
tbl = ds.Tables.Add("Customers");
tbl.Columns.Add("CustomerID", typeof(string));
tbl.Columns.Add("CompanyName", typeof(string));
tbl.PrimaryKey = new DataColumn[] {tbl.Columns["CustomerID"]};

tbl = ds.Tables.Add("Orders");
tbl.Columns.Add("OrderID", typeof(int));
tbl.Columns.Add("CustomerID", typeof(string));
tbl.Columns.Add("OrderDate", typeof(DateTime));
ForeignKeyConstraint fk;
fk = new ForeignKeyConstraint("FK_Customers_Orders",
                ds.Tables["Customers"].Columns["CustomerID"],
                tbl.Columns["CustomerID"]);
tbl.Constraints.Add(fk);

ds.Relations.Add("Customers_Orders",
                ds.Tables["Customers"].Columns["CustomerID"],
                ds.Tables["Orders"].Columns["CustomerID"]);

//Verify that only one constraint exists per table
Console.WriteLine("The parent DataTable has {0} constraint(s)",
                ds.Tables["Customers"].Constraints.Count);
Console.WriteLine("The child DataTable has {0} constraint(s)",
                ds.Tables["Orders"].Constraints.Count);
```

Foreign Key Constraints and Null Values

You might be surprised by what you learn in the course of writing a book. For example, I had no idea that even with a foreign key constraint defined, you can have orphaned data both in your database and in your *DataSet*.

You don't believe me? You can run the following query against your favorite Northwind database. (Don't run queries such as this against your production database while you're building applications or learning about ADO.NET.)

```
UPDATE Orders SET CustomerID = NULL WHERE CustomerID = 'ALFKI'
```

> The query will succeed, and you'll have orders in your Orders table that don't belong to
> a customer in the Customers table. To set the rows back to the appropriate customer, run
> the following query:
>
> ```
> UPDATE Orders SET CustomerID = 'ALFKI' WHERE CustomerID IS NULL
> ```
>
> To prove that there is a foreign key constraint on the Orders table, run the following
> query, which will fail if your Customers table has no row with a CustomerID of ZZZZZ:
>
> ```
> UPDATE Orders SET CustomerID = 'ZZZZZ' WHERE CustomerID = 'ANTON'
> ```
>
> Rows that contain *Null* values in at least one of the columns defined in the foreign
> key constraint are exempt from the database constraint. Similarly, the *DataSet* allows
> orphaned child rows if the values in the *DataColumns* used to define the relationship are
> set to *DBNull.Value*. Keep this in mind when you define the schema for your database
> and *DataSet*.

Look, Ma! No Constraints!

You've learned that when you create a *DataRelation*, ADO.NET will by default ensure that your
DataSet contains a *UniqueConstraint* and a *ForeignKeyConstraint* whose signatures match that of
your new *DataRelation*. If such constraints already exist within the *DataSet*, the new *DataRelation*
will reference them. Otherwise, ADO.NET will create the new constraints implicitly.

However, there's another option. Earlier, when we discussed the *DataRelation* class's
constructors, I mentioned that there are constructors that let you specify that you do not want
ADO.NET to create constraints for your *DataRelation*. These constructors look like the ones
we've already used, but they take an additional Boolean parameter, which indicates whether
you want the *DataRelation* to create constraints. You can use these constructors when you
want to use a *DataRelation* but do not want the corresponding constraints in your *DataSet*.
Here's an example that creates the *DataRelation* for Customers and Orders without creating
constraints:

Visual Basic

```vb
'Add a DataRelation between the two tables.
ds.Relations.Add("Customers_Orders", _
                ds.Tables("Customers").Columns("CustomerID"), _
                ds.Tables("Orders").Columns("CustomerID"), _
                False)
```

Visual C#

```csharp
//Add a DataRelation between the two tables.
ds.Relations.Add("Customers_Orders",
                ds.Tables["Customers"].Columns["CustomerID"],
                ds.Tables["Orders"].Columns["CustomerID"],
                false);
```

Self-Referencing *DataRelationship* Objects

Sometimes the parent and child tables in a relationship are one and the same. Take the Employees table in the Northwind database. This table has an EmployeeID column that contains the employee's ID and a ReportsTo column that contains the ID of the employee's manager. The Employees table also has a foreign key constraint defined on the ReportsTo column to ensure that it accepts values from only the EmployeeID column.

The following sample code retrieves data from the Employees table into a *DataSet* and creates a self-referencing *DataRelation*:

Visual Basic
```vbnet
Dim ds As New DataSet()
Dim tbl As DataTable = ds.Tables.Add("Employees")
tbl.Columns.Add("EmployeeID", GetType(Integer))
tbl.Columns.Add("LastName", GetType(String))
tbl.Columns.Add("ReportsTo", GetType(Integer))

ds.Relations.Add("Manager_DirectReports", tbl.Columns("EmployeeID"), _
                tbl.Columns("ReportsTo"))
```

Visual C#
```csharp
DataSet ds = new DataSet();
DataTable tbl = ds.Tables.Add("Employees");
tbl.Columns.Add("EmployeeID", typeof(int));
tbl.Columns.Add("LastName", typeof(string));
tbl.Columns.Add("ReportsTo", typeof(int));

ds.Relations.Add("Manager_DirectReports", tbl.Columns["EmployeeID"],
                tbl.Columns["ReportsTo"]);
```

Creating the *DataRelation* is only half the battle. The actual goal is to display all employees as a tree, as shown in Figure 7-4. Traversing the hierarchy to display the employees according to their manager is a bit of a challenge, especially if you've never written recursive code. If that's the case, you'd be best served by searching the documentation for your language of choice for information about recursion because that topic is beyond the scope of this book.

Figure 7-4   Displaying the contents of the Employees table using a self-referencing *DataRelation*

The code snippet that follows fills the *DataTable* created in the previous snippet, and then loops through the contents of the *DataTable* to locate and display the highest-level employee. In the Employees table, this is the row whose ReportsTo column is set to *Null*. For more information about *Null* values and foreign key constraints, see the sidebar "Foreign Key Constraints and Null Values" earlier in the chapter.

After locating the highest-ranking employee, the code displays that employee's direct reports, printing a tab character before each employee's name. After displaying an employee's name, it uses recursion to display that employee's direct reports. The process continues until there are no more direct reports to display.

Enough explaining—bring on the code!

Visual Basic

```vb
'Fill the DataTable with employee information
Dim strConn, strSQL As String
strConn = "Data Source=.\SQLExpress;" & _
          "Initial Catalog=Northwind;Integrated Security=True;"
strSQL = "SELECT EmployeeID, LastName + ', ' + FirstName AS EmployeeName, " & _
         "ReportsTo FROM Employees"
Dim da As New SqlDataAdapter(strSQL, strConn)
Dim ds As New DataSet()
Dim tbl As DataTable = ds.Tables.Add("Employees")
da.Fill(tbl)
Dim rel As DataRelation = ds.Relations.Add("Manager_DirectReports", _
                                    tbl.Columns("EmployeeID"), _
                                    tbl.Columns("ReportsTo"))


'Display the employee hierarchy
For Each row As DataRow In tbl.Rows
    If row.IsNull("ReportsTo") Then
        DisplayRow(row, rel, "")
    End If
Next row

Private Sub DisplayRow(ByVal row As DataRow, ByVal rel As DataRelation, _
                       ByVal intent As String)
    Console.WriteLine(indent & row("EmployeeName"))
    For Each rowChild As DataRow In row.GetChildRows(rel)
        DisplayRow(rowChild, rel, indent & "    ")
    Next rowChild
End Sub
```

Visual C#

```csharp
//Fill the DataTable with employee information
string strConn, strSQL;
strConn = @"Data Source=.\SQLExpress;" +
          "Initial Catalog=Northwind;Integrated Security=True;";
strSQL = "SELECT EmployeeID, LastName + ', ' + FirstName AS EmployeeName, " +
         "ReportsTo FROM Employees";
SqlDataAdapter da = new SqlDataAdapter(strSQL, strConn);
DataSet ds = new DataSet();
DataTable tbl = ds.Tables.Add("Employees");
da.Fill(tbl);
DataRelation rel = ds.Relations.Add("Manager_DirectReports",
                               tbl.Columns["EmployeeID"],
                               tbl.Columns["ReportsTo"]);


//Display the employee hierarchy
```

```
foreach (DataRow row in tbl.Rows)
    if (row.IsNull("ReportsTo"))
        DisplayRow(row, rel, "");

static void DisplayRow(DataRow row, DataRelation rel,
                       string indent)
{
    Console.WriteLine(indent + row["EmployeeName"]);
    foreach (DataRow rowChild in row.GetChildRows(rel))
        DisplayRow(rowChild, rel, indent + "    ");
}
```

> **Note**   The highest-ranking employee in the Employees table has a value of *Null* in the ReportsTo column. Another option is to have the employee report to himself or herself. You would need to change the sample code slightly if you're working with a table that handles self-referencing relationships in that fashion.

Many-to-Many Relationships

Most database relationships are one-to-many. A customer can have multiple orders. An order can have multiple order details. An employee can have multiple direct reports. Many-to-many relationships exist, but they're a little more difficult to define in a database. To understand why, let's take a look at the authors and titles tables in the SQL Server pubs database.

The relationship between the data in these two tables can be considered many-to-many because an author might have written multiple titles and a title might have multiple authors. However, these two tables are not directly related through a foreign key constraint because a foreign key constraint requires a unique key. This level of indirection prevents a child row from having multiple parent rows in the related table, which means we don't have a direct many-to-many relationship.

The pubs database includes another table called titleauthor (shown in Figure 7-5) that helps create an indirect many-to-many relationship. The titleauthor table has a compound primary key made up of the au_id and title_id columns—the primary key columns of the authors and titles tables, respectively.

Let's say that a title has two authors. The titleauthors table will contain two rows for that title, one for each author. So you can use the titleauthors table to find the primary key values for all the authors of a particular title. Similarly, you can also use the table to locate the primary key values for all titles that an author has written or coauthored.

The following code retrieves data from all three tables. It adds *DataRelation* objects between the authors and titleauthor tables and the titles and titleauthor tables. It then loops through the rows in the authors *DataTable*, displaying each author and then using the two *DataRelation* objects to display each author's titles.

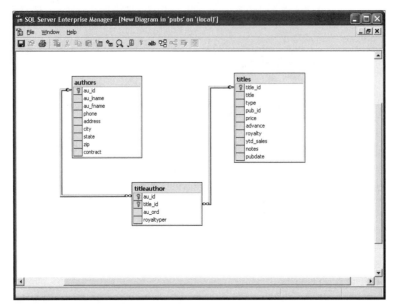

Figure 7-5   The authors, titles, and titleauthor tables in the SQL Server pubs database

Visual Basic

```vb
Dim strConn, strSQL as string
strConn = "Data Source=.\SQLExpress;" & _
          "Initial Catalog=pubs;Integrated Security=True;"
strSQL = "SELECT Au_ID, Au_LName, Au_FName FROM Authors;" & _
         "SELECT Title_ID, Title FROM Titles;" & _
         "SELECT Au_ID, Title_ID FROM TitleAuthor"
Dim da As New SqlDataAdapter(strSQL, strConn)
da.TableMappings.Add("Table", "Authors")
da.TableMappings.Add("Table1", "Titles")
da.TableMappings.Add("Table2", "TitleAuthor")

Dim ds As New DataSet()
da.Fill(ds)

ds.Relations.Add("Authors_TitleAuthor", _
                 ds.Tables("Authors").Columns("Au_ID"), _
                 ds.Tables("TitleAuthor").Columns("Au_ID"), _
                 False)

ds.Relations.Add("Titles_TitleAuthor", _
                 ds.Tables("Titles").Columns("Title_ID"), _
                 ds.Tables("TitleAuthor").Columns("Title_ID"), _
                 False)

Dim rowAuthor, rowTitle, rowTitleAuthor As DataRow
For Each rowAuthor In ds.Tables("Authors").Rows
    Console.WriteLine("{0}, {1}", rowAuthor("Au_LName"), _
                      rowAuthor("Au_FName"))
    For Each rowTitleAuthor In _
```

```
                rowAuthor.GetChildRows("Authors_TitleAuthor")
        rowTitle = rowTitleAuthor.GetParentRow("Titles_TitleAuthor")
        Console.WriteLine("  {0}", rowTitle("Title"))
    Next rowTitleAuthor
    Console.WriteLine()
Next rowAuthor
```

Visual C#

```csharp
string strConn, strSQL;
strConn = @"Data Source=.\SQLExpress;" +
          "Initial Catalog=pubs;Integrated Security=True;";
strSQL = "SELECT Au_ID, Au_LName, Au_FName FROM Authors;" +
         "SELECT Title_ID, Title FROM Titles;" +
         "SELECT Au_ID, Title_ID FROM TitleAuthor";
SqlDataAdapter da = new SqlDataAdapter(strSQL, strConn);
da.TableMappings.Add("Table", "Authors");
da.TableMappings.Add("Table1", "Titles");
da.TableMappings.Add("Table2", "TitleAuthor");

DataSet ds = new DataSet();
da.Fill(ds);

ds.Relations.Add("Authors_TitleAuthor",
                 ds.Tables["Authors"].Columns["Au_ID"],
                 ds.Tables["TitleAuthor"].Columns["Au_ID"],
                 false);

ds.Relations.Add("Titles_TitleAuthor",
                 ds.Tables["Titles"].Columns["Title_ID"],
                 ds.Tables["TitleAuthor"].Columns["Title_ID"],
                 false);

foreach (DataRow rowAuthor in ds.Tables["authors"].Rows) {
    Console.WriteLine("{0}, {1}", rowAuthor["Au_LName"],
                      rowAuthor["Au_FName"]);
    foreach (DataRow rowTitleAuthor in
                     rowAuthor.GetChildRows("Authors_TitleAuthor"))
    {
        DataRow rowTitle =
                rowTitleAuthor.GetParentRow("Titles_TitleAuthor");
        Console.WriteLine("  {0}", rowTitle["Title"]);
    }
    Console.WriteLine();
}
```

Using *DataRelation* Objects in Expression-Based *DataColumn* Objects

In Chapter 6, you learned how to use the *DataColumn* class's *Expression* property to create *DataColumn* objects that display the results of equations such as *Quantity * UnitPrice*. You can also use expression-based *DataColumn* objects in conjunction with *DataRelation* objects to calculate aggregate information such as the number of child rows and the sums and averages of child data.

The following code snippet includes two examples of using a *DataRelation* in a *DataColumn* object's *Expression* property. The code first creates a *DataRelation* between the Orders and Order Details *DataTable* objects, and then it adds the calculated ItemTotal *DataColumn* to the Order Details *DataTable*, as described earlier. Finally the code adds two expression-based *DataColumn* objects that rely on the new *DataRelation*.

The first of these two *DataColumn* objects returns the number of child rows. To gather this information, the code sets the *Expression* property of the *DataColumn* to the following:

```
Count(Child.ProductID)
```

You can use this syntax to refer to child data if the *DataTable* has only one related child *DataTable*. If you have multiple related child *DataTable* objects, you can use the following syntax:

```
Count(Child(RelationName).ProductID)
```

The final expression-based *DataColumn* that the code creates returns the sum of the ItemTotal *DataColumn* in the child *DataTable*. The value of this *DataColumn* object's *Expression* property is similar to the previous *DataColumn*:

```
Sum(Child.ItemTotal)
```

Visual Basic

```vb
'Create and fill a DataSet with order information for a customer
Dim ds As New DataSet()
Dim strConn, strSQL As String
strConn = "Data Source=.\SQLExpress;" & _
          "Initial Catalog=Northwind;Integrated Security=True;"
strSQL = "SELECT OrderID, OrderDate FROM Orders " & _
         "WHERE CustomerID = 'ALFKI';" & _
         "SELECT OD.OrderID, OD.ProductID, OD.UnitPrice, OD.Quantity " & _
         "FROM [Order Details] OD, Orders O WHERE " & _
         "OD.OrderID = O.OrderID AND O.CustomerID = 'ALFKI'"
Dim da As New SqlDataAdapter(strSQL, strConn)
da.TableMappings.Add("Table", "Orders")
da.TableMappings.Add("Table1", "Order Details")
da.Fill(ds)

'Add expression-based columns
Dim rel As DataRelation
rel = ds.Relations.Add("Orders_OrderDetails", _
                       ds.Tables("Orders").Columns("OrderID"), _
                       ds.Tables("Order Details").Columns("OrderID"))

ds.Tables("Order Details").Columns.Add("ItemTotal", GetType(Decimal), _
                                       "Quantity * UnitPrice")
ds.Tables("Orders").Columns.Add("NumItems", GetType(Integer), _
                                "Count(Child.ProductID)")
ds.Tables("Orders").Columns.Add("OrderTotal", GetType(Decimal), _
                                "Sum(Child.ItemTotal)")
```

```
'Display data using the expression-based columns
For Each rowOrder As DataRow In ds.Tables("Orders").Rows
    Console.WriteLine("OrderID: {0}  NumItems: {1}  OrderTotal: {2:C}", _
                      rowOrder("OrderID"), rowOrder("NumItems"), _
                      rowOrder("OrderTotal"))
    For Each rowDetail As DataRow In rowOrder.GetChildRows(rel)
        Console.WriteLine("  Quantity: {0,2}  UnitPrice: {1,7:C}  " & _
                          "ItemTotal: {2,7:C}", rowDetail("Quantity"), _
                          rowDetail("UnitPrice"), rowDetail("ItemTotal"))
    Next rowDetail
    Console.WriteLine()
Next rowOrder
```

Visual C#

```csharp
//Create and fill a DataSet with order information for a customer
DataSet ds = new DataSet();
string strConn, strSQL;
strConn = @"Data Source=.\SQLExpress;" +
          "Initial Catalog=Northwind;Integrated Security=True;";
strSQL = "SELECT OrderID, OrderDate FROM Orders " +
         "WHERE CustomerID = 'ALFKI';" +
         "SELECT OD.OrderID, OD.ProductID, OD.UnitPrice, OD.Quantity " +
         "FROM [Order Details] OD, Orders O WHERE " +
         "OD.OrderID = O.OrderID AND O.CustomerID = 'ALFKI'";
SqlDataAdapter da = new SqlDataAdapter(strSQL, strConn);
da.TableMappings.Add("Table", "Orders");
da.TableMappings.Add("Table1", "Order Details");
da.Fill(ds);

//Add expression-based columns
DataRelation rel;
rel = ds.Relations.Add("OrdersOrderDetails",
                       ds.Tables["Orders"].Columns["OrderID"],
                       ds.Tables["Order Details"].Columns["OrderID"]);

ds.Tables["Order Details"].Columns.Add("ItemTotal", typeof(Decimal),
                                       "Quantity * UnitPrice");
ds.Tables["Orders"].Columns.Add("NumItems", typeof(int),
                                "Count(Child.ProductID)");
ds.Tables["Orders"].Columns.Add("OrderTotal", typeof(Decimal),
                                "Sum(Child.ItemTotal)");

//Display data using the expression-based columns
foreach (DataRow rowOrder in ds.Tables["Orders"].Rows) {
    Console.WriteLine("OrderID: {0}  NumItems: {1}  OrderTotal: {2:C}",
                      rowOrder["OrderID"], rowOrder["NumItems"],
                      rowOrder["OrderTotal"]);
    foreach (DataRow rowDetail in rowOrder.GetChildRows(rel))
        Console.WriteLine("  Quantity: {0,2}  UnitPrice: {1,7:C}  " +
                          "ItemTotal: {2,7:C}", rowDetail["Quantity"],
                          rowDetail["UnitPrice"], rowDetail["ItemTotal"]);
    Console.WriteLine();
}
```

You can also use expression-based *DataColumn* objects to gather information from the parent *DataTable* in a relationship. Earlier in the chapter, we looked at a many-to-many relationship between author and title information in the pubs database. The goal of the code snippet was to list the titles that each author wrote or co-wrote.

We can simplify that code slightly by having the middle table in the relationship (titleauthor) use expression-based columns to retrieve author and title information from the related *DataTables*.

Visual Basic

```
Dim strConn, strSQL As String
strConn = "Data Source=.\SQLExpress;" & _
          "Initial Catalog=pubs;Integrated Security=True;"
strSQL = "SELECT Au_ID, Au_LName, Au_FName FROM Authors;" & _
         "SELECT Title_ID, Title FROM Titles;" & _
         "SELECT Au_ID, Title_ID FROM TitleAuthor"
Dim da As New SqlDataAdapter(strSQL, strConn)
da.TableMappings.Add("Table", "Authors")
da.TableMappings.Add("Table1", "Titles")
da.TableMappings.Add("Table2", "TitleAuthor")

Dim ds As New DataSet()
da.Fill(ds)

ds.Relations.Add("Authors_TitleAuthor", _
                 ds.Tables("Authors").Columns("Au_ID"), _
                 ds.Tables("TitleAuthor").Columns("Au_ID"), _
                 False)

ds.Relations.Add("Titles_TitleAuthor", _
                 ds.Tables("Titles").Columns("Title_ID"), _
                 ds.Tables("TitleAuthor").Columns("Title_ID"), _
                 False)

'Use expression based columns and the middle table in the
'many-to-many relationship to display author and title information
Dim strExpression As String
Dim tbl As DataTable = ds.Tables("TitleAuthor")
strExpression = "Parent(Titles_TitleAuthor).Title"
tbl.Columns.Add("Title", GetType(String), strExpression)
strExpression = "Parent(Authors_TitleAuthor).Au_LName + ', ' + " & _
                "Parent(Authors_TitleAuthor).Au_FName"
tbl.Columns.Add("Author", GetType(String), strExpression)

For Each rowAuthor As DataRow In ds.Tables("Authors").Rows
    Console.WriteLine("{0}, {1}", rowAuthor("Au_LName"), _
                      rowAuthor("Au_FName"))
    For Each rowTitleAuthor As DataRow In _
            rowAuthor.GetChildRows("Authors_TitleAuthor")
        Console.WriteLine("  {0}", rowTitleAuthor("Title"))
    Next rowTitleAuthor
    Console.WriteLine()
Next rowAuthor
```

Visual C#

```csharp
//Create and fill a DataSet with author and title information
string strConn, strSQL;
strConn = @"Data Source=.\SQLExpress;" +
          "Initial Catalog=pubs;Integrated Security=True;";
strSQL = "SELECT Au_ID, Au_LName, Au_FName FROM Authors;" +
         "SELECT Title_ID, Title FROM Titles;" +
         "SELECT Au_ID, Title_ID FROM TitleAuthor";
SqlDataAdapter da = new SqlDataAdapter(strSQL, strConn);
da.TableMappings.Add("Table", "Authors");
da.TableMappings.Add("Table1", "Titles");
da.TableMappings.Add("Table2", "TitleAuthor");

DataSet ds = new DataSet();
da.Fill(ds);

ds.Relations.Add("Authors_TitleAuthor",
                 ds.Tables["Authors"].Columns["Au_ID"],
                 ds.Tables["TitleAuthor"].Columns["Au_ID"],
                 false);

ds.Relations.Add("Titles_TitleAuthor",
                 ds.Tables["Titles"].Columns["Title_ID"],
                 ds.Tables["TitleAuthor"].Columns["Title_ID"],
                 false);

//Use expression based columns and the middle table in the
//many-to-many relationship to display author and title information
string strExpression;
DataTable tbl = ds.Tables["TitleAuthor"];
strExpression = "Parent(Titles_TitleAuthor).Title";
tbl.Columns.Add("Title", typeof(string), strExpression);
strExpression = "Parent(Authors_TitleAuthor).Au_LName + ', ' + " +
                "Parent(Authors_TitleAuthor).Au_FName";
tbl.Columns.Add("Author", typeof(string), strExpression);

foreach (DataRow rowAuthor in ds.Tables["authors"].Rows)
{
    Console.WriteLine("{0}, {1}", rowAuthor["Au_LName"],
                      rowAuthor["Au_FName"]);
    foreach (DataRow rowTitleAuthor in
                     rowAuthor.GetChildRows("Authors_TitleAuthor"))
        Console.WriteLine("  {0}", rowTitleAuthor["Title"]);
    Console.WriteLine();
}
```

For an exhaustive list of available aggregate functions in the *Expression* property, see the MSDN documentation.

Cascading Changes

Sometimes the changes you make to one row have, or should have, repercussions on related data. For example, when you delete an order, you probably want to delete the line items associated with the order as well.

Different database systems allow you to handle this situation in various ways. The Order Details table in the SQL Server Northwind database uses a foreign key constraint to prevent users from deleting rows from the Orders table if there are related rows in the Order Details table. SQL Server 2000 introduced support for cascading changes using a foreign key constraint. You can define your foreign key constraints so that when a user updates or deletes a row, the changes automatically cascade to the rows in the related table. Figure 7-6 shows the SQL Server 2005 user interface for setting these properties on a foreign key constraint.

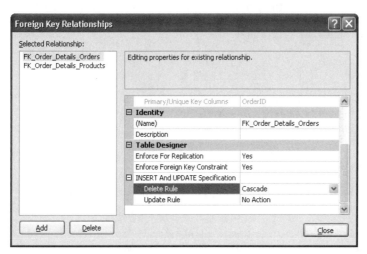

Figure 7-6 Setting a foreign key constraint's cascading update attributes in SQL Server 2005

The ADO.NET *ForeignKeyConstraint* class has similar features. It exposes *DeleteRule* and *UpdateRule* properties that you can set to control what happens when you modify rows of data in the parent table in a foreign key constraint.

The *ForeignKeyConstraint* Class's *DeleteRule* and *UpdateRule* Properties

The *DeleteRule* and *UpdateRule* properties accept values from the *Rule* enumeration in the *System.Data* namespace. By default, both properties are set to *Cascade*. This means that when you delete a row in a *DataTable*, the child rows in the related *DataTable* will be deleted as well. If you change the value of the column in the parent *DataTable* on which the foreign key constraint is defined—for example, if you change the value of the CustomerID column in the Customers *DataTable*—the value of that column will also be updated in the related rows in the child *DataTable*.

You can also set either property to *None*, *SetDefault*, or *SetNull*. Setting the *DeleteRule* property to *None* will prevent the deletion from affecting data in the child *DataTable*. If you want the process of deleting a parent row to set the constraint's columns of related child rows to *Null*, set the *DeleteRule* property of the *ForeignKeyConstraint* object to *SetNull*. Similarly, setting the *UpdateRule* property of the *ForeignKeyConstraint* object to *SetNull* will cause a change to the constraint's columns in the parent row to set the corresponding columns of related child rows to *Null*. Setting the DeleteRule or UpdateRule properties to *SetDefault* will reset the constraint's columns in the child table to the value set in the *Default* property.

Moving Away from Join Queries

Many developers have relied on join queries to retrieve data from multiple tables. You can use a *DataTable* to store the results of a query that returns data from multiple tables, but I generally wouldn't recommend it. As you'll see in Chapter 10, the *SqlDataAdapter* class is designed to examine the changes stored in a single *DataTable* and submit them to a specific table in your database. Thus, if you want to modify the contents of your *DataTable* objects, you'll want to separate the data into distinct *DataTable* objects that parallel the tables in your database.

So, what to do with join queries?

The simple answer is to split them into queries that return data from distinct tables. However, this is often easier said than done. In the snippets of sample code, we've used very simple queries that return all rows from the table in the query. Things get more complex when you're working with a query that uses a filter such as this:

```
SELECT CustomerID, CompanyName, ContactName, Phone
       FROM Customers WHERE Country = 'Canada'
```

If you want to retrieve data from the related Orders table, you'll want to retrieve only the orders that correspond to the customers returned by this query. Because the Orders table does not contain a Country column, you have to use a query that references the Customers table, such as this:

```
SELECT O.OrderID, O.CustomerID, O.EmployeeID, O.OrderDate
       FROM Customers C, Orders O
       WHERE C.CustomerID = O.OrderID AND C.Country = 'Canada'
```

Creating *DataRelation* Objects in Microsoft Visual Studio

Now that you understand the major features of the *DataRelation* class, let's see how to create *DataRelation* objects in Visual Studio.

Adding a *DataRelation* to a Strongly Typed *DataSet*

We'll discuss strongly typed *DataSets* in Chapter 9. If you've worked with them in prior versions of Visual Studio, you'll be pleased to learn that the designer now queries SQL Server for foreign key information to automatically create *DataRelations* when related tables are included in a strongly typed *DataSet*.

Adding a *DataRelation* to an Untyped *DataSet*

You can also add *DataRelation* objects to untyped *DataSet* objects. In the previous chapter, you learned how to add an untyped *DataSet* to a designer, such as a Windows form, and then add *DataTable* and *DataColumn* objects to that new *DataSet*. Adding a new *DataRelation* is just as easy.

Select the *DataSet* in the designer's components tray, and then select the Relations property in the Properties window. You'll see a button to the right of the property that you can click to launch the Relations Collection Editor, as shown in Figure 7-7.

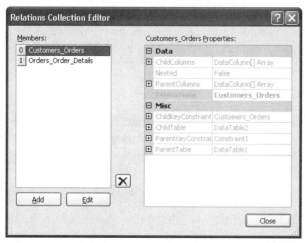

Figure 7-7 The untyped *DataSet's* Relations Collection Editor

The Relations Collection Editor lets you add, edit, and remove *DataRelation* objects. If you choose to add a new *DataRelation* or edit an existing *DataRelation*, you'll see the Edit Relation dialog box shown in Figure 7-8.

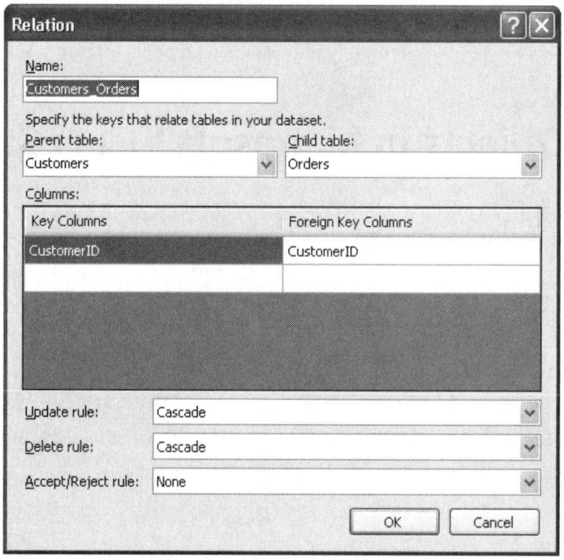

Figure 7-8 Adding a *DataRelation* to an untyped *DataSet* in the Relations Collection Editor

The Edit Relation dialog box mirrors the constructors for the *DataRelation* class, letting you specify the parent and child *DataTable* and *DataColumn* objects for the new *DataRelation*. You can also specify values for the *UpdateRule*, *DeleteRule*, and *AcceptRejectRule* properties of the *ForeignKeyConstraint* that will be associated with the new *DataRelation*.

DataRelation Object Reference

The reference information for the *DataRelation* object isn't terribly interesting. The object exposes no methods and no events—only properties. However, to leave these out would somehow feel like cheating.

Properties of the *DataRelation* Class

Most of the *DataRelation* class's properties are read-only. You can set their value only using the *DataRelation* class's constructors. The commonly used properties are described in Table 7-1.

Table 7-1 Commonly Used Properties of the *DataRelation* Class

Property	Data Type	Description
ChildColumns	Array of *DataColumn* objects	Indicates the child columns that define the relation. This property is read-only.
ChildKeyConstraint	ForeignKeyConstraint	Indicates the foreign key constraint in the child table in the relation. This property is read-only.
ChildTable	DataTable	Indicates the child table in the relation. This property is read-only.
DataSet	DataSet	Indicates the *DataSet* in which the *DataRelation* resides. This property is read-only.
ExtendedProperties	PropertyCollection	Indicates a collection of dynamic properties.
Nested	Boolean	Indicates whether the child rows are child elements when the *DataSet* is stored as XML.
ParentColumns	Array of *DataColumn* objects	Indicates the parent columns that define the relation. This property is read-only.
ParentKeyConstraint	UniqueConstraint	Indicates the unique constraint in the parent table in the relation. This property is read-only.
ParentTable	DataTable	Indicates the parent table in the relation. This property is read-only.
RelationName	String	Indicates the name of the relation.

ChildColumns Property

The *ChildColumns* property returns an array that contains the *DataColumn* object or objects from the child *DataTable* in the *DataRelation*. This property is read-only.

ChildKeyConstraint Property

The *ChildKeyConstraint* property returns the *ForeignKeyConstraint* referenced by the *DataRelation*. If you created a *DataRelation* that does not use constraints, this property returns *Nothing* or *null*, depending on your language of choice. The *ChildKeyConstraint* property is read-only.

ChildTable Property

The *ChildTable* property returns the child *DataTable* in the *DataRelation*. This property is read-only.

DataSet Property

The *DataSet* property returns the *DataSet* in which the *DataRelation* resides. This property is read-only.

ExtendedProperties Property

Like the *DataSet*, *DataTable*, and *DataColumn* objects, the *DataRelation* object also exposes an *ExtendedProperties* property in which you can store additional information.

Nested Property

The *Nested* property controls the location of the contents of the child *DataTable* when the *DataSet* is stored in XML format using the *DataSet* object's *WriteXml* method. This is one of the few read-write properties of the *DataRelation* object.

If the *Nested* property is set to *False*, which is the default, the data in the child *DataTable* will be separate from the data in the parent *DataTable*. As you can see here, without looking at the schema information for the *DataSet*, you wouldn't know that there is a *DataRelation* between the *DataTable* objects:

Not Nested
```
<Customers>
    <CustomerID>ALFKI</CustomerID>
    <CompanyName>Alfreds Futterkiste</CompanyName>
</Customers>
<Customers>
    <CustomerID>ANATR</CustomerID>
    <CompanyName>Ana Trujillo Emparedados y helados</CompanyName>
</Customers>
...
<Orders>
    <OrderID>10308</OrderID>
    <CustomerID>ANATR</CustomerID>
</Orders>
<Orders>
    <OrderID>10355</OrderID>
    <CustomerID>AROUT</CustomerID>
</Orders>
...
```

Setting the *Nested* property to *True* causes ADO.NET to embed the data from the child *Data-Table* within the data for the parent *DataTable*, as shown here:

Nested
```
<Customers>
    <CustomerID>ALFKI</CustomerID>
    <CompanyName>Alfreds Futterkiste</CompanyName>
    <Orders>
        <OrderID>10643</OrderID>
        <CustomerID>ALFKI</CustomerID>
    </Orders>
    <Orders>
        <OrderID>10692</OrderID>
        <CustomerID>ALFKI</CustomerID>
    </Orders>
    ...
</Customers>
<Customers>
    <CustomerID>ANATR</CustomerID>
    <CompanyName>Ana Trujillo Emparedados y helados</CompanyName>
    <Orders>
        <OrderID>10308</OrderID>
        <CustomerID>ANATR</CustomerID>
    </Orders>
    <Orders>
        <OrderID>10625</OrderID>
        <CustomerID>ANATR</CustomerID>
    </Orders>
    ...
</Customers>
...
```

ParentColumns Property

The *ParentColumns* property returns an array that contains the *DataColumn* objects from the parent *DataTable* in the *DataRelation*. This property is read-only.

ParentKeyConstraint Property

The *ParentKeyConstraint* property returns the *UniqueConstraint* referenced by the *DataRelation*. If you created a *DataRelation* that does not use constraints, this property returns *Nothing* or *null*, depending on your language of choice. The *ParentKeyConstraint* property is read-only.

ParentTable Property

The *ParentTable* property returns the parent *DataTable* in the *DataRelation*. This property is read-only.

RelationName Property

The *RelationName* property is read-write and can be used to set or retrieve the name of the *DataRelation*.

Questions That Should Be Asked More Frequently

Q   When should I create my *DataRelation* objects without constraints?

A   Let's say that your application queries your database for customer and order data and displays that information on a simple Windows form. The application allows the user to view the data but not modify it.

In such an application, a *DataRelation* is useful because it lets you easily display the orders for a particular customer. However, you probably don't want to use constraints within your *DataSet*. Why? Constraints are used to validate your data, and validating data takes time. If the data in the application is read-only and the database has already validated the data through its own set of constraints, there's no need for ADO.NET to revalidate the data.

Q   I want to work with data from multiple tables, but I'm not going to retrieve all rows from the parent table. The queries you showed that retrieve only the related child rows look complex and inefficient. Wouldn't a single join-based query that returned data from all tables at once be faster?

A   During the Microsoft .NET Framework beta, a thread in one of the newsgroups focused on this issue. A couple of developers felt that fetching the data from separate queries was inefficient. Their premise made sense and piqued my curiosity, so I set out to see how working with separate queries would affect performance. I built applications in Visual Basic using ADO.NET and Visual Basic 6 using ADO 2.6 to query the SQL Server Northwind database for customer, order, and order detail information for all customers in the United States. I wrote various routines for each application that used a specific type of query to retrieve this information from the database.

The routine that tested the join query simply retrieved the data and stored it in a single *DataTable* that had no validation. The queries I used were as follows:

Join-Based Query
```
SELECT C.CustomerID, C.CompanyName, C.ContactName, C.Phone,
       O.OrderID, O.EmployeeID, O.OrderDate,
       D.ProductID, D.Quantity, D.UnitPrice
       FROM [Order Details] D, Orders O, Customers C
       WHERE D.OrderID = O.OrderID AND O.CustomerID = C.CustomerID
           AND C.Country = N'USA'
```

Separate Queries
```
SELECT CustomerID, CompanyName, ContactName, Phone
       FROM Customers WHERE C.Country = N'USA'

SELECT O.OrderID, O.CustomerID, O.EmployeeID, O.OrderDate
       FROM Orders O, Customers C
       WHERE O.CustomerID = C.CustomerID AND C.Country = N'USA'

SELECT D.OrderID, D.ProductID, D.Quantity, D.UnitPrice
```

```
       FROM [Order Details] D, Orders O, Customers C
       WHERE D.OrderID = O.OrderID AND O.CustomerID = C.CustomerID
              AND C.Country = N'USA'
```

Parameterized Queries

```
SELECT CustomerID, CompanyName, ContactName, Phone
       FROM Customers WHERE C.Country = N'USA'

SELECT OrderID, CustomerID, EmployeeID, OrderDate
       FROM Orders WHERE CustomerID = @CustomerID

SELECT OrderID, ProductID, Quantity, UnitPrice
       FROM [Order Details] WHERE OrderID = @OrderID
```

Like the others in the newsgroup, I had expected the join-based query and the parameterized queries to be faster than the separate queries. Thankfully, I ran the tests before sharing my opinion on what method of retrieving the data would be fastest. It turned out that retrieving the data using separate queries was fastest. The separate queries were on average 20 percent faster than the join-based query and between six and eight times faster than the parameterized queries.

Why? Well, optimizing queries is not my strong suit, but I believe I can explain the behavior. Retrieving data using separate queries was faster than using the single join query because the single join query returned more data. A join query returns redundant data. There might be 100 entries in the Order Details table that correspond to a single row in the Customers table, but that same customer information appears in each of those 100 rows.

I used the *DataSet* class's *WriteXml* method, which we'll discuss in Chapter 12, to store the contents of the *DataSet* in an XML file. The XML file that corresponded to the *DataSet* that I filled with the results of the join-based query was nearly three times as large as the XML file that corresponded to the *DataSet* I filled using the separate queries. The join-based query might look and feel more efficient because it's simpler, but it's actually less efficient because it returns more data.

To test the parameterized queries, I executed the simple query against the Customers table, retrieved the results, and stored them in a *DataTable*. I then looped through the results of that query and executed the parameterized query against the Orders table once for each customer. Finally, I looped through each of the combined results of the queries against the Orders table and executed the parameterized query against the Order Details table once for each order. This process required executing a separate query for each customer and for each order. The structure of the parameterized queries is simple, but executing these queries over and over for each customer and order proved inefficient and the performance was lousy.

That's not a knock on parameterized queries in general. They're simply not the best solution for retrieving data from large filtered hierarchies such as the one I tested in this scenario.

Even if you're going to work with read-only data from multiple tables, you should consider breaking up your join queries into separate queries that return data from distinct tables.

> **Note**   I also ran two additional routines, one that used IN subqueries and one that bundled the separate queries into a batch. The performance of the IN subqueries was comparable to the routine that used separate queries. Bundling the separate queries into a batch improved performance by about 8 percent.

Q   I'm fetching data from stored procedures, but unfortunately I can't change the join queries inside the stored procedures. Is there a simple way to split the results into separate *DataTable* objects?

A   There is no such method in the ADO.NET object model—at least not yet. However, you can construct code to split the results using a *DataReader* and the *Find* method on the *DataTable* class's *Rows* collection (a feature we'll discuss in the next chapter).

The following code snippet executes a join query against the Customers and Orders tables, retrieving information for Canadian customers. It then loops through the data returned in the *DataReader* and appends new rows to separate Customers and Orders *DataTable* objects.

Visual Basic

```vb
'Create the DataSet structure
Dim ds As New DataSet()
Dim tblCustomers, tblOrders As DataTable
tblCustomers = ds.Tables.Add("Customers")
tblCustomers.Columns.Add("CustomerID", GetType(String))
tblCustomers.Columns.Add("CompanyName", GetType(String))

tblOrders = ds.Tables.Add("Orders")
tblOrders.Columns.Add("OrderID", GetType(Integer))
tblOrders.Columns.Add("CustomerID", GetType(String))
tblOrders.Columns.Add("OrderDate", GetType(DateTime))

'Create a primary key on the customers DataTable
'  to enable lookups using the primary key column
tblCustomers.PrimaryKey = _
    New DataColumn() {tblCustomers.Columns("CustomerID")}

'Add the DataRelation
Dim rel As DataRelation
rel = ds.Relations.Add("Customers_Orders", _
                       tblCustomers.Columns("CustomerID"), _
                       tblOrders.Columns("CustomerID"))

'Connect and execute the query
Dim strConn, strSQL As String
strConn = "Data Source=.\SQLExpress;" & _
          "Initial Catalog=Northwind;Integrated Security=True;"
strSQL = "SELECT C.CustomerID, C.CompanyName, O.OrderID, O.OrderDate " & _
         "  FROM Customers C INNER JOIN Orders O ON C.CustomerID = O.CustomerID " & _
         "  WHERE C.Country = 'Canada'"
Dim cn As New SqlConnection(strConn)
cn.Open()
```

```vb
Dim cmd As New SqlCommand(strSQL, cn)
Dim rdr As SqlDataReader = cmd.ExecuteReader(CommandBehavior.CloseConnection)

'Loop through the results and add DataRows
Dim objNewCustomer, objNewOrder As Object()
Dim strCustomerID As String
Do While rdr.Read
    'Retrieve the value for CustomerID
    strCustomerID = rdr.GetString(0)

    'If the customers DataTable does not contain that CustomerID
    'Retrieve the rest of the customer information
    '  and add a new row to the customers DataTable
    If tblCustomers.Rows.Find(strCustomerID) Is Nothing Then
        objNewCustomer = New Object() {strCustomerID, rdr.GetString(1)}
        tblCustomers.LoadDataRow(objNewCustomer, True)
    End If

    'Retrieve the order information and add it to the orders DataTable
    objNewOrder = New Object() {rdr.GetInt32(2), strCustomerID, rdr.GetDateTime(3)}
    tblOrders.LoadDataRow(objNewOrder, True)
Loop
rdr.Close()

'Display the retrieved information
For Each rowCustomer As DataRow In tblCustomers.Rows
    Console.WriteLine("{0} - {1}", rowCustomer("CustomerID"), _
                        rowCustomer("CompanyName"))
    'Loop through the related orders.
    For Each rowOrder As DataRow In rowCustomer.GetChildRows(rel)
        Console.WriteLine("  {0} - {1:d}", rowOrder("OrderID"), _
                            rowOrder("OrderDate"))
    Next rowOrder
    Console.WriteLine()
Next rowCustomer
```

Visual C#

```csharp
//Create the DataSet structure
DataSet ds = new DataSet();
DataTable tblCustomers, tblOrders;
tblCustomers = ds.Tables.Add("Customers");
tblCustomers.Columns.Add("CustomerID", typeof(string));
tblCustomers.Columns.Add("CompanyName", typeof(string));

tblOrders = ds.Tables.Add("Orders");
tblOrders.Columns.Add("OrderID", typeof(int));
tblOrders.Columns.Add("CustomerID", typeof(string));
tblOrders.Columns.Add("OrderDate", typeof(DateTime));

//Create a primary key on the customers DataTable
//  to enable lookups using the primary key column
tblCustomers.PrimaryKey = new DataColumn[] {tblCustomers.Columns["CustomerID"]};

//Add the DataRelation
DataRelation rel;
```

```csharp
rel = ds.Relations.Add("Customers_Orders",
                        tblCustomers.Columns["CustomerID"],
                        tblOrders.Columns["CustomerID"]);

//Connect and execute the query
string strConn, strSQL;
strConn = @"Data Source=.\SQLExpress;" +
            "Initial Catalog=Northwind;Integrated Security=True;";
strSQL = "SELECT C.CustomerID, C.CompanyName, O.OrderID, O.OrderDate " +
         "  FROM Customers C INNER JOIN Orders O ON C.CustomerID = O.CustomerID " +
         "  WHERE C.Country = 'Canada'";
SqlConnection cn = new SqlConnection(strConn);
cn.Open();
SqlCommand cmd = new SqlCommand(strSQL, cn);
SqlDataReader rdr = cmd.ExecuteReader(CommandBehavior.CloseConnection);

//Loop through the results and add DataRows
object[] objNewCustomer, objNewOrder;
string strCustomerID;
while (rdr.Read()) {
    //Retrieve the value for CustomerID
    strCustomerID = rdr.GetString(0);

    //If the customers DataTable does not contain that CustomerID
    //Retrieve the rest of the customer information
    //  and add a new row to the customers DataTable
    if (tblCustomers.Rows.Find(strCustomerID) == null) {
        objNewCustomer = new object[] {strCustomerID, rdr.GetString(1)};
        tblCustomers.LoadDataRow(objNewCustomer, true);
    }

    //Retrieve the order information and add it to the orders DataTable
    objNewOrder = new object[] {rdr.GetInt32(2), strCustomerID, rdr.GetDateTime(3)};
    tblOrders.LoadDataRow(objNewOrder, true);
}
rdr.Close();

//Display the retrieved information
foreach (DataRow rowCustomer in tblCustomers.Rows) {
    Console.WriteLine("{0} - {1}", rowCustomer["CustomerID"],
                    rowCustomer["CompanyName"]);
    //Loop through the related orders.
    foreach (DataRow rowOrder in rowCustomer.GetChildRows(rel))
        Console.WriteLine("  {0} - {1:d}", rowOrder["OrderID"],
                        rowOrder["OrderDate"]);
    Console.WriteLine();
}
```

Chapter 8
Sorting, Searching, and Filtering

In Chapter 5, you learned how to use a *SqlDataAdapter* object to fetch the results of queries into a *DataSet* object. In Chapter 6, which covered the *DataSet* class and the objects it contains, you learned how to examine the results of such queries by looping through the *DataRow* objects in a *DataTable*.

But how do you locate a specific row in your *DataTable* by a value or set of values? How do you apply a filter so that only rows that satisfy the specified criteria are visible? And how do you control the sort order for the rows you want to access or display?

This chapter will answer these questions and more as it covers the *Find* method of the *DataRowCollection* class and the *Select* method of the *DataTable* class and introduces the *DataView* and *DataRowView* classes.

Using the *DataTable* Class's Searching and Filtering Features

The *DataTable* class exposes two methods that you can use to locate data based on search criteria. One method, *Find*, lets you locate a row based on its primary key values. The other, *Select*, acts as more of a filter, returning multiple rows of data based on more flexible search criteria.

Locating a Row by Its Primary Key Values

When you're querying your database for information, you'll often want to retrieve a specific row of data based on the values of its primary key columns, using a query such as this one:

```
SELECT CustomerID, CompanyName, ContactName, Phone
    FROM Customers WHERE CustomerID = 'ALFKI'
```

You can also locate a *DataRow* in a *DataTable* based on the row's primary key values. You might have noticed that the final code snippet in Chapter 7, which split the results of a JOIN query into distinct *DataTables*, looped through the results of a query and had to determine whether a row of data already existed in the *DataTable*. This code used the *Find* method to perform a search of the contents of the *DataTable* based on the primary key value.

Although the *Find* method is designed for *DataTable* objects, it's actually exposed by the *DataRowCollection* class. The *Find* method accepts an object that contains the primary key value for the row you want to locate. Because primary key values are unique, the *Find* method can return at most one *DataRow*. The following code snippet attempts to locate a customer row by its primary key value and then determines whether the search located a row.

Visual Basic

```
Dim strConn, strSQL As String
strConn = "Data Source=.\SQLExpress;" & _
          "Initial Catalog=Northwind;Integrated Security=True;"
strSQL = "SELECT CustomerID, CompanyName FROM Customers " & _
         "WHERE CustomerID LIKE 'A%'"
Dim da As New SqlDataAdapter(strSQL, strConn)
Dim tbl As New DataTable("Customers")
da.Fill(tbl)
tbl.PrimaryKey = New DataColumn() {tbl.Columns("CustomerID")}
Dim row As DataRow = tbl.Rows.Find("ALFKI")
If row Is Nothing Then
    Console.WriteLine("Row not found!")
Else
    Console.WriteLine(row("CompanyName"))
End If
```

Visual C#

```
string strConn, strSQL;
strConn = @"Data Source=.\SQLExpress;" +
          "Initial Catalog=Northwind;Integrated Security=True;";
strSQL = "SELECT CustomerID, CompanyName FROM Customers " +
         "WHERE CustomerID LIKE 'A%'";
SqlDataAdapter da = new SqlDataAdapter(strSQL, strConn);
DataTable tbl = new DataTable("Customers");
da.Fill(tbl);
tbl.PrimaryKey = new DataColumn[] {tbl.Columns["CustomerID"]};

DataRow row = tbl.Rows.Find("ALFKI");
if (row == null)
    Console.WriteLine("Row not found!");
else
    Console.WriteLine(row["CompanyName"]);
```

Note   Technically, your *DataTable* can contain multiple rows that have the same primary key values. If you set the *EnforceConstraints* property of the *DataSet* to *False*, the *DataTable* will not throw an exception if you violate the primary key constraint. In such a scenario, the *Find* method will return the first row it finds with the desired primary key values.

The *Find* method is overloaded for scenarios in which the primary key for your *DataTable* consists of multiple *DataColumn* objects. This is often referred to as a compound key. If you're working with a compound key, pass an object array to the *Find* method where the items in the array correspond to the *DataColumns* that comprise the primary key. For example, the primary key for the Order Details table is based on the OrderID and ProductID columns. So, the first entry in the object array will correspond to the OrderID column, and the second entry will correspond to the ProductID column, as shown in the following code:

Visual Basic

```
Dim strConn, strSQL As String
strConn = "Data Source=.\SQLExpress;" & _
          "Initial Catalog=Northwind;Integrated Security=True;"
strSQL = "SELECT OrderID, ProductID, Quantity, UnitPrice " & _
          "FROM [Order Details]"
Dim da As New SqlDataAdapter(strSQL, strConn)
Dim tbl As New DataTable("Order Details")
da.Fill(tbl)
tbl.PrimaryKey = New DataColumn() {tbl.Columns("OrderID"), _
                                   tbl.Columns("ProductID")}

Dim objCriteria As New Object() {10643, 28}
Dim row As DataRow = tbl.Rows.Find(objCriteria)
If row Is Nothing Then
    Console.WriteLine("Row not found!")
Else
    Console.WriteLine("{0} - {1}", row("Quantity"), _
                      row("UnitPrice"))
End If
```

Visual C#

```
string strConn, strSQL;
strConn = @"Data Source=.\SQLExpress;" +
           "Initial Catalog=Northwind;Integrated Security=True;";
strSQL = "SELECT OrderID, ProductID, Quantity, UnitPrice " +
          "FROM [Order Details]";
SqlDataAdapter da = new SqlDataAdapter(strSQL, strConn);
DataTable tbl = new DataTable("Order Details");
da.Fill(tbl);
tbl.PrimaryKey = new DataColumn[] {tbl.Columns["OrderID"],
                                   tbl.Columns["ProductID"]};

object[] objCriteria = new object[] {10643, 28};
DataRow row = tbl.Rows.Find(objCriteria);
if (row == null)
    Console.WriteLine("Row not found!");
else
    Console.WriteLine("{0} - {1}", row["Quantity"],
                      row["UnitPrice"]);
```

Conducting More Dynamic Searches

Locating a row based on its primary key values is efficient, but not all searches are that straightforward. What if you want to locate all customers in the United States who are not in the city of Seattle? You can add such criteria to a database query using a WHERE clause, as shown here:

```
SELECT CustomerID, CompanyName, ContactName, Phone, City, Country
    FROM Customers WHERE Country = 'USA' AND City <> 'Seattle'
```

You can use the *DataTable* class's *Select* method to locate rows based on similar criteria. Let's say you retrieve the entire contents of the Customers table and store it in a *DataTable*. You can use the same search criteria as in the WHERE clause in the previous example to locate just the customers from the United States who are not in Seattle:

Visual Basic

```
Dim strConn, strSQL, strFilter As String
strConn = "Data Source=.\SQLExpress;" & _
          "Initial Catalog=Northwind;Integrated Security=True;"
strSQL = "SELECT CustomerID, CompanyName, City, Country " & _
          "FROM Customers"
Dim da As New SqlDataAdapter(strSQL, strConn)
Dim tbl As New DataTable("Customers")
da.Fill(tbl)
strFilter = "Country = 'USA' AND City <> 'Seattle'"
For Each row As DataRow In tbl.Select(strFilter)
    Console.WriteLine("{0,-35} {1}, {2}", row("CompanyName"), _
                       row("City"), row("Country"))
Next row
```

Visual C#

```
string strConn, strSQL, strFilter;
strConn = @"Data Source=.\SQLExpress;" +
           "Initial Catalog=Northwind;Integrated Security=True;";
strSQL = "SELECT CustomerID, CompanyName, City, Country " +
          "FROM Customers";
SqlDataAdapter da = new SqlDataAdapter(strSQL, strConn);
DataTable tbl = new DataTable("Customers");
da.Fill(tbl);

strFilter = "Country = 'USA' AND City <> 'Seattle'";
foreach (DataRow row in tbl.Select(strFilter))
    Console.WriteLine("{0,-35} {1}, {2}", row["CompanyName"],
                       row["City"], row["Country"]);
```

Conducting Wildcard Searches

The following SQL query returns all customers that have a value for the CustomerID column that begins with the letter *A*:

```
SELECT CustomerID, CompanyName, ContactName, Phone
    FROM Customers WHERE CustomerID LIKE 'A%'
```

ADO.NET allows you to perform similar searches using wildcards. You can use either % or * as a wildcard at the beginning or the end of the search string. For example, using the following filter with the *DataTable*'s *Select* method would return customers in New Hampshire, New Jersey, New Mexico, and New York:

```
"State LIKE 'New %'"
```

The following filter returns customers from North and South Dakota:

```
"State LIKE '% Dakota'"
```

> **Note**   ADO.NET does not let you use a single-character wildcard such as ? or _.

Working with Delimiters

You might have noticed that in both the database query example and the *DataTable.Select* example, we specified criteria for string-based columns. In each case, we surrounded the value with single quotes. This process appears simple in an example but can pose a bit of a problem for developers.

You can't simply surround a string with single quotes in your search criteria. Well, actually, you can, but you shouldn't. Say your application allows the user to locate an employee based on the employee's last name. When the application prompts the user for the last name, the user enters **O'Malley**. If you simply surround the literal value with single quotes in your search criteria, your string will look like this:

```
"LastName = 'O'Malley'"
```

As with most database queries, if the delimiter appears in the literal string, you have to double it. In this situation, the search criteria should look like this:

```
"LastName = 'O''Malley'"
```

If you build search criteria dynamically, you must be sure to search your strings for delimiters. Use the *Replace* method of the *String* class to handle such situations. The following code snippet builds a string for the *Select* method and uses the *Replace* method of the *String* class to replace single quotes with two single quotes in the string:

Visual Basic
```vb
Dim strLastName, strCriteria As String
strLastName = "O'Malley"
strCriteria = String.Format("LastName = '{0}'", _
                            strLastName.Replace("'", "''")) Console.WriteLine(strCriteria)
```

Visual C#
```csharp
string strLastName, strCriteria;
strLastName = "O'Malley";
strCriteria = string.Format("LastName = '{0}'",
                            strLastName.Replace("'", "''"));
Console.WriteLine(strCriteria);
```

How do you delimit dates in search criteria? You surround the date with pound symbols, as shown here. (Thankfully, you don't have to worry about delimiters appearing in your dates.)

```
"OrderDate >= #01/01/2002# AND OrderDate < #02/01/2002#"
```

In some scenarios, you'll need to delimit your column names in your search criteria—perhaps because you have a space or another non-alphanumeric character in your column name or because your column name is a reserved word such as *LIKE* or *SUM*. ADO.NET uses square brackets as column delimiters. So, if your column name is *Space In Name* and you're looking for all rows that have a value of 3 in that column, you can use this string to locate those rows:

```
"[Space In Name] = 3"
```

What if you have a column delimiter in your column name? You can use an escape character (\) before the closing bracket (]) in your criteria string. For example, if your column name is *Bad]Column[Name* and you're looking for all rows that have a value of 5 in that column, you can construct the following criteria string:

Visual Basic
```
strCriteria = "[Bad\]Column[Name] = 5"
```

Visual C#
```
strCriteria = @"[Bad\]Column[Name] = 5";
```

> **Note** Remember that in C#, the \ character is an escape character. You can preface the string with the @ symbol so that C# will know that a \ is just a \, or you can double it as shown here:
> ```
> strCriteria = "[Bad\\]Column[Name] = 5";
> ```

Before (finally) moving on from delimiters, let's take a look at a code snippet that handles a really horrible scenario fairly elegantly. The *DataTable* in the code snippet contains a hideously named column that accepts strings. The code performs a search against that string, successfully delimiting the column name as well as the value to locate. First, the code uses the *String* class's *Format* function to surround the column name in brackets and the value in single quotes. Then the code uses the *String* class's *Replace* function to preface any closed bracket characters in the column name with a slash, and to double any single quotes that appear in the value. Finally, the code uses the new filter to find the desired row.

Visual Basic
```
Dim tbl As New DataTable()
tbl.Columns.Add("ID", GetType(Integer))
tbl.Columns.Add("Why]would[you ever\use.this#column/name?", _
                GetType(String))
tbl.LoadDataRow(New Object() {1, "Thompson"}, True)
tbl.LoadDataRow(New Object() {2, "O'Malley"}, True)
```

```
Dim strFilter, strColumnName, strValue As String
strColumnName = "Why]would[you ever\use.this#column/name?"
strValue = "O'Malley" strFilter = String.Format("[{0}] = '{1}'", _
                        strColumnName.Replace("]", "\]"), _
                        strValue.Replace("'", "''"))
For Each row As DataRow In tbl.Select(strFilter)
    Console.WriteLine(row(strColumnName))
Next row
```

Visual C#

```
DataTable tbl = new DataTable();
tbl.Columns.Add("ID", typeof(int));
tbl.Columns.Add(@"Why]would[you ever\use.this#column/name?",
                typeof(string));
tbl.LoadDataRow(new object[] {1, "Thompson"}, true);
tbl.LoadDataRow(new object[] {2, "O'Malley"}, true);

string strFilter, strColumnName, strValue;
strColumnName = @"Why]would[you ever\use.this#column/name?";
strValue = "O'Malley";
strFilter = string.Format("[{0}] = '{1}'",
                        strColumnName.Replace("]", @"\]"),
                        strValue.Replace("'", "''"));
foreach (DataRow row in tbl.Select(strFilter))
Console.WriteLine(row[strColumnName]);
```

> **Note**   After reading the previous few paragraphs, I hope you've figured out the simple and elegant way to avoid problems with delimiters and reserved words in column names: Don't use them!

Using the Additional *Select* Methods

Like many methods in the ADO.NET object model, the *Select* method is overloaded. You can supply just a search string, but you can also include a sort order as well as a parameter to control the state of the rows you want to search (only added rows, for example, or only modified rows). Let's look at these overloaded methods briefly.

Including a Sort Order

In our initial *Select* method code snippet, we searched a *DataTable* that contained customer information to locate the customers from the United States that are not located in Seattle. We can control the order of the *DataRow* objects that the *Select* method returns by using one of the overloaded method signatures.

In a SQL query, you control the sort order of the data returned by the query using the ORDER BY clause. For example, the following query returns customers sorted by city:

```
SELECT CustomerID, CompanyName, ContactName, Phone, City
    FROM Customers ORDER BY City
```

To sort by city in descending order, you simply change *ORDER BY City* to *ORDER BY City DESC*.

The overloaded *Select* method accepts a sort order, just as the SQL ORDER BY clause does. Here, we've modified our initial code snippet so that the *DataRow* objects returned by the *Select* method are sorted by the City column in descending order:

Visual Basic

```
Dim strConn, strSQL, strFilter, strSortOrder As String
strConn = "Data Source=.\SQLExpress;" & _
          "Initial Catalog=Northwind;Integrated Security=True;"
strSQL = "SELECT CustomerID, CompanyName, City, Country " & _
         "FROM Customers"
Dim da As New SqlDataAdapter(strSQL, strConn)
Dim tbl As New DataTable("Customers")
da.Fill(tbl)
strFilter = "Country = 'USA' AND City <> 'Seattle'"
strSortOrder = "City DESC"
For Each row As DataRow In tbl.Select(strFilter, strSortOrder)
    Console.WriteLine("{0,-35} {1}, {2}", row("CompanyName"), _
                      row("City"), row("Country"))
Next row
```

Visual C#

```
string strConn, strSQL, strFilter, strSortOrder;
strConn = @"Data Source=.\SQLExpress;" +
          "Initial Catalog=Northwind;Integrated Security=True;";
strSQL = "SELECT CustomerID, CompanyName, City, Country " +
         "FROM Customers";
SqlDataAdapter da = new SqlDataAdapter(strSQL, strConn);
DataTable tbl = new DataTable("Customers");
da.Fill(tbl);

strFilter = "Country = 'USA' AND City <> 'Seattle'";
strSortOrder = "City DESC";
foreach (DataRow row in tbl.Select(strFilter, strSortOrder))
    Console.WriteLine("{0,-35} {1}, {2}", row["CompanyName"],
                      row["City"], row["Country"]);
```

Specifying the *RowState* of the Rows to Search

As you learned in Chapter 6, the *DataSet* supports caching changes. What if you want to perform a search against just the modified rows in a *DataTable*?

You can use an overloaded *Select* method to specify a value from the *DataViewRowState* enumeration. Think of this value as an added filter to your search criteria. Say you want to examine just the modified and deleted rows in a *DataTable*. The following code snippet modifies only the *DataRows* whose Country column is set to "USA", thanks to the *Select* method. The code then uses the *Select* method again, but the *FilterExpression* and *Sort* parameters are set to empty strings, the default. If the code only used those parameters, the *Select* method would return all rows in the *DataTable*. Instead, the code uses the *RecordStates* parameter to indicate that only modified rows should be returned.

Visual Basic

```vb
Dim strConn, strSQL As String
strConn = "Data Source=.\SQLExpress;" & _
          "Initial Catalog=Northwind;Integrated Security=True;"
strSQL = "SELECT CustomerID, CompanyName, City, Country " & _
         "FROM Customers"
Dim da As New SqlDataAdapter(strSQL, strConn)
Dim tbl As New DataTable("Customers")
da.Fill(tbl)
Console.WriteLine("DataTable contains {0} rows", tbl.Rows.Count)
Console.WriteLine()

For Each row As DataRow In tbl.Select("Country = 'USA'")
    row("CompanyName") = "Modified Value"
Next row

Dim dvrs As DataViewRowState
dvrs = DataViewRowState.ModifiedCurrent
Console.WriteLine("Modified rows")
For Each row As DataRow In tbl.Select("", "", dvrs)
    Console.WriteLine("  {0}", row("CompanyName", _
                                   DataRowVersion.Original))
Next row
```

Visual C#

```csharp
string strConn, strSQL;
strConn = @"Data Source=.\SQLExpress;" +
            "Initial Catalog=Northwind;Integrated Security=True;";
strSQL = "SELECT CustomerID, CompanyName, City, Country " +
         "FROM Customers";
SqlDataAdapter da = new SqlDataAdapter(strSQL, strConn);
DataTable tbl = new DataTable("Customers");
da.Fill(tbl);
Console.WriteLine("DataTable contains {0} rows", tbl.Rows.Count);
Console.WriteLine();

foreach (DataRow row in tbl.Select("Country = 'USA'"))
    row["CompanyName"] = "Modified Value";

DataViewRowState dvrs = DataViewRowState.ModifiedCurrent;
Console.WriteLine("Modified rows");
foreach (DataRow row in tbl.Select("", "", dvrs))
    Console.WriteLine("  {0}", row["CompanyName",
                                 DataRowVersion.Original]);
```

 Note Remember that with deleted rows, you can examine only the original version of the row.

What Is a *DataView* Object?

The *DataTable* class's *Select* method is powerful and flexible, but it's not always the best solution. It has two major limitations. First, because it accepts such dynamic search criteria, it's not terribly efficient. Also, neither Windows nor Web forms support binding to the *Select* method's return value—an array of *DataRow* objects. The ADO.NET solution to both limitations is the *DataView* class.

The ADO.NET *DataTable* class is roughly equivalent to a table in a database, so you might assume that the *DataView* class is similar to a view in a database. Although there are some similarities between *DataView* objects and views in a database, they are not as closely related as *DataTable* objects and tables in a database are.

Changes to Indexes in ADO.NET 2.0

The internal indexing logic used in ADO.NET has changed in version 2.0. For the most part, this is a change for the better.

In versions 1.x, ADO.NET uses *ArrayLists* to maintain index information. Creating and navigating these lists was simple, but they were difficult and potentially extremely expensive to maintain. For example, if you set a *DataTable*'s *PrimaryKey* property, the *DataTable* creates an index to keep track of those values so that it can enforce the constraint. The values are sorted and then added to the *ArrayList*. While looking for an existing value in the *ArrayList* is a simple binary search, inserting a new entry is costly. Some developers noticed that when inserting rows into a *DataTable* that had a *Primary-Key*, performance degraded severely as the size of the *DataTable* grew.

ADO.NET 2.0 now uses red-black trees for indexes. If you're not familiar with a red-black tree, it's a self-balancing binary tree. The new indexes are much easier to maintain with large *DataTables*, but they're more expensive to construct. As a result, you might see some performance degradation when creating indexes.

Speaking of indexes, ADO.NET 2.0 handles index creation and maintenance differently than ADO.NET 1.x when calling *DataTable.Select*. Calling the *Select* method might require the *DataTable* to use internal indexes to perform the search, sorting, or both. If those indexes already exist, the *DataTable* will use them; otherwise, the *DataTable* will create them. The change in behavior from 1.x to 2.0 is this: With ADO.NET 1.x those indexes are maintained while with ADO.NET 2.0 any indexes created by the call to *Select* are discarded at the end of the method call. As a result, repeated searches using *DataTable.Select* can result in poor performance if those indexes are created each time the *Select* method is called.

If you want to maintain those indexes to improve performance, create a *DataView* and set its *Sort* property to the columns involved in your search. When you set the *Sort* property on a *DataView*, the corresponding *DataTable* creates an index on the column (or columns) referenced by the property. Repeated searches that require indexes for those columns will yield better performance.

DataView Objects Return Data from a *DataTable*

The *DataView* class does not maintain its own copy of data. When you access data through a *DataView*, the *DataView* returns data stored in the corresponding *DataTable*.

Views in a database behave the same way. When you query a view, the database returns data from the table or tables referenced in the view.

DataView Objects Are Not SQL Queries

A view in a database is really just a query. When you create a view in a database, you supply the query that the database will execute in order to return data for that view:

```
CREATE VIEW ViewCustomersAndOrders AS
    SELECT C.CustomerID, C.CompanyName, C.ContactName, C.Phone,
           O.OrderID, O.EmployeeID, O.OrderDate
    FROM Customers C, Orders O WHERE C.CustomerID = O.CustomerID
```

ADO.NET *DataView* objects let you filter, sort, and search the contents of *DataTable* objects, but they are not SQL queries. You cannot use a *DataView* to join data between two *DataTable* objects. *DataView* objects do support filtering rows based on dynamic criteria, but they can access only a single *DataTable*, and all columns in the *DataTable* are available through the *DataView*. In ADO.NET 2.0, the *DataView* does offer some support for hiding columns through the *ToTable* method, which we'll cover later in the chapter.

Simulating Joins Using a *DataRelation*

You can use a *DataRelation* and an expression-based column to simulate a join. For example, if you have *DataTable* objects for customer and order information, you can create a relationship between the two *DataTable* objects and then add an expression-based *DataColumn* in the orders *DataTable* to display a column from the customer's *DataTable*:

Visual Basic
```
Dim strConn, strSQL, strFilter, strSortOrder As String
strConn = "Data Source=.\SQLExpress;" & _
          "Initial Catalog=Northwind;Integrated Security=True;"
strSQL = "SELECT CustomerID, CompanyName FROM Customers;" & _
          "SELECT OrderID, CustomerID, OrderDate FROM Orders"
Dim da As New SqlDataAdapter(strSQL, strConn)
da.TableMappings.Add("Table", "Customers")
da.TableMappings.Add("Table1", "Orders")
Dim ds As New DataSet()
da.Fill(ds)

'Create the DataRelation between the DataTables
ds.Relations.Add("CustomersOrders", _
                ds.Tables("Customers").Columns("CustomerID"), _
                ds.Tables("Orders").Columns("CustomerID"))

'Create a column in the orders DataTable
'that shows data from the customers DataTable
```

```
ds.Tables("Orders").Columns.Add("CompanyName", GetType(String), _
                            "Parent(CustomersOrders).CompanyName")


'Use the DataRelation/expression based column
'in the search criteria
strFilter = "CompanyName LIKE 'A%'"
strSortOrder = "OrderDate"
For Each row As DataRow In _
    ds.Tables("Orders").Select(strFilter, strSortOrder)
    Console.WriteLine("{0,-35} {1} {2:d}", row("CompanyName"), _
                    row("OrderID"), row("OrderDate"))
Next row
```

Visual C#
```
string strConn, strSQL, strFilter, strSortOrder;
strConn = @"Data Source=.\SQLExpress;" +
            "Initial Catalog=Northwind;Integrated Security=True;";
strSQL = "SELECT CustomerID, CompanyName FROM Customers;" +
            "SELECT OrderID, CustomerID, OrderDate FROM Orders";
SqlDataAdapter da = new SqlDataAdapter(strSQL, strConn);
da.TableMappings.Add("Table", "Customers");
da.TableMappings.Add("Table1", "Orders");
DataSet ds = new DataSet();
da.Fill(ds);

//Create the DataRelation between the DataTables
ds.Relations.Add("CustomersOrders",
                ds.Tables["Customers"].Columns["CustomerID"],
                ds.Tables["Orders"].Columns["CustomerID"]);

//Create a column in the orders DataTable
//that shows data from the customers DataTable
ds.Tables["Orders"].Columns.Add("CompanyName", typeof(string),
                            "Parent(CustomersOrders).CompanyName");

//Use the DataRelation/expression based column
//in the search criteria
strFilter = "CompanyName LIKE 'A%'";
strSortOrder = "OrderDate";
foreach (DataRow row in ds.Tables["Orders"].Select(strFilter, strSortOrder))
    Console.WriteLine("{0,-35} {1} {2:d}", row["CompanyName"],
                    row["OrderID"], row["OrderDate"]);
```

For more information on using expression-based columns that reference DataRelations,
see "Using *DataRelation* Objects in Expression-Based *DataColumn* Objects" section in
Chapter 7.

Working with *DataView* Objects in Code

The *DataView* class offers functionality similar to that of the *DataTable* class's *Select* method.
Let's take a closer look at this functionality and compare it to the *Select* method as we go.

Creating *DataView* Objects

To use a *DataView* object to view data in a *DataTable*, you must associate it with a *DataTable* object. You can specify the *DataTable* that the *DataView* will use in one of two ways: by setting the *DataView* object's *Table* property or by using the *DataView*'s constructor. The following code snippets are equivalent:

Visual Basic
```
Dim tbl As New DataTable("TableName")
Dim vue As DataView

'Create the DataView and associate it with the DataTable
vue = New DataView()
vue.Table = tbl

'Perform both operations through the DataView's constructor
vue = New DataView(tbl)
```

Visual C#
```
DataTable tbl = new DataTable("TableName");
DataView vue;

//Create the DataView and associate it with the DataTable
vue = new DataView();
vue.Table = tbl;

//Perform both operations through the DataView's constructor vue = new DataView(tbl);
```

> **Note**   If you set the *DataView* object's *Table* property to a *DataTable*, the *DataTable* must have its *TableName* property set to something other than an empty string (the default). This restriction is not enforced in the *DataView* class's constructor.

The *DataView* class also has a constructor whose signature more closely matches the *DataTable* class's *Select* method. This more advanced constructor sets the *Table*, *RowFilter*, *Sort*, and *RowStateFilter* properties of the *DataView* in a single line of code. Thus, the following code snippets are equivalent:

Visual Basic
```
Dim strConn, strSQL, strFilter, strSortOrder As String
strConn = "Data Source=.\SQLExpress;" & _
        "Initial Catalog=Northwind;Integrated Security=True;"
strSQL = "SELECT CustomerID, CompanyName, City, Country " & _
        "FROM Customers"
Dim da As New SqlDataAdapter(strSQL, strConn)
Dim tbl As New DataTable("Customers")
da.Fill(tbl)
Dim dvrs As DataViewRowState
dvrs = DataViewRowState.ModifiedOriginal Or _
       DataViewRowState.Deleted
Dim vue As DataView
'Set Table, RowFilter, Sort and RowStateFilter separately
vue = New DataView
vue.Table = tbl
vue.RowFilter = "Country = 'USA'"
```

```
vue.Sort = "City DESC"
vue.RowStateFilter = dvrs
'Set all properties at once via the DataView's constructor
vue = New DataView(tbl, "Country = 'USA'", "City DESC", dvrs)
```

Visual C#

```csharp
string strConn, strSQL, strFilter, strSortOrder;
strConn = @"Data Source=.\SQLExpress;" +
            "Initial Catalog=Northwind;Integrated Security=True;";
strSQL = "SELECT CustomerID, CompanyName, City, Country " +
        "FROM Customers";
SqlDataAdapter da = new SqlDataAdapter(strSQL, strConn);
DataTable tbl = new DataTable("Customers");
da.Fill(tbl);
DataViewRowState dvrs = DataViewRowState.ModifiedOriginal |
                    DataViewRowState.Deleted;
DataView vue;

//Set Table, RowFilter, Sort and RowStateFilter separately
vue = new DataView();
vue.Table = tbl;
vue.RowFilter = "Country = 'USA'";
vue.Sort = "City DESC";
vue.RowStateFilter = dvrs;

//Set all properties at once via the DataView's constructor
vue = new DataView(tbl, "Country = 'USA'", "City DESC", dvrs);
```

Using the *RowStateFilter* Property

The *RowStateFilter* property accepts values from the *DataViewRowState* enumeration. (See Table 8-1.) You can think of the enumeration as a combination of the *RowState* property of the *DataRow* object and the *DataRowVersion* enumeration.

The property acts as a dual filter. For example, setting the *DataView* object's *RowStateFilter* property to *ModifiedOriginal* means that only modified rows will be visible through the *DataView* and that you'll see the original values of those rows.

Table 8-1   *DataViewRowState* Enumerations

Value	Description
Added	Added rows are included.
CurrentRows	Non-deleted rows are included. (Default)
Deleted	Deleted rows are included.
ModifiedCurrent	Modified rows are included; current values are visible.
ModifiedOriginal	Modified rows are included; original values are visible.
None	No rows are included.
OriginalRows	Deleted, modified, and unmodified rows are included; original values are visible.
Unchanged	Unmodified rows are included.

Using the *DataRowView* Class

If you use the *DataTable* class's *Select* method and specify *ModifiedOriginal*, the method will return only modified rows. However, as you saw in the earlier code snippet illustrating the *Select* method, we still had to specify that we wanted to retrieve original values from the row in calls to the *DataRow* objects returned.

This extra step is not required when you use the *DataView* because the *DataView* returns data using its own specialized class: a *DataRowView*. The *DataRowView* offers much of the same functionality as the *DataRow*. It exposes a default *Item* property that you can use to access the contents of a column by supplying either a column name or the index of a column. You can examine and modify the contents of a row using the *Item* property, but only one version of the row's data is available through the *DataRowView*–the version you specify in the *DataView* class's *DataRowVersion* property.

The following code snippet shows how to use the *DataView* class to return a *DataRowView* object and how to use the *DataRowView* class to examine data from a row:

Visual Basic

```
Dim strConn, strSQL As String
strConn = "Data Source=.\SQLExpress;" & _
          "Initial Catalog=Northwind;Integrated Security=True;"
strSQL = "SELECT CustomerID, CompanyName FROM Customers"
Dim da As New SqlDataAdapter(strSQL, strConn)
Dim tbl As New DataTable("Customers")
da.Fill(tbl)  Dim vue As New DataView(tbl)
Dim row As DataRowView = vue(0)
Console.WriteLine(row("CompanyName"))
```

Visual C#

```
string strConn, strSQL;
strConn = @"Data Source=.\SQLExpress;" +
          "Initial Catalog=Northwind;Integrated Security=True;";
strSQL = "SELECT CustomerID, CompanyName, City, Country " +
         "FROM Customers";
SqlDataAdapter da = new SqlDataAdapter(strSQL, strConn);
DataTable tbl = new DataTable("Customers");
da.Fill(tbl);
DataView vue = new DataView(tbl);
DataRowView row = vue[0];
Console.WriteLine(row["CompanyName"]);
```

If you find that the *DataRowView* class doesn't give you the functionality you need, you can use the *DataRowView* class's *Row* property to access the corresponding *DataRow* object.

Changes to the *DataRowView* Class in ADO.NET 2.0

In ADO.NET 1.x, the *DataRowView* class maintains a reference to a *DataRow* object. If you change the *DataView*'s *RowFilter* property or change the contents of the *DataTable*, the data returned by your *DataRowView* will not change.

In ADO.NET 2.0, the *DataRowView* class maintains a reference to an entry in the *DataView*. If the contents of the *DataView* change, the *DataRowView* might return different data.

For example, the next code snippet adds two rows to a *DataView* and then uses a *DataRowView* to access the first available row of data. The code then changes the *DataView's Sort* property before writing the contents of that same *DataRowView* to the *Console* window.

Visual Basic

```
'Create and populate the DataTable
Dim tbl As New DataTable("Customers")
tbl.Columns.Add("CustomerID", GetType(String))
tbl.Columns.Add("CompanyName", GetType(String))
tbl.Rows.Add(New Object() {"ALFKI", "Alfreds Futterkiste" })
tbl.Rows.Add(New Object() {"WOLZA", "Wolski Zajazd" })

'Create the DataView
Dim vue As New DataView(tbl)
vue.Sort = "CompanyName ASC"

'Use a DataRowView to write the contents of
'the first row in the DataView to the Console window
Dim row As DataRowView = vue(0)
Console.WriteLine(row("CompanyName"))

'Change the DataView's Sort property
vue.Sort = "CompanyName DESC"

'Re-write the contents to the DataRowView to the Console window
Console.WriteLine(row("CompanyName"))
```

Visual C#

```
//Create and populate the DataTable
DataTable tbl = new DataTable("Customers");
tbl.Columns.Add("CustomerID", typeof(string));
tbl.Columns.Add("CompanyName", typeof(string));
tbl.Rows.Add(new object[] {"ALFKI", "Alfreds Futterkiste" });
tbl.Rows.Add(new object[] {"WOLZA", "Wolski Zajazd" });

//Create the DataView
DataView vue = new DataView(tbl);
vue.Sort = "CompanyName ASC";

//Use a DataRowView to write the contents of
//the first row in the DataView to the Console window
DataRowView row = vue[0];
Console.WriteLine(row["CompanyName"]);

//Change the DataView's Sort property
vue.Sort = "CompanyName DESC";

//Re-write the contents to the DataRowView to the Console window
Console.WriteLine(row["CompanyName"]);
```

> If you use ADO.NET 1.x, the *DataRowView* will continue to reference the same *DataRow* of information and will write "Alfreds Futterkiste" to the *Console* window. If you use ADO.NET 2.0, the *DataRowView* will return different information as soon as the *Data-View*'s *Sort* property is changed and will write "Wolski Zajazd" to the *Console* window.

Examining All Rows of Data Available Through a *DataView*

Using a *DataView* to access data in a *DataTable* is slightly different from accessing the *DataTable* directly. The *DataTable* exposes its rows of data through the *Rows* property, which allows you to scroll through its contents with a *For Each* loop. The *DataView* class does not have a corresponding property, but you can still access all available *DataRowViews* using a *For Each* loop.

The *DataView* class also exposes a *Count* property that returns the number of rows visible through the *DataView*. You can use this property to construct a simple *For Each* loop to examine all of the rows.

Visual Basic

```
'Create and fill a DataTable
Dim strConn, strSQL As String
strConn = "Data Source=.\SQLExpress;" & _
          "Initial Catalog=Northwind;Integrated Security=True;"
strSQL = "SELECT CustomerID, CompanyName FROM Customers"
Dim da As New SqlDataAdapter(strSQL, strConn) Dim tbl As New DataTable("Customers")
'Create a DataView  'and access the DataTable's contents using DataRowViews
Dim vue As New DataView(tbl) For Each rowview As DataRowView in vue
    Console.WriteLine(rowview("CompanyName"))
Next rowview
```

Visual C#

```
//Create and fill a DataTable
string strConn, strSQL;
strConn = @"Data Source=.\SQLExpress;" +
            "Initial Catalog=Northwind;Integrated Security=True;";
strSQL = "SELECT CustomerID, CompanyName, City, Country " +
         "FROM Customers";
SqlDataAdapter da = new SqlDataAdapter(strSQL, strConn);
DataTable tbl = new DataTable("Customers"); da.Fill(tbl);
//Create a DataView
//and access the DataTable's contents using DataRowViews
DataView vue = new DataView(tbl);
foreach (DataRowView rowview in vue)
    Console.WriteLine(rowview["CompanyName"]);
```

Searching for Data in a *DataView*

You've already seen how the *DataView* class supports filtering using the *RowFilter* and *RowStateFilter* properties. It also supports searching using the *Find* and *FindRows* methods. These methods are similar to the *Find* method of the *DataTable* class's *Rows* collection.

The *Find* Method

Once you've set the *Sort* property on a *DataView* object, you can call its *Find* method to locate a row based on the columns specified in the *Sort* property. As with the *Find* method of the *DataRowCollection* object, you can supply a single value or an array of values.

The *DataView* class's *Find* method does not, however, return a *DataRow* or a *DataRowView* object. Instead, it returns an integer value that corresponds to the index of the desired row in the *DataView*. If the *DataView* cannot locate the desired row, the *Find* method returns a value of –1.

The following code snippet shows how to use the *DataView* class's *Find* method to locate a customer based on the value of the ContactName column. First, set the *DataView*'s *Sort* property to the column used in the search. Then pass the value to search for in the *Find* method. The code also uses the return value of the *Find* method to determine whether the *Find* method located the desired row.

Visual Basic

```
Dim strConn, strSQL As String strConn = "Data Source=.\SQLExpress;" & _
        "Initial Catalog=Northwind;Integrated Security=True;"
strSQL = "SELECT CustomerID, CompanyName, ContactName " & _
        "FROM Customers"
Dim da As New SqlDataAdapter(strSQL, strConn)
Dim tbl As New DataTable("Customers")
da.Fill(tbl)
Dim vue As New DataView(tbl)

vue.Sort = "ContactName"
Dim intIndex As Integer = vue.Find("Fran Wilson")
If intIndex = -1 Then
    Console.WriteLine("Row not found!")
Else
    Console.WriteLine(vue(intIndex)("CompanyName"))
End If
```

Visual C#

```
string strConn, strSQL; strConn = @"Data Source=.\SQLExpress;" +
        "Initial Catalog=Northwind;Integrated Security=True;";
strSQL = "SELECT CustomerID, CompanyName, ContactName " +
        "FROM Customers";
SqlDataAdapter da = new SqlDataAdapter(strSQL, strConn);
DataTable tbl = new DataTable("Customers");
da.Fill(tbl);
DataView vue = new DataView(tbl);

vue.Sort = "ContactName";
int intIndex = vue.Find("Fran Wilson");
if (intIndex == -1)
    Console.WriteLine("Row not found!");
else
    Console.WriteLine(vue[intIndex]["CompanyName"]);
```

The *FindRows* Method

The *DataRowCollection* class's *Find* method performs a search based on the column(s) specified in the *DataTable* object's *PrimaryKey* property. Because a primary key is also associated with a unique key constraint, one row at most will satisfy the criteria specified in the *DataRow-Collection* object's *Find* method.

The *DataView* class's *Find* method performs searches based on the column or columns specified in the *DataView* object's *Sort* property. Multiple rows of data might have the same values for the columns used to sort the data in the *DataView*. For example, you can sort customers based on the Country column, and multiple rows have a value of *Spain* in the Country column. But you can't use the *DataView* class's *Find* method to locate all customers in Spain because the *Find* method returns only an integer.

Thankfully, the *DataView* class also exposes a *FindRows* method. You call the *FindRows* method just as you call the *DataView* class's *Find* method, but the *FindRows* method returns an array of *DataRowView* objects that contains the rows that satisfied the criteria you specified.

The following code snippet shows how to use the *FindRows* method and checks whether the method found any rows:

Visual Basic

```
Dim strConn, strSQL As String
strConn = "Data Source=.\SQLExpress;" & _
          "Initial Catalog=Northwind;Integrated Security=True;"
strSQL = "SELECT CustomerID, City, Country FROM Customers"
Dim da As New SqlDataAdapter(strSQL, strConn)
Dim tbl As New DataTable("Customers")
da.Fill(tbl)
Dim vue As New DataView(tbl)

vue.Sort = "Country"
Dim aRows As DataRowView() = vue.FindRows("Spain")
If aRows.Length = 0 Then
    Console.WriteLine("No rows found!")
Else
    For Each row As DataRowView In aRows
        Console.WriteLine(row("City"))
    Next row
End If
```

Visual C#

```
string strConn, strSQL; strConn = @"Data Source=.\SQLExpress;" +
          "Initial Catalog=Northwind;Integrated Security=True;";
strSQL = "SELECT CustomerID, City, Country FROM Customers";
SqlDataAdapter da = new SqlDataAdapter(strSQL, strConn);
DataTable tbl = new DataTable("Customers");
da.Fill(tbl);
DataView vue = new DataView(tbl);

vue.Sort = "Country";
```

```
DataRowView[] aRows = vue.FindRows("Spain");
if (aRows.Length == 0)
    Console.WriteLine("No rows found!");
else
    foreach (DataRowView row in aRows)
        Console.WriteLine(row["City"]);
```

Modifying *DataRowView* Objects

Modifying a row of data using a *DataRowView* object is similar to modifying the contents of a *DataRow* object. The *DataRowView* class exposes *BeginEdit*, *EndEdit*, *CancelEdit*, and *Delete* methods, just as the *DataRow* class does.

Creating a new row of data using a *DataRowView* object is slightly different from creating a new *DataRow*. The *DataView* has an *AddNew* method that returns a new *DataRowView* object. The new row is not actually added to the underlying *DataTable* until you call the *EndEdit* method of the *DataRowView* object.

The following code snippet shows how to create, modify, and delete a row of data using the *DataRowView* class:

Visual Basic
```
Dim tbl As New DataTable("Customers")
tbl.Columns.Add("CustomerID", GetType(String))
tbl.Columns.Add("CompanyName", GetType(String))
tbl.Columns.Add("ContactName", GetType(String))
Dim vue As New DataView(tbl)

'Add a new row.
Dim row As DataRowView = vue.AddNew()
row("CustomerID") = "ABCDE"
row("CompanyName") = "New Company"
row("ContactName") = "New Contact"
row.EndEdit()

'Modify a row.
row.BeginEdit()
row("CompanyName") = "Modified"
row.EndEdit()

'Delete a row.
row.Delete()
```

Visual C#
```
DataTable tbl = new DataTable("Customers");
tbl.Columns.Add("CustomerID", typeof(string));
tbl.Columns.Add("CompanyName", typeof(string));
tbl.Columns.Add("ContactName", typeof(string));
DataView vue = new DataView(tbl);
```

```
//Add a new row.
DataRowView row = vue.AddNew();
row["CustomerID"] = "ABCDE";
row["CompanyName"] = "New Company";
row["ContactName"] = "New Contact";
row.EndEdit();

//Modify a row.
row.BeginEdit();
row["CompanyName"] = "Modified";
row.EndEdit();

//Delete a row.
row.Delete();
```

Using a *DataView* to Create a New *DataTable*

The ADO.NET team received countless requests to give the *DataView* class the ability to create a new *DataTable* that contained just the rows currently visible in the *DataView*. This request was made primarily by developers who are using the *DataSet* to maintain cached data, often in a Web service, and who wanted to return just the rows visible through a filter.

So, the ADO.NET team added a *ToTable* method on the *DataView* class. This method returns a *DataTable* that contains just the rows visible through the *DataView*'s *RowFilter* property and offers a number of overloads. You can use the various overloads to control the new *Data-Table*'s *TableName* property, the *DataColumns* that will appear in the resulting *DataTable*, and even whether or not the resulting *DataTable* contains only unique rows based on those *DataColumns*.

Let's start by looking at some code that retrieves information for all customers into a *Data-Table*, then uses a *DataView* to find just the customers in a particular country (Spain), and then uses the *ToTable* method to create a new *DataTable* containing just those customers:

Visual Basic
```
Dim strConn, strSQL As String
strConn = "Data Source=.\SQLExpress;" & _
        "Initial Catalog=Northwind;Integrated Security=True;"
strSQL = "SELECT CustomerID, CompanyName, City, Country " & _
        "FROM Customers"
Dim da As New SqlDataAdapter(strSQL, strConn)
Dim tblAllCustomers As New DataTable("Customers")
da.Fill(tblAllCustomers)

'Create a DataView so only the Spanish customers are available
Dim vue As New DataView(tblAllCustomers)
vue.RowFilter = "Country = 'Spain'"

'Create a new DataTable based on the DataView and show its contents
Dim tblSpanishCustomers As DataTable = vue.ToTable("SpanishCustomers")
Console.WriteLine("TableName: {0}", tblSpanishCustomers.TableName)
```

```
Console.WriteLine("Rows:")
For Each row As DataRow In tblSpanishCustomers.Rows
    Console.WriteLine("  {0}, {1}", row("City"), row("Country"))
Next row
```

Visual C#

```
//Create and fill a DataTable
string strConn, strSQL;
strConn = @"Data Source=.\SQLExpress;" +
          "Initial Catalog=Northwind;Integrated Security=True;";
strSQL = "SELECT CustomerID, CompanyName, City, Country " +
         "FROM Customers";
SqlDataAdapter da = new SqlDataAdapter(strSQL, strConn);
DataTable tblAllCustomers = new DataTable("Customers");
da.Fill(tblAllCustomers);
//Create a DataView so only the Spanish customers are available
DataView vue = new DataView(tblAllCustomers);
vue.RowFilter = "Country = 'Spain'";
//Create a new DataTable based on the DataView and show its contents
DataTable tblSpanishCustomers = vue.ToTable("SpanishCustomers");
Console.WriteLine("TableName: {0}", tblSpanishCustomers.TableName);
Console.WriteLine("Rows:");
foreach (DataRow row in tblSpanishCustomers.Rows)
    Console.WriteLine("  {0}, {1}", row["City"], row["Country"]);
```

The previous code snippet displayed only the City and Country columns, but the *DataTable* we created by calling *ToTable* also contained other columns—*CustomerID* and *CompanyName*. We can control the columns in the resulting *DataTable* by using one of two overloads of the *ToTable* method that take an array of strings for the column names to include in the new *DataTable*. Both overloads also expose a *Boolean* parameter to indicate whether you want the resulting *DataTable* to contain only unique values for the collection of columns. The previous code snippet returned multiple customers from Madrid.

The following code uses the *DataView* class's *ToTable* method to restrict the columns returned in the resulting *DataTable*. The original *DataTable* contains *DataColumns* for CustomerID, CompanyName, City, and Country. The resulting *DataTable* contains *DataColumns* only for City and Country. The code snippet also uses the *Distinct* parameter in the *ToTable* method to make sure that only distinct sets of values for City and Country are returned.

The uniqueness restriction is applied to the entire row in the new *DataTable*. In other words, the combination of City and Country must be unique. There's a city named Vancouver in the Canadian province of British Columbia (BC) and one in the American state of Washington (WA). If we were searching for customers in North America and set the *Distinct* parameter in the *ToTable* method to true, the resulting *DataTable* could contain one customer row from Vancouver, BC, as well as one from Vancouver, WA.

Yes, I know that's a fairly roundabout explanation, especially because the filter in our sample looks for customers in Spain. Let's get back to the code. In the previous example, there were multiple customers from Madrid. We can use the overloaded *ToTable* method to return unique sets of values for the City and Country columns:

Visual Basic

```vbnet
'Create and fill a DataTable
Dim strConn, strSQL As String
strConn = "Data Source=.\SQLExpress;" & _
          "Initial Catalog=Northwind;Integrated Security=True;"
strSQL = "SELECT CustomerID, CompanyName, City, Country " & _
         "FROM Customers"
Dim da As New SqlDataAdapter(strSQL, strConn)
Dim tblAllCustomers As New DataTable("Customers")
da.Fill(tblAllCustomers)
'Create a DataView so only the Spanish customers are available
Dim vue As New DataView(tblAllCustomers)
vue.RowFilter = "Country = 'Spain'"
'Create a new DataTable based on the DataView
'that contains only the City and Country columns
'and only unique sets of values for those columns
Dim tblSpanishCustomers As DataTable
tblSpanishCustomers = vue.ToTable("SpanishCustomers", True, _
                                  New String() { "City", "Country" })
Console.WriteLine("TableName: {0}", tblSpanishCustomers.TableName)
Console.WriteLine("Columns:")
For Each col As DataColumn In tblSpanishCustomers.Columns
    Console.WriteLine("  {0}", col.ColumnName)
Next col
Console.WriteLine()
Console.WriteLine("Rows:")
For Each row As DataRow In tblSpanishCustomers.Rows
    Console.WriteLine("  {0}, {1}", row("City"), row("Country"))
Next row
```

Visual C#

```csharp
//Create and fill a DataTable
string strConn, strSQL;
strConn = @"Data Source=.\SQLExpress;" +
          "Initial Catalog=Northwind;Integrated Security=True;";
strSQL = "SELECT CustomerID, CompanyName, City, Country " +
         "FROM Customers";
SqlDataAdapter da = new SqlDataAdapter(strSQL, strConn);
DataTable tblAllCustomers = new DataTable("Customers");
da.Fill(tblAllCustomers);
//Create a DataView so only the Spanish customers are available
DataView vue = new DataView(tblAllCustomers);
vue.RowFilter = "Country = 'Spain'";
//Create a new DataTable based on the DataView
//that contains only the City and Country columns
//and only unique sets of values for those columns
DataTable tblSpanishCustomers;
tblSpanishCustomers = vue.ToTable("SpanishCustomers", true,
                          new string[] { "City", "Country" });
Console.WriteLine("TableName: {0}", tblSpanishCustomers.TableName);
Console.WriteLine("Columns:");
foreach (DataColumn col in tblSpanishCustomers.Columns)
    Console.WriteLine("  {0}", col.ColumnName);
Console.WriteLine();
```

```
Console.WriteLine("Rows:");
foreach (DataRow row in tblSpanishCustomers.Rows)
    Console.WriteLine("  {0}, {1}", row["City"], row["Country"]);
```

Creating *DataView* Objects in Microsoft Visual Studio

Creating a *DataView* object is much simpler than creating a *DataTable*. You don't have to add columns and data types. You simply point the *DataView* at a *DataTable* and set the desired properties (*RowFilter*, *RowStateFilter*, *Sort*, and so on).

Adding a New *DataView* Object to Your Designer

With the release of Visual Studio 2005, the *DataView* is no longer on the Toolbox by default. However, you can right-click the Toolbox, select "Choose Items…" from the context menu, and then select *DataView* from the list of .NET Framework Components and it will once again appear on the Data tab of the Toolbox.

Once the *DataView* is available on the Toolbox, you can add a new *DataView* object to your designer by dragging the DataView item from the Toolbox and dropping the item onto the designer or the component tray. You can also simply double-click the DataView item in the Toolbox.

Setting Properties of Your *DataView* Object

Once you've created your new *DataView* object, you'll want to set a few of its properties. Visual Studio simplifies this process. As you can see in Figure 8-1, you can use the Properties window to select an available *DataTable* and set other available properties of the *DataView* object, such as *RowFilter*, *RowStateFilter*, and *Sort*.

Figure 8-1   Setting properties of the DataView object in Visual Studio

That's really all there is to it.

DataView Object Reference

In Table 8-2, you'll find all the properties of the *DataView* class.

Table 8-2   Properties of the *DataView* Class

Property	Data Type	Description
AllowDelete	*Boolean*	Specifies whether rows in the *DataView* can be deleted. (Default = True)
AllowEdit	*Boolean*	Specifies whether rows in the *DataView* can be edited. (Default = True)
AllowNew	*Boolean*	Specifies whether rows can be added to the *DataView*. (Default = True)
ApplyDefaultSort	*Boolean*	Specifies whether the default sort (primary key) is used. (Default = False)
Count	*Integer*	Returns the number of rows visible in the *DataView*. (Read-only)
DataViewManager	*DataViewManager*	Returns a reference to the *DataView* object's *DataViewManager*. (Read-only)
IsInitialized	*Boolean*	Indicates whether the *DataView* has been initialized.
Item	*DataRowView*	Returns a *DataRowView* that encapsulates a row of data visible through the *DataView*. (Read-only)
RowFilter	*String*	Contains a filter that specifies which rows in the *DataTable* are visible through the *DataView*. Similar to the WHERE clause in a SQL query. (Default = empty string)
RowStateFilter	*DataViewRowState*	Specifies what rows can be visible through the *DataView* as well as the version of the rows. (Default = Data-ViewRowState.CurrentRows)
Sort	*String*	Specifies the sort order of the rows visible through the *DataView*. (Default = empty string)
Table	*DataTable*	Returns the corresponding *DataTable* to which the *DataView* is bound.

AllowDelete, *AllowEdit*, and *AllowNew* Properties

DataView objects are often used in conjunction with bound controls. The *AllowDelete*, *AllowEdit*, and *AllowNew* properties simplify the process of restricting the types of changes that the user can make using the bound controls. Rather than setting properties on each of the bound controls, you can set these properties on just the *DataView*.

By default, each of these properties is set to *True* on the *DataView* object.

ApplyDefaultSort Property

The *ApplyDefaultSort* property is set to *False* by default. Setting it to *True* will sort the contents of the *DataView* according to the primary key of the *DataView* object's *DataTable*. If you set *ApplyDefaultSort* to *True*, the *DataView* object's *Sort* property will be set to the columns in the *DataTable* object's primary key. For example, if a *DataView* is bound to a *DataTable* that contains order detail information and whose primary key is the combination of the OrderID and ProductID columns, setting *ApplyDefaultSort* to *True* will implicitly set the *Sort* property of the *DataView* to *OrderID, ProductID.*

Count and *Item* Properties

The *Item* property returns a *DataRowView* object and is parameterized. When you call the *Item* property, you supply an integer that represents the row you want to retrieve. The following code snippet loops through the contents of the *DataView* by using the *Count* and *Item* properties:

Visual Basic

```vb
'Create and fill a DataTable
Dim strConn, strSQL As String
strConn = "Data Source=.\SQLExpress;" & _
          "Initial Catalog=Northwind;Integrated Security=True;"
strSQL = "SELECT CustomerID, CompanyName FROM Customers"
Dim da As New SqlDataAdapter(strSQL, strConn)
Dim tbl As New DataTable("Customers")
da.Fill(tbl)
'Create a DataView and display its contents
'Using DataRowViews and a For loop with the Count property
Dim vue As New DataView(tbl)
Dim row As DataRowView
For intCounter As Integer = 0 To vue.Count - 1
    row = vue(intCounter)
    Console.WriteLine(row("CompanyName"))
Next intCounter
```

Visual C#

```csharp
//Create and fill a DataTable
string strConn, strSQL;
strConn = @"Data Source=.\SQLExpress;" +
          "Initial Catalog=Northwind;Integrated Security=True;";
strSQL = "SELECT CustomerID, CompanyName FROM Customers";
SqlDataAdapter da = new SqlDataAdapter(strSQL, strConn);
DataTable tbl = new DataTable("Customers");
da.Fill(tbl);
//Create a DataView and display its contents
//Using DataRowViews and a for loop with the Count property
DataView vue = new DataView(tbl);
DataRowView row;
for (int intCounter = 0; intCounter < vue.Count; intCounter++)
{
    row = vue[intCounter];
    Console.WriteLine(row["CompanyName"]);
}
```

DataViewManager Property

If you created your *DataView* using the *CreateDataView* method of an instance of a *DataView-Manager* object, the *DataViewManager* property will return the *DataViewManager* object that created the *DataView*. Otherwise, the property will return an uninitialized *DataViewManager*.

For more information on the *DataViewManager* object, see the section titled "Questions That Should Be Asked More Frequently" later in the chapter.

IsInitialized Property

The *DataView* class supports the *IsInitialized* property as part of its implementation of the *ISupportInitializeNotification* interface. For more information, see the sidebar that describes the *ISupportInitializeNotification* interface following the *BeginInit* and *EndInit* methods of the *DataSet* class in Chapter 6.

RowFilter Property

The *RowFilter* property is similar to a WHERE clause in a SQL query. Only rows that satisfy the criteria in the property are visible through the view. The default for the *RowFilter* property is an empty string.

Simple filter that uses a column containing strings:
```
vue.RowFilter = "Country = 'Spain'"
```

Filter that uses a wildcard (displaying only rows whose CustomerID starts with *A*):
```
vue.RowFilter = "CustomerID LIKE 'A%'"
```

Delimiting dates:
```
vue.RowFilter = "OrderDate >= #01/01/2002# AND OrderDate < #02/01/2002#"
```

Delimiting the column name and handling the delimiter in the column value:
```
vue.RowFilter = "[Spaces In Column Name] = 'O''Malley'"
```

RowStateFilter Property

The *RowStateFilter* property affects the data visible through a *DataView* in two ways. It filters rows based on their *RowState*, and it controls the version of the row that's visible through the *DataView*. The *RowStateFilter* property accepts values and combinations of values from the *DataViewRowState* enumeration, as described earlier in the chapter.

You can set the *RowStateFilter* property using the *DataView* class's constructor. The default value for the *RowStateFilter* property is *CurrentRows*, which causes the view to display the current version of all rows in the *DataTable* that satisfy the criteria specified in the *DataView* object's *RowFilter* property and are not marked as deleted.

Sort Property

The *Sort* property controls the sort order of data visible in the *DataView*; it works much like the ORDER BY clause in a SQL query. You can create a sort order based on a single column or a combination of columns. By default, the rows are sorted in ascending order. To sort columns in descending order, you add the keyword *DESC* after the column name. Remember to delimit your column name if it contains a nonalphanumeric character (such as a space) or if the column name is a reserved word.

Simple sort by two columns (Country and then City):
```
vue.Sort = "Country, City"
```

Sorting in descending order:
```
vue.Sort = "OrderDate DESC"
```

Delimiting the column name:
```
vue.Sort = "[Space in ColumnName]"
```

By default, the *Sort* property is set to an empty string, which will display the contents of the *DataView* in the same order that they appear in the underlying *DataTable*. You can set this property using the *DataView* class's constructor.

Table Property

You use the *DataView* class's *Table* property to set or access the *DataTable* to which the *DataView* is bound. Changing the value of the *Table* property resets the *RowFilter* and *RowStateFilter* properties of the *DataView* to their respective default values.

You can also set the *Table* property using the *DataView* class's constructors.

As of this writing, setting the *Table* property to a *DataTable* whose *TableName* property is an empty string generates an exception.

Methods of the *DataView* Class

Table 8-3 lists the methods of the *DataView* class.

Table 8-3   Methods of the *DataView* Class

Method	Description
AddNew	Creates a new *DataRowView* object
BeginInit	Temporarily caches changes to the *DataView* object
CopyTo	Copies *DataRowView* objects to an array
Delete	Marks a *DataRowView* as deleted
EndInit	Commits cached changes to the *DataView* object
Find	Searches the *DataView* for a row of data
FindRows	Searches the *DataView* for multiple rows of data
ToTable	Creates a new *DataTable* that contains only the rows currently visible through the *DataView*

AddNew and *Delete* Methods

You can use the *AddNew* and *Delete* methods to add rows of data to and remove rows of data from the underlying *DataTable*. The *AddNew* method returns a new *DataRowView* object. Once you've set the values of the desired columns, you can call the *DataRowView* object's *EndEdit* method to add the row of data to the underlying *DataTable*.

You can use the *Delete* method to delete a row if you know the index of the row within the *DataView*. If you have a reference to the *DataRow* or the *DataRowView*, you can call the *Delete* method of the *DataRow* or *DataRowView* object instead. Remember that using the *Delete* method of any of these objects simply marks the row as deleted. To remove the row from the *DataTable*, you call the *AcceptChanges* method (of the *DataRow* or of the *DataTable* or *DataSet* that contains the row) or submit the change to your database using a *SqlDataAdapter*.

BeginInit and *EndInit* Methods

The *DataView* class supports the *BeginInit* and *EndInit* methods as part of its implementation of the *ISupportInitializeNotification* interface. For more information, see the sidebar that describes the *ISupportInitializeNotification* interface following the *BeginInit* and *EndInit* methods of the *DataSet* class in Chapter 6.

CopyTo Method

The *DataView* class exposes a *CopyTo* method that behaves like the *CopyTo* method of the *Array* object. You can copy the *DataRowView* objects available through the *DataView* to an array using the *CopyTo* method.

> **Note**   Developers who have experience using DAO, RDO, and ADO might assume that the *CopyTo* method behaves like *GetRows*, which returns the contents of the data structure as a two-dimensional array. Alas, this is not the case.

To be honest, I'm not sure how having an array of *DataRowView* objects helps. However, let's look at a code snippet that demonstrates using this method, on the off chance that someone will find a groundbreaking use for the feature. That person might remember how helpful this code snippet was and thank me profusely. I also accept cash.

Visual Basic
```
Dim strConn, strSQL As String
strConn = "Data Source=.\SQLExpress;" & _
        "Initial Catalog=Northwind;Integrated Security=True;"
strSQL = "SELECT CustomerID, CompanyName FROM Customers"
Dim da As New SqlDataAdapter(strSQL, strConn)
Dim tbl As New DataTable("Customers")
da.Fill(tbl)
Dim vue As New DataView(tbl)
Dim aRows As DataRowView()
```

```
aRows = CType(Array.CreateInstance(GetType(DataRowView), vue.Count), _
            DataRowView())
vue.CopyTo(aRows, 0)
For Each row As DataRowView In aRows
    Console.WriteLine(row("CompanyName"))
Next row
```

Visual C#
```
string strConn, strSQL;
strConn = @"Data Source=.\SQLExpress;" +
            "Initial Catalog=Northwind;Integrated Security=True;";
strSQL = "SELECT CustomerID, City, Country FROM Customers";
SqlDataAdapter da = new SqlDataAdapter(strSQL, strConn);
DataTable tbl = new DataTable("Customers");
da.Fill(tbl);

DataView vue = new DataView(tbl);
DataRowView[] aRows;
aRows = (DataRowView[]) Array.CreateInstance(typeof(DataRowView),
                                            vue.Count);
vue.CopyTo(aRows, 0);
foreach (DataRowView row in aRows)
    Console.WriteLine(row["CompanyName"]);
```

Find and *FindRows* Methods

The *DataView* allows you to locate one or more rows of data using its *Find* and *FindRows* methods. Both methods are overloaded to accept a single value or an array of values. The *DataView* uses the values specified to search its contents based on the columns specified in the *Sort* property, as shown here:

Visual Basic
```
Dim strConn, strSQL As String
strConn = "Data Source=.\SQLExpress;" & _
          "Initial Catalog=Northwind;Integrated Security=True;"
strSQL = "SELECT CustomerID, CompanyName, ContactName, " & _
          "Phone, City, Country FROM Customers"
Dim da As New SqlDataAdapter(strSQL, strConn)
Dim tbl As New DataTable("Customers")
da.Fill(tbl)
Dim vue As New DataView(tbl)

Console.WriteLine("Use the Find method to locate a row " & _
                  "based on the ContactName column")
vue.Sort = "ContactName"
Dim intIndex As Integer = vue.Find("Fran Wilson")
If intIndex = -1 Then
    Console.WriteLine("  Row not found!")
Else
    Console.WriteLine("  {0}", vue(intIndex)("CompanyName"))
End If
Console.WriteLine()

Console.WriteLine("Use the FindRows method to locate rows " & _
                  "based on the Country column")
```

```
vue.Sort = "Country"
Dim aRows As DataRowView() = vue.FindRows("Spain")
If aRows.Length = 0 Then
    Console.WriteLine("  No rows found!")
Else
    For Each row As DataRowView In aRows
        Console.WriteLine("  {0}", row("City"))
    Next row
End If
```

Visual C#

```
string strConn, strSQL;
strConn = @"Data Source=.\SQLExpress;" +
            "Initial Catalog=Northwind;Integrated Security=True;";
strSQL = "SELECT CustomerID, CompanyName, ContactName, " +
            "Phone, City, Country FROM Customers";
SqlDataAdapter da = new SqlDataAdapter(strSQL, strConn);
DataTable tbl = new DataTable("Customers");
da.Fill(tbl);
DataView vue = new DataView(tbl);

Console.WriteLine("Use the Find method to locate a row " +
                    "based on the ContactName column");
vue.Sort = "ContactName";
int intIndex = vue.Find("Fran Wilson");
if (intIndex == -1)
    Console.WriteLine("  Row not found!");
else
    Console.WriteLine("  {0}", vue[intIndex]["CompanyName"]);
Console.WriteLine();

Console.WriteLine("Use the FindRows method to locate rows " +
                    "based on the Country column");
vue.Sort = "Country";
DataRowView[] aRows = vue.FindRows("Spain");
if (aRows.Length == 0)
    Console.WriteLine("  No rows found!");
else
    foreach (DataRowView row in aRows)
        Console.WriteLine("  {0}", row["City"]);
```

ToTable Method

The ADO.NET team received countless requests to give the *DataView* class the ability to create a new *DataTable* that contained just the rows currently visible in the *DataView*. This request was made primarily by developers who are using the *DataSet* to maintain cached data, often in a Web service, and who wanted to return just the rows visible through a filter.

You can also use the *ToTable* method to control which *DataColumns* appear in the resulting *DataTable*, and apply uniqueness for those columns. For more information, see the examples earlier in the chapter.

Events of the *DataView* Class

Table 8-4 lists the events of the *DataView* class.

Table 8-4   Events of the *DataView* Class

Event	Description
Initialized	Fires when the *DataView*'s *EndInit* method is called
ListChanged	Fires when the *DataView*'s contents change

Initialized Event

The *DataView* class supports the *Initialized* event as part of its implementation of the *ISupport-InitializeNotification* interface. For more information, see the sidebar that describes the *ISupportInitializeNotification* interface following the *BeginInit* and *EndInit* methods of the *DataSet* class in Chapter 6.

ListChanged Event

The *DataView* class supports the *ListChanged* event as part of its implementation of the *IBindingList* interface. The *DataView* class's *ListChanged* event fires when the contents of the *DataView* change—such as when a row visible through the *DataView* is added, deleted, or modified; when a *SqlDataAdapter* fills the underlying *DataTable*; or when the *DataView* object's *RowFilter*, *RowStateFilter*, *Sort*, or *Table* property changes. Here's one example:

Visual Basic
```
'Imports System.ComponentModel
Dim vue As New DataView()
AddHandler vue.ListChanged, vue_ListChanged

Private Sub vue_ListChanged(ByVal sender As Object, _
                            ByVal e As ListChangedEventArgs)
    Console.WriteLine("ListChanged: {0}", e.ListChangedType)
End Sub
```

Visual C#
```
//using System.ComponentModel;

DataView vue = new DataView();
vue.ListChanged += new ListChangedEventHandler(vue_ListChanged);

private void vue_ListChanged(object sender, ListChangedEventArgs e)
{
    Console.WriteLine("ListChanged: {0}", e.ListChangedType);
}
```

Properties of the *DataRowView* Class

Apart from the Item property, the properties of the *DataRowView* class are read-only. Table 8-5 summarizes these properties.

Table 8-5   Properties of the *DataRowView* Class

Property	Data Type	Description
DataView	*DataView*	Returns the *DataView* to which the *DataRowView* belongs. (Read-only)
IsEdit	*Boolean*	Indicates whether the row is currently being modified. (Read-only)
IsNew	*Boolean*	Indicates whether the row is a new, pending row. (Read-only)
Item	*Object*	Sets or returns the contents of a column.
Row	*DataRow*	Returns the corresponding *DataRow* object for the *DataRowView*. (Read-only)
RowVersion	*DataRowVersion*	Returns the *RowVersion* of the corresponding *DataRow* that is visible via the *DataViewRow*. (Read-only)

DataView Property

The *DataView* property returns the *DataView* to which the *DataRowView* object belongs.

IsEdit and *IsNew* Properties

You can use the *IsEdit* and *IsNew* properties to determine whether the *DataRowView* object is currently being edited and what type of edit is being made.

If you're in the process of editing a new row (that is, you've created the new *DataRowView* using *DataView.AddNew* but haven't called *EndEdit* to add the row to the underlying *Data-Table*), *IsNew* will return *True* and *IsEdit* will return *False*. If you're editing a row that already exists in the table, *IsEdit* will return *True* and *IsNew* will return *False*.

Item Property

The *DataRowView* class's *Item* property offers much of the same functionality as the *DataRow* class's *Item* property. You can use the *DataRowView* class's *Item* property to modify or examine the contents of a column of data for that row. You can access the column by using its name or its ordinal value in the *Item* property.

Row Property

This property returns the *DataRow* object that corresponds to the *DataRowView* object. The *DataRowView* class doesn't offer all of the functionality available through the *DataRow* class.

For example, the *DataRowView* class doesn't expose methods such as *AcceptChanges* and *GetChanges*. If you need to work with features of the *DataRow* interface, you can use the *DataRowView* class's *Row* property.

RowVersion Property

If you're working with a row of data using the *DataRowView* interface and you want to determine which version of the data you're seeing through the *Item* property, you can check the *RowVersion* property of the *DataRowView*.

The *RowVersion* property is read-only and returns a value from the *DataRowVersion* enumeration.

Methods of the *DataRowView* Class

Table 8-6 summarizes the methods that the *DataRowView* class exposes.

Table 8-6   Methods of the *DataRowView* Class

Method	Description
BeginEdit	Begins the process of editing the row
CancelEdit	Cancels pending changes for the row
CreateChildView	Creates a new *DataView* containing only the child rows for the current row
Delete	Marks the row as deleted
EndEdit	Saves pending changes for the row

BeginEdit, *CancelEdit*, and *EndEdit* Methods

The *BeginEdit*, *CancelEdit*, and *EndEdit* methods of the *DataRowView* class work the same way as the corresponding methods of the *DataRow* class. If you call the *BeginEdit* method before modifying the row, your changes will not be committed to the row until you call *EndEdit*. If you want to discard the changes instead, you can call *CancelEdit*.

CreateChildView Method

Let's say you want to create a *DataView* object that displays only the related child rows for a particular row. If you're working with the customers and orders relation we've used throughout this book, setting up the new *DataView* is simple. You set the *Table* property to the orders *DataTable* and then set the *RowFilter* property to a string such as *CustomerID = 'ALFKI'*.

That sounds very straightforward. But what if you also need to check the column value (CustomerID) for delimiters? Or what if you're working with a relationship that's based on a combination of columns?

The *DataRowView* class offers a simpler and more elegant solution—using the *CreateChildView* method. You can call this method and supply either a relation name or a *DataRelation* object (such as the *GetChildRows* method on the *DataRow* object). The *CreateChildView* method will return a new *DataView* object that uses that relation as its filter.

The following code snippet shows how to use the *CreateChildView* method:

Visual Basic

```vb
'Create and fill a DataSet with customer and order information
Dim strConn, strSQL As String
strConn = "Data Source=.\SQLExpress;" & _
          "Initial Catalog=Northwind;Integrated Security=True;"
strSQL = "SELECT CustomerID, CompanyName FROM Customers " & _
         "      WHERE CustomerID LIKE 'A%';" & _
         "SELECT OrderID, CustomerID, OrderDate FROM Orders " & _
         "      WHERE CustomerID LIKE 'A%'"
Dim da As New SqlDataAdapter(strSQL, strConn)
da.TableMappings.Add("Table", "Customers")
da.TableMappings.Add("Table1", "Orders")
Dim ds As New DataSet()
da.Fill(ds)
Dim tblCustomers, tblOrders As DataTable
tblCustomers = ds.Tables("Customers")
tblOrders = ds.Tables("Orders")
Dim rel As DataRelation
rel = ds.Relations.Add("Customers_Orders", _
                       tblCustomers.Columns("CustomerID"), _
                       tblOrders.Columns("CustomerID"))
'Use a DataView to find the entry for a customer
'Then use DataRowView.CreateChildView to access the child rows
Dim vueCustomers, vueOrders As DataView
Dim rowCustomer As DataRowView
vueCustomers = New DataView(tblCustomers)
vueCustomers.Sort = "CustomerID"
rowCustomer = vueCustomers(vueCustomers.Find("ANTON"))
vueOrders = rowCustomer.CreateChildView(rel)
For Each rowOrder As DataRowView In vueOrders
    Console.WriteLine("{0} - {1:d}", rowOrder("CustomerID"), _
                      rowOrder("OrderDate"))
Next rowOrder
```

Visual C#

```csharp
//Create and fill a DataSet with customer and order information
string strConn, strSQL;
strConn = @"Data Source=.\SQLExpress;" +
          "Initial Catalog=Northwind;Integrated Security=True;";
strSQL = "SELECT CustomerID, CompanyName FROM Customers " +
         "      WHERE CustomerID LIKE 'A%';" +
         "SELECT OrderID, CustomerID, OrderDate FROM Orders " +
         "      WHERE CustomerID LIKE 'A%'";
SqlDataAdapter da = new SqlDataAdapter(strSQL, strConn);
da.TableMappings.Add("Table", "Customers");
da.TableMappings.Add("Table1", "Orders");
DataSet ds = new DataSet();
da.Fill(ds);
DataTable tblCustomers, tblOrders;
tblCustomers = ds.Tables["Customers"];
tblOrders = ds.Tables["Orders"];
DataRelation rel;
```

```
rel = ds.Relations.Add("Customers_Orders",
                       tblCustomers.Columns["CustomerID"],
                       tblOrders.Columns["CustomerID"]);
//Use a DataView to find the entry for a customer
//Then use DataRowView.CreateChildView to access the child rows
DataView vueCustomers, vueOrders;
DataRowView rowCustomer;
vueCustomers = new DataView(tblCustomers);
vueCustomers.Sort = "CustomerID";
rowCustomer = vueCustomers[vueCustomers.Find("ANTON")];
vueOrders = rowCustomer.CreateChildView(rel);
foreach (DataRowView rowOrder in vueOrders)
    Console.WriteLine("{0} - {1:d}", rowOrder["CustomerID"],
                      rowOrder["OrderDate"]);
```

Note   When you use the *CreateChildView* method to create a new *DataView*, the *RowFilter* property will return an empty string. However, only the expected child rows will be visible. How is this possible? Well, the new *DataView* object uses a feature that technical people like to refer to as "magic."

Delete Method

You can use the *DataRowView* class's *Delete* method to delete a row. Remember that the row will still exist in the *DataTable* and will be marked as deleted. The row will not actually be removed from the *DataTable* until you call *AcceptChanges* or submit the pending deletion to your database using a *SqlDataAdapter*.

Questions That Should Be Asked More Frequently

Q   How can I use ADO.NET features to generate a distinct list of values? I know I can use the *DataTable*'s Select method or the *DataView*'s *RowFilter* property to apply filters like "Country = 'Spain'" and I can use either feature to list values for the corresponding rows, but in each case the resulting list of values can contain duplicates. Is there any way to use ADO.NET to generate lists that omit duplicate values?

A   The *DataView* class's new *ToTable* method is designed to help you handle this scenario, which we covered earlier in the chapter. I've spoken with a number of developers who hadn't noticed the new method and/or did not realize it could be used to generate distinct values, so I figured it was worth covering again here.

If you were writing a pure SQL query, you could use the DISTINCT clause in the query. For example, if you wanted to list the cities for customers in Spain and omit duplicates, you could execute the following query:

```
SELECT DISTINCT City FROM Customers WHERE Country = 'Spain'
```

Using ADO.NET, you can display the desired values using a two-step process. First, construct a *DataView* whose *RowFilter* property applies the desired filter. Then, call the *DataView*'s *ToTable* method and specify *True* for the *Distinct* parameter, and the list of column names to include in the results. The following code snippet uses this process to display the distinct list of cities for customers in Spain:

Visual Basic

```
Dim strConn, strSQL As String
strConn = "Data Source=.\SQLExpress;" & _
          "Initial Catalog=Northwind;Integrated Security=True;"
strSQL = "SELECT CustomerID, City, Country FROM Customers"
Dim da As New SqlDataAdapter(strSQL, strConn)
Dim tbl As New DataTable()
da.Fill(tbl)
Dim vue As New DataView(tbl)
vue.RowFilter = "Country = 'Spain'"
For Each row As DataRow In vue.ToTable(True, "City").Rows
    Console.WriteLine(row("City"))
Next row
```

Visual C#

```
string strSQL, strConn;
strConn = @"Data Source=.\SQLExpress;" +
            "Initial Catalog=Northwind;Trusted_Connection=Yes;";
strSQL = "SELECT CustomerID, City, Country FROM Customers";
SqlDataAdapter da = new SqlDataAdapter(strSQL, strConn);
DataTable tbl = new DataTable();
da.Fill(tbl);

DataView vue = new DataView(tbl);
vue.RowFilter = "Country = 'Spain'";
foreach (DataRow row in vue.ToTable(true, "City").Rows)
    Console.WriteLine(row["City"]);
```

Q   How do I determine which method to use to search for data in my *DataTable*?

A   That depends on what type of search you want to perform and what you want to do with the results of the search. Here's a simple set of guidelines:

- ■   If you need to locate a row based on its primary key value(s), use *DataTable.Rows.Find*.

- ■   If you need to bind controls to the rows that satisfy your search criteria, use a *DataView*.

- ■   If you're going to perform repeated searches against a non-key column or combination of columns, use *DataView.Find*.

- ■   In all other situations, use the *DataTable.Select* method.

Q   Setting up a *DataView* in code is relatively simple, so is there really any benefit to setting it up at design time using Visual Studio?

A   I'm so glad you asked. Creating *DataView* objects using Visual Studio offers two major benefits over creating them in code. First, if you're creating the *DataView* for use with bound controls, you can bind the controls to the *DataView* at design time if you also create the *DataView* at design time. Personally, I'd rather set these properties at design time with mouse clicks than write code.

Visual Studio actually creates a *DataView* for you behind the scenes, which leads us to the second major benefit. As you set properties using the Properties window, Visual Studio applies your input to the *DataView* object you created. If you set a property incorrectly by making a typo in the column name or by forgetting to include that column in the *DataTable*, Visual Studio will alert you to this at design time. Believe it or not, the information in the alert, shown in Figure 8-2, is actually helpful. If you make a similar mistake in straight code, the code will compile successfully and you won't realize your error until you run your application.

Figure 8-2   An alert generated by an invalid column name entered in a *DataView* at design time in Visual Studio

Q   What is the purpose of the *DataViewManager* class?

A   The *DataViewManager* class is a container that contains *DataViewSetting* objects, which are somewhat similar to *DataView* objects but have less functionality. I've yet to see a significant scenario in which you can use the *DataViewManager* but not the *DataView*. For that reason, I'm not covering the *DataViewManager* class in more detail in this book, except for the brief example of the *DataSet*'s *DefaultViewManager* property in the reference section of Chapter 6.

Q   How do I locate a row in a *DataView* if I need to perform a search on a column other than the one that's referenced in the *DataView* object's *Sort* property?

A   This is a fairly common scenario when you're using bound controls on a *Windows form*. Unfortunately, neither the *DataView* nor the *Windows form*'s data binding objects offer functionality to handle this scenario elegantly.

Let's say you have a grid bound to a *DataView* that shows customer information sorted by the Country column. You want to let the user locate a customer based on another column such as *ContactName*. Figure 8-3 shows such a form.

Figure 8-3   Customer information sorted by country

Remember that the goal is to programmatically locate the desired row in the grid, not just to locate the desired *DataRow*. In the figure, the currently selected row has a value of *Aria Cruz* for the ContactName column and a value of *Brazil* for the Country column.

So, first we need to find the row whose ContactName column contains Aria Cruz. Then we need to find the value for the Country column in that row. Last, we need to look through the rows in the *DataView* that have the desired value for the Country column until we find the row we're looking for.

We can perform the first step, finding the row whose ContactName contains Aria Cruz, by using the *Select* method of the *DataTable* or using the *Find* method of a *DataView*. Let's opt for the latter. We'll need a new *DataView* whose *Sort* property is set to the *ContactName* column. Then we can use the *Find* method to determine the index of the desired row within the *Data-View*. With that information, we can access the desired *DataRow* and determine the country for that customer as well. The following code snippet does all this:

Visual Basic

```
'Fill the DataTable with customer information
Dim strConn, strSQL As String
strConn = "Data Source=.\SQLExpress;" & _
          "Initial Catalog=Northwind;Integrated Security=True;"
strSQL = "SELECT CustomerID, CompanyName, ContactName, " & _
          "Phone, City, Country FROM Customers"
Dim da As New SqlDataAdapter(strSQL, strConn)
Dim tbl As New DataTable("Customers")
da.Fill(tbl)
'To locate the row based on the contact name
'Create a DataView, sorted by the ContactName column
'Then use the DataView's Find method to find the index
Dim vueByContactName As New DataView(tbl)
vueByContactName.Sort = "ContactName"
Dim indexContactName As Integer
indexContactName = vueByContactName.Find("Aria Cruz")
```

```vb
'Use the DataRowView's Row property to find the desired DataRow
Dim rowToFind As DataRow = vueByContactName(indexContactName).Row
Dim strCountry As String = CStr(rowToFind("Country"))
...
```

Visual C#

```csharp
//Fill the DataTable with customer information
string strConn, strSQL;
strConn = @"Data Source=.\SQLExpress;" +
          "Initial Catalog=Northwind;Integrated Security=True;";
strSQL = "SELECT CustomerID, CompanyName, ContactName, " +
         "Phone, City, Country FROM Customers";
SqlDataAdapter da = new SqlDataAdapter(strSQL, strConn);
DataTable tbl = new DataTable("Customers");
da.Fill(tbl);
//To locate the row based on the contact name
//Create a DataView, sorted by the ContactName column
//Then use the DataView's Find method to find the index
DataView vueByContactName = new DataView(tbl);
vueByContactName.Sort = "ContactName";
int indexContactName = vueByContactName.Find("Aria Cruz");
//Use the DataRowView's Row property to find the desired DataRow
DataRow rowToFind = vueByContactName[indexContactName].Row;
string strCountry = (string) rowToFind["Country"];
...
```

This is only half the job. Remember that the goal is to find the desired entry in a *DataView* sorted by Country. As you can see in Figure 8-3, there are multiple rows with the same value for the Country column as our desired row. Since the Country column is not unique, we'll need to use the *DataView*'s *FindRows* method. We'll then need to iterate through the array of *DataRowViews* returned by *FindRows* until we find a *DataRowView* whose *Row* property matches the *DataRow* we found earlier.

Visual Basic

```vb
...
'Find the desired DataRowView in the DataView sorted by Country
Dim vueByCountry As New DataView(tbl)
vueByCountry.Sort = "Country"
Dim rowviewFound As DataRowView = Nothing
For Each rowview As DataRowView In vueByCountry.FindRows(strCountry)
    If rowview.Row Is rowToFind Then
        rowviewFound = rowview
        Exit For
    End If
Next rowview

'Write the CustomerID column for the DataRowView to the Console
Console.WriteLine(rowviewFound("CustomerID"))
...
```

Visual C#

```csharp
...
//Find the desired DataRowView in the DataView sorted by Country
DataView vueByCountry = new DataView(tbl);
vueByCountry.Sort = "Country";
```

```
DataRowView rowviewFound = null;
foreach (DataRowView rowview in vueByCountry.FindRows(strCountry))
    if (rowview.Row == rowToFind) {
        rowviewFound = rowview;
        break;
    }

//Write the CustomerID column for the DataRowView to the Console
Console.WriteLine(rowviewFound["CustomerID"]);
...
```

Now, for a little bit of extra credit, we can also find the index of the entry within the *DataView* sorted by Country. Knowing the index can be helpful if you want to set the *Position* property of a *CurrencyManager* class, part of the *Windows forms* data binding feature set. The *DataView* class implements the *IList* interface, which is in the *System.Collections* namespace. We can cast the *DataView* to an *IList* and use its *IndexOf* method to find the index of the desired entry, as shown in the following code:

Visual Basic

```
...
'Imports System.Collections
'Cast the DataView to IList and call IndexOf to find the index
Dim indexCountry As Integer
indexCountry = CType(vueByCountry, IList).IndexOf(rowviewFound)

'Write the index to the Console window
'Then use the index to prove it's correct
Console.WriteLine(indexCountry)
Console.WriteLine(vueByCountry(indexCountry)("CustomerID"))
```

Visual C#

```
...
//using System.Collections;
//Cast the DataView to IList and call IndexOf to find the index
int indexCountry = ((IList) vueByCountry).IndexOf(rowviewFound);

//Write the index to the Console window
//Then use the index to prove it's correct
Console.WriteLine(indexCountry);
Console.WriteLine(vueByCountry[indexCountry]["CustomerID"]);
```

Chapter 9

Working with Strongly Typed *DataSet* Objects and *TableAdapters*

In this chapter, you'll learn about features built into Microsoft Visual Studio that can simplify the process of filling a *DataSet* and accessing its contents. Strongly typed *DataSets*, which were introduced in Visual Studio 2002 and version 1.0 of the .NET Framework, extend the basic *DataSet* class and make tables and columns of information available through properties and methods. *TableAdapters*, introduced in Visual Studio 2005, complement strongly typed *DataSets* by offering *Fill* and *Update* methods intended for specific *Data-Tables* within a strongly typed *DataSet*.

This chapter will cover the major features and scenarios for both strongly typed *DataSets* and *Table-Adapters*. Along the way, you'll learn how to add your own code to these classes to extend their functionality. As with many designer-generated classes, strongly typed *DataSets* and *TableAdapters* have their own strengths and weaknesses. This chapter will help identify those strengths and weaknesses so that you can make intelligent decisions about when (or if) to use these features.

Strongly Typed *DataSets*

Over the past three chapters, you've learned how to create and use *DataSet* objects. The code used to access the contents of a *DataSet* is programmatically similar to code for accessing earlier objects such as the ADO and DAO *Recordset* objects, as you can see by comparing the following examples:

ADO.NET and Visual Basic

```
Dim strCompanyName As String
strCompanyName = CStr(tblCustomers.Rows(0)("CompanyName"))
```

ADO.NET and Visual C#

```
string strCompanyName;
strCompanyName = (string) tblCustomers.Rows[0]["CompanyName"];
```

ADO, DAO, and Visual Basic "Classic"

```
Dim strCompanyName As String
strCompanyName = rs.Fields("CompanyName").Value
```

Developers have been writing this kind of code since the early days of Visual Basic. Technically, there's nothing wrong with this code; it works. But that doesn't mean we can't improve on the old coding techniques.

To help you write data access code more easily, Microsoft Visual Studio 2002 introduced strongly typed *DataSet* objects, allowing you to write code that looks like this instead:

Visual Basic

```
Dim strCompanyName As String
strCompanyName = ds.Customers(0).CompanyName
```

Visual C#

```
string strCompanyName;
strCompanyName = ds.Customers[0].CompanyName;
```

In this code, the *CompanyName* property returns the contents of the CompanyName column as a string.

You can think of a strongly typed *DataSet* as a *DataSet* with class. More specifically, a strongly typed *DataSet* is a class that inherits from the *DataSet* class and also includes properties and methods based on the schema you specify. This class also contains other classes for your *DataTable* objects and *DataRow* objects.

These classes, combined with the Microsoft IntelliSense drop-downs available in Visual Studio, enable you to write data access code more efficiently. For example, each strongly typed *DataTable* class includes strongly typed *Add* and *Find* methods. If you're working with customer information, the *Add* method would accept parameters for each column in the *DataTable* (CustomerID, CompanyName, and so on) and the *Find* method would accept a value for the CustomerID column.

You can also build user interfaces more quickly in Visual Studio by using strongly typed *DataSets*. The schema for a strongly typed *DataSet* is already defined at design time, so you can create bound controls at design time without having to write any code. We'll take a closer look at creating bound controls for Microsoft Windows applications in Chapter 13, and for Web applications in Chapter 14.

Visual Studio 2005 has taken the concept of the strongly typed *DataSet* further by adding *TableAdapters*, classes that roughly resemble strongly typed *SqlDataAdapters*. You can use a *TableAdapter* to quickly fill a strongly typed *DataSet* with the results of a query, or submit the pending changes stored in a strongly typed *DataSet*. The *TableAdapter* already knows how to connect to your database, execute the query to retrieve data, and submit pending changes. We'll discuss *TableAdapters* in more detail later in the chapter.

Creating Strongly Typed *DataSet* Objects

So how do you create a strongly typed *DataSet* class? You can choose one of two basic approaches. One involves writing code and using a command-line tool that's part of the .NET Framework SDK. The other approach, which is much simpler, relies on the Visual Studio development environment and doesn't require you to open a Command window.

The Hard Way

The .NET Framework SDK includes a command-line utility called the XML Schema Definition Tool, which helps you generate class files based on XML schema (.xsd) files. You can use this utility in conjunction with the *DataSet* class's *WriteXmlSchema* method to translate your *DataSet* into a strongly typed *DataSet* class.

Using the *DataSet* Class's *WriteXmlSchema* Method

Later in this text, in Chapter 12, we'll take a closer look at the *DataSet* class's *WriteXmlSchema* method. You can use this method to create a file that contains schema information (tables, columns, constraints, and relationships) about your *DataSet*. The following code snippet builds a *DataSet* using columns from the Customers and Orders tables in the sample Northwind database. It also adds a *DataRelation* between the two *DataTable* objects before writing the schema for the *DataSet* to a file.

Visual Basic

```
Dim strConn, strSQL As String
strConn = "Data Source=.\SQLExpress;" & _
          "Initial Catalog=Northwind;Integrated Security=True;"
strSQL = "SELECT CustomerID, CompanyName FROM Customers;" & _
         "SELECT OrderID, CustomerID, OrderDate FROM Orders"
Dim da As New SqlDataAdapter(strSQL, strConn)
da.TableMappings.Add("Table", "Customers")
da.TableMappings.Add("Table1", "Orders")
Dim ds As New DataSet("NorthwindDataSet")
da.FillSchema(ds, SchemaTable.Mapped)
ds.Relations.Add("Customers_Orders", _
                 ds.Tables("Customers").Columns("CustomerID"), _
                 ds.Tables("Orders").Columns("CustomerID"))
ds.WriteXmlSchema("C:\NorthwindDataSet.XSD")
```

Visual C#

```
string strConn, strSQL;
strConn = @"Data Source=.\SQLExpress;" +
           "Initial Catalog=Northwind;Integrated Security=True;";
strSQL = "SELECT CustomerID, CompanyName FROM Customers;" +
         "SELECT OrderID, CustomerID, OrderDate FROM Orders";
```

```
SqlDataAdapter da = new SqlDataAdapter(strSQL, strConn);
DataSet ds = new DataSet("NorthwindDataSet");
da.FillSchema(ds, SchemaType.Mapped);
ds.Relations.Add("Customers_Orders",
                ds.Tables["Customers"].Columns["CustomerID"],
                ds.Tables["Orders"].Columns["CustomerID"]);
ds.WriteXmlSchema(@"C:\NorthwindDataSet.XSD");
```

> **Note**   The preceding code snippet uses the *SqlDataAdapter* class's *FillSchema* method.
> I generally advise developers to avoid using this method in their applications whenever
> possible. The purpose of the code snippet is to generate an .xsd file that contains *DataSet*
> schema information, so I consider it to be "design-time" code, which is exactly the type of
> scenario for which the method was created.

Using the XML Schema Definition Tool

The XML Schema Definition Tool is simply a file in the bin directory called XSD.exe. The
tool can generate class files based on XML schema (.xsd or .xdr) files. It can also create XML
schema files from libraries (.dll) and executables (.exe).

In the previous code snippet, we saved the schema for a *DataSet* to an .xsd file. Now let's use
the XML Schema Definition Tool to generate a class file based on this file. Open a Command
window and type the following:

> **Note**   To open a Command window, choose Programs, Accessories, Command Prompt
> from the Start menu. Or you can choose Run from the Start menu and then type **cmd.exe**.

Visual Basic
```
C:\>XSD.exe NorthwindDataSet.XSD /d /l:VB
```

Visual C#
```
C:\>XSD.exe NorthwindDataSet.XSD /d
```

> **Note**   You can either enter the full path to the XSD.exe file or add the .NET Framework
> SDK's bin directory to your system's *Path* environment variable. You'll also need to supply the
> appropriate path to your XML schema file.

The first parameter is the path to the XML schema file. The second parameter indicates that
the class we want to create is derived from the *DataSet* class. The Visual Basic example uses a
third parameter to specify the language for the output file. By default, the tool generates Visual
C# class files.

The XML Schema Definition Tool also offers other options that are documented in the .NET
Framework SDK. You can type **XSD /?** in the Command window to list the available options.

Now simply add your new class file to your project and then you can create an instance of your strongly typed *DataSet* class, as shown in the following code snippet:

Visual Basic
```
Dim ds As New NorthwindDataSet()
```

Visual C#
```
NorthwindDataSet ds = new NorthwindDataSet();
```

> **Note**   The name of your class is based on the *DataSetName* property of the *DataSet* used to generate your .xsd file. In the code snippet that generated the .xsd file, the *DataSetName* property is set to *NorthwindDataSet*, so that's also the name of our new strongly typed *DataSet* class.

The Easy Way

Creating a strongly typed *DataSet* class in Visual Studio is much simpler than the approach you saw in the previous example. There's no code to write and, best of all, no Command window.

To demonstrate how much easier it is to create a strongly typed *DataSet* class in Visual Studio, let's build the same strongly typed *DataSet* class that we built using code and the Command window in the previous section. Like the previous *DataSet*, the new *DataSet* will include two *DataTable* objects and a *DataRelation*.

The steps involved will be roughly equivalent to the ones we followed in Chapter 2, except that we'll skip the Data Source Configuration Wizard.

First, create a new Console application in your language of choice. In the screenshots that follow, I called the project Chapter09. Now select Project and then Add New Item from the Visual Studio menu. You'll see the dialog box shown in Figure 9-1. Select *DataSet* from the list of available items, and call the new item NorthwindDataSet.xsd before clicking Add.

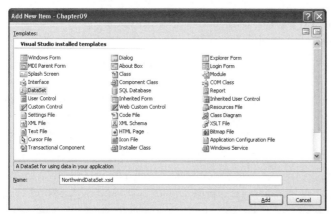

Figure 9-1   Adding a new *DataSet* to your project

You will now see an empty designer named NorthwindDataSet.xsd. We will then add tables and columns from the Server Explorer window to this designer. Doing so requires that you have a connection to your database established in Server Explorer. Just in case you do not already have a connection to your database established in Server Explorer, let's review how to create that connection.

Creating a Database Connection in Server Explorer

In Server Explorer, select the Data Connections node. Right-click this node and select Add Connection from the context menu. You could also click the Connect To Database button just above the Data Connections node. If this is the first time you've performed this action, you'll see the dialog box shown in Figure 9-2, which prompts you for information about the type of database to which you want to connect.

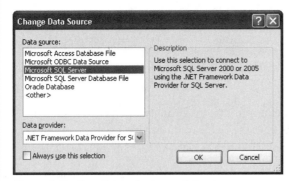

Figure 9-2   Specifying the type of database

This chapter will focus on working with the Northwind database on the local installation of Microsoft SQL Server Express, a Microsoft SQL Server database. If you do not have the sample Northwind database installed, see the "SQL Server for the Masses" sidebar in Chapter 2 to learn how to add this database to an instance of SQL Server. If you're not working with a Microsoft SQL Server database, select the type of database you want to use from the list and follow the subsequent dialog boxes.

If you've specified that you want to connect to a Microsoft SQL Server database, you'll see the dialog box shown in Figure 9-3.

To connect to the local instance of SQL Express, select ".\SQLExpress" in the Server Name drop-down list. The "." character is a shortcut of sorts that translates to the local machine. You could supply the machine name or the "(local)" shortcut, but the "." character requires less typing and takes up less space in code snippets. The "\" character separates the machine name from the name of the SQL Server instance, and the name of the SQL Express instance is "SQLExpress."

The dialog box assumes you'll connect to the SQL Server database using Windows Authentication. By default, installations of SQL Server 2005 and SQL Express require users to connect using their current Windows credentials rather than supplying a user name and password. If you want to log in using this second option, often called *SQL Server authentication*, select the Use SQL Server Authentication option and supply a user name and a password.

Figure 9-3   Connecting to a Microsoft SQL Server database

The dialog box also provides a drop-down list of available catalogs for the server. To connect to the Northwind database, select Northwind from this drop-down list. You could also select the Attach a database file option to supply your own database file.

There's a wealth of other options available when connecting to SQL Server. Clicking the Advanced button allows you to set additional properties for the connection—packet size, connection pooling information, and so on—using the dialog box shown in Figure 9-4. You can also click the Test Connection button and the dialog box will attempt to connect to the database by using the information you've provided. Once you've supplied information to connect to your database, click OK. Your new connection is now available in Server Explorer.

Now that you have a connection in Server Explorer, let's see how to add information to the strongly typed *DataSet*: Expand the connection node in Server Explorer and then expand the Tables folder and the Customers table. You could select the Customers table, and then drag the node over to the strongly typed *DataSet*'s designer. This would add a *DataTable* to your strongly typed *DataSet* that would include all columns from the Customers table. Adding all columns may be simple, but it may also be overkill if you're not interested in every column. Another option is to hold the Control button down and select just the columns you want in Server Explorer, and then drag those nodes onto the strongly typed *DataSet*'s designer. Select the CustomerID and CompanyName columns this way, and add them to your strongly typed *DataSet*.

Figure 9-4   Advanced connection options

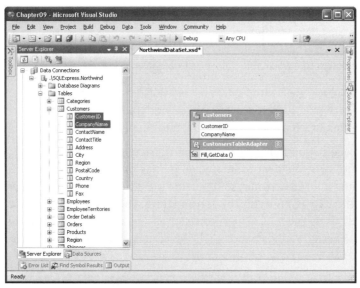

Figure 9-5   Adding customer columns to the strongly typed *DataSet*

Once you've performed this action, you'll see a new item in your strongly typed *DataSet*, as shown in Figure 9-5. The top half of this item is the Customers *DataTable*, which contains *DataColumns* for the columns you selected—CustomerID and CompanyName. The bottom half of this item, called *CustomersTableAdapter*, is something that Visual Studio calls a *TableAdapter*, a class that contains (rather than derives from) a *DataAdapter* such as a *SqlDataAdapter*. We'll talk about *TableAdapter*s later in this chapter.

Now let's add order information to the strongly typed *DataSet*. Drill down into the Orders table in Server Explorer. Multiselect the OrderID, CustomerID, and OrderDate columns, and drag the columns onto the strongly typed *DataSet*'s designer. Once you've completed this task, the strongly typed *DataSet*'s designer will look like the one shown in Figure 9-6.

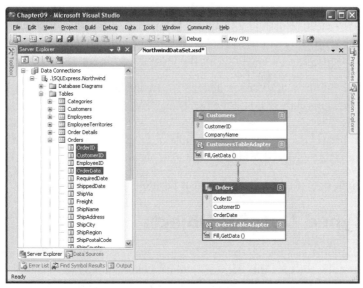

Figure 9-6   Adding related order information to the strongly typed *DataSet*

> **Note**   If you've used previous versions of Visual Studio, you may have noticed that the strongly typed *DataSet*'s designer now recognizes the relationship between the Customers and Orders table in the database.

That's it. No muss, no fuss. No oily residue. You can now create instances of your new strongly typed *DataSet* class in code, as you saw earlier.

When you generated your *DataSet*, Visual Studio went through the following steps to create your new strongly typed *DataSet* class:

1. Created a new instance of the *DataSet* class

2. Called the *FillSchema* method of all the *SqlDataAdapter* objects implicitly created by dragging columns from Server Explorer onto the strongly typed *DataSet* designer

3. Called the *WriteXmlSchema* method of the *DataSet*

4. Added the .xsd file to the project

5. Used the XML Schema Definition Tool to generate the strongly typed *DataSet* class based on the .xsd file

6. Added the new class file to the project

Where Is the Class File?

But where is the class file for the strongly typed *DataSet*? The schema file for your *DataSet* (NorthwindDataSet.xsd) will have three files associated with it. (If you do not see these files listed under the strongly typed *DataSet* node, click the Show All Files button at the top of the Solution Explorer window.) The first file will be the designer-generated class file for your strongly typed *DataSet*–either NorthwindDataSet.Designer.vb or NorthwindDataSet .Designer.cs, depending on your language of choice. The other files will have .xsc and .xss extensions, and they simply contain settings for the layout of your *DataSet* in the designer.

The class file actually contains many classes. There's the main class, NorthwindDataSet, which is derived from *DataSet*. This class exposes the two *DataTable* objects–Customers and Orders, each of which returns a class derived from *DataTable*, *CustomersDataTable*, and *OrdersDataTable*, respectively. Each of these classes (*CustomersDataTable* and *OrdersDataTable*) exposes rows through table-specific classes derived from *DataRow*, *CustomersRow*, and *OrdersRow*.

Now let's take a look at how to use a strongly typed *DataSet*.

Using Strongly Typed *DataSet* Objects

Strongly typed *DataSet* objects simplify the development process, making it easier to write code to access and modify the contents of your *DataSet*. Let's look at a few examples that compare working with data in a standard untyped *DataSet* versus working with a strongly typed *DataSet*.

Adding a Row

Each class for the *DataTable* objects in your *DataSet* offers two ways to add a new row to the *DataTable*. Calling *New<TableName>Row* returns a new strongly typed *DataRow* for your *DataTable*. You can then set values for columns in the row using properties of the strongly typed *DataRow*, as shown in the following code snippet:

Visual Basic
```
Dim ds As New NorthwindDataSet()
Dim tblCustomers As NorthwindDataSet.CustomersDataTable = ds.Customers

'Strongly-typed example
Dim rowCustomer As NorthwindDataSet.CustomersRow
rowCustomer = tblCustomers.NewCustomersRow()
rowCustomer.CustomerID = "NEWCO"
rowCustomer.CompanyName = "New Company"
tblCustomers.AddCustomersRow(rowCustomer)

' --or--

'Untyped example
Dim rowCustomer As DataRow = tblCustomers.NewRow()
rowCustomer("CustomerID") = "NEWCO"
rowCustomer("CompanyName") = "New Company"
tblCustomers.Rows.Add(rowCustomer)
```

Visual C#

```csharp
NorthwindDataSet ds = new NorthwindDataSet();
NorthwindDataSet.CustomersDataTable tblCustomers = ds.Customers;

//Strongly-typed example
NorthwindDataSet.CustomersRow rowCustomer = tblCustomers.NewCustomersRow();
rowCustomer.CustomerID = "NEWCO";
rowCustomer.CompanyName = "New Company";
tblCustomers.AddCustomersRow(rowCustomer);

// --or--

//Untyped example
DataRow rowCustomer = tblCustomers.NewRow();
rowCustomer["CustomerID"] = "NEWCO";
rowCustomer["CompanyName"] = "New Company";
tblCustomers.Rows.Add(rowCustomer);
```

The benefits of using the strongly typed *DataRow* in this example may not be clear when you see the code in print. Seeing this code in the Visual Studio development environment will provide a better demonstration.

Figure 9-7 is a snapshot of the development environment. It shows that the columns of the strongly typed *DataRow* are easily accessible through statement completion. I was thrilled when statement completion first appeared in Visual Basic version 5. However, statement completion does not automatically help you code strings. Our preceding untyped examples relied on supplying column names as strings. If you use this approach and forget or mistype a column name (say, "ConpanyName instead of "CompanyName"), you would not discover that mistake until you ran your application. Strongly typed *DataSet* objects and statement completion can all but eliminate such problems in the development cycle because the columns are available as properties on the strongly typed *DataRow*.

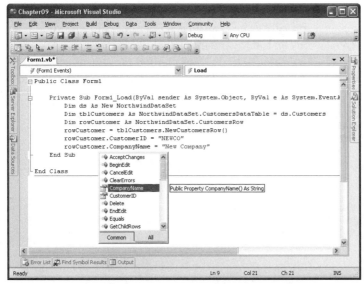

Figure 9-7   Using a strongly typed *DataSet* in code in Visual Studio

Like the *Add* method of the *DataRowCollection*, the *Add<TableName>Row* method of the strongly typed *DataTable* is overloaded. The following code snippet uses the Customers *DataTable* in the strongly typed *DataSet* we created earlier in the chapter:

Visual Basic

```
Dim ds As New NorthwindDataSet()
Dim tblCustomers As NorthwindDataSet.CustomersDataTable = ds.Customers

'Strongly typed example
tblCustomers.AddCustomersRow("NEWCO", "New Company")

'Untyped example
tblCustomers.Rows.Add(New Object() {"NEWCO", "New Company"})
```

Visual C#

```
NorthwindDataSet ds = new NorthwindDataSet();
NorthwindDataSet.CustomersDataTable tblCustomers = ds.Customers;

//Strongly typed example
tblCustomers.AddCustomersRow("NEWCO", "New Company");

//Untyped example
tblCustomers.Rows.Add(new object[] {"NEWCO", "New Company"});
```

Again, thanks to IntelliSense and statement completion, this is a feature that looks more impressive as you write code. In the Visual Studio development environment, the names of the parameters of the method appear as you type, so you don't have to jump back to other parts of your code to figure out the names and order of your columns.

Finding a Row

With a standard untyped *DataSet*, you can use the *Find* method of the *DataTable* object's *Rows* collection to locate a particular row based on its primary key value, or values. Using that *Find* method can be confusing, especially if the *DataTable* has a multicolumn primary key. For example, the Order Details table in the Northwind database uses the OrderID and ProductID columns as its primary key. Code that uses the *Find* method for a corresponding *DataTable* would therefore look like this:

Visual Basic

```
Dim tblDetails As DataTable
'Initialize the DataTable

Dim rowDetail As DataRow
rowDetail = tblDetails.Rows.Find(New Object() {10245, 7})
```

Visual C#

```
DataTable tblDetails;
//Initialize the DataTable

DataRow rowDetail;
rowDetail = tblDetails.Find(new object[] {10245, 7});
```

This code works, but it can be confusing to write. More importantly, it is difficult to read, which makes it challenging to maintain. If you've had some experience with the sample Northwind database, you may remember that the primary key for the Order Details table is defined by both the OrderID and ProductID columns, and that the first value supplied in the *Find* method represents an OrderID and the second value represents a ProductID. However, to someone who is not as familiar with the schema for the Northwind database, this code is fairly difficult to write and maintain.

Strongly typed *DataSets* make such code much easier to write and maintain because each *DataTable* class in a strongly typed *DataSet* exposes its own *Find* method if the *DataTable* has a primary key defined. In fact, the name of the strongly typed *Find* method includes the name or names of the column or columns defined in the *DataTable's PrimaryKey*. The following code snippet assumes you've added a *DataTable* for the Order Details table to your strongly typed *DataSet*.

Visual Basic

```
Dim ds As New NorthwindDataSet()
'Assume the DataSet has been filled with Order Detail rows

Dim tblDetails As NorthwindDataSet.Order_DetailsDataTable
tblDetails = ds.Order_Details
Dim rowDetail As NorthwindDataSet.Order_DetailsRow
rowDetail = tblDetails.FindByOrderIDProductID(10245, 7)
If rowCustomer Is Nothing Then
    Console.WriteLine("Row not found!")
Else
    Console.WriteLine("Item found with quantity {0}", _
                    rowDetail.Quantity)
End If
```

Visual C#

```
NorthwindDataSet ds = new NorthwindDataSet();
//Assume the DataSet has been filled with Order Detail rows

NorthwindDataSet.Order_DetailsDataTable tblDetails;
tblDetails = ds.Order_Details;
NorthwindDataSet.Order_DetailsRow rowDetail;
rowDetail = tblDetails.FindByOrderIDProductID(10245, 7);
if (rowDetail == null)
    Console.WriteLine("Row not found!");
else
    Console.WriteLine("Item found with quantity {0}",
                    rowDetail.Quantity);
```

Editing a Row

Editing rows in a strongly typed *DataSet* is similar to editing rows in a standard *DataSet*. You still have the option of using the *BeginEdit*, *EndEdit*, and *CancelEdit* methods. However, you can access the values of columns of the *DataRow* using properties of the strongly typed *DataRow*, as shown here:

Visual Basic

```
Dim ds As New NorthwindDataSet()
'Assume the DataSet contains Customer rows
Dim rowCustomer As NorthwindDataSet.CustomersRow = ds.Customers(0)

'Strongly typed example
rowCustomer.CompanyName = "Modified Company Name"

'Untyped example
rowCustomer("CompanyName") = "Modified Company Name"
```

Visual C#

```
NorthwindDataSet ds = new NorthwindDataSet();
//Assume the DataSet contains Customer rows
NorthwindDataSet.CustomersRow rowCustomer = ds.Customers[0];

//Strongly typed example
rowCustomer.CompanyName = "Modified";

//Untyped example
rowCustomer["CompanyName"] = "Modified";
```

Working with Null Data

In Chapter 6, you saw that you can use the *DataRow* class's *IsNull* function to check for null values and use *DBNull.Value* to assign null values to columns. The *IsNull* method is handy, but it still requires passing either the name, ordinal, or reference *DataColumn* you wish to check.

Strongly typed *DataSets* also make working with null values easier. Each strongly typed *DataRow* that can contain null values also includes two methods per column—one to check whether the column contains a null value, and one to set the column's value to null. The following code snippet works with the OrderDate column for a row of order information, so these methods are named *IsOrderDateNull* and *SetOrderDateNull*. The code checks to see if the value of the OrderDate column for the row is null. The code then sets the value to null if it was not previously set to null.

Visual Basic

```
Dim ds As New NorthwindDataSet()
'Assume the DataSet contains Order rows
Dim rowOrder As NorthwindDataSet.OrdersRow = ds.Orders(0)

'Strongly typed example
If Not rowOrder.IsOrderDateNull() Then
    rowOrder.SetOrderDateNull()
End If

'Untyped example
```

```
If Not rowOrder.IsNull("OrderDate") Then
    rowOrder("OrderDate") = DBNull.Value
End If
```

Visual C#

```
NorthwindDataSet ds = new NorthwindDataSet();
//Assume the DataSet contains Order rows
NorthwindDataSet.OrdersRow rowOrder = ds.Orders[0];

//Strongly typed example
if (!rowOrder.IsOrderDateNull()) then
    rowOrder.SetOrderDateNull();

//Untyped example
if (!rowOrder.IsNull("OrderDate"))
    rowOrder["OrderDate"] = DBNull.Value;
```

Working with Hierarchical Data

The *DataRow* class exposes two methods that let you navigate through your hierarchical data—*GetChildRows* and *GetParentRow*. These methods require you to supply either the name of the *DataRelation* you want to reference or the object itself.

If your strongly typed *DataSet* contains *DataRelation* objects, it will also contain methods that let you navigate through your hierarchical data without having to specify the *DataRelation* or its name. In the strongly typed *DataSet* we built, Visual Studio "automagically" added a *DataRelation* to relate the Customers and Orders *DataTable* objects. As a result, the *CustomersDataTable* class exposes a *GetOrdersRows* method and the *OrdersDataTable* class exposes a *GetCustomersRow* method.

The following code snippet uses the *GetOrdersRows* method to display all customers, as well as the orders for each customer.

Visual Basic

```
Dim ds As New NorthwindDataSet()
'Assume the DataSet contains Customer and Order rows
'and a DataRelation named FK_Orders_Customers

'Strongly typed example
Dim rowCustomer As NorthwindDataSet.CustomersRow
Dim rowOrder As NorthwindDataSet.OrdersRow
For Each rowCustomer In ds.Customers
    Console.WriteLine("Orders for {0}", rowCustomer.CompanyName)
    For Each rowOrder In rowCustomer.GetOrdersRows()
        Console.WriteLine("  {0} - {1:d}", rowOrder.OrderID, _
                          rowOrder.OrderDate)
    Next rowOrder
Next rowCustomer

' --or--
```

```
'Untyped example
Dim rowCustomer, rowOrder As DataRow
Dim rel As DataRelation = ds.Relations("FK_Orders_Customers")
For Each rowCustomer In ds.Tables("Customers").Rows
    Console.WriteLine("Orders for {0}", rowCustomer("CompanyName"))
    For Each rowOrder In rowCustomer.GetChildRows(rel)
        Console.WriteLine("  {0} - {1:d}", rowOrder("OrderID"), _
                          rowOrder("OrderDate"))
    Next rowOrder
Next rowCustomer
```

Visual C#

```
NorthwindDataSet ds = new NorthwindDataSet();
//Assume the DataSet contains Customer and Order rows
//and a DataRelation named FK_Orders_Customers

//Strongly typed example
foreach (NorthwindDataSet.CustomersRow rowCustomer in ds.Customers) {
    Console.WriteLine("Orders for {0}", rowCustomer.CompanyName);
    foreach (NorthwindDataSet.OrdersRow rowOrder
            in rowCustomer.GetOrdersRows())
        Console.WriteLine("   {0} - {1:d}", rowOrder.OrderID,
                          rowOrder.OrderDate);
}

// --or--

//Untyped example
DataRelation rel = ds.Relations["FK_Orders_Customers"];
foreach (DataRow rowCustomer in ds.Tables["Customers"].Rows) {
    Console.WriteLine("Orders for {0}", rowCustomer["CompanyName"]);
    foreach (DataRow rowOrder in rowCustomer.GetChildRows(rel))
        Console.WriteLine("    {0} - {1:d}", rowOrder["OrderID"],
                          rowOrder["OrderDate"]);
}
```

Other *DataSet*, *DataTable*, and *DataRow* Features

The classes that are part of the strongly typed *DataSet* derive from the *DataSet*, *DataTable*, and *DataRow* classes. This means you can also treat the classes as their untyped counterparts.

For example, the strongly typed *DataSet* classes do not have their own methods for reading and writing XML data and schema information. But because the classes are derived from the *DataSet* class, they still expose methods such as *ReadXml* and *WriteXml*. So for all other tasks, such as using a strongly typed *DataSet* in conjunction with *DataViews*, you can treat the strongly typed *DataSet* just like any other *DataSet*.

Adding Your Own Code

The component that generates strongly typed *DataSets* can't anticipate all your needs. You may want to add your own code to provide additional functionality. In this section, we'll look at an example of how you can add code to the strongly typed *DataSet* to improve performance. The actual increase in performance in this example is small, but that's not the point. Instead, the goal is to understand how you can add functionality. Thankfully, adding functionality to a strongly typed *DataSet* is now easier than it has ever been.

Partial Classes and Designer-Generated Code

Many developers added code or modified code to strongly typed *DataSet*s in Visual Studio 2002 and 2003 with mixed results. The main problem with this approach was that every change to the structure of the strongly typed *DataSet* caused Visual Studio to discard the existing class file and generate a new one. Thus, any changes made to the previous class file were lost.

Visual Studio 2005 now leverages partial classes to make scenarios like this one easier to handle. Partial classes, in case you're not familiar with them, represent a fairly simple concept. A partial class can span multiple files. For example, let's say you're building a Windows application. Visual Studio will maintain all designer-generated code (such as the creation and layout of all controls) in one file. The code you add to handle the *Load* event of the *Form* or the *Click* event of a *Button* will be stored in a separate file. This approach can make it easier to focus on just *your* code, and it makes it easier for Visual Studio to separate designer-generated code from developer-supplied code. For more information on partial classes, see the .NET Framework SDK.

In Chapter 2, I pointed out that you can often write better code than the Visual Studio designers. Let's look at an example of how you can apply the knowledge you've gained from previous chapters and improve on the designer-generated code in the strongly typed *DataSet*.

You may remember that in Chapter 7 we discussed the various overloads for the *DataRow* class's *GetChildRows* method. You could pass either a *DataRelation* object or a string that corresponds to the *RelationName* property on a *DataRelation* object. If you pass a string, you're forcing the *DataRow* to implicitly find the *DataRelation* in the *DataSet*'s collection of *Data-Relations* based on that string. In other words, in the following example, the first code snippet will run faster than the second one because the string lookup is done only once:

Visual Basic

```
Dim ds As New DataSet()
Dim strRelName As String = "FK_Orders_Customers"
Dim intNumOrders As Integer
'Assume the DataSet contains Customer and Order rows

'More performant
Dim rel As DataRelation = ds.Relations(strRelName)
For Each rowCustomer As DataRow In ds.Tables("Customers").Rows
    intNumOrders = rowCustomer.GetChildRows(rel).Length
Next rowCustomer
```

```
'Less performant
For Each rowCustomer As DataRow In ds.Tables("Customers").Rows
    intNumOrders = rowCustomer.GetChildRows(strRelName).Length
Next rowCustomer
```

Visual C#

```
DataSet ds = new DataSet();
string strRelName = "FK_Orders_Customers";
int intNumOrders;
//Assume the DataSet contains Customer and Order rows

//More performant
DataRelation rel = ds.Relations[strRelName];
foreach (DataRow rowCustomer in ds.Tables["Customers"].Rows)
    intNumOrders = rowCustomer.GetChildRows(rel).Length;

//Less performant
foreach (DataRow rowCustomer in ds.Tables["Customers"].Rows)
    intNumOrders = rowCustomer.GetChildRows(strRelName).Length);
```

Generally speaking, the code within the strongly typed *DataSet* is more efficient. For example, the code that returns the value for a column in a *DataRow* through a strongly typed property (*CustomerID*, *CompanyName*, and so on) performs a lookup using a reference to the *Data-Column* rather than the name of the column.

Unfortunately, the code to access related rows relies on string-based lookups using the name of the relation. You can see this code for yourself if you select the *GetOrdersRows* method in the sample from the "Working with Hierarchical Data" section earlier in the chapter, and then right-click the method and select Go To Definition.

The designer-generated code does a lot in one line of code, so it may be a little difficult to follow. I've made the logic a little easier to follow in the following code snippet. The code first locates the desired *DataRelation* using a string-based lookup, and then passes that *DataRelation* into the base *DataRow*'s *GetChildRows* method. Finally, the code casts the array of *DataRow* objects returned by *GetChildRows* to an array of strongly typed *DataRows*.

Visual Basic

```
Public Function GetOrdersRows() As OrdersRow()
    Dim rel As DataRelation
    rel = Me.Table.ChildRelations("FK_Orders_Customers")
    Return CType(MyBase.GetChildRows(rel), OrdersRow())
End Function
```

Visual C#

```
public OrdersRow[] GetOrdersRows() {
    DataRelation rel;
    rel = this.Table.ChildRelations["FK_Orders_Customers"];
    return ((OrdersRow[])(base.GetChildRows(rel)));
}
```

We can do better. The strongly typed *DataSet* already has a private field that contains the *DataRelation*, called *relationFK_Orders_Customers*. So we could change this code to access the *DataRow*'s *DataSet*, cast that *DataSet* to the strongly typed *DataSet* class, and access the private field to avoid the string-based lookup. That code would look like this:

Visual Basic

```
Public Function GetOrdersRows() As OrdersRow()
    Dim ds As NorthwindDataSet
    ds = CType(Me.Table.DataSet, NorthwindDataSet)
    Dim rel As DataRelation = ds.relationFK_Orders_Customers
    Return CType(MyBase.GetChildRows(rel), OrdersRow())
End Function
```

Visual C#

```
public OrdersRow[] GetOrdersRows() {
    NorthwindDataSet ds = (NorthwindDataSet) this.Table.DataSet;
    DataRelation rel = ds.relationFK_Orders_Customers;
    return ((OrdersRow[])(base.GetChildRows(rel)));
}
```

> **Note** In my tests, I found that changing the code this way increased the performance of the method by about 10 percent.

We could simply apply the changes to the designer-generated code. However, because this code was generated by the Visual Studio designers, any change to this code would be lost the next time the structure of the strongly typed *DataSet* changes. Instead, we can add this code to a partial class for the strongly typed *DataSet*. We'll also need to give the function a new name (such as *FasterGetOrdersRows*) so that it does not conflict with the designer-generated *GetOrdersRows* method. Because both methods are part of the same class, we can't simply override the designer-generated one.

To add the new method, right-click NorthwindDataSet.xsd in Solution Explorer and select View Code to create the partial class file. Once you've pasted the following code into the editor, you can call *FasterGetOrdersRows* rather than *GetOrdersRows* on your *CustomersRow* class from your code.

Visual Basic

```
Partial Public Class NorthwindDataSet
    Partial Public Class CustomersRow
        Public Function FasterGetOrdersRows() As OrdersRow()
            Dim ds As NorthwindDataSet
            ds = CType(Me.Table.DataSet, NorthwindDataSet)
            Dim rel As DataRelation = ds.relationFK_Orders_Customers
            Return CType(MyBase.GetChildRows(rel), OrdersRow())
        End Function
    End Class
End Class
```

Visual C#

```
partial public class NorthwindDataSet {
    partial public class CustomersRow {
        public OrdersRow[] FasterGetOrdersRows() {
            NorthwindDataSet ds = (NorthwindDataSet) this.Table.DataSet;
            DataRelation rel = ds.relationFK_Orders_Customers;
            return ((OrdersRow[])(base.GetChildRows(rel)));
        }
    }
}
```

When to Use Strongly Typed *DataSet* Objects

Every developer, both inside and outside of Microsoft, with whom I've spoken about strongly typed *DataSets* has been impressed by how strongly typed *DataSets* can simplify the development process. However, many developers still have reservations about using strongly typed *DataSets* in their applications.

Most of these developers have not looked at the code that the XML Schema Definition Tool generates, nor have they compared the performance of untyped and strongly typed *DataSet* objects. And you know what? I was one of those skeptical developers before I researched this chapter for the first edition. (What did I find? I'll get to that shortly.)

Software Components and Pocket Knives

A decade or three ago, I was a Boy Scout. There's an unwritten rule that every Boy Scout must own a pocket knife. Pocket knives came in handy on our camping trips. Most of the food we ate came out of cans, so the can opener blade got a lot of use. And you'd always find Scouts whittling wood around the campfire.

Some pocket knives have more gadgets than others. Thankfully, at least one Scout always had a knife that came with a pair of tweezers, because when you combine young boys and wood, you're bound to get splinters. At one point, I owned a pocket knife that had 20-some gadgets. It had everything but a squeegee to wash a car's windshield. I probably used two or three gadgets regularly, but the rest got little use because I had no need for them or they didn't work well.

Another unwritten rule says that children will lose small items and that the chances of the child losing an item are proportional to the cost of the item. At the end of any camping trip, at least one Scout would have lost a knife. When I lost my super-sized knife, I bought a nice but much more basic model. In fact, that knife lasted 20 years until the corkscrew, which saw more use in recent years than when I purchased the knife, broke. Luckily for me, the manufacturer replaced the entire knife as guaranteed by the warranty.

Why didn't I buy another knife with a plethora of gadgets when I was still a Boy Scout? Simple. The larger one, with a ton of features I never used, was more expensive and heavier.

I didn't buy the very simplest knife, however, because I did occasionally need a couple gadgets. So I bought a mid-size knife with just the gadgets I thought I would find useful.

Strongly typed *DataSets* definitely expose more functionality than do untyped *DataSets*. However, as with pocket knives, you won't always need the advanced features. If you're not going to use the additional gadgets, you're better off sticking with a more basic model.

The same premise holds true with software components. Simpler components are generally faster than the ones that offer a long list of features.

With that said, let's take a closer look at some benefits of using strongly typed *DataSets*.

Design-Time Benefits

I've already covered the most obvious design-time benefit of strongly typed *DataSet* objects: Writing code to access data in a strongly typed *DataSet* is much easier than with a standard untyped *DataSet*, thanks to statement completion and IntelliSense in Visual Studio.

There's also less code to write because the strongly typed *DataSet* class contains code to build the schema and to create the necessary *DataTable*, *DataColumn*, *DataRelation*, and *Constraint* objects in the class's initialization code. If you're using an untyped *DataSet*, you have three options for adding schema information to your *DataSet*: writing the code yourself, loading the schema from an .xsd file using the *DataSet* object's *ReadXmlSchema* method, or using a *SqlDataAdapter* object's *FillSchema* method. Of these three options, using *FillSchema* requires the least amount of work at design time (because *ReadXmlSchema* requires that you build your .xsd file). However, in Chapter 5, we discussed why you should avoid using this feature in your code whenever possible.

If you're building a Windows or Web application that uses data binding, it will be much easier to bind your controls at design time if you're using a strongly typed *DataSet*. Why? Because the strongly typed *DataSet* contains its own schema information, Visual Studio can provide you with a list of tables and columns to which you can bind your control.

Figure 9-8 shows the form created in Chapter 2 using the Data Source Configuration Wizard. As mentioned in Chapter 2, this wizard actually created a strongly typed *DataSet*. The designer added an instance of the strongly typed *DataSet* to the Form's components tray, along with an instance of a *BindingSource* (which we'll discuss in Chapter 13) for each *Data-Table* in the strongly typed *DataSet*. If you select the *TextBox* control for the Customer ID column and then go to the Properties window, expand the (DataBindings) node, and click the drop-down list for available values for *Text*, you'll see a list of available columns, as shown in the figure.

Strongly typed *DataSets* aren't just for data binding. Developers who build multitiered applications can gain design-time benefits by using strongly typed *DataSets*. When you add a reference to a class library or a Web service that returns a strongly typed *DataSet*, your project will have its own copy of the .xsd file and the class file for the strongly typed *DataSet*. Thus, the client application can still take advantage of the design-time benefits of strongly typed *DataSet* objects.

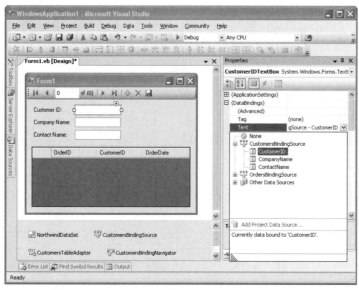

Figure 9-8   Binding a *TextBox* on a Windows Form to a column in a strongly typed *DataSet*

Run-Time Benefits

What are the run-time implications of using strongly typed *DataSet* objects? How do they affect the performance of your applications? Not only is it easier to write code to access the contents of a strongly typed *DataSet*, but that code can also improve the performance of your application. The following code snippet shows the standard way to assign the contents of a column to a string, using both an untyped and a strongly typed *DataSet*:

Visual Basic

```
Dim strCompanyName As String

'Untyped
Dim dsUntyped As New DataSet()
'Assumes the DataSet contains Customer rows
strCompanyName = dsUntyped.Tables("Customers").Rows(0)("CompanyName")

'Strongly typed
Dim dsTyped As New NorthwindDataSet()
'Assumes the DataSet contains Customer rows
strCompanyName = dsTyped.Customers(0).CompanyName
```

Visual C#

```
string strCompanyName;

//Untyped
DataSet dsUntyped = new DataSet();
//Assumes the DataSet contains Customer rows
strCompanyName =
  (string) dsUntyped.Tables["Customers"].Rows[0]["CompanyName"];
```

```
//Strongly typed
NorthwindDataSet dsTyped = new NorthwindDataSet();
'Assumes the DataSet contains Customer rows
strCompanyName = dsTyped.Customers[0].CompanyName;
```

The strongly typed code yields better performance. Exactly how much better will depend on your code. In the first edition of the book, I estimated that the code using the strongly typed *DataSet* ran nearly twice as fast. To verify that claim for the second edition, I wrote code that filled a *DataSet* with all rows and all columns from the Customers and Orders tables in the Northwind database. After filling the *DataSet*, I wrote code to access the values in all columns of all rows, comparing the performance of code that accesses the strongly typed *DataSet* to standard code that uses an untyped *DataSet*. Here's a snippet of that code that checks for *Null* values and uses the *Nullable* types new to version 2.0 of the .NET Framework to handle *Null* values in value data types such as *Integer*:

Visual Basic

```
Dim intOrderID As Integer
Dim strCustomerID As String
Dim intEmployeeID As Nullable(Of Integer)

'Strongly typed code
Dim dsStronglyTyped As New NorthwindDataSet()
'Fill the DataSet...

For Each rowOrder As NorthwindDataSet.OrdersRow _
                In dsStronglyTyped.Orders
    intOrderID = rowOrder.OrderID
    If rowOrder.IsCustomerIDNull() Then
        strCustomerID = Nothing
    Else
        strCustomerID = rowOrder.CustomerID
    End If
    If rowOrder.IsEmployeeIDNull() Then
        intEmployeeID = Nothing
    Else
        intEmployeeID = rowOrder.EmployeeID
    End If
    '...continue for all columns
Next rowOrder

'Untyped code
Dim dsUntyped As New DataSet()
'Fill the DataSet ...

For Each rowOrder As DataRow In dsUntyped.Tables("Orders").Rows
    intOrderID = CInt(rowOrder("OrderID"))
    If rowOrder.IsNull("CustomerID") Then
        strCustomerID = Nothing
    Else
        strCustomerID = CStr(rowOrder("CustomerID"))
    End If
    If rowOrder.IsNull("EmployeeID") Then
        intEmployeeID = Nothing
```

```
        Else
            intEmployeeID = CInt(rowOrder("EmployeeID"))
        End If
        '...continue for all columns
Next rowOrder
```

Visual C#

```csharp
int intOrderID;
string strCustomerID;
Nullable<int> intEmployeeID;

//Strongly typed code
NorthwindDataSet dsStronglyTyped = new NorthwindDataSet();
//Fill the DataSet ...

foreach (NorthwindDataSet.OrdersRow rowOrder in
        dsStronglyTyped.Orders) {
    intOrderID = rowOrder.OrderID;
    if (rowOrder.IsCustomerIDNull())
        strCustomerID = null;
    else
        strCustomerID = rowOrder.CustomerID;
    if (rowOrder.IsEmployeeIDNull())
        intEmployeeID = null;
    else
        intEmployeeID = rowOrder.EmployeeID;
    //...continue for all columns
}

//Untyped code
DataSet dsUntyped = new DataSet();
//Fill the DataSet ...

foreach (DataRow rowOrder in dsUntyped.Tables["Orders"].Rows) {
    intOrderID = (int) rowOrder["OrderID"];
    if (rowOrder.IsNull("CustomerID"))
        strCustomerID = null;
    else
        strCustomerID = (string) rowOrder["CustomerID"];
    if (rowOrder.IsNull("EmployeeID"))
        intEmployeeID = null;
    else
        intEmployeeID = (int) rowOrder["EmployeeID"];
    //...continue for all columns
}
```

As of this writing, version 2.0 of the .NET Framework has shipped, and, in the tests I've run, typical code that uses the strongly typed *DataSet* runs approximately four times as fast as typical code that uses the untyped *DataSet*! I use the term "typical" here because I see developers constantly writing code that uses string-based lookups to locate the desired *Data-Table* or the desired column value inside a *DataRow*. The larger the collection of *DataTables* or *DataColumns*, the less efficient this code becomes.

How does the strongly typed *DataSet* provide improved performance? In Chapter 6, you learned that the *DataRow* object allows you to access the contents of a column by supplying the name of the column, the ordinal for the column, or the *DataColumn* object itself. Code that uses the actual *DataColumn* object yields the best performance, but it's the most difficult to write and maintain. Supplying the column name as a string results in code that's easy to write and maintain, but it also results in the worst performance.

The code generated by the XML Schema Definition Tool gives you the best of both worlds. The code you write is easy to maintain, and the code that the tool generates uses the *Data-Column* object. If you look at the definition of the *OrderID* property on the strongly typed *DataSet*'s *OrdersRow* class, you'll see the following code:

Visual Basic
```
Public Property OrderID() As Integer
    Get
        Return CType(Me(Me.tableOrders.OrderIDColumn),Integer)
    End Get
    Set
        Me(Me.tableOrders.OrderIDColumn) = value
    End Set
End Property
```

Visual C#
```
public int OrderID {
    get {
        return ((int)(this[this.tableOrders.OrderIDColumn]));
    }
    set {
        this[this.tableOrders.OrderIDColumn] = value;
    }
}
```

We can achieve comparable performance with the untyped *DataSet* code by referencing the *DataColumn* objects outside of the loop, and then accessing the contents of the *DataRows* using those *DataColumn* objects, as shown in the following code:

Visual Basic
```
Dim intOrderID As Integer
Dim strCustomerID As String
Dim intEmployeeID As Nullable(Of Integer)

'Untyped code
Dim dsUntyped As New DataSet()
'Fill the DataSet ...

'Reference each of the DataColumns
Dim tblOrders As DataTable = dsUntyped.Tables("Orders")
Dim colOrderID As DataColumn = tblOrders.Columns("OrderID")
Dim colCustomerID As DataColumn = tblOrders.Columns("CustomerID")
Dim colEmployeeID As DataColumn = tblOrders.Columns("EmployeeID")
'...
```

```
For Each rowOrder As DataRow In tblOrders.Rows
    intOrderID = CInt(colOrderID)
    If rowOrder.IsNull(colCustomerID) Then
        strCustomerID = Nothing
    Else
        strCustomerID = CStr(rowOrder(colCustomerID))
    End If
    If rowOrder.IsNull(colEmployeeID) Then
        intEmployeeID = Nothing
    Else
        intEmployeeID = CInt(rowOrder(colEmployeeID))
    End If
    '...continue for all columns
Next rowOrder
```

Visual C#

```
int intOrderID;
string strCustomerID;
Nullable<int> intEmployeeID;

//Untyped code
DataSet dsUntyped = new DataSet();
//Fill the DataSet ...

//Reference each of the DataColumns
DataTable tblOrders = dsUntyped.Tables["Orders"];
DataColumn colOrderID = tblOrders.Columns["OrderID"];
DataColumn colCustomerID = tblOrders.Columns["CustomerID"];
DataColumn colEmployeeID = tblOrders.Columns["EmployeeID"];
//...

foreach (DataRow rowOrder in dsUntyped.Tables["Orders"].Rows) {
    intOrderID = (int) rowOrder[colOrderID];
    if (rowOrder.IsNull(colCustomerID))
        strCustomerID = null;
    else
        strCustomerID = (string) rowOrder[colCustomerID];
    if (rowOrder.IsNull(colEmployeeID))
        intEmployeeID = null;
    else
        intEmployeeID = (int) rowOrder[colEmployeeID];
    //...continue for all columns
}
```

In fact, this code ran about 35 percent faster than the code that used the strongly typed *DataSet* and approximately six times faster than the original code that used the untyped *DataSet*. This brings up an important point. There's nothing in the code for the strongly typed *DataSet* class that you can't write yourself. In fact, anything a strongly typed *DataSet* can do, you can do just as well, and probably even better! But writing your own code can take time. To access the contents of an untyped *DataSet* with the same performance as a strongly typed *DataSet*, you must avoid performing string-based lookups in your collections. Instead, use index-based lookups or maintain references to the columns in your untyped *DataSet*.

Because of the added overhead that comes with a strongly typed *DataSet*, creating, filling, and accessing strongly typed *DataSet* objects takes more time. In tests I've run, efficiently written code (code with no string-based lookups) that uses untyped *DataSet* objects provided slightly better performance (usually between 8 and 10 percent) than code using strongly typed *DataSet* objects.

Additional Considerations

Strongly typed *DataSet* objects can simplify your coding and help save a modicum of sanity. Here are a few more matters for you to consider if you decide to use strongly typed *DataSet* objects.

Making Structural Changes

If you need to change the structure of your strongly typed *DataSet* by adding or changing some of the *DataColumn* objects, you have to regenerate your strongly typed *DataSet*. Keep this in mind if you build a multitiered application in which the middle tier returns strongly typed *DataSet* objects. If you regenerate the strongly typed *DataSet* that the middle tier returns, you'll also need to rebuild the client application after refreshing the reference to the middle-tier object. However, if you're going to change the structure of the data returned by your server, you'll probably need to change the client code that accesses that structure anyway, regardless of whether you're using strongly typed *DataSet* objects.

Converting *DataSet* Objects

Because strongly typed *DataSet* objects inherit from the standard *DataSet* class, the following code that accesses a strongly typed *DataSet* through an untyped *DataSet* interface is valid:

Visual Basic
```
Dim dsStronglyTyped As New NorthwindDataSet()
Dim dsUntyped As DataSet
dsUntyped = CType(dsStronglyTyped, DataSet)
```

Visual C#
```
NorthwindDataSet dsStronglyTyped = new NorthwindDataSet();
DataSet dsUntyped;
dsUntyped = (DataSet) dsStronglyTyped;
```

However, you can cast an untyped *DataSet* to a strongly typed *DataSet* class only if the untyped *DataSet* was originally created as an instance of that same strongly typed *DataSet* class. Otherwise, the cast to the strongly typed *DataSet* will throw an *InvalidCastException*. The following code snippet should help clarify this behavior:

Visual Basic
```
Dim dsStronglyTyped1, dsStronglyTyped2 As NorthwindDataSet
Dim dsUntyped As DataSet
```

```
'This code will succeed.
dsStronglyTyped1 = New NorthwindDataSet()
dsUntyped = CType(dsStronglyTyped1, DataSet)
dsStronglyTyped2 = CType(dsUntyped, NorthwindDataSet)

'This code will throw an exception.
dsUntyped = New DataSet()
dsStronglyTyped2 = CType(dsUntyped, NorthwindDataSet)
```

Visual C#

```
NorthwindDataSet dsStronglyTyped1, dsStronglyTyped2;
DataSet dsUntyped;

//This code will succeed.
dsStronglyTyped1 = new NorthwindDataSet();
dsUntyped = (DataSet) dsStronglyTyped1;
dsStronglyTyped2 = (NorthwindDataSet) dsUntyped;

//This code will throw an exception.
dsUntyped = new DataSet();
dsStronglyTyped2 = (NorthwindDataSet) dsUntyped;
```

What if you have an untyped *DataSet* and you want to access its contents using a strongly typed *DataSet* class? If the untyped *DataSet* object was created as an untyped *DataSet*, you cannot cast the object to a strongly typed *DataSet*. However, you can use the *Merge* method of the strongly typed *DataSet* to import the data from the untyped *DataSet*, as the following code snippet illustrates:

Visual Basic

```
Dim dsStronglyTyped As New NorthwindDataSet()
Dim dsUntyped As New DataSet()
dsStronglyTyped.Merge(dsUntyped)
```

Visual C#

```
NorthwindDataSet dsStronglyTyped = new NorthwindDataSet();
DataSet dsUntyped = new DataSet();
dsStronglyTyped.Merge(dsUntyped);
```

The *Merge* method is also useful if you need to move data back and forth between instances of two different strongly typed *DataSet* classes. You can also use the *WriteXml* and *ReadXml* methods to move data back and forth between different strongly typed *DataSet* classes if you include the XML schema in the calls to *WriteXml* and *ReadXml*.

Untyped Features of Strongly Typed *DataSet* Objects

Let's say your application uses strongly typed *DataSet* objects and you want to send a *DataSet* back to your middle-tier server to submit changes to your database. You can use the strongly typed *DataSet* object's *GetChanges* method to create a new *DataSet* that contains only modified rows. However, the *GetChanges* method returns an untyped *DataSet*. Can you cast the untyped

DataSet returned by the *GetChanges* method to a strongly typed *DataSet*? Absolutely. The following code snippet demonstrates this functionality:

Visual Basic
```
Dim dsStrongAllRows As New NorthwindDataSet()
'Fill the strongly typed DataSet and modify some of its rows.
Dim dsUntyped As DataSet
dsUntyped = dsStrongAllRows.GetChanges()
Dim dsStrongModifiedRows As NorthwindDataSet
dsStrongModifiedRows = CType(dsUntyped, NorthwindDataSet)
```

Visual C#
```
NorthwindDataSet dsStrongAllRows = new NorthwindDataSet();
//Fill the strongly typed DataSet and modify some of its rows.
DataSet dsUntyped;
dsUntyped = dsStrongAllRows.GetChanges();
NorthwindDataSet dsStrongModifiedRows;
dsStrongModifiedRows = (NorthwindDataSet) dsUntyped;
```

The strongly typed *DataSet* has other methods that return untyped data. For example, the *Select* method returns an array of *DataRow* objects. You can't cast the array to an array of strongly typed *DataRow* objects, but you can cast the individual *DataRow* objects to their strongly typed counterparts.

Similar rules apply to the *DataView*. You can't access its contents directly through the strongly typed classes, but you can convert the *DataRow* returned by the *DataRowView* object's *Row* property to a strongly typed class as in the following code snippet:

Visual Basic
```
Dim dsStronglyTyped As New NorthwindDataSet()
'Fill the strongly typed DataSet and modify some of its rows.
Dim vueCustomers As New DataView(dsStronglyTyped.Customers)
Dim rowCustomer As NorthwindDataSet.CustomersRow
rowCustomer = CType(vueCustomers(0).Row, NorthwindDataSet.CustomersRow)
```

Visual C#
```
NorthwindDataSet dsStronglyTyped = new NorthwindDataSet();
//Fill the strongly typed DataSet and modify some of its rows.
DataView vueCustomers = new DataView(dsStronglyTyped.Customers);
NorthwindDataSet.CustomersRow rowCustomer;
rowCustomer = (NorthwindDataSet.CustomersRow) vueCustomers(0).Row;
```

Manually Adding Tables and Columns

While dragging and dropping columns (or entire tables) from the Server Explorer window is the easiest way to add schema to a strongly typed *DataSet*, it's not the only way.

Creating a *DataTable* Manually

There are a number of ways to manually add a new *DataTable* to your strongly typed *DataSet*. You can manually add a *DataTable* to your *DataSet* by selecting Data from the Visual Studio menu, choosing Add, and then selecting DataTable. You can also add a *DataTable* by right-clicking the strongly typed *DataSet* designer and selecting Add and DataTable from the resulting context menu. You can also drag and drop a *DataTable* from the *DataSet* tab on the Toolbox.

Once you've added your new *DataTable*, you can change the name of the *DataTable* from Data-Table1 to whatever you'd like by clicking once on the name of the *DataTable* at the top of the item. You could also rename the *DataTable* by selecting the *DataTable* and then changing the value of the *Name* property in the Properties window.

Adding *DataColumn*s

Now that you have a new *DataTable*, you'll want to add *DataColumn*s to the *DataTable*. To add a *DataColumn* to an existing *DataTable*, select the *DataTable* and then use either the Data portion of the Visual Studio menu or the context menu shown by right-clicking the *DataTable*, and then choose Add and DataColumn.

Setting Properties on a *DataColumn*

The strongly typed *DataSet* designer makes it easy to see and modify names for your *Data-Columns*, though you'll likely want to access more than just the *ColumnName* property. The simplest way to view and modify properties on a *DataColumn* is to select the *DataColumn* in the strongly typed *DataSet* designer and then select the Properties window, as shown in Figure 9-9.

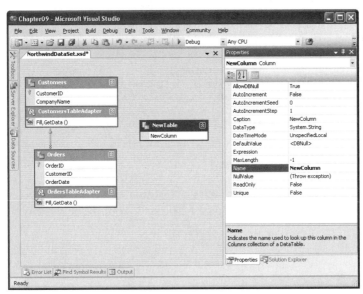

Figure 9-9 Viewing properties on a *DataColumn* using the Properties window

Setting the *DataTable*'s *PrimaryKey* Property

To set the *PrimaryKey* property on a *DataTable*, select the *DataColumn* (or *DataColumns*) that constitutes the primary key. Then right-click one of the *DataColumns* (or select Data from the Visual Studio menu) and select Set Primary Key. If you later want to modify or remove the primary key, these options are also available through the menu.

Adding *DataRelations*

When you create a new *DataTable* by dragging and dropping columns from the Server Explorer window, Visual Studio will automatically add *DataRelations* based on the foreign key information it retrieves from the database. If, however, you're creating your *DataTables* manually, you'll also need to create your *DataRelations* manually.

To add a *DataRelation*, right-click any item in the strongly typed *DataSet* designer (or select Data from the Visual Studio menu) and select Add and then Relation. This action will launch the dialog box shown in Figure 9-10.

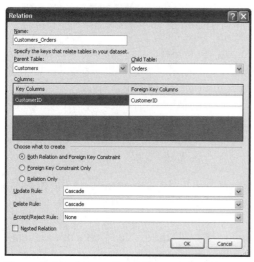

Figure 9-10   Manually adding a *DataRelation* to a strongly typed *DataSet*

You can select the parent and child *DataTables* using the drop-down lists at the top of the dialog box. The name of the *DataRelation* will change as you change the tables involved in the *DataRelation*. Once you've selected the parent and child *DataTables*, select the *DataColumns* for the *DataRelation* in the grid just below the drop-down lists.

The lower half of the dialog box lets you control whether the action will create a *DataRelation*, a *ForeignKeyConstraint*, or both. The default is to create just a *DataRelation*—a default that can cause problems for many developers, as we'll see shortly. If you specify that the action will create a *ForeignKeyConstraint* (or a *DataRelation* and a *ForeignKeyConstraint*), you can also specify values for the *UpdateRule*, *DeleteRule*, and *AcceptRejectChangesRule* properties on the *ForeignKeyConstraint*. The dialog box will default to *Cascade*, *Cascade*, and *None*, respectively.

Creating a *DataRelation* without a *ForeignKeyConstraint* can improve the performance of your code. If you know you're working with read-only data and that you're only retrieving rows from a database that has already validated that the data using a similar foreign key constraint, there's no need to have a *ForeignKeyConstraint* object in the *DataSet* revalidate that data. Under those circumstances, there's no problem using a *DataRelation* that is not associated with a *ForeignKeyConstraint*.

However, if you're going to allow changes to the data in your *DataSet*, you should have *ForeignKeyConstraints* associated with your *DataRelations*. As we learned in Chapter 7, it's the *ForeignKeyConstraint* that cascades changes between parent and child rows in the *DataSet*. Let's look at two common scenarios where not having a *ForeignKeyConstraint* object associated with a *DataRelation* in a *DataSet* that allows changes could cause problems.

If you delete a parent row in the *DataSet*, the child rows will automatically be marked as deleted if (and only if) the *DataRelation* is associated with a *ForeignKeyConstraint* whose *Delete-Rule* is set to *Cascade*. Otherwise, the child *DataRows* will not be marked as pending deletions. If you try to submit the pending changes back to the database, the database might disallow the attempt to delete the parent row because the child rows still exist.

Another potential problem could arise if you query the child table for information. Let's assume the *DataSet* contains order and order detail information for a particular customer. The user marks an order as a pending deletion and then uses the *Compute* method on the order detail *DataTable* to determine the total cost of all orders placed by the customer. Because marking the order as a pending deletion did not cascade that change down to the related order details, the value returned by the *Compute* method will include the cost of the order that's marked as deleted.

Similarly, changes to a key value in a parent row will automatically trickle down to the related child rows if (and only if) the *DataRelation* is associated with a *ForeignKeyConstraint* whose *UpdateRule* is set to *Cascade*. For the moment, let's assume that you're working with auto-increment values in your *DataSet* and a *DataRelation* that's not associated with a *ForeignKeyConstraint*. When you retrieve the new database-generated key values for newly submitted parent rows, those values will not trickle down to the related child rows. The values for the foreign key column for those child rows will still be set to the ADO.NET-generated placeholder values when you submit those rows to the database. If you're lucky, the placeholder values that ADO.NET generated do not exist in the database, and the operation will fail because of a foreign key constraint violation. If you're unlucky, the placeholder values that ADO.NET generated will already exist in the database and correspond to an entirely different row of data, and the operation succeeds although the child rows now correspond to the wrong parent rows.

> **Important**   I strongly recommend creating both a *DataRelation* and a *ForeignKeyConstraint* unless you're absolutely positively sure that you will not need to validate data at the client. The *ForeignKeyConstraint* should have its *UpdateRule*, *DeleteRule*, and *AcceptRejectRule* properties set to *Cascade*, *Cascade*, and *None*. Note that these are the default values when creating *DataRelations* programmatically, but not when creating *DataRelations* by dragging and dropping tables from Server Explorer onto the strongly typed *DataSet* designer, or when creating a strongly typed *DataSet* via the Data Source Configuration Wizard.

Improving on the *DataSet*s (De)Faults

At the end of Chapter 2, I pointed out that with a strong understanding of ADO.NET, you can often improve on the code generated by tools such as Visual Studio. Let's take a look at a couple of areas in which the strongly typed *DataSet* designer could use such improvements.

Associate Autogenerated *DataRelations* with *ForeignKeyConstraints*

Recently, when we covered manually creating new *DataRelations* in a strongly typed *DataSet*, I covered some examples of why associating the *DataRelation* with a *ForeignKeyConstraint* is recommended. Unfortunately, the *DataRelations* that Visual Studio automatically generates when dragging and dropping tables and columns from the Server Explorer window are not associated with *ForeignKeyConstraints*.

I strongly recommend that you manually associate your *DataRelations* with *ForeignKey-Constraints*. Right-click each *DataRelation*, and select Edit Relation from the context menu. In the resulting dialog box, previously shown in Figure 9-10, select Both Relation And Foreign Key Constraint. You'll also need to set the options for the Update Rule and Delete Rule drop-down lists to *Cascade*. These options are set to *None* by default for autogenerated *DataRelations*. Leave the Accept Reject Rule set to its default of *None*.

Force Auto-Increment Columns to Generate Negative Placeholder Values

Earlier, when I mentioned some potential problems that can arise from working with *Data-Relations* that are not associated with *ForeignKeyConstraints*, I covered a scenario involving auto-increment values. The worst-case portion of the scenario occurs when the placeholder values that ADO.NET generates for the auto-increment column correspond to rows that already exist within the database.

The best way to avoid this scenario is to have ADO.NET generate negative placeholder values, such as −1, −2, −3, and so on. You can force ADO.NET to generate placeholder values this way by setting the *AutoIncrementSeed* and *AutoIncrementStep* properties to −1 for auto-increment columns in your *DataSet*. Simply select each *DataColumn*, and then set the two properties to −1 in the Properties window.

Introducing *TableAdapters*

Earlier in the chapter, when you first constructed your *DataSet*, you saw that each *DataTable* you created by dragging and dropping columns from Server Explorer also created something called a *TableAdapter*. Now it's time to take a closer look at *TableAdapters*.

A *TableAdapter* provides some of the basic logic associated with *DataAdapter* classes such as the *SqlDataAdapter*. You can use a *TableAdapter* to fill a *DataTable* in a strongly typed *DataSet*, or to submit the pending changes stored in a *DataTable*. We'll take a closer look at using *SqlDataAdapters* to submit pending changes in Chapters 10 and 11. *TableAdapters* offer similar overloads for the *Update* method, so much of the information covered there applies to *Table-Adapters* as well.

Creating a *TableAdapter*

There are two main ways to create a *TableAdapter*—dragging and dropping items from Server Explorer, and using the Visual Studio menu system.

Drag and Drop from Server Explorer

When you dragged the CustomerID and CompanyName columns from the Customers table in Server Explorer onto the strongly typed *DataSet*'s designer, Visual Studio added a *Data-Table* for the Customers table with *DataColumns* for the CustomerID and CompanyName columns. Visual Studio also created a *TableAdapter* that contains a *SqlDataAdapter* configured to execute the query:

```
SELECT CustomerID, CompanyName FROM Customers
```

Similarly, dragging columns from the Orders table added a *DataTable* to the strongly typed *DataSet* for those columns and a *SqlDataAdapter* to retrieve those columns of information from the SQL Server table into the *DataTable*.

Adding a *TableAdapter* from the Visual Studio Menu

You can also use the Visual Studio menu to add a *TableAdapter*. Simply select Data, choose Add, and then select TableAdapter. You can also right-click the designer surface and select Add and then TableAdapter. Either action will launch the TableAdapter Configuration Wizard, which will guide you through the process of creating your *TableAdapter*.

The first page for the wizard, shown in Figure 9-11, prompts you for information about your connection. You can select connections available from Server Explorer in the drop-down list at the top of the page. You can also click the New Connection button to establish a new connection, which will launch the dialog box discussed earlier in the chapter and shown in Figure 9-3.

When you select a connection that contains sensitive data such as password information, the wizard lets you control whether or not you save this information in the connection string.

There's also a +/− button next to the Connection String label at the bottom of the page. You can click this button to display or hide the connection string for the connection you've selected. For security reasons, the wizard will not display the connection string for the connection, by default—just in case your connection string uses a password that you don't want someone peering over your shoulder to see. The wizard also provides an option to exclude that sensitive information from the connection string for the *TableAdapter*.

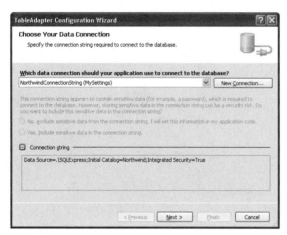

Figure 9-11   Specifying connection information in the TableAdapter Configuration Wizard

Once you've specified the connection information, the wizard asks you what type of command the *TableAdapter* will execute. As you can see in Figure 9-12, you can specify a SQL statement, create a new stored procedure based on a query, or use an existing stored procedure. The final two options are available only if you're working with a SQL Server database. The second option will create stored procedures to retrieve, insert, update, and delete rows of data based on a SQL query. The third option allows you to select stored procedures to retrieve, insert, update, and delete rows of data.

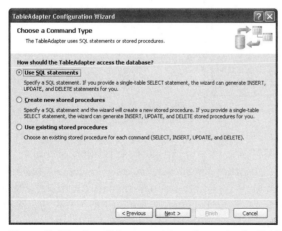

Figure 9-12   Specifying a command type in the TableAdapter Configuration Wizard

If you specify that you want your *TableAdapter* to execute a SQL statement, the next page in the wizard prompts you for that query, as shown in Figure 9-13. If you're comfortable typing your SQL statement by hand, this wizard page is perfectly fine. However, you can also select a graphical design tool, the Query Builder, by clicking the Query Builder button.

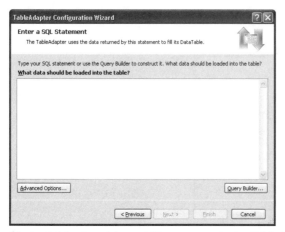

Figure 9-13   Supplying a SQL statement in the TableAdapter Configuration Wizard

When you click the Query Builder button, the wizard will display the dialog box shown in Figure 9-14, which lets you select a table, view, function, or synonym.

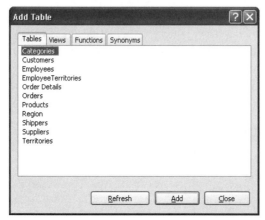

Figure 9-14   Adding a table for the SQL statement

Once you've selected a table for your SQL statement, the Query Builder gives you a graphical way to define your query. As Figure 9-15 shows, you can easily select the columns you want to retrieve. The second pane lets you add sort orders and query criteria without having to type the corresponding SQL query manually. The Query Builder displays the SQL for your query and lets you execute the query by clicking the Execute Query button. Once you're satisfied with your query, click the OK button.

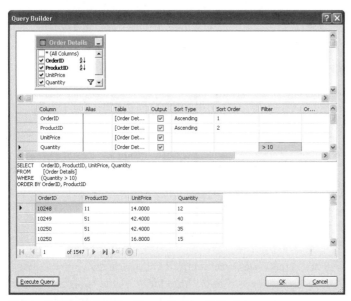

Figure 9-15   Using the Query Builder to build your query

The TableAdapter Configuration Wizard provides advanced options for scenarios involving updates. You can access these options by clicking the Advanced Options button on the page in the wizard (shown in Figure 9-13) that prompts you for the SQL statement. Clicking this button will display the dialog box shown in Figure 9-16. We'll discuss these options and the effect they have on the updating logic in more detail in Chapters 10 and 11.

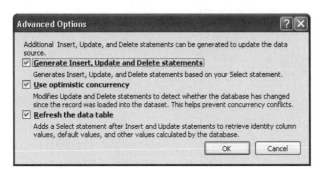

Figure 9-16   Advanced options in the TableAdapter Configuration Wizard

Once you've supplied your SQL statement, the wizard lets you control the methods available on your *TableAdapter*. By default, the wizard will create a *Fill* method that will fill an existing corresponding *DataTable* in the strongly typed *DataSet* with the results of the query. The wizard will also add a *GetData* method that will return a new instance of the strongly typed *DataTable* that contains the results of the query. The wizard lets you specify whether or not you want these methods, and it lets you control the names of these methods, as shown in Figure 9-17.

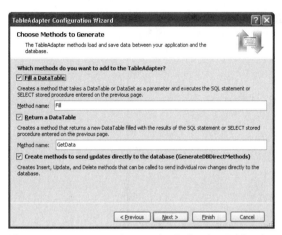

Figure 9-17   Generating methods for the *TableAdapter*

By default, the wizard will also create *DBDirect* methods, if the query you've constructed references a single table with a primary key, and if the query includes all columns that comprise the primary key. These methods—*Insert*, *Update*, and *Delete*—allow you to submit new rows or modify existing rows of data in your database directly without forcing you to have a corresponding *DataRow* in your strongly typed *DataSet*. We'll discuss this feature in more depth later in the chapter.

Finally, the TableAdapter Configuration Wizard displays the results, shown here in Figure 9-18, explaining what functionality the wizard provided in your new *TableAdapter*.

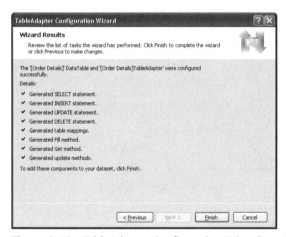

Figure 9-18   TableAdapter Configuration Wizard results

Using a *TableAdapter*

Now that you understand how to create a *TableAdapter* through Visual Studio, let's examine how to use a *TableAdapter* through code.

Instantiating a *TableAdapter* at run-time is simple. *TableAdapter* classes require no additional initialization. With a *SqlDataAdapter*, for example, you need to supply query and connection information either through the *SqlDataAdapter*'s constructor or through its properties. When you created your *TableAdapter* at design time, you supplied all of this information. As a result, as soon as you instantiate your *TableAdapter*, it's ready to use.

Fill (and *ClearBeforeFill*)

TableAdapters make filling a strongly typed *DataSet* simple. As soon as you instantiate the *Table-Adapter*, it's ready to go. You don't need to pass any parameters to the constructor. You don't need to set any properties. Just instantiate the *TableAdapter* and pass an instance of the corresponding strongly typed *DataTable* to the *Fill* method, as shown in the following code snippet:

Visual Basic

```
Dim dsNorthwind As New NorthwindDataSet()
Dim daCustomers As NorthwindDataSetTableAdapters.CustomersTableAdapter

'Create the TableAdapter
daCustomers = New NorthwindDataSetTableAdapters.CustomersTableAdapter()

'Fill the strongly typed DataTable
daCustomers.Fill(dsNorthwind.Customers)

'Display the results
For Each rowCustomer As NorthwindDataSet.CustomersRow _
    In dsNorthwind.Customers
    Console.WriteLine(rowCustomer.CompanyName)
Next rowCustomer
```

Visual C#

```
NorthwindDataSet dsNorthwind = new NorthwindDataSet();
NorthwindDataSetTableAdapters.CustomersTableAdapter daCustomers;

//Create the TableAdapter
daCustomers = new NorthwindDataSetTableAdapters.CustomersTableAdapter();

//Fill the strongly typed DataTable
daCustomers.Fill(dsNorthwind.Customers);

//Display the results
foreach (NorthwindDataSet.CustomersRow rowCustomer in tblCustomers)
    Console.WriteLine(rowCustomer.CompanyName);
```

As you may have guessed from looking at the preceding code snippet, the *TableAdapters* reside in a separate namespace that's based on the name of the strongly typed *DataSet* class. In this case, the strongly typed *DataSet* class is named *NorthwindDataSet*, so the *TableAdapters* reside in the *NorthwindDataSetTableAdapters* namespace.

Like the *Fill* method on the *SqlDataAdapter*, the *TableAdapter*'s *Fill* method returns an integer that corresponds to the number of rows retrieved.

The *TableAdapter*'s *Fill* method differs slightly from the *SqlDataAdapter*'s *Fill* method in other ways. Unlike the *SqlDataAdapter*'s *Fill* method, a *TableAdapter*'s *Fill* method is not overloaded. A *TableAdapter*'s *Fill* method will only accept an instance of the strongly typed *DataTable* to which it is associated. The *TableAdapter* documentation implies that it can accept a strongly typed *DataSet*, but that scenario does not work, at least in the initial release of Visual Studio 2005.

In other words, each of the calls to *Fill* in the following code snippet will result in an error at compile time:

Visual Basic

```
Dim dsNorthwind As New NorthwindDataSet()
Dim daCustomers As NorthwindDataSetTableAdapters.CustomersTableAdapter
daCustomers = New NorthwindDataSetTableAdapters.CustomersTableAdapter()

'Fill the wrong strongly typed DataTable (ERROR)
daCustomers.Fill(dsNorthwind.Orders)

'Fill with a strongly typed DataSet (ERROR)
daCustomers.Fill(dsNorthwind)

'Fill with an untyped DataTable or DataSet (ERROR)
Dim dsUntyped As New DataSet()
Dim tblUntyped As New DataTable()
daCustomers.Fill(dsUntyped)
daCustomers.Fill(tblUntyped)
```

Visual C#

```
NorthwindDataSet dsNorthwind = new NorthwindDataSet();
NorthwindDataSetTableAdapters.CustomersTableAdapter daCustomers;
daCustomers = new NorthwindDataSetTableAdapters.CustomersTableAdapter();

//Fill the wrong strongly typed DataTable (ERROR)
daCustomers.Fill(dsNorthwind.Orders);

//Fill with a strongly typed DataSet (ERROR)
daCustomers.Fill(dsNorthwind);

//Fill with an untyped DataTable or DataSet (ERROR)
DataSet dsUntyped = new DataSet();
DataTable tblUntyped = new DataTable();
daCustomers.Fill(dsUntyped);
daCustomers.Fill(tblUntyped);
```

> **Note**   The Visual Basic example that tries to fill an untyped *DataTable* will only create a compilation error if you're using Option Strict On. Otherwise, this will result in an *InvalidCast-Exception* at run time.

The *TableAdapter*'s *ClearBeforeFill* Property   Each *TableAdapter* has a *ClearBeforeFill* property, which is initially set to *True*. If the property is set to *True* when the *Fill* method is called, the *TableAdapter* will clear the rows available in the strongly typed *DataTable* by calling its *Clear* method prior to filling it with the results of the query.

If you want to add to the existing contents of your *DataTable*, make sure you set this property to *False* prior to calling *TableAdapter.Fill*.

GetData

Each *TableAdapter* also exposes a *GetData* method that returns a new strongly typed *Data-Table* that contains the results of the query. Using the *GetData* method can save you a line of code because it does not require you to create an instance of the strongly typed *DataTable*.

Visual Basic

```
Dim daCustomers As NorthwindDataSetTableAdapters.CustomersTableAdapter
Dim tblCustomers As NorthwindDataSet.CustomersDataTable

daCustomers = New NorthwindDataSetTableAdapters.CustomersTableAdapter()
tblCustomers = daCustomers.GetData()
For Each rowCustomer As NorthwindDataSet.CustomersRow In tblCustomers
    Console.WriteLine(rowCustomer.CompanyName)
Next rowCustomer
```

Visual C#

```
NorthwindDataSetTableAdapters.CustomersTableAdapter daCustomers;
NorthwindDataSet.CustomersDataTable tblCustomers;

daCustomers = new NorthwindDataSetTableAdapters.CustomersTableAdapter();
tblCustomers = daCustomers.GetData();
foreach (NorthwindDataSet.CustomersRow rowCustomer in tblCustomers)
    Console.WriteLine(rowCustomer.CompanyName);
```

Controlling the *TableAdapter*'s Connection

By default, each *TableAdapter* uses its own *Connection* object. Even if you have multiple *TableAdapters* that are designed to communicate with the same database, they will still each receive their own *Connection* object. However, *TableAdapters* do expose a *Connection* property that you can use to control the *Connection* it uses to communicate with their database. The availability of this property is controlled through the strongly typed *DataSet* designer. Select a *TableAdapter* in the designer and you'll see a property in the Properties window called *ConnectionModifier*. This property controls the availability of the *Connection* property on the *TableAdapter*. By default, the property is marked as Friend or Internal for Visual Basic and C#, respectively, so it is available to other classes within your assembly, but is not available from other assemblies.

You could also create your own *SqlConnection* and then assign it to one or multiple *TableAdapters* using the *Connection* property. For example, you could use the following code to have two *TableAdapters* use the same *Connection* object.

Visual Basic

```
Dim daCustomers As NorthwindDataSetTableAdapters.CustomersTableAdapter
Dim daOrders As NorthwindDataSetTableAdapters.OrdersTableAdapter

daCustomers = New NorthwindDataSetTableAdapters.CustomersTableAdapter()
daOrders = New NorthwindDataSetTableAdapters.OrdersTableAdapter()

daOrders.Connection = daCustomers.Connection
```

Visual C#

```
NorthwindDataSetTableAdapters.CustomersTableAdapter daCustomers;
NorthwindDataSetTableAdapters.OrdersTableAdapter daOrders;

daCustomers = new NorthwindDataSetTableAdapters.CustomersTableAdapter();
daOrders = new NorthwindDataSetTableAdapters.OrdersTableAdapter();

daOrders.Connection = daCustomers.Connection;
```

Remember that by default, a *SqlDataAdapter* will open a *SqlConnection* prior to filling a *Data-Table* if the *SqlConnection* is closed when the *Fill* method is called. The same behavior is true of *TableAdapters*. So, even after associating both *TableAdapters* with the same *SqlConnection*, executing the previous code snippet will cause that *SqlConnection* to be opened and closed on each call to *Fill*.

The implicit connection state management is great in simple scenarios, but it can cause problems as you add more functionality to your application. Thanks to connection pooling, there's only a small performance hit associated with the implicit calls to *Connection.Open* and *Connection .Close*, but that's beside the point. Consider a scenario where you want to call *Fill* on multiple *TableAdapters* and have each query run within the same *SqlTransaction*. Doing so requires that the *TableAdapters* use the same *SqlConnection* and that the *SqlConnection* remains open through all calls to *Fill*.

> **Note** Yes, the scenario I'm describing is a bit contrived. You're more likely to want multiple calls to *Update* to use the same *SqlConnection* for a transaction (either *SqlTransaction* or *System.Transaction*), but the concept is the same and we haven't discussed submitting updates yet.

A better approach is to explicitly open the *SqlConnection* prior to calling the *Fill* methods on the *TableAdapters* that use the *SqlConnection*, as shown in the following code snippet:

Visual Basic

```
Dim dsNorthwind As New NorthwindDataSet()
Dim daCustomers As NorthwindDataSetTableAdapters.CustomersTableAdapter
Dim daOrders As NorthwindDataSetTableAdapters.OrdersTableAdapter

daCustomers = New NorthwindDataSetTableAdapters.CustomersTableAdapter()
daOrders = New NorthwindDataSetTableAdapters.OrdersTableAdapter()
```

```
daOrders.Connection = daCustomers.Connection

daCustomers.Connection.Open()
daCustomers.Fill(dsNorthwind.Customers)
daOrders.Fill(dsNorthwind.Orders)
daCustomers.Connection.Close()
```

Visual C#

```
NorthwindDataSet dsNorthwind = new NorthwindDataSet();
NorthwindDataSetTableAdapters.CustomersTableAdapter daCustomers;
NorthwindDataSetTableAdapters.OrdersTableAdapter daOrders;

daCustomers = new NorthwindDataSetTableAdapters.CustomersTableAdapter();
daOrders = new NorthwindDataSetTableAdapters.OrdersTableAdapter();

daOrders.Connection = daCustomers.Connection;

daCustomers.Connection.Open();
daCustomers.Fill(dsNorthwind.Customers);
daOrders.Fill(dsNorthwind.Orders);
daCustomers.Connection.Close();
```

Update

The *TableAdapter* has an overloaded *Update* method that accepts an instance of the strongly typed *DataSet* or *DataTable*, a single *DataRow*, or an array of *DataRows*. These overloads roughly correspond to overloads of the *SqlDataAdapter*'s *Update* method. The *TableAdapter* offers an additional overload to the *Update* method, called a *DBDirect* method, which we'll cover shortly.

You use the *Update* method on a *TableAdapter* just like you do on a *SqlDataAdapter*. We'll cover submitting updates using *SqlDataAdapters* in Chapters 10 and 11.

Using the *DBDirect* Methods

As you'll see in Chapter 10, a standard *SqlDataAdapter* is designed to submit the pending changes stored in a *DataRow* to a database using parameterized queries. A *TableAdapter* lets you modify the contents of the database without even having to create a *DataRow*.

If the TableAdapter Configuration Wizard is able to find a primary key in the database table in your query, it will generate logic to submit pending inserts, updates, and deletes to your database. This logic will be stored in the *InsertCommand*, *UpdateCommand*, and *DeleteCommand* for the *SqlDataAdapter* that's stored inside the *TableAdapter*.

The *TableAdapter* also makes that logic available through *Insert*, *Update*, and *Delete* methods that are specifically designed for your strongly typed *DataTable*. For example, you could use the following code to submit a new customer using the *CustomersTableAdapter* configured earlier. The following code also deletes the newly created row so that you can run the code repeatedly without generating an exception. If you want to verify that the row was actually created in the database, set a breakpoint at the call to *Delete* and then use Server Explorer to check the contents of the database table prior to the call to *Delete*.

Visual Basic

```
Dim daCustomers As NorthwindDataSetTableAdapters.CustomersTableAdapter
daCustomers = New NorthwindDataSetTableAdapters.CustomersTableAdapter()
'Insert a new row in the Customers table in the database
daCustomers.Insert("NEWCO", "New Company")
'Delete that newly created row
daCustomers.Delete("NEWCO", "New Company")
```

Visual C#

```
NorthwindDataSetTableAdapters.CustomersTableAdapter daCustomers;
daCustomers = new NorthwindDataSetTableAdapters.CustomersTableAdapter();
//Insert a new row in the Customers table in the database
daCustomers.Insert("NEWCO", "New Company");
//Delete that newly created row
daCustomers.Delete("NEWCO", "New Company");
```

The *Insert* method executes a parameterized INSERT query, using the parameters to the *Insert* method as the values for the parameterized query. In the preceding example, the parameters correspond to the CustomerID and CompanyName *DataColumns* in the strongly typed *DataTable*.

Visual Studio calls these parameterized *TableAdapter* methods *DBDirect* methods because the values are sent directly to the database without creating a *DataRow*.

The parameters for the *DBDirect* methods depend on the parameters for the updating logic stored in the *TableAdapter*'s internal *SqlDataAdapter*. Input parameters in the updating logic are translated to input parameters on the *DBDirect* methods. Output parameters in the updating logic are translated to output parameters on the *DBDirect* methods. Concurrency checks are honored—the *DBDirect Update* method on the *CustomersTableAdapter* takes current and original values for the CustomerID and CompanyName columns. Nullable parameters for value types (such as the .NET *Int32* and *DateTime* data types) are translated into the Nullable types new to .NET 2.0 (*Nullable<Int32>* and *Nullable<DateTime>* for C# developers, and *Nullable(Of Int32)* and *Nullable(Of DateTime)* for Visual Basic developers.

BaseClass

At design time, you can control the base class that the *TableAdapter* derives from through the *BaseClass* option in the Properties window. This sounds like a great idea. You could have all your *TableAdapters* derive from the same base class. However, I've yet to find an effective way to use this option to use features of the *TableAdapter* (or the internal *SqlDataAdapter*) using the *BaseClass* option without resorting to *Reflection*.

Adding More Queries

Whereas a *SqlDataAdapter* can support a single query—the *SqlCommand* specified in the *SqlDataAdapter*'s *SelectCommand* property—a *TableAdapter* can contain multiple queries. Let's look at how you can add more queries to the *TableAdapter*, and how you can use those additional queries.

The *OrdersTableAdapter* class we created by dragging and dropping columns from the Orders table in Server Explorer retrieves all rows from the Orders table. Let's add a parameterized query that returns just the orders for a particular customer.

Open the *NorthwindDataSet* class in the strongly typed *DataSet* designer and select the *OrdersTableAdapter*. Right-click the *TableAdapter* and select Add Query from the context menu. This will relaunch the TableAdapter Query Configuration Wizard shown earlier in the chapter.

Figure 9-19   Supplying a new query for a *TableAdapter*

For the first page of the wizard, specify that you want to use a SQL query. In the second page of the wizard, specify the *SELECT* Which Returns Rows option. Then modify the SQL query as shown in Figure 9-19, adding **WHERE CustomerID = @CustomerID**. Then, on the next page of the wizard, change the names of the *Fill* and *GetData* methods to *FillByCustomerID* and *GetDataByCustomerID*, as shown in Figure 9-20.

The *TableAdapter* now contains two queries—one that returns all order rows, and one that returns just the orders for a particular query. If you examine the code generated for the *Table-Adapter*, you'll find that it has a private property called *CommandCollection* that is an array of *SqlCommands*. Each time you call one of the *Fill* or *GetData* methods, the *TableAdapter* assigns the appropriate *SqlCommand* to the *SqlDataAdapter*'s *SelectCommand* property before calling the *SqlDataAdapter*'s *Fill* method.

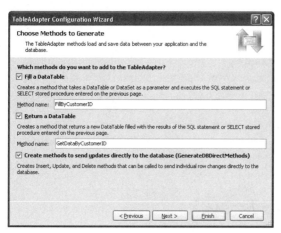

Figure 9-20   Naming the *Fill* and *GetData* methods for the new *TableAdapter* query

We can now use the new parameterized query by executing the following code:

Visual Basic

```
Dim daOrders As NorthwindDataSetTableAdapters.OrdersTableAdapter
Dim tblOrders As NorthwindDataSet.OrdersDataTable

daOrders = New NorthwindDataSetTableAdapters.OrdersTableAdapter()
tblOrders = daOrders.GetDataByCustomerID("ALFKI")

For Each rowOrder As NorthwindDataSet.OrdersRow In tblOrders
    Console.WriteLine("{0} - {1} - {2:d}", rowOrder.OrderID, _
                    rowOrder.CustomerID, rowOrder.OrderDate)
Next rowOrder
```

Visual C#

```
NorthwindDataSetTableAdapters.OrdersTableAdapter daOrders;
NorthwindDataSet.OrdersDataTable tblOrders;

daOrders = new NorthwindDataSetTableAdapters.OrdersTableAdapter();
tblOrders = daOrders.GetDataByCustomerID("ALFKI");

foreach (NorthwindDataSet.OrdersRow rowOrder in tblOrders)
    Console.WriteLine("{0} - {1} - {2:d}", rowOrder.OrderID,
                    rowOrder.CustomerID, rowOrder.OrderDate);
```

Adding Your Own Code

The designer-generated code for the *TableAdapters* resides in the same code file as the code for the strongly typed *DataSet*. And like the strongly typed *DataSet*, the designer-generated code for the *TableAdapters* uses partial classes. So you can add your own code for the *TableAdapters* without having to worry about having Visual Studio overwrite your code.

If, for example, you wanted to add a public property that returns the *SqlDataAdapter* for a *TableAdapter*, you could add the following code:

Visual Basic

```
Namespace NorthwindDataSetTableAdapters
    Partial Public Class CustomersTableAdapter
        Public ReadOnly Property GetDataAdapter() As SqlDataAdapter
            Get
                Me.Adapter.SelectCommand = Me.CommandCollection(0)
                Return Me.Adapter
            End Get
        End Property
    End Class
End Namespace
```

Visual C#

```
namespace NorthwindDataSetTableAdapters {
    partial class CustomersTableAdapter {
        public SqlDataAdapter GetDataAdapter {
            get {
                this.Adapter.SelectCommand = this.CommandCollection[0];
                return this.Adapter;
            }
        }
    }
}
```

TableAdapter Limitations

TableAdapters can make filling your strongly typed *DataSet* a snap. However, they have some limitations.

A Component, Not a *DbDataAdapter*

TableAdapters do not derive from the base class for *DataAdapters*–*DbDataAdapter*. Instead, *TableAdapters* derive from the *Component* class in the *System.ComponentModel* namespace.

There are two main drawbacks to this approach. There is no way to write code that accepts a *TableAdapter* as a parameter and calls methods or accesses properties on the *TableAdapter* unless you access the *TableAdapter* through .NET Reflection–a feature that's somewhat similar to late binding in COM. Also, some features that are readily available on any *DataAdapter* are not available directly on *TableAdapters*. Using *TableAdapters* in scenarios where you need to set properties on the actual *DataAdapter* can pose a problem.

For example, say you've accessed the *Connection* property for the *TableAdapter* and created a *SqlTransaction*. How can you associate the *TableAdapter*'s queries with the transaction? Thankfully, this is a scenario that can be handled by adding a method to a partial class file for your *TableAdapter*, as shown here:

Visual Basic

```
Namespace NorthwindDataSetTableAdapters
    Partial Public Class CustomersTableAdapter
        Friend Sub SetTransaction(ByVal txn As SqlTransaction)
            For Each cmd As SqlCommand In Me.CommandCollection
                cmd.Transaction = txn
            Next cmd

            Me.Adapter.InsertCommand.Transaction = txn
            Me.Adapter.UpdateCommand.Transaction = txn
            Me.Adapter.DeleteCommand.Transaction = txn
        End Sub
    End Class
End Namespace
```

Visual C#

```
namespace NorthwindDataSetTableAdapters {
    partial class CustomersTableAdapter {
        internal void SetTransaction(SqlTransaction txn) {
            foreach (SqlCommand cmd in this.CommandCollection)
                cmd.Transaction = txn;

            this.Adapter.InsertCommand.Transaction = txn;
            this.Adapter.UpdateCommand.Transaction = txn;
            this.Adapter.DeleteCommand.Transaction = txn;
        }
    }
}
```

In other cases, there might not be a simple solution. For example, let's assume that you build a *TableAdapter* that encapsulates an *OleDbDataAdapter* that communicates with a Microsoft Access database. You might need to retrieve database-generated values (defaults, auto-increments) from the database after submitting new rows—a scenario we'll cover in depth in Chapter 11. If you were using a true *OleDbDataAdapter*, you would add code to handle the *RowUpdated* event. Unfortunately, *TableAdapters* do not expose events.

Visual Basic developers can add code to the *TableAdapter* class to provide a default for the *RowUpdated* event for the *DataAdapter* encapsulated by the *TableAdapter* using the *Handles* keyword as in code like the following:

Visual Basic

```
Namespace NorthwindDataSetTableAdapters
    Partial Public Class OrdersTableAdapter
        Private Sub HandlesRowUpdated(ByVal sender As Object, _
                                      ByVal e As SqlRowUpdatedEventArgs) _
                                      Handles _adapter.RowUpdated
            'To understand what code to execute when handling the event,
            '  see Chapter 11
        End Sub
    End Class
End Namespace
```

Unfortunately for C# developers, there are no default handlers in C#. While C# developers can programmatically supply their own handlers, there is no appropriate place to for that code.

Row Refresh Logic Not Compatible with Batch Updates

Enabling batch updating with a *TableAdapter* can be quite a challenge. While some properties of the *SqlDataAdapter* stored inside the *TableAdapter* are available through the Visual Studio designer, the *UpdateBatchSize* property is not. Partial classes do not offer a simple solution for where to place code to change designer-generated values. Unless you want to manually change the code in the designer-generated partial class file for the *TableAdapter*, the best solution is to expose the underlying *SqlDataAdapter* through a method or property, such as the *GetDataAdapter* property shown earlier.

If you're working with a SQL Server database, the TableAdapter Configuration Wizard will automatically include logic to refresh the contents of your *DataRow* after inserts and updates against the database. The TableAdapter Configuration Wizard returns this information by appending a SELECT query to the INSERT or UPDATE query to return the current contents of the row in the database. This feature is extremely handy if the database may generate values for your rows through defaults, triggers, or auto-increment columns.

While this approach works quite well in scenarios where you're submitting changes to the database one row at a time, which was the only way to submit changes in ADO.NET via a *SqlDataAdapter* prior to version 2.0, this approach is not compatible with the batch updating features added in ADO.NET 2.0. Returning values during update operations is supported only through output parameters. We'll discuss batch updating and ways to return server-generated values in batch updates in detail in Chapter 11.

Choosing Your Path

Strongly typed *DataSet* objects can help you build your application more quickly. They can also help you write efficient code more easily. But they don't offer the best possible performance. You can build an application that will run faster if you use untyped *DataSet* objects along with intelligent code.

If you decide to use strongly typed *DataSets*, *TableAdapters* can simplify the process of retrieving data and submitting pending changes. While *TableAdapters* hide some of the complexity of *SqlDataAdapters*, they also hide some of the functionality you might want to access directly.

So what's the right choice for you?

It all depends on the needs of your application. If performance and control of your application are the absolute highest priorities, you should use only untyped *DataSet* objects and *SqlData-Adapters*. However, if saving a few hours of development time is worth a small performance hit, you should consider using strongly typed *DataSet* objects, and perhaps *TableAdapters* as well.

Questions That Should Be Asked More Frequently

Q   When I try to submit changes using a *TableAdapter*'s *Update* method, I get an exception stating that "*Update* requires a valid *UpdateCommand* when passing a *DataRow* collection with modified rows." What went wrong?

A   This is the same exception you would receive if you called the *Update* method on a *Sql-DataAdapter* without having supplied updating logic. The TableAdapter Configuration Wizard does not display any warnings or errors if it fails to generate the logic required to submit changes to the database. There are three common scenarios where the *TableAdapter* lacks updating logic:

   ❑   You neglected to include the primary key column or columns in the *TableAdapter*'s query.

   ❑   The table you used in the *TableAdapter*'s query does not contain a primary key.

   ❑   You included multiple tables in the *TableAdapter*'s query.

Q   I need to get the best possible performance out of my middle-tier components, so I'm using untyped *DataSet* objects on the server. But strongly typed *DataSet* objects are so handy when I build the client portion of the application. Is there a way to get the best of both worlds?

A   Yes. Have your middle tier return and accept untyped *DataSet* objects. Use instances of strongly typed *DataSet* objects in the client application, and use either the *Merge* or *Load* method to import the contents of the untyped *DataSet* objects returned by the middle tier.

Q   *DataSet* objects offer limited validation features. I can't set properties on either an untyped or a strongly typed *DataSet* to ensure that the value of a column falls between certain limits. Can I add my own code to the class file for added validation?

A   Of course. You can add validation code to the desired properties of your strongly typed classes, but this scenario is not simple to handle with a strongly typed *DataSet*, even after introducing partial classes.

Partial classes can help you extend the classes generated by the strongly typed *DataSet* designer, helping you add properties and methods in a separate file that Visual Studio will not overwrite if you modify your strongly typed *DataSet* using the designer. However, partial classes won't help you override or change the behavior of existing properties and methods. The "best" option may be to add the validation routine to your partial class, and call that routine from the designer-generated code. Keep in mind that changing the structure of your strongly typed *DataSet* through the designer will delete and regenerate the designer-generated code file, forcing you to re-add the call to your validation routine.

Q   Kurt Meyer, one of the editors of this book, asked: In the discussion of null values, why did you check the Is<ColumnName>Null function before calling Set<ColumnName>Null?

Wouldn't it have been more efficient to simply call the Set<ColumnName>Null method since you'll end up using fewer machine operations?

A   The answer actually has more to do with the *DataRow*'s behavior than strongly typed *DataSets*. If the *RowState* of the *DataRow* is initially Unchanged and you set the column's value to *DBNull.Value*, the *DataRow* will now have a *RowState* of *Modified*, even if the column already contained *DBNull.Value*. So, the check prevents you from otherwise unnecessarily marking the *DataRow* as containing a pending change.

Q   What other options do I have when I use the XML Schema Definition Tool to generate a class?

A   If you check the "Using Annotations with a Typed DataSet" topic in the .NET Framework SDK, you'll find various options for controlling the names of some of the strongly typed classes generated by the tool. You'll also discover how to control how the properties on your strongly typed *DataRow* classes react when they contain null values. The XML Schema Definition Tool checks your .xsd file for the annotations listed in the documentation.

The XML Schema designer does not let you add annotations to your *DataSet* object's .xsd file through the designer's user interface. You can switch to XML view and add the annotations by hand. Or you can add annotations to your *DataSet* class in code and then save the *DataSet* object's schema to an .xsd file using the *DataSet* object's *WriteXmlSchema* method.

Adding annotations to your *DataSet* in code is actually simple if you use the *Extended-Properties* collection of the *DataTable* and *DataColumn* objects. The following code snippet is an example:

Visual Basic

```vbnet
Dim ds As New DataSet()
ds.DataSetName = "NameForYourNewClass"
Dim tbl As DataTable = ds.Tables.Add("Table1")
Dim col As DataColumn

'Set the name of the strongly typed DataRow for the DataTable.
tbl.ExtendedProperties.Add("typedName", "MyTable1Row")

'Set the name of the DataTable property of the DataSet.
tbl.ExtendedProperties.Add("typedPlural", "MyTable1Rows")

col = tbl.Columns.Add("StringColumn", GetType(String))
'Have the class return "<Null>" if the column contains null.
col.ExtendedProperties.Add("nullValue", "<Null>")

col = tbl.Columns.Add("StringColumn2", GetType(String))
'Have the class return String.Empty if the column contains null.
col.ExtendedProperties.Add("nullValue", String.Empty)

col = tbl.Columns.Add("IntegerColumn", GetType(Integer))
'Have the class return 0 if the column contains null.
col.ExtendedProperties.Add("nullValue", "0")

ds.WriteXmlSchema("C:\Desired\Path\To\YourNew.XSD")
```

Visual C#

```csharp
DataSet ds = new DataSet();
ds.DataSetName = "NameForYourNewClass";
DataTable tbl = ds.Tables.Add("Table1");
DataColumn col;

//Set the name of the strongly typed DataRow for the DataTable.
tbl.ExtendedProperties.Add("typedName", "MyTable1Row");

//Set the name of the DataTable property of the DataSet.
tbl.ExtendedProperties.Add("typedPlural", "MyTable1Rows");

col = tbl.Columns.Add("StringColumn", typeof(string));
//Have the class return "<Null>" if the column contains null.
col.ExtendedProperties.Add("nullValue", "<Null>");

col = tbl.Columns.Add("StringColumn2", typeof(string));
//Have the class return String.Empty if the column contains null.
col.ExtendedProperties.Add("nullValue", String.Empty);

col = tbl.Columns.Add("IntegerColumn", typeof(int));
//Have the class return 0 if the column contains null.
col.ExtendedProperties.Add("nullValue", "0");

ds.WriteXmlSchema(@"C:\Desired\Path\To\YourNew.XSD");
```

Chapter 10

Submitting Updates to Your Database

"When you believe in things that you don't understand, then you suffer. Superstition ain't the way."

–Stevie Wonder

In this chapter:

Although Stevie Wonder probably wasn't talking about submitting updates, the quote is still relevant to the topic. ADO.NET gives database programmers unprecedented power and control over submitting updates. However, based on the questions I've handled personally on internal and external newsgroups and at conferences, I'd say that few developers really understand how to wield this control and power effectively.

So many of the ADO.NET code snippets I've seen rely on the *SqlCommandBuilder* class to generate updating logic. Sometimes the code snippet comes with a warning that says you should generate your own updating logic instead, but those comments rarely explain why or how this is done.

How many times have you asked someone how he got his code to work, only to have him shrug, smile, and say, "It just works"? That's the sort of superstition I want to dispel in this chapter and the following chapter.

The more you understand how you can use ADO.NET to submit updates, the more comfortable you'll become generating your own updating logic and submitting updates through stored procedures. This chapter will help you understand how to use a *SqlDataAdapter* to submit the pending changes from your *DataSet* to your database. Along the way, you'll also learn how and when to use tools to save time without sacrificing performance or control.

If you've been reading the chapters of this book in sequence, you should already be comfortable creating untyped and strongly typed *DataSet* objects to store the data returned by *SqlData-Adapter* objects. You should also be comfortable modifying the contents of a *DataSet*. This chapter will help you understand the basics of using *SqlDataAdapter* objects to submit the changes stored in your *DataSet* to your database.

Let's look at an order from the sample Northwind database. Figure 10-1 shows the query issued in Microsoft SQL Server Query Analyzer to retrieve information for the order. For the sake of argument, let's say that the customer calls and wants to change the order. The customer no longer wants to order tofu because it isn't selling in the store. Instead, the customer wants to order more bottles of hot sauce, which are flying off the shelves, and begin stocking some chai tea. The sales representative will look up the customer's order and modify it using a Microsoft Windows application written in .NET.

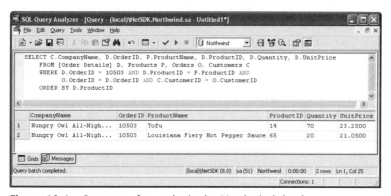

Figure 10-1   Contents of an order in the Northwind database

You're building the application that the sales representative will use to modify such orders. Thanks to the knowledge you gained in Chapter 5, you know how to fetch the contents of the customer's order and put it into a *DataSet* using a parameterized *SqlDataAdapter*. Based on what you learned in Chapter 6, you can enable your application to modify the data in the *DataSet* according to the customer's instructions. In this scenario, the sales representative deletes the *DataRow* for tofu, modifies the *DataRow* for hot sauce, and adds a new *DataRow* for chai tea. As noted earlier, changing the contents of a *DataSet* doesn't change the corresponding rows in the database. Now you need to provide the logic to submit these changes in the order back to the database.

In Chapter 5, you learned that the *SqlDataAdapter* exposes an *Update* method that you can use to submit pending changes to your database. So you can build an application that uses code such as the following to try to submit the changes to the order:

Visual Basic

```
'Retrieve the contents of the order into a DataTable.
Dim strConn, strSQL As String
strConn = "Data Source=.\SQLExpress;" & _
          "Initial Catalog=Northwind;Integrated Security=True;"
strSQL = "SELECT OrderID, ProductID, Quantity, UnitPrice " & _
         "FROM [Order Details] WHERE OrderID = @OrderID " & _
         "ORDER BY ProductID"
Dim da As New SqlDataAdapter(strSQL, strConn)
da.SelectCommand.Parameters.AddWithValue("@OrderID", 10503)
Dim tbl As New DataTable("Order Details")
da.Fill(tbl)


'Modify the contents of the order.
Dim rowToDelete, rowToUpdate, rowToInsert As DataRow
'Delete the tofu DataRow
rowToDelete = tbl.Rows(0)
rowToDelete.Delete()
'Double the quantity for hot sauce
rowToUpdate = tbl.Rows(1)
rowToUpdate("Quantity") = CShort(rowToUpdate("Quantity")) * 2
'Add a new DataRow for chai
rowToInsert = tbl.Rows.Add(New Object() {10503, 1, 24, 18})

'Submit the pending changes.
Try
    da.Update(tbl)
    Console.WriteLine("Successfully submitted new changes")
Catch ex As Exception
    Console.WriteLine("Call to SqlDataAdapter.Update " & _
                      "threw exception: {0}", ex.Message)
End Try
```

Visual C#

```
//Retrieve the contents of the order into a DataTable.
string strConn, strSQL;
strConn = @"Data Source=.\SQLExpress;" +
            "Initial Catalog=Northwind;Integrated Security=True;";
strSQL = "SELECT OrderID, ProductID, Quantity, UnitPrice " +
         "FROM [Order Details] WHERE OrderID = @OrderID " +
         "ORDER BY ProductID;";
SqlDataAdapter da = new SqlDataAdapter(strSQL, strConn);
da.SelectCommand.Parameters.AddWithValue("@OrderID", 10503);
DataTable tbl = new DataTable("Order Details");
da.Fill(tbl);

//Modify the contents of the order.
DataRow rowToDelete, rowToUpdate, rowToInsert;
//Delete the tofu DataRow
rowToDelete = tbl.Rows[0];
```

```
rowToDelete.Delete();
//Double the quantity for hot sauce
rowToUpdate = tbl.Rows[1];
rowToUpdate["Quantity"] = (short) (rowToUpdate["Quantity"]) * 2;
//Add a new DataRow for chai
rowToInsert = tbl.Rows.Add(new object[] {10503, 1, 24, 18});

//Submit the pending changes.
try
{
    da.Update(tbl);
    Console.WriteLine("Successfully submitted new changes");
}
catch (Exception ex)
{
    Console.WriteLine("Call to SqlDataAdapter.Update " +
                    "threw exception: {0}", ex.Message);
}
```

This code will successfully compile, but it will not successfully submit the changes to the order to your database. Instead, you'll receive an exception that says, "Update requires a valid DeleteCommand when passed DataRow collection with deleted rows."

Developers who are new to ADO.NET are often puzzled by this exception, especially because previous Microsoft data-access technologies, such as ADO, include features that let you submit changes automatically. With ADO.NET, you can submit changes using the *SqlDataAdapter* class, but the *SqlDataAdapter* does not automatically include the logic required to submit changes.

So how do you add the necessary updating logic to your ADO.NET *SqlDataAdapter*? There are two main options: you can write your own code or explicitly ask ADO.NET to generate the updating logic for you. There's a third option that's essentially a hybrid of the first two options—you can use a code-generation tool such as Microsoft Visual Studio to generate the updating logic for you and store that logic in your application. This chapter explores all three options and explains the pros and cons of each.

Because the code we'll examine in this chapter is designed to modify the contents of a particular order in the database, you might find it helpful to have simple code snippets that display the contents of the order and that reset the contents of the order. Here are procedures you can call to perform each of these operations:

Visual Basic

```
Private Sub DisplayOrder()
    Dim strConn, strSQL As String
    strConn = "Data Source=.\SQLExpress;" & _
            "Initial Catalog=Northwind;Integrated Security=True;"
    Using cn As New SqlConnection(strConn)
        cn.Open()

        strSQL = "SELECT P.ProductName, D.Quantity, D.UnitPrice " & _
                " FROM [Order Details] D JOIN Products P " & _
```

```
                    "          ON D.ProductID = P.ProductID " & _
                    "    WHERE D.OrderID = @OrderID"
            Dim intOrderID As Integer = 10503
            Dim cmd As New SqlCommand(strSQL, cn)
            cmd.Parameters.AddWithValue("@OrderID", intOrderID)

            Console.WriteLine("Contents of order {0}", intOrderID)
            Using rdr As SqlDataReader = cmd.ExecuteReader()
                Do While rdr.Read()
                    Console.WriteLine("  {0,-32}    {1}    {2:c}", _
                                        rdr.GetString(0), rdr.GetInt16(1), _
                                        rdr.GetDecimal(2))
                Loop
                rdr.Close()
            End Using
            Console.WriteLine()

            cn.Close()
        End Using
    End Sub

    Private Sub ResetOrder()
        Dim strConn, strSQL As String
        strConn = "Data Source=.\SQLExpress;" & _
                "Initial Catalog=Northwind;Integrated Security=True;"
        Using cn As New SqlConnection(strConn)
            cn.Open()

            'Delete the current contents of the order
            strSQL = "DELETE [Order Details] WHERE OrderID = @OrderID"
            Dim cmd As New SqlCommand(strSQL, cn)
            cmd.Parameters.AddWithValue("@OrderID", 10503)
            cmd.ExecuteNonQuery()

            strSQL = "INSERT INTO [Order Details] " & _
                    "  (OrderID, ProductID, Quantity, UnitPrice) VALUES " & _
                    "  (@OrderID, @ProductID, @Quantity, @UnitPrice)"
            cmd.CommandText = strSQL

            'Re-add the tofu
            cmd.Parameters.AddWithValue("@ProductID", 14)
            cmd.Parameters.AddWithValue("@Quantity", 70)
            cmd.Parameters.AddWithValue("@UnitPrice", 23.25)
            cmd.ExecuteNonQuery()

            'Re-add the hot sauce
            cmd.Parameters("@ProductID").Value = 65
            cmd.Parameters("@Quantity").Value = 20
            cmd.Parameters("@UnitPrice").Value = 21.05
            cmd.ExecuteNonQuery()

            cn.Close()
        End Using
    End Sub
```

Visual C#

```csharp
static void DisplayOrder()
{
    string strConn, strSQL;
    strConn = @"Data Source=.\SQLExpress;" +
            "Initial Catalog=Northwind;Integrated Security=True;";
    using (SqlConnection cn = new SqlConnection(strConn))
    {
        cn.Open();

        strSQL = "SELECT P.ProductName, D.Quantity, D.UnitPrice " +
                "  FROM [Order Details] D JOIN Products P " +
                "      ON D.ProductID = P.ProductID " +
                "  WHERE D.OrderID = @OrderID";
        int intOrderID = 10503;
        SqlCommand cmd = new SqlCommand(strSQL, cn);
        cmd.Parameters.AddWithValue("@OrderID", intOrderID);

        Console.WriteLine("Contents of order {0}", intOrderID);
        using (SqlDataReader rdr = cmd.ExecuteReader())
        {
            while (rdr.Read())
                Console.WriteLine("  {0,-32}    {1}    {2:c}",
                                rdr.GetString(0), rdr.GetInt16(1),
                                rdr.GetDecimal(2));
            rdr.Close();
        }
        Console.WriteLine();

        cn.Close();
    }
}

static void ResetOrder()
{
    //Reset the order.
    string strConn, strSQL;
    strConn = @"Data Source=.\SQLExpress;" +
            "Initial Catalog=Northwind;Integrated Security=True;";
    using (SqlConnection cn = new SqlConnection(strConn))
    {
        cn.Open();

        //Delete the current contents of the order
        strSQL = "DELETE [Order Details] WHERE OrderID = @OrderID";
        SqlCommand cmd = new SqlCommand(strSQL, cn);
        cmd.Parameters.AddWithValue("@OrderID", 10503);
        cmd.ExecuteNonQuery();

        strSQL = "INSERT INTO [Order Details] " +
                "  (OrderID, ProductID, Quantity, UnitPrice) VALUES " +
                "  (@OrderID, @ProductID, @Quantity, @UnitPrice)";
        cmd.CommandText = strSQL;

        //Re-add the tofu
```

```
cmd.Parameters.AddWithValue("@ProductID", 14);
cmd.Parameters.AddWithValue("@Quantity", 70);
cmd.Parameters.AddWithValue("@UnitPrice", 23.25);
cmd.ExecuteNonQuery();

//Re-add the hot sauce
cmd.Parameters["@ProductID"].Value = 65;
cmd.Parameters["@Quantity"].Value = 20;
cmd.Parameters["@UnitPrice"].Value = 21.05;
cmd.ExecuteNonQuery();

cn.Close();
    }
}
```

Submitting Updates Using Parameterized *SqlCommands*

Let's set aside the *SqlDataAdapter* class for just a moment. As in the preceding simple snippets, you can already submit updates using parameterized *SqlCommands*.

Submitting a New Row

You can execute the following parameterized INSERT query to add a new row to your table. The syntax is straightforward. Specify the table name, a parameterized list of column names, and a parameterized list of parameters. For more information about the various options available on an INSERT query, see the documentation for your database's query language.

```
INSERT INTO [Order Details] (OrderID, ProductID, Quantity, UnitPrice)
    VALUES (@OrderID, @ProductID, @Quantity, @UnitPrice)
```

In Chapter 4, you learned how to create a *SqlCommand* to execute this type of query, setting the *SqlCommand*'s *CommandText* property and appending *SqlParameters*. The following code snippet contains logic to submit a new order detail from the rowToInsert DataRow.

Visual Basic
```
Dim strConn, strSQL As String
strConn = "Data Source=.\SQLExpress;" & _
          "Initial Catalog=Northwind;Integrated Security=True;"
Dim cn As New SqlConnection(strConn)
cn.Open()
strSQL = "INSERT INTO [Order Details] " & _
         "  (OrderID, ProductID, Quantity, UnitPrice) VALUES " & _
         "  (@OrderID, @ProductID, @Quantity, @UnitPrice)"
Dim cmdInsert As New SqlCommand(strSQL, cn)
cmdInsert.Parameters.AddWithValue("@OrderID", rowToInsert("OrderID"))
cmdInsert.Parameters.AddWithValue("@ProductID", rowToInsert("ProductID"))
cmdInsert.Parameters.AddWithValue("@Quantity", rowToInsert("Quantity"))
cmdInsert.Parameters.AddWithValue("@UnitPrice", rowToInsert("UnitPrice"))
Try
```

```
    cmdInsert.ExecuteNonQuery()
    rowToInsert.AcceptChanges()
    Console.WriteLine("Query executed successfully")
Catch ex As Exception
    Console.WriteLine("Query failed: {0}", ex.Message)
End Try
```

Visual C#

```
string strConn, strSQL;
strConn = @"Data Source=.\SQLExpress;" +
        "Initial Catalog=Northwind;Integrated Security=True;";
SqlConnection cn = new SqlConnection(strConn);
strSQL = "INSERT INTO [Order Details] " +
        " (OrderID, ProductID, Quantity, UnitPrice) VALUES " +
        " (@OrderID, @ProductID, @Quantity, @UnitPrice)";
SqlCommand cmdInsert = new SqlCommand(strSQL, cn);
cmdInsert.Parameters.AddWithValue("@OrderID", rowToInsert["OrderID"]);
cmdInsert.Parameters.AddWithValue("@ProductID", rowToInsert["ProductID"]);
cmdInsert.Parameters.AddWithValue("@Quantity", rowToInsert["Quantity"]);
cmdInsert.Parameters.AddWithValue("@UnitPrice", rowToInsert["UnitPrice"]);
try {
    cmdInsert.ExecuteNonQuery();
    rowToInsert.AcceptChanges();
    Console.WriteLine("Query executed successfully");
} catch (Exception ex) {
    Console.WriteLine("Query failed: {0}", ex.Message);
}
```

Note   If the query executes successfully, the code calls the *AcceptChanges* method on the *DataRow*, so it is marked as an unchanged row rather than a pending insertion.

Because this code only needs to submit a single row, it takes a bit of a shortcut—the *AddWith-Value* method—to create each *SqlParameters* and set its *Value* property in a single line of code. If you needed code to execute the INSERT query multiple times, you should create the *SqlParameters* using the *Add* method and then set the *Value* property for each *SqlParameter* prior to executing each query.

Well, that was simple enough, but submitting new rows is relatively straightforward. Now let's look at a more complex scenario.

Updating an Existing Row

The syntax for the UPDATE query is more complex. Here's an example of an UPDATE query that you can execute to submit a change to a row in the Order Details table:

```
UPDATE [Order Details]
  SET OrderID = @OrderID_New, ProductID = @ProductID_New,
      Quantity = @Quantity_New, UnitPrice = @UnitPrice_New
  WHERE OrderID = @OrderID_Old AND ProductID = @ProductID_Old
    AND Quantity = @Quantity_Old AND UnitPrice = @UnitPrice_Old
```

Modifying Values in the SET Clause

The SET clause in the UPDATE query looks similar to the first half of the UPDATE query, including all column names and parameters for each *DataColumn* in the *DataTable*. Do we *really* need to include all these columns? If you look back at the code that modified the *DataRow* for hot sauce, you'll see that it modified only the Quantity column. In theory, the UPDATE query could have included just the Quantity column. However, the sales representative may want to modify other columns based on the customer's request.

If you do not know which columns in a *DataRow* will be modified, you have two choices: include all updatable columns, or compare the values for the columns in the *DataRow*. The second approach is definitely an appealing option because it involves passing less data to your database and requires less work for your database to perform. However, this approach greatly increases the complexity of your code because it requires not just changing the values of parameters for each row, it also involves changing the text of the query, including only the columns that have been modified.

Key Columns in the WHERE Clause

It's the WHERE clause that makes this query so much more complex than the INSERT query. When you want to modify a particular row, you must provide enough information for the database to find that row. The primary key for the Order Details table consists of the OrderID and ProductID columns. Because the primary key enforces uniqueness within the database, referencing these columns in the WHERE clause for the query guarantees that the query cannot modify more than one row in the table.

Multiple *SqlParameters* for a Column

You might have noticed that the parameters for the OrderID and ProductID columns in the WHERE clause are not the same as the parameters in the SET clause. With updating logic, you may want (or need) to submit multiple "versions" of a particular column in the parameterized query.

The sales representative might have decided that the best way to satisfy the customer request of removing one item from the order and adding another was to simply modify the *DataRow* for the unwanted item—changing the values for the ProductID, Quantity, and UnitPrice columns to reflect the desired item. In that scenario, you want to pass two different versions of the ProductID column to the query. You need to pass the original value that you retrieved into the ProductID column in your *DataRow* in the WHERE clause so that the database can find the row to modify. For the SET clause, you want to pass the current version for that column to modify the row.

In Chapter 6, we discussed how to access both the current and original values for columns in a *DataRow*. The *DataRow*'s default indexer returns the current value, but you can explicitly request the original value for a column using code such as the following:

Visual Basic

```
Dim row As DataRow = ...
Console.WriteLine("Current ProductID:  {0}", row("ProductID"))
Console.WriteLine("Original ProductID: {0}", _
                  row("ProductID", DataRowVersion.Original))
```

Visual C#

```
DataRow row = ...;
Console.WriteLine("Current ProductID:  {0}", row["ProductID"]);
Console.WriteLine("Original ProductID: {0}",
                  row["ProductID", DataRowVersion.Original]);
```

We can combine the UPDATE query with logic to assign values from the current and original versions of columns in the *DataRow* to parameters in the query using the following code:

> **Warning** The logic to submit this change is incomplete, as you'll discover shortly. Do not use the logic shown here in your code.

Visual Basic

```
Dim strConn, strSQL As String
strConn = "Data Source=.\SQLExpress;" & _
          "Initial Catalog=Northwind;Integrated Security=True;"
Dim cn As New SqlConnection(strConn)
cn.Open()
strSQL = "UPDATE [Order Details] " & _
         "  SET OrderID = @OrderID_New, ProductID = @ProductID_New, " & _
         "      Quantity = @Quantity_New, UnitPrice = @UnitPrice_New " & _
         "  WHERE OrderID = @OrderID_Old AND ProductID = @ProductID_Old " & _
         "    AND Quantity = @Quantity_Old AND UnitPrice = @UnitPrice_Old"
Dim cmdUpdate As New SqlCommand(strSQL, cn)
cmdUpdate.Parameters.AddWithValue("@OrderID_New", _
                     rowToUpdate("OrderID"))
cmdUpdate.Parameters.AddWithValue("@ProductID_New", _
                     rowToUpdate("ProductID"))
cmdUpdate.Parameters.AddWithValue("@Quantity_New", _
                     rowToUpdate("Quantity"))
cmdUpdate.Parameters.AddWithValue("@UnitPrice_New", _
                     rowToUpdate("UnitPrice"))
cmdUpdate.Parameters.AddWithValue("@OrderID_Old", _
                     rowToUpdate("OrderID", DataRowVersion.Original))
cmdUpdate.Parameters.AddWithValue("@ProductID_Old", _
                     rowToUpdate("ProductID", DataRowVersion.Original))
cmdUpdate.Parameters.AddWithValue("@Quantity_Old", _
                     rowToUpdate("Quantity", DataRowVersion.Original))
cmdUpdate.Parameters.AddWithValue("@UnitPrice_Old", _
                     rowToUpdate("UnitPrice", DataRowVersion.Original))
Try
```

```
    cmdUpdate.ExecuteNonQuery()
    rowToUpdate.AcceptChanges()
    Console.WriteLine("Query executed successfully")
Catch ex As Exception
    Console.WriteLine("Query failed: {0}", ex.Message)
End Try
```

Visual C#

```
string strConn, strSQL;
strConn = @"Data Source=.\SQLExpress;" +
            "Initial Catalog=Northwind;Integrated Security=True;";
SqlConnection cn = new SqlConnection(strConn);
strSQL = "UPDATE [Order Details] " +
         "  SET OrderID = @OrderID_New, ProductID = @ProductID_New, " +
         "      Quantity = @Quantity_New, UnitPrice = @UnitPrice_New " +
         "  WHERE OrderID = @OrderID_Old AND ProductID = @ProductID_Old " +
         "    AND Quantity = @Quantity_Old AND UnitPrice = @UnitPrice_Old";
SqlCommand cmdUpdate = new SqlCommand(strSQL, cn);
cmdUpdate.Parameters.AddWithValue("@OrderID_New",
                    rowToUpdate["OrderID"]);
cmdUpdate.Parameters.AddWithValue("@ProductID_New",
                    rowToUpdate["ProductID"]);
cmdUpdate.Parameters.AddWithValue("@Quantity_New",
                    rowToUpdate["Quantity"]);
cmdUpdate.Parameters.AddWithValue("@UnitPrice_New",
                    rowToUpdate["UnitPrice"]);
cmdUpdate.Parameters.AddWithValue("@OrderID_Old",
                    rowToUpdate["OrderID", DataRowVersion.Original]);
cmdUpdate.Parameters.AddWithValue("@ProductID_Old",
                    rowToUpdate["ProductID", DataRowVersion.Original]);
cmdUpdate.Parameters.AddWithValue("@Quantity_Old",
                    rowToUpdate["Quantity", DataRowVersion.Original]);
cmdUpdate.Parameters.AddWithValue("@UnitPrice_Old",
                    rowToUpdate["UnitPrice", DataRowVersion.Original]);
try {
    cmdUpdate.ExecuteNonQuery();
    rowToUpdate.AcceptChanges();
    Console.WriteLine("Query executed successfully");
} catch (Exception ex) {
    Console.WriteLine("Query failed: {0}", ex.Message);
}
```

Warning   The logic to submit this change is incomplete, as you'll discover shortly. Do not use the logic shown here in your code. Yes, it bears repeating.

Additional Concurrency Checks

Earlier, we discussed why the columns that constitute the table's primary key—OrderID and ProductID—appear in the query's WHERE clause. The WHERE clause also includes logic to check the contents of the other columns—Quantity and UnitPrice. Including these columns in the WHERE clause dictates what happens if multiple users want to modify the same row of data.

For a moment, let's assume that this order comes from a large customer. Increasing the quantity of hot sauce in the order is vitally important to the customer's business. (Some people are really passionate about hot sauce.) In fact, the order is so important that two people from the company call at the same time to change the order. The order currently calls for 20 boxes of hot sauce. ContactA wants to increase the order to 40 units, and ContactB wants to increase the order to 50 units.

Each contact simultaneously speaks with a different sales representative. Each sales representative accesses the order, makes the requested change, and clicks the application's Save button to save the changes. What happens when the second sales representative tries to save the change on her screen?

To better understand what might happen in a scenario such as this, let's take another look at the sample UPDATE query from earlier in the chapter:

```
UPDATE [Order Details]
  SET OrderID = @OrderID_New, ProductID = @ProductID_New,
      Quantity = @Quantity_New, UnitPrice = @UnitPrice_New
  WHERE OrderID = @OrderID_Old AND ProductID = @ProductID_Old
    AND Quantity = @Quantity_Old AND UnitPrice = @UnitPrice_Old
```

Let's assume that the change that ContactA requested (changing Quantity from 20 to 40) is saved first. Using this UPDATE query, the change will succeed. ContactB's requested change will not succeed.

To understand why the second change will fail to update the row in the database, look more closely at the WHERE clause. The query checks the current value of each column in the row. Because ContactA and ContactB each called at the same time, the original value in the Quantity column in each sales representative's application is 20. When the sales representative for ContactB tries to save the change to the order, the Quantity column in the row within the database has a value of 40 (as a result of ContactA's change to the order). Thus, when ContactB's sales representative tries to submit the change, the query does not modify the desired row in the database.

Alternative Concurrency Options   Had the UPDATE query included only the primary key columns, ContactB's change would have succeeded and overwritten ContactA's change. Using only the primary key columns in updating logic is often referred to as "last in wins," for obvious reasons. This logic might make sense in some scenarios, but it's not an approach that I recommend in general.

Another approach is to use the primary key and a row version column that changes with each successive update. SQL Server's timestamp column was designed specifically for this approach. Each time you modify the contents of the row, the server generates a new timestamp value for the row. If you're working with a database that does not have such a column, you can work with globally unique identifiers (GUIDs) instead, storing either their binary or string representation.

> **Note**   If you rely on timestamp columns in concurrency checks, you'll likely want to retrieve the new database-generated timestamp values after successful updates, a topic that I explain in Chapter 11.

Determining the Success or Failure of Your Update Attempt

The code snippet that showed how you could execute the UPDATE query came with a warning, and it's time to explain why.

In the multi-user scenario described earlier, ContactB's desired change to the order would not succeed. Because the value assigned to the parameter for the Quantity column in the WHERE clause does not match the current contents of the column in the corresponding row in the database, the query did not modify any rows. However, executing the query would not generate an exception. The database did what the query asked, modifying all rows that matched the criteria specified in the WHERE clause. There just weren't any rows that matched.

If you're submitting changes by writing your own updating logic, you need to take scenarios like this into consideration. Thankfully, you can use the return value of the *ExecuteNonQuery* method to determine how many rows were affected by the query. The desired outcome is for the query to affect one row. Let's modify the previous code snippet to account for this possible outcome:

Visual Basic

```
Try
    Dim intRecordsAffected As Integer
    intRecordsAffected = cmdUpdate.ExecuteNonQuery()
    If intRecordsAffected = 1 Then
        rowToUpdate.AcceptChanges()
        Console.WriteLine("Success - Query affected one row")
    ElseIf intRecordsAffected = 0 Then
        Console.WriteLine("Failure - Query affected no rows")
    Else
        Console.WriteLine("Query affected {0} rows?!?", _
                        intRecordsAffected)
    End If
Catch ex As Exception
    Console.WriteLine("Query failed: {0}", ex.Message)
End Try
```

Visual C#

```
try {
    int intRecordsAffected = cmdUpdate.ExecuteNonQuery();
    if (intRecordsAffected == 1) {
        rowToUpdate.AcceptChanges();
        Console.WriteLine("Success - Query affected one row");
    } else if (intRecordsAffected == 0)
        Console.WriteLine("Failure - Query affected no rows");
    else
```

```
        Console.WriteLine("Query affected {0} rows?!?",
                          intRecordsAffected);
} catch (Exception ex) {
    Console.WriteLine("Query failed: {0}", ex.Message);
}
```

Additional Logic: @@ROWCOUNT and NOCOUNT   There are some circumstances in which the *ExecuteNonQuery* method will not return the number of rows modified by your query. For example, you may have configured your *SqlCommand* to call a stored procedure that performs multiple actions, such as inserting a row into a logging table to indicate that a user called the stored procedure, or you might have similar logic in a trigger in the database. The additional logic can affect the value returned by the call to *ExecuteNonQuery*.

Let's assume for a moment that the code snippet calls a stored procedure to submit the change to the order, rather than just using a simple UPDATE query. And let's assume that the stored procedure inserts a row into some log table to keep track of who is calling the stored procedure and when. If the call to the stored procedure updates the desired row in the Order Details table, the *ExecuteNonQuery* method will return 2 because the call to *ExecuteNonQuery* inserted a row into the log table and modified a row in the Order Details table. If the call to the stored procedure does not update the desired row in the table, the *ExecuteNonQuery* method will return 1 because the call to *ExecuteNonQuery* inserted a row into the log table.

You can tell SQL Server when to return (or not return) information about modified rows by using the NOCOUNT setting. This stored procedure definition tells SQL Server not to report information about the row inserted into the log table:

```
CREATE PROCEDURE Proc_UpdateOrderDetail
  (@OrderID_New int, @ProductID_New int, @Quantity_New smallint,
   @UnitPrice_New money, @OrderID_Old int, @ProductID_Old int,
   @Quantity_Old smallint, @UnitPrice_Old money) AS
BEGIN
  SET NOCOUNT ON
  INSERT INTO LoggedOrderChanges (OrderID, ModifiedDate)
    VALUES (@OrderID_New, GetDate())
  SET NOCOUNT OFF
  UPDATE [Order Details]
    SET OrderID = @OrderID_New, ProductID = @ProductID_New,
        Quantity = @Quantity_New, UnitPrice = @UnitPrice_New
  WHERE OrderID = @OrderID_Old AND ProductID = @ProductID_Old
    AND Quantity = @Quantity_Old AND UnitPrice = @UnitPrice_Old
END
```

Thanks to the use of the NOCOUNT setting, the stored procedure will report only the number of rows affected by the UPDATE query that it executes.

If you cannot use NOCOUNT to force SQL Server to report the number of records affected by just the desired queries, you could use the @@ROWCOUNT function, which returns the number of rows affected by the last query. The following stored procedure demonstrates this approach, returning the number of rows affected by just the UPDATE query through an output parameter. Using this approach does require you to check the value for the output parameter rather than the return value for the *ExecuteNonQuery* method because that method call will return the total number of rows affected by the stored procedure—including both the INSERT and UPDATE queries.

```
CREATE PROCEDURE Proc_UpdateOrderDetail
  (@OrderID_New int, @ProductID_New int, @Quantity_New smallint,
   @UnitPrice_New money, @OrderID_Old int, @ProductID_Old int,
   @Quantity_Old smallint, @UnitPrice_Old money,
   @RowsAffected int OUTPUT) AS
BEGIN
  INSERT INTO LoggedOrderChanges (OrderID, ModifiedDate)
    VALUES (@OrderID_New, GetDate())
  UPDATE [Order Details]
    SET OrderID = @OrderID_New, ProductID = @ProductID_New,
        Quantity = @Quantity_New, UnitPrice = @UnitPrice_New
  WHERE OrderID = @OrderID_Old AND ProductID = @ProductID_Old
    AND Quantity = @Quantity_Old AND UnitPrice = @UnitPrice_Old
  SET @RowsAffected = @@ROWCOUNT
END
```

> **Note** If you return the number of rows modified by the stored procedure, the *SqlDataAdapter* will not be able to determine whether an update attempt succeeded without your help. You'll need to handle the *RowUpdated* event and check the value of the output parameter to determine whether the update succeeded. If you determine the update failed, set the *Status* property of the *SqlRowUpdatedEventArgs* parameter to *ErrorsOccurred* and set the *Errors* property to a new *DBConcurrencyException*. Otherwise, set the *Status* property to *Continue* and the *Errors* property to *null* or *Nothing*, depending on your language of choice.

Working with Null Values

The Customers table in the Northwind database contains a Region column that accepts strings of up to 15 characters and also accepts null values. A number of rows in the Region column have a null value. Many developers will try to use a query such as the following to retrieve those rows:

```
SELECT COUNT(CustomerID) FROM Customers WHERE Region = NULL
```

If you use this query in ADO.NET or run this query in SQL Query Analyzer, you'll find that it returns zero rows.

Null values are a special case in the database world, especially when it comes to comparing null values in a query. According to ANSI standards, you can't compare null values using the equal to (=) operator. Instead, you must use IS NULL in your query. The following query returns the rows in the Customers table that have null values for the Region column:

```
SELECT COUNT(CustomerID) FROM Customers WHERE Region IS NULL
```

What do null values have to do with submitting changes to your database? You want the concurrency checks in the WHERE clause to succeed as long as the current values in the row in the database match the original values in the *DataRow*. If the value for a column is null for both the database row and the *DataRow*, testing for equality will still fail. You need to treat this as a special case and check for null values in both the database and the *DataRow*. In other words, you want the concurrency check for a column that can be null to succeed if the database and *DataRow* columns are equal, or if they are both null.

The updating logic for the Order Details table does not require null checks because none of the columns can contain null values. For the moment, let's assume that the Quantity column could be set to null. According to ANSI standards, the following comparison would return false if both the column and parameter values were set to null:

```
Quantity = @Quantity_Old
```

So we would need to treat this scenario as a special case when comparing values for the column and parameter. The following line of code shows what that logic would look like:

```
(@Quantity_Old IS NULL AND Quantity IS NULL) OR Quantity = @Quantity_Old
```

Deleting an Existing Row

Deleting a row via a DELETE query is similar to modifying a row via an UPDATE query, except that there are no new values to submit, so there's no SET clause. We can use the following query to delete an existing row in the Order Details table:

```
DELETE [Order Details]
  WHERE OrderID = @OrderID AND ProductID = @ProductID
    AND Quantity = @Quantity AND UnitPrice = @UnitPrice
```

We can use this updating logic to submit the pending deletion using the following code:

Visual Basic
```
strSQL = "DELETE [Order Details] " & _
        "   WHERE OrderID = @OrderID AND ProductID = @ProductID" & _
        "     AND Quantity = @Quantity AND UnitPrice = @UnitPrice"
Dim cmdDelete As New SqlCommand(strSQL, cn)
cmdDelete.Parameters.AddWithValue("@OrderID ", _
                    rowToDelete("OrderID", DataRowVersion.Original))
cmdDelete.Parameters.AddWithValue("@ProductID", _
                    rowToDelete("ProductID", DataRowVersion.Original))
cmdDelete.Parameters.AddWithValue("@Quantity", _
                    rowToDelete("Quantity", DataRowVersion.Original))
cmdDelete.Parameters.AddWithValue("@UnitPrice", _
                    rowToDelete("UnitPrice", DataRowVersion.Original))
Try
    Dim intRecordsAffected As Integer
    intRecordsAffected = cmdDelete.ExecuteNonQuery()
    If intRecordsAffected = 1 Then
        rowToDelete.AcceptChanges()
```

```vb
            Console.WriteLine("Success - Query affected one row")
        ElseIf intRecordsAffected = 0 Then
            Console.WriteLine("Failure - Query affected no rows")
        Else
            Console.WriteLine("Query affected {0} rows?!?", _
                            intRecordsAffected)
        End If
    Catch ex As Exception
        Console.WriteLine("Query failed: {0}", ex.Message)
    End Try
```

Visual C#

```csharp
strSQL = "DELETE [Order Details] " +
        "  WHERE OrderID = @OrderID AND ProductID = @ProductID" +
        "    AND Quantity = @Quantity AND UnitPrice = @UnitPrice";
SqlCommand cmdDelete = new SqlCommand(strSQL, cn);
cmdDelete.Parameters.AddWithValue("@OrderID ",
                    rowToDelete["OrderID", DataRowVersion.Original]);
cmdDelete.Parameters.AddWithValue("@ProductID",
                    rowToDelete["ProductID", DataRowVersion.Original]);
cmdDelete.Parameters.AddWithValue("@Quantity",
                    rowToDelete["Quantity", DataRowVersion.Original]);
cmdDelete.Parameters.AddWithValue("@UnitPrice",
                    rowToDelete["UnitPrice", DataRowVersion.Original]);
try {
    int intRecordsAffected = cmdDelete.ExecuteNonQuery();
    if (intRecordsAffected == 1) {
        rowToDelete.AcceptChanges();
        Console.WriteLine("Success - Query affected one row");
    } else if (intRecordsAffected == 0)
        Console.WriteLine("Failure - Query affected no rows");
    else
        Console.WriteLine("Query affected {0} rows?!?",
                        intRecordsAffected);
} catch (Exception ex) {
    Console.WriteLine("Query failed: {0}", ex.Message);
}
```

What More Could You Need?

You already have all the functionality you need to take the pending changes from a database and submit them to your database. What more could you need?

Actually, submitting changes requires...well, a little more code. You'll still need to do the following:

- Create a procedure (or function) that accepts multiple *DataRows*.

- Look for *DataRows* that contain pending changes.

- Access a *SqlCommand* that contains the updating logic that corresponds to the *DataRow*'s *RowState* property.

- Assign values from the *DataRow*'s columns to the *Value* property on the corresponding *SqlParameters*.

- Execute the *SqlCommand*.

- Check the number of records affected and indicate failure scenarios, possibly by raising an exception.

- Call the *DataRow*'s *AcceptChanges* method if submitting the pending change in the *DataRow* succeeded.

Actually, forget what I said earlier about submitting changes requiring just a little more code. Submitting changes requires a lot more code. Thankfully, the *SqlDataAdapter* can help simplify the process of submitting changes. Let's see how.

Submitting Updates Using a *SqlDataAdapter*

The *SqlDataAdapter* class's *Update* method covers all the items from the preceding list.

Create a procedure (or function) that accepts multiple *DataRows*.

The *Update* method is overloaded. You can pass in a *DataTable* or an array of *DataRows*. You can also pass in a *DataSet*; however, the *SqlDataAdapter* will submit the pending changes stored in just one *DataTable*.

Look for *DataRows* that contain pending changes.

The *Update* method walks through the *DataRows* submitted, checking each *DataRow*'s *RowState* property.

Access a *SqlCommand* that contains the updating logic that corresponds to the *DataRow*'s *RowState* property.

The *SqlDataAdapter* class exposes properties—*InsertCommand*, *UpdateCommand*, and *Delete-Command*—to store this updating logic. The *Update* method checks each *DataRow*'s *RowState* property to determine which *SqlCommand* to execute.

Assign values from the *DataRow*'s columns to the *Value* property on the corresponding *SqlParameters*.

The *SqlDataAdapter* relies on properties set on the *SqlParameter* to determine how to assign a value to the *SqlParameter* based on the contents of the corresponding column in the *DataRow*.

SqlParameter.SourceColumn   The *SqlParameter* class contains a *SourceColumn* property. The *SqlDataAdapter* uses this property to associate the *SqlParameter* with the *DataColumn* of the same name in the *DataRow*'s *DataTable*.

SqlParameter.SourceVersion   The *SqlParameter* class also exposes a *SourceVersion* property. The *SqlDataAdapter* uses this property to determine whether to assign the current or original value in the desired column in the *DataRow* to the *SqlParameter*'s *Value* property. By default, the *SourceVersion* property is set to *Current*.

SqlParameter.SourceColumnNullMapping   ADO.NET 2.0 adds a *SourceColumnNullMapping* property to the *SqlParameter* class. This property is designed as a shortcut to help developers handle null value concurrency checks.

The *SqlClient* .NET Data Provider supports named parameters, which allows you to create a single parameter that can be used multiple times in a query, such as in a concurrency check against a nullable column, as shown here:

```
(@Column IS NULL AND Column IS NULL) OR Column = @Column
```

The database matches the parameter values you supply to the parameter markers in the query based on their names rather than their position.

Not all providers support named parameters. For example, the .NET Data Providers for ODBC and OLE DB support only positional parameters. With positional parameters, parameter values are matched to the parameter markers based on their position. For providers that support only positional parameters, each parameter marker in the query is assumed to be a different parameter, so there is no way to indicate that an existing parameter should be reused. As a result, that same concurrency check would require two separate parameters that receive the same value from the *DataRow*:

```
(? IS NULL AND Column IS NULL) OR Column = ?
```

While this comparison makes sense and is valid according to ANSI standards, passing the same parameter value multiple times to the database might not be the best use of your network resources. You can determine whether the value in the *DataRow* is null before executing the query. You can pass a *Boolean* or an integer to the database to indicate whether the value within the *DataRow* is null, and your logic would look like this instead:

```
(? = 1 AND Column IS NULL) OR Column = ?
```

If you set the *SourceColumnMapping* property for a *Parameter* class such as *SqlParameter* to *True*, this is exactly the behavior you'll get. The *SqlParameter* will not send the value specified to the database when you execute the query. Instead, the *SqlParameter* will pass a value of 1 if the value dictated by *SourceColumn* and *SourceVersion* properties is equal to *DBNull.Value* and 0 otherwise.

If you check the updating logic generated by the *SqlCommandBuilder*, you'll see that it uses the *SourceColumnNullMapping* property.

Execute the *SqlCommand*.

After the *SqlDataAdapter* assigns values to the various *SqlParameters* based on the *SourceColumn*, *SourceVersion*, and *SourceColumnNullMapping* properties, the *SqlDataAdapter* executes the *SqlCommand* to submit the pending changes stored in a *DataRow*.

Check the number of records affected and indicate failure scenarios, possibly by raising an exception.

The *SqlDataAdapter* determines the number of records affected by executing the query and throws a *DBConcurrencyException* if the query did not modify any rows. If the database does not report how many records were affected by the query (reporting −1 instead), the *SqlData-Adapter* still assumes success.

> **Note**   If the database reports that the query affected more than one record, the *SqlData-Adapter* still assumes success. But because you're using primary key columns in your concurrency checks, this scenario should never occur. Right?

Call the *DataRow*'s *AcceptChanges* method if submitting the pending change in the *DataRow* succeeded.

If the *SqlDataAdapter* determines that the attempt to update the row in the database succeeded, the *SqlDataAdapter* calls the *AcceptChanges* method on the *DataRow*, so it no longer contains a pending change.

But wait! There's more. The *SqlDataAdapter* also offers the following functionality.

Events Before and After Update Attempts

The *SqlDataAdapter* fires *RowUpdating* and *RowUpdated* events that you can use to add more logic before and after update attempts.

The Ability to Assign Retrieved Values Back to *DataRows*

After you submit a change to the database, you might want to retrieve database-generated values such as defaults, timestamps, and auto-increment values. You can configure your updating logic to return this information by using output parameters or by returning a row of data, and the *SqlDataAdapter* will assign those values to the corresponding columns in your *DataRow*. For more information about this scenario, see the discussion of refreshing a row after submitting an update in Chapter 11.

Batch Updates

By default, the *SqlDataAdapter* will perform a round-trip call to the database for each pending change. In ADO.NET 2.0, you can submit updates in batches, so a single call to the database can submit changes in multiple rows. You can enable batched updates by setting the *Update-BatchSize* property to a value other than 1, its default. For more information about batch updates, see the discussion of this topic in Chapter 11.

Using *SqlDataAdapter* Objects to Submit Updates

You have the following three choices when it comes to generating the updating logic that your *SqlDataAdapter* objects use to submit changes to your database:

- Use code to manually configure your *SqlDataAdapter* objects.
- Use a *SqlCommandBuilder* at run time.
- Use the Visual Studio wizards at design time.

Each of these methods has benefits and drawbacks. In the following sections, I explain both in detail.

Manually Configuring Your *SqlDataAdapter* Objects

The *SqlDataAdapter* class exposes four properties that contain *Command* objects. You've already learned that the *SelectCommand* property contains the *Command* that the *SqlData-Adapter* uses to fill your *DataTable*. The other three properties—*UpdateCommand*, *Insert-Command*, and *DeleteCommand*—contain the *Command* objects that the *SqlDataAdapter* uses to submit pending changes.

This architecture represents a major change from previous Microsoft data-access technologies, such as ADO. There is no magical "black box" technology involved. You control the logic the *SqlDataAdapter* uses to submit pending changes because you supply the *SqlCommand* objects that the *SqlDataAdapter* uses.

The *SqlDataAdapter* class's *Update* method is very flexible. You can supply a *DataSet*, a *DataSet* and a table name, a *DataTable*, or an array of *DataRow* objects. Regardless of how you call the *SqlDataAdapter* class's *Update* method, the *SqlDataAdapter* will attempt to submit the pending changes through the appropriate *SqlCommand*.

We can simply use the *SqlCommands* we created earlier in the chapter to submit pending inserts, updates, and deletes by assigning those *SqlCommands* to a *SqlDataAdapter*'s *Insert-Command*, *UpdateCommand*, and *DeleteCommand* properties. However, we won't want to manually assign values from columns in the *DataRow* to the parameters prior to submitting the changes in the *DataRow*.

Bound Parameters

As mentioned earlier in the chapter, the *SqlDataAdapter* uses the *SourceColumn*, *SourceVersion*, and *SourceColumnNullMapping* properties on the *SqlParameters* in conjunction with the *DataRow* to determine what values to submit to the database. Once we set these properties on the *SqlParameters* used in the *InsertCommand*, *UpdateCommand*, and *DeleteCommand* properties, the *SqlDataAdapter* will have all the information it needs to submit the pending changes:

Visual Basic
```
Dim pc As SqlParameterCollection
```

```vb
Dim p As SqlParameter

'Set the InsertCommand
strSQL = "INSERT INTO [Order Details] " & _
        " (OrderID, ProductID, Quantity, UnitPrice) VALUES " & _
        " (@OrderID, @ProductID, @Quantity, @UnitPrice)"
da.InsertCommand = New SqlCommand(strSQL, cn)
pc = da.InsertCommand.Parameters
pc.Add("@OrderID", SqlDbType.Int, 0, "OrderID")
pc.Add("@ProductID", SqlDbType.Int, 0, "ProductID")
pc.Add("@Quantity", SqlDbType.SmallInt, 0, "Quantity")
pc.Add("@UnitPrice", SqlDbType.Money, 0, "UnitPrice")

'Set the UpdateCommand
strSQL = "UPDATE [Order Details] " & _
        " SET OrderID = @OrderID_New, ProductID = @ProductID_New, " & _
        "     Quantity = @Quantity_New, UnitPrice = @UnitPrice_New " & _
        " WHERE OrderID = @OrderID_Old AND ProductID = @ProductID_Old " & _
        "     AND Quantity = @Quantity_Old AND UnitPrice = @UnitPrice_Old"
da.UpdateCommand = New SqlCommand(strSQL, cn)
pc = da.UpdateCommand.Parameters
pc.Add("@OrderID_New", SqlDbType.Int, 0, "OrderID")
pc.Add("@ProductID_New", SqlDbType.Int, 0, "ProductID")
pc.Add("@Quantity_New", SqlDbType.SmallInt, 0, "Quantity")
pc.Add("@UnitPrice_New", SqlDbType.Money, 0, "UnitPrice")
p = pc.Add("@OrderID_Old", SqlDbType.Int, 0, "OrderID")
p.SourceVersion = DataRowVersion.Original
p = pc.Add("@ProductID_Old", SqlDbType.Int, 0, "ProductID")
p.SourceVersion = DataRowVersion.Original
p = pc.Add("@Quantity_Old", SqlDbType.SmallInt, 0, "Quantity")
p.SourceVersion = DataRowVersion.Original
p = pc.Add("@UnitPrice_Old", SqlDbType.Money, 0, "UnitPrice")
p.SourceVersion = DataRowVersion.Original

'Set the DeleteCommand
strSQL = "DELETE [Order Details] " & _
        " WHERE OrderID = @OrderID AND ProductID = @ProductID " & _
        "     AND Quantity = @Quantity AND UnitPrice = @UnitPrice"
da.DeleteCommand = New SqlCommand(strSQL, cn)
pc = da.DeleteCommand.Parameters
p = pc.Add("@OrderID", SqlDbType.Int, 0, "OrderID")
p.SourceVersion = DataRowVersion.Original
p = pc.Add("@ProductID", SqlDbType.Int, 0, "ProductID")
p.SourceVersion = DataRowVersion.Original
p = pc.Add("@Quantity", SqlDbType.SmallInt, 0, "Quantity")
p.SourceVersion = DataRowVersion.Original
p = pc.Add("@UnitPrice", SqlDbType.Money, 0, "UnitPrice")
p.SourceVersion = DataRowVersion.Original
```

Visual C#

```csharp
SqlParameterCollection pc;
SqlParameter p;
```

```
//Set the InsertCommand
strSQL = "INSERT INTO [Order Details] " +
        " (OrderID, ProductID, Quantity, UnitPrice) VALUES " +
        " (@OrderID, @ProductID, @Quantity, @UnitPrice)";
da.InsertCommand = new SqlCommand(strSQL, cn);
pc = da.InsertCommand.Parameters;
pc.Add("@OrderID", SqlDbType.Int, 0, "OrderID");
pc.Add("@ProductID", SqlDbType.Int, 0, "ProductID");
pc.Add("@Quantity", SqlDbType.SmallInt, 0, "Quantity");
pc.Add("@UnitPrice", SqlDbType.Money, 0, "UnitPrice");

//Set the UpdateCommand
strSQL = "UPDATE [Order Details] " +
        " SET OrderID = @OrderID_New, ProductID = @ProductID_New, " +
        "    Quantity = @Quantity_New, UnitPrice = @UnitPrice_New " +
        " WHERE OrderID = @OrderID_Old AND ProductID = @ProductID_Old " +
        "    AND Quantity = @Quantity_Old AND UnitPrice = @UnitPrice_Old";
da.UpdateCommand = new SqlCommand(strSQL, cn);
pc = da.UpdateCommand.Parameters;
pc.Add("@OrderID_New", SqlDbType.Int, 0, "OrderID");
pc.Add("@ProductID_New", SqlDbType.Int, 0, "ProductID");
pc.Add("@Quantity_New", SqlDbType.SmallInt, 0, "Quantity");
pc.Add("@UnitPrice_New", SqlDbType.Money, 0, "UnitPrice");
p = pc.Add("@OrderID_Old", SqlDbType.Int, 0, "OrderID");
p.SourceVersion = DataRowVersion.Original;
p = pc.Add("@ProductID_Old", SqlDbType.Int, 0, "ProductID");
p.SourceVersion = DataRowVersion.Original;
p = pc.Add("@Quantity_Old", SqlDbType.SmallInt, 0, "Quantity");
p.SourceVersion = DataRowVersion.Original;
p = pc.Add("@UnitPrice_Old", SqlDbType.Money, 0, "UnitPrice");
p.SourceVersion = DataRowVersion.Original;

//Set the DeleteCommand
strSQL = "DELETE [Order Details] " +
        " WHERE OrderID = @OrderID AND ProductID = @ProductID " +
        "    AND Quantity = @Quantity AND UnitPrice = @UnitPrice";
da.DeleteCommand = new SqlCommand(strSQL, cn);
pc = da.DeleteCommand.Parameters;
p = pc.Add("@OrderID", SqlDbType.Int, 0, "OrderID");
p.SourceVersion = DataRowVersion.Original;
p = pc.Add("@ProductID", SqlDbType.Int, 0, "ProductID");
p.SourceVersion = DataRowVersion.Original;
p = pc.Add("@Quantity", SqlDbType.SmallInt, 0, "Quantity");
p.SourceVersion = DataRowVersion.Original;
p = pc.Add("@UnitPrice", SqlDbType.Money, 0, "UnitPrice");
p.SourceVersion = DataRowVersion.Original;
```

Once you've set up this updating logic, you need only call the *Update* method on the *SqlData-Adapter* and supply the *DataTable* as a parameter.

Using Stored Procedures to Submit Updates

A common complaint of developers who used previous Microsoft data-access technologies, such as ADO, was that they couldn't submit updates using stored procedures.

Earlier, I mentioned that the *SqlDataAdapter* lets you define your own updating logic. The previous code snippets showed how you can build your own *SqlCommand* objects that the *Sql-DataAdapter* can then use to submit pending changes. We can use similar code to submit updates using stored procedures.

First we need to define stored procedures in the Northwind database that can modify, insert, and delete rows from the Order Details table. You can paste and then execute the following code in SQL Server Management Studio or SQL Query Analyzer to create the stored procedures that we're going to call in our code. If you don't have access to either of these tools, you can call a procedure named *CreateSprocs* (which appears in a later code snippet) to create the desired stored procedures.

```
CREATE PROCEDURE procInsertDetail
    (@OrderID int, @ProductID int,
     @Quantity smallint, @UnitPrice money)
AS
INSERT INTO [Order Details]
    (OrderID, ProductID, Quantity, UnitPrice)
    VALUES (@OrderID, @ProductID, @Quantity, @UnitPrice)
GO
CREATE PROCEDURE procUpdateDetail
    (@OrderID_New int, @ProductID_New int,
     @Quantity_New smallint, @UnitPrice_New money,
     @OrderID_Old int, @ProductID_Old int,
     @Quantity_Old smallint, @UnitPrice_Old money)
AS
UPDATE [Order Details]
    SET OrderID = @OrderID_New, ProductID = @ProductID_New,
        Quantity = @Quantity_New, UnitPrice = @UnitPrice_New
    WHERE OrderID = @OrderID_Old AND ProductID = @ProductID_Old
      AND Quantity = @Quantity_Old AND UnitPrice = @UnitPrice_Old
GO
CREATE PROCEDURE procDeleteDetail
    (@OrderID int, @ProductID int,
     @Quantity smallint, @UnitPrice money)
AS
DELETE FROM [Order Details]
    WHERE OrderID = @OrderID AND ProductID = @ProductID AND
          Quantity = @Quantity AND UnitPrice = @UnitPrice
```

Now that we have stored procedures that we can call to submit changes to the Order Details table, we can write *SqlCommand* objects to call those stored procedures automatically when we call the *SqlDataAdapter* object's *Update* method.

The following code snippet contains functions that create *SqlCommand* objects that contain calls to the stored procedures just described. It also contains a procedure you can call to create those stored procedures in your database. All that's left to do to submit updates using stored procedures is to wire up our new *Command* objects to the *SqlDataAdapter*, which we can do in the *SubmitChangesViaStoredProcedures* procedure.

Visual Basic

```vb
'Create the stored procedures
CreateSprocs(cn)

Dim pc As SqlParameterCollection
Dim p As SqlParameter

'Set the InsertCommand
da.InsertCommand = New SqlCommand("procInsertDetail", cn)
da.InsertCommand.CommandType = CommandType.StoredProcedure
pc = da.InsertCommand.Parameters
pc.Add("@OrderID", SqlDbType.Int, 0, "OrderID")
pc.Add("@ProductID", SqlDbType.Int, 0, "ProductID")
pc.Add("@Quantity", SqlDbType.SmallInt, 0, "Quantity")
pc.Add("@UnitPrice", SqlDbType.Money, 0, "UnitPrice")

'Set the UpdateCommand
da.UpdateCommand = New SqlCommand("procUpdateDetail", cn)
da.UpdateCommand.CommandType = CommandType.StoredProcedure
pc = da.UpdateCommand.Parameters
pc.Add("@OrderID_New", SqlDbType.Int, 0, "OrderID")
pc.Add("@ProductID_New", SqlDbType.Int, 0, "ProductID")
pc.Add("@Quantity_New", SqlDbType.SmallInt, 0, "Quantity")
pc.Add("@UnitPrice_New", SqlDbType.Money, 0, "UnitPrice")
p = pc.Add("@OrderID_Old", SqlDbType.Int, 0, "OrderID")
p.SourceVersion = DataRowVersion.Original
p = pc.Add("@ProductID_Old", SqlDbType.Int, 0, "ProductID")
p.SourceVersion = DataRowVersion.Original
p = pc.Add("@Quantity_Old", SqlDbType.SmallInt, 0, "Quantity")
p.SourceVersion = DataRowVersion.Original
p = pc.Add("@UnitPrice_Old", SqlDbType.Money, 0, "UnitPrice")
p.SourceVersion = DataRowVersion.Original

'Set the DeleteCommand
da.DeleteCommand = New SqlCommand("procDeleteDetail", cn)
da.DeleteCommand.CommandType = CommandType.StoredProcedure
pc = da.DeleteCommand.Parameters
p = pc.Add("@OrderID", SqlDbType.Int, 0, "OrderID")
p.SourceVersion = DataRowVersion.Original
p = pc.Add("@ProductID", SqlDbType.Int, 0, "ProductID")
p.SourceVersion = DataRowVersion.Original
p = pc.Add("@Quantity", SqlDbType.SmallInt, 0, "Quantity")
p.SourceVersion = DataRowVersion.Original
p = pc.Add("@UnitPrice", SqlDbType.Money, 0, "UnitPrice")
p.SourceVersion = DataRowVersion.Original

Private Sub CreateSprocs(ByVal cn As SqlConnection)
    Dim cmd As SqlCommand = cn.CreateCommand
    Dim strSQL As String

    'Drop any pre-existing stored procedures with these names
    cmd.CommandText = "DROP PROCEDURE procInsertDetail"
    Try : cmd.ExecuteNonQuery() : Catch : End Try
    cmd.CommandText = "DROP PROCEDURE procUpdateDetail"
    Try : cmd.ExecuteNonQuery() : Catch : End Try
```

```
cmd.CommandText = "DROP PROCEDURE procDeleteDetail"
Try : cmd.ExecuteNonQuery() : Catch : End Try

strSQL = "CREATE PROCEDURE procInsertDetail " & _
         "   (@OrderID int, @ProductID int, " & _
         "    @Quantity smallint, @UnitPrice money) AS " & _
         "INSERT INTO [Order Details] " & _
         "   (OrderID, ProductID, Quantity, UnitPrice) " & _
         "   VALUES (@OrderID, @ProductID, @Quantity, @UnitPrice)"
cmd.CommandText = strSQL
cmd.ExecuteNonQuery()

strSQL = "CREATE PROCEDURE procUpdateDetail " & _
         "   (@OrderID_New int, @ProductID_New int, " & _
         "    @Quantity_New smallint, @UnitPrice_New money, " & _
         "    @OrderID_Old int, @ProductID_Old int, " & _
         "    @Quantity_Old smallint, @UnitPrice_Old money) AS " & _
         "UPDATE [Order Details] " & _
         "   SET OrderID = @OrderID_New, ProductID = @ProductID_New, " & _
         "       Quantity = @Quantity_New, UnitPrice = @UnitPrice_New " & _
         "   WHERE OrderID = @OrderID_Old AND " & _
         "         ProductID = @ProductID_Old AND " & _
         "         Quantity = @Quantity_Old AND " & _
         "         UnitPrice = @UnitPrice_Old"
cmd.CommandText = strSQL
cmd.ExecuteNonQuery()

strSQL = "CREATE PROCEDURE procDeleteDetail " & _
         "   (@OrderID int, @ProductID int, " & _
         "    @Quantity smallint, @UnitPrice money) AS " & _
         "DELETE FROM [Order Details] " & _
         "   WHERE OrderID = @OrderID AND ProductID = @ProductID AND " & _
         "         Quantity = @Quantity AND UnitPrice = @UnitPrice"
cmd.CommandText = strSQL
cmd.ExecuteNonQuery()
End Sub
```

Visual C#

```
//Create the stored procedures
CreateSprocs(cn);

SqlParameterCollection pc;
SqlParameter p;

//Set the InsertCommand
da.InsertCommand = new SqlCommand("procInsertDetail", cn);
da.InsertCommand.CommandType = CommandType.StoredProcedure;
pc = da.InsertCommand.Parameters;
pc.Add("@OrderID", SqlDbType.Int, 0, "OrderID");
pc.Add("@ProductID", SqlDbType.Int, 0, "ProductID");
pc.Add("@Quantity", SqlDbType.SmallInt, 0, "Quantity");
pc.Add("@UnitPrice", SqlDbType.Money, 0, "UnitPrice");

//Set the UpdateCommand
da.UpdateCommand = new SqlCommand("procUpdateDetail", cn);
```

```
da.UpdateCommand.CommandType = CommandType.StoredProcedure;
pc = da.UpdateCommand.Parameters;
pc.Add("@OrderID_New", SqlDbType.Int, 0, "OrderID");
pc.Add("@ProductID_New", SqlDbType.Int, 0, "ProductID");
pc.Add("@Quantity_New", SqlDbType.SmallInt, 0, "Quantity");
pc.Add("@UnitPrice_New", SqlDbType.Money, 0, "UnitPrice");
p = pc.Add("@OrderID_Old", SqlDbType.Int, 0, "OrderID");
p.SourceVersion = DataRowVersion.Original;
p = pc.Add("@ProductID_Old", SqlDbType.Int, 0, "ProductID");
p.SourceVersion = DataRowVersion.Original;
p = pc.Add("@Quantity_Old", SqlDbType.SmallInt, 0, "Quantity");
p.SourceVersion = DataRowVersion.Original;
p = pc.Add("@UnitPrice_Old", SqlDbType.Money, 0, "UnitPrice");
p.SourceVersion = DataRowVersion.Original;

//Set the DeleteCommand
da.DeleteCommand = new SqlCommand("procDeleteDetail", cn);
da.DeleteCommand.CommandType = CommandType.StoredProcedure;
pc = da.DeleteCommand.Parameters;
p = pc.Add("@OrderID", SqlDbType.Int, 0, "OrderID");
p.SourceVersion = DataRowVersion.Original;
p = pc.Add("@ProductID", SqlDbType.Int, 0, "ProductID");
p.SourceVersion = DataRowVersion.Original;
p = pc.Add("@Quantity", SqlDbType.SmallInt, 0, "Quantity");
p.SourceVersion = DataRowVersion.Original;
p = pc.Add("@UnitPrice", SqlDbType.Money, 0, "UnitPrice");
p.SourceVersion = DataRowVersion.Original;

static void CreateSprocs(SqlConnection cn)
{
    SqlCommand cmd = cn.CreateCommand();
    string strSQL;

    //Drop any pre-existing stored procedures with these names
    cmd.CommandText = "DROP PROCEDURE procInsertDetail";
    try {cmd.ExecuteNonQuery();} catch {}
    cmd.CommandText = "DROP PROCEDURE procUpdateDetail";
    try {cmd.ExecuteNonQuery();} catch {}
    cmd.CommandText = "DROP PROCEDURE procDeleteDetail";
    try {cmd.ExecuteNonQuery();} catch {}

    strSQL = "CREATE PROCEDURE procInsertDetail " +
            "    (@OrderID int, @ProductID int, " +
            "     @Quantity smallint, @UnitPrice money) AS " +
            "INSERT INTO [Order Details] " +
            "    (OrderID, ProductID, Quantity, UnitPrice) " +
            "    VALUES (@OrderID, @ProductID, @Quantity, @UnitPrice)";
    cmd.CommandText = strSQL;
    cmd.ExecuteNonQuery();

    strSQL = "CREATE PROCEDURE procUpdateDetail " +
            "    (@OrderID_New int, @ProductID_New int, " +
            "     @Quantity_New smallint, @UnitPrice_New money, " +
            "     @OrderID_Old int, @ProductID_Old int, " +
            "     @Quantity_Old smallint, @UnitPrice_Old money) AS " +
```

```
                            "UPDATE [Order Details] " +
                            "    SET OrderID = @OrderID_New, " +
                            "        ProductID = @ProductID_New, " +
                            "        Quantity = @Quantity_New, " +
                            "        UnitPrice = @UnitPrice_New " +
                            "    WHERE OrderID = @OrderID_Old AND " +
                            "          ProductID = @ProductID_Old AND " +
                            "          Quantity = @Quantity_Old AND " +
                            "          UnitPrice = @UnitPrice_Old";
            cmd.CommandText = strSQL;
            cmd.ExecuteNonQuery();

            strSQL = "CREATE PROCEDURE procDeleteDetail " +
                        "    (@OrderID int, @ProductID int, " +
                        "     @Quantity smallint, @UnitPrice money) AS " +
                        "DELETE FROM [Order Details] " +
                        "    WHERE OrderID = @OrderID AND " +
                        "          ProductID = @ProductID AND " +
                        "          Quantity = @Quantity AND UnitPrice = @UnitPrice";
            cmd.CommandText = strSQL;
            cmd.ExecuteNonQuery();
        }
```

Supplying Your Own Updating Logic

Now let's look at the benefits and drawbacks of supplying your own updating logic in code.

Benefits

The two biggest benefits of supplying your own updating logic are control and performance. The ADO.NET *SqlDataAdapter* offers you more control over your updating logic than any previous Microsoft data-access technology, such as ADO. You're no longer restricted to submitting updates directly against tables; you can finally leverage your stored procedures quickly and easily.

Moreover, because you're not relying on the data-access technology to determine the origin of your data, you can treat any result set as updatable. With ADO.NET, you can fill your *DataSet* with the results of a stored procedure call, a query against a temporary table, or the union of multiple queries—or fill it in any other way you see fit—and still be able to submit changes to your database.

Supplying updating logic in your code improves the performance of your application. ADO, by comparison, "automagically" generated updating logic for you. Although using ADO to submit updates might result in fewer lines of code, that code requires ADO to query the database for metadata that's not normally part of the results of your query—the source table name, source column names, and primary key information for the source table. Querying database system tables for metadata and then using that metadata to generate updating logic takes more time than simply loading it from local code.

Drawbacks

The primary drawback to supplying your own updating logic is that it requires more code than using "automagically" generated logic. Take a quick peek back and look at the total number of lines of code it took to supply updating logic for the *SqlDataAdapter*. Writing that code is time consuming and rather tedious.

The other drawback is that many developers are not comfortable writing their own updating logic. They would rather not have to ponder such questions as: Do I need to delimit the table name in the query? What type of parameter markers should I use? Which columns should appear in the WHERE clause of the *CommandText* for the *UpdateCommand* and *DeleteCommand*? What is the appropriate setting for the *SqlDbType* property for a parameter that contains a date /time value?

Thankfully, there are simpler ways to generate your updating logic, as I'll explain in the upcoming sections.

Using a *SqlCommandBuilder* to Generate Updating Logic

The ADO.NET object model not only allows you to define your own updating logic, but it also provides dynamic updating logic generation similar to that of the ADO cursor engine, using the *SqlCommandBuilder* class. If you instantiate a *SqlCommandBuilder* object and associate it with a *SqlDataAdapter* object, the *SqlCommandBuilder* will attempt to generate updating logic based on the query contained in the *SqlDataAdapter* object's *SelectCommand*.

To demonstrate how the *SqlCommandBuilder* works, I'll use it to generate updating logic for our sample code that queries the Order Details table. The following code snippet instantiates a *SqlCommandBuilder*, supplying a *SqlDataAdapter* in the constructor. It then writes the text of the *Command* that the *SqlCommandBuilder* generated to submit new rows.

Visual Basic

```
Dim strConn, strSQL As String
strConn = "Data Source=.\SQLExpress;" & _
          "Initial Catalog=Northwind;Integrated Security=True;"
strSQL = "SELECT OrderID, ProductID, Quantity, UnitPrice " & _
         "FROM [Order Details] WHERE OrderID = @OrderID " & _
         "ORDER BY ProductID"
Dim da As New SqlDataAdapter(strSQL, strConn)
da.SelectCommand.Parameters.AddWithValue("@OrderID", 10503)
Dim cb As New SqlCommandBuilder(da)
Console.WriteLine(cb.GetInsertCommand().CommandText)
```

Visual C#

```
string strConn, strSQL;
strConn = @"Data Source=.\SQLExpress;" +
          "Initial Catalog=Northwind;Integrated Security=True;";
strSQL = "SELECT OrderID, ProductID, Quantity, UnitPrice " +
         "FROM [Order Details] WHERE OrderID = @OrderID " +
```

```
          "ORDER BY ProductID";
SqlDataAdapter da = new SqlDataAdapter(strSQL, strConn);
da.SelectCommand.Parameters.AddWithValue("@OrderID", 10503);
SqlCommandBuilder cb = new SqlCommandBuilder(da);
Console.WriteLine(cb.GetInsertCommand().CommandText);
```

You'll notice that the text of this query looks remarkably similar to the queries we built earlier in the chapter to submit new rows, as shown here:

```
INSERT INTO [Order Details]
    ( [OrderID] , [ProductID] , [Quantity] , [UnitPrice] )
    VALUES ( @p1 , @p2 , @p3 , @p4 )
```

> **Note**   For more information about why the *SqlCommandBuilder* names parameters in this fashion, see the discussion of the *GetInsertCommand*, *GetUpdateCommand*, and *GetDeleteCommand* in the reference section of this chapter.

How the *CommandBuilder* Generates Updating Logic

The logic that the *SqlCommandBuilder* uses to generate UPDATE, INSERT, and DELETE queries isn't terribly complex. The *SqlCommandBuilder* queries the database to determine base table and column names as well as key information for the results of your query. The *SqlCommandBuilder* can generate updating logic if all the following are true:

- Your query returns data from only one table.
- That table has a primary key.
- The primary key is included in the results of your query.

As we discussed earlier, the primary key ensures that the query-based updates that the *SqlCommandBuilder* generates can update one row at most. Why does the *SqlCommandBuilder* place a restriction on the number of tables referenced in the results of your query? We'll discuss that later in the chapter.

The *SqlCommandBuilder* object uses the *SqlDataAdapter* object's *SelectCommand* to fetch the metadata necessary for the updating logic. Actually, we discussed this feature briefly in Chapter 4. The *SqlCommand* class's *ExecuteReader* method allows you to request this type of metadata with the results of your query. The following code snippet demonstrates this feature:

Visual Basic
```
Dim strConn, strSQL As String
strConn = "Data Source=.\SQLExpress;" & _
        "Initial Catalog=Northwind;Integrated Security=True;"
strSQL = "SELECT OrderID, ProductID, Quantity, UnitPrice " & _
        "FROM [Order Details] WHERE OrderID = @OrderID " & _
        "ORDER BY ProductID"
Dim cn As New SqlConnection(strConn)
Dim cmd As New SqlCommand(strSQL, cn)
```

```
cmd.Parameters.AddWithValue("@OrderID", 10503)
cn.Open()
Dim rdr As SqlDataReader
rdr = cmd.ExecuteReader(CommandBehavior.SchemaOnly Or _
                        CommandBehavior.KeyInfo)
Dim tbl As DataTable = rdr.GetSchemaTable
rdr.Close()
cn.Close()

For Each row As DataRow In tbl.Rows
    For Each col As DataColumn In tbl.Columns
        Console.WriteLine("{0}: {1}", col.ColumnName, row(col))
    Next col
    Console.WriteLine()
Next row
```

Visual C#

```
string strConn, strSQL;
strConn = @"Data Source=.\SQLExpress;" +
            "Initial Catalog=Northwind;Integrated Security=True;";
strSQL = "SELECT OrderID, ProductID, Quantity, UnitPrice " +
         "FROM [Order Details] WHERE OrderID = @OrderID " +
         "ORDER BY ProductID";
SqlConnection cn = new SqlConnection(strConn);
SqlCommand cmd = new SqlCommand(strSQL, cn);
cmd.Parameters.AddWithValue("@OrderID", 10503);
cn.Open();
SqlDataReader rdr;
rdr = cmd.ExecuteReader(CommandBehavior.SchemaOnly |
                        CommandBehavior.KeyInfo);
DataTable tbl = rdr.GetSchemaTable();
rdr.Close();
cn.Close();

foreach (DataRow row in tbl.Rows)
{
    foreach (DataColumn col in tbl.Columns)
        Console.WriteLine("{0}: {1}", col.ColumnName, row[col]);
    Console.WriteLine();
}
```

If you run this code, you'll see all the data that the *SqlCommandBuilder* needs for each column so that it can generate updating logic. What's the name of the column? What are the base table and base column names for the column? Is the column part of the base table's primary key? Does the column contain a long data type (large text or binary)? What is the scale and precision of that floating point column? And so on.

Concurrency Options Using the *SqlCommandBuilder*

The *SqlCommandBuilder*, by default, will use all comparable columns in the WHERE clause of the *CommandText* for the *UpdateCommand* and *DeleteCommand*. This ensures that a call to submit a pending change will result in a *DBConcurrencyException* if another user has modified any of these columns between the time you retrieved the original values for the row and submitted new values for the row.

In ADO.NET 2.0, the *SqlCommandBuilder* class exposes a *ConflictOptions* property that you can use to control the concurrency checks that it generates. By default, this property is set to *CompareAllSearchableValues*. If you set this property to *OverwriteChanges*, the *SqlCommand-Builder* will use a "last in wins" approach by including only the primary key column or columns in the WHERE clause. You can also set the property to *CompareRowVersion*, which will cause the *SqlCommandBuilder* to rely on timestamp and primary key column or columns in the updating logic.

Benefits and Drawbacks of Using the *SqlCommandBuilder*

You can see the two major benefits of using the *SqlCommandBuilder* class if you compare the code snippet that created the *SqlCommandBuilder* with the code that we used to generate our own updating logic. Using the *SqlCommandBuilder* class requires less code. It also allows you to generate updating logic without requiring you to have in-depth knowledge of the SQL syntax for UPDATE, INSERT, and DELETE queries.

The *SqlCommandBuilder* can also be helpful if you're having problems generating your own updating logic. If the *SqlCommandBuilder* can generate the updating logic successfully, you can check the value of the *CommandText* property of the *SqlCommand* objects it generated or the various properties on the *SqlParameter* objects it constructed.

The *SqlCommandBuilder* is also extremely handy for any application in which you need to support updating but you won't know the structure of your queries at design time.

Because the *SqlCommandBuilder* generates updating logic for you at run time by querying for additional metadata, it does not offer the best possible run-time performance. You can supply your own updating logic in code in less time than it takes the *SqlCommandBuilder* to request and process the metadata required to generate similar updating logic. The *SqlCommandBuilder* doesn't offer options to provide the same level of control over the updating logic. For example, a *SqlCommandBuilder* will not help you submit updates using stored procedures.

If only there were a way to generate updating logic quickly and easily at design time . . . .

Using the Visual Studio TableAdapter Configuration Wizard to Generate Updating Logic

In Chapter 9, you saw that you could use the TableAdapter Configuration Wizard to create *TableAdapter* classes for the *DataTables* in your strongly typed *DataSet*. The wizard also generates updating logic and stores that logic in your code.

One purpose of the TableAdapter Configuration Wizard is to generate updating logic for you at design time to let you build efficient updating code quickly and easily. Obviously, that's an ambitious goal. Although the wizard is not foolproof (what wizard is?), it actually achieves this goal in the vast majority of situations.

Let's take a closer look at a TableAdapter's updating logic by creating a new strongly typed *DataSet*. Open a project in Visual Studio, and add a new item to the project. In the resulting Add New Item dialog box, select *DataSet*. Web-based projects will automatically launch the TableAdapter Configuration Wizard. If you created a Windows-based project, add a new *TableAdapter* to the strongly typed *DataSet* designer to launch the TableAdapter Configuration Wizard. Specify a connection to your favorite Northwind database, and then enter the following query in the SQL statement page of the wizard:

```
SELECT OrderID, ProductID, UnitPrice, Quantity
    FROM [Order Details]
    WHERE OrderID = @OrderID ORDER BY ProductID
```

Click Next. On the View Wizard Results screen, you'll see the output shown in Figure 10-2.

Figure 10-2   The View Wizard Results screen of the TableAdapter Configuration Wizard

Examining the *TableAdapter*'s Updating Logic

As you can see in Figure 10-2, the wizard generated UPDATE, INSERT, and DELETE queries for the new *TableAdapter*. Click the wizard's Finish button. Select the new *TableAdapter* in the strongly typed *DataSet* designer, and then go to the Properties window and drill down into the *TableAdapter* object's *DeleteCommand*. Select the *CommandText* property, and then click the ellipsis button (...) to the right of the property's value. This will bring up the Query Builder and display the *CommandText* for the *TableAdapter* object's *DeleteCommand*, as shown in Figure 10-3.

As you can see, the query that the TableAdapter Configuration Wizard generated to submit pending deletions is identical to the one we manually created earlier in the chapter. You can also drill down into the *TableAdapter* object's *InsertCommand* and *UpdateCommand* to view the rest of the updating logic that the wizard generated.

Options for Building Updating Logic

The SQL Statement screen of the wizard has an Advanced Options button that you can click to display a dialog box that offers a series of options, as shown in Figure 10-4. These options offer you a small level of control over the updating logic that the TableAdapter Configuration Wizard generates.

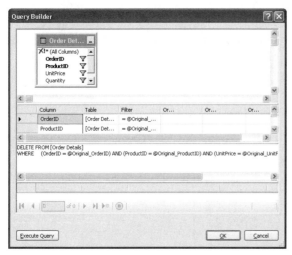

Figure 10-3   The wizard-generated *DeleteCommand*

If you're using your *TableAdapter* only to fetch data from your database, you can deselect the Generate Insert, Update And Delete Statements option. This will prevent the wizard from generating logic and storing that logic as code in the strongly typed *DataSet*'s code file at design time, and it can prevent you from having to execute that code at run time.

The TableAdapter Configuration Wizard gives you some options for how you generate your updating logic. The wizard defaults to the most defensive concurrency option available. If you leave the Use Optimistic Concurrency box selected, the wizard will try to generate concurrency checks that rely on primary key and timestamp columns. If that fails, the wizard will try to generate concurrency checks that rely on the primary key column or columns and all non-BLOB columns (because data types such as image, text, and ntext cannot be compared by SQL Server). If you deselect the Use Optimistic Concurrency option, the wizard will include only primary key columns in the WHERE clauses for these queries.

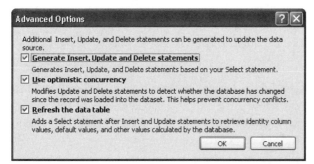

Figure 10-4   Advanced options offered by the TableAdapter Configuration Wizard

Some databases, such as SQL Server, support batched queries that can return rows of data. If you're using the TableAdapter Configuration Wizard to build a *TableAdapter* that talks to such a database, the Refresh The Data Table option will be enabled and selected. When this option is selected, the wizard will generate queries to refetch the contents of your modified row immediately after submitting that change. This means that new server-generated values such as timestamp and autoincrement values will be available in your *DataRow* after you call *Table-Adapter.Update.*

This functionality is extremely handy, and the scenario is not supported by the *SqlCommand-Builder* class. We'll discuss this scenario in more depth in the next chapter, including how you can refresh the *DataRow* using databases that don't support batched queries.

Using Stored Procedures to Submit Updates

The TableAdapter Configuration Wizard can also help you build *TableAdapter* objects that submit updates to your SQL Server database using stored procedures. On the Choose A Command Type screen of the wizard, you'll see a Use Existing Stored Procedures option, as shown in Figure 10-5. Select this option, and then click Next.

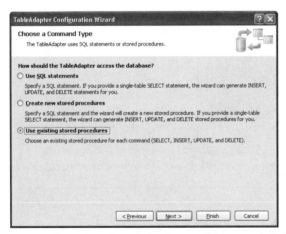

Figure 10-5   The Choose A Command Type screen of the TableAdapter Configuration Wizard

The next screen allows you to select the stored procedures for each of the *Command* objects of your *TableAdapter*. The first step is to select the stored procedure for your *TableAdapter* object's *SelectCommand*. The drop-down list will contain the available stored procedures, as shown in Figure 10-6. When you select a stored procedure, the columns that the stored procedure returns will appear in the list to the right.

Once you've set the *TableAdapter* object's *SelectCommand*, you can specify the stored procedures for the updating *Command* objects. To set the *SourceColumn* property for the parameters of your updating stored procedures, use the drop-down lists on the right side of the wizard screen, as shown in Figure 10-7.

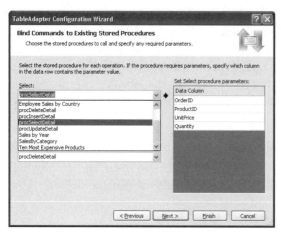

Figure 10-6   Selecting a stored procedure for the *TableAdapter* object's *SelectCommand*

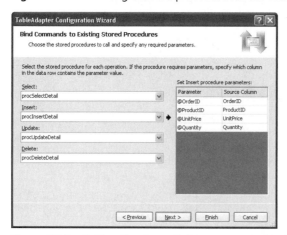

Figure 10-7   Setting the *SourceColumn* property for the parameters of the *InsertCommand*

> **Note**   The TableAdapter Configuration Wizard still does not give you the option to set the *SourceVersion* property for the *Parameter* objects. Because the default value for this property is *Current*, you must change the value of this property using the Properties window for all parameters that must be bound to the original value of your modified columns.

If you have the Professional edition of Visual Studio 2005 installed, you can also supply a SQL query and the TableAdapter Configuration Wizard will generate new SQL Server stored procedures for your *TableAdapter* object's *SelectCommand*, *UpdateCommand*, *InsertCommand*, and *DeleteCommand*. Select the Create New Stored Procedures option on the Choose A Command Type screen of the TableAdapter Configuration Wizard, and the wizard will prompt you for the SQL query that returns data from your database, as shown in Figure 10-8.

The next wizard screen lets you supply names for the stored procedures that the wizard generates. This screen also includes a Preview SQL Script button, which you can click to bring up a dialog box showing the SQL script that the wizard generated to create your stored procedures (as shown in Figure 10-9). If you're building your application against a sample database, you can use the dialog box to save the SQL script to a file so that you can run the script later against your production database.

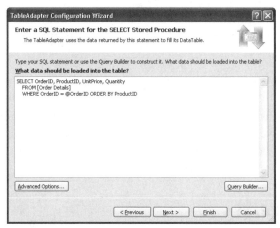

Figure 10-8   Specifying a SQL query for your new stored procedures

Figure 10-9   Viewing the SQL script for creating your new stored procedures

Once you've completed the wizard, you'll have new stored procedures in your database and your new *TableAdapter* will be set to use those stored procedures.

Benefits and Drawbacks of Using the Wizard

I mentioned that one of the TableAdapter Configuration Wizard's goals is to generate updating logic to let you build efficient updating code quickly and easily. The wizard offers some options that are not available in the *SqlCommandBuilder* class. It also generates the tedious code that most developers would rather not write by hand (or keyboard).

The wizard requests the same schema information from your database to generate updating logic that the *SqlCommandBuilder* class does. In fact, the wizard actually uses the *Command-Builder* class for the .NET Data Provider you use. However, unlike a *CommandBuilder*, the wizard requests this information once at design time and then stores the newly generated logic in your code so that your code does not query for this schema information at run time. Thus, your application avoids the run-time performance penalty that goes with using the *SqlCommandBuilder* class.

The TableAdapter Configuration Wizard does a great job generating logic, but it is not perfect—few wizards are. The logic that the wizard uses to retrieve values does not work with batched updates. There's a more efficient way to refresh the *DataRow* after performing an INSERT or UPDATE using SQL Server and other databases. The wizard also generates a *Table-Adapter*. If you want to generate updating logic for a *SqlDataAdapter* (or an *OdbcDataAdapter*, an *OracleDataAdapter*, and so on) you're out of luck. Or are you?

Return of the *DataAdapters*!

Consider the following basic scenario. You want to create a simple data-access layer—a component that lets you connect to your database, returns information about a particular order, and can submit pending changes back to the database. You want a simple way to create this component—one that allows you to write a minimum of code—but you don't want to rely on *TableAdapters* for reasons we've previously discussed.

You can create a strongly typed *DataSet* and remove the *TableAdapters*. No major challenge there.

You already know how to create *SqlConnections* and *SqlDataAdapters* in code. You also know that you can create *SqlCommandBuilders* to generate updating logic, but that this approach involves (needlessly) querying the database for schema information every time the *SqlCommandBuilder* needs to generate updating logic at run time. There has to be a better way....

Thankfully, the TableAdapter Configuration Wizard is not the only way to generate updating logic at design time using Visual Studio, just the most obvious. If you would prefer to create *DataAdapter* objects (*SqlDataAdapters*, *OracleDataAdapters*, and so on), you can still use its cousin, the Data Adapter Configuration Wizard from Visual Studio 2002/2003.

Invoking the Data Adapter Configuration Wizard

Invoking the older wizard the first time involves a little work, but the results are worthwhile.

The various *DataAdapter* classes are not available on the Visual Studio toolbox by default, but you can add them to the toolbox by right-clicking on the toolbox and selecting Choose Items from the context menu. You can also select Tools and then Choose Toolbox Items from the Visual Studio menu. In the resulting dialog box, select the items you want to appear on the toolbox. If you're working with SQL Server databases, selecting the *SqlConnection*, *SqlCom-*

mand, and *SqlDataAdapter* classes would be a good start. Once you've added the desired items, they will appear on whichever toolbox tab you clicked to launch the Choose Toolbox Items dialog.

You can now drag and drop the items from the toolbox onto most designers for many project items, including Windows Forms, Components, and Web Services. Web Forms will not support these drag-and-drop operations. We'll talk about options for building Web applications in more depth in Chapter 14.

Creating a Simple Data Access Layer with *SqlDataAdapters*

Now let's take a closer look at how we can build that simple data-access layer using the Data Adapter Configuration Wizard as a starting point.

Imagine the following situation. You want to instantiate your data-access layer component, supplying a connection string in the constructor. Then you want to call a method that accepts an OrderID and returns information about that order and its line items. Later, you'll want to submit pending changes for the customer back to the database.

The Component project item is perfect for this work. It exposes a designer, like a Windows Form, but it offers no user interface at run time such as a standard class. You can drag and drop various *Connection*, *Command*, and *DataAdapter* classes onto the designer for the Component.

When you drag and drop a *DataAdapter* class (*SqlDataAdapter*, *OracleDataAdapter*, and so on) onto the designers listed previously, you'll launch the Data Adapter Configuration Wizard. This wizard looks remarkably similar to its cousin, the TableAdapter Configuration Wizard. Like its cousin, the Data Adapter Configuration Wizard lets you specify connection information, a query, and various options for generating updating logic. The main difference is that this wizard does not generate a new *TableAdapter* class that encapsulates the *DataAdater* you create.

Let's walk through a very quick demonstration of this approach.

Adding *DataAdapters* (and a Connection)

Add a new Component to your project, and call it MyDataAccessLayer. Drag and drop a *SqlData-Adapter* onto the Component's design surface. In the Data Adapter Configuration Wizard, specify a connection to the Northwind database on your local installation of SQL Express. Then specify the query to return just customer information using the following query:

```
SELECT OrderID, CustomerID, OrderDate FROM Orders
  WHERE OrderID = @OrderID
```

Once you've completed this wizard, you'll see a *SqlConnection* and a *SqlDataAdapter* on the Component's component tray. Select the new *SqlConnection* object, and name it northwind-Connection. Then rename the new *SqlDataAdapter* ordersAdapter.

Drag and drop another *SqlDataAdapter* onto the designer surface. In the Data Adapter Configuration Wizard, use the same connection information and supply the following query to return just the orders for a particular customer:

```
SELECT OrderID, ProductID, Quantity, UnitPrice FROM [Order Details]
  WHERE OrderID = @OrderID
```

Rename the new *SqlDataAdapter* detailsAdapter.

Create a Strongly Typed *DataSet*

You can build a new strongly typed *DataSet* based on these *SqlDataAdapters*. Select Data on the Visual Studio menu, and then select GenerateDataSet. If this option is not available, try selecting only the two *SqlDataAdapters* on the design surface before returning to the Visual Studio menu. Once you've selected this menu option, you'll see the dialog box shown in Figure 10-10. Select the New option and name the new strongly typed *DataSet* class NorthwindDataSet.

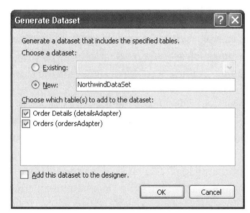

Figure 10-10   Creating a strongly typed *DataSet* based on *SqlDataAdapters*

Open the new *DataSet*'s designer and you'll see the *DataTables* for orders and order detail information. You won't see a *DataRelation* defined between the two *DataTables*; they're automatically generated only when adding *TableAdapters*. Right-click the design surface, and select Add and then Relation from the context menu. Select Orders as the Parent Table, Order Details as the Child Table, and the OrderID column as the key for each table. Specify that you want to create Both Relation And Foreign Key Constraint, and select Cascade, Cascade, and None for the Update Rule, Delete Rule, and Accept/Reject Rule, respectively, as shown in Figure 10-11.

Note   Don't forget to set the *AutoIncrementSeed* and *AutoIncrementStep* properties on the OrderID column in the Orders *DataTable* to –1 to ensure that ADO.NET will generate placeholder values such as –1, –2, –3, and so on for pending inserts generated in the *DataSet*.

Figure 10-11   Creating a *DataRelation* for the strongly typed *DataSet*

Add Code to Your Data-Access Layer Component

Now it's time to add some code to the data-access layer component. Right-click the component's designer, and select View Code from the context menu to see the partial class file that's for you rather than for the designers. You can hide the public constructors that the designer automatically created by changing their modifiers from *public* to *private* or from *Public* to *Private*, depending on your language of choice.

Visual Basic

```vb
Public Sub New(ByVal ConnectionString As String)
    'Initialize the items in the component class
    InitializeComponent()

    'Assign the specified connection string to the SqlConnection
    northwindConnection.ConnectionString = ConnectionString
End Sub

Public Function GetOrder(ByVal OrderID As Integer) As NorthwindDataSet
    Dim ds As New NorthwindDataSet

    'Assign the OrderID specified to the parameter for each SqlDataAdapter
    ordersAdapter.SelectCommand.Parameters(0).Value = OrderID
    detailsAdapter.SelectCommand.Parameters(0).Value = OrderID

    'Connect, retrieve the results of each query, and disconnect
    northwindConnection.Open()
    ordersAdapter.Fill(ds.Orders)
    detailsAdapter.Fill(ds.Order_Details)
    northwindConnection.Close()

    'Return the new DataSet
    Return ds
```

```
End Function

Public Function SubmitChanges(ByVal DataSet As NorthwindDataSet) As Integer
    'Warning: This is a very simplistic example of submitting changes
    '         stored in related DataTables.  This approach will NOT work
    '         if there are deleted orders involved.  For more information
    '         on the right way to submit such changes, see the discussion
    '         of hierarchical updates in Chapter 11
    Dim intRowsAffected As Integer

    'Connect, submit pending changes, and disconnect
    northwindConnection.Open()
    intRowsAffected = ordersAdapter.Update(DataSet.Orders)
    intRowsAffected += detailsAdapter.Update(DataSet.Order_Details)
    northwindConnection.Close()

    'Return the total number of changes submitted
    Return intRowsAffected
End Function
```

Visual C#

```
public MyDataAccessLayer(string ConnectionString) {
    //Initialize the items in the component class
    InitializeComponent();
    //Assign the specified connection string to the SqlConnection
    northwindConnection.ConnectionString = ConnectionString;
}

public NorthwindDataSet GetOrder(int OrderID) {
    NorthwindDataSet ds = new NorthwindDataSet();

    //Assign the OrderID specified to the parameter for each SqlDataAdapter
    ordersAdapter.SelectCommand.Parameters[0].Value = OrderID;
    detailsAdapter.SelectCommand.Parameters[0].Value = OrderID;

    //Connect, retrieve the results of each query, and disconnect
    northwindConnection.Open();
    ordersAdapter.Fill(ds.Orders);
    detailsAdapter.Fill(ds.Order_Details);
    northwindConnection.Close();

    //Return the new DataSet
    return ds;
}

public int SubmitChanges(NorthwindDataSet dataSet) {
    //Warning: This is a very simplistic example of submitting changes
    //         stored in related DataTables.  This approach will NOT work
    //         if there are deleted orders involved.  For more information
    //         on the right way to submit such changes, see the discussion
    //         of hierarchical updates in Chapter 11
    int intRowsUpdated;

    //Connect, submit pending changes, and disconnect
    northwindConnection.Open();
```

```
intRowsUpdated = ordersAdapter.Update(dataSet.Orders);
intRowsUpdated += detailsAdapter.Update(dataSet.Order_Details);
northwindConnection.Close();

//Return the total number of changes submitted
return intRowsUpdated;
}
```

> **Warning**   This is a very simplistic example of submitting changes stored in related *DataTables*. This approach will *not* work if there are deleted orders involved. For more information about the correct way to submit such changes, see the discussion of hierarchical updates in Chapter 11.

Now that we have our data-access layer component, we can use it to retrieve and display the contents of an order, as well as submit changes to an order using the following code:

Visual Basic
```
Dim strConn As String
strConn = "Data Source=.\SQLExpress;" & _
          "Initial Catalog=Northwind;Integrated Security=True;"

'Reset the order
ResetOrder(strConn)

'Retrieve and display the order
Dim myDal As New MyDataAccessLayer(strConn)
Dim ds As NorthwindDataSet = myDal.GetOrder(10503)
Dim tblDetails As NorthwindDataSet.Order_DetailsDataTable
tblDetails = ds.Order_Details
Dim rowOrder As NorthwindDataSet.OrdersRow = ds.Orders(0)
Dim rowDetail As NorthwindDataSet.Order_DetailsRow
Console.WriteLine("Original details for {0} placed on {1:d}", _
                   rowOrder.OrderID, rowOrder.OrderDate)
For Each rowDetail In rowOrder.GetOrder_DetailsRows
    Console.WriteLine("  ProductID: {0}  Quantity: {1}  UnitPrice: {2:c}", _
                       rowDetail.ProductID, rowDetail.Quantity, _
                       rowDetail.UnitPrice)
Next rowDetail
Console.WriteLine()

'Modify the contents of the order
'Note: Assumes knowledge of ProductIDs

'Delete the tofu DataRow
rowDetail = tblDetails.FindByOrderIDProductID(10503, 14)
rowDetail.Delete()

'Double the quantity for hot sauce
rowDetail = tblDetails.FindByOrderIDProductID(10503, 65)
rowDetail.Quantity *= 2

'Add a new DataRow for chai
tblDetails.AddOrder_DetailsRow(rowOrder, 1, 24, 18)
```

```vb
'Submit the pending changes
myDal.SubmitChanges(ds)

'Re-Retrieve and display the order
ds = myDal.GetOrder(10503)
rowOrder = ds.Orders(0)
Console.WriteLine("New details for {0} placed on {1:d}", _
                  rowOrder.OrderID, rowOrder.OrderDate)
For Each rowDetail In rowOrder.GetOrder_DetailsRows
    Console.WriteLine("  ProductID: {0}  Quantity: {1}  UnitPrice: {2:c}", _
                      rowDetail.ProductID, rowDetail.Quantity, _
                      rowDetail.UnitPrice)
Next rowDetail
Console.WriteLine()

Sub ResetOrder(ByVal ConnectionString As String)
    'Reset the order.
    Dim strSQL As String
    Dim cn As New SqlConnection(ConnectionString)
    cn.Open()

    'Delete the current contents of the order
    strSQL = "DELETE [Order Details] WHERE OrderID = @OrderID"
    Dim cmd As New SqlCommand(strSQL, cn)
    cmd.Parameters.AddWithValue("@OrderID", 10503)
    cmd.ExecuteNonQuery()

    strSQL = "INSERT INTO [Order Details] " & _
             " (OrderID, ProductID, Quantity, UnitPrice) VALUES " & _
             " (@OrderID, @ProductID, @Quantity, @UnitPrice)"
    cmd.CommandText = strSQL

    'Re-add the tofu
    cmd.Parameters.AddWithValue("@ProductID", 14)
    cmd.Parameters.AddWithValue("@Quantity", 70)
    cmd.Parameters.AddWithValue("@UnitPrice", 23.25)
    cmd.ExecuteNonQuery()

    'Re-add the hot sauce
    cmd.Parameters("@ProductID").Value = 65
    cmd.Parameters("@Quantity").Value = 20
    cmd.Parameters("@UnitPrice").Value = 21.05
    cmd.ExecuteNonQuery()

    cn.Close()
End Sub
```

Visual C#

```csharp
string strConn;
strConn = @"Data Source=.\SQLExpress;" +
          "Initial Catalog=Northwind;Integrated Security=True;";

//Reset the order
ResetOrder(strConn);
```

```
//Retrieve and display the order
MyDataAccessLayer myDal = new MyDataAccessLayer(strConn);
NorthwindDataSet ds = myDal.GetOrder(10503);
NorthwindDataSet.Order_DetailsDataTable tblDetails;
tblDetails = ds.Order_Details;
NorthwindDataSet.OrdersRow rowOrder = ds.Orders[0];
NorthwindDataSet.Order_DetailsRow rowDetail;
Console.WriteLine("Original details for {0} placed on {1:d}",
                  rowOrder.OrderID, rowOrder.OrderDate);
foreach (NorthwindDataSet.Order_DetailsRow row in
         rowOrder.GetOrder_DetailsRows())
   Console.WriteLine("  ProductID: {0}  Quantity: {1}  UnitPrice: {2:c}",
                     row.ProductID, row.Quantity, row.UnitPrice);
Console.WriteLine();

//Modify the contents of the order
//Note: Assumes knowledge of ProductIDs

//Delete the tofu DataRow
rowDetail = tblDetails.FindByOrderIDProductID(10503, 14);
rowDetail.Delete();

//Double the quantity for hot sauce
rowDetail = tblDetails.FindByOrderIDProductID(10503, 65);
rowDetail.Quantity *= 2;

//Add a new DataRow for chai
tblDetails.AddOrder_DetailsRow(rowOrder, 1, 24, 18);

//Submit the pending changes
myDal.SubmitChanges(ds);

//Re-Retrieve and display the order
ds = myDal.GetOrder(10503);
rowOrder = ds.Orders[0];
Console.WriteLine("New details for {0} placed on {1:d}",
                  rowOrder.OrderID, rowOrder.OrderDate);
foreach (NorthwindDataSet.Order_DetailsRow row in
         rowOrder.GetOrder_DetailsRows())
   Console.WriteLine("  ProductID: {0}  Quantity: {1}  UnitPrice: {2:c}",
                     row.ProductID, row.Quantity, row.UnitPrice);

Console.WriteLine();

static void ResetOrder(string ConnectionString) {
    //Reset the order.
    string strSQL;
    SqlConnection cn = new SqlConnection(ConnectionString);
    cn.Open();

    //Delete the current contents of the order
    strSQL = "DELETE [Order Details] WHERE OrderID = @OrderID";
    SqlCommand cmd = new SqlCommand(strSQL, cn);
    cmd.Parameters.AddWithValue("@OrderID", 10503);
    cmd.ExecuteNonQuery();
```

```
strSQL = "INSERT INTO [Order Details] " +
        " (OrderID, ProductID, Quantity, UnitPrice) VALUES " +
        " (@OrderID, @ProductID, @Quantity, @UnitPrice)";
cmd.CommandText = strSQL;

//Re-add the tofu
cmd.Parameters.AddWithValue("@ProductID", 14);
cmd.Parameters.AddWithValue("@Quantity", 70);
cmd.Parameters.AddWithValue("@UnitPrice", 23.25);
cmd.ExecuteNonQuery();

//Re-add the hot sauce
cmd.Parameters["@ProductID"].Value = 65;
cmd.Parameters["@Quantity"].Value = 20;
cmd.Parameters["@UnitPrice"].Value = 21.05;
cmd.ExecuteNonQuery();

cn.Close();
}
```

As you can see, if you're at all frustrated with *TableAdapters*, you can still use the Data Adapter Configuration Wizard to quickly and easily build *DataAdapters* and the updating logic required to submit pending changes.

Submitting Updates in *SqlTransactions*

What if you want to submit all your updates as a single unit of work so that either all the updates succeed or none of them does? You could create a *SqlTransaction* for your *SqlConnection* and wrap the updates in that transaction. However, the *SqlDataAdapter* does not expose a *Transaction* property. What to do?

Remember that the *SqlDataAdapter* does not actually submit the updates. It simply hands the work off to the *SqlCommand* objects in its *UpdateCommand*, *InsertCommand*, and *DeleteCommand* properties. The *SqlCommand* object exposes a *Transaction* property, so to submit the changes using the *SqlDataAdapter*, you must set the *Transaction* property of the *SqlCommand* objects that the *SqlDataAdapter* will use.

The following code snippet shows one way to accomplish this task:

Visual Basic
```
Dim strConn, strSQL As String
strConn = "Data Source=.\SQLExpress;" & _
        "Initial Catalog=Northwind;Trusted_Connection=Yes;"
strSQL = "SELECT OrderID, ProductID, Quantity, UnitPrice " & _
        "FROM [Order Details] WHERE OrderID = @OrderID " & _
        "ORDER BY ProductID"
Dim tbl As New DataTable()
Dim cn As New SqlConnection(strConn)
Dim da As New SqlDataAdapter(strSQL, cn)
da.SelectCommand.Parameters.AddWithValue("@OrderID", 10503)

'Define updating logic for the SqlDataAdapter.
...
```

```
'Open the connection and fetch the results of the query.
cn.Open()
da.Fill(tbl)

'Modify the contents of the DataTable.
tbl.Rows(0).Delete()
tbl.Rows(1)("Quantity") = CShort(tbl.Rows(1)("Quantity")) * 2
tbl.Rows.Add(New Object() {10503, 1, 24, 18})

'Create a new transaction.
Using txn As SqlTransaction = cn.BeginTransaction()
    'Set the Transaction property of the DataAdapter's Commands.
    da.UpdateCommand.Transaction = txn
    da.InsertCommand.Transaction = txn
    da.DeleteCommand.Transaction = txn

     'Submit the changes.
    da.Update(tbl)

     'Commit the changes and close the connection.
    txn.Commit()
End Using
cn.Close()
```

Visual C#

```
string strConn, strSQL;
strConn = @"Data Source=.\SQLExpress;" +
          "Initial Catalog=Northwind;Integrated Security=True;";
strSQL = "SELECT OrderID, ProductID, Quantity, UnitPrice " +
         "FROM [Order Details] WHERE OrderID = @OrderID " +
         "ORDER BY ProductID";
DataTable tbl = new DataTable();
SqlConnection cn = new SqlConnection(strConn);
OleDbDataAdapter da = new OleDbDataAdapter(strSQL, cn);
da.SelectCommand.Parameters.AddWithValue("@OrderID", 10503);

//Define updating logic for the SqlDataAdapter.
...

//Open the connection and fetch the results of the query.
cn.Open();
da.Fill(tbl);

//Modify the contents of the DataTable.
tbl.Rows[0].Delete();
tbl.Rows[1]["Quantity"] = (short) tbl.Rows[1]["Quantity"] * 2;
tbl.Rows.Add(new object[] {10503, 1, 24, 18});

//Create a new transaction.
using (SqlTransaction txn = cn.BeginTransaction()) {
    //Set the Transaction property of the DataAdapter's Commands.
    da.UpdateCommand.Transaction = txn;
    da.InsertCommand.Transaction = txn;
    da.DeleteCommand.Transaction = txn;

    //Submit the changes.
    da.Update(tbl);
```

```
    //Commit the changes and close the connection.
    txn.Commit();
}
cn.Close();
```

> **Note** The *DataSet* is unaware of the transaction. It does not keep track of the pending changes submitted on the transaction. Rolling back the transaction does not revert the *DataSet* to its state prior to the transaction. We'll take a look at ways of handling this scenario in Chapter 11 when we discuss distributed transactions.

It's slightly more challenging to submit changes in a *SqlTransaction* if you're relying on the *SqlCommandBuilder* object to generate your updating logic. The *SqlCommandBuilder* does not actually generate the updating logic when you instantiate it. If you instantiate a *SqlCommand-Builder* object and later call *SqlDataAdapter.Update*, the *SqlCommandBuilder* will not actually build the updating logic until you call the *SqlDataAdapter* object's *Update* method. To build that updating logic, the *SqlCommandBuilder* needs to query the database for information about the resultset generated by the *SelectCommand*.

This behavior poses a slight problem if you want to use the *SqlCommandBuilder* to submit changes in a transaction. If you start your transaction before the *SqlCommandBuilder* has retrieved that schema information, you must associate the *SelectCommand* with the transaction, as shown in this code snippet:

Visual Basic
```
Dim strConn, strSQL As String
strConn = "Data Source=.\SQLExpress;" & _
          "Initial Catalog=Northwind;Trusted_Connection=Yes;"
strSQL = "SELECT OrderID, ProductID, Quantity, UnitPrice " & _
          "FROM [Order Details] WHERE OrderID = @OrderID " & _
          "ORDER BY ProductID"
Dim tbl As New DataTable()
Dim cn As New SqlConnection(strConn)
Dim da As New SqlDataAdapter(strSQL, cn)
da.SelectCommand.Parameters.AddWithValue("@OrderID", 10503)

cn.Open()
da.Fill(tbl)

'Modify the contents of the DataTable.
tbl.Rows(0).Delete()
tbl.Rows(1)("Quantity") = CShort(tbl.Rows(1)("Quantity")) * 2
tbl.Rows.Add(New Object() {10503, 1, 24, 18})

'Submit the changes in a transaction
Using txn As SqlTransaction = cn.BeginTransaction()
    Dim cb As New SqlCommandBuilder(da)

    'Associate the SqlDataAdapter's SelectCommand
    'with the SqlTransaction so the SqlCommandBuilder can
```

```
    'retrieve schema using the transaction on the call to
    'SqlDataAdapter.Update
    da.SelectCommand.Transaction = txn

    da.Update(tbl)
    txn.Commit()
End Using

cn.Close()
```

Visual C#

```
string strConn, strSQL;
strConn = @"Data Source=.\SQLExpress;" +
        "Initial Catalog=Northwind;Integrated Security=True;";
strSQL = "SELECT OrderID, ProductID, Quantity, UnitPrice " +
        "FROM [Order Details] WHERE OrderID = @OrderID " +
        "ORDER BY ProductID";
DataTable tbl = new DataTable();
SqlConnection cn = new SqlConnection(strConn);
SqlDataAdapter da = new SqlDataAdapter(strSQL, cn);
da.SelectCommand.Parameters.AddWithValue("@OrderID", 10503);
cn.Open();
da.Fill(tbl);

//Modify the contents of the DataTable.
tbl.Rows[0].Delete();
tbl.Rows[1]["Quantity"] = (short) tbl.Rows[1]["Quantity"] * 2;
tbl.Rows.Add(new object[] {10503, 1, 24, 18});

//Create a new transaction.
using (SqlTransaction txn = cn.BeginTransaction()) {
    SqlCommandBuilder cb = new SqlCommandBuilder(da);

    //Associate the SqlDataAdapter's SelectCommand
    //with the SqlTransaction so the SqlCommandBuilder can
    //retrieve schema using the transaction on the call to
    //SqlDataAdapter.Update
    da.SelectCommand.Transaction = txn;

    da.Update(tbl);
    txn.Commit();
}

cn.Close();
```

Another option is to force the *SqlCommandBuilder* to generate updating logic prior to starting your *SqlTransaction* (by calling one of the *Get<Insert/Update/Delete>Command* methods) and then associating the *SqlTransaction* with the *SqlCommands* that the *SqlCommandBuilder* constructed, as shown here:

Visual Basic

```
Dim strConn, strSQL As String
strConn = "Data Source=.\SQLExpress;" & _
        "Initial Catalog=Northwind;Trusted_Connection=Yes;"
```

```
strSQL = "SELECT OrderID, ProductID, Quantity, UnitPrice " & _
         "FROM [Order Details] WHERE OrderID = @OrderID " & _
         "ORDER BY ProductID"
Dim tbl As New DataTable()
Dim cn As New SqlConnection(strConn)
Dim da As New SqlDataAdapter(strSQL, cn)
da.SelectCommand.Parameters.AddWithValue("@OrderID", 10503)

cn.Open()
da.Fill(tbl)

'Modify the contents of the DataTable.
tbl.Rows(0).Delete()
tbl.Rows(1)("Quantity") = CShort(tbl.Rows(1)("Quantity")) * 2
tbl.Rows.Add(New Object() {10503, 1, 24, 18})

'Create the SqlCommandBuilder and force it to retrieve schema
Dim cb As New SqlCommandBuilder(da)
cb.GetInsertCommand()

'Submit the changes in a transaction
Using txn As SqlTransaction = cn.BeginTransaction()

    'Associate the SqlCommands built by the SqlCommandBuilder
    'with the SqlTransaction
    cb.GetInsertCommand().Transaction = txn
    cb.GetUpdateCommand().Transaction = txn
    cb.GetDeleteCommand().Transaction = txn

    da.Update(tbl)
    txn.Commit()
End Using

cn.Close()
```

Visual C#

```
string strConn, strSQL;
strConn = @"Data Source=.\SQLExpress;" +
        "Initial Catalog=Northwind;Integrated Security=True;";
strSQL = "SELECT OrderID, ProductID, Quantity, UnitPrice " +
         "FROM [Order Details] WHERE OrderID = @OrderID " +
         "ORDER BY ProductID";
DataTable tbl = new DataTable();
SqlConnection cn = new SqlConnection(strConn);
SqlDataAdapter da = new SqlDataAdapter(strSQL, cn);
da.SelectCommand.Parameters.AddWithValue("@OrderID", 10503);
cn.Open();
da.Fill(tbl);

//Modify the contents of the DataTable.
tbl.Rows[0].Delete();
tbl.Rows[1]["Quantity"] = (short) tbl.Rows[1]["Quantity"] * 2;
tbl.Rows.Add(new object[] {10503, 1, 24, 18});
```

```
//Create the SqlCommandBuilder and force it to retrieve schema
SqlCommandBuilder cb = new SqlCommandBuilder(da);
cb.GetInsertCommand();

//Create a new transaction.
using (SqlTransaction txn = cn.BeginTransaction()) {

    //Associate the SqlCommands built by the SqlCommandBuilder
    //with the SqlTransaction
    cb.GetInsertCommand().Transaction = txn;
    cb.GetUpdateCommand().Transaction = txn;
    cb.GetDeleteCommand().Transaction = txn;

    da.Update(tbl);
    txn.Commit();
}

cn.Close();
```

Using the *TableMappings* Collection

In Chapter 5, you learned how the *SqlDataAdapter* class's *TableMappings* collection affects how the *SqlDataAdapter* populates a *DataSet* using the *Fill* method. In the following code, calling the *Fill* method of the *SqlDataAdapter* creates a new *DataTable* whose *TableName* property is set to *Table*:

Visual Basic

```
Dim strConn, strSQL As String
strConn = "Data Source=.\SQLExpress;" & _
          "Initial Catalog=Northwind;Integrated Security=True;"
strSQL = "SELECT OrderID, ProductID, Quantity, UnitPrice " & _
         "FROM [Order Details] WHERE OrderID = @OrderID " & _
         "ORDER BY ProductID"
Dim da As New SqlDataAdapter(strSQL, strConn)
da.SelectCommand.Parameters.AddWithValue("@OrderID", 10503)
Dim ds As New DataSet()
da.Fill(ds)
Console.WriteLine(ds.Tables(0).TableName)
```

Visual C#

```
string strConn, strSQL;
strConn = @"Data Source=.\SQLExpress;" +
          "Initial Catalog=Northwind;Integrated Security=True;";
strSQL = "SELECT OrderID, ProductID, Quantity, UnitPrice " +
         "FROM [Order Details] WHERE OrderID = @OrderID " +
         "ORDER BY ProductID";
OleDbDataAdapter da = new OleDbDataAdapter(strSQL, strConn);
da.SelectCommand.Parameters.AddWithValue("@OrderID", 10503);
DataSet ds = new DataSet();
da.Fill(ds);
Console.WriteLine(ds.Tables[0].TableName);
```

If we want our new *DataTable* to have a *TableName* of Order Details, we can change our code in one of two ways. The first option is to use the overloaded *Fill* method to supply the desired *TableName*:

Visual Basic

```
Dim da As New SqlDataAdapter(strSQL, strConn)
Dim ds As New DataSet()
da.Fill(ds, "Order Details")
```

Visual C#

```
SqlDataAdapter da = new SqlDataAdapter(strSQL, strConn);
DataSet ds = new DataSet();
da.Fill(ds, "Order Details");
```

The other option is to add an entry to the *SqlDataAdapter* object's *TableMappings* collection so that the *SqlDataAdapter* knows that it's associated with the Order Details *DataTable*:

Visual Basic

```
Dim da As New SqlDataAdapter(strSQL, strConn)
da.TableMappings.Add("Table", "Order Details")
Dim ds As New DataSet()
da.Fill(ds)
```

Visual C#

```
SqlDataAdapter da = new SqlDataAdapter(strSQL, strConn);
da.TableMappings.Add("Table", "Order Details");
DataSet ds = new DataSet();
da.Fill(ds);
```

The *TableMappings* collection has a similar effect when you submit updates. If you supply just a *DataSet* object in the *SqlDataAdapter* object's *Update* method, the *SqlDataAdapter* will rely on its *TableMappings* collection to determine which *DataTable* in the *DataSet* to examine.

If you have not populated the *SqlDataAdapter* object's *TableMappings* collection, you must either use the *Update* method that accepts a *DataSet* and a table name or use the *Update* method that accepts a *DataTable* object. As a general rule, you should use the same logic to control the *DataTable* you're referencing in both *SqlDataAdapter.Fill* and *SqlData-Adapter.Update*.

Visual Basic

```
Dim da As New SqlDataAdapter(strSQL, strConn)
'Define updating logic.
'...
Dim ds As New DataSet()
da.Fill(ds, "Order Details")
'Modify a series of rows.
'...
da.Update(ds, "Order Details")
```

```
'or

Dim da As New SqlDataAdapter(strSQL, strConn)
'Define updating logic.
'...
Dim tbl As New DataTable()
da.Fill(tbl)
'Modify a series of rows.
'...
da.Update(tbl)
```

Visual C#

```
SqlDataAdapter da = new SqlDataAdapter(strSQL, strConn);
//Define updating logic.
//...
DataSet ds = new DataSet();
da.Fill(ds, "Order Details");
//Modify a series of rows.
//...
da.Update(ds, "Order Details");

//or

SqlDataAdapter da = new SqlDataAdapter(strSQL, strConn);
//Define updating logic.
//...
DataTable tbl = new DataTable();
da.Fill(tbl);
//Modify a series of rows.
//...
da.Update(tbl);
```

The Best Way to Update

ADO.NET gives you many options for submitting changes. You can generate updating logic at run time using *SqlCommandBuilder* objects. You can supply your own updating logic in code, submitting changes via INSERT, UPDATE, or DELETE queries or via stored procedure calls. You can also use the TableAdapter Configuration Wizard to generate such code easily at design time. Which of these options is right for you? The answer really depends on the parameters of your application.

Should you rely on *TableAdapters* or *DataAdapters*? Personally, I love the fact that the *Table-Adapters* add strongly typed *Fill* and *Get* methods that can simplify your code. At the same time, the fact that the *TableAdapters* hide the *DataAdapters* they use internally can be frustrating if you want to use functionality that's not part of a *TableAdapter*. I've found that the frustration outweighs the benefits, but I'm curious to see the overall reaction to *TableAdapters* within the .NET community.

Regardless of whether you use *TableAdapters* or *DataAdapters*, you'll get the best performance by submitting updates using stored procedure calls. However, if your application must work with databases, such as Microsoft Access, that don't support stored procedures, that solution is not appropriate. You'd be better off using INSERT, UPDATE, and DELETE queries. You'll need to consider such factors when deciding what's appropriate for your application.

From a general standpoint, I strongly recommend submitting changes using stored procedures whenever possible. If the ability to work with multiple back ends is a greater priority, use query-based updates (INSERT, UPDATE, DELETE) instead. Regardless of which option you choose, generate your own updating logic. Use the TableAdapter Configuration Wizard or a similar code-generation tool to save development time, but avoid generating updating logic at run time whenever possible. If you remember only one thing from this chapter, remember this: Don't rely on *SqlCommandBuilder* objects in your applications unless absolutely necessary.

There are a number of more advanced updating scenarios that we've yet to discuss. How do you fetch newly generated auto-increment values? How do you submit changes from a *DataSet* that contains new and deleted rows to multiple related tables? How do you detect and handle failed update attempts? How can you use ADO.NET with distributed transactions? We'll discuss these and other more advanced updating scenarios in the next chapter.

SqlCommandBuilder Object Reference

Because this chapter introduces the ADO.NET *SqlCommandBuilder* class, now is a great time to review the properties and methods of the *SqlCommandBuilder* class.

If you worked with different *CommandBuilder* classes in ADO.NET 1.x, you might have noticed that they did not share a common base class (other than *System.Component*). ADO.NET 2.0 introduces the *DbCommandBuilder* base class that all *CommandBuilder* classes should derive from. This change will help developers who want to use *CommandBuilders* from different .NET Data Providers through a common set of properties and methods.

Properties of the *SqlCommandBuilder* Class

Table 10-1 lists the properties of the *SqlCommandBuilder* class.

Table 10-1   Properties of the *SqlCommandBuilder* Class

Property	Data Type	Description
ConflictOption	*ConflictOption*	Controls the type of concurrency checks the *SqlCommandBuilder* adds to the WHERE clause in the *UpdateCommand* and *DeleteCommand* it generates. (The default is *CompareAllSearchableValues*.)
DataAdapter	*SqlDataAdapter*	Returns the *SqlDataAdapter* for which the *SqlCommandBuilder* is generating updating logic.
SetAllValues	*Boolean*	Controls whether the *SqlCommandBuilder* submits values for all columns or just the modified ones, when submitting modified rows. (The default is *False*.)

ConflictOption

The *ConflictOption* property controls the type of concurrency checks the *SqlCommandBuilder* uses in the WHERE clause for the *UpdateCommand* and *DeleteCommand*. By default, this property is set to *CompareAllSearchableValues*. The three possible settings are:

- *CompareAllSearchableValues*   Causes the *SqlCommandBuilder* to include all *searchable* (non-BLOB) columns in the WHERE clause. It's worth noting that the more searchable columns that appear in your original query, the longer it takes for the database to compare the values before determining whether or not to update the row. As the number of columns increases, you should consider using a row version column in your table and query.

- *CompareRowVersion*   Causes the *SqlCommandBuilder* to include just the primary key and row version (also known as the timestamp data type for SQL Server) columns in the WHERE clause. Comparing just the primary key and row version columns is more efficient for the database than comparing all non-BLOB columns.

Remember that SQL Server automatically modifies the row version column for a row (if one exists) when any value in the row changes. This is important to keep in mind for two reasons:

If another user modifies the value of a column that does not appear in the resultset you retrieved, the concurrency check will fail.

If you modify the row successfully, you will need to fetch the new server-generated row version for the row in order to submit another change to the row at a later time.

> **Note**   If you set *ConflictOption* to *CompareRowVersion* but the query does not return a row version column, the *SqlCommandBuilder* will throw an *InvalidOperationException*.

- *OverwriteChanges*   Causes the *SqlCommandBuilder* to include only the primary key column or columns in the WHERE clause. This approach is often referred to as "last in wins." All update attempts succeed as long as the row continues to exist in the database. If you use this approach, a user might overwrite another user's changes without ever having seen those changes.

DataAdapter

The *SqlCommandBuilder* class's *DataAdapter* property allows you to examine or change the *SqlDataAdapter* with which the *SqlCommandBuilder* object is associated. You can also set this property in the *SqlCommandBuilder* class's constructor.

SetAllValues

By default, the *SqlCommandBuilder* will submit modified columns to the database only when submitting a *DataRow* with a *RowState* of *Modified*. If you set the *SetAllValues* property to *True*, the *SqlCommandBuilder* will submit values for all columns to the database when the *DataRow*'s *RowState* is *Modified*.

Methods of the *SqlCommandBuilder* Class

Table 10-2 lists the methods of the *SqlCommandBuilder* class.

Table 10-2   Methods of the *SqlCommandBuilder* Class

Method	Description
DeriveParameters	Retrieves parameter information for a *SqlCommand* that calls a stored procedure.
GetDeleteCommand	Returns the *SqlCommand* that contains the logic for the *SqlDataAdapter* object's *DeleteCommand*.
GetInsertCommand	Returns the *SqlCommand* that contains the logic for the *SqlDataAdapter* object's *InsertCommand*.
GetUpdateCommand	Returns the *SqlCommand* that contains the logic for the *SqlDataAdapter* object's *UpdateCommand*.
QuoteIdentifier	*SqlCommandBuilder* returns the string supplied surrounded by square brackets.
RefreshSchema	Tells the *SqlCommandBuilder* that it will need to regenerate its updating logic.
UnquoteIdentifier	*SqlCommandBuilder* returns the supplied string, removing square brackets from the leading and trailing characters.

DeriveParameters

The *SqlCommandBuilder* object can do more than just generate updating logic for *SqlData-Adapter* objects. You can also use a *SqlCommandBuilder* to fetch parameter information for stored procedures. The following code snippet uses the *SqlCommandBuilder* class's static *DeriveParameters* method to retrieve and display parameter information for a stored procedure call:

Visual Basic

```
Dim strConn As String
strConn = "Data Source=.\SQLExpress;" & _
          "Initial Catalog=Northwind;Integrated Security=True;"
Dim cn As New SqlConnection(strConn)
Dim cmd As New SqlCommand("CustOrdersOrders", cn)
cmd.CommandType = CommandType.StoredProcedure
Dim cb As New SqlCommandBuilder()
cn.Open()
cb.DeriveParameters(cmd)
cn.Close()
For Each param As SqlParameter In cmd.Parameters
    Console.WriteLine("Name: {0}", param.ParameterName)
    Console.WriteLine("  Direction: {0}", param.Direction)
    Console.WriteLine("  SqlDbType: {0}", param.SqlDbType)
```

```
    Console.WriteLine()
Next param
```

Visual C#

```
string strConn;
strConn = @"Data Source=.\SQLExpress;" +
          "Initial Catalog=Northwind;Integrated Security=True;";
SqlConnection cn = new SqlConnection(strConn);
SqlCommand cmd = new SqlCommand("CustOrdersOrders", cn);
cmd.CommandType = CommandType.StoredProcedure;
cn.Open();
SqlCommandBuilder.DeriveParameters(cmd);
cn.Close();
foreach (SqlParameter param in cmd.Parameters)
{
    Console.WriteLine("Name: {0}", param.ParameterName);
    Console.WriteLine("  Direction: {0}", param.Direction);
    Console.WriteLine("  SqlDbType: {0}", param.SqlDbType);
    Console.WriteLine();
}
```

If you're trying to build the parameters collection for a command that calls a stored procedure but you're unsure of what value to set for the *Size*, *Precision*, and *Scale* properties, you might want to use this type of code once at design time.

There is no way to differentiate between input/output and output-only parameters in a SQL Server stored procedure. SQL Server reports all parameters that include the OUTPUT keyword as input/output.

> **Note**   For you to use the *DeriveParameters* method, the *SqlConnection* for the supplied *SqlCommand* object must be open and available.

GetDeleteCommand, *GetInsertCommand*, and *GetUpdateCommand*

The *SqlCommandBuilder* class's *GetUpdateCommand*, *GetInsertCommand*, and *GetDelete-Command* methods let you examine the logic that the *SqlCommandBuilder* generated.

These methods can also prove helpful at design time. You can create a *SqlCommandBuilder* in code in a small sample application and then use these methods to display the *Command-Text* and parameter information that the *SqlCommandBuilder* generated. You can then use that same updating logic using the same query and parameter information in your code.

By default, the *SqlCommandBuilder* generates parameters named *@p1*, *@p2*, *@p3*, and so on. You might have noticed that the code samples in this book and the TableAdapter Configuration Wizard use parameter names that are based on the columns they reference, such as *@CustomerID*, *@CompanyName*, and so on. If you want to generate parameter names based on the corresponding column names, use the overloaded *Get<Insert/Update/Delete> Command* method that takes a *Boolean* parameter and pass in *True*.

These parameter names are more meaningful and easier to follow in code samples but they are not recommended when building parameterized queries at run time. If you build your parameterized queries based on column names, a malicious user could (in theory) inject his own logic into the INSERT, UPDATE, or DELETE queries generated by the *SqlCommandBuilder* (or any similar query generating component).

Although I'm not aware of any scenarios that are susceptible to this type of attack, I recommend using the default (and less interesting) naming convention *@p1*, *@p2*, *@p3*, and so on.

QuoteIdentifier and *UnquoteIdentifier*

Quoting identifiers is generally optional, unless you have a space or a special character in the identifier name, or if your identifier is a reserved word such as SELECT, FROM or ORDER. Quoting the identifier helps the database recognize that the quoted value is actually an identifier.

If you have an identifier name (column, table, and so on) and you want to quote the identifier for a query, use the *QuoteIdentifier* method. For example, most of the samples in this chapter use the Order Details table. Because of the space in the name, the identifier must be quoted when it appears in a query:

```
SELECT ... FROM [Order Details]
--or
SELECT ... FROM "Order Details"
```

Use one of the preceding formats rather than the following:

```
SELECT ... FROM Order Details
```

When you pass a string into the *QuoteIdentifier* method, the method assumes the value you've passed in represents an identifier within the database and "quotes" it accordingly. I used quotation marks around the word *quotes* because the *QuotedIdentifier* doesn't actually use quotes. Instead, it uses the square bracket characters. So Order Details becomes [Order Details].

Similarly, the *UnquoteIdentifier* assumes the value you've passed in represents a quoted identifier and returns the unquoted identifier.

Most databases support quoting identifiers, though they don't all use the same characters. SQL Server, by default, supports quoted identifiers using square brackets or the double quote character–[Order Details] or "Order Details". Access supports square brackets and the 'character–[Order Details] or 'Order Details'. Oracle supports only the double quote character–"Order Details".

CommandBuilder classes that are designed for a specific database, such as the *SqlCommand-Builder* and *OracleCommandBuilder*, can quote (and unquote) identifiers easily using the guidelines for their database. *CommandBuilder* classes that support various databases, such as the *OleDbCommandBuilder* and *OdbcCommandBuilder*, need a little help. These *Command-Builder* classes expose *QuotePrefix* and *QuoteSuffix* properties that you should set to help the *CommandBuilder* understand how to quote (and unquote) identifiers prior to calling the *QuoteIdentifier* or *UnquoteIdentifier* methods.

Of course, you would not have to worry about quoting if you make sure your table and column names don't require quoting. In fact, I've yet to hear a developer say, "Boy, I sure am glad we put spaces in our table and column names. That made my life so much easier." But I digress.

For more information, see the documentation for your database on quoted identifiers.

RefreshSchema

If you're changing the structure of your *SqlDataAdapter* object's query in your application, you'll probably need to use the *SqlCommandBuilder* object's *RefreshSchema* method.

The *SqlDataAdapter* object does not fire an event when the *CommandText* property of its *Select-Command* changes. Once the *SqlCommandBuilder* object has generated your updating logic, as far as it knows, its work is done. If you've changed the structure of the *SqlDataAdapter* object's query so that the *CommandBuilder* needs to regenerate the updating logic, you can call the *RefreshSchema* method of the *SqlCommandBuilder* object.

Calling the *SqlRefreshSchema* method does not force the *CommandBuilder* to regenerate its updating logic immediately. It simply sets a flag within the *SqlCommandBuilder* to indicate that the current logic is no longer accurate. The *SqlCommandBuilder* will regenerate the updating logic when you call the *SqlDataAdapter* object's *Update* method or when you call one of the *SqlCommandBuilder* object's *Get<Update/Insert/Delete>Command* methods.

Questions That Should Be Asked More Frequently

Q   So the *SqlDataAdapter* can fill a *DataSet* with the results of a query and submit changes stored in a *DataSet* to my database. Do I have to use the same object to accomplish both tasks? I'm working with multi-tiered applications, and it sounds like I need to keep my *SqlDataAdapter* objects alive in the middle tier between calls from the client application. Is that the case?

A   You *can* use the same *SqlDataAdapter* to fill your *DataSet* and submit changes to your database, but that's not a requirement.

Suppose that your middle-tier object has two simple methods—one to return a new *DataSet* and one to submit the pending changes in your *DataSet* to your database. You can use separate *SqlDataAdapter* objects for each of the methods. When you're simply filling a *DataSet*, the

SqlDataAdapter does not need updating logic. Conversely, if you're using a *SqlDataAdapter* only to submit updates, the *SqlDataAdapter* does not require you to define a *SelectCommand*.

The *SqlDataAdapter* really needs *SqlCommand* objects defined for only the types of commands it will need to execute. For example, if you know that your *SqlDataAdapter* will submit only new rows (rather than modify or delete existing rows), you will need only an *InsertCommand*. Because the *SqlDataAdapter* will not execute the *Command* objects stored in its *SelectCommand*, *UpdateCommand*, and *DeleteCommand* properties, you won't need to set those properties.

The one caveat to this rule is if you use a *SqlCommandBuilder* object to define the updating logic in your *SqlDataAdapter*. The *SqlCommandBuilder* cannot generate your updating logic if you do not have a *SelectCommand* defined for the *SqlDataAdapter*.

Q   I want to fill a *DataTable* based on the results of a join query, modify the data in the *DataTable*, and then submit the changes back to the database using a *SqlDataAdapter*. In the example you've used throughout the chapter, showing the line items for an order, I want to show the ProductName column from the Products table in each row. Neither the TableAdapter/Data Adapter Configuration Wizard nor the *SqlCommandBuilder* object will build this logic for me if I include the Products table in my query. What should I do?

A   My first recommendation is to reread the section about join queries in Chapter 7, but we'll get back to this in a moment.

The reason that neither the *SqlCommandBuilder* nor the wizard generates updating logic is that it's not clear what modifying the data returned by a join query truly means. Let's say that we take the query we've been using to retrieve order detail information and change it slightly so that the query also returns the name of the product in the line item:

```
SELECT D.OrderID, P.ProductName, D.ProductID,
      D.Quantity, D.UnitPrice
    FROM [Order Details] D, Products P
    WHERE D.OrderID = 10503 AND D.ProductID = P.ProductID
    ORDER BY P.ProductID
```

When we fetch the results of this query, place it into a *DataTable*, and modify a *DataRow* to reference a different product (changing the ProductID and ProductName columns), how do we want to change the contents of the database? The answer is clear to us. We want to modify the corresponding row in the Order Details table in the database, submitting a change for just the ProductID column. But that's not clear to the TableAdapter/Data Adapter Configuration Wizard or the *SqlCommandBuilder* object.

The old ADO cursor engine generates updating logic for you automatically, even with join queries, but this logic has frustrated most developers. If you generate an ADO *Recordset* using this query and modify only columns that correspond to the Order Details table, the ADO cursor engine will try to modify only the corresponding row in the Order Details table.

But if you want to change the product that the line item references and you change both the ProductID column (Order Details table) and the ProductName column (Products table) so that the row of data looks correct on your screen, the ADO cursor engine will try to modify the ProductID column in the Order Details table and the ProductName in the Products table. Chances are that isn't what you want the ADO cursor engine to do.

Thankfully, ADO.NET is not a black box technology like ADO. You can supply your own updating logic. In this scenario, you want to submit changes only to the Order Details table, so you can define your updating logic to ignore changes stored in the ProductName column.

How can you generate that updating logic? As noted earlier, neither the *SqlCommand-Builder* nor the TableAdapter/Data Adapter Configuration Wizard will be of much help with the actual join query. But you can temporarily leave off the ProductName column, use either tool to generate the desired updating logic, and then re-add the ProductName column to your query. Devious, yet effective.

Let's get back to my first recommendation. The section in Chapter 7 titled "Using *DataRelation* Objects in Expression-Based *DataColumn* Objects" includes a code snippet that shows how you can use multiple *DataTable* objects and a *DataRelation* to simulate the results of a join query, adding an expression-based *DataColumn* to display data from the related *DataTable*. The other major benefit to this approach is that you've greatly simplified your updating logic. The data in each *DataTable* corresponds to a single table in your database, so the *SqlCommandBuilder* and TableAdapter/Data Adapter Configuration Wizard can generate the appropriate updating logic for you.

Q You talked about optimistic concurrency only. How do I handle pessimistic concurrency in ADO.NET?

A With pessimistic concurrency, you lock the row before you start making your changes. Because the contents of the *DataSet* are disconnected from the database, there is no simple way to lock the data in the database before you modify a row in a *DataSet*. However, you can achieve similar functionality using transactions.

Let's say that you want to lock data in your database before the user modifies data on the screen to ensure that the user's changes will succeed. You could open a transaction and lock those rows in the database so that other users cannot modify those rows by issuing the following query within the transaction:

```
SELECT * FROM [Order Details] HOLDLOCK WHERE OrderID = 10503
```

> **Note**   This query was written specifically for SQL Server 2000/SQL Server 2005. Not all databases support this query syntax. If you're working with another database, see your database's documentation for information about how to lock data in a query.

This approach has some major drawbacks. What if your user forgets to click the Submit Changes button in your application and strolls off to the kitchen to grab a donut and some caffeine? Those rows in the database are locked. The more data you lock and the longer you maintain those locks, the less scalable your application becomes.

It's time for me to confess. I've made some mistakes in my life. I used a similar approach in an application years ago, but not because I was young or needed the money. It was because the users requested this feature. They didn't want to run into a situation in which the changes they made on the screen could not be committed to the database and they would have to reenter those changes later.

One employee, whom I'll call Steve (half the people in the company were named Steve), would repeatedly forget to commit his changes. When other users could not modify data in the database, they'd find me and then I'd have to find Steve, which sometimes took a while. Trying to explain that this was the functionality they had asked for didn't make anyone any happier.

Hey, I was in college. That's when kids are supposed to experiment with things like pessimistic locking. I learned my lesson, and no one got hurt. Not even a Steve.

Q   What if I want to submit updates when my *DataSet* contains BLOB columns?

A   The short answer is that you should take the initial query and break it out into separate queries—one that retrieves your non-BLOB columns, and one that retrieves just the primary key columns and your BLOB column.

Because the structure of the queries that the *SqlDataAdapter* uses to submit changes is static, the values from all columns are used in the SET clause of the *UpdateCommand* object's *CommandText*, even if only one column contains changed data. This is a small nuisance for most queries (and a necessary evil when you submit changes using a stored procedure), but it can be a major pain if you're working with BLOB columns. Why?

Let's say that we're working with employee information and the database contains an Employees table with columns for the employee's name, identification number, title, and photo. The photo column holds large amounts of binary information—the contents of a JPEG file.

If you have a *DataTable* that contains all these columns and you modify just the title column for a row, the *SqlDataAdapter* will include the current values for all columns in the query to update the row in the database. This means that even though you've only modified a small string-based column, you'll still pass the binary contents of the employee photo across the wire to your database.

Another approach is to split the data into separate tables, as shown in Figure 10-12. The figure shows two *DataTable* objects linked by a *DataRelation*. The parent *DataTable* includes the main columns for the Employees table—*EmployeeID*, *LastName*, and *FirstName*. The child *DataTable* contains the BLOB column photo as well as the EmployeeID column so that it can maintain the relationship to the parent *DataTable*.

If you use a *DataSet* with this architecture with separate *SqlDataAdapter* objects for each *DataTable*, a change to the LastName column will result in a query-based update that does not include the Photo column. The only time the contents of the Photo column will be sent back to the database in this architecture is when the contents of the Photo column change.

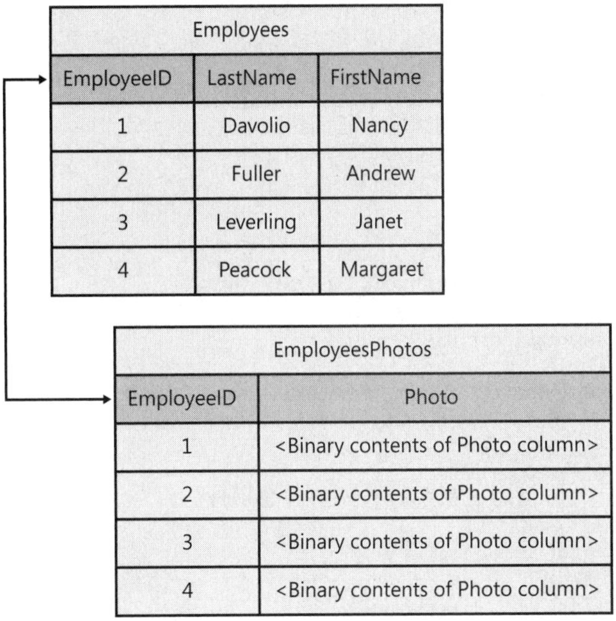

Employees		
EmployeeID	LastName	FirstName
1	Davolio	Nancy
2	Fuller	Andrew
3	Leverling	Janet
4	Peacock	Margaret

EmployeesPhotos	
EmployeeID	Photo
1	\<Binary contents of Photo column\>
2	\<Binary contents of Photo column\>
3	\<Binary contents of Photo column\>
4	\<Binary contents of Photo column\>

Figure 10-12   Splitting a *DataTable* based on a BLOB column

Of course, this entire discussion would be moot if you were to store the binary data in a file and use the database to maintain the location of the file rather than the actual binary data.

Q   I built a small application that uses the OLE DB .NET Data Provider to work with a Jet (Access) database. My application works great, except when I try to submit changes to the Order Details table using the *OleDbCommandBuilder*, where my code fails with an error about "Incorrect syntax near the keyword 'Order.'" What happened?

A   As noted earlier in the discussion of the *QuoteIdentifier* and *UnquoteIdentifier* methods, the *SqlCommandBuilder* class knows that it's talking to a SQL Server database, so it automatically quotes all the identifiers (table, column, and catalog names) using square brackets. The *OleDbCommandBuilder* does not query the database to determine the characters that the database uses to delimit table and column names that are reserved words or that contain spaces and other mischievous characters. If you use the *OleDbCommandBuilder* to generate updating logic for a query that includes such table or column names, your update attempts will fail unless you specify values for the *OleDbCommandBuilder* object's *QuotePrefix* and *QuoteSuffix* properties.

What if you're not comfortable supplying values for those properties because you're writing code that must run successfully against various back ends? If you're working with the OLE DB .NET Data Provider, you might be able to use the *OleDbConnection* object's *GetOleDbSchemaTable* method to fetch the proper delimiters from the database. I've tested the following code, and it has worked successfully using the Microsoft OLE DB providers that communicate with SQL Server, Oracle, and Access:

Visual Basic

```vb
'Imports System.Data.OleDb
Dim strConn, strSQL As String
strConn = "Provider=SQLOLEDB;Data Source=.\SQLExpress;" & _
          "Initial Catalog=Northwind;Trusted_Connection=Yes;"
strSQL = "SELECT OrderID, ProductID, Quantity, UnitPrice " & _
         "FROM [Order Details] WHERE OrderID = ? " & _
         "ORDER BY ProductID"
Dim cn As New OleDbConnection(strConn)
Dim da As New OleDbDataAdapter(strSQL, cn)
da.SelectCommand.Parameters.AddWithValue("@OrderID", 10503)
cn.Open()
Dim cb As New OleDbCommandBuilder(da)
Dim tblSchema As DataTable
tblSchema = cn.GetOleDbSchemaTable(OleDbSchemaGuid.DbInfoLiterals, _
                                   New Object() {})
cn.Close()
tblSchema.PrimaryKey = New DataColumn() _
                       {tblSchema.Columns("LiteralName")}
Dim row As DataRow
row = tblSchema.Rows.Find("Quote_Prefix")
If Not row Is Nothing Then
    cb.QuotePrefix = CStr(row("LiteralValue"))
End If
row = tblSchema.Rows.Find("Quote_Suffix")
If Not row Is Nothing Then
    cb.QuoteSuffix = CStr(row("LiteralValue"))
End If
```

Visual C#

```csharp
//using System.Data.OleDb;
string strConn, strSQL;
strConn = @"Provider=SQLOLEDB;Data Source=.\SQLExpress;" +
          "Initial Catalog=Northwind;Trusted_Connection=Yes;";
strSQL = "SELECT OrderID, ProductID, Quantity, UnitPrice " +
         "FROM [Order Details] WHERE OrderID = ? " +
         "ORDER BY ProductID";
OleDbConnection cn = new OleDbConnection(strConn);
OleDbDataAdapter da = new OleDbDataAdapter(strSQL, cn);
da.SelectCommand.Parameters.AddWithValue("@OrderID", 10503);
cn.Open();
OleDbCommandBuilder cb = new OleDbCommandBuilder(da);
DataTable tblSchema;
tblSchema = cn.GetOleDbSchemaTable(OleDbSchemaGuid.DbInfoLiterals,
                                   new object[] {});
cn.Close();
tblSchema.PrimaryKey = new DataColumn[]
                       {tblSchema.Columns["LiteralName"]};
DataRow row;
row = tblSchema.Rows.Find("Quote_Prefix");
if (row != null)
    cb.QuotePrefix = (string) row["LiteralValue"];
row = tblSchema.Rows.Find("Quote_Suffix");
if (row != null)
    cb.QuoteSuffix = (string) row["LiteralValue"];
```

Of course, you can avoid such problems by making sure your table and column names do not require delimiters.

Q   When I submit new rows using an ADO.NET *Sql*DataAdapter, I see null values in the new row in my database rather than the default values I defined for those columns in my database. When I submitted changes via ADO, I got default values. What gives?

A   SQL Server, and other databases, lets you define default values for columns in your database. As we saw in Chapter 6, the *DefaultValue* property of the ADO.NET *DataColumn* class is not an exact match for this functionality. So ADO.NET will not generate your database's default values for you automatically. There's also another factor involved.

Databases generate default values for columns in your new rows if you use an INSERT query that either omits the column or specifies the keyword DEFAULT rather than a value for the column. ADO.NET will not omit the column from its updating logic, nor will it use the keyword DEFAULT.

ADO.NET's predecessor, ADO, generated dynamic updates on a per-row basis. When submitting updates, it omitted unmodified columns from the INSERT statements that it generated. Thus, the new rows in your database that you created with ADO might automatically contain the default values, whereas the ones you create with ADO.NET will not.

The simplest solution in ADO.NET is to add code to your application so that when you create a new row, you automatically supply the desired default values for your columns.

Advanced Updating Scenarios

In Chapter 10, you learned how to use the updating features of the *SqlDataAdapter* class to submit changes to your database. At this point, you should be comfortable generating updating logic by using either the Microsoft Visual Studio TableAdapter or Data Adapter Configuration Wizard or the *SqlCommandBuilder* object. You should also feel comfortable with the UPDATE, INSERT, and DELETE SQL queries that these tools generate to translate the pending changes stored in your *DataSet* into changes in your database.

All the examples in Chapter 10 involve simple updating scenarios. You will likely face more challenging updating scenarios in your applications. For example, if you're working with tables that have auto-increment columns, you'll want to retrieve the auto-increment values that your database generates for new rows. In other situations, you'll want to refetch the contents of your row after you submit an update, such as when you're relying on timestamp columns to enforce optimistic concurrency. You may decide to use the *System.Transactions* functionality, new to version 2.0 of the Microsoft .NET Framework, to manage transactions without needing to rely on *System.EnterpriseServices*.

The more complex your application is, the more complex the updating scenarios you'll likely face. Submitting changes to hierarchical data can prove challenging. Multi-tiered applications pose their own special set of problems—such as transmitting *DataSet* objects that contain only the data required to submit updates to your database and reintegrating newly fetched values such as timestamps and auto-increment values into a preexisting *DataSet*.

Optimistic update attempts don't always succeed. For example, your update attempts might fail if another user has modified the rows you wanted to update. You're probably better off learning to handle such failures elegantly rather than going to extreme lengths to try to prevent the failures in the first place.

Microsoft ADO.NET 2.0 introduces support for other updating scenarios. By default, ADO.NET will submit pending changes to your database one row at a time. Using ADO.NET 2.0, you can submit pending changes in batches using a *SqlDataAdapter* or the Microsoft SQL Server bulk copy functionality. ADO.NET 2.0 also includes support for *System.Transactions*, new to version 2.0 of the .NET Framework.

This chapter will examine each of these scenarios in detail. The sample code for this chapter contains working code for each scenario.

Refreshing a Row After Submitting an Update

In Chapter 10, you learned how to construct and use INSERT, UPDATE, and DELETE queries to submit changes to your database. These queries are basically one-way streets. The database modifies the contents of the row based on the information you supply in the query. Although the database reports how many rows the query affected, it does not return the new contents of the modified rows.

Sometimes submitting an update to your database needs to be a two-way street. In Chapter 10, we discussed using the Microsoft SQL Server timestamp data type to ensure that you don't unintentionally overwrite another user's changes to the database. When the contents of the row change, the database generates a new value for the timestamp column for that row. Consider the following scenario.

Your application is used by representatives who take orders over the phone from customers. The SQL Server table that contains the line items for the orders includes a timestamp column, and the updating logic in the application uses this timestamp column when submitting modified or deleted line items.

The customer describes the order to the phone representative, who enters the order. Once the customer is satisfied with the order, the phone representative clicks the Commit Changes button to commit the order to the database. While the phone representative reads back the order number and sets the customer's expectations as to when the order should arrive, the customer changes his or her mind and wants to change the quantity for a particular item. The information from the order remains on the screen, so the phone representative modifies the quantity for the line item, clicks the Commit Changes button, and . . . .

What happens next depends on the logic used to submit the order. If the application simply submitted the new line items to the database and did not refresh the contents of the row, the subsequent change to the order will fail. As noted earlier, the logic used to submit modified or deleted line items uses the timestamp column in concurrency checks. If the *DataRow* does not contain the same value for the timestamp column as the database row, submitting the change will fail.

Let's look at various ways to refresh the contents of a row after submitting a pending change using the *SqlDataAdapter* class.

Refreshing the Contents of a *DataRow* After Submitting Changes

In the following examples, we'll use a hypothetical table called OrderDetailsWithTimestamp that, as its name implies, looks like the Order Details table in the sample Northwind Traders database, except that the table also contains a timestamp column.

Let's say that the initial query to retrieve data from the table looks like this:

```
SELECT OrderID, ProductID, Quantity, UnitPrice, TimestampColumn
    FROM OrderDetailsWithTimestamp WHERE OrderID = @OrderID
```

You learned in the previous chapter that you can submit updates to the table using the following parameterized query:

```
UPDATE OrderDetailsWithTimestamp
    SET OrderID = @OrderID_New, ProductID = @ProductID_New,
        Quantity = @Quantity_New, UnitPrice = @UnitPrice_New
    WHERE OrderID = @OrderID_Old AND ProductID = @ProductID_Old
      AND TimestampColumn = @TimestampColumn_Old
```

We can issue the following query to refresh the contents of the row after submitting the change:

```
SELECT Quantity, UnitPrice, TimestampColumn
    FROM OrderDetailsWithTimestamp
    WHERE OrderID = @OrderID_New AND ProductID = @ProductID_New
```

Sure, you could manually execute this query after submitting an update, but what if you have a series of changes to submit? You'd need to keep track of all the *DataRow* objects whose pending updates succeeded, retrieve the new timestamp values for those *DataRow* objects, and be sure to call *AcceptChanges* on the *DataRow* objects so that the change to the timestamp values is not seen as a pending change to submit to the database.

Let's look at how we can simplify this process using ADO.NET features.

Caution   In the scenario described, the only value we need to retrieve to submit subsequent changes is the timestamp column. You might have noticed that the preceding query retrieves data for all the non-key columns. Why retrieve data for all these columns?

The goal is to refresh the entire row, not just the timestamp column. In fact, retrieving just the timestamp column could be dangerous. Consider a scenario in which the database administrator has added a trigger to the table that might modify the data you've submitted so that the values in the database differ from the values in your *DataRow*. If you retrieve just the timestamp value, you now have all the information you need to make further changes to the *DataRow* and submit those changes successfully. However, this means that you could potentially overwrite values you've never seen.

> As a general rule, you should refresh the contents of the entire *DataRow* rather than just the timestamp column. The key columns are not returned in the SELECT query because they are used in the WHERE clause.

Using Batch Queries to Retrieve Data After You Submit an Update

In Chapter 5, you learned how to use a *SqlDataAdapter* to fetch the results of a batch query such as this one:

```
SELECT CustomerID, CompanyName FROM Customers;
SELECT OrderID, CustomerID, OrderDate FROM Orders
```

You can also use batched queries to retrieve data after you submit an update. You can combine the update query and the query to retrieve the new timestamp value by using a batched query. Set the *CommandText* of the *SqlDataAdapter* object's *UpdateCommand* to the following parameterized query:

```
UPDATE OrderDetailsWithTimestamp
    SET OrderID = @OrderID_New, ProductID = @ProductID_New,
        Quantity = @Quantity_New, UnitPrice = @UnitPrice_New
    WHERE OrderID = @OrderID_Old AND ProductID = @ProductID_Old
      AND TimestampColumn = @TimestampColumn_Old;
SELECT Quantity, UnitPrice, TimestampColumn
    FROM OrderDetailsWithTimestamp
    WHERE OrderID = @OrderID_New AND ProductID = @ProductID_New
```

> **Note**   Not all databases support row-returning batch queries. Microsoft SQL Server supports this functionality. Microsoft Access does not. Oracle supports this functionality through ref cursors. For more information on handling this scenario with Oracle, see Appendix A. Check your database's documentation to determine whether it supports this functionality.

You could execute this query yourself by calling the *ExecuteReader* method on the *SqlCommand*. You could then use the *RecordsAffected* property on the resulting *SqlDataReader* to determine the number of rows affected by the UPDATE query. If the query affected a single row, you would call the *SqlDataReader*'s *Read* method, check the contents of the *SqlDataReader*, apply the newly retrieved values to the *DataRow*, and then call the *DataRow*'s *AcceptChanges* method.

Or you could rely on features of the *SqlDataAdapter* and *SqlCommand* to handle this logic and apply values for you automatically.

The *SqlCommand* Class's *UpdatedRowSource* Property

The *SqlDataAdapter* uses the *SqlCommand* objects stored in its *InsertCommand*, *UpdateCommand*, and *DeleteCommand* properties to submit updates to your database. The *SqlDataAdapter* then checks the number of rows affected by the *SqlCommand* to determine whether the update attempt succeeded. If the *SqlDataAdapter* determines that submitting the pending change in a

DataRow succeeded, the *SqlDataAdapter* checks the *SqlCommand*'s *UpdatedRowSource* property to determine how (or whether) it should apply values returned by the *SqlCommand* to the *DataRow*.

The *UpdatedRowSource* property accepts a value from the *UpdateRowSource* enumeration. (The available values are listed in Table 11-1.) By default, the *SqlCommand* will fetch new data for the modified row by checking for output parameters and the first row returned by the query.

Table 11-1 Members of the *UpdateRowSource* Enumeration

Constant	Value	Description
Both	3	Tells the *SqlCommand* to fetch new data for the row using both the first returned record and output parameters. This is the default.
FirstReturnedRecord	2	Tells the *SqlCommand* to fetch new data for the row through the first returned record.
None	0	Tells the *SqlCommand* not to fetch new data for the row upon execution.
OutputParameters	1	Tells the *SqlCommand* to fetch new data for the row using output parameters.

If the *SqlCommand*'s *UpdatedRowSource* property is *FirstReturnedRecord* or *Both* and the *SqlCommand* reports that the update attempt succeeded, the *SqlDataAdapter* will look for the first record returned by the query in the *SqlCommand* and apply values in that record to the *DataRow*, matching values from the query results to columns in the *DataRow* using the column names in the query results and the *DataTable*'s *Columns* collection.

Similarly, if the *SqlCommand*'s *UpdatedRowSource* property is set to *OutputParameters* or *Both* and the *SqlCommand* reports that the update attempt succeeded, the *SqlDataAdapter* will apply values in the *SqlCommand*'s output parameters to the *DataRow*, matching output parameters to columns in the *DataRow* based on the *SourceColumn* property on the *SqlParameters*.

Tip   You can improve the performance of your update by setting the value of the *UpdatedRow-Source* property to the appropriate value. The *SqlCommand* does not parse the query it is about to execute, and it has no idea whether the query will return data through a SELECT query or output parameters. If you leave the *SqlCommand* object's *UpdatedRowSource* property set to *Both* (its default), the *SqlDataAdapter* will check for both output parameters and a record returned. There is a small performance hit incurred in performing this check. By setting the *SqlCommand* object's *UpdatedRowSource* property to the appropriate value, you can improve the performance of your code by avoiding unnecessary checks for output parameters or returned records.

I performed a small, informal test using this property. I used a *Sql*DataAdapter to retrieve the contents of the Order Details table and insert all the rows in a new table with the same structure. Initially, I left the *UpdatedRowSource* property at its default value, *Both*.

In my test, the *InsertCommand* simply submitted the new row. It does not include a batch query to refetch the contents of the row after the update is submitted, so there's no need to have the *InsertCommand* property's *UpdatedRowSource* property set to anything other than *None*. When I set the property to *None* and ran the test again, the test ran between 1 and 2 percent faster.

We'll take a closer look at output parameters in a moment, but first let's look at how we can improve on the batch query used in the previous example.

Improving the Batch Query

We can improve on the logic in the batch query used to submit the pending change and return the contents of the modified row. Currently, the query looks like this:

```
UPDATE OrderDetailsWithTimestamp
    SET OrderID = @OrderID_New, ProductID = @ProductID_New,
        Quantity = @Quantity_New, UnitPrice = @UnitPrice_New
    WHERE OrderID = @OrderID_Old AND ProductID = @ProductID_Old
      AND TimestampColumn = @TimestampColumn_Old;
SELECT Quantity, UnitPrice, TimestampColumn
    FROM OrderDetailsWithTimestamp
    WHERE OrderID = @OrderID_New AND ProductID = @ProductID_New
```

What happens if the UPDATE query does not affect any rows? If you execute this query in an ad hoc query tool such as SQL Server Management Studio, you'll find that the SELECT query can return a row of data even if the UPDATE query did not modify any rows.

The *SqlDataAdapter* knows to check for this possible outcome. The *SqlDataAdapter* calls the *ExecuteReader* method on the *SqlCommand* object stored in its *UpdateCommand* property, and it checks the *RecordsAffected* property of the resulting *SqlDataReader* to determine whether to apply values from the *SqlDataReader* to the *DataRow*. In other words, you don't have to worry about how this scenario affects the *DataRow*.

But what about how this scenario affects SQL Server? You're asking SQL Server to execute the SELECT query even if the UPDATE query affects no rows. You can make this batch query more efficient by using the SQL Server system function @@ROWCOUNT, which returns the number of rows affected by the previous query. If the UPDATE query affected no rows, there's no need to execute the SELECT query.

We can use the @@ROWCOUNT function in an IF block to make sure we execute the SELECT query only if the UPDATE query affected a row, as shown here.

```
UPDATE OrderDetailsWithTimestamp
    SET OrderID = @OrderID_New, ProductID = @ProductID_New,
        Quantity = @Quantity_New, UnitPrice = @UnitPrice_New
    WHERE OrderID = @OrderID_Old AND ProductID = @ProductID_Old
      AND TimestampColumn = @TimestampColumn_Old;
IF @@ROWCOUNT <> 0
    SELECT Quantity, UnitPrice, TimestampColumn
        FROM OrderDetailsWithTimestamp
        WHERE OrderID = @OrderID_New AND ProductID = @ProductID_New
```

Retrieving New Data Using Output Parameters

The *UpdatedRowSource* property also lets you specify that you will retrieve new data using output parameters. Retrieving new information via output parameters is more efficient than returning data in a SELECT query. Parameters require less overhead than a resultset, so this approach may improve the performance of your code when submitting changes. More important, returning server-generated values via parameters can work with the new batch updating features of ADO.NET, which we'll cover later in the chapter.

Here, we've taken the previous batch query but returned the new values through output parameters:

```
UPDATE OrderDetailsWithTimestamp
    SET OrderID = @OrderID_New, ProductID = @ProductID_New,
        Quantity = @Quantity_New, UnitPrice = @UnitPrice_New
    WHERE OrderID = @OrderID_Old AND ProductID = @ProductID_Old
      AND TimestampColumn = @TimestampColumn_Old;
IF @@ROWCOUNT <> 0 THEN
    SELECT @Quantity_New = Quantity, @UnitPrice_New = UnitPrice,
           @TimestampColumn_New = TimestampColumn
        FROM OrderDetailsWithTimestamp
        WHERE OrderID = @OrderID_New AND ProductID = @ProductID_New
```

To use this updating logic and refresh the contents of the *DataRow*, we need to do two things. First, we need to bind *SqlParameters* to the appropriate *DataColumns*, with their *Direction* property set to the appropriate value for the *SqlParameters*. The *@Quantity_New* and *@Unit-Price_New* parameters are used to submit values to the database, and to return the contents of the columns after submitting the change. Therefore, the *Direction* property on these *SqlParameters* should be set to *InputOutput*. The *@TimestampColumn_New* parameter returns only data, so its *Direction* property should be set to *Output*. Second, we need to make sure the *UpdateCommand*'s *UpdatedRowSource* property is set to *OutputParameters*.

We can build a stored procedure that uses a similar UPDATE query to modify a row in the Order Details table and return the new timestamp value using an output parameter, as shown here:

```
CREATE PROCEDURE spUpdateDetail
(@OrderID_New int, @ProductID_New int,
 @Quantity_New smallint OUTPUT, @UnitPrice_New money OUTPUT,
 @OrderID_Old int, @ProductID_Old int, @TimestampColumn_Old timestamp,
 @TimestampColumn_New timestamp OUTPUT)
AS
UPDATE OrderDetailsWithTimestamp
    SET OrderID = @OrderID_New, ProductID = @ProductID_New,
        Quantity = @Quantity_New, UnitPrice = @UnitPrice_New
    WHERE OrderID = @OrderID_Old AND ProductID = @ProductID_Old
      AND TimestampColumn = @TimestampColumn_Old;
IF @@ROWCOUNT <> 0
    SELECT @Quantity_New = Quantity, @UnitPrice_New = UnitPrice,
           @TimestampColumn_New = TimestampColumn
        FROM OrderDetailsWithTimestamp
        WHERE OrderID = @OrderID_New AND ProductID = @OrderID_New
```

All that's left to do is set the *UpdateCommand* property's *CommandText* to the stored procedure, build the *SqlCommand* object's *Parameters* collection, and set the *SqlCommand* object's *UpdatedRowSource* property to *OutputParameters*. It's really that easy.

Using the *SqlDataAdapter* Class's *RowUpdated* Event to Retrieve Data After You Submit an Update

Some databases, such as Microsoft Access, don't support batch queries and output parameters on stored procedures. If you're using such a database, the two previous methods of retrieving data after performing an update aren't available. However, you do have one option, apart from moving to a database that supports more functionality.

Each *DataAdapter* class exposes two events that it throws when it submits the changes cached in a *DataRow*: *RowUpdating* and *RowUpdated*. As their names imply, the former occurs just before you submit the change and the latter occurs immediately after you submit the change.

If you submit the changes in multiple rows, the *RowUpdating* and *RowUpdated* events will fire for each row. You won't get all the *RowUpdating* events and then all the *RowUpdated* events. If you add logging code to the events, you'll see entries such as the following in your log file:

```
RowUpdating event fired for row #1
RowUpdated event fired for row #1
RowUpdating event fired for row #2
RowUpdated event fired for row #2
RowUpdating event fired for row #3
RowUpdated event fired for row #3
```

> **Note**   The behavior is slightly different if you set the *DataAdapter*'s *UpdateBatchSize* property to submit changes in batches. In that case, the *RowUpdating* event fires for each row in the batch prior to submitting the changes in the batch. After submitting the changes in the batch, the *RowUpdated* event fires once. We'll discuss batch updates later in the chapter.

We can use the *RowUpdated* event to fetch the new value that the database generates for the updated row. The following code snippet includes such an example. The code demonstrates how to handle the *RowUpdated* event. For the sake of brevity, it references imaginary functions that create the *DataTable*, the *OleDbDataAdapter*, and the *OleDbCommand* used to refresh the contents of the timestamp, quantity, and unit price columns in the *DataRow* after successful updates.

Note that in the *RowUpdated* event handler, the code tests to make sure the update succeeded and that the change stored in the row constituted an insert or an update. Obviously, if we've just deleted a row from the database, there's no need to query for server-generated values.

Visual Basic

```vb
Imports System.Data.OleDb
Dim da As OleDbDataAdapter
Dim cmdRefresh As OleDbCommand
da = CreateMyDataAdapter()
cmdRefresh = CreateRefreshAfterUpdateCommand()
AddHandler da.RowUpdated, AddressOf HandleRowUpdated
Dim tbl As DataTable = CreateMyDataTable()
```

```
da.Fill(tbl)
⋮
da.Update(tbl)

Private Sub HandleRowUpdated(ByVal sender As Object, _
                            ByVal e As OleDbRowUpdatedEventArgs)
    If e.Status = UpdateStatus.Continue AndAlso _
      (e.StatementType = StatementType.Insert OrElse _
      e.StatementType = StatementType.Update) Then
        cmdRefresh.Parameters("@OrderID").Value = e.Row("OrderID")
        cmdRefresh.Parameters("@ProductID").Value = e.Row("ProductID")
        Using rdr As OleDbDataReader = cmdRefresh.ExecuteReader()
            rdr.Read()
            e.Row("Quantity") = rdr("Quantity")
            e.Row("UnitPrice") = rdr("UnitPrice")
            e.Row("TimestampColumn") = rdr("TimestampColumn")
            rdr.Close()
        End Using
    End If
End Sub
```

Visual C#

```
//using System.Data.OleDb;
OleDbDataAdapter da;
OleDbCommand cmdRefresh;
da = CreateMyDataAdapter();
cmdRefresh = CreateRefreshAfterUpdateCommand();
da.RowUpdated += new OleDbRowUpdatedEventHandler(HandleRowUpdated);
DataTable tbl = CreateMyDataTable();
da.Fill(tbl);
⋮
da.Update(tbl);

private void HandleRowUpdated(object sender,
                             OleDbRowUpdatedEventArgs e) {
    if ((e.Status == UpdateStatus.Continue) &&
        ((e.StatementType == StatementType.Insert) ||
        (e.StatementType == StatementType.Update)))          {
        cmdRefresh.Parameters["@OrderID"].Value = e.Row["OrderID"];
        cmdRefresh.Parameters["@ProductID"].Value = e.Row["ProductID"];
        using (OleDbDataReader rdr = cmdRefresh.ExecuteReader()) {
            rdr.Read();
            e.Row["Quantity"] = rdr["Quantity"];
            e.Row["UnitPrice"] = rdr["UnitPrice"];
            e.Row["TimestampColumn"] = rdr["TimestampColumn"];
            rdr.Close();
        }
    }
}
```

The code manually retrieves the new values and assigns them to the appropriate columns in the *DataRow*.

This approach is very flexible because it will work with any database, but you pay a price in performance. In the tests I've run, using events to retrieve timestamp values proved to be about 35 percent slower than the batch query approach and about 50 percent slower than using output parameters on stored procedures.

RefreshAfterUpdate Sample Code

The sample code for this chapter includes examples, in both Microsoft Visual Basic and Microsoft Visual C#, that demonstrate how to refresh a row after submitting an update using *UpdateRowSource.FirstReturnedRecord*, *UpdateRowSource.OutputParameters*, and the *Row-Updated* event.

Retrieving Newly Generated Auto-Increment Values

SQL Server, Access, Sybase, MySQL, and other databases use auto-increment columns, also referred to as *identity columns*. (Oracle offers similar scenarios through its sequences.) You can insert a new row into a table, and the database will generate a new value for the auto-increment column for that row. Many tables in the Northwind database—such as Employees, Orders, and Products—use auto-increment columns for their primary keys.

How does working with auto-increment columns differ from general scenarios that require refreshing the conents of the row after performing an update? In the previous examples, the query executed to refresh the contents of the row used the value of the primary key columns in the *DataRow* as input parameters. In the auto-increment scenario, the primary key values are generated by the database and are not available in the *DataRow*.

So how do you use the ADO.NET object model to retrieve the newly generated auto-increment value for your row?

> **Note** As noted earlier, you should refresh the contents of the entire row rather than just the auto-increment column, and returning the data via output parameters is faster than returning the data through a query that returns a row. For the sake of brevity, the samples in this section will retrieve values for just the auto-increment column.

Working with SQL Server

For the moment, imagine that you're not submitting changes to your database using a *SqlData-Adapter*. Let's say that you're building your own queries to submit changes.

If you're working with order information from the Northwind database, you might use the following query to retrieve data from your table:

```
SELECT OrderID, CustomerID, OrderDate FROM Orders
```

To insert a new row into your table, you might issue a query such as this:

```
INSERT INTO Orders (CustomerID, OrderDate)
    VALUES (@CustomerID, @OrderDate)
```

If you're working with a flavor of SQL Server 2005 (including SQL Express) or SQL Server 2000 (including MSDE), you'll probably use the following query to retrieve the auto-increment value:

```
SELECT SCOPE_IDENTITY()
```

> **Note**   Why "probably use" rather than "should use"? See the discussion on SCOPE_IDENTITY() vs. @@IDENTITY later in the chapter.

For earlier versions of SQL Server, use the following query instead:

```
SELECT @@IDENTITY
```

This query is the key to retrieving the new auto-increment value. We can use this query in the ADO.NET object model the same way we used the query to retrieve the timestamp value in the previous example.

We can modify the *CommandText* of the *SqlDataAdapter* object's *InsertCommand* to refresh the contents of the row by using SCOPE_IDENTITY() in the query after each insert:

```
INSERT INTO Orders (CustomerID, OrderDate)
    VALUES (@CustomerID, @OrderDate);
SELECT @OrderID = SCOPE_IDENTITY()
```

As with the previous scenarios, we can also refresh the row using a stored procedure and output parameters, as shown here:

```
CREATE PROCEDURE spOrdersInsert
(@OrderID int OUTPUT, @CustomerID nchar(5),
 @OrderDate datetime)
AS
INSERT INTO Orders (CustomerID, OrderDate)
    VALUES (@CustomerID, @OrderDate)
SELECT @OrderID = SCOPE_IDENTITY()
```

Finally, we can use the *SqlDataAdapter* object's *RowUpdated* event to execute a query to fetch the new auto-increment value, as shown in the following code samples:

Visual Basic

```
Dim da As SqlDataAdapter = CreateMyDataAdapter()
Dim cn As SqlConnection = da.SelectCommand.Connection
Dim strSQL As String
strSQL = "SELECT @OrderID = SCOPE_IDENTITY()"
Dim cmdRefresh As New SqlCommand(strSQL, cn)
Dim p As SqlParameter
p = cmdRefresh.Parameters.Add("@OrderID", SqlDbType.Int)
```

```
p.Direction = ParameterDirection.Output
AddHandler da.RowUpdated, AddressOf HandleRowUpdated
Dim tbl As DataTable = CreateMyDataTable()
da.Fill(tbl)

'Changes made to the contents of the DataTable
⋮

da.Update(tbl)

Private Sub HandleRowUpdated(ByVal sender As Object, _
                            ByVal e As OleDbRowUpdatedEventArgs)
    If e.Status = UpdateStatus.Continue AndAlso _
        e.StatementType = StatementType.Insert Then
          cmdRefresh.ExecuteNonQuery()
          e.Row("OrderID") = cmdRefresh.Parameters("@OrderID").Value
    End If
End Sub
```

Visual C#

```
SqlDataAdapter da = CreateMyDataAdapter();
SqlConnection cn = da.SelectCommand.Connection;
string strSQL;
strSQL = "SELECT @OrderID = SCOPE_IDENTITY()";
SqlCommand cmdRefresh = new SqlCommand(strSQL, cn);
SqlParameter p;
p = cmdRefresh.Parameters.Add("@OrderID", SqlDbType.Int);
p.Direction = ParameterDirection.Output;
da.RowUpdated += new OleDbRowUpdatedEventHandler(HandleRowUpdated);
DataTable tbl = CreateMyDataTable();
da.Fill(tbl);

//Changes made to the contents of the DataTable
⋮

da.Update(tbl);

private void HandleRowUpdated(object sender, OleDbRowUpdatedEventArgs e)
{
    if ((e.Status == UpdateStatus.Continue) &&
        (e.StatementType == StatementType.Insert)) {
        cmdRefresh.ExecuteNonQuery();
        e.Row["OrderID"] = cmdRefresh.Parameters["@OrderID"].Value;
    }
}
```

SCOPE_IDENTITY() vs. @@IDENTITY

The SELECT @@IDENTITY query returns the last identity value generated on your connection. This means that work done by other users on other connections will not affect the results of your query. However, that does not mean you'll receive the value you expected.

Database administrators often use their own audit tables to track changes made to the database. To track those changes, they generally rely on triggers or stored procedures. Figure 11-1 shows an example.

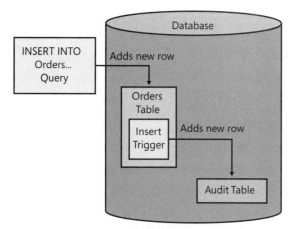

Figure 11-1   Tracking changes using audit tables

Why have I drifted into a discussion of audit logs and triggers in the middle of a discussion of retrieving auto-increment values? Let's assume that the audit table that the trigger shown in Figure 11-1 references has an auto-increment column. If you insert a new row into the Orders table and then issue the SELECT @@IDENTITY query, you'll receive the auto-increment value that the trigger generated for the new row in the audit table, rather than the value generated for the new row in the Orders table. Remember that SELECT @@IDENTITY returns the last auto-increment value generated for your connection.

To address this type of scenario, SQL Server introduced a new way to retrieve auto-increment values in SQL Server 2000: SCOPE_IDENTITY(). If you issue a SELECT SCOPE_IDENTITY() query in this situation, you'll receive the auto-increment value generated for the new row in the Orders table.

If you're working with SQL Server 2000, SQL Server 2005, or later, you should use SCOPE_IDENTITY() instead of @@IDENTITY. There's one minor exception to this rule. If you insert the new row using a stored procedure but you want to retrieve that value after calling the stored procedure, SCOPE_IDENTITY() will return *Null*. According to SQL Server Books Online, SCOPE_IDENTITY returns the last auto-increment value generated in the current scope, and the stored procedure is executed in a different scope. As I said, this is a minor exception. If you're going to insert new rows using stored procedures and you want to retrieve the newly generated auto-increment value, you should return this information using an output parameter.

For more information on the differences between SCOPE_IDENTITY() and @@IDENTITY, see SQL Server Books Online.

Working with Access Databases

If you're working with an Access database, you can also use the SELECT @@IDENTITY query to retrieve new auto-increment values. This feature was added in version 4.0 of the Jet OLE DB provider and works only with databases formatted for Access databases version 2000 or later. Like its SQL Server counterpart, the SELECT @@IDENTITY query returns the last auto-increment value generated on your connection.

Access databases do not support output parameters on QueryDefs—stored queries that are similar to views and stored procedures. The Jet OLE DB provider does not support batch queries. So the only way to fetch newly generated auto-increment values is to use the *OleDbDataAdapter* object's *RowUpdated* event, as shown earlier in the chapter.

Working with Oracle Sequences

Oracle databases do not support auto-increment columns, but they do support a similar construct—a sequence. With SQL Server, you mark a column as an auto-increment column and SQL Server will automatically generate new values for the column when you insert a new row.

An Oracle sequence is slightly different. You generally create a sequence to generate new values for a column in your table, but there is no direct link between the sequence and the table or column. There is no way for a technology such as ADO.NET to know to associate a table with a sequence.

The following query creates a new Oracle sequence:

```
CREATE SEQUENCE MySequence
```

You can set a number of options when you create an Oracle sequence, such as the minimum and maximum values for the sequence.

> **Note**   Some developers who work with Oracle databases prefer querying the sequence prior to executing the INSERT query; others prefer referencing the sequence in the INSERT query or in the table's trigger. For more information on Oracle sequences, see your Oracle documentation.

You can use the sequence in two ways. You can reference the sequence in your INSERT query, as shown here:

```
INSERT INTO MyTable (ID, OtherColumn)
    VALUES (MySequence.NEXTVAL, 'New Row')
```

The sequence returns a new value each time you call NEXTVAL. Once you've inserted the new row, you can query the sequence to determine the last value you used, as shown here:

```
SELECT MySequence.CURRVAL FROM DUAL
```

As with using the SCOPE_IDENTITY() and @@IDENTITY features of SQL Server and Access databases, the results of this query are not affected by other users referencing the sequence to insert new rows.

How do you retrieve the new sequence values into your *DataRow* objects? The simplest option is to use a batch query that returns the new key value through an output parameter. Query the sequence for the new value, assign the value to an output parameter, and then reference the parameter in the INSERT INTO query, as shown in the following code snippet:

Visual Basic

```
Imports System.Data.OracleClient
Dim da As OracleDataAdapter = CreateMyDataAdapter()
Dim cn As OracleConnection = da.SelectCommand.Connection
Dim strSQL As String
strSQL = "BEGIN " & _
        "    SELECT MySequence.NEXTVAL INTO :ID FROM DUAL;" & _
        "    INSERT INTO MyTable (ID, SomeColumn) VALUES " & _
        "        (:ID, :SomeColumn);" & _
        "END;"
Dim cmd As New OracleCommand(strSQL, cn)
Dim p As OracleParameter
p = cmd.Parameters.Add(":ID", OracleType.Int32, 0, "ID")
p.Direction = ParameterDirection.Output
cmd.Parameters.Add(":SomeColumn", OracleType.NVarChar, 255, "SomeColumn")
cmd.UpdatedRowSource = UpdateRowSource.OutputParameters
da.InsertCommand = cmd
```

Visual C#

```
//using System.Data.OracleClient
OracleDataAdapter da = CreateMyDataAdapter();
OracleConnection cn = da.SelectCommand.Connection;
string strSQL;
strSQL = "BEGIN " +
        "    SELECT MySequence.NEXTVAL INTO :ID FROM DUAL;" +
        "    INSERT INTO MyTable (ID, SomeColumn) VALUES " +
        "        (:ID, :SomeColumn);" +
        "END;";
OracleCommand cmd As new OracleCommand(strSQL, cn);
OracleParameter p;
p = cmd.Parameters.Add(":ID", OracleType.Int32, 0, "ID");
p.Direction = ParameterDirection.Output;
cmd.Parameters.Add(":SomeColumn", OracleType.NVarChar, 255, "SomeColumn");
cmd.UpdatedRowSource = UpdateRowSource.OutputParameters;
da.InsertCommand = cmd;
```

If you're working with Oracle 10g, you don't even have to use a batch query. You can simply use the RETURNING clause in the INSERT INTO query, as shown here:

```
INSERT INTO MyTable (ID, SomeColumn) VALUES
    (MySequence.NEXTVAL, :SomeColumn)
    RETURNING ID INTO :ID
```

As with SQL Server, you can call a stored procedure and return the new key value through an output parameter. The procedure uses that value to insert the new row using an INSERT INTO query.

```
CREATE PROCEDURE MyStoredProc
    (pOtherCol IN VARCHAR2, pID OUT NUMBER) IS
BEGIN
    SELECT MySequence.NEXTVAL INTO pID FROM DUAL;
    INSERT INTO MyTable (ID, OtherCol)
        VALUES (pID, pOtherCol);
END;
```

The stored procedure returns the new sequence value using an output parameter. You can use this type of stored procedure in your *DataAdapter* object's *InsertCommand* to insert new rows. If you bind the output parameter to the corresponding column in your *DataRow* object, the *DataRow* will contain the new value immediately after you've submitted the new row to your database.

> **Note**   Remember that there is no direct link between the sequence and the column in the table. You don't have to use the sequence when you insert a new row into the table. If users insert new rows without referencing the sequence, the sequence might generate new values that already exist in your database. To avoid the problem, make sure that the only way to insert new rows into your table is to call a stored procedure that references the sequence.

Generating Placeholder Values for Your Sequence *DataColumn* Objects

Sequences are not auto-increment columns, but you can have ADO.NET generate placeholder values for new rows by setting the *AutoIncrement* property of the corresponding *DataColumn* objects to *True*. However, you must do this manually. There is no direct link between the sequence and the table. If you use the *OracleDataAdapter* object's *FillSchema* method or the Visual Studio Data Adapter (or TableAdapter) Configuration Wizard to retrieve database schema information, ADO.NET won't know that the column in your table is associated with a sequence.

You'll face similar problems no matter how you generate updating logic for your *OracleData-Adapter* objects. The *OracleCommandBuilder* object and the Data Adapter Configuration Wizard won't know to omit the column from the logic in the *InsertCommand*. If you're going to rely on such tools to generate your updating logic, you must make some minor changes to the logic they generate.

It might sound like I'm knocking these tools. I'm not. There is no schema information that links the column in the table to the sequence, so the tools are doing the best they can to generate the appropriate code.

The fact that you can treat a column that's indirectly linked to an Oracle sequence as an auto-increment column and control how and when you retrieve new sequence values into your *DataSet* is a testament to the power and control that the ADO.NET object model gives to developers. Such functionality was not an option in previous Microsoft data access object models.

Sample Applications That Retrieve Auto-Increment Values

The sample code includes examples, in both Visual Basic and Visual C#, that demonstrate how to retrieve new auto-increment values from SQL Server, Access, and Oracle, using *Update-RowSource.OutputParameters* for SQL Server and Oracle, and using the *RowUpdated* event for Access.

Submitting Hierarchical Changes

When you modify data in multiple levels of a hierarchical *DataSet*, you will face two challenges when you submit those changes to your database. Let's take a look at these scenarios.

Submitting Pending Insertions and Deletions

Say that you're dealing with a hierarchy that contains orders and order details. The application you've built is an order entry system. The user has made a number of changes to the data and now wants to submit those changes to your database. The modified data in the *DataSet* contains new orders and new order details. The *DataSet* also contains orders and order details that are marked for deletion.

The challenge is to submit these changes in the proper order to comply with the referential integrity constraints in your database. The Northwind database contains referential integrity constraints that require all orders to refer back to customers in the database.

If the *DataSet* contains new orders and new order details for those orders, we must submit those new orders before submitting the new order details for them. As a general rule, you should submit new rows in a top-down approach.

The opposite is true for deleted rows, however. You can't delete orders in the Northwind database that have order details. You must delete the details first.

Assuming you have both added and deleted orders, the following code will not work because it will attempt to delete orders that still have pending order details. Even if we reverse the order of the updates, the first update attempt will fail because the *DataAdapter* for the Order Details table will attempt to submit new order details for orders that do not yet exist in the database.

Visual Basic

```
OrdersAdapter.Update(MyDataSet.Tables("Orders"))
OrderDetailsAdapter.Update(MyDataSet.Tables("Order Details"))
```

Visual C#

```csharp
OrdersAdapter.Update(MyDataSet.Tables["Orders"]);
OrderDetailsAdapter.Update(MyDataSet.Tables["Order Details"]);
```

What's a poor programmer to do? We need a way to control the order of updates in a hierarchical *DataSet* to submit the changes in the following order:

1. Submit new orders.

2. Submit new order details.

3. Submit modified orders.

4. Submit modified order details.

5. Submit deleted order details.

6. Submit deleted orders.

Using the *DataTable* Object's *Select* Method to Submit Hierarchical Changes

In Chapter 7, I discussed the *Select* method of the *DataTable* object as a way to locate *DataRow* objects that satisfy the desired criteria. For example, the following line of code returns an array of the pending new *DataRow* objects whose City column contains Seattle. The *DataRow* objects are sorted based on the value of the ContactName column.

```
tbl.Select("City = 'Seattle'", "ContactName", DataViewRowState.Added)
```

The *Select* method returns an array of *DataRow* objects. And one of the overloaded *Update* methods on the various *DataAdapter* classes accepts an array of *DataRow* objects. What a pleasant coincidence.

The following code snippet uses the *Select* method to isolate just the desired changes and submit them to the database in the proper order:

Visual Basic

```vb
Dim ds As DataSet = CreateDataSet()
Dim tblOrders As DataTable = ds.Tables("Orders")
Dim tblDetails As DataTable = ds.Tables("Order Details")
Dim daOrders As SqlDataAdapter = CreateOrdersAdapter()
Dim daDetails As SqlDataAdapter = CreateOrderDetailsAdapter()

FillDataSetAndModifyItsContents(ds)

Dim rowstate As DataViewRowState

'Submit the new orders and then the new order details.
rowstate = DataViewRowState.Added
daOrders.Update(tblOrders.Select("", "", rowstate))
daDetails.Update(tblDetails.Select("", "", rowstate))
```

```
'Submit the modified orders and then the modified order details.
rowstate = DataViewRowState.ModifiedCurrent
daOrders.Update(tblOrders.Select("", "", rowstate))
daDetails.Update(tblDetails.Select("", "", rowstate))

'Submit the deleted order details and then the deleted orders.
rowstate = DataViewRowState.Deleted
daDetails.Update(tblDetails.Select("", "", rowstate))
daOrders.Update(tblOrders.Select("", "", rowstate))
```

Visual C#

```csharp
DataSet ds = CreateDataSet();
DataTable tblOrders = ds.Tables["Orders"];
DataTable tblDetails = ds.Tables["Order Details"];
SqlDataAdapter daOrders = CreateOrdersAdapter();
SqlDataAdapter daDetails = CreateOrderDetailsAdapter();

FillDataSetAndModifyItsContents(ds);

DataViewRowState rowstate;

//Submit the new orders and then the new order details.
rowstate = DataViewRowState.Added;
daOrders.Update(tblOrders.Select("", "", rowstate));
daDetails.Update(tblDetails.Select("", "", rowstate));

//Submit the modified orders and then the modified order details.
rowstate = DataViewRowState.ModifiedCurrent;
daOrders.Update(tblOrders.Select("", "", rowstate));
daDetails.Update(tblDetails.Select("", "", rowstate));

//Submit the deleted order details and then the deleted orders.
rowstate = DataViewRowState.Deleted;
daDetails.Update(tblDetails.Select("", "", rowstate));
daOrders.Update(tblOrders.Select("", "", rowstate));
```

Using the *GetChanges* Method to Submit Hierarchical Changes

You can also use the *GetChanges* method of the *DataSet* or *DataTable* to control the order of updates. The following code snippet creates a new *DataTable* that contains just the pending new rows in the initial *DataTable*:

```
tblNewOrders = tblOrders.GetChanges(DataRowState.Added)
daOrders.Update(tblNewOrders)
tblNewDetails = tblDetails.GetChanges(DataRowState.Added)
daCustomers.Update(tblNewDetails)
```

I find this code easier to read and write than the approach that uses the *Select* method. However, I don't recommend using this approach.

When you use the *GetChanges* method of the *DataSet* or *DataTable* object, you're creating a new and separate object. The previous code snippet submits new rows to the Orders and Order

Details tables in the database. In the Northwind database, the Orders table has an auto-increment column: OrderID. If the *SqlDataAdapter* that submits the changes to the Orders table includes logic to fetch the newly generated values for the OrderID column, the values will be inserted into the *DataTable* used in the *Update* method—*tblNewOrders*. However, this *DataTable* object is separate from the main *tblOrders DataTable*, so those new *OrderID* values will not appear in the main *DataTable*.

This scenario will make more sense when we discuss isolating and reintegrating changes later in the chapter.

If, instead, you use the *Select* method to submit modified rows, the changes returned by the *SqlDataAdapter* will be applied to your main *DataTable* because the *Select* method returns an array of *DataRow* objects. The *DataRow* objects in the array are actually pointers to the *DataRow* objects in the *DataTable*, so changes you make to the contents of the array will be implemented in the main *DataTable*.

Working with Auto-Increment Values and Relational Data

Let's shift the focus of our hierarchical *DataSet* slightly. In this example, the user will enter two new orders as well as details for each new order.

In Chapter 6, I recommended that you set the *AutoIncrementSeed* and *AutoIncrementStep* properties of the *DataColumn* object to −1 when you work with auto-increment columns. If you follow that recommendation and add new orders and details to your hierarchy, your *DataSet* will look something like the depiction in Figure 11-2 before you submit the new orders to your database.

To successfully submit the new orders and the details for each new order, we need to submit the new orders, retrieve the new auto-increment values for the new orders, apply those values to the appropriate order details, and then submit the new order details to the database. This process sounds complicated, but it's actually fairly simple.

You already know how to submit the new orders. If you need to submit only new orders, you use the *Select* method of the *DataTable* that contains order information, as we discussed earlier in the chapter. You can also fetch your new auto-increment values using any of the options we discussed earlier in the chapter.

But how do you apply the new auto-increment values to the pending new order details? Actually, you don't. You let ADO.NET do the work for you through the *DataRelation*, which was covered in Chapter 7. By default, the *DataRelation* object will cascade changes through your *DataSet*. If you've set up a *DataRelation* between the orders and order details *DataTable* objects in your *DataSet*, as soon as you've submitted the new orders and fetched the new auto-increment values, the *DataRelation* will cascade the new auto-increment values to the order details *DataTable*, as shown in Figure 11-3.

Orders			
OrderID	CustomerID	EmployeeID	OrderDate
10268	GROSR	8	7/30/1996
10785	GROSR	1	12/18/1997
-1	GROSR	7	1/14/2002
-2	GROSR	7	1/14/2002

Order Details			
OrderID	ProductID	Quantity	UnitPrice
10268	29	10	99.00
10268	72	4	27.80
10785	10	10	31.00
10785	75	10	7.75
-1	1	12	18.00
-1	67	24	14.00
-2	4	6	22.00
-2	65	8	21.05

Figure 11-2   A *DataSet* with pending new orders and details

Once the new rows in the order details *DataTable* contain the appropriate values for the OrderID column, you can successfully submit the pending new rows to your database. Thanks to the functionality in the *DataRelation* class, cascading the new auto-increment values throughout your hierarchy is the simplest part of the process.

> **Important**   If you find that the newly retrieved auto-increment values do not cascade down to the related child rows, this behavior may be due to how Visual Studio's design-time features configured your strongly typed *DataSet*. As Chapter 9 points out, *DataRelations* that are generated automatically by Visual Studio 2005 are not associated with a *ForeignKey-Constraint*, which will prevent changes to parent rows from cascading down to related child rows. If you run into this problem, double-click the *DataRelations* in your strongly-typed *DataSet*, and indicate in the resulting dialog box that you want both a *DataRelation* and a *ForeignKeyConstraint* and that you want the *Update* and *Delete* rules to be set to *Cascade*. Leave the *Accept Reject* rule as *None*.

Orders			
OrderID	CustomerID	EmployeeID	OrderDate
10268	GROSR	8	7/30/1996
10785	GROSR	1	12/18/1997
12000	GROSR	7	1/14/2002
12001	GROSR	7	1/14/2002

Order Details			
OrderID	ProductID	Quantity	UnitPrice
10268	29	10	99.00
10268	72	4	27.80
10785	10	10	31.00
10785	75	10	7.75
12000	1	12	18.00
12000	67	24	14.00
12001	4	6	22.00
12001	65	8	21.05

Figure 11-3   Cascading the auto-increment values into the child table in your hierarchy

Isolating and Reintegrating Changes

Say that you're building a multi-tiered application with a Microsoft Windows client user interface that accesses your database via a Web service. The Web service returns *DataSet* objects that contain the requested information to clients. The client application allows the user to modify the contents of the *DataSet*. After modifying the data, the user can click a button and the client will submit the changes to the database via the Web service. The simplest way to submit these changes is to send the *DataSet* back to the Web service and have the Web service use *DataAdapter* objects to submit the changes.

To get the best possible performance out of your application, you'll want to make the best possible use of your bandwidth. The less data you pass back and forth between the client application and the Web service, the faster your application will run.

Limiting the amount of data that the Web service returns is fairly simple and intuitive. Don't design your Web service to return the entire contents of your tables if they might contain thousands or millions or rows; if you do, the performance of your application will suffer. Also make sure that the Web service returns only the data that the client application needs.

What about limiting the amount of data that the client application passes back to the Web service? You can pass a *DataSet* back to the Web service to have the Web service submit changes to your database. But if that's the goal of calling the Web service, you probably don't want to pass the entire *DataSet*. If the *DataSet* contains a few hundred rows and the user has modified only a handful of those rows, passing the entire *DataSet* back to the Web service will be extremely inefficient. How can we improve upon this process?

Saving Bandwidth Using the *GetChanges* Method

As mentioned previously in the chapter, the *DataSet* and *DataTable* objects each expose an overloaded *GetChanges* method. When you call a *DataSet* object's *GetChanges* method, you receive a new *DataSet* object that has the same structure as the original *DataSet* but contains only the modified rows from the original *DataSet*.

If you're calling your Web service to submit changes to your database, you might gain a significant improvement in performance by first calling the *GetChanges* method on your *DataSet* and sending the results to your Web service because there's no need to submit unmodified rows back to the Web service.

> **Note** When I said that the *DataSet* object's *GetChanges* method returns a new *DataSet* object that contains only the modified rows, I bent the truth a tiny bit. The new *DataSet* that the *GetChanges* method returns has the same structure as the original *DataSet* and contains the modified rows that you requested, but it might also contain other rows needed to maintain referential integrity. For example, say that you have a *DataSet* that contains *DataTable* objects for orders and order detail information with a *DataRelation* defined between the two *DataTable* objects. If you add some new order details and then call the *DataSet* object's *GetChanges* method, the *DataSet* that the method returns will contain those new rows as well as the corresponding rows from the orders *DataTable*. Otherwise, the new *DataSet* would violate the constraint associated with the *DataRelation*.

In Chapter 10, we covered using timestamp columns to make sure your update attempts don't accidentally overwrite changes from another user. Earlier in this chapter, we discussed how to refresh the contents of a row after a successful update, a process that is required if you're using timestamp columns and want to submit subsequent changes to *DataRow* objects. This process gets a little more complicated in a multi-tiered application. Let's say that you're using timestamp concurrency checks in the *SqlDataAdapter* object's updating logic in your Web service. You're also retrieving the new timestamp values using one of the options we discussed earlier in the chapter. But what happened to those new timestamp values?

You retrieved the new values and stored them in the *DataSet* in the Web service. But that *DataSet* is separate from the one in your client application. How can you get the new timestamp values into the *DataSet* in your client application?

You could simply have the Web service return a new *DataSet* that contains all the same data as the client application. But even though this approach will ensure that the client application has more up-to-date data, it might not be the best use of your bandwidth.

A more economical solution, shown in Figure 11-4, is to have the Web service return the *DataSet* it received, with the new timestamp values included.

Main DataSet with original data			
CustomerID	CompanyName	ContactName	TSCol
ALFKI	Alfreds Futterkiste	Maria Anders	<Original Value>
ANATR	Ana Trujillo	Ana Trujillo	<Original Value>
ANTON	Antonio Moreno	Antonio Moreno	<Original Value>
AROUT	Around the Horn	Thomas Hardy	<Original Value>

Main DataSet with modified rows			
CustomerID	CompanyName	ContactName	TSCol
ALFKI	Alfreds Futterkiste	New Contact #1	<Original Value>
ANATR	Ana Trujillo	Ana Trujillo	<Original Value>
ANTON	Antonio Moreno	Antonio Moreno	<Original Value>
AROUT	Around the Horn	New Contact #2	<Original Value>

DataSet returned by GetChanges and sent to Web service			
CustomerID	CompanyName	ContactName	TSCol
ALFKI	Alfreds Futterkiste	New Contact #1	<Original Value>
AROUT	Around the Horn	New Contact #2	<Original Value>

Figure 11-4   Returning new server-generated values via a Web service

But that solves only part of the problem. The client application now has the new timestamp values, but how can you integrate the *DataSet* that the Web service returns into the client application's *DataSet*?

The *Merge* Method of the *DataSet* Class

The simple answer is to use the *Merge* method of the *DataSet* class. The *DataSet* class's *Merge* method lets you merge the contents of a *DataSet*, a *DataTable*, or an array of *DataRow* objects into an existing *DataSet*. Figure 11-5 shows a basic example of this functionality.

Each *DataSet* initially contains a single *DataTable* with the same name. After you call the *Merge* method on the main *DataSet* and supply the second *DataSet*, the main *DataSet* will contain all its original columns plus those from the second *DataSet*. The main *DataSet* will also contain the rows from the second *DataSet*.

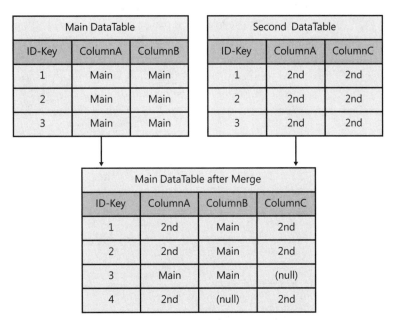

Main DataTable	
ColumnA	ColumnB
A1	B1
A2	B2

Second DataTable	
ColumnC	ColumnD
C1	D1
C2	D2

Main DataTable after Merge			
ColumnA	ColumnB	ColumnC	ColumnD
A1	B1	(null)	(null)
A2	B2	(null)	(null)
(null)	(null)	C1	D1
(null)	(null)	C2	D2

Figure 11-5   Basic example of the results of the *DataSet* class's *Merge* method

This example is not terribly useful, however. Few developers will combine two *DataSet* objects that contain *DataTable* objects with the same name but that have completely different structures. Figure 11-6 shows a more typical example. The two *DataSet* objects contain *DataTable* objects with similar structures. In each *DataTable*, the ID column is the primary key.

Main DataTable		
ID-Key	ColumnA	ColumnB
1	Main	Main
2	Main	Main
3	Main	Main

Second DataTable		
ID-Key	ColumnA	ColumnC
1	2nd	2nd
2	2nd	2nd
3	2nd	2nd

Main DataTable after Merge			
ID-Key	ColumnA	ColumnB	ColumnC
1	2nd	Main	2nd
2	2nd	Main	2nd
3	Main	Main	(null)
4	2nd	(null)	2nd

Figure 11-6   A more typical example of the results of the *DataSet* class's *Merge* method

After the call to the *Merge* method, the main *DataSet* will contain an additional column from the second *DataSet*. The contents of the main *DataSet* will also have changed as a result of the call to the *Merge* method. In the previous example (shown in Figure 11-5), the *Merge* method simply appended existing rows to the main *DataSet*. In this example, the *Merge* method combines the contents of the two *DataSet* objects.

The difference in this example is the primary key. If ADO.NET encounters rows that have the same primary key values while it is merging data, it combines the contents into a single row. In this example, both *DataSet* objects have rows that have primary key values of 1 and 2. Each *DataSet* also has an additional row that has no counterpart in the other *DataSet*.

Notice that in the results of the *Merge* method, the data from the *DataSet* that's being merged in takes precedence. The values for Column A in the second *DataSet* replace the corresponding values from the main *DataSet* when ADO.NET combines rows. In the diagram, these are rows whose ID value is 1 or 2.

Now that you're armed with a better understanding of how the *Merge* method works, let's recap the scenario.

Our client application retrieves customer information from a Web service. The user modifies the contents of that *DataSet*. The client application uses the *GetChanges* method to create a new *DataSet* that contains only the modified rows and sends this smaller *DataSet* back to the Web service.

The Web service submits the changes to the database using timestamp values in the updating logic to enforce optimistic concurrency. The Web service also retrieves the new timestamp values for the modified rows (using one of the techniques we discussed earlier in the chapter) and stores that information in its *DataSet*. After the Web service completes this operation, it returns the *DataSet* with those new timestamp values included. The client application receives this *DataSet* and merges it into the main *DataSet*, as shown in the following code snippet, to integrate the new timestamp values in the main *DataSet*, as shown in Figure 11-7.

Visual Basic

```
Dim objWebService As New WebServiceClass()
Dim dsMain As DataSet = objWebService.GetDataSet()
ModifyDataSetContents(dsMain)
Dim dsChanges As DataSet = dsMain.GetChanges()
dsChanges = objWebService.SubmitChanges(dsChanges)
dsMain.Merge(dsChanges)
```

Visual C#

```
WebServiceClass objWebService = new WebServiceClass();
DataSet dsMain = objWebService.GetDataSet();
ModifyDataSetContents(dsMain);
DataSet dsChanges = dsMain.GetChanges();
dsChanges = objWebService.SubmitChanges(dsChanges);
dsMain.Merge(dsChanges);
```

Main DataSet with modified rows			
CustomerID	CompanyName	ContactName	TSCol
ALFKI	Alfreds Futterkiste	New Contact #1	<Original Value>
ANATR	Ana Trujillo	Ana Trujillo	<Original Value>
ANTON	Antonio Moreno	Antonio Moreno	<Original Value>
AROUT	Around the Horn	New Contact #2	<Original Value>

DataSet returned by Web service with new timestamp values			
CustomerID	CompanyName	ContactName	TSCol
ALFKI	Alfreds Futterkiste	New Contact #1	<New Value>
AROUT	Around the Horn	New Contact #2	<New Value>

Main DataSet after merging DataSet returned by Web service			
CustomerID	CompanyName	ContactName	TSCol
ALFKI	Alfreds Futterkiste	New Contact #1	<New Value>
ANATR	Ana Trujillo	Ana Trujillo	<Original Value>
ANTON	Antonio Moreno	Antonio Moreno	<Original Value>
AROUT	Around the Horn	New Contact #2	<New Value>

Figure 11-7 Merging newly fetched data into an existing *DataSet*

The *Merge* Method and the *RowState* Property

We're almost done, but not quite. If you checked the contents of the rows that we originally modified in the main *DataSet*, you'd see that they do have the new timestamp values. However, those rows still have a *RowState* of *Modified*.

If the user clicks a button in the application to submit changes to the database, the *DataSet* that the *GetChanges* method returns will still contain the rows that the user previously modified. When the Web service receives this *DataSet* and tries to submit the changes, the update attempt will generate an exception because the database already contains those changes.

We know that we've submitted those changes to the database, but ADO.NET doesn't understand this. When the Web service submits the changes, ADO.NET changes the *RowState* of the modified rows from *Modified* to *Unmodified*. But that change occurs in the Web service's *DataSet*. ADO.NET does not change the *RowState* of the modified rows in the client application's main *DataSet* because there is no link between these two *DataSet* objects.

Merging the *DataSet* that the Web service returns will not change the *RowState* property of the modified rows in the main *DataSet*. That's definitely what we want to have happen, but ADO .NET will not do this for us automatically. However, because we know that we successfully submitted the changes that currently reside in the main *DataSet*, we can change the *RowState* of the modified rows back to *Unmodified* by calling the *AcceptChanges* method on the main *DataSet* after we call *Merge*, as shown in the following code:

Visual Basic

```
Dim objWebService As New WebServiceClass()
Dim dsMain As DataSet = objWebService.GetDataSet()
ModifyDataSetContents(dsMain)
Dim dsChanges As DataSet = dsMain.GetChanges()
dsChanges = objWebService.SubmitChanges(dsChanges)
dsMain.Merge(dsChanges)
dsMain.AcceptChanges()
```

Visual C#

```
WebServiceClass objWebService = new WebServiceClass();
DataSet dsMain = objWebService.GetDataSet();
ModifyDataSetContents(dsMain);
DataSet dsChanges = dsMain.GetChanges();
dsChanges = objWebService.SubmitChanges(dsChanges);
dsMain.Merge(dsChanges);
dsMain.AcceptChanges();
```

The *Merge* Method and Auto-Increment Values

Let's change the example slightly. Instead of working with customer information, let's work with order information. In this example, the database table that contains the order information will use an auto-increment column as its primary key, like the Orders table in the Northwind database does.

As in the previous example, the client application will communicate with the database through a Web service. Let's say that the user retrieves two orders for an existing customer, adds two new orders for the customer, and then submits those new orders to the database. You already know how to use the *GetChanges* method to pass just the modified rows to the Web service, as shown in Figure 11-8.

You also know how to retrieve new auto-increment values into the *DataSet* that the Web service uses to submit new orders to the database. These values are included in the *DataSet* that the Web service returns after you submit the modified orders to the database. However, if we merge this *DataSet* into our main *DataSet*, we won't get the desired behavior, even if we call *AcceptChanges* on the main *DataSet* immediately afterward.

Main DataSet with original data			
OrderID	CustomerID	EmployeeID	OrderDate
10643	ALFKI	6	09/22/1997
10692	ALFKI	4	10/31/1997

Main DataSet with new rows			
OrderID	CustomerID	EmployeeID	OrderDate
10643	ALFKI	6	09/22/1997
10692	ALFKI	4	10/31/1997
-1	ALFKI	7	02/24/2002
-2	ALFKI	7	02/24/2002

DataSet returned by GetChanges and sent to Web service			
OrderID	CustomerID	EmployeeID	OrderDate
-1	ALFKI	7	02/24/2002
-2	ALFKI	7	02/24/2002

Figure 11-8   Using the *GetChanges* method to submit just the pending new orders to a Web service

Instead, we'll get the results shown in Figure 11-9. The main *DataSet* will contain the original pending orders with the placeholder values for the OrderID column as well as the orders returned by the Web service with the actual values for the OrderID column. What's going wrong?

This *Merge* method relies on the *DataTable* object's primary key to match up the rows from the different *DataSet* objects. The rows that we want the *Merge* method to combine do not have the same values for their primary key columns. The *Merge* method does not realize that the orders in the *DataSet* returned by the Web service match existing pending orders in the main *DataSet*. As a result, the *Merge* method simply adds the rows from the Web service's *DataSet* to the main *DataSet*.

Obviously, this is not the behavior we want, but a couple of solutions are available to us.

Purge Before *Merge*   Look again at the results of the call to the *Merge* method in Figure 11-9. Our goal was to combine the contents of the two *DataSet* objects and pull the new Order-ID values into the existing *DataSet*. The results really aren't that far off. We have the new OrderID values, but we also have copies of those new orders with the placeholder OrderID values.

We can achieve the desired results by removing the new orders from the main *DataSet* just before we merge in the *DataSet* returned by the Web service. The following code snippet uses the *Select* method of the *DataTable* object to loop through the rows whose *RowState* property is *Added*, and it removes those rows from the *DataSet* before merging in the *DataSet* that the Web service returns:

Main DataSet with new rows			
OrderID	CustomerID	EmployeeID	OrderDate
10643	ALFKI	6	09/22/1997
10692	ALFKI	4	10/31/1997
-1	ALFKI	7	02/24/2002
-2	ALFKI	7	02/24/2002

DataSet returned by Web service with new values			
OrderID	CustomerID	EmployeeID	OrderDate
12000	ALFKI	7	02/24/2002
12001	ALFKI	7	02/24/2002

Main DataSet after merging DataSet returned by Web service			
OrderID	CustomerID	EmployeeID	OrderDate
10643	ALFKI	6	09/22/1997
10692	ALFKI	4	10/31/1997
-1	ALFKI	7	02/24/2002
-2	ALFKI	7	02/24/2002
12000	ALFKI	7	02/24/2002
12001	ALFKI	7	02/24/2002

Figure 11-9 The results of merging the *DataSet* returned by the Web service into the main *DataSet*

Visual Basic

```
Dim objWebService As New WebServiceClass()
Dim dsMain As DataSet = objWebService.GetDataSet()
ModifyDataSetContents(dsMain)
Dim dsChanges As DataSet = dsMain.GetChanges()
dsChanges = objWebService.SubmitChanges(dsChanges)

'Remove the pending new orders from the main DataSet
'before merging the orders returned by the Web service.
Dim tbl As DataTable = dsMain.Tables("Orders")
Dim row As DataRow
For Each row in tbl.Select("", "", DataRowViewState.Added)
    tbl.Rows.Remove(row)
Next row
```

```
dsMain.Merge(dsChanges)
dsMain.AcceptChanges()
```

Visual C#

```csharp
WebServiceClass objWebService = new WebServiceClass();
DataSet dsMain = objWebService.GetDataSet();
ModifyDataSetContents(dsMain);
DataSet dsChanges = dsMain.GetChanges();
dsChanges = objWebService.SubmitChanges(dsChanges);

//Remove the pending new orders from the main DataSet
//before merging the orders returned by the Web service.
DataTable tbl = dsMain.Tables["Orders"];
foreach(DataRow row in tbl.Select("", "", DataRowViewState.Added))
    tbl.Rows.Remove(row);
dsMain.Merge(dsChanges);
dsMain.AcceptChanges();
```

Looping through the main *DataSet* and removing the pending inserts isn't terribly elegant, but it definitely solves the problems.

Changing the Primary Keys in Your *DataSet* Objects   There's another possible solution, but it's not for the weak of code. You now understand how the *Merge* method works and why it doesn't combine the *DataSet* objects from our example in the way we want. The rows that we want to combine do not have the same primary key values.

What if we change the primary key? Just before merging the two *DataSet* objects, we can change the primary key of each *DataTable* to a different column. If the corresponding rows in the *DataSet* have the same values in this column, we'll get the desired results when we merge the *DataSet* objects. After merging them, we can reset the primary keys to their original values.

Let's add a new column to the original *DataTable* and call it PseudoKey. It's just an arbitrary column. It does not map back to an actual column in the database. It's just there to help force the results of the *Merge* method to suit our needs. Figure 11-10 shows an example.

But what about the contents of the PseudoKey column? How can we generate unique values for this column when it does not correspond to a column in the database? We can use another auto-increment column or a globally unique identifier (GUID) column.

How can we programmatically change the primary key on each table just before merging and reset the primary key afterward? The following sample code accomplishes the task nicely:

Visual Basic

```vbnet
Dim objWebService As New WebServiceClass()
Dim dsMain As DataSet = objWebService.GetDataSet()
ModifyDataSetContents(dsMain)
Dim dsChanges As DataSet = dsMain.GetChanges()
dsChanges = objWebService.SubmitChanges(dsChanges)

'Change the primary key in each table to be the pseudokey.
Dim tblMain As DataTable = ds.Tables("Orders")
Dim pkOriginal As DataColumn() = tblMain.PrimaryKey
tblMain.PrimaryKey = New DataColumn() {tblMain.Columns("PseudoKey")}
```

```
Dim tblChanges As DataTable = dsChanges.Tables("Orders")
tblChanges.PrimaryKey = New DataColumn() {tblChanges.Columns("PseudoKey")}

dsMain.Merge(dsChanges)

'Set the primary key in the main table back to its original value.
tblMain.PrimaryKey = pkOriginal

dsMain.AcceptChanges()
```

Main DataSet with new rows				
OrderID	CustomerID	EmployeeID	OrderDate	PseudoKey
10643	ALFKI	6	09/22/1997	1
10692	ALFKI	4	10/31/1997	2
-1	ALFKI	7	02/24/2002	3
-2	ALFKI	7	02/24/2002	4

DataSet returned by Web service with new values				
OrderID	CustomerID	EmployeeID	OrderDate	PseudoKey
12000	ALFKI	7	02/24/2002	3
12001	ALFKI	7	02/24/2002	4

Main DataSet after merging DataSet returned by Web service				
OrderID	CustomerID	EmployeeID	OrderDate	PseudoKey
10643	ALFKI	6	09/22/1997	1
10692	ALFKI	4	10/31/1997	2
12000	ALFKI	7	02/24/2002	3
12001	ALFKI	7	02/24/2002	4

Figure 11-10 Adding a pseudokey to the *DataSet* to merge in new auto-increment values

Visual C#
```csharp
WebServiceClass objWebService = new WebServiceClass();
DataSet dsMain = objWebService.GetDataSet();
ModifyDataSetContents(dsMain);
DataSet dsChanges = dsMain.GetChanges();
dsChanges = objWebService.SubmitChanges(dsChanges);

//Change the primary key in each table to be the pseudokey.
DataTable tblMain = ds.Tables["Orders"];
DataColumn[] pkOriginal = tblMain.PrimaryKey;
tblMain.PrimaryKey = new DataColumn[] {tblMain.Columns["PseudoKey"]};
```

```
DataTable tblChanges = dsChanges.Tables["Orders"];
tblChanges.PrimaryKey = new DataColumn[] {tblChanges.Columns["PseudoKey"]};

dsMain.Merge(dsChanges);

//Set the primary key in the main table back to its original value.
tblMain.PrimaryKey = pkOriginal;

dsMain.AcceptChanges();
```

Reviewing Your Options   Personally, I don't like either solution. The solution that involves changing the primary key can become overly complex, especially if the table in question has related child *DataTable* objects in the *DataSet*. If I had to pick one, I'd choose the one that removes the pending inserts from the original *DataSet* before calling *Merge*. However, I will say this: these solutions are a major step forward from previous data access technologies, such as ADO, in which there were no solutions to this scenario.

One final option for this scenario is to avoid the problem altogether by structuring your data so that you know the primary key values for your new rows before you submit them to the database. A growing number of developers are using GUIDs for primary key columns in their databases. Although you might not want to use a GUID column as the primary key for your database table, you can use it as the primary key for your *DataTable* to help the *Merge* method match related rows, as described earlier.

Isolating and Reintegrating Changes Sample Code

The sample code for this chapter includes examples, in both Visual Basic and Visual C#, that demonstrate how to refresh a row after submitting an update using *UpdateRowSource.First-ReturnedRecord*, *UpdateRowSource.OutputParameters*, and the *RowUpdated* event. Two samples relate to this topic: *SubmitHierarchicalChanges* and *IsolateAndReintegrateChanges*. Each sample follows the same basic premise. A customer called in to complain about the first order she received. The code deletes the first order, re-issues all remaining orders with a 10-percent discount, and enters two new orders with a 25-percent discount. There are changes to orders and order details for each order. In each case, the added and modified rows must be submitted top-down (orders before order details), while pending deletions must be submitted bottom-up (order details before orders).

The *SubmitHierarchicalChanges* sample submits those pending changes using the *SqlData-Adapter*'s *Update* method in conjunction with the *DataTable*'s *Select* method as described earlier in the chapter.

The *IsolateAndReintegrateChanges* sample contains all the same changes, but it also contains orders and details for other customers. This sample uses the *DataSet*'s *GetChanges* method to create a *DataSet* that contains just the pending changes before submitting changes (simulating a scenario in which you would want to pass just the pending changes to a Web service). The sample purges the pending new orders, merges in the *DataSet* that contains new OrderID values, and then calls *AcceptChanges*.

Handling Failed Update Attempts

ADO.NET is designed to work with disconnected data. When a user modifies the contents of a *DataSet*, he does not directly modify the contents of the database. Instead, ADO.NET caches the change in the modified *DataRow* object or objects. You can submit the changes to the database later using a *SqlDataAdapter* object.

However, there are no guarantees that the data in the database won't be changed after the user runs the initial query. The updating logic that *SqlDataAdapter* objects use to submit changes uses optimistic updating logic. As with being an optimist in life, things don't always turn out the way you'd like.

Consider the following scenario. User A retrieves customer information from your database into a *DataSet*. That user modifies information for a particular customer. Between the time that User A queries the database and attempts to submit the new customer data, User B modifies that same row of data in your database. As a result, User A's update attempt fails.

Many developers see this behavior as a major headache, but consider the alternative. What if User A's update attempt were to succeed? User A would overwrite the changes that User B made. Neither User A nor User B would realize that User A had overwritten User B's data.

Planning Ahead for Conflicts

If you're building a multiuser application that works with disconnected data and relies on optimistic concurrency to submit changes, there's a chance that update attempts will fail. You should plan ahead and determine how your application should respond to such situations.

Say that you modify the contents of 10 rows and attempt to submit those changes. The *SqlDataAdapter* successfully submits the changes in the first three rows, but the attempt to submit the change stored in the fourth row fails. How should your application respond? Should the *SqlDataAdapter* attempt to submit the remaining pending changes? Will you prompt the user to let her know that a failure occurred? Will you help the user try to recover from the problem?

The *SqlDataAdapter* Class's *ContinueUpdateOnError* Property

You can control how the *SqlDataAdapter* responds to a failed update attempt by using the *ContinueUpdateOnError* property. By default, this property is set to *False*, which means that the *SqlDataAdapter* will throw an exception when it encounters a failed update attempt. If you want the *SqlDataAdapter* to attempt to submit the remaining changes, set its *ContinueUpdateOnError* property to *True*.

If you set this property to *True* and one or more of the update attempts fail, the *SqlDataAdapter* will not throw an exception. When the *SqlDataAdapter* encounters a failed update attempt, it will set the *HasErrors* property of the corresponding *DataRow* object to *True* and set the *RowError* property of the *DataRow* to the exception message. You can check the

HasErrors property of your *DataSet* or *DataTable* after calling *SqlDataAdapter.Update* to determine whether any of the update attempts failed. Of course, this will not be a valid test if your *DataSet* or *DataTable* has errors before you call *SqlDataAdapter.Update*.

Some developers will want to submit changes in a transaction and commit the changes only if all update attempts succeed. In such scenarios, you'll probably want to leave the *ContinueUpdateOnError* property set to its default value of *False* and roll back the transaction if the *Update* method throws an exception.

Informing the User of Failures

It's important to inform the user if an update attempt fails. Some components will help you show the user which rows did not update successfully. For example, if you modify a number of rows in a Windows *DataGridView* control and the attempt to submit those modified rows fails, the rows that did not update successfully will be marked with a warning icon in the row header. If you move the mouse over the icon, the grid will display a ToolTip that shows the contents of the error.

If you're not using a bound Windows *DataGridView*, you can use code like the following to provide information about the rows whose updates failed:

Visual Basic
```vb
'Imports System.Text
Try
    MyDataAdapter.ContinueUpdateOnError = True
    MyDataAdapter.Update(MyDataTable)
    If MyDataTable.HasErrors
        Dim sb As New StringBuilder()
        sb.AppendLine("The following row(s) were not " & _
                    "updated successfully:")
        Dim row As DataRow
        For Each row In MyDataTable.Rows
            If row.HasErrors Then
                sb.AppendFormat("{0}: {1}", row("ID"), row.RowError)
                sb.AppendLine()
            End If
        Next row
        MessageBox.Show(sb.ToString())
    Else
        MessageBox.Show("All updates succeeded")
    End If
Catch ex As Exception
    MessageBox.Show("The following exception occurred:" & vbCrLf & _
                    ex.Message)
End Try
```

Visual C#
```csharp
try {
    MyDataAdapter.ContinueUpdateOnError = true;
    MyDataAdapter.Update(MyDataTable);
```

```
    if (MyDataTable.HasErrors) {
        StringBuilder sb = new StringBuilder();
        sb.AppendLine("The following row(s) were not " +
                      "updated successfully:");
        foreach (DataRow row in MyDataTable.Rows)
            if (row.HasErrors) {
                sb.AppendFormat("{0}: {1}", row["ID"], row.RowError);
                sb.AppendLine();
            }
        MessageBox.Show(sb.ToString());
    } else {
        MessageBox.Show("All updates succeeded");
    }
} catch (Exception ex) {
    MessageBox.Show("The following exception occurred: \n\r" +
                    ex.Message);
}
```

Users can be demanding. If an update attempt fails, they don't just want to know that it failed. They generally want to know why the update attempt failed and how to make the update successful. First, let's focus on determining why an update attempt failed.

What if we could extract the information shown in Figure 11-11 for each failed update attempt?

	CustomerID	CompanyName	BalanceDue
You tried to submit the following data:	ABCDE	ABCDE Inc.	$200.00
The original data for the row was:	ABCDE	ABCDE Inc.	$100.00
The row in the database now contains:	ABCDE	ABCDE Inc.	$125.00

Figure 11-11 Displaying information about failed update attempts

You already know how to use the *DataRow* object to access the current and original contents of a row.

Visual Basic
```
Dim tbl As DataTable = CreateFillAndModifyTable()
Dim row As DataRow = tbl.Rows(0)
Console.WriteLine("Current  Balance Due: {0:c}", row("BalanceDue"))
Console.WriteLine("Original Balance Due: {0:c}", _
                  row("BalanceDue", DataRowVersion.Original))
```

Visual C#
```
DataTable tbl = CreateFillAndModifyTable();
DataRow row = tbl.Rows[0];
Console.WriteLine("Current  Balance Due: {0:c}",  row["BalanceDue"]);
Console.WriteLine("Original Balance Due: {0:c}",
                  row["BalanceDue", DataRowVersion.Original]);
```

But how can we fetch the current contents of the desired rows in the database?

Fetching the Current Contents of Conflicting Rows

To fetch the current contents of the desired rows, we can use the *SqlDataAdapter* class's *RowUpdated* event. The following code snippet determines whether the *SqlDataAdapter* encountered an error on the update attempt. If the error is a concurrency exception, the code will use a parameterized query to fetch the current contents of the corresponding row in the database.

To make the code snippet concise and readable, I've omitted the definition of the *SqlData-Adapter* objects and *DataSet* objects. The *ConflictAdapter* variable is a *SqlDataAdapter* that contains a parameterized query that retrieves the contents of a row in the database. The parameter for this query is the primary key column for the database. That column in the *DataTable* is ID. The code uses the value of the ID column for the row whose update failed as the value for the parameter, executes the query using that parameter, and stores the results into a separate *DataSet*.

There's also the chance that the row you tried to update no longer exists in the database. The code determines whether the query retrieved a row and sets the *DataRow* object's *RowError* property appropriately.

Visual Basic

```
Private Sub HandleRowUpdated(ByVal sender As Object, _
                             ByVal e As OleDbRowUpdatedEventArgs)
    If e.Status = UpdateStatus.ErrorsOccurred AndAlso _
       TypeOf e.Errors Is DBConcurrencyException Then
         ConflictAdapter.SelectCommand.Parameters(0).Value = e.Row("ID")
         Dim intRowsReturned As Integer
         intRowsReturned = ConflictAdapter.Fill(ConflictDataSet)
         If intRowsReturned = 1 Then
             e.Row.RowError = "The row has been modified by another user."
         Else
             e.Row.RowError = "The row no longer exists in the database."
         End If
         e.Status = UpdateStatus.Continue
    End If
End Sub
```

Visual C#

```
private void HandleRowUpdated(object sender, OleDbRowUpdatedEventArgs e)
{
    if ((e.Status == UpdateStatus.ErrorsOccurred) &&
        (e.Errors.GetType == typeof(DBConcurrencyException))
    {
        ConflictAdapter.SelectCommand.Parameters[0].Value = e.Row["ID"];
        int intRowsReturned = ConflictAdapter.Fill(ConflictDataSet);
        if (intRowsReturned == 1)
            e.Row.RowError = "The row has been modified by another user.";
        else
            e.Row.RowError = "The row no longer exists in the database.";
        e.Status = UpdateStatus.Continue;
    }
}
```

> **Note**   The *SqlDataAdapter* will automatically append text to the *RowError* property on a failed update attempt if you do not change the event's *Status* property to *Continue* or *SkipCurrentRow*.

This code snippet fetches the current contents of the corresponding rows in the database into a separate *DataSet* so that you can examine the data after the update attempt. You now have all the data you need to construct a dialog box similar to Figure 11-11.

If at First You Don't Succeed . . .

Telling the user why an update attempt failed is helpful, but your users probably don't want to requery your database and reapply the same set of changes to the new data in order to try to resubmit their changes. How can we use the ADO.NET object model to simplify the process?

Let's think back to why the update attempt failed in the first place. The data that the *SqlData-Adapter* used in its concurrency checks no longer matches the current contents of the row in the database. The *SqlDataAdapter* uses the original content of the *DataRow* object in the updating logic's concurrency checks. Until we refresh the original values in the *DataRow* object, we will not be able to submit the changes stored in that *DataRow* to the database no matter how many times we call the *SqlDataAdapter* object's *Update* method.

If we can change the original content of a *DataRow* object without losing the current content of the *DataRow*, we can successfully submit the changes stored in that *DataRow*, assuming that the contents of the corresponding row in the database don't change again.

Importing "New Original" Values into a *DataRow*

Earlier in the chapter, you learned how to use the *DataSet* class's *Merge* method to combine the contents of two *DataSet* objects. If the *Merge* method detects that two rows have the same primary key values, it will combine the contents of the two rows into one. The *Merge* method also lets you specify that you want to preserve the changes stored in your *DataSet*.

In the previous code snippet, we trapped for the *SqlDataAdapter* object's *RowUpdated* event. If the current row did not update successfully, the code retrieved the current contents of the corresponding row in the database into a new *DataSet* called *ConflictDataSet*. Assuming that the main *DataSet* is called *MainDataSet*, we can use the following line of code to merge the contents of *ConflictDataSet* into *MainDataSet*:

Visual Basic
```
MainDataSet.Merge(ConflictDataSet, True)
```

Visual C#
```
MainDataSet.Merge(ConflictDataSet, true);
```

Passing in *True* for the second parameter tells the *DataSet* to preserve the current values in the "main" *DataSet* when combining rows. The method overwrites only the original values of the *DataRow* objects with the data in the conflict *DataSet*.

With this "new original" data in the main *DataSet*, we can attempt to submit the remaining pending changes to the database. If the contents of the corresponding rows have not changed again since we retrieved them in the *RowUpdated* event, our updates will succeed.

> **Caution**   I describe this process of retrieving values from the database and overwriting the original values in the *DataRow* to show how you *could* resubmit pending changes. Performing this operation automatically is the same as using only the primary key values in updating logic—you'll simply overwrite other users' changes. The point of this exercise is to demonstrate how you can access the current and original values in the *DataRow* as well as the current values in the database. Depending on the goals of your application, you may want to prompt the user to determine how to proceed.

Keep in mind that you can't get "more up-to-date" information about a row that no longer exists in the database. If an update attempt fails because the row no longer exists in the database, you can't use this approach to refresh the original values in the row. If you want to re-add the current contents of the *DataRow* object to the database, you can call the *DataRow* class's *SetAdded* method to change the *DataRow* object's *RowState* to *Added*. When you use the *SqlDataAdapter* to submit the change, it will try to insert the row into the database.

The Conflicts Sample Application

The sample code for this chapter includes a sample called *HandleFailedUpdateAttempts*. The sample attempts to submit a series of changes to the database. The sample also simulates changes by another user to cause many of the update attempts to generate concurrency failures.

As described earlier, the code uses the *SqlDataAdapter* class's *RowUpdated* event to detect concurrency failures. When the code detects a concurrency failure, it adds the *DataRow* to a list of *DataRow* objects that failed to update due to concurrency failures and queries the database for the current contents of the corresponding row in the database. Once the code has attempted to submit all pending changes, it loops through all *DataRows* that failed to update due to concurrency failures, printing out the *DataRow*'s contents and *RowState*, as well as the contents of the corresponding row in the database. If there is a corresponding row in the database, the code uses the *LoadDataRow* method (similar to the *Merge* method) to overwrite the original values in the *DataRow* with the values retrieved from the database, and it resubmits the pending change in the *DataRow*.

Working with Distributed Transactions

In Chapter 4, we learned about the ADO.NET *SqlTransaction* class. You can use a *SqlTransaction* object to group the results of multiple queries on a connection as a single unit of work.

Let's say that your database contains banking information. You can transfer money from a savings account to a checking account by executing the following two queries:

```
UPDATE Savings
    SET BalanceDue = BalanceDue - 100
    WHERE AccountID = 17
UPDATE Checking
    SET BalanceDue = BalanceDue + 100
    WHERE AccountID = 17
```

To make sure you can group the two changes into a single unit of work that you can commit or roll back, you can create a new *SqlTransaction* object before executing the queries. If an error occurs or one of the queries doesn't have the desired row, you can roll back the transaction. Otherwise, you can commit the changes you made in the transaction. Figure 11-12 shows how to wrap both changes in a single transaction. (You know all this already.)

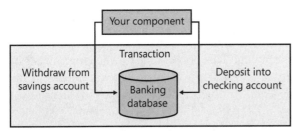

Figure 11-12   Wrapping multiple changes to a database in a transaction

But what do you do if the checking and savings accounts aren't in the same database?

You can start a transaction on each connection. Then, if you determine that the withdrawal from the savings account or the deposit into the checking account failed, you can roll back both transactions. Otherwise, you can commit them both. That sounds simple enough. Figure 11-13 depicts such an application.

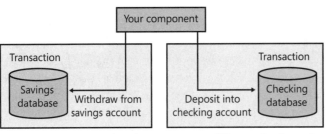

Figure 11-13   Wrapping changes to two different databases in separate transactions

Let's say that you commit the withdrawal from the savings account, but just before you commit the deposit into the checking account, you lose your network connection. The database will detect the lost connection and roll back the transaction automatically. You will have withdrawn the money from the savings account but not deposited that money into the checking account. Oops.

Maybe using a transaction on each connection isn't a completely reliable solution to the problem. To make the system more reliable, your application needs to work more closely with both databases to coordinate the transactions and resolve problems like the one I've just described. You need to use a transaction that enlists multiple database connections. A transaction that can span multiple resources is generally known as a *distributed transaction*.

> **Note** Entire books are dedicated to transaction processing or to COM+. Obviously, I can't cover either topic nearly as thoroughly over the next few pages. I will simply provide an introduction to the basics of transaction processing and working with COM+ components. For more information on transaction processing, I strongly recommend *Principles of Transaction Processing* by Philip A. Bernstein and Eric Newcomer (Morgan Kaufmann, 1997).

Transaction Coordinators and Resource Managers

Two main components are involved in a distributed transaction: the resource manager and the transaction coordinator. A resource manager performs the desired work, whether it's modifying the contents of a database or reading a message from a queue. It then reports whether it was able to complete the work.

The transaction coordinator communicates with the resource managers participating in the transaction and oversees the current state of the transaction. If one resource manager indicates that an error occurred, the transaction coordinator will receive this message and inform the other resource managers to cancel the work performed in the transaction. If all resource managers indicate that they successfully completed their tasks, the transaction coordinator will tell all the resource managers to commit the results of those tasks.

Two-Phase Commits

Each resource manager implements what's known as a *two-phase commit*. The transaction coordinator tells each resource manager to prepare the changes performed during the lifetime of the transaction. This is just the first phase of the process. The resource managers have not actually committed the changes yet. They're simply preparing to commit the changes.

Once all the resource managers indicate that they are ready to commit the changes, the transaction coordinator will tell each resource manager to do so. If, however, one or more resource managers indicate that they could not prepare the changes, the transaction coordinator will tell each resource manager to cancel the work performed in the transaction.

Let's apply this to the problem scenario. When the transaction coordinator asks the resource managers to prepare to commit the changes, they both indicate that they are ready, willing, and able to commit the changes. The transaction coordinator sends a message to the resource manager for the savings account to commit the changes, but a fatal error (such as a power outage) occurs before it can communicate with the resource manager for the checking account. What happens now?

It's up to the transaction coordinator and the resource manager for the checking account to resolve the transaction. Each component is responsible for maintaining information about the status of the transaction. The transaction coordinator must be able to recover from the failure, determine that the transaction is still pending, and contact the appropriate resource managers to resolve the transaction.

The resource manager must be able to commit all changes that it prepared in the first phase of the commit process. Let's say that the power outage that threw the resolution of the transaction into doubt occurred on the machine where the database that maintains the checking account is located. The database system needs to recover from the failure, determine that the transaction is still pending, provide the ability to commit those changes, and resolve the transaction with the coordinator.

As you can already tell, it takes a lot of work to develop a transaction coordinator or a resource manager.

Distributed Transactions in the .NET Framework

Microsoft initially introduced its transaction coordinator and supporting technologies for the Windows operating system as an add-on to Microsoft Windows NT 4. This functionality is now integrated into the Windows operating system as part of Component Services.

The beauty of this architecture is that you have to write only a small amount of code to take advantage of the transactional features in Component Services. You write your code just like you would normally. You then tell Component Services whether to commit or abort the transaction, and it will take care of the grunt work necessary to manage a distributed transaction. Figure 11-14 shows an example of working with multiple databases in a distributed transaction using Component Services.

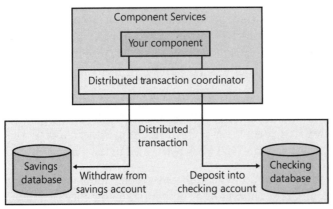

Figure 11-14   Using Component Services to wrap changes to multiple databases in a distributed transaction

Database Support for Distributed Transactions

To use distributed transactions with your database, your database system needs to have a resource manager that can communicate with the transaction coordinator that's built into Component Services.

Some database systems (such as SQL Server and Oracle) have resource managers that support this functionality, but many others (such as Access and dBASE) do not. Before you start planning an application that relies on distributed transactions, make sure you're using a database that has a resource manager that implements two-phase commits and can communicate with Component Services.

Actually, distributed transactions aren't just for databases. Microsoft Message Queuing services, for example, lets you send and receive messages as part of a distributed transaction.

Building Your Components

The first edition of this book covered using Component Services Distributed Transactions in conjunction with ADO.NET using the *ServicedComponent* class in the *System.EnterpriseServices* namespace. The tedious process of registering a component with Component Services required invoking multiple command-line tools (Sn.exe and RegSvcs.exe) and adding attributes to both the assembly and the class.

In short, the process was...well, suboptimal.

System.Transactions to the Rescue!

Thankfully, working with distributed transactions in version 2.0 of the .NET Framework is much simpler due to the *System.Transactions* namespace. This namespace includes multiple transaction classes that you can use in your code to create transactions without having to invoke command-line tools or add attributes to your assembly and class. Let's take a look at a couple of examples involving the two most commonly used classes in the *System.Transactions* namespace—*TransactionScope* and *CommittableTransaction*.

TransactionScope

The *TransactionScope* class is the simplest class to work with. Assuming the .NET Data Provider you're working with supports *System.Transactions*, opening a connection within the scope of a *TransactionScope* will automatically enlist that connection in the transaction. (All .NET Data Providers included with version 2.0 of the .NET Framework support *System.Transactions*.) Calling the *Commit* method of the *TransactionScope* commits the work performed on the transaction. If the *Dispose* method of the *TransactionScope* is called (either implicitly at the end of a *Using* block or explicitly), uncommitted work performed on the transaction is automatically rolled back.

The following code example shows how you can perform work on multiple connections within a *TransactionScope* and commit the work:

Visual Basic

```
'Imports System.Transactions
Using txn As New TransactionScope()
    Using cn1 As New SqlConnection(strConn1)
        cn1.Open()
        'Perform work on the connection
        cn1.Close()
    End Using
    Using cn2 As New SqlConnection(strConn2)
        cn2.Open()
        'Perform work on the connection
        cn2.Close()
    End Using

    'Commit the work performed within the transaction
    txn.Commit()
End Using
```

Visual C#

```
//using System.Transactions;
using (TransactionScope txn = new TransactionScope()) {
    using (SqlConnection cn1 = new SqlConnection(strConn1)) {
        cn1.Open();
        //Perform work on the connection
        cn1.Close();
    }
    using (SqlConnection cn2 = new SqlConnection(strConn2)) {
        cn2.Open();
        //Perform work on the connection
        cn2.Close();
    }

    //Commit the work performed within the transaction
    txn.Commit();
}
```

CommittableTransaction

The *CommittableTransaction* class is similar to the *TransactionScope* class, except for one major difference—you must explicitly enlist the connections you want to participate in the transaction. To enlist a connection in a *CommittableTransaction*'s transaction, pass the transaction object into the connection's *EnlistTransaction* method.

To commit or roll back the work performed in a *CommittableTransaction*, call the *Commit* or *Rollback* method, respectively. If the *Dispose* method on the *CommittableTransaction* is called (implicitly or explicitly), any uncommitted work performed on the *CommittableTransaction* is automatically rolled back.

The following code example shows how you can perform work on multiple connections within a *CommittableTransaction* and commit the work.

Visual Basic

```vb
'Imports System.Transactions
Using cn1 As New SqlConnection(strConn1), _
      cn2 As New SqlConnection(strConn2)
    cn1.Open()
    cn2.Open()
    Using txn As New CommittableTransaction()
        cn1.EnlistTransaction(txn)
        cn2.EnlistTransaction(txn)

        'Perform work on the connections

        'Commit the work
        txn.Commit()
    End Using

    'Dissociate the connections with the transaction
    cn1.EnlistTransaction(Nothing)
    cn2.EnlistTransaction(Nothing)

    cn1.Close()
    cn2.Close()
End Using
```

Visual C#

```csharp
//using System.Transactions;
using (SqlConnection cn1 = new SqlConnection(strConn1),
                     cn2 = new SqlConnection(strConn2)) {
    cn1.Open();
    cn2.Open();
    using (CommittableTransaction txn = new CommittableTransaction()) {
        cn1.EnlistTransaction(txn);
        cn2.EnlistTransaction(txn);

        //Perform work on the connections

        //Commit the work
        txn.Commit();
    }

    //Dissociate the connections with the transaction
    cn1.EnlistTransaction(null);
    cn2.EnlistTransaction(null);

    cn1.Close();
    cn2.Close();
}
```

SQL Server 2005 and Promotable Transactions

Distributed transactions are powerful, but they require more overhead than simple transactions. If only one database participates within a *System.Transaction*, in theory, the transaction does not *have* to be a distributed transaction. You could have the database work with a transaction that's local to the database, like a *SqlTransaction*. However, the database would need the ability to promote the local transaction to a distributed transaction if another resource manager participates within the *System.Transaction*.

SQL Server 2005 and the SQL Client .NET Data Provider that's included with version 2.0 of the .NET Framework support promotable transactions. If you enlist a *SqlConnection* that communicates with SQL Server 2005 within a *System.Transactions* transaction, and that *SqlConnection* is the first resource manager involved in the transaction, SQL Server will perform the work on a local transaction, which will result in better performance. If another resource manager enlists in the transaction, SQL Server will promote the local transaction to a distributed transaction.

System.Transactions Samples

The sample code for this chapter includes two *System.Transactions* samples: *SystemTransactions _TransactionScope* and *SystemTransactions_CommittableTransaction*. As their names imply, the first sample uses the *TransactionScope* class and the second sample uses the *Committable-Transaction* class.

Batch Queries

In version 1.0 of the .NET Framework, the various *DataAdapter* classes could submit only one pending change at a time to your database. In some ways, this was a step backward from ADO "Classic," which let you submit pending changes to the database in batches.

Version 2.0 of ADO.NET addresses this scenario through the *UpdateBatchSize* property on the various *DataAdapter* classes. By default, this property is set to 1, which will cause the *DataAdapter* to submit pending changes to the database one row at a time. If you want to submit pending changes to the database in batches, set the *UpdateBatchSize* property to the desired batch size. If you set the *UpdateBatchSize* property to 0, the *DataAdapter* will submit all rows in a single batch.

> **Note**   Not all *DataAdapters* support submitting updates in batches. In version 2.0 of the .NET Framework, the *SqlDataAdapter* and *OracleDataAdapter* support batch updates, but the *OdbcDataAdapter* and the *OleDbDataAdapter* do not.

The logic required to support this functionality in ADO.NET is more complex than ADO "Classic" because ADO.NET lets you define your own updating logic in a *DataAdapter*. ADO "Classic" generated its own updating logic, so it could easily examine the information returned by executing the batch query and determine which updates succeeded and which updates failed. Because the *DataAdapter* does not inherently know what the updating logic in its *InsertCommand*, *UpdateCommand*, and *DeleteCommand* will do, the task of batching together all the queries while still maintaining enough internal logic to determine which update attempts succeeded and which update attempts failed is more complicated.

The *SqlDataAdapter* adds remote procedure call (RPC) tokens to separate the queries within the batch. This approach helps the *SqlDataAdapter* identify the results of queries from the server, and it prevents the *SqlDataAdapter* from having to rename parameters within the batch.

Note If you submit updates in batches using a *SqlDataAdapter* and look at a SQL Profiler trace, it might look like the *SqlDataAdapter* submitted the changes one row at a time. SQL Profiler sees the RPC tokens and splits the batch into separate queries, giving the impression that the *SqlDataAdapter* did not really batch the queries.

The *OracleDataAdapter* has to perform more work. Because Oracle does not support returning the number of rows affected by individual queries within a batch, the *OracleDataAdapter* adds output parameters to the batch that return the number of rows affected by individual queries within the batch. The *OracleDataAdapter* also modifies the contents of the batch query to ensure that parameter names from different entries within the batch do not repeat. For example, if the *UpdateCommand* includes a parameter named ":MyColumn" and the batch will submit two pending updates, the *OracleDataAdapter* renames the parameters. You can use Oracle's tracing features if you want to take a closer look at the batch of queries that the *OracleDataAdapter* generates.

In other words, asking a *DataAdapter* to submit updates in batches rather than one row at a time is not a trivial request.

Using Transactions with Batched Updates

Simply setting the *UpdateBatchSize* property on a *DataAdapter* that supports batched updates to a value greater than 1 may improve the performance of your code, but that's not the *right* way to try to improve the performance of your application.

When you submit a batch of queries to a SQL Server database, SQL Server will (by default) handle each query separately and write the changes to disk after executing each query. Let's assume that you have 100,000 modified rows within a *DataTable*. Whether you submit the changes via a *SqlDataAdapter* one row at a time or in batches of a thousand, you're still asking SQL Server to write all the changes to disk in 100,000 separate operations.

A more efficient approach is to submit those changes in a transaction. This way, SQL Server can respond more quickly to changes and commit them all to disk at the end of the operation.

It's also wise to wrap batched updates within a transaction because handling failures can become more difficult in batched updating mode. If you submit pending changes in single-row updating mode and an attempt to submit a pending change violates a constraint in the database, it is obvious which *DataRow* corresponds to the exception. In batched updating mode, determining which *DataRow*(s) failed and what caused those failures is more challenging. The actual exception is available in the *Errors* property of the *RowUpdatedEventArgs*, but the *DataRow*(s) that correspond to that exception are not available. The *DBConcurrencyException* is an exception to the rule (no pun intended) because it exposes a *Row* property and a *CopyToRows* method you can use to find the *DataRow*(s) that caused the exception.

> **Note** You use the *CopyToRows* method by creating an array of *DataRow* objects (using the value of the *RowCount* property on the *DBConcurrencyException* to determine the appropriate length of the array) and then passing the array of *DataRow* objects into the *CopyToRows* method. The *CopyToRows* method will assign the *DataRow* objects whose update attempts modified no rows in the database to the entries in the array.

Choosing an Appropriate Value for *UpdateBatchSize*

For a moment, let's consider a scenario in which you have 100,000 pending changes within a *DataTable* and you're working with SQL Server. You look at the time it takes to submit all pending changes and wish the code would run faster.

You remember that ADO.NET 2.0 supports batch updating. You've read the preceding section about batched updates and transactions, so you wrap the changes in a *SqlTransaction*, set the *SqlDataAdapter*'s *UpdateBatchSize* property to 10, run your performance tests, and discover that your scenarios run faster. It used to take 60 seconds to submit all the changes; now it takes only 30. You set *UpdateBatchSize* to 100, re-run your performance tests, and find your scenarios ran even faster—now taking only 23 seconds.

You determine that increasing the batch size increases performance, so you set the *Update-BatchSize* property to 0, a special value that causes the *SqlDataAdapter* to submit all changes in a single batch. Running the performance tests now results in terrible performance and/or generates an exception. What went wrong?

Actually, nothing went wrong. Increasing the size of the batches can improve performance, but submitting 100,000 rows at once might not perform as well as submitting one row at a time. At some point, constructing the batch and handling the results becomes too complex. For that reason, do not set the *UpdateBatchSize* property to 0.

In my tests, I've found that the optimal batch size is somewhere between 100 and 1000 rows. Many factors can influence your scenarios, such as, but not limited to, the size of the row, the concurrency checks used in the updating logic, and constraints within the database. Your best bet is to perform your own testing.

> **Note**   Attempts to submit huge numbers of changes in a single batch might generate an exception due to a timeout. To increase the timeout interval used to submit the batch, set the *CommandTimeout* property of the *DataAdapter's SelectCommand*.

Events

The *RowUpdating* event for the *SqlDataAdapter* and *OracleDataAdapter* behave the same in single-row updating mode and in batched updating mode, with a couple of minor exceptions. In both cases, the *RowUpdating* event fires prior to submitting the pending changes in each *DataRow*. The *DataRow* that contains the change, the *Command* used to submit the change, and *TableMapping* information are all available. However, if you submit the changes in batching mode, the *RowUpdating* event will fire once for each of the *DataRow* objects in the batch prior to submitting the batch.

The *RowUpdated* event behaves differently in batched updating mode. The event does not fire on a per-*DataRow* basis. Instead, the *RowUpdated* event fires after submitting each batch. You can access the *DataRow* objects for the batch through the *CopyToRows* method on the *RowUpdatedEventArgs*. However, the *Command* (and, therefore, the *Parameters*) is not available. The total number of rows modified by the batch is available, but the number of rows modified for individual entries within the batch is not.

Refreshing Rows

Refreshing rows after update is more complex in batch updating mode. Whereas the *SqlDataAdapter* and *OracleDataAdapter* classes support refreshing the *DataRow* via output parameters, neither class supports refreshing the *DataRow* by returning a row through a basic SELECT query. In fact, these classes will throw an *InvalidOperationException* if they encounter a *Command* in batched updating mode whose *UpdatedRowSource* is set to *FirstReturnedRecord* or *Both*.

Batched Updating Samples

The sample code for this chapter includes two batched updating samples: BatchedUpdates and BatchedUpdates_RefreshAfterUpdate. The samples demonstrate how to submit updates in batches and how to refresh *DataRow* objects after updates while submitting changes, respectively.

SQL Bulk Copy

Batched updates are great, but SQL Server offers a much more efficient approach for submitting new rows to the database. SQL Server's Bulk Copy Protocol features, commonly referred to as BCP, have been available since the early days of SQL Server, predating ODBC.

BCP is powerful and extremely fast because SQL Server allows you to insert rows via BCP that bypass many SQL Server operations, such as firing triggers or enforcing constraints. However, many developers have traditionally found BCP frustrating, a bit archaic, or both because it required placing the data to import in specially formatted files.

ADO.NET 2.0 introduces a new class, *SqlBulkCopy*, specifically designed to help developers access SQL Server's BCP features. Rather than having to construct specially formatted files, you can use in-memory ADO.NET classes that you're already familiar with. The *SqlBulkCopy* class's overloaded *WriteToServer* method accepts a *DataTable*, an array of *DataRow* objects, or even a *DataReader*.

The *SqlBulkCopy* class works with both SQL Server 2005 and SQL Server 2000, as well as with SQL Server Express and MSDE.

Creating a *SqlBulkCopy* Object

The *SqlBulkCopy* class's constructor is overloaded. You can supply either a *SqlConnection* object or a connection string that the *SqlBulkCopy* class will use to construct a new *SqlConnection* object so that the *SqlBulkCopy* class can communicate with a SQL Server database.

The *SqlBulkCopy* class's constructors also let you specify a value (or combination of values) from the *SqlBulkCopyOptions* enumeration, which we'll cover shortly.

Finally, you can supply a *SqlTransaction* object if you want the *SqlBulkCopy* object to perform the work on a *SqlTransaction* that you can later commit or roll back. If you don't want to use a *SqlTransaction*, but you find you need to use the constructor that takes one, use *Nothing* or *null* (depending on your language of choice) for that parameter on the constructor.

Visual Basic
```
Dim bcp As SqlBulkCopy
Dim strConn As String
strConn = "Data Source=.\SQLExpress;" & _
          "Initial Catalog=Northwind;Integrated Security=True"
Dim cn As New SqlConnection(strConn)
Dim options As SqlBulkCopyOptions = SqlBulkCopyOptions.Default
Dim txn As SqlTransaction = Nothing

'Supply a connection string
'The SqlBulkCopy object will implicitly create and use
'a new SqlConnection object using this connection string
bcp = New SqlBulkCopy(strConn)

'Supply a connection string and a value from SqlBulkCopyOptions
bcp = New SqlBulkCopy(strConn, options)

'Supply a SqlConnection object
bcp = New SqlBulkCopy(cn)

'Supply a SqlConnection object, a value from SqlBulkCopyOptions
'and a SqlTransaction object (or Nothing)
bcp = New SqlBulkCopy(cn, options, txn)
```

Visual C#

```csharp
SqlBulkCopy bcp;
string strConn;
strConn = @"Data Source=.\SQLExpress;" +
          "Initial Catalog=Northwind;Integrated Security=True";
SqlConnection cn = new SqlConnection(strConn);
SqlBulkCopyOptions options = SqlBulkCopyOptions.Default;
SqlTransaction txn = null;

//Supply a connection string
//The SqlBulkCopy object will implicitly create and use
//a new SqlConnection object using this connection string
bcp = new SqlBulkCopy(strConn);

//Supply a connection string and a value from SqlBulkCopyOptions
bcp = new SqlBulkCopy(strConn, options);

//Supply a SqlConnection object
bcp = new SqlBulkCopy(cn);

//Supply a SqlConnection object, a value from SqlBulkCopyOptions
//and a SqlTransaction object (or null)
bcp = New SqlBulkCopy(cn, options, txn);
```

Writing Data to the Server

The *SqlBulkCopy* class writes data to the server when you call the aptly named *WriteToServer* method. Like the *SqlBulkCopy* class's constructor, the *WriteToServer* method is overloaded to help you handle various scenarios from ADO.NET. You'll need to set the *DestinationTable-Name* property on the *SqlBulkCopy* object before calling the *WriteToServer* method. We'll discuss this property shortly.

You can take a stream-based approach by passing a *DataReader* to the *WriteToServer* method. The *SqlBulkCopy* object will write all the subsequent rows available on the *DataReader* to SQL Server. This method is not limited to *SqlDataReaders*. You can use any class that implements *IDataReader—OdbcDataReader, OracleDataReader, OleDbDataReader*, and so on.

The *SqlBulkCopy* class can also handle data that's cached in a *DataTable*. If you pass just the *DataTable*, the *SqlBulkCopy* object will write all the non-deleted rows to SQL Server. You can also supply a value (or combination of values) from the *DataRowState* enumeration if you want to write just the *DataRow* objects that have a particular *RowState* (or *RowStates*).

Finally, the *SqlBulkCopy* class offers a *WriteToServer* method that accepts an array of *DataRows*. This overload is handy if you want to write just the *DataRow* objects that satisfy criteria that can be expressed through the *DataTable*'s *Select* method, as shown in the following code snippet:

Visual Basic

```vbnet
Dim bcp As SqlBulkCopy
Dim tbl As New DataTable("Customers")
```

```
'Assumes the SqlBulkCopy object has been instantiated
'And that the DataTable contains valid data
bcp.WriteToServer(tbl.Select("Country = 'Brazil'"))
```

Visual C#
```
SqlBulkCopy bcp;
DataTable tbl = new DataTable("Customers");

//Assumes the SqlBulkCopy object has been instantiated
//And that the DataTable contains valid data
bcp.WriteToServer(tbl.Select("Country = 'Brazil'"));
```

Note   At the time of this writing, the *WriteToServer* method will throw an exception if the *DataTable* contains *DataRow* objects whose *RowState* is *Deleted*.

Mapping Data to the Destination Table

By default, the *SqlBulkCopy* class implicitly maps columns from the *DataReader* (or *DataTable*) to the destination table. However, the *SqlBulkCopy* class does not implicitly determine the name of the destination table. You must set this property explicitly prior to calling the *WriteTo-Server* method. The *SqlBulkCopy* class qualifies the value you supply, enclosing it in square brackets, so you don't need to worry about whether the name of the table contains a space.

Earlier I mentioned that the *SqlBulkCopy* class implicitly maps columns. This process maps the columns from the *DataReader* (or *DataTable*) to the destination table by ordinal. In other words, the first column in the *DataReader* (or *DataTable*) will be mapped to the first column in the destination table.

You can also explicitly map columns through the *SqlBulkCopy* class's *ColumnMappings* property. The *Add* method is overloaded to allow you many different options for mapping columns. You can specify the name or ordinal of both the source and destination columns. You can even mix and match names and ordinals, specifying the name of the source column and the ordinal for the destination column, or vice versa.

The *SqlBulkCopyOptions* Enumeration

Some of the *SqlBulkCopy* class's constructors let you supply a value (or combination of values) from the *SqlBulkCopyOptions* enumeration. This enumeration gives you finer control over the behavior that occurs on the call to *WriteToServer*. Table 11-2 shows the various options.

As a general rule, sticking with the *Default* option will yield the best behavior. The one exception to this rule is the *KeepNulls* option. Specifying *KeepNulls* will increase the performance of the *WriteToServer* call slightly because this prevents SQL Server from having to check for and evaluate defaults for columns.

Table 11-2   Members of the *SqlBulkCopyOptions* Enumeration

Constant	Value	Description
Default	0	Specifies that none of the options will be used. As its name implies, this is the default behavior if you use a constructor that does not include a parameter for *SqlBulkCopyOptions*.
KeepIdentity	1	Specifies that the values supplied for identity columns should be written to the new rows; otherwise, new identity values will be generated by the database.
CheckConstraints	2	Specifies that foreign key constraints are checked when importing data; otherwise, incoming data will be validated using foreign key constraints.
TableLock	4	Specifies that SQL Server will hold a table lock during the operation; otherwise, row locks are used.
KeepNulls	8	Specifies that the null values coming from the source will be applied to the new rows even if the corresponding column in the destination table has a default value; otherwise, the default value is used.
FireTriggers	16	Specifies that creation of new rows will fire triggers; otherwise, triggers will not be fired.
UseInternalTransaction	32	Specifies that the work in each batch will be wrapped in an implicit transaction; otherwise, no transaction is created.

BulkCopy Sample Code

The sample code for this chapter includes working code that uses the *SqlBulkCopy* class in the *BulkCopy* procedure.

DataSet Objects and Transactions

Many of the scenarios discussed so far in this chapter have involved transactions. Unfortunately, as of version 2.0 of the .NET Framework, the *DataSet* class does not offer support for transactions.

If you submit pending changes via a *SqlDataAdapter*, the *SqlDataAdapter* will implicitly call the *AcceptChanges* method on *DataRow* objects whose changes were submitted successfully. If the call to *SqlDataAdapter.Update* relied on a transaction (either a *SqlTransaction* or a *System .Transaction*) and you roll back the work performed on the transaction, the database will discard the changes you made during the transaction. The *DataSet* will not revert back to its state at the time the transaction began. However, there are a couple of simple ways to address this scenario.

The general approach is to store the contents of the *DataSet* at the time the transaction starts. If you roll back the transaction, discard the *DataSet* used to perform the transaction and use the *DataSet* that you stored that still contains all the pending changes.

How you store the contents of the *DataSet* is up to you. The simplest option is to use the *Copy* method to copy the *DataSet* to another *DataSet* in memory. If you'd rather store the contents of the *DataSet* to your hard drive to conserve memory, use the *WriteXml* method, but be sure to specify *XmlWriteMode.DiffGram* so that when you reload the data via *ReadXml*, the pending changes will be preserved. Programmatically serializing and deserializing the *DataSet* is another option.

Regardless of which option you choose, this is a simple but inconspicuous way to address the *DataSet*'s lack of support for transactions.

DataSet Objects and Transactions Sample Code

The sample code for this chapter includes an example of working with *DataSet* objects and transactions, called *DataSetAndTransactions*, which creates a copy of a *DataTable* in memory before submitting updates in a transaction. The code rolls back the work in the transaction, reverts back to the *DataTable* in memory, and then resubmits the pending changes to demonstrate that the approach can succeed.

When Handling Advanced Updating Scenarios, Use ADO.NET

The *SqlCommandBuilder* class and code-generation tools such as the Data Adapter Configuration Wizard make handling basic updating scenarios simple. Unfortunately, these tools do not generate the logic required to handle more advanced updating scenarios, such as detecting and resolving failed update attempts.

However, you can use various ADO.NET features to handle the more advanced updating scenarios. Armed with the knowledge you've gained from reading this chapter, you now have the ability to handle such scenarios using the ADO.NET features described in the chapter.

Questions That Should Be Asked More Frequently

Q   How do the Data Adapter Configuration Wizard and *CommandBuilder* objects handle a scenario in which I want to refresh the contents of my row after submitting an update? Some things seem to work automatically, but others don't.

A   The wizard will include queries to refresh your data immediately after you submit a new row or modify an existing row only if you're using a *SqlDataAdapter*. If you do not want the Data Adapter Configuration Wizard to generate these refresh queries, click the Advanced Options button in the wizard and turn this feature off.

The *CommandBuilder* classes do not generate refresh queries no matter what .NET Data Provider you're using.

Q I have cascading referential integrity constraints in my database. If I delete an existing customer, the database automatically deletes the remaining orders for that customer. If I have deleted customers and orders in my *DataSet*, I get errors when I try to submit those changes, even though it looks like all the changes succeeded when I view the contents of my database. What's going on?

A If you have a *DataRelation* defined between the orders and the order details *DataTable* objects in your *DataSet* and you delete an order, ADO.NET will automatically mark the related child rows as deleted. Some databases allow you to define cascading referential integrity constraints in a similar fashion. So, when you submit the pending delete on the order, the database will delete the order and the related child rows from your database.

However, ADO.NET will not know that the database has cascaded the change. The child rows will still be marked as pending deletions in the ADO.NET *DataSet*. If you submit the pending changes stored in the child *DataTable* to your database, the *SqlDataAdapter* will attempt to delete the rows you've already deleted because of the database's cascading rules.

The simplest solution is to use the techniques for submitting pending changes from a hierarchical *DataSet* that I described earlier in the chapter. Use the *Select* method of the *DataTable* to submit new rows, starting at the top level of the hierarchy and working your way down. Submit pending deletions starting at the bottom level or levels of the hierarchy, working your way up to the top.

Another option is to use the ADO.NET object model so that when you submit the pending deleted parent item, ADO.NET cascades the *SqlDataAdapter*'s call to *AcceptChanges* on the parent *DataRow* to the corresponding child *DataRow* objects. You can accomplish this by setting the *AcceptRejectRule* property on the *ForeignKeyConstraint* to *Cascade*. However, you would want to cascade only the *AcceptChanges* call on pending deleted rows. There is no special property to cascade just those changes, but you can temporarily set the *AcceptReject-Rule* to *Cascade* just prior to submitting pending deletions.

There's a working example in the samples for this chapter called *CascadeDeletesOnServer* that demonstrates how to accomplish this using the Orders and Order Details tables in the sample Northwind database. The foreign key constraint in the database does not cascade deletions, so the example drops the existing foreign key constraint and creates a new one that matches the old one, except that it does cascade deletions.

As noted earlier, the key is to temporarily set the *AcceptRejectRule* to *Cascade* just prior to submitting pending deletions, as shown in the following snippet of code from the example:

Visual Basic
```
rel.ChildKeyConstraint.AcceptRejectRule = AcceptRejectRule.Cascade
daOrders.Update(tblOrders.Select("", "", DataViewRowState.Deleted))
rel.ChildKeyConstraint.AcceptRejectRule = AcceptRejectRule.None
```

Visual C#

```
rel.ChildKeyConstraint.AcceptRejectRule = AcceptRejectRule.Cascade;
daOrders.Update(tblOrders.Select("", "", DataViewRowState.Deleted));
rel.ChildKeyConstraint.AcceptRejectRule = AcceptRejectRule.None;
```

Q The ADO *Recordset* object has a *Resync* method that you can use to fetch information on rows that did not update successfully. What is the equivalent method in the ADO.NET object model?

A The ADO.NET object model has no direct equivalent of this feature. However, you can achieve similar functionality by filling a new *DataSet* and merging the contents into your existing *DataSet* using the *Merge* method, as described earlier in the chapter.

Chapter 12
Working with XML Data

This chapter will cover how to use ADO.NET's XML features, most notably those that allow you to read and write data in XML format. Along the way, you'll also learn about how to use SQL Server 2005's new XML data type from ADO.NET, including how to access the contents of XML columns, use XPath queries to filter the results returned, and process the results using XQuery.

Before we proceed, this chapter comes with a disclaimer. This chapter will discuss how you can use XML and related technologies (such as XML schemas, XPath expressions, and XQuery) from ADO.NET. However, this chapter is not intended to teach you all about XML. There are entire books dedicated to that task.

Although this chapter won't offer an in-depth guide to XML and related technologies, it will demonstrate some of the power of these technologies. This chapter assumes that you know the basics of working with XML, XSL, XPath, and XQuery, but this knowledge is not required. Even if you can't spell XML, this chapter can help you develop an appreciation for XML and whet your appetite for learning more.

Bridging the Gap Between XML and Data Access

XML continues to be one of the hot technologies in the development world. More and more developers are finding that passing data as XML between different service layers or different applications provides tremendous flexibility and allows for interoperability between disparate systems.

You can use an XML document to store data such as information about a series of customers and each customer's order history. In some ways, an XML document is similar to an ADO.NET *DataSet* or an ADO *Recordset*. Each object can store multiple pieces of data in a well-defined structure.

With previous development technologies such as Microsoft Visual Basic "classic" or Microsoft Active Server Pages (ASP), developers traditionally used either XML or a data access technology such as ADO, but rarely both. Why? These earlier technologies were not designed to work together. For example, you can't easily move between an XML document and an ADO *Recordset*. You cannot control the schema generated when creating XML documents from an ADO *Recordset*, and you cannot read generic XML documents into an ADO *Recordset*.

One major goal of the ADO.NET development team was to bridge the gap between XML and data access so that you can easily integrate the two technologies. Loading data from an XML document into an ADO.NET *DataSet* and vice versa is simple. If you're working with SQL Server 2005 (or 2000), you can retrieve data from your database as XML and store the results in an ADO.NET *DataSet* or an XML document. You can also synchronize an ADO.NET *DataSet* and an XML document so that the changes made in one are visible in the other.

Let's take a closer look at these features.

Reading and Writing XML Data

First let's examine the different ways we can read and write XML data using the *DataSet* class.

The *DataSet* Class's XML Methods

The *DataSet* class has a series of methods that let you examine its contents as XML, as well as load XML data into the *DataSet*.

GetXml Method

The simplest of these XML methods is the *GetXml* method, which you can use to extract the contents of your *DataSet* and place them into a string. The *GetXml* method is simple, almost to a fault. It is not overloaded and accepts no parameters.

Figure 12-1 shows the contents of a *DataSet* in the Console window. The code that generates and displays this *DataSet* follows. The code snippet retrieves orders and line items for a customer using a function we'll reuse in subsequent code snippets—*GetOrderInfoForCustomer*.

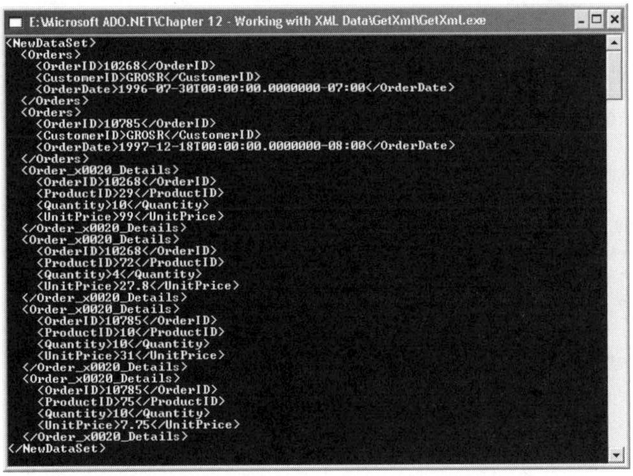

Figure 12-1   Using the *GetXml* method to view the contents of a *DataSet* as XML

Visual Basic

```
Dim ds As DataSet = GetOrderInfoForCustomer("GROSR")
Console.WriteLine(ds.GetXml())

Private Function GetOrderInfoForCustomer(ByVal CustomerID As String) _
                                    As DataSet

    Dim strConn, strSQL As String

    strConn = "Data Source=.\SQLExpress;" & _
            "Initial Catalog=Northwind;Integrated Security=True;"
    strSQL = "SELECT OrderID, CustomerID, OrderDate FROM Orders " & _
            "  WHERE CustomerID = @CustomerID;" & _
            "SELECT OrderID, ProductID, Quantity, UnitPrice " & _
            "  FROM [Order Details] " & _
            "  WHERE OrderID IN (SELECT OrderID FROM Orders " & _
            "                    WHERE CustomerID = @CustomerID)"
    Dim da As New SqlDataAdapter(strSQL, strConn)
    da.SelectCommand.Parameters.AddWithValue("@CustomerID", CustomerID)
    da.TableMappings.Add("Table", "Orders")
    da.TableMappings.Add("Table1", "Order Details")

    Dim ds As New DataSet()
    da.Fill(ds)

    Return ds
End Function
```

Visual C#

```
DataSet ds = GetOrderInfoForCustomer("GROSR");
Console.WriteLine(ds.GetXml());

static DataSet GetOrderInfoForCustomer(string CustomerID)
{
    string strConn, strSQL;
```

```
        strConn = @"Data Source=.\SQLExpress;" +
                "Initial Catalog=Northwind;Integrated Security=True;";
        strSQL = "SELECT OrderID, CustomerID, OrderDate FROM Orders " +
                " WHERE CustomerID = @CustomerID;" +
                "SELECT OrderID, ProductID, Quantity, UnitPrice " +
                " FROM [Order Details] " +
                " WHERE OrderID IN (SELECT OrderID FROM Orders " +
                "                       WHERE CustomerID = @CustomerID)";
        SqlDataAdapter da = new SqlDataAdapter(strSQL, strConn);
        da.SelectCommand.Parameters.AddWithValue("@CustomerID", CustomerID);
        da.TableMappings.Add("Table", "Orders");
        da.TableMappings.Add("Table1", "Order Details");

        DataSet ds = new DataSet();
        da.Fill(ds);

        return ds;
}
```

WriteXml and *ReadXml* Methods

As I noted earlier, the *GetXml* method is rather limited. The *DataSet* class's *WriteXml* method is more robust. It is overloaded so that you can write the contents of your *DataSet* to a file or to an object that implements the *Stream*, *TextWriter*, or *XmlWriter* interfaces.

The *WriteXml* method also lets you specify values from the *XmlWriteMode* enumeration for added control over the output. You can use this enumeration to choose whether to include the schema information for the *DataSet* and whether to write the contents of the *DataSet* in diffgram format, which we'll cover shortly.

The code snippet that follows shows how to use the *WriteXml* method to write the contents of a *DataSet* (including its schema) to a file, and it displays the contents of that file, as shown in Figure 12-2. I'd rather examine the contents of an XML document in Microsoft Internet Explorer than in the Console window because Internet Explorer will format the data nicely. The code snippet displays the XML on a Windows Form that includes a *WebBrowser* control to display the contents of the XML file, and therefore it requires a reference to the *System.Windows.Forms* namespace. The code snippet also relies on the *GetOrderInfoForCustomer* function from the previous code snippet.

Visual Basic

```
'Imports System.Windows.Forms
Dim ds As DataSet = GetOrderInfoForCustomer("GROSR")
Dim strPathToXml As String = "C:\MyData.XML"
ds.WriteXml(strPathToXml, XmlWriteMode.WriteSchema)
ShowXmlOnForm(strPathToXml, "DataSet.WriteXml")

Private Sub ShowXmlOnForm(ByVal Path As String, Caption As String)
    Using frm As New Form()
        frm.Width = 800
        frm.Height = 600
        frm.Text = Caption
```

```
        Dim browser As New WebBrowser()
        browser.Dock = DockStyle.Fill
        browser.Visible = True
        browser.Navigate(Path)
        frm.Controls.Add(browser)
        frm.ShowDialog()
    End Using
End Sub
```

Figure 12-2   Viewing the *DataSet* and its schema in a *WebBrowser* control

Visual C#

```csharp
//using System.Windows.Forms;
DataSet ds = GetOrderInfoForCustomer("GROSR");
string strPathToXml = @"C:\MyData.XML";
ds.WriteXml(strPathToXml, XmlWriteMode.WriteSchema);
ShowXmlOnForm(strPathToXml, "DataSet.WriteXml");

static void ShowXmlOnForm(string Path, string Caption)
{
    using (Form frm = new Form())
    {
        frm.Width = 800;
        frm.Height = 600;
        frm.Text = Caption;
        WebBrowser browser = new WebBrowser();
        browser.Dock = DockStyle.Fill;
        browser.Visible = true;
        browser.Navigate(Path);
        frm.Controls.Add(browser);
        frm.ShowDialog();
    }
}
```

> **Note**   The C# code snippet requires that the main thread be marked as single-threaded, which you can do by adding the following attribute to the main procedure:
>
> `[STAThread]`

The *DataSet* class has an overloaded *ReadXml* method that you can use to load data into your *DataSet*. The *ReadXml* method is basically the inverse of the *WriteXml* method. It can read XML data from a file or from an object that implements the *Stream*, *TextReader*, or *XmlReader* interfaces. You can also control how the method reads the contents of the XML data by supplying values from the *XmlReadMode* enumeration.

WriteXmlSchema, *ReadXmlSchema*, and *InferXmlSchema* Methods

The *DataSet* class also exposes *ReadXmlSchema* and *WriteXmlSchema* methods that allow you to read and write just the schema information for your *DataSet*. Each method supports working with files and objects that implement the *Stream*, *TextReader*, or *XmlReader* interface.

The *ReadXmlSchema* method can load schema information from an XML schema document using the XML Schema Definition (XSD) or XML Data Reduced (XDR) standard. It can also read an inline schema from an XML document.

The *DataSet* class also exposes an *InferXmlSchema* method, which works just like the *ReadXmlSchema* method except that *InferXmlSchema* has a second parameter. You can supply an array of strings in the second parameter to tell ADO.NET which namespaces you want to ignore in the XML document.

Inferring Schemas

Previous chapters have noted that supplying metadata or schema information in code yields better performance than generating this information programmatically at run time. The same holds true for inferring XML schemas, and the *ReadXml* method is a prime example.

Say that you use the *ReadXml* method to load data into a *DataSet* and that neither the XML document nor the *DataSet* has any schema information. You can't add rows of data to the *DataSet* if it has no schema information. The *ReadXml* method must first scan the entire XML document to determine the structure of the *DataSet* and then add the appropriate schema information to the *DataSet* before it adds the contents of the document to the *DataSet*. The larger the XML document, the greater the performance penalty incurred by inferring the schema from the document.

This approach can lead to another problem: You might not get the schema you want. ADO .NET will assume that all data types are strings, and it won't create any constraints. Why?

Imagine that your XML document contains a list of contacts and addresses (XML tags omitted) in the following format:

```
<MailingLabel>
  <First_Name>Randall</First_Name>
  <Last_Name>Stevens</Last_Name>
  <Address>123 Main St.</Address>
  <City>Sometown</City>
  <Region>MA</Region>
  <PostalCode>01234</PostalCode>
</MailingLabel>
```

Let's say that the contents of the document represent a small sampling of the actual data in your database. In other entries in your database, the contact might have a second address line or an address outside of the United States with a postal code in a different format. You must remember that if you ask ADO.NET to infer a schema from the contents of an XML document that contains no schema information, it will do its best to build an appropriate schema. You should therefore supply a schema whenever possible. One option is to include the schema when you save the contents of the *DataSet* by specifying *XmlWriteMode.WriteSchema* on the call to the *WriteXml* method. Another option is to save the *DataSet*'s schema in a separate file by calling *WriteXmlSchema* and loading that schema by calling *ReadXmlSchema* before loading the contents of the *DataSet*. Either way will help you improve the performance of your application while avoiding schema inference headaches.

ADO.NET Properties That Affect the Schema of Your XML Document

You can format an XML document in more than one way. As the saying goes, the devil is in the details. Look at the XML documents in Figures 12-3 and 12-4. They contain the same information, but they differ in their schema.

```
<?xml version="1.0" standalone="yes" ?>
- <NewDataSet>
  - <Orders>
      <OrderID>10268</OrderID>
      <CustomerID>GROSR</CustomerID>
      <OrderDate>1996-07-30T00:00:00-07:00</OrderDate>
    </Orders>
  - <Orders>
      <OrderID>10785</OrderID>
      <CustomerID>GROSR</CustomerID>
      <OrderDate>1997-12-18T00:00:00-08:00</OrderDate>
    </Orders>
  - <Order_x0020_Details>
      <OrderID>10268</OrderID>
      <ProductID>29</ProductID>
      <Quantity>10</Quantity>
      <UnitPrice>99.0000</UnitPrice>
    </Order_x0020_Details>
  - <Order_x0020_Details>
      <OrderID>10268</OrderID>
      <ProductID>72</ProductID>
      <Quantity>4</Quantity>
      <UnitPrice>27.8000</UnitPrice>
    </Order_x0020_Details>
  - <Order_x0020_Details>
      <OrderID>10785</OrderID>
      <ProductID>10</ProductID>
      <Quantity>10</Quantity>
      <UnitPrice>31.0000</UnitPrice>
    </Order_x0020_Details>
  - <Order_x0020_Details>
      <OrderID>10785</OrderID>
      <ProductID>75</ProductID>
      <Quantity>10</Quantity>
      <UnitPrice>7.7500</UnitPrice>
    </Order_x0020_Details>
  </NewDataSet>
```

Figure 12-3   An XML document that contains the order history for a customer

```
<?xml version="1.0" standalone="yes" ?>
- <MyNs:NewDataSet xmlns:MyNs="http://www.microsoft.com/MyNamespace">
  - <MyNs:Orders MyNs:OrderID="10268" MyNs:CustomerID="GROSR" MyNs:OrderDate="1996-07-30T00:00:00-07:00">
      <MyNs:Order_x0020_Details MyNs:OrderID="10268" MyNs:ProductID="29" MyNs:Quantity="10" MyNs:UnitPrice="99.0000" />
      <MyNs:Order_x0020_Details MyNs:OrderID="10268" MyNs:ProductID="72" MyNs:Quantity="4" MyNs:UnitPrice="27.8000" />
    </MyNs:Orders>
  - <MyNs:Orders MyNs:OrderID="10785" MyNs:CustomerID="GROSR" MyNs:OrderDate="1997-12-18T00:00:00-08:00">
      <MyNs:Order_x0020_Details MyNs:OrderID="10785" MyNs:ProductID="10" MyNs:Quantity="10" MyNs:UnitPrice="31.0000" />
      <MyNs:Order_x0020_Details MyNs:OrderID="10785" MyNs:ProductID="75" MyNs:Quantity="10" MyNs:UnitPrice="7.7500" />
    </MyNs:Orders>
  </MyNs:NewDataSet>
```

Figure 12-4   An XML document that contains the same order history in a different format

If you try to load data into a *DataSet* that already contains schema information, ADO.NET will ignore data that does not match up with the *DataSet* object's schema. It's therefore important that you match your *DataSet* object's schema to that of the data you want to load.

You can use properties of the objects within your *DataSet* to control the format that ADO.NET uses to read and write XML documents for your *DataSet*. In fact, I used the same *DataSet* object to generate both Figure 12-3 and Figure 12-4. I simply changed the values of these properties.

Names of Elements and Attributes

Notice that the names of the elements in Figures 12-3 and 12-4 are different. ADO.NET uses the name property for each object as the name of the corresponding element or attribute. The *DataSet* object's *DataSetName* property controls the name of the root element. Similarly, the *DataTable* object's *TableName* property and the *DataColumn* object's *ColumnName* property control the names that ADO.NET will use for the elements and attributes that correspond to those tables and columns.

Choosing Elements or Attributes

The two documents also differ in how they represent the order and detail data. Figure 12-3 uses elements to store this information, and Figure 12-4 uses attributes.

You can use the *DataColumn* object's *ColumnMapping* property to control this behavior. By default, the *ColumnMapping* property is set to *Element*. You can set the property to *Attribute* if you want to store the column's data in an attribute rather than an element. You can also set the *ColumnMapping* property to *Hidden* if you don't want the contents of the column to appear in your XML document.

Nesting Relational Data

In Figure 12-3, all the line items for the orders appear at the end of the document, whereas in Figure 12-4, the line items appear within the order. You can control whether the relational data is nested by setting the *Nested* property of the *DataRelation* object. By default, the property is set to *False*, which results in the format shown in Figure 12-3. Setting the *Nested* property to *True* will cause ADO.NET to nest the relational data as shown in Figure 12-4.

Namespaces and Prefixes

The *DataSet*, *DataTable*, and *DataColumn* objects all expose *Namespace* and *Prefix* properties. Both properties contain strings and are empty by default. The *DataSet* used in Figure 12-4 has each object's *Namespace* property set to *http://www.microsoft.com/MyNamespace* and the *Prefix* property set to *MyNs*.

Caching Changes and XML Documents

Shortly after a previous data access technology added the ability to read data in XML format, I spoke to a number of developers who used the technology to build a data access layer by pulling data from the database and storing the data as XML. They would then modify the contents of the XML document and expect that they could just rehydrate the data back into objects, which would somehow be able to submit the changes back to the database. It didn't work. Here's why.

In Chapter 6 and Chapter 10, I discussed how the ADO.NET *DataRow* stores the current and original contents of the row so that you can submit the changes back to the database. If you change the contents of an element or an attribute in an XML document, the document will not retain the original value for that object. If you then read that modified document into an ADO.NET *DataSet*, ADO.NET will not be able to tell whether any rows have been modified, let alone how they've been modified.

In fact, if you modify the contents of a *DataSet* and use the *WriteXml* method to save that data in an XML document using the code shown earlier in the chapter, you'll lose the changes. By default, the *WriteXml* method writes just the current contents of the rows to the document.

ADO.NET Diffgrams

As I discussed earlier, you can supply values from the *XmlWriteMode* enumeration when calling the *WriteXml* method. One of the entries in the enumeration is *DiffGram*. If you supply this value in the call to the *XmlWriteMode* method, ADO.NET will write both the current and original contents of the *DataSet* to the document in a diffgram. Figure 12-5 shows an example of this format. You can later read this document back into your *DataSet* and submit the pending changes to your database using your *SqlDataAdapter* objects.

The following code snippet generates the XML document shown in Figure 12-5. The code modifies the *DataSet*—modifying one row, deleting another, and adding a third—and then displays the contents of the *DataSet* as an XML diffgram. By looking at the document in the figure, you can see how the changes that the code makes to the *DataSet* correspond to the entries in the diffgram. The code uses the *ShowXmlOnForm* procedure defined in an earlier code snippet and thus requires a reference to the *System.Windows.Forms* namespace.

Figure 12-5   The contents of a *DataSet* stored in diffgram format

Visual Basic

```vb
Dim strConn, strSQL As String
strConn = "Data Source=.\SQLExpress;" & _
          "Initial Catalog=Northwind;Integrated Security=True;"
strSQL = "SELECT TOP 3 CustomerID, CompanyName FROM Customers"
Dim da As New SqlDataAdapter(strSQL, strConn)
Dim ds As New DataSet()
da.Fill(ds, "Customers")
Dim tbl As DataTable = ds.Tables("Customers")

'Leave the first customer unchanged.
'Modify the second customer.
tbl.Rows(1)("CompanyName") = "Modified Company Name"

'Delete the third customer.
tbl.Rows(2).Delete()

'Add a new customer.
tbl.Rows.Add("NEWCO", "New Company Name")

'Write the contents to an XML document in diffgram format
'and display the document in a WebBrowser control on a form.
Dim strPathToXml As String = "C:\MyData.XML"
ds.WriteXml(strPathToXml, XmlWriteMode.DiffGram)
ShowXmlOnForm(strPathToXml, "DataSet.WriteXml - Diffgram")
```

Visual C#

```csharp
string strConn, strSQL;
strConn = @"Data Source=.\SQLExpress;" +
          "Initial Catalog=Northwind;Integrated Security=True;";
```

```
strSQL = "SELECT TOP 3 CustomerID, CompanyName FROM Customers";
SqlDataAdapter da = new SqlDataAdapter(strSQL, strConn);
DataSet ds = new DataSet();
da.Fill(ds, "Customers");
DataTable tbl = ds.Tables["Customers"];

//Leave the first customer unchanged.
//Modify the second customer.
tbl.Rows[1]["CompanyName"] = "Modified Company Name";

//Delete the third customer.
tbl.Rows[2].Delete();

//Add a new customer.
tbl.Rows.Add("NEWCO", "New Company Name");

//Write the contents to an XML document in diffgram format
//and display the document in WebBrowser control on a form.
string strPathToXml = @"C:\MyData.XML";
ds.WriteXml(strPathToXml, XmlWriteMode.DiffGram);
ShowXmlOnForm(strPathToXml, "DataSet.WriteXml - Diffgram");
```

New to ADO.NET 2.0: *DataTable*-level XML Features

Developers using version 1.x of the .NET Framework were occasionally frustrated that XML methods were available only on the *DataSet* class. In version 2.0 of the .NET Framework, the ADO.NET team has added those methods to the *DataTable* class, as well. Using these methods on the *DataTable* class, you can now read or write the contents of a single *DataTable* rather than the entire *DataSet*. You can also use these methods with a *DataTable* that does not reside within a *DataSet*.

DataSet + XmlDocument = XmlDataDocument

The previous code snippets used some of the *DataSet* class's XML features, but they weren't terribly exciting. If you're using these features simply to store the contents of a *DataSet* in a file and later to read that data back into your *DataSet*, the fact that ADO.NET is storing the data as XML is irrelevant.

If you're really interested in working with the contents of a *DataSet* in XML format, you might want to consider loading the data into an *XmlDocument* object. This class has a *Load* method that you can use to load the contents of an XML file, so you could use a *DataSet* object's *WriteXml* method to create your XML file and then call an *XmlDocument* object's *Load* method to load the file. That might sound fine at first, but you'll have two objects storing the same data and you'll have no simple way to synchronize them. If you want to keep the objects synchronized and you change the contents of one object, you'll need to locate and modify the corresponding data in the other object. What a hassle!

Using the *XmlDataDocument* Class

The simple solution to this problem is to use an *XmlDataDocument* object. You can think of an *XmlDataDocument* as an *XmlDocument* that knows how to communicate with a *DataSet* object. The *XmlDataDocument* class is derived from the *XmlDocument* class, so an *XmlDataDocument* object exposes all the same features as an *XmlDocument*.

The *XmlDataDocument* class adds two key features. First, it lets you easily load the contents of a *DataSet* into an *XmlDocument*, and vice versa. Second, the *XmlDataDocument* also synchronizes itself with the *DataSet*. If the *DataSet* object contains data, that same data will be available through the *XmlDataDocument* object. Also, when you change the contents of one object, that change will affect the other.

Accessing Your *DataSet* as an XML Document

If you're an XML programmer who's used to working with XML documents to access data, you'll find it easy to use the *XmlDataDocument* object to access the contents of a *DataSet* through XML interfaces.

For example, you can create an *XmlDataDocument* synchronized with your *DataSet* to use XPath queries to examine the contents of the *DataSet*. The following code snippet creates an *XmlDataDocument* synchronized with a *DataSet* that contains order and line item information for a customer. The code then uses XPath queries to extract the contents of an order from the *XmlDataDocument* object. It uses the *GetOrderInfoForCustomer* function from previous code snippets, and it requires you to use the appropriate construct for the language to reference the *System.Xml* namespace.

Visual Basic

```
'Imports System.Xml

Dim ds As DataSet = GetOrderInfoForCustomer("GROSR")
Dim xmlDataDoc As New XmlDataDocument(ds)
Dim strXPathQuery As String
strXPathQuery = "/NewDataSet/Orders[OrderID=10268]"
Dim nodOrder As XmlNode = xmlDataDoc.SelectSingleNode(strXPathQuery)
Console.WriteLine("OrderID: {0}  CustomerID: {1}  OrderDate: {2:d}", _
                  nodOrder.ChildNodes(0).InnerText, _
                  nodOrder.ChildNodes(1).InnerText, _
                  DateTime.Parse(nodOrder.ChildNodes(2).InnerText))
Console.WriteLine("Line Items:")
strXPathQuery = "/NewDataSet/Order_x0020_Details[OrderID=10268]"
For Each nodDetail As XmlNode In xmlDataDoc.SelectNodes(strXPathQuery)
    Console.WriteLine("  ProductID: {0,2}, Quantity: {1,2}, " & _
                  "UnitPrice: {2:c}", _
                  nodDetail.ChildNodes(1).InnerText, _
                  nodDetail.ChildNodes(2).InnerText, _
                  Decimal.Parse(nodDetail.ChildNodes(3).InnerText))
Next nodDetail
```

Visual C#

```
//using System.Xml;

DataSet ds = GetOrderInfoForCustomer("GROSR");
XmlDataDocument xmlDataDoc = new XmlDataDocument(ds);
string strXPathQuery = "/NewDataSet/Orders[OrderID=10268]";
XmlNode nodOrder = xmlDataDoc.SelectSingleNode(strXPathQuery);
Console.WriteLine("OrderID: {0}  CustomerID: {1}  OrderDate: {2:d}",
                  nodOrder.ChildNodes[0].InnerText,
                  nodOrder.ChildNodes[1].InnerText,
                  DateTime.Parse(nodOrder.ChildNodes[2].InnerText));
Console.WriteLine("Line Items:");
strXPathQuery = "/NewDataSet/Order_x0020_Details[OrderID=10268]";
foreach (XmlNode nodDetail in xmlDataDoc.SelectNodes(strXPathQuery))
    Console.WriteLine("  ProductID: {0,2}, Quantity: {1,2}, " +
                      "UnitPrice: {2:c}",
                      nodDetail.ChildNodes[1].InnerText,
                      nodDetail.ChildNodes[2].InnerText,
                      Decimal.Parse(nodDetail.ChildNodes[3].InnerText));
```

> **Note**   The XPath query in the preceding code may look odd since it references "Order_x0020
> _Details". "Order Details" is not a valid name for an XML node because it contains a space. The
> *DataSet* automatically encodes the name to generate a valid name. You can manually encode
> names using the *EncodeName* method on the *XmlConvert* class. *XmlConvert.EncodeName*("Order
> Details") returns "Order_x0020_Details".

Caching Updates to the XML Document

Earlier in the chapter, I pointed out that XML documents don't maintain state in a way that
lets you later submit changes to your database. The *XmlDataDocument* class actually provides
this functionality by synchronizing the XML document and the *DataSet*. As you modify the
contents of the XML document, the *XmlDataDocument* object modifies the corresponding
data in the *DataSet* object. The *DataSet* object then has all the information it needs to submit
the change to the database.

The following code snippet demonstrates this functionality. The code uses an XPath query to
locate an order and modifies the contents of the child node that corresponds to the CustomerID
for the order. The code then examines the contents of the corresponding *DataRow* to show
that both the current and original values for the order's CustomerID are available in the
DataRow. You can use a *SqlDataAdapter* with the necessary updating logic to submit this
change to your database.

Just before modifying the contents of the XML document, the code sets the *EnforceConstraints*
property of the *DataSet* object to *False*. Without this line of code, the snippet would generate
an exception. You will receive an error if you modify the contents of a *DataSet* using an *Xml-
DataDocument* if the *DataSet* associated with the *XmlDataDocument* has its *EnforceConstraints*
property set to *True*.

Visual Basic

```
'Imports System.Xml
Dim ds As DataSet = GetOrderInfoForCustomer("GROSR")
Dim tblOrders As DataTable = ds.Tables("Orders")
tblOrders.PrimaryKey = New DataColumn() {tblOrders.Columns("OrderID")}
Dim xmlDataDoc As New XmlDataDocument(ds)
Dim strXPathQuery As String = "/NewDataSet/Orders[OrderID=10268]"
Dim nodOrder As XmlNode = xmlDataDoc.SelectSingleNode(strXPathQuery)
ds.EnforceConstraints = False
nodOrder.ChildNodes(1).InnerText = "ALFKI"
ds.EnforceConstraints = True
Dim row As DataRow = tblOrders.Rows.Find(10268)
Console.WriteLine("OrderID: {0}", row("OrderID"))
Console.WriteLine("  Current  CustomerID: {0}", row("CustomerID"))
Console.WriteLine("  Original CustomerID: {0}", _
                  row("CustomerID", DataRowVersion.Original))
```

Visual C#

```
//using System.Xml;
DataSet ds = GetOrderInfoForCustomer("GROSR");
DataTable tblOrders = ds.Tables["Orders"];
tblOrders.PrimaryKey = new DataColumn[] {tblOrders.Columns["OrderID"]};
XmlDataDocument xmlDataDoc = new XmlDataDocument(ds);
string strXPathQuery = "/NewDataSet/Orders[OrderID=10268]";
XmlNode nodOrder = xmlDataDoc.SelectSingleNode(strXPathQuery);
ds.EnforceConstraints = false;
nodOrder.ChildNodes[1].InnerText = "ALFKI";
ds.EnforceConstraints = true;
DataRow row = tblOrders.Rows.Find(10268);
Console.WriteLine("OrderID: {0}", row["OrderID"]);
Console.WriteLine("  Current  CustomerID: {0}", row["CustomerID"]);
Console.WriteLine("  Original CustomerID: {0}",
                  row["CustomerID", DataRowVersion.Original]);
```

As you can see, the changes are now cached in the *DataSet*. We could then use a *SqlData-Adapter* to submit those cached changes back to the database.

Using SQL Server 2005's XML Features

All databases support XML, sort of. You can generally store XML data in a text-based field, but that's nominal support at best.

SQL Server 2005 provides rich server-side XML features and we'll cover these features in the "SQL Server 2005's XML Type" section later in the chapter. But first, let's briefly review the XML features available in SQL Server 2000.

SQL Server 2000 added the ability to take data stored in typical relational columns and return the data as a stream of XML through SELECT ... FOR XML queries. However, SQL Server 2000 did not provide truly rich server-side XML features. For example, there was no way to say that a column had to contain XML, let alone XML that conformed to a particular schema. SQL Server 2000 could not directly handle an XPath query, let alone support indexes to improve the performance of such a query. Finally, SELECT ... FOR XML queries provide very limited options over how you format the results of your query. SQL Server 2000 addressed this limitation through rich client-side XML features such as template queries and the SQL XML .NET Data Provider.

SQL Server 2005 addresses all of these limitations. XML is now a fully supported SQL Server data type. You can create database columns of XML type. You can also register XML schemas and require that a column conforms to a particular schema. You can use XPath, a language designed to query XML documents, when querying SQL Server 2005 XML columns. SQL Server 2005 also supports indexing XML columns to provide better performance for XPath queries. Finally, SQL Server supports Xquery, a rich XML querying language that lets you construct queries that return data as XML. XQuery allows you to include both XML columns and standard columns (int, nvarchar, and so on) in the query results. With XQuery, you have fine-grained control over the format of the query results without having to transform the data from within your client code.

This portion of the chapter will provide an introduction to those features and, hopefully, whet your appetite for more. There are entire books devoted to SQL Server 2005's XML features.

SQL Server 2005's XML Type

You can create an XML column in a SQL Server 2005 table just as easily as you would any other column via the CREATE TABLE query:

```
CREATE TABLE MyTable (MyIntColumn int PRIMARY KEY,
                      MyXmlColumn xml)
```

The *MyXmlColumn* in the table can now contain XML data, but SQL Server 2005 does not validate that data. The simplest way to validate the data is to register an XML schema, and then associate the column with the XML schema.

```
CREATE XML SCHEMA COLLECTION MyXmlSchema AS ...
CREATE TABLE MyTable (MyIntColumn int PRIMARY KEY,
                      MyXmlColumn xml (MyXmlSchema))
```

For the sake of brevity, I've omitted the actual schema here in the CREATE XML SCHEMA COLLECTION statement. You can specify the schema as an in-line static value, or you can supply a parameter.

SQL Server will now validate incoming data to ensure that the data conforms to the schema specified. By default, SQL Server will allow a value in the column to contain multiple documents that conform to the specified schema. If you want to ensure that values in the column can contain only a single document that conforms to the specified schema, use the DOCUMENT keyword, as shown here:

```
CREATE TABLE MyTable (MyIntColumn int PRIMARY KEY,
                      MyXmlColumn xml (DOCUMENT MyXmlSchema))
```

Retrieving XML Data via ADO.NET

XML data that's retrieved by a *SqlCommand* or *SqlDataAdapter* will be returned as a .NET *String* by *default*. In other words, you can simply call the *GetString* method on the *SqlData-Reader* without having to add specialized code to cast the data to another type.

If you'd prefer to use a stream-based approach to access your XML data, you can use the new *SqlXml* class in the *System.Data.SqlTypes* namespace.

Retrieving data into this type from a *SqlDataReader* follows the same pattern as with other types in the *SqlTypes* namespace, as explained in Chapter 4. Specifically, to retrieve data from a *SqlDataReader* using the *SqlXml* type, use the *GetSqlXml* method.

Once you've retrieved the contents of a column into a *SqlXml* object, you can call the *SqlType* object's *CreateReader* method to access the contents of the column as an *XmlReader*.

As with other classes in the *SqlTypes* namespace, the *SqlXml* class exposes *IsNull* and *Value* properties. The *SqlXml* class's constructor accepts either a *Stream* or an *XmlReader* and, once instantiated, its contents cannot be changed.

Submitting XML Data via ADO.NET

Submitting XML data via ADO.NET is just as straightforward. Say that you have the following parameterized query that you want to execute to insert a new row into the table defined earlier:

```
INSERT INTO MyTable (MyIntColumn, MyXmlColumn)
    VALUES (@MyIntColumn, @MyXmlColumn)
```

As with the XML data-retrieval scenarios, you can supply the value for the XML parameter as either a simple .NET *String* or as a *SqlXml* object, as shown in the following code snippet:

Visual Basic
```
'Imports System.Xml
'Imports System.Data.SqlTypes

'Create the parameterized query
Dim cn As SqlConnection
'Supply a connection string
'...
cn.Open()
Dim cmd As SqlCommand = cn.CreateCommand()
cmd.CommandText = "INSERT INTO MyTable (MyIntColumn, MyXmlColumn) " & _
                "    VALUES (@MyIntColumn, @MyXmlColumn)"
cmd.Parameters.AddWithValue("@MyIntColumn", 1)

'Supply an XML value using a simple string
Dim strValue As String = "<Tag>Value</Tag>"
```

```
cmd.Parameters.AddWithValue("@MyXmlColumn", strValue)

'Or supply an XML value using the SqlXml class
Dim strPathToXml As String
'Specify the path to the XML file to load
'...
Dim sqlxmlValue As New SqlXml(New XmlTextReader(strPathToXml ))
cmd.Parameters.AddWithValue("@MyXmlColumn", sqlxmlValue)

'Execute the query
cmd.ExecuteNonQuery()
```

Visual C#

```
//using System.Xml;
//using System.Data.SqlTypes;

//Create the parameterized query
SqlConnection cn;
//Supply a connection string
//...
cn.Open();
SqlCommand cmd = cn.CreateCommand();
cmd.CommandText = "INSERT INTO MyTable (MyIntColumn, MyXmlColumn) " +
                "    VALUES (@MyIntColumn, @MyXmlColumn)";
cmd.Parameters.AddWithValue("@MyIntColumn", 1);

//Supply an XML value using a simple string
string strValue = "<Tag>Value</Tag>";
cmd.Parameters.AddWithValue("@MyXmlColumn", strValue);

//Or supply an XML value using the SqlXml class
string strPathToXml;
//Specify the path to the XML file to load
//...
SqlXml sqlxmlValue = new SqlXml(new XmlTextReader(strPathToXml));
cmd.Parameters.AddWithValue("@MyXmlColumn", sqlxmlValue);

//Execute the query
cmd.ExecuteNonQuery();
```

Adding an OrderDetailsAsXml Column to the Northwind Orders Table

The previous code snippet was a theoretical one—the table does not really exist in the database (unless you ran the CREATE TABLE query to create it), and the XML file to load does not exist. The majority of samples in this book have focused on the Northwind sample database, but that database does not make use of SQL Server 2005's XML features.

Rather than switch gears and use a different sample database, consider the following scenario. The order detail information for each order, previously stored in the Order Details table, is stored in an XML column in the corresponding row in the Order table. The XML schema for the column is defined as follows:

```
<schema id='OrderDetail' xmlns='http://www.w3.org/2001/XMLSchema'>
  <element name='OrderDetail'>
    <complexType>
      <attribute name='ProductID' type='int' use='required' />
      <attribute name='UnitPrice' type='decimal' use='required' />
      <attribute name='Quantity' type='short' use='required' />
      <attribute name='Discount' type='float' use='required' />
    </complexType>
  </element>
</schema>
```

Given that schema, a query for order information for a particular customer would return the information in the following table:

OrderID	CustomerID	OrderDetailsAsXml
10268	GROSR	`<OrderDetail ProductID="29" Quantity="10" UnitPrice="99" Discount="0" /><OrderDetail ProductID="72" Quantity="4" UnitPrice="27.8" Discount="0" />`
10785	GROSR	`<OrderDetail ProductID="10" Quantity="10" UnitPrice="31" Discount="0" /><OrderDetail ProductID="75" Quantity="10" UnitPrice="7.75" Discount="0" />`

Note We could get more precise with the schema—specifying that the attributes cannot be negative, that values for ProductID must be unique, and so on—but this is intended to be a simple introductory example. For more information on XML schema features available, see SQL Server Books Online.

Now that we have this column, what will we do with it? A fairly common SQL query example is to list orders that contain a particular product. The SQL for that query looks like this:

```
SELECT O.OrderID, C.CompanyName, OD.Quantity
  FROM Orders O
    JOIN Customers C ON C.CustomerID = O.CustomerID
    JOIN [Order Details] OD ON OD.OrderID = O.OrderID
    JOIN Products P ON P.ProductID = OD.ProductID
  WHERE P.ProductName = @ProductName
```

If you run this query and specify a product name of "Chocolade", you'll get the results shown in Figure 12-6.

Now that the line items for the order are contained as XML in the OrderDetailsAsXml column, the query required to retrieve this information must change. We'll look at two examples of how we can use SQL Server 2005's new XML features to retrieve this information. First, we'll retrieve the same data using an XPath query. Second, we'll use the power of XQuery to format the results of the query as XML.

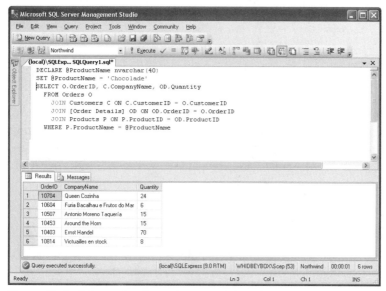

Figure 12-6   Information for orders containing Chocolade

Example: Adding the OrderDetailsAsXml Column to the Northwind Orders Table

The downloadable sample code for this chapter includes a procedure called *"SqlServer2005-Xml_CreateOrderDetailsAsXmlColumn"* that creates this column and populates it with the appropriate order information. The code also creates and registers the XML schema described, associating the column with the schema so that SQL Server will ensure incoming data conforms to the specified schema. You'll need to run this code once to create the column before running the other SQL Server 2005 XML Data Type samples.

Executing an XPath Query to Retrieve Data

Information about the line items for an order (ProductID, Quantity, UnitPrice, Discount) are now stored as XML in the OrderDetailsAsXml column. So how do we find the orders that contain a particular product?

XPath is a language designed to query XML documents. In fact, the following XPath could be used to query for the line items that contain a ProductID of 48—Chocolade:

```
/OrderDetail[@ProductID=48]
```

SQL Server 2005 supports XPath queries through different methods on the XML data type. In this case, we want to use the XPath query in the WHERE clause to find just the orders that contain such line items. The *exist* method on the XML data type is designed to be used from within the WHERE clause in just this type of situation. The method returns 1 if the XPath query was satisfied, 0 if it was not, and NULL if the XML data was NULL. In this case, we would want to check for columns for which calling the *exist* method and specifying the XPath query returns 1. So our query would look like this:

```
SELECT O.OrderID, C.CompanyName
  FROM Orders O
    JOIN Customers C ON O.CustomerID = C.CustomerID
    WHERE O.OrderDetailsAsXml.exist('/OrderDetail[@ProductID=48]') = 1
```

In the scenario described, we don't know the ProductID for the product, only the product name. We can query the Products table for the ProductID value supplying the product name. Thankfully, SQL Server provides a way for us to reference values from other columns in the XPath query using the *sql:column* function. For example, this XPath query uses the value from the ProductID column in the resultset and compares it against the ProductID attribute in the XML column:

```
/OrderDetail[@ProductID=sql:column("P.ProductID")]
```

We can modify the previous query to include the Products table and supply the product name through a variable and then use the *sql:column* function to reference the ProductID value in the XPath query, as shown here:

```
SELECT O.OrderID, C.CompanyName
  FROM Orders O
    JOIN Customers C ON O.CustomerID = C.CustomerID
    CROSS JOIN Products P
  WHERE P.ProductName = @ProductName AND
        O.OrderDetailsAsXml.exist(
           '/OrderDetail[@ProductID=sql:column("P.ProductID")]') = 1
```

Now we only need to add the Quantity of the product ordered in the line item.

The XML data type also supports *shredding*, which means ripping apart the XML content for specific values, via XPath. In this case, we want to return just the *Quantity* attribute for the OrderDetail element that contains the desired product, so we can use the following XPath query to access that value:

```
/OrderDetail[@ProductID=sql:column("P.ProductID")]/@Quantity
```

SQL Server supports shredding XML through the *value* method on the XML data type. The first parameter for the method takes an XPath query, and the second parameter takes the name of the desired SQL data type. SQL Server might require you to modify the XPath query slightly to ensure it returns only a single value, by enclosing the XPath query in parentheses and then appending [1] to the end, as shown here:

```
(/OrderDetail[@ProductID=sql:column("P.ProductID")]/@Quantity)[1]
```

If you omit the [1] from the query, SQL Server will return an error message saying "'value()' requires a singleton (or empty sequence)", indicating that SQL Server expects the XPath query to return at most single value, which is what the [1] in the query accomplishes.

We can now include the quantity of items ordered in the results of the query by using the value method on the OrderDetailsAsXml column, as shown here:

```
SELECT O.OrderID, C.CompanyName,
       O.OrderDetailsAsXml.value(
'(/OrderDetail[@ProductID=sql:column("P.ProductID")]/@Quantity)[1]',
                                 'smallint') AS Quantity
  FROM Orders O
    JOIN Customers C ON O.CustomerID = C.CustomerID
    CROSS JOIN Products P
  WHERE P.ProductName = @ProductName AND
        O.OrderDetailsAsXml.exist(
            '/OrderDetail[@ProductID=sql:column("P.ProductID")]') = 1
```

Using *sql:variable* to Avoid Potential SQL Injection

The *exist* and *value* methods on the XML data type accept only string literals. You cannot pass parameters into these methods. As a result, there might be a natural tendency to concatenate strings to construct the literal strings to pass to these methods. Do not add input from the user directly into these values. Instead, use the *sql:variable* function, which is similar to the *sql:column* function.

Imagine for a moment that the OrderDetailsAsXml column contained product names, rather than ProductID. The user still specifies the product name. You should not trust the user input to construct an XPath query like the following:

```
'/OrderDetail[@ProductName="Chocolade")]'
```

Rather, you should assign the user input to the *@ProductName* parameter, as in previous examples, and then reference that parameter using the *sql:variable* function as shown here:

```
'/OrderDetail[@ProductName=sql:variable("@ProductName"))]'
```

> **Note**   The product name does not contain a typo. The product in the sample Northwind database is Belgian chocolate—thus, chocolade.

Improving Performance of XPath Queries via XML Indexes

The preceding query will, by default, require a table scan of the Orders table. Why? Because there's no way for SQL Server to know which rows in the Orders table contain the desired product without examining the contents of the OrderDetailsAsXml column for each row.

We can improve the performance of this query by indexing the XML column using a query like this:

```
CREATE PRIMARY XML INDEX IDX_OrderDetailsAsXml
    ON Orders(OrderDetailsAsXml)
```

The sample code used to create the OrderDetailsAsXml column also creates an XML index on the column using this query. For more information on XML indexes, see SQL Server Books Online.

Example: Querying the OrderDetailsAsXml Column Using XPath

The sample code for this chapter includes a procedure called *"SqlServer2005Xml_GetOrders-ContainingProduct_XPath"* that uses the XPath expression described earlier to retrieve information about orders that contain a particular product, given its name.

Retrieving Query Results as XML Using XQuery

The previous examples demonstrated how to use the power of XPath to query XML columns in a SQL Server 2005 database and return the data in a standard resultset. But what if you want to return data as XML rather than as rows and columns?

SQL Server 2000 introduced a "FOR XML" clause that allows you to convert a standard result into XML. Although the "FOR XML" clause is a powerful feature, it's also rather limited in the options it provides for the schema for the results. Trying to get the results into the desired schema generally required client-side processing, using template queries, an XSL transform, or both.

SQL Server 2005 supports XQuery, an XML language that allows users to query and format data. It's the second portion of the definition, formatting, that distinguishes it from XPath. XQuery is a very powerful and flexible language. This section will show how you can use XQuery to format the results of the previous query as XML. In some ways, the example is akin to writing "Hello, World!" to a Console window in C# or Visual Basic.

Format for the Desired Results

To demonstrate just some of the power of XQuery, let's stick with the same scenario described earlier where we want to return information about orders that contain a particular product but add the following twist—we want the results to be returned as a stream of XML data that looks like this:

```
<Order OrderID="10403" CompanyName="Ernst Handel" Quantity="70" />
<Order OrderID="10453" CompanyName="Around the Horn" Quantity="15" />
...
```

Thankfully, formatting query results with XQuery is a breeze.

XQuery is, in many ways, similar to technologies such as ASP.NET or ASP. With ASP.NET, you create HTML that includes server-side scripting code. XQuery takes a similar approach, letting you combine XML content and XQuery code. The XQuery code is delimited between curly braces { }. The goal is to generate the following content for each row found using the XPath query described earlier:

```
<Order OrderID="{ Value from OrderID column }"
       CompanyName="{ Value from CompanyName column }"
       Quantity="{ Value from Quantity attribute in OrderDetail }" />
```

We can use the *sql:column* function from the previous example in XQuery to assign values from the CompanyName and OrderID columns to the corresponding attributes, as shown here:

```
<Order OrderID="{ sql:column("O.OrderID") }"
       CompanyName="{ sql:column("C.CompanyName") }" />
```

We can also construct the XML nodes programmatically. For example, the following XQuery expression is equivalent to the previous one:

```
element Order {
  attribute CompanyName { sql:column("C.CompanyName") },
  attribute OrderID { sql:column("O.OrderID") }
}
```

I find this second approach to be clearer for examples.

Merely formatting columns from the resultset as attributes is unimpressive because you can get the same results from a SELECT ... FOR XML query. So let's do something a little more complex. Let's make sure the value that appears in the *CompanyName* attribute contains, at most, 20 characters from the CompanyName column. If the CompanyName column is longer than 20 characters, we'll trim the value to 20 characters and append "..."; otherwise, we'll just return the full value. We can accomplish this using an *if* statement and the *string-length*, *concat*, and *substring* functions, as shown here:

```
element Order {
  attribute CompanyName {
    if (string-length(sql:column("C.CompanyName")) <= 20)
      then sql:column("C.CompanyName")
      else concat(substring(sql:column("C.CompanyName"), 0, 20), "...")
  },
  attribute OrderID {
    sql:column("O.OrderID")
  }
}
```

Now that's a little more impressive. Hopefully, this example helps convey the fact that XQuery is a powerful language.

All that's left to do is add the value from the *Quantity* attribute in the OrderDetail element that contained the desired product. The previous section of the chapter demonstrated how to find that element using the following XPath query:

```
/OrderDetail[@ProductID=sql:column("P.ProductID")]
```

XQuery supports XPath queries, so we can use this XPath query and specify that we want to return the value of the *Quantity* attribute for the OrderDetail element. Now the XQuery expression looks like this:

```
element Order {
  attribute CompanyName {
    if (string-length(sql:column("C.CompanyName")) <= 20)
      then sql:column("C.CompanyName")
      else concat(substring(sql:column("C.CompanyName"), 0, 20), "...")
  },
  attribute OrderID { sql:column("O.OrderID") },
  attribute Quantity {
    /OrderDetail[@ProductID=sql:column("P.ProductID")]/@Quantity
  }
}
```

Now it's time to use this XQuery expression. SQL Server 2005's XML data type supports executing XQuery expressions via the *query* method. Like the *exist* and *value* methods, the *query* method takes a string literal. If we combine the XQuery expression with our SQL and XPath queries, the result is the following:

```
SELECT OrderDetailsAsXml.query(
'element Order {
  attribute CompanyName {
    if (string-length(sql:column("C.CompanyName")) <= 20)
      then sql:column("C.CompanyName")
      else concat(substring(sql:column("C.CompanyName"), 0, 20), "...")
  },
  attribute OrderID { sql:column("O.OrderID") },
  attribute Quantity {
    /OrderDetail[@ProductID=sql:column("P.ProductID")]/@Quantity
  }
}') AS OrderDetail
  FROM Orders O
    INNER JOIN Customers C ON C.CustomerID = O.CustomerID
    CROSS JOIN Products P
  WHERE P.ProductName = @ProductName AND
        O.OrderDetailsAsXml.exist(
            '/OrderDetail[@ProductID=sql:column("P.ProductID")]') = 1
```

Executing this query will now return the desired results, which are shown in Figure 12-7.

Figure 12-7   Information for orders containing Chocolade formatted as XML by an XQuery expression

Example: Retrieving Order Information as XML Using XQuery

The downloadable sample code for this chapter includes a procedure called "*SqlServer2005-Xml_GetOrdersContainingProduct_XQuery*". The procedure constructs and executes a query using the XQuery and XPath expressions described to display the desired orders as XML as shown in Figure 12-7.

Retrieving XML Data from SQL Server 2000 via SELECT...FOR XML

After covering the XML features included with SQL Server 2005, discussing SELECT ... FOR XML queries is somewhat anticlimactic. I've included the information here for developers who are still using SQL Server 2000 in their applications and therefore can't use SQL Server 2005's XML features.

Executing a SELECT ... FOR XML Query in SQL Server Query Analyzer

The simplest way to execute such a query and examine the results is to execute the query in SQL Server Query Analyzer. Let's take a simple query that retrieves the values of the CustomerID and CompanyName columns for the first two rows in the Customers table:

```
SELECT TOP 2 CustomerID, CompanyName FROM Customers
```

And then let's append the following code to the query:

```
FOR XML AUTO, ELEMENTS
```

The FOR XML portion tells SQL Server to return the results of the query in XML format. AUTO tells SQL Server to name the element for each row in the result set after the table that is referenced in the query. ELEMENTS tells SQL Server to store the value of each column in an element. By default, SQL Server would return this information in attributes rather than in elements.

> **Note**   If you're using a SELECT ... FOR XML query with SQL Server 2005, you can also include a ROOT clause in the query. The ROOT clause adds a single top-level element to the result using the name specified. Adding a top-level element can be helpful because a series of XML nodes that does not contain a top-level element is an XML fragment rather than an XML document.
>
> ```
> SELECT TOP 2 CustomerID, CompanyName FROM Customers
>     FOR XML AUTO, ELEMENTS, ROOT('RootNode')
> ```

Choose Results In Text from the Query menu, and then execute the query. The results will look like those shown in Figure 12-8, except that in the figure, I've manually formatted the data to make it easier to read.

Of course, fetching XML data into SQL Server Management Studio isn't terribly helpful. Let's look at how to retrieve this data into more accessible objects using ADO.NET.

The *SqlCommand* class is designed to help handle results of SQL Server SELECT ... FOR XML queries by exposing an *ExecuteXmlReader* method that returns an *XmlReader* object, which you can use to access the results of the query. The OLE DB, ODBC, and OracleClient .NET Data Providers that are included with the .NET Framework do not offer a similar method.

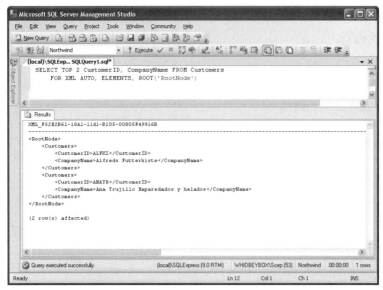

Figure 12-8   Executing a FOR XML query in SQL Server Management Studio

Loading the Results of Your Query into an *XmlDocument* Object

You can take the *XmlReader* returned by the call to *ExecuteXmlReader* and use it to populate an *XmlDocument* with the following code:

Visual Basic

```vbnet
'Imports System.Xml
Dim strConn, strSQL As String
strConn = "Data Source=.\SQLExpress;" & _
          "Initial Catalog=Northwind;Integrated Security=True;"
strSQL = "SELECT TOP 2 CustomerID, CompanyName FROM Customers " & _
          "FOR XML AUTO, ELEMENTS"

Dim doc As New XmlDocument
Dim root As XmlNode = doc.CreateElement("ROOT")
doc.AppendChild(root)
Using cn As New SqlConnection(strConn)
    cn.Open()
    Dim cmd As New SqlCommand(strSQL, cn)
    Using rdr As XmlReader = cmd.ExecuteXmlReader()
        Do While Not rdr.EOF
            root.AppendChild(doc.ReadNode(rdr))
        Loop
        rdr.Close()
    End Using
    cn.Close()
End Using

Dim strPathToXml As String = "C:\MyData.XML"
doc.Save(strPathToXml)
ShowXmlOnForm(strPathToXml, "SqlCommand.ExecuteXmlReader")
```

Visual C#

```csharp
//using System.Xml;
string strConn, strSQL;
strConn = @"Data Source=.\SQLExpress;" +
          "Initial Catalog=Northwind;Integrated Security=True;";
strSQL = "SELECT TOP 2 CustomerID, CompanyName FROM Customers " +
         "FOR XML AUTO, ELEMENTS";

XmlDocument doc = new XmlDocument();
XmlNode root = doc.CreateElement("ROOT");
doc.AppendChild(root);
using (SqlConnection cn = new SqlConnection(strConn))
{
    cn.Open();
    SqlCommand cmd = new SqlCommand(strSQL, cn);
    using (XmlReader rdr = cmd.ExecuteXmlReader())
    {
        while (!rdr.EOF)
            root.AppendChild(doc.ReadNode(rdr));
        rdr.Close();
    }
    cn.Close();
}

string strPathToXml = @"C:\MyData.XML";
doc.Save(strPathToXml);
ShowXmlOnForm(strPathToXml, "SqlCommand.ExecuteXmlReader");
```

This code would be simpler if the query returned an XML document rather than an XML fragment. As noted earlier, if you're using SQL Server 2005, you can use the ROOT clause in your SELECT ... FOR XML query and then simplify the code that loads the data into the *XmlDocument*, changing it to the following:

Visual Basic

```vb
Dim doc As New XmlDocument
Using cn As New SqlConnection(strConn)
    cn.Open()
    Dim cmd As New SqlCommand(strSQL, cn)
    Using rdr As XmlReader = cmd.ExecuteXmlReader()
        doc.Load(rdr)
        rdr.Close()
    End Using
    cn.Close()
End Using
```

Visual C#

```csharp
XmlDocument doc = new XmlDocument();
using (SqlConnection cn = new SqlConnection(strConn))
{
    cn.Open();
    SqlCommand cmd = new SqlCommand(strSQL, cn);
    using (XmlReader rdr = cmd.ExecuteXmlReader())
    {
```

```
        doc.Load(rdr);
        rdr.Close();
    }
    cn.Close();
}
```

The SQL XML .NET Data Provider

There's another way to process the results of SELECT ... FOR XML queries–the SQL XML .NET Data Provider. This provider was originally built for SQL Server 2000 to help developers generate SELECT ... FOR XML queries and process their results. Thanks to the XML features included with SQL Server 2005, there's really little need to use the SQL XML .NET Data Provider. This portion of the chapter is here for developers who need to use the provider because their applications have to work with SQL Server 2000 databases.

The SQL XML .NET Data Provider is not included in the .NET Framework, but it is installed as part of the SQL XML features included with SQL Server 2005. You can use the SQL XML .NET Data Provider in your applications by adding a reference to the *Microsoft.Data.SqlXml* namespace.

 Note A previous version of the SQL XML .NET Data Provider is part of the SQLXML download for SQL Server 2000. This version of the SQL XML .NET Data Provider was not tested with, nor is it supported on, version 2.0 of the .NET Framework.

The SQL XML .NET Data Provider is very different from the other providers because SQL Server's XML features aren't traditional data-access features. The SQL XML .NET Data Provider consists of only three objects from the "traditional" .NET Data Provider: *SqlXml-Command*, *SqlXmlAdapter*, and *SqlXmlParameter*. These classes do not derive from the base classes that other .NET Data Providers do–such as *DbCommand*, *DbDataAdapter*, and *DbParameter*–nor can the classes be used within a *Using* block because they do not implement *IDisposable*. The SQL XML .NET Data Provider does not include classes to manage connections, connection strings, or transactions.

It's also worth noting that the SQL XML .NET Data Provider relies on the native OLE DB technology to communicate with SQL Server. You need to supply an OLE DB connection string to connect to SQL Server.

Using a *SqlXmlCommand* to Load Data into an *XmlDocument*

Storing the results of a SQL Server XML query into an *XmlDocument* object is simpler than using a *SqlXmlCommand*. The *SqlXmlCommand* object offers a single constructor that requires a connection string to your SQL Server database. You can therefore use the same connection string that you would use for an *OleDbConnection* object.

As with the *SqlCommand* and *OleDbCommand* classes, you use the *CommandText* property to specify the query you want to execute. You can then use the *ExecuteXmlReader* object to execute the query and fetch the results in an *XmlReader* object.

I noted earlier that the SQL XML .NET Data Provider is specifically designed to help developers work with the results of XML queries. The *SqlXmlCommand* class has a *RootTag* property that you can use to add a top-level node to the results of a query, which means that the results will constitute a well-formed document without having to rely on the ROOT clause in the SELECT ... FOR XML query. This is especially handy if you're connecting to a SQL Server 2000 database. You can thus use the *XmlDocument* class's *Load* method as shown here rather than programmatically adding a top-level node to the *XmlDocument* and then adding the results of the query one node at a time:

Visual Basic

```vb
'Imports Microsoft.Data.SqlXml
'Imports System.Xml

Dim strConn, strSQL As String
strConn = "Provider=SQLOLEDB;Data Source=.\SQLExpress;" & _
        "Initial Catalog=Northwind;Integrated Security=SSPI;"
strSQL = "SELECT TOP 2 CustomerID, CompanyName FROM Customers " & _
        "FOR XML AUTO, ELEMENTS"
Dim cmd As New SqlXmlCommand(strConn)
cmd.CommandText = strSQL
cmd.RootTag = "RootNode"
Dim doc As New XmlDocument()
Dim rdr As XmlReader = cmd.ExecuteXmlReader()
doc.Load(rdr)
rdr.Close()
Dim strPathToXml As String = "C:\MyData.XML"
doc.Save(strPathToXml)
ShowXmlOnForm(strPathToXml, "SqlXmlCommand.ExecuteXmlReader")
```

Visual C#

```csharp
//using Microsoft.Data.SqlXml;
//using System.Xml;

string strConn, strSQL;
strConn = @"Provider=SQLOLEDB;Data Source=.\SQLExpress;" +
        "Initial Catalog=Northwind;Integrated Security=SSPI;";
strSQL = "SELECT TOP 2 CustomerID, CompanyName FROM Customers " +
        "FOR XML AUTO, ELEMENTS";
SqlXmlCommand cmd = new SqlXmlCommand(strConn);
cmd.CommandText = strSQL;
cmd.RootTag = "RootNode";
XmlDocument doc = new XmlDocument();
XmlReader rdr = cmd.ExecuteXmlReader();
doc.Load(rdr);
rdr.Close();
string strPathToXml = @"C:\MyData.XML";
doc.Save(strPathToXml);
ShowXmlOnForm(strPathToXml, "SqlXmlCommand.ExecuteXmlReader");
```

The *SqlXmlCommand* class also allows you to pass the results of an XML query to a stream, either to create a new stream for the results via the *ExecuteStream* method or to write the results to an existing stream via the *ExecuteToStream* method.

If you want to execute a query that does not return results, the *SqlXmlCommand* class offers an *ExecuteNonQuery* method. This method behaves like the *ExecuteNonQuery* method on the *SqlCommand* class except for one difference. Unlike the method on the *SqlCommand* class, the *SqlXmlCommand* class's *ExecuteNonQuery* method does not return a value.

Unlike the *SqlCommand* class, the *SqlXmlCommand* class does not offer a method to return standard SELECT query results through a *DataReader* class.

Using a *SqlXmlAdapter* to Load Data into a *DataSet*

You could use the same process to load the contents of the *XmlReader* object into a *DataSet*, but the SQL XML .NET Data Provider offers a simpler way—the *SqlXmlAdapter* class. Just as you can easily store the results of a standard SQL query in a *DataSet* using a *SqlDataAdapter*, you can store the results of a FOR XML query in a *DataSet* using a *SqlXmlAdapter*.

You use the same code to create your *SqlXmlCommand*, and then you create a *SqlXmlAdapter*, specifying your *SqlXmlCommand* in the constructor. You can then fill your *DataSet* with the results of your query by calling the *SqlXmlAdapter* object's *Fill* method, as shown in the following code snippet:

Visual Basic
```
'Imports Microsoft.Data.SqlXml

Dim strConn, strSQL As String
strConn = "Provider=SQLOLEDB;Data Source=.\SQLExpress;" & _
          "Initial Catalog=Northwind;Integrated Security=SSPI;"
strSQL = "SELECT TOP 2 CustomerID, CompanyName FROM Customers " & _
          "FOR XML AUTO, ELEMENTS"
Dim cmd As New SqlXmlCommand(strConn)
cmd.CommandText = strSQL
cmd.RootTag = "RootNode"
Dim da As New SqlXmlAdapter(cmd)
Dim ds As New DataSet()
da.Fill(ds)
For Each row As DataRow In ds.Tables(0).Rows
    Console.WriteLine("  CustomerID: {0}  CompanyName: {1}", _
                      row("CustomerID"), row("CompanyName"))
Next
```

Visual C#
```
//using Microsoft.Data.SqlXml;

string strConn, strSQL;
strConn = @"Provider=SQLOLEDB;Data Source=.\SQLExpress;" +
          "Initial Catalog=Northwind;Integrated Security=SSPI;";
strSQL = "SELECT TOP 2 CustomerID, CompanyName FROM Customers " +
          "FOR XML AUTO, ELEMENTS";
```

```
SqlXmlCommand cmd = new SqlXmlCommand(strConn);
cmd.CommandText = strSQL;
cmd.RootTag = "RootNode";
SqlXmlAdapter da = new SqlXmlAdapter(cmd);
DataSet ds = new DataSet();
da.Fill(ds);
foreach (DataRow row in ds.Tables[0].Rows)
    Console.WriteLine(" CustomerID: {0}  CompanyName: {1}",
                      row["CustomerID"], row["CompanyName"]);
```

Working with Template Queries

To give you greater control over the format of the results of your queries, the SQL XML .NET Data Provider supports XML template queries. Basically, a template query is an XML document that contains queries. When you execute such a query, the SQL XML .NET Data Provider combines the XML in the query along with the results of your query.

Let's look at an example of a template query. The template query that follows contains two SELECT ... FOR XML queries that retrieve order and line item information for a particular customer:

```
<ROOT xmlns:sql='urn:schemas-microsoft-com:xml-sql'>
  <sql:query>
    SELECT OrderID, CustomerID, OrderDate FROM Orders
        WHERE CustomerID = 'GROSR'
        FOR XML AUTO, ELEMENTS
  </sql:query>
  <sql:query>
    SELECT OrderID, ProductID, Quantity, UnitPrice
        FROM [Order Details] WHERE OrderID IN
        (SELECT OrderID FROM Orders WHERE CustomerID = 'GROSR')
        FOR XML AUTO, ELEMENTS
  </sql:query>
</ROOT>
```

The query itself is an XML document. The SQL XML .NET Data Provider examines the elements that reside in the *sql* namespace and executes the text in the query elements. The rest of the elements are treated simply as XML and appear in the results as such.

You can execute this query using the SQL XML .NET Data Provider, and you'll receive the XML document shown in Figure 12-9. As you can see in the figure, the root element in the template query appears in the results.

Executing a Template Query Using a *SqlXmlCommand*

To tell the *SqlXmlCommand* object that you're working with a template query using the *SqlXml-Command* object, you set the *SqlXmlCommand* object's *CommandType* property to the appropriate value in the *SqlXmlCommandType* enumeration. If you supply the path to the file that contains your query, set the *CommandType* property to *TemplateFile*. If, instead, you supply the actual text of the query, you should set the *CommandType* property to *Template*.

Figure 12-9 The results of an XML template query

You can then execute the query to store the results in an XML document or a *DataSet*, as shown in the previous examples. The following code snippet stores the results in a *DataSet*. Note that the code that creates the file for the template query uses classes in the *System.IO* namespace and requires a reference to the namespace.

Visual Basic

```
'Imports Microsoft.Data.SqlXml
'Imports System.IO
Dim strPathToTemplateQuery As String = "C:\TemplateQuery.xml"
Using writer As TextWriter = File.CreateText(strPathToTemplateQuery)
    writer.WriteLine("<ROOT xmlns:sql='urn:schemas-microsoft-com:xml-sql'>")
    writer.WriteLine("  <sql:query>")
    writer.WriteLine("    SELECT OrderID, CustomerID, OrderDate")
    writer.WriteLine("      FROM Orders WHERE CustomerID = 'GROSR'")
    writer.WriteLine("      FOR XML AUTO, ELEMENTS")
    writer.WriteLine("  </sql:query>")
    writer.WriteLine("  <sql:query>")
    writer.WriteLine("    SELECT OrderID, ProductID, Quantity, UnitPrice")
    writer.WriteLine("      FROM [Order Details] WHERE OrderID IN")
    writer.WriteLine("      (SELECT OrderID FROM Orders")
    writer.WriteLine("         WHERE CustomerID = 'GROSR')")
    writer.WriteLine("      FOR XML AUTO, ELEMENTS")
    writer.WriteLine("  </sql:query>")
    writer.WriteLine("</ROOT>")
    writer.Close()
End Using

Dim strConn As String
strConn = "Provider=SQLOLEDB;Data Source=.\SQLExpress;" & _
        "Initial Catalog=Northwind;Integrated Security=SSPI;"
```

```
Dim cmd As New SqlXmlCommand(strConn)
cmd.CommandText = strPathToTemplateQuery
cmd.CommandType = SqlXmlCommandType.TemplateFile
Dim doc As New XmlDocument()
Dim rdr As XmlReader = cmd.ExecuteXmlReader()
doc.Load(rdr)
rdr.Close()
Dim strPathToXml As String = "C:\MyData.XML"
doc.Save(strPathToXml)
ShowXmlOnForm(strPathToXml, "SqlXmlCommand - Template Query")
```

Visual C#

```
//using Microsoft.Data.SqlXml;
//using System.IO;

string strPathToTemplateQuery = @"C:\TemplateQuery.xml";
using (TextWriter writer = File.CreateText(strPathToTemplateQuery))
{
    writer.WriteLine("<ROOT xmlns:sql='urn:schemas-microsoft-com:xml-sql'>");
    writer.WriteLine("  <sql:query>");
    writer.WriteLine("    SELECT OrderID, CustomerID, OrderDate");
    writer.WriteLine("        FROM Orders WHERE CustomerID = 'GROSR'");
    writer.WriteLine("        FOR XML AUTO, ELEMENTS");
    writer.WriteLine("  </sql:query>");
    writer.WriteLine("  <sql:query>");
    writer.WriteLine("    SELECT OrderID, ProductID, Quantity, UnitPrice");
    writer.WriteLine("        FROM [Order Details] WHERE OrderID IN");
    writer.WriteLine("        (SELECT OrderID FROM Orders)");
    writer.WriteLine("            WHERE CustomerID = 'GROSR')");
    writer.WriteLine("        FOR XML AUTO, ELEMENTS");
    writer.WriteLine("  </sql:query>");
    writer.WriteLine("</ROOT>");
    writer.Close();
}

string strConn;
strConn = @"Provider=SQLOLEDB;Data Source=.\SQLExpress;" +
         "Initial Catalog=Northwind;Integrated Security=SSPI;";
SqlXmlCommand cmd = new SqlXmlCommand(strConn);
cmd.CommandText = strPathToTemplateQuery;
cmd.CommandType = SqlXmlCommandType.TemplateFile;
XmlDocument doc = new XmlDocument();
XmlReader rdr = cmd.ExecuteXmlReader();
doc.Load(rdr);
rdr.Close();
string strPathToXml = @"C:\MyData.XML";
doc.Save(strPathToXml);
ShowXmlOnForm(strPathToXml, "SqlXmlCommand - Template Query");
```

Parameterized Template Queries

What happens if you need to programmatically supply a value to the template query prior to execution? If you were using a *SqlCommand* or *SqlDataAdapter*, you would construct a parameterized query. Thankfully, you can do the same with a template query.

Creating and executing parameterized template queries is fairly straightforward. First, you define the parameter in the template query, specifying its name. (Make sure you omit the "@" character.) Then use the parameter in the queries inside the template, as you would in a *SqlCommand*, specifying the parameter's name (including the "@" character).

The following template query retrieves the same information—orders and line item information for a customer—except the query contains a parameter marker for the value of the CustomerID column rather than specifying that value explicitly:

```
<ROOT xmlns:sql='urn:schemas-microsoft-com:xml-sql'>
  <sql:header>
    <sql:param name='CustomerID'/>
  </sql:header>
  <sql:query>
    SELECT OrderID, CustomerID, OrderDate
        FROM Orders WHERE CustomerID = @CustomerID
        FOR XML AUTO, ELEMENTS
  </sql:query>
  <sql:query>
    SELECT OrderID, ProductID, Quantity, UnitPrice
        FROM [Order Details] WHERE OrderID IN
        (SELECT OrderID FROM Orders WHERE CustomerID = @CustomerID)
        FOR XML AUTO, ELEMENTS
  </sql:query>
</ROOT>
```

To set the value of this parameter programmatically, you use the *SqlXmlParameter* class. You can't create a *SqlXmlParameter* using the *New* keyword. The only way to create one is to use the *CreateParameter* method of the *SqlXmlCommand* object. There is no need to append the *SqlXmlParameter* object to the *SqlXmlCommand* object's parameters collection. (In fact, the *SqlXmlCommand* class does not expose its parameters collection through a property.) Once you have your *SqlXmlParameter* object, you set its *Name* and *Value* properties accordingly before executing your query, as shown in the following code snippet:

Visual Basic

```
Dim strConn As String
strConn = "Provider=SQLOLEDB;Data Source=.\SQLExpress;" & _
        "Initial Catalog=Northwind;Integrated Security=SSPI;"
Dim cmd As New SqlXmlCommand(strConn)
Dim param As SqlXmlParameter = cmd.CreateParameter()
param.Name = "@CustomerID"
param.Value = "GROSR"
```

Visual C#

```
string strConn;
strConn = @"Provider=SQLOLEDB;Data Source=.\SQLExpress;" +
        "Initial Catalog=Northwind;Integrated Security=SSPI;";
SqlXmlCommand cmd = new SqlXmlCommand(strConn);
SqlXmlParameter param = cmd.CreateParameter();
param.Name = "@CustomerID";
param.Value = "GROSR";
```

Working with XPath Queries

If we had an XML document that contained all the orders in the Northwind database, we could use the following XPath query to examine just the orders for the customer whose CustomerID is GROSR:

```
Orders[CustomerID='GROSR']
```

If you look at the *SqlXmlCommandType* enumeration, you'll find an XPath entry. You could set the *CommandType* property of a *SqlXmlCommand* to XPath, supply the XPath query in the *CommandText*, and then execute the query, but doing so would throw an exception stating that the query is invalid.

The SQL Server database engine doesn't really know what to do with an XPath query. The SQL XML .NET Data Provider supports XPath queries, but what it actually does is translate XPath queries into SELECT ... FOR XML queries. Although you can interpret the query and perform this translation, the SQL XML .NET Data Provider needs a little help.

Adding Schema Information

You can help the SQL XML .NET Data Provider translate this XPath query by supplying an XML schema that defines the tables and columns in your database to include in the query as well as the structure for the results, as shown here:

```xml
<?xml version="1.0" ?>
<xsd:schema xmlns:xsd="http://www.w3.org/2001/XMLSchema"
            xmlns:sql="urn:schemas-microsoft-com:mapping-schema">
  <xsd:annotation>
    <xsd:appinfo>
      <sql:relationship name="relOrdersDetails"
                        parent="Orders"
                        parent-key="OrderID"
                        child="[Order Details]"
                        child-key="OrderID" />
    </xsd:appinfo>
  </xsd:annotation>
  <xsd:element name="Orders">
    <xsd:complexType>
      <xsd:sequence>
        <xsd:element name="OrderID" type="xsd:int" />
        <xsd:element name="CustomerID" type="xsd:string" />
        <xsd:element name="OrderDate" type="xsd:dateTime"
                    sql:datatype="datetime" />
        <xsd:element name="Order_x0020_Details"
                    sql:relation="[Order Details]"
                    sql:relationship="relOrdersDetails">
          <xsd:complexType>
            <xsd:sequence>
              <xsd:element name="ProductID" type="xsd:int" />
              <xsd:element name="Quantity" type="xsd:int" />
              <xsd:element name="UnitPrice" type="xsd:decimal" />
```

```
            </xsd:sequence>
          </xsd:complexType>
        </xsd:element>
      </xsd:sequence>
    </xsd:complexType>
  </xsd:element>
</xsd:schema>
```

The schema has entries that reference tables and columns, that relate data from two tables (*sql:relationship*), and that help the SQL XML .NET Data Provider understand the SQL data type for a column (*sql:datatype*). However, this schema demonstrates just a fraction of the features that you can use in an XML schema file with the SQL XML .NET Data Provider. For more information on all the features, see the "Using Annotations in XSD Schemas" topic in the documentation for SQL XML.

Once you've created your schema file, you set the *SchemaPath* property of your *SqlXml-Command* object to the file that contains this schema information. The following code snippet executes the XPath query described earlier to retrieve the orders and line items for a particular customer using this schema. The code then stores the results of the query in an *XmlDocument* object.

Visual Basic

```
'Imports Microsoft.Data.SqlXml
'Imports System.Xml

Dim strConn As String
strConn = "Provider=SQLOLEDB;Data Source=.\SQLExpress;" & _
          "Initial Catalog=Northwind;Integrated Security=SSPI;"
Dim cmd As New SqlXmlCommand(strConn)
cmd.SchemaPath = "C:\MySchema.XSD"
cmd.CommandText = "Orders[CustomerID='GROSR']"
cmd.CommandType = SqlXmlCommandType.XPath
cmd.RootNode = "RootNode"
Dim rdr As XmlReader = cmd.ExecuteXmlReader()
Dim doc As New XmlDocument()
doc.Load(rdr)
rdr.Close()
Dim strPathToXml As String = "C:\MyData.XML"
doc.Save(strPathToXml);
ShowXmlOnForm(strPathToXml, "SqlXmlCommand - XPath Query");
```

Visual C#

```
//using Microsoft.Data.SqlXml;
//using System.Xml;

string strConn;
strConn = @"Provider=SQLOLEDB;Data Source=.\SQLExpress;" +
          "Initial Catalog=Northwind;Integrated Security=SSPI;";
SqlXmlCommand cmd = new SqlXmlCommand(strConn);
cmd.SchemaPath = @"C:\MySchema.XSD";
cmd.CommandText = "Orders[CustomerID='GROSR']";
cmd.CommandType = SqlXmlCommandType.XPath;
```

```
cmd.RootNode = "RootNode";
XmlReader rdr = cmd.ExecuteXmlReader();
XmlDocument doc = new XmlDocument();
doc.Load(rdr);
rdr.Close();
string strPathToXml = @"C:\MyData.XML";
doc.Save(strPathToXml);
ShowXmlOnForm(strPathToXml, "SqlXmlCommand - XPath Query");
```

Applying an XSL Transform

Earlier in the chapter, I said that you could format an XML document in more than one way and that it's possible for two XML documents to contain the same data, differing only in their schema. You can use a companion technology called XSL to transform the structure of your XML documents.

XSL stands for Extensible Stylesheet Language. You can think of an XSL transform as an XML document that contains a set of instructions describing how to transform the contents of another XML document. XSL transforms are handy if you want to change the structure of your document. You can also use an XSL transform to translate XML into HTML.

If you have an XSL transform and you want to apply it to the results of your SQL XML query, you can set the *XslPath* property of the *SqlXmlCommand* object to a string that contains the path to your XSL transform.

We'll touch on this feature again shortly.

Submitting Updates

The SQL XML .NET Data Provider lets you submit updates to your database. The *SqlXml-Adapter* class has an *Update* method that you can use to submit the changes stored in your *DataSet* to your database. If you've read Chapter 10, you're probably not surprised to see an *Update* method on a *DataAdapter* class.

However, the *SqlXmlAdapter* class doesn't handle updating in the same way that other *Data-Adapter* classes do. Most *DataAdapter* classes (such as *OleDbDataAdapter*, *SqlDataAdapter*, and *OdbcDataAdapter*) expose properties that contain *Command* objects that contain the logic necessary to submit changes to your database. These *Command* objects generally contain a number of parameters that are bound to columns in the *DataTable*. When you call the *Update* method on most *DataAdapter* classes, the *DataAdapter* looks at the rows in a particular *Data-Table*. Each time the *DataAdapter* discovers a modified row, it uses the appropriate *Command* object to submit the pending change before calling the *DataRow* object's *AcceptChanges* method. (Note: The *DataAdapter* might group the updates into batches based on the setting of the *UpdateBatchSize* property.)

The *SqlXmlAdapter* takes a different approach. Earlier in the chapter, you learned a little about diffgrams. Figure 12-5 shows the contents of a diffgram. Rather than locating pending changes in a *DataSet* by looping through *DataRow* objects one row at a time, the *SqlXml-Adapter* processes the pending changes in a *DataSet* by generating a diffgram for the *DataSet*. The SQL XML .NET Data Provider then processes the entire diffgram, creating a complex batch query to submit all the changes to your database at once.

If you look at the contents of the diffgram in Figure 12-5, you can probably figure out how to generate a series of INSERT, UPDATE, and DELETE queries to submit the pending changes to your database. The SQL XML .NET Data Provider cannot generate those queries without a little help.

Remember the annotated XML schema file that we used to help the SQL XML .NET Data Provider translate an XPath query into a SQL query? Different challenge, same solution. When we were working with the XPath query, we set the *SchemaPath* property of the *SqlXml-Command* to the path to our schema file. You can use the *SqlXmlAdapter* to submit changes to your database by making sure that the *SqlXmlAdapter* object's *SqlXmlCommand* object has a schema file that contains all the necessary table and column information for the data in the diffgram.

In fact, you can submit the update by using a *SqlXmlCommand* whose *CommandText* property is set to *DiffGram*. You simply use the *DataSet* object's *WriteXml* method to create your diffgram. Then you set up a *SqlXmlCommand* to use that diffgram and a schema file and...voilà! The following code snippet demonstrates this functionality:

Visual Basic

```vb
'Imports Microsoft.Data.SqlXml
'Imports System.Xml
'Imports System.IO

Dim strConn As String
strConn = "Provider=SQLOLEDB;Data Source=.\SQLExpress;" & _
          "Initial Catalog=Northwind;Integrated Security=SSPI;"
Dim cmd As New SqlXmlCommand(strConn)
cmd.SchemaPath = "C:\MySchema.XSD"
cmd.CommandText = "Orders[CustomerID='GROSR']"
cmd.CommandType = SqlXmlCommandType.XPath
cmd.RootTag = "RootNode"
Dim da As New SqlXmlAdapter(cmd)
Dim ds As New DataSet()
da.Fill(ds)

ds.Tables("Orders").Rows(0)("CustomerID") = "ALFKI"
ds.Tables("Orders").Rows(1)("CustomerID") = "ALFKI"

Dim strPathToDiffGram As String = "C:\MyDiffGram.XML"
ds.WriteXml(strPathToDiffGram, XmlWriteMode.DiffGram)
cmd = New SqlXmlCommand(strConn)
cmd.SchemaPath = strPathToSchema
cmd.CommandType = SqlXmlCommandType.DiffGram
cmd.CommandStream = New FileStream(strPathToDiffGram, _
                                  FileMode.Open, FileAccess.Read)
```

```
cmd.ExecuteNonQuery()

'Undo the changes.
Dim strSQL As String
strSQL = "UPDATE Orders SET CustomerID = 'GROSR' " & _
    "    WHERE OrderID = 10268 OR OrderID = 10785"
cmd = New SqlXmlCommand(strConn)
cmd.CommandText = strSQL
cmd.CommandType = SqlXmlCommandType.Sql
cmd.ExecuteNonQuery()
```

Visual C#

```
//using Microsoft.Data.SqlXml;
//using System.Xml;
//using System.IO;

string strConn;
strConn = @"Provider=SQLOLEDB;Data Source=.\SQLExpress;" +
    "Initial Catalog=Northwind;Integrated Security=SSPI;";
SqlXmlCommand cmd = new SqlXmlCommand(strConn);
cmd.SchemaPath = @"C:\MySchema.XSD";
cmd.CommandText = "Orders[CustomerID='GROSR']";
cmd.CommandType = SqlXmlCommandType.XPath;
cmd.RootTag = "RootNode";
SqlXmlAdapter da = new SqlXmlAdapter(cmd);
DataSet ds = new DataSet();
da.Fill(ds);

ds.Tables["Orders"].Rows[0]["CustomerID"] = "ALFKI";
ds.Tables["Orders"].Rows[1]["CustomerID"] = "ALFKI";

string strPathToDiffGram = @"C:\MyDiffGram.XML";
ds.WriteXml(strPathToDiffGram, XmlWriteMode.DiffGram);
cmd = new SqlXmlCommand(strConn);
cmd.SchemaPath = strPathToSchema;
cmd.CommandType = SqlXmlCommandType.DiffGram;
cmd.CommandStream = new FileStream(strPathToDiffGram, FileMode.Open,
                                    FileAccess.Read);
cmd.ExecuteNonQuery();

//Undo the changes.
string strSQL  = "UPDATE Orders SET CustomerID = 'GROSR' " +
    "    WHERE OrderID = 10268 OR OrderID = 10785";
cmd = new SqlXmlCommand(strConn);
cmd.CommandText = strSQL;
cmd.CommandType = SqlXmlCommandType.Sql;
cmd.ExecuteNonQuery();
```

Note   The code also executes an action query to undo the changes to the database. This ensures that you can run the code snippet multiple times. To verify that the *SqlXmlCommand* submitted the changes stored in the diffgram, you can set a breakpoint so that you can pause the execution of the code before the execution of this last query.

SqlXmlCommand Updating Logic

Before we move on, I'd like to show you some of the logic that the *SqlXmlCommand* generates to submit changes to your database. This information might help you better understand the benefits and drawbacks of using the SQL XML .NET Data Provider to submit changes.

When the previous code snippet called the *SqlXmlCommand*'s *ExecuteNonQuery* method to submit the changes stored in the diffgram, the SQL XML .NET Data Provider generated and submitted the following batch query to SQL Server:

```
SET XACT_ABORT ON
BEGIN TRAN
DECLARE @eip INT, @r__ int, @e__ int
SET @eip = 0

UPDATE Orders SET CustomerID=N'ALFKI' WHERE  ( OrderID=10268 )  AND
( CustomerID=N'GROSR' )  AND  ( OrderDate=N'1996-07-30 00:00:00' ) ;
SELECT @e__ = @@ERROR, @r__ = @@ROWCOUNT
 IF (@e__ != 0 OR @r__ != 1) SET @eip = 1
 IF (@r__ > 1) RAISERROR ( N'SQLOLEDB Error Description: Ambiguous update,
                unique identifier required  Transaction aborted ', 16, 1)
 ELSE IF (@r__ < 1) RAISERROR ( N'SQLOLEDB Error Description: Empty update,
                no updatable rows found  Transaction aborted ', 16, 1)

UPDATE Orders SET CustomerID=N'ALFKI' WHERE  ( OrderID=10785 )  AND
( CustomerID=N'GROSR' )  AND  ( OrderDate=N'1997-12-18 00:00:00' ) ;
SELECT @e__ = @@ERROR, @r__ = @@ROWCOUNT
 IF (@e__ != 0 OR @r__ != 1) SET @eip = 1
 IF (@r__ > 1) RAISERROR ( N'SQLOLEDB Error Description: Ambiguous update,
                unique identifier required  Transaction aborted ', 16, 1)
 ELSE IF (@r__ < 1) RAISERROR ( N'SQLOLEDB Error Description: Empty update,
                no updatable rows found  Transaction aborted ', 16, 1)

IF (@eip != 0) ROLLBACK ELSE COMMIT
SET XACT_ABORT OFF
```

The batch query starts off by telling SQL Server to abort the current transaction if it raises an error, and then it starts a transaction and defines some variables to store data. Once this preparation work is done, the code executes the first UPDATE query and then pulls data into variables to determine whether an error occurred and how many rows the query affected. If the query affected one row and did not generate an error, the code continues, issuing action queries and determining whether the updates succeeded. After issuing all the action queries, the code commits the work in the transaction if all the updates succeeded and turns off the setting that tells SQL Server to abort transactions in case of an error.

This is impressive and well-designed code. It's a large and complex batch of queries, but this query minimizes the number of round-trips required to submit changes and determine the success or failure of those changes. If you're looking to provide similar functionality in your application by generating your own queries, this is a great example to reference.

Although it's not important that you understand the individual queries in this batch, you must understand the following points if you're going to rely on this provider to submit changes:

- The SQL XML .NET Data Provider wraps this batch of updates in a transaction and will roll back the transaction if it detects that an error occurred or if any individual query reports that it did not update exactly one row. This means that you'll submit either all the updates or none of them.

- The SQL XML .NET Data Provider does not retrieve data from your database while submitting changes. You will not see any new auto-increment or timestamp values after you submit your updates.

- Generally speaking, *DataAdapter* classes implicitly call the *AcceptChanges* method on *DataRows* after successfully submitting pending changes in those *DataRows*. The *SqlXmlAdapter* behaves somewhat differently. If you submit changes to your database using the *SqlXmlAdapter* object's *Update* method, the *SqlXmlAdapter* will call your *DataSet* object's *AcceptChanges* method after successfully submitting your changes.

A Simple ADO.NET and XML Sample

We've looked at snippets of code that demonstrate isolated features. Now it's time to put some of these features into a small sample application that shows off the power of XML and of ADO.NET's XML features. To do this, I'll pull together functionality from many of the previous code snippets.

The sample will use parameterized queries to retrieve an order history for a particular customer. Before you roll your eyes, note that we're going to collect more information in this set of queries. The queries will retrieve data from four related tables: Customers, Orders, Order Details, and Products. In this way, our order history will be more robust. We'll see company names as well as the names of the products ordered.

The sample turns the results of the queries into XML, uses an XSL transformation to turn that XML data into HTML, and then displays this HTML data in Internet Explorer, as shown in Figure 12-10.

The sample is a console application that launches an instance of Internet Explorer. Using a console application as a starting point makes the sample less flashy but easier to use as a resource. You can apply the same logic in two scenarios in which turning the results of queries into HTML can be extremely helpful: building Web applications and generating reports. I think that these are the most compelling uses of ADO.NET's XML features.

To create a very simple HTML page, I built a very simple Web page using Microsoft FrontPage. Then I compared the structure of that page's HTML with the structure of the XML document I created using ADO.NET, which contained my date and constructed an XSL transform to describe how to get from point X to point H.

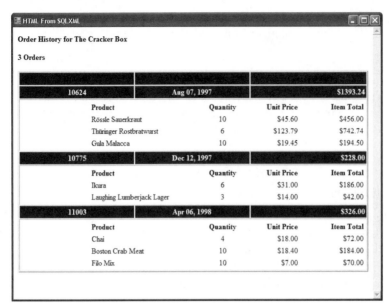

Figure 12-10   The Web page generated by the XML sample application

Two Paths, One Destination

Actually, I lied. I didn't create a sample. I created two of them. Both samples rely on the same XSL transform and produce the same HTML, but they differ in how they generate an XML document that contains data from the standard Northwind database.

The first sample, called *GenerateHtml_FromDataSet*, connects to the local Northwind database and uses standard SQL queries, and it stores the results in a *DataSet*. To access this data as an XML document to perform the XSL transform and generate HTML, the sample creates an *XmlDataDocument* object linked to the *DataSet*.

The second sample, called *GenerateHtml_FromSqlXml*, relies on the SQL XML .NET Data Provider and an XML template query that uses the same Northwind tables but uses the FOR XML syntax. The *SqlXmlCommand* object that this sample uses has its *XslPath* property set to the location of the XSL transform.

ADO.NET and XML: A Happy Couple

ADO.NET offers robust support for XML. ADO.NET's XML features allow programmers to easily move back and forth between traditional data access objects and XML objects. You can use the features of the *DataSet* object to read and write data, schema information, or both as XML. The *XmlDataDocument* object allows you to easily access the contents of a *DataSet* as XML.

SQL Server 2005's new XML features all but eliminate the need for developers to use SELECT ... FOR XML queries through SQL Server's support for the XML data type, XPath queries, and the XQuery language. For developers who still need to use SELECT ... FOR XML queries to work with SQL Server, the SQL XML .NET Data Provider is still helpful for retrieving the results of queries in XML format to files, XML documents, and *DataSet* objects.

Questions That Should Be Asked More Frequently

Q   The *DataSet*, *DataTable*, and *DataColumn* objects give me some flexibility in the structure of the XML document I create in the *WriteXml* method, but I need even more control. I want to add a processing instruction to my XML that references my XSL transformation. How do I do this?

A   You can use the *XmlDataDocument* object to access the contents of the *DataSet* as an *XmlDocument*. You set the *EnforceConstraints* property of the *DataSet* to *False* and then use the *XmlDataDocument* object to customize the structure of your XML document as you see fit. In this case, you can use the *CreateProcessingInstruction* method of the *XmlDataDocument* object, as shown in the following code snippet. Once you're done, you call the *XmlDataDocument* object's *Save* method to create your file.

Visual Basic

```
Dim ds As New DataSet()
'Initialize DataSet
'...
ds.EnforceConstraints = False
Dim xmlDoc As New XmlDataDocument(ds)
Dim strPI As String = "type='text/xsl' href='MyTransform.XSLT'"
Dim xmlPI As XmlProcessingInstruction
xmlPI = xmlDoc.CreateProcessingInstruction("xml-stylesheet", strPI)
xmlDoc.InsertBefore(xmlPI, xmlDoc.DocumentElement)
Dim strPathToXmlFile As String = "C:\MyData.XML"
xmlDoc.Save(strPathToXmlFile)
```

Visual C#

```
DataSet ds = new DataSet();
//Initialize DataSet
//...
ds.EnforceConstraints = false;
XmlDataDocument xmlDoc = new XmlDataDocument(ds);
string strPI = "type='text/xsl' href='MyTransform.XSLT'";
XmlProcessingInstruction xmlPI;
xmlPI = xmlDoc.CreateProcessingInstruction("xml-stylesheet", strPI);
xmlDoc.InsertBefore(xmlPI, xmlDoc.DocumentElement);
string strPathToXmlFile = @"C:\MyData.XML";
xmlDoc.Save(strPathToXmlFile);
```

Q   I want to retrieve the results of my queries as XML, but I'm calling stored procedures that already exist. Is there anything I can do to fetch the results as XML?

A   You can ask the SQL XML .NET Data Provider to format the results of the query as XML by setting the *SqlXmlCommand* object's *ClientSideXml* property to *True*. The following code snippet demonstrates this functionality:

Visual Basic

```
Dim strConn, strSQL As String
strConn = "Provider=SQLOLEDB;Data Source=.\SQLExpress;" & _
          "Initial Catalog=Northwind;Integrated Security=SSPI;"
strSQL = "EXEC CustOrdersOrders 'ALFKI' FOR XML NESTED"
Dim cmd As New SqlXmlCommand(strConn)
cmd.CommandText = strSQL
cmd.ClientSideXml = True
cmd.RootTag = "ROOT"

Dim xmlDoc As New XmlDocument()
Dim xmlRdr As XmlReader = cmd.ExecuteXmlReader
xmlDoc.Load(xmlRdr)
xmlRdr.Close
Console.WriteLine(xmlDoc.InnerXml)
```

Visual C#

```
string strConn, strSQL;
strConn = @"Provider=SQLOLEDB;Data Source=.\SQLExpress;" +
           "Initial Catalog=Northwind;Integrated Security=SSPI;";
strSQL = "EXEC CustOrdersOrders 'ALFKI' FOR XML NESTED";
SqlXmlCommand cmd = new SqlXmlCommand(strConn);
cmd.CommandText = strSQL;
cmd.ClientSideXml = true;
cmd.RootTag = "ROOT";

XmlDocument xmlDoc = new XmlDocument();
XmlReader xmlRdr = cmd.ExecuteXmlReader();
xmlDoc.Load(xmlRdr);
xmlRdr.Close();
Console.WriteLine(xmlDoc.InnerXml);
```

For more information on using client-side XML formatting with the SQL XML .NET Data Provider, see the "Comparing Client-Side XML Formatting to Server-Side XML Formatting" topic in the SQL XML help file.

Q   How can I tell what XML schema is associated with a SQL Server 2005 XML column?

A   I've yet to find a way to retrieve this information through *SqlConnection.GetSchema*. However, there are ways of retrieving this information. Create a *SqlCommand* that references the desired column. Call *ExecuteReader* to create a *SqlDataReader*, and specify *SchemaOnly* so that you don't return any data. Then call *GetSchemaTable* to get the schema for the fields that appear in the *SqlDataReader*. In the resulting *DataTable*, you'll see *DataColumns* with *ColumnNames* of "XmlSchemaCollectionDatabase", "XmlSchemaCollectionOwning-Schema", and "XmlSchemaCollectionName". These columns contain the XML schema information for XML columns. Here's some sample code that returns XML schema information for the OrderDetailsAsXml column created and used in samples earlier in the chapter:

Visual Basic

```
Dim strConn, strSQL As String
strConn = "Data Source=.\SQLExpress;" & _
```

```vbnet
                    "Initial Catalog=Northwind;Integrated Security=True;"
    strSQL = "SELECT OrderID, OrderDetailsAsXml FROM Orders"

    Dim cn As New SqlConnection(strConn)
    cn.Open()
    Dim cmd As New SqlCommand(strSQL, cn)
    Dim rdr As SqlDataReader = cmd.ExecuteReader(CommandBehavior.SchemaOnly)
    Dim tbl As DataTable = rdr.GetSchemaTable()
    For Each row As DataRow In tbl.Rows
        If CType(row("ProviderType"), SqlDbType) = SqlDbType.Xml Then
            Console.WriteLine("Found XML column {0}", row("ColumnName"))
            If Not row.IsNull("XmlSchemaCollectionName") Then
                Console.WriteLine("  Schema defined in [{0}].[{1}].[{2}]", _
                                  row("XmlSchemaCollectionDatabase"), _
                                  row("XmlSchemaCollectionOwningSchema"), _
                                  row("XmlSchemaCollectionName"))
            End If
        End If
    Next row
    rdr.Close()
    cn.Close()
```

Visual C#

```csharp
    string strConn, strSQL;
    strConn = @"Data Source=.\SQLExpress;" +
              "Initial Catalog=Northwind;Integrated Security=True;";
    strSQL = "SELECT OrderID, OrderDetailsAsXml FROM Orders";

    SqlConnection cn = new SqlConnection(strConn);
    cn.Open();
    SqlCommand cmd = new SqlCommand(strSQL, cn);
    SqlDataReader rdr = cmd.ExecuteReader(CommandBehavior.SchemaOnly);
    DataTable tbl = rdr.GetSchemaTable();
    foreach (DataRow row in tbl.Rows) {
        if ((SqlDbType) row["ProviderType"] == SqlDbType.Xml) {
            Console.WriteLine("Found XML column {0}", row["ColumnName"]);
            if (!row.IsNull("XmlSchemaCollectionName"))
                Console.WriteLine("  Schema defined in [{0}].[{1}].[{2}]",
                                  row["XmlSchemaCollectionDatabase"],
                                  row["XmlSchemaCollectionOwningSchema"],
                                  row["XmlSchemaCollectionName"]);
        }
    }
    rdr.Close();
    cn.Close();
```

Q   How can I define additional constraints on a SQL Server 2005 XML column?

A   In most cases, you can define the desired constraint through an XML schema, and associate the XML column with that XML schema. If you want to define a constraint that you can't describe through an XML schema, you can create a user-defined function to validate the data in the XML document and then define a CHECK constraint on the XML column that calls that user-defined function.

Part IV
Building Effective Applications with ADO.NET 2.0

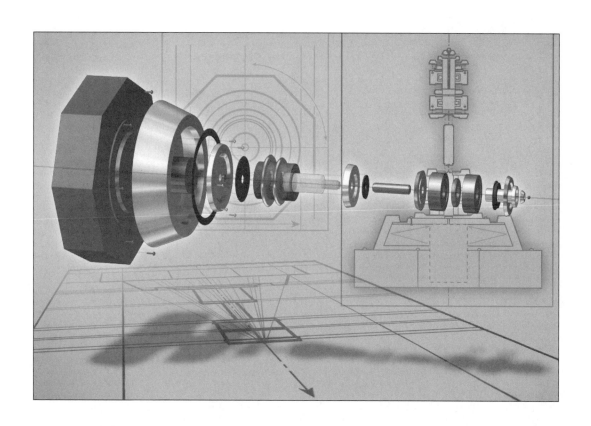

Chapter 13
Building Effective Microsoft Windows–Based Applications

You should now feel comfortable working with the various objects in the ADO.NET object model. Need to create a *DataSet* and store the results of a query in a *DataTable* using a *SqlDataAdapter*? No problem. Need to add a *DataRelation* so you can navigate between parent and child data in two related *DataTable* objects? Child's play. Need to create the logic required to submit changes back to the database? Piece of cake.

Although these skills are important, they're still not enough to build an application that allows a user to view and modify the contents of a database. You also need to build a user interface.

In this chapter, we'll use the knowledge you gained from previous chapters to discuss building effective Windows-based applications. In the first part of the chapter, we'll look at the stages of building a sample application that is similar to the one we created in Chapter 2 using the Data Source Configuration Wizard and Data Source window.

This chapter will also cover the new features that are part of Windows Forms data binding. We'll take a closer look at how to use drag-and-drop data binding from the Data Source Window. This chapter will also cover new classes in the *System.Windows.Forms* namespace—the *BindingNavigator*, *BindingSource*, and *DataGridView* classes—designed to help you build interactive data user interfaces more quickly. We'll also look at enhancements to existing features, such as the properties available on the *Binding* class.

This chapter will demonstrate how you can use data binding to save time while you're developing the user interface for your application. We'll also examine different strategies for updating and connection strategies. Finally, we'll discuss different ways to work with binary large object (BLOB) data in a Windows-based application.

Building a User Interface Quickly by Using Data Binding

So you want to build a user interface? You can write code that retrieves data from your database and submits changes, but you need to display data on a form and allow users to interact with that data by adding, modifying, and deleting rows of data. You also want to develop this user interface quickly.

Obviously, you can write code to read the contents of a *DataRow* and display that data in *TextBox* controls on a form. You can also write code that gives the user the ability to navigate through different rows of data, as well as the ability to add, modify, and delete rows in your *DataSet*. If you wrote a series of applications that all shared these same basic goals but differed only in the type of data they handled, you'd find yourself writing the same basic routines in each application.

The Windows Forms package that's part of the Microsoft .NET Framework includes support for data binding. Data binding offers functionality similar to the routines I described in earlier chapters for displaying the contents of a *DataSet* in various controls, and it includes features that allow users to modify that data. In short, data binding allows you to build data-access applications more quickly and easily by reducing the amount of code required to develop the user interface.

> **Note**   Data binding actually supports more than just *DataSet* objects. You can bind controls to ADO.NET structures such as *DataSet* objects and *DataTable* objects, to arrays, or to any object that implements the *IList* interface. Because this book is dedicated to ADO.NET, I'll focus on using data binding with ADO.NET structures. For more information on using data binding with other structures, see the corresponding documentation in the .NET Framework SDK.

That's enough preliminary talk about data binding. Let's use data binding to develop a fairly simple order entry application. The application, shown in Figure 13-1, allows users to view and modify orders for a customer. We'll build the application in phases to demonstrate the various data-binding features needed to develop an application.

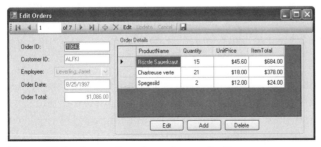

Figure 13-1   A sample order entry application

The sample code for this chapter includes the final version of this application, which relies on bound controls to interact between user input and the contents of the *DataSet*. You'll find versions of the application built in Microsoft Visual Basic as well as Microsoft Visual C#.

Step 1: Creating Your Strongly Typed *DataSet*

Because this is a Windows-based application, you start by creating a new Windows project in your language of choice. Name the application Chapter13. Rename the default form Orders-Form, and change the caption to Edit Orders.

The application will display order information for a particular customer, including data from the Orders, Order Details, Products, and Employees tables. We'll want to access data from each of these related tables in various portions of the application based on foreign key constraints that exist in the database. To simplify the process of accessing all this related data, we will create a strongly typed *DataSet* that contains *DataTables* for each of these related database tables. We'll start with only the data we want to work with initially—in this case, the Orders table—and build the strongly typed *DataSet*'s schema incrementally.

There are a couple of options for creating the strongly typed *DataSet* at design time. The simplest option is to invoke the Data Source Configuration Wizard by clicking the Add New Data Source button or link in the Data Sources window or by selecting Add New Data Source from the Data portion of the Visual Studio menu.

Once you've invoked the Data Source Configuration Wizard, specify that you want to build your new data source based on a database and select the connection string that will let you connect to your SQL Server Northwind database. If you do not already have a connection to a SQL Server Northwind database, you can create one using the wizard.

The Data Source Configuration Wizard makes the process of selecting tables and columns of information for your strongly typed *DataSet* a snap. Let's start by selecting the OrderID, CustomerID, EmployeeID, and OrderDate columns from the Orders table. Simply drill down into the Orders table and select these columns, as shown in Figure 13-2. The wizard will automatically generate a default name for the strongly typed *DataSet* based on the connection string. You can specify your own name or simply accept the default. Click the Finish button and voilà! Your strongly typed *DataSet* is ready for use.

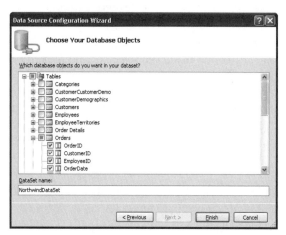

Figure 13-2   Selecting columns in the Data Source Configuration Wizard

You don't need to create a *SqlDataAdapter* separately. The Data Source Configuration Wizard will create a separate *TableAdapter*, which encapsulates the *SqlDataAdapter*, automatically for each table (or view) you select in the wizard. For more information on *TableAdapters*, see the discussion of *TableAdapters* in Chapter 9.

> **Note**   The *TableAdapter* that the Data Source Configuration Wizard generated retrieves data from all rows in the table. Keep this in mind when using the wizard. We'll add a query to retrieve just the orders for a particular customer in Step 3, later in the chapter.

The OrderID column in the Orders table is an auto-increment column. In Chapter 6, I recommended setting both the *AutoIncrementSeed* and *AutoIncrementStep* properties to –1 on auto-increment columns in a *DataSet*. Let's set these properties on the OrderID column in the strongly typed *DataSet* class that we just created. Double-click the strongly typed *DataSet* schema file in Solution Explorer (NorthwindDataSet.xsd). Select the OrderID column. Set the *AutoIncrementSeed* and *AutoIncrementStep* properties to –1. Then save the changes and close the *DataSet* designer window.

Step 2: Adding Simple Bound Controls to the Form

You now have a strongly typed *DataSet* class for your project. Now let's add some bound controls to the form so that we can display the data for a particular order. To make the user interface more intuitive, we'll also add a *Label* control for each bound control to help the user understand what data the bound controls contain.

The process of creating bound controls is much easier in Visual Studio 2005 than in previous versions of Visual Studio. Creating a *Label* and a bound *TextBox* for a column in a strongly typed *DataSet* used to require multiple (and fairly tedious) steps. You used to have to drag and drop a *Label* and *TextBox* control for each column that you wanted to display on the *Form* and then set multiple properties on each control through the Properties window.

With Visual Studio 2005, the process involves dragging the desired column from the Data Source window. That's all. No muss, no fuss, no oily residue. Drag and drop the OrderID, CustomerID, and EmployeeID columns onto the form, one at a time. Visual Studio takes care of the rest—creating a *Label* and *TextBox* control and using the selected column name to set the *Name* property on each control (such as orderIDTextBox and orderIDLabel) and the *Text* property on the *Label* control (Order ID). You can change the values of these properties through the Properties window, but thankfully Visual Studio provides intelligent defaults so that you don't *have* to set these properties yourself. Visual Studio also binds the *TextBox* control's *Text* property to the column in the *DataSet*. We'll take a closer look at how you can bind a *TextBox*, both through the Properties window and through pure code, shortly.

Once you've dragged and dropped the OrderID column from the Data Source window onto your Form, your Form will look like the one shown in Figure 13-3.

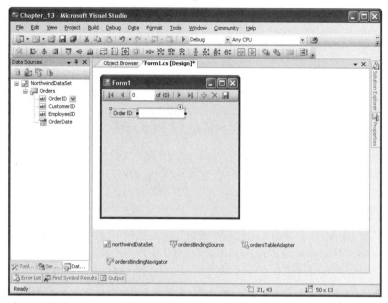

Figure 13-3   Creating bound controls using Visual Studio

Introducing the *BindingSource* Class

The first time you drag a column from the Data Source window onto your form, Visual Studio does more than just add controls to the form. Visual Studio also adds a series of components to the form's Components Tray, as shown in Figure 13-3. Two of these components are instances of classes that should already be familiar to you: the strongly typed *DataSet* and the *TableAdapter*. The other two components are instances of classes that are new to version 2.0 of the .NET Framework: the *BindingSource* class and the *BindingNavigator* control. We'll take a closer look at the *BindingNavigator* control in Step 4.

You may remember from Chapter 6 and Chapter 8 that there is no "current" position in the *DataTable* or *DataView*. All rows of data are available at all times. Although this concept works well when programmatically accessing the contents of a *DataTable* or *DataView*, it does not translate well to a Windows Forms application. The user might expect that there's a current row of information that's available in a series of controls on the form and that she has the ability to navigate back and forth through the available rows of data.

In version 1.0 of the .NET Framework, the *CurrencyManager* class managed the current row of data, serving as a middleman between the bound controls and the *DataView*. (Note that attempts to bind controls to a *DataTable* actually bound the controls to the *DataView* returned by the *DataTable*'s *DefaultView* property.) Giving the user the ability to navigate through the available data required adding your own controls to the form and having them modify the *Position* property on the *CurrencyManager* object associated with the bound controls. Binding controls to the *DataView* implicitly created a *CurrencyManager* object. There are countless posts to .NET forums from developers who struggled trying to access the *CurrencyManager* objects they created programmatically by binding controls.

The *BindingSource* class derives from the *CurrencyManager* class, providing additional functionality while simplifying the process of writing code to interact with bound controls. Let's look at some of the ways the *BindingSource* class makes life easier for developers.

Explicit Creation   You can create instances of the *BindingSource* class explicitly through the class's constructor. This represents a major step forward for Windows Forms data binding. Explicitly creating *BindingSource* objects and then binding your controls to the *BindingSource* objects requires an extra line of code, but it removes a great deal of confusion.

Indirection   The *BindingSource* class involves an added layer of indirection, which lets you separate the controls from the data. You bind your *BindingSource* to the source of the data while binding your controls to the *BindingSource* object. You can also bind your controls to a *BindingSource* object before your application actually receives the data.

This added level of indirection is extremely helpful if your application receives data from a component such as a Web service. Imagine that when the user clicks a button in your application, your code calls a Web service to execute a query and retrieve the results in a *DataSet*. After retrieving the results, you simply set the *DataSource* and *DataMember* properties on the *BindingSource* object so that it can access the data and alert the bound controls that data is available. You do not need to rebind all your controls to the newly retrieved *DataSet*, which was required to handle this scenario in version 1.0 of the .NET Framework.

Navigation Methods   The *BindingSource* class exposes simple navigation methods: *MoveFirst*, *MovePrevious*, *MoveNext*, and *MoveLast*. These methods simplify the process of programmatically changing the current position. Changing the current position using a *Currency Manager* object involves changing the value of the *Position* property. It's not actually difficult to write code like the following to move to the last available row of data:

```
CurrencyManager.Position = CurrencyManager.Count - 1
```

However, I'd still rather write the following code instead:

```
BindingSource.MoveLast()
```

Surfacing Properties from the *DataView*   The *BindingSource* class surfaces many properties that are already on the *DataView* class, though the actual property names differ in some cases. Surfacing these properties allows developers to work with just the *BindingSource* class. Prior to adding the *BindingSource* class, developers were forced to set properties on the *CurrencyManager* object to navigate through results but set properties on the *DataView* object to control which rows were visible and/or the order of those rows.

The *Filter* and *Sort* properties on the *BindingSource* class correspond to the *RowFilter* and *Sort* properties on the *DataView* class, respectively. The *AllowAdd*, *AllowEdit*, and *AllowRemove* properties on the *BindingSource* class correspond to the *AllowNew*, *AllowEdit*, and *AllowDelete* properties on the *DataView* class, respectively.

Creating a *BindingSource*

The *BindingSource* is available as an item on the Data tab of the Toolbox window. You can add a *BindingSource* to your form at design time by dragging and dropping a *BindingSource* from the Toolbox onto either the form or its Components Tray.

To bind the *BindingSource* to a *DataTable* in your *DataSet*, set the *BindingSource*'s *DataSource* property to the *DataSet* using the Properties window. Then set the *DataMember* property to the desired *DataTable*.

There are two ways to accomplish the same task in code. You can create a *BindingSource* object and set its *DataMember* and *DataSource* properties separately, or you can set those properties when calling the *BindingSource*'s constructor. In the following code snippets, sections A and B are equivalent:

Visual Basic

```
Dim bindingSource As BindingSource

'Section A
bindingSource = New BindingSource()
bindingSource.DataMember = "TableName"
bindingSource.DataSource = dataSet

'Section B
bindingSource = New BindingSource(dataSet, "TableName")
```

Visual C#

```
BindingSource bindingSource;

//Section A
bindingSource = new BindingSource();
bindingSource.DataMember = "TableName";
bindingSource.DataSource = dataSet;

//Section B
bindingSource = new BindingSource(dataSet, "TableName");
```

Now that you understand what the *BindingSource* class is for and how to create an instance of one, let's look at how you can bind simple controls such as the *TextBox* to a *BindingSource*.

Binding Simple Controls Using the Properties Window

Binding a simple control, such as a *TextBox*, using the Properties window is simple, though not terribly intuitive. While you want the *Text* property on the control to display the value from the desired column for the current row of data, you don't directly set the *Text* property on the control using the Properties window.

Instead, you use the *DataBindings* section of the Properties window. First, select the control you want to bind. Then expand the *DataBindings* of the Properties window. For most controls, the property you want to bind will be listed in this section. If the property is listed, click the property and then select the desired column in the drop-down list, as shown in Figure 13-4. If the property you want to bind does not appear in the short list under *DataBindings* in the Properties window, click the ellipsis (...) button in the (Advanced) item under (DataBindings), and then select the desired property to bind from the resulting dialog box.

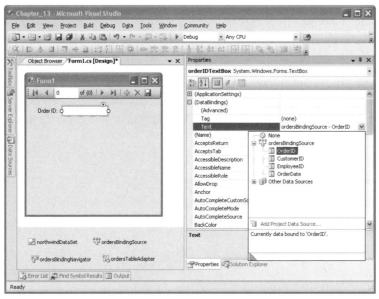

Figure 13-4   Binding a *TextBox* using the Properties window

Binding Simple Controls Programmatically

You can also bind controls through code. Each control exposes a *DataBindings* property that you can use to bind the control to a *BindingSource* or directly to a *DataView*. You could use the following code to bind a *TextBox* control's *Text* property to the OrderID column available through a *BindingSource*:

Visual Basic
```
OrderIDTextBox.DataBindings.Add("Text", OrdersDataSource, "OrderID")
```

Visual C#
```
orderIDTextBox.DataBindings.Add("Text", ordersDataSource, "OrderID");
```

In fact, this is the code that Visual Studio generates when you bind the control at design time, either by dragging and dropping the column from the Data Sources window or by binding the control using the (*DataBindings*) portion of the Properties window.

Changing the Control Type Associated with a Column

The OrderDate column in the Orders table, as its name implies, contains the date the order was placed. When you create a strongly typed *DataSet*, the OrderDate column in the strongly typed *DataSet* is of type *DateTime*. By default, Visual Studio associates this data type with the

DateTimePicker control. If you drag and drop the column onto your form, Visual Studio will add a *Label* and *DateTimePicker* onto your form.

Let's look at how we can change this behavior.

If you look at the column in the Data Sources window, you'll see the icon for the *DateTime-Picker* control to the left of the OrderDate column. Select the OrderDate column, click the down arrow to the right of the column name, and you'll see a list of controls that you can use to bind to the column, as shown in Figure 13-5. Select the *TextBox* control from the list. Then drag and drop the OrderDate column onto your form, and Visual Studio will create a *Label* and a *TextBox* rather than a *Label* and a *DateTimePicker*.

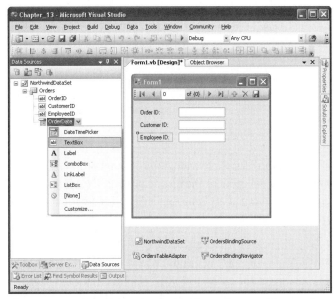

Figure 13-5   Specifying the desired bound control for a column

The *DateTimePicker* control is a very handy control because it allows the user to view and change *DateTime* values easily. However, the *DateTimePicker* control does not handle null values well. If you move to a row that contains a null value, the *DateTimePicker* control continues to display the *DateTime* value from the previous row. If your application might have to handle null values for *DateTime* columns, you're probably best served using *TextBox* controls instead.

Step 3: Retrieving Data

You now have a strongly typed *DataSet* and some *TextBox* controls bound to columns in the Orders table for the *DataSet*. If you run your project, you'll see your form with its *Label* and *TextBox* controls and the *TextBox* controls will contain information about the first order in the Orders table.

How did the project know how to retrieve order information? Did the strongly typed *DataSet* automagically fill itself?

There's no real magic occurring. Visual Studio automatically added code to help retrieve information when the form appears. If you examine the code in the Form's *Load* event, you'll see the following:

Visual Basic
```
Private Sub Form1_Load(ByVal sender As System.Object, _
                       ByVal e As System.EventArgs) Handles MyBase.Load
        'TODO: This line of code loads data into
        '     the 'NorthwindDataSet.Orders' table.
        '     You can move, or remove it, as needed.
        Me.OrdersTableAdapter.Fill(Me.NorthwindDataSet.Orders)
End Sub
```

Visual C#
```
private void Form1_Load(object sender, EventArgs e) {
    // TODO: This line of code loads data into
    //       the 'northwindDataSet.Orders' table.
    //       You can move, or remove it, as needed.
    this.ordersTableAdapter.Fill(this.northwindDataSet.Orders);
}
```

How did this code get here?

You might have noticed that in Step 2, dragging the first column of information onto the form created an instance of the *TableAdapter* for the Orders table. Visual Studio realized that you were adding a column from the Orders table in the strongly typed *DataSet*, so it added an instance of the corresponding *TableAdapter* and automatically added code to the form's *Load* event to call the *TableAdapter*'s *Fill* method.

As the comment suggests, you can change this code as you see fit. In fact, I'd argue that you *should* change the code. When you used the Data Source Configuration Wizard, Visual Studio automatically generated *TableAdapters* for each table you referenced in the wizard, and those *TableAdapters* don't perform any filtering. In other words, the *TableAdapters* retrieve all rows from their corresponding tables when you call their *Fill* methods.

This approach might be just fine in small applications that interact with tables that contain a small number of rows. However, as the size of the table in the database grows, the application is requesting more information from the database—tying up the database, using additional bandwidth, and consuming additional memory at the client, not to mention increasing the time it takes for the application to load.

A better approach is to add a filter to the query. In this case, you could add a parameterized query to the *TableAdapter* to request just the orders for a particular query by asking the user to supply the name or ID for the desired customer or selecting the customer from a list. Chapter 9 demonstrates how to add queries to a *TableAdapter*. The sample application for this chapter relies on a parameterized query that uses the CustomerID column, as shown in the following code. When I created the query, I used the Choose Methods To Generate page of the wizard to add *FillByCustomerID* and *GetDataByCustomerID* methods. The query to retrieve the orders based on that parameter is simple because the column appears in both the Customers and Orders tables.

Visual Basic
```vb
Dim customerID As String = "ALFKI"
Me.OrdersTableAdapter.FillByCustomerID(Me.NorthwindDataSet.Orders, _
                                       customerID)
```

Visual C#
```csharp
string customerID = "ALFKI";
this.ordersTableAdapter.FillByCustomerID(this.northwindDataSet.Orders,
                                         customerID);
```

For a moment, let's imagine that you wanted to apply a filter using a column that appears only in the Customers table, such as the CompanyName column. You could add a query to the *TableAdapter* for the Orders table and add the Customers table in the query, but use the CompanyName column only in the WHERE clause, comparing it to a parameter, as shown in Figure 13-6.

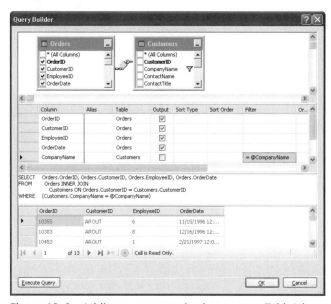

Figure 13-6   Adding a parameterized query to a *TableAdapter*

On the Choose Methods To Generate page of the *TableAdapter* Configuration Wizard, you could name the *Fill* and *GetData* methods for the query *FillByCompanyName* and *GetDataByCompanyName*, respectively. Once that's done, you could change the code in the form's *Load* event to use the new *FillByCompanyName* method to retrieve just the orders for the desired customer, as shown in the following code:

Visual Basic
```vb
Me.OrdersTableAdapter.FillByCompanyName(Me.NorthwindDataSet.Orders, _
                                        "Around The Horn")
```

Visual C#

```
this.ordersTableAdapter.FillByCompanyName(this.northwindDataSet.Orders,
                                          "Around The Horn");
```

The new query returns the same columns of information as the original query for the *Table-Adapter*. So there's no need to change the structure of the strongly typed table for the Orders information. This also means that Visual Studio does not need to try to build updating logic based on the query.

Step 4: Navigating Through the Results

Visual Studio automatically added a *BindingNavigator* control to the form when you dragged and dropped the first column of information from the Data Source window onto the form. Let's take a closer look at this control.

What Is a *BindingNavigator* Control?

The *BindingNavigator* control, which is new to version 2.0 of the .NET Framework, is designed to help developers build applications that let users navigate through data without having to write large amounts of code. In version 1.0 of the .NET Framework, developers routinely had to add a series of buttons to forms, and they had to add code to the buttons' *Click* events to move back and forth through available rows of data. The process of adding these buttons, and the code for the buttons, was tedious and developers often found themselves writing the same code over and over. Thanks to the *BindingNavigator* control, developers no longer need to create their own navigation buttons.

The *BindingNavigator* control derives from the *ToolStrip* control. It contains a series of buttons preconfigured to let users navigate through the data available through a *BindingSource* object, and it allows users to add items to and remove items from that *BindingSource*.

How Does It Work?

The *BindingNavigator* control exposes a series of properties—*AddNewItem, CountItem, DeleteItem, MoveFirstItem*, and so on—each of type *ToolStripItem*. Figure 13-7 shows the *BindingNavigator* at design time, with the Properties window adjusted to show the properties. By default, the *BindingNavigator* includes a *ToolStripItem* for each of these properties and associates each *ToolStripItem* with the corresponding property, as shown in the figure.

The *BindingNavigator* control listens to the *Click* events for these *ToolStripItems* and performs the appropriate action based on the item that was clicked. In other words, if the user clicks the *ToolStripItem* contained in the *BindingNavigator*'s *MoveFirstItem*, the *BindingNavigator* automatically calls the *MoveFirst* method on the *BindingSource* object to which it is associated.

The *BindingNavigator* control also listens to events broadcast by the *BindingSource*. If the position of the *BindingSource* changes, the *BindingNavigator* control automatically reflects this change—updating the area of the control that displays the position (or row number), as well as enabling and disabling the appropriate navigation based on the current position.

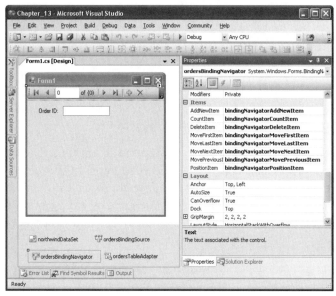

Figure 13-7   The *BindingNavigator* control

How Can I Create a *BindingNavigator* Control at Design Time?

You can simply drag a *BindingNavigator* from the Data tab of the Toolbox onto your form. Associating a *BindingNavigator* control with a *BindingSource* is just as simple. With the *Binding-Navigator* control selected, click the *BindingSource* property in the Properties window and select an available *BindingSource* from the drop-down list.

How Can I Create a *BindingNavigator* Control in Code?

Creating a *BindingNavigator* control in code is almost as easy. Pass the desired *BindingSource* object into the *BindingNavigator*'s constructor, as shown in the following code:

Visual Basic
```
Dim OrdersBindingNavigator As BindingNavigator
OrdersBindingNavigator = New BindingNavigator(OrdersBindingSource)
Me.Controls.Add(ordersBindingNavigator)
```

Visual C#
```
BindingNavigator ordersBindingNavigator;
ordersBindingNavigator = new BindingNavigator(ordersBindingSource);
this.Controls.Add(ordersBindingNavigator);
```

Note   Don't forget to add the *BindingNavigator* to the form's *Controls* collection.

Can I Customize the *BindingNavigator*?

Absolutely! You can add your own code to existing buttons. You can also add your own buttons. We'll take a closer look at each of these options in the upcoming steps.

Step 5: Adding and Deleting Items

The *BindingNavigator* control automatically includes buttons that allow the user to add and delete items. It's almost too easy. However, there's plenty of room for customization.

Adding Custom Logic to a *ToolStripItem's Click* Event

In this order entry form that we're building, you might want to set the OrderDate for the new order to today's date. One possible approach would be to trap for the *DataTable*'s *TableNewRow* event and generate the value there. A more intuitive approach would be to add code to the *Click* event for the *Add* button on the *BindingNavigator* and assign today's date to the *TextBox* that's bound to the OrderDate column. Let's take a look at a third approach that's a hybrid of the first two.

By the time the *Click* event fires, the *BindingNavigator* has already called the *AddNew* method on the *BindingSource* object. That means that the *Current* property on the order's *BindingSource* object is set to a *DataRowView* object that contains the new row of data. We can assign today's date to the OrderDate column in the *DataRowView*. We can then use the *BindingSource* object's *ResetCurrentItem* method to alert the controls bound to the *BindingSource* that there is new information available for the current item. The following code demonstrates this approach:

Visual Basic
```
Private Sub BindingNavigatorAddNewItem_Click(ByVal sender As Object, _
                                   ByVal e As EventArgs) _
                          Handles BindingNavigatorAddNewItem.Click
    Dim currentRow As DataRowView
    currentRow = DirectCast(Me.OrdersBindingSource.Current, DataRowView)
    currentRow("OrderDate") = DateTime.Today
    Me.ordersBindingSource.ResetCurrentItem()
End Sub
```

Visual C#
```
private void bindingNavigatorAddNewItem_Click(object sender, EventArgs e) {
    DataRowView currentRow = (DataRowView) this.ordersBindingSource.Current;
    currentRow["OrderDate"] = DateTime.Today;
    this.ordersBindingSource.ResetCurrentItem();
}
```

The best part of this hybrid approach is that it does not directly interact with the bound control or controls. Why is this a good thing? Let's say that you started out with a *DateTimePicker* control for the OrderDate column and later changed to a *TextBox* (or vice versa). This specialized code to handle adding a new row of data will still work. If you set the property of a control, you'll have to change that code if you change the control you're using.

This example demonstrates that you can add your own code to enhance a feature of the *Binding-Navigator*. But what if you want to override or change the behavior associated with clicking an item?

Changing the Behavior of an Item on a *BindingNavigator*

The *BindingNavigator* control includes a *Delete* button. You might want to change the behavior associated with this button, displaying a dialog box asking the user to confirm the deletion of the current item. That sounds simple enough, except for one minor problem—by the time your code executes, the *BindingNavigator* has already implicitly called the *RemoveCurrent* method on the corresponding *BindingSource* object. There's no simple way to cancel that action after it has already occurred. There is, however, a simple solution.

The *BindingNavigator* object exposes a *DeleteItem* property. Whenever the *ToolStripItem* associated with this property is clicked, the *BindingNavigator* will call the *RemoveCurrent* method on the corresponding *BindingSource* object. Clearing the *BindingNavigator*'s *Delete-Item* property will prevent the *BindingNavigator* from implicitly calling the *BindingSource* object's *RemoveCurrent* method. In the Properties window, select the *BindingNavigator*'s *DeleteItem* property. Then click the drop-down arrow and select (none) at the top of the list, as shown in Figure 13-8.

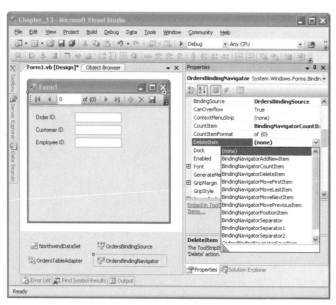

Figure 13-8   Clearing the *BindingNavigator*'s *DeleteItem* property

Now that you've prevented the *BindingNavigator* from removing items from the data source, it's up to you to handle the removal of items. Double-click the *Delete ToolStripButton* on the

BindingNavigator control and Visual Studio will create a procedure to handle the *Click* event for the *ToolStripButton*. You can add the following code to the *Click* event of the *Delete Tool-StripButton* to display a confirmation dialog box and remove the current item only if the user clicks the *Yes* button on the dialog box:

Visual Basic

```
Dim result As DialogResult
result = MessageBox.Show("Are you sure you want to delete this order?", _
                         "Confirmation Dialog", MessageBoxButtons.YesNo)
If result = Windows.Forms.DialogResult.Yes Then
    this.ordersBindingSource.RemoveCurrent()
End If
```

Visual C#

```
DialogResult result;
result = MessageBox.Show("Are you sure you want to delete this order?",
                         "Confirmation Dialog", MessageBoxButtons.YesNo);
if (result == DialogResult.Yes)
    this.ordersBindingSource.RemoveCurrent();
```

Some developers and users find confirmation dialog boxes annoying, but that's not the point of this exercise. The point is that you can use this approach to turn off the default behavior associated with clicking an item on the *BindingNavigator* and replace it with your own logic.

Step 6: Submitting Changes

You might have noticed the button on the far right of the *BindingNavigator* with the floppy disk icon. If you move the mouse cursor over this button while your application is running, you'll see a ToolTip that says Save Data. Clicking this button will save the pending changes to the database. Let's find out how the *BindingNavigator* accomplished this.

If you double-click the button at design-time, you'll see the following code in the *Save Tool-StripButton*'s *Click* event:

Visual Basic

```
Me.Validate()
Me.OrdersBindingSource.EndEdit()
Me.OrdersTableAdapter.Update(Me.NorthwindDataSet.Orders)
```

Visual C#

```
this.Validate();
this.ordersBindingSource.EndEdit();
this.ordersTableAdapter.Update(this.northwindDataSet.Orders);
```

If you've read Chapters 10 and 11, the last line of code should be familiar. The *Update* method submits the pending changes stored in the Orders *DataTable*.

The two prior lines of code might not be familiar. The call to the *Validate* method on the form causes the form to validate the data. Calling the *EndEdit* method on the Orders' *BindingSource* object requires a bit of an explanation.

If you modified a row of data by changing the contents of at least one bound control and then called the *HasChanges* method on the strongly typed *DataSet*, you'd find that it returned *False*. The *BindingSource* has not written the changes made in the bound controls to the current row of data. The *BindingSource* object lets you control whether you want to write or discard the changes through the *EndEdit* and *CancelEdit* methods, respectively. Moving to another row will implicitly call the *EndEdit* method if you've made changes through bound controls. So, prior to submitting changes, the code in the *Save* button calls the *EndEdit* method on the *BindingSource* object.

Adding Items to a *BindingNavigator* Control

The *BindingNavigator* control does not actually include a Save button. Visual Studio added the *ToolStripButton* for you and added the code we just examined at the same time it added the *TableAdapter* to the form's components tray when you dragged the first column of information onto the form.

I mention this for two reasons: first, to explain why you won't see a Save button if you create a *BindingNavigator* control yourself; and second, to demonstrate that you can add new items to a *BindingNavigator* control.

To add a new item to the *BindingNavigator* control, first select the control in the designer. You'll see a small drop-down arrow just to the right of the last item on the control. (Make sure your form is wide enough to display the entire control.) Click that drop-down arrow and you'll see a list of available item types—such as a *Button*, a *Label*, and so on—as shown in Figure 13-9.

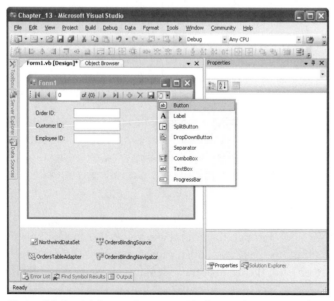

Figure 13-9   Adding an item to a *BindingNavigator* control

The various item types offer different properties and events. Once you've added your new item, set the properties on the item and add handlers to its events as appropriate. In particular, you'll need to name the controls to match the code in the *SetOrderEditMode* procedure shown in the next section.

In fact, let's add a few more items.

Step 7: Adding Edit, Accept, and Reject Buttons

The application we have so far lets the user start editing any row without explicitly entering edit mode. Changes made in bound controls are implicitly written to the row of data when the user moves to a different row.

This approach makes it easy for the user to modify a number of rows, but it might not be the best approach. Depending on the application and the users you're targeting, you might want the process of editing a row to be more explicit. A simple way to make the editing process more explicit is to force the user to click an Edit button to edit the contents of the current item.

The sample project for this chapter contains a *SetOrderEditMode* procedure. This procedure accepts a *Boolean* value that indicates whether the user can edit the current order. When the form initially loads, the *Load* event calls *SetOrderEditMode* and specifies that the user cannot edit the order, which locks down all the bound controls, as shown in Figure 13-10. The code in the *SetOrderEditMode* sets the *ReadOnly* property of the bound *TextBoxes* for the editable columns to *True* or *False*, depending on the value passed into the procedure.

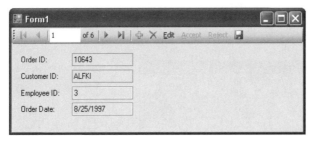

Figure 13-10 Adding Edit, Accept, and Reject buttons to the form

Unfortunately, not all controls offer a *ReadOnly* property. However, the base *Control* class does offer an *Enabled* property. I prefer relying on the *ReadOnly* property for *TextBoxes* rather than the *Enabled* property because I like giving the user the ability to select the text stored in a *TextBox* even if the user is not allowed to change that text. When you set a control's *Enabled* property to *False*, the user cannot select the control.

If you're going to force the user to explicitly enter edit mode, you should also force the user to accept or reject the changes made through the bound controls. The sample application also includes Accept and Reject buttons. You can choose your own names (Accept and Reject, Update and Cancel, and so on), but the basic premise remains the same—clicking one button accepts the changes, clicking the other button discards the changes. The code in the *Click* events of the Accept button calls the *EndEdit* method on the *BindingSource* object to accept the changes to the current row, and then it calls the *SetOrderEditMode* to prevent further changes. The code in the *Click* event of the Reject button calls the *CancelEdit* method to reject the changes prior to calling *SetOrderEditMode* to prevent further changes.

The *SetOrderEditMode* procedure also modifies many of the items on the *BindingNavigator* control. Once the user enters edit mode, the user should be able to exit edit mode only by clicking the Accept or Reject buttons. The *SetOrderEditMode* procedure (shown below) enables or disables the items responsible for navigation, adding, deleting, and saving changes, depending on whether the user is entering or exiting editing mode.

Visual Basic

```vb
Private Sub SetOrderEditMode(ByVal IsEditing As Boolean)
    'TextBoxes should be read only if not in editing mode
    Me.OrderIDTextBox.ReadOnly = Not IsEditing
    Me.CustomerIDTextBox.ReadOnly = Not IsEditing
    Me.EmployeeIDTextBox.ReadOnly = Not IsEditing
    Me.OrderDateTextBox.ReadOnly = Not IsEditing

    'Navigation/Add/Delete/Save enabled if not in editing mode
    Me.BindingNavigatorMoveFirstItem.Enabled = Not IsEditing
    Me.BindingNavigatorMovePreviousItem.Enabled = Not IsEditing
    Me.BindingNavigatorMoveNextItem.Enabled = Not IsEditing
    Me.BindingNavigatorMoveLastItem.Enabled = Not IsEditing
    Me.BindingNavigatorPositionItem.Enabled = Not IsEditing
    Me.BindingNavigatorAddNewItem.Enabled = Not IsEditing
    Me.BindingNavigatorDeleteItem.Enabled = Not IsEditing
    Me.OrdersBindingNavigatorSaveItem.Enabled = Not IsEditing

    'Edit enabled if not in edit mode
    Me.OrdersBindingNavigatorEditItem.Enabled = Not IsEditing

    'Accept and Reject if not in edit mode
    Me.OrdersBindingNavigatorAcceptItem.Enabled = IsEditing
    Me.OrdersBindingNavigatorRejectItem.Enabled = IsEditing
End Sub
```

Visual C#

```csharp
private void SetOrderEditMode(bool IsEditing) {
    //TextBoxes should be read only if not in editing mode
    this.orderIDTextBox.ReadOnly = !IsEditing;
    this.customerIDTextBox.ReadOnly = !IsEditing;
    this.employeeIDTextBox.ReadOnly = !IsEditing;
    this.orderDateTextBox.ReadOnly = !IsEditing;

    //Navigation/Add/Delete/Save enabled if not in editing mode
    this.bindingNavigatorMoveFirstItem.Enabled = !IsEditing;
    this.bindingNavigatorMovePreviousItem.Enabled = !IsEditing;
    this.bindingNavigatorMoveNextItem.Enabled = !IsEditing;
    this.bindingNavigatorMoveLastItem.Enabled = !IsEditing;
    this.bindingNavigatorPositionItem.Enabled = !IsEditing;
```

```
    this.bindingNavigatorAddNewItem.Enabled = !IsEditing;
    this.bindingNavigatorDeleteItem.Enabled = !IsEditing;
    this.ordersBindingNavigatorSaveItem.Enabled = !IsEditing;

    //Edit enabled if not in edit mode
    this.ordersBindingNavigatorEditItem.Enabled = !IsEditing;

    //Accept and Reject if not in edit mode
    this.ordersBindingNavigatorAcceptItem.Enabled = IsEditing;
    this.ordersBindingNavigatorRejectItem.Enabled = IsEditing;
}
```

Adding this functionality requires just a few minutes of coding, but I think it's time well spent. As a result of these changes, the application's behavior is much more intuitive. Users won't encounter problems submitting changes due to uncommitted changes. Plus, you won't be left scratching your head trying to figure out how and when the *BindingSource* object commits changes to the *DataSet*.

Step 8: Viewing Child Data

Our application now allows users to view and modify data from the Orders table. However, that functionality isn't terribly helpful unless we also allow the user to view and modify the line items for those orders.

Figure 13-11 shows the user interface for the next phase of the sample application. As you can see, I've added a grid that displays data from the Order Details table. As you move from one order to the next, the grid displays just the related rows.

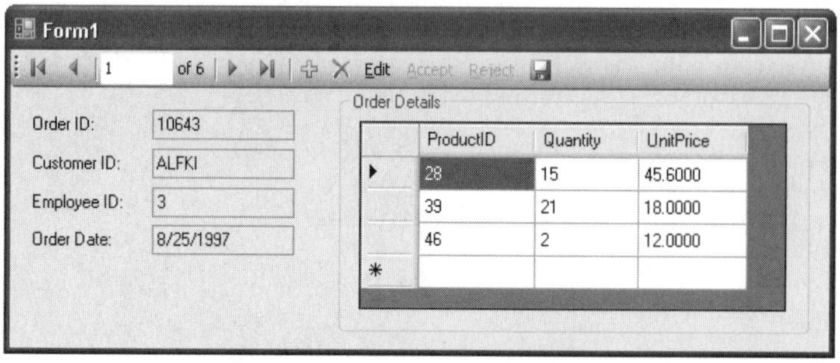

Figure 13-11   Displaying an order and its line items

To add this functionality to the application, we'll do the following in the next sections:

1. Add a *DataTable* to the strongly typed *DataSet* for order detail information.

2. Add a parameterized query to the *TableAdapter* to retrieve just the order details for a single customer, and execute that query when the form loads.

3. Add a *DataGridView* to the form to display just order details for the current order.

4. Add logic to the procedure for the Save button to submit changes from both *DataTable* objects.

Adding Order Detail Information to the Strongly Typed *DataSet*

Visual Studio 2005 makes adding data from a related table simple. Open the strongly typed *DataSet* in the designer. Select the OrderID, ProductID, Quantity, and UnitPrice columns from the Order Details table in Server Explorer. Then drag the columns onto the strongly typed *DataSet*. This will add a related Order Details table to the strongly typed *DataSet*.

The strongly typed *DataSet* designer will automatically add a *DataRelation* between the two tables in the *DataSet*. However, the designer will not associate the new *DataRelation* with a *ForeignKeyConstraint*. Chapters 7 and 9 discuss reasons why you should associate your *DataRelations* with *ForeignKeyConstraints*. One such reason is to ensure that marking a parent row as deleted also marks the related child rows as deleted. Double-click the *DataRelation* in the designer, select the Both Relation And Foreign Key Constraint option, and set both Update Rule and Delete Rule to *Cascade*.

Adding a Query to the *TableAdapter* to Retrieve Just the Order Details for a Customer

Adding columns from the Order Details table to the strongly typed *DataSet* also added a *Table-Adapter* configured to fill the *DataSet* with data from those columns in the Order Details table. The *TableAdapter*'s query will not, however, apply any filter to the query. It will retrieve all rows from the table.

Adding a query to retrieve just the order details for a particular customer is easy. Right-click the new *TableAdapter*, and select Add Query from the context menu. You can use the Query Builder to add the Orders table and add a filter to the CustomerID column on the Orders table using a parameter, or you can simply paste the following query into the query pane:

```
SELECT [Order Details].OrderID, [Order Details].Quantity,
       [Order Details].ProductID, [Order Details].UnitPrice
    FROM [Order Details]
        INNER JOIN Orders ON [Order Details].OrderID = Orders.OrderID
    WHERE Orders.CustomerID = @CustomerID
```

Name the new methods *FillByCustomerID* and *GetDataByCustomerID*, and save the changes to the strongly typed *DataSet*.

Adding a *DataGridView* That Displays Child Data

Now look at the contents of the strongly typed *DataSet* in the Data Sources window. You'll see two separate Order Details nodes, as shown in Figure 13-12. As you can see in the figure, one Order Detail node is a sibling of the Orders node, and the other is a child of the Orders node.

If you drag either node onto the form, you'll create a *TableAdapter* to retrieve information from the database, a *DataGridView* to display the information retrieved, and a *BindingSource* to handle the interaction between the grid and the data. The difference between the two operations is in how Visual Studio sets properties on the *BindingSource* object. If you drag the Order Details node that's a sibling of the Orders node, Visual Studio will set the new

BindingSource object's *DataSource* property to the strongly typed *DataSet* and the *DataMember* property to the name of the *DataTable*. These properties will cause the *DataGridView* control to display all rows in the Order Details table. If you drag the Order Details node that's a child of the Orders node, Visual Studio will set the new *BindingSource* object's *DataSource* property to the Orders *BindingSource* and the *DataMember* property to the name of the *DataRelation* between the Orders and Order Details tables in the strongly typed *DataSet*. These properties will cause the *DataGridView* control to display just the Order Details rows for the currently visible Order.

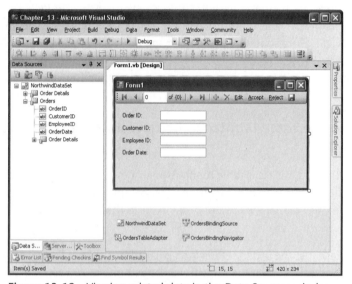

Figure 13-12   Viewing related data in the Data Sources window

Changing the *TableAdapter.Fill* Code in the Form's *Load* Event

Earlier in the chapter, you associated the *DataRelation* between the Orders and Order Details *DataTables* with a *ForeignKeyConstraint*. As a result, the *DataSet* now requires that the rows in the value for the OrderID column for rows in the Order Details *DataTable* must correspond to a value in the Orders *DataTable*.

If you run the form as is, you'll receive a *ConstraintException*. The exception occurs on the call to the *Fill* method on the *TableAdapter* for the Order Details *DataTable*. Visual Studio added this line of code when you dragged the Order Details node onto the form. To prevent the *ConstraintException*, we need to do two things. First, modify the code so that it retrieves only order details that correspond to the orders retrieved. Second, move the code to retrieve order detail information so that it appears after the call to retrieve order information. The resulting code should look like this:

Visual Basic

```vb
Dim customerID As String = "ALFKI"
OrdersTableAdapter.FillByCustomerID(NorthwindDataSet.Orders, _
                                    customerID)
Order_DetailsTableAdapter.FillByCustomerID(NorthwindDataSet.Order_Details, _
                                    customerID)
```

Visual C#

```
string customerID = "ALFKI";
ordersTableAdapter.FillByCustomerID(northwindDataSet.Orders,
                                    customerID);
order_DetailsTableAdapter.FillByCustomerID(northwindDataSet.Order_Details,
                                           customerID);
```

Submitting Changes to Both Tables

Chapter 11 discusses the complexities involved in submitting hierarchical changes to a database. Basically, you need to submit new rows starting at the top of the hierarchy (orders before order details) but deleted rows starting at the bottom (order details before orders). As a result, you can't simply supply the entire *DataTable* when you call the *TableAdapter* objects' *Update* methods.

First you submit the new and modified orders. Then you can submit all the changes to the Order Details table. After that, you can submit the deleted orders. If you look at the code in the procedure for the Save button's *Click* event in the sample, you'll see that it is based on the following:

Visual Basic

```
Dim ordersTable As DataTable = Me.NorthwindDataSet.Orders
Dim detailsTable As DataTable = Me.NorthwindDataSet.Order_Details

Dim rows() As DataRow
'Submit new or modified orders
rows = ordersTable.Select("", "", DataViewRowState.Added Or _
                                  DataViewRowState.ModifiedCurrent)
Me.OrdersTableAdapter.Update(rows)

'Submit new or modified order details
rows = detailsTable.Select("", "", DataViewRowState.Added Or _
                                   DataViewRowState.ModifiedCurrent)
Me.Order_DetailsTableAdapter.Update(rows)

'Submit deleted order details
rows = detailsTable.Select("", "", DataViewRowState.Deleted)
Me.Order_DetailsTableAdapter.Update(rows)

'Submit deleted orders
rows = ordersTable.Select("", "", DataViewRowState.Deleted)
Me.OrdersTableAdapter.Update(rows)
```

Visual C#

```
DataTable ordersTable = this.northwindDataSet.Orders;
DataTable detailsTable = this.northwindDataSet.Order_Details;

DataRow[] rows;
```

```
//Submit new or modified orders
rows = ordersTable.Select("", "", DataViewRowState.Added |
                                   DataViewRowState.ModifiedCurrent);
this.ordersTableAdapter.Update(rows);

//Submit new or modified order details
rows = detailsTable.Select("", "", DataViewRowState.Added |
                                   DataViewRowState.ModifiedCurrent);
this.order_DetailsTableAdapter.Update(rows);

//Submit deleted order details
rows = detailsTable.Select("", "", DataViewRowState.Deleted);
this.order_DetailsTableAdapter.Update(rows);

//Submit deleted orders
rows = ordersTable.Select("", "", DataViewRowState.Deleted);
this.ordersTableAdapter.Update(rows);
```

The actual code in the *Click* event is more complex, employing a Try/Catch block, tracking the number of changes, and so on. I've removed the other code here to focus on submitting the changes from the related tables in the appropriate order.

Step 9: Binding a Second Form to the Same Data Source

Trying to bind controls on multiple forms to the same data source is challenging but possible. Before I explain how to accomplish this, I want to make a quick detour to show you how to improve the user interface to help even novice users edit data easily.

The *DataGridView* is a helpful and powerful tool. I regularly use *DataGridView* controls to display the contents of multiple rows. However, I'm not a big fan of having users modify data in a *DataGridView*.

The goal of Step 7 was to make the editing process as explicit and predictable as possible. The *DataGridView* control does not work well in such environments. You can't force the user to remain on a single row within the grid.

I would rather have users edit data in more basic controls, such as *TextBoxes* and *ComboBoxes*, for another reason. The simple controls are easier to manage. If you want to add code to validate changes made in one control and apply appropriate changes to related controls or change the appearance of controls based on their contact (to make negative values appear in a red font, for example), that process is fairly straightforward with simple controls.

The *DataGridView* exposes 170 events. As I mentioned before, the *DataGridView* is a helpful and powerful tool. With enough time, patience, and documentation, you can probably figure out how to achieve the same level of control with a *DataGridView*. If you do, be sure to let the rest of us know.

If you need true fine-grained control over how the user modifies multiple rows of data, such as the order detail information on the form we're building in this chapter, I recommend using the *DataGridView* strictly for display purposes. You can prevent users from modifying data through the *DataGridView* control by setting its *AllowUserToAddRows* and *AllowUserToDelete-Rows* properties to *False* and its *ReadOnly* property to *True*. Then provide buttons so that the user can add, modify, or remove rows from the grid. If the user clicks a button to add or edit a row, display the row to modify on a separate form shown as a modal dialog box, as in Figure 13-13.

Figure 13-13   Editing related data in a modal dialog box

The sample project for this chapter includes a second form named *DetailForm* that lets the user edit a row from the Order Details table through its *EditDetail* method. The controls on the *DetailForm* are already bound to a *BindingSource* object. The *DetailForm* exposes an *Edit-Detail* method that the main form can call, passing in the main form's order details *Binding-Source*. The code inside the *EditDetail* method associates its *BindingSource* with the main form's *BindingSource*. The code then displays the *DetailForm* in a modal dialog box and calls the *EndEdit* or *CancelEdit* method on the *BindingSource*, depending on whether the user clicks the OK or Cancel button. This approach keeps the two forms in sync simply and easily.

Step 10: Improving the User Interface

We now have an application that lets users view and edit order information for a customer, but we can do a couple more things to improve the overall user experience.

Given the choice, most users would rather see descriptive information than cryptic key information on a form. For example, the child form that allows the user to modify a line item forces the user to know the key value rather than the name of the product. Also, the formatting for the unit price and item total for each line item looks unprofessional.

Let's see how we can present the data in a more user-friendly format, as shown in Figure 13-14. The three key improvements shown on the form are the Employee *ComboBox* control to simplify changing foreign key values, better formatting for numeric values, and expression-based columns (ProductName and ItemTotal) to display helpful calculated values. Let's examine how you can make each of these improvements yourself.

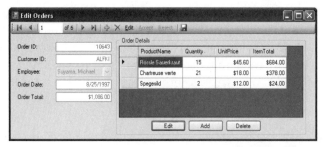

Figure 13-14   Presenting data in a more user-friendly format

Adding Lookup Functionality Using a *ComboBox* Control

If you look at Figure 13-14, you'll see that I replaced the *TextBox* that listed the EmployeeID for the current order with a *ComboBox* control that shows the employee's name. Adding this functionality is really quite simple. In fact, you need to set only four properties on the *ComboBox*.

The form will allow the user to associate an order with a different employee, but it does not actually modify values in the employee table. Because we do not have to worry about generating updating logic for employee information, we can use a query to construct friendly employee names based on the LastName and FirstName columns in the Employees table with a query such as the following one:

```
SELECT EmployeeID, LastName + ', ' + FirstName AS EmployeeName
    FROM Employees
```

First, you'll need to add employee information to the strongly typed *DataSet*. Right-click the *DataSet* designer, select Add TableAdapter, and enter the previously described query. Because the EmployeeName column in the query results is calculated, the TableAdapter Configuration Wizard will not be able to generate logic to submit new or modified employee information. Because the form will not make changes to the *DataTable* of employee information, that limitation of the wizard is not a problem. Visual Studio will automatically add an Employees *DataTable* to the strongly typed *DataSet*.

Visual Studio will recognize the database's foreign key constraint that links the Orders and Employees tables, and it will create a *DataRelation* for the two *DataTables* in the strongly typed *DataSet*. Visual Studio will not associate the *DataRelation* with a *ForeignKeyConstraint*, but because the form will not let users modify the contents of the Employees DataTable, there's no need to create a *ForeignKeyConstraint*. Similarly, there's no need to set the *AutoIncrement-Seed* and *AutoIncrementStep* properties on the EmployeeID column to –1 because the form will not allow the user to enter new employee rows.

Now that the strongly typed *DataSet* contains employee information, replacing the *TextBox* that displays the EmployeeID column from the Orders table with the EmployeeName column from the corresponding row in the Employees table is actually quite simple. Delete the

TextBox that displayed the EmployeeID column. Now drag and drop a *ComboBox* from the Toolbox onto the form. Click the small arrow just above the *ComboBox*, and specify that you want to use data-bound items. The dialog box entitled ComboBox Tasks will expand to appear as shown in Figure 13-15. In the Data Source drop-down list, select the Employees table under Other Data Sources, Project Data Sources, NorthwindDataSet. This action will add a *BindingSource* and a *TableAdapter* for the Employees table to the form, add a call to the *TableAdapter*'s *Fill* method in the form's *Load* event, and set the *ComboBox*'s *DataSource* property to the new *BindingSource*. Now set the Display Member to EmployeeName and the Value Member to EmployeeID. Finally, set the Selected Value to the EmployeeID column in the Orders *BindingSource*. You'll also need to update the SetOrderEditMode procedure to disable the new *ComboBox* control instead of setting the Employee *TextBox* to *ReadOnly*.

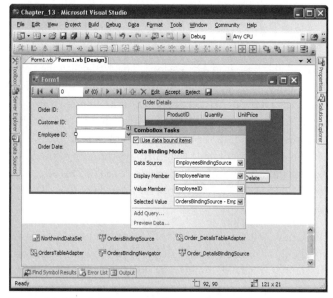

Figure 13-15   Setting properties on a bound *ComboBox* in Visual Studio

You can accomplish these same steps at run time by executing the following code:

Visual Basic

```
Me.EmployeeIDComboBox.DataSource = Me.EmployeesBindingSource
Me.EmployeeIDComboBox.DisplayMember = "EmployeeName"
Me.EmployeeIDComboBox.ValueMember = "EmployeeID"
Me.EmployeeIDComboBox.DataBindings.Add("SelectedValue", _
                      Me.OrdersBindingSource, "EmployeeID")
```

Visual C#

```
this.employeeIDComboBox.DataSource = this.employeesBindingSource;
this.employeeIDComboBox.DisplayMember = "EmployeeName";
this.employeeIDComboBox.ValueMember = "EmployeeID";
this.employeeIDComboBox.DataBindings.Add("SelectedValue",
                      this.ordersBindingSource, "EmployeeID");
```

The end result of all these actions is that the *ComboBox* will display the EmployeeName for the employee associated with the current order, and it will allow the user to change the value of the EmployeeID column in the current order row by selecting a different employee name from the *ComboBox*'s list.

Adding Expression-Based Calculated Columns

Chances are that the person using this application would like to see the total amount for each item in the order, as well as for the entire order. We could modify the queries in the *Table-Adapter* queries to return this information, but that would cause two problems. First, the TableAdapter Configuration Wizard would get confused and would not be able to generate updating logic to submit changes back to the database. Second, this approach would cause the values to be calculated only once, when the queries are executed, and would not reflect changes in the *DataSet*.

In Chapter 6, you learned that the *Expression* property on a *DataColumn* can be used to create columns whose values are calculated based on expressions. The Order Details table contains columns for Quantity and UnitPrice. We can add an ItemTotal *DataColumn* to the Order Details table to display the total cost of the item by setting the *DataColumn*'s *Expression* property to `"Quantity * UnitPrice"`. (Yes, the true total cost of the item should include the Discount column, but we'll use this simpler calculation for the purposes of the sample.) We can also add an OrderTotal *DataColumn* to the Orders table that displays the sum of the ItemTotals for the order by setting the *DataColumn*'s *Expression* property to `"Sum(Child(FK_Order_Details_Orders).ItemTotal)"`. Set the *DataType* property on each of these *DataColumns* to *System.Decimal*.

We can then add each of these new columns to the form. To create a new OrderTotal *TextBox*, drag and drop the OrderTotal column from the Data Sources window onto the form. To add an ItemTotal column to the *DataGridView*, right-click the grid, select Add Column, and then select the ItemTotal column.

The sample application also adds a ProductName *DataColumn* to the Order Details *DataTable* that references the ProductName *DataColumn* in the Products *DataTable*.

Controlling the Format of Bound Data

The data type of the new OrderTotal column is *System.Decimal*. As a result, the *TextBox* on the details form that's bound to the OrderTotal column will display the contents of that column using the standard numerical formatting. If the total cost for the order is $491.20, the *TextBox* will display 491.2000. Let's change the formatting for this column so that the data is formatted as currency.

With version 1.x of the .NET Framework, changing the display of this data required adding code to handle the *Format* event on the *Binding* object created when binding the *TextBox* to the column. Now with version 2.0 of the .NET Framework and Visual Studio 2005, you can change the formatting simply and easily at design time.

Let's look at how we can change the formatting for the OrderTotal *TextBox*. Select the *TextBox* on the form in Visual Studio. Then go to the Properties window, expand the (*DataBindings*) entry near the top of the window, select (Advanced), and click the ellipsis (...) button. This action will display the Formatting And Advanced Binding dialog box shown in Figure 13-16. Simply set the Format Type to Currency. Now the *TextBox* will display the contents of the column as units of currency ($491.20, €491.20, and so on) using your system's settings instead of 491.2000. As you can see in Figure 13-16, this dialog box can be used to apply standard or custom format strings to various data types.

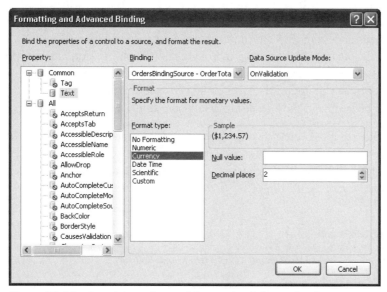

Figure 13-16   Supplying advanced formatting information for a *TextBox*

You can also use this dialog box to control what value is associated with null values. For example, if you launched this dialog box for the OrderDate *TextBox* and set the *Null* value for the *TextBox* to "<Null>", then "<Null>" would appear if the OrderDate column for the current order contained *DBNull.Value*. Similarly, entering "<Null>" into the *TextBox* would assign *DBNull.Value* to the column.

The *DataGridView* also lets you specify formatting strings for the columns in the grid, though this option is somewhat difficult to discover. Select the *DataGridView* on your form, right-click the control, and then select Edit Columns from the context menu. In the resulting dialog box, select the column whose format you want to change, select the *DefaultCellStyle* property, and click the ellipsis (...) button. In the resulting CellStyle Builder dialog box, select the *Format* property, and click the ellipsis (...) button. Finally, in the resulting Format String dialog box, specify the desired formatting. What could be simpler?

If you need more control over the formatting, you can supply your own formatting and parsing code. Earlier in the chapter, I showed an example of code that binds the *Text* property of a *TextBox* to a column in a *BindingSource*:

Visual Basic
```
OrderIDTextBox.DataBindings.Add("Text", OrdersDataSource, "OrderID")
```

Visual C#
```
orderIDTextBox.DataBindings.Add("Text", ordersDataSource, "OrderID");
```

The *Add* method returns a *Binding* object, which responds to the *BindingSource* object's events and moves data back and forth between the *TextBox* and the column to which the *TextBox* is bound. The *Binding* class exposes two events—*Format* and *Parse*. The *Format* event fires when the *Binding* object loads data from the data source into the property to which it's bound. The *Parse* event fires when the *Binding* object reads data from the bound property and assigns this data to the data source. We can use these two events to change the format of the data displayed in the bound *TextBox* controls. This approach works best for complex formatting and parsing scenarios, where the options available in the formatting dialog box simply aren't enough.

The following code snippet from the sample shows how it formats the data in the *TextBox* for the OrderTotal column as currency. The code uses an overloaded *ToString* method of the *Decimal* class to format the decimal as currency. For more information on using these events, see the documentation of the *Binding* class in the .NET Framework SDK.

Visual Basic
```
'Imports System.Globalization
Dim b As Binding
b = OrderTotalTextBox.DataBindings.Add("Text", OrdersDataSource, _
                                       "OrderTotal")
AddHandler b.Format, AddressOf FormatDecimalToCurrency
AddHandler b.Parse, AddressOf ParseCurrencyToDecimal

Private Sub FormatDecimalToCurrency(ByVal sender As Object, _
                                    ByVal cevent As ConvertEventArgs)
    If Not cevent.DesiredType Is GetType(String) Then
        Exit Sub
    End If

    If cevent.Value Is DBNull.Value Then
        cevent.Value = CDec(0).ToString("c")
    Else
        cevent.Value = CDec(cevent.Value).ToString("c")
    End If
End Sub

Private Sub ParseCurrencyToDecimal(ByVal sender As Object, _
                                   ByVal cevent As ConvertEventArgs)
    If Not cevent.DesiredType Is GetType(Decimal) Then
        Exit Sub
    End If
```

```
        cevent.Value = Decimal.Parse(cevent.Value.ToString, _
                                NumberStyles.Currency, _
                                Nothing)
End Sub
```

Visual C#

```
//using System.Globalization;
Binding b;
b = orderTotalTextBox.DataBindings.Add("Text", ordersDataSource, "OrderTotal");
b.Format += new ConvertEventHandler(FormatDecimalToCurrency);
b.Parse += new ConvertEventHandler(ParseCurrencyToDecimal);

private void FormatDecimalToCurrency(object sender,
                                    ConvertEventArgs cevent) {
    if (!cevent.DesiredType.Equals(typeof(string)))
        return;

    if (cevent.Value == DBNull.Value)
        cevent.Value = ((Decimal) 0).ToString("c");
    else
        cevent.Value = ((Decimal) cevent.Value).ToString("c");
}

private void ParseCurrencyToDecimal(object sender,
                                    ConvertEventArgs cevent) {
    if (!cevent.DesiredType.Equals(typeof(Decimal)))
        return;

    cevent.Value = Decimal.Parse(cevent.Value.ToString(),
                                NumberStyles.Currency,
                                null);
}
```

Step 11: If You Want Something Done (Just) Right...

Let's take a short break and look at the sample application we've built. Thanks to data-binding features, it took very little code to let users view and edit data from two related *DataTable* objects through bound controls. That's the whole point of the data-binding features—providing basic functionality so that you can build user interfaces with minimal code.

When we initially bound the controls, we had little control over how the controls interacted with the data in our *DataSet*. In step 10, we added code to control the format of data in bound *TextBox* controls. You can add more code to gain more control over the bound controls, but remember that the more code you write, the less benefit you'll really get from using data binding in the first place.

Here's an example. I finished step 10 and started using the sample application, looking for ways to improve the application. I discovered that on the Edit Detail form, changing the contents of the Quantity and UnitPrice *TextBox* controls did not update the contents of the ItemTotal *TextBox*. I started looking for a way to automatically update the ItemTotal *Text-Box* when the contents of the Quantity or UnitPrice *TextBox* controls changed. I tried setting the *Text* property for the ItemTotal *TextBox* in the *Leave* event of the Quantity and UnitPrice *TextBox* controls. I tried calling the *Refresh* method of the *BindingSource* object. I tried relying on the *SuspendBinding* and *ResumeBinding* methods of the *BindingSource* object. No matter what I tried, I couldn't get the functionality I was looking for. Although I think it's possible to accomplish this task with data binding, this isn't the type of scenario that data binding was designed to address.

The more functionality we add to this application through code, the more we relegate the data-binding features to three simple tasks—navigation through the available rows, displaying the contents of the current row in a series of controls, and saving user input to the current row. That's not terribly complex code to write.

If you rely on your own code to display data in controls and write changes back to the data structure, you take control of and responsibility for the interaction between the user interface and your data structures. The sample application includes a form called OrdersForm_DIY, where *DIY* stands for "Do It Yourself." The only data-binding code in this form involves showing the contents of the current order in the *DataGridView* and the list of employees in the *ComboBox*. The remaining functionality—letting the user navigate through the available orders, displaying the current order in the controls, and applying changes from the controls to the current order—relies on simple "do it yourself" code.

Although this approach requires more time and coding, it can give you increased flexibility and control over the behavior of your application.

Data Binding Summary

As you've seen in the various steps in the sample application, the data-binding features in the Windows forms package allow you to create a powerful and robust user interface with minimal code. However, as you try to take more control of the user interface and add more and more code to your application, you might find that your code is battling data binding rather than complementing it. In such cases, you might be better off writing your own code to manage the interaction between your data and the user interface.

Application Design Considerations

Creating a helpful and intuitive user interface is just one of many facets of building an effective Windows-based application. Let's discuss some important application design considerations.

Fetching Only the Data You Need

As you develop your application, it's important that you consider how your database will grow. Executing a SELECT ... FROM MyTable query when your application starts up might seem fine while you're developing the application, but as the table grows in size, fetching the results of the query will take more time. The more data you retrieve, the more time your application will take to retrieve that data.

Take our sample order entry application. As the application starts, it issues queries to retrieve information for all the orders that a customer has placed. Is that the right call? Perhaps retrieving all orders for a customer is overkill. Maybe the users of the application are primarily interested in viewing the orders that have not yet shipped. Maybe the application should fetch only orders that a particular customer has placed in the past three months.

The application's environment can also be a factor in determining which data to fetch. Perhaps the user needs to be able to download data onto a laptop using a 28-Kbps modem, access and modify that data off line while at a remote site, and then reconnect using the same modem at the end of the day to transmit changes back to the database. You won't want to waste any bandwidth because the pipeline is so thin, but because of the environment, the application will require you to download all the necessary data from the database.

Updating Strategies

The sample application cache changes and relies on optimistic locking to submit updates. Let's discuss some other updating strategies.

Immediate Updates vs. Cached Updates

Whether you decide to submit changes immediately or cache those changes and submit them later should depend on what's appropriate for your application.

When the user modifies an order in the sample application, the application does not immediately submit the change to the database. The application relies on ADO.NET to cache the update until the user clicks the Save button.

We could easily change the application so that it submits the change to an order when the user clicks the Update button. When the user clicks the Edit button, the application will allow the user to modify the order and its line items. If the user clicks the Cancel button, the application will discard the changes. If the user clicks the Update button instead, the application will save the changes and then use the *TableAdapter* to submit the changes to the database.

One benefit of working with data off line and caching changes is that the application does not need to communicate with the database as frequently. However, the longer the user waits to submit cached changes, the greater the chances that another user will have modified the same data in the database, which can cause the update attempt to fail.

You should weigh the pros and cons of each approach to determine what's appropriate for your application. If the users of our sample application will handle incoming phone orders from customers with slow-moving inventory, caching the changes will probably suffice. But that approach isn't appropriate for an airline ticket reservation system. You wouldn't want a user to try to save a traveler's itinerary only to discover that the last seat on the return flight was sold while the traveler was trying to find his or her frequent flyer number.

Re-Fetching Before Allowing Changes

When you retrieve data into a disconnected structure such as a *DataSet*, the data can become stale. But unlike a carton of milk, your *DataSet* does not come with an expiration date. The *DataSet* does not fire an event when the corresponding rows in your database change. By the time the user modifies data in your application and attempts to submit the changes to your database, another user might have modified that same row of data, and the update attempt will fail.

Take our sample application. It fetches data when the application starts. The user might click the Edit button within seconds of starting the application. The longer the application is open, the more stale the data becomes. In fact, the user might wait minutes or hours before modifying the contents of a row.

By the time the user clicks the Edit button, another user might have modified the corresponding row in the database. If you're developing an application that might face this scenario, you might want to re-fetch the contents of the corresponding row from the database when the user clicks the Edit button.

To re-fetch the contents of the row, you can create a *SqlDataAdapter* (or an added query in a *TableAdapter*) that executes a parameterized query that looks like this:

```
SELECT ... FROM MyTable WHERE KeyCol = @KeyCol
```

If you've set the *PrimaryKey* property of your *DataTable*, the *SqlDataAdapter* (or *TableAdapter*) will update the contents of the *DataRow* with data from your database. Remember that this query will not generate an exception if another user has deleted the corresponding row in the database. In that case, the query will just return no rows. The *Fill* method of both the *SqlData-Adapter* and *TableAdapter* returns an integer that contains the number of rows that the database fetched. If the *Fill* method returns 0, you know that the row no longer exists in the database. You can trap for that scenario and elegantly inform the user that the row that he or she wanted to edit no longer exists.

ADO.NET and Pessimistic Locking

One drawback to being an optimist is that things don't always work out the way you'd like. Imagine you're the user of an application who clicks a button to execute a query and retrieve a row of data. After you fetch the results of the query, you modify the data on the form and click a button to submit your changes. If the application is using optimistic updating, the data you want to modify is not locked on the server. So another user might have submitted a change to the same row of data between the time you fetch the results of the query and the time you submit your change, in which case, your update attempt will fail, assuming that the other user has modified columns that appear in the WHERE clause of the UPDATE or DELETE query used to submit your change. You can use pessimistic locking to ensure that an update attempt will never fail due to concurrency issues.

> **Warning**   Pessimistic locking is a powerful and somewhat dangerous feature. Be afraid. Be very afraid.
>
> This is an advanced topic, intended for developers who really understand the impact of locking data on their servers. Only a small number of applications, such as airline reservation systems, require pessimistic locking.
>
> I don't recommend using pessimistic locking as a general way of avoiding failed update attempts. For most applications, it's better to have optimistic update attempts occasionally fail than to have queries to retrieve data fail because the data on the server is locked.

Updating data using pessimistic locking involves locking the row in the database before editing its contents, which ensures that the update attempt will not fail as a result of changes made by another user. The ADO.NET object model is designed to submit changes through optimistic updates. As you learned in Chapter 10 and Chapter 11, the *SqlDataAdapter* class lets you submit pending changes stored in a *DataSet*. The *DataSet* object does not lock data on the database when you modify the contents of a *DataRow* object. There are no properties you can set on ADO.NET objects to achieve pessimistic locking, at least not in the current release of ADO.NET.

You can still achieve pessimistic locking through the use of *Transaction* objects. However, you'll probably need to do more than issue a simple SELECT query from within a transaction. Whether issuing a SELECT query from within a transaction locks the rows returned by the query depends on the database, the type of query, and the isolation level for the transaction.

A transaction's isolation level controls how the work performed on a transaction will affect work performed on other transactions. SQL Server uses "read committed" as its default transaction isolation level. With this isolation level, rows are locked once they're modified in the transaction. Simply retrieving the contents of a row in a SELECT query will not lock the row. If, however, you use an isolation level of "repeatable read" or "serializable," you lock the rows you retrieve in a SELECT query.

Some databases support the use of locking hints in a query. With SQL Server, you can issue the following query to lock a row of data in a transaction, regardless of the transaction's isolation level:

```
SELECT CustomerID, CompanyName, ContactName, Phone FROM Customers
    WITH (UPDLOCK) WHERE CustomerID = 'ALFKI'
```

See your database's documentation to find out what types of transaction isolation levels and locking hints it supports.

The following code snippet pessimistically locks a row in a SQL Server database through the use of a *SqlTransaction* object and the use of locking hints in the SELECT query. As soon as the code retrieves the results of the query, the row of data is locked on the server. You can set a breakpoint after the call to the *SqlDataAdapter* object's *Fill* method to verify that the data is locked. At this point, you can examine the contents of the row in an ad hoc query tool such as SQL Server Management Studio, but attempts to modify the contents of the row will fail.

Visual Basic

```vb
Dim strConn, strSQL As String
strConn = "Data Source=.\SQLExpress;" & _
          "Initial Catalog=Northwind;Integrated Security=True;"
strSQL = "SELECT CustomerID, CompanyName FROM Customers " & _
         "WITH (UPDLOCK) WHERE CustomerID = 'ALFKI'"
Using cn As New SqlConnection(strConn)
    cn.Open()
    Using txn As SqlTransaction = cn.BeginTransaction()
        Dim cmd As New SqlCommand(strSQL, cn, txn)
        Dim da As New SqlDataAdapter(cmd)
        Dim cb As New SqlCommandBuilder(da)
        Dim tbl As New DataTable()
        da.Fill(tbl)
        Dim row As DataRow = tbl.Rows(0)
        row("CompanyName") = "Modified"
        da.Update(tbl)
        txn.Rollback()
    End Using
    cn.Close()
End Using
```

Visual C#

```csharp
string strConn, strSQL;
strConn = @"Data Source=.\SQLExpress;" +
          "Initial Catalog=Northwind;Integrated Security=True;";
strSQL = "SELECT CustomerID, CompanyName FROM Customers " +
         "WITH (UPDLOCK) WHERE CustomerID = 'ALFKI'";
using (SqlConnection cn = new SqlConnection(strConn)) {
    cn.Open();
    using (SqlTransaction txn = cn.BeginTransaction()) {
        SqlCommand cmd = new SqlCommand(strSQL, cn, txn);
        SqlDataAdapter da = new SqlDataAdapter(cmd);
        SqlCommandBuilder cb = new SqlCommandBuilder(da);
        DataTable tbl = new DataTable();
        da.Fill(tbl);
        DataRow row = tbl.Rows[0];
        row["CompanyName"] = "Modified";
        da.Update(tbl);
        txn.Rollback();
    }
    cn.Close();
}
```

Note   I use a *SqlCommandBuilder* in the sample code solely for the sake of brevity. Chapters 10 and 11 discuss why you're better off supplying your own updating logic.

Connection Strategies

You can choose between two connection strategies. The appropriate approach will depend on the parameters of your application.

Connecting and Disconnecting

The simplest approach to connecting to your database is to let *SqlDataAdapter* (and *Table-Adapter*) objects open the connection implicitly. The *SqlDataAdapter* objects implicitly open the connection on calls to the *SqlDataAdapter* object's *Fill* and *Update* methods and close the *Connection* object at the end of the calls. This approach is simple, but it's not always the best approach.

Connection pooling can help limit the number of connections used by this default implicit connection management behavior. For example, imagine that you have two *SqlDataAdapter* objects that retrieve data from separate tables in your database. The code you execute to construct the *SqlDataAdapters* uses the same connection string. This code will create a separate *SqlConnection* object for each *SqlDataAdapter*. If you call the *Fill* method of each *SqlDataAdapter* and look at a SQL Profiler trace, you'll find that your code still used a single connection to the database to retrieve the results of both queries.

Let's examine what happened, step by step. Each call to the *Fill* method implicitly opened the *SqlConnection* associated with the *SqlDataAdapter*'s *SelectCommand* and closed the *SqlConnection* after retrieving the results of the query. Calling the *Fill* method on the first *SqlDataAdapter* established a new physical connection to the database. When the *SqlDataAdapter* implicitly closed the *SqlConnection* that used that physical connection, the connection pooling code in the SQL Client .NET Data Provider pooled the physical connection rather than closing it. The second *SqlDataAdapter* re-uses this pooled physical connection to execute its query before returning it to the pool. Pretty slick, no?

With that said, you're still better off associating the *SqlDataAdapters* with the same *SqlConnection* object and explicitly opening and closing the *SqlConnection*. Although the *Fill* scenario might work just fine with separate *SqlConnections* and implicit connection state management, the *Update* scenario is more complex and more likely to encounter problems.

Imagine that same scenario (two *SqlDataAdapters* using the same connection string but different *SqlConnections*), but now you want to submit changes from both *DataTables* in a single transaction. If you're using a *SqlTransaction*, this approach simply won't work. You need to explicitly open the *SqlConnection* before starting the transaction, and you can't share the *SqlTransaction* against different *SqlConnections* even if they connect to the same SQL Server database.

You could use *System.Transactions* instead and have your code work, but it might not do what you expect. You can create a *TransactionScope* object and then implicitly open a *SqlConnection* inside the *TransactionScope*'s scope. If the *SqlConnection* is the only participant in the transaction (so far) and is talking to SQL Server 2005, this will implicitly create a local transaction

(*SqlTransaction*) rather than a distributed transaction. In fact, that is the behavior you'd get when you called the *Update* method on the first *SqlDataAdapter*. Due to logic inside *Sql-Connection*'s pooling code, the call to the *Update* method on the second *SqlDataAdapter* would not re-use the physical connection established by the first *SqlDataAdapter*. Instead, the second *SqlDataAdapter* would establish a second physical connection to the SQL Server database. The local transaction created by the first *SqlDataAdapter* would be promoted to a distributed transaction, and the second physical connection would enlist in that distributed transaction.

If, instead, you have both *SqlDataAdapters* use the same *SqlConnection* and you explicitly open the *SqlConnection* before calling the *Fill* or *Update* methods of the *SqlDataAdapters*, you'll get better performance and more predictable results. The sample order entry application discussed earlier in the chapter follows this approach, and it's the one I recommend.

Connection Pooling

Connection pooling can greatly improve the performance of your multi-tiered applications. In fact, because connection pooling is enabled by default, you might be taking advantage of connection pooling without even realizing it. Connections are only reused if both the connection string and the credentials match. Imagine a Web service where the service connects to a SQL Server database using integrated security and impersonates the current user. If connection pooling reused connections based on just the connection string, that would mean that UserB might reuse a connection opened by UserA, which might have different database privileges.

Some developers rely on their database to enforce security in their multi-tiered applications. Because the middle-tier components use the users' credentials to connect to the database, applications that use this approach will not benefit from connection pooling. To get the full benefit of connection pooling, you should have your middle-tier components rely on their own specific credentials. Use network security to make sure that only users who have the appropriate credentials can access the middle-tier components, rather than forcing the database to determine whether the user has rights to the functionality in the components.

Although connection pooling is primarily geared toward multi-tiered applications, it can also improve the performance of your simple two-tiered application. When the sample application closes its *SqlConnection* object, implicitly or explicitly, the physical connection to the database is cached in the connection pool. If the application reopens the *SqlConnection* object before the connection times out in the pool, the connection will be reused.

If you're working with the SQL Client .NET Data Provider and you don't want to use connection pooling in your application, add the following attribute to your connection string:

```
Pooling=False;
```

Developers working with the OLE DB .NET Data Provider can use the following attribute to ensure that their connections are not pooled when the *OleDbConnection* object is closed:

```
OLE DB Services=-4;
```

Working with BLOB Data

You'll get better performance by storing BLOB data in files on your server and storing the location of those files in your database. Operating systems are better suited to working with files. Storing that same data in a database is less efficient. SQL Server, for example, breaks up BLOB data that's greater than 8 KB in size into multiple pages in the database. That means that storing the contents of a 40-KB file involves separating the contents of that file into five separate pieces.

Although I'm not a big fan of storing BLOB data in databases, I can definitely see the appeal. Storing some data in a database and other data in files increases the number of technologies involved. Keeping the data secure and backing up your data becomes more complex.

In case you do decide to store BLOB data in your database, here are some tips for working with BLOB data in ADO.NET.

Delaying BLOB Fetching

If your query fetches a hundred rows and the query includes BLOB columns, do you really want to retrieve all that data along with the results of your query? SQL Server BLOB columns can contain up to 2 GB of data. Do you know how much BLOB data your query will return?

One way to improve the performance of your application is to avoid fetching BLOB data from your database until you need it. Fetch the non-BLOB data ahead of time, and then fetch the BLOB data as necessary. This technique is especially helpful when the user will access the BLOB data only for the currently visible row.

Handling BLOBs in *DataSet* Objects

Accessing and modifying the contents of a BLOB column in a *DataSet* is actually very straight-forward. ADO.NET stores BLOBs of text as strings and binary BLOBs as byte arrays. The *DataRow* object does not expose *GetChunk* or *AppendChunk* methods as in previous data access models. You must retrieve or modify the entire contents of the column.

You treat a BLOB of text just as you would any other text-based column.

Visual Basic
```
Dim row As DataRow
Dim strBlob As String
'Initialize the DataRow object
'...

'Accessing the contents of a BLOB of text
strBlob = CStr(row("TextBlob"))
'Modifying the contents of a BLOB of text
row("TextBlob") = strBlob
```

Visual C#

```
DataRow row;
string strBlob;
//Initialize the DataRow object
//...

//Accessing the contents of a BLOB of text
strBlob = (string) row["TextBlob"];
//Modifying the contents of a BLOB of text
row["TextBlob"] = strBlob;
```

Similarly, you treat binary BLOB columns just as you would smaller binary columns.

Visual Basic

```
Dim row As DataRow
Dim aBinaryBlob As Byte()
'Initialize the DataRow object
'...

'Accessing the contents of a BLOB
aBinaryBlob = CType(row("BinaryBlob"), Byte())
'Modifying the contents of a BLOB row("BinaryBlob") = aBinaryBlob
```

Visual C#

```
DataRow row;
Byte[] aBinaryBlob;
//Initialize the DataRow object
//...

//Accessing the contents of a BLOB
aBinaryBlob = (Byte[]) row["BinaryBlob"];
//Modifying the contents of a BLOB
row["BinaryBlob"] = aBinaryBlob;
```

Handling BLOBs Using *DataReader* Objects

The *DataReader* object offers you a choice: you can access the contents of a BLOB column all at once, or you can fetch data from the column in chunks.

The following code snippet uses a single call to the *DataReader* to retrieve the contents of a BLOB column:

Visual Basic

```
Dim cmd As SqlCommand
Dim rdr As SqlDataReader
Dim intTextBlobColumnNo, intBinaryBlobColumnNo As Integer
Dim strTextBlob As String
Dim aBinaryBlob As Byte()
'Initialize the SqlCommand
'...
```

```
rdr = cmd.ExecuteReader(CommandBehavior.SequentialAccess)
Do While rdr.Read
    strTextBlob = rdr.GetString(intTextBlobColumnNo)
    aBinaryBlob = CType(rdr(intBinaryBlobColumnNo), Byte())
Loop
rdr.Close
```

Visual C#

```
SqlCommand cmd;
SqlDataReader rdr;
int intTextBlobColumnNo, intBinaryBlobColumnNo;
string strTextBlob;
Byte[] aBinaryBlob;
//Initialize the SqlCommand
//...

rdr = cmd.ExecuteReader(CommandBehavior.SequentialAccess);
while (rdr.Read())
{
    strTextBlob = rdr.GetString(intTextBlobColumnNo);
    aBinaryBlob = (Byte[]) rdr[intBinaryBlobColumnNo];
}
rdr.Close()
```

> **Note** The preceding code snippet retrieves the contents of the text BLOB column using the strongly typed *GetString* method but retrieves binary BLOB data by implicitly calling the untyped *Item* property and then converting the return value to a byte array. The *DataReader* object does expose a *GetBytes* method, but it returns data in chunks rather than in a single call.

BLOB columns can be rather large. Storing the entire contents of a BLOB column in a single string or byte array might not be the best idea if the column contains a couple hundred megabytes of data. In such cases, your best bet is to fetch the BLOB data a chunk at a time, write the contents to the hard drive, and access the contents when appropriate.

The *DataReader* object exposes two methods—*GetBytes* and *GetChars*—that let you retrieve binary data in chunks. The following code snippet demonstrates how you can use the *GetBytes* method to retrieve the contents of a binary BLOB column from a *DataReader* in 8-KB chunks and write that data to a file. You can follow the same logic to retrieve text BLOB data using the *GetChars* method instead.

Visual Basic

```
'Imports System.IO

Dim cmd As SqlCommand
Dim rdr As SqlDataReader
Dim intBlobColumnNo As Integer = 1
Dim intChunkSize As Integer = 8192
Dim intOffset As Integer = 0
Dim intBytesReturned As Integer
Dim aBinaryBlob(intChunkSize) As Byte
Dim strPathToFile As String = "C:\GetBytes.jpg"
```

```
Dim filOutput As New FileStream(strPathToFile, FileMode.Create)
'Initialize the SqlCommand
'...
rdr = cmd.ExecuteReader(CommandBehavior.SequentialAccess)
rdr.Read()
Do
    intBytesReturned = CInt(rdr.GetBytes(intBlobColumnNo, intOffset, _
                                    aBinaryBlob, 0, intChunkSize))
    If (intBytesReturned > 0) Then
        filOutput.Write(aBinaryBlob, 0, intBytesReturned)
    End If
    intOffset += intBytesReturned
Loop Until intBytesReturned <> intChunkSize
filOutput.Close()
rdr.Close()
```

Visual C#

```
//using System.IO;

SqlCommand cmd;
SqlDataReader rdr;
int intBinaryBlobCol = 1;
int intChunkSize = 8192;
int intOffset = 0;
int intBytesReturned;
Byte[] aBinaryBlob = new Byte[intChunkSize];
string strPathToFile = @"C:\GetBytes.jpg";
FileStream filOutput = new FileStream(strPathToFile, FileMode.Create);
//Initialize the SqlCommand
//...
rdr = cmd.ExecuteReader(CommandBehavior.SequentialAccess);
rdr.Read();
do
{
    intBytesReturned = (int) rdr.GetBytes(intBinaryBlobCol, intOffset,
                                    aBinaryBlob, 0, intChunkSize);
    if (intBytesReturned > 0)
        filOutput.Write(aBinaryBlob, 0, intBytesReturned);
    intOffset += intBytesReturned;
} while (intBytesReturned == intChunkSize);
filOutput.Close();
rdr.Close();
```

Binary BLOBs in the Northwind Database

You might have noticed that the Northwind database includes BLOB columns. For example, the Employees table includes a column called Photo, which contains a picture of the employee.

Unfortunately, the Photo column also contains some extra bytes in the form of an Access OLE header. This header allows Microsoft Access to know what type of data the BLOB column contains—such as a .jpg file, a Microsoft Office Word document, or a Microsoft Office Excel spreadsheet. As a result, if you try to fetch the contents of the Photo column using ADO.NET (or ADO, or RDO, or...), you won't be able to load that data into a *PictureBox* control or view the contents of the file in an imaging program such as Paint.

How can you discard the Access OLE header so that you're left with just the desired data? In short, you can't. The format of the Access OLE header is proprietary and is not documented.

However, the companion CD includes a sample application called *LoadEmployeePhotos* that can help you replace the default contents of the Photo column in the Employees table with pure .jpg images. In the application's directory, you'll find .jpg files that contain pictures of the employees. The application loads this data into the Northwind database by executing a series of parameterized queries.

You can also look to this application as an example of how to load the contents of files into a database using parameterized queries.

A Sample BLOB Application

Now that you have actual pictures in the Employees table, let's take a brief look at a sample application that retrieves this data and displays it on a Windows form. This application, ShowEmployeesPhotos, which is on the companion CD, retrieves employee information from the Northwind database into a *DataSet*. Figure 13-17 shows the user interface for the sample application.

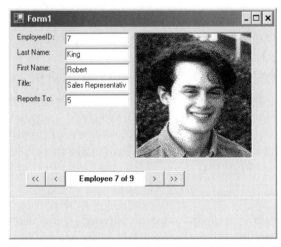

Figure 13-17   Retrieving binary BLOB data and displaying it in a *PictureBox* control

To build the application more quickly, I relied on a *BindingSource* and bound controls to manage the current position and simplify the process of displaying employee information.

The *DataSet* that the sample application uses has two separate *DataTable* objects—one for the non-BLOB data and one for the BLOB data. The child *DataTable* also includes the primary key column (EmployeeID) to simplify the process of moving from a row in the parent *DataTable* to the corresponding row in the child *DataTable*. I added a column called FetchedPhoto to the parent *DataTable* to keep track of whether I've fetched the photo for that employee.

When the application starts up, it retrieves non-BLOB employee information (EmployeeID, LastName, FirstName, and so on) from the Employees table. The application then retrieves the contents of the Photo column the first time the user navigates to a particular employee. (The photos are small in size—only 22 KB—so the application wouldn't incur a large performance hit if it had loaded this data on startup, especially if the size of the table remains small.) This approach can greatly improve the performance of applications in which the user can view only a fraction of the rows that the application retrieves.

User Interfaces Built with ADO.NET Power

You've seen how the data-binding features that are intrinsic to Windows forms can help you build user interfaces quickly and easily. You've also learned that you can achieve greater control over your user interface by relying on your own code rather than on bound controls. You now also know the pros and cons of different strategies for connecting to your database, querying your database, submitting updates, and working with BLOB data.

Questions That Should Be Asked More Frequently

Q Should I rely on data binding in an application that I plan to distribute?

A I rely on data binding when I build the user interface for an application. It lets me develop the basic user interface quickly with a small amount of code. Once I'm comfortable with the layout of the user interface and the schema of the data that the application uses, I consider whether to continue relying on data binding. If I need more control than I can achieve using data binding, or if I decide that relying on data binding will not save time in completing the application, I replace the data-binding functionality with my own code.

You'll notice that step 11 in the chapter's main sample application still relies on a bound *DataGridView* control to display the contents of an order. I disabled the *DataGridView*'s updating features, but I felt that trying to replace the *DataGridView*'s functionality would require a great deal of time without providing enough value to make that effort worthwhile.

Q Can I bind controls with an untyped *DataSet*?

A Absolutely. You can still bind controls at design time with untyped *DataSet* objects whose schemas you define at design time through the Property pages. You can also bind controls at run time with *BindingSource* objects using the code I showed you earlier in the chapter.

Visual Basic
```vb
'Creating a BindingSource
Dim bindingSource As New BindingSource(dataSet, "TableName")

'Binding a TextBox
textBox.DataBindings.Add("Text", bindingSource, "ColumnName")

'Binding a DataGridView
dataGridView.DataSource = bindingSource
```

Visual C#

```
//Creating a BindingSource
BindingSource bindingSource;
bindingSource = new BindingSource(dataSet, "TableName");

//Binding a TextBox
textBox.DataBindings.Add("Text", bindingSource, "ColumnName");

//Binding a DataGridView
dataGridView.DataSource = bindingSource;
```

Q I have to load a lot of data when my application starts up. Any recommendations?

A Make sure you really need all that data. Obviously, if you can retrieve fewer rows and/or columns, it will take less time to fetch the results of your queries. Another option is to rely on the *BackgroundWorker* class that's new to the *System.Windows.Forms* namespace in version 2.0 of the .NET Framework. You can use this class to write code that runs asynchronously in the background as the application starts up. For more information, see the documentation for the *BackgroundWorker* class in the .NET Framework SDK.

Q Why does the code in step 11 use a *DataView* rather than the *DataTable* to determine the position of the current order?

A If you mark a *DataRow* as deleted, it will still reside in the *DataTable* object's *Rows* collection. The application allows the user to mark an order as deleted. If the application were to rely solely on the *DataTable* object, it would require a great deal more code to skip orders that are marked as deleted while navigating through the remaining orders.

Instead, the application uses the *DataView* object. With the default setting for the *Data-View* object's *RowStateFilter* property, rows marked as deleted are not visible through the *DataView*, which simplifies the process of navigating through the remaining orders. The *BindingSource* object behaves in the same way.

Q How can I achieve pessimistic locking in a multi-tiered application that relies on a stateless middle tier?

A As I stated earlier in the chapter, only a small percentage of applications truly require pessimistic locking. Pessimistically locking data in a multi-tiered application with a stateless middle tier is definitely an advanced scenario. Airline reservation systems require this functionality. The user requests a seat on a flight, and the application locks that seat so that no one else can purchase it.

Consider the architecture for a moment. Because the application accesses the database through a stateless middle tier, this means that the application must allow the user to maintain locks on data without a live connection. Offhand, I don't know of any database that lets you persist a lock on data so that you can disconnect and later reconnect while the lock remains.

However, you could devise your own locking scheme to achieve this functionality. I haven't deployed large multi-user applications that rely on this type of architecture, but if my livelihood depended on developing such applications using SQL Server as the back end, here's what I'd do:

1. Set the database's security so that users can modify the contents of the table only through calls to stored procedures.

2. Add two columns to the table—one to contain a unique lock key and one to indicate the date and time the user successfully locked the row.

3. Create a stored procedure that allows the user to request a lock on a row. The stored procedure will take the row's primary key and a globally unique identifier (GUID) as input parameters. The stored procedure marks the row of data as locked if it is not already locked. Here's an example of such a stored procedure:

```
CREATE PROCEDURE spPessimisticLockAcquireLock
(@ID int, @LockID uniqueidentifier)
AS
UPDATE tblPessimisticLock
    SET LockAcquired = GetDate(), LockID = @LockID
    WHERE ID = @ID AND LockAcquired IS NULL
```

4. Create a stored procedure that lets the user modify the contents of the row. The stored procedure takes parameters for the row's primary key columns, the new data for the column, and the lock key. The stored procedure updates the row only if the lock key supplied matches the one in the database. If the stored procedure successfully updates the row, it will mark the row as available.

```
CREATE PROCEDURE spPessimisticLockUpdateRow
(@ID int, @DescCol varchar(32), @LockID uniqueidentifier)
AS
UPDATE tblPessimisticLock
    SET DescCol = @DescCol
    WHERE ID = @ID AND LockID = @LockID
IF @@ROWCOUNT = 1
BEGIN
    SET NOCOUNT ON
    UPDATE tblPessimisticLock
        SET LockAcquired = NULL, LockID = NULL
        WHERE ID = @ID AND LockID = @LockID
END
```

5. Create a stored procedure that the user can call to mark the row as available again.

```
CREATE PROCEDURE spPessimisticLockReleaseLock
(@ID int, @LockID uniqueidentifier)
AS
UPDATE tblPessimisticLock
    SET LockAcquired = NULL, LockID = NULL
    WHERE ID = @ID AND LockID = @LockID
```

6. Create a job that will clean up all the locks that have not been released in a timely fashion. The following query locates rows marked as locked that have been locked for more than five minutes and marks those rows as available:

```
UPDATE tblPessimisticLock
    SET LockAcquired = NULL, LockID = NULL
    WHERE DateAdd(mi, 5, LockAcquired) <= GetDate()
```

With this approach, a user might start the process of editing a row of data only to find that if he lollygagged, he can no longer commit the changes he made. Although this might seem rude, this general approach is used in many applications. For example, many high-traffic Web sites that sell tickets for flights, concerts, and sporting events reserve tickets for the user. However, the sites only make those tickets available to the user for a brief period of time. If the allotted time expires before the user has completed the ticket purchasing process, there is no guarantee that the user will be able to purchase those tickets. In such situations, the user might need to restart the process.

Chapter 14
Building Effective Web Applications

Now that you've learned about building Microsoft Windows data applications, let's look at their Web counterparts—Microsoft ASP.NET applications.

The new data access features in ASP.NET 2.0 make it even easier to build Web applications that interact with databases. You can now create Web pages that retrieve data from a database, display data in a Web browser, allow the user to modify that data, and submit changes back to the database, all without writing a single line of code!

This chapter will take an in-depth look at the *SqlDataSource* control, the centerpiece of the new data access features in ASP.NET, and at the new "code-free" data-binding scenarios available in ASP.NET 2.0. We'll look at how you can use the *SqlDataSource* control in conjunction with some of the new bound controls to build simple Web applications that allow the user to display the results of a query, make changes, and submit those changes to the database.

For developers who might not be familiar with building Web applications by using ASP.NET, this chapter will also discuss what you need to know about connecting to your database, as well as various options for caching data between roundtrips and partitioning large queries into individual pages of data. Along the way, we'll introduce two features new to Microsoft SQL Server 2005: Notification Services, which allows you to request to be notified when the results of a query change in the database, and the ROW_NUMBER function, which you can use in your queries to retrieve a single page of data.

Brief Introduction to Web Applications

This chapter will serve as an introduction to Web applications. It will provide some basic background to building Web applications that use Microsoft ADO.NET to communicate with your database. Along the way, we'll learn a little about data binding, the pros and cons of various ASP.NET caching options, paging, and submitting updates. Most of the examples will focus on the most powerful and flexible of the ASP.NET data-bound controls: the *GridView* control, which is the successor to the *DataGrid* control from ASP.NET 1.0.

ASP.NET Makes Building Web Applications Easier

To build a Web application, you write code that runs in a Web server that generates HTML that the browser will translate into a Web page. You also need to include functionality in the Web page that allows the user to click buttons or links to post data back to the server. Finally, you need to write code to allow your Web server to respond to those post-back events and interpret the information that the user posted.

ASP.NET greatly simplifies the process of building Web applications. You can write ASP.NET code in your language of choice—Microsoft Visual Basic or Microsoft Visual C#. Simply set properties on ASP.NET Web controls as you would with standard Windows controls, and the controls automatically translate those settings into HTML. If you place an ASP.NET button on your Web Form and add code to the *Button* control's *Click* event, ASP.NET will automatically add HTML to the corresponding Web page so that the Web server will run the code for the *Click* event when the user clicks the button. Thanks to the metadata that ASP.NET adds to the page, your code can access settings on your controls to collect the information that the user posted.

Many developers who have built ASP.NET applications aren't even aware of the ASP.NET features that make building Web applications so simple. That's part of the power of ASP.NET. For example, some developers might not truly understand that the ASP.NET code and the HTML user interface are running on separate machines. Many more developers are not aware that most ASP.NET applications use a stateless middle tier; some might not even know what a stateless middle tier is.

The Good and Bad of Statelessness

When a user directs his or her browser to an ASP.NET page (*.aspx), Internet Information Services (IIS) hands off the request to ASP.NET, which loads the compiled library for that page if it's not already in memory. Once ASP.NET responds to the request, it releases the resources for the page. When the user posts information back to that page, ASP.NET re-creates the page and responds to the post-back event. By default, ASP.NET does not maintain any information about the user's session between requests.

This statelessness makes your ASP.NET applications more scalable, but it can also prove challenging to developers who might not have experience building applications that rely on a stateless middle tier.

Forgetful Server, Dumb Client

In some ways, Web applications are similar to traditional mainframe applications. The Web server performs the majority of the actual processing. The Web browser might offer helpful features such as allowing you to bookmark sites, but its primary job is to transform the data that the Web server returns into a simple user interface.

For example, say you write ASP.NET code that uses a *SqlDataAdapter* to fetch product information from your database and place it into a *DataTable*. You then bind a *GridView* control to the *DataTable* to display the product information on your Web page. Let's also assume that you've added a button or a link for each product to the Web page so that the user can add that particular product to a shopping cart.

ASP.NET helped you convert the results of the query into HTML that the Web browser then displayed. But once ASP.NET finished responding to the page request, it released the page's resources, including the *DataTable* of product information. The Web browser displays a visual representation of the results, but it didn't actually receive the *DataTable* object. In fact, even if the browser did receive the *DataTable* object, it wouldn't know what to do with it; it's not .NET aware, so to speak.

ASP.NET Caching Features

ASP.NET offers robust caching features that allow you to store and retrieve data. You can cache data on the server side on either a per-session or per-application basis. You can also store the data in an ASP.NET page's *ViewState*—writing the data to a hidden field in the page, which ASP.NET then reconstitutes back into the original data on the next round trip to the server.

I use the term *reconstitute* because the process is similar to turning orange juice into juice concentrate and then back into orange juice. If you don't need the orange juice to be 100 percent fresh, storing the juice concentrated and later adding water to convert it back into "regular" juice can be cost effective.

The same logic applies to data in many Web applications. There are many scenarios in which you don't need to re-execute the query every time the user clicks a link on a page. In such cases, storing relatively small amounts of data in the page's *ViewState* can improve the performance of your application.

We'll take a closer look at the ASP.NET caching options later in the chapter.

Connecting to Your Database

Connecting to your database in a Web application is similar to connecting to your database in Windows applications. You still use an instance of the *Connection* class for your .NET Data Provider to manage the connection to your database. However, there are some slight differences to keep in mind when connecting in a Web application.

Connecting with Integrated Security

Throughout this text, we've used trusted connections to connect to the local SQL Express installation on your development machine:

```
Data Source=.\SQLExpress;
Initial Catalog=Northwind;Integrated Security=True;
```

You can use this same connection string at design time in a Web application, but you might encounter problems using this connection string at run time. Say you create a new Web application and add the following code to your Web Form's *Load* event:

Visual Basic
```
Dim strConn As String
strConn = "Data Source=.\SQLExpress;" & _
          "Initial Catalog=Northwind;Integrated Security=True;"
Using cn As New SqlConnection(strConn)
    cn.Open()
```

Visual C#
```
string strConn;
strConn = @"Data Source=.\SQLExpress;" +
          "Initial Catalog=Northwind;Integrated Security=True;";
using (SqlConnection cn = new SqlConnection(strConn)) {
    cn.Open();
```

If you execute this code from a Web application, your code might generate an exception with the following message:

```
Cannot open database "Northwind" requested by the login. The login failed.
Login failed for user 'MyMachine\ASPNET'.
```

This behavior confuses many developers new to building Web applications in Microsoft Visual Studio, especially because the same connection string works fine in Windows applications or in Console applications, as well as at design time in Visual Studio features such as Server Explorer. Why would the attempt to connect fail in the Web application?

By specifying integrated security in the connection string, you're stating that you want to try to connect to SQL Server using the current user credentials. Using integrated security in a Windows or Console application or Visual Studio, Server Explorer attempts to connect with the current user's credentials because the code is running under the current user's account. For an HTTP Web site, the code is actually running in IIS under the ASP.NET account listed in the error message. So success or failure of the connect attempt using integrated security hinges on the ASP.NET account's permissions in the SQL Server database.

> **Note**   Visual Studio 2005 and Visual Web Developer let you create File System Web Sites that run in ASP.NET Development Server under the current user's account. The samples for this chapter will use File System Web Sites. For more information on this option, see the Visual Studio or Visual Web Developer documentation.

For developers working with SQL Server 2005, SQL Server Management Studio makes granting database access to an account simple. Expand the Security folder for the server, right-click Logins, and select New Login. Add the desired account through the dialog box. Then select the User Mapping page in the "Select a page" area. On the right of the Login – New dialog box, specify the databases the account can connect to, and for each database, specify the Database Role Membership for the account. If you don't have access to SQL Server Management Studio, you could execute the following queries to create a login for the local ASP.NET account and allow the account to connect to the Northwind database and execute SELECT queries:

```
USE Northwind
CREATE LOGIN [MyMachine\ASPNET] FROM WINDOWS WITH
        DEFAULT_DATABASE=[Northwind]
CREATE USER [MyMachine\ASPNET] FOR LOGIN [MyMachine\ASPNET]
GRANT SELECT TO [MyMachine\ASPNET]
```

Impersonating Users

What if you want to use the actual user's credentials from your Web application to log in to your database?

ASP.NET makes impersonating users relatively straightforward. You can configure your Web application by changing the settings in the application's Web.config file. If your application does not already have a Web.config file, you can add one easily by selecting Add New Item from Visual Studio's Website menu and then selecting Web Configuration File from the resulting dialog box.

The configuration file is an XML document. In the <System.Web> section of the document, you can add the following elements to have the application impersonate the current user and deny anonymous logins:

```
<authorization>
    <deny users="?" />
</authorization>
<identity impersonate="true" />
```

For more information on Web application configuration options, see the .NET Framework SDK.

Once you've made these changes, attempts to connect to your database using trusted connections rely on the actual user's network credentials. However, I'm not a big fan of using trusted connections in this fashion for Web applications for a number of reasons.

This architecture does not benefit from connection pooling. If three different users connect to a Web application that relies on impersonation and trusted connections, each of these connections has a different security context. As a result, ADO.NET can't pool User A's connection and then reuse it for User B. In fact, connection pooling can adversely affect the performance of this type of application. Each user's connection will remain open until it's removed from the pool, but it can be reused only by that particular user.

I don't like the idea of relying on the database to enforce security in an application. If you're familiar with trusted connections to your database, it's tempting to rely on this feature rather than learn about different ASP.NET authentication options. There's no need to incur a network roundtrip to your database to authenticate the current user. ASP.NET offers plenty of options for enforcing security in your application—Windows authentication, Passport authentication, and Forms authentication.

Working with Microsoft Office Access Databases

Many developers are accustomed to communicating with Access databases and plan on relying on them in their ASP.NET applications. I understand the appeal of Access databases in small applications. They're extremely simple to create and manage. But unlike database systems such as SQL Server and Oracle, Access databases are not intended to support large numbers of simultaneous users. For example, to increase performance, the Jet engine does not write changes to the .mdb file immediately but instead maintains those changes in memory for a period of time. As a result, changes made on one connection might not be visible on other connections. There are multiple Knowledge Base articles on Microsoft's Web site that explain other reasons why Jet databases should not be used in Web applications.

Even though the ASP.NET team has created a data source control (a concept we'll cover shortly) specifically designed to interact with Access databases, I strongly discourage developers from using Access databases in Web applications. However, I'd be performing a disservice if I didn't talk briefly about working with Access databases in ASP.NET applications.

When you open an Access database, the Jet database engine uses a locking file associated with the database to keep track of the various locks (both read and write) that users have placed on various rows and pages. As a result, the user who is accessing the database needs read/write permissions on the directory in which the Access database resides. If you receive either of the following exceptions,

```
The Microsoft Jet database engine cannot open the file
'C:\Path\To\MyDatabase.mdb'. It is already opened exclusively by another
user, or you need permission to view its data.
```

or

```
Operation must use an updateable query.
```

the likely cause of the problem is that the ASP.NET account cannot write to the lock file. Make sure that the ASP.NET account has read/write access to the directory in which your Access database resides. Another option is to move to a database that's better suited for Web applications, such as one of the different editions of SQL Server. (Nudge, nudge.)

Challenges Interacting with Databases in ASP.NET 1.0

Visual Studio 2002 (and 2003) made it easy to create queries at design time using the various *Command* and *DataAdapter* classes. You could even configure a strongly typed *DataSet* based on your *DataAdapters* and bind controls to the *DataSet*.

However, you could not execute a query or display the results of the query in bound controls without adding your own code. Executing the query required a call to either *Command* *.ExecuteReader* or *DataAdapter.Fill*. Displaying the results of your query in bound controls required a call to the *DataBind* method on either the page or the desired controls to display the contents of the *DataReader* or *DataSet* to which they were bound, even after setting the *DataSource* property of your controls.

Once you successfully displayed data on a Web page, allowing the user to interact with that data required more code. The *DataGrid* control let you add links to the data displayed in the browser for editing and deleting rows, sorting and paging easily at design time through a property builder. Unfortunately, all the property builder did was help generate the user interface. You still had to write code for the events to handle editing, deleting, sorting, and paging through data.

That's not to knock the features in the initial release of ASP.NET, but they definitely left room for improvement.

Introducing Data Source Controls

ASP.NET 2.0 includes a series of data source controls that all derive from the same base *Data-SourceControl* control. These controls, shown in the following list, are designed to help you retrieve, display, and interact with different types of data:

- The *SqlDataSource* control uses ADO.NET to connect to your database, execute queries, retrieve data, and submit changes.

- The *AccessDataSource* control derives from the *SqlDataSource* control and is designed to work with Access databases.

- The *ObjectDataSource* control is designed for developers who want to work with collections of objects rather than *DataSets* and *DataReaders*, allowing you to supply methods to select, insert, update, and delete objects.

- The *XmlDataSource* control is designed to interact with XML documents.

- The *SiteMapDataSource* control lets you retrieve and display information about your site to help users navigate through the site.

This chapter covers scenarios that use the *SqlDataSource* control. For information on the other data source controls, see the documentation in the .NET Framework SDK.

Despite what its name might imply, the *SqlDataSource* control is designed to work with any database that can be accessed by a .NET Data Provider that supports the ADO.NET 2.0 provider factory model, described in Appendix A. The *SqlDataSource* control does offer some features that are supported only when working with SQL Server databases, but the basic features can be used with other databases, such as Oracle, DB2, and MySQL. The *Sql* in the *SqlDataSource* control's name is intended as a generic database term.

Displaying Data by Using a *SqlDataSource* Control

Let's build a simple Web page that uses a *SqlDataSource* to connect to your database, executes a simple query, and displays the results on the page by using the *GridView* control.

Getting Started

To create a new ASP.NET application, choose File, New, and Web Site from the Visual Studio menu. Select ASP.NET Web Site from the list of available templates, specify File System (instead of HTTP or FTP) as the location, and then select the language of your choice.

Adding a *SqlDataSource* Control

The *SqlDataSource* control is available on the Data portion of the Toolbox, along with the other data source controls. This is the sole starting point for creating *SqlDataSource* controls. There is no Data Sources window in Visual Studio (or Visual Web Developer) when building ASP.NET applications, nor is there a Data portion of the Visual Studio menu.

To add a *SqlDataSource* to your page, drag the *SqlDataSource* item from the Toolbox onto your page in Design view. When you drop the *SqlDataSource* item onto the page, Visual Studio will add a new *SqlDataSource* control to the page. You'll see a context menu that includes an option to configure the data source. Click that option and you'll launch a wizard similar to the TableAdapter Configuration Wizard described in Chapter 9.

Connecting to Your Database

The initial page of the SqlDataSource Configuration Wizard prompts you for connection information, as shown in Figure 14-1. The page includes a drop-down list of the connections available in Server Explorer. You can select one of these connections or create a new one by clicking the New Connection button—here we are connecting to the Northwind database—and then clicking the Next button.

Visual Studio stores connection strings in the application's Web.config file. If you've specified a connection that you've yet to use in the current application, Visual Studio will ask you to provide a name for the connection string, as shown in Figure 14-2.

We'll take a closer look at where Visual Studio stores the connection string and how you can access this information programmatically shortly. But for now, on with the wizard.

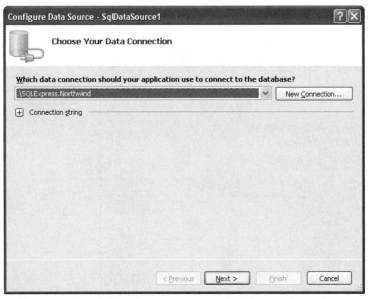

Figure 14-1   Specifying connection information for the *SqlDataSource* control

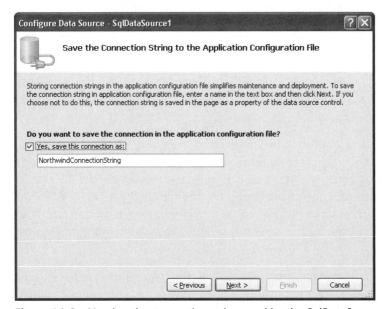

Figure 14-2   Naming the connection string used by the *SqlDataSource* control

Constructing Your Query

The SqlDataSource Configuration Wizard offers multiple options for specifying your query, as shown in Figure 14-3. The wizard lists the tables and views available on the specified connection. Select a table or view and the wizard displays the columns available on that table or view. You can select the "*" box to include all columns or select the boxes of individual columns to retrieve. At the bottom of the page, the wizard displays the SELECT query it will execute based on your input.

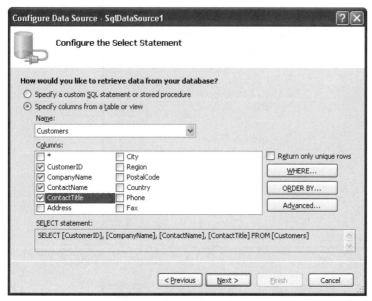

Figure 14-3   Specifying columns from a table or view to be used by the *SqlDataSource* control

On the right side of the page, you'll find additional options. You can specify that you want only unique rows. You can also specify a WHERE clause, an ORDER BY clause, and other advanced options for your query by clicking the corresponding buttons. We'll revisit these features later in the chapter.

If you don't want to rely on the wizard to generate your query, you can supply your own. There's an option at the top of the page that allows you to construct your own query through a custom SQL query or a stored procedure. If you select this option and then click the Next button, you'll see the page shown in Figure 14-4. You can enter your own SELECT, UPDATE, INSERT, and DELETE queries by hand on the corresponding tabs of the page. If you don't want to manually type the queries, you can click the Query Builder button to invoke the Query Builder.

Click the Previous button to go back to the page that lets you choose a table or view and select the desired columns. Specify the Customers table and the first four columns in the table (CustomerID, CompanyName, ContactName, and ContactTitle) as shown earlier in Figure 14-3. Then click the Next button.

Testing Your Query

The next page of the SqlDataSource Configuration Wizard lets you test the query you've built. Simply click the Test Query button. If the query includes parameters, the wizard will display a dialog box that lets you supply values for the parameters prior to executing the query. Once the wizard executes the query, it displays the results on the page, as shown in Figure 14-5.

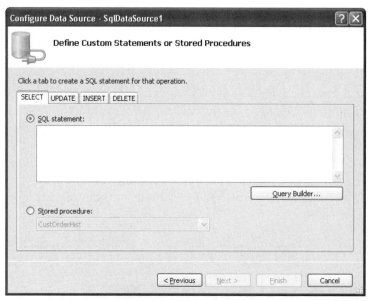

Figure 14-4   Supplying your own SQL queries for the *SqlDataSource* control

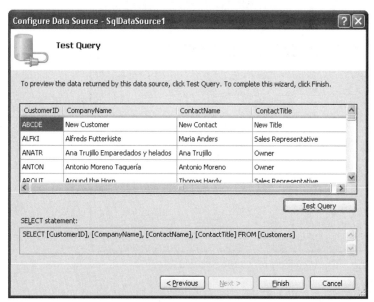

Figure 14-5   Testing your query in the SqlDataSource Configuration Wizard

If your query does not return the expected results, you can click the Previous button to move back to the previous page and modify your query. Otherwise, click the Finish button to accept the query and exit the wizard.

Displaying the Query Results on Your Page

If you build your project and display your page in your Web browser, the page will be blank. The page will not open a connection to your database, nor will it execute your query, because there are no controls bound to the *SqlDataSource* control. We can remedy that situation quickly and easily by adding a *GridView* control to the page and binding it to the *SqlDataSource* control.

Drag a *GridView* item from the Data tab on the Toolbox and drop the item onto the page to add a *GridView* control to the page. Like the *SqlDataSource* control, the *GridView* control offers a set of options in a context menu when you add a *GridView* control to the page. Select the *SqlDataSource* (generally named *SQLDataSource1* by default) that you created earlier in the drop-down list that appears next to the Choose Data Source option. Once you've selected the *SqlDataSource*, you'll see the columns from the *SqlDataSource*'s query appear in the *GridView* control. You can also add formatting for the grid by clicking the Auto Format option.

Once you've bound the *GridView* control to the *SqlDataSource* and, optionally, added formatting to the *GridView* control, your page will look like the one shown in Figure 14-6.

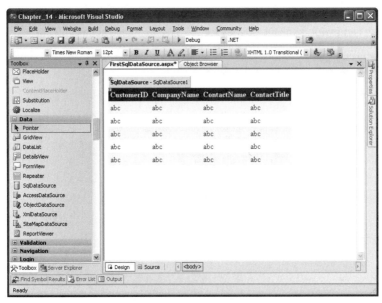

Figure 14-6 Binding a *GridView* control to the *SqlDataSource*

Now if you build the project and launch the application by pressing the F5 key, you'll see the results of your query in the resulting page in your Web browser, as shown in Figure 14-7.

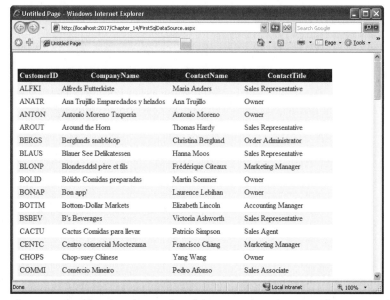

Figure 14-7   Showing the results of the query by using a *GridView* control

Features of the *SqlDataSource* Control

Now that you've created a very simple Web page that uses a *SqlDataSource* control to execute a query, let's take a quick look at the features offered by the *SqlDataSource* control.

Code-Free Data Binding

The Web page we constructed earlier required no code. Binding the *GridView* control to the *SqlDataSource* control causes the *SqlDataSource* control to execute the query and the *GridView* control to display the results without your having to write a single line of code. You do not have to add code to call the *ExecuteReader* method on a *SqlCommand* or the *Fill* method on a *SqlDataAdapter*. You do not have to call the *DataBind* method on the *GridView* control or the Page. This is a major step forward from ADO.NET and ASP.NET 1.0.

We'll take a closer look at more advanced code-free data-binding scenarios later in this chapter.

Connection String Management

Earlier I mentioned that Visual Studio stores the connection string in the application's Web.config file. If you examine the contents of the Web.config file, you'll find an entry in the *connectionString* section that includes the name, connection string, and provider name for the connection you specified in the SqlDataSource Configuration Wizard that is similar to the following:

```
<connectionStrings>
  <add name="NorthwindConnectionString"
       connectionString="Data Source=.\SQLExpress;
```

```
                        Initial Catalog=Northwind;
                        Integrated Security=True"
        providerName="System.Data.SqlClient" />
</connectionStrings>
```

Visual Studio does not directly reference the connection string in the *SqlDataSource* control's *ConnectionString* property. Instead, Visual Studio references the connection string entry in the configuration file by using the "<%$ ... %>" ASP.NET expression, as shown here:

```
<asp:SqlDataSource ID="SqlDataSource1" runat="server"
    ConnectionString="<%$ ConnectionStrings:NorthwindConnectionString %>"
    SelectCommand="SELECT [CustomerID], ... FROM [Customers]">
</asp:SqlDataSource>
```

The contents inside the "<%$ ... %>" tag are evaluated when the application is compiled, and it is roughly the equivalent of the following code:

Visual Basic

```
Dim strConn, strKey As String
strKey = "NorthwindConnectionString"
strConn = ConfigurationManager.ConnectionStrings(strKey).ConnectionString
Me.SqlDataSource1.ConnectionString = strConn
```

Visual C#

```
string strConn, strKey;
strKey = "NorthwindConnectionString";
strConn = ConfigurationManager.ConnectionStrings[strKey].ConnectionString;
this.SqlDataSource1.ConnectionString = strConn;
```

For more information on the "<%$ ... %>" syntax, see the .NET Framework SDK.

Integrating External Input in the Query's WHERE Clause

The *SqlDataSource* control makes it easy to add user input to the WHERE clause of the control's query so that your query retrieves just the desired data.

The page we constructed earlier retrieves information for all customers in the Northwind database's Customers table. What if the user wants to see just the rows that have a specific value for the ContactTitle column? You can prompt the user for the desired value of the ContactTitle column by adding a *Label* control to the page that has a value of "ContactTitle" for its *Text* property, followed by a *TextBox* control in which the user can specify the desired value.

In Chapter 4, you learned that rather than appending the user-specified value on the WHERE clause of the query, you should use a parameterized query like the following:

```
SELECT CustomerID, CompanyName, ContactName, ContactTitle
    FROM Customers WHERE ContactTitle = @ContactTitle
```

Once you've constructed the query, you assign the user-specified value to the *Value* property on the *SqlParameter* and execute the query. However, thanks to the *SqlDataSource* control's code-free binding support, you don't have to write that code.

You might remember that the page of the SqlDataSource Configuration Wizard that lets you build your query by selecting a table and columns also has a WHERE button, as shown earlier in Figure 14-3 If you reconfigure your *SqlDataSource* control and click this button, you'll see the dialog box shown in Figure 14-8.

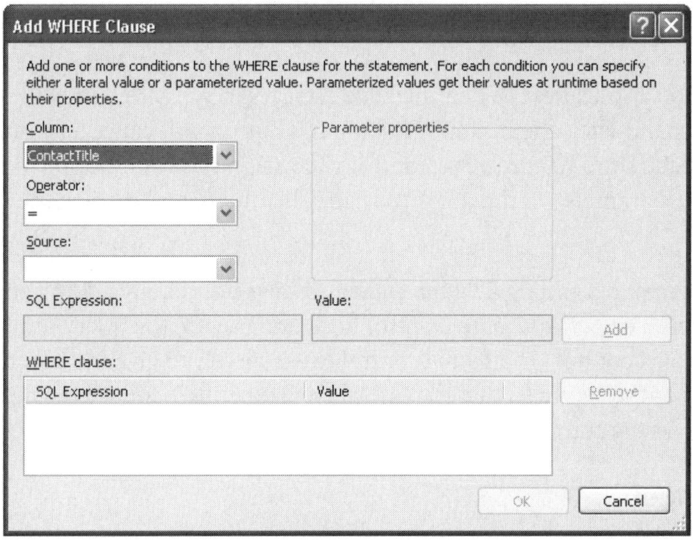

Figure 14-8   Adding a WHERE clause to the *SqlDataSource* control's query

This dialog box can do more than just help you add a parameterized WHERE clause to your *SqlDataSource* control's query. You can use this dialog box to bind that parameter to a value from another area of your application, such as a control, a cookie, the page's query string, a field on the form, a profile property, or an entry in session state (a feature we'll examine in more detail later in the chapter). Let's build an example that relies on a value supplied in a control.

First, add a few controls to the top of the page. Add a *Label* control, and set its *Text* property to "ContactTitle:". Then add a *TextBox* control with its ID property set to "Contact-TitleTextBox". Finally, add a *Button* control with its *Text* property set to "Get Customers". Now let's add the parameterized WHERE clause to the query and bind the parameter to the *TextBox* control.

To relaunch the SqlDataSource Configuration Wizard, right-click the *SqlDataSource* control and select Configure Data Source from the context menu. Select the *SqlDataSource* control on your page. When you reach the page that constructs the SELECT query based on user input, click the WHERE button to launch the Add WHERE Clause dialog box.

Now let's use the dialog box to add a parameterized WHERE clause and bind the parameter to the contents of the *TextBox*. Once you've launched the dialog box, select the column you want to reference in the WHERE clause. For this example, select the ContactTitle column. Next, select the desired operator for the comparison (=, <, >, <=, >=, <>, IS NULL, IS NOT NULL, LIKE, NOT LIKE, or CONTAINS) from the drop-down list of operators. For this example, stick with the default comparison, =. Then select the desired source for the value of the comparison. For this example, specify Control from the list of possible source options, and then select the ContactTitle *TextBox* from the list of available controls. You can also specify a default value for the parameter. Finally, click the Add button to add the comparison to the WHERE clause.

Now build and run the application. When the page appears in your Web browser, type **Owner** in the *TextBox* and click the button. Clicking the button will cause a roundtrip to the server, at which time the *SqlDataSource* control will assign the value supplied in the *TextBox* control to the parameter in the query, execute the query, and display the results in the *GridView* control.

Although this sample requires adding a *Button* control, it does not require adding any code to the *Button*'s *Click* event. The *SqlDataSource* control does not execute the query until a value is supplied in the *TextBox* control. The *Button* control exists merely to give the user the ability to post the page back to the server so that the *SqlDataSource* control can use the input to the *TextBox* control and execute the query.

Submitting Changes

Like the TableAdapter Configuration Wizard, the SqlDataSource Configuration Wizard can help you generate the updating logic necessary to submit changes to your database. By default, the SqlDataSource Configuration Wizard does not generate this updating logic. You can ask the wizard to generate this logic by clicking the Advanced button on the same page as the WHERE button, which launches the dialog box shown in Figure 14-9.

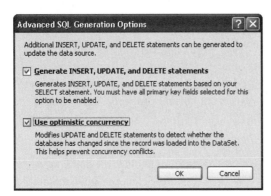

Figure 14-9   Advanced options in the SqlDataSource Configuration Wizard

Adding Updating Logic to the *SqlDataSource*   To enable editing and deleting items in the *GridView* control, you must first tell the SqlDataSource control to generate updating logic. Selecting the Generate INSERT, UPDATE And DELETE Statements check box in the dialog box will cause the wizard to generate the parameterized INSERT, UPDATE, and DELETE queries needed to submit pending changes to your database. By default, the UPDATE and DELETE queries will include only the key columns in the WHERE clause. Note that including only the key columns corresponds to "last in wins" updating logic or the OverwriteChanges concurrency option available through the *CommandBuilder* classes, both described in Chapter 10. In other words, update attempts will automatically overwrite other users' changes. Selecting the UseOptimisticConcurrency option will include all comparable columns in the WHERE clause, which corresponds to the CompareAllSearchableValues concurrency option available through the *CommandBuilder* classes. This ensures that your update attempts do not overwrite other users' changes.

Enabling Updates in the *GridView*   The *GridView* control is aware of the features available in the *SqlDataSource* control. If you bind a *GridView* control to a *SqlDataSource* that has updating logic specified, the *GridView* will let you enable updates through the grid. Now that you've added updating logic to the *SqlDataSource* control, all you need to do is to right-click the *GridView* control and select Show Smart Tag. Then select the Enable Editing and Enable Deleting boxes in the smart tag.

Now when you build and run the application, you'll see two new links for each row: Edit and Delete. To edit the contents of a row, click the Edit button. The *GridView* control will replace the contents of the editable columns with *TextBox*es that let you modify the contents of the row, as shown in Figure 14-10. The *GridView* also replaces the Edit and Delete links with links that allow you to update the row or cancel the changes.

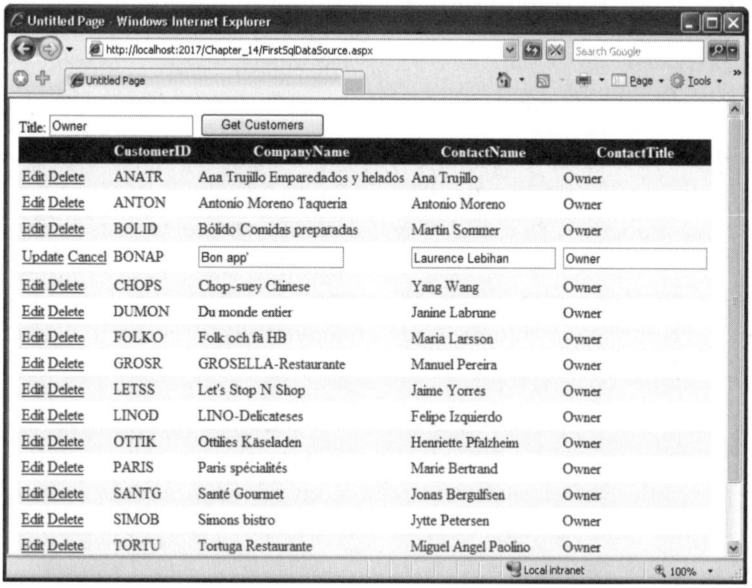

Figure 14-10   Editing the contents of a row by using the *GridView* control

As the text contained in the links implies, clicking the Update link submits the changes to the database, clicking the Cancel button cancels the pending changes to the row, and clicking the Delete link deletes the selected row. If you click a link that corresponds to updating or deleting a row, the *GridView* control instructs the *SqlDataSource* control to submit the change.

> **Warning** The *SqlDataSource* is optimistic to a fault when submitting changes. As noted earlier, the *SqlDataSource* includes by default only key columns in the WHERE clause for the UPDATE and DELETE queries. The *SqlDataSource* control does include logic to detect the scenario in which the query executes successfully but does not update any rows. However, the *SqlDataSource* does not throw an exception. Instead, it treats the scenario as if the user clicked the Cancel button rather than trying to submit the change. If you feel that you need a strong enough indication to the user that the update attempt failed, you can trap for this scenario by adding code to handle the *SqlDataSource* control's *Updated* and *Deleted* events and examining the *SqlDataSourceStatus-EventArgs* object. If the *AffectedRows* property returns zero, the update attempt did not modify any rows.

Caching

The *GridView* control stores information in the page's *ViewState* so that it can pass original and modified row information to the *SqlDataSource* control to submit pending changes. However, the *SqlDataSource* control caches no information and executes the query each time the page is generated, assuming that the ContactTitle *TextBox* contains a value.

The *EnableCaching* and *EnableViewState* Properties   Enabling caching on the *SqlData-Source* control is straightforward. To have the *SqlDataSource* cache information, simply set the *EnableCaching* property to *True*. The *SqlDataSource* then checks the value of the control's *EnableViewState* property to determine where to store the results of the query. By default, this property is set to *True*, causing the *SqlDataSource* to store the results in the page's *ViewState*. Setting the *EnableViewState* property to *False* causes the *SqlDataSource* control to store the information in the server-side Application cache.

The *CacheDuration* and *CacheExpirationPolicy* Properties   You can also control the amount of time the data is cached by setting the *SqlDataSource* control's *CacheDuration* and *CacheExpirationPolicy* properties. By default, a *SqlDataSource* control with its *EnableCaching* property set to *True* will cache the results of the query indefinitely because the *CacheDuration* property is set to *Infinite*. If you set the *CacheDuration* property to an integer, the *SqlDataSource* will use that value in conjunction with the *CacheExpirationPolicy* property to determine the amount of time it will cache the results of the query.

If you set the *CacheDuration* property to 30 and leave the *CacheExpirationPolicy* property set to its default value, *Absolute*, the *SqlDataSource* control will cache the results for 30 seconds. Until that time elapses, the *SqlDataSource* control will rely on the cached data. Once that time elapses, the next attempt to access data from the *SqlDataSource* control will cause the control to re-execute the specified query.

Setting the *CacheExpirationPolicy* property to *Sliding* changes the behavior slightly. Let's say that the *CacheDuration* property is set to 30 and the *SqlDataSource* executes the query it contains to display data in a *GridView* control. The *SqlDataSource* will store the results of the query in the appropriate cache, as dictated by the *EnableViewState* property. Now let's assume that the user clicks a link on the page, causing a post-back event that forces the *GridView* control to re-request the results of the query from the *SqlDataSource* control. Because fewer than 30 seconds have elapsed, the *SqlDataSource* control will reuse the cached results. The *SqlDataSource* control will reset the amount of time the control will cache the results of the query. As long as the *SqlDataSource* control receives requests for the query results in 30 seconds or fewer, it will continue to cache the results of the query rather than re-execute the query.

Using SQL Server 2005 Query Notifications with the *SqlDataSource* Control   The *SqlDataSource* control is also designed to work with SQL Server 2005 Query Notifications. You can configure the *SqlDataSource* so that it will continue to cache the results of the query until that data changes in the database. At that point, SQL Server 2005 will notify the *SqlDataSource* of the change. The *SqlDataSource* will then invalidate the results from the cache, causing it to re-execute your query the next time the *SqlDataSource* is used on the page.

We'll take a closer look at using SQL Server 2005 Query Notifications later in this chapter.

Linking Multiple *SqlDataSource*s and Multiple Bound Controls

The ASP.NET 2.0 "code-free" data-binding support lets you build simple Web pages quickly and easily, but this approach is not restricted to just simplistic Web pages. To prove my point, let's take a look at a scenario that's a little more challenging.

Let's construct a new page that displays the company name for each customer, one page at a time. To add a new page, select Website and Add New Item from the Visual Studio menu. Then select Web Form from the resulting dialog box. Like the previous page, the new page will display customer information. However, when the user selects a customer on this new page, the page should display more detailed information for that customer. The detail portion of the page should give the user the ability to modify or delete the current customer as well as to enter a new customer. This is a fairly straightforward master/detail Web page, as shown in Figure 14-11. Believe it or not, you can handle this scenario without writing a single line of code.

First, let's build the portion of the page that displays the company names. Add a *SqlDataSource* control to your new page and call it *CompanyNamesDataSource,* specified in the (ID) property box. Configure the *SqlDataSource* so that it retrieves the CustomerID and CompanyName columns from the Customers table. Now add a *GridView* control to the page, call its ID *CompanyNamesGridView*, and then bind it to the *CompanyNamesDataSource*.

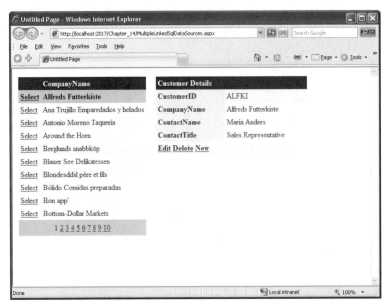

Figure 14-11 A sample master/detail Web page

We want the grid to display just the CompanyName column. The query includes the CustomerID column, which we will use to retrieve more detailed information about the currently selected column. Removing a column from the *GridView* control is simple. Click the EditColumns link on the *GridView*'s smart tag, and remove the CustomerID column from the selected fields (select CustomerID and then select the red X for deletion).

The *GridView* control includes built-in support for paging and selection. Enabling these features is straightforward. On the *GridView* control's smart tag, select the boxes for Enable Paging and Enable Selection.

When you enable paging on the *GridView* control, the *GridView* partitions the results into pages of rows based on the *GridView*'s *PageSize* property. By default, this property is set to *10*. The *GridView* control will display a single page's worth of results and build a series of links to let the user navigate to other pages. When the user clicks one of the links, the *GridView* control displays the appropriate page of data. The *SqlDataSource* will re-execute the query unless you've configured it to cache the results.

Although this is the simplest way to achieve paging in a Web application, it's not the most efficient solution. We'll take a closer look at various paging options later in the chapter. For the purposes of this sample, relying on *GridView* paging in this way is fine.

The *GridView* selection feature is a little more straightforward. The *GridView* control displays a Select link next to each row. Clicking the Select link highlights the selected row. If the *GridView* is configured to cache data in *ViewState*, a feature we'll discuss later in the chapter, it will be able to highlight the current row without having to re-execute the query.

Now let's add another *SqlDataSource* and another bound control to display detailed information about the currently selected customer. Add another *SqlDataSource* control, and call its ID *Edit-CustomerDataSource*. Configure the *SqlDataSource* to retrieve the CustomerID, CompanyName, ContactName, and ContactTitle fields from the Customers table. Add a parameter to the WHERE clause by using the SqlDataSource Configuration Wizard. Using the Add WHERE Clause page in the wizard, specify the CustomerID column, "=" as the operator, Control as the source, and the CompanyNamesGridView as the Control ID. Then click the Add button to add the bound parameter and click the OK button to return to the Configure The Select Statement page of the wizard. Because we want to give the user the ability to modify the data returned by this *SqlDataSource*, click the Advanced button and specify that you want the wizard to generate updating logic and include optimistic concurrency checks.

ASP.NET 2.0 includes a new *DetailsView* control specifically designed to let the user view and modify the contents of a single row of data. First, add a *DetailsView* control to the page, and name the ID *EditCustomerDetailsView*. Then bind the new *DetailsView* control to the *Edit-CustomerDataSource SqlDataSource* control. Finally, select the Enable Inserting, Enable Editing, and Enable Deleting check boxes on the *DetailsView* control's smart tag. Now run your project and your page will display the desired data.

The sample files for Chapter 14 include a page called *MultipleLinkedSqlDataSources* that was built by following these same steps. The sample includes some additional cosmetic changes—placing the *GridView* and *DetailsView* in different cells in a table so that they appear side by side on the Web page. The sample also sets the *SelectedIndex* property of the *GridView* control to *0* so that the *DetailsView* displays information about the first customer when the page is initially created.

Caching Data Between Roundtrips

So now you know how to display data on a Web page by using the *SqlDataSource* and bound controls such as *GridView* and *DetailsView*. What if you don't want to execute the same queries every time someone hits your Web server? Maybe you want to cache the results of a process-intensive query. Maybe you want to store the contents of the user's shopping cart.

ASP.NET offers many caching features that let you control how you maintain data for your application or for each separate session. The features themselves are very straightforward. However, there's no single universal right or wrong way to cache data. Relying on a particular caching feature in one application might improve performance, whereas using the same feature in another application might hinder performance.

To understand which, if any, caching feature you should use in your application, you need to understand the architecture of the application you're building, as well as how each caching feature works and its pros and its cons. Rather than make sweeping statements such as, "Caching data in the *Application* object is a lousy idea," this text will quickly cover the basics of the various ASP.NET caching features, as well as some of the pros and cons for each feature.

The Stateless Approach—Maintaining No State

There's no programming law requiring you to cache data. You can have your Web application's ASP.NET code be completely stateless.

You can have your ASP.NET code execute queries and convert the results to HTML by using bound controls. If you're working with an order-entry application in which the user stores items in a shopping cart, you can store the contents of the current user's shopping cart in your database, relying on the session ID as a way to locate which rows in the database belong to the current user.

Benefits to Statelessness

This approach has obvious merits. By not caching data in your ASP.NET code, the application requires a minimum of memory per user. In terms of memory, this approach is the most scalable.

Drawbacks to Statelessness

However, that's a very simplistic view of building scalable applications. Suppose that the application is an online catalog and you're displaying a list of product categories on all pages. Do you really want to query your database for the list of product categories each and every time a user accesses a page?

Caching Data at the Client

If you want to cache data but don't want to maintain that data on your servers, you can use various options to cache data at the client.

Cookies

Many Web sites use cookies to store user information at the client. The ASP.NET *Request* and *Response* objects each expose a *Cookies* collection that you can use to store and retrieve information between roundtrips. For example, you could add the following code to the Load event of a Form in your ASP.NET application to track the date and time of the user's last visit in a cookie. You can get the *Form_Load* event by double-clicking on the Design view empty space. This will bring you to the Source view of the *Page_Load* event where you can paste the following code:

Visual Basic

```
If Request.Cookies("LastVisit") Is Nothing Then
    Response.Write("This is your first visit!  Welcome!")
    Response.AppendCookie(New HttpCookie("LastVisit", Now.ToString()))
Else
    Response.Write("Welcome back.  Your last visit was: " & _
                   Request.Cookies("LastVisit").Value)
    Response.Cookies("LastVisit").Value = Now.ToString()
End If
```

Visual C#

```csharp
if (Request.Cookies["LastVisit"] == null)
{
    Response.Write("This is your first visit!  Welcome!");
    Response.AppendCookie(new HttpCookie("LastVisit",
                                DateTime.Now.ToString()));
}
else
{
    Response.Write("Welcome back.  Your last visit was: " +
                Request.Cookies["LastVisit"].Value);
    Response.Cookies["LastVisit"].Value = DateTime.Now.ToString();
}
```

Benefits to Maintaining State by Using Cookies   ASP.NET makes working with cookies simple. Storing data at the client allows your ASP.NET code to be stateless, which improves your application's scalability. Cookies are also configurable. You can control when the cookie expires by setting the *HttpCookie* object's *Expires* property.

Drawbacks to Maintaining State by Using Cookies   Cookies are designed to store small pieces of information. Most browsers will not let you store more than a couple kilobytes of data in a cookie, so they're not terribly handy for caching the results of a query that returns more than a couple rows.

Web application developers are becoming less reliant on cookies for multiple reasons. Depending on the browser's settings, the browser might reject the cookie. Plus, cookies aren't completely secure. The user can modify the contents of the cookie. Keep that in mind before deciding to use cookies to store user settings.

Hidden Fields

You can store information in a hidden field on your Web page. This process is somewhat analogous to a hidden control on a Windows Form. You can store data in a *HiddenField* control in your ASP.NET code and later examine the contents of the control the next time the page is posted back to the server. You can store large quantities of data in hidden fields on a Web page, but reconstituting the contents of the hidden fields back into the desired objects can be cumbersome. So let's move along to a similar feature in ASP.NET that's much more developer-friendly—*ViewState*.

ViewState

The *Page* class in the *System.Web.UI* namespace exposes a *ViewState* property, which contains a *StateBag* object. Essentially, a *StateBag* object is similar to a collection of name/value pairs. You use it to store information, similar to the *Cookies* collections on the *Request* and *Response* objects.

You can store data in a page's *ViewState* and then retrieve that data in the next post-back event for the page. Working with the page's *ViewState* is as simple as working with cookies, as shown in the following code sample:

Visual Basic

```
If ViewState("LastVisit") Is Nothing Then
    Response.Write("This is your first visit!  Welcome!")
    ViewState("LastVisit") = Now.ToString()
Else
    Response.Write("Welcome back.  Your last visit was: " & _
                ViewState("LastVisit"))
    ViewState("LastVisit") = Now.ToString()
End If
```

Visual C#

```
if (ViewState["LastVisit"] == null)
{
    Response.Write("This is your first visit!  Welcome!");
    ViewState["LastVisit"] = DateTime.Now.ToString();
}
else
{
    Response.Write("Welcome back.  Your last visit was: " +
                ViewState["LastVisit"]);
    ViewState["LastVisit"] = DateTime.Now.ToString();
}
```

Figure 14-12 shows the source for a page that uses the preceding code snippet to maintain the date and time of the user's last visit in the page's *ViewState*. If you look closely at the page's HTML, you'll see that the *ViewState* is maintained in a hidden field. Because all browsers support hidden fields regardless of their configuration, you can use the *ViewState* to store data for many scenarios in which using cookies would cause problems.

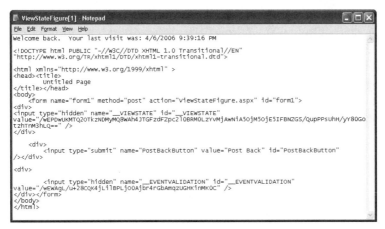

Figure 14-12   Examining a page's *ViewState*

Benefits to Maintaining State in *ViewState*   As with cookies, storing data in a page's *ViewState* allows the ASP.NET code to remain stateless, which improves your code's scalability. Because *ViewState* is implemented as a hidden field, you can store and retrieve data from a page's *ViewState* regardless of the browser's security settings. And unlike cookies, the page can hold much larger items in its *ViewState*.

Drawbacks to Maintaining State in *ViewState*   The data you store in a page's *ViewState* is sent down to the browser, so the more data you store, the longer it takes to load pages and post back to the server. Also, although the data stored in *ViewState* is hashed, it's still possible for the user to decrypt the data stored there. Thus, it's not completely secure.

You can't store just any data in *ViewState*. You can store only data that your ASP.NET code knows how to serialize. You can store simple data types such as strings and integers. However, you can't store generic objects in *ViewState* because ASP.NET doesn't know how to store and re-create generic objects. Classes that support the *ISerializable* interface, such as *DataSet* objects and *DataTable* objects, can be written to *ViewState*.

Maintaining State in Your Web Server

ASP.NET also gives you various options for maintaining state on the Web server, as follows:

Session

The *Page* class exposes a *Session* property, which returns an instance of an *HttpSessionState* class. You can store data in the page's *Session*, just as you can in the page's *ViewState*. However, the data that you store in the page's *Session* is kept on the server rather than sent down to the browser along with the HTML for the page.

ASP.NET maintains the settings stored in *Session* until the user's session ends. Also, these settings are kept separate from those of other sessions. So the information stored in the page's *Session* is specific to that session.

Benefits to Maintaining State in *Session*   Because the data is maintained by the Web server rather than by the browser, the data is secure. The user cannot access or modify the contents of the *Session* object through the browser. Also, because the data is maintained on the server, you can rely on the *Session* object regardless of the user's browser settings.

Drawbacks to Maintaining State in *Session*   Storing data in the page's *Session* means that your ASP.NET code might be less scalable as a result. Maintaining state in *Session* requires resources for each session of your application.

Say the user searches your product catalog and you maintain the results of that search in *Session* so that the user can page back and forth through the results without having to re-execute the query with each change of a page. Estimate how much memory is required to store the results of that query. 5 KB? 50 KB? 500 KB? Now multiply that by the number of people accessing this feature of your Web application. 10? 100? 1000? More? Make sure you consider the total server resources you're likely to consume if you decide to maintain state in *Session* scope.

Application

The *Application* object is similar to the *Session* object except that the data available through the page's *Application* property is shared across all sessions. Thus, data you store in *Application* is available to all users.

Benefits to Maintaining State in *Application*   As with data that you store in *Session*, the data you store in *Application* is secure because it's maintained on the server and the functionality is available regardless of the user's browser settings.

Because the data stored in *Application* is global to all sessions of the application, it's an ideal place to store nonvolatile data that's used in all sessions, such as a list of product categories.

Drawbacks to Maintaining State in *Application*   Data that you store in *Application* uses resources on your server. Storing too much data in *Application* can adversely affect the performance of your application.

Cache

The *Page* object exposes a *Cache* property, which returns an instance of the *Cache* object. You can think of the *Cache* object as a more robust *Application* object. The data stored in *Cache* is available in all sessions of the application. You can access and modify the contents of the *Cache* object just as you can the *Application* object, but the *Cache* object gives you the following additional functionality when you add an item to the *Cache* via the *Add* or *Insert* method:

- You can specify when that item will be removed from the cache by supplying either a specific (*DateTime*) value or a relative (*TimeSpan*) value.

- You can specify a *CacheDependency*, which will force the item to be removed from the cache when the dependent item changes. For example, you can supply a *SqlDependency* object that will force the item in the cache to be removed when the data returned by a query against SQL Server 2005 changes. We'll take a closer look at using *SqlDependency* with SQL Server 2005 shortly.

- You can specify a callback function that ASP.NET will call when the item is removed from the cache.

The benefits and drawbacks to using the *Cache* object are the same as those for the *Application* object, except that the *Cache* object offers the additional cache-removal features previously listed.

Output Caching

Imagine that all pages in your Web application will show a list of site options along the left margin of the page. This list might contain the available product categories, or it might simply list the various areas of your Web site. In either case, let's say that the data that you use to construct this list is stored in your database somewhere and rarely changes.

You might decide to retrieve this data into a *DataSet* and store this *DataSet* in the *Application* object. This way your ASP.NET code does not need to fetch that data from the database each time it serves up a page. That would probably save a lot of network traffic, but you still wind up converting the contents of the *DataSet* to HTML each time you serve up a page of data.

ASP.NET offers another option: output caching. You can cache the output for a page or a portion of a page. You can also cache full or partial pages based on parameters. If you're looking to cache data to HTML for a page or a portion of the page, you should take a look at this powerful feature.

Benefits to Using Output Caching   If you need to repeatedly generate the same HTML based on the contents of the *DataSet*, output caching is more efficient because it requires less processing at the server. Just as with the *Cache* object, you can control how long the output remains cached.

Drawbacks to Using Output Caching   As with other server-side caching features, output caching still consumes resources on your server.

Using SQL Server 2005 Notification Services

One of the most powerful features of SQL Server 2005 is Notification Services. Notification Services allows applications to subscribe to various events. When those events occur, Notification Services notifies all subscribers that the event occurred.

The standard example for this architecture is a stocks application. The user submits an entry to buy or sell a number of shares of a particular stock when it reaches a specific price. The application must then continue to poll that stock price and execute the order when (or if) the stock specified reaches the desired price. Notification Services makes building this type of application straightforward.

Using Notification Services from ADO.NET

You can use Notification Services from ADO.NET to receive notification when the results of the query change in the database. The SQL Server .NET Data Provider that's included in version 2.0 of the .NET Framework also includes classes designed to work with Notification Services: *SqlDependency* and *SqlNotification*. We'll take a closer look at these classes shortly.

Enabling Notification Services   The most common Notification Services question on developer forums is, "What are the minimum security privileges required to use Notification Services in an application?" Many developers find that they can use Notification Services in their applications when the applications run under an account that has database administrator privileges but not a less privileged account. Chances are you won't want to grant administrator privileges to your users.

Two steps, each with different privileges, are required to enable Notification Services within an application to receive notifications when the results of queries change in the database. The first step is to listen for notifications by opening a connection to the database and waiting for messages from the notification queue. The second step is to specify that you want to subscribe to receive notifications for the queries you're executing. We'll look at how you perform each of these steps shortly.

The connection used to listen for notification messages requires different privileges than the connection used to subscribe to receive notifications. The account that's used to listen for notification messages must have the ability to create stored procedures and queues—permissions that are not required to subscribe to notifications.

The *FirstSqlDependencyTest* sample included with this chapter includes a SQL script that creates accounts for both the subscriber and listener and that grants those accounts the necessary privileges.

The *SqlNotificationRequest* Class   The *SqlNotificationRequest* class resides in the *System .Data.Sql* namespace and is the low-level interface for working with Notification Services. Using the *SqlNotificationRequest* class requires that you create the low-level database structures (queue, service, etc.) and that you reference these structures within your application's code.

Few, if any, developers should need to use the *SqlNotificationRequest* class or even the low-level database structures in an ADO.NET application. In fact, the *SqlNotificationRequest* class is in the *System.Data.Sql* namespace, so developers will be less tempted to use it directly. The *SqlDependency* class provides a simpler approach, preventing developers from having to worry about queues, services, or routes.

Earlier I pointed out that there are two steps in using Notification Services from an ADO.NET application: listening for notification messages and subscribing to receive notifications when query results change. The *SqlNotificationClass* handles only the second step. If you rely on the *SqlNotificationClass*, you'll still need to open a separate *SqlConnection* and query the correct queue in the database to listen for the desired notification messages.

The *SqlDependency* Class   The *SqlDependency* class is a higher-level implementation of Notification Services within ADO.NET, and it uses the *SqlNotificationRequest* class internally.

The *SqlDependency* class handles both steps required to use Notification Services from an ADO.NET application. To start listening for notification messages, you simply call the static *Start* method on the *SqlDependency* class and pass in a connection string for your database that uses an account that has the necessary privileges to listen for notification messages, as shown here:

Visual Basic
```
Dim strConn As String
strConn = "Data Source=.\SQLExpress;Initial Catalog=MyDatabase;" & _
```

```
            "User ID=Listener_User;Password=L!st3n3r_Pwd;"
SqlDependency.Start(strConn)
```

Visual C#

```csharp
string strConn;
strConn = @"Data Source=.\SQLExpress;Initial Catalog=MyDatabase;" +
          "User ID=Listener_User;Password=L!st3n3r_Pwd;";
SqlDependency.Start(strConn)
```

The call to the static *Start* method opens a new *SqlConnection* based on the connection string supplied, and it executes a series of queries to create a stored procedure, a queue, and a service. It then executes a query to wait for notification messages from the queue. The *Sql-Dependency* class generates a GUID value and uses that value in the names of the structures to ensure uniqueness. After creating the necessary objects on the server, the *SqlDependency* class executes a query to listen for notification messages. That query is set to time out after 120 seconds, and the *SqlDependency* class re-executes the query every 60 seconds to ensure that it will continue to receive messages. If you want to take a closer look at how this works, execute the code while running SQL Profiler.

Calling the *Start* method multiple times using the same connection string will not throw an exception. The first call will create the *SqlConnection* and execute the queries necessary to start listening for notification messages. Subsequent calls will be disregarded.

The *SqlDependency* class will maintain the *SqlConnection* it uses to listen for notification messages for the lifetime of the process or until you call the *Stop* method and supply the same connection string. Calling the *Stop* method also drops the service, queue, and procedure that the *Start* method created. Calling the *Stop* method multiple times will not cause a failure, nor will supplying a connection string that has not been used to start receiving notification messages.

Once you've started listening for notification messages, the next step is to subscribe to change notification messages for your queries. Let's say that you have a *SqlCommand* for which you want to receive notification messages when the results of the query change in the database. Simply create a new *SqlDependency* object and pass the *SqlCommand* object into the *Sql-Dependency*'s constructor. Next, add a handler for the new *SqlDependency* object's *OnChange* event. Then call the *SqlCommand*'s *ExecuteReader* method.

Visual Basic

```vbnet
Dim strConn, strSQL As String
strConn = "Data Source=.\SQLExpress;Initial Catalog=MyDatabase;" & _
          "User ID=Subscriber_User;Password=Subscr!b3r_Pwd;"
strSQL = "SELECT ... FROM MySchema.MyTable WHERE ..."
Using cn As New SqlConnection(strConn)
    Using cmd As New SqlCommand(strSQL, cn)
        Dim dependency As New SqlDependency(cmd)
        AddHandler dependency.OnChange, AddressOf MyOnChangeHandler

        cn.Open()
```

```
        Using rdr As SqlDataReader = cmd.ExecuteReader()
            Do While rdr.Read()
                'Process the query results
                '...
            Loop
            rdr.Close()
            cn.Close()
        End Using
    End Using
End Using

Private Sub MyOnChangeHandler(ByVal sender As Object, _
                                ByVal e As SqlNotificationEventArgs)
    Dim status As New System.Text.StringBuilder()
    status.AppendLine("SqlDependency.OnChange fired!")
    status.AppendLine("  Info: " & e.Info.ToString())
    status.AppendLine("  Source: " & e.Source.ToString())
    status.Append("  Type: " & e.Type.ToString())
    Console.WriteLine(status.ToString())
End Sub
```

Visual C#

```
string strConn, strSQL;
strConn = @"Data Source=.\SQLExpress;Initial Catalog=MyDatabase;" +
            "User ID=Subscriber_User;Password=Subscr!b3r_Pwd;";
strSQL = "SELECT ... FROM MySchema.MyTable WHERE ...";
using (SqlConnection cn = new SqlConnection(strConn)) {
    using (SqlCommand cmd = new SqlCommand(strSQL, cn)) {
        SqlDependency dependency = new SqlDependency(cmd);
        dependency.OnChange += new OnChangeHandler(MyOnChangeEventHandler);

        cn.Open();
        using (SqlDataReader rdr = cmd.ExecuteReader())
            while (rdr.Read()) {
                //Process the query results
                //...
            }
            rdr.Close();
            cn.Close();
        }
    }
}

void MyOnChangeHandler(object sender, SqlNotificationEventArgs e) {
    System.Text.StringBuilder status = new System.Text.StringBuilder();
    status.AppendLine("SqlDependency.OnChange fired!");
    status.AppendLine("  Info: " + e.Info.ToString());
    status.AppendLine("  Source: " + e.Source.ToString());
    status.Append("  Type: " + e.Type.ToString());
    Console.WriteLine(status.ToString());
}
```

Note If you're using a *SqlDataAdapter* to execute your query, pass the *SqlDataAdapter*'s *Select-Command* into the *SqlDependency*'s constructor before calling the *SqlDataAdapter*'s *Fill* method.

The *OnChange* event handler will fire when (or if) there's a change to the database that affects the results of the query. The *SqlNotificationEventArgs* event includes information about the reason the event fired. The *Info* property returns a value from the *SqlNotificationInfo* enumeration to indicate the reason the event fired. The values in the enumeration are very specific—with values such as *Insert*, *Update*, and *Delete* as well as *Truncate*, *Drop*, *Alter*, and so on. You can also check the *Type* property to determine whether the event fired because of an actual change in the data or a failure to subscribe to receive notification messages for the query. The *Source* property returns a value from the *SqlNotificationSource* enumeration to indicate the source of the event—a change to the data, a change to the structure of the database, a timeout of the subscription to receive notification messages, and so on. In most cases, this property will return *SqlNotification-Source.Data*, which means that a change to data on the server caused the event to fire.

Once the *OnChange* event fires for a *SqlDependency*, it will not fire again even if subsequent changes are made to the data in the database. You'll need to re-execute the query by using either the same *SqlDependency* object or a new *SqlDependency* object if you want to receive a notification message when the results of the query again change.

How you handle the *OnChange* event is up to you. In some applications, the appropriate action might be to note that the results previously retrieved for the query are no longer accurate but to delay re-executing the query. In some applications, the appropriate action might be to re-execute the query immediately to display the most current query results to the user and then to listen for further changes to the data. You can also check the *SqlDependency* object's *HasChanges* property to determine whether the *OnChange* event has fired.

The samples for this chapter include a small project called *FirstSqlDependencyTest*. This project consists of a Windows form with buttons that let you call the *Start* method on the *SqlDependency* class and execute a *SqlCommand* with a *SqlDependency* to ensure that the application receives a notification message when the results of the query change. Executing the query also displays the results in a *DataGridView* and modifies the data in the database on a separate *SqlConnection* to simulate changes made by another user. The project also includes a SQL script that creates a new database with new logins, and it grants those logins (one to listen to notification messages and one to subscribe to receive notification messages) only the privileges they need to listen and subscribe, respectively.

Warning   Notification Services is geared towards middle-tier scenarios such as ASP.NET cache dependencies that require a limited number of subscriptions, and it is not intended to be used by widely distributed Windows applications. Relying on Notification Services from within a Windows application requires a dedicated live connection to the database while waiting for messages from a queue. Although this approach is valid for a small number of simultaneous users (fewer than 10), it is not a scalable approach for larger numbers of simultaneous users. The *FirstSql-DependencyTest* sample is intended as your first attempt to use Notification Services from ADO.NET, and it is not intended to guide you towards using Notification Services from Windows applications that will support large numbers of simultaneous users.

***SqlDependency* and the ASP.NET Cache**   The most common use of the *SqlDependency* class is to interact with the ASP.NET cache.

Each time the page loads, the code checks to see whether there's an entry in the cache that contains the desired results, generally in a *DataTable*. If the entry exists, the code simply relies on that entry and displays the contents of the *DataTable* rather than re-querying the database. If the entry does not exist, the code queries the database, caches the results in the ASP.NET cache, and then displays the results.

Prior to SQL Server Notification Services, the problem with this approach boiled down to a single question: How long should the query results reside in the cache? A minute? An hour? A week? Pick too brief an interval and you'll needlessly re-query your database for results that have not changed. Pick too great an interval and the results you display in your application are no longer accurate.

SQL Server Notification Services and the *SqlDependency* class greatly simplify the scenario. Prior to executing the query, you create a *SqlDependency* object that references the query. You also add a handler for the *SqlDependency*'s *OnChange* event. In the handler, you simply remove the query results from the ASP.NET cache. Now your ASP.NET application will continue to rely on the cached results until the results of the query change.

The following code snippet demonstrates this approach:

Visual Basic

```
Dim key As String = "CategoryNames"

Protected Sub Page_Load(ByVal sender As Object, ByVal e As EventArgs) _
                        Handles Me.Load
    Dim tbl As DataTable = Cache(key)
    If tbl Is Nothing Then
        Response.Write("Executing query<P>")
        tbl = FetchAndCacheCategories()
    Else
        Response.Write("Using cached data<P>")
    End If
    CategoryNamesGrid.DataSource = tbl
    CategoryNamesGrid.DataBind()
End Sub

Private Function FetchAndCacheCategories() As DataTable
    Dim strConn, strSQL As String
    strConn = "Data Source=.\SQLExpress;Initial Catalog=Northwind;" & _
              "Integrated Security=True;"
    strSQL = "SELECT CategoryName FROM dbo.Categories"
    SqlDependency.Start(strConn)
    Dim da As New SqlDataAdapter(strSQL, strConn)
    Dim dep As New SqlDependency(da.SelectCommand)
    AddHandler dep.OnChange, AddressOf MyOnChangeHandler
    Dim tbl As New DataTable()
    da.Fill(tbl)
```

```
      Cache(key) = tbl
      Return tbl
End Function

Protected Sub MyOnChangeHandler(ByVal sender As Object, _
                                ByVal e As SqlNotificationEventArgs)
      Cache.Remove(key)
End Sub
```

Visual C#

```
string key = "CategoryNames";

protected void Page_Load(object sender, EventArgs e) {
    DataTable tbl = (DataTable)Cache[key];
    if (tbl == null)
    {
        Response.Write("Executing query<P>");
        tbl = FetchAndCacheCategories();
    }
    else
    {
        Response.Write("Using cached data<P>");
    }
    categoryNamesGrid.DataSource = tbl;
    categoryNamesGrid.DataBind();
}

private DataTable FetchAndCacheCategories() {
    string strConn, strSQL;
    strConn = "Data Source=.\SQLExpress;Initial Catalog=Northwind;" +
            "Integrated Security=True;";
    strSQL = "SELECT CategoryName FROM dbo.Categories";
    SqlDependency.Start(strConn);
    SqlDataAdapter da = new SqlDataAdapter(strSQL, strConn);
    SqlDependency dep = new SqlDependency(da.SelectCommand);
    dep.OnChange += new OnChangeEventHandler(MyOnChangeHandler);
    DataTable tbl = new DataTable();
    da.Fill(tbl);
    Cache[key] = tbl;
    return tbl;
}

void MyOnChangeHandler(object sender, SqlNotificationEventArgs e) {
    Cache.Remove(key);
}
```

The *SqlCacheDependency* Class   There's one minor drawback to the *SqlDependency* class in the previously described scenario: You may find that you use the class so often to interact with the ASP.NET cache that writing the code to handle the *OnChange* event to remove the item from the cache can become tedious.

The ASP.NET team created a class to help address this problem—the *SqlCacheDependency* class. You can create instances of the *SqlCacheDependency* class just as you can the *SqlDependency* class—by supplying the *SqlCommand* you're going to execute. The *SqlCacheDependency* class does not expose an *OnChange* event, or any events, for that matter. In fact, there's no need for you to handle any events, and there's no need to create a handler and remove the item yourself.

The *SqlCacheDependency* class, which resides in the *System.Web.Caching* namespace, derives from the *CacheDependency* class, which is designed to interact with the ASP.NET cache. So, when you add the *DataTable* to the ASP.NET cache and supply the *SqlCacheDependency* object, the *DataTable* is automatically removed from the cache when the results of the query change.

We can use the *SqlCacheDependency* class to replace the FetchAndCacheCategories procedure with the following simpler code:

Visual Basic

```
Private Function FetchAndCacheCategories() As DataTable
    Dim strConn, strSQL As String
    strConn = "Data Source=.\SQLExpress;Initial Catalog=Northwind;" & _
            "Integrated Security=True;"
    strSQL = "SELECT CategoryName FROM dbo.Categories"
    SqlDependency.Start(strConn)
    Dim da As New SqlDataAdapter(strSQL, strConn)
    Dim dep As New SqlCacheDependency(da.SelectCommand)
    Dim tbl As New DataTable()
    da.Fill(tbl)
    Cache.Add(key, tbl, dep, Caching.Cache.NoAbsoluteExpiration, _
            Caching.Cache.NoSlidingExpiration, _
            CacheItemPriority.Default, _
            Nothing)
    Return tbl
End Function
```

Visual C#

```
private DataTable FetchAndCacheCategories() {
    string strConn, strSQL;
    strConn = "Data Source=.\SQLExpress;Initial Catalog=Northwind;" +
            "Integrated Security=True;";
    strSQL = "SELECT CategoryName FROM dbo.Categories";
    SqlDependency.Start(strConn);
    SqlDataAdapter da = new SqlDataAdapter(strSQL, strConn);
    SqlCacheDependency dep = new SqlCacheDependency(da.SelectCommand);
    DataTable tbl = new DataTable();
    da.Fill(tbl);
    Cache.Add(key, tbl, dep, Caching.Cache.NoAbsoluteExpiration,
            Caching.Cache.NoSlidingExpiration, CacheItemPriority.Default,
            null);
    return tbl;
}
```

Maintaining State in Your Database

No one says you must maintain state in your Web server. Database servers are designed to maintain and serve up data. You can use your database to store global and session-specific data for your Web application, such as the contents of each user's shopping cart.

Your application might execute a query that's so complex or time consuming that you'd rather store the results of the query in a separate table than execute the query each time the user requests the next page worth of results. For example, the user might supply input to query your inventory database to find CD burners under $200 that are capable of writing at 20x or greater, that support USB and FireWire, and that are available at stores within a 30-mile radius of the user's home. The query might look something like this:

```
SELECT ProductID, ProductName, Description, UnitPrice, ... FROM Products
    WHERE UnitPrice < 200 AND Description LIKE '%USB%' AND
        Description LIKE '%FireWire%' AND ...
```

Suppose that query returns 50 records and the user will see 10 items per page. You can execute the query each time the user requests another page of results, or you can store the results in a table in your database. You could create a table to store the results of queries against this table by using an INSERT INTO query and including the user's session ID so that you can keep track of which results belong to which session:

```
INSERT INTO ProductsQueryCache
SELECT @SessionID AS SessionID, ProductID, ProductName, Description, UnitPrice, ...
    FROM Products
    WHERE UnitPrice < 200 AND Description LIKE '%USB%' AND
        Description LIKE '%FireWire%' AND ...
```

Then you could simply retrieve the next page's rows from this results table rather than executing the original query against your main catalog table. This particular example might not do the technique justice, but it can prove helpful when working with queries that you'd rather not execute repeatedly.

> **Note**   If you use this technique, be sure to remove the cached rows from the database in the *Session* object's *End* event or wherever is appropriate.

Benefits to Maintaining State in Your Database

By storing state in your database, your ASP.NET code can remain stateless. Data that you store in your database is durable. If your Web server crashes for whatever reason, the data that you've stored in your database will still be available once you get the Web server back on line. The data that you store in the database is secure because it is not readily available to the user except through your ASP.NET code. Databases are designed to handle large result sets. If you absolutely must maintain large result sets between page requests, storing that data in your database is probably your best bet.

Drawbacks to Maintaining State in Your Database

Maintaining state in your database is more complex than storing data in simple objects and collections such as *Session*, *Application*, *Cache*, *ViewState*, or a cookie.

Guidelines for Maintaining State

How and where you maintain your state can have an enormous impact on the performance, scalability, and security of your Web applications. There are no absolute guidelines to determining if, how, and where you should maintain state for your Web application. However, here are some general guidelines.

Storing Data in *ViewState*

Store data in *ViewState* if you're working with small result sets and you're OK with the user being able to view this data. If you're concerned about security and don't want to take any chances on the user modifying this data, store it in the *Session* object or in your database. Remember that the data you store in *ViewState* is passed back and forth between the server and the client on each roundtrip. The more data you store in *ViewState*, the longer each roundtrip will take.

Storing Data in the *Application* Object

Store in the *Application* object small amounts of data that's global to all sessions for the application. Remember that the more data you store in the *Application* object, the more you'll adversely affect performance.

Storing Data in the *Session* Object

Store in the *Session* object small amounts of data that are critical to that particular session and that you're not comfortable storing in *ViewState* for security reasons. Remember that the more data you store in the *Session* object, the more you'll adversely affect performance, and at a more accelerated rate than with the *Application* object. For example, storing 100 KB of data in a *Session* doesn't sound like much until you multiply that by the number of sessions that ASP.NET will maintain at any given time. Store large amounts of session-specific data in your database instead.

Storing Data in the Database

Store large amounts of session-specific data in your database. Accessing data from memory is obviously faster than retrieving the same information from your database. But if you need to store large amounts of session-specific data, maintaining that data in your database lowers the total amount of memory in use on your server at any given time.

Using Output Caching

If you want to generate the same static HTML over and over again, use ASP.NET output caching rather than caching the data required to generate that HTML.

Paging

Few companies' catalogs can fit on a single Web page. Say you set up a search engine for your product catalog and a hundred items fit the search criteria that the user specified. Rather than provide links to all products on the resulting Web page, you'll probably want to break up the results into a series of pages and display the contents of only the first page.

Displaying just the first page is generally simple. But how do you supply functionality to allow the user to move to the next page of the result set or to move to a specific page?

ASP.NET and ADO.NET offer features that can help you serve up the results of your queries one page at a time. Let's look at those features now.

Paging Features of the *GridView* Control

As shown earlier in the chapter, the *GridView* control includes rich paging functionality, making it possible to display the results of queries one page at a time and offer the user links to other pages in the results.

Paging is another "code-free" ASP.NET data-binding scenario. There's no need to handle events raised by the links. The *GridView* control simply asks the *SqlDataSource* for the data each time the user clicks a link.

AllowPaging

The simplest way to enable paging on a *GridView* control is to open the smart tag for the control and click the Allow Paging option, which will set the *AllowPaging* property to *True*. You can also set the *AllowPaging* property directly in the Properties window. By default, *AllowPaging* is set to *False*.

Once you've enabled paging, the *GridView* will partition the results into distinct pages and use the *PageIndex* property to determine which page of data to display. The *GridView* control will also include links to other pages of results at the bottom of the grid. Clicking one of these links will cause a *PostBack* event and set the *GridView* control's *PageIndex* property accordingly. The *GridView* will then requery its data source and display the desired page of data.

PageSize

The *PageSize* property controls the number of rows of data per page within the grid. By default, this property is set to *10*.

PagerSettings

By default, the *GridView* will display up to 10 links to pages. If the results of the query return more than 10 pages, the *GridView* will add "..." links to move to the next or previous set of 10 pages. You can change this behavior by drilling into the *PagerSettings* property on the

GridView in the Properties window, as shown in Figure 14-13. You can change the location of the page links, the type of links generated (numeric or next/previous with the option to include or exclude first/last links for either option), the maximum number of page links, and the text and images for first/last/next/previous links.

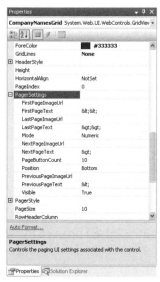

Figure 14-13   Viewing the *GridView* control's *PagerSettings* in the Properties window

Paging Features of the *DataAdapter* Classes

In Chapter 5, you learned about the features of the *SqlDataAdapter* class. You might remember that the *SqlDataAdapter* class's *Fill* method is overloaded and that one of the signatures lets you retrieve a subset of the results returned by the *SqlDataAdapter*. In this particular method, which is implemented by most *DataAdapter* classes, the second parameter controls the number of rows you skip before you start fetching data, and the third parameter controls the maximum number of rows to retrieve.

Let's say that you want to display only 10 rows per page. So, to fetch just the rows for the fifth page, you would skip the first 40 rows and fetch the next 10. The following code would retrieve that fifth page of rows into a *DataSet*:

Visual Basic

```
Dim strConn, strSQL As String
strConn = "Data Source=.\SQLExpress;" & _
          "Initial Catalog=Northwind;Integrated Security=True;"
strSQL = "SELECT CustomerID, CompanyName, " & _
          "  ContactName, ContactTitle FROM Customers"
Dim da As New SqlDataAdapter(strSQL, strConn)
Dim ds As New DataSet()
da.Fill(ds, 40, 10, "Customers")
```

Visual C#

```
string strConn, strSQL;
strConn = @"Data Source=.\SQLExpress;" +
          "Initial Catalog=Northwind;Integrated Security=True;";
strSQL = "SELECT CustomerID, CompanyName, " +
         " ContactName, ContactTitle FROM Customers";
SqlDataAdapter da = new SqlDataAdapter(strSQL, strConn);
DataSet ds = new DataSet();
da.Fill(ds, 40, 10, "Customers");
```

Although this code is very simple, there's a major drawback to the approach. In this example, you're still asking the database to return data for all rows in the table. You're still paying the performance penalty of fetching those 40 rows even though the *SqlDataAdapter* isn't adding those rows to the *DataSet*.

Building Queries That Return a Page of Data

SQL Server supports the TOP clause in a query. You can use the TOP clause to return just the first *n* rows from a query. So you could use the following query to return just the first 10 rows from the Customers table, ordered by the ContactTitle and CustomerID columns:

```
SELECT TOP 10 CustomerID, CompanyName, ContactName, ContactTitle
    FROM Customers
    ORDER BY ContactTitle, CustomerID
```

If you want to break the results into pages, you can use this syntax to return just the rows for that particular page. For example, if you want to return the rows for the fifth page, you would want to retrieve rows 41 through 50 from the Customers table.

```
SELECT TOP 10 CustomerID, CompanyName, ContactName, ContactTitle
    FROM Customers WHERE CustomerID NOT IN
    (SELECT TOP 40 CustomerID FROM Customers
        ORDER BY ContactTitle, CustomerID)
    ORDER BY ContactTitle, CustomerID
```

This query includes a subquery that locates the first 40 rows ordered by the ContactTitle and CustomerID columns and then looks for the first 10 rows that do not appear in that subquery, again ordered by the Country and CustomerID columns. Here's a more generic way to write the query:

```
SELECT TOP PageSize Column1, Column2, ... FROM MyTable
    WHERE KeyColumn NOT IN
    (SELECT TOP RowsToSkip KeyColumn FROM MyTable
        ORDER BY SortOrder)
    ORDER BY SortOrder
```

This approach has a few major drawbacks. First, you can't use parameters to replace *PageSize* and *RowsToSkip* elements in the query, which means that you have to modify the text of the query each time you want to retrieve a different page of data. Second, this approach requires a single unique key column to use the NOT IN clause.

Building SQL Server 2005 Page-Specific Queries by Using ROW_NUMBER

Thankfully, SQL Server 2005 introduced a new query construct to help generate page-specific queries. You can use the ROW_NUMBER clause to generate sequential row numbers for a query.

The following query returns customer information ordered by the ContactTitle and CustomerID columns, and it includes row numbers:

```
SELECT ROW_NUMBER() OVER(ORDER BY ContactTitle, CustomerID) AS RowNum,
      CustomerID, CompanyName, ContactName, ContactTitle
   FROM Customers
```

You can use this query in a subquery to retrieve a specific set of rows based on their row numbers:

```
SELECT RowNum, CustomerID, CompanyName, ContactName, ContactTitle FROM
(SELECT ROW_NUMBER() OVER(ORDER BY ContactTitle, CustomerID) AS RowNum,
      CustomerID, CompanyName, ContactName, ContactTitle FROM Customers)
   AS CustomersWithRowNum
   WHERE RowNum > 40 AND RowNum <= 50
```

The Visual Studio Query Builder does not handle queries that include the ROW_NUMBER clause, but you can execute these queries from ADO.NET and SQL Server Management Studio, as shown in Figure 14-14.

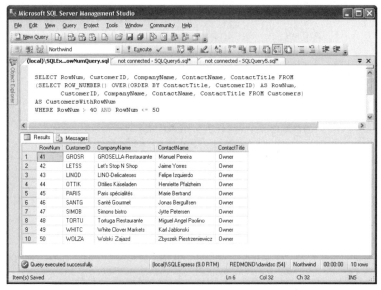

Figure 14-14   Executing a page-specific query by using the ROW_NUMBER function in SQL Server Management Studio

Because the range for the desired row numbers is supplied in the WHERE clause, you can easily convert this into a parameterized query:

```
SELECT RowNum, CustomerID, CompanyName, ContactName, ContactTitle FROM
(SELECT ROW_NUMBER() OVER(ORDER BY ContactTitle, CustomerID) AS RowNum,
     CustomerID, CompanyName, ContactName, ContactTitle FROM Customers)
  AS CustomersWithRowNum
  WHERE RowNum > ((@PageNumber - 1) * @PageSize)
    AND RowNum <= (@PageNumber * @PageSize)
```

Building Page-Specific Oracle Queries

Oracle supports a somewhat analogous feature: *rownum*. Oracle numbers the rows that the query returns, and you can use *rownum* to retrieve just the first *n* rows that the query returns. However, Oracle generates the row numbers before applying the sort order for the query, so it's a little tricky to use *rownum* to return a page of data for a query in which you want to use a sort order. With a little cajoling and an extra subquery, you can use the *rownum* feature to return a specific page of data for a query that uses a sort order. The following Oracle query returns the same page (rows 41 through 50) of the Customers table:

```
SELECT CustomerID, CompanyName, ContactName, ContactTitle FROM
    (SELECT CustomerID, CompanyName, ContactName, ContactTitle,
            rownum AS Row_Num FROM
        (SELECT CustomerID, CompanyName, ContactName, ContactTitle
            FROM Customers ORDER BY ContactTitle, CustomerID)
        WHERE rownum <= 10)
    WHERE Row_Num > 40
```

> **Note**   I don't claim to be an Oracle guru. There might be an easier way to build such queries for Oracle.

Integrating Custom Paging with the *SqlDataSource* and *GridView* Controls

Now that you know how to build page-specific queries for SQL Server and Oracle databases, let's see how you can use those queries with the *SqlDataSource* and *GridView* controls without giving up the powerful features associated with these controls.

You can easily configure the *SqlDataSource* control to use the parameterized page-specific query. Create the query in SQL Server Management Studio, and then paste it into the Define Custom Statements page of the SqlDataSource Configuration Wizard, previously shown in Figure 14-4. On the Define Parameters page of the SqlDataSource Configuration Wizard, be sure to click the Show Advanced Properties link and then specify the appropriate data type for each parameter (as shown in Figure 14-15).

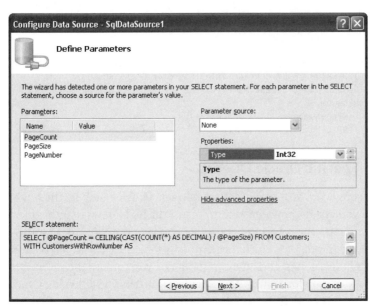

Figure 14-15 Specifying parameter information in the SqlDataSource Configuration Wizard

Using this approach presents a few challenges. This query does not return the number of pages. The *SqlDataSource*'s parameters aren't quite dynamic enough to handle the parameters required to return page information. The *GridView* will not generate links to the other pages. Finally, the *SqlDataSource* will not generate updating logic based on this query, meaning that the *GridView* control will not allow users to modify the data that appears on the Web page.

Let's look at how we can address these issues.

Adding a Query to Retrieve the Number of Pages You can prepend your page-specific query with another query that returns the number of total rows in the table:

```
SELECT COUNT(*) FROM Customers
```

We can modify this query slightly, passing the page size into the query as an input parameter, using the CEILING function to determine the number of pages, and returning this value through an output parameter:

```
SELECT @PageCount = CEILING(CAST(COUNT(*) AS DECIMAL) / @PageSize)
  FROM Customers
```

Adding this query to the original query gives us the following:

```
SELECT @PageCount = CEILING(CAST(COUNT(*) AS DECIMAL) / @PageSize)
  FROM Customers;
WITH CustomersWithRowNumber AS
```

```
  (SELECT ROW_NUMBER() OVER (ORDER BY ContactTitle, CustomerID) AS RowNum,
         CustomerID, CompanyName, ContactName, ContactTitle
   FROM Customers)
SELECT CustomerID, CompanyName, ContactName, ContactTitle
  FROM CustomersWithRowNumber
  WHERE RowNum > (@PageNumber - 1) * @PageSize
    AND RowNum <= @PageNumber * @PageSize
```

Interacting with the Parameters in the *SqlDataSource*'s Query   The *SqlDataSource* control exposes both a *Selecting* and a *Selected* event. The *Selecting* event fires just before executing the query to retrieve rows. The *Selected* event fires just after executing that query. You can use these events to programmatically assign values to input parameters and access values from output parameters, as shown in the following code:

Visual Basic

```vb
Dim pageSize, pageNumber, pageCount As Integer

Protected Sub SqlDataSource1_Selecting(ByVal sender As Object, _
                            ByVal e As SqlDataSourceSelectingEventArgs)
    e.Command.Parameters("@PageNumber").Value = Me.pageNumber
    e.Command.Parameters("@PageSize").Value = Me.pageSize
End Sub

Protected Sub SqlDataSource1_Selected(ByVal sender As Object, _
                            ByVal e As SqlDataSourceStatusEventArgs)
    Me.pageCount = CInt(e.Command.Parameters("@PageCount").Value)
End Sub
```

Visual C#

```csharp
int pageSize, pageNumber, pageCount;

protected void SqlDataSource1_Selecting(object sender,
                                SqlDataSourceSelectingEventArgs e)
{
    e.Command.Parameters["@PageNumber"].Value = this.pageNumber;
    e.Command.Parameters["@PageSize"].Value = this.pageSize;
}

protected void SqlDataSource1_Selected(object sender,
                                SqlDataSourceStatusEventArgs e)
{
    this.pageCount = (int)e.Command.Parameters["@PageCount"].Value;
}
```

Programmatically Adding Links to Other Pages   You can trap for the *GridView* control's *DataBound* event and programmatically add a series of *HyperLink* controls that include a query string in their links to pass the desired page number back to ASP.NET. This approach also requires adding code to the *Page*'s *Load* event to retrieve this information from the query string, as shown here:

Visual Basic

```vb
Protected Sub Page_Load(ByVal sender As Object, ByVal e As EventArgs)
    Dim newPageNumber As Integer
```

```
        If Integer.TryParse(Request.QueryString("Page"), newPageNumber) Then
            pageNumber = newPageNumber
        ElseIf Me.ViewState("Page") Is Not Nothing Then
            pageNumber = CInt(Me.ViewState("Page"))
        End If

        Me.ViewState("Page") = pageNumber
End Sub

Protected Sub GridView1_DataBound(ByVal sender As Object, _
                                  ByVal e As EventArgs)
    Me.GridView1.ShowFooter = True
    Dim pagerRow As GridViewRow = Me.GridView1.FooterRow
    For i As Integer = 1 to Me.pageCount
        Dim link As New HyperLink()
        If i <> Me.pageNumber Then
            link.NavigateUrl = String.Format("{0}?Page={1}", Request.Path, i)
        End If
        link.Text = i.ToString()
        link.Visible = True
        pagerRow.Cells(0).Controls.Add(link)

        Dim space As New Label()
        space.Text = " "
        space.Visible = True
        pagerRow.Cells(0).Controls.Add(space)
    Next i
    pagerRow.Visible = True
End Sub
```

Visual C#

```
protected void Page_Load(object sender, EventArgs e)
{
    int newPageNumber;
    if (int.TryParse(Request.QueryString["Page"], out newPageNumber))
        pageNumber = newPageNumber;
    else if (this.ViewState["Page"] != null)
        pageNumber = (int)this.ViewState["Page"];

    this.ViewState["Page"] = pageNumber;
}

protected void GridView1_DataBound(object sender, EventArgs e)
{
    this.GridView1.ShowFooter = true;
    GridViewRow pagerRow = this.GridView1.FooterRow;
    for (int i = 1; i <= this.pageCount; i++) {
        HyperLink link = new HyperLink();
        if (i != this.pageNumber)
            link.NavigateUrl = string.Format("{0}?Page={1}", Request.Path, i);
        link.Text = i.ToString();
        link.Visible = true;
        pagerRow.Cells[0].Controls.Add(link);
```

```
        Label space = new Label();
        space.Text = " ";
        space.Visible = true;
        pagerRow.Cells[0].Controls.Add(space);
    }
    pagerRow.Visible = true;
}
```

Adding Updating Logic for Page-Specific Queries in the *SqlDataSource*   When you supply your own query in the SqlDataSource Configuration Wizard, the wizard will not generate updating logic for you. Of course, you can generate INSERT, UPDATE, and DELETE queries yourself, but this process of supplying the queries can be tedious.

Earlier in the chapter, we saw that if we use the wizard to generate the query by selecting the desired table and columns, the wizard can generate the updating logic for you. We can use the wizard to build a query that retrieves the desired table and columns of information without all the paging logic, and we can ask the wizard to generate the updating logic for that query. That updating logic will still work for the paging query every bit as well as it works for the basic wizard-generated SELECT query. However, if you change the *SelectCommand* through the wizard, the wizard will discard the updating logic it previously generated and will not generate new logic for you.

Now it's time to get a little...well, devious.

Start by using the wizard to build the page-specific query, including the parameters for page size, page number, and page count. Then open the source for the Web page. Find your *SqlDataSource* control, and copy the contents of the *SqlDataSource* control to the clipboard, pasting the text into a high-tech text editor such as Notepad. Next, reconfigure the *SqlData-Source* control, use the wizard to create a SELECT query that returns just the desired columns from the table, and then ask the wizard to generate updating logic. Open the source for the Web page again. Replace the *SelectCommand* and *SelectParameters* entries with the text you kept in Notepad.

The wizard has no idea that you changed the *SelectCommand*. I won't tell the wizard if you won't.

Custom Paging Sample   The sample code for this chapter includes a page called *Custom-Paging* that combines all the steps listed. The page uses a parameterized ROW_NUMBER query in a *SqlDataSource* to retrieve a single page of data, and it displays the results of the query in a *GridView* control. The *GridView* control also displays custom-generated links to other pages of data. The *SqlDataSource* contains wizard-updating logic that I pasted into the page's source as described earlier, and the *GridView* control is configured to allow users to modify the data displayed on the page and submit changes.

Questions That Should Be Asked More Frequently

Q I've executed a query to create a *SqlDataReader*. How can I determine whether my query returned rows of data before I bind my *SqlDataReader* to my bound control?

A This was a very common question for Web developers in version 1.0 of the .NET Framework. Since that time, thankfully, much has changed.

In ADO.NET 1.1, the *DataReader* classes added a *HasRows* property, which returns *False* if the query returned no rows of data. So you can check this property programmatically before binding and then take the appropriate action.

The new ASP.NET data-bound controls (*GridView*, *FormView*, and *DetailsView*) have properties that you can set (*EmptyText*, *EmptyDataRowStyle*, and *EmptyDataTemplate*) that dictate how the controls behave when they're bound to an empty data source.

Q I'm working with a *DataSet* that contains two *DataTable* objects related by a *DataRelation* object. How do I display just the child rows for a particular parent row in a bound *Grid-View*?

A The *DataRow* object has a *GetChildRows* method that returns an array of *DataRow* objects with only the child rows in the array. However, you can't bind controls such as the *GridView* to an array of *DataRow* objects. You could create a *DataView* object, initialize it to the child *DataTable*, and then set the *RowFilter* property on the *DataView* so that only the desired child rows are visible through the *DataView*. Thankfully, there's an easier way.

Create a *DataView* object that's initialized to the parent *DataTable*. Then locate the desired parent row in the *DataView* and call the *CreateChildView* method to create a *DataView* that contains just the child rows. Bind that *DataView* to the *GridView* control, as shown here:

Visual Basic
```vb
Dim dsCustomersOrders As New DataSet()
'Initialize the DataSet
'...
Dim vueCustomers, vueOrders As DataView
vueCustomers = New DataView(dsCustomersOrders.Tables("Customers"))
vueCustomers.Sort = "CustomerID"
Dim intCustomerIndex As Integer = vueCustomers.Find("ALFKI")
If intCustomerIndex >= 0 Then
    'Located the desired parent row
    Dim drvCustomer As DataRowView = vueCustomers(intCustomerIndex)
    vueOrders = drvCustomer.CreateChildView("CustomersOrders")
    gridOrders.DataSource = vueOrders
    gridOrders.DataBind()
Else
    'Could not locate the desired parent row
End If
```

Visual C#

```csharp
DataSet dsCustomersOrders = new DataSet();
//Initialize the DataSet
//...
DataView vueCustomers, vueOrders;
vueCustomers = new DataView(dsCustomersOrders.Tables["Customers"]);
vueCustomers.Sort = "CustomerID";
int intCustomerIndex = vueCustomers.Find("ALFKI");
if (intCustomerIndex >= 0)
{
    //Located the desired parent row
    DataRowView drvCustomer = vueCustomers[intCustomerIndex];
    vueOrders = drvCustomer.CreateChildView("CustomersOrders");
    gridOrders.DataSource = vueOrders;
    gridOrders.DataBind();
}
else
{
    //Could not locate the desired parent row
}
```

Chapter 15

SQL Server 2005 Common Language Runtime Integration

In this chapter:

One of the most anticipated features of Microsoft SQL Server 2005 is its support for the .NET common language runtime (CLR). You can now write stored procedures, aggregate functions, user-defined functions, and triggers using Microsoft Visual Basic, C#, or any other .NET language. You can also use these languages to construct user-defined types that SQL Server can use to store the values in your database.

The Transact SQL language (commonly referred to as T-SQL) that SQL Server supports for queries and stored procedures is powerful and gives you the ability to write complex stored procedures that interact with your database. However, T-SQL is not as rich a programming language as C++ or C#. Many developers wanted to write routines that would allow the database to interact with external systems, or to perform complex mathematical operations for which T-SQL is ill suited.

Extending SQL Server the Old Way—Extended Stored Procedures

To help developers extend the power of SQL Server, SQL Server 7.0 added support for *extended stored procedures*, giving developers the ability to build their own assemblies in C or C++ and call them from SQL Server. Extended stored procedures opened up a new world for developers and database administrators, allowing them to perform complex tasks in languages better suited to handle those challenges.

However, extended stored procedures are now considered part "black box" and part "Pandora's box." The code inside extended stored procedures is, for the most part, ignorant of SQL Server.

For example, you cannot write an extended stored procedure that can access the contents of the SQL Server database to which it belongs without using a technology such as OLE DB to establish a new connection from the extended stored procedure back to SQL Server. Extended stored procedures also rely on their own infrastructure (for memory, threads, and synchronization) rather than SQL Server's. Similarly, SQL Server is ignorant of what goes on inside the extended stored procedure. An administrator cannot restrict the type of operations performed by the extended stored procedure.

The other main drawback to extended stored procedures is that they have to be written in C or C++, which limits the number of developers who can write them. As many database administrators will concur, this further limits the number of developers who can write an extended stored procedure without keeping the database administrator up at night worrying about memory leaks and scalability.

Extending SQL Server the New Way—CLR Integration

SQL Server 2005 introduces a new way to allow developers to extend the power of SQL Server—by integrating the CLR.

Now when you're faced with a task you need to accomplish for which either T-SQL or the native SQL Server data types are ill-equipped, you can write code in your .NET language of choice to tackle that task. Need a new aggregate function? Write one using the .NET Framework. Need a stored procedure that performs mathematical computations? Write one using the .NET Framework. Need to store data in a data type that SQL Server is not natively equipped to handle? Create one using the .NET Framework. Need to write a user-defined function or a trigger that goes beyond T-SQL's capabilities? You get the general idea.

This chapter will lead you through various examples of using the .NET Framework within SQL Server 2005. The chapter includes an example of building an aggregate function, stored procedure, and user-defined data type in both Visual Basic and C#. The chapter will also cover T-SQL-based alternatives to the aggregate function and stored procedure, comparing the performance and flexibility of the two approaches.

Note   SQL Server 2005 does not enable CLR integration by default. You can enable CLR integration in one of two ways. You can execute the following script in SQL Server Management Studio:

```
sp_configure 'clr enabled', 1
GO
RECONFIGURE
GO
```

or you can enable CLR integration by launching the SQL Server 2005 Surface Area Configuration tool, clicking the Surface Area Configuration for Features link and then checking the Enable CLR integration checkbox, as shown in Figure 15-1.

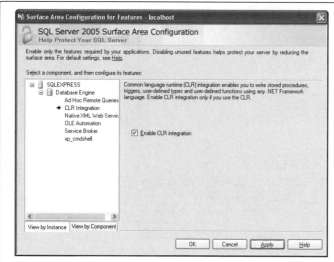

Figure 15-1   Enabling CLR integration using the SQL Server 2005 Surface Area Configuration tool

Using Microsoft Visual Studio 2005 to Simplify Building SQL CLR Code

During the early betas of SQL Server 2005, the most frequently asked questions on developer forums were the following: "How do I build my .NET assembly?" "How do I deploy my .NET assembly to SQL Server?" "How do I register my assembly so that I can access my new stored procedure, function, or type?" The most frequent answer to these questions started with "Open a SQL Server Project in Visual Studio 2005."

If you have both Visual Studio 2005 and SQL Server 2005 installed on the same machine, there's a new project template available to Visual Basic and C# developers—the SQL Server project. Working with a SQL Server project from Visual Studio 2005 can greatly simplify the process of building a SQL CLR assembly, deploying it to your SQL Server, and registering the procedures, functions, and types. Visual Studio 2005 also makes it easy to test your new SQL CLR assembly by letting you run SQL scripts and allowing you to step directly into your .NET code.

Setting Properties on Your SQL Server Project

To create a new SQL Server project, use the Visual Studio menu to launch the New Project dialog box. Then drill down into the project types for your language of choice and select Database. You'll see the SQL Server Project template as an available option, as shown in Figure 15-2. The sample for this chapter includes a project named, aptly enough, Chapter_15.

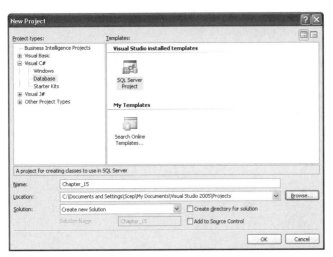

Figure 15-2   Creating a new SQL Server Project in Visual Studio 2005

Note   The first time you try to debug a SQL Server Project, Visual Studio will display a dialog asking if you want to enable CLR debugging. SQL Server Books Online recommends enabling CLR debugging only on test servers and not on production servers because when you enable CLR debugging and hit a breakpoint in CLR code, all CLR code execution on the server freezes. For more information on CLR debugging, see SQL Server Books Online.

Visual Studio will associate the new SQL Server project with a SQL Server connection string so that it can communicate with your SQL Server. When you create the project, Visual Studio will display a list of connections from Server Explorer that are connected to SQL Server 2005 databases, as shown in Figure 15-3.

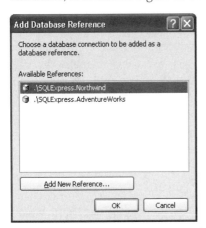

Figure 15-3   Selecting a connection for your new SQL Server Project

You can change properties on your SQL Server project by double-clicking the Properties item in Solution Explorer and choosing Database. From this dialog box, shown in Figure 15-4, you can change the connection string for the project.

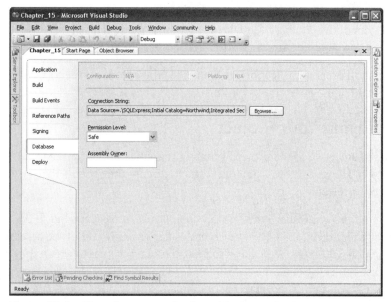

Figure 15-4   Changing properties for a SQL Server Project

From the properties page for the project, you can also change the permission level for the assembly. By default, the assembly generated for a SQL Server project is marked as Safe, meaning that your code is not allowed to access external resources—files, registry entries, network connections, or environment variables. Marking the assembly as External allows you to access these external resources.

Whether you mark your assemblies as Safe or External, your .NET code relies on SQL Server's infrastructure for memory, threads, and synchronization, which gives SQL Server the ability to manage these resources in your .NET code the same way it manages these resources for standard SQL Server features. SQL Server can suspend threads within your .NET code to perform other operations.

The .NET Framework added a series of attributes that allow a class to describe features that the class uses that might cause problems if the class is hosted in other processes. These attributes are called *HostProtectionAttributes*. This information helps hosting processes, such as SQL Server, determine whether they want to allow loading the assembly. For example, the *Timer* class manipulates threads other than its own and synchronizes those threads, so it has *HostProtectionAttributes* of *ExternalThreading* and *Synchronization*.

SQL Server relies on *HostProtectionAttributes* to ensure that the assemblies it loads will not affect the server's reliability. For example, the SQL Server will not allow you to load assemblies relying on features that are marked with the *MayLeakOnAbort HostProtectionAttribute* to ensure that thread aborts will not leak memory from the server process. SQL Server also disallows loading assemblies with *HostProtectionAtttributes* of *SharedState*, *Synchronization*, or *ExternalProcessMgmt*. If you attempt to load an assembly marked as Safe or External that relies on one of these disallowed attributes, SQL Server will throw a *HostProtectionException*.

There's a third permission level for SQL Server CLR assemblies: Unsafe. SQL Server does allow administrators of the database to register assemblies marked as Unsafe, which include no restrictions for *HostProtectionAttributes*.

For more information on host protection attributes, see the entries on the topic in the .NET Framework SDK and SQL Server Books OnLine.

Building and Deploying Your Project

We have not added any code to the project, so it might seem a bit premature to talk about building the project. However, now is a perfect time to discuss the process that Visual Studio uses to deploy your project.

When you build your project, Visual Studio merely compiles the project and builds the assembly. When you deploy the project, Visual Studio compiles the project to build the assembly, registers the assembly with SQL Server, and makes all functions, procedures, types, and so on available through SQL Server. Visual Studio also runs the test scripts that are part of the project. You can set breakpoints in the test script and step into your code as it's running in SQL Server.

Keep in mind that to register the assembly you just built, Visual Studio instructs SQL Server to drop the previous build of the assembly. This step will fail if your database depends on portions of that assembly. For example, if there's a table in your database that references a user-defined type from your assembly, the next attempt to deploy the assembly will fail.

Adding Items to Your Project

At this point, the project contains no code. You could add classes and structs to your project, and then add attributes to the classes and structs to indicate what functions, procedures, and types you want to make available in your database, but that requires a deep understanding of the SQL CLR attributes and rules. A faster and simpler way to add items to your project is to use the Project portion of the Visual Studio menu and select the type of item you want to add to your project, as shown in Figure 15-5.

Testing Your Project Using a SQL Script

Visual Studio will add a SQL script item to your project that you can use to test your the assembly for your project. This default script, called Test.SQL, includes commented-out sample queries that create tables and call stored procedures and functions to help you build your own queries. You can also set breakpoints in the script. When you run the project with debugging enabled, Visual Studio will stop at the breakpoints in your script and allow you to step into your .NET code to make it easier to debug your code.

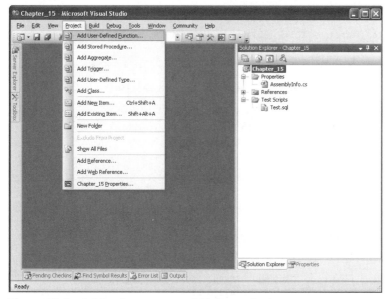

Figure 15-5   Adding items to your SQL Server Project

SQL CLR Scenarios

Now let's look at some examples of how you can use some of the features that are available through SQL CLR integration.

Creating a Scalar Function to Validate Data

What if you want to add a check constraint to perform complex validation on data coming into your database? You could build a scalar function, a function which returns a single value, such as a string or integer. For example, you could construct a scalar function to validate incoming postal code values based on the specified country and return a value to indicate whether the incoming value is valid. The goal is to accept values like *12345*, *123456789*, and *12345-6789* but not *1234567890* for United States addresses and to accept *A1B-2C3* but not *1A2-B3C* for Canadian addresses.

Regular expressions are designed to handle this type of validation. I wouldn't want to try to write this validation logic without using regular expressions. However, you can't use regular expressions directly from T-SQL.

A developer who is familiar with regular expressions can easily build a .NET function to validate postal codes for various countries. The following function validates postal codes from the United States and Canada:

Visual Basic

```
Imports System.Text.RegularExpressions
Public Function IsValidPostalCode(ByVal PostalCode As String, _
                        ByVal Country As String) As Boolean
```

```vb
    Dim patternUSA, patternCanada As String

    'United States formats - 12345, 123456789, 12345 6789, 12345-6789
    patternUSA = "^\d{5}((([ \-]{0,1})\d{4}){0,1})$"

    'Canadian formats - A1B2C3, A1B 2C3, A1B-2C3
    patternCanada = "^[a-zA-Z]\d[a-zA-Z]([ \-]{0,1})\d[a-zA-Z]\d$"

    Select Country.ToUpper()
        Case "USA" : Return Regex.IsMatch(PostalCode, patternUSA)
        Case "CANADA" : Return Regex.IsMatch(PostalCode, patternCanada)
        Case Else : Return True
    End Select
End Function
```

Visual C#

```csharp
//using System.Text.RegularExpressions;
public bool IsValidPostalCode(string PostalCode, string Country) {
    string patternUSA, patternCanada;

    //United States formats - 12345, 123456789, 12345 6789, 12345-6789
    patternUSA = @"^\d{5}((([ \-]{0,1})\d{4}){0,1})$";

    //Canadian formats - A1B2C3, A1B 2C3, A1B-2C3
    patternCanada = @"^[a-zA-Z]\d[a-zA-Z]([ \-]{0,1})\d[a-zA-Z]\d$";

    switch (Country.ToUpper()) {
        case "USA": return Regex.IsMatch(PostalCode, patternUSA);
        case "CANADA": return Regex.IsMatch(PostalCode, patternCanada);
        default: return true;
    }
}
```

Now how can we leverage this code in the SQL CLR? This code translates to a SQL Server scalar-valued function. So, let's add a user-defined function by selecting Add User-Defined Function from the Project item on the Visual Studio menu. The class file that Visual Studio adds includes a simple scalar-valued function with the appropriate syntax and attribute. I like to comment that function out but not delete the code so that I can refer back to the syntax and attributes later.

Next we add a function that's the equivalent of the previous one but instead uses *SqlTypes* for the parameters and return values. Finally, we add the *SqlFunction* attribute as shown in the sample code that appeared in the class that Visual Studio added. The result will look something like this:

Visual Basic

```vb
'Imports System.Text.RegularExpressions
<SqlFunction()> _
Public Shared Function IsValidPostalCode(ByVal PostalCode As SqlString, _
                                ByVal Country As SqlString) _
```

```
                                        As SqlBoolean
    If PostalCode.IsNull OrElse Country.IsNull Then
        Return SqlBoolean.Null
    End If

    Dim patternUSA, patternCanada As String

    'United States formats - 12345, 123456789, 12345 6789, 12345-6789
    patternUSA = "^\d{5}((([ \-]{0,1})\d{4}){0,1})$"

    'Canadian formats - A1B2C3, A1B 2C3, A1B-2C3
    patternCanada = "^[a-zA-Z]\d[a-zA-Z]([ \-]{0,1})\d[a-zA-Z]\d$"

    Select Case Country.Value.ToUpper()
        Case "USA"
            Return New SqlBoolean(Regex.IsMatch(PostalCode.Value, _
                                        patternUSA))
        Case "CANADA"
            Return New SqlBoolean(Regex.IsMatch(PostalCode.Value, _
                                        patternCanada))
        Case Else
            Return SqlBoolean.Null
    End Select
End Function
```

Visual C#

```
//using System.Text.RegularExpressions;
[SqlFunction]
public static SqlBoolean IsValidPostalCode(SqlString PostalCode,
                                    SqlString Country) {
    if (PostalCode.IsNull || Country.IsNull)
        return SqlBoolean.Null;

    string patternUSA, patternCanada;

    //United States formats - 12345, 123456789, 12345 6789, 12345-6789
    patternUSA = @"^\d{5}((([ \-]{0,1})\d{4}){0,1})$";

    //Canadian formats - A1B2C3, A1B 2C3, A1B-2C3
    patternCanada = @"^[a-zA-Z]\d[a-zA-Z]([ \-]{0,1})\d[a-zA-Z]\d$";

    switch (Country.Value.ToUpper()) {
        case "USA":
            return new SqlBoolean(Regex.IsMatch(PostalCode.Value,
                                        patternUSA));
        case "CANADA":
            return new SqlBoolean(Regex.IsMatch(PostalCode.Value,
                                        patternCanada));
        default:
            return SqlBoolean.Null;
    }
}
```

> **Note**   I modified the example slightly so that the function returns *Null* for countries other than the United States and Canada or if the value of the PostalCode column is *Null*.

Once you've deployed this assembly to SQL Server, you can use this function from a check constraint by executing the following query:

```
ALTER TABLE Customers ADD CONSTRAINT PostalCodeCheck
    CHECK (dbo.IsValidPostalCode(PostalCode, Country) <> 0)
```

Now when you modify data in the PostalCode column, SQL Server will use your function from the check constraint to validate the data. The following query will violate the check constraint and will prevent SQL Server from inserting the new row into the database:

```
INSERT INTO Customers (CustomerID, CompanyName, PostalCode, Country)
    VALUES ('Test2', 'Customer With Invalid PostalCode', 'Bad Value', 'USA')
```

Regular expressions are just the tip of the iceberg. You could use the External permission level and call a Web service to validate credit card information. In short, whatever validation you can perform from your .NET code, you can now perform in SQL Server.

Creating an Aggregate Function

Let's say that you want to return a comma-separated list of the product names contained in a particular order. You could construct a scalar function that accepts a parameter that corresponds to a value in the OrderID column in the Orders and Order Details tables. You could then open a cursor based on a parameterized query that joins the Order Details and Products tables, continually appending values to a variable and returning that variable after you've examined all data in the cursor.

Now what if you want to return a comma-separated list of the company names for customers in a given country? You could create another scalar function, but the code would be almost identical to the previous one you created. A more flexible solution would be to create an aggregate function.

You can't create an aggregate function using T-SQL. However, you can create one using the SQL CLR. Using the Visual Studio menu, select Add Aggregate from the Project tab. If you take a look at the sample code Visual Studio included, you'll see that the new aggregate includes four basic functions: *Init*, *Accumulate*, *Merge*, and *Terminate*. SQL Server will call the *Init* function before the aggregate begins processing the first record in a group. SQL Server then calls the *Accumulate* method to add new items to the aggregate, and finally it calls the *Terminate* function when the work is done. SQL Server might also partition the work into separate pieces, in which case it will populate separate aggregates and then combine them by calling the *Merge* method.

Writing this logic in .NET code is straightforward. You can use the *StringBuilder* class to continue to aggregate new comma-separated values and then return the contents of the *String-Builder* by calling the *ToString* method when aggregation is complete. You only need to change that logic to accept *SqlStrings* rather than .NET *Strings*. The result is the following code:

Visual Basic

```
'Imports System.Text
<Serializable()> _
<SqlUserDefinedAggregate(Format.Native)> _
Public Structure CommaSeparatedList
    Dim builder As StringBuilder

    Public Sub Init()
        builder = New StringBuilder()
    End Sub

    Private Sub AppendString(ByVal Value As String)
        If builder.Length = 0 Then
            builder.Append(Value)
        Else
            builder.Append(", " + Value)
        End If
    End Sub

    Public Sub Accumulate(ByVal value As SqlString)
        If Not value.IsNull Then
            AppendString(value.Value)
        End If
    End Sub

    Public Sub Merge(ByVal value As CommaSeparatedList)
        If Not value.builder Is Nothing Then
            AppendString(value.builder.ToString())
        End If
    End Sub

    Public Function Terminate() As SqlString
        If builder Is Nothing Then
            Return SqlString.Null
        Else
            Return New SqlString(builder.ToString())
        End If
    End Function
End Structure
```

Visual C#

```
//using System.Text;
[Serializable]
[SqlUserDefinedAggregate(Format.Native)]
public struct CommaSeparatedList
{
    StringBuilder builder;
    public void Init()
    {
```

```
        builder = new StringBuilder();
    }

    private void AppendString(string Value)
    {
        if (builder.Length == 0)
            builder.Append(Value);
        else
            builder.Append(", " + Value);
    }

    public void Accumulate(SqlString Value)
    {
        if (!Value.IsNull)
            AppendString(Value.Value);
    }

    public void Merge(CommaSeparatedList Group)
    {
        if (Group.builder != null)
            AppendString(Group.builder.ToString());
    }

    public SqlString Terminate()
    {
        if (builder == null)
            return SqlString.Null;
        else
            return new SqlString(builder.ToString());
    }
}
```

Although this code will compile, you will not be able to deploy it to a SQL Server database. SQL Server requires that the function has the ability to serialize its contents of the structure to disk. SQL Server can serialize the contents of your .NET class or struct only if all members are value types. This aggregate function includes a member that's a *SqlString*, which is a reference type. SQL Server needs help serializing and deserializing the contents of the structure.

You provide this help by implementing the *IBinarySerialize* interface and then providing additional information in the *SqlUserDefinedAggregate* attribute. The following snippet shows the code you need to add and omits the code from the previous snippet for brevity's sake.

Visual Basic

```
'Imports System.IO
<Serializable()> _
<SqlUserDefinedAggregate(Format.UserDefined, MaxByteSize:=8000)> _
Public Structure CommaSeparatedList
    Implements IBinarySerialize
    '...
    Private Sub Write(ByVal w As BinaryWriter) _
                            Implements IBinarySerialize.Write
        w.Write(builder.ToString())
    End Sub
```

```
        Private Sub Read(ByVal r As BinaryReader) _
                                    Implements IBinarySerialize.Read
            builder = New StringBuilder(r.ReadString())
        End Sub
    End Structure
```

Visual C#

```csharp
//using System.IO;
[Serializable]
[SqlUserDefinedAggregate(Format.UserDefined, MaxByteSize = 8000)]
public struct CommaSeparatedList : IBinarySerialize {
    //...
    void IBinarySerialize.Write(BinaryWriter w) {
        w.Write(builder.ToString());
    }

    void IBinarySerialize.Read(BinaryReader r) {
        builder = new StringBuilder(r.ReadString());
    }
}
```

Adding Information via the *SqlUserDefinedAggregate* Attribute

The attributes tell SQL Server to allow the structure to serialize and deserialize itself through the *IBinarySerialize* interface, and that the maximum size of the structure is 8000 bytes. SQL Server will not allow you to specify a larger value for the *MaxByteSize* attribute.

There are other attributes that you can add to your aggregate. The code included here discards *Null* values. We could specify `IsInvariantToNulls = True`. The benefit to adding this information through an attribute is that SQL Server can decide not to call the *Accumulate* method on the aggregate for *Null* values. Similarly, we could specify `IsNullIfEmpty = True`. SQL Server can then know that if there are no values to pass to the aggregate function, it can assume that the aggregate function returns *Null* and can avoid creating the structure altogether.

IsInvariantToDuplicates   Some aggregate functions, such as *min* and *max*, are unaffected by duplicate values. If we want to exclude duplicate values from the aggregate function, we could add code to track previously processed entries in a *List* or *Dictionary* object and then use that *List* or *Dictionary* to see whether the aggregate has already processed the incoming value. We can then also specify `IsInvariantToDuplicates = True`, which tells SQL Server that if it is able to detect duplicate values, it can discard those duplicate values rather than pass them into the aggregate function's *Accumulate* method.

IsInvariantToOrder   If we want the aggregate function to be invariant to order, we could store previously processed values in a *SortedList* or *SortedDictionary* and then specify `IsInvariantToOrder = True`. SQL Server can perform further optimizations on aggregate functions that are invariant to order.

Name   By default, the aggregate function you've created has the same name as the name of the struct. You can specify a different name through the *Name* property on the attribute.

Testing Your New Aggregate Function

You can execute the following query to test your new aggregate function from Visual Studio Query Builder or SQL Server Management Studio:

```
SELECT O.OrderID, dbo.CommaSeparatedList(P.ProductName) AS ProductList
  FROM Customers C
    JOIN Orders O ON O.CustomerID = C.CustomerID
    JOIN [Order Details] OD ON OD.OrderID = O.OrderID
    JOIN Products P ON P.ProductID = OD.ProductID
  WHERE C.CustomerID = 'ALFKI'
  GROUP BY O.OrderID
```

You can also execute this query from the test script in your project to step into the code.

Querying the Current Database Using the Context Connection

The previous examples demonstrate some of the power of the SQL Server CLR, but don't rely on ADO.NET. Let's take a look at an example that creates a scalar function that uses ADO.NET to query the current database.

We can create a scalar function that accepts a value from the CustomerID column that appears in the Customers and Orders tables and returns the number of orders placed for that customer. Granted, you could accomplish this task just as easily by writing a scalar function in T-SQL, but the goal here is to demonstrate how to query the current database.

If you wanted to write an *OrderCount* function in a basic .NET application, you'd use code like the following:

Visual Basic

```
Public Function OrderCount(ByVal CustomerID As String) As Integer
    Dim strConn, strSQL As String
    strConn = "Data Source=.\SQLExpress;" & _
            "Initial Catalog=Northwind;Integrated Security=True;"
    strSQL = "SELECT @OrderCount = COUNT(*) FROM Orders " & _
            "   WHERE CustomerID = @CustomerID"

    Using cn As New SqlConnection(strConn)
        Using cmd As New SqlCommand(strSQL, cn)
            Dim p As SqlParameter
            p = cmd.Parameters.Add("@OrderCount", SqlDbType.Int)
            p.Direction = ParameterDirection.Output
            cmd.Parameters.AddWithValue("@CustomerID", CustomerID)

            cn.Open()
            cmd.ExecuteNonQuery()
            cn.Close()
```

```
            returnValue = DirectCast(p.Value, Integer)
        End Using
    End Using

    Return returnValue
End Function
```

Visual C#

```
public int OrderCount(string CustomerID)
    string strConn, strSQL;
    strConn = @"Data Source=.\SQLExpress;" +
            "Initial Catalog=Northwind;Integrated Security=True;";
    strSQL = "SELECT @OrderCount = COUNT(*) FROM Orders " +
            "    WHERE CustomerID = @CustomerID";

    using (SqlConnection cn = new SqlConnection(strConn)) {
        using (SqlCommand cmd = new SqlCommand(strSQL, cn)) {
            SqlParameter p;
            p = cmd.Parameters.Add("@OrderCount", SqlDbType.Int);
            p.Direction = ParameterDirection.Output;
            cmd.Parameters.AddWithValue("@CustomerID", CustomerID);

            cn.Open();
            cmd.ExecuteNonQuery();
            cn.Close();

            returnValue = (int) p.Value;
        }
    }

    return returnValue;
}
```

As noted earlier, extended stored procedures written in C or C++ had to loop back to the current database by using a technology such as OLE DB, ODBC, DB-Library. You can access the current database via the *SqlConnection* class from your SQL CLR code using a special connection string:

```
Context Connection=True;
```

The *Context Connection* keyword tells the *SqlConnection* object to use the current connection to the database. The current connection is often referred to in the SQL CLR documentation as the *context connection*.

Converting the previous example to run in the SQL CLR and use the context connection requires using the *SqlTypes* (*SqlString* and *SqlInt32*) rather than the .NET *String* and *Integer* types, adding attributes, and changing the connection string, as shown here:

Visual Basic

```
<SqlFunction(DataAccess:=DataAccessKind.Read)> _
Public Shared Function OrderCount(ByVal CustomerID As SqlString) As SqlInt32
    Dim returnValue As SqlInt32
```

```
            Dim strSQL As String = "SELECT @OrderCount = COUNT(*) FROM Orders " & _
                                    "  WHERE CustomerID = @CustomerID"
        Using cn As New SqlConnection("Context Connection=True")
            Using cmd As New SqlCommand(strSQL, cn)
                Dim p As SqlParameter
                p = cmd.Parameters.Add("@OrderCount", SqlDbType.Int)
                p.Direction = ParameterDirection.Output
                cmd.Parameters.AddWithValue("@CustomerID", CustomerID)

                cn.Open()
                cmd.ExecuteNonQuery()
                cn.Close()

                returnValue = DirectCast(p.SqlValue, SqlInt32)
            End Using
        End Using

        Return returnValue
    End Function
```

Visual C#

```
[SqlFunction(DataAccess=DataAccessKind.Read)]
public static SqlInt32 OrderCount(SqlString CustomerID)
{
    SqlInt32 returnValue;

    string strSQL = "SELECT @OrderCount = COUNT(*) FROM Orders " +
                    "  WHERE CustomerID = @CustomerID";
    using (SqlConnection cn = new SqlConnection("Context Connection=True"))
    {
        using (SqlCommand cmd = new SqlCommand(strSQL, cn))
        {
            SqlParameter p;
            p = cmd.Parameters.Add("@OrderCount", SqlDbType.Int);
            p.Direction = ParameterDirection.Output;
            cmd.Parameters.AddWithValue("@CustomerID", CustomerID);

            cn.Open();
            cmd.ExecuteNonQuery();
            cn.Close();

            returnValue = (SqlInt32)p.SqlValue;
        }
    }

    return returnValue;
}
```

Note that the *DataAccess* property in the *SqlFunction* attribute is set to *DataAccessKind.Read* to indicate that the function reads data.

Building SQL CLR Table Valued Functions

SQL Server also supports *table valued functions*, sometimes referred to as *TVFs*, which are functions that return a table of information. You can create table valued functions using .NET code, though this process might seem slightly counterintuitive at first.

The .NET function you construct and expose through the SQL CLR is not required to return a *DataTable* or a *DataReader*. The SQL CLR requires only that your function return *IEnumerable* or a type that implements *IEnumerable*. We'll refer to this function as your enumerating function. Think of the return value of this function as a set of keys rather than the actual desired results. The SQL CLR also requires that you supply a *row filling function*, which is an additional .NET function that accepts an individual item returned by your enumerating function and returns values for the columns in the new row through the function's parameters. SQL Server calls this row filling function for each item returned by the enumerating function to populate the values for the new row of data.

SQL CLR table valued functions also require additional metadata in the *SqlFunction* attribute. The *FillRow* property tells SQL Server what function to call to populate values for individual rows. The *TableDefinition* property defines the structure of the table returned by the table valued function.

The following code snippet creates a table valued function that returns order information for the specified customer. The function sets the *DataAccess* property on the *SqlFunction* attribute to *Read* because the function uses the context connection to query the database. The row enumerating function uses a *SqlDataAdapter* to fill a *DataTable* with the desired data and then returns a reference to the *Rows* collection for that *DataTable*. The row filling function then accesses the contents of the *DataRow* supplied and returns values for the individual columns. Because the row filling function will return values for individual columns using the *SqlTypes* namespace, the row enumerating function sets the *SqlDataAdapter* object's *ReturnProvider-SpecificTypes* property to *True*.

Visual Basic

```vb
<SqlFunction(FillRowMethodName:="GetOrdersTVF_FillRow", _
            TableDefinition:="OrderID int, OrderDate datetime", _
            DataAccess:=DataAccessKind.Read, _
            Name:="GetOrdersTVF")> _
Public Shared Function GetOrdersTVF_Enumerator _
                    (ByVal CustomerID As SqlString) As IEnumerable
    Dim tbl As New DataTable()
    tbl.Columns.Add("OrderID", GetType(SqlInt32))
    tbl.Columns.Add("OrderDate", GetType(SqlDateTime))

    Dim strSQL As String = "SELECT OrderID, OrderDate FROM Orders " & _
                    " WHERE CustomerID = @CustomerID"
    Dim da As New SqlDataAdapter(strSQL, "Context Connection=True;")
    da.SelectCommand.Parameters.AddWithValue("@CustomerID", CustomerID)
    da.ReturnProviderSpecificTypes = True
    da.Fill(tbl)

    Return tbl.Rows
End Function

Private Shared Sub GetOrdersTVF_FillRow(ByVal OrderRow As Object, _
            ByRef OrderID As SqlInt32, ByRef OrderDate As SqlDateTime)
    Dim row As DataRow = DirectCast(OrderRow, DataRow)
```

```
        OrderID = DirectCast(row(0), SqlInt32)
        OrderDate = DirectCast(row(1), SqlDateTime)
End Sub
```

Visual C#

```csharp
[SqlFunction(FillRowMethodName = "GetOrdersTVF_FillRow",
             TableDefinition = "OrderID int, OrderDate datetime",
             DataAccess = DataAccessKind.Read,
             Name = "GetOrdersTVF")]
public static IEnumerable GetOrdersTVF_Enumerator(SqlString CustomerID) {
    DataTable tbl = new DataTable();
    tbl.Columns.Add("OrderID", typeof(SqlInt32));
    tbl.Columns.Add("OrderDate", typeof(SqlDateTime));

    string strSQL = "SELECT OrderID, OrderDate FROM Orders " +
                    "   WHERE CustomerID = @CustomerID";
    string strConn = "Context Connection=True;";
    SqlDataAdapter da = new SqlDataAdapter(strSQL, strConn);
    da.SelectCommand.Parameters.AddWithValue("@CustomerID", CustomerID);
    da.ReturnProviderSpecificTypes = true;
    da.Fill(tbl);

    return tbl.Rows;
}

private static void GetOrdersTVF_FillRow (
        object OrderRow, out SqlInt32 OrderID, out SqlDateTime OrderDate) {
    DataRow row = (DataRow)OrderRow;
    OrderID = (SqlInt32)row[0];
    OrderDate = (SqlDateTime)row[1];
}
```

In this example, the row filling function simply accesses the contents of the *DataRow* to return individual column values through parameters. However, there is no requirement that states that the row enumerating function has to make all these individual column values available to the row filling function. The row enumerating function needs to supply only enough information for the row filling function to return the column values for each row.

We could have constructed the row enumerating function to return just the contents of the OrderID column. The row filling function could then use the context connection to get the values of the OrderDate column. Although that would be an inefficient use of the context connection in this example, this approach might be valid in other scenarios.

For example, let's say that you're trying to build a table valued function that returns information about computers running in a lab. Let's also assume that the lab manager built a series of WebServices that return status information about the machines. There's one WebService that accepts two parameters—the desired operating system name, and the desired build number— and it returns the names of the machines that match the supplied criteria. Another WebSer- vice returns information about individual machines (IP address, processor architecture and speed, hard drive size, and so on), but it returns this information on a per-machine basis.

In this hypothetical scenario, your row enumerating function would call the WebService that returns the list of machine names and return those values through a type that implements *IEnumerable*, such as *List<String>* in the *System.Collections.Generic* namespace. Your row filling function could then call the WebService that returns detailed information about the machine.

I say "could" rather than "would" because you could also make all the WebService calls from within the row enumerating function and store all results in a *DataTable*. This approach requires caching all the results in a *DataTable*, whereas calling the WebService to return detailed machine information from the row filling function is more of a streaming solution. Which approach would be more efficient? That would depend on how staggering the calls to the WebService affects performance, as well as how much memory you would need to store all the machine information in the *DataTable*. Your best bet is to write some proof-of-concept code and test the performance of each option.

Returning Query Results from a Stored Procedure

Now that you've seen how to use a *SqlConnection* to execute a query on the context connection, and you've seen examples that return data through a scalar function, let's explore how to return the results of a query from a CLR stored procedure.

SQL Server stored procedures can return query results, just like a simple SELECT query. You can use ADO.NET inside a SQL CLR stored procedure and return results through this interface by relying on two classes in the *Microsoft.SqlServer.Server* namespace: *SqlPipe* and *SqlContext*.

The .NET Framework SDK aptly describes the *SqlPipe* class as conceptually similar to the ASP.NET *Response* class. The *SqlPipe* class represents the output "pipe" that the stored procedure uses to return rows of results, messages, or both. To access the *SqlPipe* for a stored procedure, check the *Pipe* property on the static *SqlContext* object. The *SqlPipe* class exposes overloaded *Send* methods that accept a string (for a message), a *SqlDataReader*, or a *SqlDataRecord*. If you want to send the entire results of a query, you can simply pass the *SqlCommand* to the *ExecuteAndSend* method as shown here:

Visual Basic

```
<SqlProcedure()> _
Public Shared Sub GetOrderDetails(ByVal OrderID As SqlInt32)
    Dim strSQL As String
    strSQL = "SELECT ProductID, Quantity, UnitPrice, Discount " & _
             "   FROM [Order Details] WHERE OrderID = @OrderID"
    Using cn As New SqlConnection("Context Connection=True")
        Using cmd As New SqlCommand(strSQL, cn)
            cmd.Parameters.AddWithValue("@OrderID", OrderID)
            cn.Open()
            SqlContext.Pipe.ExecuteAndSend(cmd)
            cn.Close()
        End Using
    End Using
End Sub
```

Visual C#

```csharp
[SqlProcedure]
public static void GetOrderDetails(SqlInt32 OrderID)
{
    string strSQL;
    strSQL = "SELECT ProductID, Quantity, UnitPrice, Discount " +
             "   FROM [Order Details] WHERE OrderID = @OrderID";
    using (SqlConnection cn = new SqlConnection("Context Connection=True"))
    {
        using (SqlCommand cmd = new SqlCommand(strSQL, cn))
        {
            cmd.Parameters.AddWithValue("@OrderID", OrderID);
            cn.Open();
            SqlContext.Pipe.ExecuteAndSend(cmd);
            cn.Close();
        }
    }
}
```

The *SqlPipe* object is also capable of handling more dynamic results. Perhaps you want to process the contents of a *SqlDataReader* and select which rows of data to return from the stored procedure. Maybe your stored procedure is a gateway of sorts, retrieving data from another database system via the ODBC, OLE DB, or OracleClient .NET Data Providers. You might even want to construct results by hand without communicating with a database.

If you're not sending results from a *SqlDataReader*, or you want to apply a filter to the results, you'll need to write a little more code. The first step is to define the structure of the results by creating an array of *SqlMetaData* objects and then use the array of *SqlMetaData* objects in the *SqlDataRecord* class's constructor to create a new *SqlDataRecord* object. Pass the new *SqlDataRecord* object into the *SqlPipe* object's *SendResultsStart* method. This method call initializes the *SqlPipe* so that it can handle the results to follow.

You can then reuse the *SqlDataRecord* to populate the results. Modify the *SqlDataRecord* by calling its various *Set* methods, which are the rough equivalents of the *Get* methods on the *SqlDataReader*. For example, to set a field in the record to a 32-bit integer, you would call the *SetInt32* method and pass in the ordinal for the field number and the desired value. Once you've assigned values for all columns in the *SqlDataRecord*, pass the *SqlDataRecord* into the *SqlPipe*'s *SendResultsRow* method. Finally, once you've submitted all rows of data to the *SqlPipe*, call the *SendResultsEnd* method.

To demonstrate how flexible this approach is, I built a sample that generates prime numbers, up to the maximum value specified, using a simple function. Then I created a SQL CLR stored procedure that calls that function and returns the results as a resultset.

Visual Basic

```vbnet
'Imports System.Collections.Generic
<SqlProcedure()> _
Public Shared Sub GetPrimes(ByVal MaxValue As Integer)
    Dim pipe As SqlPipe = SqlContext.Pipe
```

```
    Dim metadata(1) As SqlMetaData
    metadata(0) = New SqlMetaData("ID", SqlDbType.Int)
    metadata(1) = New SqlMetaData("Prime", SqlDbType.Int)
    Dim record As New SqlDataRecord(metadata)
    pipe.SendResultsStart(record)

    Dim counter As Integer = 0
    For Each prime As Integer In InternalPrimeGenerator(MaxValue)
        counter += 1
        record.SetSqlInt32(0, New SqlInt32(counter))
        record.SetSqlInt32(1, New SqlInt32(prime))
        pipe.SendResultsRow(record)
    Next prime

    pipe.SendResultsEnd()
End Sub

Private Shared Function InternalPrimeGenerator(ByVal MaxValue As Integer) _
                                        As List(Of Integer)
    Dim confirmedPrimes As New List(Of Integer)
    Dim potentialPrimes As New List(Of Integer)(MaxValue)
    For i As Integer = 2 To MaxValue
        potentialPrimes.Add(i)
    Next i

    Do
        Dim newPrime As Integer = potentialPrimes(0)
        potentialPrimes.RemoveAt(0)
        confirmedPrimes.Add(newPrime)

        Dim valuePosition As Integer = 1
        Do While valuePosition < potentialPrimes.Count
            If potentialPrimes(valuePosition) Mod newPrime = 0 Then
                potentialPrimes.RemoveAt(valuePosition)
            Else
                valuePosition += 1
            End If
        Loop
    Loop Until potentialPrimes.Count = 0

    Return confirmedPrimes
End Function
```

Visual C#

```
//using System.Collections.Generic;
[SqlProcedure]
public static void GetPrimes(int MaxValue)
{
    SqlPipe pipe = SqlContext.Pipe;
    SqlMetaData[] metadata = new SqlMetaData[2];
    metadata[0] = new SqlMetaData("ID", SqlDbType.Int);
    metadata[1] = new SqlMetaData("Prime", SqlDbType.Int);
    SqlDataRecord record;

    record = new SqlDataRecord(metadata);
```

```
        pipe.SendResultsStart(record);

        int counter = 0;
        foreach (int prime in InternalPrimeGenerator(MaxValue))
        {
            counter++;
            record.SetSqlInt32(0, new SqlInt32(counter));
            record.SetSqlInt32(1, new SqlInt32(prime));
            pipe.SendResultsRow(record);
        }

        pipe.SendResultsEnd();
    }

    private static List<int> InternalPrimeGenerator(int Max)
    {
        List<int> confirmedPrimes = new List<int>();

        List<int> potentialPrimes = new List<int>(Max);
        for (int i = 2; i <= Max; i++)
            potentialPrimes.Add(i);

        do
        {
            int newPrime = potentialPrimes[0];
            potentialPrimes.RemoveAt(0);
            confirmedPrimes.Add(newPrime);

            int valuePosition = 1;
            while (valuePosition < potentialPrimes.Count)
            {
                if (potentialPrimes[valuePosition] % newPrime == 0)
                    potentialPrimes.RemoveAt(valuePosition);
                else
                    valuePosition++;
            }
        } while (potentialPrimes.Count != 0);

        return confirmedPrimes;
    }
```

I decided to create a similar T-SQL stored procedure using the same basic logic, relying on roughly similar logic using a temporary table, to compare performance numbers. Here's the stored procedure definition:

```
CREATE PROCEDURE GetPrimes_TSQL (@MaxPrime int) AS
BEGIN
  SET NOCOUNT ON

  DECLARE @Counter int, @PreviousPrime int, @NextPrime int, @Continue bit

  CREATE TABLE #PrimeCheck (Prime int PRIMARY KEY)
```

```
  SET @Counter = 2
  WHILE @Counter <= @MaxPrime
  BEGIN
    INSERT INTO #PrimeCheck (Prime) VALUES (@Counter)
    SET @Counter = @Counter + 1
  END

  SELECT @Continue = 1, @NextPrime = 2

  WHILE @Continue = 1
  BEGIN
    DELETE #PrimeCheck WHERE Prime > @NextPrime AND Prime % @NextPrime = 0
    SET @PreviousPrime = @NextPrime
    SET @NextPrime = NULL
    SELECT TOP 1 @NextPrime = MIN(Prime)
      FROM #PrimeCheck
      WHERE Prime > @PreviousPrime
    IF @NextPrime IS NULL SET @Continue = 0
  END

  SELECT ROW_NUMBER() OVER (ORDER BY Prime) AS ID, Prime FROM #PrimeCheck

  DROP TABLE #PrimeCheck

  SET NOCOUNT OFF
END
```

As I compared performance numbers, the results were somewhat surprising. For very small resultsets, the SQL CLR stored procedure greatly outperformed the T-SQL stored procedure by at least an order of magnitude, likely due to the fact that using the *List<int>* in the CLR requires less overhead than a temporary table in SQL Server. On average, generating prime numbers up to 1000 took 10 milliseconds via the SQL CLR, compared to 150 milliseconds via T-SQL. The SQL CLR stored procedure still ran faster for larger resultsets, but by a smaller factor, outperforming the T-SQL only by a factor of 2 to 1 to generate prime numbers up to 250,000. I had expected the SQL CLR stored procedure to outperform the T-SQL stored procedure by an even larger factor in larger resultsets. The lesson to be learned is that when in doubt, you should test both approaches with sets of values that approximate the expected user scenarios before determining which approach is the right one.

Returning Data Through Stored Procedure Parameters

The preceding SQL CLR stored procedure example focused on using the *SqlPipe* available as part of the stored procedure's context. You can also build stored procedures that return data through parameters—output parameters, input/output parameters, or the stored procedure's return value. Defining parameters on a SQL CLR stored procedure to return information is a natural extension of defining parameters on functions and methods in Visual Basic or C#.

Here's an example of a SQL CLR stored procedure that uses an input parameter, an input/output parameter, an output parameter, and a return value. The procedure writes the contents of the values it receives to the *SqlPipe* so that you can verify that the procedure received those values.

Visual Basic

```
<SqlProcedure()> _
Public Shared Function ParamTest(ByVal InParam As SqlString, _
                                 ByRef InOutParam As SqlString, _
                                 ByRef OutParam As SqlString) As SqlInt32
    SqlContext.Pipe.Send("Received InParam: " & InParam.Value)
    SqlContext.Pipe.Send("Received InOutParam: " & InOutParam.Value)

    InOutParam = New SqlString("Outgoing value for InOutParam")
    OutParam = New SqlString("Outgoing value for OutParam")

    Return New SqlInt32(42)
End Function
```

Visual C#

```
[SqlProcedure]
public static SqlInt32 ParamTest(SqlString InParam,
                                 ref SqlString InOutParam,
                                 out SqlString OutParam) {
    SqlContext.Pipe.Send("Received InParam: " + InParam.Value);
    SqlContext.Pipe.Send("Received InOutParam: " + InOutParam.Value);

    InOutParam = new SqlString("Outgoing value for InOutParam");
    OutParam = new SqlString("Outgoing value for OutParam");

    return new SqlInt32(42);
}
```

You can test this SQL CLR stored procedure by including the following T-SQL code in your test script:

```
DECLARE @InParam nvarchar(32), @InOutParam nvarchar(32)
DECLARE @OutParam nvarchar(32), @RetVal int
SELECT @InParam = 'Incoming InParam Value',
       @InOutParam = 'Incoming InOutParam Value'

EXEC @RetVal = dbo.ParamTest @InParam, @InOutParam OUTPUT, @OutParam OUTPUT
SELECT @RetVal, @InParam, @InOutParam, @OutParam
```

When you execute this T-SQL code, the results will appear in your project's Output window.

Specifying Size Information for Parameters Using the *SqlFacet* Attribute

The procedure parameters are defined as *SqlStrings* but don't include information about their size. You can supply this information by using the *SqlFacet* attribute. For example, if you want the input parameter to have a maximum length of 12 characters, you could change the definition of the parameter in the procedure as shown here:

Visual Basic

```
<SqlFacet(MaxSize:=12)> ByVal InParam As SqlString
```

Visual C#

```
[SqlFacet(MaxSize=12)] SqlString InParam
```

The *SqlFacet* attribute also lets you specify whether a parameter can accept *Null* and whether a string parameter is of fixed length, as well as the scale and precision for numeric types.

Creating a SQL CLR User-Defined Type

Thanks to the SQL CLR, you can write .NET code to store your own custom data types in a SQL Server 2005 database.

Not all data can be represented in data types that SQL Server natively supports. Perhaps you want to store a date/time value that includes a time zone. Maybe you want a column in a table to contain values that represent a point in three-dimensional space or a location based on very precise GPS coordinates. If you can describe the structure of your type using .NET code, you can store data in a SQL Server 2005 database using that code.

This portion of the chapter will construct a user-defined SQL CLR type that contains the line items for an order and store that data in a column in the Orders table. Of course, that's not the most impressive use of the SQL CLR, but the point of the example is to work with a data type that is easy to grasp and can demonstrate the main scenarios when working with user-defined types in the SQL CLR.

The *OrderDetailsType* type we're going to construct needs to store multiple rows of data. We'll want to provide the ability to add and remove items, check to see whether the order already includes a product, and report the total cost of the order. We'll also want to use a structure that can be serialized, and we should be able to cache changes, so we can decide later whether we want to accept or reject those changes. Rather than build such a class from scratch, the example will rely on a *DataSet* to manage the order details information for the order.

What's in a SQL CLR User-Defined Type?

To create a SQL CLR user-defined type, you really need to support only three sets of features in your structure: null handling, representing the type as a string, and serializing the contents of the type.

Testing for Null

You might have noticed that all the types in the *System.Data.SqlTypes* namespace expose an *IsNull* property that you can use to determine whether the value is *Null*, and a static read-only *Null* property that you can use to represent a *Null* value for the type. You're required to provide the same support for SQL CLR user-defined types. When you add a new user-defined type item to your SQL Server project, you'll see that Visual Studio includes stubs for the *IsNull* property and static *Null* property.

The key is to make sure that the instance of your type you return through the static *Null* property will return *True* if you check that instance's *IsNull* property. One approach is to use a Boolean member to track whether the instance represents *Null*. The following example uses a slightly different approach. The type contains a *DataSet* member that is initialized once the type contains order details, so testing to see whether the *DataSet* is initialized can serve as the *Null* check, as shown here:

Visual Basic

```
Dim orderDetailsDataSet As DataSet

Public Shared ReadOnly Property Null() As OrderDetailsType
    Get
        Return New OrderDetailsType
    End Get
End Property

Public ReadOnly Property IsNull() As Boolean Implements INullable.IsNull
    Get
        Return (Me.orderDetailsDataSet Is Nothing)
    End Get
End Property
```

Visual C#

```
DataSet orderDetailsDataSet;

public static OrderDetailsType Null {
    get {
        return new OrderDetailsType();
    }
}

public bool IsNull {
    get {
        return (this.orderDetailsDataSet == null);
    }
}
```

Representing the Type as a String

SQL Server requires that user-defined types implement a *Parse* method that accepts a *SqlString*. Users can then create instances of your type using the CAST and CONVERT functions in T-SQL:

```
DECLARE @myVariable MyType;
SELECT @myVariable = CAST('Value' AS MyType);
SELECT @myVariable = CONVERT(MyType, 'Value');
```

SQL Server also requires that user-defined types implement a *ToString* method that returns a representation of the type as a *SqlString*. There is no requirement that the *SqlString* returned by the *ToString* method be equivalent to the one supplied in the *Parse* method.

Because we're using a *DataSet* to store the order detail information, we can use the *DataSet*'s *LoadXml* and *GetXml* methods in the *Parse* and *ToString* methods, respectively. The *Parse* method calls a static method that adds the appropriate schema information to the *DataSet* before loading its contents based on the string supplied.

Visual Basic

```vb
Public Overrides Function ToString() As String
    If Me.IsNull Then
        Return "<Null>"
    Else
        Return Me.orderDetailsDataSet.GetXml()
    End If
End Function

Public Shared Function Parse(ByVal s As SqlString) As OrderDetailsType
    If s.IsNull Then
        Return Null
    End If

    Dim u As New OrderDetailsType
    u.orderDetailsDataSet = LoadOrderDetails(s.Value)
    Return u
End Function

Public Shared Function LoadOrderDetails(ByVal value As String) As DataSet
    Dim ds As New DataSet("OrderDetails")
    Dim tbl As DataTable = ds.Tables.Add("OrderDetail")
    Dim col As DataColumn
    col = tbl.Columns.Add("ProductID", GetType(Integer))
    col.ColumnMapping = MappingType.Attribute
    tbl.PrimaryKey = New DataColumn() {col}
    col = tbl.Columns.Add("Quantity", GetType(Short))
    col.ColumnMapping = MappingType.Attribute
    col = tbl.Columns.Add("UnitPrice", GetType(Decimal))
    col.ColumnMapping = MappingType.Attribute
    col = tbl.Columns.Add("Discount", GetType(Single))
    col.ColumnMapping = MappingType.Attribute
    col = tbl.Columns.Add("ItemTotal", GetType(Decimal), _
                          "(Quantity * UnitPrice) * (1 - Discount)")
    col.ColumnMapping = MappingType.Hidden

    If value.Length > 0 Then
        Try
            Using rdr As StringReader = New StringReader(value)
                ds.ReadXml(rdr)
            End Using
        Catch
            ds.AcceptChanges()
        End Try
    End If
    Return ds
End Function
```

Visual C#

```csharp
public override string ToString() {
    if (this.IsNull)
        return "<Null>";
    else
        return this.orderDetailsDataSet.GetXml();
}

public static OrderDetailsType Parse(SqlString s) {
    if (s.IsNull)
        return OrderDetailsType.Null;

    OrderDetailsType u = new OrderDetailsType();
    u.orderDetailsDataSet = LoadOrderDetails(s.Value);
    return u;
}

static DataSet LoadOrderDetails(string value) {
    DataSet ds = new DataSet("OrderDetails");
    DataTable tbl = ds.Tables.Add("OrderDetail");
    DataColumn col;
    col = tbl.Columns.Add("ProductID", typeof(int));
    col.ColumnMapping = MappingType.Attribute;
    tbl.PrimaryKey = new DataColumn[] { col };
    col = tbl.Columns.Add("Quantity", typeof(short));
    col.ColumnMapping = MappingType.Attribute;
    col = tbl.Columns.Add("UnitPrice", typeof(decimal));
    col.ColumnMapping = MappingType.Attribute;
    col = tbl.Columns.Add("Discount", typeof(Single));
    col.ColumnMapping = MappingType.Attribute;
    col = tbl.Columns.Add("ItemTotal", typeof(decimal),
                          "(Quantity * UnitPrice) * (1 - Discount)");
    col.ColumnMapping = MappingType.Hidden;

    if (value.Length > 0) {
        try {
            using (StringReader rdr = new StringReader(value))
                ds.ReadXml(rdr);
        }
        catch { }
        ds.AcceptChanges();
    }
    return ds;
}
```

Serializing the Contents

SQL Server must be able to serialize the contents of the type to disk. SQL Server can natively serialize a user-defined type only if its members are value types from the *System.Data.SqlTypes* namespace (*SqlBoolean, SqlByte, SqlDateTime, SqlInt16*, and so on) or their .NET equivalents (*Boolean, Byte, DateTime, Int16*, and so on). Otherwise, you need to specify *Format.UserDefined* in the *SqlUserDefinedType* attribute and implement the *IBinarySerialize* interface.

Because the *OrderDetailsType* contains a member of type *DataSet*, we must implement *IBinary-Serialize*. The *BinaryWriter* and *BinaryReader* classes offer a *Write* method that accepts a *String* method and a *ReadString* method that returns a *String*. We can call these methods and reuse the code from the *ToString* and *Parse* methods as shown here:

Visual Basic

```
Imports System.IO

<Serializable()> _
<SqlUserDefinedType(Format.UserDefined, MaxByteSize:=8000)> _
Public Structure OrderDetailsType
    Implements INullable, IBinarySerialize
    '...
    Private Sub Write(ByVal w As BinaryWriter) _
                Implements IBinarySerialize.Write
        w.Write(Me.ToString())
    End Sub

    Private Sub Read(ByVal r As BinaryReader) _
                Implements IBinarySerialize.Read
        Me.orderDetailsDataSet = LoadOrderDetails(r.ReadString())
    End Sub
End Structure
```

Visual C#

```
//using System.IO;
[Serializable]
[SqlUserDefinedType(Format.UserDefined, MaxByteSize = 8000)]
public struct OrderDetailsType : INullable, IBinarySerialize {
    //...
    void IBinarySerialize.Write(BinaryWriter w) {
        w.Write(this.ToString());
    }

    void IBinarySerialize.Read(BinaryReader r) {
        this.orderDetailsDataSet = LoadOrderDetails(r.ReadString());
    }
}
```

Exposing Methods and Properties on the User-Defined Type

We now have a working user-defined type. However, the only methods or properties the type surfaces are *Parse* and *ToString*. In other words, we don't have a terribly interesting user-defined type, at least not yet.

Exposing Methods

Because the type represents the line items for an order, we should add methods that allow the user to add a line item to the order, remove a line item from the order, clear all line items from the order, and change the quantity for a particular product in the order.

For the moment, let's assume that we've already added an *AddItem* method to the type that accepts values that correspond to the ProductID, Quantity, UnitPrice, and Discount columns from the Order Details table we're replacing via the user-defined type. If we construct the *AddItem* method so that it modifies the contents of the existing structure, we can call the method in the SET clause of an UPDATE query, as shown here:

```
UPDATE Orders
    SET OrderDetailsColumn.AddItem(1, 12, 18.00, 0.00)
    WHERE OrderID = 10248
```

Some developers prefer to use immutable types, such as the *SqlTypes*, that cannot be modified directly once they have been created. In such cases, calling the *AddItem* method would leave the object unchanged, but it would return a new object that contains all the original line items, plus the line item specified in the method. If you were to construct the *AddItem* method following this pattern, you would use it in the SET clause of an UPDATE query using a syntax that might feel more familiar:

```
UPDATE Orders
    SET OrderDetailsColumn = OrderDetailsColumn.AddItem(1, 12, 18.00, 0.00)
    WHERE OrderID = 10248
```

Any methods that you want to expose through the SQL CLR must have the *SqlMethod* attribute. If the method modifies the contents of the structure, set the *IsMutator* property on the attribute to *True*. If the method will not accept null input parameters, set the *OnNullCall* property of the attribute to *False*.

Visual Basic

```
<SqlMethod(IsMutator:=True, OnNullCall:=False)> _
Public Sub AddItem(ByVal ProductID As Integer, ByVal Quantity As Short, _
                   ByVal UnitPrice As Decimal, ByVal Discount As Single)
    If Not Me.FindProductID(ProductID) Is Nothing Then
        Throw New ArgumentException("Order already contains this product")
    End If

    Me.orderDetailsDataSet.Tables(0).Rows.Add(ProductID, Quantity, _
                                              UnitPrice, Discount)
End Sub

<SqlMethod(IsMutator:=True, OnNullCall:=False)> _
Public Sub RemoveItem(ByVal ProductID As Integer)
    Dim row As DataRow = Me.FindProductID(ProductID)
    If row Is Nothing Then
        Throw New ArgumentException("Order does not contain this product")
    End If

    row.Delete()
End Sub

<SqlMethod(IsMutator:=True)> _
Public Sub Clear()
    Me.orderDetailsDataSet.Clear()
End Sub
```

```vbnet
<SqlMethod(IsMutator:=True, OnNullCall:=False)> _
Public Sub AddQuantity(ByVal ProductID As Integer, ByVal Quantity As Short)
    Dim row As DataRow = Me.FindProductID(ProductID)
    If row Is Nothing Then
        Throw New ArgumentException("Order does not contain this product")
    End If

    row("Quantity") = CShort(row("Quantity")) + Quantity
End Sub


<SqlMethod(OnNullCall:=False)> _
Public Function ContainsProductID(ByVal ProductID As Integer) As Boolean
    Return Not Me.FindProductID(ProductID) Is Nothing
End Function


Private Function FindProductID(ByVal ProductID As Integer) As DataRow
    Return Me.orderDetailsDataSet.Tables(0).Rows.Find(ProductID)
End Function
```

Visual C#

```csharp
[SqlMethod(IsMutator = true, OnNullCall=false)]
public void AddItem(int ProductID, short Quantity,
                    decimal UnitPrice, Single Discount) {
    if (this.FindProductID(ProductID) != null)
        throw new ArgumentException("Order already contains this product");

    this.orderDetailsDataSet.Tables[0].Rows.Add(ProductID, Quantity,
                                                UnitPrice, Discount);
}


[SqlMethod(IsMutator = true, OnNullCall=false)]
public void RemoveItem(int ProductID) {
    DataRow row = this.FindProductID(ProductID);
    if (row == null)
        throw new ArgumentException("Order does not contain this product");

    row.Delete();
}


[SqlMethod(IsMutator = true)]
public void Clear() {
    this.orderDetailsDataSet.Clear();
}


[SqlMethod(IsMutator = true, OnNullCall=false)]
public void AddQuantity(int ProductID, short Quantity) {
    DataRow row = this.FindProductID(ProductID);
    if (row == null)
        throw new ArgumentException("Order does not contain this product");

    row["Quantity"] = (short)row["Quantity"] + Quantity;
}


[SqlMethod(OnNullCall=false)]
public bool ContainsProductID(int ProductID) {
    return (this.FindProductID(ProductID) != null);
}
```

```
private DataRow FindProductID(int ProductID) {
    return this.orderDetailsDataSet.Tables[0].Rows.Find(ProductID);
}
```

Exposing Properties

We can also expose properties on the type. Users might want to retrieve the total cost of the order or the total number of items ordered without having to retrieve the entire contents of the type by using a query such as the following:

```
SELECT OrderID, OrderDetailsColumn.ItemCount AS ItemCount,
       OrderDetails.OrderTotal As OrderTotal
    FROM Orders WHERE CustomerID = 'ALFKI'
```

Creating properties that return the appropriate values for *ItemCount* and *OrderTotal* properties is relatively straightforward because the line items are stored in a *DataSet*. Even though SQL CLR properties are used like normal .NET properties in the T-SQL query, you must use the *SqlMethod* attribute in the property getters and/or setters to expose them through the SQL CLR. The code uses the IsDeterministic attribute, which we'll discuss shortly.

Visual Basic

```
Public ReadOnly Property ItemCount() As SqlInt32
    <SqlMethod(IsDeterministic:=True)> _
    Get
        If Me.IsNull Then
            Return SqlInt32.Null
        Else
            Dim tbl As DataTable = Me.orderDetailsDataSet.Tables(0)
            Return New SqlInt32(tbl.Select("", "", _
                                DataViewRowState.CurrentRows).Length)
        End If
    End Get
End Property

Public ReadOnly Property OrderTotal() As SqlMoney
    <SqlMethod(IsDeterministic:=True)> _
    Get
        If Me.IsNull Then Return SqlMoney.Null

        Dim tbl As DataTable = Me.orderDetailsDataSet.Tables(0)
        Dim total As Object = tbl.Compute("SUM(ItemTotal)", "")
        If total Is DBNull.Value Then
            Return SqlMoney.Null
        Else
            Return New SqlMoney(CDec(total))
        End If
    End Get
End Property
```

Visual C#

```
public SqlInt32 ItemCount {
    [SqlMethod(IsDeterministic = true)]
    get     {
```

```
        if (this.IsNull)
            return SqlInt32.Null;
        else {
            DataTable tbl = this.orderDetailsDataSet.Tables[0];
            return new SqlInt32(tbl.Select("", "",
                            DataViewRowState.CurrentRows).Length);
        }
    }
}

public SqlMoney OrderTotal {
    [SqlMethod(IsDeterministic = true)]
    get {
        if (this.IsNull) return SqlMoney.Null;

        DataTable tbl = this.orderDetailsDataSet.Tables[0];
        object total = tbl.Compute("SUM(ItemTotal)", "");
        if (total == DBNull.Value)
            return SqlMoney.Null;
        else
            return new SqlMoney((decimal)total);
    }
}
```

Deterministic Functions in the SQL CLR   SQL Server has no implicit knowledge of how SQL CLR functions generate the values they return. By default, SQL Server assumes that SQL CLR functions are not deterministic. If the function is called on the same value elsewhere in the query, rather than assume the function will return the same value, SQL Server calls the function again.

The *ItemCount* and *OrderTotal* properties are deterministic. Calling either function on an instance of an *OrderDetailsType* will return the same value until the contents of the *OrderDetailsType* changes. Marking the properties as deterministic allows SQL Server to perform optimizations in queries. Once you mark the properties as deterministic, you can use the properties to create persisted computed columns. You can then build indexes on those computed columns to improve the performance of your queries. Here are sample T-SQL queries you could use to build the computed columns and indexes:

```
ALTER TABLE Orders ADD
  ItemCount AS OrderDetailsColumn.ItemCount PERSISTED,
  OrderTotal AS OrderDetailsColumn.OrderTotal PERSISTED
CREATE INDEX IDX_Orders_ItemCount ON Orders (ItemCount)
CREATE INDEX IDX_Orders_OrderTotal ON Orders (OrderTotal)
```

Once you've defined these computed columns and indexes, you can refer to the *ItemCount* and *OrderTotal* properties on the *OrderDetailsColumn* as basic columns. Because the values are indexed, SQL Server can leverage those indexes to improve performance of queries such as the following one:

```
SELECT TOP 10 OrderID, OrderDate, ItemCount, OrderTotal
  FROM Orders
```

```
WHERE ItemCount BETWEEN 5 AND 10
ORDER BY OrderTotal DESC
```

Without these indexes, the preceding query would require a table scan, causing the query to run much more slowly.

Using Your User-Defined Type in a Client Application

We've covered a few examples of how you can use a SQL CLR user-defined type in T-SQL queries—how to create new instances of the type as well as how to access methods and properties of the type from a query—but we have not examined how to use the type from a client application.

You can also execute a query that returns a SQL CLR user-defined type in a query through a *SqlDataReader* or a *SqlDataAdapter*. If the SQL Client .NET Data Provider finds the assembly for the type registered in the global assembly cache, it will make the contents of the column available as instances of the type. From there, you simply access the contents of the column using the .NET type from within your code. Your code would look something like this:

Visual Basic

```
Dim strConn, strSQL, strOutputFormat As String
strConn = "Data Source=.\SQLExpress;" & _
          "Initial Catalog=Northwind;Integrated Security=True;"
strSQL = "SELECT OrderDate, OrderDetailsColumn FROM Orders " & _
         "  WHERE OrderID = @OrderID"
strOutputFormat = "Order {0} placed on {1:d} contains {2} line items, " & _
                  "with a total cost of {3:c}"
Using cn As New SqlConnection(strConn)
    Dim cmd As New SqlCommand(strSQL, cn))
    cmd.Parameters.AddWithValue("@OrderID", 10248)
    cn.Open()
    Using rdr As SqlDataReader = cmd.ExecuteReader()
        If rdr.Read() Then
            Dim orderID As Integer = rdr.GetInt32(0)
            Dim orderDate As DateTime = rdr.GetDateTime(1)
            Dim orderDetails As OrderDetailsColumn
            orderDetails = DirectCast(rdr.GetValue(2), OrderDetailsColumn)
            Console.WriteLine(strOutputFormat, orderID, orderDate, _
                             orderDetails.ItemCount, _
                             orderDetails.OrderTotal);
        End If
        rdr.Close()
        cn.Close()
    End Using
End Using
```

Visual C#

```
string strConn, strSQL, strOutputFormat;
strConn = @"Data Source=.\SQLExpress;" +
          "Initial Catalog=Northwind;Integrated Security=True;";
```

```
strSQL = "SELECT OrderDate, OrderDetailsColumn FROM Orders " +
         "  WHERE OrderID = @OrderID";
strOutputFormat = "Order {0} placed on {1:d} contains {2} line items, " +
                  "with a total cost of {3:c}";
using (SqlConnection cn = new SqlConnection(strConn)) {
    SqlCommand cmd = new SqlCommand(strSQL, cn))
    cmd.Parameters.AddWithValue("@OrderID", 10248);
    cn.Open();
    using (SqlDataReader rdr = cmd.ExecuteReader()) {
        if (rdr.Read()) {
            OrderID orderID = rdr.GetInt32(0);
            DateTime orderDate = rdr.GetDateTime(1);
            OrderDetailsType orderDetails;
            orderDetails = (OrderDetailsType) rdr.GetValue(2);
            Console.WriteLine(strOutputFormat, orderID, orderDate,
                              orderDetails.ItemCount,
                              orderDetails.OrderTotal);
        }
        rdr.Close();
        cn.Close();
    }
}
```

Think about that for a second. You can construct your own user-defined types in .NET code and use those types in a consistent fashion through T-SQL queries, .NET code running in a SQL CLR stored procedure, and .NET code running in your client applications. Powerful stuff.

Now that you've seen how to use your user-defined type in a .NET client application, let's take a look at a couple common client scenarios and how we can support those scenarios in the user-defined type.

Change Tracking

In Chapter 6, you saw that you can modify the contents of a *DataSet* and the *DataSet* will track those changes. You can modify the contents of the *DataSet* and later decide to accept or reject those changes. You can also check the state of an individual *DataRow* to determine whether the contents of the row contain a pending change. The *DataSet* accomplishes this by maintaining "original" copies of the values in the *DataRow* and either discarding those values or reverting to those values, depending on whether you call the *AcceptChanges* or *RejectChanges* method on the *DataRow* or *DataSet*.

The *DataSet* will not maintain a copy of the original value of a user-defined type such as the *OrderDetailsType* we've created, and it has no mechanism for determining whether an instance of the type has changed since the last call to the *AcceptChanges* method on the *DataRow*. However, we can help the *DataSet* provide this functionality by implementing the *IChangeTracking* and *IRevertibleChangeTracking* interfaces. The *IChangeTracking* interface exposes an *IsChanged* property and an *AcceptChanges* method. The *IRevertibleChangeTracking* interface derives from the *IChangeTracking* interface and adds a *RejectChanges* method. Each of these interfaces resides in the *System.ComponentModel* namespace.

Implementing these interfaces in the *OrderDetailsType* is simple. Because the type maintains its state in a *DataSet*, we can handle the property and methods by using the corresponding features of the *DataSet* class:

Visual Basic

```vb
'Imports System.ComponentModel
ReadOnly Property IsChanged() As Boolean _
        Implements IChangeTracking.IsChanged
    Get
        If Me.IsNull Then
            Return False
        Else
            Return Me.orderDetailsDataSet.HasChanges
        End If
    End Get
End Property

Sub AcceptChanges() Implements IChangeTracking.AcceptChanges
    If Me.IsChanged Then Me.orderDetailsDataSet.AcceptChanges()
End Sub

Sub RejectChanges() Implements IRevertibleChangeTracking.RejectChanges
    If Me.IsChanged Then Me.orderDetailsDataSet.RejectChanges()
End Sub
```

Visual C#

```csharp
//using System.ComponentModel;
bool IChangeTracking.IsChanged {
    get {
        if (this.orderDetailsDataSet == null)
            return false;
        else
            return this.orderDetailsDataSet.HasChanges();
    }
}

void IChangeTracking.AcceptChanges() {
    if (((IChangeTracking) this).IsChanged)
        this.orderDetailsDataSet.AcceptChanges();
}

void IRevertibleChangeTracking.RejectChanges() {
    if (((IChangeTracking)this).IsChanged)
        this.orderDetailsDataSet.RejectChanges();
}
```

XML Serialization

To write the contents of a *DataSet* to a file or serialize the *DataSet* through a WebService, the *DataSet* must be able to serialize the type used to store each *DataColumn*'s contents. If the *DataSet* does not inherently know how to serialize the type of a *DataColumn*, it will check to see whether that type implements the *IXmlSerializable* interface, which resides in the *System.Xml.Serialization* namespace. The *IXmlSerializable* interface exposes a *GetSchema* method that returns the schema for the type as an *XmlSchema* object, as well as *WriteSchema* and *ReadSchema* methods that write the contents of the type to and read the contents of the type from an *XmlWriter* and an *XmlReader*, respectively.

Because our *OrderDetailsType* stores the contents of an instance of the type in a *DataSet*, which also implements *IXmlSerializable*, we can rely on the *DataSet*'s implementation of these methods, as shown here:

Visual Basic

```
'Imports System.Xml
'Imports System.Xml.Schema
'Imports System.Xml.Serialization
Function GetSchema() As XmlSchema Implements IXmlSerializable.GetSchema
    Return DirectCast(Me.orderDetailsDataSet, IXmlSerializable).GetSchema()
End Function

Sub ReadXml(ByVal reader As XmlReader) Implements IXmlSerializable.ReadXml
    Me.orderDetailsDataSet.ReadXml(reader)
End Sub

Sub WriteXml(ByVal writer As XmlWriter) Implements IXmlSerializable.WriteXml
    Me.orderDetailsDataSet.WriteXml(writer)
End Sub
```

Visual C#

```
//using System.Xml;
//using System.Xml.Schema;
//using System.Xml.Serialization;
XmlSchema IXmlSerializable.GetSchema() {
    return ((IXmlSerializable) this.orderDetailsDataSet).GetSchema();
}

void IXmlSerializable.ReadXml(XmlReader reader) {
    this.orderDetailsDataSet.ReadXml(reader);
}

void IXmlSerializable.WriteXml(XmlWriter writer) {
    this.orderDetailsDataSet.WriteXml(writer);
}
```

Congratulations, we now have a robust user-defined type that we can leverage within a SQL Server database, as well as within .NET client applications.

Summary

You've now seen examples of SQL CLR functions, stored procedures, and user-defined types. The examples are fairly straightforward, but I hope they serve to clearly demonstrate that you can now leverage your .NET expertise to extend the power of your SQL Server 2005 database.

Questions That Should Be Asked More Frequently

Q   Given a scenario that could be solved with either T-SQL or the SQL CLR, how should I determine which to use?

A   The best advice I can offer is this: when in doubt, write some proof-of-concept code, test it in an environment that will approximate the desired scenario, and see what happens. Take the prime-number-generating stored procedure as an example. For small sets of numbers, I expected that the two approaches would yield similar performance numbers and that the overhead of switching to the SQL CLR would be roughly equivalent to the overhead of creating the temporary table. For larger sets of numbers, I expected that the SQL CLR could would be more efficient. I further expected that as the size of the set of numbers grew, the SQL CLR code would outperform the T-SQL code by a larger and larger factor. In short, I was wrong. When in doubt, write a proof-of-concept test and check the results.

For the sake of argument, let's assume that the T-SQL and SQL CLR solutions to the scenario are equally efficient. Two additional factors to keep in mind are the developer's skill set and maintainability of the code. You might find that matching the developer's skill sets and keeping that code easy to maintain outweighs a (relatively small) performance hit.

Is the person who is going to solve the problem a .NET guru but a T-SQL novice, or vice versa? Consider the stored procedures we created earlier in the chapter to generate prime numbers. There might be more efficient ways to construct those functions in .NET or T-SQL. I continually tweaked the code and improved the performance of both solutions, but I have no doubt that further improvements could save a few cycles in each approach. Perhaps there's a solution to one approach that's vastly superior to the one I created that skewed my results. In some ways, that's irrelevant. Given my knowledge, the SQL CLR stored procedure was the more efficient one.

Who will maintain the code if or when the developer leaves? Let's say that you work at a large company and you need a prime-number-generating stored procedure like the one described. Slightly cocky developers might say that they could build a T-SQL stored procedure that greatly outperforms even the most efficient SQL CLR version of the same stored procedure. Even if the developers are right and your company relies on the extremely efficient T-SQL stored procedure, what happens if you need to modify the stored procedure to accept a minimum value as well as a maximum value but the developers who have that expertise have left the company? Do you have other developers on your team who can make sense of the T-SQL stored procedure and make the appropriate changes?

> **Note**   T-SQL gurus, take no offense. The same questions could be raised with a SQL CLR stored procedure.

Q   How can I access the assembly for a SQL CLR type that's registered on my SQL Server machine if it's not already installed on my target client machine?

A   This information is not available directly through Visual Studio Server Explorer or through the schemas supported by SqlConnection.GetSchema. However, you can retrieve this information by querying SQL Server's system tables. The following query returns the assembly name and the contents of the assembly based on the classname supplied via the @ClassName parameter:

```
SELECT types.assembly_class AS udt_name,
       assemblies.name AS assembly_name,
       files.content AS file_contents
   FROM sys.assemblies AS assemblies
   JOIN sys.assembly_types AS types
     ON assemblies.assembly_id = types.assembly_id
   JOIN sys.assembly_files AS files
     ON assemblies.assembly_id = files.assembly_id AND
        assemblies.name = files.name
      WHERE types.assembly_class = @ClassName
```

You can use this query to write the contents of the assembly to a local file based on the assembly name using the following code:

Visual Basic

```
'Imports System.IO
Dim strConn, strSQL As String
strConn = "Data Source=.\SQLExpress;Initial Catalog=Northwind;" & _
          "Integrated Security=True;"
strSQL = "SELECT types.assembly_class AS udt_name, " & _
         "       assemblies.name AS assembly_name, " & _
         "       files.content AS file_contents " & _
         "    FROM sys.assemblies AS assemblies " & _
         "    JOIN sys.assembly_types AS types " & _
         "      ON assemblies.assembly_id = types.assembly_id " & _
         "    JOIN sys.assembly_files AS files " & _
         "      ON assemblies.assembly_id = files.assembly_id AND " & _
         "         assemblies.name = files.name " & _
         "       WHERE types.assembly_class = @ClassName"

Dim cn As New SqlConnection(strConn)
cn.Open()
Dim cmd As New SqlCommand(strSQL, cn)
cmd.Parameters.AddWithValue("@ClassName", "OrderDetailsType")
Dim rdr As SqlDataReader = cmd.ExecuteReader()
If Not rdr.Read() Then
    'Type not found!
    Return
End If
Dim buffersize As Integer = 8912
Dim buffer(buffersize) As Byte
Dim bytesreturned As Long = -1
Dim fieldoffset As Long = 0
Dim filename As String = String.Format("C:\{0}.dll", rdr.GetString(1))
Dim file As New FileStream(filename, FileMode.Create)
Do While bytesreturned <> 0
    bytesreturned = rdr.GetBytes(2, fieldoffset, buffer, 0, buffersize)
    fieldoffset += bytesreturned
```

```
            file.Write(buffer, 0, CInt(bytesreturned))
Loop


'Cleanup
file.Flush()
file.Close()
rdr.Close()
cn.Close()
```

Visual C#

```csharp
//using System.IO;
string strConn, strSQL;
strConn = @"Data Source=.\SQLExpress;Initial Catalog=Northwind;" +
          "Integrated Security=True;";
strSQL = "SELECT types.assembly_class AS udt_name, " +
         "       assemblies.name AS assembly_name, " +
         "       files.content AS file_contents " +
         "   FROM sys.assemblies AS assemblies " +
         "   JOIN sys.assembly_types AS types " +
         "     ON assemblies.assembly_id = types.assembly_id " +
         "   JOIN sys.assembly_files AS files " +
         "     ON assemblies.assembly_id = files.assembly_id AND " +
         "        assemblies.name = files.name " +
         "   WHERE types.assembly_class = @ClassName";

SqlConnection cn = new SqlConnection(strConn);
cn.Open();
SqlCommand cmd = new SqlCommand(strSQL, cn);
cmd.Parameters.AddWithValue("@ClassName", "OrderDetailsType");
SqlDataReader rdr = cmd.ExecuteReader();
if (!rdr.Read())
{
    //Type not found!
    return;
}
int buffersize = 8912;
byte[] buffer = new byte[buffersize];
long bytesreturned = -1;
long fieldoffset = 0;
string filename = string.Format(@"C:\{0}.dll", rdr.GetString(1));
FileStream file = new FileStream(filename, FileMode.Create);
while (bytesreturned != 0)
{
    bytesreturned = rdr.GetBytes(2, fieldoffset, buffer, 0, buffersize);
    fieldoffset += bytesreturned;
    file.Write(buffer, 0, (int)bytesreturned);
}

//Cleanup
file.Flush();
file.Close();
rdr.Close();
cn.Close();
```

Part V
Appendixes

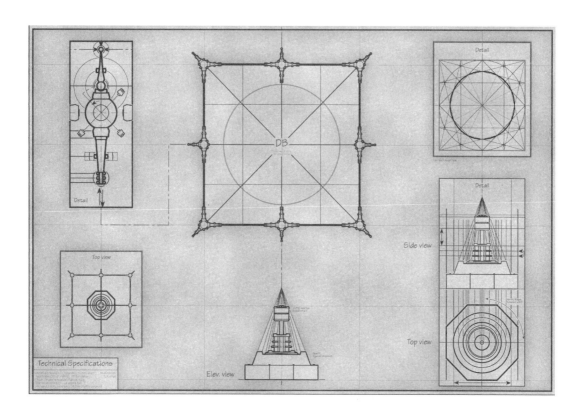

Appendix A
Using Other .NET Data Providers

The chapters in this book focus primarily on using ADO.NET to connect to Microsoft SQL Server databases using *SqlClient*–the .NET data provider designed specifically to communicate with SQL Server databases. Version 2.0 of the .NET Framework includes three other .NET data providers. Developers working with Oracle databases can use *OracleClient*, which is the Microsoft .NET data provider designed to communicate with Oracle databases. There's also a .NET data provider that can interact with databases through an ODBC driver, and a .NET data provider that can interact with databases through an OLE DB provider.

ADO.NET 2.0 introduces a new starting point for interacting with various .NET data providers– the *DbProviderFactories* class–as well as a set of base classes that is shared by all .NET data providers that have been updated to the ADO.NET 2.0 model. This appendix will start by covering this new set of common features and then cover the three .NET data providers previously described.

The .NET data providers that are referenced in the machine.config file should also be added to the .NET global assembly cache (GAC) so that they are available via the provider factory model. For .NET data providers that are not available in machine.config, you can manually add an entry to the application's configuration file and include that .NET data provider's assembly in the application's path.

> **Note** At the time of this writing, installing the SQL Server Mobile provider adds an entry to machine.config but does not register the assembly in the GAC, causing attempts to load the SQL Server Mobile provider via *GetFactory* to fail. You can work around this behavior by either manually adding the SQL Server Mobile provider to the GAC or including it in your application's path.

The Provider Factory Model

ADO.NET 2.0 introduces a provider factory model, as well as common base classes (*DbConnection*, *DbCommand*, and so on) for the various ADO.NET classes. Before we take a closer look at the new features, let's take a brief look at why the interfaces (*IDbConnection*, *IDbCommand*, and so on) that were already available in ADO.NET version 1.0 left room for improvement.

Limitations of the ADO.NET Common Interfaces

Each *Connection* class (*SqlConnection*, *OracleConnection*, and so on) in the initial releases of ADO.NET implemented a common interface—*IDbConnection*. You could cast any *Connection* class to the *IDbConnection* interface and perform common tasks (such as setting the *Connection-String* property or opening or closing the connection by calling the *Open* or *Close* methods, respectively) without having to know the exact *Connection* class you were using. ADO.NET 1.0 included interfaces for many classes—*IDbCommand*, *IDbDataAdapter*, *IDataParameter*, *IDataReader*, and so on. Although these interfaces were helpful in many scenarios, there are three major limitations with this approach.

Interfaces Aren't Easily Extensible

In version 1.0 of the .NET Framework, there was no way to determine whether a *DataReader* object contained rows prior to calling the *Read* method. Many ASP.NET developers wanted to handle a query that returned no rows as a special case. Calling the *Read* method to determine whether the query returned rows caused problems when binding ASP.NET controls to the *DataReader*, causing the first row of data (if one was returned) not to appear in the bound controls.

Microsoft addressed this scenario by adding a *HasRows* property to each *DataReader* class in version 1.1 of the .NET Framework. However, there was no way to check this property without knowing which .NET data provider you were using. Each *DataReader* class implements the *IDataReader* interface, which was introduced in .NET 1.0, but the *HasRows* property was not added to the interface in .NET 1.1. Why not? Interfaces aren't easily extensible because there's no way to offer a default implementation of new features. There isn't even a way to have the new feature do something as simple as throw a *NotImplementedException*.

The only way to extend an interface-based model like this is to introduce new interfaces each time you want to introduce a new feature to the common model. Early builds of version 1.1 of the .NET Framework included an *IDataReader2* interface. Microsoft removed the *IDataReader2* interface prior to releasing version 1.1 of the .NET Framework. Had Microsoft continued with this approach, the development team would currently be planning what properties and methods to expose on the *IDataReader4* interface for the next version of the .NET Framework.

ADO.NET 1.1 Does Not Provide a Way to Create Instances of Some Classes

Once you have an instance of a *Connection* class, you can cast it to the *IDbConnection* interface and still create an instance of the .NET data provider's *Command* class by calling the *Create-Command* method. Similarly, you can create *Parameter* objects by calling the *CreateParameter* method offered by the *IDbCommand* interface.

However, there is no provider-agnostic way to create instances of *Connection*, *DataAdapter*, or *CommandBuilder* classes in ADO.NET 1.1.

ADO.NET 1.1 Offers No Way to Determine the Available .NET Data Providers

Although previous data access technologies such as ODBC and OLE DB provided ways to programmatically access the available ODBC drivers and OLE DB providers, ADO.NET 1.1 does not offer any way to determine what .NET data providers are available.

How the Provider Factory Model Addresses Previous Limitations

Now let's look at how the provider factory and abstract base classes introduced in ADO.NET 2.0 address these limitations in ADO.NET 1.0.

Extending the ADO.NET Model via Abstract Base Classes

Although the ADO.NET 1.0 interfaces still exist in ADO.NET 2.0, the ADO.NET 2.0 object model follows a slightly different approach—abstract base classes. Each *Connection* class in ADO.NET 2.0 derives from the *DbConnection* abstract base class.

Abstract base classes provide a more extensible way to add functionality to common object models in future releases. For example, let's assume that Microsoft wants all *Connection* classes to expose a *VerifyIsStillAlive* method that you can call to see whether the connection is still alive. Microsoft could add a default implementation to the *DbConnection* class and allow .NET data providers to override that implementation if they so choose.

Using the *DbProviderFactory* Class to Create Objects

ADO.NET 2.0 allows you to create instances of all ADO.NET classes (with two minor exceptions, which we'll cover shortly) through the *DbProviderFactory* class. The name of the *DbProviderFactory* class might remind some developers of the factory pattern, a commonly used pattern in various application frameworks. Once you obtain a reference to a factory object, you use that object to create instances of other classes.

Each .NET data provider that supports the ADO.NET 2.0 model includes a factory class that allows you to create instances of other classes. Once you have accessed the factory class for your .NET data provider, you can create instances of the other classes (*Connection*, *Command*,

DataAdapter, and so on) using the factory class without having to know which .NET data provider you're using.

> **Note** You cannot use a *DbProviderFactory* object to create instances of *DbDataReader* or *DbTransaction* classes. However, you can still create instances of these classes using the provider factory model by calling methods on other classes. You can create *DbDataReader* objects by calling the *ExecuteReader* method on a *DbCommand* object. Similarly, you can create *DbTransaction* objects by calling the *BeginTransaction* method on a *DbConnection* object.

For example, the following code sample creates a *SqlDataAdapter* object (as well as other related objects along the way) to fill a *DataTable* with the results of a query:

Visual Basic

```
Dim strConn As String
strConn = "Data Source=.\SQLExpress;" & _
          "Initial Catalog=Northwind;Integrated Security=True;"

'Use the SqlClient provider's shared DbProviderFactory object
Dim fact As DbProviderFactory = SqlClientFactory.Instance

'Create a Connection object and set its ConnectionString property
Dim cn As DbConnection = fact.CreateConnection()
cn.ConnectionString = strConn

'Create a Command object, associate it with the Connection object
'and set its CommandText property
Dim cmd As DbCommand = fact.CreateCommand()
cmd.Connection = cn
cmd.CommandText = strSQL

'Create a DataAdapter object, set its SelectCommand property
Dim da As DbDataAdapter = fact.CreateDataAdapter()
da.SelectCommand = cmd

'Use the DataAdapter object to fill a DataTable
Dim tbl As New DataTable()
da.Fill(tbl)
```

Visual C#

```
string strConn, strSQL;
strConn = @"Data Source=.\SQLExpress;" +
          "Initial Catalog=Northwind;Integrated Security=True;";
strSQL = "SELECT CustomerID, CompanyName FROM Customers";

//Use the SqlClient provider's static DbProviderFactory object
DbProviderFactory fact = SqlClientFactory.Instance;

//Create a Connection object and set its ConnectionString property
DbConnection cn = fact.CreateConnection();
cn.ConnectionString = strConn;

//Create a Command object, associate it with the Connection object
```

```
//and set its CommandText property
DbCommand cmd = fact.CreateCommand();
cmd.Connection = cn;
cmd.CommandText = strSQL;

//Create a DataAdapter object, set its SelectCommand property
DbDataAdapter da = fact.CreateDataAdapter();
da.SelectCommand = cmd;

//Use the DataAdapter object to fill a DataTable
DataTable tbl = new DataTable();
da.Fill(tbl);
```

The only reference to the *SqlClient* .NET data provider is in the line of code that accesses the provider's factory object. Apart from that line of code, this example is provider agnostic.

Once you have your provider factory object, you can call the various *Create* methods the class *DbProviderFactory* class exposes to create *Connections*, *ConnectionStringBuilders*, *Commands*, *DataAdapters*, *Parameters*, and *CommandBuilders*. You might also be able to create data source enumerators—objects that allow you to list the available data sources—if the *CanCreateData-SourceEnumerator* property returns *True*.

Accessing Provider Factories   There are three ways to access provider factory objects using ADO.NET. If you know which .NET data provider you want to use as you're writing your code, call the static *Instance* property on the desired provider factory class, as shown in the preceding code sample. The provider factory class for each .NET data provider that's included in version 2.0 of the .NET Framework exposes a static *Instance* property that you can use.

If you don't know which .NET data provider you want to access as you're writing your code, you can still access the provider factory class for the desired provider given its provider invariant name. For the .NET data providers that are included with version 2.0 of the .NET Framework, the provider invariant name is the provider's namespace—*System.Data.SqlClient*, *System.Data.OracleClient*, *System.Data.Odbc*, or *System.Data.OleDb*. Simply call the static *Get-Factory* method on the *DbProviderFactories* class, and supply the provider invariant name, as shown in the following code:

Visual Basic

```
Dim fact As DbProviderFactory
fact = DbProviderFactories.GetFactory("System.Data.SqlClient")
'is equivalent to
fact = SqlClientFactory.Instance
```

Visual C#

```
DbProviderFactory fact;
fact = DbProviderFactories.GetFactory("System.Data.SqlClient");
//is equivalent to
fact = SqlClientFactory.Instance;
```

You might have noticed that the *GetFactory* method is overloaded. There's a third way to access a .NET data provider's provider factory, which we'll cover shortly.

Discovering Available .NET Data Providers

The *DbProviderFactories* class used in the previous code sample also serves as a discoverability mechanism, allowing you to discover the .NET data providers available via the *GetFactory* method. The *DbProviderFactories* class exposes a static *GetFactoryClasses* method. The method name is slightly misleading, implying that the method returns a collection of provider classes. In fact, the method returns a *DataTable* that contains information about the various provider factory classes.

Once you've called the *GetFactoryClasses* method, you can display information about the various factory classes by accessing the various *DataRows* available through the *DataTable*. The *DataTable* includes *DataColumns* that describe the name of the provider, its description, its invariant name, and the assembly-qualified name of the factory class. You can write this information to the Console window using the following code:

Visual Basic
```
Dim tbl As DataTable = DbProviderFactories.GetFactoryClasses()
For Each row As DataRow In tbl.Rows
    Console.WriteLine("Name = {0}", row("Name"))
    Console.WriteLine("Description = {0}", row("Description"))
    Console.WriteLine("InvariantName = {0}", row("InvariantName"))
    Console.WriteLine("AssemblyQualifiedName = {0}", _
                    row("AssemblyQualifiedName"))
    Console.WriteLine()
Next row
```

Visual C#
```
DataTable tbl = DbProviderFactories.GetFactoryClasses();
foreach (DataRow row in tbl.Rows) {
    Console.WriteLine("Name = {0}", row["Name"]);
    Console.WriteLine("Description = {0}", row["Description"]);
    Console.WriteLine("InvariantName = {0}", row["InvariantName"]);
    Console.WriteLine("AssemblyQualifiedName = {0}",
                    row["AssemblyQualifiedName"]);
    Console.WriteLine()
}
```

If you want to allow the user to select the desired .NET data provider to use, you could use the information returned by the *GetFactoryClasses* method to display information about the available providers. Once the user selects the desired provider, you can use the *DataRow* for that provider to access the corresponding factory class for the provider by passing the *DataRow* to the *GetFactory* method. The following code example uses the *GetFactory* method to access the factory class for each provider described via the *GetFactoryClasses* method:

Visual Basic
```
For Each row As DataRow In DbProviderFactories.GetFactoryClasses().Rows
    Dim name As String = CStr(row("InvariantName"))
    Dim fact As DbProviderFactory = DbProviderFactories.GetFactory(name)
    Console.WriteLine("  {0} - {1}", name, fact.GetType().Name)
Next row
```

Visual C#

```
foreach (DataRow row in DbProviderFactories.GetFactoryClasses().Rows) {
    string name = (string) row["InvariantName"];
    DbProviderFactory fact = DbProviderFactories.GetFactory(name);
    Console.WriteLine(" {0} - {1}", name, fact.GetType().Name);
}
```

The *GetFactoryClasses* method might not return information about all .NET data providers installed on your machine. This method examines only the contents of the *DbProviderFactories* element in the system.data section of the application's configuration.

The machine.config file that's installed with version 2.0 of the .NET Framework contains the following information in the system.data section:

```
<system.data>
  <DbProviderFactories>
    <add name="Odbc Data Provider" invariant="System.Data.Odbc"
        description=".Net Framework Data Provider for Odbc"
        type="System.Data.Odbc.OdbcFactory, System.Data,
            Version=2.0.0.0, Culture=neutral,
            PublicKeyToken=b77a5c561934e089"/>
    <add name="OleDb Data Provider" invariant="System.Data.OleDb"
        description=".Net Framework Data Provider for OleDb"
        type="System.Data.OleDb.OleDbFactory, System.Data,
            Version=2.0.0.0, Culture=neutral,
            PublicKeyToken=b77a5c561934e089"/>
    <add name="OracleClient Data Provider"
        invariant="System.Data.OracleClient"
        description=".Net Framework Data Provider for Oracle"
        type="System.Data.OracleClient.OracleClientFactory,
            System.Data.OracleClient, Version=2.0.0.0,
            Culture=neutral, PublicKeyToken=b77a5c561934e089"/>
    <add name="SqlClient Data Provider" invariant="System.Data.SqlClient"
        description=".Net Framework Data Provider for SqlServer"
        type="System.Data.SqlClient.SqlClientFactory, System.Data,
            Version=2.0.0.0, Culture=neutral,
            PublicKeyToken=b77a5c561934e089"/>
  </DbProviderFactories>
</system.data>
```

There are no guarantees the entry for each of these .NET data providers will be available via your application's configuration. A developer could add the following entry to the application's configuration file to make the OLE DB .NET Data Provider unavailable via the *GetFactoryClasses* or *GetFactory* methods:

```
<system.data>
  <DbProviderFactories>
    <remove invariant="System.Data.OleDb"/>
  </DbProviderFactories>
</system.data>
```

There's also no requirement for a .NET data provider's installer to add entries to your computer's machine.config file. You might need to add entries to your computer's or application's configuration file if you want to access other .NET data providers using the *GetFactoryClasses* or *GetFactory* methods.

Provider Factory Model Limitations

Although the ADO.NET 2.0 provider factory model is a major step forward, it does have some limitations.

Many Query Constructs Are Database-Specific

Not all databases support the same query constructs. For example, you can use a TOP clause in a query against a SQL Server or Microsoft Office Access database to limit the number of rows returned by a query, but Oracle and other databases do not support the TOP clause. The provider factory model is not designed to help you generate database-agnostic queries.

Setting *CommandText* for Parameterized Queries Might Require Provider-Specific Code

Different .NET data providers support different parameter constructs in queries. For example, the .NET data providers for SQL Server and Oracle support named parameters, whereas the .NET data providers for ODBC and OLE DB support only parameter markers. If you want to construct a parameterized query that returns the value of the CompanyName column in the Customers row given a value for the CustomerID column, the value for the *CommandText* property will depend on the *Command* class you're using, as shown here:

- *SqlCommand.CommandText*

  ```
  SELECT CompanyName FROM Customers WHERE CustomerID = @CustomerID
  ```

- *OracleCommand.CommandText*

  ```
  SELECT CompanyName FROM Customers WHERE CustomerID = :CustomerID
  ```

- *OleDbCommand.CommandText* or *OdbcCommand.CommandText*

  ```
  SELECT CompanyName FROM Customers WHERE CustomerID = ?
  ```

The provider factory model *almost* helps you determine how to generate the value for the *CommandText* property If you look at the contents of the ParameterMarkerFormat column in the DataSourceInformation schema returned by a *Connection* object, you should be able to use this information to generate the appropriate string for the parameter using the *String* class's static *Format* method. The .NET data providers for ODBC and OLE DB report a parameter marker format of "?", whereas the .NET data provider for Oracle reports ":{0}". If you use the parameter marker format in code like the following:

```
String.Format(parameterMarkerFormat, "CustomerID")
```

you'll receive "?", "?", and ":CustomerID" for the .NET data providers for ODBC, OLE DB, and Oracle, respectively. Each value corresponds to the parameter marker that should appear in the *Command*'s *CommandText* property.

Unfortunately, the .NET data provider for SQL Server reports a parameter marker format of "{0}" instead of "@{0}". You can work around this behavior by *special casing* this provider in a function like the following:

Visual Basic

```
Function GetParameterMarkerFormat(ByVal providerInvariantName As String, _
                                  ByVal connectionString As String, _
                                  ByVal parameterName As String) As String
    If providerInvariantName.ToUpper() = "SYSTEM.DATA.SQLCLIENT" Then
        Return "@{0}"
    End If

    Dim fact As DbProviderFactory
    Dim tbl As DataTable
    fact = DbProviderFactories.GetFactory(providerInvariantName)
    Using cn As DbConnection = fact.CreateConnection()
        cn.ConnectionString = connectionString
        cn.Open()
        tbl = cn.GetSchema(DbMetaDataCollectionNames.DataSourceInformation)
        cn.Close()
        Return CStr(tbl.Rows(0)("ParameterMarkerFormat"))
    End Using
End Function
```

Visual C#

```
string GetParameterMarkerFormat(string providerInvariantName,
                                string connectionString,
                                string parameterName) {
    if (providerInvariantName.ToUpper() == "SYSTEM.DATA.SQLCLIENT")
        return "@{0}";

    DbProviderFactory fact;
    DataTable tbl;
    fact = DbProviderFactories.GetFactory(providerInvariantName);
    using (DbConnection cn = fact.CreateConnection()) {
        cn.ConnectionString = connectionString;
        cn.Open();
        tbl = cn.GetSchema(DbMetaDataCollectionNames.DataSourceInformation);
        cn.Close();
        return (string)tbl.Rows[0]["ParameterMarkerFormat"];
    }
}
```

Specifying Parameter Data Types Might Require Provider-Specific Code

If you construct your parameterized query using the common provider base classes (*DbConnection*, *DbCommand*, and so on), you might still need to use provider-specific code when setting the data types for your parameters.

There are two provider-agnostic ways to set the data type for a parameter. You can simply set the *Value* property and ask the parameter class to infer the appropriate data type based on the value supplied. You can also set the *DbType* property exposed by the *DbParameter* class. The *DbType* property accepts values from the *DbType* enumeration, which resides in the *system.Data* namespace, and it includes values for many .NET-specific data types (Boolean, DateTime, Int32, String, and so on).

The parameter class for each provider exposes a provider-specific type property that can be set to a provider-specific enumeration. In some cases, you'll need to explicitly set the provider-specific data type property. For example, if you want to use the *OracleClient* .NET data provider and return results through an Oracle REF cursor, you'll need to set the *OracleParameter* object's *OracleType* property to *OracleType.Cursor*.

You might find situations in which you're building a parameterized query and you're unsure what value to set for the provider-specific type property. In most cases, the parameter corresponds to a column in a table in your database. You can use ADO.NET to retrieve schema information about that column, using features described in Chapter 4 of this book. Use a *Command* whose *CommandText* references the desired column or columns. Pass *CommandBehavior.SchemaOnly* into the *ExecuteReader* method to retrieve schema information for the query without actually executing the query. Then use the resulting *DataReader* object's *GetSchemaTable* method to access a *DataTable* that contains detailed schema information for the columns in the query. You can then cast the contents of the ProviderType column to the provider-specific type enumeration.

Visual Basic

```
Dim strConn, strSQL As String
strConn = "Data Source=.\SQLExpress;" & _
        "Initial Catalog=Northwind;Integrated Security=True;"
strSQL = "SELECT * FROM [Order Details]"
Dim tbl As DataTable tbl
Using cn As New SqlConnection(strConn)
    Dim cmd As New SqlCommand(strSQL, cn)
    cn.Open()
    Using rdr As SqlDataReader = _
                cmd.ExecuteReader(CommandBehavior.SchemaOnly)
        tbl = rdr.GetSchemaTable()
        rdr.Close()
    End Using
    cn.Close()
End Using

For Each row As DataRow In tbl.Rows
    Console.WriteLine("{0}: SqlDbType.{1}", row("ColumnName"), _
                    CType(row("ProviderType"), SqlDbType))
Next row
```

Visual C#

```
string strConn, strSQL;
strConn = @"Data Source=.\SQLExpress;" +
        "Initial Catalog=Northwind;Integrated Security=True;";
strSQL = "SELECT * FROM [Order Details]";
DataTable tbl;
using (SqlConnection cn = new SqlConnection(strConn)) {
```

```
    SqlCommand cmd = new SqlCommand(strSQL, cn);
    cn.Open();
    using (SqlDataReader rdr =
                  cmd.ExecuteReader(CommandBehavior.SchemaOnly)) {
        tbl = rdr.GetSchemaTable();
        rdr.Close();
    }
    cn.Close();
}

foreach (DataRow row in tbl.Rows)
    Console.WriteLine("{0}: SqlDbType.{1}", row["ColumnName"],
                      (SqlDbType)row["ProviderType"]);
```

The resulting output will be:

```
OrderID: SqlDbType.Int
ProductID: SqlDbType.Int
UnitPrice: SqlDbType.Money
Quantity: SqlDbType.SmallInt
Discount: SqlDbType.Real
```

If you're not sure what .NET data provider you're using, you won't know what the type-specific property is on the parameter class or what the type-specific enumeration is. You can determine the property by using .NET Reflection and looking for the property that includes a *DbProviderSpecificTypeProperty* attribute. You can then determine the enumeration by checking the return type for that property. The following code uses this basic approach to print out the provider-specific type property on the *Parameter* class of each .NET data provider available via *DbProviderFactories.GetFactoryClasses*. The code also casts 5 to the provider-specific enumeration.

Visual Basic

```
Dim attribType As Type = GetType(DbProviderSpecificTypePropertyAttribute)
For Each row As DataRow In DbProviderFactories.GetFactoryClasses().Rows
    Console.WriteLine("  {0}", row("Name"))
    Dim fact As DbProviderFactory = DbProviderFactories.GetFactory(row)
    Dim param As DbParameter = fact.CreateParameter()
    Dim paramType As Type = param.GetType()

    Dim providerSpecificProperty As PropertyInfo = Nothing
    Dim providerSpecificEnum As Type
    For Each pi As PropertyInfo In paramType.GetProperties()
        If pi.GetCustomAttributes(attribType, True).Length <> 0 Then
            providerSpecificProperty = pi
            providerSpecificEnum = pi.PropertyType
            Exit For
        End If
    Next pi
    Console.WriteLine("    Provider-specific type property is {0}", _
                    providerSpecificProperty.Name)
    Console.WriteLine("    5 translates to {0}.{1}", _
                    providerSpecificEnum.Name, _
                    Enum.GetName(providerSpecificEnum, 5))
    Console.WriteLine()
Next row
```

Visual C#

```csharp
Type attribType = typeof(DbProviderSpecificTypePropertyAttribute);
foreach (DataRow row in DbProviderFactories.GetFactoryClasses().Rows) {
    Console.WriteLine("  {0}", row["Name"]);
    DbProviderFactory fact = DbProviderFactories.GetFactory(row);
    DbParameter param = fact.CreateParameter();
    Type paramType = param.GetType();

    PropertyInfo providerSpecificProperty = null;
    Type providerSpecificEnum = null;
    foreach (PropertyInfo pi in paramType.GetProperties())
        if (pi.GetCustomAttributes(attribType, true).Length != 0) {
            providerSpecificProperty = pi;
            providerSpecificEnum = pi.PropertyType;
            break;
        }
    Console.WriteLine("    Provider-specific type property is {0}",
                    providerSpecificProperty.Name);
    Console.WriteLine("    5 translates to {0}.{1}",
                    providerSpecificEnum.Name,
                    Enum.GetName(providerSpecificEnum, 5));
    Console.WriteLine();
}
```

Database Schema Discoverability

In version 1.0 of ADO.NET, the only *Connection* class that offers database schema discoverability through its API is the *OleDbConnection* class. You can use the *GetOleDbSchemaTable* method to return tables that contained information about various schemas—tables, columns, indexes, and so on. You can also supply values to restrict the schema information returned—for example, to return only the columns for a particular table.

Each *Connection* class in ADO.NET 2.0 exposes a *GetSchema* method that you can use to query for schema information for that connection. Different *Connection* classes expose different schemas. For example, the *OracleConnection* exposes a Sequences schema that's not available through other *Connection* classes. Some schemas are available only on specific versions of a database. For example, a *SqlConnection* that's connected to a SQL Server 2005 database will expose a UserDefinedTypes schema, whereas a *SqlConnection* that's connected to a SQL Server 2000 database will not.

Querying for Available Schemas

You can determine the available schemas by calling the parameter-less *GetSchema* method. The contents of the first column (*CollectionName*) contain the list of names of the schemas that the *Connection* supports. You can then pass this schema name as a string into the *Connection* class's *GetSchema* method.

Filter the Data Returned by *GetSchema*

Let's say that the provider you're using lets you query for column information. There might be some cases in which you want to retrieve information about all columns available in the database. A more common scenario is to request column information for a single table in the database.

One of the overloaded *GetSchema* methods accepts an array of strings that serve as filters, or restrictions, on the query that the *Connection* object will execute to retrieve schema information. For example, the columns schema of the *OdbcConnection* accepts a string array with four elements that correspond to the table catalog, table schema, table name, and column name, respectively. Specifying *null* or *Nothing*, depending on your language of choice, for an entry in the array will cause the connection to ignore that entry when generating the filter for the schema.

The following code creates a string array that you could pass to the *GetSchema* method to retrieve just the columns in the Order Details table that resides in the Northwind Traders catalog and the dbo schema:

Visual Basic

```
filter = New String() {"Northwind", "dbo", "Order Details", Nothing}
```

Visual C#

```
filter = new string[] {"Northwind", "dbo", "Order Details", null};
```

We can use that filter and retrieve information about the columns available in the Order Details table using an *OdbcConnection* object using the following code:

Visual Basic

```
Dim filter As String()
filter = New String() {"Northwind", "dbo", "Order Details", Nothing}
Dim columnsTable As DataTable

Dim strConn As String = "Driver={SQL Server};Server=.\SQLExpress;" & _
                        "Database=Northwind;Trusted_Connection=Yes;"
Dim factory As DbProviderFactory = OdbcFactory.Instance
Using cn As DbConnection = factory.CreateConnection()
    cn.ConnectionString = strConn
    cn.Open()
    columnsTable = cn.GetSchema("Columns", filter)
    cn.Close()
End Using

For Each row As DataRow In columnsTable.Rows
    Console.WriteLine("  {0,-10} - {1}", row("COLUMN_NAME"), _
                      row("TYPE_NAME"))
Next row
```

Visual C#

```
string[] filter = new string[] {"Northwind", "dbo", "Order Details", null};
DataTable columnsTable;
```

```
string strConn = @"Driver={SQL Server};Server=.\SQLExpress;" +
                    "Database=Northwind;Trusted_Connection=Yes;";
DbProviderFactory factory = OdbcFactory.Instance;
using (DbConnection cn = factory.CreateConnection()) {
    cn.ConnectionString = strConn;
    cn.Open();
    columnsTable = cn.GetSchema("Columns", filter);
    cn.Close();
}

foreach (DataRow row in columnsTable.Rows)
    Console.WriteLine("{0,-10}: {1}", row["COLUMN_NAME"],
                        row["TYPE_NAME"]);
```

The *GetSchema* method is definitely handy, but the question I expect most developers will ask is "How can I determine what the restriction array for a particular schema looks like?" The answer lies in . . . well, another schema.

There is a restrictions schema that returns *DataTable* information about the restrictions available on various schemas. You could add that *DataTable* of information, along with the *DataTable* of information about the schemas, into the same *DataSet*, and then construct a *DataRelation* to relate the data from the two *DataTable* objects based on the column that's common between the two *DataTable* objects—*CollectionName*. You could then use that *DataRelation* to find the restrictions available for a given schema.

The following code sample accepts a provider name and a connection string, using this information to construct a *Connection* object using the *DbProviderFactories* class as a starting point. Next, the code retrieves information about the available schemas and restrictions. Then, using the pattern described earlier, the code displays information about the available schemas and restrictions:

Visual Basic

```
Sub ListSchemasAndRestrictions(ByVal providerName As String, _
                                ByVal connectionString As String)
    Dim schemasTable, restrictionsTable As DataTable
    Dim fact As DbProviderFactory
    fact = DbProviderFactories.GetFactory(providerName)
    Using cn As DbConnection = fact.CreateConnection()
        cn.ConnectionString = connectionString
        cn.Open()
        schemasTable = cn.GetSchema()
        restrictionsTable = cn.GetSchema("Restrictions")
        cn.Close()
    End Using

    Dim ds As New DataSet()
    schemasTable.TableName = "Schemas"
    restrictionsTable.TableName = "Restrictions"
    ds.Tables.AddRange(New DataTable() {schemasTable, restrictionsTable})
    Dim rel As DataRelation
    rel = ds.Relations.Add(schemasTable.Columns("CollectionName"), _
                            restrictionsTable.Columns("CollectionName"))
```

```
        For Each schemaRow As DataRow In schemasTable.Rows
            Console.WriteLine("{0} schema", schemaRow("CollectionName"))
            Dim restrictionRows As DataRow()
            restrictionRows = schemaRow.GetChildRows(rel)
            If restrictionRows.Length <> 0 Then
                Console.WriteLine("  Restrictions:")
                For Each restrictionRow As DataRow In restrictionRows
                    Console.WriteLine("    {0}: {1}", _
                                    restrictionRow("RestrictionNumber"), _
                                    restrictionRow("RestrictionName"))
                Next restrictionRow
            Else
                Console.WriteLine("  No restrictions")
            End If
            Console.WriteLine()
        Next schemaRow
    End Sub
```

Visual C#

```
void ListSchemasAndRestrictions (string providerName,
                                 string connectionString) {
    DataTable schemasTable, restrictionsTable;
    DbProviderFactory fact = DbProviderFactories.GetFactory(providerName);
    using (DbConnection cn = fact.CreateConnection()) {
        cn.ConnectionString = connectionString;
        cn.Open();
        schemasTable = cn.GetSchema();
        restrictionsTable = cn.GetSchema("Restrictions");
        cn.Close();
    }

    DataSet ds = new DataSet();
    schemasTable.TableName = "Schemas"
    restrictionsTable.TableName = "Restrictions"
    ds.Tables.AddRange(new DataTable[] {schemasTable, restrictionsTable});
    Dim rel As DataRelation
    rel = ds.Relations.Add(schemasTable.Columns("CollectionName"), _
                            restrictionsTable.Columns("CollectionName"))

    foreach (DataRow schemaRow in schemasTable.Rows) {
        Console.WriteLine("{0} schema", schemaRow["CollectionName"]);
        DataRow[] restrictionRows;
        restrictionRows = schemaRow.GetChildRows(rel);
        if (restrictionRows.Length != 0) {
            Console.WriteLine("  Restrictions:");
            foreach (DataRow restrictionRow in restrictionRows)
                Console.WriteLine("    {0}: {1}",
                                restrictionRow["RestrictionNumber"],
                                restrictionRow["RestrictionName"]);
        } else {
            Console.WriteLine("  No restrictions");
        }
        Console.WriteLine();
    }
}
```

The ODBC .NET Data Provider

ADO.NET includes a .NET data provider designed to communicate with databases using ODBC drivers: the ODBC .NET Data Provider. If you want to access a database that does not have its own .NET data provider (and you're not working with an Office Access database), you should use this .NET data provider.

The ODBC .NET Data Provider was not part of the initial release of the .NET Framework, but it was integrated into the .NET Framework as of version 1.1. You no longer need to download the provider separately, nor do you need to add a project reference to the assembly because the ODBC .NET Data Provider is integrated into System.Data.dll.

The code samples in this section assume that you've added a reference to the ODBC .NET Data Provider in your code module, using the construct for your language of choice (the *Imports* command for Visual Basic developers and the *using* command for Visual C# developers).

Connecting to Your Database Using an *OdbcConnection*

To connect to your database using the ODBC .NET Data Provider, you use the *OdbcConnection* class. You instantiate an *OdbcConnection* object, set its *ConnectionString* property (either explicitly or via the object's constructor), and call the object's *Open* method.

The following list shows a few examples of connection strings that you can use to connect to your database using the *OdbcConnection* object. For more information on how to connect to your database, see the documentation for the *OdbcConnection* class's *ConnectionString* property, as well as the documentation for your ODBC driver of choice.

- Connecting to a SQL Server database with a username and password:

```
Driver={SQL Server};Server=.\SQLExpress;
    Database=Northwind;UID=MyUserName;PWD=MyPassword;
```

- Connecting to a SQL Server database using a trusted connection:

```
Driver={SQL Server};Server=.\SQLExpress;
    Database=Northwind;Trusted_Connection=Yes;
```

- Connecting to a database using an ODBC data source name (DSN):

```
DSN=MyDataSource;
```

- Connecting to a database using an ODBC file DSN:

```
FileDSN=MyFileDataSource;
```

The following code sample connects to the Northwind database on the local instance of Microsoft SQL Express:

Visual Basic
```
Dim strConn As String
strConn = "Driver={SQL Server};Server=.\SQLExpress;" & _
        "Database=Northwind;Trusted_Connection=Yes;"
```

```
Using cn As New OdbcConnection(strConn)
    cn.Open()
    cn.Close()
End Using
```

Visual C#

```csharp
string strConn;
strConn = @"Driver={SQL Server};Server=.\SQLExpress;" +
            "Database=Northwind;Trusted_Connection=Yes;";
using (OdbcConnection cn = new OdbcConnection(strConn)) {
    cn.Open();
    cn.Close();
}
```

Executing Queries Using an *OdbcCommand*

As with all classes that derive from *DbCommand*, the *OdbcCommand* class offers an *ExecuteReader* method to return the results of a query as a *DataReader*. The *ExecuteReader* method accepts values from the *CommandBehavior* enumeration. You can also return a single value using the *ExecuteScalar* method, or execute a query without handling the results by calling the *ExecuteNonQuery* method.

The *OdbcCommand* class does not offer support for asynchronous query execution, nor does it offer the ability to retrieve values using provider-specific types such as *SqlTypes*.

Examining the Results of a Query Using an *OdbcDataReader*

You create *OdbcDataReaders* just like you create *DataReaders* using other providers—by calling the *OdbcCommand* object's *ExecuteReader* method, as shown in the following code:

Visual Basic

```vb
Dim strConn, strSQL As String
strConn = "Driver={SQL Server};Server=.\SQLExpress;" & _
            "Database=Northwind;Trusted_Connection=Yes;"
strSQL = "SELECT CustomerID, OrderID, OrderDate FROM Orders " & _
            "WHERE CustomerID = 'ALFKI' ORDER BY OrderDate"
Using cn As New OdbcConnection(strConn)
    Using cmd As New OdbcCommand(strSQL, cn)
        cn.Open()
        Using rdr As OdbcDataReader = cmd.ExecuteReader()
            Do While rdr.Read()
                Console.WriteLine("  {0} {1} {2:d}", rdr.GetString(0), _
                                    rdr.GetInt32(1), rdr.GetDateTime(2))
            Loop
            rdr.Close()
        End Using
        cn.Close()
    End Using
End Using
```

Visual C#

```csharp
string strConn, strSQL;
strConn = @"Driver={SQL Server};Server=.\SQLExpress;" +
          "Database=Northwind;Trusted_Connection=Yes;";
strSQL = "SELECT CustomerID, OrderID, OrderDate FROM Orders " +
         "WHERE CustomerID = 'ALFKI' ORDER BY OrderDate";
using (OdbcConnection cn = new OdbcConnection(strConn)) {
    using (OdbcCommand cmd = new OdbcCommand(strSQL, cn)) {
        cn.Open();
        using (OdbcDataReader rdr = cmd.ExecuteReader()) {
            while (rdr.Read())
                Console.WriteLine("  {0} {1} {2:d}", rdr.GetString(0),
                                  rdr.GetInt32(1), rdr.GetDateTime(2));
            rdr.Close();
        }
        cn.Close();
    }
}
```

Working with Parameterized Queries

The ODBC .NET Data Provider supports parameterized queries using positional parameters rather than parameter names. In your query string, you use the ? parameter marker to denote a parameter, and then you add a corresponding *OdbcParameter* object to the *OdbcCommand* object's *Parameters* collection.

Most developers provide meaningful values for the *Name* properties on their parameter objects. For example, they might set the *Name* property for an *OdbcParameter* that corresponds to the CustomerID column to "@CustomerID" or "pCustomerID." This practice is helpful because it simplifies the process of finding the desired entry in the parameters collection within your code. However, this practice has no effect on how the *OdbcCommand* matches entries in the parameters collection to the parameter markers in your query. The *OdbcCommand* will match the *OdbcParameters* to the parameter markers in the query based on their position rather than on their names.

The following code sample executes a parameterized query using the SQL Server ODBC driver:

Visual Basic

```vb
Dim strConn, strSQL As String
strConn = "Driver={SQL Server};Server=.\SQLExpress;" & _
          "Database=Northwind;Trusted_Connection=Yes;"
strSQL = "SELECT CustomerID, OrderID, OrderDate FROM Orders " & _
         "WHERE CustomerID = ? ORDER BY OrderDate"
Using cn As New OdbcConnection(strConn)
    Using cmd As New OdbcCommand(strSQL, cn)
        cmd.Parameters.AddWithValue("@CustomerID", "ALFKI")
        cn.Open()
        Using rdr As OdbcDataReader = cmd.ExecuteReader()
            Do While rdr.Read()
```

```
                        Console.WriteLine("  {0} {1} {2:d}", rdr.GetString(0), _
                                    rdr.GetInt32(1), rdr.GetDateTime(2))
            Loop
            rdr.Close()
        End Using
        cn.Close()
    End Using
End Using
```

Visual C#

```
string strConn, strSQL;
strConn = @"Driver={SQL Server};Server=.\SQLExpress;" +
        "Database=Northwind;Trusted_Connection=Yes;";
strSQL = "SELECT CustomerID, OrderID, OrderDate FROM Orders " +
        "WHERE CustomerID = ? ORDER BY OrderDate";
using (OdbcConnection cn = new OdbcConnection(strConn)) {
    using (OdbcCommand cmd = new OdbcCommand(strSQL, cn)) {
        cmd.Parameters.AddWithValue("@CustomerID", "ALFKI");
        cn.Open();
        using (OdbcDataReader rdr = cmd.ExecuteReader()) {
            while (rdr.Read())
                Console.WriteLine("  {0} {1} {2:d}", rdr.GetString(0),
                            rdr.GetInt32(1), rdr.GetDateTime(2));
            rdr.Close();
        }
        cn.Close();
    }
}
```

Calling a Stored Procedure

The *OdbcCommand* class does not support the *Table* or *StoredProcedure* values from the *CommandType* enumeration. If you want to call a stored procedure using the ODBC .NET Data Provider, you have to learn the ODBC CALL syntax. Thankfully, the syntax is simple. Here's an example:

```
{? = CALL MyStoredProc(?, ?, ?)}
```

You use the keyword *CALL* before the name of the stored procedure. If you want to supply parameters for the stored procedure call—regardless of whether they're input, output, or both—you use the ? parameter marker. You separate the parameter markers with commas and enclose the list of parameter markers in parentheses. If you want to trap for the return value, preface the *CALL* keyword with ? =, just as you would to retrieve the return value of a function call in your code. Finally, surround the entire query in curly braces.

> **Note**   You do not need to specify the direction of the parameters in the *CommandText* using a keyword such as *OUTPUT*. Instead, set the *Direction* property on the *OdbcParameter* objects appropriately.

The following code example demonstrates how to call a parameterized stored procedure using the ODBC .NET Data Provider:

Visual Basic

```
Dim strConn, strSQL As String
strConn = "Driver={SQL Server};Server=.\SQLExpress;" & _
          "Database=Northwind;Trusted_Connection=Yes;"
strSQL = "{CALL CustOrdersOrders(?)}"
Using cn As New OdbcConnection(strConn)
    Using cmd As New OdbcCommand(strSQL, cn)
        cmd.Parameters.AddWithValue("@CustomerID", "ALFKI")
        cn.Open()
        Using rdr As OdbcDataReader = cmd.ExecuteReader()
            Do While rdr.Read()
                Console.WriteLine("  {0} {1:d}", rdr.GetInt32(0), _
                                  rdr.GetDateTime(1))
            Loop
            rdr.Close()
        End Using
        cn.Close()
    End Using
End Using
```

Visual C#

```
string strConn, strSQL;
strConn = @"Driver={SQL Server};Server=.\SQLExpress;" +
          "Database=Northwind;Trusted_Connection=Yes;";
strSQL = "{CALL CustOrdersOrders(?)}";
using (OdbcConnection cn = new OdbcConnection(strConn)) {
    using (OdbcCommand cmd = new OdbcCommand(strSQL, cn)) {
        cmd.Parameters.AddWithValue("@CustomerID", "ALFKI");
        cn.Open();
        using (OdbcDataReader rdr = cmd.ExecuteReader()) {
            while (rdr.Read())
                Console.WriteLine("  {0} {1:d}", rdr.GetInt32(0),
                                  rdr.GetDateTime(1));
            rdr.Close();
        }
        cn.Close();
    }
}
```

Retrieving the Results of a Query Using an *OdbcDataAdapter*

If you want to retrieve the results of a query and store them in a *DataSet* or *DataTable* object, use the *Fill* method of the *OdbcDataAdapter* class:

Visual Basic

```
Dim strConn, strSQL As String
strConn = "Driver={SQL Server};Server=.\SQLExpress;" & _
          "Database=Northwind;Trusted_Connection=Yes;"
strSQL = "SELECT CustomerID, OrderID, OrderDate FROM Orders " & _
         "WHERE CustomerID = ? ORDER BY OrderDate"
```

```
Dim da As New OdbcDataAdapter(strSQL, strConn)
da.SelectCommand.Parameters.AddWithValue("@CustomerID", "ALFKI")
Dim tbl As New DataTable("Orders")
da.Fill(tbl)
For Each row As DataRow In tbl.Rows
    Console.WriteLine("  {0} {1} {2:d}", row("CustomerID"), _
                      row("OrderID"), row("OrderDate"))
Next row
```

Visual C#

```
string strConn, strSQL;
strConn = @"Driver={SQL Server};Server=.\SQLExpress;" +
          "Database=Northwind;Trusted_Connection=Yes;";
strSQL = "SELECT CustomerID, OrderID, OrderDate FROM Orders " +
         "WHERE CustomerID = ? ORDER BY OrderDate";
OdbcDataAdapter da = new OdbcDataAdapter(strSQL, strConn);
da.SelectCommand.Parameters.AddWithValue("@CustomerID", "ALFKI");
DataTable tbl = new DataTable("Orders");
da.Fill(tbl);
foreach (DataRow row in tbl.Rows)
    Console.WriteLine("  {0} {1} {2:d}", row["CustomerID"],
                      row["OrderID"], row["OrderDate"]);
```

Retrieving Database Schema Information

The *OdbcConnection* class supports the *GetSchema* methods that allow you to query your database for available schema information. The overloaded *GetSchema* methods behave like those of other .NET data providers.

Listing Schemas and Restrictions

Earlier in the appendix, we looked at how you can display the list of schemas and restrictions given a provider name and a connection string using the *DbProviderFactories* class as a starting point. If you know you're working with the ODBC .NET Data Provider, you can simplify that code slightly by using the *OdbcConnection* class as a starting point:

Visual Basic

```
Dim schemasTable, restrictionsTable As DataTable
Dim strConn As String = "Driver={SQL Server};Server=.\SQLExpress;" & _
                        "Database=Northwind;Trusted_Connection=Yes;"
Using cn As New OdbcConnection(strConn)
    cn.Open()
    schemasTable = cn.GetSchema()
    restrictionsTable = cn.GetSchema("Restrictions")
    cn.Close()
End Using

Dim ds As New DataSet()
schemasTable.TableName = "Schemas"
restrictionsTable.TableName = "Restrictions"
ds.Tables.AddRange(New DataTable() {schemasTable, restrictionsTable})
Dim rel As DataRelation
```

```vbnet
rel = ds.Relations.Add(schemasTable.Columns("CollectionName"), _
                       restrictionsTable.Columns("CollectionName"))

For Each schemaRow As DataRow In schemasTable.Rows
    Console.WriteLine("  {0} schema", schemaRow("CollectionName"))
    Dim restrictionRows As DataRow()
    restrictionRows = schemaRow.GetChildRows(rel)
    If restrictionRows.Length <> 0 Then
        Console.WriteLine("    Restrictions:")
        For Each restrictionRow As DataRow In restrictionRows
            Console.WriteLine("      {0}: {1}", _
                              restrictionRow("RestrictionNumber"), _
                              restrictionRow("RestrictionName"))
        Next restrictionRow
    Else
        Console.WriteLine("    No restrictions")
    End If
    Console.WriteLine()
Next schemaRow
```

Visual C#

```csharp
DataTable schemasTable, restrictionsTable;
string strConn = @"Driver={SQL Server};Server=.\SQLExpress;" +
                "Database=Northwind;Trusted_Connection=Yes;";
using (OdbcConnection cn = new OdbcConnection(strConn)) {
    cn.Open();
    schemasTable = cn.GetSchema();
    restrictionsTable = cn.GetSchema("Restrictions");
    cn.Close();
}

DataSet ds = new DataSet();
schemasTable.TableName = "Schemas";
restrictionsTable.TableName = "Restrictions";
ds.Tables.AddRange(new DataTable[] {schemasTable, restrictionsTable});
DataRelation rel;
rel = ds.Relations.Add(schemasTable.Columns["CollectionName"],
                       restrictionsTable.Columns["CollectionName"]);

foreach (DataRow schemaRow in schemasTable.Rows) {
    Console.WriteLine("{0} schema", schemaRow["CollectionName"]);
    DataRow[] restrictionRows = schemaRow.GetChildRows(rel);
    if (restrictionRows.Length != 0) {
        Console.WriteLine(" Restrictions:");
        foreach (DataRow restrictionRow in restrictionRows)
            Console.WriteLine("    {0}: {1}",
                              restrictionRow["RestrictionNumber"],
                              restrictionRow["RestrictionName"]);
    } else {
        Console.WriteLine(" No restrictions");
    }
    Console.WriteLine();
}
```

Returning Filtered Schema Information

The output from the preceding code sample indicates that the connection supports a Columns schema and that it also supports restrictions for table catalog, table schema, table name, and column name, respectively. So retrieving and displaying information about columns in a particular table is a snap. Just build a string array of the same length as described by the restrictions schema, supply values for the desired restrictions, omit the rest (using *null* or *Nothing*, depending on your language of choice), and pass that string array into the *GetSchema* method along with the name of the desired schema, "Columns", as demonstrated in the following code example:

Visual Basic

```
Dim filter As String()
filter = New String() {"Northwind", "dbo", "Order Details", Nothing}
Dim columnsTable As DataTable

Dim strConn As String = "Driver={SQL Server};Server=.\SQLExpress;" & _
                        "Database=Northwind;Trusted_Connection=Yes;"
Using cn As New OdbcConnection(strConn)
    cn.Open()
    columnsTable = cn.GetSchema("Columns", filter)
    cn.Close()
End Using

For Each row As DataRow In columnsTable.Rows
    Console.WriteLine("{0,-10} - {1}", row("COLUMN_NAME"), _
                      row("TYPE_NAME"))
Next row
```

Visual C#

```
string[] filter = new String[] {"Northwind", "dbo", "Order Details", null};
DataTable columnsTable;

string strConn = @"Driver={SQL Server};Server=.\SQLExpress;" +
                  "Database=Northwind;Trusted_Connection=Yes;";
using (OdbcConnection cn = new OdbcConnection(strConn)) {
    cn.Open();
    columnsTable = cn.GetSchema("Columns", filter);
    cn.Close();
}

foreach (DataRow row in columnsTable.Rows)
    Console.WriteLine("{0,-10} - {1}", row["COLUMN_NAME"],
                      row["TYPE_NAME"]);
```

The OLE DB .NET Data Provider

ADO.NET includes a .NET data provider designed to communicate with databases using OLE DB providers: the OLE DB .NET Data Provider. I recommend using this .NET data provider only if you're working with an Office Access database.

If there is a .NET data provider specifically designed for your database, you should use that .NET data provider instead because that provider will most likely outperform the OLE DB .NET Data Provider and offer more database-specific features. Using the OLE DB .NET Data Provider from your .NET code incurs a significant performance penalty because every time the OLE DB .NET Data Provider communicates with your OLE DB provider, it has to go through the COM interop layer.

I've been surprised (and pleased) at the number of .NET data providers available through database vendors (such as IBM, Oracle, and Sybase), independent software vendors (such as DataDirect), and open source projects. In fact, there has been a shift in the database connectivity components generated by these teams. .NET data providers and ODBC drivers are still being developed and improved, but OLE DB providers are no longer in vogue. The process of creating an OLE DB provider is extremely complex, and many developers have found that there's little payoff for that effort. ODBC is a simpler and better-documented technology. Plus, ODBC drivers can be used effectively from both ADO and ADO.NET.

In fact, I'd argue that there is only one OLE DB provider available today that should be used from ADO.NET—the Jet 4.0 OLE DB provider. At the time of this writing, there is no .NET data provider for Office Access databases, so using a database-specific .NET data provider is not an option. The Jet OLE DB provider is generally considered more reliable than the corresponding ODBC driver, plus version 4.0 of the OLE DB provider offers support for retrieving the last identity value generated on a connection.

The code samples up to this point have relied on the local SQL Express installation. For the sake of consistency, other than the connection string examples, the code examples for the OLE DB .NET Data Provider will rely on SQL Express as well, even though I recommend using this provider only in conjunction with the Jet OLE DB provider.

Connecting to Your Database Using an *OleDbConnection*

To connect to your database using the OLE DB .NET Data Provider, you use the *OleDbConnection* class. You instantiate an *OleDbConnection* object, set its *ConnectionString* property (either explicitly or via the object's constructor), and call the object's *Open* method.

Here are a few examples of connection strings that you can use to connect to your database using the *OleDbConnection* object. For more information on how to connect to your database, see the documentation for the *OleDbConnection* class's *ConnectionString* property, as well as the documentation for your OLE DB provider of choice.

■ Connecting to a SQL Server database with a username and password:

```
Provider=SQLOLEDB;Data Source=.\SQLExpress;
Initial Catalog=Northwind;User ID=MyUserName;Password=MyPassword;
```

■ Connecting to a SQL Server database using a trusted connection:

```
Provider=SQLOLEDB;Data Source=.\SQLExpress;
    Initial Catalog=Northwind;Integrated Security=SSPI;
```

- Connecting to an Office Access database:

```
Provider=Microsoft.Jet.OLEDB.4.0;Data Source=C:\Data\NWind.MDB;
```

- Connecting to an Office Access database with Office Access security:

```
Provider=Microsoft.Jet.OLEDB.4.0;Data Source=C:\Data\NWind.MDB;
    Jet OLEDB:System Database=C:\Data\System.mdw;
    User ID=MyUserName;Password=MyPassword;
```

- Connecting to an Office Access database with a password-protected database:

```
Provider=Microsoft.Jet.OLEDB.4.0;Data Source=C:\Data\NWind.MDB;
    Jet OLEDB:Database Password=MyPassword;
```

- Connecting to a database using an OLE DB Data Link File:

```
File Name=MyUDLFile.UDL;
```

> **Note**   There is no way to encrypt an OLE DB Data Link File. If you're using OLE DB from within a .NET application—and, if you're reading this portion of the appendix, that seems likely—Microsoft recommends storing the connection string in a .NET configuration file instead.

The following code sample connects to the Northwind database on the local instance of SQL Express:

Visual Basic

```
Dim strConn As String
strConn = "Provider=SQLOLEDB;Data Source=.\SQLExpress;" & _
          "Initial Catalog=Northwind;Integrated Security=SSPI;"
Using cn As New OleDbConnection(strConn)
    cn.Open()
    cn.Close()
End Using
```

Visual C#

```
string strConn;
strConn = @"Provider=SQLOLEDB;Data Source=.\SQLExpress;" +
          "Initial Catalog=Northwind;Integrated Security=SSPI;";
using (OleDbConnection cn = new OleDbConnection(strConn)) {
    cn.Open();
    cn.Close();
}
```

Executing Queries Using an *OleDbCommand*

Like the *OdbcCommand* and all other classes that derive from *DbCommand*, the *OleDbCommand* class offers an *ExecuteReader* method to return the results of a query as a *DataReader*. The *ExecuteReader* method accepts values from the *CommandBehavior* enumeration. You can also return a single value using the *Execute-Scalar* method or execute a query without handling the results by calling the *ExecuteNonQuery* method.

The *OleDbCommand* class does not offer support for asynchronous query execution, nor does it offer the ability to retrieve values using provider-specific types such as *SqlTypes*.

Examining the Results of a Query Using an *OleDbDataReader*

You create *OleDbDataReaders* just like you create *DataReaders* using other providers—by calling the *OleDbCommand* object's *ExecuteReader* method, as shown in the following code:

Visual Basic

```
Dim strConn, strSQL As String
strConn = "Provider=SQLOLEDB;Data Source=.\SQLExpress;" & _
          "Initial Catalog=Northwind;Integrated Security=SSPI;"
strSQL = "SELECT CustomerID, OrderID, OrderDate FROM Orders " & _
          "WHERE CustomerID = 'ALFKI' ORDER BY OrderDate"
Using cn As New OleDbConnection(strConn)
    Using cmd As New OleDbCommand(strSQL, cn)
        cn.Open()
        Using rdr As OleDbDataReader = cmd.ExecuteReader()
            Do While rdr.Read()
                Console.WriteLine("  {0} {1} {2:d}", rdr.GetString(0), _
                                  rdr.GetInt32(1), rdr.GetDateTime(2))
            Loop
            rdr.Close()
        End Using
        cn.Close()
    End Using
End Using
```

Visual C#

```
string strConn, strSQL;
strConn = @"Provider=SQLOLEDB;Data Source=.\SQLExpress;" +
           "Initial Catalog=Northwind;Integrated Security=SSPI;";
strSQL = "SELECT CustomerID, OrderID, OrderDate FROM Orders " +
          "WHERE CustomerID = 'ALFKI' ORDER BY OrderDate";
using (OleDbConnection cn = new OleDbConnection(strConn)) {
    using (OleDbCommand cmd = new OleDbCommand(strSQL, cn)) {
        cn.Open();
        using (OleDbDataReader rdr = cmd.ExecuteReader()) {
            while (rdr.Read())
                Console.WriteLine("  {0} {1} {2:d}", rdr.GetString(0),
                                  rdr.GetInt32(1), rdr.GetDateTime(2));
            rdr.Close();
        }
        cn.Close();
    }
}
```

Working with Parameterized Queries

Like the ODBC .NET Data Provider, the OLE DB .NET Data Provider supports parameterized queries using positional parameters rather than parameter names. In your query string, you use the ? parameter marker to denote a parameter, and then you add a corresponding *OleDb-Parameter* object to the *OleDbCommand* object's *Parameters* collection.

Most developers provide meaningful values for the *Name* properties on their parameter objects. For example, they might set the *Name* property for an *OleDbParameter* that corresponds to the CustomerID column to "@CustomerID" or "pCustomerID." This practice is helpful because it simplifies the process of finding the desired entry in the parameters collection within your code. However, this practice has no effect on how the *OleDbCommand* matches entries in the parameters collection to the parameter markers in your query. The *OleDbCommand* will match the *OleDbParameters* to the parameter markers in the query based on their position rather on than their names.

The following code sample executes a parameterized query using the SQL Server OLE DB provider:

Visual Basic

```vb
Dim strConn, strSQL As String
strConn = "Provider=SQLOLEDB;Data Source=.\SQLExpress;" & _
          "Initial Catalog=Northwind;Integrated Security=SSPI;"
strSQL = "SELECT CustomerID, OrderID, OrderDate FROM Orders " & _
         "WHERE CustomerID = ? ORDER BY OrderDate"
Using cn As New OleDbConnection(strConn)
    Using cmd As New OleDbCommand(strSQL, cn)
        cmd.Parameters.AddWithValue("@CustomerID", "ALFKI")
        cn.Open()
        Using rdr As OleDbDataReader = cmd.ExecuteReader()
            Do While rdr.Read()
                Console.WriteLine("  {0} {1} {2:d}", rdr.GetString(0), _
                                  rdr.GetInt32(1), rdr.GetDateTime(2))
            Loop
            rdr.Close()
        End Using
        cn.Close()
    End Using
End Using
```

Visual C#

```csharp
string strConn, strSQL;
strConn = @"Provider=SQLOLEDB;Data Source=.\SQLExpress;" +
          "Initial Catalog=Northwind;Integrated Security=SSPI;";
strSQL = "SELECT CustomerID, OrderID, OrderDate FROM Orders " +
         "WHERE CustomerID = ? ORDER BY OrderDate";
using (OleDbConnection cn = new OleDbConnection(strConn)) {
    using (OleDbCommand cmd = new OleDbCommand(strSQL, cn)) {
        cmd.Parameters.AddWithValue("@CustomerID", "ALFKI");
        cn.Open();
        using (OleDbDataReader rdr = cmd.ExecuteReader()) {
            while (rdr.Read())
                Console.WriteLine("  {0} {1} {2:d}", rdr.GetString(0),
                                  rdr.GetInt32(1), rdr.GetDateTime(2));
            rdr.Close();
        }
        cn.Close();
    }
}
```

Calling a Stored Procedure

The *OleDbCommand* class does support the *StoredProcedure* value from the *CommandType* enumeration. So you do not have to use curly braces and "CALL" in your *OleDbCommand* *CommandText* property to call a stored procedure. Simply set the *CommandText* property to the name of the stored procedure, set the *CommandType* property to *StoredProcedure*, and supply parameter information through the *OleDbCommand Properties* collection.

The following code example demonstrates how to call a parameterized stored procedure using the OLE DB .NET Data Provider:

Visual Basic

```
Dim strConn As String
strConn = "Provider=SQLOLEDB;Data Source=.\SQLExpress;" & _
            "Initial Catalog=Northwind;Integrated Security=SSPI;"
Using cn As New OleDbConnection(strConn)
    Using cmd As New OleDbCommand("CustOrdersOrders", cn)
        cmd.CommandType = CommandType.StoredProcedure
        cmd.Parameters.AddWithValue("@CustomerID", "ALFKI")
        cn.Open()
        Using rdr As OleDbDataReader = cmd.ExecuteReader()
            Do While rdr.Read()
                Console.WriteLine("  {0} {1:d}", rdr.GetInt32(0), _
                                rdr.GetDateTime(1))
            Loop
            rdr.Close()
        End Using
    cn.Close()
    End Using
End Using
```

Visual C#

```
string strConn = @"Provider=SQLOLEDB;Data Source=.\SQLExpress;" +
                "Initial Catalog=Northwind;Integrated Security=SSPI;";
using (OleDbConnection cn = new OleDbConnection(strConn)) {
    using (OleDbCommand cmd = new OleDbCommand("CustOrdersOrders", cn)) {
        cmd.CommandType = CommandType.StoredProcedure;
        cmd.Parameters.AddWithValue("@CustomerID", "ALFKI");
        cn.Open();
        using (OleDbDataReader rdr = cmd.ExecuteReader()) {
            while (rdr.Read())
                Console.WriteLine("  {0} {1:d}", rdr.GetInt32(0),
                                rdr.GetDateTime(1));
            rdr.Close();
        }
        cn.Close();
    }
}
```

Retrieving the Results of a Query Using an *OleDbDataAdapter*

If you want to retrieve the results of a query and store them in a *DataSet* or *DataTable* object, use the *Fill* method of the *OleDbDataAdapter* class:

Visual Basic

```
Dim strConn, strSQL As String
strConn = "Provider=SQLOLEDB;Data Source=.\SQLExpress;" & _
          "Initial Catalog=Northwind;Integrated Security=SSPI;"
strSQL = "SELECT CustomerID, OrderID, OrderDate FROM Orders " & _
          "WHERE CustomerID = ? ORDER BY OrderDate"
Dim da As New OleDbDataAdapter(strSQL, strConn)
da.SelectCommand.Parameters.AddWithValue("@CustomerID", "ALFKI")
Dim tbl As New DataTable("Orders")
da.Fill(tbl)
For Each row As DataRow In tbl.Rows
    Console.WriteLine("  {0} {1} {2:d}", row("CustomerID"), _
                      row("OrderID"), row("OrderDate"))
Next row
```

Visual C#

```
string strConn, strSQL;
strConn = @"Provider=SQLOLEDB;Data Source=.\SQLExpress;" +
           "Initial Catalog=Northwind;Integrated Security=SSPI;";
strSQL = "SELECT CustomerID, OrderID, OrderDate FROM Orders " +
          "WHERE CustomerID = ? ORDER BY OrderDate";
OleDbDataAdapter da = new OleDbDataAdapter(strSQL, strConn);
da.SelectCommand.Parameters.AddWithValue("@CustomerID", "ALFKI");
DataTable tbl = new DataTable("Orders");
da.Fill(tbl);
foreach (DataRow row in tbl.Rows)
    Console.WriteLine("  {0} {1} {2:d}", row["CustomerID"],
                      row["OrderID"], row["OrderDate"]);
```

Retrieving Database Schema Information

The *OleDbConnection* class supports the *GetSchema* methods that allow you to query your database for available schema information. The overloaded *GetSchema* methods behave like those of other .NET data providers.

Listing Schemas and Restrictions

Earlier in the appendix, we looked at how you can display the list of schemas and restrictions, given a provider name and a connection string using the *DbProviderFactories* class as a starting point. If you know you're working with the OLE DB .NET Data Provider, you can simplify that code slightly by using the *OleDbConnection* class as a starting point:

Visual Basic

```
Dim schemasTable, restrictionsTable As DataTable
Dim strConn As String
strConn = "Provider=SQLOLEDB;Data Source=.\SQLExpress;" & _
          "Initial Catalog=Northwind;Integrated Security=SSPI;"
```

```
Using cn As New OleDbConnection(strConn)
    cn.Open()
    schemasTable = cn.GetSchema()
    restrictionsTable = cn.GetSchema("Restrictions")
    cn.Close()
End Using

Dim ds As New DataSet()
schemasTable.TableName = "Schemas"
restrictionsTable.TableName = "Restrictions"
ds.Tables.AddRange(New DataTable() {schemasTable, restrictionsTable})
Dim rel As DataRelation
rel = ds.Relations.Add(schemasTable.Columns("CollectionName"), _
                       restrictionsTable.Columns("CollectionName"))

For Each schemaRow As DataRow In schemasTable.Rows
    Console.WriteLine(" {0} schema", schemaRow("CollectionName"))
    Dim restrictionRows As DataRow()
    restrictionRows = schemaRow.GetChildRows(rel)
    If restrictionRows.Length <> 0 Then
        Console.WriteLine("    Restrictions:")
        For Each restrictionRow As DataRow In restrictionRows
            Console.WriteLine("        {0}: {1}", _
                              restrictionRow("RestrictionNumber"), _
                              restrictionRow("RestrictionName"))
        Next restrictionRow
    Else
        Console.WriteLine("    No restrictions")
    End If
    Console.WriteLine()
Next schemaRow
```

Visual C#

```
DataTable schemasTable, restrictionsTable;
string strConn = @"Provider=SQLOLEDB;Data Source=.\SQLExpress;" +
                "Initial Catalog=Northwind;Integrated Security=SSPI;";
using (OleDbConnection cn = new OleDbConnection(strConn)) {
    cn.Open();
    schemasTable = cn.GetSchema();
    restrictionsTable = cn.GetSchema("Restrictions");
    cn.Close();
}

DataSet ds = new DataSet();
schemasTable.TableName = "Schemas";
restrictionsTable.TableName = "Restrictions";
ds.Tables.AddRange(new DataTable[] {schemasTable, restrictionsTable});
DataRelation rel;
rel = ds.Relations.Add(schemasTable.Columns["CollectionName"],
                       restrictionsTable.Columns["CollectionName"]);

foreach (DataRow schemaRow in schemasTable.Rows) {
    Console.WriteLine("{0} schema", schemaRow["CollectionName"]);
    DataRow[] restrictionRows = schemaRow.GetChildRows(rel);
```

```
    if (restrictionRows.Length != 0) {
        Console.WriteLine("  Restrictions:");
        foreach (DataRow restrictionRow in restrictionRows)
            Console.WriteLine("    {0}: {1}",
                              restrictionRow["RestrictionNumber"],
                              restrictionRow["RestrictionName"]);
    } else {
        Console.WriteLine("  No restrictions");
    }
    Console.WriteLine();
}
```

Returning Filtered Schema Information

The output from the preceding code sample indicates that the connection supports a Columns schema and that it also supports restrictions for table catalog, table schema, table name, and column name, respectively. So retrieving and displaying information about columns in a particular table is a snap. Just build a string array of the same length as described by the restrictions schema, supply values for the desired restrictions, omit the rest (using *null* or *Nothing*, depending on your language of choice), and pass that string array into the *GetSchema* method along with the name of the desired schema, "Columns", as demonstrated in the following code example:

Visual Basic

```
Dim filter As String()
filter = New String() {"Northwind", "dbo", "Order Details", Nothing}
Dim columnsTable As DataTable

Dim strConn As String
strConn = "Provider=SQLOLEDB;Data Source=.\SQLExpress;" & _
          "Initial Catalog=Northwind;Integrated Security=SSPI;"
Using cn As New OleDbConnection(strConn)
    cn.Open()
    columnsTable = cn.GetSchema("Columns", filter)
    cn.Close()
End Using

For Each row As DataRow In columnsTable.Rows
    Console.WriteLine("{0,-10} - {1}", row("COLUMN_NAME"), _
                      DirectCast(row("DATA_TYPE"), OleDbType))
Next row
```

Visual C#

```
string[] filter = new String[] {"Northwind", "dbo", "Order Details", null};
DataTable columnsTable;

string strConn = @"Provider=SQLOLEDB;Data Source=.\SQLExpress;" +
                 "Initial Catalog=Northwind;Integrated Security=SSPI;";
using (OleDbConnection cn = new OleDbConnection(strConn)) {
    cn.Open();
    columnsTable = cn.GetSchema("Columns", filter);
    cn.Close();
}
```

```
foreach (DataRow row in columnsTable.Rows)
    Console.WriteLine("{0,-10} - {1}", row["COLUMN_NAME"],
                        (OleDbType) row["DATA_TYPE"]);
```

The Oracle Client .NET Data Provider

The .NET Framework also includes a .NET data provider designed to communicate with Oracle databases. The Oracle Client .NET Data Provider interacts with Oracle databases using Oracle's client API, commonly referred to as OCI.

The Oracle Client .NET Data Provider requires that you have Oracle's client components installed on your machine. Oracle offers a wide range of installation options for their client layer. For more information on these options, see Oracle's Web site.

The Oracle Client .NET Data Provider that is included in version 2.0 of the .NET Framework was tested extensively against 32- and 64-bit versions of both Release 1 and Release 2 of Oracle 10g databases, as well as both Release 1 and Release 2 of Oracle 9i databases and Oracle 8i databases. Oracle Client works with the basic Oracle client installation, as well as with Oracle's simplified client installation—Oracle Instant Client.

The Oracle Client provider offers support for many Oracle-specific data types, such as Number, LOBs, and BFILEs, and it allows you to fetch the contents of REF cursors.

Unlike the other .NET data providers that are part of the .NET Framework, the Oracle Client .NET Data Provider resides in a separate assembly—System.Data.OracleClient.dll. The code samples in this section assume that you've added a project reference to that assembly, as well as a reference to the Oracle Client *System.Data.OracleClient* namespace in your code using the construct for your language of choice (the *Imports* command for Visual Basic developers and the *using* command for Visual C# developers).

As noted earlier, the Oracle Client .NET Data Provider relies on the OCI layer to communicate with the database. The *OracleConnection* class passes login information from your connection string to the OCI layer. It's up to Oracle's OCI layer to establish the connection to your database based on how you've configured your Oracle client components. You might use a configuration file (TNSNames.ora) that contains aliases for multiple Oracle database servers or a centralized service (Oracle Names Server) that contains similar information.

The code samples in this portion of the appendix assume that you have configured your Oracle client components to talk to an Oracle database using the alias "Ora10gR2" using the sample login "scott". If you have trouble connecting to your Oracle database using the Oracle Client .NET Data Provider, try connecting to your Oracle database using an Oracle ad hoc query tool such as SQL*Plus. Once you can connect using such a utility, you should be able to connect using the same credentials in the *ConnectionString* property of an *OracleConnection* object.

Connecting to Your Oracle Database Using an *OracleConnection*

You'll use the *OracleConnection* object to connect to your Oracle database. As with the other .NET data providers, to connect to your Oracle database, you'll simply need to create an *OracleConnection* object, set its *ConnectString* property (either explicitly or via the object's constructor), and call its *Open* method, as shown in the following code sample:

Visual Basic

```
Dim strConn As String
strConn = "Data Source=Ora10gR2;User ID=scott;Password=tiger;"
Using cn As New OracleConnection(strConn)
    cn.Open()
    cn.Close()
End Using
```

Visual C#

```
string strConn;
strConn = "Data Source=Ora10gR2;User ID=scott;Password=tiger;";
using (OracleConnection cn = new OracleConnection(strConn)) {
    cn.Open();
    cn.Close();
}
```

Pooling Oracle Connections

The *OracleConnection* class uses the same connection pooling infrastructure that the *SqlConnection* class does, offering connection string options for *Pooling*, *MinPoolSize*, and *MaxPoolSize*. The Oracle Client .NET Data Provider does not use the OCI layer to handle connection pooling and does not offer features associated with OCI connection pooling such as a proxy login and password.

For more information on the connection pooling options available in the *OracleConnection* class, see the documentation of the various properties of the *OracleConnectionStringBuilder* class.

Executing Queries Using an *OracleCommand*

Like the *SqlCommand* and all other classes that derive from *DbCommand*, the *OracleCommand* class offers an *ExecuteReader* method to return the results of a query as a *DataReader*. The *ExecuteReader* method accepts values from the *CommandBehavior* enumeration. You can also return a single value using the *Execute-Scalar* method, or execute a query without handling the results by calling the *ExecuteNonQuery* method. The *OracleCommand* class does not offer support for asynchronous query execution.

Like the SQL Client .NET Data Provider, the Oracle Client .NET Data Provider offers a series of structures that are designed to natively handle Oracle-specific data types.

Examining Results Using an *OracleDataReader*

You create *OracleDataReaders* just like you create *DataReaders* using other providers–by calling the *OracleCommand* object's *ExecuteReader* method, as shown in the following code:

Visual Basic

```
Dim strConn, strSQL As String
strConn = "Data Source=Ora10gR2;User ID=scott;Password=tiger;"
strSQL = "SELECT EMPNO, ENAME FROM EMP"
Using cn As New OracleConnection(strConn)
    Dim cmd As New OracleCommand(strSQL, cn)
    cn.Open()
    Using rdr As OracleDataReader = cmd.ExecuteReader()
        Do While rdr.Read()
            Console.WriteLine("{0} - {1}", rdr.GetDecimal(0), _
                            rdr.GetString(1))

        Loop
    End Using
    cn.Close()
End Using
```

Visual C#

```
string strConn, strSQL;
strConn = "Data Source=Ora10gR2;User ID=scott;Password=tiger;";
strSQL = "SELECT EMPNO, ENAME FROM EMP";
using (OracleConnection cn = new OracleConnection(strConn)) {
    OracleCommand cmd = new OracleCommand(strSQL, cn);
    cn.Open();
    using (OracleDataReader rdr = cmd.ExecuteReader()) {
        while (rdr.Read())
            Console.WriteLine("{0} - {1}", rdr.GetDecimal(0),
                            rdr.GetString(1));

    }
    cn.Close();
}
```

Working with Parameterized Queries

The Oracle Client .NET Data Provider supports only named parameters, much like the SQL Client .NET Data Provider does. The one difference is that you'll have to preface your parameter names with a colon. An Oracle parameterized query looks like this:

```
SELECT EMPNO, ENAME FROM EMP WHERE DEPTNO = :DEPTNO
```

Visual Basic

```
Dim strConn, strSQL As String
strConn = "Data Source=Ora10gR2;User ID=scott;Password=tiger;"
strSQL = "SELECT EMPNO, ENAME FROM EMP WHERE DEPTNO = :DEPTNO"
Using cn As New OracleConnection(strConn)
    Dim cmd As New OracleCommand(strSQL, cn)
    cmd.Parameters.AddWithValue(":DEPTNO", 20)
    cn.Open()
```

```
    Using rdr As OracleDataReader = cmd.ExecuteReader()
        Do While rdr.Read()
            Console.WriteLine("{0} - {1}", rdr.GetDecimal(0), _
                                rdr.GetString(1))
        Loop
    End Using
    cn.Close()
End Using
```

Visual C#

```csharp
string strConn, strSQL;
strConn = "Data Source=Ora10gR2;User ID=scott;Password=tiger;";
strSQL = "SELECT EMPNO, ENAME FROM EMP WHERE DEPTNO = :DEPTNO";
using (OracleConnection cn = new OracleConnection(strConn)) {
    OracleCommand cmd = new OracleCommand(strSQL, cn);
    cmd.Parameters.AddWithValue(":DEPTNO", 20);
    cn.Open();
    using (OracleDataReader rdr = cmd.ExecuteReader()) {
        while (rdr.Read())
            Console.WriteLine("{0} - {1}", rdr.GetDecimal(0),
                                rdr.GetString(1));
    }
    cn.Close();
}
```

Calling a Stored Procedure

The *OracleCommand* class supports the *StoredProcedure* value from the *CommandType* enumeration. Simply set the *CommandText* property to the name of the stored procedure, set the *CommandType* property to *StoredProcedure*, and supply parameter information through the *OracleCommand* Properties collection.

The following code sample demonstrates how to call a parameterized stored procedure using the Oracle Client .NET Data Provider. Because the sample scott schema does not contain a stored procedure, the code creates a simple one that takes two input parameters and returns their product through an output parameter.

Visual Basic

```vbnet
Dim strConn As String
strConn = "Data Source=Ora10gR2;User ID=scott;Password=tiger;"
Using cn As New OracleConnection(strConn)
    cn.Open()
    Dim cmd As OracleCommand = cn.CreateCommand()
    cmd.CommandText = "CREATE OR REPLACE PROCEDURE TestProc " & _
                    "(pIn1 NUMBER, pIn2 NUMBER, pOut OUT NUMBER) IS " & _
                    "BEGIN pOut := pIn1 * pIn2; END;"
    cmd.ExecuteNonQuery()

    cmd.CommandText = "TestProc"
    cmd.CommandType = CommandType.StoredProcedure
    cmd.Parameters.AddWithValue("pIn1", 6)
    cmd.Parameters.AddWithValue("pIn2", 7)
    Dim pOut As OracleParameter
```

```
        pOut = cmd.Parameters.Add("pOut", OracleType.Number)
        pOut.Direction = ParameterDirection.Output
        cmd.ExecuteNonQuery()
        Console.WriteLine(pOut.Value)

        cn.Close()
End Using
```

Visual C#

```
string strConn;
strConn = "Data Source=Ora10gR2;User ID=scott;Password=tiger;";
using (OracleConnection cn = new OracleConnection(strConn)) {
    OracleCommand cmd = cn.CreateCommand();
    cmd.CommandText = "CREATE OR REPLACE PROCEDURE TestProc " +
                     "(pIn1 NUMBER, pIn2 NUMBER, pOut OUT NUMBER) IS " +
                     "BEGIN pOut := pIn1 * pIn2; END;";
    cmd.ExecuteNonQuery();

    cmd.CommandText = "TestProc";
    cmd.CommandType = CommandType.StoredProcedure;
    cmd.Parameters.AddWithValue("pIn1", 6);
    cmd.Parameters.AddWithValue("pIn2", 7);
    OracleParameter pOut = cmd.Parameters.Add("pOut", OracleType.Number);
    pOut.Direction = ParameterDirection.Output;
    cmd.ExecuteNonQuery();
    Console.WriteLine(pOut.Value);

    cn.Close();
}
```

Retrieving Oracle REF Cursors as *OracleDataReaders*

Oracle does not provide support for batched queries that return results like SQL Server does, nor does Oracle support returning results from a stored procedure call like SQL Server does. Each of these Oracle scenarios requires the explicit use of a parameter that returns a REF cursor. You can retrieve the contents of a REF cursor by creating an *OracleParameter* object whose *OracleType* property is set to *Cursor* and whose *Direction* property is set to *Output*.

There are two ways to examine the results of the REF cursors using *OracleDataReaders*. The first is to simply call the *ExecuteReader* method on the *OracleCommand* object. The *Oracle-Command* will return the contents of the first REF cursor through the resulting *OracleData-Reader* and remaining REF cursors as you call the *NextResult* method on the *OracleDataReader*, as shown in the following code:

Visual Basic

```
Dim strConn, strSQL As String
strConn = "Data Source=Ora10gR2;User ID=scott;Password=tiger;"
strSQL = "BEGIN " & _
         " OPEN :DEPT_CURSOR FOR SELECT DEPTNO, DNAME, LOC FROM DEPT " & _
         "      ORDER BY DEPTNO; " & _
         " OPEN :EMP_CURSOR FOR SELECT DEPTNO, EMPNO, ENAME FROM EMP " & _
         "      ORDER BY DEPTNO; " & _
         "END;"
```

```vb
Using cn As New OracleConnection(strConn)
    Dim cmd As New OracleCommand(strSQL, cn)
    Dim pDeptCursor, pEmpCursor As OracleParameter
    pDeptCursor = cmd.Parameters.Add(":DEPT_CURSOR", OracleType.Cursor)
    pDeptCursor.Direction = ParameterDirection.Output
    pEmpCursor = cmd.Parameters.Add(":EMP_CURSOR", OracleType.Cursor)
    pEmpCursor.Direction = ParameterDirection.Output

    cn.Open()
    Using rdr As OracleDataReader = cmd.ExecuteReader()
        Do
            Do While rdr.Read()
                Console.WriteLine("{0} - {1}", rdr(1), rdr(2))
            Loop
            Console.WriteLine()
        Loop While rdr.NextResult()
        rdr.Close()
    End Using

    cn.Close()
End Using
```

Visual C#

```csharp
string strConn, strSQL;
strConn = "Data Source=Ora10gR2;User ID=scott;Password=tiger;";
strSQL = "BEGIN " +
        " OPEN :DEPT_CURSOR FOR SELECT DEPTNO, DNAME, LOC FROM DEPT " +
        "     ORDER BY DEPTNO; " +
        " OPEN :EMP_CURSOR FOR SELECT DEPTNO, EMPNO, ENAME FROM EMP " +
        "     ORDER BY DEPTNO; " +
        "END;";
using (OracleConnection cn = new OracleConnection(strConn)) {
    OracleCommand cmd = new OracleCommand(strSQL, cn);
    OracleParameter pDeptCursor, pEmpCursor;
    pDeptCursor = cmd.Parameters.Add(":DEPT_CURSOR", OracleType.Cursor);
    pDeptCursor.Direction = ParameterDirection.Output;
    pEmpCursor = cmd.Parameters.Add(":EMP_CURSOR", OracleType.Cursor);
    pEmpCursor.Direction = ParameterDirection.Output;

    cn.Open();
    using (OracleDataReader rdr = cmd.ExecuteReader()) {
        do {
            while (rdr.Read())
                Console.WriteLine("  {0} - {1}", rdr[1], rdr[2]);
            Console.WriteLine();
        } while (rdr.NextResult());
        rdr.Close();
    }

    cn.Close();
}
```

In the preceding example, the queries return rows from tables that contain department and employee information. The queries include ORDER BY clauses so that both queries return rows ordered by department.

You can open multiple REF cursors on an Oracle connection without blocking the connection by calling the *OracleCommand* object's *ExecuteNonQuery* method and then casting the *Value* property of each *OracleParameter* that contains a REF cursor to an *OracleDataReader*.

Using this approach, you can interleave results between multiple cursors. In other words, you can read a row from the department REF cursor, read a series of rows from the employees REF cursor, and then read another row from the department REF cursor. The following code sample demonstrates this approach:

Visual Basic

```vb
Dim strConn, strSQL As String
strConn = "Data Source=Ora10gR2;User ID=scott;Password=tiger;"
strSQL = "BEGIN " & _
         "  OPEN :DEPT_CURSOR FOR SELECT DEPTNO, DNAME, LOC FROM DEPT " & _
         "    ORDER BY DEPTNO; " & _
         "  OPEN :EMP_CURSOR FOR SELECT DEPTNO, EMPNO, ENAME FROM EMP " & _
         "    ORDER BY DEPTNO; " & _
         "END;"
Using cn As New OracleConnection(strConn)
    Dim cmd As New OracleCommand(strSQL, cn)
    Dim pDeptCursor, pEmpCursor As OracleParameter
    pDeptCursor = cmd.Parameters.Add(":DEPT_CURSOR", OracleType.Cursor)
    pDeptCursor.Direction = ParameterDirection.Output
    pEmpCursor = cmd.Parameters.Add(":EMP_CURSOR", OracleType.Cursor)
    pEmpCursor.Direction = ParameterDirection.Output

    cn.Open()
    cmd.ExecuteNonQuery()

    Using deptCursor As OracleDataReader = pDeptCursor.Value, _
          empCursor As OracleDataReader = pEmpCursor.Value
        Dim isEmpCursorInitialized As Boolean = False
        Dim empCursorHasData As Boolean = False
        Do While deptCursor.Read()
            Console.WriteLine("  {0} - {1}", deptCursor.GetString(1), _
                            deptCursor.GetString(2))
            If Not isEmpCursorInitialized Then
                empCursorHasData = empCursor.Read()
                isEmpCursorInitialized = True
            End If

            Do While empCursorHasData AndAlso _
                    empCursor.GetDecimal(0) = deptCursor.GetDecimal(0)
                Console.WriteLine("    {0} - {1}", empCursor.GetDecimal(1), _
                                empCursor.GetString(2))
                empCursorHasData = empCursor.Read()
            Loop
        Loop

        empCursor.Close()
        deptCursor.Close()
    End Using
    cn.Close()
End Using
```

Visual C#

```csharp
string strConn, strSQL;
strConn = "Data Source=Ora10gR2;User ID=scott;Password=tiger;";
strSQL = "BEGIN " +
        "  OPEN :DEPT_CURSOR FOR SELECT DEPTNO, DNAME, LOC FROM DEPT " +
        "          ORDER BY DEPTNO; " +
        "  OPEN :EMP_CURSOR FOR SELECT DEPTNO, EMPNO, ENAME FROM EMP " +
        "          ORDER BY DEPTNO; " +
        "END;";
using (OracleConnection cn = new OracleConnection(strConn)) {
    OracleCommand cmd = new OracleCommand(strSQL, cn);
    OracleParameter pDeptCursor, pEmpCursor;
    pDeptCursor = cmd.Parameters.Add(":DEPT_CURSOR", OracleType.Cursor);
    pDeptCursor.Direction = ParameterDirection.Output;
    pEmpCursor = cmd.Parameters.Add(":EMP_CURSOR", OracleType.Cursor);
    pEmpCursor.Direction = ParameterDirection.Output;

    cn.Open();
    cmd.ExecuteNonQuery();

    using (OracleDataReader deptCursor =
                        (OracleDataReader)pDeptCursor.Value,
                        empCursor = (OracleDataReader)pEmpCursor.Value) {
        bool isEmpCursorInitialized = false;
        bool empCursorHasData = false;
        while (deptCursor.Read()) {
            Console.WriteLine("  {0} - {1}", deptCursor.GetString(1),
                                deptCursor.GetString(2));

            if (!isEmpCursorInitialized) {
                empCursorHasData = empCursor.Read();
                isEmpCursorInitialized = true;
            }

            while (empCursorHasData &&
                    empCursor.GetDecimal(0) == deptCursor.GetDecimal(0)) {
                Console.WriteLine("    {0} - {1}", empCursor.GetDecimal(1),
                                empCursor.GetString(2));
                empCursorHasData = empCursor.Read();
            }
        }

        empCursor.Close();
        deptCursor.Close();
    }
    cn.Close();
}
```

Retrieving Schema Information for Your Queries

When you call the *ExecuteReader* method on a *Command* and pass a value for the *Command-Behavior* argument that includes *KeyInfo*, the *Command* requests additional metadata about the columns returned by the query. You can examine this information by calling the *GetSchema-Table* method on the *DataReader* returned by the *ExecuteReader* method. If you examine the contents of this *DataTable* in a bound control such as a *DataGridView*, you can learn a lot about the tables and columns referenced by the query. You'll see table names and column names, as well as key information.

SQL Server can return this additional metadata natively along with the results of the query. Because gathering this information does incur a performance hit, this information is not returned with the results of the query by default.

Oracle does not provide a mechanism to return this additional metadata. You can use the OCI layer to execute a query and gather some metadata about the query results, such as the names and data types of the columns of data as they appear in the results. However, there is no way to use the OCI layer to request the source table and column names. And yet, if you call the *ExecuteReader* on an *OracleCommand* and specify a *CommandBehavior* of *KeyInfo*, and examine the contents of the *DataTable* returned by the *OracleDataReader GetSchemaTable* method, you'll be able to see the source table and column names.

So how does the *OracleCommand* gather this additional metadata? Brute force. The Oracle Client .NET Data Provider parses the text of the query to look for table and column names and then queries the database to learn about those tables and columns. The Oracle Client .NET Data Provider's parser is not as robust or as powerful as the one inside the Oracle database and is unable to parse many queries that the database can handle.

Retrieving Results Using Oracle-Specific Data Types

The Oracle Client .NET Data Provider includes Oracle-specific data types, much like the SQL Client .NET Data Provider does for SQL Server data types. Using these Oracle-specific data types will improve the performance of your code and allow you to retrieve data from your *OracleDataReader* more quickly because you'll be able to store data in these data types without having to perform checks for *Null* values ahead of time. Plus, many of these data types offer additional functionality not available on the corresponding .NET data type.

The following code example uses the Oracle-specific data types to retrieve and display the results of a query:

Visual Basic

```
Dim strConn, strSQL As String
strConn = "Data Source=Ora10gR2;User ID=scott;Password=tiger;"
strSQL = "SELECT EMPNO, ENAME FROM EMP WHERE DEPTNO = :DEPTNO"
Using cn As New OracleConnection(strConn)
    Dim cmd As New OracleCommand(strSQL, cn)
    cmd.Parameters.AddWithValue(":DEPTNO", 20)
    cn.Open()
    Using rdr As OracleDataReader = cmd.ExecuteReader()
        Do While rdr.Read()
            Console.WriteLine("{0} {1}", rdr.GetOracleNumber(0).Value, _
                              rdr.GetOracleString(1).Value)
        Loop
        rdr.Close()
```

```
      End Using
      cn.Close()
End Using
```

Visual C#

```csharp
string strConn, strSQL;
strConn = "Data Source=Ora10gR2;User ID=scott;Password=tiger;";
strSQL = "SELECT EMPNO, ENAME FROM EMP WHERE DEPTNO = :DEPTNO";
using (OracleConnection cn = new OracleConnection(strConn)) {
    OracleCommand cmd = new OracleCommand(strSQL,  cn);
    cmd.Parameters.AddWithValue(":DEPTNO", 20);
    cn.Open();
    using (OracleDataReader rdr = cmd.ExecuteReader()) {
        while (rdr.Read())
            Console.WriteLine("{0} {1}", rdr.GetOracleNumber(0).Value,
                              rdr.GetOracleString(1).Value);
        rdr.Close();
    }
    cn.Close();
}
```

Using the *OracleDataAdapter* Class

Now that you're comfortable executing basic and parameterized queries using the *Oracle-Command* class, let's take a look at some examples using the *OracleDataAdapter* class.

Retrieving the Results of a Query Using an *OracleDataAdapter*

Let's look at an example of code that uses an *OracleDataAdapter* to fill a *DataTable* based on the results of this parameterized query:

Visual Basic

```vb
Dim strConn, strSQL As String
strConn = "Data Source=Ora10gR2;User ID=scott;Password=tiger;"
strSQL = "SELECT EMPNO, ENAME FROM EMP WHERE DEPTNO = :DEPTNO"
Dim da As New OracleDataAdapter(strSQL, strConn)
da.SelectCommand.Parameters.AddWithValue(":DEPTNO", 20)
Dim tbl As New DataTable()
da.Fill(tbl)
For Each row As DataRow In tbl.Rows
    Console.WriteLine("{0} {1}", row("EMPNO"), row("ENAME"))
Next row
```

Visual C#

```csharp
string strConn, strSQL;
strConn = "Data Source=Ora10gR2;User ID=scott;Password=tiger;";
strSQL = "SELECT EMPNO, ENAME FROM EMP WHERE DEPTNO = :DEPTNO";
OracleDataAdapter da = new OracleDataAdapter(strSQL, strConn);
da.SelectCommand.Parameters.AddWithValue(":DEPTNO", 20);
DataTable tbl = new DataTable();
da.Fill(tbl);
foreach (DataRow row in tbl.Rows)
    Console.WriteLine("{0} {1}", row["EMPNO"], row["ENAME"]);
```

Excuting Queries That Return a Page of Rows

Chapter 14 described scenarios in which you might want to display a subset of the results of a query so that the user can examine the results one page at a time. The following code sample builds a query that uses Oracle's *RowNum* function to add a column that lists the row number for a given row in the query results, and then uses that column in the WHERE clause to return a range of rows based on the page number and page size specified as parameters:

Visual Basic

```
Dim strConn, strSQL As String
strConn = "Data Source=Ora10gR2;User ID=scott;Password=tiger;"
strSQL = "SELECT * FROM " & _
         "(SELECT RowNum AS RowNumber, EMPNO, ENAME FROM " & _
         "  (SELECT EMPNO, ENAME FROM EMP ORDER BY EMPNO)) " & _
         "WHERE RowNumber > (:PageNumber * :PageSize) " & _
         "  AND RowNumber <= ((:PageNumber + 1) * :PageSize)"
Dim da As New OracleDataAdapter(strSQL, strConn)
da.SelectCommand.Parameters.AddWithValue(":PageNumber", 1)
da.SelectCommand.Parameters.AddWithValue(":PageSize", 5)
Dim tbl As New DataTable()
da.Fill(tbl)
Console.WriteLine(" {0,5} {1,5} {2,-10}", "Row #", "EMPNO", "ENAME")
For Each row As DataRow In tbl.Rows
    Console.WriteLine(" {0,5} {1,5} {2,-10}", row.ItemArray)
Next row
```

Visual C#

```
string strConn, strSQL;
strConn = "Data Source=Ora10gR2;User ID=scott;Password=tiger;";
strSQL = "SELECT * FROM " +
         "(SELECT RowNum AS RowNumber, EMPNO, ENAME, FROM " +
         "  (SELECT EMPNO, ENAME FROM EMP ORDER BY EMPNO)) " +
         "WHERE RowNumber > (:PageNumber * :PageSize) " +
         "  AND RowNumber <= ((:PageNumber + 1) * :PageSize)";
OracleDataAdapter da = new OracleDataAdapter(strSQL, strConn);
da.SelectCommand.Parameters.AddWithValue(":PageNumber", 1);
da.SelectCommand.Parameters.AddWithValue(":PageSize", 5);
DataTable tbl = new DataTable();
da.Fill(tbl);
Console.WriteLine("{0,5} {1,5} {2,-10}", "Row #", "EMPNO", "ENAME");
foreach (DataRow row in tbl.Rows)
    Console.WriteLine("{0,5} {1,5} {2,-10}", row.ItemArray);
```

Retrieving the Contents of REF Cursors

Earlier in this appendix, we covered examples of retrieving the contents of REF cursors using the *OracleDataReader* and *OracleParameter* classes. You can also use the *OracleDataAdapter* class in conjunction with the *OracleParameter* class to store the contents of REF cursors in *DataTable* objects, as shown in the following code:

Visual Basic

```
Dim strConn, strSQL As String
strConn = "Data Source=Ora10gR2;User ID=scott;Password=tiger;"
```

```
strSQL = "BEGIN " & _
        "  OPEN :DEPT_CURSOR FOR SELECT DNAME, LOC FROM DEPT " & _
        "          ORDER BY DEPTNO; " & _
        "  OPEN :EMP_CURSOR FOR SELECT EMPNO, ENAME FROM EMP " & _
        "          ORDER BY DEPTNO; " & _
        "END;"
Dim da As New OracleDataAdapter(strSQL, strConn)
Dim cmd As OracleCommand = da.SelectCommand
Dim pDeptCursor, pEmpCursor As OracleParameter
pEmpCursor = cmd.Parameters.Add(":EMP_CURSOR", OracleType.Cursor)
pEmpCursor.Direction = ParameterDirection.Output
pDeptCursor = cmd.Parameters.Add(":DEPT_CURSOR", OracleType.Cursor)
pDeptCursor.Direction = ParameterDirection.Output
da.TableMappings.Add("Table", "DEPT")
da.TableMappings.Add("Table1", "EMP")

Dim ds = New DataSet()
da.Fill(ds)

For Each tbl As DataTable In ds.Tables
    Console.WriteLine("  {0}", tbl.TableName)
    For Each row As DataRow In tbl.Rows
        Console.WriteLine("    {0} - {1}", row(0), row(1))
    Next row
    Console.WriteLine()
Next tbl
```

Visual C#

```
string strConn, strSQL;
strConn = "Data Source=Ora10gR2;User ID=scott;Password=tiger;";
strSQL = "BEGIN " +
        "  OPEN :DEPT_CURSOR FOR SELECT DNAME, LOC FROM DEPT " +
        "          ORDER BY DEPTNO; " +
        "  OPEN :EMP_CURSOR FOR SELECT EMPNO, ENAME FROM EMP " +
        "          ORDER BY DEPTNO; " +
        "END;";
OracleDataAdapter da = new OracleDataAdapter(strSQL, strConn);
OracleCommand cmd = da.SelectCommand;
OracleParameter pDeptCursor, pEmpCursor;
pDeptCursor = cmd.Parameters.Add(":DEPT_CURSOR", OracleType.Cursor);
pDeptCursor.Direction = ParameterDirection.Output;
pEmpCursor = cmd.Parameters.Add(":EMP_CURSOR", OracleType.Cursor);
pEmpCursor.Direction = ParameterDirection.Output;
da.TableMappings.Add("Table", "DEPT");
da.TableMappings.Add("Table1", "EMP");

DataSet ds = new DataSet();
da.Fill(ds);
foreach (DataTable tbl in ds.Tables) {
    Console.WriteLine("{0}", tbl.TableName);
    foreach (DataRow row in tbl.Rows)
        Console.WriteLine("  {0} - {1}", row[0], row[1]);
    Console.WriteLine();
}
```

When you call the *OracleDataAdapter* object's *Fill* method, the *OracleDataAdapter* calls the *ExecuteReader* method on the *OracleCommand* stored in its *SelectCommand* property. The resulting *OracleDataReader* returns the contents of the REF cursors in the order in which the *OracleParameters* appear in the *OracleCommand Parameters* collection. Because the *Oracle-Parameter* that corresponds to the department REF cursor was added to the *Parameters* collection first, the initial resultset available via the *OracleDataReader* contains department information. Thus, the first *DataTable* generated by the *OracleDataAdapter Fill* method contains department information.

You can force the *OracleDataAdapter* to return employee information before department information by changing the order in which you add the parameters without changing the text of the query:

Visual Basic

```
Dim strConn, strSQL As String
strConn = "Data Source=Ora10gR2;User ID=scott;Password=tiger;"
strSQL = "BEGIN " & _
         " OPEN :DEPT_CURSOR FOR SELECT DNAME, LOC FROM DEPT " & _
         "        ORDER BY DEPTNO; " & _
         " OPEN :EMP_CURSOR FOR SELECT EMPNO, ENAME FROM EMP " & _
         "        ORDER BY DEPTNO; " & _
         "END;"
Dim da As New OracleDataAdapter(strSQL, strConn)
Dim cmd As OracleCommand = da.SelectCommand
Dim pDeptCursor, pEmpCursor As OracleParameter
pDeptCursor = cmd.Parameters.Add(":DEPT_CURSOR", OracleType.Cursor)
pDeptCursor.Direction = ParameterDirection.Output
pEmpCursor = cmd.Parameters.Add(":EMP_CURSOR", OracleType.Cursor)
pEmpCursor.Direction = ParameterDirection.Output
da.TableMappings.Add("Table", "EMP")
da.TableMappings.Add("Table1", "DEPT")

Dim ds = New DataSet()
da.Fill(ds)

For Each tbl As DataTable In ds.Tables
    Console.WriteLine(" {0}", tbl.TableName)
    For Each row As DataRow In tbl.Rows
        Console.WriteLine("    {0} - {1}", row(0), row(1))
    Next row
    Console.WriteLine()
Next tbl
```

Visual C#

```
string strConn, strSQL;
strConn = "Data Source=Ora10gR2;User ID=scott;Password=tiger;";
strSQL = "BEGIN " +
         " OPEN :DEPT_CURSOR FOR SELECT DNAME, LOC FROM DEPT " +
         "        ORDER BY DEPTNO; " +
         " OPEN :EMP_CURSOR FOR SELECT EMPNO, ENAME FROM EMP " +
         "        ORDER BY DEPTNO; " +
         "END;";
```

```
OracleDataAdapter da = new OracleDataAdapter(strSQL, strConn);
OracleCommand cmd = da.SelectCommand;
OracleParameter pDeptCursor, pEmpCursor;
pEmpCursor = cmd.Parameters.Add(":EMP_CURSOR", OracleType.Cursor);
pEmpCursor.Direction = ParameterDirection.Output;
pDeptCursor = cmd.Parameters.Add(":DEPT_CURSOR", OracleType.Cursor);
pDeptCursor.Direction = ParameterDirection.Output;
da.TableMappings.Add("Table", "EMP");
da.TableMappings.Add("Table1", "DEPT");

DataSet ds = new DataSet();
da.Fill(ds);
foreach (DataTable tbl in ds.Tables) {
    Console.WriteLine("{0}", tbl.TableName);
    foreach (DataRow row in tbl.Rows)
        Console.WriteLine("  {0} - {1}", row[0], row[1]);
    Console.WriteLine();
}
```

Batched Updating

In Chapter 11, we examined how you can use the *SqlDataAdapter* class to submit batched updates. The *OracleDataAdapter* class supports batched updating, much like the *SqlDataAdapter* class does. Simply set the *UpdateBatchSize* property to the desired batch size, and the *OracleDataAdapter* will combine the queries used to submit pending changes based on the value of the *UpdateBatchSize* property. As with the *SqlDataAdapter* class, the *OracleDataAdapter* class can support batched updates only if your updating logic does not return new values through row-returning queries. The *UpdateRowSource* property of the *OracleCommands* used to submit those changes must be set to *None* or *OutputParameters*.

Visual Basic

```
Dim strConn As String
strConn = "Data Source=Ora10gR2;User ID=scott;Password=tiger;"
Using cn As New OracleConnection(strConn)
    cn.Open()
    Console.WriteLine("Preparing database...")

    Dim cmd As OracleCommand = cn.CreateCommand()
    cmd.CommandText = "DROP TABLE BatchUpdateTest"
    Try : cmd.ExecuteNonQuery() : Catch : End Try
    cmd.CommandText = "CREATE TABLE BatchUpdateTest " & _
                      "(ID int PRIMARY KEY, OtherColumn varchar(255))"
    cmd.ExecuteNonQuery()

    cmd.CommandText = "SELECT ID, OtherColumn FROM BatchUpdateTest"
    Dim da As New OracleDataAdapter(cmd)
    Dim cb As New OracleCommandBuilder(da)
    da.UpdateBatchSize = 10

    Dim tbl As New DataTable()
    da.Fill(tbl)
```

```
    For rowCounter As Integer = 1 To 25
        tbl.Rows.Add(rowCounter, "Initial Value")
    Next rowCounter
    Console.WriteLine("Inserting rows via batch updating...")
    da.Update(tbl)

    For Each row As DataRow In tbl.Rows
        row("OtherColumn") = "Modified Value"
    Next row
    Console.WriteLine("Updating rows via batch updating...")
    da.Update(tbl)

    For Each row As DataRow In tbl.Rows
        row.Delete()
    Next row
    Console.WriteLine("Deleting rows via batch updating...")
    da.Update(tbl)

    Console.WriteLine("Done!")

    cn.Close()
End Using
```

Visual C#

```
string strConn;
strConn = "Data Source=Ora10gR2;User ID=scott;Password=tiger;";
using (OracleConnection cn = new OracleConnection(strConn)) {
    cn.Open();

    Console.WriteLine("Preparing database...");
    OracleCommand cmd = cn.CreateCommand();
    cmd.CommandText = "DROP TABLE BatchUpdateTest";
    try { cmd.ExecuteNonQuery(); } catch { }
    cmd.CommandText = "CREATE TABLE BatchUpdateTest " +
                      "(ID int PRIMARY KEY, OtherColumn varchar(255))";
    cmd.ExecuteNonQuery();

    cmd.CommandText = "SELECT ID, OtherColumn FROM BatchUpdateTest";
    OracleDataAdapter da = new OracleDataAdapter(cmd);
    OracleCommandBuilder cb = new OracleCommandBuilder(da);
    da.UpdateBatchSize = 10;

    DataTable tbl = new DataTable();
    da.Fill(tbl);

    for (int rowCounter = 1; rowCounter <= 25; rowCounter++)
        tbl.Rows.Add(rowCounter, "Initial Value");
    Console.WriteLine("Inserting rows via batch updating...");
    da.Update(tbl);

    foreach (DataRow row in tbl.Rows)
        row["OtherColumn"] = "Modified Value";
    Console.WriteLine("Updating rows via batch updating...");
    da.Update(tbl);
```

```
    foreach (DataRow row in tbl.Rows)
        row.Delete();
    Console.WriteLine("Deleting rows via batch updating...");
    da.Update(tbl);

    Console.WriteLine("Done!");
    cn.Close();
}
```

Fetching Server-Generated Key Sequence Values

Chapter 11 also covered scenarios in which you might want to retrieve new server-generated values, such as auto-increment primary key values, as you submit updates using a *SqlDataAdapter*.

Many Oracle database administrators use sequences to generate key values. The following code references the sequence in the INSERT INTO query used to submit the new rows and then returns the sequence value generated, using the RETURNING clause introduced in Oracle 10g.

An alternate approach, and one preferred by many Oracle developers and database administrators, is to query the sequence for new values prior to submitting new rows. This is a helpful approach because it means that your code knows the key values for new rows before you insert them into the database. The code references the sequence to demonstrate how you can return server-generated values for each modified row rather than to recommend referencing the sequence from the INSERT INTO query.

The code adds a series of pending new rows in a *DataTable*, using ADO.NET's auto-increment functionality to generate "placeholder" primary key values. Prior to submitting the pending inserts to the database, the code writes the contents of the rows to the Console window. The code then supplies the logic needed to submit the new rows and return the server-generated values via output parameters. (Using output parameters allows us to use the batched updating features of *OracleDataAdapter*.) The code then submits the pending new rows and writes the contents of the *DataTable* to the Console window.

Visual Basic

```
Dim strConn, strSQL As String
strConn = "Data Source=Ora10gR2;User ID=scott;Password=tiger;"
strSQL = "INSERT INTO SequenceTest_Table (ID, OtherColumn) " & _
         "VALUES (SequenceTest_Sequence.NEXTVAL, :OtherColumn) " & _
         "RETURNING ID INTO :ID"
Using cn As New OracleConnection(strConn)
    cn.Open()

    Console.WriteLine("Preparing database...")
    Dim cmd As OracleCommand = cn.CreateCommand()
    cmd.CommandText = "DROP SEQUENCE SequenceTest_Sequence"
    Try : cmd.ExecuteNonQuery() : Catch : End Try
    cmd.CommandText = "DROP TABLE SequenceTest_Table"
    Try : cmd.ExecuteNonQuery() : Catch : End Try
```

```vb
        cmd.CommandText = "CREATE TABLE SequenceTest_Table " & _
                          "(ID int PRIMARY KEY, OtherColumn varchar(255))"
        cmd.ExecuteNonQuery()
        cmd.CommandText = "CREATE SEQUENCE SequenceTest_Sequence " & _
                          "START WITH 100 INCREMENT BY 5"
        cmd.ExecuteNonQuery()

        Dim tbl As New DataTable()
        Dim col As DataColumn = tbl.Columns.Add("ID", GetType(Integer))
        col.AutoIncrement = True
        col.AutoIncrementSeed = -1
        col.AutoIncrementStep = -1
        tbl.PrimaryKey = New DataColumn() {col}
        tbl.Columns.Add("OtherColumn", GetType(String))

        For rowCounter As Integer = 1 To 15
            tbl.Rows.Add(Nothing, "Row #" & rowCounter.ToString())
        Next rowCounter
        Console.WriteLine("Before Update")
        For Each row As DataRow In tbl.Rows
            Console.WriteLine("  {0} - {1}", row("ID"), row("OtherColumn"))
        Next row
        Console.WriteLine()

        cmd.CommandText = "SELECT ID, OtherColumn FROM SequenceTest_Table"
        Dim da As New OracleDataAdapter(cmd)
        da.InsertCommand = New OracleCommand(strSQL, cn)
        da.InsertCommand.Parameters.Add(":ID", OracleType.Int32, 0, "ID")
        da.InsertCommand.Parameters(0).Direction = ParameterDirection.Output
        da.InsertCommand.Parameters.Add(":OtherColumn", OracleType.VarChar, _
                                        255, "OtherColumn")
        da.InsertCommand.UpdatedRowSource = UpdateRowSource.OutputParameters
        da.UpdateBatchSize = 10

        da.Update(tbl)
        Console.WriteLine("  After Update")
        For Each row As DataRow In tbl.Rows
            Console.WriteLine("    {0} - {1}", row("ID"), row("OtherColumn"))
        Next row

        cn.Close()
    End Using
```

Visual C#

```csharp
string strConn, strSQL;
strConn = "Data Source=Ora10gR2;User ID=scott;Password=tiger;";
strSQL = "INSERT INTO SequenceTest_Table (ID, OtherColumn) " +
         "VALUES (SequenceTest_Sequence.NEXTVAL, :OtherColumn) " +
         "RETURNING ID INTO :ID";
using (OracleConnection cn = new OracleConnection(strConn)) {
    cn.Open();

    Console.WriteLine("Preparing database...");
    OracleCommand cmd = cn.CreateCommand();
    cmd.CommandText = "DROP SEQUENCE SequenceTest_Sequence";
    try { cmd.ExecuteNonQuery(); } catch { }
```

```
cmd.CommandText = "DROP TABLE SequenceTest_Table";
try { cmd.ExecuteNonQuery(); } catch { }
cmd.CommandText = "CREATE TABLE SequenceTest_Table " +
                  "(ID int PRIMARY KEY, OtherColumn varchar(255))";
cmd.ExecuteNonQuery();
cmd.CommandText = "CREATE SEQUENCE SequenceTest_Sequence " +
                  "START WITH 100 INCREMENT BY 5";
cmd.ExecuteNonQuery();

DataTable tbl = new DataTable();
DataColumn col = tbl.Columns.Add("ID", typeof(int));
col.AutoIncrement = true;
col.AutoIncrementSeed = -1;
col.AutoIncrementStep = -1;
tbl.PrimaryKey = new DataColumn[] { col };
tbl.Columns.Add("OtherColumn", typeof(string));

for (int rowCounter = 1; rowCounter <= 15; rowCounter++)
    tbl.Rows.Add(null, "Row #" + rowCounter.ToString());
Console.WriteLine("Before Update");
foreach (DataRow row in tbl.Rows)
    Console.WriteLine("  {0} - {1}", row["ID"], row["OtherColumn"]);
Console.WriteLine();

cmd.CommandText = "SELECT ID, OtherColumn FROM SequenceTest_Table";
OracleDataAdapter da = new OracleDataAdapter(cmd);
da.InsertCommand = new OracleCommand(strSQL, cn);
da.InsertCommand.Parameters.Add(":ID", OracleType.Int32, 0, "ID")
da.InsertCommand.Parameters[0].Direction = ParameterDirection.Output;
da.InsertCommand.Parameters.Add(":OtherColumn", OracleType.VarChar,
                                255, "OtherColumn");
da.InsertCommand.UpdatedRowSource = UpdateRowSource.OutputParameters;
da.UpdateBatchSize = 10;

da.Update(tbl);
Console.WriteLine("After Update");
foreach (DataRow row in tbl.Rows)
    Console.WriteLine("  {0} - {1}", row["ID"], row["OtherColumn"]);

cn.Close();
}
```

Retrieving Database Schema Information

Like other *Connection* classes, the *OracleConnection* class supports the *GetSchema* methods that allow you to query your database for available schema information. The overloaded *GetSchema* methods behave like those of other .NET data providers.

Listing Schemas and Restrictions

Earlier in the appendix, we looked at how you can display the list of schemas and restrictions, given a provider name and a connection string using the *DbProviderFactories* class as a starting point. If you know you're working with the Oracle Client .NET Data Provider, you can simplify that code slightly by using the *OracleConnection* class as a starting point:

Visual Basic

```
Dim strConn As String
strConn = "Data Source=Ora10gR2;User ID=scott;Password=tiger;"
Dim schemasTable, restrictionsTable As DataTable
Using cn As New OracleConnection(strConn)
    cn.Open()
    schemasTable = cn.GetSchema()
    restrictionsTable = cn.GetSchema("Restrictions")
    cn.Close()
End Using

Dim ds As New DataSet()
schemasTable.TableName = "Schemas"
restrictionsTable.TableName = "Restrictions"
ds.Tables.AddRange(New DataTable() {schemasTable, restrictionsTable})
Dim rel As DataRelation
rel = ds.Relations.Add(schemasTable.Columns("CollectionName"), _
                        restrictionsTable.Columns("CollectionName"))

For Each schemaRow As DataRow In schemasTable.Rows
    Console.WriteLine("{0} schema", schemaRow("CollectionName"))
    Dim restrictionRows As DataRow() = schemaRow.GetChildRows(rel)
    If restrictionRows.Length <> 0 Then
        Console.WriteLine("  Restrictions:")
        For Each restrictionRow As DataRow In restrictionRows
            Console.WriteLine("    {0}: {1}", _
                            restrictionRow("RestrictionNumber"), _
                            restrictionRow("RestrictionName"))
        Next restrictionRow
    Else
        Console.WriteLine("    No restrictions")
    End If
    Console.WriteLine()
Next schemaRow
```

Visual C#

```
string strConn;
strConn = "Data Source=Ora10gR2;User ID=scott;Password=tiger;";
DataTable schemasTable, restrictionsTable;
using (OracleConnection cn = new OracleConnection(strConn)) {
    cn.Open();
    schemasTable = cn.GetSchema();
    restrictionsTable = cn.GetSchema("Restrictions");
    cn.Close();
}

DataSet ds = new DataSet();
schemasTable.TableName = "Schemas";
restrictionsTable.TableName = "Restrictions";
ds.Tables.AddRange(new DataTable[] { schemasTable, restrictionsTable });
DataRelation rel;
```

```
rel = ds.Relations.Add(schemasTable.Columns["CollectionName"],
                        restrictionsTable.Columns["CollectionName"]);

foreach (DataRow schemaRow in schemasTable.Rows) {
    Console.WriteLine("{0} schema", schemaRow["CollectionName"]);
    DataRow[] restrictionRows = schemaRow.GetChildRows(rel);
    if (restrictionRows.Length != 0) {
        Console.WriteLine("  Restrictions:");
        foreach (DataRow restrictionRow in restrictionRows)
            Console.WriteLine("    {0}: {1}",
                                restrictionRow["RestrictionNumber"],
                                restrictionRow["RestrictionName"]);
    }
    else {
        Console.WriteLine("  No restrictions");
    }
    Console.WriteLine();
}
```

Returning Filtered Schema Information

The output from the preceding code sample indicates that the connection supports a
Columns schema and that it also supports restrictions for owner, table name, and column
name, respectively. Note that this set of restrictions differs from the set of restrictions available
through the ODBC and OLE DB .NET Data Providers described earlier in the appendix.

Even with that difference in behavior, retrieving and displaying information about columns in
a particular table is still a snap. Just build a string array of the same length as described by the
restrictions schema, supply values for the desired restrictions, omit the rest (using *null* or
Nothing, depending on your language of choice), and pass that string array into the *GetSchema*
method along with the name of the desired schema, "Columns", as demonstrated in the following code sample:

Visual Basic
```
Dim filter As String()
Dim filter As String() = New String() {"SCOTT", "EMP", Nothing}
Dim columnsTable As DataTable

Dim strConn As String
strConn = "Data Source=Ora10gR2;User ID=scott;Password=tiger;"
Using cn As New OracleConnection(strConn)
    cn.Open()
    columnsTable = cn.GetSchema("Columns", filter)
    cn.Close()
End Using

For Each row As DataRow In columnsTable.Rows
    Console.WriteLine("{0,-10} - {1}", row("COLUMN_NAME"), row("DATATYPE"))
Next row
```

Visual C#

```
string[] filter = new String[] { "SCOTT", "EMP", null };
DataTable columnsTable;

string strConn;
strConn = "Data Source=Ora10gR2;User ID=scott;Password=tiger;";
using (OracleConnection cn = new OracleConnection(strConn)) {
    cn.Open();
    columnsTable = cn.GetSchema("Columns", filter);
    cn.Close();
}

foreach (DataRow row in columnsTable.Rows)
    Console.WriteLine("{0,-10} - {1}", row["COLUMN_NAME"], row["DATATYPE"]);
```

Appendix B
Samples and Tools

At the time of writing this appendix, the samples and tools described in this appendix are works in progress. All three are fairly ambitious projects, and I plan to periodically add new features and fix existing bugs in the months ahead. The downloadable code for the appendix includes the source code for each component as well as rudimentary documentation. Subsequent updates to the code and documentation will be available through my Web site at *http://www.DavidSceppa.net*.

Note   Disclaimer: Please understand that my plans may be forced to change and that neither Microsoft Press nor I can promise to support these extra tools.

Sample .NET Data Provider—DSP

One of the things I love most about ADO.NET is that .NET Data Providers are simple to create compared with OLE DB providers. Early in the process of writing this book, I decided to build a simple .NET Data Provider to help developers understand how to make their data stores available in ADO.NET.

The goal was to provide a (mostly) working .NET Data Provider to help provider writers understand how to build their own .NET Data Providers. If, for example, you're creating your own .NET Data Provider and you're having problems making your *CommandBuilder* class work, you can load this sample provider (source code and all) and name it *CommandBuilder*, stepping into the source code to see how it works.

Figure B-1 shows a very basic diagram of how a .NET Data Provider manages the communication between ADO.NET code and a data store. I wanted to build a sample .NET Data Provider that interacts with a data store that supports basic database features. At the same time, I wanted to minimize the amount of code required to interact with the data store, which would allow me to focus on enabling features of the .NET Data Provider without having to describe the interaction between the .NET Data Provider and the data store.

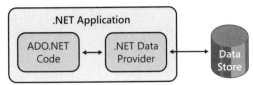

Figure B-1   .NET Data Provider managing communication between ADO.NET code and a data store

The biggest challenge was to find the right data store to target for the sample provider. I wanted to find a simple data store that handles relational data, supports returning rows and columns of data (such as a SELECT query), supports dynamic search criteria (such as a WHERE clause), provides the ability to modify rows (INSERT, UPDATE, and DELETE queries), provides the ability to cache changes and later accept or reject those changes, and provides the ability to load data from and persist data to a file (transactional features). If only there was such a powerful data store—one that was easy to access via the .NET Framework, perhaps even one that would feel familiar to developers who have experience with ADO.NET. . . .

In case my thinly veiled hints weren't transparent enough, that data store exists—the ADO.NET DataSet.

I created a simple .NET Data Provider for the *DataSet*, which I'll refer to as DSP (for DataSet Provider) because every technology needs a good acronym. DSP includes classes for each class in the Provider Factory model: *Connection, ConnectionStringBuilder, Command, Parameter, DataAdapter, CommandBuilder*, and *Transaction*. You can use DSP to load a *DataSet* from an XML file and execute queries to retrieve and/or modify the contents of the *DataSet*. DSP supports basic query syntaxes (parsing the query text using Regular Expressions), and it relies on the *DataSet* and related classes to evaluate filters in the WHERE clause.

Note   This .NET Data Provider is not intended to be used from your .NET applications. DSP is intended solely to help provider writers learn how they can enable basic ADO.NET scenarios within their .NET Data Providers.

At the time of writing this appendix, DSP handles basic query scenarios (SELECT, INSERT, UPDATE, and DELETE), generating updating logic via *CommandBuilder*, generating transactions, and returning basic schema information via *Connection.GetSchema*. I plan to add support for batch updating and perhaps *System.Transaction* support. If there's enough interest in the project, I'll continue to update DSP to enable it to work with related tools and technologies such as Microsoft Visual Studio Server Explorer.

ADO.NET Data Explorer

I love Visual Studio. The more I use each successive version, the more I dread having to write code in previous versions. I love the fact that I can create a strongly typed *DataSet* and add one to a Windows Form along with *TableAdapters*, bound controls, and a navigation control that supports submitting changes back to the database—all without being forced to write a single line of code. Visual Studio generates code that you'd probably prefer not to write by hand.

With that said, at times you might still want more control over the code in your application. The more code you write, the more you find yourself following certain patterns—the way you create *Connection* objects, the way you retrieve data from *DataReader* objects, and so on. You might even find that you create classes based on the schema of your queries and use the *DataReader* and *Generics* to create collections of objects.

I wanted to build an ad hoc query tool that could also serve as a simple and extensible starting point for generating data access code, and that could work with any .NET Data Provider. So, I created one: ADO.NET Data Explorer.

ADO.NET Data Explorer, shown in Figure B-2, lets you interact with databases using .NET Data Providers. You can examine the database's schema and execute queries. You can also modify the results of those queries and save the changes.

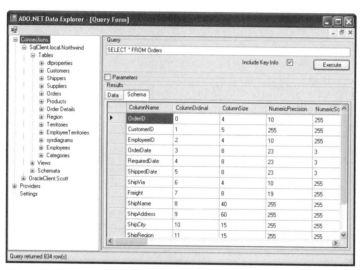

Figure B-2   ADO.NET Data Explorer

ADO.NET Data Explorer is also a starting point for generating code. At the moment, I'm working on a feature that will allow you to right-click a stored procedure in the tree-view pane and generate code that will instantiate *Connection*, *Command*, and *Parameter* objects needed to query that stored procedure. I'm also working on having the ADO.NET Data Explorer generate updating logic based on a *CommandBuilder*. As I mentioned earlier, the tools are a work in progress.

Developers are often very particular about their code—the way variables are named, the way the code is formatted, and so on. The code generation logic for the ADO.NET Data Explorer is stored in separate components that you can modify so that you can change the way the code is generated, and it lets you add your own code-generation logic.

AdapterSet

Writing code to submit changes for multiple related tables using a *DataSet* and *DataAdapters* is a nontrivial process, as Chapter 11 illustrates. That doesn't *have* to be the case. There are basic patterns to follow—inserts are top-down, deletes are bottom-up, and so on. If you build logic to submit changes to related tables in one application, you'll find that you can re-use most of that logic in other applications. You might even be able to generalize that updating logic based on the relationships and between the tables in your database.

Those database relationships might have corresponding *DataRelations* in the *DataSet*, and each *DataTable* will have a corresponding *DataAdapter*. In such cases, the generalized logic could be expressed by associating your *DataAdapters* with their *DataTables* and by relying on the *DataRelations* to dictate the order of updates submitted.

The sample code for this appendix includes a class called the *AdapterSet*, which contains basic logic that allows you to submit pending hierarchical changes based on this information. You create an *AdapterSet* and point it at a *DataSet*. Then you add your *DataAdapters* and references to their corresponding *DataTables*. The *AdapterSet* then examines the *DataRelations* defined in the *DataSet* to determine the order of updates. At the time of writing this appendix, the *AdapterSet* does not yet support submitting updates in transactions.

I've included the source code for the *AdapterSet* class, in both Microsoft C# and Visual Basic, so you can examine the logic it contains to improve on the logic or use it as a starting point for your own component.

Index

About the Author

This is David Sceppa's third book for Microsoft Press. He authored *Programming ADO*, as well as the first edition of this book. David currently works as a program manager on the Microsoft ADO.NET team, focusing on the .NET Data Provider model. He's a Microsoft Certified Solutions Developer, a regular speaker at technical conferences, a frequent contributor to the MSDN Forum on .NET Framework Data Access and Storage, and is well known for making damned good chili.

Since the completion of the first edition of this book, David has lived out two boyhood dreams. First, David watched his beloved Red Sox come back from a near sweep at the hands of the dreaded Yankees before eventually winning the World Series in 2004. To celebrate, he flew across the country to attend the World Series parade with his father and sister. Incidentally, the picture of the author with the 2004 World Series trophy that appears in this section was taken at the TechEd 2006 party at Fenway Park. Second, David attended WrestleMania with college friends and was a mere twenty feet away from Vince McMahon when he drove Hulk Hogan through the Spanish announcer's table. In fact, he still has the souvenir folding metal chair from the event, though he has not used it in the same way that professional wrestlers regularly do.

David recently joined a local adult kickball league. Thankfully, he has yet to resort to working the count to draw walks and/or wear out the opposing pitchers.

Rumors that David still expects to wake up from a dream only to find that Dave Roberts was called out at second on a Phantom Jeter Tag are, in fact, true.

Additional Resources for Developers: Advanced Topics and Best Practices

Published and Forthcoming Titles from Microsoft Press

Code Complete, Second Edition
Steve McConnell • ISBN 0-7356-1967-0

For more than a decade, Steve McConnell, one of the premier authors and voices in the software community, has helped change the way developers write code—and produce better software. Now his classic book, *Code Complete*, has been fully updated and revised with best practices in the art and science of constructing software. Topics include design, applying good techniques to construction, eliminating errors, planning, managing construction activities, and relating personal character to superior software. This new edition features fully updated information on programming techniques, including the emergence of Web-style programming, and integrated coverage of object-oriented design. You'll also find new code examples—both good and bad—in C++, Microsoft® Visual Basic®, C#, and Java, although the focus is squarely on techniques and practices.

More About Software Requirements: Thorny Issues and Practical Advice
Karl E. Wiegers • ISBN 0-7356-2267-1

Have you ever delivered software that satisfied all of the project specifications, but failed to meet any of the customers expectations? Without formal, verifiable requirements—and a system for managing them—the result is often a gap between what developers think they're supposed to build and what customers think they're going to get. Too often, lessons about software requirements engineering processes are formal or academic, and not of value to real-world, professional development teams. In this follow-up guide to *Software Requirements, Second Edition*, you will discover even more practical techniques for gathering and managing software requirements that help you deliver software that meets project and customer specifications. Succinct and immediately useful, this book is a must-have for developers and architects.

Software Estimation: Demystifying the Black Art
Steve McConnell • ISBN 0-7356-0535-1

Often referred to as the "black art" because of its complexity and uncertainty, software estimation is not as hard or mysterious as people think. However, the art of how to create effective cost and schedule estimates has not been very well publicized. *Software Estimation* provides a proven set of procedures and heuristics that software developers, technical leads, and project managers can apply to their projects. Instead of arcane treatises and rigid modeling techniques, award-winning author Steve McConnell gives practical guidance to help organizations achieve basic estimation proficiency and lay the groundwork to continue improving project cost estimates. This book does not avoid the more complex mathematical estimation approaches, but the non-mathematical reader will find plenty of useful guidelines without getting bogged down in complex formulas.

Debugging, Tuning, and Testing Microsoft .NET 2.0 Applications
John Robbins • ISBN 0-7356-2202-7

Making an application the best it can be has long been a time-consuming task best accomplished with specialized and costly tools. With Microsoft Visual Studio® 2005, developers have available a new range of built-in functionality that enables them to debug their code quickly and efficiently, tune it to optimum performance, and test applications to ensure compatibility and trouble-free operation. In this accessible and hands-on book, debugging expert John Robbins shows developers how to use the tools and functions in Visual Studio to their full advantage to ensure high-quality applications.

The Security Development Lifecycle
Michael Howard and Steve Lipner • ISBN 0-7356-2214-0

Adapted from Microsoft's standard development process, the Security Development Lifecycle (SDL) is a methodology that helps reduce the number of security defects in code at every stage of the development process, from design to release. This book details each stage of the SDL methodology and discusses its implementation across a range of Microsoft software, including Microsoft Windows Server™ 2003, Microsoft SQL Server™ 2000 Service Pack 3, and Microsoft Exchange Server 2003 Service Pack 1, to help measurably improve security features. You get direct access to insights from Microsoft's security team and lessons that are applicable to software development processes worldwide, whether on a small-scale or a large-scale. This book includes a CD featuring videos of developer training classes.

Software Requirements, Second Edition
Karl E. Wiegers • ISBN 0-7356-1879-8

Writing Secure Code, Second Edition
Michael Howard and David LeBlanc • ISBN 0-7356-1722-8

CLR via C#, Second Edition
Jeffrey Richter • ISBN 0-7356-2163-2

For more information about Microsoft Press® books and other learning products,
visit: **www.microsoft.com/mspress** *and* **www.microsoft.com/learning**

Additional SQL Server Resources for Developers

Published and Forthcoming Titles from Microsoft Press

Microsoft® SQL Server™ 2005 Express Edition
Step by Step
Jackie Goldstein ● ISBN 0-7356-2184-5

Teach yourself how to get database projects up and running
quickly with SQL Server Express
Edition—a free, easy-to-use
database product that is based
on SQL Server 2005 technology.
It's designed for building simple,
dynamic applications, with all
the rich functionality of the SQL
Server database engine and
using the same data access APIs,
such as Microsoft ADO.NET, SQL
Native Client, and T-SQL.
Whether you're new to database
programming or new to SQL Server, you'll learn how, when, and
why to use specific features of this simple but powerful database development environment. Each chapter puts you to work,
building your knowledge of core capabilities and guiding you
as you create actual components and working applications.

Microsoft SQL Server 2005 Programming
Step by Step
Fernando Guerrero ● ISBN 0-7356-2207-8

SQL Server 2005 is Microsoft's
next-generation data management and analysis solution that
delivers enhanced scalability,
availability, and security features
to enterprise data and analytical
applications while making them
easier to create, deploy, and
manage. Now you can teach
yourself how to design, build, test,
deploy, and maintain SQL Server
databases—one step at a time.
Instead of merely focusing on
describing new features, this book shows new database
programmers and administrators how to use specific features
within typical business scenarios. Each chapter provides a highly
practical learning experience that demonstrates how to build
database solutions to solve common business problems.

Microsoft SQL Server 2005 Analysis Services
Step by Step
Hitachi Consulting Services ● ISBN 0-7356-2199-3

One of the key features of SQL Server 2005 is SQL Server Analysis
Services—Microsoft's customizable analysis solution for business
data modeling and interpretation. Just compare SQL Server
Analysis Services to its competition to understand the great
value of its enhanced features. One of the keys to harnessing
the full functionality of SQL Server will be leveraging Analysis
Services for the powerful tool that it is—including creating a cube,
and deploying, customizing, and extending the basic calcula-
tions. This step-by-step tutorial discusses how to get started, how
to build scalable analytical applications, and how to use and ad-
minister advanced features. Interactivity (enhanced in SQL Server
2005), data translation, and security are also covered in detail.

Microsoft SQL Server 2005 Reporting Services
Step by Step
Hitachi Consulting Services ● ISBN 0-7356-2250-7

SQL Server Reporting Services (SRS) is Microsoft's customizable
reporting solution for business data analysis. It is one of the key
value features of SQL Server 2005: functionality more advanced
and much less expensive than its competition. SRS is powerful,
so an understanding of how to architect a report, as well as how
to install and program SRS, is key to harnessing the full functionality of SQL Server. This procedural tutorial shows how to use the
Report Project Wizard, how to think about and access data, and
how to build queries. It also walks through the creation of charts
and visual layouts for maximum visual understanding of data
analysis. Interactivity (enhanced in SQL Server 2005) and security
are also covered in detail.

Programming Microsoft SQL Server 2005
Andrew J. Brust, Stephen Forte, and William H. Zack
ISBN 0-7356-1923-9

This thorough, hands-on reference for developers and database
administrators teaches the basics of programming custom applications with SQL Server 2005. You will learn the fundamentals
of creating database applications—including coverage of
T-SQL, Microsoft .NET Framework, and Microsoft ADO.NET. In
addition to practical guidance on database architecture and
design, application development, and reporting and data
analysis, this essential reference guide covers performance,
tuning, and availability of SQL Server 2005.

Inside Microsoft SQL Server 2005:
The Storage Engine
Kalen Delaney ● ISBN 0-7356-2105-5

Inside Microsoft SQL Server 2005:
T-SQL Programming
Itzik Ben-Gan ● ISBN 0-7356-2197-7

Inside Microsoft SQL Server 2005:
Query Processing and Optimization
Kalen Delaney ● ISBN 0-7356-2196-9

Programming Microsoft ADO.NET 2.0 Core Reference
David Sceppa ● ISBN 0-7356-2206-X

For more information about Microsoft Press® books and other learning products,
visit: **www.microsoft.com/mspress** *and* **www.microsoft.com/learning**

Microsoft®
Press

Additional Resources for Web Developers

Published and Forthcoming Titles from Microsoft Press

Microsoft® Visual Web Developer™ 2005 Express Edition: Build a Web Site Now!
Jim Buyens • ISBN 0-7356-2212-4

With this lively, eye-opening, and hands-on book, all you need is a computer and the desire to learn how to create Web pages now using Visual Web Developer Express Edition! Featuring a full working edition of the software, this fun and highly visual guide walks you through a complete Web page project from set-up to launch. You'll get an introduction to the Microsoft Visual Studio® environment and learn how to put the lightweight, easy-to-use tools in Visual Web Developer Express to work right away—building your first, dynamic Web pages with Microsoft ASP.NET 2.0. You'll get expert tips, coaching, and visual examples at each step of the way, along with pointers to additional learning resources.

Microsoft ASP.NET 2.0 Programming
Step by Step
George Shepherd • ISBN 0-7356-2201-9

With dramatic improvements in performance, productivity, and security features, Visual Studio 2005 and ASP.NET 2.0 deliver a simplified, high-performance, and powerful Web development experience. ASP.NET 2.0 features a new set of controls and infrastructure that simplify Web-based data access and include functionality that facilitates code reuse, visual consistency, and aesthetic appeal. Now you can teach yourself the essentials of working with ASP.NET 2.0 in the Visual Studio environment— one step at a time. With *Step by Step*, you work at your own pace through hands-on, learn-by-doing exercises. Whether you're a beginning programmer or new to this version of the technology, you'll understand the core capabilities and fundamental techniques for ASP.NET 2.0. Each chapter puts you to work, showing you how, when, and why to use specific features of the ASP.NET 2.0 rapid application development environment and guiding you as you create actual components and working applications for the Web, including advanced features such as personalization.

Programming Microsoft ASP.NET 2.0
Core Reference
Dino Esposito • ISBN 0-7356-2176-4

Delve into the core topics for ASP.NET 2.0 programming, mastering the essential skills and capabilities needed to build high-performance Web applications successfully. Well-known ASP.NET author Dino Esposito deftly builds your expertise with Web forms, Visual Studio, core controls, master pages, data access, data binding, state management, security services, and other must-know topics—combining definitive reference with practical, hands-on programming instruction. Packed with expert guidance and pragmatic examples, this *Core Reference* delivers the key resources that you need to develop professional-level Web programming skills.

Programming Microsoft ASP.NET 2.0
Applications: *Advanced Topics*
Dino Esposito • ISBN 0-7356-2177-2

Master advanced topics in ASP.NET 2.0 programming—gaining the essential insights and in-depth understanding that you need to build sophisticated, highly functional Web applications successfully. Topics include Web forms, Visual Studio 2005, core controls, master pages, data access, data binding, state management, and security considerations. Developers often discover that the more they use ASP.NET, the more they need to know. With expert guidance from ASP.NET authority Dino Esposito, you get the in-depth, comprehensive information that leads to full mastery of the technology.

Programming Microsoft Windows® Forms
Charles Petzold • ISBN 0-7356-2153-5

Programming Microsoft Web Forms
Douglas J. Reilly • ISBN 0-7356-2179-9

CLR via C++
Jeffrey Richter with Stanley B. Lippman
ISBN 0-7356-2248-5

Debugging, Tuning, and Testing Microsoft .NET 2.0 Applications
John Robbins • ISBN 0-7356-2202-7

CLR via C#, Second Edition
Jeffrey Richter • ISBN 0-7356-2163-2

For more information about Microsoft Press® books and other learning products, visit: **www.microsoft.com/books** *and* **www.microsoft.com/learning**

What do you think of this book?
We want to hear from you!

Do you have a few minutes to participate in a brief online survey? Microsoft is interested in hearing your feedback about this publication so that we can continually improve our books and learning resources for you.

To participate in our survey, please visit:

www.microsoft.com/learning/booksurvey

And enter this book's ISBN, 0-7356-2206-X. As a thank-you to survey participants in the United States and Canada, each month we'll randomly select five respondents to win one of five $100 gift certificates from a leading online merchant.* At the conclusion of the survey, you can enter the drawing by providing your e-mail address, which will be used for prize notification *only*.

Thanks in advance for your input. Your opinion counts!

Sincerely,

Microsoft Learning

Learn More. Go Further.

To see special offers on Microsoft Learning products for developers, IT professionals, and home and office users, visit: *www.microsoft.com/learning/booksurvey*

* No purchase necessary. Void where prohibited. Open only to residents of the 50 United States (includes District of Columbia) and Canada (void in Quebec). Sweepstakes ends 6/30/2007. For official rules, see: *www.microsoft.com/learning/booksurvey*